ENCYCLOPEDIA

OF THE

FUTURE

ENCYCLOPEDIA
OF THE
FUTURE

Edited by

GEORGE THOMAS KURIAN

GRAHAM T. T. MOLITOR

VOLUME 2

MACMILLAN LIBRARY REFERENCE USA
SIMON & SCHUSTER MACMILLAN
NEW YORK

SIMON & SCHUSTER AND PRENTICE HALL INTERNATIONAL
LONDON   MEXICO CITY   NEW DELHI   SINGAPORE   SYDNEY   TORONTO

Simon & Schuster Macmillan
1633 Broadway, New York, NY 10019

PRINTED IN THE UNITED STATES OF AMERICA

printing number

2 3 4 5 6 7 8 9 10

LIBRARY OF CONGRESS CATALOGING-IN-PUBLICATION DATA
Encyclopedia of the future / edited by George Thomas
   Kurian, Graham T. T. Molitor.
            p.   cm.
      Includes bibliographical references and index.
      ISBN 0-02-897205-8 (set). — ISBN 0-02-897206-6 (v.1).
   — ISBN 0-02-897207-4 (v. 2)
      1. Forecasting—Encyclopedias. I. Kurian, George
   Thomas. II. Molitor, Graham T. T. (Graham Thomas Tate)
   CB158.E53 1996
   303.49'003—dc20   95-42003
                                                     CIP

This paper meets the requirements of ANSI/NISO Z39.48-1992
(Permanence of Paper)

L

Labor Unions.

See UNIONISM.

Land Use Planning

Land use planning is both as old as civilization and as new as bioengineering. It is practiced routinely, to varying degrees, by both governments and private organizations. It has become an established occupation and profession for individual practitioners. Many people believe it is now essential to preserving life on Earth. But it remains a highly controversial field of endeavor.

Narrowly defined, land use planning is the preparation and adoption of plans to govern the spatial pattern produced by human activities within a designated geographical area. Loosely construed, the term is used often to include, not only the plans themselves, but also the implementation of the plans over time and sometimes also the broader social purposes that the plans are intended to promote.

Land use plans typically consist of a map with text and illustrations, which together describe how each of the different subareas within the total planning area are to be "used" by human beings. The descriptive technique usually includes listing either the kind of uses encouraged or permitted in each subarea or the kind discouraged or prohib-

ited. Sometimes the uses are described in operational or functional terms, and sometimes in terms of the physical shape to which the structures housing the uses must conform.

Land use plans may be simple or complex. They may cover a parcel, a municipality, a region, or a nation. Most typical are plans for areas that coincide with the jurisdictions of particular governments. In the United States, the constitutional authority to make and implement comprehensive land use plans resides at the state level, but it has been generally delegated to the level of local government. Consequently, most land use plans are made by town, city, and county governments.

The general social purpose behind land use planning is to promote the safety, health, and welfare of the community as a whole. Beneath this commonly cited "umbrella" goal, communities often choose to emphasize certain subgoals, such as economic development, affordable housing, transportation accessibility, environmental amenity, social equity, or resource protection. Usually this choice of social goals, as well as their level of aspiration, is tempered by an assessment of how difficult or how costly it may be to achieve them.

The implementation phase of land use planning typically involves the use of two major instruments of governmental power: the police power, to regulate the activities of private citizens and corporations, and the purse power, to collect taxes to pay for the construction and operation of public works and services. When land use planning is undertaken by private corporations, a variant of these same instruments is used, involving legal covenants to govern the use of land by purchasers or tenants and commitments to repay money borrowed for construction and operational expenses.

The most controversial aspect of land use planning revolves around which of these two powers of government should be relied on more to implement the plan—the police power or the purse power. The U.S. Constitution protects private property, including land, from unwarranted intrusion or expropriation by the government without the due process of law and just compensation. Land use plans typically involve limiting the range of uses permissible on private property in certain areas to preserve public amenity and natural/cultural resources. Hence, in the United States, land use planning gives rise to a continual stream of litigation that is referred to and resolved by the judicial system.

As an occupation or profession, land use planning comprises one of a number of specializations within a broader discipline called by such various names as city, urban, or regional planning. Dating as a separate profession from the early twentieth century, this field has developed a theoretical base that combines elements from architecture, landscape architecture, civil engineering, public health, public administration, political science, and other related disciplines. Because urban planning, like medicine, involves prescription as well as description, its theoretical base is constantly evolving in response to new challenges for solutions to problems in the real world.

Largely in response to economic and civil rights problems, urban planning since 1960 has sought to expand its understanding of the "use" element (the social practices and structures of the community), while still retaining the "land" element (their geographical or physical manifestations) as a defining characteristic of the field. Today the growing awareness of the global and regional fragility of the natural environment is tending to return attention to the "land" element, as pollution, congestion, and the fragility of entire ecosystems increasingly press themselves onto to the political agenda. Thus, the challenge to integrate the functional with the physical within land use planning is increasing.

A concentration on the functional/operational aspect of planning, as contrasted with its physical/spatial aspect, is not unique to urban planning. It is true to an even greater extent for most other types of group planning activities, such as business planning, strategic planning, and policy planning. Beneath the differences, however, all these fields of planning employ a common procedural method. It involves four sequential steps: survey, analysis, choice, and implementation. Successful application of these four steps requires in most cases, an approach that combines both science and art.

For example, in land use planning, the survey and analysis steps rely heavily on scientific methods that include such sophisticated mathematical tools as geographic information systems, computer simulation models, and statistically extrapolated opinion polls. Ecological "reconnaissance" of ecosystems and populations that are to be impacted by future uses is also needed. But, in the choice of a particular plan and the sequence of actions to implement it, large measures of social intuition and political craftsmanship are necessary. Without them, plans usually fail to be accepted or implemented.

Humanity faces unprecedented changes on a global scale as it approaches the twenty-first century. The 1992 United Nations Conference on Environment and Development showed how important it is for the international community to come to grips with the effects of industry on nature. At this conference, the term *sustainable development* was adopted by the major nations of the world, to set a new goal for all future efforts to manage the built environment. Whether history will catalog this vision as the cloud castle of a Quixote or the El Dorado of a Columbus will depend greatly on how much skill the land use and urban planning profession can muster in the years ahead.

See also APPROPRIATE TECHNOLOGY; CITIES; CITIES, NORTH AMERICAN; MEGACITIES; PLANNING.

BIBLIOGRAPHY

CHAPIN, F. STUART, JR., and KAISER, EDWARD J. *Urban Land Use Planning*, 2nd ed. Chicago: University of Illinois Press, 1994.

LEUNG, HOK LIN. *Land Use Planning Made Plain*. Kingston, Ontario: P. Frye and Company, 1989.

SO, FRANK S., and GETZELS, JUDITH. *The Practice of Local Government Planning*. Washington, DC: International City Managers' Association, 1988.

SO, FRANK S., et al. *The Practice of State and Regional Planning*. Chicago: American Planning Association Planners Press, 1985.

KENT, T. J., JR. *The Urban General Plan*. Reprint. Chicago: American Planning Association Planners Press, 1990.

Richard E. Tustian

Languages

The spoken languages of humanity have always formed part of a single system of communication around the globe, the *logosphere*, the opposite ends of which were joined across the Atlantic five centuries ago. Just as the subsequent development of languages was affected by the printing revolution, so the future of languages will be increasingly determined by the electronics and telecommunications revolution.

Instant worldwide communication has helped the spoken word to regain its primacy over the printed word. Whereas the logosphere has consisted until now of sequences of links among individual spoken languages papered over by written languages, it now functions as a worldwide vehicle of human expression. In this situation, the development and wider use of English and a few other languages will be favored over that of others internationally.

English

The accelerating bandwagon of English as the unrivalled, worldwide vehicle for science and security, trade and travel, will be unstoppable. Compromise between American and British models of pronunciation and usage will lead to the increasing cultivation of a "mid-Atlantic" standard of mainstream English. There also are indications that the spread of this prestige variety will be paralleled by the worldwide spread of counterstream English, an international "youth" English associated with video-clips and teenage culture, a nonstandard English that will draw together popular elements and linguistic innovations from sources as diverse as New York, Jamaica, London, and Sydney. The increasing use of English by nonnative speakers will lead in any case to a greater tolerance of variations in English between these two extremes.

Bilingualism

Although there will be a vast increase in bilingualism throughout the non-English-speaking world, involving English as a second language, this is unlikely to be matched by a corresponding degree of bilingualism in the English-speaking world. This will be disadvantageous to native English speakers in two ways. Many of their children will miss the educational, cultural, and intellectual benefits of studying another language and culture. In many non-English parts of the world there will be hostility toward the perceived "arrogance" of monolingual English speakers.

Other Major Languages

French, although lagging far behind, is likely to remain the only language competing with English. Widespread antipathy to the idea of a linguistic monopoly in world affairs will make it easier for French to maintain its "number two" status. With a narrow base of native speakers (not more than 70 million), the international future of French will depend on its continuing as an official or auxiliary future of French will depend on its continuing as an official or auxiliary language in almost forty countries—in Africa, Europe, the Americas, and Oceania.

Certain continental or subcontinental languages will enjoy a more secure place in their coverage of specific parts of the globe: modern standard Arabic, Chinese (Mandarin and Cantonese), German, Hindi-Urdu, Japanese, Russian, Spanish-Portuguese. Their regional roles will be strengthened by their use in state-run television networks.

More Localized Languages

As English and other major languages are spread by global media, many more localized languages will also benefit from permanent recording and diffusion by audiocassettes, video, and television. Their role as vehicles of in group communication and cultural identity will often be strengthened. As the audiovisual screen lessens the impact of the printed page, speakers of one language will tend to acquire passive understanding of other closely related languages, since the spoken word permits more variation than the written.

If very closely related languages are considered together in clusters, then fewer than 10 percent of the world's total of over two thousand language-clusters are likely to fall into complete disuse during the twenty-first century. Even where this does occur, audiovisual archiving will preserve individual languages and prevent them from being totally lost.

Some languages may die for nonlinguistic reasons, if ethnic groups are exterminated on a large scale by environmental disaster, disease, famine, war, or genocide. Still, languages may survive in their spoken form even if the number of speakers is small, if those speakers struggle consciously to preserve them.

Language Policy

Thanks to international communications, nation-states will have less control over the development of languages and education. Increasingly it will be recognized that the right to one's own language is a fundamental human right. Countries with more democratic systems will give increasing recognition to minority languages, including regional forms of their official languages. Conventions on the usage and spelling of some international languages may be agreed to at the world or regional level, but there will be generally less emphasis on written standardization, except in such fields as science, law, or public health and safety.

Language Translation Machines

There will be a breakthrough in the perfection of translation machines, especially from and into English, or between closely related languages. Translation programs among non-English languages will often use English-based programs as a "go-between." Pocket translation machines will be widely available at modest cost by the early twenty-first century.

Subtitling will be an important industry, with eventual new techniques for automatic written translation from a spoken text. Computerized voice recognition will progressively be extended to the recognition of individual spoken languages, not only of major international languages and their varieties, but also of more localized languages and dialects.

See also COMMUNICATIONS; GLOBAL CULTURE; TELECOMMUNICATIONS.

BIBLIOGRAPHY

BAUERLE, RAINER, et al., eds. *Meaning, Use, and Interpretation of Languages.* Hawthorn, NY: De Gruyter, 1983.
BLEICH, DAVID. *The Double Perspective: Language, Literacy, and Social Relations.* New York: Oxford University Press, 1988.
LIEBERMAN, PHILIP. *The Biology and Evolution of Language.* Cambridge, MA: Harvard University Press, 1984.
WRIGHT, WILL. *Wild Knowledge: Science, Language, and Social Life in a Fragile Environment.* Minneapolis: University of Minnesota Press, 1992.

David Dalby

Latin America

By the mid 1990s, the nations of Latin America were well into the second decade of uninterrupted elected constitutional government. This extended period of democratic rule appeared to signal an end to military intervention in politics as the region entered the twenty-first century. The political history of Latin America following independence from Spain and Portugal consisted of brief interludes of elected civilian rule bracketed by longer periods of authoritarian rule, usually military dictatorships. In the late 1970s, the region began to break out of the particularly repressive cycle of military rule that began in Brazil in 1964 and swept through such traditionally democratic countries as Chile and Uruguay.

In sharp contrast to the previous two decades, the 1980s featured an unexpected and far reaching transition to democracy. Popularly elected civilian governments took power throughout Latin America, even in countries—Nicaragua, Paraguay, and Haiti, most notably—with virtually no democratic history.

Latin America's current transition to democracy is unprecedented in scope, longevity, and institutionalization. By 1995 nearly every country had had a second, third, or even fourth set of elections that more often than not passed the presidency from one party to another. Political scientists point to the peaceful transfer of power as a key indicator that democracy is being institutionalized as the only legitimate form of governance. An equally important development for the long-term consolidation of democratic governance is measures taken by the nations of the Americas to empower their regional organization, the Organization of American States, to promote and defend democracy as a hemispheric priority. Under its new mandate, the OAS regularly monitors elections in Latin America to assure that they are free and fair and publicly condemns threats to democracy within member countries. In 1994, it played an important role in restoring Haiti's elected president to office.

Although democracy may be stronger than it has ever been in Latin America, the transition is not complete. Cuba remains in the hands of a one-party dictatorship. The region's second largest country, Mexico, has yet to make the transition from limited democracy to a fully competitive political system. Even more disturbing, political corruption undermines popular rule throughout Latin America; transformation of the region's politics has not penetrated very deeply into societies that are profoundly undemocratic.

Economics and Society

An equally striking transformation in the region's economic policies followed on the heels of Latin

America's transition to democracy. Throughout most of this century, governments sought to develop their economies through protected, highly regulated markets with state firms controlling important segments of production. In the early 1990s, the recently elected civilian regimes began to break with this tradition and move toward free market, export-oriented development strategies. The impetus for reform was twofold: the foreign debt crisis of the 1980s and the region's worst economic recession since the Great Depression of the 1930s. International lending agencies, such as the World Bank and Inter-American Development Bank, along with private creditor banks, put pressure on Latin American governments to adopt new policies, while falling growth rates and soaring inflation undermined traditional policies. During the "lost decade" of the 1980s, Latin America's gross domestic product per capita declined at an average annual rate of 1.1 percent (compared with an annual average increase of 3.4 percent in the 1970s), while the rate of inflation for the region in 1987 was over 200 percent.

Chile and Mexico were the pioneers in economic reform, but by 1994 virtually every country in the region, including Cuba, had adopted key elements (reduced fiscal deficits, tax reforms, liberalized financial markets, exchange rate liberalization, reduced trade barriers, open investment regimes, privatization of public enterprises, and general deregulation) of the neo-liberal reform agenda. The economic liberalization of the 1990s triggered a recovery in Latin America. By 1995, the region had experienced four consecutive years of growth in per capita GDP, and inflation (excluding Brazil) had fallen to only 16 percent.

Just when Latin America seemed well on the way to achieving sustained growth under free market economics, the Mexican peso suddenly lost half of its value in late 1994, throwing Mexico into a new economic crisis. The "peso crisis" quickly spread to the rest of Latin America as foreign investors pulled funds out of Argentina, Brazil, Chile, and other countries now dependent on outside investment (direct and portfolio) to sustain the recovery. Although the region survived the crisis of 1995, bank failures in Mexico, Argentina, and Venezuela highlighted Latin America's vulnerability to shifting capital flows.

Even with the economic recovery of the first half of the 1990s, average per capita income was lower in real terms in 1994 than in 1980, and most of the region's 450 million residents benefited little from the recovery. Even though population growth and

the birthrate have declined significantly since 1970, unemployment is high, and over 40 percent of Latin America's population lives below the poverty level. Persistent widespread poverty reflects Latin America's uneven distributions of income and wealth—among the most uneven in the world. This socioeconomic inequality continues to cast a disturbing shadow over Latin America.

Latin America and the United States

At the December 1994 Summit of the Americas in Miami, the elected leaders of the Western Hemisphere agreed that the challenges of the future were to strengthen democracy, promote economic prosperity, eradicate poverty, and achieve sustainable development throughout the Americas. An underlying reality of the Miami summit—and of Latin America as it enters the twenty-first century—is that the nations of the region are drawing closer to each other and to their northern neighbors. The North American Free Trade Agreement (NAFTA), uniting Mexico, the United States, and Canada, is only one of several regional integration schemes initiated in Latin America since 1990. The Miami summit's declaration of principles and plan of action commit the governments of the region to finalize a hemispheric free trade area by the year 2005.

The forces forging closer relations between Latin America and the United States extend beyond economics. Latin American immigration is remaking U.S. society and culture. U.S. residents of Latin American origin will surpass African Americans as the largest ethnic minority in the United States, and by some estimates the United States is the sixth or seventh most populous Spanish-speaking country in the world. As the twentieth century draws to a close, the destinies of Latin America and the United States are more closely linked than any time since 1492.

See also CANADA; DEVELOPMENT, ALTERNATIVE; DEVELOPMENT: WESTERN PERSPECTIVE; FREE TRADE; MEXICO; MIGRATION, INTERNATIONAL; UNITED STATES.

BIBLIOGRAPHY

HARTLYN, JONATHAN; SHOULTZ, LARS; and VARAS, AUGUSTO, eds. *The United States and Latin America in the 1990s: Beyond the Cold War.* Chapel Hill, NC: University of North Carolina Press, 1992.
Inter-American Development Bank. *Economic and Social Progress in Latin America, 1995 Report.* Washington, DC: Johns Hopkins University Press, 1995.

WIARDA, HOWARD J., and KLINE, HARVEY F., eds. *Latin American Politics and Development*, 2nd ed. Boulder, CO: Westview Press, 1996.

Terry L. McCoy

Law Enforcement

High-tech crime, from computer-assisted theft to illegal biotech adaptations to human organ trade, will dominate the early twenty-first century. As electronic banking replaces cash and checks, muggings and armed robberies will fade, replaced by computer hackers breaking into electronic banking files and diverting funds for their own purposes. Computer terrorism, threatening to destroy vital records unless ransom is paid, can be expected along with other innovative computer fraud. As virtual reality progresses, computer fraud will take on new meaning, as illusionary worlds become "real" and elaborate ruses are perpetrated upon the unwary.

With the completion of the Human Genome Project mapping human genes, the ability to manipulate genes for profit will be performed legally and illegally. Legitimate enterprises will create new life-forms to serve humankind, microbes that eat chemical waste or viruses that attack cancer cells. Illegitimate ones will develop deadly germs that could kill massive numbers of humans if placed in water or food supplies, or oxygen-destroying organisms that could render a home or business unsuitable for human habitation and thus easy prey for pressurized-suit–wearing thieves. As human and mammal/fish/bird/plant genes are intermingled via genetic engineering, even more bizarre crimes will emerge and "genetic predisposition" may be used as a defense in the courts.

The early twenty-first century will be plagued by a severe shortage of body parts needed for transplanting. As the world population ages and human life expectancy increases through biotech advances, the demand for replacement parts will escalate rapidly. The illegal theft of body parts, a phenomenon first recognized in the 1990s, will increase if organized crime invades this lucrative field. In some cases the poor and desperate will be coerced to "sell" their body organs, though such practices are presently illegal. In other cases, donors will disappear, and their kidneys and livers will show up on the international "transplants available" black market.

Other crimes expected to escalate include land fraud as space becomes limited; environmental crimes from polluting to "speciescide"; energy crimes such as power theft by a homeowner tapping into a neighbor's sources; patent/copyright infringement, as copying machines and computer mail networks are merged; and health care quackery as desperate victims are duped into believing cures are available for exotic and deadly new illnesses.

Meanwhile, the public safety system will see massive improvements in its arsenal to control crime. The emphasis will be on prevention and behavior modification, a shift focusing on how to prevent crime rather than on how to catch criminals.

The most effective of these new approaches will be "community-oriented." As police change from crime fighters to crime preventers, the rest of the system, courts and corrections, will follow in the same direction.

Public service officers (formerly called police) will seek to identify crime-breeding situations such as homelessness, joblessness, mental illness, and truancy. They will take proactive steps to match at-risk or needy citizens with appropriate social and medical services to head off crime.

Mediation and arbitration will largely replace adversarial proceedings to settle criminal disputes. Courts will recognize a more heterogeneous society brought on by immigration and differential ethnic birth rates that result in a mosaic of races and cultures. Lifestyles and cultural differences will be reassessed and handled equitably rather than criminally. All litigants will be viewed as having rights/claims in conflict rather than designated as either victim or defendant.

Corrections will focus on the reconciliation of the offenders, assisting victims via restitution/restoration, and reclamation of the violator when appropriate and necessary. The benefits will mean both less street crime and, more significantly, less fear of crime and criminals. Corrections will also focus on reintegrating law violators into the community. It will strive to help offenders to acquire the new skills, ranging from vocational to emotional, that may be needed to help individuals live within the law and in harmony with others.

Here, too, a plethora of technologies will be available. Public service officers will be able to keep suspects, or even entire citizenry under constant surveillance via cameras and listening devices that see and hear from far away, and later from bionic eyes and ears obtained as replacement body parts. Life-to-death dossiers of "all" activities for each citizen will be available via electronic recordkeeping and networking computerized files of all government/business enterprises. Officers may "fly" patrols with jetpacks on their backs, and will never be "out of service" as their universal, instantaneous "Dick Tracy" communicators will be strapped on their wrists or possibly implanted in their larynx.

Community orientation will lower crime and fear of crime. "Smart" houses and vehicles also will protect the potential victims. Houses and motor vehicles will be equipped to deny access and even to take defensive action against unauthorized intruders, by calling the police, and releasing knockout gas into the home or vehicle.

Serious offenders will be kept under control not by costly imprisonment, but by "walking prisons,"—an "electronic bug" implanted in or affixed to their bodies so they can be kept under constant surveillance. In addition, biochemical implants that monitor emotions and aggression levels and can release soothing chemicals into the bloodstream to keep at-risk persons calm, cool, and nonthreatening. Subliminal messages intoning, "be honest, do not hurt others, do the right thing," may be used to constantly bombard and subdue the brains of the more dangerous violators.

The publicly funded criminal justice system will be supplemented by privately funded groups such as community security officers, neighborhood mediation centers, and storefront treatment programs. These phenomena accelerated in the early 1990s, when there were twice as many private police as public police in the United States. Citizens will become involved as "controllers" of the system, not just volunteers or privately paid supplements. Law and enforcement policies will be tailored to meet the needs at the individual neighborhood levels. Citizen groups, in consultation with public service departments, will set the agenda and priorities to bring order and peace to their communities.

Philosophically, it will be recognized that the key to crime control will be the scope of criminal behavior, not reducing the supply of criminals and potential criminals. Since nearly all citizens commit occasional violations of the law and thus all are potential criminals, the supply-reduction approach would mean eventually convicting and correcting everyone. More cost-effective and less intrusive into citizens' lives will be alleviation of the problems that lead citizens to desire to commit crime—from unnecessary "meddling" laws (e.g., gambling prohibitions) to greed, poverty, homelessness, truancy, fear, ignorance, mental illness, and a full range of other shortcomings. As whole communities become involved in the process, citizens in need of assistance to alleviate these problems will become easier to identify and help. The key here is the change from seeking retribution to seeking reconciliation as the desired outcome of the process.

The most difficult crime problems to bring under control in the twenty-first century will be in the "white collar" area, as the universal access to computers and networks facilitates electronic theft and fraud. If the twentieth-century attitudes toward business-related crimes—"it's just the way business operates, no real harm is done"—prevail, it will be difficult to control such offenses. But as the business community moves from the highly competitive industrial era into the heavily networked, cooperative information age, there is hope that the interdependence of individuals necessary to succeed in the twenty-first-century business world will bring recognition that such theft and fraud hurts everyone, including the violator. The world economy will be one in which everyone's self-interest is enhanced by a functioning, secure international information network that everyone can confidently use to pursue his/her own agenda for fun and profit.

Thus the twenty-first century can be a morass of greed and suppression, or it can be virtually crime-free. It depends on how policymakers progress with the reforms begun in the late twentieth century. The emerging technology is "amoral." Policy and practice will give it morality or immorality and determine whether it is used to enslave humankind or to free it.

See also CRIME, NONVIOLENT; CRIME, ORGANIZED; CRIME, VIOLENT; CRIME RATES; CRIMINAL JUSTICE; CRIMINAL PUNISHMENT; HIGH TECHNOLOGY; PRISONS.

BIBLIOGRAPHY

BENNETT, G. *Crimewarps*. Garden City, NY: Anchor/Dou bleday, 1987.

BEQUAI, A. *Technocrimes*. Lexington, MA: Lexington Books, 1987.

SCHMALLEGER, F., ed. *Computers in criminal justice*. Bristol, IN: Wyndham Hall Press, 1990.

STEPHENS, G. "Crime and the Biotech Revolution." *The Futurist* (November-December 1992): 38–42.

———. "Drugs and Crime in the Twenty-first Century." *The Futurist* (May–June 1992): 19–22.

Gene Stephens

Law of the Land

In 1927 the U.S. Supreme Court had to decide whether tapping a telephone line constituted a "search and seizure" within the meaning of the Fourth Amendment. Telephones, of course, did not exist when the founding fathers drafted the Bill of Rights. They are "objects of which the Fathers could not have dreamed," as Justice Brandeis wrote at the time. (*Olmstead* v. *United States*, 1928, p. 472). What would the founders have done if confronted with the telephone? Chief Justice (and former president) Taft wrote for the Court that the Fourth Amendment protected only the searching of physical things. It would be another forty years before the Court overruled this case and concluded that a search warrant was required for tapping a telephone line—a protection of liberty many people now take for granted.

The law, like other areas of society, faces profound challenges from the changing social, political, economic, and technological environments in which it operates. Throughout history, changing social conditions and new technologies have forced changes within the legal system. The end of the feudal system revolutionized the law of property and contract. Industrialization of the nineteenth century caused fundamental changes in personal injury law (called tort law) and gave rise to widespread workers' compensation legislation. The economic turmoil of the 1930s gave rise to new administrative agencies and increased economic regulation.

Today various forces, including new technology, computers, communications technology, biotechnology, the women's movement, multiculturalism, environmentalism—to name a few—are forcing changes in the law. Legal questions that were unimaginable twenty or thirty years ago now confront courts, legislatures, and voters. Is there a constitutional right to die? What happens to frozen embryos if the parents divorce? Is a computer network, such as the Internet, more like a newspaper and so responsible for what is "published" on its bulletin boards, or is it more like a telephone company and so not responsible for any defamatory communications? Who owns genetic information? Can international environmental issues—like the depletion of the ozone layer or the greenhouse effect—be controlled by treaties?

While these questions are new, the legal system has always had to adapt to changed circumstances. Looking at how it has responded in the past provides a basis for predicting, or at least imagining, what the future might bring.

American law consists of the U.S. Constitution, which was adopted by the original thirteen states and has been amended twenty-six times since; statutes, which are passed by the U.S. Congress and by state legislatures and local elected bodies (such as town councils); regulations, which are written by the executive branch of the government, based on the authority delegated to them by the legislature; common law, which is judge-made law; and treaties, which are negotiated by the president of the United States and ratified by the U.S. Senate. Each of these sources of law is changing in subtle and not so subtle ways.

Like other systems, the law experiences relatively long periods of stability that are interrupted by periods of rapid change or transformation, something futurists have come to call paradigm shifts. Not surprisingly, these shifts in the law parallel social transformations. For example, the social "revolution" of the 1960s brought with it many changes in the legal system, including legislation prohibiting discrimination on the basis of race or sex, environmental legislation, and greater constitutional protection for criminal defendants. And as social and technological change has accelerated, so has change in the law.

Scholars have identified three important periods of transformation in the history of U.S. law: the American Revolution and the creation of our basic system of government; the American Civil War; and the Great Depression. (It is perhaps too early to assess the importance of the transformations begun in the 1960s.) Each of these periods transformed our laws and legal systems in fundamental ways. Today's technological revolutions may be ushering in another such paradigm shift.

Despite these discontinuities, some trends have been quite steady in the development of American law. One is increasing protection for individual liberties. Another is the rising importance of the political branches of government—the legislative and the executive branches—in the creation of law. A third is expansion of the franchise: giving more people the right to vote, and to vote directly on a wider array of issues. A fourth trend, federalization, may have reached its peak as the political branches are returning programs to the states; the Supreme Court, for the first time in sixty years, invalidated a federal law regulating private activity as exceeding the powers granted to the federal government by the Constitution.

All these changes in our legal system occur within the framework of the U.S. Constitution. That this is the world's oldest written constitution speaks both to its stability and to its flexibility. While the Constitution, by definition, must consist of fixed principles, such principles must be adaptable to respond to new societal and technological developments that the founders could not have imagined. As society advances, different parts of the Constitution may take on new importance, even new meaning. As Woodrow Wilson wrote almost ninety years ago, constitutional government "does not remain fixed in any unchanging form, but grows with the growth and is altered with the change of the nation's needs and purposes." (Horwitz, 1993, pp. 51–52).

The U.S. Constitution has always stood for limited government of specified powers, but the contours of these limits and the freedoms they protect have changed during its two-hundred-year history and will continue to change in the years ahead. Imagining what the next paradigm shift might look like and how general trends may continue to operate requires a review of history.

Protection of Individual Rights

As originally conceived, the Constitution was less concerned with protecting individuals from government incursion—the focus of much Constitutional theory today—than with protecting states from the powers of the federal government. The Bill of Rights limited only the federal government from restricting speech, affecting the establishment of religion, taking of property without just compensation, and from restricting the many other rights protected by the Constitution; states, however, could pass laws affecting any of these rights, unless their own constitutions prohibited them.

This basic structure changed with the Civil War amendments to the Constitution, most importantly, the Fourteenth Amendment. The Fourteenth Amendment applies to the states and restricts the power of the states to encroach on basic liberties. However, determining which liberties are so "basic" as to be protected within the Fourteenth Amendment is a complicated endeavor and one that the Court has approached with varying methods and viewpoints over the years. It is also an area that will certainly see further changes in the future.

As the nation became increasingly industrialized toward the end of the nineteenth century, people began to see the need to regulate business and the relationship between employers and employees. Such problems had not occurred before, when more people were self-employed and did not have to rely so much on large-scale businesses for their livelihoods. In response, various labor laws were passed regulating wages and the number of hours that could be worked.

These laws were consistently struck down by the Supreme Court as unconstitutionally impinging on "liberty of contract." Using the Civil War amendments, the Supreme Court had constitutionalized common law "liberty" rights, principally liberty of property and liberty of contract. Thus state and federal governments alike could not enact laws that the Court felt would limit these freedoms—for example, minimum wage laws or maximum hours laws that the Court felt encroached on these liberties. At the same time, more and more people felt that there was no genuine liberty of contract at stake because of the unequal bargaining power between workers and industry.

With the social disruption of the Great Depression, however, the Court's view changed, and such laws were found not to violate the due process clause of the Fourteenth Amendment. The transformation engendered by the Great Depression changed many areas of society, including the law, and the change in the view of liberty of contract is just part of the changes in the legal system engendered by the Depression. The 1930s also saw the creation of large federal administrative agencies, which combined legislative, adjudicatory, and enforcement powers under one roof, and displaced much state law.

Property rights have also shifted as the ways in which people use land has changed. When the nation was founded, property rights could be closer to "absolute"—one had greater freedom to do what one wanted with his or her property. Of course, one also had much less ability to substantially alter his or her land, because the technologies either did not exist or were expensive and inefficient to build a skyscraper or drain a swamp, for example. With fewer people, large areas of undeveloped land, and limited knowledge of environmental consequences of development, most people could do as they pleased with their land and cause little inconvenience to their neighbors. But as more people lived in closer quarters, and scientists and medical doctors began to understand environmental and public health consequences of building decisions, zoning, building codes and environmental regulations were put in place to deal with these problems. The Supreme Court recognized this in a famous case about zoning almost seventy years ago, in which it noted that when "urban life was comparatively simple," intrusive zoning laws might be unconstitutional, and that "while the meaning of constitutional guaranties never varies, the scope of their application must expand or contract to meet the new and different conditions which are constantly coming within the field of their operation." (*Euclid* v. *Ambler Realty*, 1926, pp. 386–387).

While once liberty of property and contract was nearly absolute, freedom of speech barely existed. Yet in the past seventy-five years or so, freedom of speech has become a virtually absolute liberty. Perhaps free speech doctrine developed in response to a deemphasis on liberty of property and contract, as lawyers and judges sought other principles with which to protect the individual from government, or perhaps these changes were each separate responses to a changing society. Regardless, both have changed profoundly during this century and are now at the center of activity and debate again.

Some scholars predict that free speech doctrine may go through a Great Depression–type watershed—a "New Deal for speech." On this view, increasing concern about unequal distribution of "speech resources" (money to buy television time, for example) may come to justify regulations to redistribute these speech resources or to protect people from the harmful effects of speech. For example, legislatures have made attempts to equalize speech regardless of whether one is rich or poor by placing certain restrictions on financing election campaigns. Scholars and activists have sought to pass laws that would hold purveyors of pornography responsible for any harms that could linked to the pornography—such as a rapist imitating something he sees in a pornographic film. Some laws have sought to criminalize certain expressive activity if the expression is calculated to outrage the recipient. Each of these legislative efforts runs into the First Amendment. While the current Court remains committed to maximum protection for speech—a laissez-faire doctrine for the marketplace of ideas—ongoing concerns about the harmful effects of speech and the influence of money in elections are likely to bring about some changes in free speech doctrine in the next few decades.

Going in the other direction, toward greater protection of individual liberty and greater restriction on governmental authority (i.e., the right of the majority to control the minority) is a resurgence of interest in property rights. This resurgence comes both from the legislature and the courts. The Supreme Court has taken a stronger view of the takings clause of the Fifth Amendment, which forbids the taking of private property for public use without just compensation, limiting the ability of the government to regulate the use of property without compensating owners. At the same time, Congress is considering laws to require payments to landowners if the land's value is reduced by environmental regulations.

The Rising Importance of Politics in Making Law

In addition to substantive changes in the law, the process by which law is created is also changing. Historically, most law was made by judges rather than legislatures. Known as "common law," this judge-made law was derived from precedent and analogy—that is, by looking at what judges had done in similar situations in the past and trying to discern how the meaning of their prior actions should apply to the new case. But over the years the trend has been to shift policy-making authority in one subject after another from judges to legislatures. Before the Civil War, state and federal legislatures did relatively little. Judges, by default, made most law. Only after the Civil War, did the well-known "rule" that courts do not make law, they only interpret the law as it currently exists, come into existence. Legislatures then began to pass more and more laws, either to codify common law rules or to change them.

Similarly, the legislature has delegated more and more lawmaking to the executive branch, by creating regulatory agencies. The Supreme Court has granted executive agencies still more power by deferring to their interpretations of the law unless "clearly erroneous."

Finally, there is a strong trend toward "direct democracy." Seven of the sixteen amendments to the Constitution since the Bill of Rights concern expanding the franchise (the right to vote), or enhancing democracy. More and more state constitutions provide for referenda for a wide range of issues, including amending the state constitution. And public opinion polls are increasingly important in decision making by elected officials.

In recent years some of the most hard-fought elections have not been votes for candidates but votes directly on new laws, such as the California proposition to restrict public services for illegal aliens and the Colorado proposition that prohibits antidiscrimination laws from protecting homosexuals. While such direct democracy is useful in giving people a direct voice in government, it presents new challenges as well. Many people may vote on a measure about which they know very little. Such referenda may be as vulnerable or even more vulnerable to special-interest money than legislative decisions, as effective media campaigns are very expensive. Nonetheless, the trend toward direct democracy is likely to continue in the near term.

Conclusion

Stability and predictability are essential elements to a legal system; otherwise people would be unable to make sensible decisions. Thus, most changes in the law should occur relatively slowly in the years ahead. However, crises and new problems will continue to confront the legal system, and changes as dramatic as those surrounding the Civil War and the Great Depression will occur again.

See also CHANGE, PACE OF; COMMUNICATIONS: MEDIA LAW; COMMUNICATIONS: PRIVACY ISSUES; GLOBAL TURNING POINTS; JUDICIAL REFORM; LAWMAKING, JUDICIAL; LAWS, EVOLUTION OF; LAWYERS AND LEGAL PROFESSION.

BIBLIOGRAPHY

ACKERMAN, BRUCE. "Constitutional Politics/Constitutional Law." *Yale Law Journal* 99 (1989): 453–547.

CALABRESI, GUIDO. "Foreward: Antidiscrimination and Constitutional Accountability (What the Bork-Brennan Debate Ignores)." *Harvard Law Review* 105 (1990): 80–151.

"Constitutional Scholars Assess Impact of Supreme Court's 1993–94 Term." *United States Law Week* 63 (1994): 2229–2243.

HORWITZ, MORTON J.. "Foreward: The Constitution of Change: Legal Fundamentality without Fundamentalism." *Harvard Law Review* 107 (1993): 30–117.

GILMORE, GRANT. *The Ages of American Law.* New Haven: Yale University Press, 1977.

GUNTHER, GERALD. *Constitutional Law.* Westbury, N.Y.: Foundation Press, 1991.

HARRELL, MARY ANN, and ANDERSON, BURNETT. *Equal Justice Under Law: The Supreme Court in American Life.* Washington, DC: Supreme Court Historical Society, 1988.

LINOWITZ, SOL M. *The Betrayed Profession: Lawyering at the End of the Twentieth Century.* New York: Scribner, 1994.

POPE, JAMES GRAY. "Republican Moments: The Role of Direct Popular Power in the American Constitutional Order." *University of Pennsylvania Law Review* 139 (1990): 287–368.

SULLIVAN, KATHLEEN M. "Foreward: The Justices of Rules and Standards." *Harvard Law Review* 106 (1992): 24–123.

Blake M. Cornish

Lawmaking, Judicial

Most people would probably maintain that the U.S. federal government has become, over the years, significantly more powerful than any state or the states as a whole. Most people would probably also say that the powers of the American president (and many state governors) have grown at the expense of the U.S. Congress (or the state legislatures). Virtually no one would argue that the U.S. judiciary or the state judiciaries are more powerful than one or both of the other two branches, the executive and the legislative branches. Nevertheless, the importance of the state courts should not be overlooked or underestimated.

First, most U.S. citizens are more likely to come into direct and repeated contact with a state (or local) officer than a federal officer (except perhaps someone in the U.S. postal service). And that state officer is more likely to be an administrative officer of the judiciary (a police officer, prosecuting attorney, or public defender) or a member of the judiciary (a clerk or judge) than a governor, some other administrative officer, or legislative aide.

Second, because of the doctrine of judicial review, first enunciated by Chief Justice John Marshall of the U.S. Supreme Court in the case of *Marbury* v. *Madison* in 1803, all courts, federal and state, have the power to declare the law of any legislature, and actions carried out by any federal or state officer, to be contrary to the Constitution (i.e., to be unconstitutional) and thus null and void. Hence, in a very important sense, in the United States and each state, "law is what the judges say it is."

Third, for a variety of structural and political reasons, legislators and executives at both levels of government in the United States have increasingly left the most difficult policy decisions up to the courts, so that in controversial matters, public policy is made by judges, not by state legislatures or the U.S. Congress, or by presidential or gubernatorial decree. This is often decried by political commentators as inappropriate "judicial activism," and frequently denied by judges who hide behind a cloak of conservatism and legal precedence. However, it does seem to be the case that judges as a whole exercise a rather impressive degree of leadership on substantive issues within the American system.

Finally, more and more matters once left to individual discretion or private resolution have been criminalized or otherwise made justiciable. The caseloads of almost all courts have risen enormously—far faster than the number of courts and judges available to promptly resolve the conflicts fully and equitably. Allegedly in the interest of achieving fairness and decisional predictability and conformity, Congress and most legislatures also recently reduced the discretion of judges. They now require judges to hear cases that might otherwise be dismissed, and to reach specified decisions (often with specified sentences) even if a judge might prefer a different outcome in a specific case. This has been especially true of drug-related cases since the 1980s. Many criminal courts are severely backlogged as a consequence. Similarly, the increase of civil litigation means that civil courts (which deal with noncriminal conflicts between individuals or corporations) are ever more seriously backlogged.

At the same time, new technologies have emerged that are changing the way business, commerce, entertainment, religion, and all other facets of daily life are conducted. With varying degrees of enthusiasm and funding, most courts also are using new technologies in all aspects of judicial administration and decision making.

As the percentage of minorities increases in the United States and elsewhere, and as these minorities begin to insist that judicial procedures and principles follow their traditions rather than those of the historically dominant culture, choice and diversity might become more typical of the judiciary of the future than it ever was in the courts of the states. This possibility is even greater given the rising claims of the indigenous peoples of the American states.

The judicial overload and decreased relative or real funding on the one hand and the growth of new technologies and the movement for alternative dispute resolution techniques on the other is altering the judicial system. The combined effect of these developments led almost all state judiciaries during the 1980s and '90s to engage in a series of future-oriented activities aimed at more or less completely "reinventing justice" in the United States.

Taking into account the continuation of past and present trends and challenges, and the active attempts by judiciaries and members of the public generally to design new (or reinstate old) systems of conflict resolution, one can anticipate several possible future courses of development for state courts in the United States. Four of these alternatives follow:

1. *Generic justice.* The antigovernment political climate continues, even as the demand for judicial services continues to increase along with the crime rate. At the same time, the public continues to criticize all branches of government, in-

cluding the courts, and refuses to pay sufficient taxes for the services it demands. Thus, traditional guarantees of due process of law diminish (especially for the poor), and most decisions are reached in a cookie-cutter, assembly-line fashion.

2. *Judicial leadership.* The incorporation of humane, consumer-sensitive, integrated, and future-oriented methods and procedures into the administration of justice enables the formal system to regain the confidence of the public, and to settle all issues brought before it in a timely and fair manner.

3. *The multidoor dispute-resolution facility.* The formal judiciary acknowledges and/or embraces many different forms of dispute resolution, with the present monopolistic system being but one choice contestants can make in order to settle their disputes.

4. *The global virtual courthouse.* Modern and emerging communications technologies break down the barriers of time and space so that people no longer need to meet at a specific day, hour, and place to settle their disputes. Moreover, local, state, and national judiciaries give way to global dispute-resolution procedures necessary for the global world of tomorrow.

Any one of these four alternatives is not likely to encompass the totality of the future American state judiciary. Parts of each will combine with problems, opportunities, and visions as yet unforeseen to form the likely components of the American state courts of the future.

See also CRIMINAL JUSTICE; JUDICIAL REFORM; LAW OF THE LAND; LAWYERS AND THE LEGAL PROFESSION.

BIBLIOGRAPHY

DATOR, JAMES A. "The Dancing Judicial Zen Masters." *Technological Forecasting and Social Change* 46/1 (May 1994): 59–70.

DATOR, JAMES A., and RODGERS, SHARON. *Alternative Futures for the State Courts of 2020.* Chicago: State Justice Institute and the American Judicature Society, 1991.

INAYATULLAH, SOHAIL, ed. "The Futures of State Courts." Two entire issues of *Futures Research Quarterly* 9/4 (Winter 1993); 10/1 (Spring 1994).

KATSH, M. ETHAN. *Electronic Media and the Transformation of Law.* New York: Oxford University Press, 1989.

———. *Law in a Digital World.* New York: Oxford University Press, 1995.

SCHULTZ, WENDY, et al. *Reinventing Courts for the Twenty-first Century: Designing a Vision Process.* Williamsburg, VA: National Center for State Courts, 1993.

James A. Dator

Laws, Evolution of

Change is relentless and never stops. Society is constantly evolving and changing so that final fashioning of laws is simply not possible. Change assumes a ceaseless tinkering, an all-encompassing discontent with things as they are. The underlying assumption is that humans will always attempt to perfect their affairs incrementally. These assumptions entail a perpetual process of change and adaptation to evolving new circumstances.

Each new social milieu prompts new policies or revisions of previous ones. Finding the optimum balance in response to a dynamic environment requires constant adjustment and readjustment. Regulatory developments of all kinds are never-ending.

Great movements championing change alternate with periods of relative decline and quiescence. Even as basic a quest as equality comes to the fore only intermittently as injustices gather and the number of concerned persons increases. Equality is the driving force behind many ongoing quests to secure realization of the ideal society. Egalitarian quests of all kinds are always with us—movements for women's rights, minority rights, and the like will never disappear until the disparities are totally rectified and balanced. The stark reality is that humans never will fully or finally achieve perfectly balanced equality. Equality is an abstract and idealistic goal at odds with practical human experience. Furthermore, humans are destined to achieve different levels of attainment. There always will be superachievers and underachievers, haves and have-nots, geniuses and idiots, beautiful as well as ugly persons, and so on ad infinitum. Given the elusive nature of absolutes, these issues are perpetually destined to confront and confound society.

The episodic periodicity with which issues recur manifests itself in lawmaking. Laws are little more than institutional propositions that continuously are expanded to cope with life's myriad problems as they become bigger, more complicated, more technical, and so on. The larger and more complicated society becomes, there is inevitably more opportunity for variant forms of human interaction and conflict. Laws are devised to redress and minimize these conflicts.

Laws are a means for containing and institutionalizing public policy confrontations and a mechanism for implementing orderly transitions. A well-ordered and predictable society depends on rules of law as a buffer against capricious acts. Lawmaking has an evolutionary character based on its ability to re-

spond to changing circumstances. Such responses are predictable and consequently enable us to predict stages of legal development.

Environmental protection, for example, is no recent phenomenon. It evolved over a very long period of time. Fundamental philosophical and ideological concepts such as the "conservation ethic" have persisted over thousands of years. Such concerns throughout all of recorded history, up to and including contemporary times, become the subject of legislative tinkering.

Finally, we must recognize that there are no permanent solutions to society's problems. The process of change and adaptation to new circumstances is never-ending. Therefore, from this perspective we need to recognize that humanity's work is never finished. Public policy, correspondingly, is in a constant state of flux as it continually responds to altered social circumstances.

Evolutionary and devolutionary trends, such as the emergence and demise (life cycle) of social phenomena, provide a useful framework to gauge the future. These dynamics are useful in plotting the trend and direction of impending change. The process involves a kind of "staging." The staging advances in a manner similar to an unfolding set of stairs. The law establishes norms intended to constrain the excesses of human behavior that emerge from time to time. Eventually, however, the law is overtaken by events. Ingenious humans always find a way around the law. Or, structural changes introduced by new technologies give rise to a series of problems that prompt an updated response to the old circumstance. The solutions, usually in the form of a new law or regulation (although it may come about by voluntary act, custom, or some other less formal mechanism), involves the next step upward. Often remaining at a plateau for some time, there usually appears a jolt upward to the next step as the new rule of law is imposed.

Public policy issues, as they are taken up, often are considered as if they are new. Nothing could be further from the truth. There is a certain timelessness about issues. They recur again and again.

The fact is that great issues in history—such as economic equality, justice, environmental improvement, indeed, all progress, have persisted since time immemorial. Ideal philosophical concepts governing social behavior never are fully or finally realized. Detailed refinements, extensions, exceptions, and improvements of all other types continue to emerge. In relentless procession the "filigree" of an issue is fully fashioned. Basic issues tend to receive sporadic bursts of attention.

Philosophical roots of many contemporary issues can be traced all the way back to the very beginnings of recorded history. Certain age-old aspirations of humanity illuminate basic, underlying currents in ongoing public policy change. Following is a random list of sociopolitical issues, policies, and programs that date back as long as 4,000 years. Actual rhetoric surrounding debate on these issues and the statements of intended results had a familiar ring then as they have now. This tabulation strives to corroborate the conclusion that most every contemporary problem one can imagine has been and probably always will be around. They are, therefore, timeless issues.

- Taxes first imposed in Sumer, c. 3000 B.C.
- Price regulation dating back to Hittite Kingdom, c. 1300 B.C.
- Strikes used as an economic weapon to achieve concessions, Rome, 494 B.C.
- Virtually parroting today's key policy concerns, Marcus Cicero, Roman statesman and writer (106–43 B.C.), stated: "The . . . budget must be balanced. The . . . treasury should be filled. Government indebtedness must be reduced. The arrogance of the authorities must be moderated and controlled. The people should learn to work again, instead of living off the public dole."
- Titus Livius (Livy), Roman historian (c. 59 B.C.–A.D. 17), objected to greedy self-indulgence, moral rot, failure to save income, and slipping standards of conduct.
- Free food for the poor first provided by P. Claudius, Rome, 58 B.C.
- Poor aid provided by compulsory use of tithes, King Ethelred, England, A.D.1014.
- Poor law promulgated by English Parliament, A.D. 1388.
- Law to repress begging, English Parliament, A.D. 1536.
- Socrates (500–450 B.C.), Athenian philosopher, assailed earlier generations for destroying the forests and landscape.
- Graffiti adorned town walls in Pompeii prior to eruption of Mount Vesuvius in A.D. 79.
- Julius Caesar (45 B.C.), frustrated with traffic congestion, dust, and noise, banned all wheeled vehicles from Rome during daylight hours.
- Rebelling against willy-nilly town streets in Mohenjo-Daro, the area was laid out gridiron fashion, c. 2513 B.C.
- Sesotris II (1887–1849 B.C.), Egypt, was criticized for constructing mass transportation links (canals along the Nile).

- Building extensive parks under the rule of Hammurabi, king of Babylonia, was both praised and condemned, c. 1758 B.C.
- Corrupting youth of Athens was the charge leading to Socrates' death, c. 399 B.C.
- Aristotle (384–322 B.C.) criticized young people as thoughtless, unmindful of parents, and unruly in school.
- Tuition fees for students established, Sumer, 2500 B.C.
- State control of education established, Athens, 500 B.C.
- State-supported schools inaugurated by Julius Caesar, Rome, 46 B.C.
- Teachers licensed by Emperor Julian, Rome, A.D. 362.
- State-supported university established by Emperor Theodosius, Constantinople, A.D. 410.
- Written code of law established, Sumer, 2100 B.C.
- Compensation for bodily injuries written into legal texts by Ur-Namnu, king of Ur (Mesopotamia), c. 2100 B.C.
- Code of law (282 paragraphs long) published by Hammurabi, king of Babylonia, c. 1758 B.C.
- Xenophon (c. 430–354 B.C.), Greek historian, complained of litigiousness clogging the courts.
- Systematizing civil service by ordering into nine ranks undertaken, China, c. 221 B.C.
- Fed up with nepotism, court intrigue, and incompetence, competitive written civil-service exams were inaugurated, China, c. 200 B.C.
- Weights and measures standards established, Sumer, 3000 B.C.
- Racial equality (including intermarriage among Greeks, Macedonians, and Persians) decreed by Alexander the Great, 325–323 B.C.
- Divorce law, Babylon, Code of Hammurabi, 1800 B.C.
- Women's right to divorce (including recoupment of her property) accorded in Minoan Code, c. 1500 B.C.
- Adoption of children begun, Sumer, 1800 B.C.
- Prostitution regulated, Sumer, 1950 B.C.

This list, even though a bit wearying, has been gleaned from among great and small issues. The distinguished philosopher George Santayana (1863–1952) gave us good reason to heed previous trials and tribulations by noting: "Those who do not learn from history are condemned to repeat it." The Bible put it another way: "There is no new thing under the sun." (Ecclesiastes 1:9).

See also CONTINUITY AND DISCONTINUITY; ETHICS; FOOD LAWS; LAW OF THE LAND; PUBLIC POLICY

CHANGE; SOCIAL INVENTIONS; SOCIAL AND PO-
LITICAL EVOLUTION.

BIBLIOGRAPHY

ASIMOV, ISAAC. *Asimov's Chronology of the World: The History of the World From the Big Bang to Modern Times.* New York: HarperCollins, 1991.

CARRUTH, GORTON. *The Encyclopedia of American Facts and Dates*, 8th ed. New York: Harper & Row, 1987.

GOLDBERG, M. HIRSCH. *The Blunder Book: Colossal Errors, Minor Mistakes, and Surprising Slipups That Have Changed the Course of History.* New York: Quill/William Morrow, 1984.

ROBERTSON, PATRICK. *The Book of Firsts.* New York: Bramhall House, 1982.

URDAND, LAURENCE, ed. *The Timetables of American History.* New York: Simon & Schuster, 1981.

Graham T. T. Molitor

Lawyers and the Legal Profession

The law—the agreed-upon framework for acceptable human and organizational relations—will continue to evolve in scope and complexity at a dizzying speed during the next thirty to fifty years. Lawyers as counselors, advocates, and judges will be the ones to interpret, apply, and test the forces governing those fast-evolving relationships. Further, to a significant extent, it will be lawyers themselves as legislators who shape the driving forces.

By the year 2005 there will be no more debate over whether the United States has too many lawyers (especially as compared with Asian countries). The future will show that the United States was merely setting the trend for handling complex relationships. Other countries will follow, as homogeneous populations become more multicultural and international transactions increase. Thus, "lawyering" will continue to be a growth profession throughout the next century.

The Present

The number of lawyers in the United States has been increasing for more than forty years, in both constant numbers and as a ratio of lawyers to the entire population. The American Bar Association and its associated American Bar Foundation report the following statistics and projections:

TABLE 1. Numbers and Ratios of Lawyers in the United States

Year	No. of Lawyers	People/per Lawyer
1951	221,605	695/1
1960	285,933	627/1
1971	355,242	418/1
1980	542,205	403/1
1985	655,191	360/1
1988	723,189	340/1
1991	805,872	313/1
1995	896,172	290/1
1999	984,843	271/1
2000	1,005,842	267/1

In the federal trial courts, civil case filings increased 1,424 percent between 1904 and 1994, with most of that growth after 1960; criminal cases increased only 157 percent during that period, but they became much more difficult to prosecute and defend; hence, they occupy a considerably higher proportion of court time. As of 1992, for example, most federal trial courts devoted more than 50 percent of their trial dockets to criminal cases. By 1994, drug offenses accounted for 40 percent of the criminal filings. The Judicial Conference of the United States reports historical data and projections for U.S. District Courts, which are the federal trial courts of general jurisdiction (and do not include bankruptcy and other specialized courts) as shown in Table 2 below.

The most remarkable growth has occurred in the federal courts of appeals, which have experienced enormous increases generally and in appeals by prisoners seeking to reopen their cases as shown in Table 3 on the next page.

The number of federal judges in District Courts and courts of general appeal have continued to

TABLE 2. Cases Begun in U.S. District Courts

(12-Month Periods Ending June 30)

Year	Criminal Cases	Civil Cases
1940	33,401	34,734
1950	36,383	54,622
1960	28,137	59,284
1970	38,102	87,321
1980	27,968	168,789
1990	46,530	217,879
1994	44,919	235,996
2000	51,600	334,600
2010	66,000	576,500
2020	89,400	1,019,900

TABLE 3. Actual and Projected Appeals Filed In
U.S. Courts of Appeals

(12-Month Periods Ending June 30)

Year	Total Appeals	Criminal Appeals	Prisoner Petitions	Other Appeals
1940	3,505	260	65	3,180
1950	2,830	308	286	2,236
1960	3,899	623	290	2,986
1970	11,662	2,660	2,440	6,562
1980	23,200	4,405	3,675	15,120
1990	40,898	9,493	9,941	21,464
1994	48,815	11,052	12,772	24,991
2000	84,800	11,600	35,500	37,700
2010	171,600	16,000	81,900	73,700
2020	325,100	22,300	155,900	146,900

increase over the years, but less so than their case
loads, as the Judicial Conference data in Table 4
below demonstrate.

The Future

Congress will soon realize that it cannot allow the
federal court system to continue to grow at the current (and projected) rate. Alone the appointment
and confirmation process for thousands of judges
would be unworkable. By the year 2000, Congress
will have begun in earnest the difficult task of dismantling the federal court battleships and converting them to sleek missile carriers with highly defined missions. This will require state courts and
private dispute resolution systems to make up the
difference in criminal and civil cases.

TABLE 4. Federal Appellate and District Court
Judgeships

(Excluding the Specialized Federal
Circuit Court of Appeals)

Year	Appeals Court Judges	District (Trial) Judges
1940	57	191
1950	65	224
1960	68	245
1970	97	401
1980	132	516
1990	156	575
1994	167	649
2000	430	940
2010	840	1,510
2020	1,580	2,530

By 2010 Congress will have virtually eliminated
so-called general diversity jurisdiction, under
which a citizen of one state may sue a citizen of another in federal court for violation of state law.
Also by that time, the federal trial courts no longer
will be swamped by drug "busts" and other local
crime prosecutions. These courts primarily will be
venues for adjudicating matters of clear national
interest. The state and local courts will have to absorb the rest of the criminal activity, perhaps with
federal monetary assistance.

The current trend toward resolving disputes outside the courts will continue at a rapid pace in federal and state jurisdictions. By 2010, virtually all
courts will require that certain types of civil cases
undergo pre-trial alternative dispute resolution
(ADR) efforts before experienced "neutrals," who
will try to facilitate settlement through mediation.

By 2010, ADR will be the rule and litigation in
court the exception for civil cases. Competitive corporations will set up private judicial systems, with
their own professional judges and juries who will
adjudicate, on a confidential basis, controversies between competitors. ADR in the form of private, confidential arbitration will be the only form of individual relief for many disputes between employees and
employers and buyers and sellers. There will be virtually no way to appeal such decisions to any court.

By 2020, the trial of cases before federal, state,
or local government judges will in large part be
"pre-packaged." The process will be similar to the
"video trials" used in some midwestern courts
today, but the recording medium and presentations
will be much more advanced than the relatively
crude video tape presentations now made in these
courts. In video trials the entire trial will be finished and edited before the jury is selected and
seated. The jury will view the trial as it would an
instructional film and then try to reach a verdict.

A trial judge need not be present while video
cases are being presented to a jury, but he or she
could be available for unusual situations. Once the
judge or jury has seen the trial and is in the process
of trying to reach a decision or verdict, the video
record, which would include readable versions of
all written exhibits, will be made available to the
factfinder(s). The video record will be accessible
randomly and quickly, since it will contain its own
self-made index. Thus, a jury could call up a particular document and re-read it, see and listen to a
particular witness again, or accumulate and review
all evidence on a particular point.

By 2020, most exhibits and records at all levels of
adjudication will be submitted on data discs or cells,

instead of bulky paper. The new media will allow lawyers and decision makers instant access to information when they need it. Texts of legal authorities will be implanted in the cyberbriefs and cybermemoranda submitted to decision makers to allow them to create a computer window, call up, and review a cited court decision or statute at any point.

By 2020, most three-dimensional evidence will be accessible as well through video discs or cells and be capable of presentation through holographic- and virtual-reality-like presentations. Thus, a jury could be invited to "walk through" the scene of the crime or accident, rather than merely look at a photograph. Indeed, there will be computer animations and recreations designed to allow jurors to view and experience (to a degree) what happened.

See also CRIMINAL JUSTICE; JUDICIAL REFORM; LAW OF THE LAND; LAWMAKING, JUDICIAL; LAWS, EVOLUTION OF.

BIBLIOGRAPHY

BENSON, BRUCE L. *The Enterprise of Law: Justice Without the State.* San Francisco, CA: Pacific Research Institute for Public Policy, 1990.

HUBER, PETER W. *The Legal Revolution and Its Consequences.* New York: Basic Books, 1988.

KAIRYS, DAVID, ed. *The Politics of Law: A Progressive Critique.* New York: Pantheon Books, 1990.

LAMM, RICHARD D. "Lawyers and Lawyering: The Legal System and Its Cost to American Society." *Vital Speeches of the Day* 55/7 (January 15, 1989).

Richard J. Leighton

Leadership

There is not much written about leadership in the future. Out of a thousand books on leadership, only a dozen project leadership thought and practice into the future. Eight of them are discussed here.

James MacGregor Burns (1978) initiated the idea that the old models of leadership may be inadequate for the future, and he developed a theory of transformational leadership that required "leaders and followers raise one another to higher levels of motivation and morality" (p. 20). Burns also insisted that leadership produce "real, intended change" (p. 461) through a collective, dissensual process that develops mutual goals. Burns's work is viewed by many as the beginning of a new theory of leadership.

James M. Kouzes and Barry Z. Posner followed up their previous work on leadership with a book on leadership and credibility (1993). Defining leadership as "a reciprocal relationship between those who choose to lead and those who decide to follow" (p. 1), the authors argued that credibility will be the most crucial ingredient in leadership relationships in the future. Their credibility model includes six practices: (1) discovering your self, (2) appreciating constituents, (3) affirming shared values, (4) developing capacity, (5) serving a purpose, and (6) sustaining hope (p. 51). Kouzes and Posner believe that closing the credibility gap is the key to building and sustaining effective leadership relationships in the organizations of the future.

Feminist writers often call for a new paradigm of leadership for the future, an overarching view of leadership that is fundamentally different from the male models of leadership that dominated the twentieth century. Helen S. Astin and Carole Leland's work (1990) is perhaps the best example of a feminist perspective on leadership in the future. "Leadership is a process by which members of a group are empowered to work together synergistically toward a common goal or vision that will create change, transform institutions, and thus improve the quality of life" (p. 8). Throughout the book, the authors viewed leadership as a process of social change to improve the human condition. Theirs is a constructionist perspective with a generous portion of adult development to make the needed connections between research and practice.

Burt Nanus, the futurist turned leadership expert, wrote two books after his successful collaboration with Bennis in 1985. *The Leader's Edge* (1989) develops the notion of the futures-creative leader, who must develop seven megaskills, "competencies [that] are needed to exercise effective leadership in the new age" (p. 8). In his 1992 book *Visionary Leadership*, Nanus argued that twenty-first-century organizations require visionary leaders, and the book gives detailed steps for vision making.

The political mindset has made inroads into a futurist understanding of leadership. Heifetz's (1994) prescriptive understanding of leadership is the mobilizing of people and communities to do adaptive work, that is, to tackle the tough problems that must be solved in a society. While Heifetz's view of leadership has been influenced by psychology, his concept of leadership is primarily about the politics of authority and influence among people who want to solve difficult problems in a democratic society.

Joseph C. Rost (1991) constructed a prescriptive definition of leadership, one that embodies a postindustrial paradigm of leadership for the twenty-first century. "Leadership is an influence relationship among leaders and followers who intend real changes that reflect their mutual purposes" (p. 102).

Robert E. Kelley (1992) critiqued the myth of leadership for concentrating only on the leader. His book on followership looks to the future where exemplary followers will be seen as vital to the leadership process as leaders. Kelley details the skills and styles of followers and calls upon scholars and practitioners to balance the myth of leadership with the reality of followership.

In summary, there are a few scholars who are agitating for a new understanding of leadership more in tune with a postindustrial world view, but these voices have not yet become the majority view.

See also AGENTS OF CHANGE; ARTIFICIAL INTELLIGENCE; BUSINESS GOVERNANCE; CIVIL PROTEST; CONSCIOUS EVOLUTION; GOVERNANCE; MANAGEMENT; PACESETTER GOVERNMENTS; PARTICIPATIVE MANAGEMENT; PLURALISM; POLITICAL PARTIES; PUBLIC OPINION POLLS; RECORD SETTING; STRATEGIC PLANNING.

BIBLIOGRAPHY

ASTIN, HELEN S., and LELAND, CAROLE. *Women of Influence, Women of Vision*. San Francisco: Jossey-Bass, 1991.

BURNS, JAMES MACGREGOR. *Leadership*. New York: Harper & Row, 1978.

HEIFETZ, RONALD A. *Leadership without Easy Answers*. Cambridge, MA: Harvard University Press, 1994.

KELLEY, ROBERT E. *The Power of Followership*. New York: Doubleday, 1992.

KOUZES, JAMES M., and POSNER, BARRY Z. *Credibility*. San Francisco: Jossey-Bass, 1993.

NANUS, BURT. *The Leader's Edge*. Chicago: Contemporary Books, 1989.

———. *Visionary Leadership*. San Francisco: Jossey-Bass, 1992.

ROST, JOSEPH C. *Leadership for the Twenty-First Century*. New York: Praeger, 1991.

Joseph C. Rost

Legal Profession.

See LAWYERS AND LEGAL PROFESSION.

Legislative and Parliamentary Systems

Let us begin by imagining what a session of the U.S. House of Representatives might be like in decades to come. The Speaker of the House enters and takes the chair. He leads the Pledge of Allegiance. There is no chaplain present and no opening prayer. "In God We Trust" has been removed from above the rostrum.

The Speaker announces the consideration of the first bill: the federal government will give every newborn child a computer. It will be paid for by a new voluntary tax on the number of cable channels received in each home. An immediate vote is declared. There is no debate. The members of the House have already studied the issue using the vast resources of a worldwide database. The Library of Congress has compiled a list of pros and cons on the bill, complete with environmental and economic impact studies.

The members have digested these reports off their computer screens at home. In fact, there are few members even present in the chamber. Most are at home connected by a secure fiber-optic network. There are no staffers around either. The advocates of reducing staffs have succeeded beyond their wildest dreams. All committees and subcommittees are gone. The Library of Congress does all the research work and the government agencies solve all the constituent problems. The General Accounting Office and the Office of Technology Assessment have been discontinued.

No one has lobbied members on the issue. All lobbyists have been abolished. And all the members are freshmen—the term-limit advocates have won out.

The Speaker types his security code on his key pad to activate the voting machine. Members sitting at home push a button to record their votes. The Speaker asks the computer for the results. A voice-activated machine replies in a seemingly human voice: "The bill passes 435 to 0." The House adjourns.

Is this too far-fetched a scenario?

First, there is the matter of the chaplain and the opening prayer. For decades, this practice has been under attack. Those who want God out of every public ceremony have tried to abolish it. After the Supreme Court eliminated prayer in schools, the then-speaker, John McCormack, retaliated. There was a row of decorative brass stars above the rostrum. McCormack had the center ones replaced with the words "In God We Trust," declaring "This is one place where God will be present."

Congressional staff size became an issue in the 1970s when the Democrats, having lost the White House, found themselves literally outmanned by an administration that tried to preempt even the legislative process. Divided government did not mean surrender to the executive branch, congressional Democrats argued. Weren't the separate branches of government coequal? And, if they were, how many computers did the executive branch have and how many did Congress have. In an effort to level the playing field, staff and computer capacity multiplied, and the Congress felt justified. The rapid growth presented an easy target for critics of Congress, particularly by the Republicans and particularly by advocates of a strong executive.

What does the future hold? With an increasingly complex society and the federal government becoming more involved in its citizens' lives, an increase in staff for Congress is more likely than a decrease. Although there are fewer federal dollars to be spent, Congress nonetheless takes its oversight responsibility seriously and requires staff to do it.

Lobbyists are another growth occupation. As government swelled and the subjects it addressed became more intricate, experts—outside as well as inside—proliferated. Congressmen and their staff sought information about companies and their products that were changing the lives of Americans.

Industry was convinced, too, that representation in Washington was important because new federal regulations could be affected, and contracts could be won. Perhaps most important to the growth in the ranks of lobbyists, a company could help itself in Congress as well as with the administration. Divided government had emboldened the legislative branch to become a player in an area previously ceded to the executive.

Efforts to reduce the lobbying ranks took the form of limiting the activity of government workers, congressional and executive branch alike. The so-called revolving door provision prohibited lobbying one's colleagues for a specified time after moving to the private sector.

Looking to the future, lobbyists argue that they have the same constitutional right to petition the government as is granted to any citizen or group of citizens. Some further narrowing of their right is probable, but the basic right will be preserved.

Aside from formal lobbying, the United States has seen the perfection of another form of influencing the government—single-issue lobbying. A group of like-minded citizens forms around one issue. They organize, pressure their elected officials to agree with them, and threaten defeat to those who do not comply. The elected officials who do not acquiesce then try to deflect the attention from the issue by stressing other parts of their record and hoping for the best.

These single-issue groups have already become an important part of the electoral process and will likely become more so. Television lends itself to coverage of those groups that devise attention-getting gimmicks and tactics. More television in the future means more opportunity for these groups to make an impact on policy making.

If there has been any change in the Congress, it has been in the area of ethics. The future holds even more opportunity, and inevitability.

Former Speaker of the House "Tip" O'Neill preached in the 1980s that "the ethics of politics has changed." By this he meant that the closer media scrutiny of the private lives of politicians and other public figures had indelibly changed the basic machinery of governance. It was no longer possible to practice "business as usual." Increased press scrutiny and the drawing of contrasting moral values more sharply contributed to the change.

Many politicians did not understand what was happening—and they were defeated. Others changed with the times and survived. This trend is likely to continue. Lessons are being learned at the ballot box, and overall the system seems to be improving.

The big question for the Congress in the future is whether it can survive such "purification" and still perform its function of serving the people. Retention of the two-year term in the House of Representatives would ensure this. The Founding Fathers created the shortest term of any elected office in the United States to keep the representatives accountable to the people. They were not trying to fashion the most efficient form of government, only the freest. The future Congress will be measured by that standard.

See also DEMOCRATIC PROCESS; EXECUTIVE BRANCH; EXECUTIVE BRANCH: THE PRESIDENCY; GOVERNANCE; GOVERNMENT ORGANIZATION; JUDICIAL REFORM; LAWMAKING, JUDICIAL; LAW OF THE LAND; LAWS, EVOLUTION OF;

BIBLIOGRAPHY

AYDELOTTE, WILLIAM O. *History of Parliamentary Behavior.* Princeton, NJ: Princeton University Press, 1977.
CALLAHAN, DANIEL, et al. *Congress and the Media: The Ethical Connection.* Briarcliff Manor, NY: Hastings Center, 1985.
GROSS, BERTRAM, and SCHNEIER, EDWARD V. *Congress Today.* New York: St. Martin's Press, 1993.
HAYES, MICHAEL T. *Lobbyists and Legislators: A Theory of Political Markets.* New Brunswick, NJ: Rutgers University Press, 1984.

NORTON, PHILIP, ed. *Legislatures.* New York: Oxford University Press, 1990.

TRUMAN, DAVID B., ed. *Congress and America's Future.* New York: American Assembly/Columbia University, 1973.

Gary Hymel

Leisure Time

Since the 1962 publication of Sebastian de Grazia's *Of Time, Work, and Leisure,* leisure and free time are generally regarded as quite separable and different. Free time is that residual of time not required by work, maintenance of one's person and property, or compelled by some external force or need. Free time is a quantitative commodity we measure with clocks and calendars. Leisure has philosophical and spiritual dimensions clocks cannot measure. Since nearly all conversational and mass-media references to leisure relate to free time, it seems appropriate to address that first.

For the past several decades there has been a widespread belief that free time has been increasing steadily due to efficiency, productivity, labor-saving devices, and unprecedented increases in affluence and general welfare. However, that has not gone undisputed. The reduction in working hours per week from about seventy in 1850 to about forty in 1950 was, and is, de Grazia argued, largely illusory. In 1971, Swedish economist Staffan Linder argued in *The Harried Leisure Class* that increases in productivity and material wealth resulted in time becoming increasingly scarce. More recently, Harvard economist Juliet Schor's *The Overworked American: The Unexpected Decline of Leisure* (1991) became a bestseller. It reinforced both the perception people repeatedly voice of never having enough time and opinion poll reports that the workweek was increasing. Results of time-diary studies do not, however, confirm reports of a lengthened workweek during the past decade or so. Yet if the workweek is not longer than two decades ago, it is widely perceived as being so.

On other matters there is at least general agreement. Over the past 150 years, much free time has been gained via later entry into the labor force, life-expectancy increases resulting in ten to fifteen years of retirement, a shorter workweek, more holidays, and longer vacations. There is also widespread agreement that reduced hours in the workweek and work year do not necessarily translate into more free time. No one defines free time as the hours spent commuting or keeping up with increasingly rapid technological, organizational, and social change. Even "working out" is considered obligatory by many, and thus regarded as work.

The pace of work has also changed; thus, there is more stress than was the case historically. Further, the growth in labor force participation by women might lead one to conclude that there is much more work than ever before.

There is also general agreement that the workweek has not changed much since the 1950s; it has hovered between forty and forty-five hours per week. But averages may mask as much as they reveal. Hours of work per week and per year vary extensively by occupations and individuals, hours seldom reflect preferences, and quantitative measures equate migrant workers picking crops for an hour with millionaires attending a one-hour board meeting. Quite remarkable differences do not appear in our calculations. One such difference is that the potential for free time within working hours is completely masked by quantitative measures.

Despite our recent history, there are *a priori* grounds for projecting there will be more free time in the future. Whether that is chosen or imposed, and therefore realized as leisure or idleness, is at the center of our hopes and fears about the future. Authors of utopian literature have been consistent in often describing a workweek of twenty hours. Juliet Schor (1991) observed that had we been content with the standard of living of 1948, we would have a workweek of twenty hours, or six months' vacation per year, or every other year off, with pay. J. M. Keynes, in an essay published in 1930, proposed the workweek in 2030 could be fifteen hours per week, which would include a few hours we work on behalf of others.

As work becomes further deskilled, increasing numbers of workers, concluding that their jobs are not their lives, seek rewards less exclusively in work and more inclusively in all areas of life. As both Adam Smith and Karl Marx argued, the full realization of one's humanity, civility, and talent will most likely occur outside of work in time freed from work by increased productivity. "The Society for the Reduction of Human Labor" may be less quixotic than superficial appraisals suggest.

More and more people, pollsters find, would prefer to work fewer hours, even if it meant giving up some or all of the income proportionate to the reduced hours. More people identify themselves by their avocations: increasing numbers are intentionally downwardly mobile, trading off more material goods for more free time. Thus, there are a number of indicators that free time will, for that reason, increase. This portends free time realized as leisure engagements chosen because they are pleasing, intrinsically rewarding, and intuitively worthwhile. Those finding little real value in their work will continue to look for it in free time.

Alternatively, imposed idleness, unemployment and insufficient means for modest but dignified living, is a specter that haunts us when economies, increasingly global in nature, falter. The unemployed in what is now a global labor force number nearly 800 million people (Barnet, 1993). The depressing effect on wages of those in mature economies has been evident and acknowledged. The effect on rates and hours of employment is increasingly evident as well. About twice as many people work for Manpower, Inc., a temporary service agency, as for General Motors. From that and other, similar data spring our concern about the loss of "real" jobs.

The information age and the global economy are not producing jobs, at least not in the United States, Canada, and other mature, Western economies (Barnet, 1993). Japan, whose workers have the world's longest workweek and year among the developed countries, is trying diligently to reduce work hours. Political parties of both the left and right in Germany and France have recently touted the four day, thirty- to thirty-two-hour workweek as a solution to intransigent unemployment.

Television and its elaborations in multiple forms are likely to continue absorbing the lion's share of people's free time. They are comparatively inexpensive measured on a per hour basis, are convenient, and make few demands. Virtual reality and a virtually endless variety of content and interaction make them increasingly seductive, even if, as many observe, also escapist and debilitating.

Further growth in high-risk, or at least high-thrill and high-adventure activities, can also be expected. Some of this may be attributed to boredom due to unchallenging work, some to the quest for identity, some to the saturation of those slightly tamer places and activities of yesterday's adventurers.

There is a growing appreciation of leisure as intrinsically rewarding and intuitively worthwhile, which offers a source of meaning, purpose, and belongingness at all levels. Such leisure activity—including the arts, sports, hobbies, and volunteer services—is characterized by love and absorption so complete as to transcend the spatial and temporal bounds of here and now. Surgeons, chess players, dancers, journalists all experience what has been labeled "flow," otherwise described as peak or optimal experience. "Serious leisure" engaged in by dedicated amateurs will continue to grow rapidly.

Thus far, there is more hope than evidence that the individualism of recent decades has run its course and increasing amounts of free time will be devoted to reconstituting those convivial institutions of family, neighborhood, and community. Interesting evidence is mounting that peak or optimal experiences, which produce "flow," and voluntary-service activities, which produce a sense of contributing and making a difference, are healthy. Work that is stressful, unchallenging, or devoid of intrinsic worth, is unhealthy. And television, we know, is linked not only to obesity and lethargy but also to asocial, violent activity.

In short, new conditions and strong forces are imposing free time in the form of unemployment and underemployment. Much of our use of that time will remain passive and routine, but we are learning that leisure can be found in more ways and places than heretofore realized. Those who find too little meaning in work will choose leisure when they can. Imposed free time used in largely escapist fashion will remain the rule, but choosing leisure for meaning and intrinsic worth will become less the exception. Education and the distribution of jobs and income will determine how much idleness or leisure emerge. The political and economic dimensions of the amount and distribution of free time are becoming more apparent. This trend will continue in the years to come.

See also FREE TIME; GAMBLING; INTERACTIVE ENTERTAINMENT; OUTDOOR RECREATION AND LEISURE PURSUITS; SPORTS AND ACTIVITIES, SPECTATOR; SPORTS AND GAMES, COMPETITIVE; THEME PARKS AND ORGANIZED ATTRACTIONS; TOURISM.

BIBLIOGRAPHY

BARNET, RICHARD J. "The End of Jobs." *Harper's* 287 (September 1993): 47–52.
DE GRAZIA, SEBASTIAN. *Of Time, Work, and Leisure.* New York: Twentieth Century Fund, 1962.
GODBEY, GEOFFREY C. *The Future of Leisure Services.* State College, PA: Venture Publishing, 1989.
————. "Leisure in the 1990s." *The World and I* (January 1990): 95–105.
HUNNICUTT, BENJAMIN K. *Work Without End.* Philadelphia: Temple University Press, 1988.
REICH, ROBERT. *The Work of Nations.* New York: Alfred A. Knopf, 1991.
SCHOR, JULIET. *The Overworked American: The Unexpected Decline of Leisure.* New York: Basic Books, 1991.

Tom Goodale

Lethal Weapons

The production of firearms will continue to proliferate in the years ahead. More and more powerful weapons will become available to the general public. Approximately 4 million firearms were produced in the United States during 1989. Of these, 62,900 were revolvers and 1.4 million were pistols. During the twentieth century over 250 million firearms (excluding military weapons) were manufactured or imported into the United States. Sales of firearms are likely to greatly increase in both legitimate retail outlets and in the black market.

Illegal ownership will remain relatively stable because the powerful firearms manufacturers and their lobbies will eliminate many local laws presently making the possession of firearms illegal. Thus, there will be many more guns, but fewer of them will be owned illegally. As of 1990, an estimated 180–200 million firearms were in circulation. As many as 50 percent of American households own one or more guns. Only a fourth of the 200 million or so firearms in circulation during 1990 were legitimately owned according to the letter of the laws. Firearms availability and use for deadly purposes increases despite the fact that over 20,000 gun laws were on the books by the end of the 1980s.

Ownership Restrictions

Licensing, registration, mandatory waiting periods, proof of fitness to possess firearms, and marksmanship qualifications have repeatedly been prevented from enactment by powerful political lobbies. However, effective control measures of this sort seem to work well in other nations, especially in Sweden. In Japan and the United Kingdom, handguns are banned, excepting gun club members and collectors. American public opinion favors tougher controls. Gallup Poll data reveals that some 80 percent of persons polled favor stricter controls, and 95 percent support federal legislation requiring a seven-day waiting period for handgun purchases.

Laws will attempt to distinguish between automatic and semiautomatic firearms and curb the availability of guns with high firepower rates. Following the killing of five children and the wounding of thirty others by an individual wielding a semiautomatic AK-47 rifle in Stockton, California, within months fifty bills regulating the sale or possession of semiautomatic weapons had been introduced in seventeen states. Few effective laws passed. Laws regulating machine guns, assault weapons, "Saturday night specials," zip guns, and hand guns will continue to be undermined by legal challenges on definition. From 650,000 to 2 million weapons, including smuggled and stolen automatic and semiautomatic firearms, are thought to be in the hands of criminals. Firearms manufacturers and their lobbies will probably continue to be successful, at least in the United States, in getting various local jurisdictions to pass laws giving absolute liberty to possess firearms and in incrementally removing reasonable limitations.

Use Restrictions

The storage of firearm components in separate locations will be encouraged in public health and education campaigns, but they will not be legally required. Similarly, trigger locks and other safety devices will be marketed but not required. Only a very small number of firearm owners will actually acquire such devices and fewer still are likely to actually employ them. Visual tagging of firearm replicas to distinguish them from real firearms will increase, since this is not an area of concern for the firearms lobby. Laws against celebration shooting, such as on New Year's Eve or the Fourth of July, will increase, since the firearms lobby's principal interest is in selling weapons and generally not in challenging laws prohibiting their illegal use in public. There will be no increase in laws requiring weapons training and qualification, since these are successfully opposed by the firearms lobby, which fights any measures leading potential firearms purchasers to think about, or hesitate in, buying new weapons.

Ammunition

Laws regulating the possession and use of "cop-killer" bullets—teflon-coated bullets, spent uranium rounds, hollow point bullets, contact-exploding rounds, and modified slugs—will generally continue in place and perhaps increase in use. As the number of firearms, the rates of fire, and the lethal nature of bullets escalate, more police officers and more citizens will be killed by them.

The number of police officers killed in the line of duty rose from 73 in 1961 to 146 in 1989. Murders committed by handguns numbered 8,915 in the United States during 1989. In stark contrast there were only 7 murders by handguns in the United Kingdom, 8 in Canada, and 19 in Sweden during the same year. There is one final shocking statistic that may increase public clamor for tougher firearms controls: Handguns increasingly claim the lives of children, with an average of one child under fourteen years of age killed by a handgun every day. Law enforcement officers have successfully challenged the firearms lobby on these issues. Furthermore, individual states are not as economically important to the firearms manufacturers and their lobbies.

Self-Defense Paraphernalia

Bulletproof clothing, and other bullet-resistant shields will become more common as the number of firearms and shootings increases. For example, the use of metal detectors at schools and in other public buildings is rapidly increasing. Bullet-resistant civilian clothing has even been developed for children! Terrorist attacks, kidnappings, and random thrill shooting all contribute to the development of protective gear to safeguard against shootings. Bullet-proof and even bomb-proof motor vehicles, briefcase shields, and Kevlar-jacketed, bullet-deflecting bibles are on the market.

Paraphernalia such as mace, incapacitating stun-guns, and disabling high-intensity lamps will not proliferate because potential buyers will realize that many more criminals will be armed with firearms, against which mace and other merely incapacitating devices are no match.

Explosives

Dynamite, plastic, detonators, triggering devices, and bombs will continue to be heavily regulated because manufacturers have not developed effective propaganda campaigns as in the firearms industry. Consequently, control of such substances or devices arouses little public or political opposition. Ingenious microtaggants identifying sources of supply have been developed to facilitate criminal investigations. These microscopic markers survive explosions and enable investigators to track down possible users.

Other Lethal Weapons

Crossbows, bows and arrows, martial arts equipment, and killer pets will be subject to increased legal controls. Organized pro-gun lobbies do not oppose such legislation and at times support it. Representative laws go so far as to ban dart guns, pea shooters, and slingshots. By 1985 twelve states banned the sales of martial arts weapons.

Weapons controls are nothing new. Pope Innocent II, expressing fear that the newly created crossbow might wipe out Western civilization, issued a decree forbidding its use by any state against another. As new weapons are developed and come into use, efforts to prevent their illegal use and accidental deaths and injuries will continue.

See also CRIME, VIOLENT; CRIME RATES; CRIMINAL PUNISHMENT; WEAPONS OF MASS DESTRUCTION.

BIBLIOGRAPHY

DAVIDSON, OSHA GRAY. *Under Fire: The NRA and the Battle for Gun Control.* New York: Henry Holt, 1993.

LARSON, ERIK. *Lethal Passage.* New York: Crown, 1994.

SILBERMAN, CHARLES. *Criminal Violence, Criminal Justice.* New York: Random House, 1978.

WINTEMUTE, GAREN. "Firearms as a Cause of Death in the United States." *Journal of Trauma* 27 (May 1987): 5.

Joseph D. McNamara

Liberal Arts

For centuries, the liberal arts curriculum—literature, language, history, the arts, and philosophy—*was* college. These subjects, it was believed, taught students how to think, so they could be knowledgeable citizens, capable of learning specific skills suitable for any career. Introducing students to classical ideas from these many viewpoints would enable them to tie together everything life threw at them. In the last quarter of the twentieth century, however, liberal arts came under unrelenting attack by the public, business, and its own professors, for a variety of reasons. For one, the written and artistic works that formed a required "canon" were viewed as racist, sexist, and biased by class and culture. Students and faculty complained that women, minorities, and the poor were ignored. Second, the liberal arts seemed both elitist and irrelevant. Specialized studies with little bearing on key global issues cut off the liberal arts' own roots—its claim that it taught students how to be self-reliant. The business community often scorned liberal arts graduates as unskilled and impractical.

Even so, the future evolution of the liberal arts offers much hope. First, a widespread countermovement toward "critical thinking" rejects specialization in favor of teaching problem-solving, practical thinking skills—the logic, organization, and analytical thinking that create self-reliant people. This trend will expand, especially in the areas of composition, philosophy, and history.

Second, since the late 1970s, technology and liberal arts have been growing in tandem. Courses such as "Science, Technology and Society" or "Human Ecology" linked ethics, humanism, and technology. This growth is equally strong outside the United States—especially in Scandinavia, the former Soviet bloc, and Far Eastern countries. Global studies, cross-disciplinary studies, and systems thinking will be well entrenched as the twenty-first century begins, even though specialization seems destined to dominate research universities at least until around 2010.

Third, the division between a student-centered, global-minded liberal arts in liberal arts colleges and community colleges and a narrow, elitist, impersonal approach at universities will intensify. The "star system" of hiring the most published scholars at high salaries in search of prestige will accelerate into the mid-1990s. As long as such ratings prevail and students are perceived to receive a better education at mega-universities than at liberal arts colleges and community colleges, this trend will continue.

Fourth, greater diversity and inclusivity in the revised liberal arts' "canon" will accelerate. Texts are clearly moving toward greater representation of women and minority writers.

Fifth, a decisive battle over career education within the liberal arts is likely to occur before the year 2000. In the last hundred years, college education has been devoted less to "pure" thinking and more to specific job skills. In response, some liberal arts faculty retreated into a form of elitism to protect their fields from interdisciplinary "contamination." The question for the future is: Will the liberal arts accept its old role as unifier of knowledge and include job skills along with art, theory, and ethics? The liberal arts has moved too slowly to accommodate the rapid change of the knowledge explosion. In large part, it still attempts to promote a worldview that no longer exists.

History and sociology are likely to expand globally oriented courses. Global economy, ecology, energy, and empowerment issues may be integrated into existing courses, so most will emphasize internationalism or interdependence.

Literature is moving in conflicting directions. One entrenched trend of the 1990s is toward poststructuralism, an approach with a specialized vocabulary. It essentially rejects the literal world and suggests that life is a language game. The competing trend seeks integration of literary studies into society. Courses like "Technology in Literature" or "Literature and Ecology" may lead literary studies back to mainstream issues and relevance. The elite traditionalists denigrate this as "pandering" or "selling out."

Foreign languages, after a drastic loss of enrollment and faculty from the 1960s to 1980 and a watering down of programs in the United States, expanded after 1980. Languages will continue their resurgence through the twenty-first century and find greater partnerships with internationalized business. Dual business-language programs will continue to boom, as will overseas internships. Most industrial countries lead the United States in language education, but the gap should narrow by the year 2000.

The performing and creative arts—music, art, writing, dance, film, and theater—will continue to attract many more students than there are jobs available, a plight common to artists since ancient times. Since the mid-twentieth century, the trend has been toward supporting artists with university jobs and government subsidies. Only a small percentage of artists live from their creations or attract mass attention. There is no evidence that this will change.

Philosophy, once the queen of all the liberal arts, suffered in the 1970s but is poised for a revival. Courses such as "Technology and Values," "Nursing Ethics," and "Philosophy of Social Responsibility" already offer practical career training linked to "pure" thinking. Interlinked studies seem to be the long-term evolutionary prognosis for most of the liberal arts.

See also ADULT LEARNING; ELEMENTARY AND SECONDARY EDUCATION; HIGHER EDUCATION.

BIBLIOGRAPHY

BAUMAN, M. GARRETT. "Interdisciplinary Education for the Twenty-first Century." *National Forum* (Spring 1989): 38–41.

———. "Liberal Arts for the Twenty-first Century." *Journal of Higher Education* (January-February 1987): 38–45.

KNAPP, EDWARD A. "Liberal Arts Education for the Twenty-first Century." *Physics Today* (July 1984): 9ff.

TURNER, FREDERICK. "Design for a New Academy." *Harper's* (September 1986): 47–53.

M. Garrett Bauman

Liberalism, Political

From the beginning, America has been endowed with two enduring political traditions— conservatism and liberalism. Led by Secretary of State Thomas Jefferson and Secretary of the Treasury Alexander Hamilton in the opening administration of President George Washington, these rival systems of political thought competed for the nation's political soul. The creative, corrective, and balancing tension between liberalism and conservatism has been the genius of American democracy with its two-party system.

Part of the greatness of Washington, who is rightly known as "the father of his country," is that he successfully balanced the claims of Hamiltonian conservatism and Jeffersonian liberalism. The country's political balance and the health of its democracy are endangered when either of our central traditions—conservatism or liberalism—is denigrated and left undefended, as now seems to be the fate of liberalism.

It is not always easy to draw the distinction between these rival traditions, because most Americans, including our greatest leaders, have borrowed from both conservatism and liberalism. There is also an ongoing process of political realignment as historical circumstances change.

At the beginning, Hamilton—long admired as the apostle of conservatism—championed the causes of business, commerce, and the national bank, believing that the best way to serve those interests was through a strong national government. Jefferson, the apostle of liberalism, was the champion of small landholders, artisans, tradesmen, and—above all—individual liberty, believing that those concerns were best served by a limited national government with greater power in state and local hands.

With the passage of time, Andrew Jackson and other Democrats came to believe that the interests of the "common man" were better served by a stronger national government. In a sense they sought Jeffersonian ends by Hamiltonian means—the interests of the common man were advanced by a positive national governing authority.

Conservative and liberal principles were again mingled when Abraham Lincoln, the father of the Republican party, asserted that preserving the unity and the authority of the federal government was more important than states' rights. Lincoln's Republican views were so anathema to the slaveholding South that the southern states tried to withdraw from the federal union. They were prevented from doing so by Lincoln and the Union armies, but only after an incredible slaughter of Americans by Americans and the physical destruction of the South. The "solid South" remained fiercely Democratic for nearly the next century.

The Democrats found their strongest defining twentieth-century leaders in Woodrow Wilson, who shaped the progressivism and internationalism of the World War I era, and in Franklin Roosevelt, who launched the New Deal economic reforms of the 1930s and reasserted Wilsonian internationalism in the 1940s.

The liberalism and internationalism of Wilson and Roosevelt have remained the hallmarks of the Democratic party in much of the twentieth century to the present day. Although some Republicans have embraced New Deal liberalism and internationalism, most Republicans have preferred a more business-oriented, free enterprise, conservative approach. Their heroes have been McKinley, Hoover, Eisenhower, Taft, Nixon, and Reagan.

In more recent years, the composition of both the generally liberal Democratic party and the generally conservative Republican party have been changing. The civil rights movement, championed largely by northern Democrats in the last four decades, alienated much of the southern Democratic establishment and sent the once solid Democratic South into the Republican party, except for the black voters.

Other issues, such as the Vietnam War, gun control, feminism, gay rights, abortion, arms control, and affirmative action, have further convinced many Southerners as well as some northern blue-collar workers, middle Americans, and religious fundamentalists that the Republican party was a more appropriate home. Some of these concerns, along with traditional "rugged individualism," also resonated in the American West.

Thus a new political alignment finds the Republican party growing stronger among constituencies once considered safely Democratic. It is now exceedingly difficult for a Democratic liberal-internationalist to win a national election, as witness the defeats of Adlai Stevenson, Hubert Humphrey, Walter Mondale, Michael Dukakis, and the author of this article. Even more conservative southern Democratic contenders such as Jimmy Carter and Bill Clinton are said to be too liberal for what appears to be an increasingly conservative electorate. The surest applause lines these days are those that assail the federal government. Washington, D.C., is now regarded as the Sodom and Gomorrah of America. The current Speaker of the House has gone so far as to declare that the occupants of the Clinton White House are not "normal people"—that, indeed, the president and first lady are "counter-culture McGoverniks."

What constitutes liberalism and conservatism in America today? Is the now beleaguered liberal heritage of the Democratic party worth reviving, or should we give up on the old-fashioned Democratic values and become "New Democrats" of some kind or another?

Perhaps I can best define conservatism through the eyes of my father—a Wesleyan Methodist clergyman and lifelong South Dakota Republican. He believed in a limited government of laws guided by the Constitution, which he placed second only to the Bible. He was opposed to deficit financing and to any extravagance in personal or public expenditures. He and my mother were living examples of self-reliance and personal responsibility. I always think of them when I think of conservatism at its best.

Liberalism is the philosophy I generally favor—although I have frequently borrowed from the insights of my parents and the conservative tradition. Liberalism combines much of the philosophies of Jefferson, Lincoln, Wilson, and Roosevelt—my four political heroes. Liberalism holds that there is a positive role for government in American life in such activities as ending slavery, opening up the West for settlement and development, conservation, pure food and drugs, child labor protection, Social Security, Medicare, public safety, civil rights, rural electrification, collective bargaining rights, student loans, and the environment.

In recent decades, liberalism has become identified also with new controversial political and social issues that have sometimes alienated Americans of both liberal and conservative leanings: court-ordered school busing, quotas and affirmative action, gun control, abortion, feminism, gay rights—and massive protests against the Vietnam War. The emergence of these issues is associated in the public mind with the sexual revolution and youthful lifestyles that seem to be marked by permissiveness, relaxed moral standards, risqué television and movie scripts, and the decline of family stability. The proliferation of government regulations, the litigation explosion, and high tax rates are further sources of tension and conflict for which liberals are frequently blamed.

Indeed, the argument has been widely advanced in recent elections and by new, right-wing talk show hosts that since liberals have been running the country for the past half-century, liberalism is responsible for the current troubled state of the nation. In fact, if liberalism is a threat to America, the nation should have been relatively safe these past four decades, because the long list of liberal presidential contenders mentioned earlier were all defeated. The White House since the Truman administration has been in Republican hands for twenty-eight years and in Democratic hands for fourteen years.

As for Congress, since 1938 a coalition of Republicans and equally conservative southern Democrats has been running that institution. The one exception to this was in 1964 and 1965, when President Lyndon Johnson's Great Society carried the day until it was overrun by the Vietnam War, which then dominated the nation and claimed its moral, political, and economic resources for a decade marked by rancorous and divisive internal conflict.

So where do we go from here? We should first recognize that America needs to nurture and maintain both of its historic political traditions—conservatism and liberalism. Each of these political value systems has contributed so much to our way of life that every American would be threatened if our nation were to fall under the grip of a single ideology unchallenged by a competing system of thought.

Would not both Democratic liberalism and Republican conservatism be enriched today by genuine debate between contrasting views of government and rival agendas rather than by simply arguing over how much of the Republican Contract with America should be swallowed by Democrats?

See also COMMUNITARIANISM; CONSERVATISM, POLITICAL; POLITICAL CAMPAIGNING; POLITICAL CYCLES; POLITICAL PARTIES; POLITICAL PARTY REALIGNMENT; PUBLIC OPINION POLLS; SURVEYS; THIRD POLITICAL PARTIES; VOTING.

BIBLIOGRAPHY

GREEN, MARK, ed. *Changing America: Blueprints for the New Administration.* New York: Newmarket Press, 1992.

GRIFFIN, DAVID R., and FALK, RICHARD. *Postmodern Politics for a Planet in Crises: Policy, Process, and Presidential Vision.* Albany, NY: State University of New York Press, 1993.

THEOBALD, ROBERT. *Turning the Century: Personal and Organizational Strategies for Your Changed World.* Indianapolis, IN: Knowledge Systems, 1992.

WISHARD, WILLIAM VAN DUSEN. *The American Future (What Would George and Tom Do Now?).* Washington, DC: The Congressional Institute, 1992.

George McGovern

Liberation, Women's.

See WOMEN'S MOVEMENT.

Libraries

Libraries historically have been places where information is stored for use. In the future, the library will be significantly changed by the technologies

Libraries

used to store, retrieve, and present information. Its basic purpose, however, will continue to fill humanity's basic need to find answers to questions.

In the past 6,000 years, information storage has come a long way. From clay tablets that could store about one character or symbol per cubic inch we have advanced to digital storage systems capable of billions of characters per cubic inch. Along the way there was papyrus and then paper, accommodating up to five hundred characters per cubic inch. Microfilm approached the density of modern electronic storage, but it was never widely accepted by library users as a convenient means of retrieval and display. In each of these cases, the purpose of placing symbols on some medium was to preserve and communicate information—the traditional purpose of libraries.

Some of the oldest libraries known to exist were in Mesopotamia and Egypt. They were filled with material collected by various methods, including conquest and persuasion. Access to their information was often restricted to an elite population of scholars, clergy, or other intelligentsia (lack of reading skills was a major barrier to access as well). Despite the role of these ancient libraries in preserving knowledge, very little of their collections has been preserved through the ages. While fire was blamed as the culprit in the destruction of the library of Alexandria, it is unlikely that the collection was destroyed in this way because parchment does not burn. The destruction of this vast collection, and many others, most likely was due to neglect, the ravages of war, lack of political and public support, and slow deterioration of the materials.

No era typifies the traditional problem of library material deterioration more than the early twentieth century, when paper for books was made from wood pulp rather than linen or rags. This wood-pulp, high-acid paper destroys itself over time in what has been referred to as a "slow fire." Historically, libraries have not played a significant role in the long-term survival of books, which was assured by the reprinting of great works by publishers. In this century, however, major efforts have been made by libraries to stop the "slow fires" of paper deterioration and to preserve material not likely to be reprinted.

The preservation issues of interest to libraries concerned with paper deterioration, however, are paled by a new "fire" rapidly consuming other forms of library-related material. As electronic information products evolve, the mechanisms for producing, storing, and retrieving this material

evolve as well. Information stored digitally on a medium that was state-of-the-art twenty years ago is virtually unreadable today (e.g., round-hole punch cards or magnetic tape in proprietary formats from companies no longer in business). These technologically induced fires consume information at a far faster rate than the deterioration of paper ever did. The challenge of the library of today and tomorrow, then, is to preserve and provide access to all forms of information.

Just as technology is challenging libraries in their preservation role, so is it challenging them in their communication role. In the past, access was assured by physical possession of the material, and libraries measured their worth by the size of their collections. With the rapidly emerging technology of high-speed telecommunications, computing, and networking, it is no longer necessary to have material on site to have it accessible. This change in factors determining accessibility is shifting the distribution of materials from hard copy to electronic form (with the associated preservation problems mentioned above). While most material will continue to be available in print in paper form, access increasingly is in electronic form as well. Libraries must use scarce resources to assure access in traditional as well as emerging forms and formats, as long as information is published in a variety of media formats.

Librarians are struggling with maintaining three library functions or formats.

- The library of the past, focused on building collections and providing direct physical access to printed materials.
- The library of the present, with extraordinary added costs of inflation, automation, and, for many, the preservation of decaying material.
- The library of the future for which they must plan, which includes not only the development of new ideas, but the implementation of new prototypes for publishing, acquiring, storing, and providing access to information through new technology and new attitudes about such fundamental things as ownership and access.

As a result of emerging electronic information networks as well as traditional publishing expansion into new markets and interest areas, more information is available than at any time previously—so much that it would be well nigh impossible for any one person to absorb or grasp more than a fraction of what is out there. Many humans are capable of processing only a few hundred symbols per minute at best. At the same time, tools with prodigious instantaneous output focus on producing rather than absorbing and condensing information. For the librarian, the dilemma is significant: Will the profession continue to serve as an intermediary between users and information? Or will it create tools and methods to allow users to become self-sufficient?

If librarians are to build and maintain the information systems of tomorrow, they will have to collaborate with technical and business enterprises to design information delivery systems. The approach taken must be oriented to self-sufficient users capable of gleaning the information they need from the large stores of potentially relevant material. The technologies that will be applied in the library of the future may be beyond our imagination today, but not the purpose to which they will be put. They will enable citizens to be independent problem solvers, using information to address the challenges that are important to them.

See also COMMUNICATIONS; INFORMATION OVERLOAD; INFORMATION SOCIETY; INFORMATION TECHNOLOGY; LIBRARIES: ELECTRONIC FORMATS; LITERATURE; NETWORKING; ON-LINE SERVICES; PRINTED WORD.

BIBLIOGRAPHY

BUCKLAND, MICHAEL. *Redesigning Library Services.* Chicago: American Library Association, 1992.
FRYE, BILLY E. "The University Context and the Research Library." *Library Hi Tech* 40 (1992): 27–37.
GORE, DANIEL, ed. *Farewell to Alexandria.* Westport, CT: Greenwood Press, 1976.
PENNIMAN, W. DAVID. "The Library of Tomorrow." *Library Hi Tech* 40 (1992): 23–26.

W. David Penniman

Libraries: Electronic Format

Forecasts relating to future capabilities of libraries date back at least to 1907 when John Cotton Dana described, probably facetiously, a "Who, What, and Why Machine" capable of dealing automatically with the questions for which answers are most frequently sought by library users. A decade ago, Lancaster (1982) identified several forecasts characterizing the future of libraries. These ranged from the conservative—the future library looks only cosmetically different from that of today—to the radical extreme—libraries as we now know them essentially disappear. Since these various forecasts were categorized and summarized, enough changes have occurred in library and information services to make the revolutionary scenarios increasingly credible.

Systems maintain electronic records of library materials from when they are ordered to when they are discarded. Automated circulation systems yield valuable management data on how the collection is used, as well as providing the more obvious records on who has borrowed what. Card and printed catalogs of library holdings have virtually disappeared, being replaced by online catalogs that can be consulted by users in the library or remote locations in the office, home, or elsewhere. These catalogs have been expanded allowing users access to other libraries' holdings on a regional, state, national, and even international basis. Not only can users find which library owns particular items, but they can determine whether these items are immediately available, and they may even be able to use the terminal to "charge" the items and request delivery to their offices. Moreover, the terminal or workstation that gives access to the library's catalog may also provide access to other electronic resources, such as indexes to the periodical literature or even to other resources, perhaps compiled by the library itself. Examples, in the case of a public library, include calendars of local events or carpooling information. Indeed, what was once the catalog of the collection of a single library is now becoming essentially a window to a universe of information resources.

Traditionally, libraries have been judged by the size of their collections, a criterion perpetuated by agencies of accreditation and by the compilers of library statistics. It is now widely recognized that this is no longer meaningful for a variety of reasons: the continued rapid growth and diversity of the published and semipublished literature; the obsolescence of much material (collections are continuously "weeded" in some libraries); the decline of library budgets in purchasing power; and, perhaps most important, the sharing of resources among libraries facilitated by computer and telecommunications technologies—allowing access to a universe of information resources that is rapidly increasing in size and variety.

Between 1976 and 1982, Lancaster (1978, 1982), produced several scenarios that predicted the gradual "disembodiment" of the library: publications in print-on-paper form would gradually be replaced by publications in electronic form, many accessible through various networks. Carried to its logical conclusion, this would eventually result in a "library without walls" or, put somewhat differently, a situation in which every library would essentially "have" the same collection—the universe of information resources that is network-accessible.

At the time, these ideas were not widely accepted by librarians. Today, however, "access rather than ownership" has become virtually the motto of the profession.

Of course, what happens to the library in the future to a very large extent will depend on developments in related sectors, most obviously the publishing industry. The proportion of the world's publications issued in electronic form will presumably increase; thus, the proportion issued as print on paper will decline. What is less clear is the form that electronic publishing will take. How much will consist of resources that can only be accessed through networks and how much will actually be distributed, for purchase or lease, as CD-ROM, videotape, videodisk, electronic book (e.g., the Sony Data Discman), or formats yet to be devised?

While electronic resources that are distributed as physical artifacts (such as CD-ROM) can continue to be collected, those that exist only in network-accessible form present libraries with a completely different problem. Libraries have traditionally been builders of collections, but what does *collection building* really mean in an electronic world? Jutta Reed-Scott believes that "building collections will move from a static process of acquiring library resources to a more fluid position of providing access to information."

As the Internet expands into the much-publicized information superhighway, it seems reasonable to assume that present trends will continue—that electronic publishing will grow at the expense of printing on paper and that much of this output will be network-accessible rather than distributed. In such an environment, what happens to the library and what happens to the librarian?

Views on the future of the library as a physical facility range from one extreme to another. For example, the future public library might be electronically connected to all homes in the community and able to transmit recreational and informational services into these homes. Academic libraries could become mere study halls, because access to information resources would be provided directly by the various academic departments.

Some see the library as becoming a kind of switching center, possibly also having such value-added responsibilities as user education. For example, William Britten has said that "libraries should not think primarily in terms of collecting information stored on networks, but should instead pursue strategies for teaching users how to locate and retrieve this information."

This agrees with the ideas of several prominent librarians, who see the library of the future as primarily a node in a vast information network. Frederick Kilgour, for example, believes that a major function of such a node will be to build local indexes to aid users in accessing remote sources.

Other librarians disagree with the view that the library should be a mere switching center. Ross Atkinson cautions that such a role can be performed by a computer center (e.g., on campus). A library must be much more if it is to survive. Atkinson urges that libraries must go beyond the role of interface to remote resources by taking on additional functions: downloading to local storage those resources most likely to be of value to the library's constituency; building new electronic information composites for users by drawing text and illustrations from various parts of the network; and possibly acting as electronic publisher (e.g., a university library might assume the role of publisher of the institution's own research output). If the continued growth of networked electronic publishing does in fact imply the decline or demise of the library as a physical facility, does it also imply the decline or demise of the librarian?

Unfortunately for the profession, the librarian is still viewed as primarily a custodian by a large part of the general public. But the librarian of today is, or should be, primarily an information or reading consultant, diagnosing the information or reading (or viewing or listening) needs of a library user and prescribing a solution. It is in this role that the real professional expertise lies.

If librarians are seen as consultants of this type rather than managers of physical facilities, they could have very important roles to play in even a networked "virtual" information environment. In fact, their value could actually increase. This view is espoused by Mark Eagle, Karen Drabenstott, Vicki Anders, Colleen Cook, and Roberta Pitts, among others. Drabenstott states:

> A few reference staff will be physically present in the library building to assist users in person in collection navigation. Most reference staff will be posted on the network where they will respond to user calls for assistance by monitoring a user's ongoing search. Such calls could come from users who are navigating digital libraries from workstations in their home, dormitory rooms, or offices. . . . Staff could work out of their homes because they would use the capabilities of the information network to interact with users. . . . Public library environments would feature itinerant

reference staff whose duties resemble today's information brokers.

Anders put it this way:

When everyone is plugged in, the librarian becomes the "gateway." . . . Presently, there are so many gateways that one needs a gateway to the gateways. This is the librarian's job—to interpret the means of access. . . . The gateway librarian who advises on the best route to information and interprets the language of access will have job security for years to come.

Other writers see the librarian transformed into a kind of "knowledge engineer," engaged in a variety of rather sophisticated information processing activities. Ray DeBuse claims that "some librarians will become hypertext engineers. . . . They will provide intellectual connections between the works of different authors or convert linear publications to hypermedia publications."

Some librarians are already working with the technologies of artificial intelligence and expert systems in an attempt to develop programs that will perform some of the tasks now performed by skilled librarians, such as cataloging, indexing, the selection of databases, the searching of databases, and the answering of factual-type questions. Many believe that this work must continue. Others caution that it is extremely difficult to replace the true human expert and that a danger exists that such systems will emulate the mediocre librarian rather than the expert.

Even if the library as physical facility does decline in importance, there is some agreement in the profession that the librarian could continue to play an important role as information intermediary.

See also COMMUNICATIONS; INFORMATION OVERLOAD; INFORMATION SOCIETY; INFORMATION TECHNOLOGY; LIBRARIES; LITERATURE; NETWORKING; ON-LINE SERVICES; PRINTED WORD.

BIBLIOGRAPHY

ANDERS, VICKI; COOK, COLLEEN; and PITTS, ROBERTA. "A Glimpse Into a Crystal Ball: Academic Libraries in the Year 2000." *Wilson Library Bulletin* 67 (October 1992): 36–40.

ATKINSON, ROSS. "Text Mutability and Collection Administration." *Library Acquisitions: Practice and Theory* 14 (1990): 355–358.

BIRDSALL, WILLIAM F. *The Myth of the Electronic Library: Librarianship and Social Change in America.* Westport, CT: Greenwood Press, 1994.

DOUGHERTY, RICHARD M., and HUGHES, CAROL. *Preferred Futures for Libraries.* Mountain View, CA, Research Libraries Group, 1991.

KILGOUR, FREDERICK G. "The Metamorphosis of Libraries during the Foreseeable Future." In *Libraries and the Future: Essays on the Library in the Twenty-first Century*, ed., F. Wilfrid Lancaster. Binghampton, NY: Haworth Press, 1993.

LANCASTER, F. WILFRID.. *Libraries and Librarians in an Age of Electronics.* Arlington, VA: Information Resources Press, 1982.

_____. *Toward Paperless Information Systems.* New York: Academic Press, 1978.

MARTYN, JOHN; VICKERS, PETER; and FEENEY, MARY, eds. *Information UK 2000.* London: Bowker-Saur, 1990.

REED-SCOTT, JUTTA. "Information Technologies and Collection Development." *Collection Building* 9/3–4, (1989): 47–51.

RIGGS, DONALD E., and SABINE, GORDON A. *Libraries in the '90s: What the Leaders Expect.* Phoenix, AZ: Oryx, 1988.

VON WAHLDE, BARBARA, and SCHILLER, NANCY. "Creating the Virtual Library: Strategic Issues." In Laverna M. Saunders, ed. *The Virtual Library: Visions and Realities.* Westport, CT: Meckler, 1993.

F. Wilfrid Lancaster

Life on Other Planets.

See EVOLUTION: LIFE-FORMS IN THE UNIVERSE; EXTRATERRESTRIAL LIFE-FORMS.

Life Sciences

The past fifty years since the discovery of DNA have seen sweeping changes in life sciences, and the future promises more. Modern biology has been changed by the availability of close-up images of cell structure, called ultrastructure, produced by electron microscopes. Molecular biology has provided evidence for what were once considered fanciful ideas, turning theory into truths.

Outdated encyclopedias and old textbooks divide all life into either animals, the object of study of zoology, and plants, the object of study of botany. When the Dutchman Anton van Leeuwenhoek used an early version of the microscope to peer at microorganisms for the first time, he described them as minute animals. Such animals came to be known as *protozoa*, from Greek words meaning "first animals." *Protozoa* is a term whose use has only now begun to fade. All moving organisms, even the smallest, were classified as a form of animal—unless they were green, or not sufficiently rapid, in which case they were considered primitive plants.

Ernst Haeckel (1834–1919), questioning the plant/animal dichotomy, recognized a vast array of diversity in the microscopic world, especially in plankton. Considering microbes more primitive than plants and animals and assigning them their own kingdom (the *monera*), Haeckel asserted that microbes were the ancestors of all larger organisms. Enigmas such as *Euglena gracilis*, a photosynthetic swimmer that seemed to combine the traits of both plants and animals, and yet as a single cell was really neither, were accommodated in the Haeckelian kingdom of the very small.

Haeckel's three-kingdom system, never broadly adopted, has given way to the five-kingdom system, which recognizes the importance of the *bacteria*, the oldest kingdom, some of whose members combined to give rise to the other four kingdoms. Bacteria lack nuclei in their cells; they include about 15,000 described types, including 500 estimated genera of the distinctive archaebacteria. The second kingdom of organisms to appear in the fossil record of evolution, the *protoctists*, includes all organisms composed of cells with nuclei and not accommodated in the three kingdoms of larger organisms: plants, animals, and fungi.

The ancient division between plants and animals has been entirely replaced with the recognition that the biggest difference distinguishing life forms is whether their cells lack nuclei (bacteria) or not (all other organisms). If an organism is composed of cells with nuclei—either one cell with one nucleus, like an amoeba, or many cells with many nuclei, like mushrooms, rose bushes, and human beings—the organism is considered *eukaryotic*. The term *eukaryotic* comes from Greek words meaning "true" (*eu*) and "seeded" (*karyon*). Cells that do not have nuclei are called prokaryotic, from *pro*, meaning "before" in ancient Greek, and *karyon*. Prokaryotes, cells without nuclei, is another name for bacteria. The essential structural and chemical differences between bacteria (prokaryotes) and all other life-forms on Earth, eukaryotes, have been confirmed by microscopic, biochemical, and genetic studies.

Modern biology has revealed something even more startling than the essential similarities between plants and animals. We now know that all plants, animals, fungi, and protoctists—the four kingdoms of eukaryotic organisms—evolved from bacteria. Cells with nuclei also have an area around the nucleus inside the cell. This egg white–like area is called the *cytoplasm*. Inside the cytoplasm of most protoctists and all plants, animals, and fungi are structures known as *mitochondria*. The mitochon-

dria of complex, nucleated cells respire oxygen in a chemical reaction that provides cells with the energy they need to function. Although the bacterial ancestry of mitochondria was suspected in the late nineteenth century, the last two decades have revealed beyond a reasonable doubt that mitochondria are the living remnants of bacteria that invaded, or were eaten by, larger cells. In addition to mitochondria, all plants and algae (all the photosynthetic protoctists) have *plastids* in their cells. When green (they can also be red, yellow, and brown), plastids are called *chloroplasts*. Plastids of any color carry out the essential "plantlike" process of photosynthesis, in which, using the energy of the sun, carbon from carbon dioxide in the air reacts with hydrogen from water molecules. Photosynthesis assembles the carbon-hydrogen compounds forming the active chemistry of cells, simultaneously releasing the oxygen from water. Plastids, like mitochondria, are remains of captive bacteria that, trapped inside the cytoplasm of larger cells, continued to function. Molecular biology, which analyzes and compares the sequences of base pairs in DNA, has confirmed that all cells with nuclei are the result of living mergers between distinct kinds of bacteria. Like the chimera, a mythical creature of antiquity combining lion, goat, and snake, all plants and animals are highly organized bacterial monsters.

As we look to the future, lessons can be drawn from the processes of life's past. Darwin's theory once represented evolution as a bloody struggle in which each being battles others and only the strong survive. The actual scientific record of life, however, suggests just as strongly that long-term interaction, including the close physical association known as symbiosis, is required for survival. *Symbiosis*, from the Greek words meaning "to live together," is the biological term for the process in which distinct life forms are in protracted close association. *Endosymbiosis* refers to cells or animals, perhaps initially hostile, that come to dwell inside each other. Some photosynthetic algae, for example, have merged with microbes called ciliates; still others have insinuated themselves into the hair follicles of polar bears, giving the white animals a greenish tint.

As life-forms, thought to have first evolved some four billion years ago, grow into each other and the surface mineral environment of Earth, the necessity to live with other beings becomes ever more intense. As human beings trying to ensure a long-term future on this planet, we may learn from organisms such as the latter-day bacteria that still dwell as mitochondria in each of our cells: the most successful life-forms have not been isolated from the rest of life on Earth, nor have they been mere stewards magnanimously helping other life-forms. Rather, the most abundant life-forms are those that have literally embedded themselves in a living landscape and joined their destiny to the lives of beings greater than they. If we substitute ourselves for mitochondria, and the living Earth for the larger bacterial cells that the ancestors of mitochondria originally entered, we will find the lesson that our own future success may depend upon our learning to live and recycle our material waste in settings still rich in the estimated 3–30 million nonhuman life-forms with which we share this planet's surface.

See also BIODIVERSITY; EVOLUTION, BIOLOGI-CAL; EXTINCTION OF SPECIES.

BIBLIOGRAPHY

MARGULIS, LYNN, and SAGAN, DORION. *Microcosmos: Four Billion Years of Microbial Evolution.* New York: Touchstone Books, 1991.
_____. *What Is Life?* New York: Simon & Schuster, 1995.
SAGAN, DORION. *Biospheres: Reproducing Planet Earth.* New York: Bantam, 1990.
WILSON, EDWARD O. *The Diversity of Life.* Cambridge, MA: Harvard University Press, 1992.

Dorion Sagan
Lynn Margulis

Lifestyles, Alternative

Powerful trends are changing the way we live and work. Three driving trends illustrate our predicament. Within a generation, world reserves of easily accessible oil are expected to be depleted, there will be another 3 billion persons on the planet, and the world's climate is expected to heat up as a result of the greenhouse effect. Without cheap petroleum to provide the pesticides and fertilizers for high-yield agriculture, and with the real prospect of droughts due to climate changes, the likelihood of massive famines seems very high. When ozone depletion, rainforest destruction, soil erosion, acid rain, and species extinction, are factored in, it becomes all the more obvious that we face an unprecedented and intertwined pattern of challenges. Dramatic adjustments in our manner of living are indicated.

We have two options—we can adapt, either by choice or necessity. If we adapt by choice, we can mobilize our creativity and commitment to build a sustainable and satisfying future. If we ignore the trends converging around us and are forced to adapt by necessity, our future is likely to be insecure, divisive, and mean-spirited.

We face a crisis in the interconnected global system, and changes at every level are needed. At a personal level, citizens of developed nations need to adopt simple lifestyles. At a neighborhood level, we need to build new types of communities designed for sustainable living. At a national level, we need to adopt new policies with regard to energy, environment, education, and media. At a global level, economically developed nations need to forge a new partnership with developing nations. Envisioning and implementing this broad range of changes is the new global challenge.

As individuals, we need to undertake a conscious social experiment in developing simpler or more ecological ways of living. Although there is no cookbook for ecological living, certain common themes often characterize this approach to life: developing the full spectrum of one's potentials: physical, emotional, intellectual, and spiritual; reducing undue clutter by giving away or selling seldom-used things that would be useful to others; buying products that are nonpolluting, energy-efficient, and easy to repair; recycling metal, glass, and paper, and cutting back on things that use nonrenewable resources; eating foods lower on the food chain—less meat, sugar, and highly processed foods; cultivating the ability to do one thing at a time, with full attention and appreciation; and pursuing a livelihood or work that contributes to the well-being of the world.

A simpler life should not be equated with a return to the past or turning away from technological progress. The problems of the modern era require us not to move backwards but to move ahead so that we are no longer an enemy of nature but a part of it. Nor should simpler living be equated with moving to a rural area and living on a farm; to the contrary, our cities are one of the most important places for developing ecological approaches to living. An ecological way of life is not a retreat from progress; in fact, it is essential to the advance of our civilization.

To limit the damaging impact of our consumption of natural resources, persons in developed nations will have to do more than cut back at the margins. They will need to restructure their lives and design more sustainable neighborhoods or "ecovillages." For example, a city block or suburban block could be transformed from isolated houses into an organic cluster of housing types, gardens, shops, and areas for living and working. Each microcommunity could specialize in specific areas of interest to provide satisfying work for many of its inhabitants (for example, crafts, health care, child care, gardening, art, education, and so on). Each ecovillage could have a community garden for local food production, a system of recycling, a telecommuting center, and perhaps a solar energy system. If each microcommunity were designed to reflect the values and interests of different groups of people, it would foster an exciting diversity of designs for living. These ecocommunities could have the feeling and cohesiveness of a small town and would provide a strong foundation for building a sustainable future.

We also need new policies at the national level that support changes at the personal and neighborhood level. We need to develop renewable sources of energy—solar, wind, geothermal, and biomass—and make the transition away from nonrenewable energy. We need to invest in fiber-optic communications networks so people have the "information highways" essential for living and working productively in the next century. We need to invest in the education of our children and the continuing education of adults. Furthermore, we need vigorous environmental policies that protect Earth's air, land, and water.

In a sustainable economy, work will be far more purposeful—emphasizing activities that are essential to the well-being of people. Such an economy offers the intangible but immensely important benefit of generating a wide range of satisfying jobs: building renewable energy systems, retrofitting and rebuilding our neighborhoods, providing life-long education in practical skills, redesigning and rebuilding our waste recycling systems, and rebuilding our transportation systems to be as energy efficient as possible. No one should lack a meaningful job in an economy oriented toward sustainability.

Currently, television is being programmed primarily for commercial success, and as a result, our civilizational consciousness is being programmed for ecological failure. We need a new social ethic that holds the mass media accountable for how it programs our society's consciousness. Such an approach can help to break through the cultural hypnosis of consumerism and augment it with programming that fosters a sustainability consciousness. We need to use the mass media in ways that help awaken a new understanding and caring for the planet and the future. The point is not to condemn television; rather, it is to acknowl-

edge our great need for balance and perspective in our diet of images and information so we can take a healthy approach to consumption.

At a global level, we need a new partnership with and commitment to developing nations, where more than a billion persons live at the very edge of existence in absolute poverty. Just to survive, people must often take actions in the short run that result in greater environmental destruction in the longer run. More compassionate and less wasteful living by affluent nations is vital to serve the well-being of all. With simplicity, an increasing increment of national wealth can be used to provide food, housing, health care, and education to those who are homeless and otherwise in desperate need. With basic necessities assured, the whole human family can work together to restore the environment.

There are hopeful visions of a workable and meaningful future. We have but a few crucial decades in which to make essential changes, voluntarily—the blink of an eye in the lifespan of civilizations. We need leadership that calls forth a new global dream of ecological lifestyles, steady efforts to rebuild our communities at the local scale, good jobs that are satisfying and contributory, new energy policies, mature uses of the mass media, and so on. Overall, we need a "politics of sustainability" that recognizes the dramatic changes occurring in the world and the need to respond in a coherent and determined way at every level of life.

We also need a new level of citizenship. Few politicians will be willing to advocate the sweeping changes required to achieve sustainability until they are assured that their constituencies will support them. When citizens can tell their leaders with conviction where they want to go and how fast they want to get there, then leaders can do their job. Before our leaders can act with confidence, citizens need to revitalize the conversation of democracy by engaging in an entirely new level of dialogue that builds a working consensus for the future. Regular "electronic town meetings" held over television that consider a key issue in detail and then obtain feedback from a scientific sample of citizens, offer a powerful way for citizens to discover their common views and to communicate with their representatives in government.

We can prosper, live purposeful lives, advance our civilizations, enrich our cultures, and serve the well-being of the world. With an engaged citizenry, strong leadership, and ecological approaches to living, we can rise to the new global challenge of building a sustainable and satisfying future.

See also ANIMAL RIGHTS; DEFORESTATION; EN-
ERGY, RENEWABLE SOURCES OF; GLOBAL ENVI-
RONMENTAL PROBLEMS; GREEN REVOLUTION;
LIFESTYLES, VALUE-ORIENTED; NATURAL RE-
SOURCES, USE OF; SUSTAINABILITY.

BIBLIOGRAPHY

GUTKNECHT, DOUGLAS B., and BUTLER, EDGAR W. *Family,
Self and Society: Emerging Issues, Alternatives and In-
terventions.* Lanham, MD: University Press of America,
1986.
HARLAND, JOHN. *Brave New World: A Different Projection.*
Rochester, WA: Sovereign Press, 1984.
PARTRIDGE, WILLIAM L. *The Hippie Ghetto: The Natural
History of a Subculture.* Prospect Heights, IL: Wave-
land Press, 1985.

Duane S. Elgin

Lifestyles, Ethnic

The second half of the twentieth century has been characterized by political, social, and cultural movements toward localized, regionalistic, and isolationistic heterogeneity. After the end of World War II, many new, independent nations were freed from colonial subjugation. In the 1960s, two types of movements held sway in the United States: ethnic minority groups asserting their own cultures and civil rights in the form of black power, brown power, red power, and yellow power; and hippies turning inward individually or forming secluded groups with slogans such as "Drop out!" or "Tune in!" or "Turn on!" or "Grow your own potatoes!" The first movement was an assertion and revival of suppressed ethnic cultures. The second was a withdrawal. Similar withdrawal occurred in Germany during the 1950s in the form of *ohne mich*-ism ("without me-ism"), in which freedom was interpreted as freedom *from* social and political involvement. By the 1970s, the minority group movements expanded to include gray power, gay power, and women power. Then, in the early 1990s, we witnessed another surge of movements toward independence: this time within countries such as the former Soviet Union, Yugoslavia, and Czechoslovakia. All this prompted worry about the segmentation of society.

Trends in the opposite direction became gradually noticeable in the 1980s, however. The formation of the European common market was intended to increase economic interaction and mutual benefit without destroying the cultures and languages in

Europe. Less publicized was the massive migration of people in Europe; first from south to north, then from east to west. The first migrations from Turkey, Yugoslavia, and other Southern European countries to Germany and Sweden continued for several decades and were a demand-pull phenomenon: factories in Germany and Sweden needed factory workers. The number of migrants was considerable, but not threatening to the cultures of the host countries. By contrast, the post-*perestroika* migration from Eastern Europe to the West is a different phenomenon. There simply are no jobs, housing, schools, or medical facilities to accommodate even a fraction of these new immigrants. Drastic social and legal changes are inevitable. There is a new anxiety rampant in Europe, caused by these massive westward migrations, coming as they do on top of continuing migrations from the south. This time it is not the oppression of powerful governments, but poor, powerless foreign individuals that are the source of the anxiety. The xenophobic reactions sometimes take on neo-Fascist dimensions, or are reflected in the revival of the Ku Klux Klan and other racist activities in the United States fostered by rising unemployment—itself a result of the loss of international competitiveness by American business firms.

Japan, after some time lag, is now encountering similar problems. There was a shortage of engineers and factory workers in Japan, and many migrants from China, Taiwan, Iran, and Southeast Asia filled these needs, often illegally. Labor shortages still exist in some categories of work, and the Japanese immigration law has undergone successive modifications to legalize foreign workers. The number of Brazilians, Peruvians and Argentines, in particular, has increased in Japan. Yet, workers of unwanted categories arrive in large numbers, either with tourist visas (after which they stay over illegally), or in boats as fake political refugees. Japanese schools, health-care facilities, and housing cannot accommodate these legal and illegal foreigners. Some illegal foreigners behave well and cause no problems. For example, when recently, Iranians who could not find or afford living accommodations, congregated and slept in Japanese parks, they did no harm to the community. But the illegal workers are not eligible for medical insurance, and in the past, hospitals have had to absorb the costs of their care. The Japanese social system has not adjusted to such new situations.

Whatever the circumstances, one trend is unmistakable: all industrialized countries are becoming multiethnic and multicultural. The "original" inhabitants of these countries—for example, native Swedes or native Japanese—in contrast to foreigners, are individually heterogenizing themselves, choosing and taking up aspects of various foreign cultures. Even though some still believe that international contacts will lead to homogenization, the reverse is occurring, imperceptibly at first, but more and more visibly as we move toward the twenty-first century.

Fallacious Assumptions Held in the Twentieth Century

Some of the assumptions commonly held in the social sciences and psychology are incorrect. Examples are: (1) each culture is perfect and should never be changed; (2) all "normal" individuals in a given culture are acculturated and are epistemologically and psychologically homogeneous; (3) babies are born with a blank mind, to be filled with culture; (4) a culture is a mentally healthy environment for all its "normal" members; (5) rapid social change is traumatic to all persons; (6) cross-cultural or cross-national migration increases anxiety; (7) contact with many cultures will make the individual lose his/her identity.

These fallacious assumptions stem from epistemological errors made in the twentieth century. Incorrect epistemologies (i.e., knowledge theories or frameworks) were also sources of various political and social phenomena such as the colonialism that began in the sixteenth century; the isolationism, separatism, and regionalism of the twentieth century; and the seclusionistic aspects of the hippy movement in the 1960s. The interactive and interwoven cultural and individual heterogeneity of the twenty-first century will require a new epistemological framework.

Coming Decades

Massive cross-national migrations and cross-national career advancement in international business firms, and other professional and private movements of people across national boundaries are making each society more multiethnic and multicultural. The world is moving toward interwoven and interactive heterogeneity instead of localized, regionalized, and isolationistic homogeneity.

At the same time, the accessibility to information, entertainment, and lifestyles from many cultures is increasingly available to each individual, providing more opportunities for self-heterogenization and the creation of individually unique combinations

for ego identity. Self-heterogenization comes from the increased accessibility to different cultures, lifestyles, entertainments, foods, and languages. One can choose from an array of foreign books, videocassettes, and other commodities, can as it were turn them on and off and assemble one's own eclectic combinations. As a result, one is an active pattern-maker, not a passive victim of one radio station or a single newspaper as occurred at the beginning of mass-media technology. Today, there are many television channels to choose from, including programs from foreign countries.

Exposure to heterogeneity does not mean a loss of identity for individuals. It means a more unique individual identity. The same can be said of each nation. Increased immigration does not mean the loss of national identity. Rather, it provides an opportunity for making the nation more unique in redesigning its educational system, welfare system, community planning, and other systems.

Still, it requires hard work. The problems of unemployment, housing shortages, and meeting basic needs are enormous. Yet they should not be regarded as an unwelcome evil. They are a necessary step toward a new stage of our social evolution—toward an interwoven and interactive heterogeneity.

See also ETHNIC AND CULTURAL SEPARATISM; GLOBAL CULTURE; GLOBAL STATISTICS; INTERNAL MIGRATION, UNITED STATES; LIFESTYLES, ALTERNATIVE; LIFESTYLES, REGIONAL; LIFESTYLES, VALUE-ORIENTED; MIGRATION, INTERNATIONAL.

BIBLIOGRAPHY

MARUYAMA, MAGOROH. "Human Futuristics and Urban Planning." *Journal of American Institute of Planners* 29 (1973): 346–357.

———. "Interwoven and Interactive Heterogeneity in the Twenty-first Century." *Technological Forecasting and Social Change* 45 (1994): 93–102.

———. "Mindscapes and Science Theories." *Current Anthropology* 21 (1980): 589–599.

———. "The New Logic of Japan's Young Generations." *Technological Forecasting and Social Change* 28 (1985): 351–364.

Magoroh Maruyama

Lifestyles, Regional

Without fanfare, the Congressional Office of Technological Assessment in 1987 estimated that only 50,000 farms would produce 75 percent of America's food by 2000. Nothing was said about the other predictable effects of fewer farms and farm-based small towns: family breakdown, crime, failing schools, homelessness, or social polarization, all of which are likely to worsen. Societies that become too urbanized and cut off from their rural roots begin to drift toward biological and cultural extinction.

In the America of the future, regions with more farms and small towns—for example, New England and the Midwest—will stay culturally healthy longer. If farms continue to go under, farm-based small towns will either face extinction or become inhabited by culturally urbanized commuters to a city.

Lifestyles and culture are not the same thing. A culture is a ready-made design for living, with behavior and views on family, religion, work, and morality handed down from generation to generation. For example, some Jewish cultural traits go back about 160 generations to Abraham's departure from Ur. In villages the world over, race and religion aside, there is a common universal culture. Villages are made up of people who farm land. Naturally, they put prime value on property (land) and family (the work unit). Consequently, property and family are the basic rural social institutions, along with a work ethic and agricultural moral code ("You help me with my harvest, and I'll help you with yours.").

California led the shift from inherited culture to freely chosen lifestyles, followed by the South. The late twentieth century saw a great shift of farms away from the South (52 percent of the American total in 1950, half that in the 1990s) to the Midwest (32 percent to 51 percent over the same period). But California's problem is complicated—some might say alleviated—by millions of immigrants, mostly from Mexico and Latin America, but also from Asia, who do possess strong rural-based cultural traits, including high birthrates.

As in highly urbanized Russia and Europe, the birthrate among the white population of the United States declined below the replacement rate in 1972. (This is also related to farms: Over long spans of history, city dwellers fail to reproduce themselves at replacement rates while rural people fail to limit births.) In California, if existing rates of birth and migration are maintained, Americans of European descent will soon become a minority class. If Spanish-speaking immigrants keep their language and culture, California will soon be more Latino than Yankee, with a predominantly Asian professional elite.

California's biological and cultural dilemma is also complicated by the emergence of *lifestyles*, a word coined to fit a new late twentieth-century reality. Per capita GNP of $10,000–$30,000 over much of North America and Europe and the more urbanized parts of East Asia allow people to do something totally new in human society: namely, to live freely according to individual choice. Lifestyles are freely chosen; like fashions, they can be tried, kept, or discarded, something American commercial pop culture has been quick to exploit. American television and films penetrated to the world's remotest villages in the 1980s. Most people on Earth now see America as a splendid land of star treks, star wars, and stardust, where Superman swoops among skyscrapers, Batman and Dick Tracy keep the peace, and Jane Wyman fights for her vineyards and water rights.

The instant gratification and a refusal to subordinate a personal impulse to any larger social purpose or solidarity, which are implicit in lifestyles of what has been called "yuppie" behavior, help to polarize society and make cultural reproduction that much harder. As biological knowledge and computer technology explode, and galaxies and molecules are charted as never before, those in computers, semiconductors, telecommunications, robotics, electronics, politics, and the media prosper, but others do poorly.

A culture does not reproduce itself automatically from generation to generation. Families pass it on, helped by schools and churches. The experience of African Americans is illustrative. In the early 1940s, 75 percent of African Americans lived in the mainly rural South. As agriculture mechanized, 95 percent of all black-operated tenant farms—about 350,000—went under from 1950 to 1970. At the same time, white tenant farms dropped by 70 percent in the South, a decline involving about 1 million units. In 1988, 33,250 black-owned farms were left, but those families were expected to virtually disappear by 2000.

Where have they been going? To the cities of the North and West. Between 1940 and 1980 Chicago went from 8 percent to 40 percent black, Detroit from 9 percent to 63 percent, Washington, D.C. from 28 percent to 70 percent. A good many, perhaps half, made it into the middle class and accept its values. Those left behind are isolated in the ugliest, loneliest, most alienated and rootless, most crime-ridden, and most poorly educated slums in America. Many children are brought up by semiliterate teenage mothers on welfare in crowded public housing. America's 31 million African Americans in 1992, 12 percent of its people, learned less, earned less, lived worse, and died younger than anybody else. Homicide was the leading cause of death among young people. One young black man in four was either in prison, on parole, or on probation. Median black family income was 56 percent of whites, and blacks were twice as likely to be jobless. Nearly a third of all blacks, versus 10 percent of whites, lived below the poverty level, among them 45 percent of all black children.

African Americans show what could happen wherever people lose the natural apprenticeship to adult life that rural families used to give their children. In a city, the family is no longer the work unit, work itself is monetarized, teaching has shifted from parents to schools and to the mass media and to other youths, who educate peers according to their own antisocial norms. In inner-city neighborhoods, African Americans, Asians, Hispanics, and whites are caught in the same cultural trap, a subculture that produces youngsters unfit for anything but crime.

One way to solve this crisis of cultural reproduction is through a reruralization of America. This means a return to farms and small towns, to the family as the unit of both home and work to solve the problem of nurture and cultural transmission. No half-steps, like the essentially failed experiment of suburbia, which lacks a farm-based economy, can culturally work. (*See* INDIA for another perspective on the matter of reruralization.)

Without this reruralization, cultural contradictions will continue to come together, clash, ignite, and explode—as has already happened in Los Angeles.

See also CHANGE; CHANGE, CULTURAL; CHANGE, EPOCHAL; CHINA: ETHNIC REAWAKENING; CITIES, NORTH AMERICAN; ETHNIC AND CULTURAL SEPARATISM; FAMILIES AND HOUSEHOLDS; LIFESTYLES, ALTERNATIVE; LIFESTYLES, ETHNIC; LIFESTYLES, VALUE-ORIENTED; RELIGION: CHANGING BELIEFS; SOCIAL CONTROLS; VALUES CHANGE.

BIBLIOGRAPHY

CRITCHFIELD, RICHARD P. *Villagers: Changed Values, Altered Lives: The Closing of the Urban-Rural Gap*. New York: Doubleday, 1994.

Richard P. Critchfield

Lifestyles, Value-Oriented

Individual and social values are both products of their times and shaped by them. The values of the baby-boom generation, for example, stemmed largely from the increasing levels of education, affluence, and technology available in the 1950s and '60s. Those baby-boom values in turn gave shape not only to individual lifestyles but also to the social movements of those times: to the women's, minorities', consumer, and environmental movements that have endured and grown; and to the counterculture and me-generation attitudes that have largely faded.

Values and lifestyles of the future will reflect the influence of forces shaping the 1990s:

- Economic and financial concerns will play a much greater role in most Americans' daily lives as industries struggle to adapt to global competition and national economic restructuring affects employment levels.
- Demographic trends point to an aging population and increasing ethnic diversity.
- The baby-boom generation will reach middle age, pass through their own midlife crises, and emerge to assume leadership positions in business and politics.
- Women in increasing numbers will continue to assume new economic and political roles, but may opt for more flexible ways to combine their work and home lives.
- Environmentalism will spread, focusing more on local or indoor threats to human health and on planetwide concerns such as acid rain, ozone depletion, and the greenhouse effect.
- "Cocooning," a tendency to center one's life on one's home, will increase as technologies expand potentials to work and play at home and as people seek a retreat from the strains of public life.
- Time pressures, or at least individuals' perceptions of them, will intensify as the pace of change quickens and complexity increases in every facet of life.

There is no certainty as to how exactly these forces will play out, let alone what their effects on lifestyles will actually turn out to be. Speculation about the future is better focused on a range of alternative outcomes—"scenarios"—so that the full spectrum of possibilities comes to light. A framework for such speculation can be derived from the interplay of two critical dimensions of uncertainty—economic restructuring and the sociocultural environment. These uncertainties raise two key questions:

1. Will U.S. (and global) economic restructuring proceed successfully and relatively smoothly? Or will it be volatile and have only partial success?

TABLE 1.   Shifts in U.S. Consumer Lifestyle Groups, 1988–2000
(Percent of Adult Population)*

| | | Year 2000 Scenarios | | | |
Group	1988	*Freewheeling Consumption*	*Neocon- sumerism*	*Stagnation and Conflict*	*Return of Commonweal*
Actualizers	8	13	12	8	9
Fulfilleds	11	15	15	14	15
Believers	16	15	15	13	16
Achievers	13	11	12	12	12
Strivers	13	13	15	14	15
Experiencers	12	11	8	6	9
Makers	12	10	11	15	10
Strugglers	14	14	14	18	16

*Totals may not add to 100 because of rounding.

2. Will private (personal) agendas converge with or diverge from public (social and political) agendas? Such a shift is akin to Arthur Schlesinger's theme of alternating cycles between "private interest" and "public purpose."

Clearly, there will be major differences in the patterns of lifestyles, depending on which scenario develops. Stanford Research Institute's (SRI's) Values and Lifestyles typology (see Table 1) portrays the following shifts among U.S. consumers: Generally, all four scenarios provide a favorable social environment for Actualizers and especially for Fulfilleds. In large part, this development reflects the aging of the baby-boom generation and that

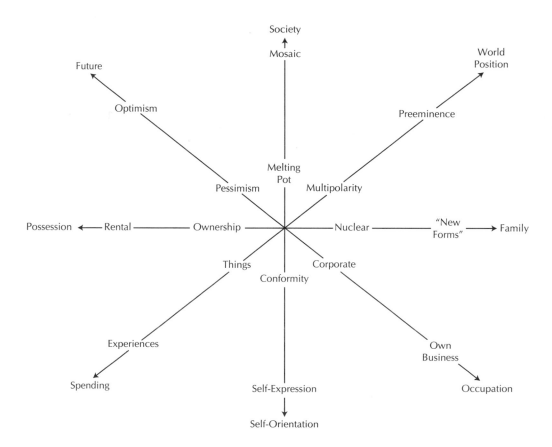

FIGURE 1.   The American Dream: axes or a reshaping. (Source: SRI International.)

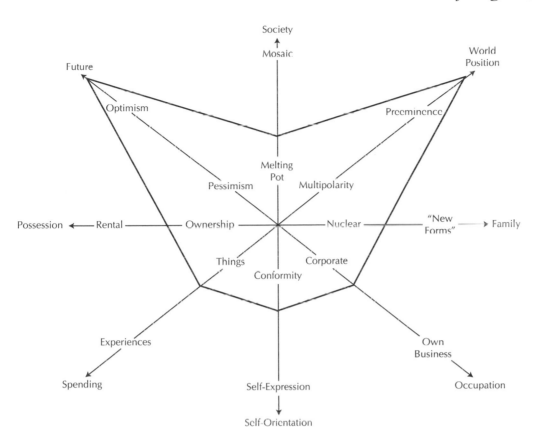

FIGURE 2.   The Old Dream. (Source: SRI International.)

large cohort's increasing access to substantially greater resources. It also reflects a warming of sociocultural concerns in America. On the other hand, the numbers of Experiencers and, to a lesser extent, Makers will most likely decline, in part because both groups represent entry points into the system for new adults; and the overall shift toward an older, more mature population will move the social focus away from the youthful experiences that have dominated the past two or three decades. Finally, the Strivers and, even more, the Strugglers will probably increase as a percentage of the adult population, reflecting the nation's struggle to deal with the problems of economic restructuring (particularly in the "Stagnation" and "Commonweal" scenarios).

Another perspective on future lifestyles can be discerned in the reshaping of the "American Dream" by these same formative forces. The post–World War II version of "the Dream" was summarized by Robert Settle and Pamela Alreck in the March 1988 issue of *Marketing Communication:*

> Knowing that they had saved the world, Americans were thoroughly immersed in optimism and confor-

mity. The good job with a large company, marriage and family, the new suburban tract home, and the station wagon and car coat to go with it. Dad worked, but Mom usually didn't. He had the job. She had the kids. It was all pretty nice. And for those baby-boom kids, it was going to be even nicer when they grew up. They firmly believed it and expected it.

We can anticipate that these forces will reshape the values and lifestyles associated with this Dream along eight axes or dimensions:

1. *Revisioning society*—from the centralizing, homogeneous tendencies of the "melting pot" to the decentralizing, diversifying "mosaic society" of the future.
2. *Reassessing U.S. world position*—from the unquestioned world dominance of the late 1940s, through confrontation with the former communist bloc, to the uncertainties of a multipolar world (as the sole remaining superpower).
3. *Redefining family*—from the Norman Rockwell nuclear family of the 1950s to the many new definitions of "family" in the 1990s.
4. *Realigning occupation*—from the aspiration of stable corporate employment to the reality of

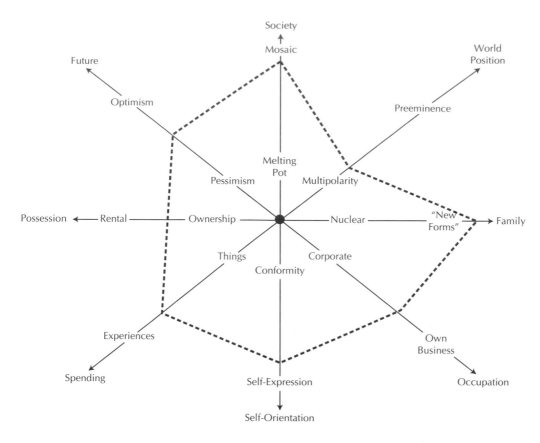

FIGURE 3.   The New Dream. (Source: SRI International.)

uncertain job restructuring and the pursuit of multiple careers in a lifetime.

5. *Reorienting self*—from outer-directed conformity to inner-directed self-actualization (*if* economic circumstances permit).

6. *Revaluing spending*—"from the acquisition of products with utility to the enjoyment of experiences with intensity," as futurist Jay Ogilvy has phrased it.

7. *Rethinking ownership*—from the pride (and status) of ownership to the growing convenience of leasing and renting.

8. *Reappraising the future*—from the boundless optimism of the postwar era to caution about an uncertain future and, in some cases, a lowering of consumer expectations.

The nature and extent of this "reshaping" can be illustrated graphically by means of three charts. This representation should not be taken too literally, but it does suggest a deeper and more serious truth: the United States is no longer the nation it was even forty years ago—in many important ways, Americans think differently, behave differently, and dream differently than we did. And these differences can only expand in the future.

SRI's Typology of Lifestyles

SRI International's Values and Lifestyles (VALS 2); program groups consumers into eight segments within a conceptual framework of "self-orientation" and "resources available." Self-orientation distinguishes between those who make decisions with a "principle-orientation" (e.g., using criteria such as quality, integrity, tradition) and those who are either "status-oriented" or "action-oriented." The eight types are as follows:

- *Actualizers* have sufficient resources to have a unique orientation—a mixture of the active and the reflective. As consumers, they are adventurous, quality-conscious, and exhibit cultivated taste for "the finer things in life."
- *Fulfilleds* turn their principle-orientation and high level of resources into a mature, self-confident outlook. As consumers, they are conservative and practical, but open to new products and services.
- *Believers*, with their principle-orientation and moderate resources, have a traditional, comfortable outlook based on family, community, and moral precepts. They are loyal and predictable

consumers, not easily persuaded to change their buying patterns.

- *Achievers*, with a status orientation and high level of resources, define their goals and valued activities in terms of their relationships with social, professional, and family groups. As consumers, they prefer established brands, and they respond to products and services that they feel will enhance their position in the eyes of their peers.
- *Strivers* are status-oriented, but their modest resources make them unsure of themselves and concerned with the opinions of others. As consumers, they follow fashions and fads and often desire products that are financially beyond their reach.
- *Experiencers* combine an action-orientation with a high level of resources, and savor the new, the offbeat, the risky. As consumers, they buy on impulse and are effectively persuaded by promises of action, variety, and adventure.
- *Makers* express their action-orientation and moderate level of resources in constructive activity, working on or building from the things that surround them. As consumers, they seek products with a practical purpose and make decisions based on considerations like comfort, durability, and utility.
- *Strugglers* have a low level of resources and little clear self-orientation. Experiencing the world as pressing and difficult, they are satisfied just to meet immediate demands. As consumers, they are extremely price-sensitive and constitute a "low yield" market.

See also BEHAVIOR: SOCIAL CONSTRAINTS; HOLISTIC BELIEFS; POPULATION GROWTH: UNITED STATES; SOCIAL CHANGE: UNITED STATES; VALUES.

BIBLIOGRAPHY

PISCATELLA, JOSEPH. *Choices for a Healthy Heart*. New York: Workman Publishing, 1987.

SETTLE, ROBERT, and ALRECK, PAMELA. "Reshaping the American Dream." *Marketing Communication* (March 1988).

WHITE, JOHN. *Lifestyle Priorities*. Wheaton, IL: Harold Shaw Publications, 1990.

Ian H. Wilson

Literacy.

See ILLITERACY.

Literature

The art of writing was invented some 5,000 years ago, and the things called books came along not many centuries after. Originally, rolls of papyrus or vellum were called *biblia* (hence the Bible) from the name of the material, while folded pages stitched together were *codices, codex* in the singular. The Jews chose the roll form for their sacred texts (and still do); Christians chose the codex form. It was not long before codices also began to be termed *books*, which they are to this day.

What is a book? Is it the physical object in your hand? Or is it the contents, the thoughts or story in your head but also in the book? The question is important for the future of books. When codices became popular, around 500 A.D., they did so because they were more convenient than rolls, which had to be rolled out—a cumbersome process with a lengthy text—in order to be read. Flipping pages was easier, especially after paper replaced parchment around 1450. Paper could also be printed on with movable type presses—Gutenberg's great invention, which ensured the triumph of that other great invention, the book itself, for the next five centuries.

Technology is ruthless; what is more convenient always wins. Today, physical volumes are becoming comparatively less easy to use than they were. Their competitors, CD-ROMs or online services, will be much preferable in the not-distant future. Parchment rolls endured for centuries after codices replaced them for most uses, and physical books are likely to endure in the future as curiosities, as lovely collector's items, and because for some purposes they remain useful. Would a CD stop a bullet as well as a Bible in your pocket? Could you fold faded flowers in an online service for a lover to come upon some day? Such trivialities apart, books will not be around much longer. In fifty years most people will live and die without ever seeing a physical book except in a museum or in churches, which both tend to be conservative.

That part is easy. It is harder to predict the effect of this change on books in the other sense of the term: on literature. The Greeks invented most of the literary forms we have today: poems, long and short; dramas, tragic and comic; novels and stories; histories; mathematical and scientific treatises; philosophy, both practical (including economics) and theoretical (including psychology). All these types of subject matter survived from rolls to codices, from codices to printed books. They will also probably survive when electronic "books" replace physical ones.

Nevertheless, there were subtle changes. Codices were read by many more people than rolls; their subject matter therefore became more popular. Cheap printed books could be used to promote new ideas and ideologies; every man, and then every woman, could be an authority if he or she published a book. Even so, there were still obstacles to communication: linguistic, economic, censorial, and others. An industry grew up, and publishers insisted that a book have an identifiable audience before they would invest in it; the bottom line was king. But it was just that sort of information monopoly Gutenberg had dreamed of overcoming. At least Luther dreamed of it, and saw in the new books the promise of a better, freer age.

Today, things (are they spiritual or material beings?) like Internet hold out a similar promise. A boy (or girl) in Des Moines can reach out to children of similar interests in Vitebsk; a girl (or boy) from Lillehammer can reach out to children in San Francisco. All the walls are coming down, and anyone will be able to publish, to say nothing of writing, his or her own book. "Writing" may not be the right word. Many of the new "books" will be spoken, felt, visualized, or dreamed, not written down. Will they be truer or less true? Perhaps truth itself will change. Will they be better or worse? Most will be worthless, like most books today: vapid, jejeune, or offensive. A few will be better than anything that has ever been, in ways it is utterly impossible to predict.

The first printed books were more private than the codices they replaced; the new technology made that possible. The new books of the near future will be intensely personal, the outpourings of lonely, naked souls seeking to touch someone, somewhere, to find a home in another human breast. We see it happening already, where authors seem to conceal nothing from readers, revealing their deepest hopes, fears, prejudices. But is this merely a new kind of concealment when such books have to be published, publicized, and sold, their authors interviewed and displayed? The publishing business demands this from its professionals. The rest of us are amateurs, and we all have one great story to tell, which we compose ceaselessly as long as we live; it is the story of our own life. Without it, we are not sane, perhaps not even human. Future authors, ourselves, will be truly private persons, awaking in the night to share our thoughts, to tell our stories to just anybody, anywhere. What of forms? There will be none, or new forms will come into being, also unpredictable. A

new, great, different literature will come into existence, and everything before it will seem stodgy and old.

As one side effect, writing, invented 5,000 years ago and for five millennia the key to power, wealth, and fame, will cease to have any importance whatsoever. Since this is inevitable, whether or not it is to be wept over is also of no importance whatsoever.

See also ARTS; ELECTRONIC PUBLISHING; LIBRARIES; PRINTED WORD.

BIBLIOGRAPHY

JAYNES, JULIAN. *The Origin of Consciousness in the Breakdown of the Bicameral Mind,* 2nd ed. Boston: Houghton Mifflin, 1989.
ONG, WALTER J. *Orality and Literacy: The Technologizing of the World.* Bradford, MA: Routledge, Chapman, & Hall, 1982.
POSTMAN, NEIL. *Technopoly: The Surrender of Culture to Technology.* New York: Alfred Knopf, 1992.
VAN DOREN, CHARLES. *A History of Knowledge.* New York: Carol Publishing Group, 1991.

Charles Van Doren

Longevity

How long on average can a child born today expect to live? Are there fixed limits on how long people can live? What are the prospects for human life extension through advances in biology and medical technology? As people become increasingly concerned with the ways in which diet, exercise, and lifestyle affect their health, can modifications in behavior result in longer, healthier lives?

Tales of extraordinarily long lives, such as the biblical Methuselah, who allegedly died at the age of 969, or the eighteenth-century British farmer Thomas Parr, who supposedly died shortly before his 153rd birthday, reflect the belief that remarkably long life may be possible.

Life Expectancy

Life expectancy refers to the average number of years a person or group of people born at a specific time can expect to live. When Julius Caesar was born, some 2,000 years ago, average life expectancy at birth was only about eighteen to twenty-two years. By 1900 life expectancy at birth was forty-nine years. In contrast, an American infant born in 1990 can expect to live an average of 75.4 years. The striking increase in life expectancy at birth during the twentieth century is primarily attributable to public-health advances that have controlled the spread of contagious diseases. Today, death before age sixty-five is way down in the United States; about seven in ten deaths occur to people age sixty-five or older.

Life expectancy of infants is affected by birth defects and infectious disease, the life expectancy of young men by war, and that of women by the number of pregnancies experienced. Life expectancy for all ages may be changed by famine and malnutrition, civil unrest, epidemics, sanitation, and the quality of medical care available.

Today females can expect to live longer than males in industrialized societies. In the United States in 1990, for example, male life expectancy at birth had increased from forty-six years in 1900 to about seventy-two years. During the same period, life expectancy for females went from forty-eight to seventy-nine years. Men who reached age sixty-five in 1990 had an average remaining life of about fifteen years, women nearly nineteen years.

African Americans and Native Americans of both sexes today have shorter life expectancies at birth than whites, reflecting their persistently lower family income. African-American males have an average life expectancy at birth of about sixty-five years; and females, seventy-four. For each racial or ethnic group, the higher the level of family income, the longer the life expectancy at birth.

In nations where the majority of the population is poor, life expectancy is much shorter. Even in a wealthy country such as the United States, in a very poor state such as Louisiana, life expectancy is several years less than for the nation as a whole.

Life Span

Although life expectancy has changed dramatically throughout industrialized nations, many scientists believe that all living beings may have a biologically fixed life span, a maximum number of years that it is theoretically possible to live. Remarkably long lives reported in the past reflect a mix of different ways of counting years, lack of accurate records, deliberate falsification of records, and wishful thinking. The longest authenticated life span is 120 years (Shigechizo Izumi, Japan). The growth in absolute numbers of old people in industrialized nations such as the United States thus re-

flects not changes in lifespan but changes in average life expectancy. In 1900 only 42 percent of Americans could expect to live until their sixty-fifth birthday; three-fourths will do so today.

Why do all living organisms age? Scientists have proposed various hypotheses. Two common categories are (1) damage or "wear-and-tear" theories, and (2) program theories. Wear-and-tear theories argue that cells or organs of the body are unable to repair themselves as they age due to inability of the immune system to resist disease. Program theories suggest that longevity is genetically controlled: a "biological clock" programs the body. The existence of a "death hormone" has also been proposed by some biologists.

Actuarial Estimates

Several nations have higher life expectancies than that of the United States. Japan has the world's highest life expectancy at birth (eighty-two for females and seventy-six for males) and at age sixty-five (eighty-five for females and eighty-one for males). Other nations with greater life expectancies at birth than that of the United States include Sweden, Iceland, the Netherlands, Australia, Canada, Norway, Spain, the United Kingdom, Italy, Switzerland, Hong Kong, Andorra, and some twenty others. Life-expectancy estimates usually rely on the premise that all current age-specific death rates will continue in force for everyone in the population throughout their lives. If health conditions of the population continue to improve, some scientists argue that this assumption underestimates actual life expectancy. If we assume that a lowering of the death rate at each age continues at the same pace as it did during the 1980s, life expectancy at birth for a child born in 1990 may increase by ten years, with the result that children born in 2015 could expect to live into their nineties.

Life Extension

TRENDS

Some scientists also argue that there is no biological limit to life itself, but only age-related physiological deterioration for which intervention may be possible in the future. Recent laboratory research on fruit flies indicates that when several inbred strains of flies are placed in different environments, some strains do not age. Such research has raised two important questions: (1) Are there biologically fixed and species-specific limits to the life span? (2) Do environmental risk factors influence longevity?

Prevention programs that reduce risk factors—lack of exercise, smoking, high-cholesterol diets implicated in heart disease, postmenopausal use of estrogen (implicated in certain types of cancer)—and adoption of a healthy lifestyle may result only in a one- or two-year increase in life expectancy.

How would life expectancy and life span be affected if all causes of death due to disease and accidents were eliminated? According to some scientists, if people were allowed to live out their lives free from heart disease, cancer, other diseases, and accidents, the average life span might be extended to about age one hundred. An opposing view offered by University of Chicago and Argonne National Laboratory scientists suggests that such gains are unrealistic, because science and medicine have pushed human life expectancy to its natural biological limit of about eighty-five years.

Closely allied to the issue of life extension is the question: What is normal aging? A promising area for investigation lies in genetics. Biologists studying simpler organisms have begun to develop frameworks to distinguish various types of genes interacting both with each other and with external factors.

A second promising area of research is the effect of dietary restriction. In the 1930s, scientists recognized that the lives of rats could be extended if their intake of calories was reduced, a finding replicated in numerous species. Caloric restriction not only prolongs life but is associated with later appearance and lower incidence of most spontaneous diseases among relatively simple species. Studies at the National Institutes of Health and elsewhere are evaluating whether restricted, nutritionally adequate diets slow aging among more complex species, such as nonhuman primates. Whether caloric restriction among human beings reduces aging, however, remains controversial.

TECHNOLOGIES

Breakthroughs in modern health care and medicine, such as antibiotics and organ transplants, have permitted more people to reach old age. If life expectancies continue to increase, issues arise about the quality of life for older people: the number of years of active life expectancy versus the number of years of chronic illness or incapacity. Merely expanding life expectancy without eradicating chronic disabilities would swell the proportion of people who are likely to suffer from dementia, arthritis, diabetes, and so forth.

Advances in biotechnology, detection methods, and ways to modify disease processes hold enormous promise. Studies in molecular biology and immunology indicate that certain molecules on cancer cells might be able to eradicate cancer cells by triggering the body's immune system. Studies in human genetics now enable discovery of many genetic disorders before their onset. By 1992, gene mapping of the DNA in cells had identified twenty-three of the twenty-four types of human chromosomes. Many diseases result from defects in specific genes. Because chromosome 21 is associated with some forms of dementia and other disorders, a clearer understanding of its genetic content is expected to have great medical relevance.

As techniques become available to repair genetic defects or replace defective genes, such diseases can be treated at their source. Searches for specific drugs that supplant the loss of genetic function and directly or indirectly regulate the rate of age-related diseases and perhaps aging itself, are underway. Research on a human growth hormone, for example, indicates that six months of injections of a genetically engineered version of the body's natural growth hormone reversed many age-related changes in the body by as much as twenty years.

If the genetic program for aging can be stopped or slowed, human life expectancy can be strikingly extended. Gene therapy, however, raises controversial social-policy issues associated with eugenics or selective breeding. Genetic engineering and gene therapy hold promise for bringing about radical changes in the physical and psychological attributes of human beings. Who should decide what normal human functioning is? If indeed the human life span can be extended so that there are no natural limits, how many years should people live? What changes in our social institutions would be required if life expectancy increases dramatically, or if there is no limit to the life span? These are challenges for the future.

See also AGING OF THE POPULATION; DEATH AND DYING; ELDERLY, LIVING ARRANGEMENTS; GENETIC ENGINEERING; GENETICS.

BIBLIOGRAPHY

ANGIER, NATALIE. "Human Growth Hormone Reverses Effects of Age." *New York Times,* July 5, 1990.
BOON, THIERRY. "Teaching the Immune System to Fight Cancer." *Scientific American* (March 1993): 83–89.

KOLATA, GINA. "Study Challenges Longevity Theory." *New York Times,* October 21, 1992.

LEWIS, PAUL. "Japanese Live Longer, the U.N. Finds." *New York Times,* April 26, 1992.

OLSHANSKY, S. JAY. "Estimating the Upper Limits to Human Longevity." *Population Today* 20/1 (1992): 6–8.

TAUBER, CYNTHIA M. "Sixty-five Plus in America." In *Current Population Reports.* Washington, DC: U.S. Department of Commerce, Bureau of the Census, 1993.

Elizabeth W. Markson

Lotteries.

See CRIME RATES; GAMBLING.

M

Macroeconomics

Macroeconomists study the complex "whole" of an economy, exploring how relationships among such factors as levels of taxes, savings, investment, and employment determine the total economic output of a nation. The goal of economists has long been to turn their field into a science, a "values-free" discipline in which the interplay of factors such as those mentioned above could be forecast as reliably as astronomers plot the motion of planets. By mid-century—thanks to computers and advanced mathematical modeling—this dream appeared realizable. To some, however, the goal remained an idealistic pipedream.

This divergence of opinion arises because economics is both a science and an ideology, concerned both with measuring what is and advocating what should be. As philosopher David Hume stated two centuries ago, it is nearly impossible to distinguish the line between descriptions of fact and prescriptions of what ought to be. The U.S. government has been caught in that muddle of confusion from the day in 1791 when Secretary of the Treasury Alexander Hamilton first attempted to macromanage the national economy. Hamilton believed that the United States would be a stronger and richer nation if it rejected Thomas Jefferson's dream of an agrarian society composed of "virtuous" farmers living in decentralized communities and, instead, embraced wholeheartedly the urban English model of industrialization. Significantly,

Hamilton did not make his case in terms of a personal vision, instead, he argued against Jefferson on "scientific" grounds, purporting to show that there was greater potential for gains in productivity in manufacturing than in agriculture. To achieve those higher levels of economic growth, Hamilton advocated a national industrial policy in which emerging industries manifesting the greatest potential for growth would be identified—and their domestic development incentivized—by means of government subsidies, tariff protection, and provision of such enabling "infrastructure" as roads, canals, and ports. He even called for the creation of a national ministry to promote the technological state of the art in the emerging industries. According to Hamilton, it was necessary to make government the partner of domestic industry because American industry needed the same kind of support that the French, Dutch, and particularly the British were giving their prime exporters.

In making this argument, Hamilton found himself directly at odds with the new economic philosophy of laissez-faire, articulated in 1776 by Adam Smith in *The Wealth of Nations*. In that influential work, Smith argued that the economy of a country would grow faster and more efficiently without governmental intervention. Thus, a debate was joined that persists to this day between economists, like Hamilton, who believe it necessary for government to take remedial and proactive measures to make economies produce at a peak level and economists, like Smith, who believe that "the invisible hand" that regulates free markets will produce the greatest overall good for society. Smith's Law of Supply and Demand, for much of American history, was the ruling principle for national economic policy, violated only as an exception—and seldom avowedly.

The Hamiltonian school achieved its moment of ascendancy during the Great Depression. John Maynard Keynes argued successfully that when levels of aggregate demand were insufficient to tap the nation's full capacity to produce goods and services, it was prudent—and probably necessary—for government to spur demand by increasing public expenditures. Keynes argued that, left to its own devices, the market was not self-regulating as Smith had claimed; rather, government must intervene when private savings and investment were insufficient to produce full employment. Thus, by manipulating the nation's fiscal (spending) policy, the Keynesian descendants of Hamilton believed government could produce a more desirable outcome than would be derived from the workings of the market alone.

In this century, the Smithian school reasserted itself in the post–World War II era, particularly in the writings of Milton Friedman and his fellow free-market economists. This school argued that the economy could be macromanaged more effectively through the manipulation of the quantity of money in circulation than through the more interventionist fiscal route. During the presidency of Ronald Reagan, these "monetarists" reached their peak of influence, advocating a minimalist role for government.

The somewhat arcane differences between those who advocate the fiscal and the monetary approaches become concrete in the matter of taxation. At times, Keynesian methods require significant tax increases, while monetarist methods usually have less impact on taxpayers' purses. To achieve what are felt to be higher-order goals—for instance, fuller employment, greater social opportunity—the Keynesians are more willing than the Smithians to spend public funds and thus either to raise taxes or to incur public debt. For their part, the followers of Smith are more willing to accept whatever social and economic outcomes—good or ill—emerge as consequences of the free play of market forces. Differences between the two philosophies are self-evident. The latter believe that the market naturally rewards the virtuous; therefore, nothing effective can be done to alter the existing order of society. The former believe that because social outcomes derive from arrangements that

were designed by humans, they do not represent a natural order; therefore, the existing order effectively can be changed by intervening.

However, among most economists, the controversy between these two schools of thought typically rages *not* over their underlying ideological differences but over what they call empirical matters: specifically, over the extent to which levels of taxation affect national economic growth. For example, the disciples of Keynes argue that, by judicious use of government spending on social welfare, underemployed humans can become more fully productive; thus, in the long run, the overall economy will grow. In contrast, the disciples of Smith argue that the economy will grow faster if money is left in the hands of those who earned it, because they will invest it more efficiently than will government officials. Both sides attempt to marshall data to buttress their respective cases. Unfortunately, it is devilishly hard to trace objective causal relationships between a nation's level of taxation and its gross domestic product (GDP)—let alone to establish a meaningful correlation between taxation and the more difficult to measure "standard of living" or "quality of life." The subjectivity of this purportedly empirical issue is illustrated by the two tables below:

Who can conclude from this data what the optimal level of taxation ought to be in order to maximize the overall wealth of a nation? As evidenced, some rich nations tax heavily, as do some poor ones; and some rich nations tax lightly, as do some poor ones. It is not simply that rates of taxation do not correlate well with per capita GDP (or with other standard economic measures, such as productivity). More to the point, among the developed nations the least-taxed people (namely, Americans) have for the last several decades been the most vociferous in proclaiming themselves "over-taxed." If nothing else, this illustrates Hume's observation about the essential confusion between what is and what ought to be.

The American feeling of being overtaxed led to a series of taxpayer revolts, the most recent beginning in the 1970s. The close of the 1980s marked the end of the Keynesian era of expanding government that had begun fifty years earlier in the New Deal. As the rate of growth in taxation slowed, there was also an increase in the growth of deficit spending. The relationship between these two factors became itself a matter of considerable controversy, with one side arguing that the deficit was caused by "taxing and spending" and the other by "borrowing and spending." What is now clearer to both sides is

TABLE 1.   Per Capita GDP of Selected Nations

RICHEST COUNTRIES (rank order based on GDP per capita)		*MOST HEAVILY TAXED* (rank order based on total tax revenue for 1992 as percent of GDP)
1. Switzerland	$33,085	20
2. Finland	27,527	14
3. Sweden	26,652	1
4. Denmark	25,150	2
5. Norway	24,924	4
6. Japan	23,801	22
7. West Germany	23,536	10
8. Iceland	22,907	19
9. Luxembourg	22,895	3
10. United States	21,449	23
11. Canada	21,418	15
12. France	21,105	7
13. Austria	20,391	8
14. Belgium	19,303	6
15. Italy	18,921	9
16. Holland	18,676	5
17. Australia	17,215	24
18. U.K.	16,985	18
19. New Zealand	13,020	16
20. Spain	12,609	17
21. Ireland	12,131	12
22. Greece	6,505	11
23. Portugal	6,085	13
24. Turkey	1,896	21

Source: OECD. GDP figures, 1990. Tax figures, 1992.

that the economy seldom behaves in practice as it is supposed to in theory. For example, the 1980s experiment with "supply-side" economics produced almost exactly the opposite of the intended effect: drastically lowering taxes produced more debt and dampened productive activity.

One constant throughout these controversies has been the self-confidence of economists that there is a "technological fix" to the problem of macromanagement. There has been nearly unlimited faith that—along with the manifest increase in the sophistication of their mathematical modeling—inevitably they will find the answer to such questions as "how much taxation will produce the optimal rate of economic growth?" Indeed, many prominent futurists share the belief that an increase in scientific knowledge will result in the ability to successfully plan for full employment. The "input-output" models of the economy pioneered by Jan Tinbergen, Wassily Leontief, Lawrence Klein, and others are often cited as an indication that economic policymaking might become a purely technical matter free of ideology. The most recent models involve hundreds of simultaneous equations describing the dynamic interactions of dozens of variables, including prices, wage, interest, tax, and investment rates, and a myriad of other factors that influence the overall wealth of a nation. Not only have these models begun to explain the causes of domestic business cycles, but they are being expanded to show the interrelationships among all the nations in the evolving world economy. These models promise not only sound scientific guidance on the best policies for domestic economies, but they also hold promise for knowledgeably addressing the more pressing problems of global economic development.

Will these promises be realized? The answers to that question are ultimately predicated on whether one believes that economics is, in the final analysis, a true science. If it is, then economies will one day be modeled successfully, and the ideology that now dominates policy debates may well disappear. But if economics proves to be the study of human behav-

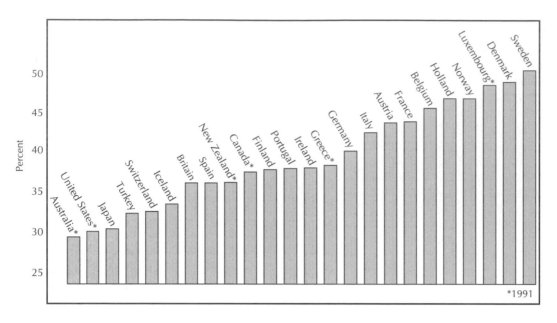

FIGURE 1.   Total tax revenue as a percentage of GNP. (Source: OECD.)

ior—infinitely varied, complex, and value-laden—then it probably will remain forever unmodelable. As a consequence, the politics of economics will continue to be as it has been: a great debate over choice among alternative visions of the good society.

Doubtless, there is a part of economics—perhaps the largest part—that is measurable and, thus, susceptible to the kind of development in terms of models and instruments of measurement found in the hard sciences. There is no question that the increased application of such tools is necessary for social progress. The complexity of history, however, lends credence to the belief that the measurement of what "is" may be the easiest part. The centuries-old debate over what "ought" to be is not only more difficult, it is the most marvelously human element in one of the most quintessentially human of all activities: the production and distribution of the fruits of society.

See also CONSERVATISM, POLITICAL; CREDIT, DEBT, AND BORROWING; DEFICITS, GOVERNMENTAL; ECONOMIC CYCLES: MODELS AND SIMULATIONS; ECONOMICS; FREE TRADE; GLOBAL BUSINESS: DOMINANT ORGANIZATIONAL FORMS; INVESTMENT; LIBERALISM, POLITICAL; MARKETPLACE ECONOMICS; PRODUCTIVITY; SAVINGS; TAXES; UNEMPLOYMENT.

BIBLIOGRAPHY

BACH, GEORGE L. *Macroeconomics: Analysis, Decision-making and Policy*. Englewood Cliffs, NJ: Prentice-Hall, 1987.

BOBER, STANLEY. *Modern Microeconomics: A Post-Keynesian Perspective*. London: Croom Helm, 1987.

BUITER, WILLEM H. *International Macroeconomics*. New York: Oxford University Press, 1990.

DERNBERG, THOMAS F. *Global Macroeconomics*. New York: HarperCollins, 1988.

FROYEN, RICHARD T. *Macroeconomics: Theories and Policies*. New York: Macmillan, 1990.

PERKINS, J. O. *General Approach to Macroeconomic Theory*. New York: St. Martin's Press, 1990.

PRATTEN, C. F. *Applied Macroeconomics*. New York: Oxford University Press, 1990.

WONNACOTT, PAUL. *Macroeconomics*. New York: John Wiley, 1990.

James O'Toole

Macroengineering

As population pressures increase, we must seek to use the vast ocean spaces to relieve congestion and meet other global needs. The future will bring many large-scale projects that utilize sites above and beneath oceans and along newly created shorelines. Such projects will be developed first by nations such as Japan, which have very high population densities, a shortage of land sites for new construction, and the available money to spend for the development of structures floating on the surface.

Floating Structures

A Japanese engineering firm has designed "an all-embracing plan for the utilization of marine space" in the form of a floating station that includes a fish farm, a marina, a convention center, shops, and restaurants. The Mediterranean principality Monaco is studying the possibility of building floating island clusters within a protective seawall to gain more development sites. This project could be completed early in the twenty-first century. Another offshore floating city, proposed for Sagami Bay, Japan, would connect the Tsukuba science city and Narita airport via a subsurface line.

Planners have long sought to create airports at midocean locations via various types of floating rafts and even icebergs. Because of environmental problems and costs, building new airports near large cities is becoming prohibitive. Consequently, interest in developing floating airports serving coastal cities has been renewed. There is also growing interest in floating hotels, power-generating stations, water treatment plants, offices, and other industrial facilities. Floating hotels can move from one site to another with the seasons or provide overflow accommodations for major events. A large pulp mill has been towed from Japan and sited on the Amazon River. Floating power plants serve at numerous locations around the world. A Norwegian firm has built a floating resort condominium. A proposed 220-meter ship providing 120 floating offices renting at one-tenth of the usual Tokyo rates could also offer recreational cruises on weekends.

Off-Shore Construction

While floating facilities are suited for deep water, there is actually more activity and planning involving shallow-water site development of structures that can be built on man-made islands or moored to the sea floor. The new Kansai airport being built in Osaka Bay, Japan, features a man-made island large enough for jet runways. Built by moving a small mountain from the nearby shore via barges, the island is linked to the shore by a bridge-causeway. This project may provide the precedent and guidelines for other offshore airports in Japan, including those already planned for Nagoya and Fukuoka and under discussion for Tokyo Bay.

In Macao, on the coast of China, a new airport is being built on a site in the Pearl River near Taipa Island. The site has been filled and pilings have been sunk more than 61 meters deep to support the runway. A development group has proposed a new airport for the Toronto area, situated in the Georgian Bay about sixteen kilometers offshore.

More ambitious is the proposed island city for Tokyo Bay, which would provide a site of 30,000 hectares in size and could support a population of 5 million. Another Japanese proposal involves diking 800 kilometers of river frontage in the Tokyo-Osaka area. This frontage would be up to 200–300 meters wide and would provide sites for housing, roads, parks, and infrastructure. The project would add 650,000 housing units by the year 2020. Singapore, another crowded nation, has added substantial areas via the reclamation of sites in shallow waters. Most noteworthy has been the huge long-term program of reclaiming land from the sea in the Netherlands, which has effectively doubled the land area of the nation!

An interesting possibility for the future involves growing new atolls by stimulating coral growth with electric currents. Development of this technology would make it possible to create many new sites where none exist today.

Undersea Habitation

Scuba diving has led to an explosive growth in tourism in many locations where the diving environment is particularly attractive. To serve this fast-growing market, entrepreneurs have developed dive centers, including underwater observation or rest facilities in tropical waters. The next step will be to develop underwater hotels and resorts. Improving technology for underwater work and travel ultimately may lead to the construction of new communities and cities under water. This technology may open a vast new world of sites twice as large as our present land areas.

Continental Links

New technology makes it possible to fulfill the centuries-old dreams of connecting the world's land masses. In 1988 Japan celebrated the connection of two main islands, Honshu and Hokkaido, via the new fifty-five-kilometer Seikan tunnel, the world's longest tunnel. More than 200 years after Napoleon proposed it, the tunnel between France and the United Kingdom nears completion. Consisting of two parallel railroad tunnels and a service tunnel, the trio of fifty-kilometer tubes extends from Calais to Folkestone. This new channel tunnel or "chunnel" will enable high-speed rail service from London to Paris. Motorists will be able to drive onto rail cars at one end and be carried quickly to interconnecting super highways on the opposite end. A long-sought link between Europe and Africa at Gibraltar, urged by the United Nations, involves a tunnel or combined tunnel-bridge-causeway. Under construction is Scanlink, which will connect Scandinavia and Europe via three interrelated projects: the Oresund Bridge between Sweden and Denmark, the Danish Great Belt tunnel-causeway among several islands, and the Fehmarn bridge/tunnel between Denmark and Germany.

Such projects are pale compared to proposals for a transatlantic tube for supersonic trains. Furthermore, Dr. Yutaka Mochida, one of the world's leading tunnel experts, proposes a global transportation system that involves tunnels under the Pacific.

Canals and Locks

Not to be overlooked among new global links are a number of canal projects. The just completed link between the Rhine and Danube rivers provides a connection between Rotterdam and the Black Sea. First undertaken by Holy Roman Emperor Charlemagne in the seventh century, this project was completed with the construction of a canal in southwestern Germany in 1992. Now, planners are talking about an even more ambitious project to link Vienna with Hamburg via a Danube-Oder-Elbe canal system.

In the Pacific Rim region a planned 102-kilometer canal across Thailand's Isthmus of Kra would shorten ocean routes by more than 1,000 kilometers for tankers moving from the Persian Gulf past Singapore to Japan. Discussions of a second Central American canal have been revived recently by a group of investors who might operate it for profit. One possible route crosses Nicaragua.

Global super projects published in *Site World* in 1992 tallied 1,334 projects, of which approximately one-third were under construction, another one-third were in the design stage, and the balance were in early planning. More and more, macro-engineering is not constrained by what minds can conjure.

See also DEVELOPMENT, ALTERNATIVE; ENGINEERING; GLOBAL ENVIRONMENTAL PROBLEMS; HIGH TECHNOLOGY; LAND USE PLANNING; NUCLEAR POWER; SCIENCE CITIES; SPACE COLONIZATION; SPACE FLIGHT; TRANSPORTATION.

BIBLIOGRAPHY

CONWAY, MCKINLEY. *Airport Cities 21*. Atlanta: Conway Data, 1993.

————. *Geo-Economics: The New Science, or The Gospel of Development According to Chairman Mac*. Atlanta: Conway Data, 1993.

————. *A Glimpse of the Future*. Atlanta: Conway Data, 1992.

McKinley Conway

Magazines.

See PRINTED WORD.

Maglev

Maglev is a new mode of transport in which passenger and freight vehicles are magnetically levitated above a guideway. The elimination of mechanical contact and the reduction of atmospheric friction enables vehicles to travel at high speeds, limited only by aerodynamic drag and route straightness. Speeds of 300 miles (500 kilometers) per hour are practical for vehicles traveling in the atmosphere; speeds of thousands of miles per hour are possible in low-pressure evacuated tunnels and tubes.

The idea of magnetically levitated transport was first described in the early 1900s by Goddard and others. Bachelet (1912) proposed levitating vehicles using the repulsive magnetic force between AC (alternating current) coils and induced currents in an aluminum sheet guideway, while Graemiger (1911) proposed using the attractive magnetic force between a vehicle's electromagnets and a guideway with iron rails.

Figure 1 illustrates the basic principles of the two types of magnetic suspensions. Repulsive force suspensions are inherently stable—if the vehicle moves toward the guideway, the magnetic force continuously increases. The vehicle then automatically levitates and stabilizes itself without external control at a distance where the upward magnetic force equals its weight. In contrast, attractive force suspensions are inherently unstable. If the vehicle starts to move closer to the guideway, the continuously increasing magnetic force pulls it upward till contact occurs.

The early Maglev concepts were not practical. The repulsive force AC coil suspension required too much electrical power, while the attractive force electromagnetic suspension could not be stabilized. The first practical Maglev system was invented by Powell and Danby in 1966. They pro-

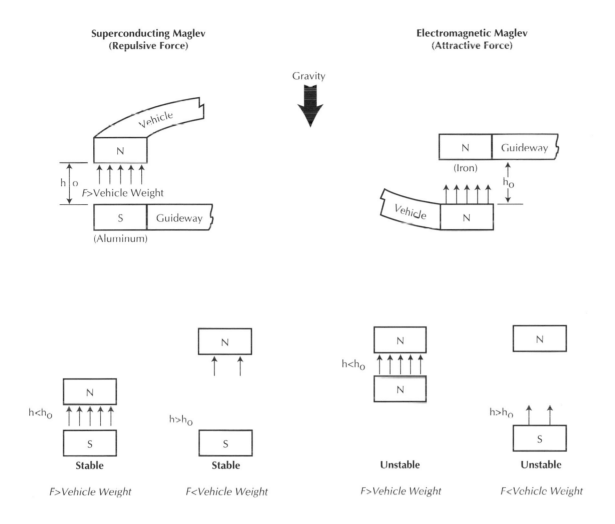

FIGURE 1. Magnetic levitation (Maglev).

posed placing an alternating sequence of powerful superconducting (SC) magnets on a vehicle. The magnets induce opposing currents in the aluminum loop guideway underneath the vehicle, which magnetically levitate and stabilize it several meters above the guideway. The guideway is designed also to stabilize the vehicle horizontally, as well as in the pitch, yaw, and roll directions. Vehicles move freely along the guideway, but cannot touch it, even when strong external forces, such as high wind gusts, act on them.

To propel the Maglev vehicles, Powell and Danby also proposed (1971) using AC current windings in the guideway. When energized by a power line, a small current in the windings magnetically interacts with the strong superconducting magnets on the vehicles, pushing it forward at a constant speed determined only by the AC frequency. This concept, called the Linear Synchronous Motor (LSM), makes all vehicles on the guideway move at the same speed, regardless of individual variations in drag force that occur due to local head or tail winds, up or down grades, and so on. Thus vehicles cannot change their relative spacing. This allows a large number of high-speed vehicles to operate safely on the same guideway.

Besides being extremely safe, the LSM is very efficient. Almost all of the input power to the guideway propels the vehicles, with only a small amount lost to I^2R heating in the windings. Not all of the guideway is continuously energized; drive power is only switched into the guideway blocks—typically, about one mile in length—that actually have vehicles. As a vehicle leaves one block, power is then switched into the next block.

Japan and Germany have both demonstrated full-scale Maglev prototypes, and are proceeding with first-generation commercial systems. Japan has developed the superconducting Maglev system originally proposed by Powell and Danby, while

Maglev

Germany has developed a modern version of the electromagnetic Maglev concept proposed by Graemiger. Although electromagnetic suspensions are inherently unstable, it is possible to use them for high-speed vehicles if the current in the conventional (room temperature) magnets is continuously controlled and adjusted by a rapid response servo system. When the vehicle magnet moves upwards to the rail from its normal position, current is reduced; conversely, when it drops below its nominal position, current is increased. The servo control system acts very quickly, in milliseconds, to keep the vehicle safely levitated.

In superconducting Maglev systems, the gap between vehicles and the guideway is large, typically six inches; in electromagnetic Maglev, the gap must be much smaller, typically one-third of an inch, in order that the magnet input power is reasonable. As a result, its guideway must be built to much tighter tolerances than those for superconducting Maglev, increasing cost.

Prototypes of a Japanese superconducting Maglev vehicle on a test track in Miyazaki (Kyotani, 1975) have operated at over 300 miles per hour. 300-mile-long route between Tokyo and Osaka is planned for operation shortly after 2000 A.D. The first thirty-mile section of the route is now under construction in Yamanishi Prefective north of Mount Fuji.

A German Transrapid electromagnetic Maglev vehicle (Miller, 1987), on its test track in Emsland has achieved speeds over 250 miles per hour. Germany plans a Hamburg–Berlin Maglev route.

Maglev may well be a major mode of transport in the twenty-first century because of its excellent energy efficiency and mobility, absence of pollution, independence from oil fuel, and low cost.

Maglev vehicles traveling in the atmosphere at 300 miles per hour use only half of the primary energy per passenger mile that is used by 60 m.p.h. automobiles, and a quarter of that used by 500 m.p.h. jet airliners. Here, primary energy refers to the thermal energy into the electric power plant that propels the Maglev vehicles, or the thermal energy in the petroleum-based fuel used by the auto or the airplane. In fact, the electricity used by Maglev could come from solar, nuclear, hydroelectric, or any nonpolluting energy source.

Maglev vehicles operating in low-pressure tunnels or tubes will be virtually frictionless, even though they travel at hypersonic speeds. One could go from New York to California in an hour, with an energy usage equivalent to less than one gallon of gasoline per passenger.

Figure 2 shows a possible national Maglev network for the United States that could be constructed along sections of the existing Interstate

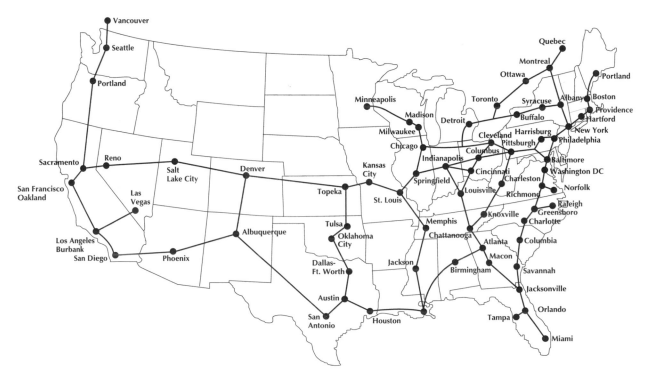

FIGURE 2.   Figure 2. A proposed national Maglev system.

Highway System. This network would carry passengers and truck-type freight at 300 m.p.h. using vehicles traveling in the atmosphere. Approximately two-thirds of the U.S. population would live within 15 miles of a Maglev station, and 95 percent within the states served.

The projected costs—energy, vehicle amortization, and system personnel—are much lower for Maglev than for other modes of transport. At 300 m.p.h., Maglev will cost approximately 3 cents per passenger mile and 7 cents per ton mile for freight, compared to 15 cents per passenger mile for auto and air travel and 30 cents per ton mile for truck freight.

Development of lightweight beam-type prefabricated guideways similar to those shown in Figure 3 will allow rapid construction of routes along existing rights of way such as highways, railroads, and power line corridors. The 20,000 mile U.S. network shown in Figure 4 could be constructed in ten to twenty years at a total cost of about $200 billion. The savings in operating costs resulting from the Maglev system could pay back its capital cost in as little as three years.

A two-way Maglev guideway can easily carry over 100,000 passengers per day, plus thousands of freight containers. It will be virtually impossible to saturate the traffic capacity of a Maglev route—unlike air travel, Maglev scheduling can be very precise, with virtually no delays due to congestion or bad weather.

By the middle of the twenty-first century, Maglev systems could carry a large fraction of the world's passenger and freight traffic. The resultant economic and energy savings, enhanced mobility, and reduced pollution, would contribute significantly to a cleaner world and a higher standard of living for its inhabitants.

See also AIR TRANSPORT; MOTOR VEHICLES; MOTOR VEHICLES, ALTERNATIVELY POWERED; RAILWAYS; TRANSPORTATION; URBAN TRANSIT.

BIBLIOGRAPHY

BACHELET, E. "Foucault and Eddy Currents Put to Service." *Engineer* 114 (1912): 420.

MILLER, L. "Transrapid 06 II—Performance and Characteristics." *Proceedings of the International Conference on Maglev and Linear Drives*. Institute of Electrical and Electronic Engineers Report 87CH2443-0, 1987, p. 129.

POWELL, JAMES R., and DANBY, GORDON T. *Cryogenics* 11 (1971): 171.

_____. "High Speed Transport by Magnetically Suspended Trains." *Mechanical Engineering* 89 (1967): 30.

James R. Powell
Gordon T. Danby

Management

Good business managers respond to the world around them. There are five key trends, or critical drivers, that have transformed market competition and will drive management practices into the twenty-first century:

- *The new consumer.* The new global consumer is richer, better educated, and much more likely to be working in the gathering, processing, and analyzing of information.
- *The new worker.* Workers will be like the new consumer, better educated, more technologically sophisticated, and more willing to accept responsibility for decisions.
- *Globalization.* All companies can operate across borders more effectively, with international firms having a vital presence in virtually every local market.
- *Technology.* The information and communication revolution creates the conditions for a wider range of choice and rapid response to varying market conditions.
- *Financial institutions.* Global financial institutions with immense resources will increasingly oversee more closely the businesses in which they invest.

Criteria for Business Success

The sophisticated new consumer and new worker will be the drivers of profound market changes. We expect to see the following types of adaptations well into the twenty-first century:

- *Growing responsiveness to markets.* If they want to gain and hold market share, the firms of the twenty-first century will have to identify and respond quickly to changing consumer needs where consumers can easily learn of alternatives.
- *Integration of knowledge.* Firms will need to gather, collect, and analyze knowledge of consumers quickly; adapt and utilize new technological options effectively; and reorganize themselves periodically to find the most productive uses of on-hand talent.
- *Ability to operate on a global scale.* Companies will have to operate not just in their local markets but increasingly across the markets of the rich consumer countries of North America and Western Europe; in the burgeoning market economies of Asia, Latin America, and Eastern Europe; and in the emerging middle-class metropolitan markets scattered through the rest of the world.

Key Management Trends

Business practices go through an unending cycle. Every year new buzzwords capture management techniques that will solve the most pressing business issues—matrix management, core competencies, reengineering, total quality, business teams, quality circles, leveraging. Yet, each year the case for the next innovative management technique seems all the more convincing.

There are, however, patterns of corporate change that endure over time that point to the underlying strategic issues. These underlying adaptations include:

DECENTRALIZATION

Decentralized organizations are those that allow a greater range of decision making to be made at more places in the organization. Decentralized decision making has two major advantages. It gives effective responsibility for decisions affecting the customer to those who are directly responsive to the customer, and it also gives the smarter, better-educated worker a greater role to play in the actions and choices that affect the customer. It empowers the worker.

Decentralized decision making will become easier because of electronic information and communications systems that allow information access to everyone at the same time. But it is important to recognize the loss of a focused response and strategic budgeting decisions by a large, centralized organization that can provide a variety of resources to solve critical problems. The greatest challenge for managers over the next decade will be to reconcile decentralization and empowerment with the proper mobilization of resources.

FOCUS AND LEVERAGING

Managers will need to help firms focus on what they do best, such as defining and utilizing core competencies of the firm in order to take full advantage of their comparative advantages. By venturing or partnering with other firms that have complementary skills, managers can leverage their own assets to bring customers and clients goods and services that more efficiently and effectively meet a wider range of needs. By leveraging—through individual contracts, consultants, partnerships, ventures, or buying ideas—managers can build a broader market role for their own firms.

The disadvantage for a leveraged firm will be the increased demand for coordination and control. The pieces of a leveraged firm are more diverse in location, organization, and work style. The ability to keep these disparate parts of a "virtual firm" focused on a single goal will be more complex than coordination within the traditional corporate structure.

WIDER REACH

All markets will be global in that every local market will be open to international influences. Thus, more firms will be counting on foreign sales for a substantial portion of their total market, and the range of foreign markets will gradually expand from the North Atlantic to the world. But each firm will also have to contend with new competitors in their local markets in the form of foreign products and services, foreign firms, foreign investments, and foreign ideas. No niche market will be immune from global competition. Hence, managers will have to take a broader strategic look at geography. Operations will cross borders and managers will have to coordinate worldwide activities of their own decentralized organizations, as well as work with a variety of venture partners and suppliers. Electronic networks and aids to group activity will be a key tool for managers. Still, the coordination time and skills needed to make global teams and partnerships effective will go up.

THE SMART FIRM

The primary goal of any large firm will be to increase its ability to pick up signals from the market and translate those signals into quick and effective actions. There are two keys to getting this done. First, managers must establish an effective means of collecting and processing information from and about the customer and get that information into the hands of those who deal with the customers. Second, managers must assure that effective decision making is in the hands of those individuals or small groups who are closest to either product development or customer service.

Corporations need to respond to the demands of a smarter, more sophisticated, affluent global consumer who has access to an almost unlimited flow of virtually free information from a variety of competing sources. Corporate managers need to create incentives for their employees to respond effectively to the varying tastes and needs of this new consumer. To do this, managers need to keep their organizations open to learning and being adaptable in responding to changing tastes. Education and retraining will be a constant need for the successful organization. Individual business units, even of the largest firms, need to be able to respond quickly to these market forces while maintaining the overall efficiencies and scale economies of large firms. Managers of both large and small businesses will face unparalleled challenges over the next several decades in reconciling decentralized empowerment and efficient resource mobilization.

See also BUSINESS GOVERNANCE; BUSINESS STRUCTURE: FORMS, IMPACTS; ENTREPRENEUR-SHIP; GLOBAL BUSINESS: DOMINANT ORGANIZATIONAL FORMS; LEADERSHIP; ORGANIZATIONAL COMPLEXITY; PARTICIPATIVE MANAGEMENT; STRATEGIC PLANNING.

BIBLIOGRAPHY

DRUCKER, PETER. *The Frontiers of Management.* New York: HarperCollins, 1987.
GUTKNECHT, DOUGLAS B. *Strategic Revitalization: Managing the Challenges of Change.* Lanham, MD: University Press of America, 1989.

Gregory Schmid

Management, Participative.

See PARTICIPATIVE MANAGEMENT.

Marketing

Businesses look to marketing and marketers to solve a small number of important problems that they face. The shorter-run problems are: which products (and services) should the business provide, what distribution channels should it choose to get them into the hands of customers, what prices should it set, and how should it communicate (by means of advertising, sales force, or sales promotion) with its customers and its distributors? The longer-run problems are: which groups of customers should it seek; and how should it adapt its products, prices, communications, and channels of distribution to likely changes in how customers buy and what they think? This article discusses likely changes in demographics and the four elements of the marketing mix—product, price, communications, and distribution.

Customer Differences

Forces altering competition continue and are likely to continue in the future: increasing international competition, accelerating technological change, the maturing or stagnating of certain markets, and continuing cycles of regulation and deregulation.

It is an inescapable truism that people differ. Marketers prefer to say, instead, that market segments differ. For most of the twentieth century, marketers directed their attention to the mass consumer. In doing so they ignored, or overlooked, differences between market segments. The singular arrogance of Henry Ford's declaration regarding color choice for his Model T, "You can have any color as long as it's black," marks the epitome of this perspective. Demographic and lifestyle changes as well as education and information have long since interceded to weaken mass marketing and erode brand loyalty. In the future, computers, scanners, and changes in payment technology will allow businesses to adapt more closely to market differences and cater to their every whim, be it ever so slight. Increasing market fragmentation will make this necessary. Hence, each business will have to learn about the specific things that make its market segments unique. "What the consumer wants, is what the consumer will get," has never been truer.

There will be more emphasis on what we now call minorities, as blacks, Hispanics, women, and the elderly assume larger roles in the economy. The elderly, in particular, have become an attractive marketing target; their relative financial well-being and access to large financial resources is accompanied by few of the obligations that attend raising a family.

Elements of the Marketing Mix

PRODUCT

Most components of product marketing strategy—presale service, after-sale service, technical marketing research, and product testing—will assume greater importance in the future. As products adapt to niche marketing, a proliferation of product offerings may increase competition to the point that the risks and costs of product failure escalate dramatically. In turn, this outcome may dampen the enthusiasm for businesses to develop new products.

Time needed to develop new products has decreased over the past few decades. It is unlikely to fall much more. Confounding this shortened product development cycle is the lengthened time requirement interposed by government regulators. Pharmaceutical products and food additives, in particular, require protracted regulatory approval periods.

PRICE

There will be increased emphasis on cost-plus pricing and pricing that conforms to government regulations. Government purchasing power constitutes the largest buyer segment for many products. Purchasing specifications, including prices, exert a powerful pressure by lowest-cost pricing.

Niche marketing is likely to bring relatively high prices and high margins, because the competition forces are weakened. Even specialty marketing is likely to give ground to the huge onslaught of deep-discount retailers; sooner or later immense mass marketers (like Wal-Mart) will make inroads on niche merchandising. Beyond domestic skirmishing, the expansion of international competition in commodities and general classes of goods will have an influence on moderating price increases in the United States and elsewhere.

MARKETING COMMUNICATIONS

The length and size of advertisements will decrease. Fifteen-second advertisements will probably become the standard on television. Thus, one will see more advertisements in a given amount of time. New electronic media will continue to emerge, and one can expect advertisements on such media as electronic bulletin boards, computer networks, home-shopping cable-TV channels, CD-ROM disks, and lengthy infomercials. There will probably be a continued increase in public skepticism toward advertising and resistance to its messages.

New systems for delivering coupons will allow marketers to focus on specific customer segments. For example, it will be possible to deliver coupons for one brand only to buyers of a competing brand (including house brands at point of purchase), and coupons for related brands of one manufacturer only to buyers of other brands of the same manufacturer.

DISTRIBUTION

Lower barriers to international trade and economic growth in developing countries will stimulate the demand for franchise services. It is likely that franchising's share will increase from one-third of all retail sales (in 1990) to one-half by 2010. The increases will be predominantly in what are called packaged franchises, those where the franchiser seeks to have franchisees reproduce in their local communities an entire business concept—products, trademarks, uniforms, and methods of operation.

Other factors likely to influence distribution strategy include: increased direct selling costs that many industries face; prominence of computerized links among manufacturers, customers, and distributors; the appearance of new channels that perform a variety of value-added services beyond those performed by traditional distributors; the growing power of the retail trade versus that of the manufacturers in consumer brand goods; and increasing concentration within channels of distribution that were long fragmented.

See also ADVERTISING; MARKETING BREAKTHROUGHS; MARKETPLACE ECONOMICS.

BIBLIOGRAPHY

DYCHTWALD, KEN, and GABLE, GREG. "Portrait of a Changing Consumer." *Business Horizons* (January/February 1990): 62–73.

LAZER, WILLIAM; LABARBERA, PRISCILLA; MACLACHLAN, JAMES M.; and SMITH, ALLEN E., eds. *Marketing 2000 and Beyond.* Chicago: American Marketing Association, 1990.

SMITH, ALLEN E.; MACLACHLAN, JAMES M.; LAZER, WILLIAM; and LABARBERA, PRISCILLA. *Marketing 2000: Future Perspectives on Marketing.* Chicago: American Marketing Association, 1990.

David L. Rados

Marketing Breakthroughs

A breakthrough is an idea that is so different it cannot be compared to any existing practices or perceptions. Employing new technology and creating new markets, breakthroughs are conceptual shifts that make history. Incremental innovation may arise through the application of new technology to an existing product, process, or system; or through the introduction of existing technology into a new market; or, sometimes merely through identifying customers' needs more effectively. Breakthroughs tend to work in all these dimensions at once.

Recognizing a marketing breakthrough is not hard: Nautilus exercise equipment, Club Med vacations, fax machines, Post-It note pads, personal copiers, compact discs, and cellular telephones readily come to mind. Successful creators of these and other breakthroughs tend to be very good at bringing about an interaction between the world of problems (situations faced by customers) and the world of solutions (technology).

A good example of this is the microwave oven, a breakthrough that began when Raytheon workers assembling radar units during World War II noticed that they could warm their hands in front of microwave-emitting magnetron tubes. In 1955, using Raytheon's magnetrons, Tappan introduced the first microwave oven for the home. These new ovens—the size of refrigerators and costing more than some new cars—did not meet the needs of customers, and not many were sold.

Across the Pacific, the Japanese quickly saw the potential of microwave cooking, but realized that the magnetron used in radar was not the appropriate one for heating soup. Several companies tried to make smaller, cheaper magnetrons, but the New Japan Radio Company (NJRC) was the only one to succeed. In 1961, Raytheon bought one-third of NJRC and thus gained access to these smaller magnetrons, but still had trouble getting the product into kitchens.

In 1965, Raytheon turned to Amana, a company with vast expertise in home appliances. The combination of Raytheon's technology, NJRC's improved magnetrons, and Amana's marketing produced a countertop microwave oven for less than $500. The solution side of the equation was now ready.

The next challenge was convincing consumers and educating wholesalers and retailers about the full range of the new product's capabilities. One of the participants recalled the role of popcorn in this process. "[Customers] would watch the molecular disturbance and the bursting of the popcorn," he said. "They would smell and hear it popping. Finally, we'd give them some, and then they'd stand around and say, 'This thing really does work!'" The microwave oven landed squarely between customers' needs and technology, and millions of them now occupy prominent places in kitchens.

Because people have long regarded such breakthroughs as the road to wealth and recognition, the creative process has been intensely analyzed. Bell Laboratories once tried to quantify the attributes of the "creative type." They found only two clearly common characteristics: an exceptional tolerance for messy work environments and a well-developed sense of humor. A wider examination of many breakthroughs, however, reveals three important elements:

The Individual

While it certainly does not hurt to have genius, the adjective more likely to describe a breakthrough originator is *obsessive*. Such a person will work on a problem twenty-four hours a day—not just from nine to five. People who bring about breakthroughs also tend to be good at what Arthur Koestler, in *The Act of Creation*, calls "bisociative" skills—the ability to connect ideas that no one has connected before. Archimedes did this when or-

dered to determine whether a king's crown was pure gold without melting it. The displacement solution to this early example of nondestructive testing finally came to this obsessed individual while he was taking a bath. A modern example of an obsessive inventor is Arthur Jones, the creator of Nautilus exercise equipment. Working for years at all hours of the day and night, he built and tested models until he perfected the kind of machines now found in fitness centers around the world.

Special Environment

Breakthroughs have come out of every imaginable workplace: basement workshops, small companies, and multinational corporations. The best environments, however, possess an aspect that can be called a sword and a shield. Inventors need someone acting as a sword to cut through red tape, change standard procedures, and thus allow something different to emerge. Akio Morita, then chairman of Sony, early on recognized the possibilities of the Walkman and wielded the sword of his position to bring it to the market. Similarly, a shield is required to protect a fledgling product from over-zealous managers who do not want to waste money on something that shows little immediate reward. The 3M Company's Post-It note pads would never have become ubiquitous in modern offices if someone had not shielded their inventor from devotees of the bottom line. Another aspect of the best environments is that they place technologists in the world of customers, thereby facilitating bisociation.

Consider the Market

Problem-solvers who think like customers are more likely to please those customers, as the development of the videocassette recorder (VCR) demonstrates. Sony hit the market first with Betamax, a technologically stunning product. However, the electronic giant did not understand that potential purchasers wanted to record shows that were two hours long. JVC did, and their VHS VCRs left Betamax in the dust.

Finally, there is one further step. Assuming an individual working in a special environment can listen to customers and come up with a breakthrough, he or she must at some point let others make their contributions to the project. Sir Godfrey Hounsfield of the United Kingdom's EMI invented the CAT scanner, yet it was John Powell's management of its marketing and manufacturing that got the device into every hospital that could afford one.

What is the best way to bring about a breakthrough? Getting customers who have needs together with people who know how to fulfill them is a start. Once an idea is hatched, companies should carefully nurture it. To produce a breakthrough, it takes many people saying "yes" to transform an idea to a success; often one "no" can kill it. The right people in the right environment—combined with a little luck—can make it happen.

See also CHANGE, PACE OF; CONTINUITY AND DISCONTINUITY; CREATIVITY; MARKETING; MATERIALS: RESEARCH AND DEVELOPMENT; NEW PRODUCTS; SCIENTIFIC BREAKTHROUGHS; SURPRISES; TECHNOLOGICAL CHANGE; WILD CARDS.

BIBLIOGRAPHY

FOSTER, RICHARD. *Innovation: The Attacker's Advantage.* New York: Summit, 1986.

MCKENNA, REGIS. *The Regis Touch: Million-Dollar Advice from America's Top Marketing Consultant.* Reading, MA: Addison-Wesley, 1985.

MILLER, JULE A. *From Ideas to Profit.* New York: Van Nostrand–Reinhold, 1986.

NAYAK, P. RANGANATH, and KETTERINGHAM, JOHN M. *Breakthroughs!* New York: Rawson, 1986.

PORTER, MICHAEL E. *Competitive Strategy—Techniques for Analyzing Industries and Competitors.* New York: Free Press, 1980.

SERVI, ITALO S. *New Product Development and Marketing.* New York: Praeger, 1990.

SOUDER, WILLIAM E. *Managing New Product Innovations.* Lexington, MA: D. C. Heath, 1987.

P. Ranganath Nayak

Marketplace Economics

In the next several decades, fundamental changes likely will be occurring in the nature of private business enterprises as they respond to the developing threats and opportunities of the global marketplace. The most domestic-oriented firm will be increasing its geographic reach because its suppliers and customers, with increasing frequency, will be located on a variety of continents.

As the intensity of global competition increases, companies will be forced to reevaluate their roles in the world economy. For some, this will entail strengthening their domestic position against competing foreign products. Others will expand their operations into foreign markets. For many,

collaborative agreements with other businesses will be an effective alternative to the more traditional approaches.

The modern enterprise will increasingly develop multinational networks composed of alliances, partially owned subsidiaries, associated firms, affiliates, licensees, and other cooperative arrangements. On a rising scale, mergers and acquisitions will involve crossing national boundaries—and dealing with several national governments, as well as with a variety of state, provincial, and local authorities.

Large enterprises that had once been content to concentrate their production, research, and exports in their home economies will be forging international ties. Often the same companies will engage in joint ventures to develop new products, coproduce existing products, serve as sources of supply for each other, share output, and compete with each other. No universal pattern will emerge. The specific ways in which companies establish their presence in overseas markets will be strongly influenced by the obstacles and incentives established by the host country and occasionally by the home country.

Companies increasingly will assume some of the functions formerly vested primarily in national governments. This will reflect the growing belief that the business firm can conduct activities more efficiently than government.

Business Responses

Many firms will take on characteristics of an open and interactive network, selectively sharing control, technology, and markets with organizations beyond their formal structure. As a result of rapid changes in technology and markets, the traditional boundaries between formal enterprises and more informal business relationships will gradually blur. For knowledge-intensive production, the distinction between maker and user is neither clear-cut nor invariant.

Many innovative forms will be utilized. In some high-technology areas, the business firm of the future will consist primarily of a central coordination center and several semiindependent internal organizations. Business activity will consequently operate on the basis of fluid ties with the internal organizations of other companies.

The predominant type of corporation will be one in which individual staff members take upon themselves the task of solving problems and revamping operations—but hopefully within an overall harmony that causes these individual efforts to converge toward the realization of the company's strategic goals. In contrast, the traditional bureaucratic organization, with its somewhat rigid hierarchies and singleminded emphasis on efficiency, was easier to manage. Yet that structure is not likely to provide the necessary decentralized autonomy, intellectual stimulation, or motivation to those engaged in creative work.

The traditional hierarchical form of business organization will not be totally abandoned. It will be appropriate for stable, slow-growth, low-tech, natural resource-based industries like metal production, oil, paper, and forest products. In contrast, the standard model is becoming obsolete in rapidly changing, high-tech markets such as computers, telecommunications, and aerospace.

The key will be to develop a subtle compromise—to allow individual employees to develop plans and programs on their own initiative while using a cooperative relationship to focus these individual efforts toward the realization of the company's goals and objectives. Fundamental to this process will be the development of a clear-cut corporate identity generated by leadership with a well-articulated vision of where the company should go. In the multinational firm of the future, the formal linkages that bind the vast corporate network will be technology, common values, and shared resources.

Government and Business

Technological progress makes possible, and economically feasible, a variety of business innovations to overcome governmental obstacles to global commerce. These barriers will continue to take many forms, ranging from tariffs and quotas on trade to restrictions on foreign ownership of domestic businesses—but the global enterprise increasingly will learn how to overcome them, albeit at a price.

In a passive mode, exporters will absorb the added costs imposed by governmental barriers to international commerce—at least to some extent. In the case of quotas imposed by the importing nations, companies can shift to higher-priced items on which unit profits are also greater. When faced with more onerous obstacles, businesses will draw on a variety of alternatives to direct exporting.

Businesses can set up new manufacturing facilities in the host nation or they can respond by acquiring existing local companies. Other alternatives that business firms will increasingly rely upon to develop positions in the markets of other nations include subcontracting production, purchasing locally, and developing products jointly with local firms.

Joint ventures, particularly those involving manufacturing operations, will often be necessary to overcome trade restrictions. On other occasions, firms will be facing sharp limits to foreign ownership of local enterprises. Barriers can include formal restrictions on investment, or less formal but often equally powerful tax and regulatory advantages limited to local companies. National antitrust laws—and their enforcement—will be geared to the global nature of the marketplace. Thus, two or three giant firms—such as the automotive industry in the United States—will be seen to be a competitive portion of a larger worldwide market for cars and trucks.

When governments restrict repatriation of earnings or foreign businesses fear future expropriation of their assets, global enterprises will frequently set up affiliate or correspondent relationships with local firms. This approach will minimize risk and liability—and also profit potentials. When other barriers are imposed by governments in the more advanced economies, licensing arrangements can be made with domestic firms in exchange for market entry. These governmental obstacles may include local political or industrial pressures and local distribution systems strongly favoring home-produced products. Enterprises in advanced economies thus will be able to respond to attractive overseas markets without directly penetrating them.

With the increasing globalization of the international economy, companies experiencing difficulty introducing products in their home country due to government requirements will license their products to firms in other countries in an effort to introduce them into markets more quickly.

It will be especially helpful under rapidly changing political circumstances to do business in several countries. When faced with rising government burdens in one nation, a firm can shift its high value-added activities to other nations in which it operates, specifically those with lower taxes and less burdensome regulation.

See also BUSINESS STRUCTURE: FORMS, IMPACTS; ECONOMICS; ENTREPRENEURSHIP; GLOBAL BUSINESS: DOMINANT ORGANIZATIONAL FORMS; INFORMAL DEMOCRACY; INTERNATIONAL TRADE AND COMMERCE; POLITICAL ECONOMY.

BIBLIOGRAPHY

JAMES, JR., HARVEY S., and WEIDENBAUM, MURRAY. *When Businesses Cross International Borders: Strategic*

Alliances and Their Alternatives. Westport, CT: Praeger Publishers, 1993.

WEIDENBAUM, MURRAY. *Business and Government in the Global Marketplace,* 5th ed. Englewood Cliffs, NJ: Prentice Hall, 1995.

————. "The Emerging Transnational Enterprise." *Business and the Contemporary World* 5/1 (Winter 1993).

Murray L. Weidenbaum

Marriage

The debate over family values makes it clear that the concept of family will continue to be important to society, to undergo change (as it always has), and to generate a great deal of controversy. The following definitions are but a sampling of the changing ways in which people are coming to view the "family":

- Webster's Ninth Collegiate Dictionary defines *family* as "the basic unit in society having as its nucleus two or more adults living together and cooperating in the care and rearing of their own or adopted children."
- A family is an institution found in many forms that provides children with legal guardianship within the larger society and with the physical and emotional nurturance that will enable them to develop into fully functioning members of society.
- The U.S. Census Bureau defines family as a group of two or more persons related by birth, marriage, or adoption and residing together.
- The New York Court of Appeals says the family can be defined by examining several factors, including "exclusivity and longevity" and the "level of emotional and financial commitment of a relationship." "It is the totality of the relationship as evidenced by the dedication, caring and self-sacrifice of the partners."

When one speaks of family, it must be remembered that families will have many common characteristics as well as many unique characteristics. Table 1 examines some of the characteristics of

TABLE 1.   Some Demographic Variables for Four Family Groups

Variable	Asian-American[†]	African-American	Hispanic	Caucasian
Percent of population*	3% (7.5 million)	12.3% (30.31 million)	9% (23 million)	75.6% (188 million
Percent of married-couple families	80%	47%	56%	83%
Birthrates per 1,000 women, ages 15–44	58%	85%	93%	67%
Birthrates per 1,000 population	18%	22%	27%	15%
Percent of women childless, ages 35–44	40%	13%	12%	18%
Out-of-wedlock births	6%	50%	25%	12%
Percent of one-parent families	14%	57%	32%	21%
Children under 18 living with:				
2 parents	84%	36%	65%	80%
1 parent	14%	57%	32%	21%
Mother only	10%	53%	28%	18%
Father only	2%	3%	4%	3%
Percent of divorced persons	2.1% (men) 5.7% (women)	8.4% (men) 11.5% (women)	6.1% (men) 8.6% (women)	7.1% (men) 8.9% (women)
Percent high school graduates	82%	68%	53%	80%
Median family income	$42,250	$21,550	$23,912	$38,909
Median income of married couples	high	$34,196	$28,515	$42,738
Percent of persons below poverty level	12.2%	30%	29.5%	11%
Percent of children below poverty level	8%	44%	40%	15%

* The population of the United States was approximately 254 million January 1, 1992.

† Some figures for the Asian-American population are estimates.

families in four different ethnic groups. The table represents group averages and does not necessarily represent individual families.

The marriage rate (marriages per 1000 population) varies over time. It was 9.1 in 1994, the lowest since 1965. This should not be taken to mean that fewer Americans in the future will want to enter into long-term intimate relationships. Well over 90 percent of Americans marry in their lifetime, and this is the highest percentage of any industrialized country. Marriage will likely remain a goal for most Americans.

The current low marriage rate results from several trends. First marriage is being postponed by young people. In 1994 the median age of first marriage was 26.8 years for men and 23.8 years for women. This is the highest median age for both sexes since 1890. Postponement of marriage partially results from women's growing interest in career work, and this interest will continue to grow in the future.

Cohabitation among unmarried couples is increasing, and is partially taking the place of marriage. When cohabitation statistics are added to marriage statistics, it would appear that the forming of intimate long-term relationships by Americans is as popular as ever, and it seems likely to continue in the future.

Research evidence about the relationship between cohabitation and future marriage stability is mixed. For never-married couples, cohabitation prior to marriage appears to reduce slightly the chances of future marital success. For previously married couples, cohabitation appears to increase the chances of future marital success. Impacts of these observations upon future marriage trends are self-evident.

Postponement of first marriage, educational advancement, and the growth of economic opportunities for women in the labor market are combining to reduce birth rates and also shift the timing of childbearing toward older ages. Birth rates declined rapidly during the 1960s and early 1970s, reaching an historical low of 1.74 births per woman in 1976. Since that time, fertility rates have leveled off at about 2.1 births per woman, which is approximately the population replacement rate. As women become more career oriented, they tend to postpone parenthood. More than in the past, women claim when young that they will not have children. But the childlessness rate for the first decade of baby boomers 35–44 years old is only running about 17 percent. Most women are opting to have fewer children rather than remaining childless.

Divorce rates are high. The rate (4.7 per 1,000 population) has dropped slightly and leveled off for

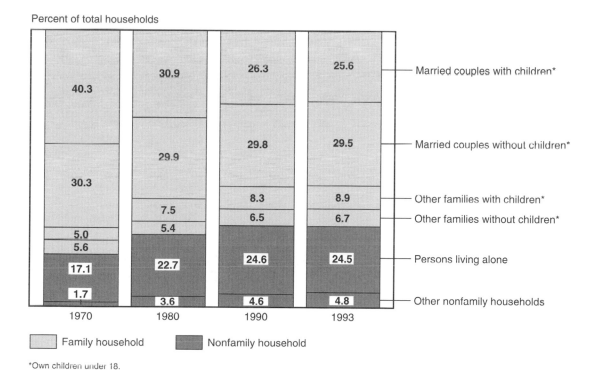

Percent of total households

*Own children under 18.

FIGURE 1.   Household Composition: 1970–1993.

the past several years from the all-time high (5.3 divorces per 1,000 population), which occurred in 1981. This high divorce rate does not mean that Americans are giving up on marriage. A high remarriage rate among divorced persons indicates that people are divorcing their spouses, not rejecting the idea of marriage itself. For several centuries, serial marriage has been a proper description of American pattern of marriage, divorce, and remarriage. Americans believe in monogamy, one spouse at a time, but often have more than one spouse over a lifetime.

Such trends mean that future marriages will more and more be between persons, one or both of whom have been married before. At this time, almost half of all marriages involve one or more previously married persons. This will create increasing numbers of "blended" families, which may have his, hers, and their children living in the family home. Partners in a blended family may have

economic obligations (such as child support payments) to prior family members. Partners may have to assume stepparent roles to the children of their previously married spouse. They may have to endure separation from their own biological children. What for a family that has remained together is a simple question (where shall we have Christmas or Thanksgiving?) becomes a logistical problem in the blended family.

These trends are reflected in the changing composition of the American family, as shown in Figures 1 and 2. The number of married couples living together with their children has diminished, while the number of men and women living alone and/or with their children is increasing.

The proportion of children living with only one parent has doubled in the past two decades, from 12 percent to 25 percent. The overwhelming majority of children in one-parent families live with their mothers (87 percent). Many of these families live

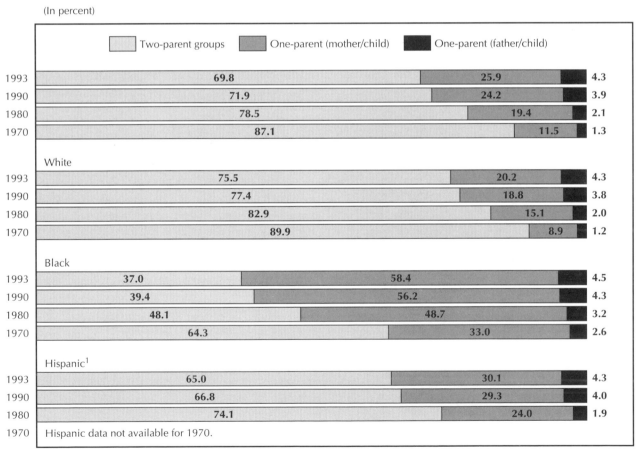

(In percent)

	Two-parent groups	One-parent (mother/child)	One-parent (father/child)
1993	69.8	25.9	4.3
1990	71.9	24.2	3.9
1980	78.5	19.4	2.1
1970	87.1	11.5	1.3
White			
1993	75.5	20.2	4.3
1990	77.4	18.8	3.8
1980	82.9	15.1	2.0
1970	89.9	8.9	1.2
Black			
1993	37.0	58.4	4.5
1990	39.4	56.2	4.3
1980	48.1	48.7	3.2
1970	64.3	33.0	2.6
Hispanic[1]			
1993	65.0	30.1	4.3
1990	66.8	29.3	4.0
1980	74.1	24.0	1.9
1970	Hispanic data not available for 1970.		

[1]Hispanic may be of any race.

FIGURE 2.   Composition of Family Groups with Children by Race and Hispanic Origin: 1970–1993 (In Percent).

below the poverty level. For many single-parent families, however, the situation is transitional, lasting only until the single-parent marries again.

Projections

It is likely that in the years ahead the creation of long-lasting intimate relationships will remain a goal for most Americans. Most Americans will fulfill this goal by marrying, although an increasing number will cohabit at least temporarily prior to marriage. As more and more women find satisfaction in the world of career work, marriage and parenthood will continue to be postponed. The increase in single-parent families will probably level off as the divorce rate levels off and remarriage remains popular. The number of blended families in which one or both of the partners have been previously married will continue to increase. Monogamy will remain as a goal and become even more important as society becomes increasingly familiar with and concerned to limit personal exposure to sexually transmitted diseases such as AIDS.

See also DEMOGRAPHICS; DIVORCE; FAMILIES AND HOUSEHOLDS; FAMILY BEHAVIOR; FAMILY PLANNING; FAMILY PROBLEMS; FAMILY VALUES; SEXUAL CODES; SEXUAL REPRODUCTION.

BIBLIOGRAPHY

U.S. Bureau of the Census. "The Asian and Pacific Islander Population in the United States: March 1991 and 1990." *Current Population Reports*. P20–459. Washington, DC: U.S. Government Printing Office, 1992.

_____. "The Black Population in the United States: March 1992." *Current Population Reports*. P20–471. Washington, DC: U.S. Government Printing Office, 1994.

_____. "Fertility of American Women: June 1992." *Current Population Reports*. P20–470. Washington, DC: U.S. Government Printing Office, 1993.

_____. "The Hispanic Population in the United States: March 1993." *Current Population Reports*. P20–475. Washington, DC: U.S. Government Printing Office, 1994.

_____. "Marital Status and Living Arrangements: March 1993." *Current Population Reports*. P20–478. Washington, DC: U.S. Government Printing Office, 1994.

_____. "Money Income of Households, Families, and Persons in the United States: 1992. *Current Population Reports*. P-60–184. Washington, DC: U.S. Government Printing Office, 1993.

_____. *Statistical Abstract of the United States: 1994*. Washington, DC: U.S. Government Printing Office, 1994.

Frank D. Cox

Mass Culture and Arts

The future of art and mass culture should take into account the many ways in which we define *art* and *culture*. We generally assume broad agreement on such definitions. In fact, they are almost as varied as the modes of expression in the arts, and as diverse as individual experiences of culture. Even the relationship of art *to* culture, though much explored, remains an open issue embracing many different and conflicting theories.

The world we now live in with its particular qualities of rapid change, physical and psychic mobility, and multiple channels of swift communications and diffusion has few historical precedents as a cultural context. Even the term *mass*, in relation to its prevailing cultural forms, may require qualification in view of the variety and heterogeneity of both its products and its participants.

The Past

The major points regarding the emergence of mass culture, and attitudes toward its growth, tend to focus for various reasons on Western culture, and to suggest that in primitive societies, the arts and culture were coextensive with the society itself, permeating all individual and social activities. As societies and civilizations developed, in complexity and functional specialization, art became more autonomous as an activity. It diverged from its linkage to religion and its direct relationship to the crafts.

The judgmental canons for high culture tended to reflect the societal beliefs and prevailing dogma within which they were created. Conceiving of such work as enduring through time, and as universally applicable expressions of the human condition, of "beauty," "truth," and so forth, these canons also carried with them ideas of permanence, uniqueness, and accessibility according to taste. They also tended to associate aesthetic pleasure with concepts and conditions of moral judgment.

The French and the Industrial Revolutions of the late eighteenth and early nineteenth century contributed significantly to a change in attitudes and focus—the former through its egalitarian principles and elevation of "mass" sentiments and taste; the latter through the mass production of vast quantities of economically cheap goods and cultural products via machine manufacture.

Views to the Future

Many recent critical assessments of the future of art and mass culture are focusing more broadly on a crisis in the relationship of culture to society, or within the concept of culture itself.

We need to broaden our definition of culture. A key proposition, therefore, in considering the future of art and mass culture is that development of the mass cultural media involves changes in the very culture itself. As Marshall McLuhan underlined, the medium is the message. This means, in terms of the electronic age, that a totally new cultural environment has been created (McLuhan, 1964). Another commentator (Alloway, 1969) suggests in more pragmatic terms:

> Acceptance of the mass media entails a shift in our notion of what culture is. Instead of reserving the word for the highest artifacts and the noblest thoughts of history's top ten, it needs to be used more widely as the description of "what a society does." Then, unique oil paintings and highly personal poems as well as mass-distributed films and group-aimed magazines can be placed in a continuum rather than frozen in layers in a pyramid.

We have, then, few historical precedents to gauge the future directions of mass culture. Many of the physical instrumentalities that render it possible have not previously existed, and the broad social changes accompanying their developments pose larger and more fundamental questions than we can address in the present discussion.

While cultural messages have traveled in the past slowly along restricted routes to equally restricted audiences, the new cultural media are broadcast to a world audience in a lavish diversity of simultaneous modes. The earlier vertical-oriented elite presenting and directing cultural preferences became simply one of a plurality of elites or "taste groups" that overlap horizontally and are as diverse as their audiences and ingroups. The apex of the taste pyramid became only one node in a mesh of interrelated cultural networks.

> . . . the high scale societies of the Western world are becoming increasingly heterogeneous, comprising thousands of minority groups, *each* joined around common interest, common value systems and shared stylistic preferences that differ from those of other groups. As the sheer value of information and knowledge increases, as technological developments farther expand the range options, and as awareness of the liberty to deviate and differentiate spreads, more variations are *possible*. Rising affluence or, even more, growing desire for at least subcultural identity induces groups to exploit these options and to invent new ones. We might almost say irregular cultural permutations are becoming the rule. (Rittel and Webber, 1973)

The increase of options and choices also entails an increase in the range of responses and value preferences. This weakens individual identification with any fixed cultural community in favor of an increasingly "privatized," temporal, and shifting range of cultural allegiances. We note one aspect of this in the increased differentiation of the individual life cycle where each age group begins to be its own subculture. The problem may, of course, not reach extreme forms due to the paradoxical quality of human proclivities. Just at the point when the increasing rapid diffusion of ideas and artifacts is creating a planetary culture, we have the parallel phenomena of increased interest in, and revival of, local cultural forms—languages, folk styles, and so on.

This *inclusive* tendency also marks the future trends in cultural values that can no longer be judged in "either/or" terms within some implicitly vertical scale. A specific characteristic of future cultural creation and participation may be its "both/and" quality. In order to create, appreciate, and participate in one form, you need not forego a whole range of others. There is no inherent value contradiction in enjoying both a comic book and a symphony.

Interesting consequences for the future of cultural products may have to be mostly questions. What is the status of an "original" work—when it may be replicated by the million or when, as an original or "masterwork," it has no unique form other than as a spool of reproducible film, magnetic tape, or a diskette?

Art Futures

Art is no longer solely in "the frame" or in the sculptured form. In many cases, it moves toward continuous formats, as in the Rauschenberg type of "combine," juxtaposing still image, live radio, and video in the same piece that characteristically spills out into the environment. Or, as in the "happening," the "event," or the conceptual artwork, what is presented *is* the experience or is a communication through which the experience may be reconstructed. The "event" is one of temporal immersion in a flow of communicated experiences, in which the technical means or media are increasingly less obtrusive or constraining. Though much has been made of the antiart quality of these latter manifestations, they probably are less "anti" than some examples of the past tradition. Instead, they are more concerned with a transformation of the idea of art in itself.

Rather than mocking the idea of the past, artistic practitioners today don't give a damn about it. The art of the past has no more to do with them than past medicine, past theology, and past plumbing . . . "art for art's sake" is no longer being discussed. Life for art's sake also seems Victorian . . . Life for life's sake, or more life for more life's sake is an aesthetic summation of current artistic expression. (Steele, 1971)

The future of art, therefore, seems not to lie so much with the creation of enduring masterworks, but, in part, with the exploration and definition of alternative social and cultural directions. It is not the isolated work that may be important but the overall context, or lifestyle and attitude, within which it is produced. An illustrative example: the late Andy Warhol, the artist, and the Rolling Stones, as a rock group, where the lifestyle of the artist or the group also becomes part of the artwork. The entire persona is presented and becomes an attitudinal model or "ikon" for its audience.

"Life styling" in itself may be viewed, in some senses, as one of the personalized artworks of the future. Such a metamorphosis of lifestyle into cultural expression and creative art is more than a mere change of external forms. It emerges from, and expresses, changes in the values of, and modes of evaluating, the core institutions of society.

The ongoing revolution in information and communications technologies and their ancillary software and interaction are creating what is virtually a new information environment. It is that new environment that is reshaping the cultural content and perception of society itself.

We may speculate, therefore, that where past societies have tended to be dominated exclusively by one measure or calculus for social or cultural worth, such measures could become more diversified in the future. Where previously, for example, the military and more recently the economic calculus were dominant measures for evaluating individual or collective activities, we may emerge into societal forms in which the aesthetic calculus becomes a dominant measure. Ancient China selected its most prestigious officials on the basis of their performance as poets or calligraphers. We may, in the future, consider the poet or painter as no less qualified for public office than the lawyer or businessman—should such fixed occupational roles still exist.

The future of art and mass culture, though treated here as a single theme, needs to be considered as only one aspect of the transformative changes through which we are passing on our way to the future. In order to understand the funda-mental bases for change in our conceptions of art and culture "we must begin with a sense of change potential in the most critical of all variables—human beings themselves," (Simon, 1973) rather than with some ultimate fixed human nature through which the expressions of art and culture are governed.

Underlying our conjectures regarding the future of art and mass culture, there are the more central questions of the ways in which personal choices and collective responses must be more consciously oriented toward broadening the imaginative reach and cultural repertory of human possibilities. Art and culture, mass or otherwise, are merely aspects of the larger challenge and long exploratory voyage which faces us—that of learning to be human.

See also ARTS; LITERATURE; MUSIC; PERFORM-ING ARTS; VISUAL ARTS.

BIBLIOGRAPHY

ALLOWAY, LAWRENCE. "The Long Front of Culture." In John Russell and Suzi Gablik, eds. *Pop Art Redefined.* New York: Praeger, 1969.

McLUHAN, MARSHALL. *Understanding Media.* New York: McGraw-Hill, 1964.

RITTEL, HORST W T , and WEBBER, MELVIN M. "Dilemmas in a General Theory of Planning." *Policy Sciences* 4/2 (June 1973).

SIMON, WILLIAM. "Future Relationships Between Man and Society." Paper presented at the Rome Special World Conference on Futures Research, September 1973.

STEELE, ROBERT. "Art, Youth Culture, and the Movies." In Bernard Rosenberg and David Manning, eds. *Mass Culture Revisited.* New York: Van Nostrand-Reinhold, 1971.

John McHale
Magda McHale

Materials: Research and Development

The history of human development can be told through changes in the use and manipulation of materials. The progress of humankind and its technological sophistication has been determined by the materials of construction available at the time. The stone age began when primitive man learned to shape stones into tools. With the dawn of the bronze age, humans learned to smelt metals and make copper and bronze tools to aid in food gathering and preparation. The development of iron technology allowed increases in the span of structures as well as decreases in their bulk. More complicated design allowed materials to be used much more efficiently. For example, truss structures made from cast iron were used by railroads to span rivers and canyons. The industrial revolution would not have been possible without the development of tough, high-strength steels. Steel expanded the scope of material designs from the truss to the cantilever beam. Lightweight metals such as aluminum, magnesium, and titanium permitted designers to build practical aircraft and aerospace structures, meeting the needs of the emerging space age in the 1950s.

Polymeric Materials

Polymeric materials have evolved to replace metals in many applications because of performance, availability, and reduced systems cost. In the early twentieth century, chemistry played a key role in the evolution of polymeric materials. Synthetic polymers were first explored in Europe in the early twentieth century. In the 1930s, the fundamental research of Wallace Carothers and his associates led to better understanding of polymeric structures and the development of neoprene synthetic rubber and nylon fibers. From that time on, progress has been swift as synthetic polymeric materials have rapidly evolved to replace older products, i.e., synthetic rubber for natural rubber, synthetic fibers for natural fibers, plastic containers and plastic bottles for metals and glass bottles, engineering plastic for die cast metals.

Synthetic polymeric materials offer several advantages over metals, among them excellent strength for equivalent weight, improved corrosion resistance, design flexibility, and easy fabrication. Polymeric materials have significantly better properties than aluminum and steel for engineering applications. Another factor important today because of limited energy resources is the energy required to produce materials (energy content). This energy is significantly higher for metals.

The world's polymer industry has undergone a remarkable period of sustained growth beginning with World War II and lasting about twenty-five years to the beginning of the 1970s. This growth was fueled by an explosion of new knowledge in macromolecular chemistry, polymerization technology, structure property relationships, and mechanical shaping technology. New monomers and new methods of polymerization were investigated, seeking new materials and properties. This led to remarkable improvements in the basic properties of polymeric materials.

Metal Replacement

The first wave of metals replacement by engineering plastics began in secondary, noncritical application with the commercialization of nylon resin in 1950. DuPont and Celanese introduced polyacetal resin in 1959 followed by polycarbonate from General Electric in 1964. In 1965, General Electric commercialized one of the first polymeric alloys, a modified phenylene oxide. Polymeric alloys became even more evident as blending, reinforcement, and toughening technology opened up hundreds of new applications. Additional generic molding resins such as PBT polyesters from Celanese, PET polyesters from DuPont, and their alloys were introduced in the 1970s. The early 1980s saw the introduction of supertough nylon and acetals and stiffened PET polyesters. Although plastic resins cost more than steel on a pound-for-pound basis, assembled and finished plastic parts often offer a total system cost savings because of lower density, lower tooling and fabrication costs, design flexibility, parts consolidation, and fewer assembly steps. The growth of engineering polymers has primarily been in metal substitution or replacement, particularly for die-cast metals and hot rolled steel.

The volume of synthetic polymers grew from 15 million in 1923 to over 60 billion pounds in 1990, representing a compound annual growth rate of 15 percent for over sixty years. DuPont in particular derived the majority of its revenue and earnings during this period by replacing traditional materials (wood, metal, cotton, wool) with synthetic polymeric materials made from petroleum. Leading this great wave of replacement was the substitution of noncellulosic fibers for cellulosic fibers.

Generically, new polymers such as Lycra® spandex, Nomex®, and Kevlar® aramids and nonwoven sheet structures such as Tyvek® fueled the substitution. A large part of the entire textile system (texturing, weaving, dyeing, permanent press washing cycles, etc.) was transformed in order to accommodate the new polymeric fibers.

The second great wave of polymeric materials substitution is the replacement of metals by engineering and reinforced plastics in critical primary structural applications. This wave of metal replacement began with the development of superstrong, superstiff, lightweight fibers such as carbon, graphite, aramid, and silicon carbide. Advanced polymeric materials based on high-performance carbon and aramid fibers have begun to replace the two primary metals aluminum and steel in demanding structural applications. The projection is mathematically calculated according to technological substitution theory. We used a volume basis in calculating this curve because in many cases it is the volume of a material that is performing a task, not its weight. This S-curve shows dramatically that the rapid takeover phase of engineering and reinforced plastics for metals is about to begin. By the year 2015, these sophisticated materials should have gained about half the market. We are now perched at the cusp of a growth surge to come. In the middle of the next century when this S-curve is coming to an end, we (or our descendants) should see the end of rust as a problem and a largely polymeric personal vehicle in every garage. The consumption of steel and aluminum is mature and declining. Metal replacement represents an enormous market potential—over 30 billion pounds in the United States and about 200 billion pounds worldwide.

Systems Thinking and the Specific Solution

What will it take to fulfill the promise of this growth curve? Many people think we should concentrate on two areas: systems thinking and specific solutions. This process is more challenging than the simple materials substitution we saw in the fibers case. As the substitution for metals continues, new, integrated engineering concepts and specifically designed polymeric composite systems will be needed. We will not simply replace metals: we will put together these materials in new ways, designing their properties to our own specifications. It will be a substitution of new, tailor-made, anisotropic, synthetic material systems for traditional isotropic materials.

Earlier ages were eras of specific solutions. Primitives built a stone ax to meet their own specific needs. Of course, it was primitive, but they knew what they wanted. The industrial revolution changed all that. As new materials and manufacturing technologies were developed, the era of the general solution was born and was exemplified by automobile manufacturer Henry Ford. He had a famous slogan during the 1920s: "Any color you want as long as it's black." This slogan symbolized mass production. Massive quantities of generic materials (steel, glass) were assembled repeatedly in the same way and huge cost savings resulted. You could not buy exactly what you wanted—it was too expensive—but you could at least get

something close. Now, and especially in the future, you can have it both ways. People will demand a specific solution to meet their needs and they will get it because it will be technically feasible at a reasonable cost.

It is the new computer technology, in the broadest sense, that makes it possible to pursue specific solutions again through flexible, intelligent manufacturing and distribution systems. In addition, some cost savings are inherent to specific solutions because only the materials needed for that specific task will be used.

In theory, everything we buy will be tailor made to meet our specific needs. It is already happening. In medicine, we can go from broad-spectrum antibiotics to disease-specific diagnosis and treatment. In agriculture, from general fertilizers and herbicides to the ability to feed and protect crops in specific soils and climates and also to design those crops for specific food industry needs. The world of structural materials is not immune to this phenomenon; what once was only isotropic steel and commodity polymer is now moving toward more use of anisotropic material systems where a particular arrangement of components solves a specific problem.

Revolutionary Material Developments

Dramatic advances in material systems will come when some level of intelligence is embedded into the system itself. Smartness in systems is entering our everyday lives today. It consists of three elements: sensing, analysis, and feedback control or response. More and more automobiles today can adjust their own brakes and carburetor fuel mixtures. Some cars give their drivers a continuous analysis of the state of their systems and recommend preventive maintenance. The continuously self-tuning internal combustion engine is being developed. Today, the smart house, where utilities are automatically monitored and adjusted to meet the needs of its residents, is almost a reality.

Embedding intelligence in material systems will help overcome current limitations holding back their pervasive substitution for metals. This materials revolution will proceed in four distinct but overlapping phases.

The first phase is already in progress; replacement occurs on a one-for-one basis, usually a polymer composite for a metal. The design of the system does not change. In the second phase, the system design is changed to take advantage of the multifunctional properties of the new materials. In both of these first two phases, the composite systems are passive, i.e., made up of basic material components in specific ways that do more than the simple sum of their parts, but that generate no useful information. The most dramatic advances will come in the third and fourth phases when material systems are developed that will be able to "sense" their environment *and* respond to such an environment by either adapting themselves (i.e., their properties) to be more productive and/or by actually changing their environment. It is during this third phase that the rapid substitution of active for passive material systems will occur. These active material systems that are responsive and adaptive are truly smart systems.

In the future, we will learn from nature and biological polymers in our design of polymeric material systems. Biological polymers have an architecture that is precisely matched to the stresses they experience. We are aware today that natural material synthesis is carried out in a very specific and precise fashion against chemical templates. These templates can be DNA itself or the chemical catalyst enzymes specified by DNA. What is perhaps less well known is that these natural materials, once synthesized, are internally programmed to self-order themselves into higher-level structures or material systems. A good example is the tendon tissue. The tendon has six distinct levels of organization starting with molecules of collagen in fibrous form assembled into a triple helix and finishing with a crimped bundle of fiber assemblages called fascicles. No synthetic material known has the strength and long-lasting three-dimensional flexibility of tendon tissue. But then, no synthetic material is assembled into such a highly ordered and complex material system—we simply do not know enough to do it. But nature does, and we must learn creatively from nature.

Our challenge is to learn how to make more efficient material systems using these natural, highly ordered systems as models. Sensors, controllers, and actuators small enough to be incorporated into composites without significantly limiting their integrity are within sight. Intelligent material systems will be a reality in the first quarter of the twenty-first century.

In conclusion, most of the new knowledge that will drive wealth-creation well into the next century is centered in three areas: advanced materials, bioscience, and information science. How we apply this knowledge to solve increasingly more difficult and important problems will determine how well we replace metals with polymeric materials. Success in the twenty-first century will demand continuously learning organizations that evolve toward multifunctional, multidisciplined technical networks to develop new technologies.

See also BATTERIES; CLOTHING; ENGINEERING; GENETIC TECHNOLOGIES; HAZARDOUS WASTES; INDUSTRIAL DESIGN; MINERALS; MOTOR VEHICLES; PETROLEUM; SCIENTIFIC BREAKTHROUGHS; SOLID WASTE; TECHNOLOGY DIFFUSION.

BIBLIOGRAPHY

Business Week, (February 9, 1987).

DHINGRA, A. K. "Metals Replacement by Composites." *Journal of Metals* (March 1986): 17.

DHINGRA, A. K.; CUNNING, J. D.; DOHERTY, T. P.; and PLETCHER, T. C. "Future Systems Integration for Development of Advanced Fibers and Composite Materials. Advanced Materials for Future Industries: Needs and Seeds." In *Proceedings of the Second Japan International SAMPE Symposium and Exhibition.* Chiba, Japan, December 11–14, 1991.

DHINGRA, A. K., and DOHERTY, T. P. "Future Trends in Advanced Fibers and Composite Materials Technology." In T. Chandra and A. K. Dhingra, eds. *Advanced Composites '93.* Minerals, Metals & Materials (TMS) Society, 1993.

MILLER, J. A. "Polymers in the 21st Century." Keynote lecture at Polymers '94 Symposium, Indian Petrochemicals Corporation Ltd, Vadodara, India, February 8–10, 1994.

MORGAN, R. J.; BAER, E.; and HILTNER, A. "Advanced Structural Multiperformance Materials for the Next Century." *SAMPE Journal,* 29/2 (March/April 1993).

TANNER, D.; DHINGRA, A. K.; COOPER, J. L.; and PIGLIACAMPI, J. "Future of Aramid Fiber Composites as a General Engineering Material." *Nippon Fukugo Zairyo Gakkaishi* 2/5 (1985).

J. A. Miller
A. J. Dahl
Ashok K. Dhingra

Media Consolidation

The media and cultural industries are joining, if not leading, the globalization of corporate enterprise. Paralleling the rapid expansion since World War II of American corporate production sites around the world, newspaper, television, film, publishing, recording, and advertising companies increasingly have been selling their product in scores of national markets.

Massive corporate conglomerates of cultural production, based in a few metropolitan centers, now produce and sell the bulk of the world's entertainment and informational (news and data) fare.

Time-Warner, Disney, Murdoch's News Corporation, Bertelsmann, Sony, Matsushita, El Globo, Hachette, Viacom, and a few other similar combines preside over what the global audience sees, hears, and reads.

Facilitating the growth of these international combines has been a continuing explosion of new information technologies—television, satellite communications, cable TV, computerization, fiber optics, and so on. These technologies provide instantaneous global (and national) transmission and reception of messages and images with economies of scale that reduce costs and allow the global media products to overwhelm local outputs.

Other large corporate enterprises engaged in producing, collecting, organizing, and disseminating information also have emerged alongside the pop culture combines. These include financial and business service companies and electronic database producers who assemble vast stockpiles of information that can be accessed electronically, worldwide, wherever terminals exist, *at a price*. Accordingly, Reuters, Dow Jones, McGraw-Hill, Reed-Elsevier, Knight-Ridder, and a handful of similar firms have become the producers and custodians of a good chunk of the world's information, and to a certain extent, the global memory. They make this available to users—governmental, corporate, and individual—who can afford to pay for it.

This institutional arrangement almost inevitably ensures a growing gap between those who can purchase information and those who cannot. No less consequential, *what* will be collected and made available in the commercial informational stockpile is largely governed by the needs of the most influential and well-off users.

There are other effects as well—not the least of which is the threat to the survival of diverse opinion and free expression.

First, the large-scale corporate entertainment and information enterprises, by their command of enormous resources, marginalize and often eliminate the smaller, less well-financed alternative sources. Secondly, the willingness of the large, heavily concentrated cultural combines to allow a full range of opinion and creative effort in their offerings is governed by financial and ideological considerations.

High production costs of programming make corporate media managers reluctant to go outside tried and tested formulaic material. Excluded almost automatically at the outset are formats and ideas that challenge routine patterns in any serious way. Reinforcing this cautiousness is an equally strong managerial suspicion of thematic material that is critical of established, dominant values and institutions.

There is a third, and perhaps the most important, structural element in the limitation of speech: the primacy of corporate sponsorship. Dependent on advertising revenue, television in the United States is essentially a conduit for the sales messages of big corporate goods-and-services providers. Their sales messages create the commercial atmosphere that pervades American TV. Since a commercial's objective is usually to encourage the consumption of this or that good or service, the omnipresence of commercials overwhelms and often trivializes whatever programming material that precedes or follows it.

The national sponsors, who are the main supporters of TV (and a good part of the other media as well), are also exceedingly sensitive to any views that they consider potentially injurious to their economic interests. All the same, open censorship in the American media is infrequent. Much more significant, though less easy to comprehend, *censorship is embedded in the institutional structures of the media*. It is implemented daily, even hourly, by decisions made by media broadcasters, journalists, editors, scriptwriters, and others, who have internalized, knowingly or not, the values of their corporate employers. Most media hands are well aware of what is expected of them. If not, they are quickly informed.

In the 1990s, many observers acknowledge the decline of U.S. power internationally. Yet, however true this may be with regard to industrial activity, it is, at least to date, totally inapplicable to American worldwide information cultural power. In fact, this power has never been stronger. U.S. exports of movies, TV programs, books and magazines, tapes and recordings, even theme parks, information from electronic databases, and *language itself* (the world increasingly speaks English) confirm the dominant position of the United States in the global cultural-media sphere.

In the 1970s, scores of nations objected to the one-way flow of American media product—from Hollywood or New York to everywhere else. These countries expressed their hope in numerous meetings and resolutions for a new international information order (NIIO). This hope has not been realized. The strength of U.S. media products in the world market—compared to that of the rest of the world—is greater than ever. The "free flow of information"—the code expression for the unrestricted global movement of the products and services of Western media conglomerates—has gained, and maintained, a global advantage for American cultural material.

United States dominance of the information realm now extends to newer information forms such as electronic databases. In 1990, the United States produced 70 percent of the world's databases. Whoever accesses these electronic data repositories, especially those holding social data, not only pays for this service, but also receives subtle but not inconsequential social perspectives that guided the compiler's selection and organization of the data.

It is difficult to predict precisely at this time how far into the future American primacy in information, entertainment, and pop culture will endure. Indeed, how long can it flourish if the economic underpinning continues to erode? Also, it is hardly likely that the widespread demand for information equality and cultural sovereignty will disappear. If anything, it is going to grow stronger. This suggests that in the cultural and information realms in the years ahead, a deepening struggle will develop, domestically and internationally, for freedom of personal and creative expression. The times are bound to be conflictive, exciting, and hopeful.

See also COMMUNICATIONS; COMMUNICATIONS: PRIVACY ISSUES; COMMUNICATIONS TECHNOLOGY; COMPUTER LINKAGE; ELECTRONIC CONVERGENCE; GLOBAL CULTURE; INFORMATION SOCIETY; MEDIA LAB; PRINTED WORD; SATELLITE COMMUNICATIONS; TELECOMMUNICATIONS; TELEVISION.

BIBLIOGRAPHY

BAGDIKIAN, BEN. *Media Monopoly*. Boston: Beacon Press, 1992.

BENNETT, JAMES R. *Control of the Media in the United States: An Annotated Bibliography*. New York: Garland, 1992.

DENNIS, EVERETT, and MERRILL, JOHN C. *Media Debates: Issues in Mass Communication*. White Plains, NY: Longman, 1991.

HERMAN, EDWARD S., and CHOMSKY, NOAM. *Manufacturing Consent*. New York: Pantheon, 1988.

SCHILLER, HERBERT. *Culture Inc.: The Corporate Takeover of Public Expression*. New York: Oxford University Press, 1989.

Herbert I. Schiller

Media of Exchange

Media of exchange (MOE) will continue to evolve—from barter to commodity money such as cattle or tobacco, to precious metals, to paper currencies backed by precious metals, to currencies backed by governments and good faith—by becoming increasingly electronic over the next generation. Cash and currency will still be with us, but they will be augmented and increasingly replaced by electronic MOE, with countertrade—in which goods are exchanged without cash changing hands—the most prominent alternative. Indeed, electronics may enable us to arrive at a global currency.

Forces Shaping the Future Media of Exchange

The technological infrastructure supporting electronic MOE is growing rapidly. The information infrastructure is flowering as the fiber-optic backbone and wireless ancillaries are put in place. Computers are becoming ubiquitous at the office and school, on the road, and in the home. On the social side, increasing time pressures in business, such as the move to just-in-time delivery, and the rise of dual-income households are are impelling the move toward faster and more convenient electronic transactions.

Banks are moving to electronic service delivery. There were about 96,000 ATMs (automatic teller machines) and 200,000 POS (point of sale) terminals in 1993, according to *Bank Network News*. Perhaps 40 percent of the country's 100,000 bank branches will be closed by the year 2000, replaced by ATMS and videoconferencing, according to Joel Friedman of Andersen Consulting. Credit and debit cards are used for a growing share of purchases—about 12.3 million households use a debit card and 66.5 million a major credit card, according to Payment Systems Incorporated.

A global economy is steadily emerging as indicated by the growing percentage of national GNPs derived from international trade. Businesses searching for new markets will require new tools for dealing with developing nations, which are often financially strapped. Increased international trade will encourage nations to harmonize disparate currencies.

Three Primary Conclusions About the Future Media of Exchange

The forces described above will lead to three significant changes in future MOE. First, money will become increasingly electronic. Today's alphabet soup of electronic money—ATM (automatic teller machines, owned both by banks and nonbanks), POS (point-of-sale), EFT (electronic funds transfer)—is an integral element moving us toward reliance on electronic MOE. Big institutional money already is electronic. Electronic wire transfers from Fedwire, the Clearinghouse International Payment System (CHIPS), and retail transactions account for a daily flow of electronic money equal to over one-third of the annual U.S. GNP (Solomon, 1993, pp. 69–70).

The progression will be as follows: first, from ATM to POS terminals at checkouts using debit and credit cards; next, to wireless, portable checkout, as used today by car rental firms, including Hertz; finally, to smart "digicash" cards. These machines or their equivalents will be readily available in public domains (kiosks in malls) and in businesses, as well as in the home. The transactions performed electronically will become increasingly sophisticated—for example, Citibank will eventually allow its customers to trade money-market and mutual fund shares at ATMs.

Cash for small transactions will be the last to go electronic. New schemes for digital cash address and strive to resolve privacy concerns and transaction costs that marred previous attempts. Companies would sell e-money refills, similar to traveler's checks, that are anonymous and untraceable using security-protected digital signatures. For example, a digicash card used to pay for a steak would allow both the merchant and the bank to record the transaction but not to link those transactions to a specific person. Other possibilities include attaching electronic money to e-mail or automatically sending the bill for renting a video as it is played (Kelly, 1993, pp. 56–57).

Secondly, a global capital market and global currency will more fully emerge. Global capital markets will enable borrowers to traverse the globe in search of the best terms. The time and space barriers that have kept financial markets and MOE local and national will be surmounted by information technology and financial networks. Global currency will gain increasing support and momentum as nations and businesses seek protection from wildly fluctuating exchange rates. Regional currency is already emerging in the EC (European Community), even as individual nations maintain their own medium of exchange.

The obstacles to global currency include national politics and the absence of a common monetary policy or credible international mechanisms for determining that policy. Economist Gary Hufbauer points out that "a common currency is the last state of a lot of other integration that takes place first."

Thirdly, countertrade will be an increasingly important mechanism for doing business in developing nations.

A key challenge for the global economy is to close the gap between rich and poor nations. Businesses in developed nations will also be searching for new markets in developing nations with growing populations and economies. In business terms, a key question is how to do business with a cash-poor or bankrupt customer.

Countertrade is accelerating as an MOE, enabling developed and developing nations to trade, as well as enhancing trade among developing nations. Such transactions account for an estimated 10–20 percent of world trade today, according to the United Nations Commission on Trade and Development (UNCTAD). Almost two-thirds of the Fortune 500 companies have used it or are using it now.

Countertrade consists mainly of barter and counterpurchase transactions that commit the exporter to buy goods from the importer. A cash value is fixed for accounting, taxation, and insurance purposes.

In summary, future MOE will be increasingly electronic and global, alongside persisting traditional mechanisms, including cash and countertrade or barter.

See also CAPITAL FORMATION; COMMUNICATIONS; COMMUNICATIONS: PRIVACY ISSUES; INVESTMENTS; MONETARY SYSTEM; TELECOMMUNICATIONS.

BIBLIOGRAPHY

KELLY, KEVIN. "Cyberpunks, E-Money, and the Technologies of Disconnection." *Whole Earth Catalog* (Summer 1993).

KURTZMAN, JOEL. *The Death of Money*. New York: Simon & Schuster, 1993.

SOLOMON, ELINOR HARRIS. "Electronic Funds Transfer: Challenges for the Computer Age." *Bankers Magazine* (January–February 1993): 69–70.

Andy Hines

Media Lab

The Media Lab at the Massachusetts Institute of Technology is the brainchild of Nicholas Negroponte, its founder, director, and chief visionary. In 1985, Negroponte, now the Wiesner Professor of Media Technology, united a group of diverse MIT research groups and gave them a common purpose: to devise new ways for people to interact with information. He was driven, in large measure, by the inadequacy and user-unfriendliness of computers and other information technologies. Personal computers, he maintained, are anything but personal. Under Negroponte's guidance, the Media Lab began to create a new world of machines that see, hear, and talk and computers that can produce a custom blend of information based on personal interests of the reader. The guiding vision was to create personalized technologies that know and serve their human masters in the manner of an English butler. Examples are refrigerators that will order milk before the carton is empty and telephones that will tell callers to try later.

Within ten years of its founding, the Media Lab has grown into a $20 million/year research and teaching organization with twenty-three faculty members and more than one hundred graduate students. Approximately 70 percent of the contract research funding comes from industrial sponsors and the balance from various agencies of the federal government. Sponsor companies range from telecommunications to advertising, from publishing to finance. Of the sponsors, 25 percent are Japanese and another 25 percent European.

One of the main areas of Media Lab research is speech recognition by machines. It is trying to build machines that could turn out whole spoken conversation into a printout and has already produced a "Dataglove" that translates hand motion into electronic instructions for a computer. It is working on ways to pump video signals down a 1.2-megabit-per-second communications channel. This would permit transmission of movies to homes using existing telephone wires, with a picture quality better than that from VHS videocassettes. It has also been instrumental in furthering the development of the graphical user interface found in home computers today and in helping to foster the ongoing evolution of the blend of text, graphics, sound manipulation, and image processing that is known as multimedia computing.

The Media Lab is engaged in a number of projects that will change the computer environment of the future and break engineering deadlocks.

- Matthew Brand is working on visual intelligence with the goal of producing robots that are visually fluent and can cooperate with humans in the design, assembly, and repair of objects.
- Justin Cassell is designing a system that integrates gesture, intonation, and facial expressions into multimodal human figure animation.

- Kenneth Haase is creating memory-based representational systems for comprehending, filtering, and summarizing news stories. Memory-based representation uses analogies between descriptions to identify semantic roles and categories. This would lead to natural-sounding computer-synthesized speech combining semantic and contextual information such as pause, intonation, rhythm, and inflection.
- Haase and Gloriana Davenport are working on storyteller systems that can produce customized stories adapted to the listener's background, preferences, and interests. Such systems transform the nature of publication; rather than producing epistles, they produce emissaries.
- Henry Lieberman is combining representation and learning techniques from artificial intelligence with interactive graphical editors to create programming by example.
- Pattie Moses has created ALIVE (Artificial Life Interactive Video Entertainment), a novel system that allows wireless full-body interaction between a human participant and a rich graphical world inhabited by autonomous agents. This is achieved through the use of interface agents or digital assistants. Interface agents may be used to select news articles, videos, music, and television shows; they also serve as personal critics and editors to recommend books, software, and videos.
- Michael Resnick, Seymour Papert, and Fred Martin have built programmable LEGO bricks that enable children to create robots and sensory rooms.
- Richard Bolt and Ronald MacNeil are building DataWall, an ultra-high-definition, seamlessly tiled, wall-sized display with which human beings can interact using natural language and gestures.
- Alex Pentland, Michael Hawley, Rosalind Picard, and Thad Starner are working on compact computers that can be "worn" like eyeglasses or clothing. With heads-up displays, unobtrusive input devices, and a host of other sensing and communication tools, wearable computers can serve as intelligent assistants. A related project is the BodyNet, a local wireless network that will integrate all the information appliances on a person—cameras, watches, calculators, notebooks, date books, checkbooks, and credit cards—connected to advanced displays, radios, and other communication systems.
- Christopher Schmandt is working on a handheld, audio note-taker, with a speech-recognition interface, as well as an interactive radio with

programs compiled from a number of sources presented on demand over the telephone or on a computer workstation.

- Barry Vercoe has built a computer-driven piano to show that computers can exhibit real-time musical behavior similar to that of skilled human performers.
- Walter Bender has devised Data-Hiding or Steganography, the process of embedding data into image and audio signals. This technique is being evaluated in the light of three applications: copyright-protection, tamper-proofing, and augmentation-data embedding.
- Michael Klug has created a holographic laser printer that allows hard-copy holograms to be generated in minutes rather than hours, automatically and without wet processing.
- V. Michael Bove has built eight systems of Cheops, including a data-flow television receiver, a compact imaging system and modular platform for acquisition, real-time processing, display of digital video sequences, and model-based representations of moving scenes.
- Michael Hawley's Media Fab is a 254-thread-per-inch multicolor printer that outputs to garments instead of photocopy paper.
- Andrew Lippman's Media Bank is a distributed web of processors that contains audio and video bits, snippets, and movies. The system is designed to synthesize programs on demand and assemble movies from multiple depositories. A Mosaic-based browser navigates through the migratory and evolving data, and an automatic page-generator depicts the current content and object location.
- The Visible Language Workshop is a seamless, sophisticated, graphical, dynamic, and interactive testbed for use in prototyping tools, editors, and scenarios.

The Media Lab is pushing the envelope in many promising directions with the goal of making technology more user-friendly and intuitive. In the world of frontier information technology it is serving as the advance guard working with ideas that will drive the future.

See also COMMUNICATIONS TECHNOLOGY; COMPUTERS: OVERVIEW; COMPUTERS: SOFTWARE; INTERACTIVE ENTERTAINMENT.

BIBLIOGRAPHY

BRAND, STEWART. *Media Lab: Inventing the Future at MIT.* New York: Viking-Penguin, 1988.

George Thomas Kurian

Media Law.

See COMMUNICATIONS: MEDIA LAW.

Medical Care Providers

In the years ahead, health professionals will be able to enhance or restore health far better than at present. However, the future boundaries, responsibilities, and reimbursement mechanisms for health care professionals are unclear. The future of the various health professions will be shaped by a variety of developments in each profession, as well as by more general trends in health care and society. Generally, the capacity of a specific health-care professional to be a healer will increase, as will the ability of consumers to handle more sophisticated self-care at home. Expert systems and advancing biological knowledge will mean a decline in the demand for some providers. The most effective health care professionals will be rewarded accordingly. As a result, providers with poor performance may not be allowed to practice. Even where certifying or licensing groups do not remove them, they may find it more difficult to get patients or jobs.

Major Trends

THE PREDICT-AND-MANAGE APPROACH

Health care, benefiting from advances in the knowledge of disease processes, aging, and genetic influences, will shift its focus from treating health conditions after they arise to preventing them or at least minimizing their impact. This predict-and-manage approach will hasten new consumer-oriented use of technologies, as well as decentralizing expert medical knowledge to primary-care providers (both doctors and nurses) and consumers.

HEALTH INFORMATION SYSTEMS

Four related developments in information systems will profoundly shape health professions. First, computer-based medical records will store all patient information including problems, test results, orders submitted, treatment plans, X rays, and other data. Over time, new types of information on genetic and biochemical proclivities to disease will be incorporated. Second, consumers will have greater access to health information through interactive learning and communication technologies, including detailed information about their own health conditions as well as information about disease prevention and health promotion. Third, expert systems will assist physicians, other health-care providers, and consumers in making therapeutic decisions. Fourth, inexpensive, non-invasive, or minimally invasive body-function monitoring devices (such as health-monitoring wristwatches) will be integral to prevention and treatment efforts.

THE BIOLOGICAL REVOLUTION

By the year 2010, the human genome will be completely sequenced, heightening the understanding of genetic influences on health and disease. Coupled with a clearer understanding of our current health, mental health, and disease states—culled from more effective medical information management—health care will use this new knowledge to develop more biochemically unique care, more refined biological markers, and better targeted therapeutics.

HEALTH OUTCOMES MEASUREMENTS

Major efforts are under way in Europe and the United States to develop and apply measures of health outcome. The implementation of electronic medical records facilitates gathering and analyzing large amounts of patient data. Better patient data will allow comparisons of individual health provider results and different therapies. Health outcome measurements will play a growing role in exposing inappropriate medical practices and enhancing therapeutic selection. Locally, consumer groups will develop comparative success statistics for physicians, nurses, and other health care providers.

THE HEALTH PROMOTION MOVEMENT

Sickness care still dominates: 96 percent of medical expenditures are related to treatment, less than 4 percent to prevention. Growing understanding that the leading causes of death and disability are greatly influenced by behavior will change this. Cost constraints will encourage health promotion as the best strategy for reducing costs in the long run, while markedly improving health.

DEMOGRAPHICS

As the baby boomer generation ages, a larger proportion of the population also will become older. This translates not only into a greater demand for elder care, but for more sophisticated prevention and better treatment services prompted by rising expectations and entitlements

LICENSURE

Health care professionals, particularly physicians, must be "licensed" to practice. Licensure of physicians was originally established as a public policy measure to protect consumers from fraudulent providers. However, licensure grants physicians a monopoly over the right to practice medicine. Other licensed health care providers (dentists, pharmacists, nurses, and less tightly regulated providers such as homeopaths and other alternative care providers) offer physicians relatively little direct competition at present. In the near future, increasing dissatisfaction with physicians, the anticipated growth of nurse practitioners, competition from alternative providers, increased access to health information through decentralizing technology, and health-outcome measures showing that some health care providers (especially nurses) are more cost-effective will elicit cries for changing medical licensure. Nurses and allied health professionals will push to gain professional status and equality through revised controls over practice. Licensure will move toward outcome-based judgments of quality, limiting the ability of physicians to limit the scope of activity of other licensed professionals.

MALPRACTICE

Direct medical liability costs (insurance premiums) were conservatively estimated in the late 1980s to represent less than 1 percent of the nation's total health care expenditures. Defensive medical procedures cost around $15 billion in 1989, for a whopping $23 billion in total costs annually, by AMA estimates. Most malpractice claims are directed at physicians. Tort laws may be modified to limit the amount of malpractice awards, which could bring about a drop in insurance premiums and unnecessary testing. Specific ways to accomplish this may include: a monetary cap on "pain and suffering" damages that a jury can award; a sliding-scale limit on attorney contingency fees; and/or a provision to allow damages over a specific amount to be paid in installments.

The Health Professions

PHYSICIANS

In the last two decades, physicians have gravitated toward specialty practices, where remuneration is high and results are immediate and clear-cut. The number of primary care physicians in the United States declined dramatically in the last decade, falling 19 percent between 1986 and 1992. Strong pressure will be applied to increase the proportion of active primary care physicians. The number of active physicians is projected to rise from around 600,000 in 1992 to 720,000 by the year 2000.

At the same time, nurses and other health practitioners will assume more responsibility for primary care. As health promotion becomes dominant, health care providers will increasingly assume the role of "health coaches."

As expert systems decentralize knowledge, there will be fewer specialty physicians needed in fields that deal largely with information rather than physical procedures (e.g., surgery). Many physical procedures may be automated and become accessible to primary care providers. Overall there will be a shift to primary care, with keener competition among types of providers and therapies. Providing favorable outcomes in cost-competitive ways will become hallmarks of success.

NURSES

Changing technology and the increased role for "healers" could dramatically alter the nurse's role. Nurses already handle many aspects of primary care more cost-effectively than physicians, and this trend will continue as demands for care increase. Recent attempts to raise academic and licensure requirements to practice nursing emphasize this expanding role. Nurses will need to demonstrate their effectiveness, measured through outcomes data, to foster these changes. Even so, a decline in the demand for nurses will come as hospital in-patient care declines.

DENTISTS

Better oral hygiene dramatically cut the demand for dentists, leading the dental profession to voluntarily limit student enrollment in dental schools. By 2000, only 3,200 dental students may graduate from dental schools, down from a peak of 5,756 in 1983. Dentists, in the past, delegated many tasks to their dental hygienists. If demand falls, dentists may seek to reclaim some of these tasks, lowering demand for dental hygienists' services. Adult orthodontics and treatment for gum disease will provide some degree of business, but professional teeth-cleaning services will continue to be dentistry's economic mainstay. However, if dental licensing changes, oral hygienists could offer these services independently.

PHARMACISTS

Pharmacy professionals created a valuable position for themselves in hospitals when they estab-

lished their role as clinical pharmacists, significantly aiding the improvement of hospital drug therapy. While pharmacists will continue to be needed in hospitals and in managed-care settings such as HMOs, overall, the hospital pharmacy business will decline as the size and number of hospitals decline. Demand for consulting pharmacists in nursing homes will grow.

As the dispensing aspects of their job become increasingly automated, community pharmacists will need to become more involved in counseling customers about drug use and related health issues. If community pharmacists—especially smaller retail pharmacists—do not reinvent their role, they will see a decline in demand for their services, left behind by technological advancement and economies of scale. With the rise of expert systems and the decentralization of health information, pharmacists will have tougher competition, particularly from mail-order firms. Also, pharmaceutical products and allied product lines will become more complex. Some pharmacies will use "designer gene machines" to develop medications uniquely suited to specific customers.

ALLIED HEALTH

Other allied health professions can be divided into those related to physical touching or personal coaching (such as physical therapy and occupational therapy) and those built around specific medical technologies.

Therapies that involve physical touch draw the greatest demand, a trend that will continue unabated into the next century; these health professions will be the last to be automated. Likewise, jobs that force allied health professionals to successfully coach their patients will also grow in demand.

While "aides" in some fields are declining, this trend could reverse. Cost-effectiveness in health care, the inability of physicians to limit the competitive roles of other providers, and the capacity for expert systems to decentralize expertise may mean that low-level, low-paying entry-level positions will remain or reappear. Workers in these positions will be dramatically assisted by expert systems and technology.

Conclusion

As society and health care undergo these transformations, persons currently exploring career opportunities might get a fatalistic feeling that nothing can be done to change the course of a particular health profession. To some degree this is true. Technology, for example, will progress regardless of how willing health professionals are to accept it. Health professions will prosper or falter depending on roles they stake out and how well they deal with change.

See also DENTISTRY; HEALTH CARE; HEALTH CARE: ALTERNATIVE THERAPIES; HEALTH CARE COSTS; HEALTH CARE FINANCING; HEALTH CARE: MORAL ISSUES; HEALTH CARE: TECHNOLOGICAL DEVELOPMENTS; MENTAL HEALTH; NURSING; PSYCHIATRY; PUBLIC HEALTH.

BIBLIOGRAPHY

BEZOLD, CLEMENT. "The Future of Health Care: Implications for the Allied Health Professions." *Journal of Allied Health* 18/5 (Fall 1989).

BEZOLD, CLEMENT, et al. *The Future of Work and Health.* Dover, MA: Auburn House, 1986.

_____. *Pharmacy in the 21st Century.* Bethesda, MD: United States Pharmacopeial Convention, 1985.

LEVINSKY, NORMAN G. "Recruiting for Primary Care." *New England Journal of Medicine* (March 4, 1993): 656–660.

Clement Bezold

Megacities

For millennia, cities have been the centers of culture and crucibles of civilization. Until recently, the vast majority of the population lived in tiny settlements, villages, and small towns, whereas only 3 percent lived in urban areas. By the year 2000, however, over 50 percent will live in cities. It is projected that twenty-three of these cities will be megacities with more than 10 million people each. Fifty years ago there was only one. Reflecting another fundamental transformation, eighteen of these megacities will be in the developing countries. By the year 2000, the urban population of developing countries will be almost twice that of developed nations; and, by the year 2025, almost four times as large.

Every city has a unique history, culture, and style. Yet in spite of differences and contrasts in demographic makeup, level of economic development, and political structure, megacities have much in common. Size alone presents a situation for which we lack collective experience. No precedent exists for feeding, sheltering, or transporting so many people in so dense an area, nor for removing their waste products or providing clean drinking water. Urban systems based on human settle-ments of 50,000 or 250,000 may accommodate urban populations of one million but break down at 4 million and become unworkable at 11 million. The infrastructural and managerial systems developed in the nineteenth century have become outmoded to handle the scale and complexity of today's cities.

Exacerbating the problem, megacities are experiencing critical environmental degradation, pushing to the limit their ability to sustain a viable quality of life. While all urbanites are affected, the urban poor are the most vulnerable, since squatter settlements are often located in the most undesirable areas of cities, such as floodplains or steep hillsides, or are adjacent to dangerous industries. Environmental degradation now represents one of the most formidable constraints on productivity for the urban poor by threatening their physical security and possessions and by increasing the incidence of diseases.

Radically new approaches are needed. They face powerful obstacles. The fragmented and overlapping structures of city agencies, departments, and divisions and the isolation of the government from both the private sector and the community are reinforced by incentive systems that discourage risk-taking by policy makers. Administrative systems' resistance to change is compounded by the persistence of outmoded assumptions among policymakers about urban development and by a paralyzing sense of hopelessness and despair about problem scale.

Megacities in developing countries bear added burdens. Although it is estimated that, by the end of the 1990s, half of the poor will be concentrated in urban areas, the international donor community has been slow to respond. Most aid agencies and development banks allocate less than 15 percent of their funds to basic needs projects in urban areas, and less than 20 percent to all other urban development projects. While there are signs of change, the focus of development assistance continues to be on the rural peasant and agricultural policy rather than on the city squatter and urban policy.

A consensus is emerging that improved resource allocation, ecological sustainability, and the acceleration of innovation processes must be policy priorities at both the international and urban levels.

1. *Improved resource allocation.* Efforts to stem cityward migration are based on a mistaken premise that urban growth is detrimental to national productivity. In fact, according to World Bank estimates, in 1989 60 percent of gross domestic product in most developing countries was gen-

erated in cities and about 80 percent of GDP growth is expected to occur in these cities." Large cities create economies of scale in public infrastructure and an investment climate that reduces capital costs, service delivery costs, maintenance costs and therefore per-unit expenditures.

In most Third World cities the informal labor market absorbs nearly one-third of the economically active urban labor force. Many workers deliberately choose informal sector jobs for their flexibility, freedom, lifestyle, and higher earnings. Because informal economies are inseparable from the formal economy, the provision of credit, training, and technical assistance to micro-enterprises and self-help efforts in low-income communities can help not only the urban poor but the entire urban and even national economy.

2. *Ecological sustainability.* Public awareness of the fragility of the planet's ecological balance has resulted in calls for limits on city size. However, experts are beginning to recognize that as the world's population increases, dense agglomerations are more efficient than space-consuming suburban style developments. Concentration in cities can save open space and natural habitats to increase food production.

3. *Accelerating innovation.* There is a desperate need to shorten the usual twenty-to-twenty-five-year lag between new ideas and their implementation. An ongoing forum that treats megacities as a global laboratory would permit this accelerated problem solving. The concept is based on mounting evidence that the most innovative urban solutions have often come not from government or academia but from the grassroots. The task is to make these innovations available to cities around the world, with the awareness that innovation transfers can flow from developing nations to advanced industrialized ones as well as the reverse.

Within cities, strategies for facilitating innovation include decentralizing some urban management functions; creating new "six sector" partnerships made up of public and private sectors, nongovernmental organizations, grassroots groups, academia, and the media; and developing mechanisms to reward innovators and disseminate local successes.

Underlying these and other strategies for improved resource allocation, ecological sustainability and accelerated innovation processes is the beginning of a powerful and profound new vision of urban life. Our ability to act on that vision will be critical in ensuring the well-being of the 322.56 million people who will live in megacities in the year 2000.

See also CITIES; CITIES, NORTH AMERICAN; ENVIRONMENT; LAND USE PLANNING; SCIENCE CITIES; URBAN TRANSIT.

BIBLIOGRAPHY

CONWAY, MCKINLEY. "Tomorrow's Supercities: For Land, Sea, and Air." *Futurist* 27/3 (May–June 1993).

DOWNS, ANTHONY. *New Visions for Metropolitan America.* Washington, DC: Brookings Institution, 1994.

GIRARDET, HERBERT. *The Gaia of Cities: New Directions for Sustainable Urban Living.* New York: Anchor/Doubleday, 1993.

KATZ, PETER. *The New Urbanism: Toward an Architecture of Community.* New York: McGraw-Hill, 1994.

PEIRCE, NEAL R. *Citystates: How Urban America Can Prosper in a Competitive World.* Washington, DC: Seven Locks Press, 1993.

SIMONDS, JOHN O. *Garden Cities 21: Creating a Livable Urban Environment.* New York: McGraw-Hill, 1994.

Janice E. Perlman

Mental Health

Of all types of human illness, mental illness is the least understood. This is especially tragic because mental illness impairs precisely those capacities that distinguish our human species, such as the faculties for abstract thought, complex language, and sophisticated social relationships. Although clinicians can already effectively treat most mental illnesses, research in mental health holds much promise to dramatically improve the quality of human life over the next fifty years.

Fifty percent of Americans suffer at least one bout with mental illness during their lifetime. Sufferers, whether or not they fully meet the formal definition of mental illness, fail to thrive because emotional conflicts block their capacity to adapt.

Mental health researchers seek both to treat illness and to improve the adaptation of humans to their environment. Investigators increasingly find the roots of mental illness in atypical biology. Those studying adaptation, on the other hand, trace most influences to experience, particularly during infancy and childhood. While biological advances in diagnosing and treating mental illness promise to transform the lives of the patients afflicted, enhancing human adaptation might help to make society itself more peaceful and productive.

Researchers studying the brain have progressed slowly, because the brain is by far the most complex organ in the body and because its physical function is difficult to measure. Scientists can study such organs as the lung or heart by observing their movements. Others, including the kidney and adrenal gland, affect easily measurable substances in the blood. The brain, in contrast, is essentially immobile, and thus far neuroscientists have been unable to find any substance that is a useful marker of its activity.

In part because of difficulty in developing a biologic understanding of mental illness, professionals heretofore have focused on the role of other factors. The currently dominant "bio-psycho-social" model, as its name suggests, seeks to balance the effect of several forces in causing mental illness. This model presumes that all human brains have some biological vulnerability to particular types of stress, but that in most cases, only those that undergo stress to which they are vulnerable develop mental illness.

Most models of psychological stress still rest on variants of the conceptual foundation laid by Sigmund Freud, who proposed that unconscious conflicts between inborn impulses and learned prohibitions lead to psychological distress. According to this view, the distress is difficult to relieve, because the conflicts are outside awareness. Freud always considered this an interim model, eventually to be supplemented or supplanted by a more biological approach.

Many contemporary psychological therapies still rest on the original Freudian model. These approaches attempt to relieve distress by making conflicts conscious so that with this "insight" the patient can actively resolve them. Other kinds of psychotherapies, such as supportive, cognitive, and behavioral, focus on helping patients to solve practical problems. These therapies usually proceed without the patient developing an understanding of any unconscious meaning.

Although the various effective types of psychotherapies differ greatly in approach, they all affect the underlying biology of the brain. Recently researchers have detected changes in brain metabolism following successful behavioral psychotherapy for obsessive-compulsive disorder. It is virtually certain that similar biological changes occur with successful psychotherapy for other psychiatric conditions.

Conversely, brain biology shapes individual experience. For example, a patient with a biological depression may inaccurately perceive people as unfriendly and work as onerous, but these distortions disappear when the depression fades. As research continues to clarify the complex interactions between experience and biology, increasingly therapists will need expertise in both psychotherapy and in biology; or they will have to work in concert with professionals possessing complementary skills.

Social stress takes many forms, but at its core is a fear of the loss of the physical and emotional supports the individual needs to survive. Social support programs attempt to provide food, shelter, and clothing, as well as companionship. In selected cases patients may be hospitalized to provide a highly supportive, albeit temporary, social setting. Improved treatments and rising costs are reducing both the frequency and duration of hospitalization for mental illness, increasing the importance of outpatient programs. This trend, which began in the 1960s, is likely to continue.

Over the past several decades researchers have developed increasingly reliable psychological tests that have helped to standardize diagnosis. Several new techniques still under development measure the brain's physical function, providing information that may eventually replace psychological tests as the standard for diagnosis. New noninvasive "imaging" techniques that produce accurate picture-like representations of living tissue give researchers and clinicians their first view of a working human brain. Several of the methods, such as computer-assisted tomography (CAT) and magnetic resonance imaging (MRI), provide images that depict detailed brain structure. More important for the future, however, are a host of new technologies that detect brain activity. Already scientists have used these methods in identifying characteristic activity that accompanies such diverse operations as performing mathematical calculations and listening to classical music. These emerging technologies include "functional" MRI, single positron emission computed tomography (SPECT), and positron emission tomography (PET).

Such advanced methods promise to reveal distinctive patterns of mental disease. Researchers have found suggestions of unique patterns, in some cases of Alzheimer's dementia, panic disorder, obsessive-compulsive disorder, and certain types of mood disorders. With such tools scientists may be able to identify activity patterns that cause anxiety or depression, or even feelings of love or security. Further, physicians treating at least some mental illnesses will base diagnoses on images of brain activity, much as X-ray images are used to diagnose a fractured bone today.

In the coming decade, brain-imaging techniques will allow exact measurements of medicines in the brain. This approach will likely replace blood tests as the preferred technique for determining proper drug dose. Such methods may also transform psychotherapy. In the future the clinician may be able to obtain objective information that correlates with the patient's thoughts and feelings. The patient and the therapist then could use this data to help them change maladaptive behaviors to more effective ones.

Another developing technology that promises to transform the field of mental health derives from molecular genetics. Research on identical twins and family genealogies indicates that many mental illnesses formerly attributed to childhood experiences, including schizophrenia and manic-depressive disorder, are substantially inherited. Although the underlying cause of most mental illnesses is currently unknown, it appears likely that genetics will play an important role in most of them.

It is probable that scientists will link at least some types of mental illness to specific genetic defects in the next decade and that genetic tests for susceptibility to these diseases will follow. Gene therapy, in which physicians repair genetic defects, holds the promise of dramatic and precise treatment by the middle of the next century, at least for those mental illnesses with genetic roots. Some may wish to use these gene alterations, not only to repair damage, but to improve on normal performance, just as some currently use anabolic steroids to build muscles beyond normal size or strength. If this happens, money may serve not only to buy happiness, but also intelligence, wit, and a magnetic personality. Unchecked, this process could lead to a widening gap between classes, as for the first time money could directly buy an increase in ability. Society will need to create regulations to ensure fairness in the availability of genetic enhancement as well as to protect consumers from possible biological side effects.

There are other opportunities—and complexities—as well. With the power to determine in childhood which children are by constitution vulnerable to specific stresses, one could develop specific child-rearing methods for minimizing the risk that these children would develop mental illness. It seems probable that a number of mental illnesses result from more than one gene, and so potential parents may be able to cross-check their genomes to assure the health of their offspring. Thoughtful approaches, including legislation, however, will be needed to prevent this information from being used in harmful ways. For example, employers might wish to screen applicants for jobs, or, in an Orwellian future, authorities might try to control the right to reproduce. Mental illness may sometimes be linked to desirable mental traits. Many of the greatest minds in history may have suffered mental illness, including Isaac Newton, Abraham Lincoln, and Vincent van Gogh. It is vital that we as a society not meddle in the natural selection of genes affecting the development of the brain until we have a much deeper knowledge of the consequences.

One might hope that in the future, studies on mental health may influence the shaping of social policy. Untreated mental illness exacts a great cost from society. In the United States 70 to 80 percent of crimes are committed by persons intoxicated with alcohol or illegal drugs, conditions considered by the American Psychiatric Association to be types of mental illness.

Mental health issues may affect society in more subtle and profound ways as well. For example, research in transcultural anthropology suggests that the social goals are primarily learned. These goals can have a marked effect on the functioning of an individual in a society, as well as on the harmony of the society as a whole. There is evidence, for example, that children raised in conflict-ridden homes, particularly those who were emotionally or physically abused, are in turn likely to be emotionally and physically abusive as adults. Children whom adults consistently love and nurture, however, generally develop into emotionally secure, cooperative, and peaceable adults themselves. As a society, we might choose to shape our educational and legal practices so as to foster more beneficent child rearing.

Biological methods for treating mental illness and techniques designed to aid adaptation hold greatest promise if harnessed together. Most "biological" mental illnesses are responsive to social stress, and their incidence will diminish if society becomes more harmonious. Untreated or undertreated mental illnesses in turn damage society. Crime and violence are the most obvious costs, but there are others: lost job productivity, alienated communities, and broken families. Repairing society and aiding the mentally ill are both vital goals. Pursuit of both is the best approach to achieve either.

See also CHANGE, PACE OF; CONSCIOUS EVOLUTION; CREATIVITY; HOLISTIC BELIEFS; INFORMATION OVERLOAD; MIND: NEW MODES OF THINKING; PSYCHIATRY; PSYCHOLOGY.

BIBLIOGRAPHY

FREEMAN, HUGH L. *Mental Health and the Environment.* New York: Churchill, 1985.

MARTIN, ALFRED. *Mental Health: Psychotherapy of Tomorrow.* Quincy, IL: Franciscan Press, 1980.

WARR, PETER. *Work, Unemployment, and Mental Health.* New York: Oxford University Press, 1987.

Joshua Friedman
Roderic Gorney

Meteorology.

See CLIMATE AND METEOROLOGY.

Mexico

Some countries of the world, because of their geographical location, serve as bridges between major cultural blocs. Mexico is one of them. Even as a bridge country, Mexico has been a victim of history. Close proximity to the United States condemned it to live in the shadow of a major power, unable to assert its identity or to exert any significant influence on hemispheric affairs. This is all the more paradoxical because Mexico was the first modern nation in the New World, and it claims some notable historical New World firsts, such as the first printing press, the first Christian church, and the first university.

Just as anatomy is destiny for a person, so is geography for a nation. (*Destiny,* used here in the classical sense, is preferable in discussing national affairs to the word *future.*) Hernando Cortés, the conqueror of Mexico, is said to have described the topography of Mexico by crumpling a piece of paper and throwing it down, saying, "This is the map of Mexico." Two thirds of the country is mountainous, and Mexicans tend to think of directions as up and down rather than as points of the compass. The mountains tend to perpetuate regionalism, and access to some areas is so difficult that they have remained culturally isolated for centuries.

Population is the second most important aspect of Mexican destiny. The dominant factors in Mexican demography have been a high birthrate and rapid urbanization. From a high of 4.8 percent in 1970, the birthrate has come down to 2.8 per 1,000 in 1990, yet remains the highest in Latin America. However, the fertility rate is declining and is expected to drop to 2.4 in 2000, whith a resulting further decline in birthrate to 1.9 percent. The 14-and-under age group will decline from 37.6 percent of the national population to 23.3 percent in 2025.

The population is expected to reach 136 million by 2025 and become stationary later in the twenty-first century at 182 million. Mexico enjoys a unique, demographic safety valve in having a permeable border with the United States across which over one million undocumented migrants move annually into the richer northern nation. The Mexicanization of many southern U.S. states is an accomplished fact and may pose extreme problems in the twenty-first century.

Urbanization is a recent problem, but the redistribution of population that it entails has hit the capital city the hardest. Nearly 25 percent of the national population is crowded into the old Aztec town that most Mexicans call "D.F.," situated at an elevation of 7,437 feet. With a metropolitan population of over 20 million, Mexico City is the second largest city in the world. Its population increased by more than 70 percent during the 1970s, is expected to reach 28 million by 2000, and 38 million by 2010. Overall, 73 percent of the population is urban; with a growth rate of 2.9 percent, this proportion is expected to reach 80 percent by 2000. By 2010, 50 percent of Mexicans will be living in cities with over 1 million inhabitants.

The third component of Mexican destiny is politics. During the first century of independence, Mexico experimented with, or was subjected to, at least forty forms of government, including federal and centralized organization, constitutional monarchy, dictatorship, and representative democratic government. The Constitution of 1917, continuously in force since adopted, has been amended more than a hundred times. The constitutional formula for continuity and relative stability in government is replete with seeming contradictions. The most prominent of these are a democracy in which political power is monopolized by a single party and universal suffrage in which the voters do not have a real choice. The Partido Revolucionaro Institucional (PRI), which has been in power since 1929, the longest such tenure in the history of democracy, in fact insists on maintaining a token opposition. The presidential election is largely ceremonial, and each president decides on his successor. As no one is allowed to hold the same elective office for more than six consecutive years, there is a turnover of approximately 20,000 elective and 30,000 appointive posts in every six-year cycle. Such a system is obviously disruptive, but contributes to stability, because participation is broad, and most PRI members have held office at some time in their lives.

The fourth dimension of Mexican destiny is the economy. With a GDP of $283 billion, the Mexican economy is about one-twentieth the size of the U.S. economy. In per capita terms, it fares worse, with $3,030 as against $22,240 for the United States. Its total external debt of $102 billion is the second largest in the world next to Brazil. The principal economic problems have been a skewed distribution of wealth, high inflation, and institutionalized corruption at all levels. The top 20 percent of the population receive 55.9 percent of the national wealth while the lowest receive only 4.1 percent. The income ratio between the poorest 10 percent and the richest 10 percent is expected to reach 50 by 2010. The annual rate of inflation from 1980 to 1991 was 66.5 percent. Unemployment is expected to become more severe.

During the next twenty years, Mexico will have to generate 800,000 to 1 million jobs every year to maintain current levels of employment. Failure to generate these jobs will provoke a higher level of social violence, political instability, reduced educational and social welfare budgets, accelerated decay of family structures, and more illegal emigration to the United States. The 1993 North American Free Trade Agreement (NAFTA) might bring some relief to the distressed economy, especially by encouraging foreign investment in the maquiladoras. If Mexican expectations about NAFTA are realized, then the economy may grow at a rate of 3 to 4 percent during the next decade. By 2010 the per capita GNP will rise to about $4,500, assuming that present demographic trends can be maintained.

The Mexican environment is not in better shape than its economy. Air, water, and land pollution are severe around all industrial areas, particularly in and around Mexico City. There are few environmental regulations, and lax controls and corruption enable the polluters to go scot-free. There is serious shortage of water, because 85 percent of the country's water resources lie at altitudes of less than 1,600 feet, yet more than half of Mexico's population and industry and much of its cropland are at higher altitudes. Other environmental problems that are likely to become more critical within the next decade are disposal of solid wastes, soil erosion, and deforestation.

Political relations with the United States have always been critical for Mexico. Porfirio Diaz is said to have lamented, "Poor Mexico. So far from God and so close to the United States." But with NAFTA a reality, these relations will become an economic boon, and may help to dissolve centuries of distrust and resentment on the part of Mexico.

As always, there are wild cards in Mexico's future. Mexico City is a time bomb, and another environmental crisis like that of the 1985 earthquake would bring it closer to disaster. A PRI debacle at the polls could usher in a period of deep political and economic instability.

See also FREE TRADE; LATIN AMERICA.

BIBLIOGRAPHY

KOSLOW, LAWRENCE, *The Future of Mexico*. Tempe, AZ: Arizona State University Press, 1978.

LADMAN, JERRY R. *Mexico: A Country in Crisis*. Austin, TX: University of Texas Press, 1987.

LOONEY, ROBERT E. *Development Alternatives of Mexico*. Westport, CT: Greenwood Press, 1982.

REYNA, JOSE L. *Understanding Mexico: Historical Perspective and Future Potential*. Atlanta: Southern Center for International Studies, 1987.

George Thomas Kurian

Microminiaturization.

See NANOTECHNOLOGY.

Middle East

The future of the Middle East will be molded by developments in the following areas:

Demographics

Present rates of growth will triple the population of the Middle East and North Africa by 2030 (from 212 million in 1990 to 635 million). Except for Israel and some oil-producing states, this will constitute an intolerable burden. Development resources will increasingly be consumed by the immediate needs of housing, education, and food imports. Even the immediate implementation of draconian measures (unlikely for cultural and religious reasons) would not ameliorate the problem. With 50 percent of the population under the age of twenty, two-child families would sustain a tremendous baby boom well into the twenty-first century.

Among Middle Eastern countries, Egypt and Iran alone are trying to implement family-planning programs. Egypt's growth rate has dropped from 3 percent to 2.5 percent a year. At this rate, the country's population will still double by 2020 (from 58 million in 1990 to close to 120 million). This has drastically skewed development priorities. Food prices are kept cheaper in the cities than in the villages to guarantee political stability. This encourages population movement from rural to urban areas, which strains inadequate infrastructures, increases social frustration, and creates a climate conducive to the rise of Islamic fundamentalism.

Two scenarios are possible:

1. Present trends will continue, leading to a social explosion and the ascendance of Muslim fundamentalists (a development which could threaten the Israeli-Egyptian peace).
2. Egypt develops a new national vision: restructures its national institutions, drives its population growth down to below 1.5 percent, and receives massive development aid from the West in order to achieve an economic stability akin to that of South Korea in recent years.

Iran, with close to 60 million people and a 3 percent growth rate, has recently justified a family-planning program by citing Islamic prohibitions against damaging the health of women. This could be a model for the entire Islamic world, since no birth control program can succeed unless it is rooted in the cultural values of the society.

The rest of the Middle East has growth rates between 3 percent and 4 percent a year. Two scenarios seem possible:

1. The population will double every seventeen years, overwhelming all hopes of development and causing extensive social and political upheaval. Cross-border wars may result as more populous Arab countries try to grab the resources of more sparsely populated Arab oil states (Sadam Hussein's incursion into Kuwait was very popular with large segments of the Arab masses).
2. Iranian-style family-planning will combine with a new regional awareness to exploit the great resources of the area for the benefit of all its residents. If this occurs in conjunction with (and perhaps as a result of) an Arab-Israeli peace, an economic miracle rivaling the Pacific Rim could occur.

Water

There are two views regarding water in the Middle East. If one is a technological and political pessimist, there is not enough water; if one is an optimist, there is.

Jordan at present has about 250 cubic meters of freshwater potential per citizen (given population growth trends, this will decline to about 125 cubic meters by 2015); Israel has 450; Egypt, 1,100; Syria, 2,800; Turkey, 4,000; and Iraq, 5,500. Again, two scenarios are possible:

1. Peace and regional cooperation will combine with Israeli water-management systems and water resources will suffice. Indeed, rational pricing might enable Turkey and Iraq to export water to other countries in the Middle East.
2. Conflict and regional competition will combine with inefficient traditional water management to create a situation wherein water wars will be inevitable. If major technological breakthroughs occur, economically viable desalinization could also play a critical role.

The key to the solution lies in the future of agriculture (which consumes about 70 percent of sweet water resources being exploited, as of 1993). Israel has begun to create what Alvin Toffler would probably call Third Wave agriculture. Half an acre under plastic with drip irrigation can produce the same amount of vegetables as five acres of industrially grown field crops, with one-thirtieth the amount of water and significantly smaller amounts of insecticides and fertilizers.

By 2010, Israel, Jordan-Palestine, and Egypt will probably be devoid of field crop agriculture. Other Middle East countries will probably evolve in the same direction. Most of the area's grain will probably come from the former communist bloc, with Middle Eastern vegetables and fruits going in the opposite direction.

Islamic Fundamentalism Versus Modernism

The internal identity crisis of Islam will dominate the Middle East as well as world politics well into the twenty-first century. One billion Muslims occupying a geographic nexus bordering on Europe, Africa, East Africa, and the former Soviet Union and controlling vast national resources are searching for a model that would enable them to preserve their cultural authenticity while modernizing.

Western commentators have cited the Iranian model and the Turkish model as two sharply differing approaches. It is not clear that there is a necessary future contradiction between Islamic devotion and modernity. Even fanatic Iranian fundamentalism might evolve into something more benign as it responds to the practical demands of running a nation-state in an increasingly complicated world.

Moreover, Iran might collapse economically, ethnically, and politically. Turkey might be split into two by a Kurdish minority that could become a majority by 2010. Twenty-first-century Islam might be dominated by the Indonesian or Kazakhstani models. Egypt might finally realize its potential and the Muslims of black Africa might create an entirely different alternative. There are no clearcut scenarios here, only contributing factors:

1. The Israeli-Palestinian conflict—if it is not resolved to the mutual satisfaction of both sides, Iranian-style fundamentalists could take over Jordan, Egypt, and the Palestinian movement itself. If it is resolved, fundamentalists in these countries will almost certainly be neutralized.
2. The status of Muslims in Europe: anti-Islamic racism and ethnic strife in Bosnia and other parts of Europe are not only local moral problems. They will affect world policy for decades.
3. The success or failure of the Muslim republics of the former Soviet Union.
4. Indonesia (the largest Muslim country in the world) becoming one of four major Asian powers (with China, Japan, and India).
5. India's treatment of its 100-million-strong Muslim minority.

Israeli-Palestinian Conflict—Two Scenarios

1. A Palestinian state is created that satisfies both Palestinian national aspirations and Israel's security requirements. Israel, Jordan, and Palestine will probably become one economic unit as an integral part of a peace settlement. Syria and Lebanon are quickly drawn into economic association (with Egypt lagging behind). The first major economic development projects will be (a) an integrated power grid (thus saving billions of dollars in energy expenses; (b) an integrated water system; and (c) promotion of tourism (with peace there is no reason why the number of tourists—now 6 million yearly—should not climb to 20 million by the first decade of the twenty-first century).

   Israel, Jordan, and Palestine will find they have more in common with one another than with other countries in the Middle East. Palestine has the potential of becoming a Middle Eastern Singapore. Palestinian social, educational, and economic characteristics are closer to Israel's than to other Arab states. International companies may see Palestine as the ideal staging area for penetration into the Middle East. This will have great spillover benefits for Israel and Jordan. Syria may become part of this development. Egypt will have difficulty finding its place unless it undergoes the transformation referred to previously.
2. The conflict will not be resolved. Political radicalism and Islamic fundamentalism will threaten

Jordan, Egypt, and the Palestinians. The very possibility of peace will wane. Given the ever-growing availability of nuclear weapons, a world-scale catastrophe could result.

Other Influencing Factors:

1. The decline of the oil states—the real-value decline of oil prices will most probably continue well into the twenty-first century as ecological concerns and technology increase productivity per energy unit. Any real increase of oil prices would probably trigger alternative energy innovations that might even replace oil as the prime energy source of the world. If nothing else, the Gulf War demonstrated that the oil states are more dependent on the West than vice versa. It is doubtful whether OPEC will ever again be a cause of political and economic instability.
2. Extremist states—the ability or inability of the West and regional moderates to neutralize or weaken the extremist states of Iran, Iraq, Libya, and possibly the Sudan will have a decisive effect on the future of the Middle East well into the twenty-first century.
3. Nuclear weapons—extremist states, Islamic fundamentalism, frightened oil states, the Israeli-Palestinian conflict, the ambition for an Islamic bomb, the ambition for an Arab bomb to offset the Israeli one—all of these factors constitute a dangerous mix.

In conclusion, the Middle East has the potential to serve as the centerweight of a new world order or to plunge the entire planet into catastrophe.

See also FUNDAMENTALISM; ISLAM; JUDAISM.

BIBLIOGRAPHY

ERES, BETH KREVITT. "Israel in the Year 2000." In *Reflection on World Problems and Future-Oriented Studies*. Paris: UNESCO Bureau of Studies and Programming, 1989.
FEILER, GIL. "Housing Policy in Egypt." *Middle Eastern Studies* 28/2 (April 1992): 295–312.

Tsvi Bisk

Migration, International

International migration—ranging from the relatively permanent movement of people across national boundaries to temporary flows involving students, business travelers, and seasonal workers—is likely to increase in the future. Migration's root causes include the push of war, ethnic repression, and economic hardship, and the pull of political freedom, better jobs, and beckoning family members. Worldwide population growth, especially in less developed countries, provides a growing pool of would-be emigrants. Since young workers migrate most, population growth today will influence international labor flows well into the first decades of the twenty-first century.

The decision to migrate is ultimately personal, but decisions are influenced by families, communities, and nations. Would-be movers weigh real and imagined job opportunities, wage scales, and personal networks in their country of origin and in potential destinations.

Future international migration depends on different types of movers and factors affecting each type. Migrants differ by length of stay (permanent versus temporary moves), distance traveled (adjacent versus intercontinental moves), reasons for moving (economic, political, or personal), and their legal status in the receiving country (documented versus undocumented). These distinctions, however, will blur. Temporary migrants often become permanent. Adjacent countries often are stepping-stones to more distant destinations. Economic migrants, once settled, often send for their families. Some legal temporary movers will overstay their visas, becoming illegal migrants. Distinctions between political asylees and economic refugees will meld for migrants whose native land provides neither freedom nor livelihood.

Cheaper communication and transportation will reduce real and perceived distances. As the world shrinks, distance as a barrier to movement declines. The global diffusion of information and cultural symbols—from the daily news to the daily reminders of popular images—plants the seeds of future immigration.

Positive as well as negative factors in countries of origin affect international migration. Severe environmental degradation and the depletion of soil, water, and forest resources can cause out-migration. About 10 percent of the world's population (500 million people) live in agricultural areas affected by natural disasters like periodic flooding, drought, and severe soil erosion. Others simply have no access to food or food-producing resources. These factors, coupled with continued rural population growth will produce a steady stream of migrants to major urban areas. Rural economic development, however, tends to increase productivity, reducing the need for farm labor and prompting the need for fewer workers in farming and an increase in rural-to-urban migration.

By 2000, developing countries will contain sixteen of the world's twenty largest cities—the megacities which are here defined as exceeding twelve million people. Vast areas of Mexico City, São Paulo, Shanghai, Calcutta, and Bombay are already economic and environmental catastrophes. International migration will flow between the megacities and the developed world in an increasingly integrated global economy. Migrants will come from professional, technical, and business classes as well as from less advantaged groups.

Economic gaps will widen between richer and poorer nations. Nearly all of the growth in per capita income from 1950 to 1990 occurred in the developed countries of Europe, Asia, and North America, but 85 percent of the world's population growth occurred in developing countries. This imbalance points to a growing potential for international migration from developing to developed countries, both within and among the major regions of the world.

Regional economic blocs (EC in Europe, NAFTA in North America, and AFTA in Asia) are likely to increase international migration in at least three ways: from less developed to more developed countries within each region; between developed countries within each region; and from developed countries in one region to developed countries in other regions. Europe (primarily the EC nations), the Far East (primarily Japan, Hong Kong, the Republic of Korea, and Singapore), and North America (primarily the United States and Canada) are likely to remain global economic development centers. As these three regions consolidate economically, they will attract international migrants: to Europe from Eastern Europe, the Middle East, and North Africa; to Japan, the Republic of Korea, and Singapore from surrounding Asian countries; to Canada and the United States from Latin America and the Caribbean.

Intercontinental migration streams are already evident and will probably grow: from China, Hong Kong, Japan, the Republic of Korea, the Philippines, and Southeast Asia, as well as from Europe to the United States and Canada; from Latin America to Spain, Portugal, and Italy; from the Caribbean and South Asia to the United Kingdom; from North Africa, the Caribbean, and the Pacific to France; and from India, Pakistan, the Republic of Korea, and the Philippines to the oil-producing Arab states. Some of these streams reflect cultural, colonial, and linguistic ties; others represent the long reach of labor demand.

Compared to world population growth and differential development in a global economy, receiving-country politics and policies exert a minor influence in the migration equation. Immigration policies are more regulatory than restrictive. Experts note, for example, that major changes in U.S. immigration legislation during 1986 and 1990 did little to decrease long-term immigration and may ultimately increase it. As of 1993, U.S. Census Bureau projections assume more, not less, immigration. The bureau's middle-series population projection indicates the year 2000 U.S. population will be 8.8 million larger than in 1991 because of permanent net increases from international migration of all types, legal and illegal. By 2050 the U.S. population will be 82 million larger than in 1991 (21 percent of the total population) due to the compound effects of net immigrants and their descendants.

Of course, politics will shape the future immigration policies. Arguments for and against immigration cross political lines. The right, in general, is split between anti-immigration and pro-growth positions. Slow growth or population decline in industrialized countries will lead to labor shortages and slow growth of consumer markets. Some economists and business leaders, therefore, argue for more immigration. Others, especially in areas of heavy immigration, argue that the cost of the cultural adaptation and public services outweigh the benefits. The left is split between those who believe that poverty and emigration result from worker exploitation, not rapid population growth, and those who believe that rapid population growth increases poverty directly. The latter promote access to health care and family planning in order to increase family welfare and decrease poverty. These fissures are not likely to subside. They will color future debates regarding population and development policies worldwide.

The collapse of communism in Eastern Europe and the former Soviet Union, as well as the adoption of market policies in China, will boost future international migration to and from those areas. The opening of borders in those states will provide for the emigration of political and economic refugees, as well as the movement of religious and ethnic groups. Redrawing a national map may change citizenship without international migration, but events in Eastern Europe suggest that shifting political boundaries often stimulates emigration and immigration.

Because characteristics of immigrants and emigrants may differ by such factors as language and skill level, two countries may experience similar net migration but experience widely differing cultural or economic effects. An equal net effect can result from large or small gross flows.

Long-term trends in international migration will depend on the success of development policies and the course of future population growth. Near-term economic development will stimulate international migration among business and professional classes as well as among the poor. But only slower population growth and sustainable, national development in the major sending regions of Asia, Africa, and Latin America will reduce the irregular, illegal, and unpredictable flows of individuals and families who would risk their lives to cross an international boundary.

In some countries today, including France, Germany, and the United States, there is a growing fear of the cultural and economic threat posed by large numbers of immigrants. Consequently, many countries may more rigorously enforce border controls to further regulate and restrict the migrant flow. Some may even enact laws restricting the citizenship of children born to guest workers in the receiving countries.

See also CHANGE, CULTURAL; ENVIRONMENTAL REFUGEES; ETHNIC AND CULTURAL SEPARATISM; GLOBAL CULTURE; INTERNAL MIGRATION: UNITED STATES; MINORITIES; POPULATION GROWTH: WORLDWIDE; RACE, CASTE, AND ETHNIC DIVERSITY; REFUGEES; SPACE COLONIZATION; TOURISM.

BIBLIOGRAPHY

APPLEYARD, REGINALD. *International Migration: Challenge for the 1990s.* Geneva: International Organization for Migration, 1991.
OECD Continuing Reporting System on Migration (SOPEMI). *Trends in International Migration.* Paris: OECD, 1992.
RUSSELL, SHARON STANTON, and TEITLEBAUM, MICHAEL. *International Migration and International Trade,* World Bank Discussion Papers, 160. Washington, DC: World Bank, 1992.
SADIK, NAFIS. *The State of World Population, 1993.* New York: UNFPA/United Nations Fund for Population, 1993.

Thomas G. Exter

Military Technologies

With the end of the massive military confrontation between the United States and what was the U.S.S.R., the nature of potential conflicts has changed significantly. Future wars are likely to be much smaller in scale, and this will be a major determinant of the course of future military technological development.

The most important new military technologies are: long-range and real-time surveillance and target identification systems—sensor and guidance systems for ultrasmart autonomous "fire-and-forget" missiles that are able to detect, identify, and effectively attack armored vehicles, combat aircraft and warships, as well as hardened, fixed targets like command-and-control centers, in all types of weather and battlefield conditions; very powerful conventional warheads; and computerized command, control, communications, and intelligence systems.

With the new surveillance and target identification technologies the military can now detect and track, in real time, enemy forces deep in their territory. Sensors on board satellites, manned aircraft, and remotely piloted vehicles (RPVs) give advance warning of preparations for attack. Rapid advances are being made in a broad range of sensors—photographic and return beam vidicon television cameras, multispectral scanners, visible and infrared radiometers and microwave synthetic aperture radars, charged couple devices, sensors sensitive to gamma rays, X-rays and electronic signals, and communications-monitoring devices.

Long-range reconnaissance equipment will be increasingly carried by remotely piloted vehicles rather than manned aircraft, because the former are less vulnerable to air defense systems. Much cheaper than manned aircraft, they can be used in relatively large numbers. They will eventually be given more battlefield roles, such as ground attack and even air combat.

Modern weapons can be guided to their targets with great accuracy by real-time, midcourse guidance and, more importantly, by terminal guidance. Accuracy is, or soon will be, virtually independent of range. Terminally guided missiles use radar or a laser system to search the area around the target, compare it with a map preprogrammed in the warhead's computer, and then guide the warhead precisely onto it.

Terminally guided submunitions—small bombs (bomblets) and mines—are being developed that can distinguish between different types of moving vehicles and attack them at their weakest point (such as the turret of a tank).

An example of a new powerful conventional warhead is the fuel air explosive. The weapon produces an aerosol cloud of a substance like propylene oxide vapor. When mixed with air, the substance is very explosive, and the aerosol cloud, ignited when at its optimum size, produces a powerful explosion. The explosion is five to ten times as effective, weight for weight, as a conventional high explosive. Fuel air explosives can be made as powerful as low-yield nuclear weapons.

Cluster bombs and fragmentation munitions are another example. Exploding fragmentation bomblets scatter small, jagged chunks of metal over a large area. The fragments have razor-sharp edges, are very hot, and travel at high speeds.

Weapon systems based on antitank, antiaircraft, and antiship missiles are particularly benefiting from the new technologies. New antitank missiles, for example, are rapidly making the main battle tank obsolete, particularly when used on helicopters.

The United States is investigating three different technologies for an advanced, light, multipurpose antitank missile. One uses a laser beam–riding guidance system. The warhead is fused to detonate at the optimum time to do maximum damage to the tank, attacking the turret from above. The second uses fiber-optics guidance and an infrared imager to acquire the target. Fiber-optics guidance is a powerful technique, useful for very long-range (tens of kilometers) missiles. The third technology is based on an autonomous missile that is locked on to the target before launch. A focal-plane infrared seeker acquires the target. Once the seeker is locked on and the missile is launched, it guides itself automatically to the target so that the operator can engage another target.

Today's helicopters have top speeds of approximately 400 kilometers per hour. Using technologies such as the Advancing Blade Concept (with two contra-rotating rotors), Tilt Rotor (in which the rotors tilt through a right angle to provide lift or thrust, or a combination of both), and the X-wing, even supersonic speeds will become possible.

Recent technological advances have considerably increased the accuracy of nuclear warhead delivery. Accuracy normally is measured by its circular error probability (CEP), defined as the radius of the circle centered on the target within which a half of a large number of warheads of the same type fired at the target will fall. For example, the CEP of a Minuteman II intercontinental ballistic missile warhead is about 370 meters; the new MX missile has a CEP of about 100 meters.

Similar developments are taking place in submarine-launched ballistic missiles. The new American Trident D-5 submarine-launched ballistic missile, for example, has a CEP of about 120 meters, whereas the CEP of the older Trident C-4 is 450 meters. Strategic missiles may eventually be fitted with terminal guidance that will reduce their CEPs to about 40 meters.

The Pentagon is planning the Phase One Strategic Defense System, known as Global Protection Against Limited Strikes (GPALS), designed to defend against a ballistic missile attack of up to 200 nuclear warheads. GPALS is a defense against an accidental attack involving one or a small number of missiles, a limited attack launched by a mad military commander, or an attack by a third world country involving a few long-range missiles.

In the space-based layer, Brilliant Pebbles missiles, now under development, are designed to destroy enemy ballistic missiles in their boost phase, before they release their warheads and decoys. Each Brilliant Pebble carries sensors to pick up radiations from rocket exhaust upon launch from their silos, to calculate speed and trajectory, and to program the missile onto an interception course, relying on the kinetic energy of impact to destroy targets. Current plans call for deploying 1,000 or so satellites orbiting at altitudes of about 960 kilometers. Each missile is about 1 meter long, 0.3 meters wide, and weighs about 45 kilograms.

During the next phase, the ground-based interceptor missiles, the High-Altitude Endoatmospheric Defense Interceptor (HEDI), will attack enemy warheads that survive the Brilliant Pebbles, shortly after they reenter Earth's atmosphere. Deployment of between 750 and 1,000 HEDI antiballistic missiles is called for.

The Boost Surveillance and Tracking System will detect enemy missile launches, track the boosters, and assess the number of missiles destroyed. The Space Surveillance and Tracking System will acquire and track postboost vehicles and reentry vehicles, satellites, and antisatellite weapons, and assess the destruction of enemy warheads. The Airborne Optical Adjunct, an infrared radiation sensor system carried on a Boeing 767 aircraft to track warheads in their midcourse and terminal stages, is in an advanced state of development. The Ground-Based Surveillance and Tracking System will discriminate between reentry warheads and decoys, track reentry vehicles and decoys, and assess the destruction of enemy warheads. The command center will link all these systems and control the space battle.

Theater antiballistic missiles are being developed to defend against attacks by tactical ballistic missiles. Current U.S. research and development programs include improvements for the existing Pa-triot surface-to-air system; the Extended Range Interceptor; the Arrow missile, a joint U.S.-Israel program to develop a high-altitude interceptor; and the Theater High Altitude Area Defense system.

See also ARMS RACE; WEAPONS OF MASS DESTRUCTION.

BIBLIOGRAPHY

MUNRO, NEIL. *Electronic Combat and Modern Warfare.* London: Macmillan, 1991.

SCHULSKY, ABRAM N. *Silent Warfare—Understanding the World of Intelligence.* London: Brassey's, 1991.

SMITH, GRAHAM. *Weapons of the Gulf War.* London: Salamander Books, 1991.

THOMPSON, JULIAN. *The Lifeblood of War—Logistics in Armed Conflict.* London: Brassey's, 1991.

WATSON, BRUCE W., ed. *Military Lessons of the Gulf War.* Novato, CA: Presidio Press, 1991.

Frank Barnaby

Mind: New Modes of Thinking

The human intellect evolved through the selection, among one branch of primates, of larger and larger brains, whose adaptiveness resides in those functional capabilities we label as "mind." The mind's most critical attribute is memory: the ability to store and recall past events, to perceive patterns, and hence to *predict* future events, such as the coming seasons. Along with detailed memory, the mind evolved a second critical ability that enormously enhanced its usefulness, namely metaphoric, or symbolic communication. At first, gestures were used to signify ideas. Then, about 200,000 years ago, symbolic vocalizations became possible, giving rise to language.

The mind, then, consists of an enlarged memory that can be recalled and shared symbolically with others. It is thus a social phenomenon, allowing the transmission of accumulated knowledge orally (and today in writing, on electronic tapes, or via films) within and between generations, greatly increasing the potential for survival-enhancing, adaptive behavior. "Learning" and "knowledge" for humans are no longer restricted to single individuals, as is largely the case with other social animals. Besides "knowledge" of the external world, the human mind is also capable of creating imagined worlds, and hence of making behavioral choices.

Factual knowledge, however, is not all that the mind encompasses. It also stores values and attitudes regarding what concerns are "important" and what actions are "right." Furthermore, it involves feelings or emotions, including not only desires for physiological needs (food, water, warmth, sex) but also powerful desires to belong to a social group (bonding) and a strong need for a sense of purpose in life (sacred meaning). Without the satisfaction of these latter needs, humans may become depressed and ill, or angry and violent.

"Mind" is never acquired outside a social context. The knowledge framework, the values, the affective behaviors needed for acceptance, and the meaning of life are all taught. Each child undergoes, through immersion in his or her culture, an apprenticeship in thinking. The world view or shared "mind" of one's culture helps one "see" and participate in its particular vision of reality, signaling what to notice and what to ignore, how to interpret, and how to behave. Shared values and meaning are thus implicit in shaping the inner mental reality that forms the map by which one is able to act effectively. Not surprisingly, we feel a strong attachment to our world view; beliefs and values and our social identity are as important to us as food and water.

Because reality—the totality of possible external information that our sensory system is actually exposed to—is far too complex, all cultures, perforce, must choose what to notice, and filter out the rest. Thus, two cultures existing side-by-side can hold dissimilar world views, based on diverse values and meanings. Each uses a different filter system. Of course, individuals within a culture can hold disparate values, too, but usually not to the same degree. Indeed, the more cohesive a culture, the more its members share values and traditions; larger, less personal societies, being less cohesive, often require complex legal systems to "govern" their divergent values and behaviors. This diversity gives rise to "politics," which is often highly emotional.

Learning, or changing the way we think, occurs at two levels. One is personal learning, by which individuals hone their understanding of their surroundings, usually in order to fit better into their own social milieu. This is the sort of learning that mostly goes on in schools and colleges. The individual adapts to the society, modifying her or his personal ways of thinking.

The other level of learning occurs when a whole society changes its way of thinking. By replacing an old way of seeing and valuing the world with a new one, it is presumably adapting to changed circumstances. It is this sort of *active search* for "new modes of thinking" that many believe is essential for humans to survive in the decades ahead.

This is historically a new activity. In the past, changes in world views have been slow, often unconscious adaptations to changing circumstances, as with the origins of agriculture. Intentional changes in world view have been rare. The Golden Age of Greece (500–400 B.C.) and the Renaissance/Enlightenment (1500–1800 A.D.) are two exceptional examples from Western history. World view changes imposed from outside a society are almost always violently opposed, often being resented for generations. Rapid, nonviolent changes in fundamental ways of thinking are historical anomalies, and most world views have not included changes in their underlying assumptions as one of their internal values. Indeed, modern Western beliefs in "progress" and "change" relate only to technical change, and presume that the underlying values of individualism, efficiency, competition, and materialism will remain intact.

Three major barriers block social change. First is our psychic attachment to the familiar map imparted to us by our own cultural world view. Even a clearly dysfunctional set of values, just like an abusive parent, is hard to disown. Second, those who hold power are usually those benefiting most from the status quo, and therefore the most difficult to persuade of the need to change. Third, changing our social thinking often means changing not only our patterns of social interaction, but also much of our physical infrastructure as well. Both bring heavy costs to a society attempting rapid change.

Change, however, appears unavoidable. Today, crises are overtaking many once stable societies whose members are being forced to abandon old assumptions and values without having had the social dialogue necessary to envision and fully develop new ones. Without a widely shared world view, a society disintegrates. The future of humankind depends on societies learning how to deliberately "change their minds" rapidly enough to adapt to crises already created and avoid creating further ones. Examples of people already doing this (e.g., the Indian state of Kerala, the Mondragon cooperatives in Spain, Grameen Bank in Bangladesh) offer visions to other societies facing the difficult process of social change. Humanity's ultimate survival may well depend on multiple world views, coexisting and adapting side-by-side, cross-fertilizing each other.

See also CREATIVITY; VALUES, NONWESTERN; VISIONARY THINKING.

BIBLIOGRAPHY

BOULDING, KENNETH E. "What Do We Know About Knowledge?" *Issues in Integrative Studies* 9 (1991): 75–89.

CLARK, MARY E. *Ariadne's Thread: The Search for New Modes of Thinking.* New York: St. Martin's, 1989.

——. "Meaningful Social Bonding as a Universal Human Need." In John W. Burton, ed. *Conflict: Human Needs Theory.* New York: St. Martin's, 1990.

DONALD, MERLIN. *The Origins of the Modern Mind.* Cambridge, MA: Harvard University Press, 1991.

ROGOFF, BARBARA. *Apprenticeship in Thinking.* New York: Oxford University Press, 1990.

Mary E. Clark

Minerals

Mineral resources—both metallic and nonmetallic—are inorganic substances taken from the earth for potential use by humans. Their diversity is remarkable. Metallic minerals are the raw materials upon which many important materials and technologies are based. Metal use is concentrated in four economic sectors: construction; transportation equipment (e.g., automobiles, airplanes, ships); capital equipment (e.g., factory machinery); and consumer durables (e.g., bicycles and refrigerators). Metals can be grouped in three broad categories: first, there are *major metals*, used in large quantities throughout the economy—e.g., iron and steel in bridges, buildings, motor vehicles, and kitchenware; aluminum in beverage containers, foil, and aircraft; copper in wiring, electronics, and plumbing; lead in batteries of all types; and zinc as a corrosion-resistant coating on various types of steel. Second, there are the so-called *minor metals* used in smaller quantities for specialized applications, including beryllium in electronic components; chromium and cobalt as alloying elements in steel; various rare-earth elements in petroleum-refining equipment and pollution-control catalysts; and zirconium as a refractory material in the process of producing metal and glass products. Third, there are *precious metals*—such as gold and silver—used primarily in jewelry and art objects.

Nonmetallic minerals make up the second large class of mineral resources. They are even more diverse than metallic minerals. At one extreme are the bulk building materials with low value per unit of weight, such as cement (made up of lime and clay), sand, and gravel. At the other extreme are gems with high unit values, such as diamonds, emeralds, and amethysts. In between are fertilizer minerals, such as phosphate rock and potash, ceramic minerals such as feldspar and clays, abrasive minerals such as sandstone and industrial diamonds, and pigments and fillers such as diatomite and barite.

Despite their diverse uses, both metallic and nonmetallic mineral resources share similarities in production, which typically takes place in the following four stages:

The first stage is *exploration*, in which mineral deposits are discovered and their technical and economic viability demonstrated. The second stage is *development*, in which mineral deposits are prepared for production; e.g., the mine and associated facilities are designed and constructed. The third stage is *extraction*, or *mining*, in which mineral-bearing rock is taken out of the ground from either underground or surface mines. Typically only a fraction of the mined rock is valuable, and thus the fourth stage, *processing*, is dedicated to upgrading the material extracted from the mine. For metallic minerals, processing usually begins with crushing, grinding, and washing of rock to facilitate separation of unwanted material from valuable rock known as ore. Ore, in turn, is upgraded or purified through a series of metallurgical processes that vary from metal to metal. Some processes use heat to upgrade the metallic ore (pyrometallurgy); others use electricity (electrometallurgy); still others use solutions (hydrometallurgy). For nonmetallic minerals, upgrading and purification also take place, but processing typically is less complicated technologically than that of metals.

An important, underappreciated source of metals is recycling. Recycled metal from scrapped batteries produces more than half of the lead used each year in the United States. For other metals, although recycling is relatively less important, it still is significant. For iron and steel, scrap metal from obsolete and discarded products probably represents one-quarter of the iron and steel used in new products each year; for copper also perhaps one-quarter; and for aluminum and zinc one-tenth to one-fifth.

As human population and the demand for minerals continue to rise, the question arises: What are the prospects for mineral availability? Are we in danger of running out of essential mineral resources? Alarming statistics allegedly show that mineral reserves—i.e., minerals known to exist and capable of being produced at a profit under current conditions—will be depleted in several decades at current rates of use. These statistical claims are misleading. Known reserves represent only a small portion of the ultimate amount of mineral resource in Earth's crust. Responding to the depletion of known deposits, exploration geologists are continuing to discover previously unknown deposits.

Mining companies are moving to higher-cost mineral deposits that are deeper below Earth's surface, located in more remote places, or contain less valuable mineral content per unit of mined rock. Engineers are discovering new ways of finding, extracting, and processing minerals that lower mineral production costs.

Society is likewise responding to the depletion of known deposits by reducing the demand for specific minerals in two ways. First, more abundant materials are being used instead of less abundant ones (material substitution). Second, engineers are reducing the material needed for specific applications (resource-saving technological change). Recent examples are thinner aluminum walls in beverage containers and thinner steel door panels in automobiles that nevertheless are designed to be more crashworthy than their thicker predecessors.

The net effect is that most mineral resources are becoming less costly to produce and less expensive for consumers to purchase. This trend has been in motion for the last century or so. Scarcity, to be sure, varies considerably from mineral to mineral. But in general, mineral resources are becoming less, rather than more, scarce in this economic sense.

The critical long-run issue for the future, therefore, is the extent to which society will be able to continue to be ingenious in its response to the depletion of known mineral deposits. To what extent will cost-reducing technologic advances in exploration, mining, and processing offset the cost-increasing effects of the depletion of known deposits and of pollution? To what extent will advances in the use of minerals allow more abundant materials to replace less abundant ones? These questions are largely unanswerable. Human ingenuity to date, combined with ongoing technologic developments, arguably allow us to be optimistic. Scientists and engineers are making great progress in commercializing new techniques of remote sensing, solution mining (including bioextraction techniques using micro-organisms to extract metal from rock), and methods of extraction permitting profitable recovery of minerals from past mining wastes. Seabeds, as well as the Moon and other extraterrestrial bodies, represent important untapped sources. Materials scientists are making great progress in designing and commercializing advanced materials—newly engineered materials using metals, ceramics, polymers, and composites of two or more of these material types. Advanced materials provide enhanced properties, such as strength, electrical conductivity, and corrosion resistance, compared to traditional materials (e.g., metals, plastics, cardboard).

For the coming decade or so, three short-run, specific issues will be key determinants of the demand for and supply of minerals. First, how fast will the developing economies grow, including most importantly those of the former Soviet Union, China, and India? The level of economic activity is perhaps the most important of the many determinants of mineral demand. These three countries arguably have the largest potential for economic growth. Second, how will mineral production evolve in the former Soviet Union and China as these countries move toward market economies and perhaps even democratic political institutions? The former Soviet Union and China have significant geologic potential, but it is unclear whether their mineral output will rise or fall in a market economy. Third, how will society's demand for a cleaner environment affect the costs of mineral production? Mining and mineral processing inevitably disturb the environment—mining requires that large amounts of earth and rock be moved, and mineral processing by its nature involves separating valuable minerals from unwanted associated material. Environmental consequences can be mitigated if we are willing to pay more for the minerals we use. Over time, however, human ingenuity and technological innovation hold forth the promise of improving the way we find, extract, and process minerals *and* of reducing the environmental damages of mineral production.

See also CHEMICALS, FINE; CHEMISTRY; COAL; HAZARDOUS WASTES; MATERIALS: RESEARCH AND DEVELOPMENT; RESOURCES.

BIBLIOGRAPHY

EGGERT, RODERICK G., ed. *Mining and the Environment: International Perspectives on Public Policy.* Washington, DC: Resources for the Future, 1994.

TILTON, JOHN E. *World Metal Demand: Trends and Prospects.* Washington, DC: Resources for the Future, 1990.

U.S. Department of the Interior, Bureau of Mines. *Minerals Yearbook.* Washington, DC: U.S. Government Printing Office, published annually.

U.S. Department of the Interior, Bureau of Mines. *The New Materials Society: Challenges and Opportunities.* Washington, DC: U.S. Government Printing Office, Vols. 1 and 2, 1990; Vol. 3, 1991.

VOGELEY, WILLIAM A., ed. *Economics of the Mineral Industries.* New York: American Institute of Mining, Metallurgical, and Petroleum Engineers, 1985.

Roderick G. Eggert

Minorities

By the middle of the next century, no single racial group will comprise majority status, given current United States demographic trends (see Table 1). This situation will have important economic and political consequences for the country. This article examines future population and employment trends for the four largest minority groups: blacks; Hispanics; Native Americans (including Eskimos and Aleutian Islanders); and Asians (including Pacific islanders) recognized by the United States Bureau of the Census.

Blacks

Blacks constitute the slowest-growing minority group in the United States and, while currently the second largest racial group, by 2020 blacks will drop to third behind whites and Hispanics. Nevertheless, by the middle of the twenty-first century, this population is expected to double from 30.6 million in 1991 to 61.6 million in 2050, according to data from the United States Bureau of the Census. Blacks also will represent a larger share of the labor force in the next century but most likely will be overtaken by Hispanics by 2020, if current United States Bureau of Labor Statistics projections hold.

The projected annual growth rate in employment for blacks is 1.9 percent for the 1990–2005 period, or slightly below the rate for the 1975–1990 period. Currently, blacks are more likely to be employed in occupations that will grow more slowly or actually decline in the future. Only in a few of the fast-growing service areas does the black share of jobs equal or exceed its share of the total population. The fastest-growing jobs are those that require at least some higher education, and currently blacks are underrepresented among college graduates.

Hispanics

Hispanics constitute the most rapidly growing minority group. Projected increases are expected to raise the Hispanic share of the total United States population from 9 percent in 1990 to 22.5 percent by 2050. The rapid growth of this population will fuel the increase in the total population, accounting for 44 percent on average of overall population growth. Hispanics are predicted to increase nearly fourfold by 2050. Much of this growth will be the result of more births. By 2050, one in three births will be Hispanic. In addition, Hispanic immigration is predicted to add 322,000 new people annually between 1990 and 2050.

In 1990, Hispanics were nearly 8 percent of the United States labor force. During the 1975–1990 period, they entered the United States workforce at an annual rate of 5.9 percent. This rate of increase is predicted to slow slightly to 3.8 percent annually by 2005. By that year, 11.1 percent of the workforce will be Hispanic. Hispanics, however, are currently underrepresented in all of the fast-growing parts of the economy, and overrepresented in the slow-growing or declining parts. This condition results from their currently low levels of education. For example, in 1990, 41 percent of Hispanic workers had not completed high school.

For many Hispanics, whether immigrants or native to the United States, Spanish is the primary language spoken in the home and English is

TABLE 1. Percent Distribution of the U.S. Population, by Race and Ethnicity, 1990 and Predicted 2050

Race or Ethnic Group	Percentage of Total Population in 1990	Percentage of Total Population Predicted in 2050
Total, United States	100.0	100.0
White, non-Hispanic	75.7	72.8
Black	12.8	15.7
Native American	0.8	1.1
Asian	3.0	10.3
Hispanic (of any race)	9.0	22.5

Source: U.S. Bureau of the Census, Population Projections of the United States, by Age, Sex, Race, and Hispanic Origin: 1993 to 2050, November 1993.

learned outside. This creates specific educational problems related to bilingual education, which is hotly debated by educators and policy planners. Most public education in the United States (and nearly all advanced technical education) is entirely in English. In addition, most Hispanic immigrants to the United States have not received extensive formal education even in their native countries, leaving them poorly equipped to undertake both the linguistic training and technical education required for increasingly technical occupations within the information economy. Thus, our rapidly increasing Hispanic population may find itself at an occupational disadvantage not simply because of language differences but also because of a lack of previous institutional empowerment and acculturation in their homelands. Unlike some other immigrants to the United States, who come with technical educations in place, Hispanic immigrants are not technically proficient.

Asians

Asians are the fastest-growing minority group, predicted to grow more than fivefold from 7.6 million people in 1990 to 41 million in 2050. As a share of the total United States population, Asians will go from 3 percent in 1990 to 10 percent in 2050. Much of the growth in the Asian population is predicted to be fueled by net immigration, not domestic births. The Census Bureau predicts that more Asians will immigrate to the United States than will be born here during the 1990–2050 period. The Asian (and other) share of the labor force is also expected to grow at an annual rate of 3.8 percent. (This group includes Asians, Pacific islanders, Native Americans, and natives of Alaska.) A higher percentage of Asians are predicted to fill positions in the fast-growing sectors of the economy than either blacks or Hispanics because of their generally higher levels of education.

Although Asian immigrants also encounter second-language problems when coming to the United States, two factors tend to mitigate their experience in this regard. First, many immigrants come with a strong background in formal education, especially in technical areas. Second, those seeking enfranchisement in technical communities find that their ethnic, linguistic, and cultural heritage is already well represented in such communities. In both academe and industry, Asian-Americans tend to occupy a sizable portion of the positions that demand advanced training in science and technology.

Native Americans

Currently, the Native American, or American Indian, population comprises less than 1 percent of the total United States population with 2.1 million people. It is predicted to grow steadily so that by 2050, the number of Native Americans is predicted to total 4.3 million or slightly more than 1 percent of the United States population. Estimates of Native American participation in the future workforce are difficult to obtain because the Department of Labor includes them in the "Asians and others" category. Currently, however, Native American educational attainment is low, and they are underrepresented in the fastest-growing jobs.

Consequences for Politics and Economy

As a result of their rates of growth, and the relative decline of the non-Hispanic white population, minority political power will probably increase. In the largest states with the most political clout—New York, California, Texas, and Florida—each minority group is getting larger. Hispanics are particularly likely to benefit politically. Combined with and undermining this likely expansion of political power, however, is the likelihood that blacks and Hispanics will be increasingly closed out of well-paying, high-status jobs in the information economy because of their currently low levels of educational attainment. One of the critical political and social issues over the next fifty years, therefore, is raising the education levels of blacks, Hispanics, and Native Americans. No society can fully participate in the Information Age if a large percentage of its population and more than half its youth lack adequate access to and understanding of information technology.

See also CHANGE, CULTURAL; CLASS AND UNDERCLASS; DEMOGRAPHY; ETHNIC AND CULTURAL SEPARATISM; ETHNIC AND RACIAL CONFLICT; ENVIRONMENTAL REFUGEES; GLOBAL CULTURE; NATIVE AMERICANS; RACE, CASTE, AND ETHNIC DIVERSITY; REFUGEES.

BIBLIOGRAPHY

ONG, WALTER J., S.J., *Orality and Literacy: the Technologizing of the Word.* New York: Routledge, 1993.

U.S. Bureau of the Census, *Current Population Report: Population Projections of the United States, by Age, Sex, Race, and Hispanic Origin: 1993 to 2050.* Washington, DC: U.S. Bureau of the Census, 1993.

U.S. Bureau of Labor Statistics, *BLS Bulletin 2402: Outlook 1990–2005.* Washington, DC: U.S. Bureau of Labor Statistics, 1992.

Robert A. Cropf
Vincent Casaregola

Modernism and Postmodernism

Future historians may say that the primary story of the twentieth century is that it marks the end of the Modern Age and the beginning of a new epoch of the human journey. The impulses that have shaped the last five hundred years are yielding to a new set of impulses. Thus we live in a century of massive dissolution of authority, of established institutions, and of patterns of life.

This shift is the essence of the turbulence that shakes America and the world. We are not simply going through a rough patch, after which life will revert to something we like to think of as normal. The old normalcy is gone. We are passing through a shift from one order of life to another.

Radical changes involving the basic principles of human life generally have happened only once in about five hundred years. Such turning points include the decline of antiquity, the surge of monasticism in the sixth century, the emergence of new intellectual currents in the Church in the eleventh century, and the arrival of the scientific outlook in the sixteenth century.

Ages of great change in world view, which can also be described as psychological reorientation, have generally displayed similar characteristics. Some of these include: a rise in general warfare; increase in internal discontent and uprisings; economic instability; a shift of emphasis in the fine arts, which lose any sense of unity; institutional exhaustion; weakening of the moral ethos and religious bonds; rise in crime; and an increase in psychological stress and in suicide.

Such characteristics have shown themselves in every major shift of world view that has taken place, from eighth century B.C. Greece to twentieth century America.

A shift of this consequence creates what Jacques Barzun termed "dissolving times." Throughout history, Barzun noted, dissolving times have manifested certain characteristics, which are once again in evidence:

- The tendency to blur distinctions of purpose, function, and form.
- A desire to simplify, to return to the innocent beginnings of things.
- The decay of public hope and common purpose.
- The fragmenting of authority, with all its consequences in terms of self-government and social order.
- In some quarters, a hatred and repudiation of the past.

- The proliferation of experimental ideas and cultural modes.
- A sense of loss, of decline.
- Institutional collapse as the cohesive force diminishes.
- The rise in general uncertainty about life.

One of the clearest signs of the end of the Modern Era is the confusion as to what to call the period we have entered. Names abound: the postindustrial, postmodern, or global age; the Pacific century; the information age; the quantum age; the post-scientific era; the era of the Earth; the age of Aquarius; and on and on . . .

It is certainly clear that we are in a postcapitalist (Drucker), postsocialist, postnationalist, postindustrial era. And as far as our culture goes, we are even in the postbelief era, because no sustaining belief now informs our culture.

Such a postbelief cultural phase has been unfolding for the past 150 years. The modernist influence held sway in Western culture from roughly 1850 to 1950, and it was followed in the 1960s by the postmodernist period.

Modernism was the cultural expression of the belief that life had lost its mystery, that men, not gods, rule the world, that tradition must yield to experimentation in every aspect of life, and that at the core of life there is nothing, just the void of nihilism.

The thrust of modernism was to substitute an aesthetic justification of life for the prevailing moral and spiritual order. Modernism, wrote Irving Howe, was "an unyielding rage against the existing order." The emphasis of modernism was a repudiation of the past with the belief that only the present has authority.

The aesthetic expression of this view demanded liberation from all inner restraints, as well as the destruction of all prevailing forms. It held that experience is the touchstone of life, that tradition is to be negated, that art must pursue the infinite along all paths, including eroticism, cruelty, and terror.

The failure of modernism was that it never understood the function of tradition. Tradition is not the sentimental attachment to the past. Tradition presupposes the timeless reality of what endures through all ages. Tradition is the carrying forward of those attitudes and forms that human experience has taught us are the highest the human spirit can attain.

Modernism waged relentless war against tradition, and consequently against the transcendent impulses that tradition manifests.

In the 1960s, the powerful current of postmodernism developed, which carried the logic of modernism to its farthermost reaches. Against the aesthetic justification of life, postmodernism substituted the instinctual. For the postmodernist, impulse and pleasure alone were real and life affirming; all else was neurosis and death. Postmodernism tore down the boundaries between art and life and insisted that acting out, instead of making distinctions, was the path to knowledge.

Despite the vitality and energy that have produced modernist and postmodernist works of art, when these two strains of expression are carried to their ultimate conclusion the result is a culture that fastens on disintegration, rage, and madness—themes that characterize so much of twentieth-century art, literature, and entertainment.

The effects of modernism and postmodernism have been so great that the "avant-garde" has disappeared, for only a minority in the culture is any longer on the side of order and tradition. Few people believe that there is any tradition left to trade for the future. Thus today we are reaping the results of a culture detached from any ethical standard or spiritual moorings.

The collapse of modernism and postmodernism has been accompanied by the exhaustion of the intellectual themes that have occupied the West for well over two centuries.

Few people any longer believe in reason as an ultimate authority in ordering life. Faith in the perfectibility of man—a cornerstone of the Enlightenment—fell victim to the wholesale slaughter of two world wars. Belief in utopias has vanished. Liberalism, having won historic gains, now languishes in exhaustion.

Socialism is discredited. Marxism has collapsed. Communism has been buried. Fascism enlists no loyalties.

Nationalism—in the nineteenth-century sense of constituting the outer limits of a people's political awareness—is on the wane. What surfaces in places such as Bosnia, Georgia, and Tajikistan is not historic nationalism, but an old ethnicity that cries out for new expression.

Even confidence in progress has substantially waned. Indeed, most of the social agenda that constituted the faith in progress has now been enacted into law. Progress has achieved its earlier goals and now needs redefinition.

While the concept of Liberty still occupies the public mind, we must ask whether such freedom is more a matter of the absence of restraint than it is the expression of some creative inner mode of being emanating from deep within the human soul. For it may well be that the idea of independence, while still obviously valid, is no longer at the cutting edge of political necessity. It has been replaced by the greater necessity of *inter*dependence.

Great motifs of life carried Western civilization through two of the most progressive—if destabilizing—centuries in history. But the end of the Modern Age and the opening up of a global era now require broader themes to encompass this fresh period of human development.

The great task now is to save progress from merely a technological interpretation, and to redefine it in terms of a new historical era, of expanding human capabilities and aspirations. We need a cultural climate that portrays the wonder and magnificence of life in all its forms; a cultural climate that helps people find deeper meanings to life, even as they struggle to make a living.

See also CHANGE; CHANGE, CULTURAL; CHANGE, EPOCHAL; CHANGE, OPTIMISTIC AND PESSIMISTIC PERSPECTIVES; CONTINUITY AND DISCONTINUITY; GLOBAL CONSCIOUSNESS; GLOBAL TURNING POINTS.

BIBLIOGRAPHY

BARRACLOUGH, GEOFFREY. *Turning Points in World History.* London: Thames and Hudson, 1979.

BELL, DANIEL. *The Winding Passage.* New York: Basic Books, 1980.

DRUCKER, PETER F. *Landmarks of Tomorrow.* New York: Harper & Row, 1957.

TOYNBEE, ARNOLD J. *A Study of History.* London: Oxford University Press, 1946.

ROBERTS, J. M. *The Triumph of the West.* Boston: Little, Brown, 1985.

SMITH, HOUSTON. *Beyond the Post-Modern Mind.* New York: Crossroads, 1989.

William Van Dusen Wishard

Monetary System

The international monetary system in the foreseeable future will evolve out of the present system. It is highly improbable that any wholly new system, which a few experts are sometimes advocating, will be introduced.

Building on the present means starting from a system in which exchange rates for the major currencies—the U.S. dollar, the Canadian dollar, the Japanese yen, and other currencies—are determined in exchange markets around the world and in which European countries try to keep their own exchange rates fixed, within limits, vis-à-vis each other through an exchange rate mechanism (ERM), which is part of the European Monetary System (EMS). This "floating rate system" has existed since March 1973.

Contrary to earlier expectations, the floating rate system has been plagued by instability. Large day-to-day and week-to-week fluctuations in exchange rates occur, as well as large longer-term swings. These changes in exchange rates usually result from sudden, massive movements of short-term capital and generally have little to do with the economic fundamentals of countries' economies or their trade and balance-of-payments positions. With the continual introduction of innovative financial instruments (most recently "derivatives"), the growth of emerging stock and bond markets in developing countries, the expansion of mutual funds in industrial countries in which even small investors put money abroad, and the increase in the use of computers and other electronic devices, money now crosses international boundaries instantaneously. It is exchanged through a variety of financial instruments offered by banks, mutual funds, and brokerage houses, in magnitudes that have grown exponentially in the last five years, reaching $1 trillion a day.

This growth and internationalization of private capital markets has made the international monetary system more vulnerable than ever to differences in the overall economic performance of both industrial and developing countries, and even to expectations of their economic performance. Since 1993, for example, sudden capital movements have exerted overwhelming pressures on the pound sterling, the Italian lira, the French franc, the Spanish peseta, the Portuguese escudo, the U.S. dollar, and the Mexican peso. The United Kingdom and Italy have had to withdraw from the ERM. Because France was unable to stay within the agreed limits, the previously narrow bands of the mechanism have been widened considerably.

To help limit exchange rate instability and uncertainty about future exchange rates, which are damaging to trade and international investment and upsetting to countries' economies and economic policy, authorities of the main industrial countries are likely to continue, and possibly enlarge and make more frequent, their interventions in exchange markets, attempting to make such interventions more effective than in the past. Central banks will hold larger reserves than they might otherwise desire of currencies under pressure and to diversify their reserves; they will increasingly supplement the dollar as a reserve currency by use of other currencies, notably the Deutschemark and the Japanese yen.

Stronger, more concerted efforts to enhance exchange rate stability and foster a more stable international monetary system, as well as to induce a more rapidly growing world economy also can be expected. It is highly unlikely, however, that any system of fixed rates—even rates that allow some fluctuation within a narrow band, such as target rates that are being advocated by several former financial officials and other experts will be introduced anytime soon. Such rates require that national economic policies and differences in the macroeconomic performance—their rates of growth and inflation—be minimal.

For any system with relatively fixed exchange rates to work, the economies in the arrangement generally have to converge. Such convergence depends on the willingness of monetary authorities to pursue policies that are in harmony with those of the other participating countries. Given the differences in the present and likely rates of growth and inflation in the main industrial countries, monetary authorities have been extremely reluctant to surrender independence over monetary policy. Monetary policy is the prime instrument though which authorities influence the performance of their domestic economies. With the prevalence of burgeoning budget deficits, alternative instruments such as fiscal policy have been delimited. In fact, it was the desire of authorities for independence of monetary policy that brought the floating rate system into effect in the first place.

Nor is it likely that any system resembling the classical gold standard will be introduced, despite its devotees. Its requirements are very much stricter, authorities are all too familiar with its potentially deflationary consequences, and many countries, especially developing countries, have no gold. On another bleak note, it is unlikely that any common currency, even that of the ECU in Europe, will be accepted.

Despite their unwillingness to agree to fixed rates, authorities of the industrial nations are also likely to intensify efforts at policy coordination, especially through the Group of Seven—Canada, France, Germany, Italy, Japan, the United Kingdom, and the United States. The G-7 may be enlarged to include Russia and some developing countries, possibly India and China, especially if developing countries continue to be dynamos of world economic growth.

The International Monetary Fund (IMF) will have an enlarged role in the policy coordination process, working more closely with the G-7 and with more clout. To prevent further financial crises like the one that hit Mexico in late 1994 and 1995, the IMF will probably initiate several measures. It may create a last-resort financial safety net for the world that is some facility for financing capital flight situations. It may develop the role of special drawing rights (SDR), the reserve asset that the IMF issues, to supplement reserves in national currencies. The IMF will reform the arrangement by which it lends money to help low-income countries, to make it better suited to these countries, by making money available for a longer time than in the past. These measures will require enlargement of the IMF's capital base. These intensified efforts by monetary authorities and the IMF will all occur simultaneously.

See also CAPITAL FORMATION; CREDIT, DEBT, AND BORROWING; DERIVATIVES; ECONOMICS; FINANCIAL INSTITUTIONS; GLOBAL STATISTICS; INTERNATIONAL TRADE: SUSTAINING GROWTH; MACROECONOMICS; MEDIA OF EXCHANGE; SAVINGS; WEALTH.

BIBLIOGRAPHY

Bretton Woods: Looking to the Future. Washington, DC: Bretton Woods Commission, 1994.

DEANE, MARJORIE, and PRINGLE, ROBERT. *The Central Banks.* London: Hamish Hamilton, 1994.

DE VRIES, MARGARET GARRITSEN. *The IMF in a Changing World.* Washington, DC: The International Monetary Fund, 1986.

FRIEDMAN, IRVING S. *Toward World Prosperity: Reshaping the Global Money System.* Lexington, MA: D. C. Health/Lexington Books, 1987.

KENEN, PETER B. *Managing Exchange Rates.* London: Royal Institute of International Affairs, 1988.

_____. *Managing the World Economy, Fifty Years After Bretton Woods.* Washington, DC: Institute for International Economics, 1994.

WILLIAMSON, JOHN, AND MILLER, MARCUS H. *Targets and Indicators: A Blueprint for the International Coordination of Economic Policies.* Washington, DC: Institute for International Economics, 1987.

Margaret de Vries

Morals

The fundamental questions of morals concern the standards of good character and social interaction: Are they merely variable cultural elements, or do they have an invariant core based in our common human nature? Are they rationally defensible? Is their focus on which specific actions we perform and their effects on others, or on the kinds of persons we become as reflected in our likes and aspirations?

Beyond Moral Skepticism

The first decades of the twenty-first century should solidify the abandonment of the skeptical conceptions of the nature of morality that predominated among twentieth-century intellectuals. Cultural relativism, noncognitivism, and both Freudian and Marxist reductionism all lost favor toward the century's turn.

Cultural relativism—the view that morality, like etiquette or civil law, is a creature of local custom—appears insufficiently to ground criticism of cultural forms as intellectuals strive to expunge nationalism, genocide, racism, and sexism from Western social orders while recognizing the near universality of these and comparable social phenomena.

Noncognitivism—the view that moral judgments are not factual claims but more akin to cries of social or personal pleasure and revulsion—is unlikely to prove itself capable of accounting for the subtlety and intricacy of moral discourse and its grammatical transformations.

Freud's system conceptualizes morality as the "superego's" internalization of the feared parent's commands to children. It stands little chance of recovering from feminist critics who fault it for sexism, for downplaying child abuse, and for psychologically manipulating analysands. Philosophers of science criticize the Freudian theory for its unfalsifiability and lack of predictive power. The spread of free markets and the collapse of Marxist political systems in Russia and Eastern Europe cast doubt on Marxist economic analyses and predictions at the same time that social theorists found alternative explanations for Marxist sociological hypotheses. It is unlikely that Marx's view of morality—as part of an elaborate ideological "superstructure," which functions merely to rationalize and facilitate capitalism's oppression of workers—will survive these challenges to the rest of the theory.

Postmodernist Morality

The new millennium begins with postmodernist trends within moral thought. These emphasize diversity of ethnicity, culture, and gender, and are skeptical about the efforts to ground morality on conceptions of universal human nature and universal reason that characterized the premodern and modern epochs respectively. It is unlikely that many of these trends will prove lasting. Anglo-American philosophy has resisted the over-attention to race, gender, and ethnicity found elsewhere in the humanities, but some moral theorists have proposed that ethnicity and, especially, gender yield special and important moral perspectives. These views face probably insurmountable problems: the growing recognition of the unscientific character of many racial classifications, the near-universality of mixed "race," and the fact that individuals manifest diversity in themselves ("microdiversity"). All of these factors undermine this line of thought. Moral perspectives do not come one to a group. Moreover, it is unclear which of the several strands of feminism that emerged near the turn of the century is most promising. Carol Gilligan claims that women's moral thinking tends toward a "care-perspective," which downplays concern over rights and instead emphasizes feelings, special connections, and maintaining relationships. However, such a view runs the risk of perpetuating gender stereotypes ("maternal thinking"). Furthermore, reducing these emphases merely to aspects of one gender's thinking may hinder our ability to see their universal centrality within ethics and the injustice of their neglect by moral philosophers.

A different strain of feminism stresses and extends political egalitarianism, as expressed in the slogan "the personal is political." This movement is useful for legitimating and facilitating cross-cultural moral critique and its opposition to gender-relativism. However, its dangers include hyper individualism, which can undermine the givenness of role obligations (such as that of father or mother), exaggeration of the very limited utility of such political concepts as justice in intimate relationships, and a tendency to replicate and even magnify the social atomism for which communitarians fault liberal individualism.

The multiculturalist movement is useful because it sensitizes us to the way overhasty universalization can misdescribe one culture's peculiarities as universal human features. Unfortunately, it threatens to degenerate into a cultural relativism that merely ratifies the status quo. In addition, any moral view that thus stresses individuals' social role and status confronts them with the choice between complacent and oppositional responses to their "station." Rationally choosing a mode of response requires appeal to something beyond culture, presumably a return either to reason or human nature. Even Hegel, regarded as a patron

saint by the multiculturalists, recognized this. His insistence on judging any social context by its place in the history of progress separates him from his multiculturalist followers, to the latter's disadvantage.

As the use of new technologies becomes more widespread, and as modern thinkers continue to demand release from the eroded values of traditional religions—especially to legitimize sexual behaviors once commonly dismissed as "deviant"—society will require more thoughtful and deeper moral inquiry. We can expect the cultural relativism that lurks behind multiculturalism to prove untenable and unappealing because multicultural society makes implausible the relativist's implicit claim that real moral disputes are few, shallow, and small.

Emerging Trends in Moral Thinking

Renewed interest in the moral virtues will grow, but ultimately will need to ground virtues either in culture or in human nature. The next few decades should see a resurgence of interest and work both in theories of human nature and in moral theories closely tied to them.

Some directions these researchers might take are indicated by sociobiology and by the rehabilitation and empirically based reconception of "moral sense" approaches from seventeenth- and eighteenth-century Britain. It seems likely that dissatisfaction with modernism's instrumentalist rationality will grow, and the absurdity of abandoning rationality (as some radical postmodernists recommend) will become manifest. Sympathetic reconsideration of premodern approaches to rationality and human nature then appears unavoidable. This should spark renewed attention to religious ethics. One important example of this revitalization near the turn of the century is the reformulation of the bases of Christian morals in the voluminous codifications, catechisms, and other documents issued from the Catholic church during the influential papacy of John Paul II, especially in his 1992 encyclical letter Veritatis Splendor.

A question asked by Alasdair MacIntyre will focus the debate among these rival approaches: Can any one of them (or combination of them) establish its rational superiority to the others by standards accepted within those other approaches?

See also BEHAVIOR: SOCIAL CONSTRAINTS; BIOETHICS; DEATH AND DYING; ETHICS; HUMAN RIGHTS; SEXUAL CODES; SEXUAL LAWS; SOCIAL CONTROLS; WOMEN'S MOVEMENT.

BIBLIOGRAPHY

CORTESE, ANTHONY. *Ethnic Ethics: The Restructuring of Moral Theory.* Albany, NY: State University of New York Press, 1990.

CREWS, FREDERICK. *Out of My System: Psychoanalysis, Ideology, and Critical Method.* New York: Oxford University Press, 1986.

ELSTER, JON. *Making Sense of Marx.* New York: Cambridge University Press, 1985.

GILLIGAN, CAROL. *In a Different Voice: Psychological Theory and Women's Development.* Cambridge, MA: Harvard University Press, 1982.

MACINTYRE, ALASDAIR. *After Virtue: A Study in Moral Theory,* 2d ed. Notre Dame, IN: University of Notre Dame Press, 1984.

OKIN, SUSAN MILLER. *Gender, Justice, and the Family.* New York: Basic Books, 1989.

RUDDICK, SARA. *Maternal Thinking: Towards a Politics of Peace.* Boston: Beacon, 1989.

SINGER, PETER. *The Expanding Circle: Ethics and Sociobiology.* New York: Farrar, Straus & Giroux, 1989.

WILSON, EDWARD O. *Sociobiology: The New Synthesis.* Cambridge, MA: Harvard University Press, 1975.

WILSON, JAMES Q. *The Moral Sense.* New York: Free Press, 1993.

J. L. A. Garcia

More, Saint Thomas (1477–1535)

English humanist and statesman. A native of London, More entered the legal profession in 1501 and soon gained recognition as a distinguished barrister, scholar, and diplomat. Under Henry VIII, he served in various high posts, including that of Lord Chancellor. In 1535 he was beheaded for his refusal to take an oath of assent to the act that established a Protestant succession. Pope Pius XI canonized him in 1935. More wrote many volumes of theology, history, and classical scholarship, but the work by which he is principally known today is his *Utopia* (1516), the tale of a visit to an imaginary ideal commonwealth. More took the name Utopia from two Greek words meaning "no place." In Utopia, the system of government is representative democracy and the economy is communist. Clergy may marry, several forms of religious belief are tolerated, and euthanasia is available for the incurably ill. *Utopia* has been interpreted in many ways. It can be read as a monkish denunciation of the materialism of the Renaissance, a learned satire poking fun at human frailty, or a blueprint for a democratic socialist future. Whatever More had in mind, his book has become the model for all subsequent utopian speculation and a classic of world literature.

See also UTOPIAS.

BIBLIOGRAPHY

BAKER-SMITH, DOMINIC. *More's Utopia.* London: Harper Collins, 1991.

HEXTER, JACK H. *More's Utopia: The Biography of an Idea.* Princeton, NJ: Princeton University Press, 1952.

LOGAN, GEORGE M. *The Meaning of More's "Utopia".* Princeton, NJ: Princeton University Press, 1983.

MARIUS, RICHARD. *Thomas More: A Biography.* New York: Alfred Knopf, 1984.

REYNOLDS, E. E. *The Field Is Won: The Life and Death of Saint Thomas More.* Milwaukee: Bruce, 1968.

W. Warren Wagar

Motion Pictures

The movies, the dominant art form of the twentieth century, evince both maturity and stability as the medium celebrates its centennial and the century comes to a close. That is the good news and the bad. For the first seventy-five years of film history, the medium was characterized by constant and repeated waves of innovation, as filmmakers in the United States, Europe, and elsewhere excitedly explored the new art, testing its limits and expanding its horizons. Constantly challenged by advances in technology, film artists devised the dramatic feature and perfected slapstick comedy in the 1910s; integrated the techniques and concerns of painters, musicians, and novelists in the 1920s, and reveled in dialogue in the 1930s, as they took on much of the artistic responsibility of modern drama. The 1940s and 1950s saw the cinema establish itself as the medium of choice for many of the major artists of the modern period: a separate art with its own newly founded traditions finally operating independent of the older pictorial and narrative arts.

By the late fifties and early 1960s, the filmmakers of the New Wave (Godard and Truffaut in particular) began to reflect the rapidly expanding legacy of movie history, integrating the work of their predecessors, and commenting on the art's past. For the first time, it became necessary for a filmgoer to have an education in the medium in order to fully appreciate new work. By the early 1970s, Hollywood had imported the New Wave's reflexive attitude. As the American sixties generation (Coppola, Lucas, Spielberg, Scorsese) established themselves in positions of power, the lengthy youth of the movies came to a close. The art had matured. While there have been occasional blooms of new talent in one national cinema or another (China in the late 1980s, Finland in the early 1990s), the genres and techniques of movies at the close of the century—in the United States, Europe, and elsewhere—are more or less what they were twenty-five years ago. The level of product is very high, and movies still hold pride of place in our culture, but the excitement of discovery and change that characterized the first seventy-five years of their history is gone. In this, film is no different from the other arts—music, painting, the novel, drama—all of which reached a point of postmodern stasis in the early seventies. As Alain Tanner put it with great prescience in *Au Milieu du Monde* (1972): "We live in a time of normalization, when exchange is permitted, but nothing changes." The idea of an avant-garde in art is now a historical curiosity.

Yet, while the esthetics of the medium haven't changed perceptibly, the technology has been preparing for the profound revolution of digitization that is now occurring, preparing us for a very different world of film in the twenty-first century. With hindsight we can see that the chemical and mechanical art of celluloid film, born of the nineteenth century, was a transitional phase. Since the 1980s, television has been the main popular dramatic medium, freeing "cinema" to evolve into an elite art. Very quickly in the 1980s, the development of videotape technology drastically changed the way most people experience movies, moving the economic locus of the art from the theater to the living room.

At the end of the 1970s, people saw movies in theaters, listened to music on records, watched one of the four national television networks (actually getting up out of their chairs to change channels on occasion), used telephones with wires tethering them to the wall, and, if they were so inclined, corresponded with each other using pens, pencils, typewriters, paper, and the U.S. Postal Service. They had been doing things this way since the turn of the century.

By the early 1990s, these same folks saw movies mainly at home on videotape, listened to digital music on compact discs (more often walking in the street than sitting at home), had their choice of forty or more cable channels from which to choose (and channel-surfed without leaving their chairs), made telephone calls in their cars or walking around, and, if they were so inclined, corresponded with each other via fax or electronic mail.

They could also, if they so chose, buy a camcorder that would let them shoot videotape of near-professional quality. They could install a home theater with a screen almost as large as the ones at the local sixplex (and with a sound system that was markedly better). They could watch videodiscs, skipping, browsing, freezing, and skimming as they might with a book; install their very own satellite dish; or buy a computer for the kids to play with that had the power of a 1980s IBM mainframe.

The continuing microcomputer revolution has prepared the ground for a further shift: from the living room to the laptop. As digital techniques are perfected, movies become individual experiences on personal screens, as easily manipulated as books, and increasingly integrated with text in a new medium called (rather unimaginatively) "multimedia." Of course, film itself was the first multimedium, combining most of the techniques (and all of the concerns) of previous media. But digitization completes the journey the Lumière brothers and Georges Méliès began more than a hundred years ago. In the context of multimedia, film for the first time is truly a personal medium, both for the producer and the consumer.

Just as television did not replace theatrical film, neither will multimedia. We can expect the mature art and business of films shown in theaters to continue throughout the next century. But the artistic innovation in the general medium and, perhaps more important, the economy of the business will shift rapidly to multimedia: cinematic/textual products privately experienced and personally controlled by individual users.

This is not necessarily good news for cinéastes. The control that multimedia gives to the user is antithetical to the rhythmic mysteries of traditional film composition. And then, too, as part of multimedia, cinema plays a necessarily subordinate role. Perhaps most important, because it is infinitely adjustable, a fully digital film sequence loses all touch with reality. We can no longer trust it as a representation of the real world: the exciting tension between film and its object disappears: Méliès, champion of pure fantasy, has won; the Lumières, proponents of verisimilitude, have lost.

Digital techniques make film a tool of pure imagination. Filmmakers are now thoroughly liberated from any dependence on reality as their subject. That is the good news for the twenty-first century—and the bad. At worst, the basic genre of the medium will become the music video. But at best, the next generation of filmmakers will discover new truths in these new techniques that will reinvent the relevance, vitality, and passion of this past century's central art.

However, in the context of not just a new century, but a new millennium, perhaps the idea of progress that visions of the future imply is itself outmoded. The challenge of the next epoch will be the achievement of a steady state, in film and culture as well as in economics and ecology. This new cultural equilibrium, paradoxically, will bring new strength to the art of the past just as the new technology will increase our intimacy with its history. Thus, to a remarkable extent the future of film is also its past.

See also BROADCASTING; COMMUNICATIONS; ELECTRONIC CONVERGENCE; INTERACTIVE ENTERTAINMENT; MEDIA LAB; PHOTOGRAPHY; RECORDING INDUSTRY; TELEVISION.

BIBLIOGRAPHY

EBERT, ROGER, and SISKEL, GENE. *The Future of the Movies*. Chicago: Andrews and McMeel, 1991.

HOLLANDER, ANNE. *Moving Pictures*. Cambridge, MA: Harvard University Press, 1991.

MILLER, MARK C. *Seeing Through Movies*. New York: Pantheon, 1990

MONACO, JAMES. *How to Read a Film*. New York: Oxford University Press, 1995

James Monaco

Motor Vehicles

In the year 2020, a Californian may order a battery-powered car on a refurbished chassis, built a decade earlier from a plant co-owned by General Motors and Toyota, directly from a personal computer. In Texas, a rancher may select a four-wheel-drive, dual fuel pickup truck fitted out with computers that calculate tailpipe emissions and gasoline usage to allow the driver to switch instantly to natural gas when pollution and gasoline consumption exceed predetermined standards. In New York, a harried executive may opt for a vehicle as fully equipped as a business office and with an onboard guidance system that lays out the routines to and from home, business, and points in between with the least amount of traffic congestion and distance control devices that prevent collisions.

Choices may differ in other parts of the world. Germans may prefer cars designed and manufactured for disassembly for mandatory recycling, while Estonians may purchase relatively inexpensive compact cars with minimal exhaust pollution.

Japanese and Koreans may seek fuel-efficient vehicles to reduce oil imports, while the Chinese and Indians may purchase all-purpose vehicles for transportation that double as tractors or as a power source for irrigating farmlands. Different national needs will induce production differentiation particularly as demand for vehicles increases among developing nations. The car of the future will hardly be a single, uniform prototype, but a variety of models with different power sources, engine designs, materials, and other features and options.

As industrializing markets continue to develop, demand for automobiles will increase in direct proportion, as has occurred, for example, in Korea, Brazil, and Mexico. Estimates of future vehicle demand worldwide up to the year 2020 appear in Table 1.

While demand for automobiles will expand in both industrialized and industrializing countries, the patterns of demand are likely to differ from market to market, depending on consumer preferences, government regulations, and local manufacturing requirements. As a consequence, the 2020 model-year vehicle in Pakistan may exhibit much different features from the same model-year vehicle in Ecuador.

In industrializing nations today, one does see vehicles typically targeted for the United States and Europe. To accommodate different market and regulatory requirements, automobile companies have achieved the capability of adapting vehicles with minor technical changes for export to both industrialized and developing markets. For example, Mercedes-Benz installs exhaust systems that satisfy U.S. environmental regulations for exports to North America while retaining conventional exhaust systems for Europe. Honda's United States plant affixes right-hand steering-wheel mechanisms for exports to the United Kingdom, Japan, and other markets with similar driving conventions.

Instead of evolving toward the uniformity of a prototype car of the future, diversity among vehicles seems to be proliferating. Even since the 1980s, automobile companies have been introducing a variety of models and styles for particular market niches. In 1994, a survey of automobile manufacturers revealed sixty different models of sport utility vehicles alone with various options. The diversity stems from changes in the traditional styling and performance characteristics—bigger or smaller engines for power or fuel efficiency, wider bodies and cargo space, larger or more compact bodies, or improvements in braking, suspension, handling, and

TABLE 1. Future Motor Vehicle Production

	Industrialized Countries			Developing Countries				
	United States	Germany	Japan	Korea	China	India	Mexico	TOTAL
	Average Growth Rate							
1970–1990	3%	2%	3%	25%	12%	8%	9%	4%
1985–1990	2%	3%	2%	35%	16%	14%	14%	4%
Est. Growth rate	2%	2%	2%	10%	12%	10%	9%	3%
	Future Production							
1990	9,782,997	4,976,552	13,486,796	1,321,630	509,242	364,181	820,558	31,261,956
1994	10,180,226	5,386,780	14,598,542	1,934,998	801,302	533,197	1,158,285	34,593,330
2000	10,806,515	6,066,389	16,440,329	3,427,968	1,581,628	944,592	1,942,559	41,209,980
2010	11,937,116	7,394,894	20,040,669	8,891,266	4,912,298	2,450,028	4,598,744	60,225,014
2020	13,186,002	9,014,335	24,429,464	23,061,654	15,256,851	6,354,741	10,886,900	102,189,946

Sources: World Automotive Market Report 1994–1995, Auto & Truck International; World Motor Vehicle Data 1992 Edition, Motor Vehicle Manufacturers Association of the United States, Inc.

Note: The total growth rates are calculated by weighting with production of 1990.

safety. Future changes are likely to embody changes in societal preferences and needs.

The extent of product diversity will surely widen. By the year 2020, industrialized markets with high per capita incomes will continue to demand variety in vehicles with costly electronic equipment, innovative materials, and differing power sources such as batteries or natural gas. The industrializing nations will seek basic transportation at affordable prices. Unless consumers in the United States and other industrialized nations are willing to freeze the level of technology in their vehicles while developing nations attain parity, the possibility of a universal world model vehicle, even one with some adaptability and variation, seems remote.

In the year 2020, cars will still look and drive much as they do today. Some cars will appear sleeker or fatter than they did in 1995. It may even seem that the styles leap backward a few decades to hot rods of the 1950s or to the Corvettes and Thunderbirds of the 1960s, while the appearance of others may seem to bypass a decade or two with lines and angles akin to a Stealth fighter. Some may accelerate faster or slower. Some may streak along the Autobahn, while others putter around city streets and culs-de-sac of suburban neighborhoods or unpaved roads in Peru or Bombay. All vehicles will brake and ride on suspension systems much improved from today and weighing between 10 and 25 percent less.

Except for cosmetic changes in body styling and modifications in performance as measured by acceleration, speed, handling, and feel of the ride, the car of the future will still look like a direct descendant of the car of today. Most people can envision these incremental improvements or engineered adaptations of existing technologies refined to reflect consumer preferences. The revolutionary changes that would radically transform the mobility for the automobile are still undergoing futuristic planning on designers' worktables or computer-aided design systems. Certainly, such chimera as steering by remote controls and videos or vehicles hovering magically over highways are not practical possibilities for the year 2020.

Overriding changes in the car of the future will pass undetected by the eye, at least at first appearance. A few vehicles, though not many, will harness batteries for electric propulsion instead of the gasoline engine. A few others will install canisters for compressed or liquefied natural gas. Most will still fill up with gasoline or diesel fuel, although these fuels may be treated with ethanol, methanol, or other chemicals that improve combustion and thus lower the expulsion of pollutants.

The significant changes will come from a set of consumer priorities emphasizing unique materials, highly efficient engine designs, and extremely crash-resistant structures and apparatus to protect driver and passengers.

The Automobile as a Symbol of Society

The automobile symbolizes the society that produces it. The Volkswagen became the car of the people; the Ferrari, the essence of Italian styling; the Chevy, Ford, and Chrysler, the manifestations of the American dream. The automobile in the United States and other countries represents the icon of society—its values, clashes, conflicts, and contradictions. People wait in traffic jams for hours rather than riding a train or subway; the internal-combustion engine pollutes the air, yet drivers putter around streets carefree. Drivers cherish safety and the sanctity of life, yet they refuse to wear seat belts and often oppose laws requiring motorists to do so.

As a symbol of society, the automobile will conform to societal values as they change. Three factors are reorganizing the social values of the United States and other countries: (1) the environment and management and resource conservation; (2) traffic congestion; and (3) the outpouring of technical innovations, particularly materials and electronics such as computers and telecommunications. While each of these factors has influenced the design, manufacture, and use of the automobile, primarily through government regulation, only in recent years have companies begun to incorporate these factors into their strategies for product development. As these factors grow in influence, they will shape consumer preferences, the economics, and the politics involved in the automobile.

Environment and Resource Conservation

For years consumers recognized the damage to the environment and depletion of natural resources inflicted by the automobile. Various regulations have attempted to curb the automobile's excesses. The U.S. government and other governments have imposed corporate average fuel efficiency (CAFE) or comparable regulations for cars to reduce the amount of energy utilized and pollutants emitted. The oil crises in 1973 and 1979 alerted consumers to the authentic concerns of resource depletion, although with lowering oil prices and additional surplus, the trend has been shifting to vehicles with increasing fuel usage. Nonetheless, the price of oil, a finite resource, will escalate, which will inevitably reduce the demand for excessive gas-guzzling engines.

Regulations, in seeking to sustain the environment, are transforming ecology into a highly prized commodity in the market. Recently the United States, Sweden, and other European countries have enacted regulations for reformulated fuel to reduce tailpipe emissions. The laws and regulations in nearly every nation imposing restraints have scheduled increasingly stringent requirements to be phased in over the next decade. In Germany, environmental concerns spawned laws about recycling the automobile.

Overall, the welling importance of the environment has become irreversible. In the worst case, environmental regulations may stall at present levels. Yet, a wholesale relaxation of environmental controls to the level of the 1950s and '60s remains improbable. Consumer awareness of environmental and resource management is evident in several pockets of demand such as vehicles that are fuel efficient, enhanced with front and side air bags, and even the nonpolluting exhaust of the electric car, which, unfortunately, may only transfer the source of pollution from individual vehicles to power-generating plants.

Congestion

Few cities in the world are exempt from traffic jams: New York; Frankfurt, Germany; Milan, Italy; Los Angeles; Tokyo; and other cities in industrialized countries all are experiencing a growing concern with traffic congestion. However, even in the developing countries, congestion is a major problem—as, for example, in such cities as São Paulo and Rio de Janeiro in Brazil, Mexico City, and Seoul, Korea. Congestion around the world will contribute to a rethinking of the entire issue of mobility. There are many implications to the congestion problem. One is the effect on the environment and on resource conservation. Waiting in traffic jams exhausts vast supplies of oil while contributing to the decline in the quality of air. Equally important is the decline in productivity of drivers and passengers. In many large cities, passengers may compensate by utilizing mobile telephones for communications or hand-held dictating machines. If the automobile can be turned into a mobile office, the productivity loss would decline. Similarly, revamping cars to consume less or perhaps no fossil fuel blunts some of the impact. Yet congestion exacts a price with delays and frustration on motorists.

Technological Advancement

By some estimates, the car of the 1990s contains more computing than the first landing craft on the moon. During the past three decades, an avalanche of technical innovation has occurred, particularly in computers, telecommunications, electronics, and materials. Samsung estimates that in the next twenty years approximately half the weight of the car will be in electronic components instead of metal body parts and engines. These present multiple benefits. Materials such as polymers, plastics, and composites contribute to lowering the weight of the car, which reduces fuel use and air pollution. Other technologies, such as fiber optics, are already in use in some cars, further lightening the weight of the automobile and reducing pollution and gas consumption without sacrificing safety.

Automobile companies as well as other technology-based companies with computers and telecommunications are investigating the intelligent vehicle highway system (IVHS), which allows drivers to determine their location and optimum routes. Such technologies may indeed allow the automobile to become a mobile office with guidance systems and mechanisms for piloting the automobile without the full attention of the driver. The electronic car may ease the congestion by circumnavigating through alternate routes. Other electronics may aid in stabilizing and braking the automobile while others correct for driver error by monitoring the distance between vehicles and automatically stopping the car to avoid a collision.

Social Choices: Preferences, Economics, and Politics

Over the next twenty-five years, it seems likely that consumer attitudes and preferences will vary over each of these social concerns as they have over other social values. These preferences will swing depending on perception of environmental damage, seriousness of resource mishandling, choices for mobility, and acceptance of new technologies. Without addressing either the economics or the politics of each of these issues, consumer preferences are likely to remain mixed. Nuclear power is an example. Many oppose nuclear power regardless of its costs; they would oppose it even if it were free. Similar controversies arise with genetic engineering, biotechnology, and even the environment itself. As technology accelerates, creating more questions than answers, consumer preferences are likely to splinter about the relative importance of these various issues.

Foreseeing the car of the future inevitably drags in economics as the yardstick of social preferences. For the most part, the issues attach themselves more to economics than to technology. Many of the technologies that may be commercialized in the future are feasible today. Examples are the electric car and IVHS. Consumers could acquire these technologies; however, they may shy away from paying the price of an electric car, including the inconvenience of recharging the battery and limited range and speed. IVHS technology exists; yet it requires a major infrastructure change to implement. Neither politicians nor consumers appear willing to invest the sums necessary for these technologies to achieve commercial application. Clearly, some technologies in the early stages of development cost more than they will after the innovations are accepted into the market and economies of scale in manufacturing kick in. Nonetheless, if consumers are willing to buy electric cars for some multiple of the price for a comparable gasoline-powered vehicle, they can do so.

Similarly, economics influences social decisions about the environment, congestion, and technology. While most people would agree that clean air is important they often balk when asked to pay for the clean environment through higher-priced fuel or increased inspections on automobiles. Others are willing to pay a higher price for the fuel, while still others want no change at all despite the preference for clean air. The same applies to congestion and technology. While many commuters may prefer to drive to work, at some point, the price of the automobile will induce those commuters to seek alternative means such as commuter rail or buses. As a consequence, economics winnows the possibilities for the car of the future.

Politics further limits the car of the future. Market failures, typified by environmental degradation and traffic congestion, invite political intervention to correct the problems. While some motorists may selflessly volunteer to drive less to save fuel and to shield the environment from further degradation, most will not without government incentive or enforcement. The political process may incorporate regulations or requirements of the automobile that reflect preferences for some as well as higher costs and specification of particular technologies and materials.

Politics affects the car of the future in other ways besides regulating characteristics and requirements for specific automobiles. Almost every government in the world seeks to attract investments in the national automobile industry. The reasoning is apparent. As the automobile often symbolizes the improvement in society for both industrialized and developing nations, the automobile industry produces thousands of jobs directly in the plant, with suppliers, and with the retail sector. Countries such as those in the EU that are trying to reject investment by Japanese auto plants in their countries may limit themselves to domestic technologies and types of cars while rejecting the innovations of the Japanese firms. Similarly, some countries attract investment, but the companies themselves may prefer to transfer vehicle models that fit the needs of the country rather than use the latest technologies.

The Company of the Future

The most significant change in the future will occur not with the automobile itself but with the companies that manufacture them. With the proliferation of models and technologies, the automobile industry will undergo a transformation of its structure. In many ways it will resemble the automobile industry before Henry Ford introduced the assembly line in Highland Park, Michigan.

In the industry's formative years, the vehicles themselves took on many different characteristics. Essentially there was no uniformity in automobile design and characteristics. Some models installed steam or electricity for power systems; others located the gasoline engines in the front, rear, or center of the chassis. Some experimented with hand brakes and throttles and an assortment of steering mechanisms. Customized for individual owners, each vehicle was distinctive and unique—no two were identical.

By 1908, a dominant design for the automobile was emerging. This design represented a consensus among consumers about the preferred features and characteristics in an automobile. Consumer experimentation with various designs and models converged into a relatively standardized, uniform automobile with rubber tires, gasoline engines, foot pedals for the throttle, brake, and the clutch, and front-end-mounted engine. Only after the design of the automobile stabilized could Henry Ford begin the assembly line to produce identical cars.

A similar fragmentation is likely to occur in the automobile industry with change in social values toward the environment, resource conservation, mobility, and new technologies. Experimentation is ongoing with battery-powered cars, natural gas combustion engines, reformulated fuels, new materials, and novel electronic and navigational technologies. Society is still pondering and debating the social value of the environment, resource management, mobility, and the direction of various technologies without having yet reached a consensus. This debate could persist for decades before being resolved. Meanwhile, the discovery of new technologies and the refinement of existing, but as yet unmarketed, technologies will influence social choices, demand patterns, and production processes, particularly as commercialization of technical alternatives affects their production costs, the environment, and the risks of society.

The technical diversity of automobiles of the future implies the necessity for equally diverse business practices for manufacturers. The rate of technological change has been accelerating so rapidly that hardly any one company holds a mastery of all the technology required for its vehicles. The pace will continue. If automobile companies do try to develop technologies solely by themselves rather than relying on specialist companies, such as suppliers or other automobile companies, these go-it-alone companies will tend to incur higher costs than they would otherwise.

Despite some adaptability in product diversity, many companies currently encounter difficulties in gaining flexibility for extensive model changes for a number of reasons—technical rigidity in the production process, organizational inertia to adapt flexible methods, unyielding labor responsiveness on the assembly line, and unmanageable sources of supply. To accomplish the technological goals, automobile companies will be engaging in joint ventures with other companies.

Some joint ventures will link horizontally, such as the present one between General Motors (GM) and Toyota in the New United Motor Manufacturing, Inc. (NUMMI). Each of the two firms are exploiting the other's competitive advantage lacking in their respective organizations. Such collaborations may include product design, marketing, manufacturing, or a set of skills such as the lean production technique that Toyota had honed, but GM lacked in the United States.

Other types of joint ventures are likely to develop vertically. Some will reach backward to suppliers. With the increasing cost of development, automobile companies are finding that suppliers' special knowledge and skills can design modular components such as suspension or braking systems at less cost and in a shorter time to meet market demands. Others will move forward to distributors and sales organizations, which themselves will employ unique marketing technologies such as computer ordering from home and virtual reality test drives of various vehicles.

See also MOTOR VEHICLES, ALTERNATIVELY POWERED; PERSONAL TRANSPORT; TRANSPORTATION; URBAN TRANSIT.

BIBLIOGRAPHY

ARNESEN, PETER J., ed. *The Auto Industry Ahead: Who's Driving?* Ann Arbor, MI: University of Michigan Center for Japanese Studies, 1989.

Automobiles and the Future: Competition, Cooperation, and Change. Warrendale, PA: Society of Automotive Engineers, 1989.

COLE, ROBERT E., ed. *The American Automobile Industry: Rebirth or Requiem?* Ann Arbor, MI: University of Michigan Center for Japanese Studies, 1984.

LAW, CHRISTOPHER M., ed. *Restructuring the Global Automobile Industry: Global, National, and Regional Impacts.* New York: Routledge, 1991.

Frank C. Schuller

Motor Vehicles, Alternatively Powered

Petroleum fuels have powered virtually all motor vehicles since the early years of this century. That is likely to change. The leading contenders are ethanol, methanol, natural gas, hydrogen, and electricity. The use of these alternative fuels would reduce petroleum consumption and provide at least some environmental advantage relative to gasoline and diesel fuel. Their relative attractiveness will depend upon the perceived importance of energy and environmental goals, the cost of producing and delivering fuels, and the cost and performance of vehicles that consume those fuels. In general, those energy options with the greatest environmental advantages face the largest start-up barriers, and those with the smallest environmental advantages face the smallest start-up barriers.

Alcohol fuels (ethanol and methanol) require the least change in vehicle design and the least investment in new infrastructure. They also provide the smallest air pollution benefits and provide few or no greenhouse gas benefits when made from natural gas, grains, and sugar crops.

Pure ethanol made from sugar cane has been used to power vehicles in Brazil since 1980. At its peak in the mid-1980s, over 90 percent of the country's new cars and light trucks were designed to burn ethanol. Ethanol's share of the new car market slowly eroded thereafter to about half the new car market by the mid-1990s. In the United States, ethanol is made mostly from corn and only used as an additive. It is mixed with petroleum in small proportions to produce a "cleaner burning" gasoline. In that form, it has accounted for about 5 to 8 percent of U.S. gasoline consumption since the early 1980s.

When made from corn, ethanol's environmental and energy advantages are virtually nonexistent. Ethanol combustion in vehicles emits somewhat fewer and less-reactive air pollutants than gasoline combustion, but large amounts of fossil fuel are used in growing, harvesting, and processing the corn. The net result is that ethanol made from corn in the United States has about the same greenhouse gas emissions as gasoline. It is also much more expensive. Ethanol is used in the United States because of generous subsidies from the federal government and various corn-growing midwestern states.

Methanol made from natural gas is widely used for a variety of industrial purposes. It is less expensive than ethanol on an energy–equivalent basis but up to 30 percent more costly in monetary terms than gasoline. It received considerable attention through the 1980s, largely because of its potential to reduce air pollution. In the early 1990s, several thousand methanol vehicles were sold in the United States by major automakers. These so-called flexible-fuel vehicles (FFVs) require minimal modification, and cost and perform about the same as gasoline vehicles. While the vehicles can operate on any mixture of gasoline and methanol, in practice the methanol fuel was sold as a 85/15 mixture with gasoline. The 15 percent gasoline was blended in for safety to assure that the fuel would burn with a visible flame, and for performance to facilitate starting in cold weather. These methanol/gasoline blends tend to have a small positive effect on vehicle emissions and little or no net effect on greenhouse gas emissions. If used as 100 percent methanol, the air quality benefits would be much greater, but the fuel would be less safe and not start well in cold weather.

Alternatively, methanol and ethanol could be made from cellulosic biomass—that is, from trees and grasses. The U.S. Department of Energy has provided substantial R&D support for this option since the 1970s. The first attraction of these biomass fuels is potentially lower cost. The second is greatly reduced greenhouse gas emissions (because cultivation is less energy intensive. (The biomass can be burned to power the processing plants, and carbon dioxide emissions resulting from combustion can be recycled through photosynthesis.) The disadvantages are large land requirements, increased soil erosion, and possible reductions in biodiversity.

Oil refiners have responded to the alcohol fuel challenge by reformulating gasoline to reduce vehicular emissions. Since first introduced in Los Angeles in 1989 by ARCO, oil refiners have made steady progress. Costing less and providing almost as much air quality benefit, reformulated gasoline has undermined interest in methanol and ethanol.

Perhaps the leading alternative fuel for internal combustion engines is natural gas. Rather than conversion to methanol, natural gas instead can be burned directly, just like gasoline and alcohol fuels. Over half a million vehicles operate on natural gas worldwide. In almost all vehicles, natural gas is stored inboard in pressurized tanks and almost all have bi-fuel capability, allowing the driver to change from natural gas to gasoline by simply flipping a switch inside the vehicle. Because they are simpler and can be optimized for a single fuel, dedicated natural gas vehicles are superior to bi-fuel vehicles in terms of cost, emissions, performance, and energy efficiency. But unless natural gas is available at many fuel stations, consumers will not buy the vehicles and manufacturers will not build or sell them. Dedicated natural gas vehicles have greater potential to reduce emissions than methanol and ethanol, would have lower life cycle costs under most conditions (the extra $1,000 for storage tanks being roughly offset by lower fuel costs), and somewhat lower greenhouse gas emissions.

Hydrogen is an attractive transportation fuel because it can be produced from a large number of renewable feedstocks and has great potential to drastically reduce all regulated automobile emissions. However, high production costs and low energy density will prevent hydrogen from being a plausible transportation fuel for many years. The first application of hydrogen fuel will probably be in electric vehicles (EVs) using fuel cells rather than direct combustion in dedicated hydrogen vehicles. Fuel cells convert hydrogen, methanol, and other fuels into electricity that can then be used to power vehicles. Fuel cells have a much higher ratio of power output to weight than batteries, but their bulkiness and high costs have so far precluded their use in automobiles. Rapid strides have been made during the 1990s in reducing the cost and size of fuel cells.

Electric vehicle research has focused on battery development for inboard electricity storage. The major international automobile manufacturers have prototype electric vehicles that can travel at freeway speeds and are capable of eighty or more miles of travel per charge. A number of smaller companies are also developing battery-powered EVs.

EV success does not hinge on battery technology advances alone. Advances being made in drivetrain efficiencies, lightweight materials, and recharging rates could make EVs a viable option for many households and business fleets within the next decade. These improvements may even make it possible to downsize EV batteries, which in turn would decrease the vehicle purchase cost (batteries are the largest cost component of an EV).

In addition to battery-powered EVs, research is also progressing on hybrid electric vehicles. These combine a small internal combustion engine (gas turbine, diesel, or spark ignition) with an electric motor and electricity storage device (probably a battery). The small combustion engine provides a longer range but with much fewer emissions and petroleum use than a gasoline vehicle.

Electric vehicles are a tantalizing prospect because of their unsurpassed potential to reduce drastically automobile emissions, greenhouse gases, and petroleum use. In most situations, even with today's relatively inefficient fossil-fuel power plants, the use of an electric vehicle would nearly eliminate hydrocarbon and carbon monoxide emissions and petroleum use, reduce nitrogen oxides by over 50 percent, and moderately reduce greenhouse gases. With fuel cells, the adavantages would be even greater.

Although it will take some years, perhaps decades, for alternative fuels to replace petroleum on a large scale, their role in transportation will be determined by decisions made today. An immediate transition to marginally cleaner fuels may be the path of least resistance, but it could come at the expensive of forestalling alternatives that offer far more substantial benefits. In any case, government intervention will play a vital role in the development of alternative fuel markets because neither energy security nor environmental issues are fully accounted for in the marketplace. No alternative fuel is a clear winner or loser (except perhaps ethanol made from corn). The fuels used to power automobiles of the future will depend on political convictions, technological advances, and the tenacity with which the petroleum industry protects the status quo.

See also ELECTRIC POWER; ENERGY, RENEWABLE SOURCES OF; MOTOR VEHICLES; PERSONAL TRANSPORT; PETROLEUM.

BIBLIOGRAPHY

AYRES, ROBERT U., AND MCKENNA, RICHARD P. *Alternatives to the Internal Combustion Engine: Impacts on Environmental Quality.* Baltimore: Johns Hopkins University Press, 1972.

Recent Advances in Electric Vehicle Technology. Warrendale, PA: Society of Automotive Engineers, 1989.

SEIFFERT, ULRICH, and WALZER, PETER. *Automobile Technology of the Future.* Warrendale, PA: Society of Automotive Engineers, 1991.

Daniel Sperling
Kevin Nesbitt

Multifold Trend

Herman KAHN was one of the great futurist thinkers of the twentieth century. Although many people disagreed with him—especially in the period just before his untimely death in 1983, when he openly supported the policies of the Reagan administration—no one ever questioned his awesome intellect or his well-informed, broad-ranging, and provocative ideas.

Perhaps the most important concept that Kahn fashioned, one that could well benefit futures thinkers of today and tomorrow, is his "basic, long-term multifold trend."

The idea of a multifold trend of interacting elements was seen as an important organizational concept—a "long-term base line which may include within it certain short-term fluctuations." It was assumed that "in most countries of the world it looks as if this Multifold Trend is going to continue, but with important differences in detail in various areas." Nor does the trend suggest beneficial progress: "This is just the way the world seems to be going in the long run, like it or not."

According to Kahn, the multifold trend "goes back about a thousand years and is one of the most basic and enduring tendencies of Western culture." It is best seen as a single entity, where every aspect is to some degree both a cause and an effect. Despite leading and lagging sectors, it goes in one direction—at least on the average and over a long period of time. But it should not be thought of as a fixed, straight railroad track: "We should allow for some curves, some switching back and forth, and even occasional changes in railroad lines."

At least three largely similar versions of the multifold trend concept were published—in 1967, 1972, and 1979. The 1979 version is presented below, slightly abbreviated:

1. *Increasingly sensate culture*—empirical, this-worldly, secular, humanistic, pragmatic, manipulative, rational, hedonistic, recently exhibiting an almost complete decline of the sacred.
2. *Accumulation of scientific and technological knowledge.*
3. *Institutionalization of technological change*, especially research, development, innovation, and diffusion.
4. *Increasing role of bourgeois, bureaucratic, "meritocratic" elites*, increasing literacy and education for everyone.
5. *Increasing military capability of Western cultures*—recently, issues of mass destruction, terrorism, and the diffusion of advanced military technologies (both nuclear and conventional) to non-Western cultures.
6. *Increasing area of world dominated or greatly influenced by Western culture*, but recent emphasis on synthesis with indigenous cultures and various "ethnic" revivals.
7. *Increasing affluence*, recently with more stress on egalitarianism.
8. *Increasing rate of world population growth*, until recently—this rate has probably passed its zenith or soon will.
9. *Urbanization*—and, recently, suburbanization and "urban sprawl"; soon the growth of megalopoli, "sun belts," and rural areas with urban infrastructure and amenities.
10. *Increasing recent attention to macroenvironmental issues*—e.g., constraints set by finiteness of Earth and limited capacity of various local and global reservoirs to accept pollution.
11. *Decreasing importance of primary and recently secondary occupations*—soon a similar decline in tertiary occupations and increasing emphasis on advanced, honorific, or desirable quaternary occupations and activities (quaternary occupations are defined by Kahn as those that render services to tertiary occupations or to each other).
12. *Emphasis on "progress" and future-oriented thinking, discussion, and planning*—recently, some retrogression in the technical quality of such activities.
13. *Increasing universality of the multifold trend.*
14. *Increasing tempo of change* in all the above areas, though this may soon peak in many areas.

Sixteen years later (1995), how does the multifold trend concept hold up?

Clearly, many of the elements still ring quite true, especially item 2, the accumulation of knowledge;

item 3, technological change; item 5, weapons proliferation; item 6, the peaking of rate of world population growth, (although the actual numbers added per year will continue at top levels for perhaps another decade); item 9, urbanization; item 10, macroenvironmental issues; item 13, the universality of the multifold trend; and item 14, the growing tempo of change.

Two of these trends deserve special comment. Technological change (item 3) as envisioned in 1967 was clearly overstated. Many of Kahn's list of "one hundred technical innovations very likely in the last third of the twentieth century" have not come about, or are not yet nearly as widespread as envisioned. In contrast, the focus on macroenvironmental issues (item 10), which was absent in the 1967 and 1972 versions of the multifold trend, may well be understated. As several authors have noted, the twenty-first century is likely to be "the Century of the Environment," in which issues of sustainability are the major driving forces of human action, and necessary actions reverse certain tendencies of industrialism and modernity.

Two of the fourteen elements have reversed direction over the past decade or so, and seem likely to continue at least in the near future: item 1, the trend to sensate culture and item 7, the increasing affluence and egalitarianism. Contrary to the widespread expectations of social science that the role of the spiritual would continue to wane—a process that Kahn thought "may be the single most important aspect of the long-term Multifold Trend"—religion has taken on new forms (fundamentalism, Pentacostalism, New Age spirituality) and is doing quite well, despite the decline of mainline Protestant denominations. If anything, it is social science that has faltered. As for the expected trend toward greater affluence, growth in real income has been stable or declining for most people over the last decade or so, and gaps between the rich and poor (both within and between countries) have been growing.

Three other elements of Kahn's multifold trend are ambiguous at best: item 4, increasing literacy and education; and item 11, the shift to "quaternary" occupations, and item 12, futures thinking and planning. Absolute progress in literacy and education for all is problematic; indeed, in view of rising standards and more-or-less constant (if not declining) levels of achievement, it could well be said that we are falling behind. A "knowledge industry" has emerged, but it does not account for much employment, nor is it in an overall robust condition at present. There has been an ongoing decline of primary (agricultural) and secondary

(manufacturing) occupations, and a decline in tertiary (service) occupations is underway, reflected in downsizing of many public and private organizations. But this is not resulting in great numbers of desirable quaternary occupations; rather, new jobs in all sectors are characterized as part-time, contingent, and generally poorly paid. Progress in "future-oriented thinking, discussion, and planning" is stagnant at best.

In sum, nine of the fourteen elements of the multifold trend still hold true, although one of these was notably overstated, and one was understated. Two of the elements have clearly reversed and three others have probably reversed. Kahn warned of "curves, switching back and forth, and occasional changes in railroad lines." The key question deserving intense ongoing debate is whether changes in the elements of the multifold trend represent temporary "switching back and forth" (perhaps over a matter of decades), or whether we have switched tracks and railroad lines, moving in a substantially new direction toward some vision of a sustainable world. Most observers would argue for the latter interpretation.

Despite falling well short of perfection, is Kahn's batting average of hits versus misses a respectable one? No judgment is possible, because futurists, unlike baseball players, have not been rated on their successes. We can say that, unlike many others, Kahn swung for the fences in pronouncing on most if not all of the big issues.

Whatever the flaws of the older versions, the multifold trend is still a key idea. If Herman Kahn were still around, he surely would have provided the needed updating.

See also CHANGE; CHANGE, PACE OF; GLOBAL CULTURE; SUSTAINABILITY; TECHNOLOGY DIFFUSION.

BIBLIOGRAPHY

KAHN, HERMAN, and WIENER, ANTHONY J. *The Year 2000: A Framework for Speculation on the Next Thirty-Three Years.* New York: Macmillan, 1967.

KAHN, HERMAN, and BRUCE-BRIGGS, B. *Things to Come: Thinking About the Seventies and Eighties.* New York: Macmillan, 1972.

KAHN, HERMAN. *World Economic Development: Projections from 1978 to the Year 2000.* Boulder, CO: Westview Press, 1979. Brief adaptation in the *Futurist* 13:3 (June 1979): 202–222.

MCKENZIE-MOHR, DOUG, and MARIEN, MICHAEL, eds. "Visions of Sustainability." *Futures* 26:2 (March 1994): 115–256.

Michael Marien

Museums

Museums are at once conservative and innovative institutions. They are conservative in their traditional functions of collecting and preserving material culture and natural history. They are innovative in their many efforts to interpret and exhibit this heritage to the public. In the future, they are likely to experience increasing tension as they attempt to fulfill long-standing missions and expand programs for public service in the face of straitened financial circumstances. How they respond will test their abilities to innovate.

While most European museums began as princely collections in search of a public purpose, American museums began as public-spirited ideas in the minds of civic leaders. The signal contribution of United States museums has been democratization.

The great institutions founded in the nineteenth century were committed to advancing and diffusing knowledge. Historical societies, art collections, natural history museums, and zoos justified their existence in terms of public service. Newer types of museums, including art centers, children's museums, nature centers, and science and technology centers, are even more clearly dedicated to education. Many of them do not own collections but borrow them for display. Others use reproductions and hands-on exhibits to promote understanding of art, nature, or technology and scientific principles. These new types of museums testify to the responsiveness of the museum as an institution to trends in scholarship and public demand for education.

Museums respond to the cultural diversity in the United States and to pressing public policy issues. Although ethnic museums are not new—the American Swedish Historical Foundation and Museum in Philadelphia, for example, was founded in 1926—specifically African-American museums are new. While black schools and colleges long collected art and artifacts, most black museums were founded in the wake of the civil rights movement. With their emphasis on contemporary problems and community service, they have pushed the museum to a further democratization. There are more than one hundred African-American museums in the United States, and the Smithsonian Institution is committed to developing an African-American museum on the National Mall.

The Smithsonian recently established the National Museum of the American Indian. Now tribal councils throughout the country are calling for museums to rethink the way they have displayed native cultures and to return human remains and sacred objects. Across the street from the Smithsonian complex in Washington is the new United States Holocaust Memorial Museum. It testifies to the sensitivity of the museum as an institution to cultural consciousness and to new exhibit techniques.

Museums of all types are increasingly responsive to social issues. Art museums with exhibits on ecology, history museums with exhibits on endangered species, university museums with exhibits on sexual abuse, or natural history museums with exhibits on garbage or waste amply demonstrate that conventional museums are engaging in public policy debates in an attempt to move visitors to action rather than mere contemplation.

Attendance is generally on the increase. In 1988 American museums had more than half a billion visits. On average, Americans visit a museum or participate in a museum program three times a year. However, financial support is not on the increase. To help cover expenses, more than half of all museums now charge admission, and many have established development offices, fund-raising programs, and endowments. Recent trends indicate that private support for museums is increasing, while the percentage of museum income from government allocations and from earned income (including admission fees) is declining.

Other forces shaping museums include the broad desire to touch, handle, and experience, not merely to see or listen. Museums are forming alliances and branches to make better use of their holdings. Most important of all will be the effects of information technology. Computers and information networks will serve to open museums to the wider world, providing endless depths of information on any artifact or work of art for the real or virtual visitor.

In the future, museums will use a variety of imaginative strategies to educate and to secure the financial support required. They will defend their traditional roles as the collectors and preservers of natural and human history at the same time that they broaden their audiences and their base of public support. They will find it financially difficult to compete in the art market for new acquisitions and will be constrained by the need to comply with legal restrictions regarding cultural materials and natural specimens.

See also ART DEALERS; ARTS; CLOTHING; INTERACTIVE ENTERTAINMENT; MASS CULTURE AND ARTS; VISUAL ARTS.

BIBLIOGRAPHY

COATES, JOSEPH F. "The Future of Museums." *The Futurist* (August 1984): 40–45.

Excellence and Equity: Education and the Public Dimension of Museums. Washington, DC: American Association of Museums, 1992.

Museums Count. Washington, DC: American Association of Museums, 1994.

Museums for a New Century: A Report of the Commission on Museums for a New Century. Washington, DC: American Association of Museums, 1984.

Ann Hofstra Grogg

Music

Music has always played a role in both shaping society and reflecting its verve. Before the widespread advent of the printed word, wandering minstrels helped communicate stories of the times. Soul singers and blues balladeers, folksingers, and rappers have sometimes exerted powerful influence over social and political change. That which artists play and sing emotes pathos, pinpoints problems, and gives meaning to people's hopes and aspirations—the very grist of social change.

Music fulfills many roles. National anthems help to unify countries. Theatrical productions like *Hair* or *Oh Calcutta!* are both a response to changing sexual mores and a stimulus for such changes. Classical music, because of the considerable expense involved in its performance (especially when larger performing forces are required), has generally been more beholden to official channels for dissemination. Even so, classical music composition today seems to be moving out of its ghetto of governmentally and corporately subsidized elitism. Contemporary works are being created in an enormous variety of styles, with a slowly growing degree of popular support. More broadly, the emergence of a global community is also serving to blur the distinctions between different types of music and to foster a true multicultural awareness, the likes of which have perhaps never been seen before.

Rock music is as good an explanation as any for the fall of the Berlin Wall. The relationship between rock music and former East German youth poignantly illustrates the complex roles of music within the overall social context. The production of music is influenced by the ongoing impact of technological change. Musical styles today are being shaped by seemingly opposite trends of increased globalization and a renewal of indigenization. The interrelated development of music and technology points toward our social future.

When the Soviet Union took over the eastern part of Germany during the late 1940s, it decided that the imposition of Soviet culture could not stamp out Nazi values. Instead, East Germans were encouraged to return to traditional German culture, including German classical music, and from those roots to forge a new East German society distinct from that of West Germany. However, unlike citizens of other authoritarian regimes such as Albania and North Korea, East Germans could not be isolated from the rest of the world. In particular, residents of East Berlin could see and hear television and radio broadcasts from West Germany and from the Western occupying forces.

Coincidentally, just as the Berlin Wall went up, rock music became a world music, and the Wall could not keep it out. The East German government, in acknowledgment of the power of this invading cultural form, encouraged its musicians to make their own rock music. At first, these musicians merely copied Western rock, but in a few years they began to incorporate elements from their own musical tradition, elements better able to accommodate the German language and sensibility, and, finally, to make uniquely East German rock with politically charged lyrics.

Bypassing state sponsorship and a state owned recording company, some peripheral East German musicians succeeded in self-producing and distributing their own inexpensive cassette tapes, as did their Soviet counterparts and other musicians around the world. Primarily in the United States and Western Europe, but also in such far-flung and impoverished places as Jamaica and Nigeria, musicians are self-producing professional-quality tapes, vinyl recordings, and, more recently, compact disks. Although distribution of these recordings in many cases remains localized, some well-known musicians distribute self-produced, high-quality material worldwide, and some types of inexpensive homemade tapes are heard throughout large regions. For example, highly politicized, self-produced tapes appear everywhere in South and Central America.

Another manifestation of the ability of musicians to work outside the recording industry and to profit directly from their own work lies in the proliferation of live music around the world as more musicians form local groups and perform for local audiences. These groups, although often culturally and politically opposed to the values of the established recording industry, are a source of innovation and raw talent for core production, a facet of the tension between increasing globalization and strengthening indigenization of cultural products.

The West has sent music, classical and popular, to the rest of the world for centuries. This music has influenced, but has not obliterated, indigenous cultural creativity. Western rock music is itself a combination of West African and European musical elements as combined by slaves, sailors, soldiers, and ministers as well as, in more recent times, direct and recorded contact among professional musicians. With the advent of recording technology and jet travel, the pace of musical experimentation has accelerated tremendously. The internationalized range of musical elements available to musicians now is further enhanced by the infinite possibilities afforded by electronic and computer technology.

Electronic technology also has separated performance of live music and production of recorded music into two distinct art forms. For decades now, recording experts have lamented their inability to reproduce accurately the ambience of live music, a gap that is rapidly closing with the development of virtual sound and digital signal processing whereby sounds can be adjusted electronically and accurately to various types of listening environments. At the same time, recording technology has made possible musical experiences that cannot be repeated on stage.

The fall of the Berlin Wall symbolizes emerging global harmony at the same time that ethnic divisions in the former Yugoslavia and Somalia indicate a desire for more localized cultural identification and control over everyday situations. Current production of music presents the same contradictory picture of the new global order where more collaborative decisions are made on an international level while, at the same time, people everywhere assume responsibility for their own affairs.

See also ARTS; LITERATURE; MASS CULTURE AND ARTS; PERFORMING ARTS; VISUAL ARTS.

BIBLIOGRAPHY

ATTALI, JACQUES. *Noise: The Political Economy of Music.* Minneapolis: University of Minnesota Press, 1985.
JONES, STEVE. *Rock Formation: Technology, Music and Mass Communication.* Newbury Park, CA: Sage Publications, 1992.
NETTL, BRUNO. *The Western Impact on World Music: Change, Adaptation, and Survival.* New York: Schirmer, 1985.
ROBINSON, DEANNA CAMPBELL; BUCK, ELIZABETH B.; CUTHBERT, MARLENE; and the International Communication and Youth Culture Consortium. *Music at the Margins: Popular Music and Global Cultural Diversity.* Newbury Park, CA: Sage Publications, 1991.
WALLIS, ROGER, and MALM, KRISTEN. *Big Sounds from Small Peoples: The Music Industry in Small Countries.* London: Constable, 1984.

Deanna Campbell Robinson

N

Naisbitt, John (1929–)

One of the world's leading trends forecasters and analysts, John Naisbitt is also a bestselling author whose books have sold in the millions. Born in 1929 in Salt Lake City, he dropped out of school in the tenth grade, and joined the Marine Corps two years later. In 1948, he enrolled in the University of Utah, graduating with academic honors in 1952. During the next fifteen years, he served in a number of corporate and government positions, notably as Assistant Commissioner of Education under President Kennedy. He formed his own company, Urban Research Corporation (later known as the Naisbitt Group), in 1967 and has been an entrepreneur ever since. Naisbitt's career as an author began in 1982 with the publication of *Megatrends*. The book presaged the coming shift from industrial to information societies, from national economies to a global economy, and from hierarchical organizations to networking organizations. Published in forty-four countries, the book has sold over 9 million copies. Almost a decade later, *Megatrends 2000* (coauthored with his wife, Patricia Aburdene) updated many of his forecasts for the 1990s and beyond. His sixth book, *Global Paradox* (1994), offers glimpses of paradoxical changes in the global village, displaying once again an ability to weave together disparate trends into simple, yet visionary futurescapes. Naisbitt is also a much sought-after public speaker and consultant to governments and corporations.

See Naisbitt's article GLOBAL PARADOX in this volume.

George Thomas Kurian

Nanotechnology

Nanotechnology is an embryonic, multidisciplinary field with the ambitious goal of manipulating matter at the atomic and molecular level. It is a speculative field, with no working models so far. Its commercial impacts, if any, are most likely a generation away.

Nanotechnology involves technology and materials at nanometer scale—one-billionth of a meter or about ten atoms long. Current technology is at the micrometer scale (one-millionth of a meter), where many experts believe it is reaching physical limits. Advocates propose nanotechnology as a new approach to reaching the nanometer scale, with the benefits of using fewer materials and less energy, and creating less waste.

Nobel Prize-winning physicist Richard Feynman anticipated the field in a 1959 speech when he asked, "What would happen if we could arrange atoms, one by one, the way we needed?" The concept became known as nanotechnology and gained popularity in the 1980s largely due to a single individual, K. Eric Drexler. The essence of Drexler's vision is that molecular machines will assemble other molecular machines and team up to do useful work, which ranges from the practical—faster computing—to the exotic—building advanced spacesuits and arresting aging processes.

Three paths are most likely for commercialization. They will be concurrent and overlapping, rather than exclusive.

- *Molecular engineering:* The human body is a living example of a nanotechnology. Nature builds self-assembling nanodevices and systems routinely, using information stored in genes to transcribe proteins for carrying out the body's functions. Biotechnology is unraveling more of nature's secrets daily. Drexler, on the other hand, takes a purely nanotechnological stance in *Unbounding the Future* (1991, pp. 19–20), stating that "nanotechnology won't be biotechnology because it won't rely on altering life. . . . Molecular nanotechnology will use molecular machinery, but unlike biotechnology, it will not rely on genetic meddling. It will be not an extension of biotechnology, but an alternative or a replacement."

- *Miniaturization of electromechanical systems:* The current approach to miniaturization is to make big things smaller—for example, by breaking down materials into their constituent parts. Micromachines, which are etched out of silicon, can operate at the micro scale. The goal is to fit them with valves, gears, and motors to carry out their tasks, perhaps as sensors in vehicles, gauges, and medical tools. Nanotechnology reverses this approach to miniaturization by seeking to make small things bigger—assembling atoms into molecules. Drexler envisions a molecular assembler, a device resembling a microscopic industrial robot arm built from rigid molecular parts, driven by motors, controlled by computers, and able to grasp and apply molecular-scale tools. Assemblers would build molecular machines and other assemblers to perform work at the nanometer scale.

- *Molecular computing:* Current semiconductor technology may be approaching its physical limits, which would mean that the doubling of computer power that has been taking place every eighteen months would slow and eventually stop. This possibility is driving interest in alternative approaches, such as molecular computing. It has been demonstrated that a bacteria molecule (bacteriodhopsin) can be used as a switch or signal transmitting device for optical computing, which uses photons (light) rather than electrons to transmit information more

rapidly. Molecules are also being investigated for data storage and as materials for flat screen displays.

Improved tools will cross the three commercialization paths. The scanning tunneling microscope (STM) can locate and arrange atoms, as IBM demonstrated when it spelled out its logo with thirty-five xenon atoms in 1990. But it is a big step from there to useful products. While manipulating individual atoms like this means that it is theoretically possible to store all human publications ever written in a credit-card-sized device, it would take billions of years using current STM technology.

The atomic force microscope adds the capability of working in open air and probing biological samples, where the STM works only in a vacuum and on conducting surfaces, such as metals. Scanning probe microscopes can create three-dimensional images of atomic structures by physically sensing surfaces instead of magnifying them. Computer simulations are increasingly useful, and as virtual reality technology improves, it should lend a boost to the field.

The most significant brakes on development are likely to be the unanticipated effects or properties of manipulating matter at the atomic scale. For example, quantum effects, in which matter at the atomic scale alternates between wave and particle form, may prove more difficult to deal with than expected. Another important consideration is what to do in the event of self-assembling nanodevices evading human control—that is, continuing to assemble despite instructions to cease.

Nanotechnology is highly multidisciplinary. It includes computer scientists and engineers, chemists, physicists, materials scientists, biotechnologists, and biophysicists. Work is going on in university and corporate research labs around the world, such as the Jet Propulsion Lab, the Naval Research Lab, and IBM. Cornell University has established a nanotechnology research institute and Japan's Ministry of International Trade and Industry is in the middle of a ten-year, $200-million Atom Technology Project.

The earliest applications of nanotechnology are likely to be in electronics and computing. Research-and-development labs are exploring the use of molecular electronic devices, in which single molecules function as computing devices. Possibilities include using atoms to represent bits of information to pack billions of electronic devices onto a single square centimeter chip or linking them to resemble neurons in the brain to form neural network computers. Other possibilities being explored take advantage of molecular magnetic properties to boost optical-disk storage by orders of magnitude. A longer-term possibility, biochips (biological computer chips), would integrate biological capabilities onto computer chips, possibly for tactile pattern recognition. Or, entering the realm of science fiction, biochips might be directly inserted into the brain.

Nanotechnology may supplement, team with, or replace biotechnology in current health areas such as diagnostics, pharmaceutical delivery, biosensors, or genetic therapies. Farther off is Drexler's oft-cited vision of millions and even billions of nanoscale devices floating through the human bloodstream to monitor and maintain health.

Nanotechnology has the potential to transform materials and manufacturing if the molecular self-assembly concept proves practical. Current research includes testing self-assembling materials as coatings to modify surfaces, such as for making a gold-surface coating uniform. The long-term vision is for structures from desks to buildings to aircraft to be built through the combination of billions of self-assembling nanodevices.

Other applications could include energy, in which nanodevices could be catalysts for producing fuel from hydrogen and carbon monoxide. In waste disposal, nanomachines could be set upon solid or hazardous waste sites to break down toxins, perhaps converting them into useful chemical or energy feedstocks.

Because the vision has arrived before the capability, nanotechnology offers society the unique opportunity to consider its potential effects and guide its development before it is in use. It has the potential to transform society, along the line of predecessors such as the steam engine, electricity, and the computer. At the same time, its prospects for being a dead end, or being subsumed into other disciplines, are perhaps equally likely within a time frame of the year 2020. The concept is sound—nature provides a working example of nanotechnology—but the challenge may take decades to meet. This potential, however, merits careful monitoring.

See also COMPUTERS: OVERVIEW; GENETIC TECHNOLOGIES; HEALTH CARE: TECHNOLOGICAL DEVELOPMENTS; ROBOTICS; SCIENTIFIC BREAKTHROUGHS; TECHNOLOGICAL CHANGE.

BIBLIOGRAPHY

DREXLER, K. ERIC. *Nanosystems: Molecular Machinery, Manufacturing, and Computation.* New York: John Wiley, 1992.

DREXLER, K. ERIC, and PETERSON, CHRIS, with Gayle Perganit. *Unbounding the Future: The Nanotechnology Revolution.* New York: William Morrow, 1991.

LANGRETH, ROBERT. "Why Scientists Are Thinking Small." *Popular Science* (May 1993).

Andy Hines

Nationalism

Despite many challenges throughout this century, nationalism remains a potent force at the end of the millennium. Both Marxist internationalism (metanationalism) and liberal democratic universalism had cast aspersions on the regressive (capitalistic) and aggressive (antidemocratic) characteristics of nationalism. Nevertheless, since the decline of the Soviet-dominated, communist satellite states in Eastern Europe in the 1980s and the collapse of the Soviet Union in 1991, nationalism in its new guise—ethnonationalism—has reemerged with extraordinary vitality and ferocity—so much so that it is safe to predict that ethnonationalism will become even more of a global issue than it already is.

In large measure, ethnonationalism is both a continuation of nineteenth-century European *völkisch* nationalism (such as the unification of Italy and Germany), as well as a reaction to the oppression endured by ethnic majorities and minorities in communist countries, in which each cultural group was exposed to intense assimilationist policies, some of them bordering on outright genocide (such as Stalin's wholesale deportation toward the end of World War II of a half dozen ethnic groups).

Independent of these forms of ethnonationalism, there has been a growing thread of separatist ethnonationalism throughout the postcolonial world (such as the mid-1960s secessionist drive by the Ibos in Nigeria and the ongoing struggles of the East Timorese against Indonesia). Worldwide, interethnic conflict, from Canada (Francophones versus Anglophones) to Sri Lanka (Hindu Tamils versus Buddhist Sinhalese) and from Northern Ireland (pro-English Anglicans versus pro-Irish Catholics) to Burundi and Rwanda (Hutus versus Tutsis), is continually threatening the present international order with a fundamental revision of international borders.

Whereas the racist monoethnicity of Nazi Germany (which culminated in the genocide of European Jewry) was long perceived as an exception, half a century later, Hitlerian German nationalism looks more like a prologue. In the light of the phenomenon of brutal, uncompromising ethnic cleansing witnessed during the recent disintegration of Yugoslavia, the genocidal danger inherent in latter-day ethnonationalist politics suggests the ferocity with which secessionist ethnic conflicts may be resolved in the future, unless the means (creative diplomacy and effective intervention) can be developed to diffuse the controversy and separate contestants. So far, however, international organizations, such as the United Nations, the North Atlantic Treaty Organization, or the European Union, and the waning superpower diplomacy of the United States, have failed to stem the rising tide of separatist ethnonationalism.

In essence, ethnonationalism calls for sovereignty—namely, the power to promote the cultural welfare of an identifiable ethnic group, or *ethnos*. That means winning a favorable climate in which to encourage its language, religion, history, customs, and so on; more often than not that means the exclusion of other minorities, which are encouraged either to assimilate or emigrate. Thus, most postcommunist and post-Soviet states are presently engaged in a chronic duel between the dominant *ethnos* and other minorities, resulting in a number of related developments: (a) *ethnoseparatism,* such as the Abkhazian secession from the former Soviet Georgia; (b) *ethnoseparatism and merger,* such as Nagorno-Karabakh, the Armenian district in Azerbaijan seeking to join with Armenia; and (c) *ethnounification,* such as the Serbian striving for a "Greater Serbia."

All three types of mono-ethnonationalism can be detected as actual or potential developments throughout the world, some of them likely to be violent. In group (a) one can include Tibet (from China), Quebec (from Canada), Wales (from Great Britain), Chechnya (from Russia), and Catalonia (from Spain); in group (b) belong the Albanians in Kosovo (Serbia), the non-Han Muslims (China), and the North and South Ossetians (Georgia and Russia, respectively); and in group (c) one can include the Kurds (in Iran, Iraq, Syria, and Turkey), the Hungarians (in Slovakia, Serbia, and Romania), the Basques (Spain and France), the Albanians (Macedonia), and the Maya Indians (Mexico and Guatemala).

At the same time one has to take note of the several, large multinational states that are most susceptible to interethnic strife and, therefore, to ethnoseparatism. Both Nigeria and India are prime targets for fragmentation along ethnoregional lines. The signs are already visible in both countries as ethnic fault lines begin to move, pressured by a combination of economic disparity, social tension, language rivalry, and religious hatred. There is little reason to believe these heavily populated countries will remain intact once the centrifugal forces of numerous ethnoseparatist nationalisms have been unleashed.

As in the past, ethnonationalism will be challenged by other modern forms of human organization. Multinational corporations, international banking institutions, electronic technology, all are meta-ethnic in their appeal and may help overcome or discourage the tendency toward ethnofragmentation. Then again, the computer is an ideal tool for a small, ethno-based body politic. Thus, as usual, the future is unclear and unpredictable; nevertheless, what remains certain is that ethnonationalism will play a prominent role in it.

Above all, ethnonationalism—which places the interests of the group over those of the individual—will remain a serious threat to societies based on liberal democratic values, in which individual rights rank first, above collective communal priorities.

To what extent, if at all, the monoethnic state can accommodate liberal principles has yet to be determined. Whether or not a bona fide, liberal (open) civil society can coexist inside a monoethnic state that grants ethnic minorities less than equality will depend upon the cultural heritage of each ethnos and a great deal on the enlightenment of its political leadership. The tensions from this conflict will affect both the internal stability of each state and also its behavior in the international arena. As is envisioned from today's perspective, international peace will be much more difficult to maintain in an era of unfettered ethnonationalism.

See also CHINA: ETHNIC REAWAKENING; ETHNIC AND CULTURAL SEPARATISM; EUROPE, CENTRAL AND EASTERN; FUNDAMENTALISM; GLOBAL CULTURE; INTERNATIONAL TENSIONS; WORLD: PROLOGUE AND EPILOGUE.

BIBLIOGRAPHY

ALTER, PETER. *Nationalism.* New York: Routledge, Chapman, and Hall, 1989.

BIRCH, ANTHONY H. *Nationalism and National Integration.* Boston: Unwin Hyman, 1989.

BREUILLY, JOHN. *Nationalism and the State.* New York: St. Martin's Press, 1982.

FEATHERSTONE, MIKE. *Global Culture: Nationalism, Globalization, and Modernity.* Newbury Park, CA: Sage, 1990.

GELLNER, ERNEST. *Nations and Nationalism.* Ithaca, NY: Cornell University Press, 1983.

Josey, Charles C. *Philosophy of Nationalism.* McLean, VA: Cliveden Press, 1984.

Kohn, Hans. *Nationalism: Its Meaning and History.* Melbourne, FL: Krieger, 1982.

Seton-Watson, Hugh. *Nations and States: An Inquiry into the Origins of Nations and the Politics of Nationalism.* Boulder, CO: Westview, 1977.

Smith, Anthony D. *Nationalism in the Twentieth Century.* New York: New York University Press, 1979.

Snyder, Louis. *Encyclopedia of Nationalism.* New York: Paragon House, 1990.

Henry R. Huttenbach

National Parks.

See FORESTRY; PARKS AND WILDERNESS.

National Security

For the first time in centuries, the very concept of national security is changing. During this historic period, fundamental forces will converge to produce new threats to the well-being of nations. National security is about protecting resources—resources that produce wealth, quality of life, and opportunity for a nation's citizens. Since the mid-seventeenth century, wealth and power have been defined primarily in terms of money, which enabled the acquisition of armed forces to project one's will. Countries went to war over economic interests: natural resources, land, boundaries, labor forces, and markets. There was an assumption that a nation could control what passed through its borders, so all national security efforts were based, in some way, on the integrity of those borders. In general, national security was understood to be about defending against threats to one's own resources and dependencies from outside of one's borders. In the future, variations of those problems will persist. However, even though the era of large, Napoleonic wars may well be over, local, ethnic and religious conflict—quite a different problem—is expanding to take its place.

Powerful new forces that include shifts in technology, science, the natural environment, and the world's population are combining with other trends to change the definitions of wealth and power—and consequently national security, particularly in the developed world. The exponential increases in the capability and ubiquity of information technology assure that future wealth and power will be derived primarily from the access to information and knowledge, rather than money. Increasingly, the ability to manipulate systems—economic, political, scientific, and military—is based on information. Information as the capital commodity of the developed world is fundamentally changing the wealth-production equation. Unlike any of the earlier resources that were central to security, information, which is difficult to control, easily crosses borders, and even when given to someone else, is still retained by the giver. Historical policies and philosophies built upon controlling limited, tangible resources are quickly beginning to erode.

The ability to easily acquire information empowers individuals at the expense of larger institutions like governments. A single person can access, through computer networks, more information faster than government can effectively control it . . . and can as well loose a computer virus that may seriously damage governments or militaries. Thus, this driving force of information technology also threatens the present forms of government. Other technologies, like molecular nanotechnology and zero-point energy, have the potential of making obsolete, within the next two decades, most manufacturing and energy production processes. If they evolve as their proponents have envisioned, the geopolitical and economic structure that supports the current notion of security will be further weakened.

Science and the practical implications of quantum mechanics are changing fundamentally the understanding of physical reality, suggesting that the human mind has a causal relationship to matter. These principles will lend credibility to many "paranormal" phenomena that have been discounted and discredited in the past. The militaries of some nations have been working in this area for some time now. Within the next two decades, these principles will shake modern civilization, and give them a new perspective of reality as much, or more so, than the discoveries of Copernicus and Galileo did in their times. The common understanding of what *contributes* to security will be turned on its end.

In both global and U.S. domestic terms, there is a clear broadening of the disparity between rich and poor. Because the exponential growth of world population is mostly in poor areas, it is producing major concerns about the migration of large numbers of poor people from their homes to wealthier countries. A number of major nations see this trend as a significant security issue that threatens the stability of their economies. Across the world, the poor are moving to large urban areas, producing local dysfunctional environments that are ridden with crime, which increasingly threatens the well-being of the larger metropolitan area. In 1993, Washington, D.C., perhaps anticipating similar considerations by other American cities, debated whether to call up the National Guard to deal with its crime problem.

The waste and pollution produced by this demographic explosion is beginning to threaten some social and physical support systems at local, regional, and global levels. Inadequate drinking water is a growing problem in many poor countries as well as in China, Russia, Israel, Saudi Arabia, and the United States. Some scientists believe the continued thinning of the ozone layer could, within the next decade, begin to kill off the ocean phytoplankton, generating in turn, a massive failure of ocean aquatic life and also eliminating the source of an estimated forty percent of the planet's oxygen-producing capability.

In addition to these fundamental shifts, exotic weapons (nuclear, chemical, biological, and radiological) and their delivery systems are proliferating dangerously in the hands of both renegade nations, and sub-and transnational terrorist groups that are not controlled by legitimate governments. As the poor get poorer, they will have no reason to avoid threatening the stability of large wealthy societies. Increasingly armed with these weapons, they will have the ability to effectively carry out these threats. There are a number of WILDCARDS, such as changing global weather patterns, increases in natural disasters, and other unanticipated events that could also radically restructure attitudes toward security.

The future security of developed countries will not be won without a significant investment of effort and funds on both the external and internal fronts. In each area, new threats as well as old ones will need to be addressed. Global and transnational issues like atmospheric pollution will need to be balanced with the need for something to be done about deteriorating inner cities, faltering or inadequate education systems, and rampant migration. National security will become much less related to borders, and be both broader and narrower in scope, addressing global as well as domestic issues.

See also ARMS RACE; COMMUNISM; ESPIONAGE AND COUNTERINTELLIGENCE; INTERNATIONAL DIPLOMACY; INTERNATIONAL TENSIONS; MILITARY TECHNOLOGIES; PEACEKEEPING; TERRORISM; WEAPONS OF MASS DESTRUCTION.

BIBLIOGRAPHY

PETERSEN, JOHN L. "New Roles for the U.S. Military." *Sloan Management Review* 34/2 (Winter 1993): 93–98.
———. *The Road to 2015: Profiles of the Future.* Corte Madera, CA: Waite Group Press, 1994.
———. "Will the Military Miss the Market?" *Whole Earth Review* (Fall 1992): 62–70.
TOFFLER, ALVIN. *Power Shift: Knowledge, Wealth, and Violence at the End of the Twenty-first Century.* New York: Bantam, 1990.
TOFFLER, ALVIN, and TOFFLER, HEIDI. *War and Antiwar: Survival at the Dawn of the Twenty-first Century.* Boston: Little, Brown, 1993.

John L. Petersen

Native Americans

Native Americans have a status unique among American minority groups. Many have the right to live on quasi-sovereign, constitutionally protected tribal lands. Members of federally recognized tribes also have unique rights to government services and other entitlements through the Bureau of Indian Affairs and the Indian Health Service. They also are the most impoverished ethnic group in the United States, with about one-third living in poverty. There are 1.9 million Americans who identify themselves as Native Americans, less than 1 percent of the population. Thirty-eight percent live on reservations, trust lands, and other recognized tribal lands. In the next twenty years, little of this legal or economic status will change for most Indian tribes. A generation from now and beyond, the possibilities for change loom larger.

Native Americans include a diverse collection of cultural groups. Though they have the common historic experiences of European colonization and domination, the 547 federally recognized tribes and other Indian groups in the United States do not speak with one voice and will not evolve in uniform ways over the next decades. This analysis can only consider the broad trends affecting most U.S. Native Americans.

In terms of current and future economic status, there are three kinds of Native Americans: those who live on reservations, urban-ghettoized, and assimilated. It is primarily reservation-living Indians who receive government benefits. A growing majority of Native Americans are urban, nonreservation dwellers, living often in Indian neighborhoods in large cities. The growth of that majority means reservation life is a shrinking force for Indians. Most Native Americans are on an inevitable track from reservation to urban ghetto to full assimilation. They are like immigrants to the United States. Forces driving this change include the following:

- A lack of jobs and other economic factors that drive migration from reservations to cities.
- American society's desire to reduce the expense of special entitlements and other social programs based on ethnic background.
- The saturation of Native-American communities with mainstream American popular culture, through television, the press, music, and retailing.

Despite the strength of forces acting to move Native Americans toward the mainstream, there are other, but weaker forces promoting Indian ways of life:

- The recent groundswell of enthusiasm among Native Americans and others for Indian culture, art, religion, and lifestyles.
- The protected legal status of Indian reservations, including exemption from taxes and other commercial restrictions. Especially important is the growth of gambling as a source of revenue.
- Treaty-protected access to key resources, including minerals, fuels, fisheries, forests, cultural, and recreational areas.

These forces ensure that a minority of Native Americans will continue to live on reservations, even if government reduces or eliminates social programs. Legal gambling, access to resources, and the ability to compete in industry with lower costs indicate that many reservations can be viable economically for the next few decades.

Federally recognized Native-American groups will not give up their sovereignty easily, and some unrecognized groups are suing to gain or regain that status. There are no strong political reasons to take sovereignty away. Most tribes will, for decades at least, maintain quasi-sovereign, constitutionally protected status. Conflicts over resources and land will only affect a minority of tribes, because most reservations have poor land and few resources.

Despite their continuing legal status, the steady economic and social development on reservations and in urban Indian neighborhoods will shake most Native Americans loose from what remains of their traditional ways over the next generation. Cultural renewal is unlikely.

Time also will threaten Indian lands. Though it is unlikely in the next decade, eventually federal recognition of some reservations could be terminated, as has been tried before. The economic and social realities of the 2010s and '20s could lead to

tribal members accepting and even promoting termination, with compensation in cash and land. With most Indians living elsewhere, there may be few resident tribal members left to object.

A more speculative scenario for Native America's future is the termination of federal tribal status across the board with money and land compensation. This could not happen without amendments to the Constitution and protracted legal action. There probably always will be Native Americans with interest in preserving their legal status. It would take fundamental rethinking of American governance to undertake such a termination, driven perhaps by severe economic hard times or fundamental political change.

See also CANADA; ETHNIC AND CULTURAL SEPARATISM; GAMBLING; HOLISTIC BELIEFS; LATIN AMERICA; MEXICO; UNITED STATES.

BIBLIOGRAPHY

JOE, JENNIE R., ed. *American Indian Policy and Cultural Values: Conflict and Accommodation.* Berkeley, CA: University of California Press, 1990.
LYNDEN, FREMONT J., and LEGTERS, LYMAN, eds. *Native Americans and Public Policy.* Pittsburgh: University of Pittsburgh Press, 1992.
TAYLOR, THEODORE W. *American Indian Policy.* Mount Airie, MD: Lomond Publications, 1983.

John B. Mahaffie

Natural Disasters

Human awareness of and responses to natural hazards (see Table 1 for a breakdown by physical process) are *not* dependent solely upon geophysical conditions, but are contingent upon the concerns, pressures, goals, and risks of society, not the least being the effectiveness of measures to reduce calamity (Hewitt, 1983). Better understanding of society, including those processes that affect the choices of society's members, is the key to defining natural hazards and determining future hazard vulnerability (Blaikie et al., 1994).

Squatters and slum dwellers, who number millions around the world, have little or no choice in their location and few options in responding to hazards. In fact, such marginalized groups often are too poor to move elsewhere. Disasters compound the difficulties for these unfortunate people and further exacerbate the poverty trap in which they exist. Crisis management, relief aid, restoration policies, and reconstruction invariably set out to re-create "normal" conditions (Hewitt, 1983).

TABLE 1.   Natural Hazards Classified by Physical Process

Meteorological	*Geological*	*Hydrological*	*Extraterrestrial*
Hurricanes	Earthquakes	Floods	Asteroids
Thunderstorms	Volcanoes	Droughts	Meteorites
Tornadoes	Landslides	Wildfire	
Lightning	Subsidence		
Hailstorms	Mudflows		
Windstorms	Sinkholes		
Ice storms	Tidal waves		
Snowstorms			
Blizzards			
Cold waves			
Heat waves			
Avalanches			
Fog			
Frost			

A simple focus on the physical world that emphasizes geophysical processes leads to an incomplete understanding of natural hazards. The human element is important, not only because humans are the victims, but also because by their exposure they define the very dimensions of natural hazards. Natural hazards constitute a complex web of physical and environmental factors interacting with the social, economic, and political realities of society.

Risk and Vulnerability

Natural hazards by definition constitute a risk to society because humans and/or their activities are constantly exposed to these extreme forces. For instance, by locating property on floodplains, by undertaking agriculture on the slopes of active volcanoes, and by developing housing in hurricane-prone coastal zones, humans are wittingly exposed to hazard risk. Given the ubiquitous nature of natural hazards, all communities face an element of risk, but not all are equally vulnerable. Some communities have adopted stringent regulations and constructed major projects to protect themselves from disasters. In this way, the vulnerability of the community has been reduced. For example, the construction of earthquake-proof structures can significantly reduce the vulnerability of a community to earthquake losses. Similarly, zoning land for low-density uses can minimize the impacts of flooding, hurricanes, and tidal waves (tsunamis).

This is not to assume that all human activities reduce the hazard risk. Indeed, there are many land-use and societal decisions that exacerbate problems and increase vulnerability. For instance, the expansion of urban areas onto floodplains, wetlands, and steep slopes has heightened the hazard risk.

Trends in Death and Damage

Every year natural hazards place a heavy toll on society, killing large numbers of people, destroying homes, and damaging property throughout the world. Assessing the number of deaths and totaling damages is no easy task, especially during the immediate post-hazard impact phase, when emergency relief and rehabilitation are priorities and general confusion prevails. Data on natural hazards can be sketchy and is frequently exaggerated, especially during the early hours of the event. It is not unusual to find initial unofficial estimates of deaths and damages to be considerably higher than final figures (Alexander, 1993). On other occasions, deaths are significantly underestimated, as in the Kobe (Japan) earthquake of 1995, when early reports put deaths below 50 but the final death toll actually exceeded 5,000 people. Similarly, estimates of economic losses are also vague and notoriously inaccurate. Despite these limitations, the data provide an indication of the impacts associated with hazard losses (see Table 2).

An important review of disaster trends by Theodore S. Glickman, Dominic Golding, and Emily D. Silverman (1992), utilizing information from more than twenty European and U.S. data sources, nevertheless underrepresents the impacts. Excluded from their analysis were pervasive hazards such as droughts, and events that did not lead

TABLE 2.   Selected Natural Disasters Worldwide, 1900–1995

Hurricanes/Typhoons/Tropical Cyclones*

Year	Location	Deaths
1900	United States	6,000
1906	Hong Kong	10,000
1928	United States	2,000
1938	United States	600
1959	Japan	4,600
1961	Hong Kong	400
1963	Bangladesh	22,000
1965	Bangladesh	17,000
1965	Bangladesh	30,000
1965	Bangladesh	10,000
1970	Bangladesh	300,000
1971	India	25,000
1977	India	20,000
1985	Bangladesh	10,000
1988	Caribbean	25,000
1989	Caribbean/U.S.	56

Volcanic Activities

Year	Location	Deaths
1902	Martinique	29,000
1902	Guatemala	6,000
1911	Philippines	1,300
1919	Indonesia	5,200
1930	Indonesia	1,400
1951	Papua New Guinea	2,900
1963	Indonesia	1,200
1980	United States	70
1982	Mexico	1,700
1985	Colombia	22,000

TABLE 2.   (continued)

Earthquakes, Tsunamis, and Associated Events

Year	Location	Deaths
1906	Taiwan	6,000
1906	United States	1,500
1908	Italy	75,000
1915	Italy	30,000
1920	China	200,000
1923	Japan	143,000
1932	China	70,000
1933	Japan	3,000
1935	India	60,000
1939	Chile	30,000
1948	USSR	100,000
1949	USSR	20,000
1960	Morocco	12,000
1962	Iran	12,000
1968	Iran	12,000
1970	Peru	70,000
1972	Nicaragua	6,000
1976	China	250,000
1976	Guatemala	24,000
1976	Italy	900
1978	Iran	25,000
1980	Italy	1,300
1985	Mexico	1,700
1988	Armenia	10,000
1990	Iran	25,000
1995	Japan	5,200

Floods

Year	Location	Deaths
1945	Japan	1,200
1949	China	57,000
1953	North Sea coast	1,800
1954	China	40,000
1993	United States	50

* The name for large tropical storms of 75 m.p.h. or greater wind intensity is hurricane in the Atlantic-Caribbean and the eastern Pacific, typhoon in the western Pacific, tropical cyclone in the Indian Ocean, and various other names in other regions.

Source: Office of Foreign Disaster Assistance (1988) and Eric Noji (1991).

to 25 deaths or more, even if they had been economically devastating. They found that, between 1945 and 1986, there were 1,267 global natural disasters that caused 2,343,000 deaths, for an average of 56,000 deaths per year. A closer examination of these statistics shows that 3 events accounted for a substantial number of deaths. Two earthquakes, one in the former Soviet Union (1948) and one in China (1976), killed 110,000 and 700,000 people respectively, and a tropical cyclone in Bangladesh (1970) killed 500,000 people. If these major catastrophes are removed from the data set, then the number of deaths per year falls to 25,000 and the average per disaster to 837.

It is also true that large-magnitude events account for the greatest number of deaths from natural hazards. Keith Smith (1992), for instance, found that there were 17 major disasters since

1949, defined as those that have killed more than 10,000. Using the Glickman et al. data, only 29 disasters (2.3 percent) met this criterion of 10,000 deaths; yet, they accounted for 1.9 million deaths (81.2 percent).

Temporal Trends

The hazard data on disasters and deaths show distinct trends over time (see Table 3). The number of

Natural Disasters

TABLE 3. Temporal Trends in Natural Disasters, 1945–1986

Period	Number of Disasters	Thousands of Deaths	Deaths per Disaster	Deaths per Year
1945–1951	107 (106)	252 (142)	2,351 (1,336)	36,000 (20,286)
1952–1958	172	92	534	13,143
1959–1965	197	239	1,212	34,143
1966–1972	244 (243)	706 (206)	2,892 (847)	100,857 (29,428)
1973–1979	244 (243)	921 (221)	3,777 (912)	131,571 (31,571)
1980–1986	303	134	441	19,143
Total	**1,267**	**2,343**	**1,849**	**55,786**

Note: Data in parentheses exclude three worst disasters for the period.
Source: Glickman, Golding, and Silverman (1992).

disasters per 7-year period has gradually risen from 107 between 1945 and 1951, to 303 between 1980 and 1986, while the number of deaths shows a similar pattern, at least until the last period. Global economic losses have also increased dramatically. For instance, losses per decade from weather-related natural disasters have risen from $400 billion in the 1950s to ninety times that value in the 1980s.

Spatial Trends

The spatial pattern of disaster deaths and damages is even more telling. Ninety-five percent of all disaster-related deaths occur among the 67 percent of the population that lives in the world's poorer nations, whereas 75 percent of the economic losses accrues to those in the wealthy nations. Data show that East Asia and the Pacific region, Southern Asia, Latin America, and the Caribbean have experienced the most deaths and disasters during the 42-year period. Controlling for size of resident populations, the Middle East and North Africa also join Latin America and the Caribbean as the worst-hit areas (see Table 4). When these data are broken down by country different patterns emerge. Between 1900 and 1988, India suffered most disasters, while the U.S.S.R. experienced most disaster-related deaths, but Italy the most economic loss (see Table 5) (OFDA, 1988). (Note that the United States was omitted from these statistics.)

These statistics, however, fail to reflect the significance of economic loss in the different countries. Greater affluence means that more property is at risk; hence, losses are often high whenever disaster strikes a wealthy community. But the loss sustained by poorer nations is actually greater in real terms than that in wealthy nations. A family in Bangladesh may lose all its possessions in a tropical cyclone and still only accrue tens of dollars in damage. In contrast, when an automobile is crushed by falling debris in a Californian earth-

TABLE 4. Spatial Patterns of Natural Disasters, 1945–1986

Region	Number of Disasters	Thousands of Deaths	Deaths per Disaster	Deaths per Million People
East Asia/Pacific	401 (400)	977 (277)	2,435 (691)	5
Latin America/Caribbean	239	239	999	21
Southern Asia	234 (233)	808 (308)	3,452 (1,321)	10
North America	149	15	104	2
Europe/U.S.S.R.	127 (126)	166 (56)	1,308 (444)	2
Middle East/North Africa	86	129	1,505	24
Sub-Saharan Africa	45	9	201	1
Total	**1,267**	**2,343**	**1,849**	

Note: Data in parentheses exclude three worst disasters for the period.
Source: Glickman, Golding, and Silverman (1992).

TABLE 5.   Disasters, Deaths, and Damage by Country

Disasters		Disaster Deaths per Event		Disaster Damage per Event (Thousands of U.S. $)	
India	199	U.S.S.R.	284,334	Italy	611,694
Philippines	134	China	80,812	Spain	374,686
Indonesia	110	India	4,379	Chile	121,505
Bangladesh	109	Bangladesh	26,981	U.S.S.R.	90,645
Japan	91	Ethiopia	16,138	Argentina	84,758
China	89	Niger	7,826	Mexico	80,563
Brazil	68	Mozambique	7,262	Colombia	51,969
Mexico	60	Italy	,949	Pakistan	39,370
Peru	55	Pakistan	2,061	China	39,296
Iran	53	Japan	2,005	Peru	32,498
Turkey	43	Peru	1,355	India	31,940
Colombia	39	Chile	1,107	Sri Lanka	31,734
Italy	39	Iran	1,103	Japan	30,416
Korea	38	Turkey	1,027	Bangladesh	26,831
Chile	37	Colombia	705	Korea	25,116
Myanmar	36	Haiti	429	Philippines	13,393
Pakistan	33	Vietnam	412	Haita	10,460
Vietnam	32	Sri Lanka	317	Mozambique	9,588
U.S.S.R.	31	Mexico	287	Ecuador	8,830
Ecuador	30	Ecuador	261	Brazil	6,964
Argentina	29	Indonesia	225	Indonesia	6,838
Sri Lanka	29	Philippines	222	Niger	4,322
Niger	27	Argentina	202	Myanmar	4,280
Haiti	26	Myanmar	176	Ethiopia	3,129
Ethiopia	25	Korea	107	Vietnam	2,296
Mozambique	25	Spain	106	Iran	1,415
South Africa	25	Brazil	99	South Africa	40
Spain	25	South Africa	73		

Source: Office of Foreign Disaster Assistance (1988) and Smith (1992).

quake, the economic loss is high but the personal costs may be low. Disaster losses as a percentage of the GNP can be much higher in poorer nations than in wealthy ones. For example, the growth of the gross domestic product (GDP) in five Central American countries was reduced by 2.3 percent annually between 1960 and 1974 as a consequence of natural disasters. Smith (1992) pointed out that hurricane losses in the Dominican Republic (1979), Haiti, St. Lucia, and St. Vincent (1980) rose to 15 percent of the gross national product (GNP). The scale of these losses means that the potential for development for many of these countries is undermined by the recurring disasters and the efforts and finance needed for recovery.

Geophysical Patterns

If these hazard data are broken down by geophysical event, then distinct patterns emerge (see Table 6). First, floods are clearly the most common natural hazard during the post-World War II period, accounting for over 30 percent of all disasters. Hurricanes and tropical cyclones make up about 20 percent; earthquakes between 15 percent and 17 percent; and tornadoes approximately 12 percent of natural hazards (Glickman et al., 1992).

In terms of deaths, the pattern is different. The Glickman, Golding, and Silverman (1992) study indicated that earthquakes and hurricanes/tropical cyclones killed more people than any other hazard, with floods dropping to third. Even when the three largest events are removed from the data, earthquakes and tropical cyclones still account for more deaths than other hazards.

Conclusions

Various hypotheses have been put forward to explain these spatial and temporal trends in hazards

TABLE 6.   Loss of Life by Selected Geophysical Event, 1945–1986

Disaster Type	Number of Disasters	Thousands of Deaths	Deaths per Disaster
Floods	395	244	618
Hurricanes/Tropical Cyclones	272 (271)	791 (291)	2,907 (1,072)
Other Storms	212	28	131
Heat Waves	23	5	223
Cold Waves	15	4	275
Earthquakes	191 (189)	1,198 (388)	6,272 (2,053)
Volcanic Eruptions	27	40	1,494
Tsunamis	7	3	271
Landslides	85	25	295
Fires	40	6	157
Total	**1,267 (1,264)**	**2,343 (1,033)**	**1,849 (837)**

data. First, it is conceivable that the frequency of extreme geophysical events has increased over the last twenty or thirty years, thus accounting for the rise in number of hazards and the jump in number of deaths. Studies of geophysical processes do not support this contention, although it is possible that certain natural hazards have increased because of human activities. Drainage of wetlands, urbanization, and deforestation have all modified the storm hydrograph, resulting in more incidents of small-scale flooding. On the other hand, it is unlikely that humans have had any significant impact on the frequency of volcanic activity, earthquakes, or tropical cyclones. Nevertheless, we can expect to see increasing impacts from human activities, at least at the local levels, for many years to come.

A second explanation for these trends might be the tremendous increase in population, rapid urbanization, and continuing development of squatter settlements in hazard-prone areas. In addition, the movement to large urban agglomerations has exacerbated the hazard problem by increasing the density of people living in certain high-risk areas. Finally, the growth of squatter settlements has also exacerbated hazards. These patterns will continue as poverty, population pressures, and other social constraints force people into these unsafe and unsavory conditions.

A third argument suggests that the spatial and temporal patterns are a product of better data collection and reporting. Certainly data collection has improved over the years as global connections have shrunk with new technological advances. Thus, pictures of famines and floods in "remote" parts of the world can be flashed instantaneously onto television screens, heightening our awareness.

Problems are no longer viewed as purely physical in nature but comprised of political, social, and economic forces, as well as natural processes. This changing focus has greatly enhanced our understanding of hazards and improved our ability to mitigate disaster losses. National governments are increasingly looking at disaster policies and how best to serve their populations. At the international level, the United Nations Disaster Relief Office, the Red Cross, and Red Crescent societies have been active in alleviating suffering. The 1990s was designated the International Decade for Natural Disaster Reduction by the United Nations, to encourage implementation of comprehensive disaster plans.

In spite of all this activity, natural hazards will continue virtually unabated. The number of deaths accruing from hazards will increase, and economic losses will jump significantly in the next fifty years. Without careful planning and major adjustments in policies, these consequences are unavoidable. There are vast numbers of people living in highly vulnerable locations, many of whom will die and others of whom will lose everything they own. Research reveals the root causes of natural hazards, but there is little evidence of political commitment or social will to change behavior that can alleviate future suffering.

See also APOCALYPTIC FUTURE; ASTRONOMY; BIODIVERSITY; DISASTERS, PLANNING FOR; EPIDEMICS; EVOLUTION, BIOLOGICAL; EXTINCTION OF SPECIES;   GLOBAL ENVIRONMENTAL PROBLEMS; GLOBAL WARMING.

BIBLIOGRAPHY

ALEXANDER, DAVID. *Natural Hazards.* New York: Chapman and Hall, 1993.

BLAIKIE, PIERS; CANNON, TERRY; DAVIS, IAN; and WISNER, BEN. *At Risk: Natural Hazards, People's Vulnerability, and Disasters*. London and New York: Routledge, 1994.

GLICKMAN, THEODORE S.; GOLDING, DOMINIC; and SILVERMAN, EMILY D. *Acts of God and Acts of Man: Recent Trends in Natural Disasters and Major Industrial Accidents*. Washington, DC: Center for Risk Management, Discussion Paper 92-02. Resources for the Future, 1992.

HEWITT, KENNETH. "The Idea of Calamity in a Technocratic Age." In *The Interpretations of Calamity*, ed. K. Hewitt. Winchester, MA: Allen and Unwin, 1983.

SMITH, KEITH. *Environmental Hazards: Assessing Risk and Reducing Disaster*. London and New York: Routledge, 1992.

TAYLOR, ANTHONY J. W. *Disasters and Disaster Stress*. Stress in Modern Society, 10. New York: AMS Press, 1989.

WHITE, GILBERT F. *Choice of Adjustments to Floods*. Department of Geography Research Paper, 93. Chicago: University of Chicago Press, 1964.

————. *Human Adjustments to Floods*. Department of Geography Research Paper, 29. Chicago: University of Chicago Press, 1945.

WHITE, GILBERT F., ed. *Papers on Flood Problems*. Department of Geography Research Paper No. 70. Chicago: University of Chicago Press, 1961.

Graham A. Tobin

Natural Gas

Methane, or natural gas as it is commonly known, has increased in importance as a fuel throughout the twentieth century. Today methane provides nearly a quarter of all of the world's primary energy, and this contribution is likely to grow even larger in the future. Although gas utilization expanded most rapidly in the industrialized countries since 1950, dramatic shifts toward increased methane usage occurred in many less developed nations over the past twenty years. Rising world oil prices in the 1970s triggered this trend. These price signals motivated nations to develop indigenous fuel resources. In many nations this indigenous fuel was methane.

Methane Reserves

One measure of the amount of methane available is the quantity of proved reserves, that is, the amount of methane that: (1) is known to exist with reasonable certainty and (2) is producible under current economic and operating conditions. A more comprehensive category of methane is the total quantity of methane estimated to comprise the potential resource base, that is, the quantity of methane thought to be economically recoverable in the foreseeable future. To illustrate the difference in these statistics, the United States has 170 quads (a quad represents a quantity of energy equal to 10^{15} British Thermal Units) of proved reserves of methane and well over 1,000 quads of recoverable resources of methane. Each year a part of these gas resources is converted into proved reserves, and some of the proved reserves are produced and used as fuels.

Producers find and make available the production from proved reserves to satisfy the demand for gas. They do this by drilling wells that penetrate geological formations beneath Earth's crust. These wells provide the gas to the pipeline systems that transport the gas to the burner or other end-use equipment.

This entire process of natural gas discovery, production, and transmission, is technically challenging. Since 1980 the technology to find and produce gas advanced very rapidly. As a result, methane production is now more efficient and many gas deposits that were not economically attractive for production twenty years ago are now being routinely developed. One consequence of this rapidly increasing efficiency is that more and more methane deposits are now being judged to be economically producible. In other words, new technology caused both the methane resource base and reserves to increase.

THE ORIGINS OF METHANE

Traditional petroleum geology postulates that most of the hydrocarbons, such as oil, methane, coal, and so on, are the transformed remains of plants and animals that lived millions of years ago. These biological remains, compressed and heated deep within rock formations, became oil, gas, or coal over time. This interpretation has physical support from the organisms found in the rocks; further, this hypothesis is the basis for most of the hydrocarbon exploration and production to date.

A more recent and still controversial theory cites the existence of methane throughout our solar system, especially in the four gas-giant planets. This theory postulates that methane is a basic building block of nature and holds that Earth's formation trapped large quantities of methane deep in the earth. The theory further stipulates that methane found today identifies a path of migration from deep methane deposits to Earth's surface. Massive quantities of methane are found in any rock formations on the migrational path that could hold the gas. One popular advocate of this theory is Thomas Gold, an astrophysicist, whose name has been used to label this hypothesis as the Gold Theory.

Despite the major differences between the traditional interpretations and the Gold Theory there are some important points that are not in dispute. Almost everyone agrees that some methane is a result of biological processes of decay. In our everyday experience we observe that methane is generated from biological decay in swamps, animal digestive tracts, and in rice paddies. Also, most scholars agree that some methane is abiogenic, that is, not of animal or plant origin. The theories differ about which is the dominant source of methane— abiogenic or biological. Additional evidence continues to be collected and analyzed from volcanoes, deep wells in nonproducing regions of the world, and in methane deposits in ice-like formations on the ocean floor. As usual in science, each newly discovered answer raises new questions.

Scientists have not been able to determine the true origin of most methane. Yet while the scholars pursue these fundamental questions, more and more people use methane as a primary fuel to heat or cool the world around them.

See also COAL; ENERGY; ENERGY, RENEWABLE SOURCES OF; MINERALS; NATURAL RESOURCES, USE OF; NUCLEAR POWER; NUCLEAR POWER: CON; PETROLEUM; PIPELINES; RESOURCES.

BIBLIOGRAPHY

OPPENHEIMER, ERNEST J. *U.S. Energy Independence.* New York: Pen and Podium Productions, 1980.

Special Energy Report Supplement. *National Geographic* 159 (February 1981): 560.

STOBAUGH, ROBERT, and YERGIN, DANIEL, eds. *Energy Future.* New York: Ballantine Books, 1980.

WEAVER, JACQUELINE. *The Case for Natural Gas, Publication No. 91–11.* Houston: Center for Public Policy, University of Houston, 1991.

Nelson Hay
Robert Kalisch

Natural Resources, Use of

In a 1968 article in *Science* magazine, biologist Garrett Hardin identified an important type of future problem in our use and management of the Earth's natural resources. He pointed out that overusing a resource usually is constrained because it is someone's property, and there is an in-herent self-interest in taking good care of it and safeguarding its use. But, Hardin asked, what about resources that no one owns and all use in common? What about shared-use resources, such as the air we breathe or the oceans that make up more than half our planet's surface? Who or what protects shared-use resources from overuse when all of us can use these resources?

Hardin cited the experience of the common pasture in preindustrial times. Everyone got milk from their own cow, which each household kept on "the commons." It was in each household's self-interest to get still more milk by adding for themselves another cow to the commons. Furthermore, any family's restraint would not stop others from making additional demands upon the commons, until the commons was degraded or destroyed.

Individual Powerlessness and Shared Destruction

What Hardin termed "the tragedy of the commons" is akin to what nonsmokers long experienced in restaurants where others were smoking: the nonsmoker was powerless to protect the air everyone breathes by restraining the behavior of smokers. The only solution Hardin saw was "mutual coercion mutually agreed upon." During the late 1980s the rise of the "Smoke-Free Movement" resulted in many public spaces becoming legally smoke-free through voluntary or government-mandated action.

Carrying this concept to an extreme, the legal scholar Christopher D. Stone has proposed also that natural objects in general should be granted legal standing in our courts, just as ships and corporations are. His intent was to provide a basis for broad and sweeping environmental protection whereby lawsuits could be brought to protect an endangered stand of trees—or a lake or stream or fishery. Currently natural objects have virtually no standing of their own and are protected only as someone's property.

Now, a generation later, the degradation of resources used in common has become a major public policy dilemma. We are facing a future in which our present actions (or inactions) are shaping the fate of basic resources. For example, the great fisheries of Georges Bank in the North Atlantic off New England and Nova Scotia were suddenly in the late 1980s overfished and out of stock, with annual fish-catches plummeting. The fishing practices of the industry were threatening the ability of a common resource to recharge or regenerate itself. Despite the declining stock, fishermen intensified their activities in order to sustain profitability. How, short of closing them down, could fisheries be protected from such overuse by all those who depend upon them for a livelihood?

Similarly, in the 1980s scientists discovered that chlorofluorocarbons (CFCs) from spray cans, air conditioning, refrigeration, and industrial solvents were being dissipated into the Earth's upper atmosphere, depleting the ozone layer, thinning out the protective sunscreen in the Northern mid-latitudes, and creating over the entire South Pole a seasonal "ozone hole" the size of all of North America. The natural sunscreen effect of the atmosphere has been degraded to such an extent that even if there is widespread restraint in the use of CFCs, the problem will persist for some time. Only a sustained effort worldwide is likely to alleviate present conditions.

On another front, rivers and lakes and oceans have been convenient dumping grounds for millennia, receiving sewage and industrial wastes and bilge wastes from ships all around the world. The present dilemma is how to protect all such shared-use resources, used by all in common but owned by none.

"The Public Interest" as a Shared Resource in Politics

In the politics of governance, the public interest is a similar kind of shared-use resource. We strive to fulfill the Kantian ideal of the greatest good for the greatest number. The long and short of it is that national well-being and the political processes of government are used by all but owned by none. Akin to exploitive and selfish use of resources, in politics and government each interest group's selfishness is driven by a stubbornly rational pattern of political and economic behavior in which the benefits it seeks are captured for itself and the costs incurred are spread diffusely to all others. From one viewpoint, the long-run advantage of every group might benefit if all groups surrendered just enough of their own self-interest to achieve a greater common good. But it makes no sense for any beneficiary to surrender unilaterally. Like fishing boat captains, the political special interests are driven by selfish—perhaps innate—behavior.

Treaties among nations to regulate CFC use and governmental regulations regarding auto emissions, clean air standards, and clean water standards have not yet succeeded in adequately diverting us from degrading these shared-use resources.

Hardin's prophetic call to resolve the tragedy of the commons remains an ongoing challenge. His "mutual coercion mutually agreed upon" is repeatedly resisted. Until the larger self-interest in everyone's common future is widely perceived and becomes the operative principle, there will be little relief for "the tragedy of the commons."

See also ACID RAIN; AGENTS OF CHANGE; CIVIL PROTEST; CLIMATE AND METEOROLOGY; DEFORESTATION; ENVIRONMENTAL BEHAVIOR; ENVIRONMENTAL ETHICS; ENVIRONMENTAL POLICY CHANGES; FISHERIES; FRESHWATER; GLOBAL ENVIRONMENTAL PROBLEMS; GLOBAL WARMING; GREEN REVOLUTION; HAZARDOUS WASTES; OZONE LAYER DEPLETION; SOLID WASTE; SUSTAINABILITY.

BIBLIOGRAPHY

HARDIN, GARRETT. "Second Thoughts on 'The Tragedy of the Commons.'" In *Economics, Ecology, Ethics*, ed., Herman E. Daly. San Francisco: W. H. Freeman, 1980.
_____. "The Tragedy of the Commons." *Science* 162 (December 13, 1968): 1243–1248. Reprinted in his *Exploring New Ethics of Survival*. New York: Viking, 1972.
HARDIN, GARRETT, and BADEN, JOHN, eds. *Managing the Commons*. San Francisco: W. H. Freeman, 1977.
STONE, CHRISTOPHER D. *Should Trees Have Standing?: Toward Legal Rights for Natural Objects*. Los Altos, CA: W. H. Freeman, 1974.

David Dodson Gray

Networking

The last frontier of exploration will not be space or the sea; it will be the silicon chip and the bits that make up computers. In this frontier, nothing is constant except change. The rate of technological change has accelerated so greatly that growth is virtually exponential. As a result, we can hardly envision clearly the networking industry in 2010. However, there are likely scenarios of how networking will affect the way we work and live in the early part of the twenty-first century.

Entertainment

The information super highway (ISH) is primarily an entertainment network for mass-produced and inexpensive entertainment. It is estimated that it will contain more than 500 entertainment channels. With the gigabit-per-second national backbone, bandwidth is not an issue, and access will be inexpensive. ISH applications will include:

- Movies on demand produced by telecable companies.
- Personal home videos made with digital cameras and built-in optical disks (videophones will grow less popular because they intrude on privacy).
- Video shopping in which people will interact directly with video catalogs, checking availability and pricing with the store's database and even trying on clothing in electronic "dressing rooms."
- Interactive games will be popular with the MTV generation.
- Education—people everywhere will have access to electronic classrooms and research materials. All large libraries, including the Library of Congress, will be fully digitized, and navigation software will make it easier to locate and download information.
- Information publishing—in interactive publishing, the information faucet can be controlled to provide customized news mixing text, photos, sound, and video in the right amount and at the right time.

The ISH will become the underpinning for business-to-business communication, particularly document transfer and videoconferencing. However, leading-edge companies will not use the ISH because of privacy and security concerns. They will use ATM2. The ATM superhighway with its ISDN on-ramps is owned by bit-pushers like Sony, Time-Warner, R. J. Reynolds/IBM/Dow Jones (RID), or by telecable companies. Nearly all businesses will have fiber connections to the ISH. In homes, television sets will have fiber-optic connections, optical disks, and digital cameras, all linked to the phone. Programming will be selected by remote PDAs (personal digital assistants) and drag-and-drop interfaces of Microsoft/Intel selectors or audiotext provided by telecable. All telephones will have integrated data-fax modems. The danger of the ISH is that people will be so bombarded with MTV-type information that they will become desensitized to substantive information.

Private Networks

The ISH as a vehicle to deliver business information will be a failure, because in a competitive world, corporations need ownership of their own dedicated networks. Large companies will bypass the ISH to build their own highly functional networks to be used not only for internal communications but also for business-to-business communi-

cations. With such networks, companies will be free to disperse their employees. Most companies will lease their wide-area bandwidth (usually ATM or clear-channel T-4) from WAN service providers. Most desktop computers will have 128-bit operating systems, such as Microsoft's RNT/4 with its integrated file/mail/print/fax services. AT&T/Novell Netware will be the main remote operating system. Desktop computers will have 155-Mbps interfaces to the internal networks. Directory services (updated on a subscription basis) will help users locate services available on their networks. The biggest advance will be application integration. People will have to buy a certain operating system, such as UNIX, but they will be able to point, click, drag, and drop, and speak from one application to another. Most simple commands will be by voice.

Portable Consumer Computing Devices

To appreciate the free-floating computers of 2010, it is necessary to look at the shortcomings of its ancestor, the PC. The PC was an uninspired machine, a square, stale heap of hardware, strapped by wires, and trapped to the desk by an overweight and clunky CPU, not to mention the keyboard and the mouse. As a result, in 1995 a mere 3 percent of the world's population used computers. By 1995, consumer electronics companies began building computers for computer-illiterates, using sophisticated electronics with no-brainer user interfaces. As a result, computers became more like television sets, available in the same price range. By 2010, companies like Sony and Sharp, rather than IBM or Apple, will be producing the most popular computers, and they will be selling portable consumer computing devices (CCDs) with a wide variety of network options and in designer colors. These devices will use the pen rather than the mouse or keyboard. These portables will be small, lightweight, and energy-efficient, running off a watch battery. Network protocols for local and remote access will be embedded into the personal operating system with infrared transmission for the short trek and spread-spectrum radio for long-distance access to public and private networks. Each CCD will be compatible with other CCDs, making it easy to exchange information and also connect peer-to-peer networks over slow ethernet. Voice annotation will be standard as well as a variety of personal security guards, such as fingerprint locks. While CCD-based consumer networks proliferate, business users will use integrated machines, such as AT&T's Personal Electronic Organizer Node (PEON) with its built-in fax, copier, scanner, phone, and printer. Pagers will have pull-down menus in which users can scan multiple incoming phone numbers.

The Work Environment

Microsoft will remain the largest player in the industry, although it will be forced to break up into a number of "Baby Bills." The trend to build up gigantic consolidated databases will bring back the IBM mainframe to its linchpin role. Whereas 100 MHz was considered fast in 1995, most computers will need 1GHz to process the vast amounts of data coming across airwaves or the wire. Voice-driven systems will become universal. While screen radiation and carpal tunnel syndrome become less serious hazards, most users in 2010 will complain of dry throats as a result of talking to their computers all day. The real winners in 2010 will be otolaryngologists and voice trainers. Fax machines will have become extinct. People will not have as many computers because there will be less need to own separate desktop and portable machines. All the off-shelf software will be downloaded automatically on-line using automatic license meters. Virtual-reality glasses will be worn like eyeglasses. These eyeglasses will take their orders wirelessly from wrist-mounted personal communicators.

Network-Driven Divisions

The rise of networks will hasten the polarization of the world into technological haves and have-nots. Even in developed societies, computer illiterates will become the new underclass. The same will be true of corporations, as information-rich companies outsmart the information-poor. Information will replace capital as the key wealth builder. As the world becomes more networked, network managers will become the new elite. Geographically, networks will reinforce the trend toward a borderless world. Inexpensive, high-speed wide-area communications will disperse databases.

See also COMMUNICATIONS; COMMUNICATIONS TECHNOLOGY; COMPUTER LINKAGE; COMPUTERS: OVERVIEW; ELECTRONIC CONVERGENCE; ELECTRONIC PUBLISHING; HIGH TECHNOLOGY; INFORMATION OVERLOAD; INFORMATION SOCIETY; INFORMATION TECHNOLOGY; INTERACTIVE ENTERTAINMENT; MEDIA LAB; ON-LINE SERVICES; TELECOMMUNICATIONS.

BIBLIOGRAPHY

KROL, ED. *Whole Internet User's Guide*, 2d ed. Petaluma, CA: O'Reilly & Associates, 1994.
MCMULLEN, MELANIE. *Networks 2000*. San Francisco: Miller Freeman, 1994.
SCHNAIDT, PATRICIA. *LAN Tutorial*, 3rd ed., San Francisco: Miller Freeman, 1994.

Melanie McMullen
The Editors of LAN Magazine

New Consumer Products

In 1994, 20,076 new supermarket and drugstore products were introduced to United States consumers—at a rate of 55 per day. (See Figure 1.) Back in 1964, the total number of new products introduced was only 1,281. New food and drug products arriving on the store shelves increased approximately 1,609 percent in the past thirty years!

New product introductions have increased virtually every year for the past three decades, with annual increases averaging 5.3 percent. This growth pattern has been due to major technological developments in the manufacture of foods and nonfoods, as well as significant lifestyle changes in American society. With important food science refinements on the immediate horizon, and with consumer attitudes toward and usage of foods and nonfoods remaining in flux, there are ample reasons to predict continuing growth of new product activity. In addition, the resurgence of private labels will compel food and drug manufacturers to resist this challenge with an increasing flow of imaginative new products. Food and drug marketers live by the axiom "innovate or die." There is nothing to suggest that, in a market share-based economic system, any company can afford to reduce its new product development efforts in the coming years. (See Figure 2.)

The palate of today's food shopper is increasingly more sophisticated. Americans currently travel more, read gourmet publications, and eat in a wide variety of ethnic restaurants. The emergence of "foodies" in the mass market has prompted an explosion of ethnic food products in supermarkets. While this category is still dominated by foods derived from Asian, Italian, and Mexican cuisines, other ethnic cuisines—Thai, Vietnamese, Caribbean, East Indian, and Cajun—will become more prominent in the future. (Note that all these fares are very spicy.) Also, there will be an upgrading of traditional ethnic offerings. Thirty years ago, Mexican food meant chili and beans. Now, consumers can find more exotic varieties, such as chimichangas, quesadillas, and black bean salsa.

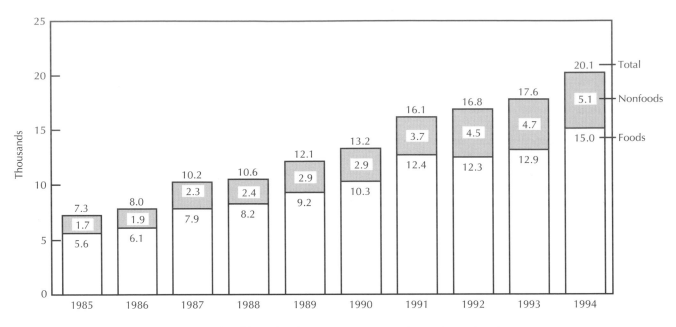

FIGURE 1. Increases in new food/nonfood consumer product introductions, 1985–1994. Source: U.S. Dept. of Agriculture (*New Product News,* January 8, 1995).

What appears on an Italian, Chinese, or Mexican restaurant menu today will be available as branded supermarket selections in the coming years. Daily response to menu changes preferred by restaurant-goers define desires that become tomorrow's packaged products.

Along with the consumer's move to more adventuresome ethnic foods has been the constant quality upgrading of basic food products. This "gourmetizing" of foods, to provide consumers with more diverse flavors and recipes, not only influences the manufacture of conventional foods, but also has led to a dramatic growth in gourmet foods. Specialty store shoppers can select from hundreds of flavored coffees, teas, preserves, mustards, or cheeses, while supermarkets also have expanded their limited specialty food selections. As the sophisticated consumer seeks out new taste experiences, it can be expected that domestic and import suppliers will continue to market new specialty food options. What today is an exotic gourmet food, tomorrow will be standard supermarket fare.

Perhaps the most dramatic impetus in new product development in the past ten years has been the growth of nutritionally oriented foods. While so-called "health foods" have been available for decades, only in the late 1980s and early '90s has the consumer interest in the enhancement of foods through the addition of useful ingredients or the subtraction of harmful ingredients produced so many new food categories. Consumers and health experts have asked for, and received, new foods that are sodium-reduced, fiber-added, calcium-fortified, cholesterol-decreased, calorie-controlled, sugar-substituted, nitrate-eliminated, or additive-excised. In 1995, the nutritional emphasis is on fat annihilation, with products such as Nabisco's fat-free, fat-reduced SnackWell becoming the best-selling cookie in the country. As long as cardiologists continue to urge fat reduction, fat-reduced products will flood the market. Also, vegetarian and organic foods will expand in the near future.

What will be the next nutritional "hot button"? Whatever emerges as a harmful food or food ingredient in the medical and popular press will be quickly followed by a variety of new products that reduce or eliminate the latest nutritional hazard. In addition, food industry researchers are working on products with far greater health implications. Words or phrases such as functional foods, nutraceuticals, pharmfoods, and designer foods now are part of a food technologist's vocabulary. While the specific definition may vary somewhat, these terms all refer to future foods containing properties believed either to help prevent diseases or heal them, or to enhance human performance. While functional foods (isotonic sports beverages, sleep-aid teas, calcium-fortified orange juice, etc.) are proliferating in Europe and Japan, they have made only limited and discreet inroads in the United

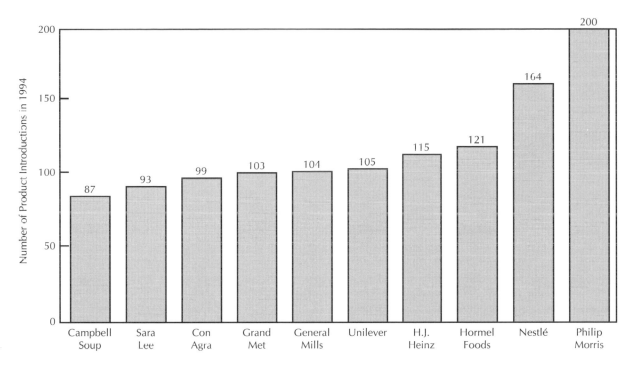

FIGURE 2.   New food product introductions, 1994. Source: U.S. Dept. of Agriculture (*New Product News,* January 8, 1995).

States. However, as scientific progress accelerates and U.S. regulatory testing produces efficacy evidence, the impact of functional foods will be influential on overall U.S. food marketing.

There has been great progress in the development of bio-engineered foods. In 1994, the government approved Calgene's Flavr Savr tomato, the first genetically manipulated food to be sold on a mass market basis. Calgene scientists slowed the ripening gene in the ordinary tomato, allowing it to stay on the vine longer before being picked. Some other genetically engineered foods we may see on stores some day include: snack cakes that provide total daily nutritional needs; potatoes with a chicken gene to better resist spoilage; instant meals that expand in the stomach, creating a sense of fullness; and canned or bottled drinks that make major nutritional claims (these are already major successes in Japan). Phytochemicals, which naturally appear in fruits and vegetables, and which may help prevent cancer and heart disease, already appear in newly marketed vitamins.

While food manufacturers have made great strides in delivering enhanced taste and improved nutrition to their products, their prediction of greater convenience in food preparation has been disappointed. Although the majority of homes have a microwave oven, only 30 percent use it for anything other than reheating food. The most common use for microwave ovens is making popcorn. However, a major technological breakthrough in microwave cooking, such as quick browning, could renew microwaves' promise.

Minor marketing moves have increased food preparation convenience somewhat. New "speed scratch" meal kits combine various ingredients so that cooks must only add fresh meat to produce a dinner entree. Specialty appliances permit easier home bread-baking, pasta preparation, and espresso coffee brewing. Other convenience products that aid meal preparers pressed for time are cooking sauces, stuffing mixes, prepackaged fresh salads, pasta, and refrigerated entrees and lunches. There will be significant increases in take-out and home delivery of food.

Although over 20,000 new food and drug products were introduced in 1994, this total includes many local, regional, and test market products, as well as many items sold only in gourmet shops, health food stores, and drugstores. The 20,000-plus total is a national conglomeration. (See Figure 3.) No retailer or consumer in the United States was exposed to all 20,000 items. It should also be noted that from 80 to 90 percent of new food and drug products can be described as line extensions—including new flavors, colors, or varieties. Few so-called "new" products are true breakthroughs—totally new to the world. Any changes in U.S.

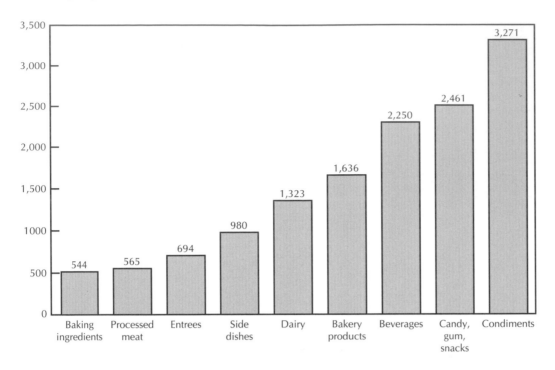

FIGURE 3. New food product introductions, leading categories in 1994. Source: U.S. Dept. of Agriculture (*New Product News,* January 8, 1995).

consumption of foods or drugs will be evolutionary rather than revolutionary, since humans are conservative about what they put in or on their bodies. Nevertheless, important changes in how we produce, distribute, prepare, and eat foods will occur in the future. Dynamic marketplace, scientific, medical, and behavioral influences will not permit any status-quo outlook.

See also ALCOHOL; BATTERIES; CHEMICALS, FINE; CLOTHING; COMIC BOOKS; FOOD ADDITIVES; FOOD CONSUMPTION; FOOD DISTRIBUTION; FOOD TECHNOLOGIES; FRAGRANCES; GENETICS, COMMERCIALIZATION OF; GRAY MARKET GOODS; NUTRITION; PHARMACEUTICALS; RECORDING INDUSTRY; TOBACCO.

BIBLIOGRAPHY

ABRAMS, MALCOLM, and BERNSTEIN, HARRIET. *Future Stuff*. New York: Viking-Penguin, 1989.
_____. *More Future Stuff*. New York: Viking-Penguin, 1991.
APPLE, L. EUGENE, and HUSTAD, THOMAS P., eds. *Product Development: Prospering in a Rapidly Changing World*. Indianapolis: Product Development Management Association, 1990.
SAUDER, WILLIAM E. *Managing New Product Innovations*. New York: Free Press, 1986.

Martin Friedman

Newspapers

Newspapers as we know them today may not even exist in the future. The general circulation newspaper of general interest, published daily, is threatened with obsolescence, as people find other methods of keeping informed.

Most people now have radios, televisions, and telephones. Many have personal computers as well. In the future, all these information technologies will be combined in integrated systems. An investor could find out how the stock market is doing and send instructions to her broker. A sports fan could read about the big game and watch a tape of the deciding play. A consumer can find out what is on sale at the local supermarket and place an electronic order for delivery.

Many of the needs now met by newspapers thus will be met with more options by the home media center. Newspapers that want to survive will be on-line and compatible with the other technologies. Nor will readers be satisfied with seeing what some editor thinks is the news. Instant access to information worldwide will enable readers to pick and choose—and to find stories on almost any subject.

Similarly, some papers have found their niche and are likely to remain there—for example, the *New York Times,* the *Wall Street Journal,* and the

Washington Post. These and other major daily newspapers have branched out beyond their original markets and have developed a loyal readership among readers elsewhere in the country—although in the future, these readers may be reading on-line rather than a printed copy delivered by a carrier.

Local newspapers may also find themselves in a better position. People care about what is happening in their community. They want to know where the neighborhood break-ins have occurred and which restaurants have been shut down for health-code violations. After all, you might not find your local classified ads or police-beat entries on the Internet. Newspapers that tailor themselves to a specific, small area could become more financially secure than the giants who attempt to grab every reader all over the country.

For similar reasons, specialty newsletters may flourish. With a few key strokes, the reader could find up-to-the-minute information on whatever is of special interest. With the whole world as a potential market, even the most obscure publications could find an audience.

Ironically, the new technology could get us back to our American journalistic roots: the pamphleteer. Anyone with a computer can become a publisher and put out the information he considers to be important. And anyone with a computer could receive it.

Specialized reading will also require specialized reporting. The job of the newspaper reporter is also likely to be quite different in the future. Instead of being a generalist knowing a little bit about a lot of topics, the reporter of the future may be an expert in a narrow field. This trend is already becoming well established.

The mechanics of reporting also will evolve. The computer has changed the way reporters do their job. Most reporters now file their stories electronically, sending their stories to their editors via a computer. Through portable computers and cellular phones, or even satellite phones, reporters can stay in touch with the office even while covering events in a remote area. This ability can only expand in the future.

Many more reporters will use the computer as a resource tool to find information on a particular issue or to find experts to quote on a particular topic. Need a political scientist to comment on declining voter turnout? Put out the message on the Internet and political scientists from around the world will respond, with no need for the reporter to work the phones. This method can only increase

as more people get on-line. Reporters could find themselves covering their beat in front of a computer screen as often as not.

Also the need actually to cover that school board meeting or zoning commission hearing in person may decline as more people get access to the event itself. Citizens who are interested will be able to call up the transcript or a video record of the proceeding. Interested citizens likewise will be able to instantly register their opinion of how public officials are doing. One could read the debate, watch the vote, and then send off a message of praise or protest.

But won't we always need "real" newspapers—printed matter that can be stuffed in a briefcase and perused on the way to work? After all, you cannot take a computer on the bus. Well, maybe someday everyone can own a computer that is light enough and portable enough to access information anywhere.

Perhaps newspaper racks will give way to computerized outlets offering passers-by a selection of reading materials, sort of like public, coin-operated copy machines of the kind that are now available everywhere, from libraries to convenience stores. Readers who like the feel of paper can simply print out whatever interests them, in whatever order they like. In effect, people will be able to construct their own newspapers, lifting a column from one source, a cartoon from another.

Regrettably, there is a growing number of people who do not find newspapers important to their lives. They catch televised news once in a while and gossip with fellow office workers. They do not see current events as relevant to their lives. Furthermore, they distrust the ability or willingness of newspapers, television, and magazines to give them the true story. Perhaps if "readers" have more discretion in what they can get access to, they will be less distrustful of the messengers. If newspapers are to survive, they will have to keep up with the technology and the changing needs of readers.

See also COMMUNICATIONS; ELECTRONIC CONVERGENCE; ON-LINE SERVICES; PRINTED WORD; TELECOMMUNICATIONS.

BIBLIOGRAPHY

TOFFLER, ALVIN. *Power Shift.* New York: Bantam Books, 1990.

STRAUSSMAN, PAUL A. *Information Pay-off.* New York: Free Press, 1985.

UNDERWOOD, DOUG. *When MBAs Rule the Newsroom.* New York: Columbia University Press, 1993.

Nora Raum

New Zealand.

See AUSTRALIA AND NEW ZEALAND.

Nongovernmental Organizations

Nongovernmental Organizations (NGOs) are non-profit associations that address public issues, social concerns, or more limited interests, but are not a part of government. In addition to providing social services, many of these organizations seek to influence governmental decisions through expert testimony, public information campaigns, and professional research. They operate at local, national, and international levels. Some NGOs, such as hospitals and universities, attempt to work for the public good with minimum government intrusion, especially in the United States. Sometimes this involvement may only be limited to registration with the government and possibly with the attainment of a tax-exempt status. In some societies, NGOs may be quasi-governmental entities.

Approximately eighty million adults work as volunteers for nonprofit organizations in the United States, such as the Girl Scouts, United Way, the Salvation Army, and others (Drucker, 1992, p. 203). From 1962 until 1993 charitable contributions to NGOs in the United States grew, in constant dollars, from $61 billion to $124 billion. This contribution level is 2.1 percent of the economy, and 88 percent of the donations came from individuals, with foundations and corporations making up the rest. NGOs have become increasingly influential to assist the more than 83,000 total governmental units in the United States, which employ fifteen million civil servants, of which three million are working for the national government (Gaebler, et al., 1992, p. xxi). In comparison, there are approximately 7.5 million people employed by NGOs in the United States.

The past four American presidents have strongly emphasized the need to streamline government bureaucracy at all levels and to privatize many government services. President Bill Clinton referred to "reinventing government," while President George H. Bush spoke of NGOs as a "thousand points of light." It seems there is a growing, nonpartisan recognition of citizen responsibility as an untapped asset that could be more effectively used in improving communities and individual lives. The number of tax-exempt, nonprofit organizations in the United States has roughly doubled in the past ten years, while the number of supporting chari-table foundations has nearly quadrupled to approximately 34,000. Only about 10 percent of these have assets greater than $5 million, and they account for 75 percent of the total amount of foundation grant money.

The advantages of NGOs, as opposed to government, often include flexible and creative response to human problems as well as the ability to channel the enthusiasm of volunteers and concerned citizens. For instance, Robert Macauley founded Americares in the 1980s to provide rapid airlift anywhere a major disaster occurred. By 1991 it had carried more than $100 million of food and medicine on short notice to seventy-five countries. Often governments require time-consuming authorizations, studies, and procedures that are ill-suited for rapidly or effectively meeting human needs. NGOs are not bound by these restrictions. Management guru Peter Drucker has praised many NGOs for their ability to define their missions and to develop cost-effective strategies in accomplishing them. Many of them are "working out policies and practices that business will have to learn tomorrow." (Drucker, 1992, p. 203)

Because NGOs often are largely dependent on charitable contributions, there are problems. First, funding may be unreliable. Further, some NGOs are not candid in regard to how they spend their money. Their descriptive literature sometimes bears little resemblance to reality. In some cases, annual reports, if available, obscure true financial status. The Better Business Bureau often keeps track of problems with such organizations. Furthermore, most reputable charitable organizations will be audited each year by an outside accounting firm, which prepares a detailed financial statement. While most NGOs undoubtedly operate at high levels of integrity, those that do not may encourage increased future government scrutiny and regulation.

In addition to charitable service organizations, NGOs also can refer to advocacy groups that tout such causes as the environment, a strong national defense, or human life. Furthermore, some NGOs may represent the interests and concerns of professions, such as attorneys, scientists, accountants, or even nonprofit association executives. The past twenty years has seen a proliferation of more than 1,000 nonprofit research organizations, or think tanks, which are a newer addition to the world of NGOs.

Think tanks often combine professional research with advocacy related to government or social policy. With the growth and complexity of government, especially after World War II, there has arisen a new group of specialists who continually research and test ideas for changes in public policies.

Some think tanks are "big concept" in focus with a high level of imagination and speculation, while others are more technical in nature and focus on methods of implementing public policy. Perhaps the most visible pioneer of think tanks was Herman Kahn, who worked for the Rand Corporation after World War II and who then founded the Hudson Institute in the early 1960s. Best known for his ideas on nuclear war, Kahn also studied a wide variety of economic and social problems

In evaluating think tank research, the prudent consumer would do well to know about funding sources, since the source of funding may influence the type of research gathered and conclusions drawn. Support can come from combinations of government, business, interest groups, foundations, or individuals, and each of these sources may have beliefs or interests they wish to advance.

The growth of NGOs in recent years is likely to continue well into the future because of their demonstrated efficiency and effectiveness at problem solving. Nonetheless, with all this growth there may also occur the threat of or need for increased government regulation.

See also INSTITUTIONS AND ORGANIZATIONS; ORGANIZATIONAL COMPLEXITY.

BIBLIOGRAPHY

DRUCKER, PETER F. *Managing for the Future: The 1990s and Beyond.* New York: Truman Talley Books/Dutton, 1992.

GALLUP, JR., GEORGE. *Forecast 2000.* New York: William Morrow, 1984.

GAEBLER, TED, and OSBORNE, DAVID. *Reinventing Government: How the Entrepreneurial Spirit is Transforming the Public Sector from Schoolhouse to Statehouse, City Hall to the Pentagon.* Reading, MA: Addison Wesley, 1992.

SMITH, JAMES A. *The Idea Brokers: Think Tanks and the Rise of the New Policy Elite.* New York: Free Press, 1991.

TEMPLETON, JOHN MARKS, ed. *Looking Forward: The Next Forty Years.* New York: K. S. Giniger Co., 1993.

Michael Y. Warder

Nonreligious Beliefs

A philosophical orientation and life stance committed to the pursuit of the human good as the ultimate concern for human beings is called human-ism. Humanism has a strong ethical focus and perceives the future as open and subject to human agency. Central to humanist ideals is an appreciation for the dignity and irreducibility of the human being. It also upholds the importance of such values as justice, compassion, reason, and cooperation as essential to creating the good society.

While there have been humanistic tendencies within both Eastern and Western religions, humanism in the narrower sense has come to be identified with a nontheistic position that either rejects the supernatural or views it as unknowable or irrelevant to the end of human flourishing. Since the middle of the nineteenth century, variants of idealism, agnosticism, and philosophical naturalism have given rise to organized associations promoting humanist thought and objectives through education, publication, and social action. Some have been explicitly secular and anti-ecclesiastical, while others have been identified as religious. Among these groups have been the Religion of Humanity founded by the French sociologist, Auguste Comte, and various "free thought" movements located primarily in Germany and England. The Ethical Culture Movement, founded by Felix Adler in 1876, and the American Humanist Association are distinctively American expressions with intellectual roots in Unitarianism, Transcendentalism, and liberal Judaism. The International Humanist and Ethical Union was founded in 1952 as a global umbrella organization. Headquartered in Utrecht, the International Humanist and Ethical Union at present unites more than ninety humanist organizations on all continents, representing hundreds of thousand of individuals. It is impossible to determine the number of humanists worldwide since humanist values overlap with other beliefs and ideologies that may not be explicitly humanist. It can be assumed, however, that there are millions of people unaffiliated with established religious organizations whose outlook is prevailingly humanistic.

Contemporary humanism is a child of the Scientific Revolution and the European Enlightenment of the seventeenth and eighteenth centuries, though precursors can be found in classical antiquity, the European Renaissance, as well as in biblical emphases on the sacredness of the human being.

Humanism carries forward the legacy of the Enlightenment in its commitment to the political values of progress, democracy, individual rights, and tolerance. Its character has been shaped by the scientific spirit and the search for universal and objective truths. It stands in opposition to obscurantism, dogmatism, and authoritarianism.

Humanism today is, therefore, closely identified with the values of modernity and sees itself as a defender of these values. Consequently, the future of humanism is tied to economic, social, political, and religious forces that threaten modernist ideals and sensibilities on a global scale. It is challenged by trends that are identified with the emergence of the postmodern era. Current trends most in conflict with humanist values include the rise of religious fundamentalisms, the emergence of particularist loyalties including xenophobic nationalism, the dominance of consumer culture, and the decline in prestige of science.

Humanism is also philosophically challenged by the epistemological assumptions of postmodernism and extreme forms of multiculturalism that deny the possibility of universal human values. To the extent that postmodernism presupposes radical subjectivity, perspectivism, and moral relativism, it runs counter to humanism's commitment to objective knowledge, however provisionally held.

As these social and intellectual forces become more acute over the next several decades, the relevance of humanism both philosophically and organizationally will intensify. If the world, and particularly the West, is heading toward an era of "neomedievalism," as the thinker Umberto Eco has speculated, then humanism will become an increasingly important redoubt for the defenders of liberal and democratic values. But if postmodernism proves to be a temporary phase within modernity, then the future will become an increasingly humanistic one. If this latter scenario triumphs, then it will validate humanism's conviction that its ideals have a universal and eternal claim and are necessary for the maintenance of any decent social order, especially on a planet with close to six billion human mouths to feed.

Despite discontent with the alienation, bureaucratization, and alleged despiritualization of modern life, there are many indicators that humanism has a promising future. The collapse of Marxism in Eastern Europe has left an ideological vacuum that humanism and humanistic organizations can fill by providing a positive alternative to both nihilism and Christian orthodoxy. Emergence of powerful free market economies on the Pacific Rim are generating conditions that are more open and democratic and, thus, may prove more consonant with humanistic values. Within the United States, organizations such as the Ethical Culture movement provide congregational structures for those who

seek to reinforce progressive moral values, without accepting the supernaturalism of traditional or conservative faiths. Within the next several decades, humanist organizations will expand, partially in response to the strength of fundamentalist religious groups espousing a reactionary political agenda.

Another source of growth for organized humanism is the result of the autonomy associated with modern life. This freedom ensures that many people today marry outside of their religion of birth. Organized humanist communities will increasingly provide attractive alternatives for those couples who intermarry and seek wider affiliation. Finally, because of the perceived social and moral breakdown in American society, humanistic organizations will have an increasingly significant role in sustaining fundamental ethical ideals. This task grows apace as more Americans come to feel that these principles cannot be sustained by the general culture alone.

See also BUDDHISM; CHRISTIANITY; GLOBAL CONSCIOUSNESS; HINDUISM; ISLAM; JUDAISM; RELIGION: CHANGING BELIEFS; RELIGION, SPIRITUALITY, MORALITY; RELIGIONS, DECLINE OR RISE OF; RELIGIONS, STATISTICAL PROJECTIONS OF.

BIBLIOGRAPHY

ERICSON, EDWARD. *The Humanist Way.* New York: Continuum, 1988.
Humanist Manifestos I and II. Buffalo, NY: Prometheus Books, 1973.
LAMONT, CORLISS. *The Philosophy of Humanism.* New York: Continuum, 1990.

Joseph Chuman

Nostradamus (Michel de Nostredame, 1503–1566)

French physician and astrologer Nostradamus is the best remembered of the many diviners of the future who practiced their art during the Renaissance. He began his professional career as a physician, rising to the rank of court physician to Charles IX of France. Blending biblical, astrological, and literary lore, he wrote a long series of cryptic verses, including nearly 1,000 rhymed quatrains grouped in "centuries" (sets of 100 quatrains) as well as a smaller number of sextains. The first edition of his *Centuries* appeared in 1555. In a prefatory letter addressed to his newborn son, Nostradamus explained that he had deliberately cast his predictions "in nebulous rather than plainly prophetic form." The apparent success of some of his forecasts gained him widespread celebrity during his lifetime. His fame continued to grow long after his death. His works were formally condemned by the Catholic Church in 1781. In the twentieth century, they have been studied exhaustively by latter-day disciples, who claim that he foresaw many of the tribulations of our time. But his ambiguous verses can be interpreted to mean almost anything; few professional futurists take them seriously.

See also APOCALYPTIC FUTURES; FUTURISM; FUTURISTS; PSEUDO-FUTURISTS.

BIBLIOGRAPHY

CHEETHAM, ERIKA, ed. and tr. *The Prophecies of Nostradamus.* London: Neville Spearman, 1974.

FONTBRUNE, JEAN-CHARLES DE. *Nostradamus: Countdown to Apocalypse.* London: Hutchinson, 1983. Translation by Alexis Lykiard of *Nostradamus: historien et prophète: les prophéties de 1555 a l'an 2000,* 1980.

W. Warren Wagar

Nuclear Power

Some time fairly early in the next century, nuclear power is likely to become the predominant source of energy throughout much of the world. The supply of fossil fuels is diminishing rapidly and alternative sources of energy are unlikely to suffice for the widespread, varying applications that will be needed in the near and short term.

Uranium Supplies and Reserves

The rich uranium deposits (i.e., concentrations of greater than 0.1 percent) utilized at present are believed to be quite limited, perhaps only enough to last for 50–100 years. There are supplies of lower grade ores (concentrations of about 0.005 percent) that could last for several centuries. Since the cost of raw uranium now represents only about 1 percent of that of nuclear electricity, the use of these lower grade ores would tend to raise the cost of electricity by perhaps 20 percent.

For the longer term, the problem can best be solved by using breeder reactors that derive 100 times as much energy from each pound of uranium. This means that it is economically feasible to use uranium costing a hundred times its current price. In turn this makes extraction of uranium from seawater an economically attractive alternative. The uranium now found in seawater could provide the world's electricity needs for a few million years. Rivers are constantly dissolving uranium out of rock and carrying it into the seas. Taking this process into account, seawater could provide all the world's uranium needs for several billion years, which is as long as Earth will be habitable.

Cold Fusion

There has been a great deal of publicity about "cold fusion," thermonuclear reactions at room temperature mediated by the absorption of hydrogen isotopes in the metallic element palladium. However, a large majority of the scientific community is convinced that there is no credible evidence that the reported effects are real. Even if such reactions were real, no one has suggested a practical method for generating large quantities of useful energy from them.

Standard Approaches

Research on the two standard approaches to thermonuclear fusion—magnetic confinement and inertial confinement—has continued, and there is a high degree of confidence that "scientific feasibility" will be demonstrated within the next several years. The significance of this is that the energy generated by thermonuclear reactions will be larger than the electrical energy input to operate the system. This condition will persist for perhaps one second and will be repeatable only about once an hour.

The next step, technical feasibility, will be a difficult and expensive one, extending over thirty years or more. The repetition rate must be greatly increased. Efficient capture of the released energy and its conversion into electricity must be developed. The technology also must breed tritium fuel to replace the fuel consumed. Maintenance problems of unprecedented severity will have to be worked out. Problems of economic feasibility in continuing these activities must be faced, and a great deal of optimism is required to believe that the outcome will be favorable. Many proponents of fusion research now concede that its application to large-scale electricity generation will not be economically feasible. Interest in pursuing these efforts is largely motivated by other potential applications.

Safety

The science of probabilistic risk analysis (PRA) for studying the safety of nuclear reactors has recently developed to the point that it is widely accepted in the technical and regulatory communities. For the present generation of 1,000-MWe (megawatt electrical output) light water reactors, the PRA indicate that we may expect one severe accident per 20,000 reactor years of operation, with an average of 400 deaths per accident, or 0.02 deaths per 1000 MWe-year. This is less than 0.1 percent of the number of deaths estimated from coal burning, and substantially less than the estimated number from any competitive technology.

However, safety can be further improved by reducing the size to 600 MWe. At this lower power level, active systems with pumps, now required to cool the reactor fuel and protect the containment structure from overpressure under accident conditions, can be replaced by passive systems with water flow driven by gravity. This approach eliminates the problem of electric power loss (including back-up diesel generators) and pump failures, which are the most prominent causes of accidents in 1,000-MWe reactors. Other simplifications allowed by the lower power reduce the cost-per-MWe, compensating for most of the economies of scale in the larger reactors. Simplicity also inherently improves safety.

In the United States, with its numerous small utilities, there are also institutional problems favoring the smaller units. The 600-MWe reactors are targeted at that market. Large national utilities like those in Britain, France, and Japan still favor plants of greater than 1,000-MWe size.

Disposal of Radioactive Waste

The technical side of radioactive waste disposal is very simple—convert it into a "rock-like" material, and bury it in the natural habitat of rocks, deep underground. There is abundant evidence on the behavior of average rock materials, and if this is applied to the radioactive waste buried at random locations, it is easy to show that health impacts will be about 0.02 eventual deaths per gigawatt electrical output–year or GWe-year (1 GWe-year = 1,000 MWe-years). This is less than 0.1 percent of the consequences of air pollution and wastes resulting from fossil fuel burning. It is also less than 0.1 percent of the deaths per GWe-year attributed to chemical carcinogens released into the ground in coal burning, or from the eventual radon emissions from uranium dispersed by coal burning. With careful siting and use of engineered safeguards, such as enclosing wastes in leach-resistant casings, the release of buried waste should be much less probable than that of materials in average rock.

The ground is full of natural radioactivity, and adding radioactive waste from nuclear energy production adds very little to the total. The fact that the waste will be concentrated in a small area does not increase its potential danger to human health.

Politics of Nuclear Energy

In the last quarter of the twentieth century, nuclear power development was adversely impacted upon and even halted by political opposition. Environmental groups attacked nuclear power, although coal burning, according to all scientific evidence, is far more harmful. Media attacks swayed public opinion to the point that politicians found opposition to be hard to resist. Approximately 1,000 extra people are condemned to a premature death each time a coal-burning plant is built instead of a nuclear plant. This is true even if we accept the risks of nuclear accidents proposed by the principal antinuclear activist organization—the Union of Concerned Scientists. Their estimates are one hundred times those given by PRAs.

It is difficult to predict how long this irrational situation will persist, but there are powerful forces at work that hopefully will overcome it. France, Japan, and other countries are maintaining strong nuclear power programs with advantages that in time will become evident. Concern over the greenhouse effect, acid rain, and air pollution will drive up the cost of coal burning and force it into a difficult competitive position. The public must eventually come to realize that solar electricity can never compete economically with nuclear power at night and in winter, and that the latter is environmentally preferable in any case.

The political problems and opposition facing nuclear power should fade away, and it will become dominant sometime in the twenty-first century. Ultimately, the dominance of nuclear power seems all but certain, since within a few hundred years available fossil fuels will become scarce and expensive. Nuclear power may well be the dominant energy source one thousand years from now, one million years from now, and even a billion years from now—for as long as intelligent beings inhabit Earth.

For a different, cautionary look at nuclear power, *see* NUCLEAR POWER: CON. *See also* ARMS RACE;

ENERGY; ENVIRONMENTAL REFUGEES; HAZARD-
OUS WASTES; TERRORISM; TRANSURANIUM ELE-
MENTS; WEAPONS OF MASS DESTRUCTION.

BIBLIOGRAPHY

COHEN, BERNARD L. *The Nuclear Energy Option.* New
York: Plenum, 1990.
_____. "Risk Analysis of Buried Waste from Electricity
Generation." *American Journal of Physics* 54 (1986):
38.
"The New Reactors." *Nuclear News* (September 1992):
65–90.
"Severe Accident Risks." Washington, DC: U.S. Nuclear
Regulatory Commission. Document NUREG-1150,
1989.

Bernard L. Cohen

Nuclear Power: Con

Approximately 112 nuclear power plants operating
in the United States generate about 20 percent of
the country's electricity. Globally, nuclear power
accounts for about 10 percent of the electricity
generated. At its inception during the 1950s and
early '60s, commercial nuclear power promised
much. Nuclear power was to generate clean, safe,
and cheap electricity. Today, with social and political attention focused on threats to the global environment posed by fossil fuels, nuclear power's future would seem bright. An energy source that did
not contribute to acid rain or ozone depletion
would seem to have a secure place in the world's
energy future. Curiously, such is not the case. In
the United States, no new nuclear power plants
have been ordered since 1978 and those ordered
since 1974 have been cancelled. Internationally, the
picture is mixed. Countries such as Japan, France,
and Germany rely on nuclear power. Elsewhere,
opposition has halted nuclear power in Australia,
New Zealand, Denmark, and Sweden.

Six key reasons for the lack of enthusiasm for
nuclear power can be reduced to a simple proposition: Nuclear power may play a significant part in
the energy future if the public perceives the cost of
nuclear power to be cheaper than that of electricity
from fossil fuels.

There are three variables in that last statement—
public perception, costs, and *fossil fuels*—which
must be explained. Public perception encompasses
questions about the perceptions of risk and the
cost of paying for nuclear-generated electricity.
Cost, in turn, encompasses both the direct and in-

direct economic costs, as well as social costs attendant on this controversial energy source. Finally,
nuclear power must be cheaper than generating
electricity from fossil fuels—coal, oil, and natural
gas—that are primarily responsible for global environmental damages.

Six Arguments Against Nuclear Power

THE DIRECT AND INDIRECT COST OF NUCLEAR POWER

Nuclear power plants, expensive to construct, were
expected to be cheap to operate relative to the cost
of fuel. Unfortunately, construction costs were
grossly underestimated. The decade of the 1970s
was financially disastrous to the industry as increasing inflation, higher labor and construction
costs, longer lead times, more regulatory burdens,
and changing public attitude raised construction
costs several factors. It was not unusual to project
a cost of $800 million for a plant and then have
that cost escalate to over $2 billion as it took eight
to twelve years to complete.

Operating costs are another matter. At one time
it was believed that a plant would last forty or fifty
years, but that figure has been revised downward
to twenty-five years or less. Construction cost over-
runs, inattention to the back end of the fuel cycle—
for example, waste disposal and plant decommis-
sion—and increasing regulatory requirements have
contributed to make nuclear-generated electricity
more expensive than coal-generated electricity as
nuclear power plants fail to achieve hoped-for
economies of scale.

While construction and operating costs are considered direct economic costs, social or external
costs include such matters as the health and environmental costs of routine and nonroutine radiation emission, and property and personal damages
caused by routine emissions and nuclear accidents.
Admittedly, these costs are difficult to quantify and
quantification relies more on modeling than empirical data. Moreover, discussion and analysis of
such environmental costs are highly politicized.

NUCLEAR SAFETY

The accidents at Three Mile Island (TMI) and
Chernobyl and plant cancellations, such as the
Shoreham fiasco, destroyed the confidence of the
public in the safety of nuclear power and became
symbolic of questions of safety and risks. Even
though risks from nuclear power are not statistically inordinate, nuclear power presents serious

problems of perception. Even the small risk of a core meltdown creates the real possibility of nuclear catastrophe. An early, and disputed, study noted that even though the chance of a serious accident was only one in 200 million reactor years, the cost of such an accident would be 3,000 to 4,000 lives and over $14 billion of property damage. In other words, while the probability of accidents is small, the costs are enormous, and these costs have captured public attention.

WASTE DISPOSAL

The nuclear industry produces radioactive waste from mining, processing, and burning the fuel. Nuclear power plants produce two forms of radioactive waste—high-level waste from spent fuel and low-level waste from reactor cooling water. Little in the United States was done to provide for the disposal of nuclear plant waste until the passage of the Nuclear Waste Policy Act in 1982 and the Low-Level Radioactive Waste Policy Act of 1980. Both acts establish complex mechanisms for the siting of nuclear waste disposal facilities; however, as of the date of this writing, no permanent storage for spent fuel has been established. To further aggravate this problem, the stockpiling of commercial nuclear waste on site as well as environmental harm caused at nuclear weapons facilities, such as Fernald in Ohio and Rocky Flats in Colorado, have made the public more suspicious of radioactive waste storage. To exacerbate matters further, the transportation of nuclear waste, both domestically and internationally, has raised further public concern.

DECOMMISSIONING

The back end of the fuel cycle not only entails the temporary storage of waste on site and the permanent storage of nuclear waste in a facility, it also involves the decommissioning of nuclear power plants. The two basic forms of decommissioning are the dismantling and long-term storage of a plant and the entombment of a plant in concrete. Decommissioning takes years, is extremely expensive, can amount to the cost of building a new plant, and presents transportation problems as well.

In some instances, decommissioning may be more expensive than building and operating a nuclear plant. A Japanese utility has estimated that decommissioning costs for a unit will be $1.2 billion, and Three Mile Island decommissioning and clean-up costs are projected at $3.2 billion.

GOVERNMENT REGULATION

Government regulation of any industry necessarily entails costs to that industry. Measures to reduce the cost of federal regulation in the nuclear field would include streamlining licensing, standardizing plants (including their safety designs), and further centralizing decision making in the federal government as opposed to the states. Some of these regulatory reform measures are part of the National Energy Security Act of 1992. Internationally, regulatory problems increase exponentially as one considers: the transboundary effects of routine and accidental radiation from plants; the need for international codes, practices, and agreements; the consequences of the international movement of wastes; and international protection for waste repositories, site selection, and decontamination and dismantling.

PUBLIC ACCEPTANCE

Over the last twenty years or more, nuclear power plants have been a cause célèbre among environmental activists. Threats of catastrophic accident, radiation effects of plant operation, and waste disposal efforts as well as transportation of nuclear fuel have caused concern among nuclear critics. While it is difficult to turn around public perception regarding the risks of radioactivity, until that perception is reversed, nuclear power prospects will be bleak. If the public perceives fossil fuel plants to be more dangerous to the global environment than nuclear power, this trend could possibly be reversed. If it becomes both technologically and economically feasible to harness the power of nuclear fusion, rather than fission, nuclear power could gain a new prominence, but this does not appear at all likely in the near term.

THE FUTURE

Although a nuclear resurgence in the near term is unlikely, the key variables for a nuclear future are clear. Direct, external, and regulatory costs must all decrease to the point that nuclear power is a more attractive energy alternative than fossil fuels, especially coal. Public attitude must adjust to the point that personal, property, and environmental risks of nuclear power are less than the risks from other energy sources.

See the essay NUCLEAR POWER preceding this one for a more favorable viewpoint on this form of energy. *See also* ARMS RACE; ENERGY; ENVIRONMENTAL REFUGEES; HAZARDOUS WASTES; TERRORISM; TRANSURANIUM ELEMENTS; WEAPONS OF MASS DESTRUCTION.

BIBLIOGRAPHY

CARTER, LUTHER J. *Nuclear Imperatives and Public Trust: Dealing with Radioactive Waste.* Washington, DC: Resources for the Future, 1987.

INTERNATIONAL ENERGY AGENCY. *Global Energy: The Changing Outlook.* Paris: Organization for Economic Cooperation and Development, 1992.

TESTER, JEFFERSON W.; WOOD, DAVID O.; and FERRARI, NANCY A., eds. *Energy and the Environment in the Twenty-first Century.* Cambridge, MA: MIT Press, 1991.

TOMAIN, JOSEPH P. *Nuclear Power Transportation.* Bloomington, IN: Indiana University Press, 1987.

Union of Concerned Scientists. *Safety Second: The NRC and America's Nuclear Power Plants.* Bloomington, IN: Indiana University Press, 1987.

Joseph P. Tomain

Nursing

Registered nurses (RNs) are independent health care practitioners who are officially recognized through licensure and registration by the individual states in which they practice. The nursing profession acknowledges an individual's competency at a specific level through the certification process. Nurses are therefore identified both officially and professionally. Nurses often collaborate with or practice in conjunction with a variety of other individuals from other disciplines, including but not limited to physicians, respiratory and physical therapists, social workers, pharmacists, and dieticians.

"Nursing is the diagnosis and treatment of human responses to actual or potential health problems" (American Nurses' Association, 1980, p. 9). One of the fundamental roles of a nurse has been to provide care to those who would ordinarily be able to care for themselves, if they had the ability to do so. Nurses are most commonly recognized for their delivery of direct "hands-on" care to individual patients, typically in hospital settings. But nurses have historically provided care everywhere people are—in the home, community, school, street, workplace, hospital, hospice, or health center. Nurses also deliver a variety of other types of therapeutic, supportive, and palliative care. Nursing's future will continue to build upon its strengths: the diversity of the profession's constituents and of the populations cared for, an ongoing flexibility in approaches to patient care, and a continuing ability to adapt to changes in diverse areas.

The nursing profession has historically been predominantly female. However, a growing number of men are entering the profession. This trend is expected to continue into the next century. The nursing profession can be expected to draw members from all segments of the population.

Nurses have always cared for those in need—whoever and wherever they are. The profession's heterogeneity has added to its ability to care for those from all walks of life and will continue to do so. The flexibility in the delivery of care is reflected through the classic nursing process—assessing a patient's condition, diagnosing the problem or need, formulating a plan of care, implementing the plan, and then evaluating it. This approach allows care to be custom-tailored to each individual situation. The consideration of each patient's unique strengths, weaknesses, support systems, and resources increases the possibility for successful intervention—whether smoking cessation or postcardiac surgery rehabilitation is involved. This holistic approach to care will help perpetuate nursing's human service ideology.

The nursing profession will be influenced by and will influence social, financial, environmental, educational, governmental, and professional forces. Any change in the demographics of the population will precipitate a concomitant change in the delivery of nursing care. As a larger segment of the population moves into the over-sixty-five category, nurses will adapt to meet the special needs of this group. This adaptation and specialization will become increasingly evident through the growing prominence of such nursing roles as the gerontological nurse practitioner.

A shift in the focus of care from the acute, tertiary care to primary, preventative care will result in a related shift in job opportunities. Nurses will continue to build the primary care foundation in the community. Acute care hospitals will continue to become places where only the most intense care is delivered. Patients will be cared for increasingly in the home, with services such as nursing being brought in. In-patient hospital nursing opportunities will shift from the general medical/surgical units to intensive care environments. Reimbursement for specific nursing interventions and intensity of care is foreseen at the service-provider level. Nursing opportunities will increase in the community and home care areas.

Technological advances will drive the need for specialization of nursing skills in some areas. The specialization will require supplemental education and will provide additional employment opportunities.

Nursing will confront the diverse preparatory routes that lead to entry into practice. Preparation at the baccalaureate level is anticipated to increase. Additional preparation at the postgraduate or master's level for advanced practice providers, such as certified nurse midwives (CNMs), clinical nurse specialists (CNSs), and nurse practitioners (NPs), is expected to sharply escalate and increase in importance.

A dramatic increase in the number of CNMs, CNSs, and NPs is anticipated to continue for several years and then level off. The scope of skills and autonomy of these advanced nurse clinicians is expected to grow. Predicted changes include direct reimbursement by patients or health-insurance plans for services at the individual-practitioner level for advanced nurse clinicians, and a new authority for such clinicians to issue medical prescriptions for specific classes of pharmacologic agents. There will be a growth in the amount of research devoted to confirming the efficacy, efficiency, and cost-effectiveness of nursing interventions. Professional certification is expected to increase in the areas of specialization. National centralization of registration and licensure is also predicted.

Health care reform on the national, state, regional, and community levels is envisioned. Nursing will be at the forefront of these reform efforts. Nursing will continue to remain at the pivotal core of the future health care system by continuing to increase its political activity and visibility. It will also continue to build upon its traditional strengths by providing an increasing majority of direct patient care—wherever, whenever, or for whomever it is needed—and by providing continual, comprehensive, coordinated care throughout each patient's life span.

By continuing to anticipate change, the profession will be able to adapt to new conditions on an "as needed" basis. This adaptability will serve to further the primary care foundation in the community-at-large. It will also give rise to an increase in the scope of advanced-practice nursing clinicians, such as certified nurse midwives, clinical nurse specialists, and nurse practitioners.

See also HEALTH CARE; HEALTH CARE: ALTERNATIVE THERAPIES; HEALTH CARE COSTS; HEALTH CARE FINANCING; HEALTH CARE: MORAL ISSUES IN; HEALTH CARE: TECHNOLOGICAL DEVELOPMENTS; MEDICAL CARE PROVIDERS.

BIBLIOGRAPHY

American Nurses' Association. *Nursing: A Social Policy Statement.* Kansas City, MO: American Nurses' Association, 1980.

_____. *Standards of Practice for the Primary Health Care Nurse Practitioner.* Kansas City, MO: American Nurses' Association, 1987.

LEE, PHILIP R., and ESTES, CARROLL L., eds. *The Nation's Health.* Boston: Jones and Bartlett, 1994.

U.S. Department of Health and Human Services. *Health Personnel in the United States: Eighth Report to Congress, 1991—Nursing.* Washington, DC: U.S. Government Printing Office, 1991.

Joseph J. Napolitano

Nutrition

As we move into an increasingly health-conscious era, we need to foster an awareness that an optimum diet consists of a variety of foods that provide (1) sufficient energy (calories) to satisfy energy needs without causing undesirable weight gain, (2) levels of essential nutrients (protein, vitamins, and minerals) to meet body needs and maintain body reserves, and (3) moderate amounts of components associated with chronic diseases (i.e., fat, saturated fat, cholesterol, sodium, and alcohol). Dietary guidelines have been devised that encourage Americans to:

- Eat a variety of foods
- Maintain a healthy body weight
- Choose a diet low in fat, saturated fat, and cholesterol
- Select a diet with plenty of vegetables, fruit, and grain products
- Consume sugars only in moderation
- Use only moderate amounts of salt and sodium
- Drink alcoholic beverages in moderation, if at all

These guidelines are based on scientific literature showing the relationship of diet to health and disease.

Macronutrition

Dietary guidelines specify that humans should consume 30 percent or less of calories as fat, less than 10 percent of calories as saturated fat, and 300 or fewer milligrams of cholesterol per day to minimize risk for certain types of cancer and heart disease. For a diet of 2,000 calories per day, this would amount to about 65 or fewer grams of fat, and 20 or fewer grams of saturated fat. One can maintain a diet low in fat by eating primarily grain products, vegetables, and fruits; using fats and oils sparingly in cooking and at the table; selecting lean cuts of meat, poultry, and fish; and using nonfat or low-fat dairy products. The use of polyunsaturated vegetable oils (e.g., safflower, sunflower, and corn oils) in place of more saturated fats (e.g., butter or shortening) helps maintain a low intake of saturated fat. Moderate intake of animal products (especially egg yolk) helps to maintain a low intake of cholesterol.

Vegetables, fruits, and grain products are good sources of complex carbohydrates (starches), and dietary fiber, as well as various vitamins and minerals. Carbohydrates should provide at least 55 percent of the daily calories (about 275 grams for a daily intake of 2,000 calories). Adults should eat at least three servings of vegetables, two servings of fruits, and six servings of grain products (breads, cereals, pasta, and rice—with an emphasis on whole grains) per day. Dietary fiber is important for proper bowel function and can reduce symptoms of chronic constipation, diverticular disease, and hemorrhoids. People with diets low in dietary fiber and complex carbohydrates and high in fat, tend to have more heart disease, obesity, and some types of cancer. Foods high in sugars (simple carbohydrates) should be consumed in moderation because they tend to be low in essential nutrients and may contribute to tooth decay.

Adequate protein is essential for growth and maintenance of body tissues. Daily intakes for women and men of 50 and 63 grams, respectively, are recommended. Moderate protein intake is recommended because there are no known benefits, and possibly some risks, in consuming diets with a high animal protein content. A strict vegetarian (vegan) diet can meet protein needs with a balance of legumes and grains.

Alcoholic beverages are not recommended because they provide calories but few nutrients, can be addictive, are linked to many health problems, and are a contributing factor in many accidents. Adults who consume alcoholic beverages should drink moderately: no more than 1 drink per day for women, and no more than 2 per day for men (1 drink is equivalent to 12 ounces of regular beer, 5 ounces of wine, or 1.5 ounces of distilled spirits). Some people should not drink alcoholic beverages, including children and adolescents, women who are pregnant or trying to conceive, individuals who engage in activities that require attention or skill, individuals using medicines, and individuals addicted to alcohol.

Improved eating habits (e.g., lower fat intake) and increased exercise are the best ways to achieve a desirable weight. Excessive amounts of body fat are associated with high blood pressure, heart disease, stroke, diabetes, and certain types of cancer. Extreme approaches to losing weight, such as induced vomiting or the use of laxatives, amphetamines, and diuretics, can be dangerous and should be avoided.

Micronutrition

An adequate intake of fruits, vegetables, grain products, dairy products, and meats supply the micronutrients (vitamins and minerals) needed for normal body functioning (see Table 1). Two minerals of special concern in U.S. diets are calcium and iron. Inadequate intake of calcium is associated with osteoporosis along with other factors including genetics, hormone levels (estrogen), and physical activity. Adults require two or more servings of dairy products per day to meet calcium requirements; children need four or more servings per day. Iron deficiency is a problem for teenage girls and women of childbearing age because of iron losses during menstruation, and the increased requirements during pregnancy. Pregnant and lactating women can help to meet their increased nutrient requirements with supplements of vitamins and minerals.

Dietary sodium intake is related to blood pressure in some individuals. Reduced sodium intake for these individuals helps to lower blood pressure. Sodium is reduced by avoiding the use of salt and sodium-containing flavoring agents (e.g., soy sauce) during cooking and at the table. Intake of processed foods to which salt has been added (e.g., potato

TABLE 1.   Vitamins and Minerals Required by Humans

Vitamins	*Minerals (atomic symbols)*
Vitamin A	Sodium (Na)
Thiamin (Vitamin B_1)	Potassium (K)
Riboflavin (Vitamin B_2)	Calcium (Ca)
Niacin	Phosphorus (P)
Vitamin B_6	Magnesium (Mg)
Folic Acid	Iron (Fe)
Vitamin B_{12}	Zinc (Zn)
Biotin	Copper (Cu)
Pantothenic Acid	Manganese (Mn)
Vitamin C (Ascorbic Acid)	Iodine (I)
Vitamin D	Selenium (Se)
Vitamin E	Molybdenum (Mo)
Vitamin K	Chromium (Cr)
	Fluoride (F)

chips, corned beef, cheeses, luncheon meats, canned foods, and crackers) also should be reduced. Grain products may be high in sodium if made with baking powder or baking soda. Commercial products identified as low-sodium or reduced-sodium provide alternatives to higher-sodium counterparts.

Enteral and Parenteral Nutrition

Enteral (tube) formulas provide nutrients in liquid form and are used in hospitals for patients who, for various reasons, cannot retain food (vomiting or obstruction), or who cannot or will not eat. Enteral formulas, which are digested and absorbed through the gastrointestinal tract, usually contain protein (or protein hydrolysates or free amino acids), fats, carbohydrates, vitamins, electrolytes, and trace minerals, and may contain dietary fiber. The tube usually extends from the nose to the esophagus, stomach, or upper small intestine. Tubes also may be surgically placed into the pharynx, esophagus, duodenum, stomach, or jejunum.

Parenteral nutrition refers to nutrients that are provided intravenously. For patients whose nutritional needs can be partially met by mouth or tube, supplementary parenteral nutrition may be a useful adjunct. Parenteral solutions usually contain water, glucose, lipid emulsions, amino acids, vitamins, electrolytes, and trace elements.

A formula selected for enteral or parenteral use should meet the specific caloric and nutrient requirements of a patient. For patients recovering from surgery, shock, trauma, burns, or other massive injuries, it is essential that the formulas meet the increased nutrient requirements needed to repair and build new tissue.

Nutrition for Animals

Nutritional requirements vary among animal species; more highly evolved creatures (i.e., primates) have more complex nutrient requirements. For example, vitamin C is required by humans, but most other animals synthesize it from glucose and do not require an exogenous source. Commercial livestock feeds and pet foods are generally designed to meet the specific requirements of each species for calories, protein, and various vitamins and minerals. One nutritional problem of domestic dogs and cats is their tendency to gain weight. A relatively new market is opening up for dog and cat foods for different life stages, with the caloric content generally decreasing for the older animals.

Public awareness of the vitamins, minerals, and nutrients considered essential to health will hopefully continue to expand in the future. Precise levels of need are continually being fine-tuned as experience with traditional foods, nutritional supplements, enteral and parenteral administration, and requirements for commercial livestock, pets, and animals of all kinds grows.

See also ALCOHOL; FISHERIES; FOOD ADDITIVES; FOOD CONSUMPTION; FOOD AND DRUG SAFETY; FOOD LAWS; FOOD TECHNOLOGIES; HEALTH CARE: TECHNOLOGICAL DEVELOPMENTS.

BIBLIOGRAPHY

Committee on Diet and Health, Food and Nutrition Board, Commission on Life Sciences, National Research Council. *Diet and Health: Implications for Reducing Chronic Disease Risk.* Washington, DC: National Academy Press, 1989.

U.S. Department of Agriculture and U.S. Department of Health and Human Services. *Nutrition and Your Health: Dietary Guidelines for Americans,* 3rd ed. Washington, DC: U.S. Government Printing Office, 1990.

U.S. Department of Health and Human Services. *The Surgeon General's Report on Nutrition and Health.* DHHS (PHS) Publication, 88-50211. Washington, DC: U.S. Government Printing Office, 1988.

Jean Pennington

Oceans

The world ocean is frequently referred to as humankind's last frontier. It may not be the last, but certainly it is a frontier space that we are discovering, exploiting, and endangering.

The scientific exploration of ocean space is an exciting adventure, involving a large number of disciplines and countries. We have discovered that oceans are born and grow, as new ocean floor wells up from Earth's mantle through the volcanic activities of the huge mountain chains (mid-oceanic ridges) that traverse the world's oceans. Seafloor spreading forces continents apart. Oceans shrink and "die" when more seafloor is swallowed, disappearing in volcanic trenches along "active" coastlines, than is produced at the mid-oceanic ridges. The lifetime of an ocean may be on the order of 800 million years. The hydrology of the whole system, covering two-thirds of the surface of our planet, and the interaction between ocean surface and atmosphere have a decisive influence on the world's climate. This interaction is as yet poorly understood. Global warming would entail the melting of polar ice masses, with a consequent sea level rise and the flooding of coastal areas and cities such as Boston, as well as the disappearance of low-lying islands such as the Maldives. This, however, is a hypothesis that has to be dealt with in the light of uncertainty.

In our age, we are witnessing the penetration of this frontier space by the industrial revolution. All traditional sea uses—fishing, shipping, tourism, waste disposal, military uses—have been drastically transformed by modern high technology. And new uses have been generated, such as seabed mining and the production of energy from tides, waves, currents, biomass, and temperature and salinity differentials. Artificial islands, whether for waste disposal or human habitation, are appearing offshore to relieve overcrowded coastal areas. Floating cities, made of new materials and organized in "modules," are conceived to eliminate the woes besetting our overgrown, decaying metropolises: crowding, traffic jams, air pollution, and unsustainable energy consumption. These ocean cities rise upward and descend below the water surface. They are still on the drawing boards of futuristic architects, in the United States, Japan, Italy, France, and the United Kingdom. They may become realities in the next century.

The wealth of the oceans is awesome and could make a far more important contribution to sustainable development in the future than it has in the past.

Fishing may have reached or passed its limits. Many stocks are overfished, and many species are endangered by unselective and destructive gear, pollution, and the destruction of habitat. About 60 percent of the world's population lives within sixty miles of the world ocean's coasts. Poor coastal management, entailing beach erosion and silting, together with poorly controlled agricultural, domestic, and industrial wastes, are a serious threat to coastal waters and enclosed and semienclosed seas; this in turn is a threat to the ocean's fauna and flora and to human health.

The end of an old and exhausted system may give way to the emergence of a new one. Fishing from the wild is coming to an end, but we are witnessing its transformation into a new system of husbanding aquatic animals and cultivating aquatic plants. Aquaculture and mariculture are already producing about 15 percent of the global fish and algae production, and this new industry is growing at a rate of about 6 percent a year. The emergence of aquaculture, making the transition from "hunting" to "culture" in the oceans, is by itself a revolutionary event comparable to the emergence of "agriculture" from the hunting and gathering that preceded it ten thousand years or so ago. What we are witnessing today, however, is a revolution within this evolution: the penetration of aquaculture by genetic engineering and bioindustrial processes. Aquaculture will be radically altered by the biotechnology revolution. This development could alleviate the hunger problem. It also opens new horizons for a number of other industries, including the pharmaceutical and chemical industries, the extraction of metals and minerals from ores or water bodies, whether for combatting pollution or processing minerals.

There are other new uses of the oceans made possible by contemporary technology. The extraction of energy, in various forms, directly from seawater, will be a key component of the diversified, renewable, and nonpolluting energy systems of the future. Desalinization and the extraction of fresh water from the oceans will play a major role in solving the world's acute and growing water problems. Ocean mineral mining will becomean important industry early in the twenty-first century.

Trillions of potato-shaped manganese nodules litter the deep seabed, at depths of about 5,000 meters. They contain nickel, copper, cobalt, and manganese. Technologies exist to lift them and to process their useful metals. The United Nations Convention on the Law of the Sea (1982) has declared that these resources, along with any other mineral resources on or under the deep seabed beyond the limits of national jurisdiction, to be a "common heritage of mankind." This important new concept in international law is fundamental to the economics of "sustainable development." Resources that are the common heritage of humankind cannot be appropriated by anybody; they must be managed for the benefit of humankind as a whole, with particular regard for the needs of poor countries; they must be managed with due regard for the conservation of the environment and reserved for exclusively peaceful purposes.

The United Nations Convention on the Law of the Sea has been called "a constitution for the Oceans." It has radically redistributed ocean space. One-third of the world ocean now falls under coastal-state jurisdiction, in the form of extended territorial seas, exclusive economic zones, and continental shelves. Tiny island states and archipelagos now enjoy sovereign rights over huge ocean spaces and their resources. This may cause boundary conflicts in a number of cases, but the convention also provides for mandatory, binding, and peaceful settlement of all disputes. It has established a new International Tribunal for the Law of the Sea, with its seat in Hamburg, Germany, to deal with these disputes.

The convention also has established an International Seabed Authority, based in Jamaica, to manage the mineral wealth of the oceans for the benefit of humankind as a whole, based on the principle of the common heritage.

The convention covers all major uses of the seas and oceans; enhances both sustainable economic development and the protection of the environment; and fosters peace, international cooperation, development of human resources, and the advancement of the marine sciences and technologies.

See also ACID RAIN; FISHERIES; FRESHWATER; GLOBAL WARMING; GENETICS.

BIBLIOGRAPHY

BORGESE, ELISABETH MANN. *The Future of the Oceans.* Montreal: Harvest House, 1986.

BORGESE, ELISABETH MANN; GINSBURG, NORTON; and MORGAN, JOSEPH, eds. *Ocean Yearbook*, Vols. 1–11. Chicago: University of Chicago Press, 1980–present.

SANGER, CLYDE. *Ordering the Oceans: The Making of the Law of the Sea.* London: Zed Books Ltd., 1986.

Elisabeth Mann Borgese

Ogburn, William Fielding (1886–1959)

American sociologist William Ogburn was born in Georgia and took his doctorate at Columbia University in 1912. From 1919 until his retirement in 1951, he taught sociology at Columbia, Barnard College, and later the University of Chicago. During the Hoover administration, he served as research director of the President's Research Committee on Social Trends, an early example of state-sponsored futurism in the United States. Later, he chaired the Subcommittee on Technology of the National Resources Committee and took a leading part in the preparation of its 1937 report, *Technological Trends and National Policy*. His pioneering interest in technology assessment was carried further in *The Social Effects of Aviation* (1946), coauthored with Jean L. Adams and S. G. Gilfillan. Ogburn's most influential book is *Social Change, With Respect to Culture and Original Nature* (1922; revised, 1950). In this and other writings he expressed confidence in the predictive powers of sociological analysis, believing that many trends could safely be extrapolated into the near future and even beyond. He is best remembered for his theory of "cultural lag," the tendency of cultures to adapt slowly and reluctantly to technological innovation and socioeconomic change.

BIBLIOGRAPHY

JAFFE, A. J. "William Fielding Ogburn." *International Encyclopedia of the Social Sciences*. New York: Macmillan, 1968.
MARTINDALE, DON. *The Nature and Types of Sociological Theory*. Boston: Houghton Mifflin, 1960.

W. Warren Wagar

Oil.

See PETROLEUM.

On-Line Services

Communication over distance by means of on-line services, though beginning in the 1970s, has cultural roots as distant as the earliest smoke signals and drumbeats. Then and now communication has been governed by access and technology. Communication around the world on self-designed schedules signals a new means of communicating and changes how and with whom we communicate. For most of the last twenty-five years, the number of users of these services has been small. In the 1990s, the number jumped into the millions, with projections of continued rapid growth.

The on-line services user base grows in size and composition as the very nature of the services and access to technology change. What has been service for a few is rapidly becoming widespread for business, education, and individuals. On-line services are a new means to communicate for most that will transform how they communicate and that promise to be as monumental in impact as the printed word, which changed communication from acoustical interaction to more restrictive print. Print is now only part of how we communicate. Gesture, sound, and image as well as text are the tools to shape the way people communicate and the services they use. The mid-1990s is at the threshold of on-line video, images, audio and virtual reality. The advanced computers that make this possible in the 1990s will gradually be replaced by low-cost devices in the next century.

Experience with computers in the 1980s strengthened the perception that "a picture is worth a thousand words." By the 1990s, applications required not only images but video, audio, as well as text. On-line services are evolving to fully mature on-line services capable of delivering different types of information (video, images, audio, and text.) By the mid-1990s improvement in transmission speeds, better software, and a greater desire to use multimedia had begun a three- to five-year process of testing and delivering a variety of fully mature on-line services.

The pace of implementation varies from one country to another. In countries such as France, on-line services are being introduced and sustained earlier than in a more market-oriented economy such as the United States. Since the pace of innovation varies from one country to another, the emphasis is focused on the United States, where there is a freer interplay of technology, access, and market acceptance.

Computer conferencing, one of the earliest kinds of on-line service, became popular in the 1970s. Predating the existence of personal computers, it depended on using "dumb" terminals connected to mainframe computers. The slow communication speeds and limited graphics capabilities restricted most of these services to text. However, a few professional services such as economic analysis provided black-and-white vector graphics.

The desire to upgrade services to include color images was central to the development of consumer videotex services delivered in the television signal or over telephone lines. Large companies such as Knight-Ridder in Miami and Bell Canada in Canada experimented in delivering and building market acceptance of videotex services with graphics in the early to mid-1980s. These experiments proved premature despite large investments of money, though they did provide experience in constructing applications, market testing, and delivering a variety of services to consumers and businesses that provided information in the 1990s for interactive television experiments.

After the demise of videotex services with graphics, videotex survived in the form of on-line services such as the Source. By the end of the 1980s, a number of on-line services were available—some already providing users with graphic access screens.

From 1985 to the early 1990s, the rapid expansion of computers, low-cost communications software, and modems served an ever larger number of sophisticated users who could access on-line services directly from their home or business. Services were designed to work with these devices and allow for the downloading of files (text and graphics). Many services such as those provided by America Online provided a user-friendly graphics interface on the user's computer for click-and-pick access. Additional graphics were downloaded when users logged on. By the mid-1990s, the most successful on-line services provided graphic access screens to make their services easier to use.

By the mid-1990s, development and acceptance of better compression techniques for video, images, and audio as well as small, inexpensive processors set the scene for the development of on-line services with video, audio, and images. The success of these technical developments and the lure of large consumer markets prompted a number of large international companies to also announce trial interactive television services. The trade-offs of speed, cost, resolution, and content—much as those of videotex a decade earlier—were again put to the test.

In 1994 and 1995, new experimentation began with a heavy emphasis on interactive video delivered to the television set. The interactive television trials continued the ongoing process of experimentation and market testing that has persistently moved industrial countries closer to the time when fully mature on-line services will be available. Service providers again needed to provide the device, now called a set-top box, for these new services. Existing personal computers did not meet the video requirements.

On-line services are usually one-on-one communications over a variety of communications transport media such as cable, fiber, twisted-pair, telephone lines, as well as a number of wireless transmission technologies. Though this early development and use of on-line services will continue, the emerging technology increasingly will grow to accommodate more group-to-group communications. Video and voice transmissions are equally well suited to group communication, as is the case in video conferencing.

Group chat sessions are common on private on-line services such as CompuServe, Prodigy, GEnie, and America Online. The Internet began in the mid-1990s to provide real-time services with most of its use reserved for the exchange of text messages. With the advent of the World Wide Web, users had Internet access to images, audio, and video. Underlying software programs are providing Web sites with productivity tools to search increasingly large multimedia databases. Once information is found, the Web services provide users with the option to download image, text, and video files.

While the technologies are more advanced, the decision that video is key to any new on-line consumer service has raised the technological threshold. The adoption of more advanced video compression standards such as the Motion Picture Experimental Group (MPEG), faster networks, and more capable set-top boxes are untested in the mid-1990s marketplace. The quest for a "killer application" eludes industry giants, but projected demand for more technology solutions for education, consumer information, and business, and the increased cost-effectiveness of computing and communications technology suggest, finally, the often heralded convergence of the necessary market conditions. Tests during the 1995–1998 period will measure whether the perceived value of on-line services is enough to encourage and economically sustain a sizable market.

On-line services are sometimes combined with devices that play compact discs. In these instances, the soon-to-be larger capacity compact discs (projected over the next three years to be able to hold more than 3.5 gigabytes of visual and audio information) will enhance these services beginning in 1997. These services will combine the benefits of large, low-cost storage and reduced transmission requirements to provide up-to-date information to users. The on-line services provide up-to-date information to complement the compact discs and can facilitate access to specific subjects.

With entire communities turning into "electronic villages," all sectors of society will begin the twenty-first century with rich opportunities to communicate and share information. The emphasis will shift from whether it can be accomplished technically to whether the content is adequately customized to meet the individual and group needs of homes and in businesses. The pace, number of users, and types of use will depend on whether access is determined on economic terms or subsidized by government and other organizations to meet specific social and political needs.

See also COMMUNICATIONS; COMMUNICATIONS TECHNOLOGY; COMPUTER LINKAGE; COMPUTERS: OVERVIEW; ELECTRONIC CONVERGENCE; ELECTRONIC PUBLISHING; HIGH TECHNOLOGY; INFORMATION OVERLOAD; INFORMATION SOCIETY; INFORMATION TECHNOLOGY; INTERACTIVE ENTERTAINMENT; MEDIA LAB; NETWORKING; TELECOMMUNICATIONS.

BIBLIOGRAPHY

CIAMPA, JOHN A. *Communication: The Living End.* New York: Philosophical Library, 1989.

GILSTER, PAUL. *The Internet Navigator.* New York: John Wiley, 1993.

MCLUHAN, MARSHALL. *Counterblast.* New York: Harcourt, Brace, & World, 1969.

RUSHKOFF, DOUGLAS. *Cyberia: Life in the Trenches of Hyperspace.* San Francisco: HarperCollins, 1994.

Richard G. Maynard

Opinion Polls.

See PUBLIC OPINION; SURVEYS.

Organizational Complexity

Predicting the future may be controversial, but one thing almost everyone can agree on is that it will be far more complex than the past. The exponential rise of information technology (IT), increasing competition in a global economy, a mounting environmental crisis, and other revolutionary trends make it clear that the world is entering a turbulent epoch of constant change, exploding diversity, and unmanageable complexity.

For instance, automation is eliminating jobs and leaving roughly half of all workers floating in a "contingency status" between temporary positions. Entire industries are being transformed. Convergence of the computer, communication, and entertainment fields is an example. Large organizations, such as AT&T and IBM, are being disaggregated at the very time they are forming alliances with other organizations.

This shift to a complex world is so striking that a new field of science has emerged devoted to the study of complexity and chaos. Institutions are in crisis because they were designed on simple, hierarchical principles. The unpleasant fact is that most organizations today share the same problem that brought about the collapse of communism: an authoritarian, centrally coordinated hierarchy that is simply too cumbersome to manage the complexity of the information age. Large corporations such as General Motors have suffered such massive financial losses that their former CEOs have been replaced. Bureaucratic governments are running unsustainable deficits and many are collapsing; communism was simply the most extreme case because it had the most rigid hierarchy. Furthermore, almost all Americans acknowledge that health care and education are badly in need of reform.

The type of organization evolving now is fundamentally different because there is a growing recognition of the shortcomings in controlling complex behavior from the top down. Emerging is an "organic" theoretical perspective. This approach creates loosely structured organizations with each unit possessing sufficient autonomy and intelligence to manage its own actions at the grass roots. This system is then guided (rather than controlled) by response to market forces and information systems. The result is a self-organizing system of small, self-managed units, enjoying wide participation, with decisions originating from the bottom up.

The principles needed to produce this organic behavior are extensions of Western ideals of free enterprise and democracy. These powerful concepts have not been applied within institutions generally, but recently the information revolution has been driving an organizational transformation toward a new system of management and economics called the "New Management" and the "New Capitalism."

The most crucial aspect of this organizational revolution focuses on the application of free market concepts. Today, many trends are under way to bring free market mechanisms *inside* organizations, resulting in the reduction or elimination of middle-management levels, the breakup of big companies like IBM into autonomous units, a new kind of company-internal entrepreneurship, and so on. Even governments are becoming entrepreneurial and are privatizing some undertakings.

Each unit in such an organization (including line and staff units, manufacturing facilities, research and development, and other functions) is being defined as a self-managed "internal enterprise." Funds are allocated in proportion to performance, and units are allowed the freedom to manage their operations as they think best. Executives focus their efforts on designing and regulating this organizational economy and providing collaborative leadership, just as government manages a national economy.

Some of the most dynamic corporations increasingly are designed along these lines. MCI, the young upstart that successfully challenged the AT&T monopoly, credits its success to a unique culture that embraces entrepreneurship and initiative. Hewlett-Packard avoided the recent difficulties of IBM, DEC, Commodore, and other computer makers by keeping each division a small, independent unit free of bureaucratic controls. Johnson & Johnson has thrived for decades using a decentralized system of 168 independent divisions. Asea Brown Boveri's 1,200 companies and 5,000 intersecting profit centers have become a model for other global corporations.

Market concepts are also spreading into government. Roughly forty states have been moving in this direction for years, and even the federal government is struggling to become entrepreneurial. The Department of Defense, the Federal Aviation Agency, and other departments are creating "information utilities" in which internal units pay for services. The trend is convincingly clear in education, where the concept of "choice" is introducing competition among schools. New York City's worst school districts have been turned around by decentralizing large schools into small, self-managed units and allowing students greater freedom in selecting the curriculum they prefer. Mexico City converted a central licensing bureau into competing offices with great improvement in service.

This transitional change poses major challenges for managers and employees. Organizations may gain accountability for performance, entrepreneurial freedom, creative solutions, rapid response time, improved quality and services, and other advantages of free enterprise—at the cost of tolerating the messy disorder that is also characteristic of markets. People can find these new work roles more financially rewarding, liberating, and satisfying—if they show the initiative that is required and are prepared to take on the risks that are unavoidable.

This should prove an unusually demanding challenge because a very different management logic is involved. Many will resist it. Most large institutions are likely to be forced in this direction, however, out of the necessity to manage an increasingly turbulent world. By accepting the loss of control over details and allowing people greater freedom as well as accountability, a different form of sophisticated, cre-

ative control is likely to be achieved. Educated people may then pursue their needs through market-based, democratic institutions, producing a more organic society better able to manage the enormous complexity that lies ahead.

See also BUSINESS GOVERNANCE; BUSINESS STRUCTURE: FORMS, IMPACTS; GLOBAL BUSINESS: DOMINANT ORGANIZATIONAL FORMS; GOVERNANCE; GOVERNMENT ORGANIZATION; INSTITUTIONS AND ORGANIZATIONS.

BIBLIOGRAPHY

FREEDMAN, DAVID. "Is Management Still a Science?" *Harvard Business Review* (November–December 1992).

HALAL, WILLIAM E.; GERANMAYEH, ALI; and POURDEHNAD, JOHN. *Internal Markets: Bringing the Power of Free Enterprise Inside Your Organization*. New York: John Wiley, 1993.

KELLY, KEVIN. *Out of Control: The Rise of Neo-Biological Civilization*. Reading, MA: Addison-Wesley, 1994.

OSBORNE, DAVID, and GAEBLER, TED. *Reinventing Government*. Reading, MA: Addison-Wesley, 1992.

WALDROP, MITCHELL. *Complexity: The Emerging Science at the Edge of Order and Chaos*. New York: Simon and Schuster, 1992.

William E. Halal

Orwell, George (1903–1950)

"George Orwell" is the pseudonym of the writer Eric Arthur Blair, who was born in Motihari, Bengal, India. He was educated at Eton (where he claimed to have learned nothing) and later joined the Burmese police force. A socialist at heart, like many of his generation, he contended by 1927 that British imperialism was "largely a racket." This conviction, plus his ill health and a desire to write, led him to return to Europe. Adopting the pen name of George Orwell, he wrote *Burmese Days* in 1934. It brought him enough income to devote himself to writing full-time. In 1928 he published his most admired book, *Homage to Catalonia*, based on his experiences as a member of the Republican Army in the Spanish Civil War. Although Orwell claimed that he was not really a novelist, he is best remembered for his two novels *Animal Farm* (1945) and *Nineteen Eighty-Four* (1949). The former was a bitter anti-Stalinist satire that shook the Socialist establishment. Orwell's main contribution to futurism was *Nineteen Eighty-Four*, a grimly dystopian warning predicting the spread of Stalinist-type tyranny throughout much of the world. Ironically, none of Orwell's predictions came true; there is more freedom half a century after his death than at any time in human history. He died in London on January 1, 1950, still committed to his own highly idiosyncratic form of Marxist socialism, which because of his own intense intellectual honesty was in no sense doctrinaire.

See also DYSTOPIAS.

BIBLIOGRAPHY

BUITENHUIS, PETER, and NADEL, IRA B. *George Orwell: A Reassessment.* New York: St. Martin's Press, 1988.

FISHMAN, ROBERT L. *Nineteen Eighty-Four in Nineteen Eighty-Four: Orwell as Prophecy.* Trenton, NJ: New Jersey State Museum, 1986.

HUNTER, LYNETTE. *George Orwell: The Search for a Voice.* London: Open University Press, 1984.

RAI, ALOK. *Orwell and the Politics of Despair.* New York: Cambridge University Press, 1990.

WILLIAMS, RAYMOND. *George Orwell.* New York: Columbia University Press, 1981.

George Thomas Kurian

Outdoor Recreation and Leisure Pursuits

Participation in outdoor recreation increased tremendously in the past generation. The most noteworthy trend was the great popularity of physically demanding activities, especially canoeing, swimming, boating, walking, bicycling, and snow-skiing. The number of canoeists grew fivefold in one twenty-year span; the number of bicyclists, almost four-fold.

This growth is expected to continue, although not at such fast rates. The U.S. Forest Service projects that between the years 2000 and 2040, canoeing will grow by 70 percent and bicycling by 120 percent.

Some of the factors contributing to this growth include the increased concern with health and physical fitness, greater accessibility of recreation areas, and equipment advances that make activities safer, more comfortable, and within the abilities of more people.

Demographics

The aging of the population will be as important to the future of outdoor recreation as to other areas of life. Participation increased in thrill-seeking sports, such as rock climbing, bungee jumping, and river running, partly because equipment that improved safety raised the level of risk that people seem willing to accept. Equipment advances may continue to pull younger people in this direction.

People continue to do many of the outdoor activities they adopted before age forty, but are less able to do some of the most strenuous activities. Consequently, activities like backpacking are down 50 percent from the 1970s, a change that coincided with baby-boomers having children of their own.

A complementary trend toward seeking activities closer to home is expected to continue, and more facilities will be developed to meet this need. The conversion of multipurpose trails from abandoned railroad lines reflects this trend.

Quality of the Experience

More conflicts over resource use are likely in the years ahead. The quality of many outdoor-recreation activities depends upon the quality of the environment in which they are enjoyed, and that quality has eroded with population and development pressures. For example, pollution has cut visibility by one-third to one-half in Western parks, and by more in the East.

At flagship national parks such as Yosemite and Yellowstone, reservations are necessary to obtain campsites. Overuse has forced the closure of some areas, and closures are likely to increase because of concerns such as harm to endangered species. This pressure could lead to the preservation of more land in the public domain and the development of more land for recreation—especially closer to population centers.

More remote areas will undoubtedly see more use as people travel farther to get away from each other. For example, the land overseen by the Bureau of Land Management, an area nearly one-eighth the size of the United States, has been largely overlooked, because it was thought of as undesirable desert. But its many beautiful areas are now being developed and marketed as alternatives to more famous destinations.

One reason that recreation supporters will win many resource conflicts is the increasing recognition of recreation's economic importance. In Colorado, tourism income outweighs the economic contributions of traditional industries, such as mining and logging; and tourists come to the Rockies for outdoor activities, such as skiing. Georgia's Chattahoochee National Forest is expected to produce $108 million from timber and $637 million from recreation over the next fifty years.

But some kinds of outdoor recreation will run into environmental conflicts of their own: Snow-skiing's popularity has led to a demand for more facilities, which may not be a problem in some parts of the country. But places like the Northeast, which is dependent on snowmaking, water availability, and quality issues, as well as land availability, could limit future developments.

Technology

Technical developments have fostered an endless number of new sports: from the introduction of ski lifts and equipment that differentiated downhill from Nordic skiing, to lightweight materials that made backpacking accessible to the average participant, to radio collars for dogs that have changed hunting, to reliable mountain-climbing equipment, to mountain bicycles allowing riders to pedal places once thought impossible, to snowboards, off-road vehicles, snowmobiles, jet skis, hang gliders, ultralight aircraft, and bungee jumping. Options have exploded in recent years and will continue to do so, in such diverse directions as fantasy baseball camps, where one can actually play the game with professional athletes, and guided trips to almost anywhere.

Of course, technical advances mean more competition for leisure time, as VCRs and cable television have demonstrated in the past decade. And who can predict the next invention—will virtual reality enable a person to experience the thrill of climbing Mount Everest without ever leaving the living room?

Some looming developments could be all-terrain skateboards and in-line skates with brakes or go-anywhere cellular phones to call for help. Global positioning system units could become so inexpensive that people would never get lost.

Some Trends

- Equipment will undoubtedly continue to evolve and become more specialized. A typical enthusiast's closet already contains a dozen shoes with particular abilities, from running to rock climbing. Inventions such as the breathable polyester fabrics that revolutionized clothing are certain to find their way to market. Materials continue to grow lighter, stronger, and more versatile.
- The line between the natural and artificial worlds will continue to blur. Climbers build walls indoors and on freeway overpass supports;

kayakers practice and compete on artificial white-water runs. Year-round skiing on the snow equivalent of Astroturf and surfing on waves generated in amusement parks are possibilities. Such developments mesh well with the increased desire for recreation closer to home.

- Trends increasing inequality in income may also be felt: Permits to climb Mount Everest are limited, expensive, and increasingly go to rich people being led by guides instead of pioneering climbers. The availability of places to hunt has decreased with suburban and exurban sprawl and the disappearance of much farmland. The decrease in opportunities could lead to an increase in the importance of hunting reserves and clubs, including exclusive ones that raise animals, then release them for patrons to shoot or fish. The majority who cannot afford those clubs may have to crowd onto public areas.
- Campgrounds and other developments in parks and forests may tend less toward the primitive and contain more amenities in keeping with the desires of older users.
- Some things remain constant through time: Despite the inroads of new sports and technology, the most low-tech activity imaginable—walking—continues to be the most popular form of outdoor recreation among Americans and shows no signs of relinquishing its primacy.

On the other hand, we may ration the unusual recreation site—those in excess demand—not by cost but by qualifications. Access to many areas may depend upon the certified ability to use that site effectively.

See also EXERCISE AND FITNESS; FREE TIME; LEISURE TIME; PARKS AND WILDERNESS; SPORTS AND ACTIVITIES, SPECTATOR; SPORTS AND GAMES, COMPETITIVE; THEME PARKS AND ORGANIZED ATTRACTIONS.

BIBLIOGRAPHY

ABRAMS, MALCOLM, and BERNSTEIN, HARRIETT. *More Future Stuff: Over 250 Inventions That Will Change Your Life by 2001.* New York: Penguin Books, 1991.

Future Vision: The 189 Most Important Trends of the 1990s. Compiled by the editors of *Research Alert.* Naperville, IL: Sourcebooks, 1991.

Report of the President's Commission on Americans Outdoors. *Americans Outdoors: The Legacy, The Challenge.* Washington, DC: Island Press, 1987.

U.S. Forest Service. *An Analysis of the Outdoor Recreation and Wilderness Situation in the U.S., 1989–2040.* Washington, DC: U.S. Department of Agriculture, 1989.

Eric Seaborg

Ozone Layer Depletion

A thin layer of ozone molecules in the stratosphere, twice as high as jet planes fly, shields the Earth's surface from the full force of the sun's hazardous ultraviolet rays. The depletion of this ozone layer is widely recognized as the first truly *global* environmental crisis. Fortunately, ozone is a "renewable resource" in the sense that it is continuously created by ultraviolet radiation striking the upper atmosphere. The ozone layer will slowly mend itself if we act quickly to halt ozone depletion.

First Evidence and Response

In 1974 two scientific papers, published independently, first suggested a threat to the ozone layer. The first study described how chlorine atoms that reach the ozone layer could act as powerful ozone destroyers. The second study reported that chemical compounds called chlorofluorocarbons (CFCs) were reaching the stratosphere, were breaking up, and were releasing chlorine atoms. Taken together, these studies suggested that harmless-seeming CFCs being widely used for propellants in aerosol cans, coolants in refrigerators and air conditioners, industrial cleaning solvents, and for many other purposes might be producing a massive depletion of stratospheric ozone.

This was alarming news because the ozone layer prevents most of a dangerous ultraviolet wavelength of the sun's light, called UV-B, from searing the Earth's surface. UV-B radiation breaks down organic molecules. If the amount of UV-B that reaches the top of the atmosphere were to penetrate to ground level, Earth would become virtually uninhabitable.

In response to this scientific alarm, environmental and consumer groups targeted aerosol spray cans, creating a symbolic ozone villain to sway public opinion. Sales of these products plunged by over 60 percent, placing heavy pressure on legislators to respond. In 1978, the United States criminalized and otherwise discouraged the use of CFCs as aerosol propellants. Unfortunately, the use of CFCs in spray cans in other countries as well as in other applications drove worldwide CFC use back to its 1975 peak use level by the mid-1980s.

The Ozone Hole

In 1984, a shocking event catapulted ozone depletion into the international limelight. Scientists of the British Antarctic Survey reported a 40 percent decrease in ozone in the stratosphere over their survey site. Initially, many scientists were skeptical. Computer models based on knowledge of atmospheric chemistry at the time could not explain such a large drop. Measurements of atmospheric ozone taken routinely since 1978 by the National Aeronautics and Space Administration's (NASA) Nimbus-7 satellite had never shown Antarctic ozone depletion.

Within a year, however, evidence for the existence of what was termed an "ozone hole" in the southern hemisphere became overwhelming. Other measuring stations in Antarctica confirmed the British findings. Checking Nimbus-7 readings, NASA scientists found that their computers had been programmed to reject very low ozone readings as instrument error. The rejected Nimbus-7 data showed that ozone levels had been dropping over the South Pole ever since the satellite measurements began, creating an ozone hole as large as the continental United States.

Scientists around the world raced to understand why the ozone hole was forming and why it was positioned over Antarctica. Dramatic evidence linking CFCs to the ozone hole was gathered in September 1987, when scientists flew a high-altitude research aircraft from Punta Arenas, Chile, toward the South Pole. As the plane entered the ozone hole, its instruments registered a jump in chlorine monoxide molecules to about 500 times normal levels, while the ozone concentration plummeted. These measurements, shown in Figure 1, are often referred to

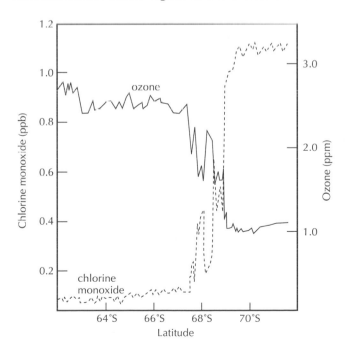

FIGURE 1. As chlorine increases, Antarctic ozone decreases.

as the "smoking gun" that convinced even CFC manufacturers that CFCs were the culprit.

Further research showed that ozone depletion is especially pronounced in the Antarctic because the continent's extremely cold, dry air is full of ice crystals that provide surfaces on which chlorine and ozone can alight and react with each other. Also, each winter the prevailing wind pattern—a circumpolar vortex—keeps Antarctic air from blending with the rest of the atmosphere, concentrating the CFCs there.

The Montreal Protocol and London Agreements

The discovery of the Antarctic ozone hole had a galvanizing impact on international discussions that were already underway to limit CFC production. The United Nations Environmental Program (UNEP) also played an important role by assembling the scientific evidence and providing a neutral forum for discussion and resolution. Responding to pressures from all sides—scientists, environmentalists, journalists, and UNEP—thirty-six nations signed the historic 1987 Montreal Protocol on Substances that Deplete the Ozone Layer. The Montreal Protocol stipulated that world production of the five most common CFCs should initially be frozen at 1986 levels, then reduced 20 percent by 1993, and cut an additional 30 percent by 1998.

When the "smoking gun" evidence (Figure 1) was published several months after the Montreal Protocol was signed, many scientists concluded that an even faster CFC phase-out was necessary. At that point, Dupont, the world's largest CFC producer, announced that it would completely phase out its CFC manufacturing. Dupont's environmental leadership brought around many of the remaining doubters in the chemical industry. After further negotiations, again led by UNEP, ninety-two countries signed the "London Agreement," which phases out all CFC production (as well as several other ozone-destroying chemicals) by the year 2000. An international fund also was created to help developing countries shift to CFC alternatives.

Alternative Ozone Futures

Figure 2 shows three different scenarios of the future concentration of ozone-destroying chlorine in the stratosphere. Scenario A shows how chlorine would build up in the stratosphere in a "no controls" situation, in which CFC emissions continue at the 1986 rate. Scenario B projects the CFC production cuts agreed to in the Montreal Protocol, which still allows a doubling of stratospheric chlorine concentrations by 2100. Scenario C projects the CFC phase-out agreed to in the London Agreement. In Scenario C, ozone depletion peaks around the year 2000 and then the ozone layer slowly starts becoming thicker. Even in Scenario C, it takes at least a century for the ozone layer to return to its normal thickness, with chlorine completely eliminated from the stratosphere. The world is on a path that is clearly much closer to Scenario C than to Scenario A. Some uncertainty remains, however, about whether our actual situation is quite as optimistic as Scenario C.

Continuing Uncertainty

One major source of uncertainty is the level of compliance with the London Agreement. Some of the signatory nations, such as the nations of the former Soviet Union, may fail to meet the agreement's phase-out schedule, pleading economic difficulties. And many of the developing nations of the southern hemisphere and elsewhere have not yet signed the agreement or may find it difficult to comply. Actions by developing countries will be critical for the ozone future. China and India, for example, are just now trying to equip most households with their first refrigerators, which will produce enormous new demands for Freon unless CFC substitutes are utilized.

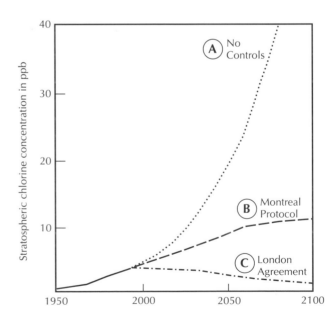

FIGURE 2.   Alternative scenarios of stratospheric chlorine concentrations due to chlorofluorocarbon emissions.

The other major source of uncertainty is our imperfect understanding of atmospheric physics and chemistry. In 1991, for example, NASA announced that new satellite measurements show that ozone depletion over populated areas in North America, Europe, and Central Asia is occurring twice as fast as previously predicted. Even more surprisingly, middle latitude ozone depletion in both the Northern and southern hemispheres is extending, for the first time, into spring and summer months when radiation damage to people, crops, and other living things is likely to be greatest.

In 1993 NASA reported a startling decrease in the average amount of ozone over the planet as a whole. Over some parts of the temperate zone, ozone loss during the winter of 1992 was as severe as 14 percent. NASA researchers attributed this sudden change to the eruption of Mount Pinatubo in 1991, which injected large quantities of particulates into the stratosphere, thereby altering stratospheric wind and temperature patterns. The researchers' computer models failed to predict the scale of Mount Pinatubo's effects on the ozone layer. As long as such large uncertainties and knowledge gaps remain, it is too soon to become complacent about having put the ozone crisis behind us.

Potential Impacts of Increased UV-B

Better instrumentation and longer periods of data collection are needed to assess how much UV radiation is actually reaching the ground as the ozone layer thins. If UV levels are increasing, they potentially pose serious health hazards for humans and other animals. The United Nations Environmental Programme predicts a 26 percent rise in the incidence of melanoma skin cancers worldwide if overall ozone levels drop 10 percent. Increased UV radiation may also suppress immune systems, reducing the body's ability to fight cancers and making people more susceptible to a wide range of infectious diseases. UV-B can also damage the retina and produce cataracts in the eye's lens, which can lead to blindness if untreated.

A growing body of evidence suggests that these potential hazards should be taken seriously. In Australia, for example, health officials report that skin cancers have tripled over the past decade. In Patagonia, at the tip of South America, there are reports of hunters finding blind rabbits and anglers catching blind fish. For many scientists, however, this kind of evidence is not yet convincing. Skin cancer rates have been climbing in many countries through most of this century, probably due to lifestyle changes such as wearing skimpier clothing in summer. As a result, it is extremely difficult to assess how much skin cancer is attributable to ozone depletion. Efforts to link the Patagonian fish and rabbit claims to ozone depletion also have failed. As the long-running debates over cigarette smoking show, it is not easy to demonstrate irrefutable links between potential health hazards and actual health impacts.

Despite the uncertainties, some governments are beginning to base policies on the assumption that actual health impacts are occurring. School children in New Zealand are urged to wear hats to school and play and eat their lunches in the shade of trees. In Australia, the government issues alerts when especially high UV levels are expected. Public service ads warn of the dangers of sunbathing, much as U.S. ads warn of the health hazards of smoking.

Just as worrisome is the threat to the world's food supply. When fifty crop varieties were exposed to a 50 percent increase in UV levels (much higher than scientists anticipate will actually occur), about two-thirds of the varieties displayed reduced yields. The most sensitive soybean varieties, for example, lost over 25 percent of their yield. UV-B can also kill phytoplankton and krill, which are at the base of most ocean food chains. Therefore large increases in UV-B could be expected to affect many populations of ocean life, possibly even causing maritime food shortages.

As in the area of health hazards, it is not clear how serious these potential threats to the food supply are in practice. The most credible claim of an effect on food systems that has already occurred comes from studies showing a 6 to 12 percent decline in planktonic organisms in the ocean surrounding Antarctica where the ozone hole is open. Some Australian scientists believe that their crops of wheat, sorghum, and peas have already been affected, but this claim remains controversial.

Fortunately, organisms are not helpless against UV radiation. Both ocean algae (eaten by planktonic animals) and land plants produce a natural "sunscreen" molecules when exposed to increased UV. Nature's ingenious self-defense strategies will protect organisms up to a point, but no one knows just what that point is.

Lessons from the Ozone Problem

Because the ozone problem is relatively uncomplicated, with one major cause (CFCs) and one major effect (ozone depletion), it is relatively easy to draw lessons from it that may apply to other global environmental problems. One lesson is that where knowledge is incomplete, good research and constant monitoring of the actual state of the environment are critical. Agreements were possible on the ozone problem largely because reliable measurements and credible research findings influenced the views of the parties involved.

Another lesson is the importance of responsible action by all major actors. In the ozone controversy, environmentalists sometimes exaggerated, but on the whole, they based their case on research findings and played a critical role alerting the public and putting pressure on governments and corporations. Chemical companies at first acted as foot-draggers, but as the evidence for the role of CFCs in ozone depletion grew more convincing, some companies displayed extraordinary responsibility and environmental leadership. International organizations, such as UNEP, while limited in power, showed they can be very effective in prodding national governments to action and helping them negotiate. Scientists from many fields shifted their research priorities to focus on the ozone problem, and many took it upon themselves to communicate directly with the media and policy makers. Today, technologists and corporations are playing an indispensable role developing and marketing CFC alternatives that will be both profitable and good for the environment.

The most important lesson is simply that global environmental problems can be solved, despite vested interests, political conflicts, underdeveloped global institutions, and imperfect scientific understanding. Response to the ozone problem holds out the promise that it is possible to create a successful, sustainable society in harmony with the Earth.

See also ACID RAIN; CHEMISTRY; DEFORESTATION; ENVIRONMENT; ENVIRONMENTAL BEHAVIOR; ENVIRONMENTAL ETHICS; FORESTRY; GLOBAL ENVIRONMENTAL PROBLEMS; GLOBAL WARMING; OCEANS; SUSTAINABILITY.

BIBLIOGRAPHY

BENEDICK, RICHARD E. *Ozone Diplomacy.* Cambridge, MA: Harvard University Press, 1991.

GLEASON, J. F., et al. "Record Low Global Ozone in 1992." *Science* 260 (1993): 523–526.

LEAF, ALEXANDER. "Potential Health Effects of Global Climatic and Environmental Changes." *The New England Journal of Medicine* 321 (1989): 1577–1583.

MATHEWS, JESSICA TUCHMAN, ed. *Preserving the Global Environment: The Challenge of Shared Leadership.* The American Assembly and World Resources Institute. New York: W. W. Norton, 1990.

MOLINA, MARIO J., and ROWLAND, SHERWOOD F. "Stratospheric Sink for Chlorofluoromethanes: Chlorine Atomic Catalyzed Destruction of Ozone." *Nature* 249 (1974): 810.

TOON, OWEN B., and TURCO, RICHARD P. "Polar Stratospheric Clouds and Ozone Depletion." *Scientific American* (June 1991): 68–74.

Robert L. Olson

P

Pacesetter Governments

Governments that consistently pioneer public policy innovations at international, state, and local government levels are known as pacesetters, bellwethers, telltales, precursors, or just leading jurisdictions. During a given period of time, an identifiable vanguard of governments consistently attains prominence as the most adventuresome, experimental, and progressive. In short, there are a few identifiable governments that consistently tend to be the first to try the new.

Shifting Concepts from Theory to Practice

Implementation of public policy transforms proposals from concept to practice, from mere discussion to actual realization. Trial-and-error experimentation tests the merit of new concepts and their capacity to resolve problems. Unsound approaches become glaringly evident and the best concepts survive. Usually it is only a matter of time until proven approaches are copied elsewhere.

Telltale Diffusion Pattern

Diffusion—lead-lag relationships among public policy leaders, followers, and laggards—varies by jurisdictional level, time, and issue. Timelines graphically displaying past and present public policy responses on specific issues indicate the likelihood of further action among the remaining nonresponding jurisdictions.

Timelines demonstrating the implementation of a specific law year by year typically show an S-curve pattern. This is so because lawmaking on any issue virtually never occurs everywhere at the same time. The sequence starts slowly with a few initial innovators, followed by a somewhat larger group of early adopters. Next comes a surge of followers during mid-sequence, and the timeline ends with a slow response or outright rejection by a relatively small group of laggards. One move is followed by another, an action-response pattern akin to a row of falling dominoes. A very few diehard holdouts may not respond at all.

State-level lawmaking by all or nearly all U.S. states typically requires a minimum of five to ten years, but the usual response period is from eleven to twenty-six years. The primary diffusion time for the surge of laws updating air pollution controls among the fifty U.S. states spanned a period of twenty-three years, for example, and the process is not entirely complete today.

Bellwether jurisdictions are not always the first to adopt every new law. Nevertheless, a pattern of early response to many issues over a long period of time is so consistent that ascertaining action taken on an issue in just a few key jurisdictions reliably indicates coming change elsewhere.

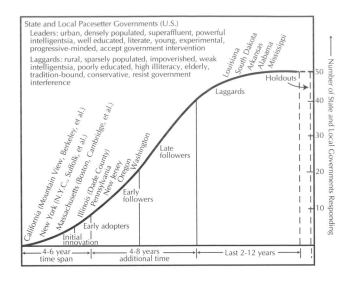

FIGURE 1. Molitor's multiple-timeline model of change—1. (Source: Graham T. T. Molitor, Public Policy Forecasting, Inc.)

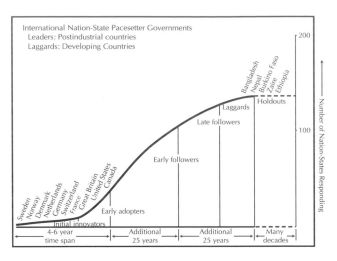

FIGURE 2. Molitor's multiple-timeline model of change—2. (Source: Graham T. T. Molitor, Public Policy Forecasting, Inc.)

State Pacesetters

The leading wedge of early-adopter states include California, New York, and Massachusetts. Additional early adopters sometimes include Pennsylvania, Illinois, and New Jersey. During colonial times, Massachusetts typically was the usual first innovator. Over time, New York moved to the forefront. Following westward expansion, California became the pacesetter and it retains that leadership role today.

In addition to the usual early adopters, a number of other bellwethers for one or more issue-specific topics can be identified. Oregon, Washington, Minnesota, and Maine, for example, are pacesetters for environmental issues. Wisconsin has been a noted leader in the area of social welfare since the Progressive party era. Maryland has become a precursor for privacy issues. State leaders on other specific topics have been identified.

Local Bellwethers

City and county bellwethers in the United States include New York, Boston, and Berkeley, California. Laggard state and local U.S. jurisdictions include Mississippi, Alabama, Arkansas, South Dakota, and Louisiana.

International Pacesetters

Outside the United States, notable local-government pacesetters include Stockholm, Oslo, Copenhagen, Amsterdam, The Hague, Bonn, London, Brussels, Zürich, Basel, Bern, and Tokyo. Internationally, state or provincial bellwethers have included North Rhine–Westphalia in Germany, Saskatchewan in Canada, New South Wales in Australia, and St. Gallen in Switzerland.

Response by nation-states also occurs in predictable patterns. Listed by region, pacesetter countries currently include Scandinavia (Sweden, Norway, Denmark); Western Europe (the Netherlands, Germany, Switzerland, France, Great Britain); North America (the United States, Canada). Developing nations in Asia (Bangladesh, Nepal, etc.) and Africa (Burkina Faso, Zaire, Ethiopia, etc.) and elsewhere are consistently among the laggards. Rank-ordered adoption of public policy frequently follows this very sequence. Principles proven effective by one nation often spread to other countries.

Additional countries occasionally among the early adopters include Australia, New Zealand, Japan, and Iceland. Eastern European nations (Poland, the Czech Republic, and the former U.S.S.R.) also have at times been leaders (at least in terms of their enactment of written laws) for some issues, such as certain environmental problems (pesticide pollution, the harmful effects of synthetic food colors, or electromagnetic field hazards).

Two Leading Bellwethers

Sweden and California are almost always in the forefront of change. By studying the responses of just these two jurisdictions, forecasters can anticipate similar developments likely to be undertaken elsewhere at a later date. Since the end of World War II, Sweden has consistently led all other jurisdictions in pioneering pacesetting public policy responses to most problems: social welfare programs, tax policies, environmental controls, consumer programs, video display tube safety, automotive safety, and prison reform. If not always first, Sweden has invariably been an early adopter. California, partly because it is a heterogeneous macrocosm for the nation as a whole, has served as the proving grounds for new policies in the United States.

Corroboration of Forecasts

Diffusion patterns among pacesetter jurisdictions pertain not only to legislation and regulation. Judicial decisions, quasi-legislative responses, self-government measures, voluntary accommodation patterns, contractual arrangements, and informal customs are among the social controls that follow similar patterns. The composite timelines of all such public policy responses among state and local, national and international jurisdictions provide an interesting study of the evolution of public policy. Change originates in creative minds, is focused by vision, advanced by deliberation, and confirmed by practical application, commencing with pacesetter jurisdictions.

See also AGENTS OF CHANGE; CHANGE; ENVIRONMENTAL POLICY CHANGES; FORECASTING, DETERMINISTIC; FORECASTING METHODS; LAWS, EVOLUTION OF; PUBLIC POLICY CHANGE; SWEDEN.

BIBLIOGRAPHY

COATES, JOSEPH F., et al. *Issues Management: How You Can Plan, Organize, and Manage for the Future.* Mt. Airy, MD: Lomond Publications, 1986.
CRAWFORD, CHARLES, and MOLITOR, GRAHAM T. T. *The Evolution of Electro-magnetic Fields as a Public Policy Issue: Analysis and Response Options.* Washington, DC: Hill and Knowlton, 1991.
MOLITOR, GRAHAM T. T. "Look Out: Here Comes Consumerism Again!" *Mobius* 8/4 (Fall 1989): 7–11.
———. "Plotting Patterns of Change." *Enterprise* 8/2 (March 1984): 4–9.
———. "Swedish Benefits Today: U.S. Benefits Tomorrow?" *Innovations* (March 1990): 6–18.

Graham T. T. Molitor

Paradigm Shift.

See GLOBAL TURNING POINT; MULTIFOLD TREND.

Parasensory Phenomena

Parasensory, "paranormal," or "psi" phenomena are phenomena that *appear to be* in some sense beyond the senses. The study of such phenomena is variously termed "parasensory investigation," "parapsychology," or "psi research."

The range of such phenomena is vast, and the boundary between "normal" and "paranormal" is somewhat indistinct. There are usually considered to be three main categories of (purported) paranormal phenomena:

1. *Entrasensory perception:* Apparent perception "beyond the senses." Examples include telepathic communication, clairvoyant remote viewing, remote diagnosis, precognition, retrocognition, and verisimilar memories of another life.
2. *Psychokinesis:* Apparent influence of the physical environment by mental states. Examples include remote actuation, poltergeist, teleportation, levitation (of one's own body), psychic surgery, and psychic healing, "thought photography."
3. *Evidence of disembodied self:* Examples include spirit possession, hauntings, spirit communication, some poltergeists, apparitions of the dead.

Parapsychology is typically assumed to be concerned with only the first two categories.

Much of the history of research in this area can be characterized as follows:

- The phenomena are considered paranormal, which in effect means that the phenomena do not appear to be explicable in known or imaginable scientific causal terms, and they tend to be sporadic in occurrence.
- Research has tended to focus on one of two types of situations—either those where a "star performer" seems to be able to produce "spectacular" phenomena more or less at will, or where low-level phenomena seemingly produced by persons not specially endowed can be studied statistically.
- Both kinds of research result tend to be unconvincing to the "tough-minded" scientist, for different reasons—the first because of nonreproducibility and the second because of methodological questions.
- The chief factor behind the unfriendly reception to research in psi phenomena by the scientific and medical communities has been the fact that the meaning and significance people tended to

attach to these experiences seemed to clash so directly with prevailing assumptions about the nature of scientific reality.

The possibility of a change in this situation seems now on the horizon. W. V. O. Quine, a major figure in the recent philosophy of science, has given us an important clue regarding what to do about these anomalous phenomena. He argued that the scientific explanation for any phenomenon is embedded in a theoretical network that involves multitudinous assumptions, including:

- assumptions involved in observation of the phenomenon
- hypotheses about the context of the phenomenon
- underlying theoretical hypotheses
- "basic laws" of the pertinent area of science
- the accepted nature of scientific methodology
- epistemological assumptions underlying scientific inquiry
- ontological assumptions about the basic nature of reality

When there is an "anomaly," or a failure of observations to conform to scientific expectations, it means that *somewhere* in that network there is a falsity. There is no way to tell just where in the theoretical network the falsity lies. Thus in the face of an anomaly we must consider revising any or all elements of the network. There is ultimately no such thing as a "crucial experiment" to "prove" a scientific hypothesis; the best that can be said is that a hypothesis is not challenged by any known anomalies. A consequence of Quine's view is that even our epistemological convictions about how we acquire knowledge, and about the nature of explanation, justification, and confirmation, are subject to revision and correction.

It is precisely to that point that we are brought by the impressive amount of empirical and anecdotal data regarding psi phenomena. For an assortment of reasons, Western science by the eighteenth century had adopted *an ontological assumption of separateness:* the separability of observer from observed; of humankind from nature; of mind from matter; of science from religion; the separateness of "fundamental particles" from one another; the separability of the parts of a system or organism with the assumption that one can understand the whole through understanding the parts; the separateness of scientific disciplines; the separateness of investigators competing over who was the first discoverer.

The assumption of separateness leads to the myth of the "objective observer" and to the search for reductionist explanations. It implies the locality of causes; that is, it precludes "action at a distance," either in space or time. It implies the *epistemological assumption* that our sole empirical basis for constructing a science is the data from our physical senses (positivism). These assumptions taken together have been termed the position of *logical empiricism.* By the middle of this century there was almost complete consensus that these are the proper foundation assumptions for science.

Scientists typically take these ontological and epistemological premises to be inviolate, to be an inherent and ineluctable part of the definition of science, rather than the optional assumptions which in fact they are. These underlying assumptions (which have been somewhat modified with the advent of quantum physics) are put in question by the data of psi research. More importantly, the worldview based on these assumptions seems to deny the validity of much of our everyday experience, including the sense of conscious awareness, of volition or "free will," of discoverable meaning and purpose in life, of apparently teleological influences in nature. Few have dared to suggest a reassessment of these most basic underlying ontological and epistemological assumptions, yet that is where we now must seek the resolution of the puzzle posed by psi phenomena.

The above arguments suggest the need for an "extended" science based upon (a) an *ontological assumption of oneness, wholeness,* the interconnectedness of everything, and (b) an *epistemological assumption that we contact reality in not one but two ways*—one of these being through physical sense data (forming the basis of normal science); the other through being ourselves part of the oneness, that is, through a deep intuitive "inner knowing." This "wholeness-based" science would regard present science as useful but having limited application.

Imagine, in accordance with this proposition, starting from the holistic assumption that everything—not only physical things but all things experienced, including sensations, emotions, feelings, motivations, thoughts—is really part of a single unity. Everything is interconnected in a *ground of being* (not really harder to imagine than everything being connected by an all-pervasive gravitational field). It is a bit like your experience of your own mind, wherein different parts of the mind may be relatively isolated from one another, each doing its own thing, and yet in the end your mind, conscious and unconscious, is experienced as a single, connected unity. One part of your mind hides things from another part of your mind (repression); different parts may be relatively autonomous with respect to one another (multiple personality syndrome being an extreme example); one part of your mind may communicate falsehood to another part—yet there is no doubt it is one mind.

Thus in a "wholeness-based" science apparent telepathic communication between two individuals does not appear as "anomalous"; rather, the puzzle is why one's mind is not perpetually cluttered by information coming in from other minds. Psychokinesis—mind affecting a remote part of the environment—is no more anomalous than volition—mind affecting the muscles in my arm and hand. Similarly, with the "oneness" assumption, one does not find other states of consciousness, teleological influences, "meaningful coincidences" (see Beloff, 1977), and so on, to be "anomalous." If volition or purpose or meaning exist in myself, then *ipso facto* they exist in the universe; there is nothing to be "explained," only explored.

If you try to imagine that the universe might be something like this, the first thing you notice is that it *feels* right. Every one of us has had trouble trying to feel at home in the universe that science pictured to us. We just never could feel as though consciousness and volition were simply illusions; as though our deeply felt values and purposes are simply made up; as though we humans exist in a meaningless universe having evolved through random mechanical processes; as though love, truth, beauty, and goodness have no more foundation than our hunger pains and sexual urges. How much more true it feels to imagine being at home in the universe, part of a meaningful whole. (Why "meaningful"? Because if I find meaning in myself, then by the basic unitive assumption, meaning exists in the universe.)

The significance of psi phenomena in the context of science has been that they seemed to challenge a view of science that some saw as inadequate. A "wholeness-based" science resolves that difficulty. Certain aspects of the unity that is the whole will continue to be quite profitably studied by means of "separateness-based science"; however, that kind of science—as only part of a more extended science—would no longer have the authority to insist that we are here, solely through random causes, in a meaningless universe. Likewise it would no longer be able to assert that our consciousness is "merely" the chemical and physical processes of the brain or to suggest that

claimed psi phenomena could not have occurred "because they violate scientific laws."

Heretofore science has started with a limiting set of assumptions and has then found it necessary to deny the validity and even the possibility of a host of reported phenomena that do not fit within those limits. A tremendous amount of effort has gone on within science defending the barricades against, or explaining away, these outcasts—a category containing paranormal events like "miraculous" healings and "psi phenomena," but also including more ordinary experiences such as volition, selective attention, and the hunger for meaning.

Rather than having to defend against the anomalous, "wholeness-based science" would incorporate the assumption that any class of inner experiences that have been reported, or of phenomena that have been observed, down through the ages and across cultures, apparently in some sense exist and have a *face validity* that cannot be denied.

See also CONSCIOUS EVOLUTION; GLOBAL TURNING POINTS; HOLISTIC BELIEFS; MIND: NEW MODES OF THINKING; PSEUDO-FUTURISTS; VALUES; VALUES, NONWESTERN.

BIBLIOGRAPHY

BELOFF, JOHN. "Psi Phenomena: Causal versus Acausal Interpretation." *Journal of the Society for Psychical Research* 49/773 (September 1977).

EISENBUD, JULE. *Parapsychology and the Unconscious.* Berkeley, CA: North Atlantic Books, 1983.

GUILEY, ROSEMARY E. *Harper's Encyclopedia of Mystical and Paranormal Experience.* San Francisco: Harper-Collins, 1991.

JAHN, ROBERT, and DUNNE, BRENDA. *Margins of Reality: The Role of Consciousness in the Physical World.* New York: Harcourt Brace Jovanovich, 1987.

LESHAN, LAWRENCE. *The Science of the Paranormal.* London: Thorsons, 1987.

MITCHELL, EDGAR D., ed. *Psychic Exploration: A Challenge for Science.* New York: G. P. Putnam's Sons, 1974.

PEAT, F. DAVID. *Synchronicity: The Bridge Between Matter and Mind.* New York: Bantam, 1987.

Willis W. Harman

Parks and Wilderness

The United States gave the world a model when it made Yellowstone Park the first national park in 1872. Since then, nations around the globe also have protected areas of outstanding natural beauty or scientific uniqueness. Earlier actions by monarchs had designated lands for their personal pleasure or for state purposes, but national parks were different in that they were established for the benefit of the people.

Overall, Americans enjoy a rich mosaic of public and private lands that provide scenery, open space, recreation, and nature protection. Congress broadened the concept of national parks over the years. Now there are national monuments, recreation areas, historical sites (or historical parks), seashores, lakeshores, trails, and wild and scenic rivers, among others. In 1964 Congress established the National Wilderness Preservation System, intended to maintain tracts of federal land in unspoiled condition. Much of this expansion was driven by the 1962 recommendations of the Outdoor Recreation Resources Review Commission (ORRRC), established by law in 1958 to make studies and recommendations that would help ensure that accessible high-quality outdoor recreation resources are available.

State and local governments also contribute many outdoor recreational resources: parks, forests, beaches, playgrounds, ball fields, and wilderness camping areas. Following ORRC recommendations, many states created river and trail systems paralleling those of the federal government.

Vast federal acreage dedicated to agricultural commodity production, forestry, or wildlife protection supplement these park and recreation lands. The national forests, wildlife refuges, and public domain lands serve both commodity and conservation roles, as well as serving the demands for outdoor recreational activities. Many designated wilderness areas, trails, or wild and scenic rivers are found on these lands managed by the U.S. departments of Agriculture and the Interior.

The private sector also contributes importantly to the variety of outdoor recreation lands. Private owners develop facilities—such as golf courses—that the federal government does not consider appropriate in national parks or recreation areas, or that local governments may find too expensive to build and maintain. Similarly, more elaborate facilities are often found at commercial campgrounds and resorts than at public areas.

Some nongovernmental organizations, such as the Nature Conservancy, Conservation Fund, and Audubon Society, also protect natural areas. These organizations, using funds from members or donors, buy lands to protect their natural resources. Some public access to these lands is allowed if it does not threaten plants, wildlife, or other fragile resources.

These private lands help fill a gap in outdoor opportunities. In the United States most federal lands are situated in the West, relatively removed from centers of population, leaving the rest of the country with generally smaller federal land units, primarily national forests and state or local parks. Private lands thus meet open space needs nearer to population concentrations.

The political process largely drives the supply and use of public land. During the 1960s and 1970s, advocates got Congress to designate significant acreages of federal land as protected; millions of acres of public-domain and national forest lands were thus converted to national parks, recreation areas, and wilderness. Congress also funded the purchase of private lands to add to the national recreation estate at federal, state, and local levels. Environmental groups supported legislation that emphasized resource protection over general recreational use of federal lands. Budget constraints and differing priorities during the Reagan administration limited federal funds available for land acquisition at all government levels.

Just as the supply and diversity of park lands has increased over time, so have the demands people place on these resources. Technology, social trends, and demographics drive these new uses; these factors are likely to cause even more changes in the future.

Technological changes include the development of new materials or applications that make outdoor recreation more convenient: lightweight tents and packs, freeze-dried foods, comfortable but protective clothing, and high-performance sporting equipment.

Crossover technology from military applications plays an important role in changing outdoor recreation. The first, perhaps, was the conversion of World War II life rafts to recreational use on whitewater rivers, now a major recreational activity for all ages. Other transfers include snowmobiles and four-wheel-drive vehicles. More recently, new night vision gear and global-positioning satellite equipment to maintain precise tabs on one's location in the wilderness or anywhere have begun to open up new areas for nocturnal recreational activity.

Social trends include a concern for protection of the environment, maintenance of health and fitness, and a perceived decline in the amount of leisure time. These trends impose differing demands pressures on park resources and their management. A major need is for more and better park and outdoor recreational opportunities closer to where people live. These demands may influence building and development patterns in the future to ensure that parks are part of any successful new real estate project.

The aging and cultural diversification of the population are dominant demographic trends affecting the use of recreation lands. In the past, an aging population made fewer demands for outdoor recreation opportunities. Now, however, health and fitness concerns are keeping individuals involved in many activities later in life. When visiting parks far from home, these older users may prefer comfortable lodge-type accommodations or facilities for recreational vehicles, amenities disliked by preservation groups. People of different ethnic and cultural backgrounds may have different expectations of parks. At the very least, there is a need for park managers to learn these expectations and communicate with these new clients.

Changes in family composition and the issue of economic disparity are other important demographic and financial considerations in assessing the demand for park and recreational resources in the next century. The growth of dual-income households has eroded the time available for recreational activities. Single-parent households often suffer from both loss of time and money; this can doubly constrain the ability to participate in many recreational activities. Increased supervised recreational activity may be an emerging response to these trends, although local budget problems may limit this amenity.

It was a political process inspired by a vision for the future that provided our heritage of federal, state, and local parks. Can that process continue to adequately provide for tomorrow's park and recreation needs?

See also AGING OF THE POPULATION; DEFORESTATION; FORESTRY; GREEN REVOLUTION; NATURAL RESOURCES, USE OF; OUTDOOR RECREATION AND LEISURE PURSUITS; RESOURCES; THEME PARKS AND ORGANIZED ATTRACTIONS.

BIBLIOGRAPHY

ENDICOTT, EVE, ed. *Land Conservation through Public/ Private Partnerships*. Washington, DC: Island Press, 1993.
FROME, MICHAEL. *Regreening the National Parks*. Tucson, AZ: University of Arizona Press, 1992.
MCNEELY, JEFFREY A. "The Future of National Parks." *Environment* (January–February 1990): 16–20.

George H. Siehl

Participative Management

The concept of participation in decision making, or PDM, was popularized in North America as a result of experiments with school children conducted by psychologist Kurt Lewin and his colleagues in the late 1930s. These studies claimed to show the superiority of groups that were democratically led over those autocratically led, especially when the leader was absent. The PDM idea was reinforced by a widely publicized study conducted in 1948 in a pajama factory by Coch and French, which claimed to show that PDM reduced resistance to change among employees. Although both claims were later disputed, these studies were widely influential.

After World War II, the idea of democratic leadership spread to Western Europe, mainly in the form of official, often legally mandated, worker representation systems, that guaranteed direct or indirect employee-representation on boards of directors or other decision-making bodies in business. These systems differ from country to country and are known by various names (e.g., codetermination, joint consultation, works councils). PDM has also been used in non-European countries. In Israel PDM was advocated mainly by the Kibbutz, as well as the labor or Histadrut sector, which owns and manages many companies. In Japan, PDM is fostered by an intensive, multidirectional communication system, although this takes place within a strongly hierarchical and status-focused organizational structure.

In Canada and the United States, the PDM movement spread informally through training managers in participative leadership methods; the use of management by objectives (MBO), with objectives being set jointly by superior and subordinate; the adoption of productivity-sharing plans such as the Scanlon Plan, which include mechanisms for increasing employee involvement; the quality movement; and employee ownership plans (e.g., ESOP's). American unions, however, were very reluctant participants in the PDM movement, fearing that it would coopt their members and undermine the unions' traditional adversarial role.

PDM Research

In the United States there now are, roughly speaking, two schools of thought about PDM. One school views it as a "moral imperative" and thus eschews any need to study the phenomenon empirically. The other school views PDM as one of many management tools and seeks to understand the actual conditions under which PDM will be most effective.

Those who favor the empirical approach find that PDM is much less effective in raising morale and productivity than has been assumed by people in academia and industry. Many PDM studies, including the early ones done in the United States and noted earlier, were widely criticized on methodological grounds. Even ignoring these criticisms, the average productivity increase resulting from PDM programs in organizational settings is only about 0.5 percent. Studies of participation in setting goals found that PDM results in no greater commitment to goals than simply telling people what goals to achieve accompanied by a rationale. PDM, however, sometimes leads to higher goals being set, thus stimulating higher productivity.

More recent studies suggest, however, that the benefits of PDM may be more cognitive than motivational—that is, PDM may foster better performance not so much by raising commitment (which can be achieved through other means such as visionary leadership and incentives) as by facilitating the exchange of information between supervisor and subordinate, leading in turn to better decision making.

This finding has an important caveat. Information exchange will be most beneficial when subordinates possess knowledge not possessed by supervisors. This contingency does not limit the effective use of PDM as much as one might think, however, because subordinates often know a lot more about many aspects of their own, specific jobs than do their bosses. It is widely believed (not without cause) that many managers underestimate the knowledge and capability of their subordinates. On the other hand, it would obviously not be very beneficial to practice PDM in cases where subordinates clearly lack relevant knowledge.

PDM Today

PDM is evolving in North America, and to an extent in other countries, toward delegation of responsibility to self-managing teams and work groups. Such groups make decisions on their own about their own jobs (e.g., scheduling, assignment of tasks) and the coordination of their work with that of other teams. After appropriate training, such groups may also discover ways to improve work processes and to improve work quality. They may also have direct contact with customers and responsibility for customer service. In addition, individual training in self-management has been used to overcome such seemingly intractable problems as absenteeism.

The trend toward self-management has coincided with the trend in organizational design toward flatter, leaner structures. Due to rapid changes in technology and increased global competition, modern organizations need to be closer to the customer, faster moving, and more flexible than in the past. Autonomous work teams, bound together by a common vision and careful measurement of work performance accompanied by clear standards, help to fulfill these needs. Thus far, the results look very promising.

The main obstacle to this trend is the reluctance of some managers to give up their traditional power, either because they like the power or because they do not trust workers to be either responsible or knowledgeable. Strong organizational leadership is needed to overcome such reluctance.

PDM in the Future

The workplace trend toward empowerment at every level is likely to continue. Not only is this virtually necessitated by the realities of modern, global business, but workers are becoming more educated and well-trained. The labor force is becoming increasingly dominated by skilled knowledge workers who need to engage routinely in creative problem-solving in order to be effective. It is reasonable to forecast that more and more business decisions will be made by small, autonomous work teams which will be connected to other parts of the organization and customers through high technology information and communication systems and held accountable for their results by means of performance standards. Of course, not everyone likes to work continuously in teams, not everyone wants responsibility, and not everyone in authority wants to give it. Thus, we should continue to see variety in organizational forms and perhaps even a backlash against too much "groupism" due to its sometimes pernicious effects on independent thinking and healthy conflict.

The irony of these changes is that PDM itself increasingly will become an inadequate concept for describing the new business realities. PDM refers to joint-decision making, but autonomous work teams are actually delegated full responsibility for their work processes and typically have no supervisors at all. Furthermore, performance standards will probably be imposed by top management based on competitive necessity (as is common now) and not set jointly. Finally, the concept of continuous communication in all directions will replace the idea of participation between supervisor and subordinate.

See also BUSINESS GOVERNANCE; DEMOCRATIC PROCESSES; GOVERNANCE; MANAGEMENT; SOCIAL DEMOCRACY.

BIBLIOGRAPHY

LATHAN, G.; WINTERS, D.; and LOCKE, E. "Cognitive and Motivational Effects of Participation: a Mediator Study." *Journal of Organizational Behavior* 15 (1994): 49–63.

LOCKE, E. and LATHAM, G. *A Theory of Goal Setting and Task Performance.* Englewood Cliffs, NJ: Prentice Hall, 1990.

LOCKE, E., and SCHWEIGER, D. "Participation in Decision Making: One More Look." In B. Staw, ed. *Research in Organizational Behavior*, vol. 1. Greenwich, CT: JAI Press, 1979.

MANZ, C., and SIMS, H. *Business Without Bosses: How Self-Managed Teams Are Producing High Performance Companies.* New York: Wiley, 1993.

Edwin A. Locke
Gary P. Lathan

Peacekeeping

The term *peacekeeping* has at least five different interpretations, each one depending on a particular concept of peace, as illustrated in Figure 1.

Peacekeeping as War Prevention

If peace is seen as the absence of war, then peacekeeping requires the use, or threat of use, of military power. During the Cold War, both the United States and the Soviet Union adopted the theory of nuclear deterrence to keep the peace. They believed this standoff was the only strategy that would prevent the other from attacking. Many analysts argued that the common policy of Mutually Assured Destruction (MAD), a policy based on the enormous destructive capability of the 50,000 nuclear warheads that were then in existence, prevented a war between the two sides. The motto of the U.S. Strategic Air Command, "Peace is our profession," enshrines this view of peacekeeping between states.

With the end of the Cold War, the world has seen a dramatic increase in internal conflicts or civil wars within states. For example, in 1992, thirty-nine of the forty armed conflicts fought in the world were internal conflicts. In states such as Somalia, Russia, Mexico, and the former Yugoslavia, military force has been used in internal conflicts, either as a deterrent, or in peacekeeping operations.

Peacekeeping and the International System

This view of peacekeeping arose in the 1960s as a result of U.N. military interventions to help maintain cease-fires, assist in troop withdrawals, or provide a buffer between opposing forces. Here peacekeeping uses armed personnel, such as the U.N. "blue helmets," but does not provide an overwhelming military force. They carry light arms and are allowed to use minimum force only in self-de-

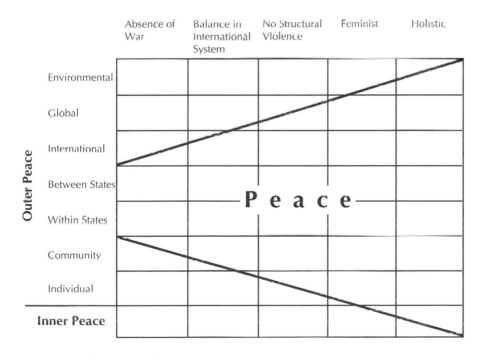

FIGURE 1. Elements of peace.

fense; their effectiveness depends on the moral authority of the United Nations and the expressed concern of the international system. This approach assumes peace requires a balance of military, political, economic, and social forces operating across a range of levels from the local community to the international system.

There has been a dramatic increase in U.N. peacekeeping operations since the end of the Cold War. From 1948 to May 1993, more than 600,000 soldiers and civilians have served in twenty-eight U.N. peacekeeping operations. Fifteen of these have been established since 1988, and the number of personnel involved has increased from a maximum of about 20,000 in any one year prior to 1990 to more than 80,000 in May 1993.

Peacekeeping and Structural Violence

There has also been a steady shift away from the primarily military goals of keeping the warring parties apart toward a concern with combating "structural violence"—the social, political, and economic structures that contribute to poverty, starvation, and diminished life expectancy. U.N. policy endorses this approach: "Complicated military tasks must be complemented by measures to strengthen institutions, encourage political participation, protect human rights, organize elections and promote economic and social development" (United Nations, 1993, p. 8).

With the emergence of truly global actors—such as transnational corporations, whose economic interests transcend those of any nation or state, and international nongovernmental organizations (INGOs), whose members act as world citizens—peacekeeping operations have broadened their mandate to include a concern for both physical and structural violence. This has meant that peacekeeping operations increasingly "require peacekeeping troops to work closely with civilian police, elected officials, human rights observers, refugee specialists and many others from a variety of nations" (Smith, 1993, p. ix).

Peacekeeping in the latter 1990s requires the participation of many different groups to both deal with immediate crises, such as humanitarian aid, and longer-term problems, such as creating conditions for peace and stability in the country concerned. It also involves international cooperation to combat terrorism.

Peacekeeping in a Feminist Framework

Feminist definitions of peace include the abolition of violence against women and children in the home and on the streets, as well as doing away with patriarchal economic, political, and social structures—structural violence—that directly affect people at the individual level. Peacekeeping in this sense includes a broad range of "conflict resolution" and counseling procedures that are designed to control, or prevent, physical violence against individual women, men, and children, as well as encourage the evolution of new customs and mores that change traditional gender roles.

Peacekeeping thus involves the police force, the courts, schools, and other community agencies that are working to stop wife beating, gang violence, and other forms of local violence that directly affect individuals. Feminist definitions also include a concern with all of the other levels of analysis, from community to global, and with all forms of violence against and between people.

Holistic Peacekeeping

Holistic interpretations can be expanded to apply the peacekeeping concept still further to include peace with the environment. This means that peacekeeping would be carried out in an environmentally sound fashion. Holistic peacekeeping would also be based on a more balanced peace concept that includes both outer and inner peace. While outer peace focuses on events in the material world, such as war, starvation, or pollution, inner peace is a spiritual state of oneness that can be developed through various spiritual practices, such as meditation or prayer.

If peace is seen as both inner and outer, balanced in harmony, then peacekeeping will require both action in the outer material world and exploration of the inner spiritual one. The relationship between inner peace and outer peace is of fundamental importance for holistic peacekeeping, as illustrated by Gandhi's approach to nonviolent action, which involved a period of inner searching and purification prior to action in the outer world.

Conclusion

Peacekeeping seems to be evolving from the mainly military interpretation associated with peace as the absence of war, to the broader structural-violence interpretation that emerged in the 1990s. In the future, the term may expand further and be based on feminist definitions of peace, in which the abolition of all forms of violence against people is required, and holistic interpretations that balance the demands of both outer and inner notions of peace.

See also INTERNATIONAL GOVERNANCE AND RE-
GIONAL AUTHORITIES; INTERNATIONAL TENSIONS.

BIBLIOGRAPHY

CHILDERS, ERSKINE, and URQUHART, BRIAN. *Renewing the
United Nations System.* Uppsala: Dag Hammarskjöld
Foundation, 1994.
DURCH, WILLIAM J. *The Evolution of UN Peacekeeping:
Case Studies and Comparative Analysis.* New York: St
Martin's Press, 1993.
SMITH, HUGH, ed. *Peacekeeping: Challenges for the Future.*
Canberra: Australian Defence Studies Centre, 1993.
United Nations Department of Public Information. *The
Blue Helmets: A Review of United Nations Peace-keep-
ing.* New York: United Nations Publications, 1985.
_____. *United Nations Peacekeeping.* New York: United
Nations Publications, 1993.

Paul Smoker

Pediatrics.

See CHILD CARE.

Pentecostalism

Pentecostalism has been the most rapidly spreading form of Christianity during the twentieth century. Pentecostalism is derived from Pentecost
(from the Greek word *pentecoste,* meaning "fiftieth
day"), a Christian feast day occurring on the seventh Sunday after Easter, commemorating the descent of the Holy Spirit upon the Apostles fifty
days after the resurrection of Christ. The Acts of
the Apostles 2:3–4 relates that there appeared to
them "parted tongues as of fire, which settled
upon each of them. And they were all filled with
the Holy Spirit and began to speak in foreign
tongues." These two phenomena—glossolalia, or
speaking in tongues, and the baptism of the Holy
Spirit—are the principal signatures of the Charismatic and Pentecostal churches, known also as
Latter Rain or the Apostolic Faith. Pentecostal
churches also stress the charisms, or gifts of the
Spirit, including those of prophecy, discernment,
and divine healing.

Characteristic of these churches is joyous, emotional worship with uplifted hands, handclapping,
use of musical instruments, and sometimes dancing. They generally exude a camp-meeting fervor.
Pentecostal churches are evangelical, or revival,
congregations, independent of any single denominational organization, and usually connected only
by a common set of beliefs. They teach sanctifica-
tion, or holiness, and premillenarianism, or the imminent return of Jesus Christ to head a literal kingdom on earth. They have a strong appeal to the
common people because they minister to not only
the spiritual but also the emotional and physical
needs of their members.

In 1900 there were 50,000 Pentecostals in all of
Latin America, by 2000 it is expected that they will
number more than 100 million and 80 percent of all
Latin American Protestants will be Pentecostal. The
five largest churches in the world are all Pentecostal:
the Full Gospel Central Church in Seoul, Korea
(800,000 members); Jotabeche Methodist Pentecostal Church in Santiago, Chile (350,000 members); Congregaçao Christo in São Paulo, Brazil
(185,000 members); Deeper Christian Life Ministry
in Lagos, Nigeria (65,000 members);and Vision del
Futuro in Buenos Aires (45,000 members).

Pentecostalism has been described as the Third
Wave of Christianity. In his book *The Household of
God,* Bishop Leslie Newbigin of the Church of
South India describes three major types of Christianity. The Catholic tradition emphasizes continuity, orthodoxy, and sacraments. The Protestant tradition emphasizes the centrality of scriptures.
Pentecostals emphasize the experience and gifts of
the Holy Spirit. The three streams together, says
Newbigin, provide the basis for a unified Christian
witness.

During the first two centuries of Christianity, the
gifts of the Holy Spirit were highly valued, and
pentecostal forms of Christianity as a separate
movement spread throughout Asia Minor and
North Africa. The first wave of this movement was
Montanism, founded by Montanus, about 160 A.D.
Despite widespread support, including that of Ter-
tullian, Montanism was ultimately condemned by
the Synod of Iconium about 230 A.D. Thereafter
Montanism went underground and lasted for a few
more centuries before disappearing altogether.
Modern Pentecostalism in the United States was
begun in Topeka, Kansas, at the turn of the century
by Charles Fox Parham, an independent Holiness
preacher. The movement grew slowly and locally
until 1906 when William Joseph Seymour, a student of Parham, carried it to Los Angeles. There a
great revival began in a warehouse known today as
Seymour's Azusa Street Mission. The revival continued there for two years attracting thousands,
some of whom were to carry the message across
the United States and around the world.

The Pentecostal renewal in the twentieth century
arrived in three surges or waves. The first wave of

1906 was followed half a century later by the Charismatic renewal within the Roman Catholic Church and a decade later by a third wave of mainstream Protestant church renewal. These three waves make up between one-quarter and one-third of Christians worldwide.

In *Restoring the Faith: The Assemblies of God, Pentecostalism, and American Culture,* Edith L. Blumhofer sees four stages of modern Penecostal development. Restorationism in the early years; fundamentalism followed by charismatic renewal in the middle years; and now the growing incorporation of popular culture, which will continue into the future. Caught in a secular materialist culture, the existing social order is changing the church rather than the other way around. There is a decreasing emphasis on the operation of prophetic and healing gifts within the church as well as a decline in the chiliastic fervor that marked the early Pentecostal movement.

Who becomes a Pentecostal? In terms of global demographics, about one-quarter are white; members are more urban than rural, more female than male, more likely to be children than adults, more Third World than Western, more poor than rich. Europe has the smallest number of Pentecostals. In East Asia, Christians have been massively "pentecostalized," with vast numbers of converts in Korea and China.

See also CHRISTIANITY; RELIGION, SPIRITUALITY, MORALITY; RELIGIONS: DECLINE OR RISE OF.

BIBLIOGRAPHY

BARRETT, DAVID. "The Twentieth Century Pentecostal/ Charismatic Renewal in the Holy Spirit with Its Goal of World Evangelization." *International Bulletin of Missionary Research* (July 1988).
SYNAN, VINCENT. *In the Latter Days.* Ann Arbor, MI, 1991.

George Thomas Kurian

Performing Arts: Dance and Theater

The performing arts mirror trends in society. Recessions, new technologies, political conservatism, an aging society, rapid social change, multiculturalism, and even a new understanding of nature all have challenged the arts and offer creative opportunities.

In *Megatrends 2000,* futurists John Naisbitt and Patricia Aburdene predicted that the 1990s would see a renaissance in the arts and that "the arts will gradually replace sports as society's primary leisure activity." Trends supporting this prediction include the increased education and economic influence of women and older people, who tend to prefer cultural activities over sports and the recognition among corporations and communities of the economic benefits of the arts, including more jobs, tax revenues, urban renewal, and tourism income.

Despite record receipts at the box office—attributable more to skyrocketing ticket prices than to increases in attendance or in numbers of new productions—the recession of the early 1990s struck fear into the hearts of arts' producers. New musicals were especially hard hit by the recession. Veteran Broadway director/producer Harold Prince has suggested that one reason musicals have suffered is that Hollywood films and television have been siphoning off the best creative talents for the past thirty years. Enormous investments are required for presenting musicals, and so there is no room for failure—and no second chances for composers, lyricists, and playwrights to learn from their mistakes. Thus, Broadway is rapidly becoming a repository for safe, familiar material, especially revivals and "musicalized" versions of such popular movies as *Sunset Boulevard* and *Kiss of the Spider Woman.*

Future creativity and growth of new audiences will come from outside Broadway, in the more than 200 professional theaters around the United States. But these smaller companies, too, face several challenges. Where will the new plays come from when all the best writers are in Hollywood? What will happen to acting when skills such as projecting the voice are being lost in the age of microphones? Where are the new audiences going to come from if parents don't take their children to the theater? Where will the leadership come from when people must devote years of life to a small theater and still have to struggle to make ends meet? And where will the money come from? Public and private support for the arts has dwindled. Another challenge is where tomorrow's actors, dancers, playwrights, choreographers, and directors will come from when so many of the most able young talents are succumbing to AIDS.

Addressing these challenges will require creativity—which is of course the lifeblood of performing artists. For instance, the challenge of AIDS has led to a burst of creativity in new plays about the disease, and the challenge of finding jobs in the theater has led to a resurgence of one-person plays.

The future of the performing arts will rely on nurturing tomorrow's artists and audiences. Many theater and dance groups work with children. For instance, former dancer Jacques d'Amboise's National Dance Institute has taught dancing to more than 100,000 schoolchildren, primarily in inner-city schools. And the 1994 Goals 2000 education program promises to sharply increase the role of the arts in U.S. school curricula.

The Future of Theater

Theater will continue to stretch its boundaries, incorporating not only dance and music but the visual and electronic arts. Advances in virtual reality will make some forms of theater interactive, allowing audiences to participate in or create an individual theatrical experience. New scenarios for plays could be written, based on psychological and behavioral databases for individual characters, and the audience could vote on Hamlet's fate: "Press 'one' for 'To Be'; press 'two' for 'Not to Be.'"

Experimental theater has challenged the formalism of the Aristotelian aesthetic for at least a century, offering a nonlinear drama of existence that more closely "imitates" what we perceive as reality. Aristotle's emphasis on plot led to the structure used in much of Western drama up to the twentieth century—that is, an action culminating in a single climactic moment. However, modern theater gives equal weight to isolated moments and keeps the audience in the present. This new "aesthetic of the event" is more in tune with the information age. Audiences raised on *Sesame Street* and MTV, where everything seems to happen at once, are becoming increasingly "omniattentive," capable of perceiving many things at once and discontinuously.

As theater moves more toward an aesthetic of experience, the text of a play, considered a work of art or literature on its own in the Aristotelian aesthetic, will increasingly be used only as a starting point. Some performances may not even begin with a script—*A Chorus Line*, for instance, was developed in workshops after an all-night discussion among some eighteen dancers. Acting styles for stage work now develop from improvisational techniques (responding to experiences as they occur) rather than Method acting (a naturalistic style more appropriate to film).

Still, the Aristotelian structure of the well-made play will not disappear, and the plays of Shakespeare will live for centuries to come, though adapted to future tastes and preferences. The text may make a comeback as tomorrow's audiences become suspicious of the image—which can be infinitely manipulated by technology—and long for great words spoken by resonant, well-trained voices.

The Future of Dance

Dance, as one top arts administrator noted, "arguably is the least popular of the art forms in terms of ticket-buying public." The challenge of bringing in audiences has led to dramatic changes in philosophy, and notable ballet companies have commissioned works by rock musicians to give dance a wider and more youthful appeal.

Like theater, dance is exploring a new aesthetic based on contemporary values. Young choreographers frequently reject gender stereotyping; the corps de ballet in Mark Morris's *The Hard Nut*—a reinterpretation of *The Nutcracker*—is an equal opportunity employer for male "snowflakes."

Choreographers have also rejected the linear progression of the Aristotelian aesthetic, using chance methods of construction and stringing disparate elements together. Merce Cunningham's *Breakers* is danced to an electronic score that the audience *and* the dancers heard for the first time on opening night, defying a clear relationship between dance, dancers, and music.

Cunningham is among those using the computer software LifeForms to store, retrieve, and manipulate movement passages. Computer and video technology will allow both the preservation of classic choreography and the creation of new works. Classically trained dancers such as Mikhail Baryshnikov have created a bridge between the old and the new. Baryshnikov, founder of the White Oak Dance Project, draws much of the troupe's repertoire from modern-dance choreographers, using his fame to widen the younger creators' circle of admirers and establish them for the future.

See also ARTS; CREATIVITY; MASS CULTURE AND ARTS; MUSIC; PRIVATE ASSISTANCE PROGRAMS; PUBLIC ASSISTANCE PROGRAMS; VISUAL ARTS.

BIBLIOGRAPHY

LARIJANI, L. CASEY. *The Virtual Reality Primer.* New York: McGraw-Hill, 1994.

NAISBITT, JOHN, and ABURDENE, PATRICIA. "Renaissance in the Arts." In *Megatrends 2000: Ten New Directions for the 1990s.* New York: Morrow, 1990.

PRINCE, HAROLD. "The Good New Days." *American Theatre* (January 1993).

SCHMITT, NATALIE CROHN. *Actors and Onlookers: Theater and Twentieth-Century Scientific Views of Nature.* Evanston, IL: Northwestern University Press, 1990.

Cynthia G. Wagner

Perfumes.

See FRAGRANCES.

Personal Transport

To many people, the phrase *personal vehicle* is synonymous with *automobile*. Yet a look at the global transportation picture reveals that far more of humanity relies not on engine power, but on human power—in the form of bicycles, cycle rickshas, and similar two- and three-wheelers. Bicycles in Asia alone outnumber the world's 460 million automobiles. This gap is sure to widen in the future, since annual car production worldwide is barely one-third that of bicycles.

The bicycle's fate has been intertwined with the automobile's ever since they were both invented in the late nineteenth century. By demanding that the government build a road network, U.S. bicyclists in the 1880s literally paved the way for the motorcar, which in subsequent decades would supersede pedal power. Today in the United States, as in most countries, the extent of bicycle use is closely tied to automobile ownership. With nearly one bicycle for every two people, the country has one of the world's largest bicycle fleets. But since even more Americans own cars, few rely on cycling for everyday transport.

Pedal power is most important in Asia, where bicycles provide personal transport in much the same manner as private cars do in the United States, rickshas provide taxi service, and heavy-duty tricycles do the work of light trucks. In many cities, nonmotorized vehicles account for up to 60 percent of total trips. Much of the goods transport in China and India is by human-powered three-wheelers—which can haul loads of up to half a ton. In Bangladesh, these vehicles transport a greater total of tonnage than motor vehicles do.

Elsewhere in the developing world, bicycles are at once indispensable and undervalued. Governments in Africa and Latin America have long ignored nonmotorized vehicles in transport policy, adopting the motorized bias of aid-donor countries and international lending banks. Still, the scarcity of other options has led to heavy reliance on bicycles in many areas for commuting to work, reaching remote rural communities, and hauling vegetables to market. Parts of Zimbabwe, Ghana, and other African countries have considerable bicycle use.

Japan and several European countries are notable for their relatively widespread use of bicycles despite high rates of auto ownership. In the Netherlands and Denmark, bicycling makes up 20 to 30 percent of all urban trips—up to half in some cities. Railway passengers in Japan and Europe rely on bicycles as a convenient, affordable way to reach train stations. On a typical weekday, nearly 3 million bicycles are parked at rail stations throughout Japan. In Denmark, 25–30 percent of commuter rail passengers set out from home on two wheels.

Bicycles are experiencing something of a comeback in North America and Australia, where car driving had all but replaced cycling in the decades after World War II. Environmental concerns and a new interest in personal fitness have helped revive these countries' interest in pedal power since the 1970s. The number of Americans who regularly commute to work by bicycle has roughly tripled since the early 1980s, to an estimated 3 million riders.

Future prospects for pedal power are bright. World bicycle production is currently about 110 million bicycles annually and continues to climb. The popularity of new, sturdier models is quickly expanding the use of bicycles for urban commuting and riding on rugged, off-road terrain. Some governments that formerly pursued strictly car-oriented policies are now promoting cycling to reduce air pollution, traffic congestion, and transport infrastructure spending. Even in the United States, local governments today have the flexibility to provide bicycle lanes and paths with much of the federal funding previously reserved for highways.

Incongruously, officials in major cities in China—where there are 250 bicycles for every automobile—have threatened to ban bicycles from selected thoroughfares in order to make way for cars and trucks. Intense public outcries so far have fended off such prohibitions. Meanwhile, the World Bank and other development institutions have supported a handful of small but highly successful nonmotorized transport projects. Several cities in Africa and Latin America are building bicycle lanes and educating people about the advantages of bicycling.

Transport planners recognize that certain conditions are necessary for pedal power to fulfill its potential role in personal transportation. A formidable obstacle in cities worldwide is the danger posed by fast-moving motorized traffic and drivers who are not trained to share the road with cyclists. Until governments treat nonmotorized vehicles as an important transport mode and invest in the provision of bicycle facilities, safety fears will continue to deter many would-be cyclists, and those who do choose to pedal will remain at risk. Making adequate provision for bicycle transportation will continue to include well-designed bicycle paths, secure parking, and ample space to accommodate bicycles on regular roads.

See also MOTOR VEHICLES; MOTOR VEHICLES, ALTERNATIVELY POWERED; TRANSPORTATION; URBAN TRANSIT.

BIBLIOGRAPHY

FORESTER, JOHN. *Bicycle Transportation: A Handbook.* Cambridge, MA: MIT Press, 1994.

LECCESE, MICHAEL, and PLEVIN, ARLENE. *The Bicyclist's Sourcebook.* Rockville, MD: Woodbine House, 1991.

LOWE, MARCIA D. "Bicycle Production Rises Again." In Lester R. Brown et al., *Vital Signs 1994: The Trends That Are Shaping Our Future.* New York: W. W. Norton, 1994.

_____. *The Bicycle: Vehicle for a Small Planet.* Worldwatch Papers, 90. Washington, DC: Worldwatch Institute, September 1989.

McGURN, JAMES. *On Your Bicycle: An Illustrated History of Cycling.* London: John Murray, 1987.

STREBEIGH, FRED. "Wheels Freedom." *Bicycling* (April 1991).

Marcia D. Lowe

Petroleum

Oil has long been one of the most important energy sources. In 1930 it provided one-fourth of total U.S. energy demand; by 1991 oil supplied 40 percent of U.S. energy (DeGolyer and MacNaughton, 1992). For most of the twentieth century, oil has played a central role in world economic development, as well as in military conflicts.

Natural gas also is an important energy source. Together, oil and natural gas account for 65 percent of U.S. primary energy supply.

As the twentieth century draws to a close, world supplies of oil are adequate to meet expected demand for at least several more decades. Oil consumption will not grow as rapidly as in the past and its share of the energy market will decline. There will be continued pressure to reduce oil consumption for environmental reasons. In the United States, oil imports increasingly pose security and trade deficit concerns. Despite these changes, oil will continue to be the primary energy source well into the next century

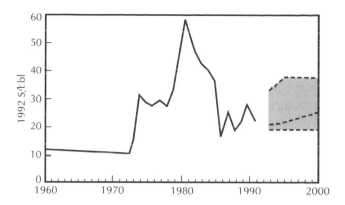

FIGURE 1. Projected petroleum prices. (Source: Conoco, *Oil & Gas Journal,* June 22, 1992. Used with permission.)

Petroleum Product Demand

Demand for all types of energy will grow at a slower pace in the 1990s and beyond in industrialized countries. Economic growth will be more modest as compared with the 1980s, and energy efficiency will continue to improve. In less developed countries, however, energy demand will grow more rapidly.

Total energy demand will increase faster than demand for oil products because environmental pressures on oil consumption will increase, and the efficiency with which petroleum is used will continue to improve. World oil demand will grow at an average rate of 1.5–1.8 percent per year through the 1990s. U.S. petroleum demand will increase at slightly more than 1 percent per year, according to most estimates. In Asia demand will grow at 4–6 percent per year.

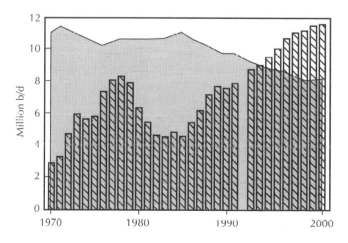

FIGURE 2. Supply sources of petroleum in the United States. (Source: Conoco, *Oil & Gas Journal,* June 22, 1992. Used with permission.)

Refineries convert crude oil into consumer oil products. On January 1, 1995, U.S. refining capacity stood at 15.3 million barrels per day, and world refining capacity totaled 74.2 million barrels per day (Rhodes, 1994).

Consumption of one of the most important petroleum products in the U.S.—gasoline—reached 7.6 million barrels per day in 1994. U.S. gasoline demand peaked earlier at 7.41 million barrels per day in 1978 (Beck, 1995). Higher prices and federal automobile mileage standards drove gasoline consumption down to 6.6 million barrels per day in 1982. When oil prices fell again in the mid-1980s, gasoline consumption began a steady increase.

Gasoline demand will grow slowly in the United States in the years ahead. Higher taxes, more use of natural gas and electricity-powered vehicles, and steady improvement in fleet fuel efficiency will combine to limit gasoline use.

U.S. consumption of other petroleum products in 1992 included 3.2 million barrels per day of distillate for home heating, truck and railroad fuel, and industry; and 1.5 million barrels per day of jet fuel (Beck, 1995).

In the early 1980s refinery shutdowns reduced excess capacity dramatically, and by 1993 U.S. refineries were operating at about 90 percent of capacity. A further reduction in U.S. refining capacity is likely in the 1990s. As a result, imports of gasoline and other petroleum products will increase.

Some smaller U.S. refineries, unable to make the large investments needed to meet the requirements of the 1990 amendments to the Clean Air Act, will be shut down, reducing capacity. Environmental restrictions make it almost impossible to build a new refinery or expand an existing plant.

Supply Fundamentals

There are two measures of crude oil supply. Reserves indicate the long-term supply, and productive capacity determines short-term availability.

Proved reserves are those that have been defined by drilling and other methods; potential reserves have not been proved. Only about one-third of the oil that has been found can be produced with today's technology and at today's prices.

Proven world reserves of crude oil stood at almost 1 trillion barrels at the beginning of 1995, enough to last 45 years at current production rates (*Oil & Gas Journal*, 1994).

Members of the Organization of Petroleum Exporting Countries (OPEC) own more than three-fourths of the world's proven oil reserves. Saudi Arabia alone has 25 percent of the world's reserves.

Much of the world's productive capacity also exists in the Middle East. Saudi Arabia's productive capacity of more than 8.5 million barrels per day will be expanded by the mid-1990s. Other OPEC producers also have plans to expand capacity.

U.S. production has declined steadily since 1985 due to reduced exploration and drilling activity. In 1995, U.S. crude oil production was expected to be 6.5 million barrels per day, the lowest level in thirty-five years. Further declines in U.S. output are expected.

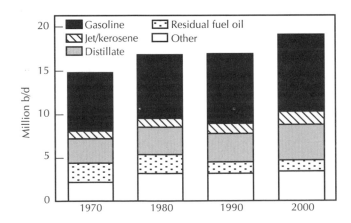

FIGURE 3. Demand in the United States by petroleum product. (Source: Conoco, *Oil & Gas Journal*, June 22, 1992. Used with permission.)

FIGURE 4. Demand worldwide by petroleum product. (Source: Conoco, *Oil & Gas Journal*, June 22, 1992. Used with permission.)

Exploration

The search for new oil and gas reserves in the U.S. reached record low levels in the early 1990s. Environmental restrictions limited access to promising areas; low prices and tax disincentives limited producers' cash flow and capital.

Many parts of the U.S. outer continental shelf (OCS) are potentially rich in oil and gas, and Alaska is likely to contain large oil reserves in areas where exploration has not yet been permitted. The lower forty-eight states also contain significant undiscovered and undeveloped reserves according to geologists.

Although more than 70 percent of U.S. offshore production is natural gas, there is still public fear that offshore development will harm the environment. As long as that fear exists, not many new areas will be opened for development.

About 12 percent of U.S. proven oil reserves of 26 billion barrels is located offshore (DeGolyer and MacNaughton, 1992).

Wells have been drilled in more than 6,000 feet of water. And production operations and drilling in several hundred feet of water are routine in offshore regions around the world.

Dependence on Foreign Supplies

As U.S. oil production declines and demand for petroleum products increases, the gap between supply and demand must be filled by importing foreign oil. In 1994, U.S. imports of crude oil and products reached 8.9 million barrels per day, or 50.4 percent of domestic demand (Beck, 1995). Imports reached their previous highest share, 48 percent of demand, in 1977. OPEC producers supplied 50 percent of U.S. imported crude in 1994; the largest contributor was Saudi Arabia.

Imports could increase further during the rest of the 1990s. But higher taxes on oil and oil products, and greater use of natural gas will slow—or even reverse—the growth in oil demand.

The United States will never be self-sufficient in oil. But the security risk associated with high import levels has lessened in recent years.

The U.S. Strategic Petroleum Reserve (SPR), for example, now contains about 600 million barrels. Foreign sources of U.S. crude are also more diverse now, lowering the risk of a critical supply interruption. In addition, crude oil markets are much more efficient at allocating available supplies than during the interruptions of the 1970s. Also, Middle East producers have integrated into refining and marketing, giving them a greater interest in market stability.

Market Control

Early in the twentieth century, the Standard Oil Trust controlled oil markets. After it was broken up, the large integrated, multinational oil companies influenced supply and therefore, prices.

Oil companies began to lose control of world oil markets when OPEC was established. Now with twelve members, OPEC exerted growing influence on the market through the 1970s and 1980s. OPEC now controls most of the world's excess producing capacity and can manipulate the price of oil by restricting or increasing production.

There are signs, however, that OPEC is interested in stabilizing the market to ensure a long-term demand for its members' oil. There is some agreement that a benchmark price of about $20 per barrel is low enough to allow demand to grow yet high enough to provide OPEC members with needed revenue.

OPEC—Saudi Arabia in particular—will continue to hold the oil market balance of power. Even as demand rises, planned capacity expansions by OPEC members will maintain an excess supply well into the future. Non OPEC production will decline.

There will be price fluctuations and political crises affecting supply. But the average cost of crude oil, in constant dollars, is likely to increase only at the rate of inflation.

Social Costs

Concern for the environment has brought many changes in oil production, processing, and consumption. The 1990 amendments to the U.S. Clean Air Act called for new transportation fuels and much stricter emissions standards. The *Valdez* tanker spill offshore Alaska in 1989 resulted in new laws concerning oil spill preparedness, tanker design, and shipper liability.

Strict environmental regulations governing offshore drilling and producing operations have dramatically lowered the risk of offshore pollution incidents. Beyond this, the Marine Spill Response Corporation in the U.S. is prepared to help industry and coastal areas deal with accidents.

Safety in refineries and in other facilities, along with attention to air and water quality, have become the top priorities of petroleum companies everywhere in the world. Typically U.S.-based companies follow U.S. standards when operating in other countries, even though local regulations may be less strict.

Environmental issues will increasingly affect oil consumption, too. Efforts to reduce the use of oil—and other fossil fuels—will continue. Higher taxes on oil and oil products, or on the carbon content of fuels, will be used to reduce the consumption of gasoline and other oil products.

See also COAL; ELECTRIC POWER; ENERGY; ENERGY, RENEWABLE SOURCES OF; HAZARDOUS WASTES; MOTOR VEHICLES, ALTERNATIVELY POWERED; NATURAL GAS; NUCLEAR POWER; NUCLEAR POWER: CON; RESOURCES; TRANSURANIUM ELEMENTS.

BIBLIOGRAPHY

BECK, ROBERT J. "Economic Growth, Low Prices to Lift U.S. Oil and Gas Demand in 1995." *Oil & Gas Journal* (January 30, 1995).
RHODES, ANNE K. "World Crude Capacity, Conversion Capability Inch Upward." *Oil & Gas Journal* (December 19, 1994).
"Worldwide Oil Flow Up, Reserves Steady in '94." *Oil & Gas Journal* (December 26, 1994).

John L. Kennedy

Pets

In the 1980s, the cat finally surpassed the dog as our most popular companion animal. The latest statistics from the American Veterinary Medical Association show that Americans have 57 million cats and 52.5 million dogs.

There are many reasons for the cat boom. Urban and suburban areas mushroomed and floor space decreased, but because felines can live comfortably without great amounts of room, they fit well into an increasingly congested world. Also, due to a dramatic rise in the number of two-income families, leisure time declined. The more self-sufficient cat—needing no outdoor exercise and less attention than a dog—became the ideal pet for busy people.

As the world becomes more crowded and regulated, will be rethinking many of our views on cat care. Roaming cats are becoming less acceptable to society, and a growing number of people are keeping their cats safely indoors. In the next few decades, cat laws will more closely mimic existing dog laws. For example, cats will not be allowed outside unless they are confined or controlled. Be-

cause indoor cats are happier with playmates, we will see a marked rise in multicat households. And as people share closer quarters with their pets, they will be tapping into an ever-widening network of resources—for example, animal behavior information—to resolve pet problems such as cats scratching furniture.

A 1990 Gallup survey demonstrated that nine out of ten Americans with pets think of their animals as family members. Hefty percentages of interviewees reported giving their pets Christmas gifts and keeping pictures of pets in their wallets. Over the last twenty years, there has been a notable trend toward treating pets as surrogate children. Statistics demonstrate that many people are marrying later and bearing fewer children: pets often wind up occupying center stage. Already, a number of businesses cater to working, pet-owning "parents." Such services, including summer camps, playgroups, and day care for dogs, are evidence of a growing demand for services similar to child care.

As people who have animal companions continue to gain clout, it could become unacceptable or maybe even illegal to summarily bar pets from rental housing. People may be allowed to list their pets as dependents to gain tax deductions. Just as some companies offer day care for children, it could become widely acceptable for employees to bring their pets to work. Pets might also be covered with health insurance through a national program as part of an employee benefits package.

In short, as cats and dogs become truly valued members of our society, their hierarchical status in the world will increase. Dogs completing obedience courses might receive access rights, much like today's guide dogs, to restaurants, hotels, and motels. With a heightened sensitivity to the invaluable gift of an animal's companionship, people will no longer think of pets as property and will replace the term *pet owner* with *animal companion*.

Studies show that pets are good for our mental and even physical well-being. Statistics document that we are living longer, and as the baby-boom generation ages, we will be faced with an enormous population of older people. Animals can help to prevent these elderly citizens from feeling depressed and isolated, and we could see an upsurge of resident pets in hospitals and nursing homes. Today, people over sixty are often reluctant to adopt pets that could outlive them. In the future, people in their seventies, eighties, and nineties will be able to rely on readoption programs or lifetime pet homes to safeguard their animals should they pass away before their pets.

As a group, people with pets can afford to give their animals the best of care. A survey commissioned by the American Veterinary Medical Association showed that people who have pets have higher than average incomes and are more likely to own their homes. A desire to pamper pets has created a market for gourmet pet foods and treats. The growth in cat popularity and the move toward keeping cats safely indoors ushered in fleets of innovative products, including the feline version of MTV: videos of lively birds. Pets in the future may keep themselves happily occupied indoors with high-tech interactive video games that have symbols they can push to produce different sounds, smells (such as aromatic food smells), or visuals.

As society continues to become more industrialized, products like commercial pet food (rather than food scraps) should gain an international market. Increased knowledge of medical care, nutrition, and animal behavior—everything from state-of-the-art surgery to more nutritious pet foods—will continue to better pets' lives.

Unfortunately, despite the bright outlook for most of our companion animals, inappropriate pets remain a problem. Although the enforcement of existing regulations and the enactment of new laws has helped to put a dent in the exotic pet trade, a demand for exotic pets (both legal and illegal) continues to devastate wildlife populations. However, humane education is the hope of the future. Already, many airlines are refusing to transport wild birds for ethical reasons. As people become more aware of the issues surrounding exotic pets, one hopes the demand for these animals will decline.

Education must also play a key role in another animal welfare problem: vicious pet dogs. In the mid 1980s and early '90s, fatal attacks on humans by pit bull terriers made international headlines. Public awareness about illegal dog fighting and aggressive, uncontrollable pet dogs (a macho status symbol) was raised, but the ensuing media frenzy obscured the fact that irresponsible people were at the root of the problem.

Laws that target human behavior, such as stiffer sentences for those who train and keep aggressive animals, have already proved far more effective deterrents than banning specific dog breeds. As such laws are strengthened, future generations should hold humans—and not abused animals—responsible for dangerous dogs.

See also ANIMAL RIGHTS; HOUSING: DEMOGRAPHIC AND LIFESTYLE IMPACTS; LEISURE TIME.

BIBLIOGRAPHY

"Crazy Over Cats." *Time* (December 7, 1981).
"Furry and Feathery Therapists." *Time* (March 30, 1987).
"Warriors in the Parrot Game." *International Wildlife* (September-October 1990).
"The Year of the Cat." *Shelter Sense* (December 1992–January 1993).

Richard Avanzino

Pharmaceuticals

By 2020, pharmaceuticals will have played an important role in curing and preventing major diseases. Pharmaceuticals will be an integrated component of health care customized for each of us as biochemically unique individuals. Pharmaceutical tools that operate at the molecular level will both effectively treat disease and play a role in health promotion. Pharmaceuticals will have evolved to include biosensors and biocontrollers that circulate in the body, monitoring conditions, manufacturing the relevant therapeutic agent in the body, and delivering it directly to the diseased cells. Responding to and anticipating scientific breakthroughs, the pharmaceutical industry will have undergone significant changes.

Prospect of Definitive Cures

According to the late Lewis Thomas, author of *Lives of a Cell*, diseases are biological puzzles that we are on the verge of solving, thus heralding a relatively disease-free society. While research has promised breakthroughs for decades, the next twenty-five years (from 1995 to 2020) are likely to see definitive control of heart disease, cancer, and some neurologic diseases. Research focusing on the molecular level is likely to uncover the role genetics plays in instigating or making us more susceptible to disease.

There are several promising approaches now on the horizon. Disarmed viruses will be used to attack diseased cells, carrying information that reprograms the diseased cells' DNA. The recognition that the cells and molecules of our immune, cardiovascular, neural, and digestive systems are valuable information centers useful in disease prevention and treatment will lead to new and profitable scientific approaches. Another promising technology is "antisense." This technology blocks the molecular information necessary for the disease to flourish. Messenger RNA is essential to the successful replication of cells. Antisense devices string together nucleic acids that define the RNA so as to be complementary or opposite to the original RNA sequence. The antisense sequence binds to the original sequence, preventing the original sequence from conveying its information, thus disabling the cellular reproduction mechanisms. This will give an accuracy for treatment far higher than in the late twentieth century. According to Stuart Davidson, director of the Center for Technology Assessment, in 1995 antisense compounds were being developed for use against Alzheimer's disease, many cancers, autoimmune disorders including rheumatoid arthritis, viral diseases, and coronary artery disease. Whether through molecular or other approaches, research will be successful in controlling major diseases in the first quarter of the twenty-first century. However, these molecular approaches are only part of the story of the future of pharmaceuticals.

Customization of Health Care with a Broader Focus

Health care will approach and treat each of us as biochemically unique individuals by 2020. The human genome will be mapped and largely understood, making "DNA fingerprints" part of a person's medical record. Health care will also recognize our unique personal and psychological characteristics and will move to take full advantage of these to enhance our health. Keep in mind that the U.S. Surgeon General's Office has argued that 50 percent of the variance in our illness over our life course is related to our behavior, 20 percent to our environment, 20 percent to our genes, and 10 percent to medical care—including pharmaceuticals as we have thought about them historically. Pharmaceuticals will be integrated into very effective preventive and therapeutic protocols that include diet, exercise, stress, and personal growth factors. These therapeutic and preventive protocols will be available in our homes, often given to us by our health care providers in whatever state-of-the-art electronic form that is available at the time. The pharmaceutical component of these protocols will include nonprescription medications; among these will be a broader range of what in the late twentieth century were considered alternative remedies, such as homeopathy. Further into the twenty-first century we will have "pharmaceuticals" in the form of small devices ingested or implanted in the body to monitor continuously our condition and to manufacture and deliver the appropriate medication as diseases begin to appear.

The pharmaceutical industry will undergo the type of consolidation the transportation sector experienced in the early part of the twentieth century. The transportation sector went from dozens of car makers to a handful worldwide. The pharmaceutical industry has begun this consolidation process. Simultaneously, the economics of pharmaceutical development will be changed. The regulatory framework that governs new drug development was put in place in the middle of the twentieth century (particularly the 1962 amendments to the U.S. Food, Drug, and Cosmetic Act). Installed at the height of the industrial era, this legislation seeks to ensure uniform standards of safety and efficacy. These will likely change in response to the shift in health care to customized medicine. Pharmaceuticals will be focused on individuals who, because of their genetic makeup or other factors, are particularly likely to respond to the drug. In the twentieth century, many "me-too" drugs were not successful because they benefited only 10, 20, or 30 percent of the people with that particular condition. In the twenty-first century, health care will target such individuals and seek out cost-effective versions of those new compounds. This will accelerate the changes already in place in pharmaceutical selection toward using pharmacoeconomics in deciding which new drug candidates to pursue.

Health care providers will take a more active part in targeting research. The development of electronic medical record keeping, consumer health approaches, personal biomonitoring, and more active consumer involvement will mean that health care providers, particularly large managed-care groups, will be able to do clinical trials at virtually no additional costs to their ongoing medical care for their customers. Health care providers will partner in clinical trials, and the cost of pharmaceutical development will plummet. As the information revolution grows, it is also possible that the prospects for drug discovery by individuals and small companies will become relatively easier. Thus, while the pharmaceutical industry will consolidate, the number of sources for new pharmaceutical discovery may remain high.

Pharmaceutical development will help redefine the meaning of health care in the twenty-first century, as pharmaceutical "tools" are used to enhance and promote health at the individual and societal level. A broader understanding of health care will blur the boundaries between markets and institutions, spawning sustained innovation and creating a "healthier" future.

See also HEALTH CARE; HEALTH CARE, ALTERNATIVE THERAPIES; HEALTH CARE, TECHNOLOGICAL DEVELOPMENTS; HEALTH CARE COSTS; MEDICAL CARE PROVIDERS.

BIBLIOGRAPHY

BEZOLD, CLEMENT; HALPERN, JEROME A.; and ENG, JACQUELINE L., eds. *2020 Visions: Health Care Information, Standards, and Technologies.* Rockville, MD: United States Pharmacopeial Convention, 1993.

BEZOLD, CLEMENT, and KNABNER, KLAUS, eds. *Health Care 2010: Health Care Delivery, Therapies, and the Pharmaceutical Industry.* Berlin and New York: Springer Verlag, 1994.

DAVIDSON, STUART. "Therapeutics for Tomorrow." *Healthcare Forum Journal* (January–February 1995): 55.

Clement Bezold

Philanthropy

As the twenty-first century approaches, it seems clear that the accelerating pace of change in society will create new challenges and unexpected opportunities for organized philanthropy. The models of organized philanthropy that have developed over the last hundred years or so—foundations and corporate giving programs—evolved as the American private sector's response to certain social and economic conditions.

The beginning of this century was a watershed moment in the transition from the age of the individual to the age of the organization. "Charity," which had been primarily individual, affective, and largely ad hoc for many of the leading families, was transformed into organized philanthropy, which was more systematic, cognitive, and strategic. The models of philanthropy pioneered by wealthy families and bankers like Frederick Goff, who formed the first community foundation in 1914, have withstood the test of time, but new models are emerging that at the beginning of the century could not have been anticipated. Who would have imagined just a few years ago, for example, that one of the largest donors in Minnesota would be the Native American Gaming Commission?

The Changing Context of Philanthropy

The first set of challenges and opportunities facing foundations and corporate givers in the coming era has to do with those changes in the social, economic, and political environment that increase the opportunity to promote the growth and protect the interest of philanthropy. Much is said and written about the intergenerational transfer of wealth, the expectation that within the next two decades as much as 8 trillion dollars may be passed down from Americans now over age fifty to their children and grandchildren. Many groups, both profit and nonprofit, are considering what needs to be done to encourage, activate, or cultivate the charitable impulse so that the intergenerational transfer of wealth includes a transfer of the charitable commitment as well.

There have been a number of recent legislative changes that could spur a major growth of interest in organized philanthropy in its varied forms, such as:

- Higher marginal tax rates. (The Revenue Act of 1993 raised the highest marginal tax rates to 39.6 percent from 31 percent.)
- Fewer available deductions. (The 1986 Tax reform Act greatly reduced the number of deductions available to higher income tax payers.)
- The increase in maximum estate and gift tax rates. (When federal and state estate taxes are combined, donors may be looking at combined tax rates for their estates nearing 70 percent.)
- Relief from the alternative minimum tax rate (ATM).

A third major change that could influence the growth of philanthropy is the changing profile of the potential donor. As the demographic makeup of the country, and the world, changes, so will the donor pool. Many of the potential donors in the next few years will be very different from the donors we know today, not only in values, lifestyles, and attitudes, but in racial and ethnic composition as well. Much of the emphasis on diversity in philanthropy has been on the "demand" side (recipients), but there will be increasing opportunity for diversity on the "supply" side (donors). Very little attention has been given to the growth in the buying power of people of color, which is projected to reach $640 billion by the year 2000. (Present purchasing power of African Americans is $211 billion, $141 billion for Hispanics, and $120 billion for Asians.) There has been considerable growth in the development of foundations and charitable funds among minorities, but as more people of color are exposed to the many options for organized giving, that growth is expected to accelerate.

The trend in foundation formation among all Americans is also favorable. More than 2,000 foundations were formed in 1994. Foundation formation peaked in the 1980s with the establishment of more than 9,000 new foundations, almost doubling the number created in the 1950s, the largest previous decade of growth. Three thousand of these were large enough for inclusion in the Foundation Center's *Foundation Directory* by qualifying with endowments of at least $1 million in assets or in charitable expenditures of at least $100,000 each year.

Two other changes in the environment can be foreseen, both representing new opportunities for collaboration. The last two decades have seen the growth and strengthening of the infrastructure supporting organized giving, particularly through nonprofit associations that promote and protect philanthropy. The next decade will likely see the growth and strengthening of profit-making alternatives, as entrepreneurs of all sorts turn their attention to this field. Many will have values and objectives widely different from the Council on Foundations and regional associations of grantmakers.

Attitudes and approaches to collaboration are also changing. The last two decades have seen a significant increase in the willingness of foundations to collaborate with each other and with the giving programs of business corporations. More recently, there has also been significant increase in the number of foundations wanting to collaborate with government or work in some other way to shape an informed public opinion. The next major growth area for collaboration is with organized religion. Many grantmakers have discovered since the Los Angeles disruptions that ethnic churches are not only the most stable organization in minority communities, but that they make good partners in implementation. A recent conference in Washington on "Religion, Philanthropy and Civil Society" focused on "models of hope," collaborative ventures between foundations and churches that were providing help and hope to those trapped in central cities.

The next major change is the increasing pluralism of the philanthropic sector. Ever since the Hudson Institute published *Workforce 2000* in 1987, the public and private sectors have been preparing for the massive demographic shifts that were predicted and that to some extent have already occurred. When the Council on Foundations issued a statement about inclusiveness in its principles and practices more than a dozen years ago, many people believed that diversity was just another euphemism for affirmative action, setting goals to recruit, retain, and promote people of color based on their representation in the labor force. What many organizations have come to realize is that simply changing the mix without changing the organizational culture is sometimes counterproductive. Diversity does not of itself create community.

Groups representing minority and women grantmakers are seeking a greater commitment to diversity on the part of foundations, but this is not unique to the field. Every major association, along with nonprofit agencies and many corporations, is seeking effective ways to promote diversity and inclusiveness. When Elizabeth Dole announced a new inclusiveness initiative at the American Red Cross, she also announced the allocation of a million dollars to provide for leadership development scholarships, a minority internship program, staff exchange programs, executive forums and a president's fund to develop additional initiatives.

While many foundations and corporate giving programs have led the way in emphasizing and practicing inclusiveness, there nevertheless is a growing frustration among minority staff in the field, about hiring practices, opportunities for professional growth and mobility, organizational culture, and openness and accessibility. Recent studies have found that the nonprofit sector lags behind business and government in the hiring of minority employees. Inclusiveness is a concern that is likely to be on the front burner of issues in the field for a while.

Another change that will have an impact on philanthropy is the increasing internationalization of society and our sector. The changing boundaries of society are changing the boundaries of philanthropy. Not only has the nation-state declined as the primary custodian of the civic culture, but an international perspective is no longer simply the concern of international foundations making what used to be called foreign or overseas grants. Community foundations are finding that they can no longer effectively address local issues or solve local problems by remaining within the limits of the old geographical boundaries. Corporate giving programs are looking beyond their headquarters communities to plant and facility communities around the world, and even small family foundations are making grants that seek to advance international understanding and cooperation.

In Eastern Europe, Central and Latin America, and South Africa, many efforts are underway not simply to develop foundations, but to preserve an intermediate space between government and business where private energy can be mobilized and deployed for the public good. The increasing globalization of philanthropy, however, should not be seen exclusively as an opportunity to promote civic values that empower people elsewhere to solve local problems locally, but as an opportunity to learn from other cultures as well.

The Changing Craft of Philanthropy

The increasing concern with public accountability has gone beyond public access and public reporting to include management and governance as well. There has been much public attention directed toward the compensation practices of foundations and other nonprofits. Yet, a primary issue for the nonprofit sector continues to be how best to attract and retain the best minds and the best managers for the sector. This will require competitive levels of compensation and other incentives, but the public must be convinced that standards of pay are closely tied to job requirements and standards of performance. Managing the multimillion dollar foundation requires managers as competent as those who run multimillion dollar businesses. It makes no sense to pretend that foundations with millions of dollars of assets have the same management requirement as the small, neighborhood organization.

Council on Foundations surveys continue to find grantmaking foundations to be among the most prudent organizations in the nonprofit sector in setting staff compensation. In reviewing what is appropriate and reasonable, many trustees ask three important questions: What functions are required and actually performed by staff? What levels of skills and experience are necessary in order to perform those functions? What is the market in which the foundation chooses to compete for the professional skills required? The questions are somewhat different for corporate giving programs where the comparison is more likely to be with other officers in the corporation.

Another area of concern is communications, including a reconsideration of what kind of public information is useful and how best to provide it. The 990 forms that nonprofit organizations submit annually to the Internal Revenue Service were developed by regulators for regulators, but they are used increasingly as a source of public information as well. Many foundations still do not publish an annual report, so perhaps the 990 could be revised, changing the kind of data required to information useful and helpful to a public that wants to know more about what drives nonprofits—how they make decisions and what shapes their priorities.

So far, much of the response to the changing public climate has focused on such external factors as myths and misinformation in the media, the increased attention to compensation practices, and the need to better educate the public on how public charities differ from the other twenty-four categories of tax-exempt organizations.

The Changing Concept of Philanthropy

Finally, as philanthropy becomes more pluralistic, public expectations of how these tax-exempt funds should be used may become even more varied. Nowhere is this likely to be more evident than in the increased public debate about how best to cultivate the moral virtues essential to good character. The concern with values has become a national obsession, creating what a national magazine recently called a new kind of politics and a new class of "virtuecrats." No organization sanctioned by the public to serve public purposes is likely to escape the scrutiny of the 76 percent of the American public who regard the erosion of values as one of the really critical issues of our time.

The problem is that the public discourse about values has become politicized. Those who talk most about good values are often those who want simply to argue that someone else has bad values. But if anyone is likely to be able to depoliticize the discussion, it is likely to be organizations with an image of neutrality and nonpartisanship.

The historian Arthur M. Schlesinger, Jr., wrote a few years ago that American society is never fixed nor final. Like every other aspect of our society, philanthropy too is changing. If foundations and corporate giving programs—the institutions of organized philanthropy that have developed over the course of this century—are to have proportionately the same impact on American life in the next century, they must commit themselves to the idea that the fear of difference is fear of the future. If they want to form a more perfect union, they must begin within themselves, striving to include all who have a stake in their endeavors. They must cultivate a passion for responsibility as well as effectiveness, and for civility as well as civic engagement.

See also INVESTMENTS; NONGOVERNMENTAL ORGANIZATIONS; PRIVATE ASSISTANCE PROGRAMS; PUBLIC ASSISTANCE PROGRAMS; VALUES; WEALTH.

BIBLIOGRAPHY

CIBA Foundation. *Future of Philanthropic Foundations.* Ann Arbor: Books on Demand, 1977.

FREEMAN, DAVID. *Handbook on Private Foundations.* Washington, DC: Council on Foundations, 1991.

JOSEPH, JAMES A. *Remaking America: How the Benevolent Traditions of Many Cultures Are Transforming Our National Life.* San Francisco: Jossey-Bass, 1995.

PIFER, ALAN. *Philanthropy in an Age of Transition.* New York: Foundation Center, 1984.

James A. Joseph

Photography

Since its introduction in 1839, silver-based photography has been the principal process for capturing, recording, and preserving images in all fields of human activity. The ever-growing demand for such images has spawned an international photographic industry, centered in the United States, Western Europe, and Japan. In 1994, the worldwide sales of imaging materials and associated special equipment and services totaled about $55 billion in U.S. dollars.

The major photography industry sectors in terms of product volume and value are (1) amateur, (2) professional, (3) medical diagnostic imaging, (4) motion picture, and (5) graphic arts. Although each sector requires somewhat different imaging materials, all have the same basic structure—they are laminates, consisting of a surface-treated support and bonded gelatin layers. The support can be transparent or translucent (cellulose triacetate or polyester film) or white opaque (mostly resin-coated paper). The gelatin layers serve one of two purposes: image formation or control of chemical reactions and/or physical characteristics. Imaging layers (called emulsions) contain millions of silver halide crystals, as well as dye formers in the case of modern color films and color papers.

The creation of an image with silver halide–type products usually involves two basic steps: (1) exposure to a pattern of light or other actinic radiation to produce a latent image; and (2) wet chemical processing that transforms the latent into a visible black-and-white silver image or a three-color dye image, and renders the image permanent.

Amateur Photography

Today, amateurs overwhelmingly take pictures with 35-mm cameras and color negative film, because they want color prints, and this is the best means to that end. Statistics for worldwide amateur photography in 1950 and 1994 attest to the remarkable growth and popularity of this system:

In 1950 there were 1.65 billion pictures taken, 9 percent of them in color, whereas in 1994 there were some 60 billion pictures taken, 92 percent in color.

A yearly 4 to 6 percent increase in the use of color negative film and color paper can be expected during the period 1995 to 2005 for the following reasons:

- Color negative images have unsurpassed information content—20,000,000 pixels per 35-mm frame compared with 350,000 to 600,000 with current sensors in amateur electronic still cameras. Also, color paper prints have excellent image quality and stability and can be mass-produced at low cost.
- Further improvements in color film performance and processing technology are in the offing.
- The system has been introduced in several of the most populous countries, including China and India. This is bound to foster increasing use.
- A new "advanced photo system" will be introduced in 1996. It includes new cameras and films with magnetic strips for encoding camera exposure data, image format selection, photofinishing instructions, and text to be recorded on the print image. These novel features are designed to stimulate picture taking and increase the demand for prints.

To date, magnetic tape recordings made with camcorders have replaced 8-mm home movies, because videotapes do not require expensive wet processing and offer the convenience of viewing on home television sets. However, electronic still cameras for amateurs have been unsuccessful so far, mainly because of inferior image quality and higher prices. These disadvantages will be reduced, but not eliminated for many years. Meanwhile, the application of hybrid systems, such as the Kodak Photo CD, will provide amateurs with many new options for manipulating, displaying, reproducing, and transmitting images captured on color film. Also, digital color printing systems will grow in importance, especially in the United States. In summary, electronic imaging systems are likely to play an increasingly important role, but continuing dominance of silver-based products well into the twenty-first century seems assured.

Professional Photography

Professional photography has two main segments: portraiture and commercial. Aggregate turnover generated in these two U.S. market sectors during

1994 was about $9 billion, or about 35 percent of the estimated world total.

Silver halide–type films and papers are the principal imaging materials in professional photography, but black-and-white and color reversal films account for more than 55 percent of total film consumption and black-and-white paper for about 25 percent. Electronic still cameras have gained acceptance in press, industrial, and military operations when rapid access and transmission of images have high priority and where the high price of 1.5 to 4 million pixel cameras is not a major deterrent. Hybrid systems are used increasingly in professional processing laboratories, including film scanners and digital workstations. The digitized images can be modified, enhanced, and combined with other images and/or text and recorded on magnetic tape or disc, or optical disc. They can then be viewed on a monitor screen prior to outputting on photographic film, or on photographic, thermal dyetransfer, ink-jet, or electrophotographic paper.

George Fisher, chairman and CEO of the Eastman Kodak Company, acknowledges that the breakneck evolution of communication technology is transforming imaging. With the remarkable drop in the cost of computing power over the past decade, "labs and photographers now have affordable access to potent image-manipulation 'horsepower' on the desktop. In addition, the huge expansion of the bandwidth accommodates photographic-quality images, which are so information-rich that they use up huge chunks of bandwidth.

Medical Diagnostic Imaging

Most medical diagnostic images are radiographs made with duplitized X-ray films (emulsion on both sides), exposed in cassettes with light emitted by fluorescent screens. Single-coated X-ray films and special cassettes and screens are used for mammography. Dental and industrial radiographs are made by direct X-ray exposure of silver-rich films. New imaging systems introduced since 1950 are displayed on blue or green fluorescing CRT screens or black-and-white video monitors that can be photographed with special single-coated films. More recently, infrared and helium-neon laser printers have been introduced for recording digitally based images on high-resolution films.

In the future, alternate systems employing optical disc technology will find more widespread acceptance. Such systems are available already. One of them can capture images from computed radiography and film radiographs and provide instant image transmission to several viewing stations within a hospital, as well as to off-site facilities via a network of fiber-optic or coaxial cables, or by infrared and microwaves, or satellite. "Jukeboxes" can be used for storage and retrieval of discs holding millions of images. Video display options include banks of monitors for primary diagnosis, for consultation and review, and display on personal computers. Film images can be generated from the optical discs with laser printers.

The main obstacles to the acquisition and use of such systems have been and will be the cost of the equipment and networking, the unaccustomed viewing mode, and the stress induced by prolonged viewing of screen images. Therefore, silver halide films will continue to be the main image capture and recording material for at least ten years. Thereafter, all-electronic imaging systems are likely to predominate in large health care facilities in wealthy countries, but universal replacement of silver halide–based systems will not occur for the foreseeable future.

Motion Pictures

Predictions of the demise of motion picture theaters in the United States seemed a sure bet when television started to invade American homes in the early 1950s. Less than ten years later, the same fate was forecast for motion picture film—that it would soon be replaced by magnetic videotape. Actually, an initial restructuring and contraction of the industry was soon followed by renewed growth of Hollywood studio operations, as they added film production for television shows to their traditional program. Movie attendance also recovered steadily, as the public rediscovered the pleasure of uninterrupted, large-screen presentations. As a result, the number of theater screens increased from 17,590 in 1980 to 26,586 in 1994, the number of admissions from about 1 billion to 1.3 billion, and ticket revenues from $2.75 billion to $5.4 billion. Also, about 80 percent of all prime-time television shows are still recorded on 35-mm motion picture film before being transferred to videotape or laser discs for broadcasting.

The main reasons for this staying power of the photographic system have been the superior image quality and stability of color film images, the substantial advantages in light output and image sharpness of optical over digital projectors, and the large investment in photographic cameras, printers, processors, and projectors. These advantages are not about to disappear, especially since continuing progress in color emulsion technology will bring further improvements in imaging efficiency and quality. Also, hybrid systems have already been developed that allow key-coding of film images during camera exposure and include film readers for scanning of the images and digital workstations for editing, production of special effects, titling, and other operations involved in converting the camera images into final print images.

Graphic Arts

Photographic films and papers are used in prepress operations—i.e., the preparation and assembly of images and/or text for imposition onto printing plates. Different products having different photographic and processing characteristics are supplied to match the requirements of the four major printing processes—letterpress, lithography, gravure, and stencil. In 1994, graphic arts films accounted for about 25 percent of worldwide film production and graphic arts papers for about 12 percent.

During the past twenty years, hybrid systems (phototypesetters, scanners, and image setters) have been used increasingly to streamline prepress operations through the reduction or elimination of multiple operations involving separate reproduction of text on photographic paper and of pictures on film, followed by manual assembly into complete page layouts. Still, the demand for photographic films has increased steadily and will continue to increase by about 4 percent per year during the next decade, due to growth in worldwide demand for printed material and a shift to color printing that requires four films instead of the one needed for black-and-white images. However, the use of photographic paper has declined substantially and will continue on a downward trend.

See also CHEMICALS, FINE; COMMUNICATIONS TECHNOLOGY; DATA STORAGE; DIGITAL COMMUNICATIONS; ELECTRONIC CONVERGENCE; ELECTRONIC PUBLISHING; INTERACTIVE ENTERTAINMENT; MEDIA LAB; MOTION PICTURES; ON-LINE SERVICES; TELEVISION; VISUAL ARTS.

BIBLIOGRAPHY

COLLINS, D. *The Story of Kodak*. New York: Harry N. Abrams, 1990.
COOTE, J. H. *The Illustrated History of Color Photography*. Surbiton, Surrey, U.K.: Fountain Press, 1993.
JAMES, T. H. *The Theory of the Photographic Process*, 4th ed. New York: Macmillan, 1977.
ROSENBLUM, N. *A World History of Photography*. New York: Abbeville Press, 1984.
STURGE, J.; WALWORTH, V.; and SHEPP, A. *Imaging Processes and Materials: Neblette's Eighth Edition*. New York: Van Nostrand Reinhold, 1989.

Tom Dufficy

Physics

In the twenty-first century the most important development in physics will be the maturity of our knowledge of reality. One hundred years from now we will know all there is to know—except for some details—about the basic structure of matter and the nature of the universe.

A glance back at the enormous increase of knowledge during the past century gives convincing evidence that the above prediction is not fantasy. As recently as 1890 most scientists doubted that matter consisted of atoms, for no direct evidence of their existence had been found. The atomic age started in 1897 with the discovery of the electron. During the next fifty years many particles believed to be fundamental had been discovered: electrons, protons and neutrons within the atom, plus many mesons (generated in high energy particle accelerators) whose status was unclear. However, as evidence continued to accumulate, it gradually became evident that most of these particles were not really fundamental, but were made of other particles named *quarks*. Starting in the 1960s a detailed model of matter emerged. This model, called *The Standard Model of Particle Physics*, is able to explain almost every phenomenon observed in particle, nuclear, and atomic physics.

In the Standard Model, matter is made up of a relatively small number of fundamental particles: six kinds of heavy particles (the quarks), and six kinds of light particles, (the electron, the muon, the tau particle, the electron neutrino, the muon neutrino, and the tau neutrino). These twelve particles and their associated antiparticles are divided into three families.

Experimental evidence accumulated during the early 1990s at the Stanford Linear Accelerator and the Large Electron-Positron Collider in Switzerland proves that the three families of particles described above include all the existing particles of matter. The Standard Model became complete when the Tevatron at the Fermi National Accelerator Laboratory in Batavia, Illinois, discovered the top quark in 1994.

Future accelerators that can reach higher energies are expected to solve a second mystery of particle physics. At the heart of the Standard Model is the idea that all the events in the universe are governed by only four different forces: gravitational, electromagnetic, nuclear, and weak. When two particles feel a force of attraction or repulsion between them, it is because these particles exchange other "messenger" particles. For example, the electromagnetic force between two electric charges is caused by an exchange of photons. The Standard Model considers the electromagnetic force and the weak force to be two aspects of a single force: the *electroweak force*. The mathematical theory of the Standard Model predicts that the electroweak force is associated with the hypothetical Higgs particle. The Higgs particle is important because in theory it causes other particles to have mass.

With this background, we can make the following predictions for the next century of particle physics:

- New machines will be built that accelerate particles to energies greater than one teravolt. One of these is the Large Hadron Collider at CERN, the European Laboratory for Particle Physics, on the border between France and Switzerland. While there has been considerable political opposition to the proposed Superconducting Supercollider, mainly because of its great cost—over $8 billion—it is likely to be completed within a few decades.
- The Higgs particle will be generated in these machines and its properties will be measured. These measurements will complete the verification of the Standard Model of Particle Physics.
- By the end of the twenty-first century particle physics will be essentially complete. We will understand all the properties of all the possible particles, and we will understand the nature of all the fundamental interactions. Furthermore, we will learn that the four forces are merely four aspects of one fundamental force. The merging of gravitation with the theory of quantum mechanics will be accomplished. The Grand Unified Theory, or an equivalent theory, will be verified.

Quantum mechanics is a mathematical system of describing particles using wave equations. There are some basic questions in quantum theory that are not understood at the present time, even though as a whole the theory is extremely successful in describing the behavior of matter and energy. One peculiar phenomenon is observed when an atom emits two photons simultaneously. If these photons travel in opposite directions and are detected by instruments located far from each other, each detector seems to know instantaneously what kind of photon is observed by the distant detector. How this happens is not understood.

The outstanding puzzles of quantum mechanics will be solved during the twenty-first century. However, the paradoxical behavior of quanta will not provide methods of sending messages faster than the speed of light, as some authors claim, and will not be found to facilitate extrasensory perception and other paranormal effects, as other authors claim.

The phenomenon of superconductivity has been known since 1911. Superconductivity occurs when certain metals and alloys are cooled to extremely low temperatures. At a certain temperature, called the critical temperature, the material loses all resistance to the flow of electricity. This property makes possible the construction of electromagnets that require no power to operate once the electric current generating the magnetic field is started. The first superconductors required cooling the wires down to the temperature of liquid helium—minus 269° Celsius, which is only four degrees above absolute zero (4° K).

High-temperature superconductivity was discovered during the 1980s. Certain compounds become superconducting when cooled to the temperature of liquid nitrogen (77° K). The advantage of this is that liquid nitrogen is much cheaper than liquid helium. The disadvantage is that most of the high-temperature superconductors investigated to date lose their superconductivity when subject to high magnetic fields. This, of course, nullifies the most important uses of superconductors. Recent progress allows us to make some predictions:

- Materials will be found within the next few decades that permit the manufacture of superconductors capable of generating intense magnetic fields at liquid nitrogen temperatures. These superconductors will be used in the construction of high energy particle accelerators and trains levitated by magnetic fields.
- A more precarious prediction is this: Materials will ultimately be found that become superconductors at ordinary room temperatures. This will allow the construction of strong magnets without the use of any cooling at all. No one knows how this will be done, but there are no laws of nature that say this development is impossible.

Superconductivity is just one area of research in solid state physics or the physics of condensed matter. In 1948, solid state physics led to the invention of the transistor, which made possible the packing of more and more electronics into smaller spaces—the miniaturization of electronics. Progress continues as we learn to make electronic components smaller and smaller.

The further miniaturization of electronics will make possible the commercialization of hand-held computers with the power of present super-computers. This will result in computers that can think essentially like human beings, giving rise to robots that behave in human ways. In this area the predictions of science fiction will come true, for we do not know enough to set limits on the possibilities of the computer.

Plasma physics is a specialty that did not exist fifty years ago. A plasma is a gas existing at such a high temperature that some or all of the electrons are stripped from the atoms that make up the gas. The study of plasma physics is important for two reasons. First, most of the matter in the universe is in the plasma state, so that astrophysics is largely about plasma physics. Second, the search for a new form of nuclear energy by the process of thermonuclear fusion requires heating a volume of deuterium gas, or deuterium plus tritium, to such a high temperature that it is rendered to the plasma state. If it can be confined by a magnetic field, or otherwise, long enough for energy-releasing reactions to take place among the deuterium nuclei, then the goal of fusion energy is reached. Devices to create fusion energy are extremely large, complex, and expensive. However, the development of a practical fusion generator would be one of the most important events in science history, since it would provide the world with an almost inexhaustible source of useful energy, without most of the drawbacks of conventional nuclear power which depends upon fission energy. During the past few decades, gradual progress has brought the promise of fusion energy close to feasibility.

- In the near future the feasibility of fusion energy will be demonstrated in a device that generates more energy than is required to run it.
- During the first half of the twenty-first century a practical fusion generating plant will be built. This will provide a source of concentrated electrical power without the pollution of coal, oil, and uranium fission, but will not be "cheap."
- Cold fusion will prove to be an unachievable dream.

Predictions are hazardous. All of the above predictions are based on developments already in the pipeline, and they represent only a fraction of what the future holds. Not mentioned for obvious reasons are unsuspected discoveries that might be made. On the other hand, predictions that violate fundamental principles are *not* going to happen. Examples of these impossibilities are: a faster-than-light spaceship or message transmitter; an antigravity machine; a perpetual motion machine; a time machine; or a satellite that hovers over one spot on Earth's surface while tethered to it with a long cable. These predictions exist only in science fiction, not in reality.

See also ASTRONOMY; BATTERIES; CHEMISTRY; DIGITAL COMMUNICATIONS; MEDIA LAB; SCIENTIFIC BREAKTHROUGHS; SEMICONDUCTORS; SUPERCONDUCTORS.

BIBLIOGRAPHY

BESANÇON, ROBERT M., ed. *The Encyclopedia of Physics.* New York: Van Nostrand Reinhold, 1985.

CAVA, ROBERT J. "Superconductors beyond 1-2-3." *Scientific American* 263 (1990): 42–49.

DAVIES, PAUL, ed. *The New Physics.* Cambridge: Cambridge University Press, 1989.

HUTH, JOHN. "The Search for the Top Quark." *American Scientist* 80 (1992): 430–443.

QUIGG, CHRIS. "Elementary Particles and Forces." *Scientific American* 252 (1985): 84–95.

ROTHMAN, MILTON. *The Science Gap: Dispelling the Myths and Understanding the Reality of Science.* Buffalo, NY: Prometheus Books, 1992.

WEINBERG, STEPHEN. "Unified Theories of Elementary Particle Interaction." *Scientific American* 231 (1974): 50–59.

Milton Rothman

Pipelines

Pipelines transport liquids, gases, and slurries of liquids and solids. Pipeline transport is the safest form of transportation, invisible to consumers (being mostly underground) and economical for many products.

Pipelines for Energy Transportation

Pipelines deliver essentially 100 percent of the natural gas used in the United States. Nearly 300,000 miles of high-pressure, long-distance transmission pipelines and over 800,000 miles of local distribution mains were in the ground in 1990. Total

Pipelines

throughput in 1991 amounted to about 20 trillion cubic feet of gas, or about 23 percent of U.S. energy consumption. Worldwide, over 500,000 miles of gas transmission lines have been constructed.

In the United States, pipelines are also the primary mode for transporting crude oil to refineries and refined products to consumers. Over 150,000 miles of liquid-carrying pipelines have been constructed in the United States and nearly 400,000 miles worldwide. In 1989 U.S. pipelines moved 53.4 percent of liquids, ships and barges moved 42.6 percent, and trucks and railroads transported the remaining 4 percent. These pipelines delivered 6.6 billion barrels (Bbbl) of crude oil and 4.8 Bbbl of refined products in 1990.

Pipelines are also in limited use for the transport of coal. Coal must first be pulverized, then mixed with water to form a slurry that is pumped through a pipeline. About 400 miles of U.S. pipelines annually carry over 8 million tons of coal from mines to electric power plants.

Other Uses

About 1 million miles of pipelines and aqueducts deliver over 300 billion gallons of water per day in the United States. Pipelines also transport mineral products from mines to product refineries, operating in the same manner as the coal slurry lines described above. Products transported include limestone, copper, iron, phosphate, zinc phosphate, gilsonite, and kaolin, as well as mine tailings for disposal. About 2,000 miles of such pipelines exist worldwide. A number of pipelines transport gases such as carbon dioxide, hydrogen, and helium.

Pipeline Economics

Construction of a high-pressure transmission pipeline is costly. However, once constructed and operating, a pipeline represents a very economical means of transport. Construction costs depend on the size and pressure of the pipeline, the terrain to be crossed, and the population density. Large-diameter (30–36 inches), high-pressure pipelines cost an average of about $800,000 per mile to construct. Smaller pipelines (8–16 inches) cost about $100,000 to $300,000 per mile.

Construction costs have remained generally constant over the past ten years. Rising labor, material, right-of-way, and permitting costs have been largely offset by improvements in construction technology.

Compressor stations, consisting of large gas turbine or reciprocating engines that drive gas compressors, are necessary to pump gas through the pipeline. Compressor stations range in size from 1,000 to 100,000 horsepower (hp), with installation costs averaging $1,200 per hp. Other pipeline system components include flow-control valves and metering stations to measure gas flow and energy content.

In 1989 pipeline operating expenses amounted to $2.6 billion. These expenses add less than fifteen cents per thousand cubic feet to the gas price, amounting to about two cents per gallon of gasoline.

Pipeline Technology Trends

The technology for pipeline construction, operation, and maintenance has evolved dramatically over the past forty years. High-strength, crack-resistant steels, advanced welding technology, corrosion protection and control, high-efficiency compressor engines, and compressor automation have had major impacts.

Hydrocarbon transport in pipelines must increase in the future to achieve the energy goals of the United States and other countries. Increased use of natural gas is a key strategy in numerous countries that are currently dependent on petroleum and coal, such as Japan, Russia, and the countries of Central Europe. In the United States the Energy Policy Act of 1992 calls for greater use of natural gas because of its relative abundance and because natural gas is the cleanest burning of the fossil fuels. Expanded uses will require new pipelines for delivery.

CONSTRUCTION AND MATERIALS.

For the next decade the material of choice for pipelines will continue to be high-strength steel. The average natural gas transmission line has 132 girth welds per mile. Continued improvements in pipeline metallurgy and welding will ensure pipeline integrity.

Looking to the future, composite pipeline materials (e.g., steel reinforced by a glass-fiber/resin composite) and entirely new, overwrapped joining techniques will become commonplace. These new materials will virtually eliminate external corrosion and stress corrosion cracking. New internal coatings or ribbed surfaces may reduce the drag in the pipe, cut pressure losses and thereby lower compressor fuel use. Planning future pipeline rights-of-way will be done using advanced geographic information systems. Satellite-based systems will optimize routing and construction that minimize environmental impact and construction cost.

719

OPERATIONS.

Federal regulations that govern pipeline operation have increased competition among pipeline operators. Liquid pipelines have already been essentially deregulated and gas pipelines are becoming partially deregulated.

Supervisory Control and Data Acquisition (SCADA) computerized systems provide operators with vital data on compressor conditions and gas-flow information, such as pressure, flow rate, and valve position. SCADA systems, electronic flow measurement, compressor station automation, diagnostic systems, and real-time pipeline computer models allow optimum operation of a pipeline system.

MAINTENANCE.

As the existing U.S. pipeline system ages (about 50 percent of the system will be greater than twenty-five years old by the year 2000), inspection and maintenance will assume greater importance. The pipeline transportation system is one of the safest modes of transportation. To maintain this record, operators will employ advanced pipeline inspection techniques, corrosion prevention technologies, and pipeline monitoring systems, as well as improved repair technologies.

Future pipeline inspection will be accomplished using so-called smart pigs. These are mechanical devices that travel through a pipeline and inspect the pipe wall, looking for cracks and areas where wall thickness has been reduced by a gouge or corrosion damage.

The Probable Future

Many changes can be expected in the next century, both in energy sources and uses and in transporta-

FIGURE 1. Part of a gas pipeline compressor station.

FIGURE 2. A "smart pig" being inserted into a pipeline to inspect for defects in the pipe wall.

tion systems. While supplies of fossil fuels, especially coal and natural gas, will be sufficient over this period, their costs will continue to rise in comparison to alternative, renewable sources. Hydrogen generated from solar energy or nuclear electric energy may begin to replace natural gas by the middle of the next century. The gas pipeline system can be used to transport hydrogen. Of course, upgraded materials or internal coatings may be necessary since hydrogen causes cracks to form in most steels.

Coal is still the most abundant energy form in the United States. However, its use creates the most pollutant emissions of the fossil fuels, including the highest level of carbon dioxide emissions, and emissions contribute to the "greenhouse" effect. Carbon dioxide emissions are likely to be restricted in the next century. But pipeline technology may play a role in allowing continued use of coal. For example, transporting coal in a slurry pipeline using a new solvent or refining chemical instead of water could actually refine the coal in the pipe to upgrade coal quality. Carbon dioxide pipelines could transport carbon dioxide captured at an electric utility generating plant from the plant to a disposal, storage, or use site.

Finally, the rising cost and environmental impact of rail and over-the-road freight shipment may stimulate entirely new applications for pipelines. It may become economically efficient to transport grains, minerals, or other products primarily by pipeline.

In conclusion, pipelines are a critical element of the world's energy transportation system. Continued advances in construction, operations, and maintenance technology will keep pipeline transport in the forefront through the next century as new concepts for energy and transportation evolve.

See also COAL; ENERGY; ENGINEERING; MATE-RIALS: RESEARCH AND DEVELOPMENT; NATURAL GAS; PETROLEUM.

BIBLIOGRAPHY

CLARK, JUDY R. "1992—A Year with a View." *Pipeline Digest* (January 1992).

HIRATSOO, J. N. H., ed. *World Pipelines and International Directory*, 1st ed. Beaconsfield, U.K.: Pipes & Pipelines International, 1983.

QUARLES, WILLIAM R. "Pipe Line Companies to Install 19,512 Miles of Lines in 1992." *Pipe Line Industry* (January 1992).

ROBINSON, RONALD C. "Computerized Monitoring Enhances Corrosion Detection." *Pipe Line Industry* (March 1992).

VINCENT-GENOD, JACQUES. *Fundamentals of Pipeline Engineering.* Houston: Gulf Publishing, 1984.

WATTS, JIM. "Dimensions of the 500 Leading U.S. Energy Pipeline Companies." *Pipeline & Gas Journal* (September 1991).

William M. Burnett

Planning

A major task of organizations involved in advancing planning and forecasting, such as the Strategic Leadership Forum, is to ensure that future directions become apparent in time to adjust social and business institutions to the desired course of action. Leaders responsible for setting direction in their organizations need access to four basic kinds of support:

1. Access to important new ideas while they are still a faint "blip" on the radar screen;
2. Access to real-world cases of practitioners at the leading edge of an applicable discipline;
3. Knowledge received just in time to be applied to unique problems;
4. A network of experts and successful peers.

The future is not anticipated through the perfect plan as much as through a powerful, evolving process that keeps leaders exposed to and aware of change.

Strategy Implementation

Successful authors of books on managing change and the future suggest various approaches to planning. William C. Finnie (1994), for example, outlines a four-cycle approach that has been success-fully used in more than a hundred corporations. The first cycle creates links among concepts about shareholder value, planning, implementation, and customer- and competitor-driven strategies. The second cycle employs strategic thinking concepts. The third promotes shared goals. The fourth keeps plans fresh and action-oriented.

Margaret Wheatley (1992) connects strategic thinking with the revolutionary discoveries being made in quantum physics, chaos theory, and evolutionary biology, conceptual breakthroughs that are changing our fundamental understanding of the universe. She proposes how to find order in a chaotic world and distinguishes order from control.

C. Davis Fogg (1994) brings us back to earth with dozens of hands-on tools that help as team-based strategy evolves, including models to forecast five-year results, keys to plotting the ongoing processes, guides for facilitators, and miscellaneous troubleshooting advice.

William A. Band (1994) reviews ten touchstones for the year 2000 and beyond: delivering superior value, revamping business processes, thriving on rapid change, developing a highly motivated workforce, building supplier and customer alliances, aligning work with strategy, creating a learning organization, building change leadership, and leveraging technologies.

Finally, Peter Senge and coauthors (1994) move from the theory of learning organizations to practical applications with an incisive workbook. The case histories in the workbook show that companies, businesses, schools, agencies, and even communities can undo their "learning disabilities" and achieve greater performance.

Tools and Techniques

Over the past decade, executives have witnessed an explosion of management tools and techniques such as reengineering, total quality management, and benchmarking, each offering to help organizations adjust to the future. Keeping up with these and deciding which ones to use have become essential parts of an executive's responsibilities.

Key findings of the Strategic Leadership Forum annual survey appraising success with strategy tools reveal that tool usage is growing but that there is no correlation between the number of tools used and the satisfactoriness of the results. Greatest satisfaction occurs when strategy tools are used to uncover new opportunities to serve customers, help build distinctive organization capabilities, and help exploit competitor vulnerabilities.

Pluralism

Human Potential

A crystal ball would reveal people becoming intensely individualistic due to the influence of technology, while continually evolving in their knowledge and becoming more flexible in their associations. Clearly, people will also require some stability—and an opportunity to touch and feel what they experience in a wired world.

With posthumous apologies to John Donne for tinkering with and perhaps contradicting his famous quote, the future holds the distinct prospect that "every man *is* an island." As it continues to evolve, technology is increasingly permitting an individual's aspirations and needs to be addressed directly; yet, paradoxically, this only intensifies the individual's need for association. As public companies give way to private enterprise and as public services shrink in their role of serving an ill-defined public good, the need heightens for voluntary associations of complementary interests.

As highly structured formal business and social institutions shrink in the future, the static concept of a career will change to a dynamic, evolutionary process of learning. So, too, the static concept of an institution containing the sum of all knowledge on a subject changes to a dynamic process of people coming together, to participate in a common task and associate the work of their team with other teams, forming flexible, vital organisms.

A Fundamentally Different World

Increasingly, labor, capital, technology, knowledge, and physical assets will transcend national boundaries. No matter where pooled, resources will be available to all through global market mechanisms. Increasingly, global business and organizational cultures will trade in knowledge and will form alliances far more than they will engage in competition and resource control. Global knowledge, experiences, and mobility will cut across boundaries of language, political geography, and property. Customers will be found everywhere and grouped around expectations that will be identified globally. Global identity may be more powerful than local identity.

Organizational Renaissance

No perfect plan or strategy is recognized, but definite progress on anticipating the future is being made. Planning and the future are not an oxymoron provided that planning is free of extensive prediction and avoids proposing highly structured solutions. Perhaps the greatest progress in understanding the future has been to avoid looking through the distorting filter of our present attempts at solutions.

At bottom it is imperative to recognize that we face a fundamentally different world, one for which we can never fully or finally prepare. Therefore, we must keep our sights set on maximal exposure to change. We also must reconnect with the fact that organizations are simply human constructs, and accord greater freedom for the coming together and breaking apart of work groups.

The complex and rapid change we face is still susceptible to management. The tools and techniques used to allow organizations to adjust to change may need constant reevaluation to produce desired results. Even as tools become obsolete or unresponsive, new authors and new ideas crop up and provide new ways to get back on track with exciting concepts to meet the challenges of a changing global society. Human creativity knows no bounds—the future is an open-ended quest.

See also CHANGE, OPTIMISTIC AND PESSIMISTIC PERSPECTIVES; CONTINUITY AND DISCONTINUITY; FORECASTING METHODS; STRATEGIC PLANNING; SURVEYS.

BIBLIOGRAPHY

BAND, WILLIAM A. *Touchstones—Ten New Ideas Revolutionizing Business.* New York: John Wiley, 1994.

FINNIE, WILLIAM C. *Hands on Strategy—The Guide to Crafting Your Company's Future.* New York: John Wiley, 1994.

FOGG, C. DAVIS. *Team-Based Strategic Planning—A Complete Guide to Structuring, Facilitating, and Implementing the Process.* New York: American Management Association, 1994.

SENGE, PETER, et al. *The Fifth Discipline Fieldbook.* New York: Doubleday, 1994.

WHEATLEY, MARGARET J. *Leadership and the New Science—Learning About Organization from an Orderly Universe.* San Francisco: Berrett-Koehler, 1992.

A. Bruce Wilson

Pluralism

The term *pluralism* has roots in philosophy, where it is contrasted with *monism*. In the social sciences, its primary use has been in political science and political philosophy, where it refers to both the analytical view that there are many sources of power in a society, state, or community, and to the normative view that this is a desirable state of affairs, which should be encouraged through the devolution of central state power to other actors—governmental and nongovernmental. The alternative viewpoints would be that empirically the power to make key decisions flows from a single ruling elite, or closely linked ruling elites, both within and outside government, and normatively that the dispersion of power that pluralists prefer is inefficient and ineffective in fulfilling the aims of government or in serving the national or community interests.

In American political science, there has been an extended debate on the nature of power in American society and government between pluralists and their opponents. Some of its leading participants have been C. Wright Mills (1956), Floyd Hunter, Robert Dahl (1961), Nelson Polsby, and Seymour Martin Lipset (1960). The variety of groups that pluralists believe actually participate in or should participate in power and decision making have included business associations, trade unions, community organizations, religious groups, the various levels of government, and indeed the whole range of associations into which men and women enter.

In the 1980s and '90s, racial and ethnic groups have become more prominent as candidates for the proper devolution of power and influence in a plural society. This has led to a debate in the United States over "multiculturalism"—that is, over the degree to which racial and ethnic groups should be recognized as distinct in their interests and culture, possessing some degree of stability and permanence, and legitimately entitled to have their distinctive interests and points of view expressed in education, the media, public ceremonies, and government. In opposition to multiculturalism is the position that racial and ethnic groups in the United States have in the past assimilated to a common American culture; that this culture is derived from England primarily, but from Europe in general; and that these groups have thus become "Americanized," and should continue to do so.

Multiculturalism was in earlier decades called *cultural pluralism*, a term coined by philosopher Horace M. Kallen during World War I, in opposition to heightened demands then made on new European immigrant groups that they become assimilated and Americanized. Kallen, along with the social critic Randolph Bourne, asserted that the United States was and should remain a society in which each group maintained its identity and contributed its distinctive strain to the common culture.

Cultural pluralism had little influence until the civil rights movement of the 1960s. Until then American Negroes, the largest minority in the United States, had fought and hoped for assimilation into American society. While this objective was not abandoned in respect to participation in the economy and government, in the course of the 1970s and '80s Negroes, whose preferred name rapidly changed first to *blacks* and then to *African Americans*, increasingly emphasized their distinctive culture and demanded that it be recognized in schools, colleges, universities, and public life. This demand became the moving force in a new cultural pluralism, labeled *multiculturalism* in the 1990s.

Black demands were echoed by other groups, in particular Mexican Americans, whose numbers expanded in the 1970s and later decades through increased immigration. Some elements among Asian-American groups, greatly expanded in numbers by immigration, also raised multicultural demands. The older European ethnic groups, whose distinctiveness had been defended by Kallen and Bourne, do not participate in the multicultural movement. Indeed, some intellectuals whose forebears came from these older European ethnic immigrant groups are among the leading critics of multiculturalism. Few from European ethnic groups protest against their cultural assimilation into American life. Seventy years after the end of mass European immigration to the United States, the identity and distinctiveness of these groups have been much altered by assimilatory forces and high rates of intermarriage.

The greatest success of multiculturalism has been in colleges and universities, where distinctive academic programs on black literature, culture, and history have been created in the hundreds, along with fewer, but still quite numerous, programs dealing with Hispanic and Asian-American culture and history; and in the elementary and high schools, where curricula in literature, history, and social science have been sharply modified to take account of multicultural demands. Multiculturalism has been strongly attacked by Arthur M. Schlesinger, Jr. (1991), and Richard Bernstein (1994), among others. It has not been defended by prominent intellectuals, but it is nevertheless solidly rooted in the educational system, higher and lower, and treated with deference in the mass media.

One success of multiculturalism has been in gaining recognition in state laws and in court decisions of the right of children speaking a foreign language to be educated for a few years in that language. The educational basis for such "bilingual" programs is educational effectiveness, on the grounds that children must have a few years to learn English before attending classes in which all teaching is in that language. But multicultural proponents would also like to see home languages maintained through school programs and to have group and homeland culture also taught, along with language. In some states those who would prefer a more rapid transition to English have tried to lessen state bilingual requirements. The great majority of those enrolled in bilingual programs are Spanish-speaking—from Mexico, Cuba, Puerto Rico, and other Spanish-speaking Latin American countries. Thus in many cities the conflict over the extent and duration of bilingual programs is drawn between Hispanic activists and community leaders and the non-Spanish-speaking majority.

The term *multiculturalism* has been broadened to cover controversies that have little to do with culture; for example, the conflict over affirmative action—preference in employment, or in bidding for government contracts, or in admission to selective college and professional schools on the basis of race, ethnicity, and sex—and the conflict over special efforts to fashion black-majority voting districts so that the number of elected black representatives can be increased. These issues and similar ones have led to important U.S. Supreme Court cases and will continue to do so.

While the controversies over pluralism and multiculturalism have received the most attention in the United States, almost identical issues have emerged in other major countries of immigration, such as Australia and Canada. Even formerly homogeneous European nations such as France, Germany, the Netherlands, and others must deal with issues of pluralism and multiculturalism because large numbers of people from different cultures have immigrated and permanently settled there. In a world in which migration, despite efforts to control it, is a permanent feature, and migrants are drawn from increasingly distant and various countries and cultures, more and more countries are dealing with the issues that have emerged so sharply in the United States, as it moves from the demand for full assimilation to some variant of multiculturalism.

See also CHINA: ETHNIC REAWAKENING; CLASS AND UNDERCLASS; DEMOCRACY; DEMOCRATIC PROCESS; ETHNIC AND CULTURAL SEPARATISM; GLOBAL CULTURE; HUMAN RIGHTS; LIFESTYLES, ETHNIC; LIFESTYLES, VALUE ORIENTED; MASS CULTURE AND ART; MINORITIES; POLITICAL PARTY REALIGNMENT; PREJUDICE, FORMS OF; RACE, CASTE, AND ETHNIC DIVERSITY; VALUES; WORKFORCE DIVERSITY.

BIBLIOGRAPHY

BERNSTEIN, RICHARD. *Dictatorship of Virtue: Multiculturalism and the Battle for America's Future.* New York: Alfred A. Knopf, 1994.
DAHL, ROBERT. *Who Governs? Democracy and Power in an American City.* New Haven, CT: Yale University Press, 1961.
GLAZER, NATHAN. *Ethnic Dilemmas, 1954–1982.* Cambridge, MA: Harvard University Press, 1983.
_____. "Is Assimilation Dead?" *The Annals* 530 (November 1993): 122–136.
HIGHAM, JOHN. "Multiculturalism and Universalism: A History and Critique." *American Quarterly* 45 (1993): 195–256.
KALLEN, HORACE M. "Democracy *Versus* the Melting Pot." *The Nation* (February 18 and 25, 1916): 190–192 and 217–220. Reprinted in Kallen, Horace M. *Culture and Democracy in the United States.* New York: Boni and Liveright, 1924.
KARIEL, HENRY S. "Pluralism." In *International Encyclopedia of the Social Sciences.* Vol. 12. New York: Macmillan, 1968.
LIPSET, SEYMOUR MARTIN. *Political Man: The Social Bases of Politics.* Garden City, NY: Doubleday, 1960.
MILLS, C. WRIGHT. *The Power Elite.* New York: Oxford University Press, 1956.
SCHLESINGER, ARTHUR M., JR. *The Disuniting of America: Reflections on a Multicultural Society.* New York: Norton, 1991.

Nathan Glazer

Polar Regions.

See ANTARCTICA.

Policy Changes.

See PUBLIC POLICY CHANGES.

Political Campaigning

Political campaigning in developed democratic nations in the twenty-first century will be affected by significant changes in the ways citizens register to vote, select candidates, cast ballots, receive both information and propaganda, and function as partisans in the election process.

Over the next fifty years, as more households become linked by national interactive computer-video-telephone-fax network grids, the process, not just of political communication but of active participation, will become increasingly home based.

Voters will be able to register, mark and record ballots, interview office seekers, attend and address campaign strategy meetings, work precincts, use credit cards to make financial contributions, and circulate literature—all from their homes.

Computer retrieval of information available in hundreds of independent data banks, as well as the material sanctioned by campaign headquarters, will permit public scrutiny of the finances, personal affairs, business involvements, and membership associations of office seekers in such detail as regularly to reopen the historic debates about appropriate privacy.

Conversely, and perhaps more important, the volumes of market research information that candidates can obtain about voters from computer research and constant interactive surveying will combine with advanced information processing to revolutionize statistical analysis in political campaigns. Pivotal voting blocs will be identified, and within these groups voters with shared, or even subliminally shared, special interests will be isolated and appealed to with tailored messages quite apart from the general campaign rhetoric.

Electronic bulletin boards and E-mail will permit quick and controlled distribution of messages to targeted groups. Closed circuit television and televised telephone conference facilities will allow candidates to speak at length to regional and national rallies of voters with specific special interests. Those in the audience who participate in these rallies will be no less responsive, and no less militant, even though they may be home alone. In fifty years a major skill of professional campaign managers will be the ability, using computer data, survey testing, and intuition, to identify and address those inconspicuous elements of shared anxiety or enthusiasm among voters who are otherwise markedly different in experience, intellect, economic position, and personal history.

The public theater that characterizes national elections will remain. Political platforms will continue to reflect common-denominator themes. But increasingly, the most productive work of a campaign in terms of winning over and galvanizing the uncommitted will be done by candidates from a single communication center. Hour after hour they will dial into and present their views to one prearranged special interest rally after the next. Comparatively silent and invisible, extremely expensive, and potentially very effective, this method of political campaigning will employ to the fullest the developing technologies in high-speed research, processing, distribution and communication.

Population dynamics will also impact on the strategy, the organization, and the cost of campaigning in the next century. Not only will populations increase, but a significantly higher percentage of citizens will register to vote and actually vote because both can be done at home. New power concentrations will emerge. In the United States, Asian Americans will continue to be the fastest-growing population group, increasing by more than 350 percent to forty-one million by mid-century. At that time African Americans will number sixty-two million, up 94 percent. Hispanics will total eighty-one million, reflecting a 24 percent increase. By the year 2050, people of color will exceed Caucasians in number for the first time; whites will be by far the slowest-growing population component and may even be in decline.

Older Americans of all races and nationalities will constitute the country's largest, most powerful, and most demanding voter bloc. By mid-twenty-first century 20 percent of the population will be sixty-five years of age or older. One of the dominant political tensions in the United States and other advanced democracies—an issue which will have to be dealt with by every political candidate in every election—will result from the demand for better and more widely distributed medical care: An increasingly older, retired citizenry with clout at the polls will need support from a steadily shrinking base of younger taxpayers.

Political debate will focus as well on institutions made obsolescent by scientific development and social change. High on this list will be the election process itself, bringing changes which will affect campaigns. Modernization in the United States will include efforts to eliminate the Electoral College; to discontinue tabulation of votes by states in presidential elections; to end the requirement of printed ballots so that all votes can be cast electronically; to permit votes to be cast at home as well as at neighborhood polling stations. There will be initiatives to set a single day for a nationwide presidential primary in each party; to reduce by half the length of all state and national election campaigns; to arrange for weekend voting with all ballots cast from East to West over precisely the same forty-eight-hour period; to stimulate voter participation by authorizing official announcement of election results, minute by minute, as they are received and recorded at electronic counting centers.

Campaigns for public office, as they will evolve in the twenty-first century, will require massive initial outlays for equipment and systems development and major year-round funding for program maintenance. This need for expensive continuing operations will produce a resurgence in political parties. It will also exacerbate the threat to democratic processes posed by wealthy special-interest organizations able to invest in the mechanics of political persuasion. Wealthy candidates will benefit disproportionately from campaigns which employ high-tech home-based electronics. Even with the greater ease by which citizens will register and vote, this electronic infrastructure will have a conservative influence on future elections and may also contribute to an electoral elite in modern democracies. These and other subtle, secondary consequences of change must not be ignored. We were not always successful in the twentieth century in providing equal opportunity for voters, guaranteeing majority rule, protecting minority voices, and avoiding fraud. The challenge will be no less great in the twenty-first century.

See also COMMUNITARIANISM; CONSERVATISM, POLITICAL; LIBERALISM, POLITICAL; POLITICAL CYCLES; POLITICAL PARTIES; POLITICAL PARTY REALIGNMENT; THIRD POLITICAL PARTIES; VOTING.

BIBLIOGRAPHY

"The Aging of the Human Species." *Scientific American* (April 1993).
"Electronic Town Halls?" *National Journal* (June 6, 1992).
"The New Computer Revolution." *Fortune* (June 14, 1993).
"Techno-Politics Is Coming of Age." *Boston Globe,* June 1, 1992.
"The Tekkie on the Ticket." *Washington Post,* October 18, 1992.
WIESENDANGER, BETSY. "Electronic Delivery and Feedback Systems Come of Age." *Public Relations Journal* (January 1993).

Richard H. Blades

Political Cycles

Ebbs and flows in politics are shaped by two types of cyclical behavior. The first is the cyclical rhythm of government involvement in public and private affairs, which follows changes in generations occurring about every thirty years. The second type of political cycle is the change in world leadership among nations based on uneven growth rates between economies as well as technological innovations that bring greater advantage to one society over the others.

The American Political Cycle

American politics alternates between what Emerson in 1841 called conservatism and innovation. Many observed this cycle, but descriptions and definitions vary. Henry Adams described an oscillation between diffusion and centralization of national purpose. Arthur M. Schlesinger, Sr., defined the cycle as a swing between conservatism and liberalism. Each of these descriptions is accurate in its own way, but these well-used terms are subject to varying definitions.

Economist Albert O. Hirschman helped to clarify this problem by characterizing the cycle as a shift in focus between the conflicting goals of private and public happiness. Arthur M. Schlesinger, Jr., further summarized the cycle as a continuing shift in national involvement between public purpose and private interest.

Periods of government action devoted to public purpose began in 1900, 1932, 1960, and 1992. Periods in this thirty-year cycle that focus on private interest followed in 1920, 1952, and 1980, with the next forecast to arrive at the end of the first decade in the next century.

Each phase in the cycle breeds contradictions. During times of public purpose, reform comes in bursts. Public action piles up change and disappointment as well. A nation is worn out by constant summons to battle and becomes weary of ceaseless political activity that produces mixed results. Individuals then turn to private action to solve problems.

Concentration on private affairs produces contradictions as well because some segments of the population do not share in the common good. Examples of excessive private acquisitiveness remind people of their public obligations and people consequently seek meaning in life beyond themselves.

Shifts in thinking between the generations is the mainspring of the political cycle. John Stuart Mill, in 1843, held that major changes in history required the appearance of a new generation open to new ideas. Ortega y Gasset, in 1961, reaffirmed the role played by successive generations and identified a thirty-year recurring pattern. It consists of a period of coming of political age challenging incumbents, followed by a period of control before the next generation takes over. As each generation attains power, it tends to repudiate the work of those it displaces and to follow the ideals of its own formative days thirty years before. This phenomenon produces a thirty-year rhythm that swings between public purpose and private interest.

The Next Cycle of Public Purpose: 1992–2000

Politics in the United States, beginning in 1992, entered a period of change dominated by public purpose. Bellwether government initiatives provide a forecast of what is likely to happen during this political cycle. Several governments in Europe—especially Sweden, as well as key state and city governments in the United States—have experimented with reforms likely to be on the United States federal government's agenda during the balance of this cycle. Among the many possibilities for change are these:

- *Employee benefits.* Longer vacations; time off; inconvenient and uncomfortable working hour pay supplements.
- *Health care.* National, universal, comprehensive, compulsory coverage; catastrophic care; right to die laws; meshing public/private benefits; health insurance courts; cooperative hospitals; environmental injury benefits; death benefits in advance of death; artificial part replacements; genetic intervention coverage.
- *Job security.* Lifetime job guarantee; industrial democratization; worker board of director membership; permanent, portable pensions; shorter pension vesting period; taxation of nonwage benefits.
- *Retirement.* Life expectancy escalators; later retirement; voluntary retirement; consolidation of government retirement programs.
- *Women.* Family leaves; universal, free, public preschooling; childcare and aging parents time-off benefits; mandatory flextime and job-sharing.

Some of these trend-setting initiatives worked well, others did not; but they point to areas where reform will be introduced in the United States during this next part of the cycle. Concurrent with the U.S. political cycle that ushered in an era of public purpose is another cyclic phenomenon driven by long waves of recurring change in the world economy.

The Long Wave

The long wave is a forty-five- to sixty-year cycle of economic growth and decline that was identified in the 1920s by a Russian economist, Nicolai Kondratieff. He presented statistical evidence of a cycle of prosperity, recession, depression, and recovery in the economies of France, Great Britain, Germany, and the United States. Closely studied since then, the cycle has completed an ebb and flow in economic development four times since the Industrial Revolution began late in the eighteenth century.

In the 1990s we will complete a transition to the next long wave. This wave, like the four previous ones, is being defined by a set of technological breakthroughs and organizational innovations that eventually will bring advantage to societies that successfully initiate and utilize them.

This will happen because downturns between each wave prompt innovation. Successful innovations become extremely profitable and form leading-edge industrial sectors that characterize the following forty-five- to sixty-year period. Prospects for increasing prosperity lead to building productive capacity beyond market need that in turn produces economic downturn until the stage has been cleared for yet another era of building.

Expansions at the start of each long wave grow around an integrated and mutually supporting combination of technologies. German economist Gerhard Mensch identified clusters of innovations that helped launch each long wave. Innovation peaked at the beginning of the Industrial Revolution in the 1770s–1780s and in the transition between long waves in the 1830s–1840s, the 1880s–1890s, and the 1930s–1940s. Once a set of innovations is established, they define the new system, and incompatible technologies are rejected as impractical. This is why innovations that define a long wave era are grouped into a ten- to fifteen-year window during the transition between long wave eras. The world is in the midst of another such transition now.

Each long wave era is fueled by an innovative industry and supporting technologies that comes to define each age. In each long wave, the nation that best capitalizes on innovation leads economic growth and through its economic power dominates world events. See Table 1.

The transition between the fourth and fifth long wave will last for the remainder of this century. It will continue to be a time of innovation. As in former transitions, new industries will build on the dominant industries of the previous era. The current age of television, plastic, and oil is being supplemented by a new age of information based on computers, silicon, and fiber optics.

New economic powers that emerge at the beginning of each wave are drawn into the power vacuum created by the relative decline of the previous wave's hegemonic power. This decline occurs because at the end of each wave the dominant power overextends itself. Attempts to fulfill commitments

TABLE 1.   Dominant Technological Forces Characterizing Economic Long Waves

	First Wave	*Second Wave*	*Third Wave*	*Fourth Wave*	*Fifth Wave*
Industry	Textile	Railroad	Automobile	Television	Computer
Material	Cotton	Iron	Steel	Plastic	Silicon
Energy	Water	Wood	Coal	Oil	Solar
Communication	Semaphore	Telegraph	Telephone	Electronic	Fiberoptic
Nation	France	United Kingdom	Germany	United States	European Community

to foreign and domestic programs deplete resources, and the wherewithal to mount new ventures, accordingly, is diminished.

The French attempt at hegemony during the first long wave, opposed by the rising economic might of Great Britain, ended in defeat at Waterloo. Britain, in turn, found itself replaced as the world's leading industrial economy by both Germany and the United States as the second wave drew to a close at the end of the nineteenth century. Germany's attempt at domination in the third wave was crushed in 1918 and 1945. The fourth wave's hegemonic power has been the United States, which until recently was constantly challenged by the old Soviet Union. The United States may surrender economic and political leadership at the end of this century as we make the transition from the fourth to the fifth long wave. In fact, part of the transition has already occurred. The nations of the European Community (EC) have constituted the world's largest economy since 1990, and Japan has become the financial capital of the world.

The United States is still the world's most open society, and that provides fertile ground for further innovation and growth. But to maintain its leadership role as the next long wave gathers speed, the United States must overcome history; the leader of the old system has rarely been the leader of the new.

Conclusion

The United States has entered a cycle dominated by public purpose, where much needs to be done to solve problems, but limited funds are available to spend for such purposes. At the same time, global political leadership is in transition, as economic power, the cornerstone of military and political influence, is shifting. The United States is the hegemonic power from the old era, weighted down with commitments that were part of its previous success, but that cannot easily be paid for in the future. Whether the United States plays the leading role in the future will be determined by how quickly it can discard the baggage of the past and embrace the future.

See also CHANGE; COMMUNITARIANISM; CONSERVATISM, POLITICAL; LIBERALISM, POLITICAL; PACESETTER GOVERNMENTS; POLITICAL PARTIES; POLITICAL PARTY REALIGNMENT; PUBLIC POLICY CHANGE; TECHNOLOGICAL CHANGE.

BIBLIOGRAPHY

ERICKSON, SCOTT W. "The Transition Between Eras: The Long Wave Cycle," *Futurist* 19/4 (1985): 40–44.
FORRESTER, JAY W. "Economic Conditions Ahead: Understanding the Kondratieff Wave," *Futurist* 19/3 (1985): 16–20.
GOLDSTEIN, JOSHUA S. *Long Cycles: Prosperity and War in the Modern Age.* New Haven: Yale University Press, 1988.
KENNEDY, PAUL. *The Rise and Fall of the Great Powers: Economic Change and Military Conflict from 1500 to 2000.* New York: Random House, 1987.
KONDRATIEFF, NIKOLAI. *The Long Wave Cycle.* Trans. Guy Daniels. New York: Richardson & Snyder, 1984.
MOLITOR, GRAHAM T. T. "Swedish Benefits Today—U.S. Benefits Tomorrow?" *Innovations* (Fall 1993): 6–18.
SCHLESINGER, ARTHUR M., JR. *The Cycles of American History.* Boston: Houghton Mifflin, 1986.
STRAUSS, WILLIAM, and HOWE, NEIL. *Generations: The History of America's Future 1584 to 2069.* New York: Quill/Morrow, 1991.

Scott W. Erickson

Political Economy

Economics and its nineteenth-century predecessor, political economy, may become academic curiosities unless their ancient meaning can be adapted to a postmodern world view in renewed systems of governance. The conditions under which they can be effective and beneficial are disappearing.

Economy is derived from a Greek compound word for household administration (a small business operation). It exemplified what Aristotle called *practical* reason, by which he meant making decisions on *what should be done*, given that there is rarely enough time, resources, or freedom to do everything. This dilemma—limited means and unlimited wants—is the essential core of economic reasoning. It implies that interpersonal conflict is inevitable and therefore raises moral issues, which Aristotle treated as topics in his *Ethics* and *Politics*.

Moral and political philosophers were the custodians of economic thought for many centuries. In the late Middle Ages, they were concerned about the *justness* of prices at a time when the rapid expansion of commerce was upsetting centuries of social-class stability. The rise of the bourgeoisie shifted the locus of political power from the allegiance of heavily armored men on horseback to an ability to pay cash for the upkeep of armies. Kings and lords were forced to collaborate with wealthy burgesses, whose assets were in coin rather than land. Moralists condemned the practice of taking interest, believing with Aristotle that the accumulation of money is an unnatural form of wealth. Profound change was imminent.

Renaissance philosophers replaced God with humankind as the *final cause*, the focus of creation. No longer inhibited by the belief that natural processes are sacrosanct, humanists began to view nature as something to be used. The new view also eroded belief in social structures as an immutable natural order. Thomas More's *Utopia* (1516) was the most systematic of their proposals for government as an instrument to promote material security, individual contentment, and civic virtue. More was original in postulating economic growth as an instrument of national policy. The belief that nature could be manipulated by technology and the presumption of a bounded nation-state were also fundamental in systems conceived by political philosophers such as Bodin, Hobbes, Bacon, Locke, and Montesquieu.

The nation-state required accounting procedures to cope with bills of exchange, deferred payments, banking, insurance, and other instruments invented by its commercial partners. This *political arithmetic* cemented the familiar but unfortunate association of economics with money. (Money appears in many *manifestations* of the economic problem, but is not of the essence.) The original meaning of economy was later applied to the nation-state in the term *political economy*, and described as the art of kings.

Enthusiastic philosophers in the eighteenth century (e.g., Godwin, Condorcet) believed that reason would assure material and social progress. Skeptical economists, however, discounted these expectations by pointing not only to the limited capacity of nature but also to human nature as self-defeating. The Malthusian theorem on population growth became a principle of classical political economy, earning it the label of *dismal science*. To counter this negative image, economists devised political structures to encourage human creative energy. At one extreme these formulas focused on freedom of action (market capitalism in the tradition of Adam Smith) and at the other on rational control by government (scientific socialism, following Karl Marx). Both sought an appropriate balance between increased production and distributive justice.

Nineteenth-century economists postulated an economic *system* that can be investigated by methods similar to those of physics, with the results used to engineer better system performance. They changed the name of their discipline to *economics* in the twentieth century and described it as a *challenge* to scarcity. So long as the focus of analysis was local, the issue of global or ultimate limits (entropic and ecological) could be ignored, and usually was. The growth-by-technology solution (use of *speculative* and *productive* reason in Aristotle's tripartite classification) is a clear departure from the original meaning of economy as part of the classical Greek quest for the "Golden Mean."

Government support for economics research has encouraged the technological focus, for material abundance is politically popular and puts off the time when uncomfortable choices are inescapable. Hence, economic studies of the kind that acknowledge limits and address the choice implications have been progressively avoided in roughly inverse proportion to the accumulating knowledge of global imbalance between population and resources. Engineers, sociologists, statisticians, computer scientists, financial analysts, management specialists, historians, and political scientists have all contributed to techniques and empirical knowledge that are useful in economics work—but without the focus on the collective choice dilemma, they are *not* economics or political economy. The confusion of money, finance, business enterprise, or decision-making technique with economics and political economy impairs the resolution of very serious problems of interpersonal, international, and human-environment relationships. Greater profits for some individuals or groups do not automatically increase the collective welfare, invocations of Adam Smith to the contrary notwithstanding.

Political economy can be useful only if its postulates hold, and they are showing signs of exhaustion today. The nation-state is weakening relative to transnational corporations, which consume collective resources relentlessly, destroying the powers of nature in the process. Access to the means for earning a living is evaporating in a new, multinational version of the sixteenth-century enclosure movement. An effective market system requires institutions of law, justice, and morality—hence governments, boundaries, and wide consensus on the purpose and nature of rules. Without these conditions, macroeconomic policy instruments are ineffective, and redistributive programs become impossible to justify or administer.

A political economy that has meaning for the future must be based in an ecological worldview and in political structures that assure that the classic concept of economy as a best possible *human* adjustment to limits is applied to means-ends decisions. In the absence of global government, a global economy will reenact the lawless frontier of nineteenth-century America in combination with massive numbers of underemployed, displaced people. Individuals and families will solve their personal economic problems in any way they can. These may involve cooperative local solutions, tribal connections, and group solidarity among geographically dispersed people held together by shared religious commitment. But even though they may have procedures, policies, and techniques for production, distribution, and exchange, these cannot by definition constitute a form of political economy.

See also BUSINESS STRUCTURE: INDUSTRIAL POLICY; CAPITAL FORMATION; CAPITALISM; ECONOMIC CYCLES: MODELS AND SIMULATIONS; ECONOMICS; ENTREPRENEURSHIP; ETHICS; EVOLUTION, SOCIAL; FREE TRADE; GLOBAL CULTURE; GOVERNANCE; INFORMATION SOCIETY; INTERNATIONAL TRADE: REGIONAL TRADE AGREEMENTS; INVESTMENTS; MARKETPLACE; MORALS; MULTIFOLD TREND; POLITICAL CYCLES; POSTINFORMATION AGE; RACE, CASTE, AND ETHNIC DIVERSITY; SOCIAL AND POLITICAL EVOLUTION; TECHNOLOGICAL CHANGE; UTOPIAS; WORKFORCE REDISTRIBUTION.

BIBLIOGRAPHY

BONAR, JAMES. *Philosophy and Political Economy.* New Brunswick, NJ: Transaction Publishers, 1991.
DALEY, HERMAN E., and COBB, JOHN B., JR. *For the Common Good.* Boston: Beacon Press, 1991.
TINDER, GLEN. "Can We Be Good Without God?" *Atlantic Monthly* (December 1989).

Keith D. Wilde

Political Parties

The best way to examine the future of American political parties is to look at trends in the past. The history of political parties in America is filled with paradoxes. Parties are not mentioned at all in the Constitution; the framers never considered them as an essential or even as particularly desirable. But parties developed immediately as a basic organizing medium for the varying political approaches and philosophies that characterized politics in the late eighteenth century. The parties of the early Congresses faded and were replaced by others, but a party system, essentially based on two major parties vying for control of state and national governmental institutions and for the allegiance of voters, has existed continuously since the beginning of the republic.

If parties have a long history, their venerability is not widely appreciated in the mid-1990s. Few people outside the parties themselves have good words to say about the parties and the party system. Fewer voters identify with either of the two major parties than at any time in the past several decades, and those who do tend to have weaker allegiances than they did several years ago. The trend toward independence among voters has been growing for more than a decade and was underscored in November 1992 by the 19 percent voter support for the independent presidential candidacy of H. Ross Perot.

Voters in focus groups talk about voting for the man (or woman) and not for the party, and decry the partisanship that has characterized policy-making in Congress. But voters also like, by a two-to-one margin, divided government, which accentuates partisan differences, and their collective judgment in November 1994 further polarized the political parties in Congress on left/right and partisan lines. The 1994 election, if a vote against divisive partisanship, also had striking partisan dimensions; while Democrats suffered serious losses for the first time in modern American history not a single Republican incumbent member of the House or Senate, or among the governors, was defeated for reelection.

What do these realities portend for the future of political parties in America? First, parties and the two-party system will not wither away. They will still be with us, in a dominant way, for some time, at least as an organizing principle in Washington and state capitals around the country. But the role of the Democratic and Republican parties will be quite fluid; the opportunity for some kind of third force, if not an organized political party, to play a major role, will be greater; and the parties will remain diffuse and decentralized entities, even if they show occasional surprising unity and strength in individual institutions, such as occurred in the House of Representatives in 1995.

Parties and the Public

Social scientists have been measuring public opinion toward the parties systematically for more than fifty years, looking particularly at partisan affiliation or party identification. For much of that time—at least from the early 1950s through the late '70s—party identification was very stable. Roughly three-fourths of Americans identified clearly with one or the other of the two parties; only one-tenth of Americans were characterized as independents or were without any identification at all with a party. Through most of that time, the Democratic party had a clear edge over the Republicans, typically running roughly 47 to 37 percent or so.

As we moved to the early 1980s, the Reagan era, Republicans moved to a stronger position, but the stability in party identification declined, as did the strength and durability of party identification generally.

In the mid-1990s, the parties moved to a position of near equity in party identification, but with both parties weaker in terms of numbers and intensity than they had been in decades past. In the summer of 1994, a major national survey found that more than one-third of Americans (35 percent) called themselves independents, while 33 percent identified as Democrats and 29 percent as Republicans. By December 1994, after the stunning 1994 election, 35 percent identified as Republicans and only 30 percent as Democrats. The turnaround in the parties' fortunes is likely to be more a demonstration of the lack of stability in partisanship than a permanent shift in party positions.

What about the future? A look at party identification trends by age group gives us clues about the future of the parties. Start with the young. The Republican party squandered an advantage it held among young voters at the beginning of George Bush's presidency in 1989. Democrats, in turn, failed to win over the young people attracted as a consequence to Bill Clinton in 1992. As of mid-1994, neither party showed any advantage among Americans under thirty, or even among those aged thirty to forty-nine.

Older voters, those over fifty, show a strong preference for the Democrats based on their generational affinity with the New Deal and John F. Kennedy. It is possible, of course, that young voters will find events or political figures in the late 1990s or the early part of the twenty-first century that will solidify their own partisan feelings. Perhaps Newt Gingrich or another Republican figure, or Al Gore or some future Democratic leader, will capture the imaginations of young voters the way FDR or JFK did. But the lack of such enduring impact by Ronald Reagan would suggest it is more likely that neither party will establish a clear growth pattern or enduring advantage in the near future—and that independence will be at least on a par with partisanship. As the older generation dies out, however, Democrats will lose a major part of their partisan base and, in a fluid atmosphere, will be at a general competitive disadvantage vis-à-vis the GOP.

Looking at other groups in the electorate does show some more significant trends that have strong political implications in the future. Racial and gender differences in partisanship are clear. Blacks overwhelmingly identify as Democrats, while Republicans have a slight lead among whites (although more whites are independents than identifiers with either party). There are some signs of a slight movement among young black voters toward the GOP, but little that would suggest a real competition between the parties for allegiance of the African-American electorate. Republicans have an advantage among men, while Democrats have an edge among women, leaving about a 10 percentage-point "gender gap" between the parties that seems quite stable looking to the future.

Republicans have made significant gains in the past decade among several significant subgroups of voters—particularly among white Southerners, white evangelicals, and white non-Hispanic Catholics. These gains clearly made some difference in the ability of the GOP to win congressional seats in 1994 and to create serious problems for Democrats in finding a winning presidential electoral coalition into at least the early part of the twenty-first century. Even so, it would take striking political developments in the next several years for these GOP advantages to develop into a long-term Republican partisan majority in the country.

Parties in Government

If parties are weaker in the electorate, they are stronger in Congress. However, they are not stronger as national forces binding a presidential party together with a congressional party. In Congress, parties are stronger largely in the House of Representatives, not in the more individualized U.S. Senate.

In Congress, the 1994 elections ushered in the first Republican-majority House of Representatives in forty years, joining a Republican-majority Senate to make the first entirely Republican-majority Congress to face a Democratic president since 1947–48. The election of a Republican House was made possible in part by extraordinary party unity by the minority Republicans in the 103rd Congress in 1993–94. The Republicans seized on their opportunity to provide more formal powers to their new Speaker, Newt Gingrich, than any Speaker since Joseph Cannon, who served as Speaker from 1903 to 1911.

Democrats had more difficulty reaching the same levels of unity, but still showed stronger solidarity than in the past several decades, brought about more by greater philosophical coherence across regions than by formal rules or procedures. The party cohesion, more generally, meant a greater number of partisan divisions on key votes than were seen in the 1960s and '70s. The Democratic party in Congress has gradually become more liberal, as conservative Southern Democrats were replaced by moderates and liberals (including some blacks) and in many cases by Republicans. The Republican party in Congress has become more conservative, as it has built a new base in the South and West, while losing its old dominance in the Northeast. These trends, toward a more liberal Democratic party, based more in the East, Midwest, and Far West, and a more conservative Republican party anchored in the South, Midwest, and Rocky Mountain region, should solidify in the next decade or so. But, to reiterate, the growing ideological and partisan gulf inside Congress does not fit any comparable set of trends in the public arena. And despite the growth in independence in the electorate, only a single independent or third party representative has been elected to Congress in nearly two decades—one Socialist from Ver-

mont serves in the House—leaving party as the sole organizing element of the legislature for the foreseeable future, as it has been throughout the past.

Parties in Campaigns and Elections

The partisan unity in Congress is in a small way a reflection of more activity by national political parties to attract, recruit, and nominate candidates for the House and Senate. But most of the candidates who run for Congress are self-starters, who win nominations in primaries without the approval of local, state, or national parties, raise most of their money on their own, win on their own, and enter elective office as individual go-getters. That fact alone makes any strong degree of partisan unity in Congress quite striking. No reforms realistically on the horizon, from campaign finance changes to party reforms, are likely to change that situation more than marginally. Parties are likely, at the level of campaigns and elections, to remain organizationally weak. The structure of the election process and the continuing high level of voter identification with the two parties make it very difficult, despite the parties' structural weaknesses, for a third party or an independent movement to develop, take root, and succeed at the state or congressional level.

However, the situation may develop differently at the gubernatorial and even presidential level. Independent candidates for governor have had some success, winning in the early 1990s in Connecticut, Alaska, and Maine, and reaching respectable vote totals in many other states. H. Ross Perot's 19 percent of the popular vote for president in 1992 was the strongest showing nationwide for an independent in eight decades, and polls showed continuing strong support for individual, independent candidacies for president, reaching in some cases over one-third of the electorate for a popular and attractive possibility such as Colin Powell.

Conclusions

Parties in the mid-1990s continued to be the major paradox in American politics, simultaneously strong and weak, important and insignificant. Their fundamental position and roles had changed only marginally in the post–World War II era, and most evidence suggested that would continue to be the case into the early part of the twenty-first century. But the marginal changes, and dramatic elections in the post–Cold War era, suggest the possibility of more signal changes in the future. If the odds remained long, even so—more than at any time in modern American history—political, social, and economic conditions created a greater opening for an independent candidacy for president to succeed. If that were to happen, it clearly would have repercussions on parties in Congress and candidacies to Congress, and would make possible the institutionalization of a new party or at least an enduring independent movement. That is perhaps the most important trend to watch in the next decade and more.

See also COMMUNITARIANISM; CONSERVATISM, POLITICAL; LIBERALISM, POLITICAL; PLURALISM; POLITICAL CAMPAIGNING; POLITICAL CYCLES; POLITICAL PARTY REALIGNMENT; SOCIAL AND POLITICAL EVOLUTION; THIRD POLITICAL PARTIES; VOTING.

BIBLIOGRAPHY

BAUMGARTNER, FRANK R., and JONES, BRYAN D. *Agendas and Instability in American Politics.* Chicago and London: University of Chicago Press, 1993.

BROWN, PETER. *Restoring the Public Trust: A Fresh Vision for Progressive Government in America.* Boston: Beacon Press, 1994.

CRAIG, STEPHEN C. *The Malevolent Leaders: Popular Discontent in America.* Boulder, CO: Westview Press, 1993.

LYNCH, WILLIAM M. *The Nationalization of American Politics.* Berkeley, CA: University of California Press, 1987.

Norman J. Ornstein

Political Party Realignment

We have reached one of those great epochal divides when new ideological distinctions reflecting the new values and a new paradigm are being defined. On the political plane, this requires rethinking fundamental assumptions about individuals, institutions, policies, and programs. What exactly do political parties stand for?

This search involves examining the underlying paradigm shift, staking out political claims on new ideologies, and setting new political landmarks to guide popular thinking. It requires a rethinking of the major issues that reflect the tempo of the times and that resonate with the majority. Voter loyalties have reached a point requiring them to be forged anew under a program that entails essential changes in direction.

Some looming themes of political party realignment address the depressing social cacophony that casts a pall over the country. The despair of these times is linked to rotten urban cores, disadvantaged youth, a growing underclass, deterioration of family values, and a pervading moral malaise. It is undergirded by age-old cyclical themes: big government versus little government; centralization versus decentralization; financial and fiscal profligacy versus restraint; and an end to tax burdens on a weary public. The philosophical principle that permeates this restructuring involves changing values and lifestyles, and balancing rights and responsibilities. At the core of this reform and rebalancing are a host of viewpoints that interminably oscillate between support for the well-to-do and support for the down-and-out, and the overall swing between the liberal and conservative perspectives.

Arthur Schlesinger, Sr., noted swings that averaged 16.5 years between increasing democracy and containing or restricting it, between shifting emphasis from the rights of a few to concerns for the wrongs of the many. Arthur Schlesinger, Jr., noted changes in U.S. political cycles averaging thirty years' duration, and asserted that political party realignment occurred at intervals of forty years.

Carrying policies too far in one direction invites a counterforce. History is characterized by an ebb and flow between extremes of all kinds. The United States is in the midst of a long sweep of the political pendulum shifting from central control to restoring state and local government responsibilities. Too heavy a hand imposing regulatory burdens invites new efforts to minimize them. Trends in the next political cycle of leadership involve shifts from:

- Big government to limited government
- Centralization to decentralization
- Control to freedom of action
- Direct to indirect control
- Oppression to liberty
- Planning to laissez-faire
- Top-down to bottom-up
- Compulsion to voluntarism
- Universality to diversity
- Dependence to independence
- Security to venturesomeness/risk taking
- Paternalism to self-help
- Individualism to communitarianism
- Protectionism to freer trade
- Egalitarian leveling to extolling excellence
- Profligate to penurious spending
- Tax increases/complexity to tax reductions/simplification

The Molitor cyclic modeling of great issues reveals that different categories of issues move at different speeds and that over the past several centuries these ebbs and flows have greatly accelerated. Molitor's cyclic models based on year-by-year counts of federal laws covering an issue category reveal bursts of new developments in laws occurring in twenty- to twenty-six-year cycles in the United States. The Molitor model places commencement of the postindustrial-era political realignment in 1980, with a serious gathering of momentum in 1988, culminating in sharp cleavage between contesting major U.S. political parties by 2000, and then tapering off between 2010 and 2018 as a new cycle gets under way.

This process of political change and adaptation generally is expressed by two points of view: (1) conservative or tradition-bound; and (2) liberal or progressive. That is one way of looking at it. Recent political history involves a continual abandonment of the status quo, a constant process of adjustment to change, and—hopefully—a steadily advancing or progressive trend. Political policy perspectives respond to change, moving along over time in a progressive mode.

U.S. history reveals an incremental progression and eventual nearly universal acceptance of liberal causes. Slowly, the nation has inched forward. Liberalism's main defining point or difference with conservatives since the New Deal has been essentially its emphasis on the welfare state. Now that liberalism has attained most of its coveted objectives, and they have become so familiar a part of the contemporary social fabric, there is little dispute over their merit. Relatively indistinguishable and undistinguished tweedledee and tweedledum positions on New Deal programs have become ingrained and no longer generate fierce debate as they once did. No longer do voters cast ballots on pro or con viewpoints involving the welfare state. Attention has shifted to other less familiar and more controversial areas.

Until the recent and resounding defeat of full-fledged socialized medicine, conservatives by and large had gone along (albeit grudgingly) with most of these paternalistic programs. But a new mood is stirring. Even the incumbent Democrat president favors reform of "welfare as we know it"—whatever that might mean. Conservatives have their own and, doubtless, more drastic version of welfare reform and advocate returning responsibility for the pottage of welfare programs back to the states. Overindulging the needy—even though sparked by a humanitarian compassion—cannot completely ignore human nature. When recipients become overly dependent and give up on helping themselves, they are more in need of a hand up than a handout. New battle lines are being drawn.

Demographically, as the elderly cohort swells, so does its political power. Political survival requires addressing health care delivery questions. When 34 to 37 percent of the public are uninsured, the issue can hardly be ignored.

Society undergoes recurring pendulumlike swings from one extreme to the other but seldom reverts to the old status quo (regression contradistinguished from progression). A good metaphor characterizing this change is that of a spiral or, better yet, a helix. The pattern is ever onward, a lifting or raising and advance.

Political policy-making in the United States is essentially confined to the two major political parties. Discernible ideological division between them has become muddled. Both political parties are searching for principles defining what they stand for and offering voters clear-cut and decisively different choices. To attract and retain voters, political parties rise and fall based on the policies and programs with which they are identified.

Meantime, both political parties scramble to hold the middle ground and try to do all things for all persons. Pandering to the amorphous middle ground lessens voter attachment to either party. When both parties stand for and occupy the common middle ground, distinctions congeal and get lost. As a result, voting hinges more on superficial aspects of the political process—personalities, campaign styles, and political "spin."

For almost a half century, U.S. government power has been divided, with Congress controlled by one party and the executive branch by the other. This state of affairs led to a virtual stalemate in a patchquilt of consensus politics that blurred distinctions between the parties. This expedient pattern, at least until the 1994 elections, stymied bold departures in ideology. Gridlocked government, with neither party able to take bold and aggressive action or reform, hobbled sweeping policy changes. Compromise—the essence of recent federal decision making—has added to voter apathy. A steady drumbeat of federal scandals, rampant pork-barrel politics, and the sophistry of national politicians have created a wave of cynicism that has dragged down voter turnout to all-time lows.

Third political parties, splinter parties, and political opportunists chime in. Their good ideas invariably get taken over by a major party. In this sense they serve a vital purpose in helping to shape, but not dominate, the new political agenda.

Confounding political change is the growing ethnicity and diversity of the population. Coupled with the growth of superzealotry—religious, ethnic, single-purpose interest groups, and so on—the discordant sway of proliferating special-interest groups has the cauldron seething. When so many diverse groups fight for individual or group advantage and their "piece of the action," the commonweal suffers. By selfishly seeking their own aims and transgressing the broader social interest, these special interests add new urgency to political agenda setting. This restatement of principles requires moderating self-interest and deferring to the broader social interest.

Central to political party realignment is the age-old question involving the best balance between individual rights and social responsibilities. These touchstones are at one of those great historic divides. In the spirit of pursuing freedom to buttress a truly democratic society, things currently have gotten out of hand. Overly zealous pursuit of individual rights is bound to interfere with somebody else's rights. Total wanton and self-centered freedom creates anarchy. Freedom left to run its full course—untrammeled freedom, extremist individualism, liberty carried to ultimate limits—can lead to tyranny. Liberty does not include unlimited license. Self-restraint is essential. Individual extremism is well suited to a single person like Robinson Crusoe living alone on a deserted island. Living in society requires accommodating and acceding to the rights of others as well. Utilitarianism—the greatest good for the greatest number—is the mediating principle. Rights must include responsibilities in a well ordered society.

At this juncture, a swing back toward communitarian values—more identified with Republicans at this point—seems to be in prospect. Willpower, self-determination, individual responsibility, self-control, social restraint, a sense of community duty, and taking responsibility for one's acts are the touchstones that grip this ongoing debate. This approach will redress the balance by emphasizing old-fashioned self-discipline and insisting on individuals taking responsibility for their own volitional acts and not seeking refuge in some excuse.

Laws are made by legislators and may be changed by them. Slavery, once the law of the land, has long since been outlawed. Dueling, once the accepted way of resolving personal disputes, has been outlawed. One of the most difficult and contentious aspects of political party reform involves rhetoric that casts privileges into rights and rights into "untouchable" entitlements. Taking without giving entails a certain self-centered, egoistic, and self-indulgent cant. Privileges must be earned. It is wrong to make demands on but not contributions to the commonweal. Society has obligations to its citizens, just as citizens have obligations to society. It is a two-way street. Providing excuses for less fortunate persons tends to eliminate incentives to step up and seek improvement. Providing aid that enables the poor to stay where they are and fatalistically resign themselves to the "hand that has been dealt them" is wrong. The time may have arrived to encourage those on welfare to do more to help themselves. The ultimate truth may be that we must expect—or even demand—from everyone the same standards of behavior we expect from one another.

The new political agenda requires a fresh vision to guide the nation along innovative paths of development. We need a better fix on where we are headed—and why. In short, we need an agenda spelling out specific goals infused with a renewed sense of national purpose and direction. Sociopolitical change, however obscure its overall design may appear to be, is neither random nor aimless. Although precise details cannot be discerned, the basic shape of things to come looms on the horizon. You cannot navigate the ship of state by staring at the wake behind the ship. We need to muster the courage and invoke the foresight of a lookout. We need to look ahead and gather information to steer us forward.

Our comprehension of domestic political trends, however imperfect it may be, must be improved. Surmising the future by mere intuition, impulse, or opinion is insufficient. Convincing proof in the form of systematic, comprehensive, accurate, and timely forecasts of public policy goals is needed. Political parties, in this sense, carry a vital, yet unfilled function. New policy directions more accurately reflecting the changed tempo of the times and the pervasive influence of the information era offer an inchoate and essentially unfulfilled opportunity.

See also AGENTS OF CHANGE; COMMUNITARIANISM; CONSERVATISM, POLITICAL; CRIME RATES; ENTITLEMENTS; HEALTH CARE COSTS; INSTITUTIONS, CONFIDENCE IN; LIBERALISM, POLITICAL; MULTIFOLD TRENDS; PLURALISM; POLITICAL CYCLES; POLITICAL PARTIES; PUBLIC POLICY CHANGE; SOCIAL AND POLITICAL EVOLUTION; SWEDEN; THIRD POLITICAL PARTIES; VOTING.

BIBLIOGRAPHY

BENNETT, WILLIAM J. *The Index of Leading Cultural Indicators: Facts and Figures on the State of American Society.* New York: Simon & Schuster/Touchstone, 1994.

ETZIONI, AMITAI. *The Spirit of Community: Rights, Responsibilities, and the Communitarian Agenda.* New York: Crown, 1993.

GINGRICH, NEWT, with DAVID DRAKE and MARIANNE GINGRICH. *Window of Opportunity: A Blueprint for the Future.* New York: Tom Doherty Associates/Baen Enterprises, 1984.

HUGHES, ROBERT. *Culture of Complaint: The Fraying of America.* New York: Oxford University Press, 1993.

MEAD, LAWRENCE M. *Beyond Entitlement: The Social Obligations of Citizenship.* New York: Free Press, 1986.

PHILLIPS, KEVIN. *Boiling Point: Democrats, Republicans, and the Decline of Middle-Class Prosperity.* New York: Harper Perennial, 1993.

Graham T. T. Molitor

Polls, Opinion.

See PUBLIC OPINION; SURVEYS.

Popularized Futures

Fascination with the future is one of the defining characteristics of the human race. It is a fascination that is born of a mixture of curiosity and dread. The urge to step beyond the thin, moving line that divides the present from the future and to part the curtains that divide the known from the unknown is inescapable.

Martin Heidegger is not generally acknowledged as a futurist, but his *Sein und Zeit* was a seminal work that explored the roots of the human concern with the future. *Dasein*, the existence into which humans are "thrown," as objects are thrown into a river, is not a state but a flow. It is a condition characterized by anxiety about and awareness of the future, as containing both the necessity and the choice of death.

Time is an arrow, and human existence is conditioned by the fact that the arrow is unidirectional and irreversible. The opposite of the future is not the past. The anguish of becoming, the dread of the disorderliness and chaos of change, makes the future a subject of interest not merely to the specialist and the intellectual, but to everyone alive.

The earliest popularized futures were religious or quasi-religious. The mantic, or prophetic, arts, which combined religion, magic, and the quest for the future, included divination, astrology, and palmistry. Roget records some sixty-nine forms of divination, including cartomancy (playing cards), pyromancy (fire), sortilege (lots), oneiromancy (dreams), lithomancy (stones), onychomancy (fingernails), geomancy (earth), hydromancy (water), and necromancy (dead bodies). In China, the I Ching was developed along with tarot cards and other esoteric means of appraising the future. Augury was the art of scanning the future by interpreting omens, especially through the study of the flight of birds, the appearance of the internal organs of sacrificed animals, and the occasion of thunder and lightning. Haruspicy involved the study of the liver for the same purpose. (The haruspices, an order of minor priests charged with this function in ancient Rome, may be considered the first group of professional futurists.) Astrology is the oldest art of predicting the future; it originated in Mesopotamia in 3000 B.C. It is also the most widespread, being found in every culture; even today it is consulted by over one billion people worldwide. Astrology is based on the belief that the stars, as Shakespeare said, govern our destinies (*King Lear*, IV, iii, 34).

The vatic (divination) arts were practiced by oracles, sibyls, and prophets. In Greece, the pythoness, a priestess of Apollo at Delphi, commonly known as the Delphic Oracle, was a national institution. Other major Greek oracles were those of Zeus at Dodona in Epirus and of Trophonius in Boeotia. The principal Egyptian oracles were at Apis and Memphis. There were also seers, such as Tiresias the blind Theban, familiar to readers of T. S. Eliot. In Hebrew culture, the tradition of prophet (literally "foreteller") was highly developed. As oracles of God, prophets enjoyed a standing almost equal to that of kings. Isaiah, the greatest of the Hebrew prophets, combined fulminations and prophecies in cadenced prose. The tradition of prophecy was preserved in the Christian church. In the stark majesty of its language, the Apocalypse of John, known also as Revelation, has no peer. Its influence is attested by the fact that over 7,000 commentaries have been written on it in more than 50 languages. One of them, *The Late Great Planet Earth* by Hal Lindsey, is the best-selling futures book in the twentieth century.

In the Middle Ages, the mantic arts and the vatic arts went underground, but one late mediaeval name stands out, that of NOSTRADAMUS. A physician by profession, and perhaps a charlatan to boot, Nostradamus has become a synonym for a forecaster. His fame rests on his book *The Centuries*, a collection of rhymed quatrains published in 1555. Many of his supposed predictions are almost Delphic in their obscurity and could be interpreted to mean almost anything.

It was only in the late twentieth century that interest in a scientific or rational—as distinguished from a personal—future became widespread. H. G. WELLS, whom W. Warren Wagar calls the father of futurism, is said to have founded the field in 1902 with his book *The Discovery of the Future*, followed in 1933 by *The Shape of Things to Come*. The future was viewed as a foreign country, an unknown timescape, that needed a few explorers to map its terrain.

A new wave of trail-blazing futurists emerged after World War II. They were responsible for shaping futurism as a profession and as an intellectual niche. (The words *futurism* and *futurist* are used here for want of a better word. There are many, like Michael Marien, who insist with good reason that futurism is neither an *-ism*, nor a science.) Futurism may be said to have come of age in the 1960s with the founding of organizations like the Club of Rome (1968), the World Future Society (1966), and Futuribles International (1960). As happens to all vigorous movements, futurism began to undergo a process known as twigging: first the trunk, then the branches, and then the twigs. One branch, led by intellectuals, like Daniel BELL, concentrated on the task of laying downthe philosophical groundwork while exploringthe frontiers. A second group, mostly business-oriented futurists, like Herman KAHN and Joseph Coates, wrote massive reports in seamless futurese. Another group turned to writing and publishing, still others to policy studies and computer modelling. "Macfuturists" also emerged by the score, popularizing a Chinese-cookie style of forecasting. They are adept at producing small nuggets of wisdom that at first seem unassailable buton closer examination prove to be of the maybe/maybe-not variety.

Popularized futures form only a twig, a small but vital part of the whole body of futurism. Pop future books are the stuff of bestsellers, the proof being John Naisbitt's *Megatrends* (1990); Alvin and Heidi Toffler's many books, including *Future Shock* (1970), *The Third Wave* (1980), and *Powershift* (1990); Frank Feather's *G Forces: Reinventing the World* (1989); Richard Carlson and Bruce Goldman's *20/20 Vision: Long View of a Changing World* (1990, 1994); Norman Myers's *The Gaia Atlas of a Changing World* (1990); and Marvin Cetron's *Crystal Globe* (1991).

Also popular are descriptions of the future, a genre in which I. F. Clarke's *Tales of the Future* lists 3,300 titles published between 1644 and 1976. The most notable among them are W. Warren Wagar's *A Short History of the Future* (1989); Alberto Villoldo's *Millennium: Glimpses into the 21st Century* (1981);

Norman Macrae's *The 2025 Report: A Concise History of the Future* (1984); Brian M. Stableford and David Langford's *The Third Millennium: A History of the World, 2000 3000* (1985); Arthur C. Clarke's *July 20, 2019: Life in the 21st Century* (1986); and Adrian Berry's *The Next 10,000 Years* (1974).

New Age futurism is represented by Marilyn Ferguson's *The Aquarian Conspiracy* (1980); Willis Harman's *The Global Mind Change* (1988); Fritjof Capra's *The Turning Point* (1982); and Mary E. Clarke's *Ariadne's Thread: The Search for New Modes of Thinking* (1989).

Panoptic futurism or global surveys abound. The best are the annual Worldwatch *State of the World Report*; the UN's *Global Outlook 2000* (1990); *Our Common Future* by the World Commission on Environment and Development (1987); and UNESCO's *World by the Year 2000*.

Panglossian futurism is exemplified by Herman Kahn's writings; Gerard K. O'Neill's *A Hopeful View of the Human Future* (1981); and Julian Simon's *The Resourceful Earth* (1983). The opposite, Cassandra futurism, has an even broader audience. In his *Terminal Visions: The Literature of Last Things* (1982), W. Warren Wagar lists 300 titles on doom, none more frightening than Jerome Deshusses' *The Eighth Night of Creation* (1982). Gee-whiz futurism, in which only technology matters, is represented by Morris Abrams and Harriet Bernstein's *Future Stuff* (1991), and eco-futurism by Al Gore's *Earth in the Balance: Ecology and the Human Spirit* (1992).

See also FORECASTING METHODS; FUTURE STUDIES; FUTURES CONCEPTS; FUTURISM; FUTURISTS; SCIENCE FICTION.

BIBLIOGRAPHY

HOWE, LEO, and WAIN, ALAN. *Predicting the Future.* New York: Cambridge University Press, 1993.
WAGAR, W. WARREN. *A Short History of the Future.* Chicago: University of Chicago Press, 1989.

George Thomas Kurian

Popular Music.

See MUSIC.

Population Growth: United States

Demographers define the "baby-boom generation" as Americans born from 1946 through 1964. During those nineteen years, 76 million people were born. Given the family-size norms of the time, this was about 17 million more people than demographers expected.

In the years immediately following World War II, births in the United States rose sharply because many Americans delayed marrying and having children until the end of the war. When the soldiers came home, marriage rates rose. Soon after, maternity wards began to fill with babies. Technically, the first baby boomers were born in June 1946, about nine months after soldiers began to return from Europe. For convenience, however, demographers include anyone born during 1946 in the "official" definition of the baby-boom generation.

By the end of 1946, American women were having 100,000 more babies each month than during the same month one year earlier. Overall, 3.4 million babies were born in 1946. In 1947, 3.8 million babies were born, fully 1 million more than in 1945.

Much to the surprise of demographers, the baby boom did not stop there. For the next seventeen years, births remained at record levels, peaking in the late 1950s. More than 4 million babies were born each year from 1954 through 1964. The birth boom lasted for nearly two decades because the young women of the 1950s chose to have larger families than their mothers did, an average of three or four children each. They gave birth to the largest generation in American history.

During the nearly two decades of record-level births, demographers began to predict that the birth boom would never end. They contended that larger families were the new American lifestyle. But the baby boom did come to an end nineteen years after it began. In 1965, births plummeted, women joined the workforce, and the baby-boom generation was complete.

The smaller generation that followed the baby boom, born from 1965 through 1976, is sometimes called the "baby-bust generation" because of the sharp drop in births during those years. In the 1960s and '70s, the fertility of American women fell dramatically, to an average of only 1.7 children per woman.

This decline in fertility to negative replacement rates surprised many. Demographers had been predicting another birth boom as the enormous baby-boom generation had children. Instead, baby-boom women went to college and embarked on careers, delaying marriage and childbearing.

In the late 1970s, the annual number of births slowly began to rise as the long-awaited "echo boom" finally appeared. Birth edged up from a low of 3.1 million in 1973 to 3.6 million in 1980. By the late 1980s, births were reaching levels not seen since the early 1960s and fertility rates were rising as well. The average number of children per woman rose to 2.1, reaching replacement level. Because of this surge in fertility, coupled with a large influx of immigrants during the 1980s, the Census Bureau projects that the American population will grow substantially during the next fifty years. The bureau's "most likely" scenario shows the total population climbing by more than 100 million over the next five decades, from 260 million in 1994 to 392 million in 2050.

Today, the baby-boom generation is a huge bulge in the American population. There are now 77 million baby boomers in the United States. This number is slightly greater than the 76 million born during the baby-boom years because immigrants of baby-boom age have arrived in the United States and raised the numbers. Baby boomers account for 29 percent of all Americans and for 42 percent of Americans aged eighteen or older. Because so many Americans crowd a nineteen-year age span, popular culture reflects and magnifies their experiences. Today the baby boom is a powerful economic and political force. It will remain so over the next thirty years.

Because baby boomers dominate the demographic landscape, they are a prime target for businesses and a mass audience for the entertainment industry. Consequently, American culture responds to their needs. When baby boomers needed schools, their communities built schools. More elementary schools were built in 1957 than in any other year before or since. Ten years later, in 1967, more colleges opened than in any year before or since. Consequently, baby boomers had the best access to education of any generation in American history. More than one-half have some college experience and one-fourth earned college degrees. When baby boomers needed cars, businesses built or imported small and inexpensive cars just for them. When baby boomers needed houses in the 1970s, housing starts rose to record levels. When baby boomers needed jobs, jobs were created by the millions.

The consequences of population growth are profound. As baby boomers joined the workforce and earned a paycheck in the 1970s, businesses saw opportunity in the numbers. There were profits to be made in giving millions of young people what they wanted. In the competition for this huge market, businesses offered baby boomers a growing variety of products and services. With so much choice available to them, baby boomers became increasingly diverse and individualistic. As baby boomers came of age, individualism became the dominant social and economic force in American society. The individualistic nature of the baby-boom generation has been transforming the United States for the past thirty years. Sociologists define individualism as the tendency to withdraw from social institutions and groups—including families, local communities, political parties, churches, and the nation. Individualists put their personal needs ahead of community needs. They make commitments for personal gain rather than for moral reasons. As individualistic baby boomers came of age over the past thirty years, voting rates fell, a rising proportion of Americans withdrew from organized religion, divorce became acceptable, materialism gained importance, and leisure was preferred to work.

The rise of individualism is the "master trend" of our time. This master trend drives a myriad of smaller trends. Individualism is behind the rise in divorce and in violent crime. It is one reason behind soaring health care costs, political gridlock, and racial tensions. It is eroding the loyalty of workers toward their employers. It is driving the accelerating pace of daily life. Individualism shapes the worldview of baby boomers and younger generations of Americans. The perspectives of these generations will shape the future of the United States.

By 2004 all baby boomers will be middle-aged. The number of people in mid-life, stretching roughly from ages thirty-five to fifty-four, will grow four times faster than the population as a whole during the 1990s. The rapid expansion of the number of people in their forties has already moved middle-aged concerns to the top of the national agenda. These concerns include family issues, health care, tax rates, crime prevention, and education. These issues will command the attention of voters and politicians well into the next century.

Middle-aged baby boomers are prominent now in politics. The first baby boomer was elected president in 1992. Baby boomers are likely to control the White House for most of the next thirty years. The baby-boom generation is becoming an important force in Congress. In the business world, few baby boomers head the nation's largest corporations today. But in ten years, most of the CEOs of the largest companies will be members of the baby-boom generation.

Baby boomers are also gaining economic power. People aged thirty-five to fifty-four spend more money than any other age group. With the baby boom increasing the number of thirty-five- to fifty-four-year-olds during the next few decades, the middle-aged will account for well over one-half of all consumer spending. They will dominate markets for nearly every category of goods and services, from shoes to insurance.

Not until boomers begin to fade from the demographic landscape, in about thirty years, will their influence begin to wane. But because younger generations (the children of the baby boom) are even more individualistic than boomers themselves, the social transformations caused by the baby-boom generation represent only the beginning of a new way of life. The individualistic perspectives of the baby-boom and younger generations of Americans are transforming the slow-moving and bureaucratic industrial economy of the mid-twentieth century into the fast-paced and diverse personalized economy of the twenty-first century.

The world of the baby-boom echo will be different. The baby boomers were born into families with large numbers of children where the mother was a homemaker. The echo babies are small numbers of children born to large numbers of families where the mother most likely works and where both parents are older, better off economically, and more mature. These changes will create a different echo generation as it matures.

Population growth also comes about from declining death rates and from immigration. Death rates are remarkably stable or slowly falling. Immigration is the big indeterminate factor in the nation's growth, in spite of the census bureau forecast.

See also AGING OF THE POPULATION; LONGEVITY; MIGRATION, INTERNATIONAL; POPULATION GROWTH: WORLDWIDE; UNITED STATES.

BIBLIOGRAPHY

RUSSELL, CHERYL. *The Master Trend: How the Baby Boom Generation Is Remaking America.* New York: Plenum, 1993.

Cheryl Russell

Population Growth: Worldwide

During the 1990s, world population will grow to a greater extent than at any previous time in history. Although the growth rate declined somewhat from the late 1960s peak (from 2.0 percent per year to 1.7 percent in the early 1990s), the number of people added has risen. This is due to the much larger base population, 5.5 billion, compared to 1965's 3.3 billion.

Population Growth: Worldwide

Long-range population projections from both the United Nations (UN) and the World Bank suggest a future world population about twice the present size. These projections assume, however, that birthrate declines occurring in many developing countries will continue. If this does not happen, total world population would not stop at the "medium" projection of about 12 billion. It could easily rise to 20 or 30 billion, or even more. It is important to note that nearly all of the future world population growth will occur in the developing countries, which already account for three-fourths of the world total.

The past fifteen years have seen rapid growth in world demographic information. Nearly every country has taken a census and the data from most are usable. Notable exceptions are Chad, Nigeria, and Saudi Arabia. Additional invaluable sources include many fertility surveys taken in Third World countries since the World Fertility Survey program began in the mid-1970s. This program, which continues today as the Demographic and Health Survey, provided a first look at actual birthrate trends in developing countries that lack vital statistics.

The most recent (1992) UN long-range projections anticipate a world population approaching 11.5 billion by the end of the next century. These projections will result in a constant world population size at some point in the future. This occurs because it is assumed that women will average two children each, meaning that each generation just replaces itself.

But projections are subject to a great deal of variation, depending on just how good the assumptions underlying them prove to be. For example, if women worldwide average not 2 but 2.5 children, world population would grow to 28 billion—not 11.5 as in the projection noted previously. This is a huge difference. Likewise, if women averaged fewer than two children each—say, 1.7—world population would be decreasing at the end of the next century, to a point less than today's total.

In the industrialized countries, birthrates have dropped so low that many of these nations—without augmenting growth by other means, such as immigration—face the prospect of population decline. A key indicator here is the total fertility rate (TFR), or the average number of children women bear during their lifetimes. If this average drops below 2.0 over a protracted period, population decrease is inevitable.

In Europe, women average only about 1.6 children each. Surprisingly, Italy's birthrate is now the world's lowest. At only 1.26 children per woman on average, it is also the lowest ever recorded. Popula-

tion projections issued by many European countries now routinely forecast population decline. The importance of the birthrate is also somewhat magnified since few European countries accept, much less welcome, many immigrants.

In the United States, fertility near the "two-child" level and continued significant immigration will, in all likelihood, result in relatively brisk population growth well into the next century. The United States gains nearly one million new legal residents a year by immigration, the highest number in the world. The most recent U.S. Census Bureau projections show that, at present levels of fertility and immigration, the population will rise from 260 million in 1994 to more than 380 million by 2050.

The greatest potential for population growth, of course, is in the developing countries. Since World War II, advances in health care have led to longer life expectancy and, as a result, lower death rates. Many developing countries found themselves with growth rates rising to 3 or 4 percent per year. Growth rates of that magnitude will double a population in only twenty years. Recognition of this record-setting growth fostered expressions such as the "population explosion."

Concern about the effects of rapid population growth led to considerable concern that the world's ability to provide sufficient food would be overburdened and Earth's ecological systems overwhelmed. Those concerns remain, but in the early 1990s, it should be noted that the spread of family planning in the Third World is making a real difference.

Family planning programs got under way in the 1960s and accelerated in the 1970s, although the number of countries involved was not large at first. There were notable success stories— Thailand, Indonesia, Taiwan, Colombia, Mexico, and Costa Rica among them. In most countries of the Third World, women averaged five or six children each during their lifetimes. Throughout Africa and the Middle East, families often average six or more children.

In many developing countries the desire for large numbers of children was, and often still is, steeped in social tradition as well as in the perceived need for security in old age that large families can provide. Higher birthrates are nearly always associated with the proportion of the population living in rural areas and engaged in agriculture. Birthrates often decrease as societies become more and more urban. But in areas such as sub-Saharan Africa, 80 percent of the population lives in the rural regions.

During the 1970s, the governments of many developing countries resisted the idea of promoting family planning. This resistance crystallized at the 1974

World Population Conference in Bucharest, Romania. Saying that "development is the best contraceptive," Third World leaders argued that birthrates would come down as a natural result of economic development, not because contraception was forced upon an often uninterested populace. Ten years later, at a similar conference in Mexico City, the situation had changed dramatically. By that time, most developing countries had adopted official policies contending with birthrates that were too high.

In Asia, the one-child policy promulgated in China often captured headlines. With over one billion people, China's numbers weigh heavily in world totals. The Chinese government recognized that the finite limits of China's arable land and other resources dictated that the country's population not be allowed to rise into the many billions. China's policy has been fraught with controversy; the rather strict programs of incentives and disincentives would probably not be appropriate or possible elsewhere. But most of the program's goals were achieved. By the early 1990s, Chinese women were averaging only about 2.2 children each, down from 5 in the 1960s.

Eastern Asia provides the most dramatic examples of sharply decreased birthrates. Innovative family planning programs have caused fertility to tumble to low levels in Thailand. Economic progress, augmented by well-organized family planning programs, are often credited with similar outcomes in Taiwan and South Korea. In South Korea, the total fertility rate is an astoundingly low 1.6 children per woman, exactly the same as Europe. In Japan, Asia's only "developed" country by the UN's classification, very low fertility is causing concern. A recent Japanese newspaper headlined "1.57 Shock" to draw attention to a story on Japan's total fertility rate dropping to that level. In Japan, the very low birthrate, it is feared, will lead to labor force shortages, already a reality, and a country topheavy with the aged. In addition, an aging labor force is expensive in Japan, since salary rates are directly tied to seniority.

In South Asia, change has come more slowly. India's population program experienced some early success, but ran into political difficulties in the late 1970s, when some aspects of it were considered overzealous. As a result, India's TFR has been about 4.0 for over a decade. In Bangladesh, a long period of high fertility that has resisted family planning efforts came to an end in the late 1980s. Although still relatively high at a TFR of about 4.9 children per woman, this represents quite a drop from 7 children per woman in the past. Unfortunately, it is likely that simple overcrowding and the lack of additional land that forced many to seek opportunities in the city partially motivated the decrease.

In other areas of Asia, there are as many stories as there are countries. In Pakistan, with a population numbering about 125 million, there has been no sign of any decrease at all. In the Philippines, the momentum has gone out of the family planning program, in part due to lack of interest by President Corazon Aquino and her successor Fidel Ramos. In Vietnam, the world's thirteenth most densely populated country, a vigorous government policy seems to be working to bring down birthrates, at least for now.

Latin America has no truly dramatic example such as China or South Korea, but birthrates are surprisingly low nonetheless. Latin America's overall TFR of 3.4 is lower than that of Asia (excluding China). Religious considerations often discourage official government policies, leaving much of the management of family planning programs to private organizations.

In Brazil, Latin America's largest country in population at 151 million, the TFR has now dropped to about 3.1. In the region, only two countries have TFRs of 5.0 or higher, Guatemala and Nicaragua. Mexico enthusiastically adopted a population program in 1974 after earlier equating population growth with prosperity. The Mexican program has featured a wide variety of novel approaches such as soap operas featuring family planning and pop songs that appeal to young adults and adolescents.

It is in Africa that the least progress has been made. Today, in sub-Saharan Africa, it is typical for women to average six or seven children. In addition, life expectancy is still quite low. As a consequence, there is great potential for very high rates of growth if death rates fall but birthrates do not.

Family planning is a new idea in many parts of Africa. There are no success stories on that continent as yet. Still, the 1980s witnessed a virtual explosion of interest. While family planning use rates are low or nonexistent in most countries of Africa, in countries such as Botswana, Zimbabwe, and Kenya, rising usage rates show that real potential does exist.

Success in lowering birthrates often leads to concerns about an aging labor force, a stagnant domestic market, the expense of old-age health care, and strains on retirement systems.

For the most part, countries rarely adopt official "pronatalist" attitudes, despite concerns that may be raised unofficially or in the press about the consequences of population decline. Still, Sweden has recently attracted attention with a striking increase in its TFR to 2.1 in 1990, up from a low of 1.6. Many feel that Sweden's generous salary support for new mothers has played a significant role. In Asia, South Korea, with very low fertility, now feels that direct support of family planning is no longer needed. Singapore also toned down its policy when fertility sank to 1.8 children per woman. Even in China, it is thought that concerns about a rapidly aging population may have caused a mid-1980s relaxation of the pressure to have only one child.

Today, we can only speculate on the world's demographic future: eleven billion? six billion? thirty billion? Any of these futures is possible. Such a wide variation in possibilities causes obvious concern for food production, the environment, and all other supportive resources, which could suffer greatly if growth occurred too quickly to be accommodated. We know that the 1990s will be the most expansive decade for world population growth in recorded history. What we cannot know is whether it will prove to be the fastest of all time.

The ultimate question is whether population growth will stop before we exceed the ability to feed, house, and cloth everyone. If it does not stop, disease, war, and natural disasters will settle the matter, resulting in a monstrously rapid population decline.

See also CHANGE, OPTIMISTIC AND PESSIMISTIC PERSPECTIVES; DEMOGRAPHY; ENVIRONMENTAL REFUGEES; FAMILY PLANNING; GLOBAL CONSCIOUSNESS; GLOBAL ENVIRONMENTAL PROBLEMS; LIFESTYLES, ALTERNATIVE; MIGRATION, INTERNATIONAL; POPULATION GROWTH: UNITED STATES; REFUGEES; SEXUAL REPRODUCTION; SEXUAL REPRODUCTION: ARTIFICIAL MEANS; SURPRISES; SUSTAINABILITY; WILDCARDS.

BIBLIOGRAPHY

BULATAO, RUDOLFO A. *World Population Projections: Short- and Long-Term Estimates.* Baltimore: Johns Hopkins University Press, 1990.

DAVIS, KINGSLEY, and BERNSTEIN, MIKHAIL S. *Resources, Environment, and Population: Present Knowledge and Future Options.* New York: Oxford University Press, 1991.

EHRLICH, PAUL R., and EHRLICH, ANNE H. *The Population Explosion.* Simon & Schuster, 1990.

KEYFITZ, NATHAN, and FLIEGER, WILHELM. *World Population Growth and Aging: Demographic Trends in the Late 20th Century.* Chicago: University of Chicago Press, 1991.

LAPPE, FRANCES MOORE, and SCHURMAN, RACHEL. *Taking Population Seriously: The Missing Piece in the Population Puzzle.* London: Earthscan, 1989.

MARDEN, PARKER G. *Population in the Global Arena: Actors, Values, Policies, and Futures.* Durham, NC: Duke University Press, 1982.

MARKS, ELI S. *Population Growth Estimation: A Handbook of Vital Statistics Measurement.* Washington, DC: Population Council, 1974.

NEWMAN, JAMES L. and MATZKE, GORDEN E. *Population Patterns, Dynamics, and Prospects.* New York: Prentice-Hall, 1984.

SALVATORE, DOMINICK. *World Population Trends and their Impact on Economic Development.* Westport, CT: Greenwood Press, 1988.

United Nations Population Fund. *State of the World's Population.* New York: United Nations, 1994.

VILLE, CLAUDE A., JR. *Fallout from the Population Explosion.* New York: Paragon House, 1986.

Carl Haub
Steven Gurley

Postal Services

By the year 2000, the U.S. Postal Service (USPS) will be delivering over 200 billion pieces of mail, about 750 pieces per person. Approximately half will be first-class letters and cards, and another 40 percent will be third-class bulk mail consisting largely of advertising and nonprofit solicitations. The remainder will be a mix of express mail, second-class publications, fourth-class parcels, and international mail.

Since 1900, the total volume of mail has grown more rapidly than the nation's real GNP and much more rapidly than its population. This persistent growth tendency is the most conspicuous long-term feature of volume trends (see Figure 1). However, mail volumes are also affected by business conditions, service offerings, competition, demographic trends, the quality of postal services, and postal rates including discounts.

The mail stream is primarily generated by the requirements of commerce. Only 7.5 percent of first-class mail is correspondence between households. Almost everything else involves a nonhousehold, either as a sender or recipient. For example, most of third-class bulk rate regular mail is direct mail advertising from businesses to households. Expenditures for direct mail are an increasing share of total advertising expenditures.

Recent studies have shown that most types of mail are relatively insensitive to increases in rates. A 1 percent increase in the rate for most mail will decrease the volume by much less than 1 percent. For example, a 1 percent increase in the rate for first-class letters will cause that volume to decrease by only about 0.2 percent.

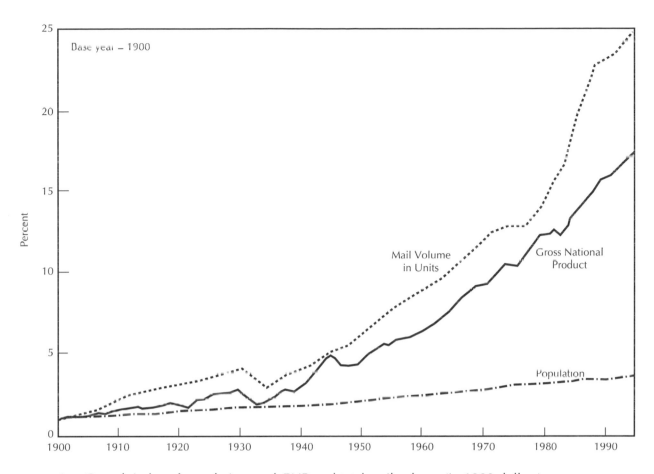

25

Base year = 1900

20

15

Percent

10

Mail Volume
in Units

Gross National
Product

5

Population

0

1900   1910   1920   1930   1940   1950   1960   1970   1980   1990

FIGURE 1.   Growth index of population, real GNP, and total mail volume (in 1982 dollars). (Source: DRI/McGraw-Hill.)

Today's large volume of mail is the result of a sustained period of growth beginning around 1977. Total mail volume approximately doubled between 1977 and 1994, from about 85 billion annually to 178 billion. Some of this growth can be attributed to the social shift that increased the proportion of women in the workforce and stimulated shopping by mail. Also, during this period the USPS introduced and enlarged discounts for work sharing. At the same time, data processing technology improved in ways that enhanced the effectiveness of direct mail. It reduced the costs of preparing mailings and made work sharing economically attractive to most bulk mailers.

Work sharing occurs when mailers perform for themselves tasks such as sorting, bar-coding, transporting, and other preparation, which reduces the Postal Service's work. Most of the growth in volume since 1977 has been in categories that receive discounts for work sharing. Ordinary nonpresorted first-class mail has grown very little, from about 50 billion to 55 billion annually. Work sharing and automation will be

prominent features of the postal system in the twenty-first century. By the year 2000, mail sorting will be fully automated, and mailers will be encouraged by discounts to presort their mail, to apply bar codes and to facilitate automated processing in other ways.

Although the overall volume of transmitted messages has grown rapidly in recent years, the Postal Service's share has decreased. Today, the USPS faces a large, varied, and growing array of competitors, many of whom are not subject to regulation. Telephone, telegraph, telex, and messenger services have always been imperfect competitors with the mail, but now, privately written messages can be sent cheaply and quickly by fax, E-mail, and electronic data interchange. Electronic funds transfers may soon become an easy substitute for the mailed check. Most newspapers are delivered directly to subscribers, and many include advertising supplements that compete directly with third-class bulk mail. The USPS's express mail, priority mail, parcel post, and money order services also have big, direct, and aggressive private competitors.

In the future, the USPS's share of the communications market will remain vulnerable to alternative services offering new and improved communications technologies. The rate of growth of both first-class mail and third-class mail has slowed in recent years. Not long after the year 2000 many observers expect the volume of first-class mail to level off, with third-class volume continuing to increase but at a slower rate.

See also COMMUNICATIONS; ON-LINE SERVICES; TELECOMMUNICATIONS.

BIBLIOGRAPHY

CREW, MICHAEL A., ed. *Competition and Innovation in Postal Services.* Norwell, MA: Kluwer, 1991.
FLEISCHMAN, JOEL L. *The Future of the Postal Service.* Westport, CT: Greenwood Press, 1983.

Robert H. Cohen
Edward S. Pearsall
Spyros S. Xenakis
Hee Sun Kim

Post–Information Age

Futurists are inclined to divide history into agricultural, industrial, and information ages. They see each age and culture as defined by its primary economic activity. These ages and cultures also tend to have their own concurrent source of social power, wealth, place of work, and sense of time. Today, advanced nations are completing the transition from the industrial to the information age. The early signs of the post-information age are barely visible, but do point to the emergence of a new age and civilization that can be anticipated.

Technological trends in microminiaturization, communications, voice recognition and synthesis, artificial intelligence, human interactivity with software, biotechnology, genetic engineering, bionics, and manufactured objects with build-in intelligence should continue and become increasingly and mutually reinforcing. The social trends in public participation, globalization, democracy, lifelong learning, and the rate of scientific inquiry and curiosity should also continue and become increasingly and mutually reinforcing. The interaction of these social and technological trends over the next century will create the *post–information age.*

In the post–information age, we will be as integrated with technology as technology is integrated with us. Distinctions between humans and machines will begin to blur. Humanity and intelligent technology will become an interrelated whole. The built environment will seem to become alive with artificial intelligence, communications, and voice recognition and synthesis. Our bodies will be augmented with technology and interconnected with global civilization. The post–information age will seem to become a "conscious technology," a continuum of human consciousness and technology.

The whole thrust of cyborg advances is to take the best of our external technology, miniaturize it, and then make it part of our bodies. We have already seen miniature pancreaslike pumps, heart pacemakers, microelectronically driven limbs, intraocular eye lenses, plastic skin, and artificial kidneys, hearts, ears, blood vessels, and bones. A cyborg is a living person who is dependent on technology for some vital function. All astronauts and scuba divers are temporary cyborgs. They use technological skins and organs to enhance abilities to move underwater and in outer space. The miniaturization of technology for both remedial purposes and the amplification of human capacity represents a strong trend toward the "cyborganization" of humanity.

Simultaneously, the whole thrust of advances in software is to take the best of our consciousness, simulate it in computer programs, and make it part of our environment. We can already talk to computers that recognize tens of thousands of words, giving us the eerie feeling that they are aware. Even buildings have sensors that make them seem alive, like the computer HAL in the movie *2001: A Space Odyssey.* This will make inanimate objects immediately responsive to our thoughts. With advancing computer power, microminiaturization, and simulated human communication, we can tell many inanimate objects what to do, and they can tell us what to do. Our whole environment will seem to change from dumb matter to one of conscious partnership as we tell our telephones to phone home, our lights to turn off, and our music to turn on.

Concurrent with the built environment becoming intelligent and humans becoming cyborgs will be the rapid growth of knowledge and the number of globally aware individuals. The time from curiosity to response is shrinking, while the scope of inquiry is expanding. Humanity is becoming a technologically interconnected, self-conscious whole. When the majority's awareness and technology are so interconnected, we will have left the information age and entered the conscious-technology age.

The primary economic activity of this new age will be the linkage of human to technology and technology to human. Just as marriage brokers connected boys and girls for marriage, and travel agents connected tourists to vacation destinations for new experiences, post-information age workers will connect themselves and others via complex technologies to invent new culture and realities.

In such a post information age, individuals become extraordinarily powerful. They can create themselves in many physical forms with technological augmentation and in even more forms in cyberspace. They grant or block access to themselves through software intelligence agents that communicate for them. This power will be like the power nations have today to grant visas. Unfortunately, like nations, others may wish to invade and manipulate others' perception without permission. The power of corporate marketing to influence behavior in the mid-1990s will seem slight compared with individuals' ability to influence human sensory systems and media upon which one bases metaphysical certainty. Information warfare and perceptual manipulation could become dominant forms of conflict waged by nations, corporations, interest groups, and individuals.

Individual power also is increased by creating barter transactions worldwide, as if each person were coining his or her own money. The exchange of virtual reality experiences will become as common as e-mail is today. Individuals will switch loyalties among corporations more easily than corporations switch capital among nations. They will invent their own nations, corporate holding companies, and religions, composed of networks of virtual realities in cyberspace, complete with software intelligence agents interacting with our technologically augmented bodies and environments.

Wealth in the post–information age becomes the quality of one's experiences, life, and being. An individual with vast expanses of land, capital, and access, but who is boring and unhappy, will be seen as less wealthy than another individual whose daily life is filled with a vastly richer set of intensely per-

sonal yet global experiences, even though the second individual might own less land, capital, and access. By agricultural age standards of wealth—land per capita—today's Japanese would be considered poor. By industrial age standards—capital per capita—today's Japanese are considered wealthy. By information age standards—access per capita—they are just beginning to get wealthy. By conscious-technology age standards—uniqueness of experience per capita—they would be poor.

In such a conscious-technology world, one will conduct his or her livelihood anywhere, with anyone, at any time. They will be viewed by others as constantly in motion. One can travel through three-dimensional space via many earthly and orbital transportation systems to reach anywhere in less than a day. One can also travel anywhere in the cyber-dimensional space almost instantaneously.

Since we will have more control over our daily reality, we can control the sequence and pace of events. This will change our sense of time. In the agricultural age, the perception of time tended to be cyclical, due to the importance of seasonal cycles so vital to agriculture. In the industrial age it tended to be more linear, with concepts of progress and increasing production efficiencies. In the information age, the perception of time has become more relativistic. As we enter the next age of increasing personal power to invent reality, time itself will seem an invention.

The table below summarizes some distinguishing characteristics of the post-information age compared with previous ages and cultures:

See also ARTIFICIAL INTELLIGENCE; CHANGE, CULTURAL; CHANGE, EPOCHAL; CHANGE, PACE OF; CHANGE, SCIENTIFIC AND TECHNOLOGICAL; COMMUNICATIONS; CONTINUITY AND DISCONTINUITY; GENETIC ENGINEERING; GENETIC TECHNOLOGIES; GLOBAL CULTURE; INFORMATION OVERLOAD; INFORMATION SOCIETY; INFORMATION TECHNOLOGY; INTERACTIVE ENTERTAINMENT; LIFESTYLES, VALUE-ORIENTED; MASS CULTURE

TABLE 1 Overview of Transition to the Post Information Age

Age	Product	Power	Wealth	Place	Time
Agricultural	Food	Religion	Land	Farm	Cyclical
Industrial	Machine	State	Capital	Factory	Linear
Information	Info/Service	Corporation	Access	Office	Relativistic
Conscious-Tech	Linkage	Individual	Being	Motion	Invented

AND ART; TECHNOLOGICAL DETERMINISM; VALUES; WORKFORCE REDISTRIBUTION.

BIBLIOGRAPHY

BELL, DANIEL. *The Coming of Post–Industrial Society.* New York: Basic Books, 1973.

CONNORS, MICHAEL. *The Race to the Intelligent State: Towards the Global Information Economy of 2005.* Cambridge: MA: Blackwell Business, 1993.

DORDICK, HERBERT S., and WANG, GEORGETTE. *The Information Society: A Retrospective View.* Newbury Park, CA: Sage Publications, 1993.

WEINBERG, NATHAN. *Computers in the Information Society.* Boulder, CO: Westview Press, 1990.

Jerome C. Glenn

Postmodernism.

See MODERNISM AND POSTMODERNISM.

Poverty, Feminization of

Between 1960 and 1990, the most significant change to take place in American society was the stark realization that single women and their children constituted the majority of all victims of poverty. In 1960 female-headed households accounted for only 23.7 percent of all poor families in America. Their percentage of all poor families grew to 37.1 percent in 1970, 47.8 percent in 1980, and 54.0 percent in 1991. As female-headed households became the dominant family type among the poor, women and children became an ever larger percentage of all the impoverished. In 1960 about 27 percent of all the poor lived in female-headed households. This percentage nearly doubled to 50 percent by 1976 and has remained at about 50 percent ever since.

Female-headed households are poor at a rate almost six times greater than the rate for intact married-couple families. In 1991 only 6.0 percent of all married couple families lived in poverty, compared to 35.6 percent of all female-headed families. Yet, female-headed families are the fastest growing household type in the nation. Between 1959 and 1991 the number of female-headed households with children tripled to 23 percent of all families with children. This included 17.5 percent of white families, 27 percent of Hispanic, and 54 percent of all black families with children. Over half of all children living in these households lived in poverty, with particularly high rates for minority children.

The poverty of so many female-headed families is the primary reason why poverty among American children has increased dramatically over the last fifteen years. More than 20 percent of American children are poor. Young single mothers form the poorest of all age groups in America.

Why are female-headed households in such jeopardy in America? There are many reasons, including the fact that females on average earn only about 71 percent of their male counterparts. The most important reason is that America's social welfare programs have not been redesigned to reflect this fact. Immense and fundamental alterations in the family structure have taken place in America over the last thirty years. Women head more households and are more often employed.

America lags behind most Western industrial nations in developing family support policies and welfare programs designed to move the poor out of poverty. A recent study showed that, using the same definition of poverty, postwelfare poverty in America averages 3.8 to 2.4 times the rates of the Western European nations. The United States is the only advanced nation with a double-digit rate of poverty. This is true despite the fact that the American poor are more likely to be employed, and that prewelfare poverty in Western Europe is actually higher. Thus, the European nations start with a higher rate of poverty, but do a much better job of reducing it through effective welfare programs. European nations spend more on welfare, target it better, and design their programs to promote economic independence.

In no small measure, the answers for dealing effectively with poverty and family supports are to be found in the laws of other advanced nations. For well over one hundred years, U.S. social policies and programs have consistently emulated those established elsewhere at earlier points in time. We can expect more of the same in the years to come.

See also FAMILIES AND HOUSEHOLDS; FAMILY PATTERNS; FAMILY VALUES; PUBLIC ASSISTANCE PROGRAMS; PUBLIC ASSISTANCE PROGRAMS: SOCIAL SECURITY; SOCIAL WELFARE PHILOSOPHIES; UNEMPLOYMENT; WOMEN AND WORK.

BIBLIOGRAPHY

COTTINGHAM, P. H., and ELLWOOD, D. T., eds. *Welfare Policies for the 1990s.* Cambridge, MA: Harvard University Press, 1989.

ELLWOOD, D. T. *Poor Support: Poverty in the American Family.* New York: Basic Books, 1988.

MCLANAHAN, S., and BOOTH, K. "Mother-Only Families: Problems, Prospects, and Politics." *Journal of Marriage and Family* 51 (August 1989): 557–580.

RODGERS, HARRELL R. *Poor Women, Poor Families: The Economic Plight of America's Female-Headed Families.* Armonk, NY: M. E. Sharpe, 1990.

RODGERS, HARRELL R., ed. *Beyond Welfare: New Approaches to the Problem of Poverty in America.* Armonk NY: M. E. Sharpe, 1988.

Harrell R. Rodgers

Preschool Education

The number of American children receiving education before age six has risen sharply in the last 25 years and will probably continue to rise in the years ahead. In 1991, 6.3 million children ages three to five were enrolled in preprimary programs, up 54 percent from 1970 when only 4.1 million were enrolled. Enrollment in kindergarten also climbed from 3.0 million in 1970 to 3.5 million in 1991, a 17 percent increase. This surge in preprimary education is all the more remarkable given that overall elementary school enrollment actually dropped slightly (.001 percent) between 1970 and 1991.

Although some day-care centers for infants and toddlers pursue no educational objectives, many do. Consequently, large numbers of the more than 1.5 million infants and toddlers in day-care centers now receive preschool instruction. Meanwhile, through government-sponsored Parents as Teachers (PAT) programs, a growing number of parents are also receiving training in how to foster the intellectual development of their children in their own homes.

Alongside the mainstream preschool programs, increasingly ambitious and sophisticated projects have emerged to meet the needs of impoverished and disadvantaged children. Designed as a preschool program to foster education receptivity and achievement among disadvantaged children, Head Start enrolled almost 714,000 children from poor households in 1993, compared to only 477,400 in 1970. However, because poverty among children has surged in recent decades, the percentage of poor preschool children enrolled in Head Start has actually dipped slightly, from 13 percent in 1970 to 12 percent in 1994. Originally launched in 1965 as part of President Lyndon Johnson's War on Poverty, Head Start has attracted strong support from both political parties as a means of helping disadvantaged children—especially minorities—break out of the cycle of poverty. In 1993, Head Start received $2.6 billion in federal money, and many child development experts feel it deserves significant increases in the years ahead.

Supporters of Head Start point to the remarkable outcomes documented for the Perry Pre-School Project (later known as High/Scope). Among young adults who were enrolled as young children in this experimental preschool project, researchers found significantly higher educational and economic attainments, and significantly lower crime rates compared to peers who were not enrolled. One analysis concluded that every dollar invested in the High/Scope program returned at least $7 (adjusted for inflation) to society by reducing the costs of remedial education, juvenile delinquency, and welfare. In light of such findings, Head Start is likely to grow in the decades ahead.

However, the growth of preschool education has not been without controversy. One such controversy concerns the longevity of positive effects from preschool. Defenders of Head Start have had to overcome American and British studies concluding that the benefits of preschool interventions largely disappear by the time students reach the third grade. Recent investigations reassure that preschool intervention benefits are long-lived, at least for the most seriously disadvantaged students. Nonetheless, the debate continues.

The hottest debates, though, have raged over the placement of infants in day-care centers. Some researchers—most prominently, psychologist Jay Belsky—have reported evidence that placement of infants below the age of one in day-care centers weakens bonding to their mothers. Evidence further indicates that infants receive less affectionate and responsive treatment in day care than at home. Although defenders of infant day care have challenged the methodologies and findings of some cautionary studies, concerns about very early placement in day-care centers also are widespread among child psychologists, many of whom recommend that one or both parents arrange for at least six months' leave of absence from their employers following the birth of a child.

Day care for preschoolers beyond infancy has been linked in some studies to heightened aggression and noncompliance. Some research indicates that the day care most likely to foster aggressive behavior—hitting, kicking, pushing, threatening, swearing, teasing, and arguing—may actually be the more "cognitively oriented" or educationally ambitious programs! On the other hand, psychologist Tiffany Field reports that "stable high-quality day care" will *reduce* subsequent aggressive behavior and improve academic performance among those enrolled.

Many Americans hope for the creation of a national day-care system based on the Scandinavian model, in which governments provide high-quality, educationally oriented day care for infants and preschoolers, free of charge. Scandinavian children coming out of these systems score high in cognitive and socio-emotional competence. Yet, the director of Denmark's highly lauded day-care system, Jacob Vedel-Petersen, laments that, in his country, "one can observe an eagerness to appropriate or monopolize the children's spare time. Childhood is about to become a phase of life thoroughly programmed from morning to night." In American day-care centers and preschools, pediatric researcher David Elkind sees a kind of "miseducation" based on the false premise that "earlier is better." Premature education may "put young children at risk for short-term stress and long-term personality problems," warns Elkind. He fears that many parents are now receptive to a dubious "conception of infantile competence," primarily because of new adult lifestyles based on dual-career marriages, not because of new research on children's educational needs.

The most intractable disputes over preschool education are, indeed, those defined by divergent attitudes toward family life. Many who view traditional family life as narrow and constraining see modern families evolving in exciting new ways. They generally regard day care and preschool as parts of a liberating formula opening new possibilities for women and new lifestyles for everyone. But others see in the increasing reliance upon day care and preschool a symptom of a broader retreat from family life. They do not see evolution in modern family life but decay—evident in high rates for divorce, cohabitation, and illegitimacy and low rates for marriage and childbearing. Exponents of this viewpoint draw upon the views of Harvard sociologist Pitirim Sorokin, who interpreted ever earlier separation of children from parents as evidence of profound cultural malaise. Some also worry that freedom from the traditional moral restraints of family life is illusory in that such freedom requires a growing number of government surrogates for the family (such as government-funded day-care centers and government-employed PAT social workers), which reduces family autonomy and increases tax burdens.

Statistical trends portend a future in which the great majority of American children will receive preprimary education. Universal publicly financed programs already abound in other advanced nations. Many Americans remain confident that simi-lar educational pathways will help pave the way to social and technological progress. Others fear that the multiplication of preschools will not mean progress if such multiplication entails further retreat from family life.

See also CHILD CARE; ELEMENTARY AND SECONDARY EDUCATION; FAMILIES AND HOUSEHOLDS; FAMILY PROBLEMS.

BIBLIOGRAPHY

Administration on Children, Youth, and Families. "Project Head Start Statistical Fact Sheet." Washington, DC: U.S. Department of Health and Human Services, 1994.

ANDERSSON, BENGT-ERIK. "Effects of Day-Care on Cognitive and Socioemotional Competence of Thirteen-Year-Old Swedish Schoolchildren." *Child Development* 63 (1992): 20–36.

BELSKY, JAY. "Infant Day Care and Socioemotional Development: The United States." *Journal of Child Psychology and Psychiatry* 29 (1988): 397–406.

ELKIND, DAVID. "Miseducation: Young Children at Risk." *Pediatrics* 83 (1989): 119–121.

FIELD, TIFFANY. "Quality Infant Day-Care and Grade School Behavior and Performance." *Child Development* 62 (1991): 863–870.

HASKINS, RON. "Public School Aggression among Children with Varying Day Care Experience." *Child Development* 56 (1985): 694–703.

MELHUISH, E. C., et al. "Type of Childcare at Eighteen Months—I. Differences in Interactional Experience." *Journal of Child Psychology and Psychiatry* 31 (1990): 849–857.

SOROKIN, PITIRIM. *Social and Cultural Dynamics: A Study of Change in Major Systems of Art, Truth, Ethics, Law, and Social Relationships*, revised and abridged ed., 1957. Reprint. New Brunswick, NJ: Transaction, 1985, pp. 700–707.

SYLVA, KATHY. "School Influences on Children's Development." *Journal of Child Psychology and Psychiatry* 35 (1994): 135–170.

TOWERS, JAMES T. "Attitudes Toward the All-Day, Everyday Kindergarten." *Children Today* (January–February 1991): 25–27.

U.S. Bureau of the Census. *Statistical Abstract of the United States, 1993*. Washington, DC: U.S. Government Printing Office, 1993.

VEDEL-PETERSEN, JACOB. "Children in Denmark: Day Care Issues." *Child Welfare* 68 (1989): 261–264.

Bryce L. Christensen

Preventive Health Care.

See HEALTH CARE.

Printed Word

One thousand years from now, our descendants will look at written records of our time and ponder how much, or perhaps how little, humans have changed. What will not have changed is the use of visual representations of sounds to signify words that express the world we perceive and our thoughts about it. The human eye is a scanner for that most convenient "computer," the human brain. Its richest data input today is the printed word. Elsewhere you will read how words will increasingly be generated electronically and be available instantaneously worldwide via computer networks. But the printed word as we know it and the process of publishing that has grown up around it will be with us for a long, long time.

Publishers in the beginning were essentially printers, manufacturers of books who owned presses to impart print images to paper. These printers subsequently became more and more involved with the authors of the works they printed and with the distribution of the finished product. Eventually, as publishers, they became in effect the bankers of the knowledge enterprise. Today their role is to select the work to be published, perfect its form, make known its appearance, provide for its availability over an extended period, and maintain the property rights of the author. These functions will continue to be essential to publishing, whether the printed word is read on a piece of paper or on a video screen, and whether the agency is called a publisher or something new like a "knowledge manager." In the academic world there is talk of a campus department that might unite a faculty author, the library, and the computer center. In this configuration, it is supposed that the author's work would be more immediately available, but by computer retrieval from a data bank rather than from a library book.

In the meantime, a seemingly endless cycle of birth, growth, and consolidation continues in conventional "trade" publishing, which produces the books we buy in stores. Many companies whose names were household words have disappeared from the publishing scene or lost their independence as media giants and foreign publishers have gobbled them up. This has been thought by some to narrow avenues of communication for unconventional writers. At the same time, however, creative entrepreneurs have continued to start up small publishing enterprises, often in some area of specialization personally close to their hearts, and some university presses have shown more interest in the experimental and the intellectually avant-garde. The cost of entry in the publishing business has always been low; basically it comprises the salaries of the staff. With the advent of computer technologies for production and distribution, the future is likely to see a vast proliferation of low-overhead publishers catering to every new intellectual and consumer interest.

Magazines and journals have always been a print avenue for very special interests, especially series in the fields of science and technology; and in recent years a far higher proportion of library budgets has been spent on these so-called "serials" than heretofore. Unfortunately, larger and larger expenditures for serials have not led to a comparable increase in the number of serials acquired; rather, serial prices have been inflated. One anticipated result will be the publication of "electronic journals," which will be more closely controlled by their intellectual sources and more readily available simply by logging onto a journal sponsor's "file server."

Often overlooked is that literary works of art and entertainment have never, as a category, been a dependable financial investment. Probably such publishing is inherently unprofitable—as with serious theater, music, and dance. Whether disseminated conventionally or electronically, artistic and scholarly compositions of the printed word will have to be subsidized by the revenues from more mundane subject matters of mass media information and instruction.

The emerging electronic transmission systems themselves may not be available to the unprofitable arts—or to education, for that matter—if government does not pay the bill as it already does in other countries. There is, however, great danger in a knowledge-transmission system dependent on the good will of a bureaucracy! What if authorities in the future decide to censor the computer network? What if funding is cut back or withdrawn? It has been much harder to shut down all the printing presses and burn all the books.

Although more books are published today than ever before, television and other distractions lead some to conclude that books and reading are losing importance. One reported result is a rise in the study of "book history" based on the premise that the book is already taking its place along with household servants and railroad trains as a quaint relic. Until recently largely taken for granted, reading itself is studied by researchers for clues to past human behavior. The influence of what we would now call "newsletters" on the French Revolution is well understood. What will be the seditious effect of e-mail? Dante's lovers were seduced by a book, but will future sweethearts kiss as they behold their computer display?

The prospect of computer-generated multimedia experiences that combine the written word with illustrations and sounds, weaving text with supplementary interactive data banks, makes the printed word alone seem tame to some. But more exciting to book devotees is the emergence of new ways to keep the printed word alive and available to readers. Xerox is pioneering a promising technology for the production of books, now called the "Docutech," which combines a scanning capability with a high-speed printing and collating function. Binding is still handled separately, but one day the process may be fully integrated. The output of this system is a short run of copies "on demand" as a means of keeping in print forever titles that heretofore could not be reprinted economically in small quantities. The system also may facilitate the publication of short runs of specialized books that could not be manufactured economically by conventional means in the first place. Similar methods may ease the production of large-type books for readers with visual impairment and even lead to new Braille technologies.

A possible loss feared by bibliophiles is the perfected aesthetic form. Originally dictated by the folding and assembly of larger sheets of printed pages, the typical six-inch-by-nine-inch object we hold in our hands, carry about, and display in our libraries has become a highly stylized art form, with its own aesthetics of proportion, typographic display, illustration, and material—even feel and smell. Fortunately the champions of new print technologies promise that these qualities, too, can be reproduced in due course—and that in any case we will eventually learn to delight in the appearance of our computer monitors.

Whether the printed word appears in a conventional book, a desktop computer printout, a Docutech edition, or transitorily on the screen, the author's manuscript ("hand-writing") will increasingly be created on a computer disk that will generate a variety of computer outputs. The revision and copyediting of the work will take place "on screen" as succeeding generations of authors, computer-literate from the primary grades, will no longer have patience with old-fashioned interlineation and crossing out. A most unfortunate loss in this proc-

ess will be the draft record of the creative changes leading to the published version that tell us so much about a work's meaning and about the mind of the author.

For all the understandable excitement generated by futuristic prospects for the printed word, a monumental 500-year investment remains in the book as we know it. In the United States alone, some 50,000 new titles are published each year, with no sign of diminishing. A universally understood method of communication, an exceedingly efficient medium, infinitely refined production processes, countless libraries, enormous investments in distribution mechanisms and an integrated process of education worldwide will be substantially transformed only after many generations that will still turn to the printed word, though in new forms of displays.

Still, one may ask why our technologically accomplished progeny would not do away entirely with printed records in favor of electronic signals. The reason is that as long as the species has eyes to see and a voice to speak, the printed word will be easily accessible. Even the most technologically adept creature in the year 3000 will not want to make the effort to arrange to display a 1995 CD, even if it should survive with its data intact by enhancement, if instead she could consult a microfilm much as we today consult the Dead Sea Scrolls. We must think of the interests of these descendants as well as our immediate convenience because their day is closer than we can comprehend.

See also ADVERTISING; ARTS; DIGITAL COMMUNICATIONS; ELECTRONIC PUBLISHING; INFORMATION OVERLOAD; INFORMATION SOCIETY; INTELLECTUAL PROPERTY; LIBRARIES; LIBRARIES: ELECTRONIC FORMATS; LITERATURE; NEWSPAPERS; PHOTOGRAPHY; POSTAL SERVICES.

BIBLIOGRAPHY

ALSTON, A. C., and FELLNER, H., eds. *Publishing, the Booktrade, and the Diffusion of Knowledge.* Cambridge, U.K.: Chadwyck-Healy, 1992.

CUMMINGS, G., et al. *University Libraries and Scholarly Communication.* Washington, DC: Association of Research Libraries, 1992.

OLMERT, MICHAEL. *The Smithsonian Book of Books.* Washington, DC: Smithsonian Books, 1992.

SMITH, DATUS C., JR. *A Guide to Book Publishing,* rev. ed. Seattle: University of Washington Press, 1989.

Peter C. Grenquist

Prisons

By the mid-twenty-first century the only prison bars will be in the minds of public offenders. Expensive cell blocks will be replaced by more intrusive mind control methods that are both cheaper and more effective in dealing with criminal behavior.

On the way to this new day in biotech behavioral control, some very old methods will be tried again and eventually discarded. When the Quakers arrived in the American colonies in the early eighteenth century, they developed a method of incarcerating offenders to give them time to repent (penitentiaries) and reform (reformatories). The idea caught on worldwide, but in no place was it more popular than in the United States. By the mid-1990s more than one million inmates were in American prisons on any given day. By the turn of the twenty-first century this number is expected to double and possibly even triple.

The idea of the reformation/rehabilitation of offenders was replaced in the latter part of the twentieth century by a focus on an even older idea—retribution and revenge. Prisons became "spartan warehouses," so prisoners would feel the pain of crime and never want to return. It was generally believed that offenders could be deterred from further crime by harsh punishment, despite empirical evidence to the contrary.

Early in the twenty-first century, the crippling cost of indiscriminate incarceration of law violators will force change in the "corrections" system. When costs of imprisonment exceed costs of education, policy will shift to accommodate the greater need. The most violent, hardened, and undeterrable offenders will still be incarcerated, but other violators will be handled in new ways.

For the minority who still must be incarcerated, undersea and space prisons will become the new method—again reviving an age-old idea of "transporting" or sending criminals somewhere else (as England transported its public offenders first to the American colonies and later to Australia). Colonies deep under the ocean will be self-supporting prisons, as inmates grow food via aquaculture. Mining asteroids may make space prisons self-sustaining as well. Both types will be easy to secure and will make escape highly unlikely.

For the moderately dangerous and incorrigible offenders, late-twentieth-century technology—electronic monitoring—will be improved and increasingly used. Using geo-based tracking systems, monitored offenders will be followed around the clock wherever they go. Eventually monitors will be implanted inside the offender's body—though only by court order—and for the most dangerous, electrodes will be attached to shock the offenders if they leave their territory. Only when a violator returns to home, work, or an approved site will the electroshock cease.

Minor offenders will be diverted from the correctional system into more productive alternatives. Community-service work will become increasingly popular, as it both forces offenders to labor and pay for their crimes and provides public services—from litter control to government building and grounds maintenance and construction—all at a savings to the taxpayer.

For offenders who are not dangerous but have no funds, homes, or skills to live on their own, old alternatives will continue to be used early in the twenty-first century. Halfway houses and group homes, along with residential drug-treatment, education, and job-training programs will be found to be cheaper and more effective than prisons.

In the early part of the twenty-first century, capital punishment will still be used for a few extreme cases—terrorists' acts causing multiple deaths, serial murders, and other isolated atrocities. Lethal injection will become the method of choice in almost all jurisdictions. New methods may emerge—such as instant death by laser ray or dematerialization by ultrasound—before capital punishment is eventually abolished as unnecessary to protect society.

Second-quarter twenty-first-century technology will make available the means to put the "bars in the minds" of offenders, as most citizens will have computer implants in their brains to increase their capacity to store and recall massive amounts of information and provide numerous types of leisure activities, from virtual reality games to soothing subliminal messages ("you are doing well"; "life is good"; "things are getting better and better"; etc.). Thus it will be a minor step further to order law violators to be "programmed" to obey—forcing compliance by eliminating alternatives. The computer inside simply will not allow the individual to disobey the law—chemical reactions will cause nausea while subliminal messages will bombard the subconscious ("obey the law"; "do the right things"; and so on).

Still, the future is one of choice. The methods described above do not have to occur, but may be reserved for a few extreme cases.

A major alternative to this high-tech scenario is a "humanized approach"—changing the basic belief about crime and justice from combating criminals on the "mean streets" to creating and maintaining "peaceful communities." Instead of reacting to crime by emphasizing "capturing criminals," the focus will change to proactively seeking to prevent crime by early identification of crime-breeding problems followed by action to remedy the situations. The bases for this approach were established in the early 1990s and will escalate in the twenty-first century. If successful, community-oriented policing combined with community-oriented justice via replacing adversarial proceedings with mediation and arbitration will mean fewer criminals and thus less need for prisons and other draconian actions. Community crime prevention will only work, however, if citizens are willing to give up their "war" mentality and adopt a "peace" approach that substitutes pragmatic restitution, restoration, and reconciliation for vindictive retribution, revenge, and retaliation. Above all else, communal attention to tender, loving care of all children ("It takes a whole village to raise a child") could ultimately eliminate the need for prisons altogether.

See also CRIME, NONVIOLENT; CRIME, ORGANIZED; CRIME, VIOLENT; CRIME RATES; CRIMINAL JUSTICE; CRIMINAL PUNISHMENT; DRUGS, ILLICIT; LAW ENFORCEMENT; LETHAL WEAPONS.

BIBLIOGRAPHY

MONTGOMERY, R. H., and MACDOUGALL, E. C. "Curing Criminals: The High-Tech Prisons of Tomorrow." *The Futurist* (January–February 1986): 36–37.
STEPHENS, GENE. "Drugs and Crime in the Twenty-first Century." *The Futurist* (May–June 1992): 19–22.
_____. "Impact of Emerging Police and Corrections Technology on Constitutional Rights." In F. Schmallenger, ed. *Computers in Criminal Justice: Issues and Applications.* Bristol, IN: Wyndham Hall Press, 1990.

Gene Stephens

Privacy Laws.

See COMMUNICATIONS: PRIVACY LAWS; COMPUTERS: PRIVACY LAWS.

Private Assistance Programs

We can generally think of private assistance programs as providing some form of tangible aid to individuals to enhance their physical, economic, and/or psychological well-being. This assistance can take various forms such as in the provision of child-care facilities, fitness centers, pension plans, health-care plans, and a host of other employee benefits. Trying to predict how any one program will evolve, let alone the entire range of programs, ignores the interdependencies and complexity of the "system" of private assistance programming. Nevertheless, although the future of private assistance programs cannot be predicted, we do know that the constellation of programs will be influenced by the interplay of choices made by individual workers, organizations, and state and federal government. These choices and actions may be made more intelligently if we consider the "forces" most likely to shape the evolution of private assistance programs.

We can picture private assistance programs as constituting an array of "employment products" needing to be offered and managed as part of an overall employment relationship. These employment products, as with other commercially available products or services, must fit the needs of an increasingly diverse and discriminating "employment consumer market." There are a host of indicators suggesting that the consumers of future employment products, the incumbent and potential employees, will be qualitatively different from consumers in the past. Several major forces will govern the evolution of the next generation of employment products:

- The increasing strategic importance of skills, knowledge, and ability to continually learn in a knowledge economy
- A growing disparity in worker skills and knowledge
- The increased diversity of workers and associated diversity of worker needs and expectations
- The increasing fluidity of organizational boundaries via mergers, acquisitions, and joint ventures
- The growing use of contingent workers
- An increasing individual worker tendency to relate financial security to employability and mobility
- Public policy actions changing constraints and incentives that affect the interplay of public and private assistance programs

Successful organizations will shape future assistance programs using an "employee as customer" and "employment as product" metaphor and apply marketing discipline and tools to manage the employment relationship. Over time this will lead to the type of "mass customization" of employment products now evident in traditional product and service markets.

The stereotypical U.S. worker—white, male, head of household—is no longer the norm. With fewer workers entering the workforce, employers will have a more diverse employee base with new entrants coming from a predominantly female and minority labor pool. As a result, organizations will be required to design and deliver "employment products" that consider the heterogeneous needs of a more diverse labor market. This diverse labor market will function within an economic system where the basis of wealth will shift from hard, "physical" assets to one that is information- and knowledge-based, and then rapidly to one that values the ability to learn in order to continually create new knowledge. This will require that individuals engage in lifelong learning. In a knowledge-learning economy, market power shifts to those organizations and individuals who can anticipate technological possibilities and consumer needs to produce the next generation of products or services.

The increasing demands of a knowledge- and learning-intensive workplace are raising the level of fundamental skills and ability that constitute the "playing stakes" in the labor market. Incumbent workers will find it increasingly difficult to maintain the skills required to stay employable, while many of the new entrants will lack even the basic skills to "get into the game." As a result, the growing diversity of worker needs will be matched or exceeded by a growing disparity in people's ability to bargain for employment products that serve their needs. This disparity in employee-bargaining power will fundamentally change the nature of the organization's employment relationships. Today, these relationships are predicated on a model that can be described as "employee as cost of production." Some of the assumptions underlying this traditional model are as follows:

- Jobs are well defined and stable.
- Skills and knowledge required to perform those jobs are well defined.
- Talented labor is in abundant supply.
- Employees are easily replaceable with insignificant loss.
- Employers have buyer power in a commodity labor market.
- Employees constitute a homogeneous group in terms of needs and expectations.

The social, political, demographic, and legal trends, however, all seem to suggest that these assumptions may no longer serve as an effective template for designing future employment offerings. A metaphor that may more appropriately embody the employment relationship of the future is that of the "employee as customer." This metaphor provides both the language and methodology to gain new insights into the employment relationship and is in stark contrast to the cost of production metaphor, which has traditionally governed the employment relationship.

Increasingly employees will become more sophisticated consumers when evaluating employment products that include any form of long-term commitment. Mergers, acquisitions, divestitures, joint ventures, alliances, insourcing, outsourcing, and comarketing agreements increasingly blur organizational boundaries and employer identities. For example, who offers the employment product supplied by a "virtual corporation"? Many in the labor force will respond to increased organizational turbulence by demanding an "open systems architecture" and easy portability for their employment product attributes.

The adaptation of an employee as customer metaphor will lead to a customization of employment products as a strategic necessity for institutions operating in a knowledge-intensive economy. The move toward mass customization of employment products and services will, however, elevate the tension between "efficient" creation and delivery of products and services, and differential notions of perceived equity. These bipolar forces will increase the urgency to apply market research methodologies for understanding the employment relationship and how to adjudicate increasingly complex human-resource issues across many dimensions of diversity and disparity.

These changes in the very nature of work and nature of the workforce that create the need to dramatically alter basic employment assumptions and metaphors are happening in an increasingly turbulent public-policy environment. Pressures to raise revenue and address increasingly complex social issues will generate legislative action directly affecting the development and management of private programs. Legislative action in the areas of health and welfare, taxation, health care access and reform, retiree health benefits, long-term care, individual savings vehicles, pension funds and portability, assistance plan administration, social security, and family benefits can quickly change the incentives, restraints, and competitive alternatives for private assistance programs.

See also ENTITLEMENT PROGRAMS; PHILANTHROPY; PUBLIC ASSISTANCE PROGRAMS; SOCIAL WELFARE PHILOSOPHIES.

BIBLIOGRAPHY

BRIDGES, W. *Job Shift*. Reading, MA: Addison-Wesley, 1994.

COATES, JOSEPH; JARRATT, JENNIFER; and MAKAFFIE, J. *Future Work*. San Francisco: Jossey-Bass, 1990.

CRAWFORD, R. *In the Era of Human Capital*. New York: HarperCollins, 1991.

REICH, R. *The Work of Nations*. New York: Alfred A. Knopf, 1991.

TREGOE, B. B.; ZIMMERMAN, J. W.; SMITH, R. A.; and TOBIA, P. M. *Vision in Action*. New York: Simon & Schuster, 1989.

Ruthann Prange

Productivity

Productivity is usually defined as the ratio of output to any or all associated inputs in real (physical volume) terms. "Total factor productivity" (TFP) is the ratio of real gross product, whether of a nation or an industry, to total real, tangible factor inputs of labor and capital (man-made and natural). Its increase over time reflects savings in real costs per unit of output due to improvements in the quality and efficiency of the factors of production. In the long run, productivity gains result from innovations in the technology and organization of production, and from human investments, especially in education and training. In modern times innovations are increasingly the result of investments in research and development (R&D).

The familiar "labor productivity" ratio (output per worker or per hour worked) reflects not only technological progress, but also increases in tangible capital goods per worker. Noninvestment forces affecting productivity generally include economies of scale, fluctuations in output, exogenous variables such as governmental fiscal and regulatory policies, and changes in social values and institutions.

The United States Record

The progress of productivity has been uneven. In the United States, as shown in Table 1, the growth rate of TFP averaged only 0.3 percent a year in the period of 1800 to 1890 before accelerating to 2.2 percent for the 1919 to 1973 period. The low growth prior to 1890 is not surprising since backcasting the twentieth-century rate would result in zero production in colonial days. The acceleration beginning in the 1890s reflected especially the beginning of research and development (R&D) as a specialized function in larger firms; the development of the field of management science and the establishment of collegiate schools of business beginning with Wharton in 1887; and increases in the average education and training of the work force.

The productivity slowdown after 1973 is a bit of a puzzle but reflects a decline in the rate of growth of intangible investments (in education, R&D, etc.) per unit of tangible input following major increases before then. Rates of return on the stocks of intangible capital designed to increase the quality and efficiency of inputs were also declining. Increasing outlays for antipollution and other social objectives likewise retarded growth, at least in the short run. Finally, the "oil shock" of 1973 ignited

TABLE 1. Real Gross Product, Population, Real Product Per Capita, Factor Inputs and Productivity Ratios

U.S. Domestic Business Economy, Selected Periods 1800–1993
(average annual percentage rates of change)

	1800–1855	1855–1890	1890–1919	1919–1948	1948–1973	1973–1993
Real gross product	4.2	4.0	3.9	3.0	4.0	2.6
Population	3.1	2.4	1.8	1.2	1.5	1.7
Real product per capita	1.1	1.6	2.1	1.8	2.5	0.9
Tangible factor inputs: total	3.9	3.6	2.2	0.8	1.8	2.2
Labor	3.7	2.8	1.8	0.6	0.9	1.7
Capital	4.3	4.6	3.1	1.2	3.9	3.5
Factor productivity ratios: total	0.3	0.3	1.7	2.2	2.2	0.3
Labor	0.5	1.1	2.0	2.4	3.4	1.3
Capital	–0.1	–0.6	0.7	1.6	0.1	–0.9

Sources: For 1800–1890: M. Abramovitz and P. David, "Economic Growth in America: Historical Parables and Realities," Stanford University, Center for Research in Economic Growth, Reprint No. 105, 1973. For 1890–1948: J. W. Kendrick, *Productivity Trends in the United States*. New York: National Bureau of Economic Research, 1961. For 1973–1993: Bureau of Labor Statistics, U.S. Department of Labor.

accelerating inflation in the later 1970s, followed by a painful disinflation.

Looking ahead, it is encouraging that the 1990 to 1994 rate of growth in TFP moved up to 1 percent a year while inflation remained low. This suggests that performance should be at least as good for the rest of the decade. Indeed, TFP growth might well accelerate further to the average 1948 to 1994 rate of 1.4 percent. It seems unlikely, however, that this country will again experience the 2.2 percent rate of 1948 to 1973 that reflected the backlogs of demand and potential innovations accumulated during the Great Depression and World War II.

Going beyond the year 2000, relatively high rates of TFP growth between 1.4 and 2 percent could be realized if strong intangible capital formation continues, and if the socioeconomic environment is favorable to entrepreneurial activity. But slowdowns such as occurred in the 1970s could happen again, moderating long-term growth rates.

There is considerable dispersion in rates of productivity change among industries. Between 1950 and 1990 average annual rates of change in real gross product per labor hour in the United States ranged from 4.8 percent in communications and 4.0 percent in agriculture down to 0.8 percent in services and a slight negative in contract construction. Manufacturing at 2.6 percent was a bit above the average of 2.1 percent for all private industry. It is generally believed that there is some downward bias in the real product and productivity trends, especially in the finance and services sectors, and in construction, because of inadequate price deflators. Real product in almost half of these sectors is assumed to move with employment, without allowance for productivity increases.

REST OF THE WORLD

Since the reconstruction following World War II, there has been impressive convergence in labor productivity levels between the United States and other industrialized nations. Between 1960 and 1992, thirteen other OECD countries increased real GDP per person at an average annual rate of 3 percent compared with 1.2 percent for the United States. Growth rates ranged from around 5 percent for South Korea and Japan, and 3.5 percent for Italy, down to 2 percent for Sweden and the United Kingdom. As a result, the average productivity level of the thirteen increased from 46.5 percent of that of the United States in 1960 to 76.6 percent in 1992. The productivity gap narrowed for two main reasons: (1) higher rates of saving and capital formation abroad and (2) technological catch-up with the United States.

As other countries come close to U.S. productivity levels, their growth rates slow down. This is already occurring since borrowing advanced technology is much cheaper than creating it through R&D. Thus, growth rates of other industrial nations will tend to converge with that of the United States, whose rate may be enhanced somewhat by increasing opportunities to borrow technology from others. But even a 1.5 percent growth rate means a doubling in less than fifty years. A major question is whether national resource and environmental constraints will slow economic progress in the new century.

There is as yet no general convergence of productivity rates and levels among the less developed countries (LDCs). Some are doing very well—for example, China since 1979. Others, such as India, are making slow progress, while the transitional economies of the former Soviet Union and Eastern Europe have had at least temporary setbacks. Fortunately, countries that seem to be mired in low-level stagnation, as are some in Southeast Asia and Central Africa, comprise only about 5 percent of world population.

In the future, an increasing proportion of LDCs should be taking off into stronger economic growth given increasing aid and investment from industrial nations, including direct investments by multinational corporations and from international organizations such as the World Bank. Public investments in infrastructure and human resources are important prerequisites to productivity growth, as are gradual increases in domestic saving and investment to supplement that from foreign sources. Development is a slow process, but it is possible that during the twenty-first century increases in planes of living made possible by productivity growth could virtually eliminate poverty in most parts of the world.

See also CAPITAL FORMATION; ENTREPRENEURSHIP; INVESTMENTS; SAVINGS; WORK; WORK, QUALITY OF.

BIBLIOGRAPHY

BAUMOL, WILLIAM J.; NELSON, RICHARD R.; and WOLFF, EDWARD M. *Convergence of Productivity: Cross-National Studies and Historical Evidence.* Oxford, U.K.: Oxford University Press, 1994.

KENDRICK, JOHN W. *Productivity Trends in the United States.* Princeton, NJ: Princeton University Press for the National Bureau of Economic Research, 1961.

KENDRICK, JOHN W., and GROSSMAN, ELLIOT. *Productivity in the United States: Trends and Cycles.* Baltimore, MD: Johns Hopkins University Press, 1980.

John W. Kendrick

Protest.

See CIVIL PROTEST.

Pseudo-Futurists

People claiming to be able to foretell the future on false bases fall into several different categories. To begin with, it is useful to distinguish between pseudo-futurists who use nonrational or even irrational arguments and those who fail to use or otherwise abuse scientific methods. Those who falsely claim a scientific basis for their predictions might properly be called pseudoscientists.

Most pseudo-futurists base the validity of their claims to foretell the future on nonscientific and often religious, metaphysical, or occult grounds. Though nonscientific, these approaches are not necessarily irrational. Nonscientific futurists include those who claim that there is a personal or charismatic basis for their authority—typically claims of precognition or divine revelation. Examples include a "psychic" counselor who "looks into your future," perhaps with the aid of a crystal ball, or someone who recalls a prophetic dream. Other nonscientific futurists claim a method of divination independent of any personal powers. Examples include such prognosticators as astrologers, numerologists, or readers of tarot cards, who claim merely to follow rules for divining with such instruments. The former usually claim they inherited such abilities, while the latter claim they learned to divine from a teacher.

Some modern, metaphysically rather than scientifically oriented claimants assert that their predictions depend upon discovering certain behavioral events or patterns. Psychoanalyst Carl Gustav Jung called such a phenomenon a *synchronicity*—a noncausal but still psychologically meaningful coincidence. Many of these claimants deny that their approach is scientific. Instead, they prefer to speak of their method as a "clinical art" (as do some psychoanalysts). It is therefore incorrect to refer to such pseudo-futurists as pseudoscientists.

An overall complicating factor in these observations is that correct predictions from a theory do not formally validate that theory. Throughout history, there have been instances of correct predictions based on false theories or of proper extrapolations from false or erroneous data. Somebody, somewhere, somehow, at some time, is likely to have guessed right.

Like the term *pseudoscientist*, the label *pseudo-futurist* is sometimes merely used pejoratively, and it may be used disarmingly and dismissively against competitive protoscientific efforts.

Some pseudo-futurists have their roots in occult traditions but also have obtained some degree of scientific legitimacy through modern research methods. One current example is parapsychology, since it offers some experimental evidence in support of precognition. Another is neo-astrology, which also has produced some positive empirical results, most notably in the correlational studies of psychologist Michel Gauquelin.

Futurism remains somewhat controversial within the broader scientific community. Furthermore, futurists sometimes seek to disassociate their modern, rational methods and hypotheses from those associated with past quackery. Most fledgling disciplines attempt to do thus. However, the history of science should make us somewhat cautious. Science today rejects some previously accepted bases for prediction. (For example, psychologists once endorsed phrenology—the study of the skull surface as an indicator of mental abilities and character traits—but today even occultists reject it. Although scientists once rejected some bases for prediction, a number of these have found new scientific backing (as with recent research findings on seasonal birth effects).

Beyond the problems involved in formal demarcation, pseudo-futurism indisputably exhibits instances of fraud and incompetence—as does any discipline or practice. Examples of fraud might include such things as the post hoc fabricated predictions attributed to Mother Shipton (c. 1486–1561); the many and varied modern reinterpretations given to the prophetic quatrains of NOSTRADAMUS; and the often strained "interpretations" given many ambiguous or unclear sources ranging from modern "seers" like Jeane Dixon and Edgar Cayce to the biblical book of Revelation. Instances of incompetence might include such things as post hoc interpretations; fallacies in logic; the misuse of statistics; spurious correlations; and especially, the presence of self-fulfilling prophecies.

Rightly or wrongly, though rotten apples may taint the entire barrel, the art of forecasting will prevail—as it has over the course of recorded history.

See also FORECASTING METHODS; FUTURISM; FUTURISTS; PARASENSORY PHENOMENA.

BIBLIOGRAPHY

EYSENCK, H. J., and NIAS, D. K. *Astrology: Science or Superstition?* London: Maurice Temple Smith, 1982.

LEONI, EDGAR. *Nostradamus and His Prophecies*. New York: Bell Publishing, 1982.

LOYE, DAVID. *The Knowable Future: A Psychology of Forecasting and Prophecy*. New York: John Wiley, 1978.

MAVEN, MAX. *Max Maven's Book of Fortunetelling*. New York: Prentice-Hall, 1992.

Marcello Truzzi

Psychiatry

The psychiatry of the future will be shaped by rapid advances in biological, psychological, and social sciences, by radical shifts in health care financing and treatment practices, and by innovations in computer technology and communication.

Scientific Advances

Advances in brain imaging using positron emission tomography (PET), magnetic resonance imaging (MRI), single photon emission tomography (SPEC), and specialized quantitative electroencephalography (QEEG) will continue providing remarkable, increasingly on-line images of the structure and physiology of the living brain. These developments will yield important information about the biological bases of the major mental disorders, particularly Alzheimer's disease, schizophrenia, manic-depressive disorder, serious depressions, anxiety and panic disorders, alcohol and drug abuse, obsessive-compulsive disorders, personality disorders, and others. As the details of the entire human genome are uncovered in the next decade, we will be able to better clarify how harmful genes, family, and social environments contribute to psychiatric disorders. Techniques of molecular genetics, neurochemistry, and neurophysiology will also unravel the nature of psychiatric symptoms, identifying involved brain pathways and chemical processes, and leading to improved laboratory testing and diagnosis. Many new psychiatric treatments can be expected, including entirely new classes of "designer" medications that may offer prevention as well as treatment with far fewer side effects.

Studies in human behavioral genetics show that many aspects of personality, such as shyness, and various features of intelligence result as much from genetic as from environmental influences. New personality theories will emerge from these findings and will examine how inborn tendencies complement and/or conflict with one another.

These theories should help explain how and why certain parenting patterns, early traumas, and adverse life events affect some children much more than others and even predict specific personality and interpersonal problems that someone is likely to develop. Medications to treat some personality disorders and to enhance memory and other intellectual functions can be expected. Improved strategies for psychotherapies, social interventions, and preventing psychiatric problems should also result.

New theories of the healthy and diseased mind will also stem from advances in computational neurobiology. Computer models of evolving neural networks, related to "complexity theory," will increasingly mimic human mental phenomena.

Psychiatric Services

As in other fields of medicine, most patients will receive psychiatric care through large, highly regulated, organized systems of "managed" care, financed by employers or public funds. Clinicians working for these systems will increasingly use treatments that have been objectively demonstrated to be efficient, effective, cost-effective, and satisfying to the patients, clients, and families. Health insurance benefits for psychiatric problems are likely to be limited to serious psychiatric disorders, with more services than at present available for biologically based psychiatric disorders such as schizophrenia and manic-depressive disease, in part due to political action by advocacy groups composed of patients and their families. Research will help show which combinations and lengths of treatment are necessary to reverse acute conditions and prevent recurrences. Much more psychotherapy in the future will be based on educationally oriented, interpersonally focused, skill and coping-style enhancing, short-term psychotherapies explicitly described in workbooks used by clinicians and patients. These therapies will emphasize ways to resolve symptoms and problems through specifically prescribed changes in thinking and behavior. Biological and psychological treatments shown through research to be ineffective will be eliminated. Officially sanctioned *practice guidelines* will be increasingly used by health care organizations to guide, if not prescribe, the types of biological treatments, psychotherapies, hospital-based, and outpatient treatments to be offered for specific sorts of problems. Studies comparing the costs and results of care for various problems as provided by psychiatrists, primary care physicians, nurses, psychologists, social workers, and other therapists, working individually or in teams, will determine what sorts of professionals will be asked to provide various aspects of care—for example, prescribing medications and/or conducting psychotherapy. In some geographic regions, psychiatric nurses and possibly psychologists with special training and licensing may be allowed to prescribe some medications independently of psychiatrists or other physicians. Because they are inexpensive to run yet relatively effective for certain problems such as alcoholism and addictions, special attention will be given to examining the cost-effectiveness of twelve-step programs based on Alcoholics Anonymous and other treatments offered by nonprofessionals. Traditional fee-for-service therapists in solo practice will still be available for those willing and able to pay out of pocket.

Computer Technology

Much more sophisticated and extensive computer-assisted psychiatric assessments and psychotherapies, based on expert systems, will provide individually tailored "virtual therapists." Virtual reality programming will be used increasingly to expose patients to provocative stimuli in the treatment of phobias, addictions, interpersonal conflicts, and other problems. Clinicians will increasingly access on-line information, ranging from past medical records to literature searches on any psychological or medical topic. At the same time, patients and their families will have access to increasing amounts of on-line information about their providers and treatments, including credentials and any malpractice histories. Patient education will be greatly facilitated by easily available interactive media. Consultations and therapies provided at a distance, teleconsultation, and teletherapy will be increasingly available due to the widespread availability of videophones.

See also GENETICS; HEALTH CARE; MEDICAL CARE PROVIDERS; MENTAL HEALTH; PSYCHOLOGY.

BIBLIOGRAPHY

MOORE-EDE, MARTIN. *The Twenty-Four Hour Society: Understanding Human Limits to a World That Never Stops.* Reading, MA: Addison-Wesley, 1993.

U.S. Congress, Office of Technology Assessment. *The Biology of Mental Disorder.* Washington, DC: U.S. Government Printing Office, 1992.

YAGER, JOEL. *The Future of Psychiatry.* Washington, DC: American Psychiatric Press, 1989.

Joel Yager

Psychology

During the past thirty years, as its base of knowledge has matured and deepened, psychology has branched into a wide array of subfields. These subfields include artificial intelligence; behavioral medicine; cognitive science; development over the life span; educational psychology; public health and wellness promotion; learning; language processing; mental health treatment and research; neuropsychology; industrial psychology and organizational behavior; perception; rehabilitation; chronic pain management; and research and treatment of sleep/wake disorders. While not a comprehensive list, these subfields are representative of the many areas in which psychology collaborates with scientists in other disciplines and about which it has generated substantial bodies of knowledge. These advances will continue to improve our understanding of human behavior. Scientific understanding of normal, abnormal, and optimal human functioning will benefit individuals who suffer from impaired functioning and will extend the benefits of normal and optimal functioning to individuals, communities, and organizations.

Two of the most significant advances in psychology that will shape the future of the discipline are (1) the demolition of the duality of cause and effect and (2) the rejection of either/or questions like those spawned by the mind/body problem. Psychologists no longer pose such questions as "What is the cause of X?" or "Which exercises the greatest influence over behavior, the body or the mind?" Such formulations are too simplistic and lead to research that can only yield incomplete answers. Psychologists recognize that the interactions that occur between physical and mental processes, or those between people and their environments, are too complex to sort into "cause" and "effect." The various factors involved influence one another. Research is now aimed at understanding the degree of influence the various factors exercise and how they affect one another. Future research in psychology will continue to investigate complex interactions. Researchers will formulate questions such as "How many and what are the factors that produced this outcome?" and "How did the factors interact with each other to produce the outcome?"

A third development that will influence the course of psychology in the future is a revolution in the method of scientific inquiry. Along with other disciplines, psychology will continue to contribute to the development of a scientific method that (1) can accommodate the study of interactions; (2) is more responsive to the needs of society rather than rigorously separated from it; and (3) is cognizant of the reciprocal relationships between the knower and the known. The adjustments necessitated by accommodation to the postmodern constructivist perspective in science will become ever more apparent in the future of psychology.

Recent advances in the behavioral sciences, along with the fruits of decades of research, explain the origins of mental disorders; how people think, reason, and make decisions; the role of emotions in behavior and health; the subtle ways in which parents and children influence one another; and how schools shape self-concept and self-esteem. Research on cultural differences in attitudes, social status, social bonds, and attitudes and beliefs will continue to improve our understanding of the role of society in the life of the individual and may in time explain why social prejudices and stereotypes are so long lasting. It is hoped that this knowledge will lead to techniques that will result in improved human relations.

Social problems and moral development will remain targets of psychological research aimed at improving the welfare of society. Occupational and industrial psychology will continue to be concerned with the effects of the dramatic changes in the world marketplace, in global competition, information technology, and the disappearance of certain types of jobs—with the effects of all these changes not only upon workers at home and in the workplace but upon the way business is conducted.

Techniques for assessing and diagnosing brain damage, autism, and mental disorders will continue to improve, as will methods of assessing academic, cognitive, and other types of human functioning. Individual differences in brain functions at the neuromolecular, neuropsychological, and neurochemical levels will be measured accurately. Differences in how individuals receive, store, and process information will also be measured with greater specificity than they can be today.

Scales for measuring good mental health will become more sophisticated, as will the means of preventing illness and promoting psychological well-being. Studies of the brain will continue to illuminate what is already known about how immune functions are influenced by the central nervous system, which is in turn affected by psychological states.

Behavioral genetics, which explores the complex interactions between constitutional factors, genetic inheritance, and the environment, will continue to yield insights into the development of schizophre-

nia and other mental disorders, leading to more effective treatment. The diathesis-stress model of mental illness will continue to point to the direction for future research on mental illness. A full understanding of mental health and illness will require the inclusion of genetic, biochemical, neurological, interpersonal, and cultural factors.

Research with animals will remain important in psychology. According to a distinguished panel of forty behavioral scientists who advise the National Institute of Mental Health (NIMH), "Behavioral studies with animals have provided many important insights into learning and the processes affecting motivation, including hunger, thirst, sleep, and sex. Studies with animals in the future will continue to permit researchers to examine fundamental behavioral processes apart from the impact of human cultures and institutions." Social influences on biological processes and interactions—such as those between nutrition and environment or those between aggressive behavior and biochemistry—will continue to emanate from research with animals.

Psychology will continue to broaden its scope in the future. Research on the long-term development of species will increase our understanding of the influence of evolution upon behavior. Advances in evolutionary theory and new discoveries about how humans have evolved will add to our understanding of why humans behave as they do. "Cross-cultural studies will yield knowledge of which aspects of human functioning represent biological imperatives and which represent cultural options" (NIMH report). Psychological study of conflicts among groups, social issues, moral exclusion, and conflict resolution will contribute to the improvement of relations between different cultures and nations. The practice of psychology and its applications to education, social issues, and the workplace will be disseminated internationally. Global dissemination will enable more people to have the most effective treatments for mental disorders and to enjoy the benefits of better techniques for education, and will encourage the application of human factors research to a wide array of environments. Research findings that are germane to public policy, the natural environment, and systems of law and adjudication will permit societies to formulate objectives and implement policies that promote well-being. Psychology will continue to participate in and contribute to the development of a scientific method that can accommodate all the facets of humans and their environments.

See also MENTAL HEALTH; PSYCHIATRY; PUBLIC HEALTH; SOCIAL SCIENCES.

BIBLIOGRAPHY

Buss, D. M. "Evolutionary Psychology: A New Paradigm for Psychological Science." *Psychological Inquiry* 6 (1995): 1–30.

Cacioppo, J. T., and Bernston, G. G. "Social Psychological Contributions to the Decade of the Brain: Doctrine of Multilevel Analysis." *American Psychologist* 47/8 (1992): 1019–1028.

Cole, J. D., et al. "The Science of Prevention: A Conceptual Framework and Some Directions for a National Research Program." *American Psychologist* 48/10 (1993): 1013–1022.

Deutsch, M. A. "Educating for a Peaceful World." *American Psychologist* 48/5 (1993): 510–517.

Maier, S. F.; Watkins, L. R.; and Fleshner, M. "Psychoneuroimmunology: The Interface between Behavior, Brain, and Immunity." *American Psychologist* 49/12 (1994): 1004–1017.

Matarazzo, J. D. "Psychological Testing and Assessment in the Twenty-First Century." *American Psychologist* 47/8 (1992): 1007–1018.

National Institute of Mental Health. *Basic Behavioral Science for Mental Health: A National Investment.* Washington, DC: U.S. Government Printing Office, 1995.

Stokols, D. "Establishing and Maintaining and Healthy Environments: Toward a Social Ecology of Health Promotion." *American Psychologist* 47/1 (1992): 6–22.

Melissa G. Warren

Public Assistance Programs

As the twentieth century draws to a close, the social landscape is shifting. In the United States and many other developed Western nations, we witness disturbing increases in economic inequality, single parenthood, homeless and ill-housed families, detached and disaffected youths, drug use, violent crime, and distrust among the races. Following "the American Century" of economic and political triumphs, we find ourselves in a state of social disarray with misgivings about the future.

At the same time, welfare state policies seem out of touch with today's and tomorrow's social issues. Public assistance or "welfare" does little except maintain poor people in their poverty, and spending for entitlements, which go mostly to the middle class, is out of control, threatening fiscal crisis in the years ahead.

Questions must be raised about the very assumptions underlying public assistance and the welfare state. During coming decades it is all but inevitable that domestic policy will undergo a fundamental transformation. While the ultimate outcome of this transformation is impossible to predict, it is likely that a new emphasis on *development* will replace the traditional welfare state emphasis on maintenance.

Public Assistance and Other Welfare State Spending

In financial terms, social spending has been the chief function of the modern state. Social spending (i.e., government payments to individuals for income security, medical care, nutrition, housing, social services, and so forth) makes up over half of federal expenditures in the United States and even more in Western Europe. This spending comes in three basic forms: public assistance, tax expenditures (or "tax benefits"), and social insurance.

PUBLIC ASSISTANCE

Public assistance or "welfare" is financial aid, food, housing, health care, or other assistance that is provided by "means test," i.e., it is targeted to people who are thought to have insufficient means to survive on their own. Although the general public seems to think of "welfare" as a huge expenditure, in fact it makes up only 16 percent of all social spending at the federal level.

By far the largest part of public assistance spending goes to the elderly and the disabled. They are the major recipients of income support through Supplemental Security Income (SSI) and the major recipients of medical care through Medicaid (see Table 1). In contrast, Aid to Families with Dependent Children (AFDC), which has been the target of heated "welfare reform" debates during the 1990s, is a comparatively modest expenditure. Also noteworthy are the small expenditures for education and training, and the even smaller expenditures for child care and other social services.

Spending trends in public assistance can be summarized succinctly: Medicaid is rising rapidly, and everything else is staying about the same. With an aging population, the rise in Medicaid is likely to continue. Because states cosponsor Medicaid, it is a growing budgetary problem in virtually all states.

At this writing, the Republican congressional majority, in its "Contract with America," is attacking public assistance for the poor. They seek to limit spending and reorganize public assistance programs into "block grants" under state control. But the proposals do not include Medicaid, which is the major budgetary problem. "Managed care" and other administrative controls will become more common in Medicaid, but these will not alter the underlying trend.

TABLE 1. Federal Spending for Means-Tested Public Assistance Programs in Billions of Dollars, 1992*

	Amount	*Percent*
Total Means-Tested Public Assistance	*178.6*	*100.0*
Income Support	32.3	18.1
Aid to Families with Dependent Children	13.6	
Supplemental Security Income	18.7	
Medical Care	75.6	42.3
Medicaid	67.8	
Medical Care for Veterans	7.8	
Food and Nutrition	30.8	17.2
Food Stamps	23.5	
School Lunch and Other	7.3	
Housing	17.3	9.7
Section 8 Rental Assistance	12.3	
Low-Rent Public Housing	5.0	
Education and Training	17.8	10.0
College Grants and Loans	11.1	
All Other	6.7	
Social Services	4.8	2.7

* Source: Ross, Jane L. *Means-Tested Programs: An Overview, Problems, and Issues.* GAO Report T-HEHS-95-76. Washington, DC: U.S. General Accounting Office (citing Congressional Research Service), 1995

TAX EXPENDITURES

The second, often overlooked leg of the welfare state is tax expenditures. In 1995, tax expenditures to individuals are estimated at $392 billion, much of this amount in housing, health care, and retirement security (see Table 2). These are hidden welfare benefits to the middle class—"hidden" because most of the public does not view them as the welfare transfers that they are. Several points about tax expenditures are important to bear in mind. First, by far the most tax expenditures go to individuals rather than to corporations. Second, almost none of the tax expenditures go to the poor. Third, tax expenditures to individuals far exceed in size all public assistance programs to the poor combined. Fourth, tax expenditures to individuals go largely into asset accumulation (mostly in homes and retirement accounts), while most other welfare state spending (in public assistance and social insurance) is oriented toward consumption. Indeed, public assistance programs for the poor do not permit asset accumulation (a very misguided policy), while tax benefits programs for the middle class promote asset accumulation.

Trends in tax expenditures are uncertain. At this writing, Republican congressional leaders and President Bill Clinton are proposing more tax cuts.

The wisdom of large tax cuts when federal spending is producing chronic deficits is much in doubt.

Also gaining momentum are proposals to replace the progressive income tax and most accompanying tax deductions with a flat tax and/or a consumption tax. If these tax reform initiatives are accompanied by (1) exclusion of tax liability for low-income households and (2) elimination of tax deductions and credits across the board (two very big ifs), tax reform would be desirable.

SOCIAL INSURANCE

By far the largest social expenditures are for social insurance or "entitlements," represented primarily by Social Security, Medicare, and federal pensions. It is important to make a few summary observations. First, at more than $600 billion in 1995, entitlement spending is about three times greater than public assistance spending. Second, this spending is not means-tested; most of it goes not to the poor but to the middle class. Third, a huge proportion of entitlement spending is for the elderly (an even bigger proportion than in public assistance spending). Fourth, up to the present, recipients of retirement and old-age medical benefits have received much more than they have put into the system (this will not be possible in the near future). Fifth, entitlement

Public Assistance Programs

TABLE 2.   Estimated Federal Tax Expenditures to Individuals and Corporations in Billions of Dollars, 1995 and 1999*

	Amount	Percent
Tax Expenditures to Individuals	*392.0*	*504.6*
Housing		
Mortgage Interest Tax Deduction	53.5	67.8
Other Home-Ownership Tax Benefits	33.4	39.8
Health Care		
Exclusion of Medical Insurance Premiums	45.8	62.6
Exclusion of Untaxed Medicare Benefits	13.1	25.2
Retirement Security		
Exclusion of Pension Contributions/Earnings	80.9	102.0
Exclusion of Untaxed Social Security and Railroad Retirement Benefits	23.1	27.1
Exclusion of Income on Life Insurance and Annuities	10.3	14.3
Capital Gains and Other Income/Property Benefits		
Exclusion of Capital Gains at Death	12.7	18.3
Maximum 28% Tax Rate on Capital Gains	9.1	13.9
Exclusion of State and Local Income and Personal Property Taxes	24.7	31.0
All Other Tax Expenditures to Individuals	85.4	102.9
Tax Expenditures to Corporations	*58.7*	*59.9*
Total Tax Expenditures	*450.7*	*564.5*

* Source: Calculated from U.S. Congress, Joint Committee on Taxation. *Estimates of Federal Tax Expenditures for Fiscal Years 1995–1999*. Washington, DC: U.S. Government Printing Office, 1994.

spending is rising rapidly; by 2003, mandatory entitlements are projected to make up 58.2 percent of all federal spending. Sixth, the tax collections ("insurance premiums") for these programs will not be enough to meet obligations in the near future: Medicare expenditures already exceed revenues, and Social Security retirement benefits will exceed revenues around 2012 (see Figures 1 and 2). Although "trust funds" have theoretically been accumulated for these programs that would carry Medicare until 2001 and Social Security until 2029, in fact this money exists only on paper. (As a population, we have voted entitlement benefits for ourselves but also voted to spend the trust fund money in other ways, all the while telling ourselves that the trust fund money is sacrosanct. In the long run, the hypocrisy of these actions cannot be painted over by self-delusion or political posturing.)

A fiscal crisis is on the horizon. Revenue shortfalls will be severe by 2012, and under current projections, entitlement spending would exceed *all* federal revenues by the year 2030. The entitlements simply cannot be paid for in their current form without grave injustice to future generations and serious harm to the U.S. economy (see Peterson, 1993). Every policy analyst and politician of substance knows this to be the case. Yet, at present, few politicians dare speak the truth lest they not be reelected. The longer this moratorium on truth prevails, the more difficult the adjustments will be when they finally arrive. Public denial may last until 2010 or 2015, when change will take place in a crisis atmosphere.

Maintenance: The Welfare State of the Twentieth Century

Overall, the welfare state of the twentieth century can be characterized as oriented toward maintenance with five distinguishing characteristics: transfer of income, passive support for the unemployed, preoccupation with problems, focus on individuals, and bureaucratic organization.

TRANSFER OF INCOME

Foremost, the welfare state is characterized by the transfer of income to support consumption. Social

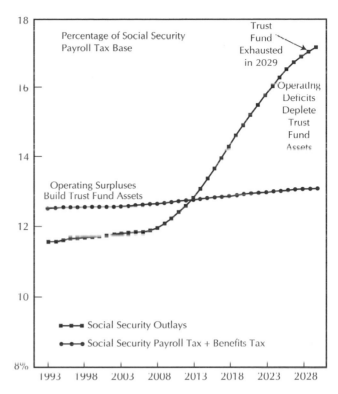

FIGURE 1. Projections for Medicare revenues and expenses.
(Source: Bipartisan Commission on Entitlement and Tax Reform. *Interim Report to the President.* Washington, DC: U.S. Government Printing Office, 1994.)

FIGURE 2. Projections for Social Security revenues and expenses.
(Source: Bipartisan Commission on Entitlement and Tax Reform. *Interim Report to the President.* Washington, DC: U.S. Government Printing Office, 1994.)

insurance and means-tested transfers make up most social spending. In this social policy scheme, an individual's "welfare" (well-being) is defined by his or her level of income, and it is assumed that this income supports a certain level of consumption. This perspective rests on flawed intellectual foundations in neoclassical economics, in which well-being derives only from consumption. But as any accountant or financial planner knows, consumption by itself does not constitute well-being. Savings and investment—asset building—must be taken into consideration as well.

PASSIVE SUPPORT FOR THE UNEMPLOYED

The origins of the welfare state were in a system of industrial capitalism wherein most employees worked productively with little education and training. Consistent with these conditions, welfare state provisions such as Social Security benefits, workers' compensation, and unemployment insurance were designed to support people off the job, but not to prepare people for new jobs. Since those days, the world of work has changed dramatically,

but U.S. social policy has not. In a postindustrial era, ever more skills—and more flexible skills—will be required to succeed in the labor market. Policies designed solely to support the unemployed and nonemployed are tragically out of date.

PREOCCUPATION WITH PROBLEMS

On the services side, the welfare state has been dominated by modern-day social work and other professions with an orientation toward problem solving. The basic idea has been to identify an individual or family "problem," and then "intervene" in an attempt to solve that problem. With this narrow focus, social workers often overlook opportunities for success.

FOCUS ON INDIVIDUALS

Despite community-oriented rhetoric, most social policies address individual issues—rental subsidies for the unhoused, food stamps for the unfed, criminal justice for the unruly, and psychotherapy for the unhinged. The vast majority of today's social workers ply their trade with individuals, in agencies and offices quite removed from community settings. The welfare state is, in reality, highly individualistic. Both income support and services have been aimed almost exclusively at individuals. Occasionally the policy focuses on families, but seldom on neighborhoods and communities. In sharp juxtaposition to this individual focus, it is apparent that the most vexing social issues of our time—alienated youth, crime, drug abuse, AIDS, homelessness, violence within families—stem from social and economic institutions, such as loss of employment, racial discrimination, weakening of community organizations, changes in family structure, and failing schools.

BUREAUCRATIC ORGANIZATION

The welfare state has been organized primarily as a public-sector, top-down, bureaucratic, and largely disconnected set of activities. To be sure, we have enacted lofty and well-intentioned policies, but we have paid too little attention to what those policies actually do when they "reach the ground" in communities and households. Programs and services are often not what they were intended to be. They are fragmented and unresponsive to genuine needs.

These five characteristics together constitute the maintenance orientation of the welfare state of the twentieth century. This emphasis on maintenance has alleviated suffering, but it has done little to build capacities that would enable people and communities to become self-sufficient. As the century draws to a close, it is clear that maintenance by itself is an inadequate foundation for constructing social policy.

Development: Domestic Policy in the Twenty-first Century

Because the fiscal problems are overwhelming, and because maintenance strategies are not responding to the most pressing social issues of our time, it is very likely that domestic policy will undergo a major transformation in the decades ahead. The nature of this transformation is impossible to predict, but it would be desirable to shift from maintenance toward development.

In contrast to the five maintenance characteristics described above, a development policy would emphasize the opposites: building assets instead of providing income for consumption, developing human capital instead of aimless support for the unemployed, enhancing capacities instead of problem-centered treatment, building communities instead of

isolating individuals, and creating responsive human service organizations instead of bureaucracies.

BUILDING ASSETS

A development policy would promote asset accumulation. This policy would recognize that individuals, families, and the nation as a whole must counterbalance income-and-consumption with savings-and-investment. Moreover, asset building would become a foundation of social policy, so that many social and economic goals—especially higher education, home ownership, small business development, retirement security, and even health care—are achieved to a significant extent through programs of asset accumulation, even for the poorest families. Work in this area has been pioneered by Sherraden (1991), who proposes a new domestic policy based on Individual Development Accounts (IDAs). This thinking has generated widespread discussion and policy initiatives (Edwards and Sherraden, 1995).

INVESTING IN PEOPLE

As the nations of East Asia are demonstrating, social policy cannot be separated from economic policy. Social policy should promote education, job skills, and labor market participation. In the United States we now realize that more attention must be paid to developing a labor force capable of competing in the international arena (Hornbeck and Salamon, 1990). We have more discussion of the importance of primary and secondary education, and effective transitions from school to work. Also, there is increasing attention to means-tested transfers as a possible deterrent to labor market participation. Little attention has yet been paid, however, to transformation of the largest social policy provisions—particularly Social Security benefits, unemployment insurance, and workers' compensation—so that they can contribute to enhancement of skills, participation, and productivity.

FOCUSING ON PERSONAL, INTERPERSONAL, AND FAMILY POTENTIAL

Instead of a narrow focus on personal problems (deviance, deficiency, abnormality), a development policy would affirm ordinary life events and opportunities. (To those who are therapy-minded, this approach may sound peculiar. Perhaps it can be understood by analogy: Peter Drucker, the management guru, has identified a common managerial error that he calls "feeding problems and starving solutions." According to Drucker, what one gets by "problem-solving" is damage containment. Only opportunities produce growth. Drucker suggests that a manager first draw up a list of opportunities facing the organization and make sure that each is adequately staffed. Only then should the manager draw up a list of problems.) The logic of development is that the best uses of energy and resources are in building social skills and strong families, promoting resilience, and striving for success. The helping professions had these traditions prior to the creation of the welfare state. Much work remains to be done in revitalizing these traditions for the twenty-first century.

PROMOTING CITIZENSHIP, MUTUALITY, AND INTERRACIAL UNDERSTANDING

However great a society's commitment to individuality and freedom, it requires a countervailing commitment to community and civic participation. Voluntary association has been a hallmark of American democracy, and mutual ties have served as an essential counterbalance to America's economic individualism. This was recognized from the outset of the republic by Jefferson, later noted by de Tocqueville, and has reappeared in calls for greater social responsibility and a stronger sense of community in work by Etzioni (1993) and others.

Although an emphasis on community is not by itself a solution (one is reminded of rather naive community action efforts during the 1960s), it is an essential starting point. Fortunately, extreme individualism in social policy and practice may be changing. Nonmilitary national service has joined military service, albeit in a small way, as a national policy (Eberly and Sherraden, 1990). In the social work profession, there is a call for a return to community-based services rather than office-based psychotherapies. Recent successes of community development corporations (CDCs) are noteworthy. Community-based youth development is being emphasized anew (Sherraden, 1992). These community-building efforts also forge ties across racial groups. In the years ahead, community-building is likely to become a stronger feature of social policy and practice in the United States.

CREATING RESPONSIVE AND EFFECTIVE HUMAN SERVICE ORGANIZATIONS

Dramatic change is needed in the administration of social policy, including fewer layers in the organizational structure, fewer forms to fill out, more integrated delivery systems, more incentives for outstanding performance, more control by those who are in the front lines, greater responsiveness to individual needs and circumstances, more emphasis on outcomes, and measurement of returns on public investment. State and local governments have been in the forefront in "reinventing" policy, organizations, programs, and services that deliver domestic policy. This thinking is beginning to emerge at the federal level. Recent innovations in areas such as public/private partnerships, collaboration across different service areas, devolution of authority to local control, client "empowerment" strategies, "one-stop shopping" for services, use of telecommunications to reduce paperwork and office visits, and return on investment accounting are all encouraging developments. But welfare-state bureaucracies are deeply entrenched. A great deal remains to be done, particularly in linking new organizational forms to family and community development.

See also ENTITLEMENT PROGRAMS; HEALTH CARE FINANCING; PRIVATE ASSISTANCE PROGRAMS; PUBLIC ASSISTANCE PROGRAMS: SOCIAL SECURITY; SOCIAL WELFARE PHILOSOPHIES; UNEMPLOYMENT; UNEMPLOYMENT INSURANCE, WORKMEN'S COMPENSATION, JOB SECURITY.

BIBLIOGRAPHY

EBERLY, DONALD, and SHERRADEN, MICHAEL, eds. *The Moral Equivalent of War? A Study of Non-Military Service in Nine Nations.* Westport, CT: Greenwood Press, 1990.
EDWARDS, KAREN, and SHERRADEN, MICHAEL. *Individual Development Accounts: Asset-Based Policy Innovation.* St. Louis: Center for Social Development, Washington University, 1995.
ETZIONI, AMITAI. *The Spirit of Community: Rights, Responsibilities, and the Communitarian Agenda.* New York: Crown Publishers, 1993.
HORNBECK, DAVID W., and SALAMON, LESTER M., eds. *Human Capital and America's Future.* Baltimore, MD: Johns Hopkins University Press, 1990.
PETERSON, PETER G. *Facing Up: How to Rescue the Economy from Crushing Debt and Restore the American Dream.* New York: Simon & Schuster, 1993.
ROSS, JANE L. *Means-Tested Programs: An Overview, Problems, and Issues.* GAO Report T-HEHS-95-76. Washington, DC: U.S. General Accounting Office, 1995.
SHERRADEN, MICHAEL. *Assets and the Poor: A New American Welfare Policy.* Armonk, NY: M. E. Sharpe, 1991.
————. *Community-Based Youth Services in International Perspective.* Washington, DC: Carnegie Council on Adolescent Development and W. T. Grant Foundation Commission on Youth and America's Future, 1992.

Michael Sherraden

Public Assistance Programs: Social Security

Social Security programs in the United States raise funds from payroll taxes to provide income support to retired or disabled workers and their dependents, as well as Medicare Hospital Insurance (HI) for those over sixty-five or suffering long-term disabilities. In addition, Medicare Supplementary Insurance (SMI) covers doctors' fees and outpatient services for this portion of the population, mainly financed through general revenues (one-fourth is paid for by premiums from those who enroll).

Operating as a chain of promises through time, Social Security is the one federal program most inescapably concerned with the future. By paying for benefits earlier promised to yesterday's workers (today's retirees), today's workers earn "entitlements" they can expect to redeem as tomorrow's beneficiaries. Since as workers they will be paying those future bills, today's children are directly involved in this chain of promises we are making for them.

Since the basic demographic patterns are already in place, there is relatively little uncertainty about the future size of the beneficiary population and the workforce that will be available to support it. Changes in fertility, immigration, and death rates can alter this picture only gradually and in the very long term. The postwar baby boomers will begin pressing on Social Security funds around 2010. Likewise, lower birthrates after the mid-1960s will produce relatively fewer workers in the early part of the next century. These established facts, along with a gradual growth of life expectancy in old age, will produce an overall aging of American society and strains on Social Security finances. The number of workers for each Social Security beneficiary will have gone from 16 in 1950 to 3.7 in 1970; 3.3 in 1990; and 1.7–2.2 workers by 2030 (depending on different assumptions).

At the other extreme of uncertainty are inherently unforeseeable developments: technological breakthroughs, pandemics, wars, culture shifts, and the like. No one can say if these will occur to produce discontinuities in demographic trends or different social understandings of dependency, aging, and obligations. At an intermediate level of uncertainty are projections in standard economic variables, such as employment, wages, and GNP growth. Greater affluence and productivity per worker can offset some of the consequences of fewer workers. Such projections give modest guidance for weighing the future, even if we have no way of finally settling on optimistic or pessimistic projections or any point in between.

Most people think about Social Security in terms of financial outlook—"Will it be there for me and my family?" In a very basic sense, the answer will be what it has always been: Social Security will be there five or fifty years from now, depending on the will of the voters and the willingness of the working population to pay the taxes that make good on promised benefit entitlements. The more complex issue thus becomes one of estimating how financially burdensome it may be to keep the chain of promises intact.

Major reforms in 1983 sought to ease the future financial burden in three ways. First, the retirement age for earning full benefits will gradually rise from 65 in 2003 to 67 in 2025. Second, beneficiaries with gross incomes over certain limits ($25,000 for single persons, $32,000 for married couples) have up to half their benefits subject to income taxation. Finally, payroll taxes were increased (from 9.35 percent in 1983 to 15.3 percent in 1990 and all years thereafter) to provide a growing surplus in the Social Security Trust Fund. The fund holdings—IOUs in the form of treasury bonds and the interest they earn—will be drawn down to help cover the gap as projected payroll tax receipts begin lagging behind spending on the growing ranks of retired baby boomers, sometime around 2016. By 2025, all of the baby boomers will have retired, the annual tax-to-spending shortfall will be $60 billion, and depletion of the fund surplus will accelerate until it is exhausted in 2036. One should note that if spending promises are to be kept, the treasury bonds redeemed from the fund from 2016 to 2036 will have to be paid for with higher taxes or further borrowing on financial markets. Once the fund is insolvent in 2036, the choices will be to cut benefits, sharply increase payroll taxes, continue funding Social Security from general revenues, or some combination of these options.

The financial outlook worsens and need for higher taxes grows when we consider the health insurance side of Social Security. Government forecasts show Medicare's HI producing a deficit of spending to payroll tax revenues in the mid-1990s and the HI Trust Fund becoming insolvent in 2002. Medicare insurance for physician services had no comparable trust fund and official projections are not made beyond 2000. But many of the same forces drive both HI and SMI spending, and forecasts are that both together will equal or exceed Social Security spending on retirement and disability by the year 2020. Yet even these projections assume that medical costs, while rising faster than general inflation, will grow substantially slower than they did in the 1970s and 1980s. Whether reform of the health system in the 1990s will produce such a slowdown in the growth of health care costs remains to be seen.

Considering Social Security and HI together, projected income should be enough to cover projected spending for perhaps the next 10 to 15 years. After about 2010, a large deficit will begin accumulating. While the future payroll tax rate is set by law at 15.3 percent of earnings (divided equally between worker and employer), projected spending will be 20 percent of payroll earnings by 2020. If the SMI portion of Medicare obligations is projected in the same way as hospital insurance, the figure grows to 26 percent in 2020, implying payroll taxes two-thirds higher than those today. This large gap between income and outgo will eventually have to be closed by enacting substantially higher taxes, lower benefits, or some combination of the two. The total of the actuarial deficit that lies ahead over the next seventy-five years is estimated at $13.2 trillion. (Actuarial deficit is defined as the amount by which projected future expenditures for benefits and administration exceed the projected income and value of the trust funds.) These projections are based on what Social Security program trustees term "intermediate" assumptions about the future. However, evidence from prevailing historical trends in birth, mortality, and productivity rates is more in line with what are conventionally labeled as the trustees' "pessimistic" alternative assumptions. If those are used, the projected deficits and need for more tax revenue would begin toward the end of the 1990s, with a total actuarial deficit estimated at $22.8 trillion. (For perspective, spending $1 million a day, it would take about 2,700 years to spend $1 trillion.)

Social Security has become institutionalized both in public beliefs about the value of the program as well as in individual and employer planning for retirement. However, there is very little public understanding of the program, the chain of promises it represents, or the immense future commitments that exist. At the same time, politicians will no doubt continue to avoid saying or doing anything controversial that could improve understanding of the program and its future commitments.

Despite the popularity of Social Security today, surveys generally show 60 percent or more of non-retired adults have little confidence that funds will

be available to pay their retirement benefits. There is a good possibility that public support for the system may slowly erode in the years ahead. First, the very high ratio of benefits received to contributions paid by those participating in the early decades of the Social Security program has now come to an end and will no longer be available to build popular support. Second, improving health, increasing wealth, and better living conditions for many older persons will help undermine once prevalent beliefs about the elderly as a homogeneous and inherently needy group. Third, the gradually emerging but huge actuarial deficit will strain the tolerance of working-age persons for ever higher payroll taxes. Fourth, economic inequality, which is greater among the elderly than among the working aged, will persist and probably grow, given prevailing inequalities in education, home ownership, occupational structure, and private employer benefits. This will increase resistance to transferring resources to elderly persons regardless of need. Finally, greater income testing of Social Security benefits will erode program support from higher income groups, whose benefits are proportionately less in relation to contributions than is the case for lower income groups. Currently, only 6 percent of workers are above the earnings ceiling at which Social Security taxes cease ($57,300 in 1993), and since this limit is indexed to constantly adjust upward with average wage increases, not many are ever likely to get beyond the tax ceiling. On the other hand, the income ceiling at which people have to start paying income tax on their Social Security benefits is unindexed; hence the current 22 percent of beneficiaries who find their entitlements subject to taxation will find their ranks constantly growing.

While Social Security will certainly provide most Americans with a minimum level of income support for many years to come, new ways of thinking about the issues are likely to be sought. Pressures will grow to use the Trust Fund surplus (projected to peak at $5.6 trillion in 2024) in more constructive ways than the current accumulation of treasury IOUs that help finance current deficit spending in the federal budget. If more active use of the surplus for public and private investment were to raise economic growth over what it would have been, future taxes to honor Social Security promises would be relatively less burdensome at the resulting higher levels of national income. Efforts will probably be made to allow individuals to apply a portion of their Social Security taxes to individual accounts for investment and future returns.

Further increases in the official retirement age are likely. Moreover, the very concept of retirement may be questioned and reformulated. It is a concept created by public policy from an earlier era of industrial factory life. Rather than compartmentalizing education, work, and leisure into sequential age categories, a postindustrial society may see these fundamental human activities as attributes of a person's security and welfare throughout a lifetime. Some form of personal account to draw upon and pay into may well be developed to allow individuals greater choice in arranging their own combinations of work, study, and leisure throughout the life cycle.

In light of existing commitments to those in and nearing old age, any such changes undoubtedly will have to be phased in gradually, as is the currently mandated increase in the retirement age after 2003. But for the 178 million Americans now under age 45, with time to adjust their retirement plans, and for the post–Cold War generation now being born, it is highly prudent and appropriate to rethink these issues.

For an overview of public assistance, see PUBLIC ASSISTANCE PROGRAMS. *See also* HEALTH CARE FINANCING; PRIVATE ASSISTANCE PROGRAMS; UNEMPLOYMENT INSURANCE, WORKMEN'S COMPENSATION, JOB SECURITY.

BIBLIOGRAPHY

AARON, HENRY J.; BOSWORTH, BARRY P.; and BURTLESS, GARY. *Can Americans Afford to Grow Old?* Washington, DC: Brookings Institution, 1989.

COOK, FAY LOMAX, and BARRETT, EDITH J. "Public Support for Social Security." *Journal of Aging Studies* 2/4 (1988): 339–356.

KOITZ, DAVID. "The Financial Outlook for Social Security and Medicare." In *CRS Report for Congress.* CRS Publication, 92-608 EPW, July 31, 1992. Washington, DC: Congressional Research Service, 1992.

KOTLIKOFF, LAURENCE J. *Generational Accounting.* New York: Free Press, 1992.

Organization for Economic Cooperation and Development. *Aging Population*s. Paris: OECD, 1988.

Hugh Heclo

Public Finance

The information revolution will continue to force dramatic changes in public finance. Still, it is not yet clear whether a powerful trend toward limited government will soon prevail over welfare state programs that are headed for fiscal disaster.

The information age has unleashed unprecedented economic competition but also cooperation between governments—cooperation because trade barriers are falling. Lower tariffs in one region of the world lead to pressures in other regions to reduce restraints on trade.

In the past, governments could charge monopolistic prices because citizens had little choice but to pay. Thanks to computer and communications technological advances, many economic transactions can now be performed anywhere in the world. This will force governments to compete by becoming more efficient by lowering taxes. Such pressures may lead to the adoption by the United States of a greatly simplified flat-rate income tax. Countries that maintain high tax rates will see capital and highly skilled entrepreneurs flee to more friendly areas.

The 1980s brought a significant decline in marginal tax rates—the tax rate paid on the last dollar earned. The cut in tax rates during President Ronald Reagan's first term was followed by the 1986 Tax Reform Act, which slashed the top tax rate to almost one-half the 70 percent rate last seen in 1980. These U.S. tax rate reductions led to tax rate cuts in many states and countries. Future elections may usher in sweeping tax reforms, such as the replacement of the current income tax with a flat-rate income tax or sales tax.

The future will also bring passage of additional constitutional limits on federal and state government taxes, spending, and debt. The Balanced Budget Amendment passed the House of Representatives for the first time ever in 1995, only to fail by one vote in the Senate. An additional attempt to pass it is likely in the near future.

The House of Representatives is expected to vote by April 1996 for the first time ever on a proposed tax limitation constitutional amendment. While the two-thirds vote necessary to approve such an amendment is unlikely, proponents may obtain over 250 of the 435 votes cast on the measure.

This tax limitation amendment would require a three-fifths vote of each house of Congress in order to pass a tax increase bill. It is similar to measures that have grown increasingly common in state constitutions, although most state limits require a two-thirds vote.

Twenty years ago, tax limits on state governments were rare. By 1995, twenty-eight states have adopted various tax or expenditure limits, and several states have adopted multiple limits. Since 1978 five states have added tax increase "supermajority" vote requirements.

Not only is the information age likely to lead to further limits on government taxes and spending, it will also shape the design of the limits. As access to information improves, voters will want to exercise more direct control over government. Since 1992, voters in five states have endorsed requirements for voter approval before certain higher taxes can become law. Several similar measures were narrowly rejected in the 1994 election, but will likely pass in future elections.

Even though there is a strong trend toward limits on government spending and taxes, the welfare state will not shrink easily. Unless current laws are changed soon, an aging population will cause spending on so-called entitlements to explode early in the next century. These entitlement programs cause government benefit checks to be written to people who meet certain criteria for age, income, or wealth.

Spending on entitlement programs, along with interest on the national debt, is projected to equal all federal taxes by the year 2012. That would leave no funds for any of the other functions of government such as defense, highways, courts, education, or law enforcement.

The two largest entitlement programs are Social Security and Medicare. The current tax rate for these two programs is 15.2 percent. Official government projections estimate that the tax rate would have to rise to between 38 and 62 percent by 2040 to pay for benefits promised under current laws. Such tax rates would crush the nation's economy and these programs are widely acknowledged to be unsustainable in their current form.

Unfunded benefit liabilities for these two programs plus federal worker pensions totaled over $14.4 trillion in 1991, or more than triple the U.S. government's debt. By the year 2025, Social Security and Medicare programs are projected to run an annual deficit of over $750 billion under current policies.

The average age of Americans is increasing, leaving fewer workers to pay the taxes that fund these old-age benefits. In 1985, there were more than five workers for each retiree. In 2030, there will be fewer than three. People are also collecting old-age benefits for a longer period of time. When Social Security began in 1935, the average life expectancy was sixty-one years. Today it is seventy-six.

Despite these ominous demographic trends, current laws promise even higher benefits. For example, if a family's wages equal $24,000, a retiree in the year 2000 will receive Social Security benefits of $11,380. With the same wages (adjusted for infla-tion to 1994 dollars), a retiree will collect $13,020 in 2030, and $14,630 in 2060.

Although changes are considered politically impossible now, that may soon change. A recent public opinion poll showed that more workers under thirty-five believed in UFOs than in the future of Social Security. Younger citizens would welcome political candor on this issue so they can properly plan for their retirement future.

Some countries have privatized their Social Security system. Chile did so in the early 1980s, and the typical Chilean worker's net worth may soon surpass that of the average American worker. When that happens, the fact will be broadly noted in the United States, further weakening public support for Social Security in its current form.

See also ARMS RACE; CREDIT, DEBT, AND BORROWING; DEFICITS, GOVERNMENTAL; ECONOMIC CYCLES; ENTITLEMENT PROGRAMS; HEALTH CARE FINANCING; MONETARY SYSTEM; PUBLIC ASSISTANCE PROGRAMS; SOCIAL WELFARE PHILOSOPHIES; TAXES.

BIBLIOGRAPHY

BARTLEY, ROBERT L. *The Seven Fat Years and How to Do It Again.* New York: Free Press, 1992.

Bipartisan Commission on Entitlement and Tax Reform: Final Report. Washington, DC: U.S. Government, Superintendent of Documents, 1995.

"The Case for Killing Social Security." *Time* (March 20, 1995).

DAVIDSON, JAMES DALE, and REES-MOGG, LORD WILLIAM. *The Great Reckoning.* New York: Summit Books, 1991.

HALL, ROBERT E., and RABUSHKA, ALVIN. *The Flat Tax.* Stanford, CA: Hoover Institution Press, 1995.

LINDSEY, LAWRENCE. *The Growth Experiment: How the New Tax Policy Is Transforming the U.S. Economy.* New York: Basic Books, 1990.

PAYNE, JAMES L. *Costly Returns: The Burdens of the U.S. Tax System.* San Francisco: Institute for Contemporary Studies Press, 1993.

"The Pension Time Bomb." *Washington Monthly* (January–February 1995).

David Keating

Public Health

Medical care has been a minor determinant of improved health over the past 150 years. Improved health has resulted primarily from better economic, environmental, and social conditions. McKeown (1979) states that improvement in health in the past was due to reduced family size, improved nutrition, hygiene, sanitation, and latterly by vaccines and antibiotics. Recent declines in deaths from heart disease in North America and Europe are ascribed mainly to lifestyle changes (quitting smoking, lower-fat diets, more exercise), and simple medical measures (control of high blood pressure) rather than to high-tech interventions such as bypass surgery and transplants. Health status will also be determined mainly by our future environmental, social, and economic situation, and by our lifestyles. Future technological and organizational developments in the delivery of medical care may play a relatively small role.

Level of Economic Development, Wealth, and Equity

Health status will vary enormously from country to country—and within countries—depending on the degree of industrialization and development. Health problems in the least developed countries will continue, at least for several decades, to include high infant mortality rates and infectious diseases. In the industrialized countries, poor health and disability (primarily among the aged) associated with chronic diseases such as heart disease, cancer, and arthritis will constitute the major health problems.

Wealth is closely associated with the level of industrialization and health. As countries industrialize, they will likely experience improved health, except among the poor as they move from rural villages to urban slums.

Overall health status in societies committed to social and economic equity is greater than in countries with a lesser degree of equity. Poverty and powerlessness are associated with poor health. Measures to alleviate poverty and ensure that everyone has access to basic prerequisites of health such as food, shelter, clean water, education, a clean, safe environment, and more control over their lives, will remain fundamental to achieving better health for all in the twenty-first century.

Global Environmental Crisis, Population Growth, and Material Expectations

Regardless of their level of economic development, all countries are likely to face a similar set of health threats in the twenty-first century, rooted in major global environmental change; only their capacity to manage these challenges will differ. Such changes are rooted in a combination of population growth, economic growth, and rising material expectations, which are having three major health-threatening impacts: global atmospheric change, resource depletion, and increasing toxification of the ecosystem.

Ozone depletion and a resultant increase in ultraviolet radiation threatens increased rates of skin cancer, cataracts, and possible interference in immune system functioning. Acid rain is associated with respiratory disease. Global warming could disrupt agricultural production, resulting in malnutrition and famine, the spread of tropical infectious diseases transmitted by insects (e.g., malaria, yellow fever); inundate heavily populated, low-lying areas (such as Bangladesh, Florida, or the Nile Delta) as a result of rising ocean levels that also could cause major population shifts aggravating the health and social problems of "eco-refugees."

Another global environmental danger arises from the impact of toxic pollution on ecosystems and the food chain (ecotoxicity). Subtle genetic, hormonal, immunological, and psychological effects of these chemicals may impose an increasing toll on health. In addition, we can expect increasing conflict within and between nations over diminishing natural resources that will result in death and disease for the civilian populations caught in the middle, many of whom will be forced to become refugees.

Population growth in the least developed countries also is of concern. Coping strategies include improving the education of women, increasing their participation in the work force, reducing infant mortality, and ensuring economic development. These steps, together with a shift toward a more environmentally sustainable form of economic development, may be among the most important strategies for achieving health for all in the twenty-first century.

Urbanization

By the year 2000, for the first time, half the world's population will live in urban areas, some inhabited by tens of millions. Urbanization poses threats as well as opportunities. Threats arise from poor environmental conditions that increase potentials for epidemic diseases and introduce the potential for social disintegration and violence. Opportunities arise from the potential to meet the human needs of large populations efficiently by harnessing the human creativity and energy. The World Health Organization's "Healthy Cities" project, developed in the 1980s, may play a vital role in igniting a new urban public health movement in the twenty-first century.

Lifestyle Changes

Lifestyles, while to some extent a matter of choice, also are significantly influenced by environmental, cultural, social, and economic circumstances. What we eat, whether we smoke or drink or use drugs, how much and how fast we drive, how much we exercise, how stressful our home and work life are—all of these and many other lifestyle behaviors affect our health.

The World Health Organization reported in 1993 that tobacco-related deaths globally rose from one million to three million annually between the 1960s and the '90s and indicated that the toll would rise to seven million annually in the Third World alone within the next two or three decades. We also can expect rising death and disability in the Third World from diseases related to alcohol use, high-fat and low-fiber diets and sedentary lifestyle associated with advanced industrialization. On the other hand, recent progress in reducing lifestyle-related death and disease in Western Europe and North America will likely continue, and in time may well diffuse to industrializing countries.

New and Old Diseases

We can be reasonably certain that we will be confronted with new diseases in the twenty-first century. Some of these will be old diseases in new places (because of the impacts of globalization and health infrastructure breakdowns), or old diseases in new forms as pathogens mutate or our immunological resistance changes. Others will be truly new diseases, either infectious like AIDS, or noninfectious, due perhaps to the impact of cumulative ecotoxicity. Nevertheless, it is likely that the broad pattern of diseases will remain much the same over the next few decades, with increasing numbers of countries undergoing the epidemiological transition to industrial patterns of disease.

Role of Health Care System and Health Technology

One of the significant developments in the 1980s was the realization that the health care system is not the major determinant of our health. Health care systems will likely evolve into more community-based and -managed arrangements, with emphasis on primary care using fewer physicians and more nurses and other allied health professionals. Technological innovations in telematics, biotechnology, and materials technology will doubtless continue at a rapid pace, but the proportionate impact of these developments on the health status of populations will remain problematic. Moreover, as life expectancy increases, the focus of the system may well shift from cure to care, ensuring a higher quality of life—and death—for an aging population.

Mental States

One final potential development that could have an impact on health involves harnessing the power of the mind. There is growing evidence of the effect the psyche can have on the body's hormonal and immunological systems and thus on disease processes. The negative side involves the effect of stress and powerlessness on physical health; the reverse aspect entails learning how to design environments, social structures, work settings, and living conditions—even hospitals—in ways that not only reduce stress but actively promote healing and maintain health. Perhaps individuals will learn to intentionally trigger the positive effects of this psychoneuroimmune system, with potential influence on immunologically related disorders such as cancer, autoimmune diseases, allergies, and infections.

Conclusion

Optimists point to the steadily rising level of health in virtually every country over the past fifty years (with the notable exception of Eastern Europe, where health status declined in the 1970s and '80s), and to a variety of positive factors that suggest this rising level of health may continue. Pessimists point to environmental challenges and to the increasing demands of our growing populations which suggest that these gains are at risk.

See also ACID RAIN; EPIDEMICS; ENVIRONMENTAL REFUGEES; FOOD ADDITIVES; FOOD AND DRUG SAFETY; FRESHWATER; GLOBAL WARMING; NUTRITION; OZONE LAYER DEPLETION; POPULATION GROWTH: UNITED STATES; POPULATION GROWTH: WORLDWIDE.

BIBLIOGRAPHY

ASHTON, JOHN, ed. *Healthy Cities*. Milton Keynes, UK: Open University Press, 1992.
Canadian Public Health Association. *Human and Ecosystem Health*. Ottawa: CPHA, 1992.

EVANS, R.; BARER, M.; and MARMORE, T. *Why Are Some People Healthy and Others Not?* New York: A. de Gruyter, 1994.

HOMER-DIXON, THOMAS; BOUTWELL, JEFFREY; and RATHIENS, GEORGE. "Environmental Change and Violent Conflict." *Scientific American* 268/2 (1993): 38–45.

KARASEK, ROBERT, and THEORELL, THORES. *Healthy Work.* New York: Basic Books, 1989.

MCKEOWN, T. *The Role of Medicine: Dream, Mirage, or Nemesis.* Oxford, U.K.: Basil Blackwell, 1979.

Trevor Hancock

Public Opinion Polls

Until general elections became common during the second half of the nineteenth century, there was essentially no linkage between what the public desired or thought and *either* political campaigning *or* political ideology. Since there were few public election campaigns (outside the United States), formal political thinking remained largely the provenance of scholars and philosophers who were principally concerned with describing a rational system of principles for explaining sociopolitical realities in the manner of the scientific enlightenment (Hobbes, Locke, the Mills and Bentham, and so forth).

The term *ideology* (*idéologie* in French) was coined around 1801 by a French philosopher, Destutt de Tracy, to describe an objective "science of ideas" that he had developed to reveal to people the sources of their biases and erroneous beliefs. But contemporary observers, including Napoleon I, dismissed de Tracy's new "science" as an artful contrivance of simplistic observations that masked dangerously "republican" underlying motives. (Napoleon himself is credited with coining the term "ideologue" to describe all those who promote simple theories for curing social and economic ills.)

The twin connotations of naïveté and hidden intentions have been associated with "ideology" since that time. The term achieved historic currency in the middle of the nineteenth century, when Marx and Engels first characterized formalized history as ideology ("a pack of lies agreed upon by the winners") and argued that all such ideologies serve to justify or rationalize a specific set of interests.

Public Opinion and Political Ideology: Separate but Equal Developments

Throughout the nineteenth century, with the exception of Marx and Engels, there continued to be a remarkable disconnection between actual public opinion and political ideology. In 1848, when the members of the Paris Revolutionary Commune had completed its Declaration of Workers' Rights, the assembly of lawyers, artists, professors, and students had to send a delegation to search the city to find at least one genuine working man to sign the document. In Britain, the first genuinely popular statement of public political desires, *The People's Charter* (drafted by the London Working Men's Association in 1838), called for voting by secret ballot, universal male suffrage, and the elimination of property qualifications for political office holders. In spite of mass demonstrations involving hundreds of thousands of protesters, all formal political parties rejected the charter repeatedly over a ten-year period.

In fact, a principal concern of most political philosophers from the seventeenth to nineteenth centuries was to devise ways that the interests of the working classes could be served without actually involving them in the governing processes. The ruling classes—the aristocracy, the entrepreneurs, the property holders, and the intellectual elite—commonly held that working class desires were driven entirely by selfish, short-term interests rather than by a coherent understanding of large-scale economic or social realities. Political philosophers, including most of America's "Founding Fathers," feared that direct involvement of the general public in governance would lead to demagoguery, mob rule, and anarchy. As a consequence, it was not until the second half of the nineteenth century, when the writings of Marx and Engels gave rise to *socialist ideology* and provided the labor movement with a formal doctrine, that general public opinion claimed a legitimate voice on such issues as foreign or economic policy.

Given the small scale of democratic processes in nineteenth-century Europe (less than 10 percent of the adult population was eligible to vote in the larger nations), it should not be surprising that the first political public opinion surveys appeared in the United States, where newspapers began conducting "show polls" or "straw votes" of their readers as early as 1824 (Harrisburg, Pa., and Raleigh, N.C.; they picked Andrew Jackson to beat John Quincy Adams, but Adams won). The increasingly frequent voter polls mounted by U.S. magazines and newspapers during the 1800s simply asked readers for their candidate of choice or party preference, *not* for their positions on specific issues. Thus, the European disconnect between public opinion and political ideology was maintained in the United States.

Post–World War I: Documenting Doctrine

A 1916 reader's survey by the *Literary Digest* on whether the United States should enter the Great War appears to have been the world's first national public opinion poll on a political issue. A majority of responses said, "Stay out," which augured well for President Woodrow Wilson's reelection under the slogan, "He kept us out of war!" But thirty days after his second inaugural, Wilson broke off diplomatic relations with Germany and asked Congress to declare war. In spite of such occasional forays into political issues, especially during the late 1930s, most opinion polls continued to solicit input *only* on party and candidate preference until after World War II.

From the mid-1950s on, the broadcast networks joined newspapers and magazines in conducting public opinion polls. These soundings increasingly solicited voter input on political issues, first on foreign policy (1950s to early 1960s); later they expanded to include domestic issues (mid-1960s to the present). National opinion polls during the late 1960s and '70s consistently showed that the great majority of Americans supported civil rights, peace in Vietnam, environmental and privacy protection, worker and consumer protection, access to information, and a wide variety of progressive agendas. This gave the impression of a de facto consensus about American ideology that made the adoption of progressive legislation in these areas not merely expedient, but a dutiful obligation for both major parties.

During the 1970s and '80s, advances in information technology made increasingly sophisticated analytical tools available to market researchers. These advances enabled manufacturers and retailers to target products and sales promotions for specific clientele with ever-greater pinpoint accuracy and effectiveness. Initially refined for the marketing of goods and services, in the early 1980s these techniques were adopted by political practitioners at all levels to package candidates and causes both for fund-raising and mobilizing constituents. In this context, opinion polls are increasingly being used not so much by political candidates to learn about the public's wishes or judgments as by interest groups to demonstrate to politicians, voters, and political contributors the extent of the electorate's support for each group's specific cause. Survey results, in other words, are being used less to *shape* political ideology and more to *promote* political ideology.

The Future

Through the mid-1990s, the increasing power of "info-com" technology has led to dramatic reductions in the costs of gathering and packaging information. The evolution of diverse new electronic distribution capabilities (e.g., cable, cellular, satellite) has made it possible for ever-smaller operators to produce and distribute high quality packages of information—talk shows, news, entertainment, etc.—for ever-smaller ideological niches. An extrapolation of the trends of the past ten to fifteen years would suggest the impending emergence of a marketplace for ideologic information segmented by the major political parties, plus dozens of continually changing special-interest groups—e.g., gays, retirees, welfare recipients, and welfare reformers. Each of these groups will use the electronic infostructure to create and sustain their ideologically based niche markets, continually polling their constituents and using psychodemographic measures to design promotions and alliances to help increase their share of the electorate and to enhance their power to influence the larger system.

Clearly, the electronic infostructure will be exploited to mobilize new interest groups and ideologies. It also has been suggested that once all Americans are connected to the information highway, legislators will be able to continually poll their constituents to find out exactly how they feel about each issue. A principal problem with voter issues polls is certain to be the ambiguity of their results. Contextual and semantic conditionalities obscure the meaning of *both* their questions *and* their outputs. To date, public issues surveys have proved to be volatile tools, both in campaigns and in drafting party platforms and policy papers.

Researchers have found that through successive interactions, it is possible for pollsters and the public to communicate genuine understanding of complex problems and to identify ranges of acceptable actions. Already, members of the U.S. Congress are connected to the information highway, as are about half of all state legislatures. The more successful legislators of the electronic age will be those who are most adept at correctly identifying their constituents' ideologic parameters and crafting actions that will satisfy those parameters. These developments could largely eliminate the need for intermediate agents, such as political parties or pollsters.

Multiple complex issues—and issues-related information—confronting the twenty-first century will create a boom in simulation models, expert systems, and information agents by which decision makers—

and voters—can optimize use of all input. It is reasonable to assume that, during the first quarter of the twenty-first century, successful elected officials will be those who master these tools. In achieving this, politicians will transcend traditional ideologies, although, no doubt, new ideologies will arise through continuing discourse in the electronic marketplace of ideas and information.

See also CHANGE, OPTIMISTIC AND PESSIMISTIC PERSPECTIVES; DEMOCRATIC PROCESS; ELECTRONIC PUBLISING; HOLISTIC BELIEFS; ON-LINE SERVICES; POLITICAL CAMPAIGNING; POLITICAL PARTIES; PREJUDICE, FORMS OF; PUBLIC POLICY CHANGES; SOCIAL CONTROLS; SURVEYS; VOTING.

BIBLIOGRAPHY

BULLOCK, ALAN, and STALLYBRASS, OLIVER. *The Harper Dictionary of Modern Thought.* New York: Harper and Row, 1977.

KAY, ALAN; GREENBERG, STANLEY; STEEPER, FREDERICK; and HENDERSON, HAZEL. *Americans Talk Issues.* St. Augustine, FL: Americans Talk Issues Foundation, 1993.

THOMPSON, DAVID. *Europe Since Napoleon.* New York: Alfred A. Knopf, 1959.

David Pearce Snyder

Public Policy Change

Public policy change rarely comes about abruptly and typically progresses through twenty to thirty distinctive steps over a period of twenty to a hundred years. (See Figure 1.) Timelines depicting each step are hallmarked by distinctive sequences. These steps and sequences constitute the "signatures of change." The characteristic sequences within each evolutionary step coalesce and reinforce each other, and the prospects for impending change may be gauged from their growth rates.

Momentum Behind Trend Extension

Forces of change steadily build over long periods and acquire a powerful momentum, like an avalanche on a mountain slope. Abrupt breaks or discontinuities in ongoing change patterns seldom occur. The cumulative force of the combined trends determines eventual outcomes. When a number of benchmark developments begin to occur and to peak simultaneously, a "critical mass" is achieved. At such "take-off points" outcomes become deterministic but not wholly fatalistic, in as much as that human will, properly and punctually directed, can alter almost any outcome.

Understanding these phenomena and their characteristic development paths provides a way to forecast public policy change with a great degree of accuracy. Public policies generally move from conception to conclusion in relatively broad time spans—twenty to a hundred years, or sometimes even longer. Such an extended time frame provides ample opportunity to grapple with public policy issues.

Public policy issues evolve through three generic phases as shown by the Multiple-Timeline Change Model (Figure 1). The three phases may be summarized as follows:

- *Framing issues.* Intellectual development of ideas gives rise to innovations that cause events from which issues emerge.
- *Advancing issue consideration.* Institutions provide a framework for publicizing and promoting issues, thereby shaping public opinion. The clamor for change may sometimes be influenced by catastrophe or cyclic phenomena.

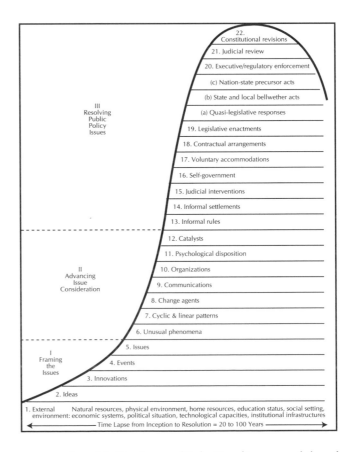

FIGURE 1. Molitor's multiple-timeline model of change, showing cumulative steps in change pattern. (Source: Graham T. T. Molitor, Public Policy Forecasting, Inc.)

• *Resolving issues.* An array of informal and formal means to contend with or resolve issues and to accommodate change.

Framing the Issues

Timelines associated with initiating change include five basic steps. Public policy commences with ideas, the wellspring of change. Ideas give rise to *innovation* (both technological *and* social, as well as practical) by which theoretical concepts are transformed into useful application. In turn, widespread implementation of new inventions introduces *events*. Disruptive effects brought on by innovative undertakings prompt the issues.

Ability to interpret steps in this process is greatly augmented by knowledge of the *external environment* in which they arise. Situational contexts provide an important frame of reference to assess evolutionary patterns in specific locales. Factors that influence the climate for change include: natural resources, human resources, educational status, social setting, economic systems, political climate, technological capabilities, and institutional infrastructure.

Advancing Issue Consideration

There are seven additional timelines during the second phase, which is characterized by on-going change. Occasionally, unusual phenomena (i.e., catastrophes) intervene to speed up the process. Change agents—ranging from victims who emote wrongs, intellectual elites who interpret developments, and crusaders who popularize them—flesh out commentary.

Responding to controversy, communications of all sorts pick up the issues, firm up findings, chronicle debate, and create widespread awareness. Communications, covering issues from development to disposition, span a minimum of twenty to thirty years, but more often forty to eighty years. Scientific and professional literature coverage typically precedes popular press coverage by many decades. When specialized journals or television specials exclusively devoted to covering or tracking an issue emerge, and books that summarize decades of wearying developments hit the marketplace, public policy response is imminent.

New organizations form, or established ones take up causes, address and sustain deliberation. Institutional frameworks provide continuity in the pursuit of change.

Public opinion polls mirror the psychological disposition of moods toward change. By piercing the veil of apathy and creating understanding, they unleash pressures for change. Catalysts, such as a major industrial accident (Bhopal or Chernobyl, for example), sometimes shock the public and provoke swift public policy response.

Cyclic and linear patterns, analogous to those in economics, may propel trends along. Social-political reform cycles, since the late 1800s, averaged twenty to twenty-six years' duration in the United States. The postindustrial political realignment cycle, underway since 1989, is projected to persist until 2010–2018 and may herald a new era of wrenching reforms akin to the previous Progressive, New Deal, and New Frontier/New Politics cycles.

The onslaught of individual actions, organizational undertakings, institutional activities, widespread communication of views, and resulting public opinion mount the drumbeat for change. The subsequent clamor escalates pressure for response.

Resolving Issues

Ten timelines, resolving confrontations during the third and final tier of steps, conclude the overall pattern of change. Informal rules—unwritten codes of behavior, values, beliefs, customs, traditions, and so forth—sometimes suffice to unofficially resolve issues. Regardless of their specific, direct effect, they nearly always influence outcomes by exerting indirect moral-ethical strictures. Case-by-case litigation also can resolve individual (or class) grievances. Sometimes self-government responses, principally by the initiative and referendum, address issues not moving fast enough through traditional channels.

Voluntary accommodation—self-policing by affected interests, for example—may be interposed to stave off formal regulatory controls. Informal settlements, including conciliation, mediation, arbitration, and other resolution approaches, mostly fall outside of official government channels, though they may be enforceable by government.

Contractual arrangements, enforceable through legal channels, provide another layer of self-help remedies. Common sense impels persons (individuals as well as other legal entities) to secure specific rights. Insurers, mortgagers, and lenders, for example, are swift to specify contract provisos that safeguard them. Labor unions secure collective bargaining contracts locking in protections for their members.

Quasi-legislative forums regulating specialized problems are likely to be in the forefront for matters under their purview. Worker compensation boards are typically the first to deal with toxic torts, and labor relations forums are the first to grapple with employee grievances.

Legislative response, wending through twenty-five to forty steps in a two-house legislature, is a time-consuming but predictable process. Legislative action almost always originates in a few bellwether jurisdictions. Initial innovators are soon followed by early adopters; then come the followers; and the laggards bring up the rear.

Lawmaking responses usually emerge first in state and local precursor jurisdictions. Implementation tests the mettle and effectiveness of specific solutions. Response by international precursor jurisdictions usually is contemporaneous with—and often ahead of—domestic precursors.

Following enactment, new laws move to implementation through executive-regulatory enforcement bureaucracies. Protracted procedural delays to fill in regulatory details or secure compliance often are interposed to extend the process.

Possible challenges posed by judicial review of laws and regulations involve last-ditch efforts to defeat, modify, or validate legislative regulatory handiwork. Court challenges, exhausting three or more levels of review, further postpone final determinations. In extreme instances, constitutional revision may be undertaken to reverse or otherwise alter fundamental principles and change outcomes. Judicial review or constitutional change efforts may bring pursuit of public policy to an end—or, the outcome may start the public policy change process anew.

See also AGENTS OF CHANGE; CHANGE; CIVIL PROTEST; CONTINUITY AND DISCONTINUITY; ECONOMIC CYCLES: MODELS AND SIMULATIONS; LAWS, EVOLUTION OF; PACESETTER GOVERNMENTS; POLITICAL CYCLES; PUBLIC OPINION POLLS; RECORD SETTING; SOCIAL CONTROLS; TECHNOLOGICAL CHANGE; TECHNOLOGY FORECASTING AND ASSESSMENT; TREND INDICATORS; VALUES; VALUES CHANGE.

BIBLIOGRAPHY

LAWLESS, EDWARD W. *Technology and Social Shock.* New Brunswick, NJ: Rutgers University Press, 1977.

MARTEL, LEON. *Mastering Change: The Key to Business Success.* New York: Simon & Schuster, 1986.

MOLITOR, GRAHAM T. T. *Evaluation of Causal Forces Related to Why Issues Emerge.* Palo Alto, CA: Electric Power Research Institue, 1989.

SCHLESINGER, ARTHUR M., JR. *The Cycles of American History.* Boston: Houghton Mifflin, 1986.

VAGO, STEVEN. *Social Change.* New York: Holt, Rinehart and Winston, 1980.

Graham T. T. Molitor

Public Relations

In the Western world, organizations and individuals carry out their activities only within the context of public acceptance. Influencing that public acceptance will be the increasingly difficult responsibility of the public relations practitioner as we move to the twenty-first century.

Edward Bernays, the "father" of public relations, established a definition for public relations practitioners that has held up for decades: "an applied social scientist who advises clients or employers on the social attitudes or actions to take to win support of the publics upon which survival of the client depends."

In his introduction to *The Engineering of Consent* (1955), one of the basic references on the theory and practice of public relations, Bernays foresaw "new instruments of transportation and mass communication, airplane, radio, movies, television [that would] accelerate the spread of ideas. People who previously had little access to them are exposed to attitudes, ideas and courses of action."

Over the following forty years, the acceleration of ideas through instantaneous global communications has transformed the world to a degree almost unimaginable in 1955: powerful minicomputers, the Internet, cable and satellite television, pocket-sized video cameras, cellular phones, and fax machines.

When Bernays edited *The Engineering of Consent,* the term *public relations* was virtually synonymous with *press relations.* It attracted many former journalists who had left that field to become "press agents." College public relations courses were mostly thought of as pathetic by both faculty and students.

Today, several hundred degree-granting colleges offer a public relations major. In many of these institutions, the public relations sequence is the largest within the journalism or communications school. But the future demands on those graduates may be quite different from what they are being taught to expect.

The practice of public relations is roughly divided into two parts: active and reactive. In *active* public relations programs, the objective is to maintain or improve the climate of acceptance within which a company, organization, agency, or individual operates. *Reactive* public relations programs attempt to influence public policy or attitudes (almost always established by someone else), or to control the damage done by an incident, and replenish the reservoir of public goodwill that any organization requires to operate effectively or profitably.

In *The Engineering of Consent*, Bernays wrote that "public relations is the attempt, by information, persuasion and adjustment, to engineer public support for an activity, cause, movement or institution."

Today, "consent engineering" is the responsibility of everyone involved with the organization. Because, in reality, the public relations profile of any company, government agency, organization, or individual is really the sum of the actions, past and present, of that organization in relation to its interaction with various groups of people or publics.

Whether that profile can be "engineered" by a public relations professional today is debatable. What that practitioner attempts to do is help shape the profile (or help reconstruct it following some kind of public disaster) by providing information geared to the interests of those groups whose knowledge and attitude can help or hurt the organization or individual the most.

Some recent examples of corporate disasters illustrate the point, such as the 1984 tragedy at a Union Carbide facility at Bhopal, India, where 3,800 died and 11,000 were injured. According to Jackson B. Browning, then a Union Carbide vice president, "the first report of the disaster reached Union Carbide executives in the United States more than twelve hours after the incident." (Two years later, it was discovered that the incident had been caused by sabotage.)

Were the Bhopal tragedy to occur today, the entire episode would be played out live to the world thorough television. Corporate executives, as well as the media and the public, would be immediately involved in their own offices and living rooms everywhere in the world on a minute-by-minute basis.

In this case, as in many others, including the Johnson & Johnson Tylenol poisoning scare and the Exxon *Valdez* oil-spill incident, the degree to which corporations were damaged was based on four factors, only two of which involve public relations: (1) the perception of the company by those public groups important to its success (stockholders, employees, customers, government regulators) before the incident and (2) efforts by communicators to restore the levels of understanding and support. The other two factors—the degree of corporate culpability in the incident itself and the company's willingness to try to prevent future occurrences—were corporate decisions that had nothing to do with public relations.

Clearly, the practice of public relations is much too important to be left up to former newspaper reporters or rosy-cheeked college graduates clutching a degree and ready to take on the world. It is not something that will be left to a corporate department, any more than obeying the law is a responsibility of only the legal department.

In *Managing Public Relations*, a textbook written the same year as the Bhopal incident, the case is made for a theoretical model that authors James Grunig and Todd Hunt describe as "two-way symmetrical," in which the public relations practitioner serves "as a mediator between organizations and their publics." According to their model, the authors argue that persuasion the purpose of most of today's public relations programs—moves two ways: (1) from the organization or individual out to the publics and (2) from the members of the various publics back to the organization or individual with the purpose of modifying programs or actions.

We are currently living in a world where the capacity of the conduits carrying information often and usually exceeds the amount of important information there is to communicate. The conduits are likely to continue to expand while the information will probably stay relatively stable.

The result will be even more far-ranging communications, ultimately surrounding each citizen of the global village with so much information at any given time that there is a very real danger of overloading the circuits.

The challenge of public relations professionals of the future will be to break through the clutter of message noise assaulting every human being on Earth to get their message even heard, much less understood and accepted. This will take a much greater understanding of how and why opinions are formed and how they can be changed. Edward Bernays's description of a public relations practitioner as a "social scientist" will be truer than it was decades ago.

See also ADVERTISING; COMMUNICATIONS; GLOBAL CULTURE; TELECOMMUNICATIONS.

BIBLIOGRAPHY

BERNAYS, EDWARD L., ed. *The Engineering of Consent.* Norman: University of Oklahoma Press, 1955.

GOTTSCHALK, JACK A. *Crisis Response.* Visible Ink Press, 1993.

GRUNIG, JAMES E., and HUNT, TODD. *Managing Public Relations.* New York: Holt, Rinehart, Winston, 1984.

James W. Plumb

Race, Caste, and Ethnic Diversity

Evolution, having clearly differentiated the human species from every other manifestation of life, went on to create a dazzling array of racial and ethnic groups. The human species then proceeded to diversify itself along national and class lines. The gender factor, the basic divide that unifies and enriches virtually every species of life, added an additional level of complexity to overall human diversity.

Viewed positively, these multiple identifying characteristics are a highly valuable facet of the human family. They testify to the essential oneness of this family, while simultaneously expanding its vistas and its creative possibilities. Over the centuries, the varying racial and ethnic groups, in developing their particular means of self-expression and achievement, have inadvertently enriched the lives of other groups with whom they have had contact. In turn, each has been enriched by the other.

At the same time, however, the very existence of these racial and ethnic differences has been a divisive factor, facilitating if not encouraging the separation of peoples along racial lines. These distinctions provide an obvious opportunity for political, economic, and social manipulation, pitting groups against one another for individual or collective aggrandizement. Indeed, the history of the human species is permeated by accounts of minor and major eruptions of animosity among various racial, ethnic, and national groups. By the same token, history is replete with accounts of personal slights, real or imagined, inflicted by and on persons of another group, often motivated by racial or ethnic hostility.

Biological science has not yet provided us the last word on whether racial and ethnic animosity has a genetic basis. Its stubborn persistence throughout human history, however, suggests that a biological basis is possible.

The social sciences have had a great deal to say about racial and ethnic friction. Economists, in particular, have provided readily understandable analyses for the observed exploitation of one racial or ethnic group by another. This has usually been achieved by technological superiority, either in weaponry or science, or by numerical superiority or treachery—and sometimes by some combination of all of the foregoing.

Paradoxically, coincident with such acts of political and economic subjugation of one group by another, the daily relations between individual members of these presumably antagonistic groups sometimes remain free of all hostility and are characterized by intermarriage and other racially and ethnically neutral behavior. This paradox suggests that the impetus for the racial and ethnic exploitation may be found in benefits that accrue to those who have the power to institute the exploitation, rather than with the general membership of the exploiting racial/ethnic group. On the other hand, the fact that the members of the group allow themselves to become passionate participants in these intergroup hostilities suggests that noneconomic factors also are involved.

In addition to *intergroup* hostilities, human history is studded with a variety of *intra*group animosities and discriminatory practices. Most prominent among these is discrimination based on caste and gender. Caste or class discrimination is clearly a type of economic behavior, for the very concepts of caste and class arise from the economic stratification of society. Although historically these concepts were not universally perceived as pejorative, largely because political and intellectual leadership has traditionally come from the upper class, their affront to human dignity has become apparent as democratic values become more widely accepted as the norm.

In India, where the caste system reached its apogee, the system was outlawed four decades ago, but it continues to survive with diminished force in much of the subcontinent. Less formalized manifestations of class antagonism continue to thrive virtually everywhere, conferring economic benefits on those in the dominant group at the expense of those who are not so favored. In the industrialized countries class antagonism may be diminishing as a social and political force as the portion of the population that perceives itself as "middle class" expands along with the ever-expanding ownership of consumer products.

Gender discrimination is even more widespread than caste/class discrimination. Almost universally, the female gender has been exploited. Here too, economics is a strong explanatory factor. In all likelihood, gender discrimination is far more complex in its origins than other types of discrimination.

In recent years the United States and some other countries have introduced affirmative action programs of various types to correct some of the more overt discriminatory practices and to help rebalance or compensate for deficiencies still borne by the victims of discrimination. Such programs have enjoyed considerable success, but are encountering increasing opposition in the United States owing to the persistent economic stagnation and declining horizons of opportunity that the general populace has been experiencing for several years.

The concepts of race and ethnic diversity have a unique history and significance in the United States. It is a country peopled overwhelmingly by immigrants from all corners of Earth who usurped a land occupied by Native Americans and simultaneously enslaved a significant portion of Africa's population in order to develop it. Centuries later, Native American and slave descendants (African Americans) remain the most economically deprived racial groups in the United States. Collectively, there is an undercurrent that condemns or disdains such groups; those attitudes are shared by a significant but diminishing portion of the population. In recent years a realization has begun to emerge that these and other marginalized racial and ethnic groups, in fact, enrich the general society in myriad ways.

As a result, diversity is currently being consciously sought, most prominently in cultural aspects. Not surprisingly, the concept of diversity as a positive societal good has both powerful detractors as well as passionate supporters. Consequently, given the recentness of its popular acceptance, it is unclear whether it should be viewed as a permanent aspect of American society.

Modern transportation and communications technology have effectively shrunk the globe, reducing all of mankind to a degree of neighborly intimacy unprecedented in human history. Racial isolation and ethnic purity are no longer possible, and encounters with the diversity of the human species are now a commonplace element of daily life for most people. Racial and ethnic diversity shares the current spotlight of heightened awareness with global ecology and human interdependence. Against this backdrop, the decision of whether the increasing proximity of human diversity is to be embraced with enthusiasm or resisted with hostility will be a powerful determinant in shaping the future.

See also CHINA: ETHNIC REAWAKENING; CLASS AND UNDERCLASS; ETHNIC AND CULTURAL SEPARATISM; LIFESTYLES, ALTERNATIVE; LIFESTYLES, ETHNIC; LIFESTYLES, REGIONAL; RACIAL AND ETHNIC CONFLICT; WORKFORCE DIVERSITY.

BIBLIOGRAPHY

ABURDENE, PATRICIA, and NAISBITT, JOHN. *Megatrends for Women.* New York: Villard Books/Random House, 1992.

DAVIDSON, ART. *Endangered Peoples.* San Francisco, CA: Sierra Club Books, 1993.

DENG, FRANCIS M. *Protecting the Dispossessed: A Challenge for the International Community.* Washington, DC: The Brookings Institution, 1993.

FRANKLIN, JOHN H. *The Color Line: Legacy for the Twenty-First Century.* Columbia, MO: University of Missouri Press, 1993.

HELD, VIRGINIA. *Feminist Morality: Transforming Culture.* Chicago: University of Chicago Press, 1993.

MAGNET, MYRON. *The Dream and the Nightmare: The Sixties' Legacy to the Underclass.* New York: William Morrow, 1993.

MASSEY, DOUGLAS S., and DENTON, NANCY A. *American Apartheid: Segregation and the Making of the Underclass.* Cambridge, MA: Harvard University Press, 1993.

PETERSON, V. SPIKE, and RUNYAN, ASSE S. *Global Gender Issues.* Boulder, CO: Westview Press, 1993.

SCHAFER, D. PAUL. "Cultures and Economics: Irresistible Forces Encounter Immovable Objects." *Futures* 26/8 (October 1994).

TAYLOR, JARED. *Paved with Good Intentions: The Failure of Race Relations in Contemporary America.* New York: Carroll & Graf, 1992.

WEST, CORNEL. *Beyond Eurocentrism and Multiculturalism.* 2 vols. Monroe, ME: Common Courage Press, 1993.

Robert S. Browne

Racial and Ethnic Conflict

Race is an anthropological reference emphasizing physical features, such as skin color, hair texture, and facial features, in the three great racial groupings of Negro, Mongol, and Caucasian races. *Ethnicity* is a reference to culture, including language, religion, family organization, social institutions, history, and heritage.

Racial and ethnic conflict will continue to be as tenacious a threat to human cooperation and development in the twenty-first century as it has been in the twentieth century. It can be defined in economic, cultural, social, and political terms of confrontation and non-cooperation, both between groups who identify themselves as distinct from their competitors and combatants *and* within groups who may be culturally homogeneous but differ on strategies of interaction with dissimilar groups. Racial and ethnic conflict is both a global phenomena with pervasive local impacts and a local phenomena capable of profound global consequences.

This essay briefly addresses demographic, historical, institutional, and economic dimensions of racial and ethnic conflict. All of these dimensions pour into the strategic actions and aspirations of racial and ethnic groups. Ted Robert Gurr argues that the Bosnians, the Kurds, the Shi'is of Iraq, and black South Africans are among the most visible of more than two hundred ethnic and religious minorities and subordinate majorities throughout the world who are contesting the terms of their incorporation into the world order. Their status in the twenty-first century largely depends upon the utilization of these dimensions to press their objectives.

The Demographic Dimension

Malappropriated demography continues to contribute to racial and ethnic conflict. The continuing trend of global economic integration is enhanced by more efficient and cheaper transportation and communication technologies and by increasing resort to large trading blocks. These trends confront 75 percent of the world's labor force, largely residing in Africa, Asia, Latin America, and islands of the Pacific, Indian, and Atlantic oceans. In the populations of nations situated in these areas the working age is younger, less experienced, and less well educated than in most "developed" nations. The developing country share of the world labor force will increase to 83 percent by 2025. Similar macro-level differences at the global level are also reflected in micro-level conflicts within "developed nations"— African and Hispanic Americans in the United States, Quebecois in Canada, African and colored populations in South Africa, and *gastarbeiders* (guest workers of color) in Holland and Germany. Lower socioeconomic status among these populations continues to stimulate conflicts and confrontations with policy-making authorities in those nations, and also divides the racial or ethnic group on issues of strategy.

The Historical Dimension

Contemporary and future demographic trends reflect the vast and complex history of racial and ethnic conflict. The legacy of the African slave trade in the sixteenth through nineteenth centuries, the colonialization of Africa, Asia, the Caribbean, and Latin America, and continuing struggles between "the North" and "South" persist. They have given way in the twenty-first century to racial and ethnic conflicts within both formerly colonized and formerly colonizing nations, and to the phenomenon of North, South, and Far East conflicts due to transitions from military to economic conflict.

However, three consequences of the historic dimension include the continuing diasporas of racial, ethnic, and language groups beyond their motherland borders, the use of historical symbols and images of oppression and exploitation as tools of conflict, and the use of history as a frame of reference for future images of racial and ethnic identity.

The Institutional Dimension

Closely connected to the historical dimension of racial and ethnic conflict is its institutional dimension. Historical patterns of racial and ethnic subordination and oppression continue to reflect their legacies in future patterns of racial and ethnic relationships. Although apartheid and segregation have been officially eliminated by the legal systems of South Africa and the United States, many institutions have yet to fully integrate. Beyond integration, the institutional policies, symbols, and practices of many racial and ethnic groups continue to alienate other groups.

Institutions based on the Sikh, Hindu, or Muslim religion or on language or cultural differences between Tamils and other Indians enflame and perpetuate racial and ethnic conflict in India. Failure of the nation-state as an institution to appropriately incorporate Bosnians, Serbs, and Croats eliminated the Yugoslav nation and led to the creation of separate Czech and Slovak nations. Often, the inability of disaffected groups to find a national home exacerbates conflict. The Zulus of South Africa, the Indians of Chiappas, Mexico, and the Sikhs and Kashmiris of India offer lurid examples of conflicts suspended between national incorporation and the creation of new, racially or ethnically homogenous nations.

Without significant reorientation of many global, regional, and national institutions, the sheer force of institutional patterns, reflexes, instincts, and symbols hurl themselves forcefully into twenty-first-century racial and ethnic relations.

The Economic Dimension

Clearly, racial and ethnic conflict will continue to be driven by scarce financial, human, technological, and infrastructural resources. Continued differences in economic status persist between African Americans and others in the United States, the Chinese minority in Indonesia, the Arab minority in Israel, and the Kurdish populations in Turkey and Iraq. The lack of educational or wage-labor job opportunities, entrepreneurial development, collective bargaining on the terms and conditions of employment, exploitation of natural resources, and quality-of-life differentials provide clear and convincing evidence to some racial and ethnic groups that they are involved in a long-term struggle for economic equity and opportunity. The revision of affirmative action policies in the United States and the insistence of the World Bank on structural adjustment of the debt, civil service, private sector, and center-periphery relations in developing nations will further exacerbate conflict as the public sector role in racial and ethnic conflict resolution continues to diminish.

A Final Word

Global economic integration, the inculcation of positive values of racial and ethnic diversity, the economic uplifting of more disadvantaged racial and ethnic groups, and the restructuring of the global, regional, national, and local labor force contribute to the emergence of a vibrant racial and ethnic middle class. This middle class is a key variable in twenty-first-century racial and ethnic conflicts. It can facilitate or catalyze integrative, cooperative tendencies or provoke more insular, conflict tendencies. The subdivision of the world into economic trading blocs, the burgeoning telecommunications and information systems technology, and the perennial tension of global commercial and social values with localized traditional religious and humanistic values are key instruments of various racial and ethnic groups, and their constituent economic classes. These factors surely will play key roles for either conflict-resolving or conflict-exacerbating strategies in the twenty-first century.

See also CHINA: ETHNIC REAWAKENING; CLASS AND UNDERCLASS; ETHNIC AND CULTURAL SEPARATISM; EUROPE, CENTRAL AND EASTERN; RACE, CASTE, AND ETHNIC DIVERSITY.

BIBLIOGRAPHY

BLOOM, DAVID E., and BRENDER, ADI. *Labor and the Emerging World Economy.* Washington, DC: Population Reference Bureau, 1993.

GURR, TED ROBERTS. *Minorities at Risk: A Global View of Ethnopolitical Conflicts.* Washington, DC: United States Institute of Peace, 1993.

HARRIS, JOSEPH E., ed. *Global Dimensions of the African Diaspora,* 2nd ed. Washington, DC: Howard University Press, 1993.

HENDERSON, LENNEAL J. "Africans in Search of Work." *The Urban League Review* (September 1983): 56–71.

Lenneal J. Henderson

Radio.

See BROADCASTING; ELECTRONIC CONVERGENCE.

Railways

Forecasters may be wrong, but they never are in doubt. For instance, the March 1825 issue of England's *Quarterly Review* asserted: "What could be more palpably absurd than the prospect held out of locomotives travelling twice as fast as stagecoaches." London's first public railway, which began operating in 1803, used horses to haul passengers and freight at a speed of about five miles per hour, hardly a match for stagecoaches. Horse-drawn coaches could attain top speeds of about ten miles per hour (m.p.h.). But technological advances quickly altered the existing state of affairs. Richard Trevithick invented a high-pressure steam engine in 1800, used it to power a road carriage in 1801, a locomotive in 1804, and a rail-mounted locomotive in 1804. By 1830, the first successful steam railroad providing public service was inaugurated in England. The mode and speed of travel was about to be transformed. Steam engines, largely because of their roles in powering railways, ships, motorcars, and providing energy for the machines of modern industrial production were poised to play a major role in ushering in the Industrial Revolution.

Even as these events were transforming the way people traveled, Professor Dionysus Lardner of London's University College asserted: "Rail travel at high speed is not possible because passengers, unable to breathe, would die of asphyxia." Not until 1938 was the record speed for a steam locomotive—125 miles per hour (m.p.h.)—achieved. Today the world's fastest railway (the French TGV) set a record speed of 320.2 m.p.h. in 1990. Going far beyond these accomplishments, an unmanned railed rocket sled achieved a speed of 6,121 m.p.h. in 1982, and railguns capable of accelerating projectiles to speeds sufficient to escape Earth's gravity (about 20,000 m.p.h.) are under development. This a far cry from the beginning of rail systems, termed "wagonways" (essentially wagons run on wooden tracks serving mines that carried freight and miners), that date back as early as the fifteenth century. Considering the threshold presented by these new technological advances, rail systems may be poised for greater things.

Diesel

Approximately 99 percent of all locomotive horsepower within the United States today is diesel-electric. In this process, a diesel-powered prime mover turns a generator or alternator to produce electrical power for traction. The horsepower generated by such an arrangement can vary, with modern mainline locomotives producing up to 4,400-horsepower each, and 6,000-horsepower models planned for release by the end of 1995.

Traditionally, this electrical native power has been at 600 volts DC, but recent technology makes the use of AC power preferable. Amtrak made use of such locomotives beginning in the early 1990s. The Burlington Northern was the first U.S. freight railroad to order large numbers of the AC-powered engines, and they began receiving AC-powered freight locomotives in 1994. Currently, both of the major U.S. manufacturers of diesel locomotives, General Electric and EMD, include such locomotives in their production plans.

Electrified

The straight electric locomotive draws its power directly from an overhead wire or a third rail immediately adjacent to the track. This type of locomotive is limited to an area where a system has been constructed for such power distribution. This system is expensive to build and requires heavy use to be economically justified. Electrification is common in much of Europe, in the northeast part of the United States, and on heavily traveled lines in Russia and China. Electrified rail generally has a longer life span and is more economically and environmentally sensitive once built.

Magnetically levitated

Magnetic levitation, or Maglev, is a technology first proposed in the 1950s whereby a vehicle is magnetically propelled and levitated along a fixed guideway. The magnetic field used for such a system is produced electrically, which has sparked great interest and research into a superconducting material. Reduced military requirements have redirected some government research efforts to develop a U.S. maglev system for civilian use.

Germany and Japan have tested such systems; however, critics of Maglev point out that both countries ultimately built only traditional high-speed rail systems, and stress that Maglev is not compatible with existing transportation systems. Environmental issues stemming from Maglev involve right-of-way, material needs, and health concerns supposedly associated with exposure to high-power electromagnetic fields.

Superfast (200–380 m.p.h.)

Considered by many to be the future of medium-distance transportation, high-speed rail (HSR) is currently operating at speeds approaching 200 m.p.h. on dedicated routes. Japan, Germany, and France are the leaders in the field with extensive operating systems. However, a number of other countries have such systems under development. Test runs in Germany already have exceeded 252 m.p.h., and 321 m.p.h. has been reached in Japan.

One concern of HSR has been keeping trains on the track and its level of safety in the event that a derailment might occur. On December 21, 1993, the first major test of the safety aspects of an HSR operation occurred when an in-service French TGV train derailed at its maximum normal operating speed of 185 m.p.h. Although such a train takes more than a mile to stop under normal conditions, the entire train remained together and upright after the derailment, primarily due to the design of the car-coupling system. No serious injuries were reported to either the crew or passengers.

Monorail

The monorail is a rail transportation system generally used as a theme park ride. Despite practical attributes, these systems have found limited use. The major advantages of a monorail are the reduction in the number of needed rails for the guideway, and the elimination of the need to level and gauge the parallel guideway rails. Disadvantages include the lack of static stability, the loss of carrying capacity when base supported, the complex arrangements needed to switch from one route to another and to provide carrying support when suspended.

Roadrailer

The Roadrailer is one of several techniques used by railroads to compete with intermodal freight carriers. Essentially, the Roadrailer is a truck trailer that can be placed on a railroad track and hauled behind a locomotive without the use of a flatcar or other carrying device. Two types are currently in use. The older style has its own railroad wheels permanently attached, which reduces the carrying capacity of the trailer on the highway. The newer trailer design has wheels attached at the rail site. Currently, the use of Roadrailers is limited to the eastern half of the United States. However, rail carriers in other parts of the world are looking at the technology.

Regulatory environment

PRIVATIZATION

Most of the world's railroads are owned and operated by national governments. The United States and several other Western countries are the major exceptions to this rule. However, recent move-

Statistics for Railroads Around the World

Country	Data Year	Diesel	Locomotives Steam	Electric	Freight Cars	Passenger Coaches	KM of Line
Argentina	1991	986	0	6	32,823	1,702	34,059
Australia	1990	771	0	0	13,167	240	14,288
Brazil	1991	1,780	27	179	53,646	1,176	26,944
Canada	1990	2,672	0	14	106,334	565	54,771
China	1991	6,111	5,986	1,809	370,000	27,612	53,416
Czechoslovakia	1991	2,562	14	1,586	134,074	6,250	13,116
France	1991	3,297	0	2,244	141,800	9,647	33,446
India	1991	3,905	2,492	1,871	346,394	29,501	62,458
Italy	1991	1,167	26	1,976	97,323	1,701	16,066
Japan	1991	664	8	1,018	30,231	2,169	20,252
Mexico	1991	1,700	0	0	44,003	1,263	20,324
Poland	1992	3,928	12	2,406	140,885	7,690	23,399
Romania	1991	2,278	989	1,061	142,222	6,520	11,365
South Africa	1992	1,442	181	2,321	153,396	3,776	21,635
Soviet Union (Former)	1991	20,767	0	13,399	1,657,400	56,287	147,500
Spain	1991	666	0	593	36,073	1,878	12,570
Sweden	1991	373	0	591	24,993	1,183	10,970
United Kingdom	1991	2,243	56	263	30,888	2,722	16,584
United States	1992	18,004	0*	59*	1,173,136	4,045	227,113
West Germany	1991	3,359	0	2,535	244,287	11,636	27,079

*Class I railroads only.

Source: World Bank Railway Database, Association of American Railroads.

ments toward railroad privatization have occurred in New Zealand, the United Kingdom, and a number of countries in South America and continental Europe.

SAFETY

U.S. rail regulation changed from one of economic regulation to safety regulation pursuant to the Staggers Rail Act of 1980 and other deregulation statutes passed at that time. These acts greatly reduced the Interstate Commerce Commission's role to provide oversight to the transportation industry. Antitrust legislation also plays a role in preventing discriminatory practices within the industry. Additionally, the Federal Railroad Administration (FRA) plays a major role in safety enforcement. Similar regulatory frameworks are in place worldwide.

Safety is a major advantage for railroads. Compared to motor carriers, railroads are more than four times safer based upon ton/miles. Vehicles at grade crossings and pedestrian trespassers account for the vast majority of accidents involving U.S. railroads. To combat this problem, Operation Lifesaver has been formed to provide public education. The success of this and other measures is resulting in a declining accident rate even as total train miles operated continue to increase.

ABANDONMENTS

Within the United States, deregulation made it easier for a railroad to abandon trackage. At the same time, economic changes resulting from deregulation also made it easier for small, specialized carriers to operate many of these lines, resulting in an increase in the number of Class III, or shortline, carriers. Worldwide, track abandonment has been a concern in developed countries, especially when government subsidy reductions or privatization has been proposed.

RIGHTS-OF-WAY

The obtainment of a railroad right-of-way can be through purchase, lease, or easement. Each provides a linear route which is ideal for joint use with communication and pipeline systems.

ENVIRONMENTAL PROBLEMS

Railroads are considered to be more environmentally friendly than other modes of transportation due to their better fuel efficiency, greater carrying capacity, and ability to be fully electrified. An additional improvement has been the introduction of locomotives which use cleaner-burning natural gas.

See also AIR TRANSPORT; ENERGY CONSERVATION; ENVIRONMENT; MAGLEV; MOTOR VEHICLES; MOTOR VEHICLES, ALTERNATIVELY POWERED; PERSONAL TRANSPORT; PETROLEUM; PIPELINES; TRANSPORATION; URBAN TRANSIT.

BIBLIOGRAPHY

GOMEZ-IBAÑEZ, JOSÉ A., and MEYER, JOHN R. *Going Private: The International Experience with Transport Privatization.* Washington, DC: Brookings Institution, 1993.
LOWE, MARCIA. *Back on Track: The Global Rail Revival.* Washington, DC: Worldwatch Institute, 1994.

Research assistance provided by Barton Jennings, University of Tennessee.

Rosalyn A. Wilson

Recording Industry

Three trends will affect all recording technologies in the future: miniaturization, increasing power and capability, and declining cost. These trends apply to both the professional recording industry as well as the consumer audio and video technology. At the same time, digital recording and playback equipment will be the preeminent audio and video technology by the late 1990s and into the twenty-first century.

Digital recording is a computer-based technology. Like other such computer technologies, it involves the capture and storage of data onto various types of magnetic hard or floppy computer discs, cartridges, tapes, or perhaps eventually integrated circuits themselves. Unlike earlier (and still widely used) recording technology, optical information is encoded directly onto the storage medium—a master disc or, for consumer use, a compact disc (CD) for music and other sound recordings, or a laser disc for audiovisual images. Both formats are played on a system that uses a laser for scanning and decoding the audio or visual information encoded on the disc.

As is usually the case with new technology, audio compact disc technology was initially prohibitively expensive for most consumers—both for playback equipment and for the CDs themselves. However, prices for CD players had plummeted by the end of the 1980s, and the cost of CDs fell somewhat as well. At the same time, CD players and professional recording equipment shrank in size, leading to portable units, and grew in capability, leading to such innovations as programmable CD players and multi-CD units. As the prices fell and the capabilities expanded, sales of both CD players and CDs grew considerably.

The second half of the 1980s saw a rapid and dramatic move away from the use of the phonograph record toward digital technology in the form of the CD. While the professional recording industry has been using digital technology in the studio for nearly two decades, the full effect of its clarity and depth was usually lost on vinyl phonograph records. The sound reproduction capability of phonograph records degrades by repeated playing. CDs, on the other hand, provide a near-optimum means of reproducing digital recordings, and are far more durable than phonograph records. Sophisticated LP turntables and accessories were developed, but they were never as user-friendly as CD players, requiring fine-tuning and nimble fingers to ensure optimal performance. By the mid-1990s, the vast majority of recordings were available only on CD or on magnetic audio cassette tape.

Cassette tapes provide reasonably high quality sound reproduction. Moreover, they are recordable—even editable—by consumers, something not possible with LPs or CDs (although blank CDs and CD players with once-only recording capabilities have been developed and sold, and may become available at reasonable prices within a few years). However, the sound-reproducing quality of cassette tapes is inferior to CDs. Cassette tapes are also very slow to rewind, and they lack the rapid access to specific points typical of CDs. Moreover, cassette tapes are far more fragile than CDs or even LPs, and will degrade with time or be ruined if exposed to magnetic fields. While magnetic audio cassette tapes likely will remain a popular, convenient format throughout the 1990s, they will continue to lose ground to the increasingly affordable CD.

Digital audio taping (DAT) is a hybrid between magnetic audio cassette tapes and digital technology. DAT encodes digital information onto a smaller cassette than the standard audio cassette and, like the CD, is played on a laser scanning and playback system. Unlike the CD, DAT tapes are recordable and editable. DAT tapes have superior sound reproduction capabilities, less distortion, rewind more quickly, and are more durable than magnetic audio cassettes.

DAT, already popular in Japan and Europe, has been obstructed from entering the U.S. market through the efforts of the professional recording industry. The recording industry fears widespread problems with piracy, resulting in a loss of royalties to both artists and recording companies. DAT players are also significantly more expensive on average than either magnetic audio cassette or CD players. Nonetheless, the growth of DAT will continue worldwide throughout the 1990s. DAT, or some other, similar format likely will replace traditional magnetic audio cassette tapes eventually, as costs fall and availability grows.

Digital technology will transform video recording in the same manner that it has transformed the consumer audio industry. Consumer home video recording and playback, like the compact disc, experienced explosive growth in the 1980s. Videotape rental stores, unknown in 1980, were a feature of every shopping center by 1990. However, this thriving industry stands at a crossroads, as it moves inexorably from magnetic videotape to optical discs that can utilize digital technology.

Magnetic videotape, like magnetic audiotape, presents problems with the quality of visual and sound reproduction, and it degrades with use. Optical discs, on the other hand, offer superior audio and visual reproduction and are far more durable than magnetic videotapes. Equally important, they are far smaller than magnetic videotapes, meaning that both cameras and playback units are smaller as well. As sales and rentals of such discs continue to grow rapidly, a growing number of video rental outlets also rent optical laser discs.

On-line video communications also may threaten the now booming video rental business. The growth of fiber optic communications in the United States, Europe, and Asia will make possible the transmission of visual as well as audio information via telephone lines. New signal compression techniques that enormously increase the carrying capacity of both wired (fiber optical, copper, or coaxial) and broadcast transmissions hasten this shift. This means that consumers could "rent" videos by dialing a number and having the video transmitted electronically to their playback unit. Federal regulators already have authorized phone companies to provide a "video dial tone." Using special receivers, an entire feature-length movie could be "burst-loaded" to a home in less than ten seconds for viewing at the consumer's pleasure. It would eliminate the need to pick up or return a videocassette, and it would solve such problems as tapes jamming or poor image/sound quality due to overuse by renters.

The large investment already made by businesses in the form of videotapes and rental outlets and by consumers in the form of videotape cameras and players creates something of a dilemma. Optical discs are clearly superior to magnetic videotapes in terms of sound and visual reproduction capability, durability, and even size. Furthermore, the on-line transmission of audio and visual information offers many advantages over video rental. But the transition to optical disc technology would be very costly in terms of replacing current consumer videotape equipment, and a move to on-line video communications and rentals has the potential to put an entire industry—videotape sales and rentals—out of business.

For these reasons, videotapes and the surrounding industry are likely to be with us for the next decade or more. Nonetheless, digital recording technology—for both audio and visual applications—will continue to grow throughout the 1990s and, in the early twenty-first century, is very likely to be the predominant professional and consumer recording and playback technology.

See also COMMUNICATIONS; COMMUNICATIONS TECHNOLOGY; DIGITAL COMMUNICATIONS; ELECTRONIC CONVERGENCE; INTERACTIVE ENTERTAINMENT; TELECOMMUNICATIONS; TELEVISION.

BIBLIOGRAPHY

BRAND, STEWART. *The Media Lab: Inventing the Future at MIT.* New York: Viking, 1987.

FREESE, ROBERT P. "Optical Disks Become Erasable." *IEEE Spectrum* 26:2, February 1988.

HAKANEN, ERNEST A. "Digital Audio Broadcasting: Promises and Policy Issues in the USA." *Telecommunications Policy* 15:6, December 1991.

LATAMORE, G. BERTON. "Smart Cards Get Smarter." *Technology Business* 7:9, September 1987.

LEVY, MARK R. *The VCR Age: Home Video and Mass Communication.* Newbury Park, CA: Sage Publications, 1989.

MILES, IAN. *Home Informatics: Information Technology and the Transformation of Everyday Life.* London: Pinter Publishers (distributed in U.S. by Columbia University Press), 1988.

PROVENZO, EUGENE F. *Video Kids: Making Sense of Nintendo.* Cambridge, MA: Harvard University Press, 1991.

ROBINSON, DEANNA C. and BUCK, ELIZABETH B. *Music at the Margins: Popular Music and Global Cultural Diversity.* Newbury Park, CA: Sage Publications, 1991.

TWITCHELL, JAMES B. *Carnival Culture: The Trashing of Taste in America.* New York: Columbia University Press, 1992.

Timothy Willard

Record Setting

Almost any aspect of society, at any given moment, seems to have reached an apparent end, the "brick-wall" finality of an absolute. History reveals, however, that these apparent limits, time and time again, have been surpassed. Each step along the way tends to be hailed as an "ultimate" achievement. In other words, there are few, if any, absolutes.

Constant upgrading is easily explained. No matter what subject one looks at, close and careful scrutiny invariably bares shortcomings of one sort or another. Nothing is ever good enough. Humans never seem fully or finally satisfied with contemporary accomplishments, but pursue new standards of excellence. There is always room for improvement. Something better can always be achieved. Human inspiration is driven by an all-consuming desire not only to better but to refine, elaborate, and extend that which has gone before.

Human affairs incessantly are being constructed only to be redesigned, then rebuilt anew. Human endeavors and the social order are open-ended, not closed. Most accomplishments, no matter how impressive they may seem at the time, represent only a continuing succession of interim advancements, a part of the overall progression and evolution of society itself.

In almost every field of human endeavor and experience there is an eternal effort under way to achieve still higher levels of perfection. Perfection, as an absolute, may eternally be just out of our grasp. Nonetheless, there is always someone out there somewhere who will strive to better the previous mark.

Pace-setting records are established only to be broken. Record setting provides a convenient benchmark for measuring the limits of earthly experiences and human capabilities. Records do represent pinnacles of achievement, at least for the moment. Invariably they turn out to be jumping-off points for going one step farther, a target to shoot at and surmount.

Field-and-track events demonstrate that nearly any human endeavor constantly is being improved upon. The world record for the mile at the turn of the century was just under five minutes. An arbitrary limit—the "impossible" four-minute mile—was taken for granted for many years. Athletes, however, never gave up the quest. Marks of any one record setter simply set the next person's aspirations that much higher. In 1954 Roger Bannister surpassed that benchmark by running the mile in a pace-setting 3:59.4. Those following him relentlessly and single-mindedly strove to better the mark. Now the world record holder has shaved nearly fifteen seconds off the "impossible" four-minute mile. The world's fastest miler and current record holder, Steven Cram (U.K.), has run the distance in 3:46.832.

In the pole vault, the pattern is much the same. When bamboo and aluminum poles were supplanted by fiberglass and boron-reinforced composites, the additional whipsaw helped catapult vaulters to add nearly two feet to previous world records. Sometimes collateral changes in materials "chime in" to push records higher yet. The current all-time record holder, Sergei Bubka (U.S.S.R.), cleared the bar at 20'½" in 1992.

Here is one final example in the sports field. High jumpers had never cleared over seven feet until 1956. Shortly thereafter, the "Fosburg Flop" was introduced at the 1968 Olympic Games. Instead of the classic scissor or forward-roll that always had been the style, Fosburg arched his back over the bar and soared 7'4.25". So the process or procedure accompanying endeavors can augment the capacity to shatter previous records. Since 1989, Javier Sotomayur (U.S.) cleared the eight-foot mark. The long and the short of it is that "the best never rest."

Record setting sometimes verges on the unbelievable. All-time world fuel economy records for passenger-carrying motor vehicles stagger the imagination. The world's record, set in Switzerland at the 1979 International Fuel Saving Competition for cars and special vehicles, a three-wheel diesel driven by Franz Maier (Germany), was an impressive 3,020.28 miles per gallon (mpg)! By 1994 a 50 percent increase in that astounding record was accomplished when Canada's Challenge X, constructed by University of Saskatchewan engineering students, achieved a mind-shattering 4,738 mpg. For commercial vehicles, one Japanese diesel compact automobile, a regular production model in the early 1980s, was getting 68 mpg. German automakers agreed in 1995 to raise fuel economy standards for passenger automobiles, set in 1990 at 31.4 mpg, to 39.9 mpg by 2005. In the United States, domestic new car fuel efficiency topped out at 27.4 mpg in 1991, then dropped to 26.9 mpg in 1992. American automobile manufacturers obviously have a long way to go. These impressive records indicate how far we can go. Thus, they provide solid evidence and a stimulus for improving everyday efficiencies.

Examples of impressive records abound in almost any other field of interest. Average U.S. corn production of 28.9 bushels per acre in 1940–1941 had risen to 131 bushels by 1992. Hens running in the wild might annually lay one or more clutches of eggs for a total of six to ten eggs. The current record-holder hen laid 361 eggs in 364 days. The green revolution has worked miracles, agricultural chemistry adds further enhancement, and genetic engineering promises to push records higher still.

Life expectancy itself has dramatically increased, rising from an average of eighteen years back in 1 B.C. to more than seventy-five years in modern times. Scientific advances, augmented by genetic engineering, portend substantial and accelerating increases in life expectancies to 125, or perhaps even 160 years, according to some forecasters. On the basis of this steady evolutionary increase and projected further increases, we can surmise that human longevity, while it has come a long way, has a much longer way to go.

Similar achievements and advancements could go on interminably. The phenomena described here apply, in principle, to virtually every other human endeavor. History is replete with examples of triumphs over the seemingly impossible. Society is open-ended, encouraging, if not necessitating, a dynamic system in which the event and levels of accomplishment will be ever-changing. Forecasting social and cultural change assumes a ceaseless tinkering and a benign dissatisfaction with things as they are. It assumes that humans will always attempt to upgrade and perfect their affairs. Human beings just cannot be complacent. The sky is the limit.

See also CHANGE, PACE OF; CHANGE, SCIENTIFIC AND TECHNOLOGICAL; CONTINUITY AND DISCONTINUITY; INFORMATION OVERLOAD; LONGEVITY; SCIENTIFIC BREAKTHROUGHS.

BIBLIOGRAPHY

ASH, RUSSELL. *The Top 10 of Everything.* New York: Dorling Kindersley, 1994.
HARVEY, EDMUND H., JR., ed. *The Reader's Digest Book of Facts.* Pleasantville, NY: The Reader's Digest Association, 1987.
KRANTZ, LES, ed. *The Best and Worst of Everything.* New York: Prentice Hall, 1991.
LEE, STAN. *The Best of the World's Worst: World Class Blunders: Screw-Ups, Oddballs, Misfits, and Rotten Ideas.* Los Angeles, General Publishing, 1994.
MATTHEWS, PETER, ed. *The Guiness Book of Records 1995.* New York: Bantam Books, 1995.

Graham T. T. Molitor

Recreation, Outdoor.

See OUTDOOR RECREATION.

Refugees

As long as human conflict occurs, refugees will flee their homelands, leaving behind most everything they hold dear. But the post–Cold War world will respond to them in different, and not always better, ways than in recent decades.

Millions of people leave their home countries each year for many reasons. Refugees do not want to leave, but do so because of persecution and/or violence, often perpetrated by their own government. By seeking asylum in another country, refugees qualify for important protections under international law. Only limited protection exists for internally displaced people, those who are uprooted by violence but who remain in their home country. People whose flight is caused by poverty, natural disaster, or environmental degradation—key determinative factors in future migrations—also do not benefit from the international system of refugee protection.

Most refugees who need protection and assistance are in the developing world, often seeking safety in some of the world's poorest countries, such as Malawi, Pakistan, and Bangladesh. Of the seventeen million refugees in such need in 1992, less than one million were in Europe and North America. Most of the world's more than twenty million internally displaced people are also located in the developing world—in Mozambique, Rwanda, Sudan, Myanmar, and other impoverished, war torn countries.

Undoubtedly, this picture of refugee demographics will remain true in coming years. The poorest of people and nations will continue to suffer the most from upheaval and displacement. Whether the developed world will continue to assist them, now that their strategic value has diminished, is the larger question for the 1990s and beyond.

Despite the relatively small numbers seeking asylum in Western developed nations, recent trends show a fortress mentality. Europe, especially, is shutting the doors on asylum seekers. Germany, in particular, encountered a violent reaction by political extremists to all foreigners, including asylum seekers. Many countries in Europe refused in the early 1990s to accept refugees from genocidal violence in the former Yugoslavia. This trend runs against the letter and spirit of the international protocols signed by those nations after World War II intended to prevent just such reactions.

The United States has a history different from Europe. Because of that history, the United States will remain far more open to refugees and asylum seekers than Europe. However, the changing demographics of American society will raise the priority of debates on immigration generally, including questions involving refugee resettlement and asylum.

Since 1951, the office of the UN High Commissioner for Refugees (UNHCR) has been at the center of the international refugee protection system. It is charged with protecting refugees and assisting them until there is a solution to their homelessness. Those solutions include refugees returning voluntarily to their home country, integrating into the country that has given them asylum, or resettling in a third country, usually in the developed world. The majority of refugees wish only to return home when it is safe to do so. Resettlement outside their region is a last resort for UNHCR, for governments, and for most refugees.

For the great majority of refugees, however, the last several decades produced no solutions. Instead, refugees endured years of forced exile, often in large, dehumanizing, and often dangerous camps or settlements with minimal services and opportunities. Refugee children often had no formal education, refugee women endured brutal mistreatment, and refugee men were unable to fulfill traditional family roles.

How will these conditions change with the demise of the Cold War? As many of the long proxy wars that created these refugees inch toward resolution, millions of refugees are finally daring to dream of going home. In most cases, however, their homelands are entirely devastated. A sudden, ill-planned, underfunded repatriation may result in desperate refugees moving home spontaneously, only to compete with internally displaced people for meager resources. The fragile peace accords of Afghanistan, Cambodia, Angola, Mozambique, and other major refugee-producing conflicts can quickly shatter under such strain. One critical prerequisite for lasting repatriation is sufficient international support and planning. The superpowers invested billions of dollars in the wars that uprooted these civilians. Will the world community have the wisdom to invest in their healing during the coming years?

Conversely, the demise of the Cold War has accelerated the disintegration of old states and the creation of new ones. Fundamental change of this nature will almost always involve violence. The raging nationalism obvious in the debris of the former Soviet Union and Yugoslavia, also highly visible in Africa and elsewhere, is likely to continue to flare for some years. One obvious result will be an increase in the number of sovereign states. However, this trend can also be expected to produce large numbers of refugees and internally displaced people. This result can be contained if the United Nations is allowed to become an effective force in peacemaking and peacekeeping.

One important, clearly visible trend, within the international community generally and the UN specifically, is a willingness for international bodies to intervene, militarily or otherwise, in conflicts where massive numbers of civilians are at risk, or in instances of massive human rights abuse where a recognized government is itself the abuser, or where there is no recognized government. The early 1990s saw international military intervention to protect Kurdish civilians in Iraq, and to halt mass starvation in Somalia. This controversial trend is exacerbated in part because the UN structure is dominated by the five permanent members of the Security Council. It is likely that superpower accommodation will be reached on this. It is also likely that regional intergovernmental bodies such as the Organization of African Unity will move in a similar direction. This is important because it will help clarify international responsibility for internally displaced people and help establish the principle that sovereign governments not only have rights but also responsibilities toward all their citizens.

The international community will be compelled by events to confront continuing large-scale populations of uprooted people. How the world community responds to refugee flows in the future will depend on whether or not it perceives refugees as the problem or understands that they are the victims of problems, such as persecution or violence.

The refugee situation may worsen worldwide if two trends continue. First, violent conflict is likely to increase over the next decade or so in balkanizing and irredentist struggles as well as from civil wars, border conflicts, and rebellions. ("Balkanization" is a process of political fragmentation along narrowly religious or ethnic lines; "irredentism" refers to the tendency of one group to exercise political power in an area over another group that has deep social and cultural roots in that area.) These conflicts, primarily in the developing world, will create tens of millions of refugees. Second, with general population growth stressing the resources of many economies, there will be vigorous rejection of masses of refugees from adjacent countries.

See also ENVIRONMENTAL REFUGEES; ETHNIC AND CULTURAL SEPARATISM; HUMAN RIGHTS; MIGRATION, INTERNATIONAL.

BIBLIOGRAPHY

DENG, FRANCES M. *Protecting the Dispossessed: A Challenge for the International Community.* Washington, DC: Brookings Institution, 1993.

LOESCHER, GIL. *Beyond Charity: International Cooperation and the Global Refugee Crises.* New York: Oxford University Press, 1993.

Roger P. Winter

Refugees, Environmental.

See ENVIRONMENTAL REFUGEES

Regional Trade Agreements.

See INTERNATIONAL TRADE: REGIONAL TRADE AGREEMENTS.

Religion: Changing Beliefs

Historians note that the great world religions are experiencing a diminution of their primary role as the cohesive, culture-shaping force in society. Resurgent fundamentalism notwithstanding, the church, mosque, and temple seem less able to provide the eternal certainties that once gave people an anchor in life and that bound people together in a clear sense of their place in the universal order.

Psychologically, religions can be understood as projections of the unconscious mind, as containers of eternal images of the soul that ascribe an order to life. Such symbols express the deepest of unarticulated meaning. Our historic spiritual disciplines are systems for psychic healing and wholeness. Their evident practical function has been to maintain the inner balance of the individual and to provide coherence and anchorage to human lives.

The emergence of the religious mind may have been part of a seminal shift of history—the appearance of consciousness as we now experience it.

We tend to view the past in terms of the present, to project backward what we are like today. But there was a time when consciousness, as we experience it, did not exist. Humans did not always have the same capacity for subjectivity, reflection, introspection, assimilation, and the capacity for willing, as we have today. Rather, "thoughts" were the result of some inner revelation; they simply *appeared*. People heard internal voices that said, "Do this, do that." Parts of the Old Testament reflect this type of mind, as does the *Iliad*, where you do not get reasoned thought, but rather gods giving commands on the field of battle.

But there came a period when the capacity for reflection, for willing, and for purposive thinking began to evolve. As Aeschylus had Prometheus say, "I gave them understanding." In biblical terms, man ate the fruit of the tree of knowledge. A major psychological reorientation took place.

Thus many of the Greek myths and Biblical texts can be interpreted as the emergence of consciousness as we now experience it. It was at this point that man changed from being merely an object of creation, and, in a sense, became a co-creator with the Divine.

With the emergence of consciousness came the recognition of good and evil as distinct choices in life, choices that either advance or retard the quality of the human condition. This evolution of good and evil as conscious choice can be seen as the birth of freedom. In this sense, consciousness, good, evil, and freedom are inextricably bound together.

During different phases of this period, the great religions of the world were born, save for Islam, which emerged in the seventh century. The great religions of the world became metaphors by which humankind could experience the transcendent mystery of life. Religions became the symbol/systems of psychic wholeness that emanate from the collective unconscious. At this same time came the concept of human-hearted caring and compassion as the desirable bonding force of social cohesion.

But in the past two centuries, and especially in the twentieth century, our awareness of the natural order has vastly expanded. So have our powers of technology. As this has happened, our defining reality has become the awareness of the human community as a single entity. The basic referent is no longer "my tribe," "my nation," or even "my civilization."

In this new era, we are incorporating the planetary dimensions of life into the fabric of our economics, politics, international relations, and culture. For the first time in human history, we are forging an awareness of our existence that embraces humanity as a whole. We may now have a unifying language out of which we can begin to organize ourselves on the level of a specie. What is emerging is a new context for all discussion of value, meaning, purpose, or ultimacy of any sort.

In light of a change on this scale, the ability of the historic world religions to carry living meaning has weakened over the past two centuries. As a container of divine significance, the soul seems to have become enfeebled. A similar process took place at the time of the Roman Caesars, when the gods lost their living force.

As the historical spiritual images of wholeness have been withdrawn as living projections, the archetypal contents of the unconscious have been activated and projected as contemporary images in our culture. As the eminent cultural historian Christopher Dawson wrote, "When the prophets are silent and society no longer possesses the channel of communication with the divine world, the way to the lower world is still open, and man's frustrated spiritual powers will find their outlet in the unlimited will to power and destruction." These other images have given rise to the psychic content of twentieth-century culture, with its portrayal of the American dream gone awry as in *The Great Gatsby*, or the negation of any life-affirming impulse as in the film *Pulp Fiction*.

We tend to take such cultural images as ominous forebodings of doom. But it is a psychological fact that every increase in consciousness derives from a creative encounter with darkness. As chaos prevails, the law of compensating opposites is engaged and eventually new projections of light and life emanate from the psyche.

We see this process expressed in literature in Odysseus' trip to the Underworld before he was able to return home to Ithaca and Penelope. In like manner, Dante's descent into the Inferno was but the prelude to Paradise. In this sense, the wasteland—the Underworld—of contemporary American culture can be seen as a prelude to a rebirth, a fresh spiritual advance to be experienced in the coming century.

It is against this background that the metaphors by which we experience transcendent reality, by which we express the deepest unknown mysteries of life, must be reinterpreted to accommodate a new stage of human development. This does not necessarily imply rejection of the spiritual metaphors and disciplines that have served us thus far. But the life of the spirit is dynamic, not static. It must be eternally renewed, and never frozen in time or form.

What we are engaged in is the soul's search for a greater expression of life. We seek a legitimizing vision of life that expresses the spiritual essence of the human journey with such force and resonance so as to define world purposes and standards of conduct for a new epoch of human development. Only by the unyielding pursuit of its inner creativeness and the texture of its truth can the human soul advance. This is, in fact, the divine process of continuous creation and recreation through human maturation.

It is impossible to predict how this spiritual search will ultimately manifest itself. We are not engaged in a rational, objective process. Nor is this a search that has to do with any particular religion. It involves all of us as individuals, and it is the most hopeful portent of the future.

While we tend to focus on the collapse of old forms, in point of fact, we are beginning to see the emergence of new expressions of eternal images of spiritual wholeness that will enable consciousness to be reborn on a higher level.

See also GLOBAL CONSCIOUSNESS; MIND: NEW MODES OF THINKING; RELIGION, SPIRITUALITY, MORALITY; RELIGIONS, DECLINE OR RISE OF.

BIBLIOGRAPHY

ARMSTRONG, KAREN. *The History of God.* New York: Ballantine Books, 1993.

CAMPBELL, JOSEPH. *The Inner Reaches of Outer Space.* New York: Harper & Row, 1986.

EDINGER, EDWARD F. *Ego and Archetype.* Boston: Shambhala, 1972.

DAVIES, PAUL. *The Mind of God.* New York: Simon & Schuster, 1992.

JUNG, C. G. *Psychology and Religion: West and East.* Vol. 11 of *Collected Works.* Princeton, NJ: Princeton University Press, 1969.

SWIMME, BRIAN, and BERRY, THOMAS. *The Universe Story.* New York: HarperCollins, 1992.

William Van Dusen Wishard

Religion: Institutions and Practices

Until recently, most social scientists would have agreed with the eminent anthropologist Anthony F. C. Wallace, when he said:

> The evolutionary future of religion is extinction. Belief in supernatural beings and in supernatural forces that affect nature without obeying nature's laws will erode and become only an interesting historical memory. To be sure, this event is not likely to occur in the next generation; the process will very likely take several hundred years, and there will always remain individuals, or even occasional small cult groups, who respond to hallucination, trance, and obsession with a supernatural interpretation. But as a cultural trait, belief in supernatural powers is doomed to die out, all over the world, as a result of the increasing adequacy and diffusion of scientific knowledge (Wallace, 1966, p. 264).

Since Wallace wrote, however, the continued vigor of American churches, coupled with the proliferation of new religious movements around the world, has brought this secularization thesis into grave doubt. As outlined by sociologists Rodney Stark, William Sims Bainbridge, and Roger Finke, the dominant current model of secularization notes that the most liberal denominations in all periods of history tend to lose their faith and thus their adherents. The close connection these denominations enjoy with secular powers is a chief reason for their loss of faith, but it also gives them some capacity to suppress competing sects. Eventually, revival movements arise within the dominant religious tradition, often in the form of sects that erupt from the denominations through disruptive schisms.

In time, the most successful of these sects will develop connections with the secular elites, transform into moderate denominations, and set the stage for a new generation of schismatic sects. Over the very long haul, an entire religious tradition can become secularized, but this only clears the social landscape for entirely new traditions that emerge in the form of radical cults.

In the United States, from 1971 to 1990, the Episcopal church lost 19 percent of its membership and the United Church of Christ (Congregationalists) lost 12 percent even as the general population was growing. At the same time that these liberal denominations were shrinking, the conservative Mormons gained 66 percent, and the Seventh-Day Adventists, 68 percent. Projected into the future, these trends predict decline for the liberal denominations, more than balanced by growth in evangelical ones. However, the growing religious movements will probably moderate, and the net result may be overall stability for decades to come.

Since colonial times, the United States has been home to many innovative cults, and a few, such as Christian Science and Scientology, have claimed to be especially well designed for the modern era. However, Pitirim SOROKIN was probably right when he argued that entirely new religious traditions succeed only when standard traditions have been discredited, and widespread social chaos drives multitudes of people to seek radical solutions to life's problems. These conditions currently exist in China and the former Soviet Union—a basis for some speculative thinking.

In Russia, three generations have grown up under a repressive regime that was resolutely atheistic. It is perhaps too much to hope that their newfound freedoms will continue indefinitely, but for the present they suddenly are able to create any kind of religion they wish. Because Marxism broke the power of the Orthodox church, and few citizens have been securely socialized into any particular faith, we can expect to see the wildest possible experimentation with radical sects and cults. New dictatorships may arise upon the ashes of the old, and their orientation to religion is highly unpredictable. In the 1930s and '40s the Nazis indulged deeply in Wagnerian cultism and attempted the eradication of Jews; conceivably Russia will become a religious battleground, with Baptists the victims and pseudo-Orthodox Rasputins the villains. Alternatively, like Judea two thousand years earlier, Russia may give birth to an entirely new benevolent world religion, perhaps healing the wounds of ethnic and national wars from the Caucasus to Capetown.

The secrets of success for a new religion are relatively simple, although most cults go out of existence when the founder loses his or her grip, or the first generation of members die off. To instill faith, a religion must first inspire hope. This means it must compellingly promise to solve the major life problems faced by potential recruits, but it must not claim to deliver the desired rewards immediately in the material world, because such claims are too easy to disprove. Faith is strengthened when religious activities offer considerable experiential rewards, such as fellowship and ecstasy.

A cult or sect grows through development and activation of social bonds linking members to nonmembers, and much of its strength comes from emotional attachments linking members with each other. A person is easier to recruit if weak in social relationships. In such a circumstance, sect members can more readily form friendships with these persons and draw them into the group. In addition, such persons lack countervailing friendships with nonmembers that might seek to pull them away. However, a new recruit who possesses friendships with nonmembers can be used as a bridge to recruit them as well. This means that the most successful religious movements recruit socially connected people and spread outward through their friendship and family networks. Thus, they become locked in fierce competition with other movements that are doing the same thing, and they must be exceedingly well organized to win.

Ecstasy is both a blessing and a curse. It inspires members with great commitment, but it also places a few of them in control of powerful emotional resources that may be used to challenge the leadership. Frequently this leads to fragmentation of the group. Partly in consequence, most cults are remarkably dull and uncreative. A sectlike cult that innovates only moderately, combining much of the traditional religion of the society with carefully chosen new elements, has the advantage of exploiting existing faith and can plausibly claim to be an improved version. American examples include Mormonism, Adventism, and Christian Science. Christianity itself was originally a Jewish cult, as Buddhism was a Hindu one.

Given the preeminence of science in the modern world, wholly new religious traditions may draw upon scientific metaphors, especially if science succeeds in discrediting older religious traditions and then slumps into a malaise of its own as fresh scientific discoveries become ever more expensive and remote from the everyday world of human existence. Thus, the future of religion depends to some extent upon the future of science.

The essential question is not whether religion will continue to be a potent force in human affairs, for it will. Instead, the question is how long the currently popular religions will hold dominance until being replaced by radically different religious visions that today can hardly be imagined.

See also CHURCH-STATE AFFAIRS; FUNDAMENTALISM; RELIGION, CHANGING BELIEFS; RELIGION, SPIRITUALITY, MORALITY; RELIGIONS, DECLINE OR RISE OF; RELIGIONS, STATISTICAL PROJECTIONS OF.

BIBLIOGRAPHY

FINKE, ROGER, and STARK, RODNEY. *The Churching of America: 1776–1990.* New Brunswick, NJ: Rutgers University Press, 1992.

SOROKIN, PITIRIM A. *Social and Cultural Dynamics.* New York: American Book Company, 1937.

STARK, RODNEY, and BAINBRIDGE, WILLIAM SIMS. *The Future of Religion.* Berkeley, CA: University of California Press, 1985.

WALLACE, ANTHONY F. C. *Religion: An Anthropological View.* New York: Random House, 1966.

William Sims Bainbridge

Religion, Spirituality, Morality

Protestant theologian Paul Tillich (1886–1965) contended that every human being has a religion, at least of a kind, for each of us has an "ultimate concern." Religions can be classified in various ways. Distinction can be drawn between revealed religions, which claim that God has revealed divinity and divine purposes to us in ways that can be understood, and religions based on human inquiry, philosophical speculation, and mystical experience.

The major revealed religions are Judaism, Christianity, and Islam. These three are related historically. Christianity accepts the validity of Jewish revelation, the Hebrew Scriptures; Islam accepts at least some elements of both Judaism and Christianity. Revealed religions typically propound doctrines (statements regarded as objectively true that adherents are expected to believe) and commandments (a way of life based on rules considered binding on all members or, in some cases, on people in general).

The development of religion, spirituality, and morality depends on whether the revealed religions will be able to defend their distinctive doctrines and ways of life in an increasingly multicultural world or will have to yield to nondogmatic kinds of spirituality. If so, they will survive and grow; if not, they will decline and the others will grow.

Prospects for the revealed religions indicate that many adherents will make a concerted stand in defense of their beliefs and associated ways of life. Such people are called "orthodox," "traditionalists," or sometimes "fundamentalists." Also included are many more people than those in the groups and sects within Judaism, Christianity, and Islam who are also commonly called "fundamentalists." Other people will move in the direction of mysticism or nondogmatic spirituality, or may drop out of organized religion altogether. Adherents of the revealed religions will defend their doctrines energetically. They will demand of themselves, and sometimes of others, adherence to the rules of conduct that grow out of those doctrines. This probably will lead to an intensification of the conflict that James Davison Hunter calls "culture wars" in his 1991 book of that title, namely, to a conflict that pits traditional ways and believers on one side against "liberal" ways and believers and nonbelievers on the other.

For those who emphasize tradition, faith and conduct are interdependent. Especially for traditional Christians, it is on the doctrines they hold to be true that they see the commandments prescribing moral conduct. Thus, the first of the Ten Commandments reads: "I am the LORD thy God, that brought thee up out of the land of Egypt. . . . Thou shalt have none other gods before me" (Exodus 20:2).

Traditional believers cannot give up their doctrines, on which both their pattern of conduct in this world and their hope of salvation hereafter are based. They feel themselves threatened by both scientific and pseudo-scientific views that question the factual basis of their revelation, as well as by widely practiced behaviors that they find immoral. One example is the theory of evolution when it is interpreted to deny the existence of God as well as of any divine design or purpose. Another example is the kind of psychology which asserts that behavior urged or prohibited by religion is psychologically or genetically determined and not subject to human moral control—for example, behavior involving sex (especially homosexuality) and violence. These doctrines imply that some people, or even people in general, simply cannot be expected to behave as the traditional revealed religions demand.

In reaction, we can expect traditionalists to continue to set up rival institutions of science and learning to defend their positions, and to make an effort to see their moral convictions made a part of the civil law. Conservative Christians already have attempted this in the United States. In Israel, orthodox Judaism makes similar efforts to make Israeli law conform to religious law, and Muslims frequently establish *Sharia* (Islamic law) in societies where they are dominant.

Morality for religious adherents is tied to religion. The culture can be viewed as the fulfillment of God's intentions and embraced, or the religious adherents can separate more and more from the rest of society to the extent that they view society as secular, pluralistic, and permissive—which, in the eyes of those adherents, means immoral. Ernst Troeltsch and later H. Richard Niebuhr made the study of this variety of relationships between "Christ and culture" their life work.

Much revealed religion is characterized by apocalypticism, which claims to have revelation that accurately predicts the impending end of the world and divine judgment. Orthodox Christianity believes in the return of Christ and the Last Judgment, but does not claim to know the day and hour of these events. Apocalyptic movements, claiming to know when all this will happen, arise and gain a following in times of social, political, and economic troubles. These movements suddenly flourish and usually fade even more suddenly when the dates set by their predictions pass without incident. The popular fundamentalist Christian author Hal Lindsey's record-breaking bestseller *The Late Great Planet Earth* (1971) is a contemporary example of this phenomenon. Such apocalyptic phenomena will probably increase, especially as the twentieth century draws to a close.

Traditionalism and orthodoxy, with their doctrines that have to be believed and rules that must be obeyed, will appeal only to a minority of people. Religious feminists also will continue to put pressure on Judaism, Christianity, and Islam, criticizing them as "male-dominated" and patriarchal. In fact, the status of women in late antiquity, in the first three centuries after Christ, was far higher in Judaism and especially in Christianity than it was in the surrounding religions of that time.

Most human beings seem to be unable to live entirely without religion. Where the traditional religions of the West decline, the great world religions based on philosophy and mysticism, notably Hinduism and Buddhism, will continue to gain adherents in the West, including former Christians, Jews, and people who grew up with no religion. However, these religions from Asia frequently entail codes of conduct and spiritual disciplines that are very demanding. Consequently, they do not appeal to people increasingly eager for instant gratification and in pursuit of unbridled individualism.

Hinduism and Buddhism will be less attractive than what the late Francis A. Schaeffer (1912–1984) called "contentless mysticism," an expression to be seen as descriptive rather than pejorative. Instead of claiming roots in objectively true divine revelation, or in the intensely demanding spiritual disciplines of religious giants such as the Buddha, many varieties of New Age spirituality, rather like the early Christian heresy called gnosticism, present an elaborate structure of concepts and teachings but do not base them on biblical, historical, or scientific evidence. They appeal to a group that sees itself as a kind of spiritual elite.

Feminist concepts and female leaders are prominent in this New Age movement, dating back to Helena Blavatsky (1831–1891), and Annie Besant (1847–1933). Although both Hinduism and Buddhism arose in highly patriarchal cultures, their modern offshoots, grouped under the heading New Age, are characterized by feminist activism, often by goddess worship, and sometimes by great sexual freedom, which their critics call licentiousness and degeneracy. Some New Age and related movements claim to be resurrecting ancient beliefs, for example, the worship of Gaia, meaning the Earth personified as a goddess, and Wicca, a modern form of witchcraft claiming very ancient origins. Traditional Hindu and Buddhist concepts, such as reincarnation, will continue to gain popularity, especially when they are presented in a nondemanding kind of "pop" religion without the moral and spiritual requirements of the Asian religions.

In conclusion, human beings are and will remain religious by nature. Even worldviews that are supposedly based on objective science have a strong "belief" component, one that cannot be documented scientifically but must be taken by faith. See, for example, the worldview presented by Cornell University astronomer Carl Sagan in his book *Cosmos* (1980). The traditional revealed religions demand loyalty and impose standards of belief and/or conduct to which adherents of New Age and other movements, as well as nonreligious people, will object.

Unless the future brings a great spiritual renewal across whole societies, or a great "falling away" from faith—both of which are mentioned in biblical prophecy—we can expect continuing "culture wars." This conflict will rage on between traditionalist believers and moralists in Judaism, Christianity, and Islam on the one hand, the secularizing Western culture of technology, New Agers, and moral relativists on the other.

See also APOCALYPTIC FUTURES; BUDDHISM; CHRISTIANITY; EVOLUTION, BIOLOGICAL; FUNDAMENTALISM; HINDUISM; HOLISTIC BELIEFS; ISLAM; JUDAISM; PENTECOSTALISM; RELIGION: INSTITUTIONS AND PRACTICES; RELIGIONS, DECLINE OR RISE OF; RELIGIONS, STATISTICAL PROJECTIONS OF; WOMEN AND RELIGION.

BIBLIOGRAPHY

ELLUL, JACQUES. *The Technological Bluff.* Grand Rapids, MI: Eerdmans, 1990.

GRENZ, STANLEY. *The Millennial Maze: Sorting Out Evangelical Options.* Downers Grove, IL, and Grand Rapids, MI: Inter-Varsity Press, 1992.

MARTIN, RALPH. *The Catholic Church at the End of an Age.* San Francisco: Ignatius, 1994.

SAGAN, CARL. *Cosmos.* New York: Random House, 1980.

SCHWARZ, HANS. *The Way to the Future.* Minneapolis: Augsburg, 1972.

SUCHOCKI, MARJORIE. *The End of Evil: Process Eschatology in the Light of Current Trends in Religion.* Albany, NY: State University of New York Press, 1988.

TOFFLER, ALVIN. *Powershift: Knowledge, Wealth and Violence at the Edge of the 21st Century.* New York: Bantam, 1990.

Harold O. J. Brown

Religions, Decline or Rise of

Writing about the future of religion has always been a hazardous business. Those brave enough to venture into this realm are drawn inexorably to two visions of the religious future of mankind—from fanciful predictions of religious utopia (such as Bellamy, *Looking Backward, 2000–1887*, a long-term future scenario of utopia as the result of mankind's obedience to Christian principles) on the one side, to predictions of inexorable decline and collapse (such as Lorie and Murray-Clark, *History of the Future: a Chronology*, which predicts the collapse of organized religion beginning in 2006—the Age of Aquarius) on the other. Perhaps this is due to the strong opinions of the authors—either as devout religionists or as those opposed to organized religion.

"Religion—it's hard to kill" sums up the feeling of many futurists (*What Futurists Believe*, Coates and Jarratt, 1989). In this book, the two authors demonstrate that most futurists do not take religion seriously or are interested in only its aberrations or extremes (e.g., fanaticism, fundamentalism). Stark and Bainbridge begin their book *The Future of Religion* with the following observation: "The most illustrious figures in sociology, anthropology, and psychology have unanimously expressed confidence that their children, or surely their grandchildren, would live to see the dawn of a new era in which, to paraphrase Freud, the infantile illusions of religion would be outgrown" (Stark and Bainbridge, 1985, p. 1). The fourth major trend in social scientist Burnham Beckwith's *The Next 500 Years* is "the decline of religion and superstition." Beckwith includes this in a list of thirty-one major trends he believes will shape the next few centuries. Sociologist Brian M. Stableford and weapons physicist David Langford also see religion on the decline. In their masterful *The Third Millennium: a History of the World, AD 2000–3000*, by the middle of the twenty-first century, the last great "religion," Marxism, is on the decline (Stableford and Langford, 1985, p. 24). The world's old faiths have all but disappeared.

Equally prolific are the writers expounding a future where religion is central to the destiny of mankind. This ranges from pseudo-humanistic utopias (still based on religion) to Christian, Muslim, or Buddhist eschatological visions to New Age "cosmic consciousness" sans organized religion. It should be noted that the bestselling futurist work in the 1970s was Hal Lindsey's *Late Great Planet Earth* (Lindsey and Carlson, 1976) with 25 million copies in print and still selling strong in the 1990s. The most widely read futurist work of any kind in history is *The Revelation of John* (c. A.D. 90), which has been translated into over 1,000 languages. It is also important to note a new attitude among Muslims about their future. "At the beginning of the 20th century, Islam—colonized, defeated, stagnant—could easily have been written off from history and the future. At the dawn of the 21st century, Islam—resurgent, confident, 'militant,' 'fundamentalist,' very much alive—is poised to become a global force" (Sardar, 1991, p. 223).

Futurist H. Gerjouy in "The Most Significant Events of the Next Thousand Years" (Gerjouy, 1992, p. 6) counters pessimistic views of the future by stating that "there will be a radiation and proliferation of religions, and new important religions will spring up that will attract many adherents."

Hiley H. Ward set out a scenario of religion in the twenty-second century in his 1975 work *Religion 2102 A.D.* Ward suggests that "Christianity is likely to be around for a long time to come in some form." He then surveys the current literature on futurism, drawing out its implications for religion in the future with such interesting applications as telepathic sermons, God as supermachine, and pluralistic Christianity.

L. E. Browne, writing in the *International Review of Missions* in 1949, ventured his opinion under the title "The Religion of the World in AD 3000." Browne predicts the extinction of not only polytheism (including Hinduism) but also of all major religions except Christianity. He goes on to say that the only competitor to Christianity will be materialism, which is essentially a belief that man does not need God or ethics.

Perhaps the Christian theologian to write most seriously on the future is the German Catholic Hans Küng. His major treatise *Theology for the Third Millennium* deals with a paradigm shift that represents a narrowing of the perceived chasm between the various Christian traditions (particularly Catholicism, Orthodoxy, and Protestantism). Christianity in the future need not be polarized, as differences in theology are often artificially accentuated by the political and structural context. The new paradigm is an ecumenical one, but without sacrificing distinctions of faith and tradition. He extends this to include solidarity with all of the world's religious traditions—always searching for a common ground in solving mankind's problems.

In conclusion, the reader of literature on the future of religion is confronted with a dizzying range of opinions. Writing from a wide range of disciplines and personal perspectives, scholars, economists, environmentalists, and science fiction writers paint a future for religion ranging from its extinction to its central role for human survival. Perhaps futurist Warren Wagar put it best: "As futurists, we are really out of our depth in trying to chart the far future of religion" (1991:140).

See also RELIGION: INSTITUTIONS AND PRACTICES; RELIGION, SPRITUALITY, MORALITY; RELIGIONS, STATISTICAL PROJECTIONS OF.

BIBLIOGRAPHY

BECKWITH, BURNHAM. *The Next 500 Years*. New York: Harper & Row, 1967.

BELLAMY, EDWARD. *Looking Backward, 2000–1887*. Boston: Houghton Mifflin Company, 1887.

BROWNE, L. E. "The Religion of the World in AD 3000." *International Review of Missions* 38/104 (1949); 463–468.

COATES, JOSEPH F., and JARRATT, JENNIFER. *What Futurists Believe*. Mt. Airy, MD: Lomond, 1989.

GERJOUY, HERBERT G. "The Most Significant Events of the Next Thousand Years." *Futures Research Quarterly*. 8/3 (Fall 1992): 5–21.

KÜNG, HANS. *Theology for the Third Millennium: An Ecumenical View*. New York: Doubleday, 1988.

LINDSEY, HAL, and CARLSON, C. C. *The Late Great Planet Earth*. Grand Rapids, MI: Zondervan, 1976.

LORIE, PETER, and MURRAY-CLARK, SIDD. *History of the Future: a Chronology*. New York: Doubleday, 1989.

SARDAR, ZIAUDDIN, ed. Special issue. "Islam and the Future." *Futures* 23/3 (April 1991): 223–332.

STABLEFORD, BRIAN M., and LANGFORD, DAVID. *The Third Millennium: A History of the World: AD 2000–3000*. London: Sidgwick & Jackson, 1985.

STARK, RODNEY, and BAINBRIDGE, WILLIAM SIMS. *The Future of Religion: Secularization, Revival, and Cult Formation*. Berkeley, CA: University of California Press, 1985.

WAGAR, W. WARREN. *The Next Three Futures: Paradigms of Things to Come*. New York: Praeger, 1991.

WARD, HILEY H. *Religion 2101 A.D.* Garden City, NY: Doubleday, 1975.

Todd M. Johnson

Religions, Statistical Projections of

The opportunity to project the future of religious affiliation has presented itself for the first time with the recent availability of four publications and two databases. Foundational demographic data for every country in the world are available for the years 1950–2025 through the United Nations Demographic Database (see United Nations, 1994). Data on religions and Christianity for every country are available through the World Evangelization Database (see *World Christian Encyclopedia* [1982] and *Our Globe and How to Reach It*

[1990]). Data beyond 2025 for the world's nine major continental areas are available for the first time in the UN's publication *Long-Range World Population Projections: Two Centuries of Population Growth, 1950–2150* (1992).

The intersection of these data form the starting point for a quantitative analysis of the future of religion. The demographic projections of the United Nations provide a foundation on which religious data can be compared. This can be described as a five-stage process.

Stage One

Christian data are more complete globally than data on other religions. A detailed analysis can be performed by matching data on Christianity with the population projections for every country of the world. If none of the 1990 percentages are adjusted but assumed to remain static, the demographic effects on Christian affiliation can be analyzed on both regional and global levels. This reveals the differential growth of adherents to Christianity depending on population growth where they live. This is the first stage of demographic analysis by country.

Stage Two

A more realistic application is to use current trends to make adjustments to the Christian data. Thus, if evidence exists that the Christian church is in decline in a particular country, then the percentage to be matched to that country at a future date will be lowered to an appropriate level. With adjustments made to Christian populations in each country a second stage of analysis is added. Now one can view the effects of not only demographic change but change in religious adherence.

But these first two stages of analysis have two important limitations. First, they only analyze the Christian situation. Without reference to other religions and nonreligions, it is easy to miss the overall context of religious change either by country, region, or globally. Second, they only take us to the year 2025. Our next stages will, therefore, have to overcome both of these limitations.

Stage Three

The most detailed table of religions by United Nations regions is published yearly by *Encyclopaedia Britannica* in its *Britannica Book of the Year*. This table includes all religions by major region and is thus suited perfectly for demographic manipulation.

It overcomes the first limitation of the first two stages—all major religions are included. The second limitation is overcome in that regional projections have been published by the United Nations for the years 2025–2200.

Analysis of the *Britannica* tables begins by using the 1990 table as a base from which to project all future tables (to 2200) using only demographic tools. Thus, the regional totals reflect United Nations projections while all religious percentages within a region remain unchanged. This allows us to examine how demographic growth or decline alone within a particular region affects the global total. This yields remarkable insights into what we can expect from the most consistent source of growth and decline of religious and nonreligious adherence—births and deaths. This amounts to our third stage of analysis of the future of religion.

Stage Four

The fourth stage allows us to use results from our country-by-country analysis to update the *Britannica* tables to 2025. From this base, more reasonable demographic future projections can be made. In addition, for the first time we can see our Christian projections in the context of the world's religions and nonreligions.

Stage Five

The fifth stage of analysis completes our methodology by making adjustments to the end of our study period, A.D. 2200, based on conservative assumptions about religious change. The adjustments yield what could be considered our most likely scenario.

Conclusions

The results from the fifth stage are presented in Table 1, "Scenarios for Adherents of World Religions, 1900–2200." This table shows Christianity increasing from 33.2 percent in 1990 to 37.9 percent by 2200 while Islam also increases from 17.7 percent in 1990 to 22.6 percent in 2200. Nonreligious persons and atheists, on the other hand, grew rapidly over the period 1900–1990, then decrease from a combined percentage of 19.6 percent in 1990 to 16.1 percent by A.D. 2200.

These results could be revised simply by modifying either the assumptions or the actual figures used to calculate religious change. For illustrative purposes, two additional scenarios have been added to Table 1. First, a plausible future is one in which Islam makes unprecedented inroads into the Western world. (See columns labeled "Muslim revival"). The assumption is made that 1 percent of the Christians in Europe, North America, and Oceania defect to Islam every twenty-five years. In this scenario Christians lose 0.9 percent of the world's population (dropping from 37.9 to 37.0 percent while Muslims gain from 22.6 to 23.5 percent) over the 175-year period 2025–2200.

A second alternative scenario is constructed by assuming that Muslims in Asia are hard hit by secularization, losing 0.5 percent every twenty-five years from 2025 to 2200. The result, presented under "Nonreligious" in Table 1, is that Muslims lose 1.2

TABLE 1 Scenarios for Adherents of World Religions, 1900–2200

	1900	%	1950	%	1990	%	2000	%	2020	%
Christians	558,056,000	34.5%	849,352,000	33.8%	1,757,206,000	33.2%	2,090,417,000	33.4%	3,022,623,000	35.5%
Muslims	200,102,000	12.4%	379,295,000	15.1%	935,331,000	17.7%	1,159,901,000	18.5%	1,716,091,000	20.2%
Nonreligious	2,923,000	0.2%	332,170,000	13.2%	857,708,000	16.2%	1,005,109,000	16.1%	1,279,525,000	15.0%
Hindus	203,033,000	12.5%	326,269,000	13.0%	705,000,000	13.3%	840,792,000	13.4%	1,113,103,000	13.1%
Buddhists	127,159,000	7.8%	171,118,000	6.8%	307,219,000	5.8%	366,265,000	5.9%	484,432,000	5.7%
Atheists	226,000	0.0%	100,658,000	4.0%	229,000,000	4.3%	233,301,000	3.7%	237,257,000	2.8%
Chinese folk-religionists	380,404,000	23.5%	208,865,000	8.3%	180,000,000	3.4%	210,313,000	3.4%	233,813,000	2.7%
New-Religionists	5,910,000	0.4%	27,379,000	1.1%	138,000,000	2.6%	164,418,000	2.6%	217,314,000	2.6%
Tribal religionists	106,340,000	6.6%	83,729,000	3.3%	102,242,000	1.9%	96,677,000	1.5%	77,026,000	0.9%
Sikhs	2,961,000	0.2%	6,515,000	0.3%	18,100,000	0.3%	21,522,000	0.3%	28,370,000	0.3%
Jews	12,270,000	0.8%	11,641,000	0.5%	16,500,000	0.3%	17,473,000	0.3%	21,468,000	0.3%
Shamanists	11,341,000	0.7%	8,558,000	0.3%	10,100,000	0.2%	12,015,000	0.2%	15,849,000	0.2%
Confucians	640,000	0.0%	1,752,000	0.1%	5,800,000	0.1%	6,913,000	0.1%	9,142,000	0.1%
Baha'is	9,000	0.0%	251,000	0.0%	5,300,000	0.1%	6,485,000	0.1%	9,544,000	0.1%
Jains	1,323,000	0.1%	1,871,000	0.1%	3,650,000	0.1%	4,357,000	0.1%	5,795,000	0.1%
Shintoists	6,720,000	0.4%	3,519,000	0.1%	3,100,000	0.1%	3,698,000	0.1%	4,892,000	0.1%
Other religionists	470,000	0.0%	2,861,000	0.1%	17,938,000	0.3%	21,144,000	0.3%	27,978,000	0.3%
Total population	1,619,887,000	100.0%	2,516,443,000	100.0%	5,292,194,000	100.0%	6,260,800,000	100.0%	8,504,222,000	100.0%

TABLE 1   (CONTINUED)

	Demographic from 1990		Demographic from 2025		Most likely		Muslim revival		Nonreligious	
	2200	%	2200	%	2200	%	2200	%	2200	%
Christians	3,779,997,000	32.6%	4,257,919,000	36.7%	4,397,929,000	37.9%	4,291,467,000	37.0%	4,397,929,000	37.9%
Muslims	2,582,642,000	22.3%	2,607,061,000	22.5%	2,624,567,000	22.6%	2,730,478,000	23.5%	2,485,513,320	21.4%
Nonreligious	1,609,929,000	13.9%	1,580,647,000	13.6%	1,626,497,000	14.0%	1,626,497,000	14.0%	1,764,999,680	15.2%
Hindus	1,398,329,000	12.1%	1,398,329,000	12.1%	1,398,329,000	12.1%	1,398,329,000	12.1%	1,398,329,000	12.1%
Buddhists	607,601,000	5.2%	607,601,000	5.2%	607,601,000	5.2%	607,601,000	5.2%	607,601,000	5.2%
Atheists	409,408,000	3.5%	291,083,000	2.5%	249,000,000	2.1%	249,000,000	2.1%	249,000,000	2.1%
Chinese folk-religionists	356,278,000	3.1%	293,297,000	2.5%	253,162,000	2.2%	253,162,000	2.2%	253,162,000	2.2%
New-Religionists	272,280,000	2.3%	272,280,000	2.3%	272,280,000	2.3%	272,280,000	2.3%	272,280,000	2.3%
Tribal religionists	426,416,000	3.7%	136,010,000	1.2%	15,416,000	0.1%	15,416,000	0.1%	15,416,000	0.1%
Sikhs	35,434,000	0.3%	35,434,000	0.3%	35,434,000	0.3%	35,434,000	0.3%	35,434,000	0.3%
Jews	26,035,000	0.2%	24,697,000	0.2%	24,697,000	0.2%	24,697,000	0.2%	24,697,000	0.2%
Shamanists	19,859,000	0.2%	19,859,000	0.2%	19,859,000	0.2%	19,859,000	0.2%	19,859,000	0.2%
Confucians	11,459,000	0.1%	11,459,000	0.1%	11,459,000	0.1%	11,459,000	0.1%	11,459,000	0.1%
Baha'is	14,559,000	0.1%	14,559,000	0.1%	14,559,000	0.1%	14,559,000	0.1%	14,559,000	0.1%
Jains	7,351,000	0.1%	7,351,000	0.1%	7,351,000	0.1%	7,351,000	0.1%	7,351,000	0.1%
Shintoists	6,138,000	0.1%	6,138,000	0.1%	6,138,000	0.1%	6,138,000	0.1%	6,138,000	0.1%
Other religionists	36,273,000	0.3%	36,273,000	0.3%	36,273,000	0.3%	36,273,000	0.3%	36,273,000	0.3%
Total population	**11,600,000,000**	100.0%	**11,600,000,000**	100.0%	**11,600,000,000**	100.0%	**11,600,000,000**	100.0%	**11,600,000,000**	100.0%

Source: *World Christian Encyclopedia*; future figures projected and adjusted.

percent of the world's population over the 175-year period.

A secondary side effect of this study is the evidence it provides for the quantitative resiliency of religion over the next two hundred years. Purely demographic changes do not show a massive decline in religious adherence. The onus would be on the person putting forth such a statement to prove that massive defections from religious adherence represent a plausible assumption.

See also RELIGION: INSTITUTIONS AND PRACTICES; RELIGION, SPIRITUALITY, MORALITY; RELIGIONS, DECLINE OR RISE OF.

BIBLIOGRAPHY

BARRETT, DAVID B. *World Christian Encyclopedia: a Comparative Survey of Churches and Religions in the Modern World, AD 1900–2000.* New York: Oxford University Press, 1982.

——. "World Religious Statistics" (annual compilation). In *Britannica Book of the Year.* Chicago: Encyclopaedia Britannica, 1994.

BARRETT, DAVID B., and JOHNSON, TODD M. *Our Globe and How to Reach It: Seeing the World Evangelized by AD 2000 and Beyond.* Birmingham, AL: New Hope, 1990.

United Nations. *Long-Range World Population Projections: Two Centuries of Population Growth, 1950–2150.* New York: United Nations, 1992.

—— *World Population Prospects 1992.* New York: United Nations, 1994.

Todd M. Johnson

Religious Fundamentalism.

See FUNDAMENTALISM.

Research and Development

There is a clear link between technological progress and economic growth. This link, long recognized by economists, accounts for the strong interest of many governments in promoting the creation of new technology, primarily by investing in research and development (R&D). Neither invention nor innovation absolutely requires R&D. Some important historical inventions and a larger number of new applications of old ideas have resulted from pure inspiration. Others, mostly in the past, undoubtedly occurred almost by accident. Archaeologists speculate, for example, that the uses of fire for cooking meat and making pottery may have evolved in this way, thousands of years ago. However, inspiration and lucky accidents occur too seldom to be reliable sources of new discoveries or inventions. In the modern world it is necessary to search both intensively and systematically. The search process may be quite informal, in some cases, but when it is carried out by trained engineers and scientists, it is called R&D.

It has been shown quite conclusively that industrial R&D yields very high returns compared to other types of investments. Studies have shown that there is a very close statistical correlation between R&D per employee, sales per employee, and profit margins when firms in the same type of business are compared. To be sure, R&D could well be a consequence of high profit margins and sales. Yet the weight of evidence suggests strongly that applied R&D on average yields high returns.

The case for fundamental research is less easy to document statistically. Yet it is fundamental scientific research that pays some of the biggest dividends for society as a whole, even though the immediate sponsors may not gain any direct or immediate economic benefit. For this reason, fundamental research tends to be carried out primarily in universities, where the primary justification is educational.

Most firms do not invest in fundamental research because of the long lags before commercial payoff and the difficulty in capturing a significant portion of the benefits. There have been a few exceptions. Bell Telephone Labs, GE, and IBM have supported a modest amount of fundamental research of Nobel Prize caliber in their own corporate laboratories, especially in solid-state physics.

R&D at the National Level

Since World War II, governments have increasingly realized the importance of technology as the basis of economic power without which there is no military power. In recent decades R&D expenditures at the national level as well as public financing, for civilian and military purposes, have become increasingly important. The greatest proportion of

basic research is financed by national governments. Governments also finance both a major part of applications-oriented research and development in areas that have a public character. In most countries these include defense, public safety, energy, transportation, communication, health—all areas that have a major political component. In the United States, however, the federal government has concentrated its R&D overwhelmingly on defense, health, and space.

Overall, between 1978 and 1988, the United States, the United Kingdom, France, Japan, and West Germany devoted roughly the same percentage of their GDP to R&D—around 2.5 percent. In the United States and the United Kingdom the total has traditionally been slightly higher, but "defense" accounted for a large portion of the total. In Japan and West Germany, by contrast, the civilian portion was by far the larger. (See Table 1.)

The distribution of R&D expenditures among the various sectors in major OECD countries in 1987 is shown in Figure 1: It is notable that the first two sectors, defense and civilian space, represented 40 percent of the total. They benefitted, to be sure, by receiving the lion's share of government aid. This situation is not confined to France. However, industrial participation in the financing of R&D in these two sectors was a great deal more important in Japan (around 65 percent), and West Germany (around 60 percent), than in the United States (around 50 percent).

The lower level of defense-oriented R&D in Germany and Japan has released engineers and scientists for other purposes. This job concentration provides a plausible explanation of the competitive

TABLE 1. R&D Expenditure in OECD Countries

Country	Percentage share of gross output		Percentage share of value added		Percentage share of fixed investment in manufacturing sector	
	1981	1985	1981	1985	1981	1985
Denmark	1.0	1.2	2.5	2.9	28.2	25.5
Finland	0.8	1.1	2.2	3.2	13.2	19.9
FRG	2.0	2.3	4.3	5.2	47.8	55.8
Japan	1.5	2.1	4.3	5.6	43.0	51.5
Norway	0.7	1.0	2.6	3.7	12.3	22.2
Sweden	2.2	3.1	5.3	7.6	41.5	56.7
UK	2.0	2.0	4.9	5.0	58.1	50.6
USA	2.5	3.3	6.0	7.6	63.2	91.0

Source: OECD.

FIGURE 1.   The distribution of R&D expenditures among the various sectors in major OECD countries, as of 1987.

strength of Japan and Germany, particularly in the manufacture of sophisticated capital goods.

In Japan, most R&D is application-oriented and is carried out either in industrial laboratories or in universities with direct industrial support. Even the universities do not yet do much fundamental research, although this is gradually changing. An important government function in Japan, performed mainly by the Ministry of International Trade and Industry (MITI), is to organize consortia of private firms to carry out major R&D tasks, using relatively small amounts of "seed money" from the government to leverage much larger amounts of corporate money.

States and provinces play a significant role in supporting R&D in several countries. In Germany, states (*Länder*) provide approximately half the public funding for all applied R&D, much of it through the Frauenhofer Institutes. The individual German states provide a lesser, but still significant portion of the support for basic research, through the vari-

ous universities (state supported) and through the Max Planck Institutes for research.

In the United States many of the larger universities are state supported, especially in the Midwest and Western states, where so-called land-grant agricultural and mechanical (A&M) colleges were created in the nineteenth century to train agronomists and engineers. Some state universities, such as the universities of California (Berkeley), Illinois, Michigan, Minnesota, and Wisconsin, have reached world-class status as research centers. Most agricultural research in the United States is still carried out through these and similar institutions.

R&D at the Business Level

Nations, taken as a whole, typically spend 2–3 percent of gross output and 5–7.5 percent of value added on R&D. Firms in mature commodity and service industries tend to spend less (often 0.5–1 percent of gross output). Firms in newer technologies and more dynamic activities—such as microelectronics, information technology, robotics, specialty chemicals, biotechnology, and pharmaceuticals—typically devote a greater percentage of their total budget to R&D. For instance, in the data-processing (computer) field for the year 1986, 55 (of 64) U.S. firms spent $28.5 billion on R&D (7.1 percent of revenues), 13 (of 15) Japanese firms spent $9.6 billion on R&D (5.8 percent of revenues), while 2 (of 4) German firms spent $2.7 billion on R&D, which was 11.3 percent of revenues. For other high-tech firms, especially genetic engineering and software firms, R&D expenditures are even higher. For instance, the first and largest of the genetic engineering firms, Genentech, was spending 38 percent of total revenues on R&D as recently as 1989.

Total industrial R&D financed by U.S.-based firms reached $65 billion (1989 dollars) in 1989, up 10 percent from the previous year. This was roughly equal to the total of industrial R&D expenditures for the rest of the OECD countries. Japanese firms spent $26.3 billion on R&D. The leaders (excluding Toyota, for which figures were not available) were Hitachi ($2.9 billion), Matsushita ($2.4 billion), Fujitsu, Toshiba, NTT, NEC, and Honda. German firms spent $11.4 billion, led by Siemens ($3.7 billion), and the three chemical giants (Bayer, Hoechst, and BASF) with a total of $3.8 billion among them. Other countries' firms contributed as follows: the United Kingdom ($5.7 billion); France ($4.9 billion, excluding Peugeot, for which data were not available); the Netherlands ($3.5 billion, of which Phillips alone accounted for $2.2 billion); Switzerland ($3 billion); Sweden ($2.9 billion); Italy ($2.9 billion); and Canada ($2 billion).

Most international firms do not perform all of their R&D in their own countries. (The Japanese are the exception in this respect.) A business, even a large multinational firm, must consult in a regular and timely fashion with technical centers, universities, and other outside sources in order to keep up with the increasing complexity and variety of areas encountered in a program of R&D. Industry contributions to university R&D increased nearly fivefold (to $900 million) from 1979 to 1989. Joint ventures now account for as much as 25 percent of total R&D. The rapid growth of international R&D joint-venturing is largely due to the fact that nowadays even the very largest firms can no longer afford to be fully aware—still less, on the frontier—of every technology that affects them. A business must thus provide financing not only for direct R&D expenditures in its own laboratories, but also indirect R&D expenditures through other organizations.

R&D at the Supranational Level

In Western Europe, a coordinating function similar to that performed by MITI in Japan, is performed by the supranational European Union (EU), headquartered in Brussels. It is possible for a European-based business in association with one or more other businesses from other countries, to obtain financing from the EU to cover the cost of "pre-competitive" R&D programs in a core set of well-defined areas. The EU's research budget accounts for only 4 percent of total civilian R&D in the European Union however.

The European Strategic Program for R&D in Information Technology (ESPRIT) program was launched in 1984. It was designed as a ten-year program with three major objectives: (1) to develop industrial technologies in the information technology area, (2) to promote European industrial cooperation, and (3) to promote the development of international standards for information technology. It is focused mainly on microelectronics, information processing systems, and applications such as computer-integrated manufacturing (CIM). In the first phase (1984–1989), more than 200 projects were initiated. As of mid-1992, ESPRIT claimed to have generated 700 information technology prototypes, tools, or standards, including some commercial successes.

In addition to the EU programs there are a number of broader cooperative programs in both science and technology, encompassing nineteen Western European countries. These include "big science" efforts such as the European Center for Nuclear Research (CERN) in Geneva, the European Organization for Astronomical Research in the Southern Hemisphere, the European Space Agency, the European Science Foundation, and the European Molecular Biology Laboratory.

The most ambitious supranational program is EUREKA, which began in 1985 as a response to the U.S. Strategic Defense Initiative. It represents 19 countries plus the Commission of the EU. The approved budget (1989) for 297 EUREKA-sponsored projects was $6.5 billion, of which 25 percent to 50 percent represented public funding. Annual spending (1989) was about $1 billion. No money crossed national borders.

The general patterns shown above will continue. More newly industrialized countries will commit to R&D. In all countries the focus of private and public research will be more consciously directed at practical uses and competitive advantage. In the United States, defense budgets will decline to the advantage of civil sector research.

See also APPROPRIATE TECHNOLOGY; CHANGE, SCIENTIFIC AND TECHNOLOGICAL; HEALTH CARE: TECHNOLOGICAL DEVELOPMENTS; INTELLECTUAL PROPERTY; RECORD SETTING; SCIENCE CITIES; SCIENTIFIC BREAKTHROUGHS; TECHNOLOGICAL CHANGE; TECHNOLOGICAL INNOVATION.

BIBLIOGRAPHY

AYRES, ROBERT U. *Technological Forecasting and Long-Range Planning.* New York: McGraw-Hill, 1969.
BOTKIN, JAMES, and DIMANESCU, DAN. *The New Alliance: America's R & D Consortia.* Cambridge, MA: Ballinger, 1986.
ROMAN, DANIEL D. *Research and Development Management: The Economics and Administration of Technology.* New York: Appleton-Century-Crofts, 1968.
SOUDER, WILLIAM E. *Managing New Product Innovations.* Lexington, MA: Lexington Books/D. C. Heath, 1987.

Robert U. Ayres

Resources

Global industrialization has been resource-intensive. Quite naturally, concerns about the adequacy of the world's resource base to support future industrialization have been raised. The contemporary controversy received a strong impetus from the publication of *The Limits to Growth* in 1972 (updated in 1992 as *Beyond the Limits*; see bibliography). Publication of the book was soon followed by the OAPEC (Organization of Arab Petroleum Exporting Countries) oil embargo, which triggered rapid increases in the prices of fuels and many other basic commodities. These developments fostered the perception that the world would soon run out of the resources required for future industrialization. Over the two decades that followed, perceptions of scarcity varied along with estimates of the strength of global economic growth.

Natural resources are defined as anything required by a population to facilitate growth. Thus, commodities such as coal, oil, minerals, water, and food have been the focus of concern in debates over the future of industrial growth. More recently, the worldwide circulation of water and air through the hydrosphere and atmosphere have been recognized as providing not unlimited environmental waste dispersal services, and thus are also recognized as scarce resources.

Concern over resource limits to growth has focused on energy, particularly world reserves of oil, because energy can be used to overcome other resource shortages. For example, an abundant supply of energy would permit arid Middle Eastern countries to desalinate sea water and overcome freshwater limitations. Oil is particularly critical since so much of world production enters into international trade.

Patterns of world resource consumption are currently undergoing an important transformation. At present, the world's industrialized countries consume the vast majority of resources. It is estimated, for example, that each person living in the industrialized countries consumes between ten and twenty times as much commercial energy as his or her counterparts living elsewhere. To meet these demands, resources generally flow from the less to the more industrialized parts of the world. However, a structural transformation of the industrialized countries from the production of goods to provision of services, combined with materials conservation and recycling, is reducing the resource intensity of economic growth. Still, continued industrialization of the world's less wealthy countries will account for the biggest increases in future resource consumption.

Largely because of slower economic growth and the structural transformation of the industrial countries, worldwide commercial energy consumption has been growing very slowly in recent years. According to the World Resources Institute, consumption grew only 18 percent from 1979 to 1989. On a per capita basis this represented a 1 percent decline in energy usage. Worldwide commercial production of solid fuels, which accounted for 31 percent of all energy produced, was up 26 percent in the 1979–1989 period. Natural gas production accounted for 22 percent of energy produced and was up 33 percent during the period. However, worldwide production of oil and other liquid fuels, accounting for 42 percent of commercial energy production, actually fell by 4 percent. The rest of the world's energy production is split almost equally between renewables and nuclear that accounts for only 5 percent of the total. A substantial increase in energy prices would give a significant boost to supplies of fossil fuels, and would also make renewable energy sources more attractive. In the early 1990s, energy production and consumption growth continued to slow and was nearly flat by 1994.

Anxieties about the adequacy of world energy and nonfuel mineral reserves have recently given way to concern over future market stability. Proven world petroleum reserves have grown steadily to nearly one trillion barrels in recent years, which represents about forty-six years of consumption at current rates. Add to this a considerable surplus of petroleum in storage as well as much excess production capacity around the world and a potential for discovering more reserves. The World Resources Institute reports a 200-year supply of aluminum in current reserves, a 175-year reserve of iron ore, and a 36-year supply of copper (all at present production rates).

These reserve figures may well understate the magnitude of future supplies since they are based on reserves that are known and economically recoverable at current prices. If a larger "reserve base" is used, composed of what is known to exist but not economically recoverable at today's prices, the depletion horizons are much extended. These perspectives should not be cause for complacency, however, because recent consumption figures have been gathered during years of economic stagnation. Should the global economy suddenly surge forward, resource consumption could quickly rise and depletion horizons would shorten dramatically.

World food production over the last two decades has kept slightly ahead of population growth. Production increases in many less industrialized countries, however, have not kept up with population. Expanded agricultural production in the industrial countries created large surpluses. Even as technology increases yields and more crops are grown on marginal lands, the specter of future global warming threatens possible major dislocations in world agricultural productivity.

Freshwater is likely to be the resource that most limits future food production. While the world has a tremendous supply of water, only 3 percent of it is fresh, the rest being saltwater in the world's oceans and inland seas. Of the small amount of freshwater available, 87 percent is locked in polar ice caps, glaciers, or other unreachable places. While there is still enough water to meet human needs on a global scale, local shortages are already apparent. The North China plain, which includes Beijing, could face a shortage of 6 percent of demand in only a few years. The Sahel region of West Africa has repeatedly suffered from severe drought and related famine, and the Middle East is a tinderbox of disputes over scarce water. The western part of the United States faces significant problems as the growing population presses up against available water supplies.

One future partial solution to freshwater scarcity is desalinization, but water gained from such processes currently can cost up to four times the price of water from other sources. Still, the World Resources Institute reports a doubling of desalinization plants, from 3,527 at the beginning of 1987 to 7,536 at the beginning of 1990.

The original pessimism about running out of raw materials, expressed in *The Limits to Growth*, now has been replaced by more sophisticated understanding of the problems of basic commodity markets. The major future resource threat to global economic security is maintaining a reliable and sustainable flow of natural resources from producing to consuming countries. If producing countries interrupt the flow of important basic commodities, particularly oil, prices would rise dramatically and destabilize the importing countries' economies. But if the importers cut back substantially on resource consumption, the less industrialized producers would be devastated.

The recent demise of the former Soviet Union has been a major destabilizing factor in resource markets. The tremendous decline in the economies of the former Soviet republics has lessened domestic resource requirements and spurred foreign sales. Thus, the Russian aluminum industry has been exporting into a glutted world market well below the costs of production among established Western manufacturers, thus creating a crisis in the aluminum market.

The current apparent abundance of fuels, food, and minerals should not give rise to complacency about the future. An upturn in the global economy, a major war, or a revolution in the Middle East could quickly destabilize resource markets. But even successfully meeting the industrialization goals to produce jobs for the growing populations of poorer countries would substantially alter future resource requirements and severely strain environmental services. Imagine, for example, the global resource impact of a future China elevated to just half the United States level of living.

Concern continues to mount over the ability of the atmosphere and hydrosphere, important "environmental sinks," to sustain future industrial growth. The build-up of carbon dioxide in the atmosphere, closely related to burning fossil fuels, threatens to increase global temperatures by one to three degrees Celsius over the next century. This could lead to major dislocations in world agriculture as well as a rise in sea level due largely to polar thawing.

Projected global warming, water shortages, and other natural resource problems have raised concern over the sustainability of the model of industrial progress that is now being emulated, more or less successfully, by many of the world's less industrialized countries. Questions about the long-term sustainability of the industrial way of life in a more densely populated world began to grow in the mid-1970s, and received official acknowledgement in the Bruntland Commission Report of 1987. The commission officially sanctioned a debate over the nature of sustainable development, defined as that which "meets the needs of the present without compromising the ability of future generations to meet their own needs." Some consider sustainable development a contradiction in terms. Others appropriated the term to their own causes, making sustainability an umbrella sheltering many different points of view.

Sustainability dialogue will occupy scholars and politicians well into the next century. The dialogue grows from a concern that future development take place within the long-term constraints of nature, and that the welfare of future generations be enhanced by current patterns of economic growth. The focus is on environmentally benign growth which uses fewer nonrenewable resources, shifts to renewables where possible, and stresses recycling as a way of easing environmental burdens. A transformation of values is also implicit in sustainable development, since meeting human needs while limiting human wants is part of the future agenda.

The 1992 United Nations Conference on the Environment and Development (UNCED) sharpened the dialogue between the industrially developed countries of the North and the less industrialized countries of the South. The debate over sustainable development now centers on the course of future industrial development in the South, the transfer of environmentally benign technologies from North to South, and proposed transfers of wealth to compensate the less industrialized countries that forego future development opportunities.

See also ENERGY; ENERGY CONSERVATION; ENERGY, RENEWABLE SOURCES OF; FRESHWATER; GLOBAL WARMING.

BIBLIOGRAPHY

BROWN, LESTER R., et al. *State of the World 1993*. New York: W. W. Norton, 1993.
MEADOWS, DONELLA H., et al. *Beyond the Limits*. Post Mills, VT: Chelsea Green, 1992.
REPETTO, ROBERT C., ed. *The Global Possible: Resources, Development, and the New Century*. New Haven: Yale University Press, 1985.
World Commission on Environment and Development. *Our Common Future*. New York: Oxford University Press, 1987.
World Resources Institute. *World Resources 1994 95*. New York: Oxford University Press, 1994.

Dennis Pirages

Right to Life.

See ABORTION; FAMILY PLANNING.

Robotics

Oscar Wilde contended that humankind required slavery. Indeed, Greek philosophers claimed that without someone to do the slow and boring work, in order to release the rest of humankind to dream and create, civilization would come to a standstill. Since the slavery of sentient beings is considered evil, immoral, and demoralizing, the advance of civilization depends upon the slavery of machines! Karel Čapek gave these machines a name. He called them *robota*, Czech for "obligatory work" or "servitude."

There were 500,000 robots in the world in 1992 compared to 16,000 in 1980; 400,000 of these were in Japan with only 40,000 in the United States. The growth of the service economy, the increased competition in the industrial economy and downsizing of corporations will increase the robot population as they replace humans. In the industrial area alone current trends indicate a worldwide work force of 1.2 to 1.5 million robots by 2001. This will result in a loss of 3 to 4 million jobs as robots continue to replace humans in the boring repetitive activities like assembly, welding, and painting, among others; and hazardous jobs such as, environmental cleanup, bomb disposal, oil rig maintenance, and so forth. It is estimated that robots will virtually replace humans in the manufacturing sector early in the twenty first century.

There is a simple reason for this: Robots markedly increase productivity because they do not take personal or sick leave, require much less energy, do not quit, and can work twenty-four hours a day. Several automated factories in Japan already operate "lights out" with only a few humans present to monitor and maintain the computers and robots. New factories being built in the United States require much fewer workers than in the past as well.

In addition, as U.S. manufacturers upgrade, they are replacing outmoded machinery with flexible manufacturing systems (FMS) that employ robots to operate, service, and maintain high-tolerance advanced machine tools, and to assemble and package the finished products.

Processes such as computer-aided design and computer-aided manufacturing (CAD/CAM) are incorporating robots when planning the manufacturing process. Computer-integrated manufacturing (CIM) is bringing the factory under direct control of management through desktop manufacturing, and under indirect control of the customer through feedback. These advancements enable U.S. factories to produce customized products at lower costs than manufacturing with cheap labor in developing countries. Robots are making inroads in the service industry. They will eventually perform most janitorial activities. Robots will largely replace humans in the food service industry too, as increasing wages force owners to automate. MacDonalds will be replaced by MacRobot and will become a robotic automat. Banking also is being transformed; automated teller machines (ATMs)—robot tellers are everywhere.

Meanwhile, robots (under human tutelage) are building robots, *and* robots are building the robots that build robots. Feedback systems enable the robot-building robots to improve on the design; hence robots are evolving. Ongoing research and development (R&D) efforts are investigating the creation of self-replicating robots and factories. These self-replicating devices can be deposited in remote areas to literally grow a manufacturing facility and make specific products, using local raw materials, while getting power directly from the sun.

None of this bodes well for the unskilled worker; however, there are solutions to the worker displacement problem. Specifically by educating workers to design, develop, manufacture, supervise, and maintain the automation systems and robots that replaced them. These replacement jobs will be superior in quality to the assembly line jobs that are lost. In general, schools will prepare people for the service industry and other jobs created for the age of automation, information and knowledge. A unique process for coping with automation is presented in James Albus's book *People's Capitalism*, in which he outlines a program to replace people with robots slowly and with the least disruption through reeducation, government involvement, changes in monetary policy, changes in tax policies, and new approaches for people to obtain income.

Robots are encroaching on skilled jobs as well. Several chores in health care will be performed by robots. These include patient rehabilitation, assistance, and entertainment, as well as routine functions now performed by nurses and orderlies. Robots will assist doctors in performing delicate operations like eye surgery, brain surgery, and parts replacement. Eventually micro-robots (microbots) will be injected into a vein. These microbots will scurry through our bodies, keeping them clean and functioning as they probe for signs of deterioration and affect repairs. Other microbots will be programmed to seek out specific sites in the body, like the brain, the heart, the liver, or individual cells, and implant themselves. They will then monitor the functions or products of that site, and transmit this information to the outside world.

Eventually robots will be inexpensive enough to be used in the home. These robots will not be humanoid, using tools designed for humans; rather, they will be designed to perform particular tasks. Robots in general will not resemble the popular picture presented by movies and television; instead, they will be formed to fulfill a function: janitor robots may resemble large vacuum cleaners, robots that haul things will look like wagons, space robots will look like space ships, and so on. An outdoor robot could be a snow blower, a hedge trimmer, or a fertilizer spreader depending on the attachment installed. An indoor robot will vacuum, clean rugs, or polish floors, and with a little ingenuity maybe even wash windows. There will not be a kitchen robot per se, rather the kitchen *will be* a robot that will plan and prepare meals, and clean up afterward. Once they become affordable and useful, robots will multiply exponentially, like the telephone and the personal computer. Within ten years of introduction there could be 20 to 25 million robots in U.S. homes.

Other skilled tasks performed by robots will include: flying airplanes, with pilots acting as flight supervisors; driving trucks, with dispatchers controlling them from their home; or operating farm machinery (with a little positional information from satellites to ensure they are in the right field), under the management of the farmer sitting in her/his living room. In schools robots will be teaching assistants with the teachers being facilitators. The secretary or receptionist will be a virtual robot residing in an information system. A virtual traveler may use robots to tour distant lands.

Robots are already venturing into space. Early in the twenty-first century the self-replicating robots will build colonies and manufacturing facilities on the Moon, then mine asteroids and deliver raw materials to these colonies. Someday robots may terraform Mars and make it habitable for humans. Meanwhile, back on Earth, robots will be diving and trudging around on the ocean floors to retrieve the large nuggets of pure minerals that have formed there. Robots will build and maintain underwater colonies and assist humans in these colonies to monitor and operate underwater farms.

Robots of the future will have the power of vision, touch, speech, and speech recognition. They will ingest, digest, and incorporate information from these senses using signal processing, pattern recognition, inference machines, and learning attributes to make decisions and take action. Researchers are experimenting with neural network processing techniques that will provide the robot with learning and memory capabilities similar to humans. Further, these senses will enable robots to communicate easily with human beings. Robots will replace the seeing eye dog; they will talk for the mute; they will be able to feel and judge objects, weights, and textures with enough precision to lift a brick or an egg. Advanced medical techniques will permit a human to become a cyborg (a being part human and part machine), either by necessity or by choice. Using nanotechnology scientists will create devices that can be used to replace human parts: eyes, ears, internal organs, and skin to name a few. Implanted math chips, language chips, telecommunications chips, and on-board expert systems chips will enhance the powers of the human brain. Exoskeletons will provide strength for those who need it: an arm, a leg, and even a whole body.

During the next century nanotechnology may produce the first android (a programmable robot biologically or chemically grown), either through the manipulation of molecules or the programming of DNA. Imagine creating a special-purpose android, equipped with gills and a functional tail for mobility, to work underwater. Including features such as eyes, ears, and arms will allow this android to farm and mine the ocean for human masters. Will these androids be human? Will they have feelings, emotions, desires? Will they rise in revolt and overthrow their masters? Will they replace the human race? All of these things are possible. All of them have been the stuff of science fiction for decades.

The robots around today are a small hint of the things to come. The robots of the future will truly become servants of human beings. They will provide the manual labor to provide all of the material things humans require and additional brain power to assist humans in things of the mind. They will finally release humans from the drudgeries of life and give them the freedom to do as they please, to exist in harmony, to create, to enjoy, to explore the universe.

See also FACTORIES AND MANUFACTURING; GENETIC ENGINEERING; GENETICS; NANOTECHNOLOGY; PRODUCTIVITY; SCIENCE FICTION; SPACE TRAVEL.

BIBLIOGRAPHY

ALBUS, JAMES S. *People's Capitalism: Economics of the Robot Revolution.* College Park, MD: New World Books, 1976.

———. *Brains, Behavior, and Robotics.* Peterborough, NH: BYTE Books, 1981.

ASIMOV, ISAAC, and FRENKEL, KAREN A. *Robots: Machines in Man's Image.* New York: Harmony Books, 1985.

CONNEL, JONATHAN H., and MAHADAVAN, SRIDHAR, eds. *Robot Learning.* Boston: Kluwer Academic Publishers, 1993.

KOSKO, BART. *Fuzzy Thinking: The New Science of Fuzzy Logic.* New York: Hyperion, 1993.

SAFFORD, EDWARD L., Jr. *The Complete Handbook of Robotics.* Blue Ridge Summit, PA: TAB Books, 1980.

TZAFESTAS, SPYROS G., ed. *Intelligent Robotic Systems.* New York: Marcel Dekker, 1991.

Brian K. Toren

Rocketry.

See SPACE FLIGHT.

Russia

The political future of Russia is vitally important but difficult to predict. The forces of nationalism which disintegrated the Soviet Union also threaten the Russian Federation. Russians constitute 82 percent of the population, but there are over 100 other ethnic groups and 20 areas with ethnic populations sufficiently large to constitute autonomous republics. In addition to Chechnya, where there has been bloody fighting, secessionist movements also exist in Tatarstan, Dagestan, the Tuva Republics, and Northern Ingushetia. Besides ethnic separatism, the desire for independence is sometimes fueled by the desire to fully control rich natural resources, such as the oil in Tatarstan or the diamonds, natural gas, timber, and other natural resources of Siberia.

These forces for independence, however, are countered by long associations with Moscow, strong economic interdependence with the rest of Russia, the cost and weakness of a small state providing for its own national security, and the frequent absence of clear ethnic boundaries. Moscow's role in regional affairs will continue to decrease, allowing local cultures to prevail and administration of public sector activities to improve, but few if any splinter states are likely to emerge because of the forces mentioned above and Russian determination to hold key areas. Over time, economic progress will reduce ethnic tensions and secessionist tendencies.

These same centripetal forces will probably bring closer ties between Russia and other republics of the former Soviet Union. The relationship which emerges between Russia and Ukraine will be particularly important to both republics. Many sources of tension exist, including a predominantly Russian population in the Crimean portion of Ukraine, but economic interdependence, particularly Ukraine's need for Russian oil, will encourage increasing cooperation.

Extreme Russian nationalists and unreformed Communists might conceivably reestablish an authoritarian government if economic hardships and rampant crime continue or separatism grows stronger. However, there also are signs favorable to democracy. The August 1991 coup attempt had little popular support. A large, well-educated middle class has been exposed to Western ideas, and younger Russians are less inclined than their elders to accept state authority. Independent media and democratic elections have taken hold.

Despite Soviet military disarray after the U.S.S.R. breakup, Russia is likely to remain a major military power. Lengthy borders, uncertain relations with neighbors, a large, well-trained officer corps, advanced equipment, and a long military tradition point to continuing prominence. Nuclear forces, though reduced to a fraction of Cold War levels, will be retained as a deterrent.

Its seat on the UN Security Council and powerful military forces will keep Russia a major player in international relations. Because economic and political interests go hand-in-hand, Russia will seek to maintain good relations with the United States, Europe (particularly Germany), Japan, China, Korea, and the Middle East.

Fertility rates for ethnic Russians are likely to remain at or below the replacement rate; the non-Russian population has had higher fertility rates, but these are decreasing and probably will continue to do so. Some increase in the present population of just under 150 million will probably result from inward migration by some of the 26 million Russians in the other former Soviet republics. This migration could reach millions if economic hardship in neighboring republics or discrimination against Russians living there worsens. In twenty years the population may reach 160 million—with the percentage of Russians remaining about the same. Political turbulence, however, could also spur large-scale migration to the West.

Urbanization will continue, following the worldwide pattern for developed countries. As agriculture becomes more productive and the infrastructure improves, the large gap in living conditions between urban and rural areas will decrease.

The Russian economy is as difficult to predict as the political future. Privatization appears irreversible, but questions remain about the level of government regulation, the pace of macroeconomic reform, and how to soften the impact of change.

In the past, Russia needed to import large amounts of food. The high ratio of arable land to people, provides the potential for Russia to become an agricultural net exporter—as it was before World War I. Privatization will increase motivation; technical assistance from the West can increase yields and, coupled with infrastructure improvements, decrease spoilage losses.

The outlook for manufacturing is not so good. Few factories are capable of competing in global markets. To build a modern industrial base will require investing hundreds of billions of dollars.

The future of the Russian economy will be determined by how well the Russian government creates a climate attractive to foreign investment and how well it encourages savings and investment over consumption as the economy grows. Aided by its enormous natural resources—oil, natural gas, coal, forests, and mineral deposits—the Russian economy could approach Western European performance levels within twenty-five years.

A very pessimistic economic scenario also is possible. To date, Russia has attracted little foreign investment—and the technology and know-how which come with it—because of uncertainties over ownership of assets, shifting regulations and laws (including taxes), and overlapping jurisdiction among levels of government. Xenophobia, lack of understanding of the value of capital, and the absence of a developed banking system also impede foreign investment. In a country where unemployment has been virtually unknown, creating efficient enterprises will require tolerating levels of unemployment, which could lead to labor unrest and work stoppages. Another problem that could get worse is the occurrence of production shutdowns due to a lack of raw materials or components previously supplied by other republics.

The well-educated Russian workforce favors economic growth. Under communism no attention was paid to productivity, cost reduction, or quality. Privatization and foreign investment will change this—and experience has shown that young Russian workers perform very well when given proper training and incentives. New programs will teach managerial skills and nurture the work ethic necessary in a market economy.

Women in Russia traditionally have been relegated to lower-paid jobs, and their ability to compete with men has been crippled by the time required for shopping and household chores. As managers, pressured by competition, pay more attention to who performs best, opportunities for women will improve. While women will continue to do most household chores, these will become less time-consuming as shopping becomes more efficient, convenience foods become available, and household appliances become better and more reliable.

The large network of scientific and research institutes will undergo major changes in the next few years because of less government funding. Part of the expected downsizing will result from emigration of scientists, part from attrition. In the past, members of these institutes did little teaching or nonmilitary research; in the future, most will work part-time or full-time in higher education or industrial research. Despite transitional problems, Russian science will remain world-class in areas like theoretical physics, mathematics, nuclear science, and astronomy.

Major environmental policy changes will take place. In the past, little attention was paid in the U.S.S.R. to the environmental consequences of the single-minded pursuit of economic growth. Chernobyl is the most infamous environmental disaster, but there have been many others. Huge investments must be made to prevent further damage, and the cost of cleanups to improve health conditions will be very large.

Environmental neglect has created a strong environmental movement, which not only prevented construction of new facilities that would cause environmental problems (e.g., a plant to destroy chemical weapons), but has shut down existing polluting facilities. Past environmental disasters may make Russia insistent on balancing economic development with long-range environmental needs—in much the same way that Hiroshima made Japan so opposed to nuclear weapons.

One safe prediction is that health care will improve. Even special clinics previously reserved for elites lack equipment routinely available in the West, and most Russians cannot get medicines available to the poorest Western patients. The abysmal state of health care has become widely recognized in Russia; while it will be many years before the care available to ordinary citizens will approach that in the West, widespread public knowledge of this need and the enormous market for improved health care products should result in improvements within a relatively short time.

In many areas what happens in Russia will largely parallel what happens in the rest of the world. A global culture (in the broadest sense) is emerging as a result of mass media, and over 90 percent of Russian homes have television sets connecting them to the outside world.

BIBLIOGRAPHY

CONQUEST, ROBERT, ed. *The Last Empire: Nationality and the Soviet Future.* Stanford, CA: Hoover Institution Press, 1986.

FESHBACH, MURRAY, and FRIENDLY, ALFRED JR. *Ecocide in the U.S.S.R.* New York: Basic Books, 1992.

HECHT, JAMES L., ed. *Rubles and Dollars.* New York: Harper Business, 1991.

HOSKING, GEOFFREY. *The Awakening of the Soviet Union.* Cambridge, MA: Harvard University Press, 1990.

HOUGH, JERRY. *Russia and the West.* New York: Simon & Schuster, 1988.

SMITH, HEDRICK. *The New Russians.* New York: Random House, 1990.

YERGIN, DANIEL, and GUSTAFSON, THANE. *Russia 2010 and What It Means for the World.* New York: Random House, 1993.

(The views expressed in this article are the opinions of the authors and do not necessarily represent the opinions or positions of the U.S. government or of any of its agencies.)

James L. Hecht
Lawrence E. Modisett

Safety, Food and Drug.

See FOOD AND DRUG SAFETY; FOOD LAWS.

Satellite Communications

Most communications satellites are placed in a geostationary orbit 22,300 miles (36,000 kilometers) above the equator, a concept first envisioned by Arthur C. CLARKE in 1945. At this altitude the geostationary satellite takes twenty-four hours to travel around Earth, appearing to remain stationary as Earth rotates on its axis. Signals are transmitted from Earth stations to the satellite and back to one or more receiving stations. Typically, the satellite simply receives and amplifies the signal, changes its frequency, and retransmits it to Earth. More intelligent satellites have "on-board processing" in which the signal may be switched to a specific site or data may be stored. Future satellites will relay the signal from one satellite to another, avoiding the delay required when a signal must "double-hop" through two satellites or from a small station to a master station and again through the satellite to another small station to reach its destination.

Some satellites, known as "LEOs" (low Earth-orbiting satellites), operate in much lower orbits, appearing to pass overhead several times per day. An example of a simple LEO is the Oscar satellite used by radio amateurs. Small, inexpensive terminals transmit data to the satellite when it passes overhead. The satellite then reads the address of the message, stores the data, and forwards the message to the receiving terminal. Several companies have proposed to operate multiple-satellite LEO systems that would be accessible by small, hand-held receivers from virtually anywhere on Earth.

Since the first commercial satellite transmissions in the early 1960s, communications satellites have come to be taken for granted. Live global television coverage of the Olympics and the World Cup, as well as of natural disasters and political upheavals, reaches hundreds of millions of viewers. Nightly television news programs carry stories from around the world. Less obvious are the many satellite networks that carry information about orders, sales transactions, and inventory levels from thousands of retailers to their headquarters or command centers. Satellites also have extended the range of education: Students in rural schools can take high school science and foreign language courses via satellite; professionals can watch televised lectures delivered via satellite to study for advanced degrees without leaving their workplace.

Satellites are used for a wide range of applications that can be divided into point-to-point and point-to-multipoint or broadcasting communications. Point-to-point applications include: transmitting telephone traffic from one location to another (for example, to link villages in remote areas, and to link developing countries where terrestrial networks are very limited); transmitting data (such as financial transactions for banks, airline reservations, and credit card verifications); and transmitting video signals from one place to another (such as for a video teleconference or for a video feed from a remote location to a television station). Broadcasting applications include: distribution of television programs to numerous television stations or cable television head-ends, and transmission of data such as stock market reports and weather forecasts to multiple receiving sites. Transmission of television programs directly to households equipped with small receiving antennas is called direct broadcasting via satellite (DBS). DBS systems are now used in Western Europe and Japan, and are on the verge of being introduced in North America.

Satellites are particularly important to developing countries, where they can bring telephone and broadcasting services to villages far from urban centers. Some developing countries and regions such as the Arab states, Brazil, India, Indonesia, and Mexico have their own domestic satellites; other countries and regions in Africa, Latin America, Southeast Asia, and the South Pacific are planning to get satellites of their own. These satellites will help to overcome the isolation of millions of people by providing them with reliable communications for the first time.

Satellite Earth stations vary in diameter from nearly 100 feet for large INTELSAT stations that carry thousands of channels of voice or data traffic between countries or continents to very small-aperture terminals (VSATs) as small as two feet in diameter. VSATs may be installed on rooftops or even in windowsills to pick up television or data signals. Some VSATs are used for interactive data communications, such as transmitting point-of-sale data from department stores and gas stations. Somewhat larger Earth stations approximately ten feet in diameter have been installed in backyards and on hotels in North America to pick up television signals from satellites in areas where there are no cable systems, or to pick up specialized programming, or for videoconferencing. In some locations, zoning restrictions may make it difficult to install such antennas; however, the smallest VSATs are very unobtrusive and unlikely to be aesthetically objectionable.

As terrestrial optical-fiber-based networks become more widespread, some people wonder whether satellites will become obsolete. It is more likely, however, that they will become increasingly specialized and used for several growing applications:

- basic telecommunications to remote locations, particularly in the developing world, where terrestrial facilities are cost-prohibitive and not available
- broadcasting of video or data to multiple locations through pay television channels to millions of homes and through news service information to thousands of offices
- interactive, low-volume data communications from multiple sites or remote locations, such as point-of-sale and inventory data from hundreds of stores, and monitoring data from remote pipelines and oil rigs
- mobile and eventually personal communications from small transceivers mounted on vehicles or carried in a briefcase, or even in one's purse or pocket
- transmission of very-high-quality broadcast signals such as digital audio for direct reception by small radio receivers, and reception of high-definition television (HDTV), including digitized video that will have very high resolution

Communications satellites will continue to be important for services that take advantage of their assets that include cost insensitivity to distance; wide coverage of countries, continents, or oceans; and flexibility in the location of facilities without the need for terrestrial links. As Arthur C. Clarke has forecast, every call will be "local" and long-distance charges will be eliminated.

See also COMMUNICATIONS; COMMUNICATIONS TECHNOLOGIES; COMPUTER LINKAGE; DIGITAL COMMUNICATIONS; ELECTRONIC CONVERGENCE; MEDIA CONSOLIDATION; SPACE SATELLITES; TELECOMMUNICATIONS; TELEPHONES.

BIBLIOGRAPHY

BAYLIN, FRANK. *Satellites Today: The Guide to Satellite Television.* Indianapolis, IN: Howard A. Sams, 1986.

CODDING, GEORGE A., JR. *The Future of Satellite Communications.* Boulder, CO: Westview, 1990.

HUDSON, HEATHER E. *Communication Satellites: Their Development and Impact.* New York: Free Press, 1990.

REES, DAVID W. *Satellite Communications: The First Quarter Century of Service.* New York: John Wiley & Sons, 1990.

Heather E. Hudson

Savings

Economists have been warning for years that the rate of savings in the United States may be too low to sustain the level of investment and economic growth needed to produce a desirable future. Net domestic investment is currently about 3.8 percent of gross domestic product, about half the level of the 1960s. Household saving as a percentage of disposable income is about 4.6 percent, down from 9.1 percent in 1981 and far below that of other OECD countries (for example, 14.6 percent in Japan, 12.1 percent in Germany).

Why is saving so low in the United States? One reason is the method of measurement: under current practices, different forms of saving, like business investment, consumer durables, education, research and development, are not counted as such. Another reason is simply the fact that the United States is such a wealthy country: a high ratio of capital to labor means a lower rate of return on capital (and therefore on saving). A third reason lies in the tax code: through high marginal tax rates on corporate dividends, capital gains, estates, profits, retirement, investment and interest income, the government double-taxes, and even triple-taxes, saving.

On the other hand, maybe it is mostly a matter of demographics. According to the life cycle hypothesis of saving, people save more as they age, and the American population *is* aging. By the year 2020, one out of every six Americans will be sixty-five or over; by 2050, one in every five. Indeed, according to a recent McKinsey & Company analysis, the United States and most of the rest of the developed world is about to experience an incredible saving surge, due to aging populations and an integrating global capital market (which places real limits on government indebtedness and inflationary inclinations).

In the United States the baby-boom cohort—those Americans born between 1946 and 1964—are entering the period in their life cycle when they will save at higher rates. This means that they will enter their peak years for financial asset accumulation over the next two decades. In fact, high-savers as a percentage of the total workforce will peak at 55 percent in the year 2010.

What will these savings add up to? McKinsey projected that the supply of net household financial assets in the developed world will increase by nearly $12 trillion in real terms over a ten-year period. And because the global capital market is increasingly acting as one single market operating under the law of one price, it seems likely that these savings will be well invested.

In other words, the discipline that a unified global market brings to bear on investors means that money will flow to where it has the best

prospects for healthy returns at comparatively lower risk. This will induce developing nations to grow and modernize faster to attract and retain investment, and it will induce *all* governments to limit indebtedness that either funds consumption or creates inflation.

McKinsey concluded that the returns from these investments may be sufficient to provide the baby-boom generation with comfortable retirements while at the same time stimulating worldwide economic growth. Indeed, they view this "best case" scenario as the most likely outcome.

An analysis by economists at the New York Federal Reserve Bank is not so sanguine. They examine the demographic argument—that baby boomers will start to save more as they age through the life cycle's saving stages—and find it inadequate. They argue that any rise in baby-boomer saving rates will be offset by a continued high rate of early retirement and an increasing share of households headed by people over sixty-five and under thirty-five—those who usually save little.

In 1990, when boomers were twenty-five to forty-four, they headed 41 million households, about 44 percent of the total. By 2010, when baby boomers will be between forty-five and sixty-four, they will head about 46 million households, or only 39 percent of the total. This relative decline will diminish baby boomers' potential impact on the aggregate savings rate, according to New York Fed economists.

But perhaps they are too pessimistic. A recent survey for the Employee Benefit Research Institute found that 61 percent of today's workers are saving for retirement, and started saving at an average age of thirty. By comparison, only 55 percent of today's retirees saved for retirement, and those savers did not start saving until they were thirty-eight.

According to the U.S. Department of Labor, more than 25 million workers have 401(k) income deferment accounts, up from only 2.7 million ten years ago. There is about $500 billion invested in 401(k) plans, with about $50 billion a year in new money pouring in. The higher the age and wage, the more likely the participation. But it is not just older, better paid workers who are stashing it away: at companies offering 401(k) plans, nearly 70 percent of workers of ages thirty-one to fifty participate, as do 50 percent of workers with salaries under $20,000—both shares up sharply from just five years ago.

To ensure a future of savings sufficient to guarantee investment and economic growth, we need to restore incentives to saving. Reducing the federal deficit, a highly likely prospect by 2002, with or without a balanced budget amendment to the Constitution, would be the swiftest and most certain way to boost national savings. The most effective way to promote savings by families and individuals would be to scrap the income tax and replace it with a consumption tax, a real possibility within the next ten years. Short of that, a broad expansion of Individual Retirement Account (IRA) and 401(k) plans would be a good place to start.

Congress adopted IRAs in 1981; every worker could put $2,000 a year, deductible from income for tax purposes, into an IRA. Couples with just one wage earner could save $3,000. But just five years later Congress passed the Tax Reform Act of 1986, which severely restricted tax-deductible contributions to IRAs. Congress adopted 401(k)s in 1978, but it has also more recently restricted the amounts that can be contributed to the plans.

The tax code is plainly one of the major reasons Americans do not save more. High tax rates reduce the ability and incentive to save, as does the Social Security payroll tax, which has been hiked 32 percent since 1980 and 60 percent since 1970. Social Security taxes depress saving because people have come to rely on the Social Security program to fund their retirements. But Social Security was designed to be a small, supplemental source of need-based income, not a general retirement fund. Besides, there *is* no trust fund: recipients are paid out of current income.

Eighty-two percent of Americans aged eighteen to thirty-four want the freedom to invest all or part of their Social Security payments in private retirement accounts. Most senior citizens also endorse the idea. A private Social Security system would boost savings, restrain interest rates, and provide the economy with hundreds of billions of dollars yearly for investments. This could happen by 2010, the year the first baby boomers turn sixty-five.

See also CAPITAL FORMATION; CREDIT, DEBT, AND BORROWING; DEFICITS, GOVERNMENTAL; ECONOMICS; ESTATE AND FINANCIAL PLANNING; FINANCIAL INSTITUTIONS; HUMAN RESOURCES DEVELOPMENT; INSURANCE; INVESTMENTS; WEALTH.

BIBLIOGRAPHY

BRYAN, LOWELL, and FARRELL, DIANA. "The Savings Surge." *The Wall Street Journal*, November 7, 1994.

EHRBAN, AL. "How Washington Can Stop Its War on Savings." *Fortune* (March 6, 1995).

MODIGLIANI, FRANCO. "Life Cycle, Individual Thrift, and the Wealth of Nations." *The American Economic Review* (June 1986).

NOVAK, JANET. "Hey, Big Saver." *Forbes* (December 19, 1994).

"Whatever Happened to That Rainy Day?" *The Economist* (January 21, 1995).

"Why Do People Really Save?" *Business Week* (February 27, 1995).

Roger Selbert

Scandinavia.

See EUROPE, WESTERN; SWEDEN.

Scanning

Scanning is a futures research tool that allows us to integrate our understanding of various sectors of the external environment and their relationships with systematically collected macroenvironmental information to obtain early warning of change. Scanning provides strategic intelligence useful in determining strategic options. In the context of strategic planning, scanning is one analytic component. Analysis consists of scanning environments to identify changing trends and potential developments, monitoring them, forecasting their future patterns, and assessing their impacts. Combined with an internal analysis of an organization's vision, mission, strengths, and weaknesses, external analysis assists in planning.

Fahey and Narayanan (1986) describe three environmental levels. The *task environment* refers to a set of customers. The *industry environment* comprises all enterprises within a particular industry. At the broadest level is the *macroenvironment*, which includes the Social, Technological, Economic, Environmental, and Political (or STEEP) sectors. Changes in one sector at any level (local, national, or global) may lead to changes in another. A war in the Middle East may cause the price of oil to increase, thus stimulating a recession, in turn resulting in budget cuts. Technological developments in California that enable the conversion of wind power to low-cost energy may be introduced worldwide, thereby reducing the costs of fossil fuel energy, with concomitant economic ramifications. Thus, developments in the macroenvironment can affect developments in the task and industrial environments. This point underscores the necessity of scanning the macroenvironment, as well as the task and industrial environments, to pick up the early signals of change that may affect one's organization or activities.

Scanning can be conceptualized in a number of ways. Aguilar (1967) identified four collection modes:

- *Undirected viewing* consists of reading a variety of publications for no specific purpose other than to be informed.
- *Conditioned viewing* consists of responding to this information in terms of assessing its relevance to the organization.
- *Informal searching* consists of actively seeking specific information but in a relatively unstructured way.
- *Formal searching* is a more actively organized attempt to devise methodologies for obtaining information for specific purposes.

Morrison, Renfro, and Boucher (1984) describe two modes: passive and active scanning. *Passive scanning* is what most people do when they read journals and newspapers. For serious news coverage, many read the same kinds of materials: a local newspaper, perhaps a national newspaper like the *New York Times* or *Wall Street Journal*, and an industry or trade newspaper. People are less inclined to read narrow-interest periodicals when passively scanning. The organizational consequences of passive scanning are that we do not systematically use the information as intelligence to benefit the organization, and, furthermore, we may miss ideas signalling changes in the macroenvironment that could affect the organization. Consequently, to broaden our perspectives and to fight inherent myopia, a more active scanning is required. Such active scanning focuses attention on information resources that span a broad area of concern, including the technological, economic, social, and political sectors, at the local, regional, national, and global level.

Fahey, King, and Narayanan (1981) have defined the typology of active scanning. *Irregular* scanning systems are used on an ad hoc basis and are often initiated by specific crises. This approach is used when planners need information for making assumptions, and is conducted for that purpose only. *Periodic* systems are invoked when periodically required to update previous scans, perhaps in preparation for a new planning cycle. *Continuous* systems use the active scanning mode of data collection to systematically inform users. This mode limits potentially relevant "data" only in terms of one's conception of the relevant macroenvironment. Scanning data derived from a host of varied sources is inherently scattered, vague, and imprecise. Because early signals often show up in unexpected places, the scanning purview must be broad, ongoing, and sufficiently comprehensive to cover the environments important to users or to an organization.

The important criterion for literature selection is diversity. Information can be obtained from books, newspapers, magazines, journals, television and radio programs, computer bulletin boards and other on-line services, and from knowledgable individuals. There is no lack of available information resources. *Future Survey Annual 1988–1989* lists some 454 futures-relevant periodicals, including 46 publications in international economics and development, 45 in environment/resources/energy, and 31 in health and human services (Marien, 1991, p. 86).

Existing environmental scans provide ready-made surveys. United Way of America publishes *What Lies Ahead* on a biennial basis. The World Future Society publishes *Future Survey*, a monthly abstract of books, articles, and reports containing forecasts, trends, and ideas about the future. The Global Network publishes *John Naisbitt's Trend Letter*, and Kiplinger Washington Editors publish the *Kiplinger Washington Letter*.

Other general-interest sources are as follows:

- Newspapers—*New York Times, Washington Post, Wall Street Journal, Miami Herald, Chicago Tribune, Los Angeles Times, Christian Science Monitor*, and *The Times* (of London).
- Magazines—*Vital Speeches of the Day, Across the Board, Time, Newsweek, U.S. News and World Report, Atlantic, The Nation, Ms, The Futurist*, and *Whole Earth Review*.

Adequate scanning of the macroenvironment requires identifying specific information resources for each STEEP category. Some information sources organized by category for the macroenvironment should include the following:

1. Social/demographic/values/lifestyles literature—*American Demographics, Public Opinion* and data from periodic publications or statistics from the Census Bureau, other federal, state, and local governmental agencies, and university sociology departments or population study centers. The Department of Labor and the National Technical and Information Services generate specific types of demographic analyses. The National Center for Health Statistics provides data on trends in areas such as fertility and life expectancy. The U.S. League of Savings Associations studies changes in home-buyer demographics, and the American Council of Life

Insurance's Social Research Services conducts demographic studies. The UN and OECD publish periodic reports detailing international developments in these areas.

2. Technological literature—*Technology Review, Datamation, Byte, Computer World, Discover, InfoWorld, Science, Scientific American, Proceedings of the National Academy of Sciences,* and *Issues in Science and Technology.*

3. Economic literature—*Business Week, The Economist, Fortune, Forbes, Money, Inc.,* and *The Monthly Labor Review.* Data may also be obtained from Department of Commerce Bureau of Economic Analysis monthly reports as well as reports from the Departments of Labor, Energy, and Treasury. State and local governmental agencies provide regional economic data.

4. Environmental literature—*Ecodecision* (Royal Society of Canada) and *Environment.* Several organizations publish future-oriented reports on the environment—the Global Tomorrow Coalition, the Worldwatch Institute, the World Resources Institute, the Audubon Society, and the Sierra Club.

5. Political literature—*New Republic, The National Review, The Nation, The National Journal, In These Times, Mother Jones, Federal Register, Congressional Quarterly, Weekly Report,* and *Digest of Public General Bills.* Other sources include public opinion leaders, social critics, futures-oriented research establishments (e.g., the Hudson Institute, the Institute for the Future), public policy research centers (e.g., Brookings Institution, the American Enterprise Institute), governmental documents (e.g., public hearings, congressional hearings), proposed bills to the legislature, and statements or opinions by experts or activists. *State Legislatures* (National Conference of State Legislatures) or provides a periodic summary of pertinent legislation being considered in state legislatures throughout the country.

Information resources for scanning the task environment include local, state, and regional newspapers, local and state government reports as well as experts in demography, sociology, and political science departments in local colleges and universities. Perhaps one of the most useful information resources consists of networks of friends and colleagues within the organization and in the industry. Electronic databases containing up-to-date descriptions of articles (by title and, many times, by abstract) are available by subscription. Abstracted

Business Information (ABI Inform) and Public Affairs Information Service (PAIS) are two such databases. Two database services, Dialogue and BRS, contain hundreds more databases specializing in many areas. Many libraries already subscribe to these databases and database services.

In conclusion, most everyone does passive scanning. However, active scanning is required to enhance abilities to understand, anticipate, and respond to the threats and opportunities posed by changes in the external environment. Active scanning is a part of any level of scanning—irregular, periodic, or continuous.

Environmental scanning is only one component of external analysis. However, it is the starting point for identifying critical trends and potential events, monitoring them, and forecasting where they are going. Comprehensive external analysis is not only an enriching development experience; more importantly, it provides a basis for discerning the strategic direction of your organization from which you may plan far more effectively.

See also DATA STORAGE; FORECASTING METHODS; ON-LINE SERVICES; PLANNING.

BIBLIOGRAPHY

AGUILAR, FRANCIS. *Scanning the Business Environment.* New York: Macmillan, 1967.

FAHEY, LIAM; KING, WILLIAM R.; and NARAYANAN, V. K. "Environmental Scanning and Forecasting in Strategic Planning: The State of the Art." *Long Range Planning* 14 (1981): 32–39.

FAHEY, LIAM, and NARAYANAN, V. K. *Macroenvironmental Analysis for Strategic Management.* New York: West Publishing Company, 1986.

MARIEN, MICHAEL. "Scanning: An Imperfect Activity in an Era of Fragmentation and Uncertainty." *Futures Research Quarterly* 7 (1991): 82–90.

MORRISON, JAMES L.; RENFRO, WILLIAM L.; and BOUCHER, WAYNE I. *Futures Research and the Strategic Planning Process.* Washington, DC: Association for the Study of Higher Education, 1984.

James L. Morrison

Scenarios

Today's organizations face tremendous structural change and uncertainty: globalization, multiculturalism, internal diversity, technological innovation, and decisions with huge risks and consequences. Anticipating the future in this volatile environment calls for more than systematic analysis: it demands creativity, insight, and intuition. Scenarios—stories or story outlines about possible futures—combine these elements to create robust strategies. The test of a good scenario is not whether it portrays the future accurately but whether it helps an organization to learn and adapt.

By definition, a scenario is a tool for ordering one's perceptions about alternative future environments in which today's decisions might play out. In practice, scenarios resemble a set of stories built around carefully constructed plots. Stories are an old way of organizing knowledge; as planning tools, they discourage denial by enabling the willing suspension of disbelief. Stories can express multiple perspectives on complex events; scenarios give meaning to these events.

Scenarios are powerful precisely because the future is unpredictable. Unlike traditional forecasting or market research, which extrapolate from current trends, scenarios present alternative images. Scenarios also embrace qualitative perspectives and potential discontinuities that econometric models exclude. Consequently, creating scenarios requires decision makers to question their broadest assumptions about how the world works so they can foresee the consequences of decisions that might be missed or denied; what has not been foreseen is unlikely to be seen in time. Organizationally, scenarios add value by providing a common vocabulary and effective basis for communicating complex—sometimes paradoxical—conditions and options.

Scenario planning is a highly intense and imaginative process that follows systematic and recognizable phases. It begins by isolating the decision to be made and rigorously challenging the mental maps that shape one's perceptions. The next steps are more analytical: identifying and prioritizing the driving forces (social, technological, economic, environmental, political, and technological), the predetermined elements (i.e., what is inevitable, like demographics already "in the pipeline"), and the critical uncertainties (i.e., what is unpredictable or willfully chosen, such as matters of public policy).

These exercises culminate in two or three carefully constructed scenario "plots"—typically an evolutionary and extrapolative business-as-usual approach buttressed by an optimistic as well as a pessimistic speculation. Another perspective might involve scenarios that are preferable, probable, and possible. If the scenarios are to function as useful learning tools, the lessons they teach must be relevant to the key decision. Whatever the framework, only a few scenarios can be developed fully and remembered; these should represent credible alternative futures, not a best case/worst case/most

likely continuum. Once the scenarios are embellished and woven into a narrative, their implications are identified along with the leading indicators to be monitored.

Good scenarios are plausible and surprising; they have the power to break old stereotypes; and their creators assume ownership and put them to work. Using scenarios is rehearsing the future; by recognizing the warning signs and the unfolding drama, one can avoid being overwhelmed by surprises and consequently can adapt and act effectively. Decisions that have been pretested against a range of what the future may offer are more likely to stand the test of time, to produce robust and resilient strategies, and to create a competitive advantage. The act of scenario planning is a mainstay in anticipating the future and planning strategically in an uncertain and rapidly changing world. Ultimately, the legacy of scenarios is not a more accurate picture of tomorrow, but the ability to help make better long-term decisions today.

See also FORECASTING, DETERMINISTIC; FORECASTING METHODS; SURPRISES; TECHNOLOGY FORECASTING AND ASSESSMENT; TREND INDICATORS, WILDCARDS.

BIBLIOGRAPHY

COATES, JOSEPH F. "A Chrestomathy of Flawed Forecasts." *Technology Forecasting and Social Change* 45/3 (March 1994).

COYLE, R.G., CRAWSHAY, W. and SUTTON, L. "Futures Assessment by Field Anomaly Relaxation: A Review and Appraisal." *Futures* 26/1 (January–February 1994).

DRUCKER, PETER F. *The Ecological Vision: Reflections on the American Condition.* New Brunswick, NJ: Transaction Publishers, 1993.

GODET, MICHEL. *Scenarios and Strategic Management.* London and Stoneham, MA: Butterworths, 1987.

HEILBRONER, ROBERT. *Visions of the Future: The Distant Past, Yesterday, Today, and Tomorrow.* New York: The New York Public Library/Oxford University Press, 1995.

MAKRIDAKIS, SPYROS G. *Forecasting, Planning, and Strategy for the 21st Century.* New York: The Free Press, 1990.

MORRISON, J. IAN. "The Futures Tool Kit." *Across the Board* 31/1 (January 1994).

SCHNAARS, STEVEN P. "How to Develop and Use Scenarios." *Long Range Planning* 20/1 (February 1987).

SCHWARTZ, PETER. *The Art of the Long View: Planning for the Future in an Uncertain World.* New York: Doubleday/Currency Book, 1991.

WAGAR, WARREN W. "A Funny Thing Happened on My Way to the Future: Or, The Hazards of Prophecy." *The Futurist* 28/3 (May–June 1994).

Peter Schwartz

Schumpeter, Joseph A. (1883–1950)

The American economist Joseph Schumpeter was born in what is now the Czech Republic. Educated in Vienna, he taught at the universities of Graz and Bonn. He moved to the United States in 1932, where he joined the faculty of Harvard University and became a naturalized American citizen. His earlier theoretical works offered an analysis of capitalism as a dynamic system fueled by the innovations of bold entrepreneurs. The less daring, faceless organization men who take their place, he argued, are ultimately responsible for the slumps that follow times of prosperity. In his most important futures-oriented book, *Capitalism, Socialism, and Democracy* (1942), Schumpeter foresaw the recovery of modern capitalism from the Great Depression of the 1930s, but he did not believe it could survive in the long run. Abandoned by the intelligentsia and subject to decay from within, capitalism would eventually give way to socialism or some other form of public control of wealth. Among Schumpeter's other major works are *Theorie der wirtschaftlichen Entwicklung* (1912; in English, *The Theory of Economic Development*, 1934) and a massive two-volume study, *Business Cycles: A Theoretical, Historical, and Statistical Analysis of the Capitalist Process* (1939).

BIBLIOGRAPHY

ALLEN, ROBERT LORING. *Opening Doors: The Life and Work of Joseph Schumpeter.* New Brunswick, NJ: Transaction Publishers, 1991.

BOTTOMORE, TOM. *Between Marginalism and Marxism: The Economic Sociology of J. A. Schumpeter.* New York: St. Martin's Press, 1992.

SWEDBERG, RICHARD. *Schumpeter: A Biography.* Princeton, NJ: Princeton University Press, 1991.

WOOD, JOHN CUNNINGHAM, ed. *J. A. Schumpeter: Critical Assessments.* New York: Routledge, 1991.

W. Warren Wagar

Science Cities

The present concept of the science city or technopolis began with Silicon Valley and was followed some thirty years later by Sophia Antipolis in the South of France (1969), and Tsukuba Science City in Japan (1970). The technopolis is a city of acceptable size that can be part of an international community but still retain the capability to organize and focus activities locally. Its overall success will depend on the socioeconomic conditions of the international community. The technopolis concept is an attempt to reinvent the city, but its development remains outside the mainstream of urban change and in its current form it is not seen as a solution for major urban problems.

The core concept is stated in Kozmetsky's *Technopolis Phenomenon*: "The technopolis is an innovative approach to economic development that involves linking technology commercialization with effective public- and private-sector initiatives to create new infrastructures for economic growth, diversification, and global competitiveness."

Silicon Valley in the suburbs of San Francisco, California, with its legendary garage startups, such as Hewlett Packard and Apple, became a magnet to attract many other new companies, and by the 1960s it had become the envy of other countries. In 1983 Japan's Ministry of International Trade and Industry (MITI) succeeded in passing legislation for its technopolis concept.

Japan, seeking solutions for population distribution and urban/rural problems, began planning in 1958, but started construction in 1970 of Tsukuba Science City at the heart of an area expected to reach 700,000 in population by the year 2000. Tsukuba Science City includes research universities, science centers (technocenters), industrial research parks, R&D consortiums, venture capital foundations, office complexes, international convention centers, and residential new towns. By 1986, the MITI core concept included twenty-eight regional cities.

Sophia Antipolis in France was founded with a focus on cross-fertilization of ideas, high quality of life, and close contact and interaction with the region and its constituencies. In twenty years it became the largest technopolis of its kind in Europe. If Silicon Valley was a first-generation science city, Tsukuba and Sophia Antipolis are part of the second generation, with the latter hovering on the edge of the third generation. In the United States there are a number of newer "Silicon Valleys." These include Route 128 around Boston; Telecom Belt (Princeton, New Jersey); Satellite Valley (Gaithersburg, Maryland); Research Triangle, North Carolina (consisting of Chapel Hill, Durham, and Raleigh); Silicon Plain (Ft. Worth and Dallas, Texas); Silicon Forest (Portland, Oregon); and Silicon Mountain (Denver, Boulder, and Colorado Springs, Colorado).

For over twenty years, the concept of the science city, or technopolis, has evolved. Each technopolis reflects the demands of the culture and the circumstances under which it was conceived. From a growing number of technopolises, there emerges a richer set of experiences about what does and does not work. This experience, combined with the rapid expansion of information generation and transfer technologies, new transportation systems, and exploitable new technologies, shapes the technopolises that have already begun and new ones still in some stage of planning.

The success of a science city hinges on how well it invents new products and the adequacy of transportation and communications technologies to meet changing socioeconomic conditions. Economic success is increasingly determined by information and how people think, by airports, and by communications—not by access to raw materials or sea lanes. Learning from earlier experiences, future generations of science cities are expected to exhibit greater responsiveness to changing socioeconomic changes.

Science cities emerge from the cultural, economic, and political circumstances of the governments, corporations, and individuals that create them. The creators bring elements of their past experience as well as new expectations to their task. Current experience suggests that their success depends on whether the invented city is structured for self-learning and can achieve rapid enough change to overcome any limiting aspects of the initial vision.

Science cities are expected to evolve to increasingly higher levels of maturity. Level three science cities, which are emerging today, demonstrate more self-learning and capacity for change than level two cities such as Tsukuba and the early stages of Sophia Antipolis. Level four cities will evolve adequate self-learning and achieve responsive enough change to be self-sustaining in the twenty-first century.

Learning and communications are key to future successes in the development of viable science cities. Research and application of new processes and products are at the forefront of the science city. Rapid dissemination of information provides all segments of the city with the opportunity to contribute and participate in making necessary changes. Emerging communications technology and the integration of voice, images, data, and sound for delivery of information anywhere in the city by anyone promises the fullest opportunity for information sharing and learning. Disparities in learning will need to be minimized across economic groups in order to continuously attract resi-dents and provide for a citywide response to changing conditions.

Movement of people, materials, and products will need to adapt to shifts in economic and social activity. The various modes of transportation will need to be more customized to allow individuals and organizations the capability to modify their use and rapidly respond to transportation changes required to sustain the viability of the city. Because of the central role of science and technology in national prosperity, most countries of the world will eventually have their science cities.

See also CITIES; CITIES, NORTH AMERICAN; SCIENCE ISSUES.

BIBLIOGRAPHY

BURKE, JAMES. *Connections.* Boston: Little, Brown, 1978.
GIBSON, DAVID V.; KOZMETSKY, GEORGE; and SMILOR, RAYMOND W., eds. *The Technopolis Phenomenon.* Lanham, MD: Rowman & Littlefield, 1992.
_____. *Creating the Technopolis.* Cambridge, MA: Ballinger, 1988.
TATSUNO, SHERIDAN M. *The Technopolis Strategy.* Englewood Cliffs, NJ: Prentice Hall, 1986.

Richard G. Maynard

Science Fiction

Science fiction—sometimes called "sci-fi," but not by most of the people who read or write it—is notoriously hard to define, though easy enough for its devotees to recognize. Although most science fiction is about the future and much of it has to do with space travel, robots, super-computers, and alien intelligent life, there are many classic stories with none of those ingredients that nevertheless are still clearly science fiction. One of the most illuminating attempts at clarification comes from the English scholar of science fiction Tom Shippey. After listing more than a dozen proposed definitions of the subject, Shippey concluded by saying: "Perhaps science fiction is impossible to define since, being the literature of change, it changes as you try to define it." But there is an excellent definition within that disclaimer: science fiction is indeed the literature of change, particularly of the changes brought about—and especially those still to come—by the explosive growth of science and technology.

Although stories that have some claim to be included in the science fiction canon date back for centuries—with examples as early as *The True History* by

Lucian of Samosata, written in the second century A.D.—the real flowering of science fiction could not come before science itself began to assume its present form. Accordingly, the first authors to make a career of writing in this form were Jules Verne and H. G. WELLS. Wells in particular deserves recognition as the master who laid out the pattern of subject matter for future science fiction writers to explore. Still, when their works were published the field did not yet have a name, nor was there any publication devoted entirely to the new kind of literature.

Both those needs were supplied when Hugo Gernsback launched his magazine, *Amazing Stories,* in April 1926. Other magazines followed, and for more than twenty years thereafter almost all science fiction published in America first appeared in one or another of the science fiction "pulps." Among the major writers of the early magazine period were E. E. "Doc" Smith, who with his *The Skylark of Space* essentially invented the "space opera" (now most frequently found in such box-office film successes as *Star Wars*), and David H. Keller, best known for such satirical short stories as "The Revolt of the Pedestrians."

In the transitional period, from about 1950 to the end of the 1960s, the dominant writers were Isaac ASIMOV, Ray Bradbury, Robert A. Heinlein, and Arthur C. CLARKE. All four began their careers in the science fiction magazines (all of them but Bradbury being closely identified with *Astounding Science Fiction,* edited by that dominant figure among science fiction editors, John W. Campbell) but went on to succeed as authors of many best-selling books. Since then book publication has provided the major outlet for most of the current writers. Among the best known of these are John Varley, Samuel R. Delany, and the two "cyberpunk" writers, Bruce Sterling and William Gibson, as well as a host of prominent female writers such as Ursula K. LeGuin, Anne McCaffrey, Suzie McKee Charnas, Joan Slonjewski, and Sherri S. Tepper.

Another significant development in current science fiction is its large place in film and television production. In television, pride of place must go to the pioneering series *Star Trek,* originally described by its creator, Gene Roddenberry, as "a sort of *Wagon Train* in space." The original *Star Trek* series was canceled by its network after the second year because of poor ratings, but a blizzard of angry letters from viewers caused the network to give it one more year before the axe fell. Its real popularity began only after that cancellation. For years afterward *Star Trek* was the most repeated series in syndication; there was said to be one small city (in

Texas) where the series could be viewed eight times a day, from different stations. A Saturday-morning animated version came next, but failed quickly; since then its successor *Star Trek: The Next Generation,* with a new cast of characters, has outlasted the original and spawned two spin-off series and one more darkly toned imitator (*Babylon 5*). A series of feature films has appeared with the old standby actors. Other important feature motion pictures have included *THX 1138,* the *Star Wars* films, *ET, Close Encounters of the Third Kind, 2001* and its sequel, and *Alien,* as well as a steady diet of lower-budget productions every year.

Although science fiction has become predominantly an Anglo-American literature in this century, there are hundreds of writers and many thousands of fans in other countries, including a few non-English-speaking writers, such as Poland's Stanisłau Lem, Japan's Sakyo Komatsu, and Russia's collaborating brothers Boris and Arkady Strugatsky, who have become world famous. The best-known American writers are almost invariably widely published abroad, with translations of works into forty or more languages. Since 1980 the international organization World SF has been a forum for persons who are professionally concerned with science fiction, whether as authors, editors, critics, teachers, artists, filmmakers, or in any other professional capacity. World SF now has members in thirty-eight countries and although most of its annual general meetings have taken place in European countries, they have also been held in Canada and the People's Republic of China.

Science fiction stories do not ordinarily claim to predict the future, since a single writer will frequently write many stories with completely different future histories. Still, they do provide a sort of general catalog of possible future events. The field has been called a useful prophylactic against future shock, since almost all the important technological and social changes of the twentieth century have been prefigured in science fiction. In recognition of this fact, many science fiction writers have been asked to contribute to "futurological" studies conducted by universities, research establishments, large corporations, and even the American military services.

Science fiction and science, too, have enjoyed a similar synergistic relationship. Although there are many excellent science fiction stories that contain little or no real science, it is also true that many science fiction writers are trained scientists, or laymen who keep abreast of scientific theories and discoveries. These accomplishments are often reflected in their stories, while a significant number of scientists, including some of the world's leading scientific authorities, such as Marvin Minsky, Freeman J. Dyson, and Stephen Hawking, first became interested in science through reading science fiction and often still continue both to read it and occasionally to write it. Among well-known scientists and mathematicians who have written science fiction stories (sometimes under pen-names) are Minsky, Eric Temple Bell (writing as "John Taine"), Robert Forward, Carl Sagan, and Fred Hoyle.

One of the most unusual features of the science-fiction field lies in the cohesiveness of its adherents, both readers and writers. Collectively known as "science fiction fandom," these individuals support a regular program of "cons," short for "conventions," unknown to any other literature. More than 500 of these cons occur ever year in the United States alone (with nearly as many again in the rest of the world). The largest is usually the annual "worldcon," the first of which took place in New York City in 1939, and since then, though usually in some city of the United States, it has been held also in England, Canada, Australia, Germany, and the Netherlands. At these meetings, ranging in attendance from a few hundred to more than ten thousand, writers, readers, artists, editors, and others discuss every aspect of the field. Many close friendships arise between people who meet only at such cons; marriages occur; individuals who live thousands of miles apart maintain close touch with each other; in the argot of the field, FIAWOL (an acronym for "Fandom Is A Way Of Life") is an accurate description.

See also APOCALYPTIC FUTURE; DYSTOPIAS; GLOBAL CONSCIOUSNESS; POPULARIZED FUTURES; UTOPIAS. In addition, see CHRONOLOGY OF FUTURISM AND THE FUTURE in the Appendix.

BIBLIOGRAPHY

ALDISS, BRIAN W. *Trillion Year Spree: The History of Science Fiction.* New York: Atheneum, 1986.

AMIS, KINGSLEY. *New Maps of Hell.* New York: Harcourt, Brace, 1960.

BLEILER, E. F., ed. *Science Fiction Writers.* New York: Scribner, 1982.

NICHOLLS, PETER, and CLUTE, JOHN, eds. *The Science Fiction Encyclopedia,* 2nd ed. New York: St. Martin's Press, 1993.

PANSHIN, ALEXEI, and PANSHIN, CORY. *The World Beyond the Hill: Science Fiction and the Quest for Transcendence.* Los Angeles: Jeremy Tarcher, 1989.

POHL, FREDERIK. *The Way the Future Was.* New York: Ballantine, 1978.

Frederik Pohl

Science Issues

Advancing science through investments in research and development (R&D) is expensive. Annually, the United States spends over $180 billion for R&D, which is carried out by industry, academia, and government laboratories. Academia and some government laboratories focus on fundamental research, while industry and other government laboratories focus on applied research and on developing technological products, processes, and systems.

How much should be spent on various fields of science and in pursuit of the various societal objectives that R&D will help us achieve? Because they study the unknown, researchers are uncertain about what they might learn. Cost-benefit and financial analysis help little in deciding what to spend and on what projects, so experienced researchers must help decide.

In the United States, industry pays for over half of R&D, and the federal government pays for most of the rest. Thus, decisions about what to study also involve industry managers and leaders in Congress and the executive branch. While rarely expert in science, they establish the broad economic and social objectives that motivate large R&D expenditures.

This discussion of how science priorities are set raises a key issue for science in a democracy: How can ordinary citizens influence decisions about scientific research and technological applications that will importantly affect their lives, work, and pocketbooks? Some argue that science and technology are "out of control"—that the combination of the special expertise required to understand new advances and the enormous financial and political advantages that can accrue to those who know how to take advantage of them means that science and technology are inherently undemocratic. Others argue that advances in communications have enhanced the abilities of everyone to learn about and participate in the decisions that affect them. So, just as industrialization required reading, writing, and arithmetic, the new information and biotechnologies demand that we become more conversant with science and with how technologies work. The need for improved public understanding has motivated major efforts to upgrade mathematics and science education, not only for the few who hope for careers in science and engineering, but for everyone.

Modern societies spend lavishly on R&D in hopes that material and social progress will come from improved understanding. We have learned how to prevent and cure disease; grow more and more nutritious foodstuffs; enhance our economy; sometimes prevent and when necessary win wars; and provide ourselves with an expanding array of entertainments.

However, we have also learned that applications of new knowledge can challenge traditional values and bring us grief. The telecommunications technologies that enhance education, entertainment, and edification provide platforms for poisonous dialogue and expose us to violence, real and imaginary. The synthetic ammonium nitrate that fertilizes our crops is fashioned into the bomb used at the federal building in Oklahoma City. Automobiles that whisk us across town or the nation emit air pollutants and kill thousands each year in accidents.

It is hard to anticipate the impacts of newly introduced technologies. Even if undesirable consequences are foreseen, we don't always have appropriate and democratic ways to manage them. Sometimes the lure of the benefits clouds our judgment of the costs. Technology assessment is one approach to anticipating and managing the unexpected and undesirable consequences of new technologies. Environmental and safety regulations can help control some of the undesirable impacts of new technologies.

Despite its awesome powers, science has limitations. Some things are too big, hot, fast, or far away to be studied easily. The history of science is about attempts to measure what was not measurable before, through the invention of ever more powerful telescopes, microscopes, chemical analyzers, and the like.

Projects to develop very large instruments are often called "big science"—the billion-dollar Hubble space telescope and the multi-billion-dollar superconducting super-collider (cancelled in 1993) are illustrations. Whereas "little science" is conducted by individuals and small groups, "big science" demands bureaucratic management, major budget commitments, and coordinated scientific programs. In big projects it is often impossible to determine individual responsibility for discoveries, a scientific practice for centuries. It is news when big projects fail or are terminated, and political pressures often keep them going.

Some natural phenomena have proven too complex for satisfactory scientific study. We still know very little about how an embryo becomes an adult being, and a full understanding of the causes of earthquakes still eludes us. Some phenomena cannot be studied in controlled experiments and are studied instead from indirect and historical evidence. We cannot rerun history to do experiments

on the Earth's geology, the evolution of species, or the factors that drive national and world economies. Studies of these unique phenomena are no less scientific than those that can be conducted in a laboratory, but they demand different standards of evidence and they yield a different sort of truth.

Fraud in science receives a lot of attention. A few researchers have faked experiments, misrepresented findings, or made outlandish, insupportable claims. However, science is a remarkable social instrument for exposing fraud. Several mechanisms operate. Typically, other scientists, or "peers," review planned projects and examine carefully the claims made in papers submitted for publication. Scientists often attempt to repeat or extend the work of those who came before, and this exposes work done poorly or falsified.

When new scientific results are put to immediate practical use, however, as sometimes occurs in medicine, environmental regulation, or the design of new technologies, scientific fraud can pose immediate threats to the public. It is imprudent for society to take important actions using brand-new scientific results without subjecting them to great scrutiny, especially if the more traditional approaches to validation don't have time to work. Engineers know this about science, so they are often accused of being slow to use new findings. Those working in other fields would be advised to heed the engineers' example.

See also RESEARCH AND DEVELOPMENT; SCIENTIFIC BREAKTHROUGHS; TECHNOLOGY AND SCIENCE.

BIBLIOGRAPHY

GOLDMAN, STEVEN, and CUTCLIFFE, STEPHEN, eds. *Science, Technology and Social Progress*. Bethlehem, PA: Lehigh University Press, 1988.

National Science Board. *Science and Engineering Indicators–1993*. Washington, DC: U.S. Government Printing Office, 1993.

TEICH, ALBERT H.; NELSON, STEPHEN D.; and MCENANEY, CELIA, eds. *Science and Technology Policy Yearbook–1994*. Washington, DC: American Association for the Advancement of Science, 1994.

Christopher T. Hill

Scientific Breakthroughs

Science is the single most important source of contemporary and future products, processes, and services that will enhance individual well-being, enlarge our understanding of the world around us, and prepare us to manage that world. Some breakthroughs in individual sciences will come about from applying already existing knowledge in unanticipated ways. Other breakthroughs will depend upon combining already available capabilities to do new things. Still others will create new capabilities.

Ecology over the next generation will become the central science in our understanding and management of the environment. Quantitative models of the biota and ecosystems will be the tools to effectively manage natural environments and guide the managed environments of farms, forests, and grazing land.

Brain science will flower in two directions as a result of understanding genetic links to mental health and disease and to individual human mental capabilities. First will be the elimination of mental disorders, such as schizophrenia and psychotic depression. Second will be the capability to improve our cognitive capabilities and give us better emotional balance and more fulfilling lives.

In agriculture, the ability to directly manipulate plant genes will lead to at least two breakthroughs. The first will be fully nutritionally balanced plants. For example, the native Mexican diet consists largely of rice and beans, each of which provides different essential proteins. The future will permit plants to have more complete protein content (so-called protein-efficiency ratios that assure human metabolic availability), as well as trace materials and other necessary dietary components. The second breakthrough will be a diet with double or triple the number of food plants. Many nutritional plants with undesirable characteristics will be changed into edible, marketable commodities. Ocean science will lead to the effective farming and ranching of the oceans.

Medical genetics will discover the heritable linkages to several thousand human diseases and disorders. Interventions for disease prevention or genetic correction will be common by supplying what is missing or removing what is harmful. Less clear in the future is whether medicine and biological research will identify the genes that determine our natural lifetime and manipulate them to extend human life. Whether that will be socially or even personally desirable is unclear even if the extension of life were accompanied by the maintenance of essential human faculties. More likely than extending our species's lifetime will be the applications of medicine to allow more of us to live out our full biological lifetime—to square off the death curve—giving most of us healthier, happier lives until our genetic time limit of about eighty-five years is reached.

Genetic knowledge will allow us to move beyond the control and prevention of disease to increasing our physical, intellectual, emotional, and social abilities. We are on the brink of being able to influence, if not shape, our own evolution as well as the evolution of the rest of the biota. It is plausible that early in the twenty-first century, some nations will have a program of raising the average IQ of their population by a few points per generation.

Every aspect of biology will be changed from genetics research. Two of the most striking will be the revival of extinct species. Far more likely than a Jurassic Park of animals extinct for tens of millions of years is the revival of more recently extinct animals like the woolly mammoth and the passenger pigeon. Every museum is a repository of species to revive. The primary scientific breakthrough to make the revival possible is learning to release from the DNA (genetic material) in every single somatic (body cell) of every living thing the ability to reproduce. At the time of this writing, among higher animals only reproductive cells (sperm and ova), not somatic cells, can reproduce.

Geology will help us to prevent some catastrophic earthquakes. Since earthquakes result from the sudden release of stress as the plates of Earth rub against each other or one passes under the other, we should be able to lubricate those stress points to allow a continuous stress release by low-level Richter-scale tremblors, thereby avoiding stress buildup and catastrophic release.

Several developments in economics could well lead to a genuine breakthrough. The world now has an urgent need to reconceptualize the economics of information. Similarly, as the structure of work changes and we move into an information-based society, the concept of what work is and how it should be compensated will be reconceptualized.

The third breakthrough in economics will be the introduction of a new system of national accounts that will factor in disease, disasters, unemployment, illness, accidents, pollution, resource loss, and other undesirable developments to create a more realistic and reliable measure of national welfare. These fundamental changes in economic thinking will carry us beyond the constraints and limitations of the economics of the industrial era and fashion the economic tools for understanding and managing the postindustrial society.

Chemistry will evolve in many new directions. One of the most important will be the development of materials based on the concept of biomimetics—

that is, the imitation of the processes that nature uses to create complex material with desirable characteristics. As we better understand how these natural materials, such as wood and seashells, are produced, we should be able to imitate their structures. A quite different line of development will be the flourishing of inorganic chemistry to accomplish many of the functions for which we now use organic materials.

Environmental science, should the threat of greenhouse warming prove to be valid, will move to radical remedies. To reduce the melting of the Antarctic ice cap, we may attempt to control the currents that flow around the South Pole that annually eat away at the ice sheets. Even more likely are processes to increase snowfall in Antarctica in order to compensate for any ocean rise resulting from the warming of the ocean. Another macroengineering response may be to increase the albedo—that is, the reflectivity of Earth. Today, Earth reflects into space about 53 percent of the sunlight that hits it. If we could increase the reflection from some portions of Earth, such as unpopulated, desert, and semidesert areas of the world, we might be able to compensate for the effects of greenhouse warming.

Macroengineering—civil works on a scale so large that they exceed the budgets of most governments and affect many nations—will be part of the growing pattern of a totally managed globe. Among the most likely macroengineering projects will be the harvesting of Antarctic icebergs, perhaps a mile by a quarter of a mile on edge to move to the west coast of South America, the Australian Outback, or Baja California, or Saudi Arabia. That enormous amount of water will transform the local environment and literally allow the deserts to bloom. Massive desalinization of ocean water could provide similar results.

Robots, based on research in space and military programs, will go outdoors, be weatherized, and have some on-board intelligence and mobility. They will do heavy and dangerous work, changing the nature of farming, mining, ocean activities, and the operation of risky facilities. They will also be utilized in dangerous situations such as disasters and fires.

Architecture may experience the development of the third paradigm for construction. Today, all structures depend upon one of two principles for their stability, either compression or tension. The fusion of the technologies of lightweight composite materials, reliable sensors, and artificial intelligence for appropriate and quick responses, and

motors and cable for strength will allow for the first time the construction of dynamic buildings. These structures in real time will respond to changes in their environment—wind, rain, even earthquakes. For the first time, we may be on the brink of having truly lightweight or temporary structures that could be easily dismantled like Lego blocks.

Artificial intelligence in several different forms will bring us devices capable of understanding the spoken word and speaking in a variety of languages with extensive vocabularies. Expert systems will be at the disposal of people in a suitable software package. On a larger scale, artificial intelligence will allow less skilled workers to undertake the tasks normally done by more highly trained and skilled workers. Artificial intelligence will be used to test systems. Are they foolproof? Are they fail-safe? Will they do their job? Are they free of viruses?

Artificial intelligence will also make possible currently unprecedented services, such as a health kiosk, where people could puncture the finger for a blood sample to put on a slide, urinate into a bottle, and drop that in the analytical machines, spit in the vial and drop that in a different machine, using artificial intelligence programs to explore symptoms, conditions, disease concerns, and so on. This evolution of an alternative or countermedicine could stimulate people's interest in their health and provide a useful and widely recognized needed check on traditional medical practice.

Asteroids have been striking Earth from time to time since the formation of the solar system. We now have the capability to identify potentially hazardous asteroids far enough away to take active and preventive measures. Early in the next century, we should see an internationally institutionalized asteroid watch, and we will probably begin on a trial basis the first intervention involving a large object outside Earth with a view to changing its course. If we can establish the practicality of doing that with a nonthreatening asteroid, we will be in better shape for the inevitable hazard.

There is no limit to what breakthroughs science will bring to us. We can be confident that an endless frontier that knows no bounds is still ahead of us.

See also ARCHITECTURAL DESIGN; ARTIFICIAL INTELLIGENCE; ASTRONOMY; CHEMISTRY; DISASTERS, PLANNING FOR; GENETIC ENGINEERING; GENETICS: AGRICULTURAL APPLICATIONS; GLOBAL WARMING; MACROENGINEERING; ROBOTICS; SURPRISES; WILDCARDS.

BIBLIOGRAPHY

BALLARD, STEVEN. *Innovation Through Scientific and Technical Information.* Westport, CT: Greenwood, 1989.

CARSON, J. W. *Innovation. A Battle Plan for the 1990s.* Brookfield, VT: Gower, 1989.

DIEBOLD, JOHN. *Innovators: The Discoveries, Inventions and Breakthroughs of Our Time.* New York: NAL-Dutton, 1990.

FORIDA, RICHARD. *The Breakthrough Illusion: Corporate America's Failure to Move from Innovation to Mass Production.* New York: Basic Books, 1990.

GABOR, DENNIS. *Innovations: Scientific, Technological and Social.* New York: Oxford University Press, 1970.

HAMMOND, A. L. *Twenty Discoveries That Changed Our Lives.* Washington, DC: American Association for the Advancement of Science, 1984.

McLOUGHLIN, IAN, and CLARK, JON. *Technological Change at Work.* Washington, DC: Taylor and Francis, 1988.

NAYAK, P. RANGANATH. *Breakthroughs!* New York: Rosen, 1986.

PARKINSON, CLAIRE. *Breakthroughs: A Chronology of Great Achievements in Science and Mathematics, 1200–1930.* Boston: G. K Hall, 1985.

POTTER, STEPHEN. *On the Right Lines? The Limits of Technological Innovation.* New York: St. Martin's Press, 1987.

Joseph F. Coates

Semiconductors

Semiconductors are the foundation of today's information age. They enable and underlie virtually every system involved in the manipulation and movement of information, from laptop computers to satellite-based global communications networks. Moreover, the manipulation and movement of information are rapidly becoming as vital to world economic growth as were once the generation and movement of food (the agricultural age) and the development and powering of machine tools (the industrial age). Semiconductor materials are becoming as vital (or more) to world economic growth as were once other materials such as stone and wood, metals and coal.

Semiconductor Materials: Characteristics and Families

What are some of the characteristics of semiconductors that enable them to excel at information manipulation and movement?

A primary characteristic, from which they derive their name, is that they are "lukewarm" electrical conductors. Neither highly insulating nor highly conducting, they were not initially believed to be particularly useful. However, because their conductivity is not only lukewarm, but also extremely sensitive to the introduction of impurities and the application of electric fields, they can easily be precision engineered into the basic building blocks of microelectronics: current or voltage-controlled switches and amplifiers.

A secondary (but also crucial) characteristic is that their electrical conductivity is based on two "effective" carrier types, negatively charged electrons and positively charged holes. The interaction between these carrier types is very strong and in many cases is either caused by the absorption, or results in the emission, of light (photons). Then, by precision engineering of the interaction between electrons and holes in compact devices, they can be used to form the basic building blocks of photonics: light-absorbing and -emitting devices such as detectors, lasers, and light-emitting diodes (LEDs).

What are some of the families of semiconductors from which these microelectronic and photonic devices are built? The dominant semiconductors are inorganic and can be divided into three major families, according to whether they are composed of elements from column IV, columns III and V, or columns II and VI of the periodic table. Although they all have the two unique characteristics described above, all their other physical and chemical properties vary widely both from family to family, as well as within each family. For example, at one extreme, carbon (C) in its diamond form has a very small lattice constant, is transparent into the ultraviolet, and is mechanically hard with a high thermal conductivity. At the other extreme, HgCdTe has a very large lattice constant, is transparent only in the far infrared, and is mechanically soft with a low thermal conductivity.

The column IV family is composed of silicon (Si), germanium (Ge), carbon (C), and silicon carbide (SiC). Of these, Si is by far the most important and is the material from which perhaps 95 percent of all semiconductor devices (by dollar volume) are produced. Due to its unmatched combination of robustness, performance, low cost, and integrability with high-quality passivating oxides, Si is overwhelmingly likely to continue to be the most important semiconductor for the foreseeable future. Although Ge was the material in which the first transistor was demonstrated in 1948, and although SiC and C have important current and future niche applications (e.g., in severe-environment electronics and as coatings for heat sinks and field-emission devices), none is likely to ever play as important a role as Si as an active device material in mainstream applications.

The column III-V family contains permutations of the column III elements aluminum (Al), gallium (Ga), and indium (In), and the column V elements nitrogen (N), phosphorus (P), arsenic (As), and antimony (Sb). Of these, GaAs-related materials are the most important and are the materials from which perhaps 75 percent of all III-V devices are produced. The relative importance of GaAs within the column III-V family of materials is less pronounced than that of Si within the column IV family of materials. The reason is that though GaAs is characterized by a reasonable balance between robustness, cost, and performance, other materials have important advantages in particular areas. InP-related materials, for example, emit light in the 1.3–1.55 μm wavelength range important to fiber-based optical communications and have high-field transport properties superior to GaAs-based materials. GaN-related materials, for example, though difficult to grow, are extremely robust and emit light in the blue-green wavelength range important to displays, illumination sources, and high-resolution optical storage and printing. Both InP- and GaN-related materials are likely to increase in importance relative to GaAs-related materials in the future.

The column II-VI family contains permutations of the column II elements magnesium (Mg), zinc (Zn), cadmium (Cd), and mercury (Hg), and the column VI elements sulfur (S), selenium (Se), and tellurium (Te). These semiconductors are not used widely for active devices, but are important as passive phosphor materials for cathode-ray-tube devices such as television monitors. They are particularly noteworthy, however, because of their wide range of energy gaps. At the same time that ZnSSe-related materials are currently being explored for blue-green lasers, HgCdTe-related materials are the high-performance material of choice for long-wavelength (8–14 μm) infrared radiation detectors. None of these materials, though, is likely to be a very important active device material in mainstream applications.

All of the semiconductors mentioned thus far have been inorganic. Recently a new family of semiconductor materials has been developed, based on organic polymers. Although these materials are very immature, they promise a new generation of ultra-inexpensive devices fabricated from polymer coatings on low-temperature substrates such as glass and plastics. Indeed, both transistors and light-emitting devices have recently been demonstrated, though a major challenge will be achieving the performance and reliability required for wide acceptance.

A related family of materials from which extremely dense three-dimensionally-packed circuitry can clearly be formed are biological materials. Although biological devices are much slower (with switching times measured in microseconds rather than nanoseconds) than semiconductor devices, their ability to "self-assemble" could enable artificial circuits of unprecedented complexity. Ethical issues regarding artificial life will surely arise, but they presumably already will have for complex, ultradense networks of computers as well.

Si Materials: Information Manipulation

As discussed above, Si-based materials will likely continue to dominate semiconductor applications in information manipulation (logic and memory) for the foreseeable future. Much of that dominance is based on the expected continued increase in functionality of Si-based integrated circuits (ICs). Historically, that increase in functionality has obeyed Moore's Law and has doubled approximately every three years. A continuation of that rate of increase through the year 2015 is not unlikely and will enable applications that are as difficult to imagine now as today's applications were difficult to imagine yesterday.

Nevertheless, this continued increase in functionality will require major changes in the manner in which ICs are fabricated. Among the major technological challenges are those anticipated by the Semiconductor Industry Association in its 1994 national technology road map for semiconductors. In design and test, a major challenge will be to develop and integrate a hierarchy of tools spanning high-level system issues all the way to low-level packaging and chip issues. In process integration, devices and structures, a major challenge will be to develop and integrate radically new devices with ultra-high packing densities. In lithography, a major challenge will be to move from 0.5 μm to 0.1 μm linewidths and below, and to develop new short-wavelength compact optical sources. Soon, quantum effects will become important and may lead to a new generation of coherent-electron-effect devices and circuits. In metal interconnects, a major challenge will be both to increase interconnect complexity and bandwidth without introducing additional crosstalk as well as eventually to understand and harness inevitable traveling-wave effects as lumped elements become distributed elements. In materials and bulk processes, a major challenge will be to understand and control impurity profiles and interfaces at the nanoscale through improved wafer- and equipment-level physical models and simulations. In assembly and packaging, a major challenge will be to move from perimeter- connected single-chip modules to area-connected multichip modules, perhaps through a new generation of optoelectronic interconnects and stacked (three-dimensional) packaging. In factory integration, a major challenge will be to move from an environment in which processes are optimized individually to one in which they are optimized collectively through more comprehensive modeling, sensing, and control of the overall factory environment.

Along with this continued increase in functionality will likely come a decrease in the need for today's vast array of different kinds of ICs. A limited set of standard ICs (such as today's Pentium and PowerPC chip families) will become so inexpensive, powerful, and general-purpose, that it will gradually become easier to reprogram them using software or "ROMware" than to manufacture costly, low-volume lots of "hardware-programmed" application-specific ICs. Customization of IC function will increasingly occur at higher and higher (software rather than hardware) levels and will decrease or eliminate the need for "agile manufacturing" of low volume IC lots.

III-V Materials: Information Movement

As discussed above, column III-V-based materials are and will continue to be a much smaller market than Si-based materials. Nevertheless, information manipulation is only half of what is necessary; information movement (communications and display) is the other half, and it is that half that will place increasing demands on III-V materials. Indeed, it is likely that, as communications technology finally "catches up" (and ultimately surpasses) computation technology in tomorrow's ultra-high-bandwidth networks of distributed intelligence, the III-V versus Si dollar-volume ratio will grow significantly from today's 1:20. It will do so because III-V materials are crucial to both types of tomorrow's dominant forms of high-speed communication: wireless and optoelectronic.

In wireless communications, the key ingredient is the ability to efficiently receive, modulate/demodulate, amplify, and transmit radio and microwave (0.8–100 GHz) frequency signals. In all of these areas, III-V semiconductors dominate now and are likely to continue to dominate in the future. Their efficiencies at all of these functions will always exceed those of Si due to their higher electron mobilities and hence their higher switching speed × switching power product. This will be particularly the case as carrier frequencies continue to increase, both to accommodate higher data transmission rates as well as to decrease interference between adjacent cells in tomorrow's ultradense global grid of wireless base stations.

In optoelectronic communications, the key ingredient is the ability to emit and detect light efficiently. Because of their direct energy gaps, column III-V semiconductors will always be far more efficient at both of these than column IV semiconductors. One important trend will be the increased use of devices in which light is absorbed or emitted vertically rather than horizontally. Light-emitting diodes (LEDs), for example, will continue to grow in importance, particularly as a wider spectrum of wavelengths is made available by the development of new materials. Blue, green, and red (0.4–0.7 µm wavelength) LEDs enabled by AlGaInN and AlGaInP materials will find applications in high-brightness, robust illumination sources and displays; and mid-infrared (2.0–5.0 µm wavelength) LEDs enabled by AlGaInAsSb materials will find applications in environmental sensing. Due to their performance and cost advantages, vertical cavity surface emitting lasers will displace conventional horizontal-cavity, edge-emitting lasers in most applications, including as high-bandwidth sources for fiber-optic communications and as low-bandwidth sources for peripherals such as laser printers and optical disks.

Integrated Materials: Systems on a Chip

A final major trend will be the integration of materials, each matched to a particular function, for systems on a chip. At an evolutionary level, this kind of integration has been going on for some time. The integration of polycrystalline Si and metals for interconnects, for example, with single-crystal Si for active transistors, is at the heart of Si integrated circuits. Mainstream Si technology will continue to incorporate new materials for enhanced performance. SiGe, SiGeC, and SiC alloys and compounds can enable more sophisticated heterojunction devices by improving carrier confinement in field-effect transistors and injection efficiency in bipolar transistors. Other variants of Si itself, such as amorphous and polycrystalline Si, will also gradually increase in importance, particularly as devices shrink and as the carrier mobilities of the material used to fabricate the device becomes less and less important. Silicon-on-insulator may also increase in importance, as device packing density increases and cross talk becomes more difficult to suppress.

At a revolutionary level, the continued integration of other materials may enable radically new applications in which entire systems are miniaturized and placed on single chips or wafers. The integration of polycrystalline Si with glass-based flat-panel displays will enable entire computer systems to become "part of" the display, rather than the other way around. The integration of Si logic and wireless transmitters/receivers with microelectromechanical devices fabricated by precision selective etching will enable a new generation of smart manipulators, chemical microlaboratories, sensors, displays, and perhaps even autonomous microrobots. The integration of organic materials with semiconductors will enable a new generation of smart chips that can sense and control biological functions. The integration of III-V and other optically active materials with Si will enable a new generation of "smart" optoelectronics and a new generation of "talkative" logic.

Conclusion

Semiconductors are, and will continue to be, the critical material enabling the manipulation and movement of information. Insofar as information is rapidly becoming the dominant commodity fueling world economic growth, semiconductors will likely continue to be one of our most important materials. Unlike during the past several decades, though, commercial rather than military markets will drive their further evolution and development. It is likely to be several decades before another

class of materials, perhaps biotechnology materials, in turn eclipses semiconductors in importance.

See also CHEMICALS, FINE; CHEMISTRY; COMMUNICATIONS TECHNOLOGY; COMPUTER HARDWARE; COMPUTER LINKAGE; COMPUTERS; COMPUTERS: SOFTWARE; DATA STORAGE; HIGH TECHNOLOGY; NANOTECHNOLOGY; PARASENSORY PHENOMENA; SCIENTIFIC BREAKTHROUGHS; SUPERCONDUCTORS; TELECOMMUNICATIONS.

BIBLIOGRAPHY

GILDER, GEORGE. *Telecosm.* New York: Simon & Schuster, 1996.

"The Incredible Shrinking Laboratory." *Science* 268 (1995): 26.

The National Technology Roadmap for Semiconductors. San Jose, CA: Semiconductor Industry Association, 1994.

STREETMAN, B. *Solid State Electronic Devices,* 3rd ed. Englewood Cliffs, NJ: Prentice Hall, 1990.

"Towards Point One." *Scientific American* (February 1995).

"U.S. Display Industry on the Edge." *IEEE Spectrum* 32 (1995): 62.

J. Y. Tsao

Sexual Behavior

The twentieth century has witnessed a transition from the dogmatic sexual Victorianism of the nineteenth century to a more tolerant sexual pluralism. Americans have had difficulty adjusting to this change. As a result, the United States has the highest rate in the Western world of almost every sexual problem, including HIV/AIDS, rape, teenage pregnancy, and child sexual abuse (Reiss, 1990). Despite this atrocious record, we are now finally learning how to better deal with our sexuality.

Premarital sexual behavior changed radically from the 1960s to the '90s. The trend is most clearly seen in teenage sexual behavior. In 1960 slightly over 20 percent of teenage young women fifteen to nineteen years old were not virgins; by 1970 the rate was 30 percent, and by 1980 it was about 50 percent (Hofferth, et al., 1987; Reiss, 1990, chapter 3). Since then, although the age at first coitus has dropped some, the overall percentage who are not virgins has changed very little. Women have made most of the changes in sexuality and are now close to men's nonvirginity rates. For nineteen-year-olds, by the late 1980s about 75 percent of women and 85 percent of men were nonvirginal (Sonenstein, et al., 1989; *Morbidity and Mortality Weekly Reports,* 1991).

TABLE 1 Elements From Which Inorganic Semiconductors Are Derived

II*	III	IV	V	VI
		C	N	
Mg	Al	Si	P	S
Zn	Ga	Ge	As	Se
Cd	In	Sn	Sb	Te
Hg				

*Roman numeral heads refer to sections of the Periodic Table.

Since the 1960s there have also been extraordinary changes in attitudes toward premarital sexuality. In June 1963 the National Opinion Research Center (NORC) at the University of Chicago administered a questionnaire to a representative national sample inquiring about their personal acceptance of premarital sexual intercourse in four types of relationships: engaged, love, strong affection, and relationships with no particular affection (Reiss, 1967). The results indicated that in 1963 less than 25 percent of adult Americans accepted premarital intercourse under any of the conditions asked about (Reiss, 1967, p. 27). Since this study was conducted just before the start of the "sexual revolution" that erupted later in the 1960s, it provides a base from which to judge what has changed.

In 1970 Albert Klassen and his colleagues posed a comparable set of questions in another NORC representative national sample. They found that over 55 percent of adult Americans replied that premarital intercourse was acceptable under one or more of their conditions (Klassen, et al., 1989, p. 18). In 1975 another national survey conducted by NORC reported that the percent of adults finding premarital intercourse to *not* be "always wrong" had risen to almost 70 percent (National Opinion Research Center, 1989, p. 769). Since that time this percentage has increased only a few percentage points.

The 1963–1975 change, from less than 25 percent to almost 70 percent accepting premarital intercourse under some condition, is phenomenal for such a short time period. When we combine these attitudinal changes with the changes mentioned above for sexual behavior, going from 20 percent of teenage females not being virginal in 1960 to 50 percent by 1980, we do indeed have strong evidence for the popular view that we underwent a sexual revolution starting in the late 1960s.

Western Europeans experienced similar changes at about the same time, but they did a far better job of adjusting. In America when young people first engage in sexual behavior, they often have many qualms and confusions about sexuality. We have relatively little societal preparation for making wise sexual choices, because so much effort is expended trying to get teens to avoid sex altogether. This inadequate preparation for sexual decision making is one of the major reasons for our very high rate of unwanted sexual outcomes, such as pregnancy, rape, HIV/AIDS, and child sexual abuse (Reiss, 1990).

Sexual choices are complicated further for women by the additional restraints our society imposes on female sexuality. The far lower rates of teenage pregnancy in every other Western country, with the same proportion of young people sexually active, shows clearly what a poor job we are doing in preparing our children for sexual choices (Reiss, 1990). Nevertheless, change is taking place. For example, in a representative national study of women it was found that the proportion of women who used a contraceptive method at first intercourse rose from about half in the 1970s to about two-thirds during the 1980s (Mosher and McNally, 1991). This is a very important change, because it shows increased protection at the very first coital experience and this helps prevent pregnancies that often occur during the start of new sexual relationships.

Increased use of condoms was a major part of the greater use of contraception. In national studies of teenage males it was found that youths aged seventeen to nineteen reported that condom use at last intercourse more than doubled, from less than one in four in 1979 to more than one in two in 1988 (Sonenstein, et al., 1989). Both the changes in contraception at first coitus and the increased condom usage indicates that sexuality is increasingly becoming something that we prepare for rather than an urge that we impulsively act upon.

This more positive approach to sexuality does not exclude abstinence, but neither does it view abstinence as the only moral choice. Starting about 1990 the New York City public schools and other school districts began forming programs encouraging condom use for sexually active teenagers. We finally recognized that vows of abstinence break far more often than do condoms. In this age of AIDS, it may be best to prepare young people for the choices they may make and try also to give them some ethical guidelines for carrying on appropriate consensual sexual relationships.

Another important factor in our move toward greater sexual tolerance has been the rise in gender equality since the 1960s. Women who have more economic and political power feel freer to assert their sexual rights and raise their daughters to do the same. We find today that 40 percent of condoms are bought by women and more women are letting their partners know that they will not have sex without a condom.

Old romantic myths slow our progress toward safer sexuality. There is a belief that if you are in love, then you can stop using condoms because a lover would not infect you with a sexually transmitted disease. But we now know that most of the women with AIDS, who became infected from heterosexual intercourse, were involved in monogamous, not casual, relationships (Reiss, 1990: chapter 5). Unfortunately for them, either their partners were not faithful, or in many cases, were former or current intravenous drug users. Love is not always a good indicator of safe sexuality.

There is a new sexual ethic that is sweeping the Western world, replacing dogmatic Victorianism with a *pluralistic* view of sexuality. Americans believe in pluralism in almost all areas of life. Our society accepts more than one religion, political party, or type of family. Still, sexual pluralism does not mean that absolutely anything goes; rather, pluralism stresses concern for one's sexual partner and rejects the use of force or exploitation in sexuality.

The new guidelines model the sexual relationship on friendship or other important relationships and they are based on three key values: Honesty, Equality, and Responsibility (HER) (Reiss, 1990, chapter 1). These HER principles are increasingly popular among youth in America and Europe. Women as well as men are more and more feeling that they have the right to seek such a HER relationship.

As women's rights grow into the twenty-first century, the support for this new sexual ethic will increase (Reiss, 1986, 1990). We see this blossoming gender equality in our country in the greater wage equality and greater political power of women. Furthermore, there are pressures on religious organizations to adopt more of a pluralistic stance on sexuality and to give women more rights in the churches and synagogues of America. Women now make up over one-half of our college students. In city after city, our sex education programs are gradually becoming more open to discussing the full meaning of sexuality without trying to suggest either that only abstinence or only straight sex is truly moral.

Today's major social trends support the view that HER sexual pluralism will flourish in the twenty-first century. The sexual revolution of the late 1960s was predicted by some social scientists (Reiss, 1960, pp. 235–250) and the societal changes noted above are a reasonable basis for now predicting that we will increasingly adopt the new HER sexual ethic (Reiss, 1990, chapter 10). It was the lack of such a guiding ethic that was a key factor in maintaining our high rates of sexual problems and so we can expect that those problems will gradually be brought under better control. Just as the Russians will look back at the late twentieth century and wonder how they could ever have endorsed communism for so long, we Americans will look back and wonder how we could ever

have endorsed the remnants of Victorianism for so long.

See also ABORTION; BEHAVIOR: SOCIAL CONSTRAINTS; CHILD ABUSE; FAMILY PATTERNS; FAMILY PLANNING; FAMILY VALUES; MORALS; SEXUAL CODES; SEXUAL HARASSMENT; SEXUAL LAWS; SEXUAL REPRODUCTION; SEXUAL REPRODUCTION: ARTIFICIAL MEANS; SOCIAL CONTROLS.

BIBLIOGRAPHY

HOFFERTH, SANDRA L.; KAHN, JOAN R.; and BALDWIN, WENDY. "Premarital Sexual Activity Among U.S. Teenage Women Over the Past Three Decades." *Family Planning Perspectives* 19 (1987): 46–53.

KLASSEN, ALBERT D.; WILLIAMS, COLIN J.; and LEVITT, EUGENE E. *Sex and Morality in the U.S.: An Empirical Enquiry Under the Auspices of the Kinsey Institute.* Middletown, CT: Wesleyan University Press, 1989.

MOSHER, WILLIAM D., and MCNALLY, JAMES W. "Contraceptive Use at First Premarital Intercourse: United States, 1965–1988." *Family Planning Perspectives* 23 (1991): 108–116.

National Opinion Research Center. *General Social Survey Trends Tape Marginals: 1972–1989.* Chicago: National Opinion Research Center, 1989.

"Premarital Sexual Experience Among Adolescent Women: U.S., 1970–1988." *Morbidity and Mortality Weekly Reports (MMWR)* 39 (1991): 929–932.

REISS, IRA L. *An End To Shame: Shaping Our Next Sexual Revolution.* Buffalo, NY: Prometheus Books, 1990.

_____. *Journey Into Sexuality: An Exploratory Voyage.* New York.: Prentice Hall, 1986.

_____. *Premarital Sexual Standards in America.* New York: Free Press, 1960.

_____. *The Social Context of Premarital Sexual Permissiveness.* New York: Holt, Rinehart, and Winston, 1967.

SONENSTEIN, FREYA L.; PLECK, JOSEPH H.; and KU, LEIGHTON C. "Sexual Activity, Condom Use, and AIDS Awareness Among Adolescent Males." *Family Planning Perspectives* 21 (1989): 152–158.

Ira L. Reiss

Sexual Codes

Every society regulates sexual relationships to protect the next generation, facilitate the proper passage of property to offspring, and avoid conflicts and maintain the moral and social order. Twice in human history sexual codes have experienced a global, root-wrenching revolution. We are in the midst of the second of these two revolutions. See Table 1 for a summary of this process.

TABLE 1. Evolutionary Stages of Self-Awareness, Human Consciousness and Sexual Codes

Time Line Era	Before 10,000 B.C. *Pre-axial* *Matrical/* *Matriarchal*	3000 B.C. to Recent Times *Axial* *Patriarchal*	1900s on into Future *Second Axial Period* *Contextual-* *Transformation*
Lifestyle	Nomadic Hunter/gatherer	City life Agriculture, technology, industrial revolution, science	Global village, GAIA Information/service
Fundamental Human Unit	Clan and family egalitar- ian council	Patrilineal hierarchical structures and rankings	Matrices and networks ever-changing, dynamic
Personal Identity	Emergence of tribal identity No true individuality	Male versus female identity Individual as distinct from the other, differ- ences contrasted	Global organism, GAIA Independently centered selves, contextually rooted
Style of Consciousness	Participation mystic	Objective, analytical, dis- criminating, lineal	Contextual, holistic dialogic
Relationship of Ego and Unconsciousness	Ego carried by or encompassed by larger psyche; no clear differentiation	Oppositional, confron- tational frontier between ego and unconscious psyche	Dialogical inter- connection. Each is context for the other, the birther of the other.
What Constitutes a Whole	The whole is collectively generated by the sum of its parts.	The whole is individual unit differentiated out of chaos.	Multiple levels of wholes; perpetual birthing of new wholes
Gender Relations	Gender equality	Patriarchy	Gender differences but equality
Pair-Bonding Unit	Egalitarian pair-bonding for childrearing	Patriarchal marriage to guarantee legitimacy of heirs to family property; arranged marriages yield romantic marriages based on couple choice.	Long- and short-term pair-bonding more for personal needs than for reproduction; marital households, LATs, cohabitation
Sexual Imagery	Fertility and its cycles	Phallic, genital, coital, male performance confirmed by female orgasm	Whole body sensuality, ecstasy, union with the cosmic self- transcendence; con- nectedness; oceanic awareness
Sexual Networks	Nonexclusive pair- bonding within the clan or tribe	Premarital virginity at least for female; sex limited to marriage; sexual exclusivity at least for wife (double standard); nuclear families	Intentional families with sexual intimacy allowed among a fluid network of friends
Religious Focus	Goddesses and gods	Patriarchal gods; male monotheism	???

TABLE 1. (CONTINUED)

Time Line Era	Before 10,000 B.C. *Pre-axial* *Matrical/* *Matriarchal*	3000 B.C. to Recent Times *Axial* *Patriarchal*	1900s on into Future *Second Axial Period* *Contextual-* *Transformation*
Style of Power and Source of Value	Power of participation and inclusion; value lies in participating in the collective.	Power over other or the situation; value lies in one's superiority.	Power of self-transcendence; centered self in multiple context
How Growth Is Characterized and Promoted	Natural growth; proliferation; nurturance and cyclicity	Linear progress; ascent; competition and mastery over; begetting upon another	Transformations rooted in context; multi directional, fluid, unexpected

The Pre-Axial Period

In our "pre-axial period," as philosopher Karl Jaspers labeled our prehistoric millennia, sexual codes were quite different from those that have prevailed for the past five thousand years or so. Our earliest ancestors lived in scattered, nomadic clans and tribes of twenty to thirty adults: male hunters of carrion and small game, female gatherers of fruits and roots, and a few young. Within the clans, men and women shared equal power. If anything, women held the edge, honored both as the source of life and as the teachers of the art of love, joining spiritual love of the heart with passionate, sexual love. Their spirit world echoed with gods and goddesses, priests and priestesses.

In that precarious world where each life lasted but a brief few decades, men and women were drawn to bond in pairs for mutual support and to rear their offspring. Within the clan, women formed supportive, cooperative networks to help them nurture the young, while the men were out competing in the hunt. Evidence of a prevailing pattern of sexual matings within and outside the pair bond among our nearest primate relations—the bonobo dwarf chimpanzees—and indeed of most mammals suggests that human pair-bonding in this long-forgotten era was not sexually exclusive. That characteristic of our sexual code did not emerge until males assumed social dominance some six thousand to ten thousand years ago, when men became concerned about the inheritance of their property through legitimate heirs born to a virgin bride or faithful wife.

The Axial Period

The world of our ancestors and our sexual codes entered a global, wrenching transition some ten thousand years ago, with the advent of agriculture, the domestication of dogs and horses, the smelting of metal plows and weapons, and the invention of the wheel. Males consolidated their new power, first in the manly art of war and physical strength, and then more subtly with the invention of writing and alphabets to record the wealth they accumulated in war and trade. Written legal codes centralized male power in political and business hierarchies. In ancient Sumer, Egypt, Babylon, Greece, and Rome, males increasingly celebrated the rational and the analytical, scientific knowledge that allowed them to understand, manipulate, and, yes, exploit the natural world. Male gods moved to the fore as goddesses faded, and eventually a single, male God was revealed by male prophets in Judaism, Christianity, and Islam.

The new sexual codes that emerged in this axial period endorsed highly defined, rigid gender roles and male/female stereotypes, with many strong socially imposed roles and rules for male/female relationships. Sex was clearly defined and measured in male terms as a genital activity with coitus resulting in offspring. Female sexuality and needs were ignored—or simply denied. In this patriarchal, hierarchical world, rational, analytical males were superior to emotional, passionate females, who were obviously designed by God for motherhood and to be obedient to their men and cater to male needs. Sexual exclusivity was important, much more so for females than males. Sex—and women—posed a danger to male dominance, and so sexual activity was hedged in by sex-negative attitudes, by taboos on nudity, fear of the body, emotions, and senses.

Toward a Second Axial Period: Sexual Codes in Transition

Many observers of the human story in fields as diverse as theology, history, sociobiology, feminist studies, sociology, sexology, anthropology, and chaos theory, have independently suggested that human culture is already in transition to a new societal structure and value system. Thirty years ago, anthropologist Margaret Mead described America as a "pre-figurative culture," a culture whose patriarchal myths and archetypes handed down from biblical times are no longer meaningful or supportive of the male-defined sexual codes of the axial period.

The power of our traditional myths and archetypes has faded because Copernicus, Galileo, Darwin, and Einstein have pushed us out of the ancient fixed worldview with its unchanging hierarchy of the Great Chain of Being into a world of process and evolution. Ever accelerating, radical changes in our social environment have in this century made it impossible for us to deny that we are moving into a new environment that will require a new sexual code. Our life expectancy has doubled from forty-seven years in the 1900s to close to eighty; the United States is graying and those over age one hundred are our fastest-growing group. Increased leisure, mobility, an information superhighway that by the year 2000 will connect 200 million people, reliable and safe contraceptives, reproductive technologies that separate sex and reproduction, smaller families with many couples opting for no children, challenges to organized religion and its authority over sexual behavior, and television are part of this new environment. Around the world, but most evident in the Euro-American scene, women are entering men's domains, the salaried workforce, dealing with men on their own level, and regaining some of the power they enjoyed in the pre-axial era. The emergence of feminism has brought new challenges to the phallocentric, coital male model of sex and a growing shift to a holistic model that emphasizes sensual pleasure and transcendence as well as orgasm—with orgasm not limited to coital penetration.

The value of pair-bonding, often long-term despite the availability of easy divorce and our in-creasing life expectancy, will continue to hold priority in our emotions and sexual code. Whether this pair-bonding will be dominated by one-household marital bonding or by adults living alone together (LAT) and maintaining two households while in a long-term intimate relationship, remains to be seen. Whether this pair-bonding will be expressed more often in a series of sexually exclusive monogamies or in a flexible, more or less sexually open, long-term, even lifelong pair-bonding, likewise remains to be seen. More than likely, as blood kinships shrink in the nomadic life of the 1990s and beyond, their role in supporting a stable and dynamic society will be increasingly replaced by intentional families created by pair-bonding individuals to accept and include emotional and sexual intimacies within a fluid matrix of more or less intimate friendships that increasingly cuts across the spectrum of gender orientations.

The sexual codes of the future are already breaking out of the dichotomies and clear distinctions that have dominated our axial cultures. The rigidity of the male/female sexual dichotomy, in which physicians routinely performed surgery to assign the roughly 4 percent of babies born with hermaphrodite and pseudohermaphrodite status to either the male or female sex, is being challenged by the affected individuals and their advocates who increasingly demand to be left in their intersex status and accepted as such (Fausto-Sterling, 1993). More obvious in recent decades has been the social and legal recognition of the gender-orientation spectrum of gay, straight, and all shades in-between. Similarly, we are experiencing an increasing fluidity in our gender role behaviors, the near infinite varied spectrum of masculine-androgynous-feminine (butch-androgynous-fem in the gay culture), even as neurobiologists identify anatomical and physiological differences in the brains of males and females.

At this point in human history, we have only faint hints of how the new sexual code will emerge and what its character will be. We can hope that it will preserve the best of what humans have achieved in the pre-axial and axial periods—the benefits those cultures have brought us—and incorporate these into the new sexual code.

See also ABORTION; BEHAVIOR: SOCIAL CONSTRAINTS; CHILD ABUSE; FAMILY PATTERNS; FAMILY PLANNING; FAMILY VALUES; GENETICS; MORALS; SEXUAL BEHAVIOR; SEXUAL LAWS; SEXUAL REPRODUCTION: ARTIFICIAL MEANS; SOCIAL CONTROLS; WOMEN'S MOVEMENT; WOMEN'S RIGHTS.

BIBLIOGRAPHY

ABRAHAM, RALPH. *Chaos, Gaia, Eros.* San Francisco: HarperCollins, 1994.

CHAPELLE, DELORES LA. *Sacred Land, Sacred Sex, Rapture of the Deep.* Silverton, CO: Finn Hill Arts, 1988.

COUSINS, EWERT. "Male-Female Aspects of the Trinity in Christian Mysticism." In *Sexual Archetypes: East and West,* ed., Bina Gupta. New York: Paragon, 1987, pp. 37–50.

FAUSTO-STERLING, ANNE. "The Five Sexes: Why Male and Female Are Not Enough." *The Sciences* (March–April 1993): 20–24.

FRANCOEUR, ROBERT T. *Becoming a Sexual Person.* New York: John Wiley & Sons, 1982, pp. 473–476, 679–692.

_____. *Hot and Cool Sex: Cultures in Conflict.* New York: Harcourt Brace & Jovanovich, 1974.

HADDON, GENIA PAULI. *Uniting Sex, Self, and Spirit.* Scotland, CT: Plus Publications, 1993.

JASPERS, KARL. *The Origin and Goal of History.* New Haven, CT: Yale University Press, 1953.

OGDEN, GINA. *Women Who Love Sex.* New York: Simon & Schuster/Pocket Books, 1994.

Robert T. Francoeur

Sexual Harassment

Unwanted sexual attention has long been an indignity suffered by less powerful groups, especially women and children. Traditionally the most visible and frequent abuse has involved men harassing women. But with a greater diversity of people in power in the workplace, corporations are finding that men can also harass other men in this way; or women in positions of power can harass men; or women can harass other women. The key feature in any form of sexual harassment is unwanted sexual attention.

In the United States since 1980, the personal indignity of being subjected to unwanted sexual attention at work has been addressed by a number of legal steps. These offenses now are legally actionable. Sexual harassment complaints filed with state and federal governments rose from 6,892 in 1991 to 12,537 in 1993. Over the same period, compensation awards rose from $7.1 million to $25.7 million. Sexual and gender harassment, no matter how measured, now is viewed by the courts as a major form of employment discrimination. By 1994 the courts recognized two basic types of sexual harassment: quid pro quo involving explicit threats of "Do this or else," and a less-extreme form involving a hostile or abusive work environment.

In 1980 the U.S. Equal Employment Opportunity Commission (EEOC) regulations defined harassment in this way: "Unwelcome sexual advances, requests for sexual favors, and other verbal or physical conduct of a sexual nature constitute harassment when (1) submission to such conduct is made either explicitly or implicitly a term or condition of an individual's employment, (2) submission to or rejection of such conduct by an individual is used as the basis for employment decisions affecting such individual, or (3) such conduct has the purpose or effect of unreasonably interfering with an individual's work performance or creating an intimidating, hostile, or offensive working environment" (29 C.F.R. #1604.11). Then in 1986 the Supreme Court ruled in *Meritor Savings Bank, FSB* v. *Vinson* that sexual harassment constituted an act of sexual discrimination.

The quid pro quo aspects of sexual harassment (items 1 and 2 above) are relatively clear. But establishing that a hostile environment constitutes sexual harassment has been more controversial. In 1993 the EEOC proposed guidelines indicating that a hostile environment can occur in the form of (1) "epithets, slurs, negative stereotyping, or threatening, intimidating, or hostile acts" (1609.1); or (2) "written or graphic material that denigrates or shows hostility or aversion on the employers's premises or circulated in the workplace" (1609.1).

Building on Title VII of the Civil Rights Act of 1964, the Supreme Court also ruled, in *Harris* v. *Forklift Systems, Inc.* (1993) that sexual harassment included not only unwanted explicit sexual behavior but *gender harassment or harassment of women in general* as well. The rationale is that sex discrimination laws preclude unequal treatment based on sex. Sexually harassing work environments also can be created by sex-based comments related to women's bodies and by allowing expression of supposed intellectual or other hostile differences between the sexes.

Establishing the existence of a hostile sexual or gender environment is difficult. The Supreme Court required that several criteria be met (*Meritor Savings,* 1986). Specific circumstances surrounding each case must be examined to verify that the conduct is persistent, severe, physically threatening or humiliating, and actually interferes with work performance.

Moreover, an assessment must be made as to whether the behavior would be considered "reasonable" in the given circumstances. While different work environments (e.g., road crews as contrasted with a bank office) are likely to produce different standards, these variations are compounded and further complicated by the 1991 ruling in *Ellison* v. *Brady*. That case maintained that determinations of sexual or gender harassment could be ascertained by a "reasonable woman" (rather than a "reasonable man") standard.

Subsequently EEOC proposed in 1993 to expand the "reasonable person" standard to include "consideration of the perspective of persons of the alleged victim's race, color, religion, gender, national origin, age, or disability" (1609 1). The Supreme Court ruling in the 1993 *Harris* case reaffirmed that women can see harm in cases where men will see only offensive behavior. In this case the court also ruled that it was not necessary to demonstrate psychological injury or a quid pro quo situation in order to show that sexual or gender harassment had occurred.

Who is responsible whenever such harassment occurs? The EEOC has consistently affirmed that it is employers who are responsible for the sexual and gender harassment perpetrated by their representatives. Such responsibility has been extended since the 1980s to include harassment by coworkers and even by nonemployees.

Key questions in determining responsibility include whether the employer can be considered to have known or should have known what was happening, and whether supervisors with control over the situation were acting as the employer's agent. Employers can protect themselves by (1) having an explicit policy against sexual harassment and (2) by establishing readily available procedures for victims to lodge and pursue remedy for complaints of harassment.

As the diversity of the workforce expands, harassment of all forms, whether racial, ethnic, sexual, gender, or other, although potentially omnipresent, will be less tolerated. The trend is toward enforcing existing laws on such matters and—in a preventive mode—encouraging greater sensitivity on all fronts.

See also BEHAVIOR: SOCIAL CONSTRAINTS; CHILD ABUSE; FAMILY PATTERNS; FAMILY PROBLEMS; FAMILY VALUES; POVERTY, FEMINIZATION OF; SEXUAL CODES; SEXUAL LAWS; WOMEN'S MOVEMENT; WOMEN'S RIGHTS.

BIBLIOGRAPHY

BAXTER, RALPH H. *Sexual Harassment in the Workplace*. New York: Executive Enterprises Publications, 1989.

RUSSELL, DIANE E. *Sexual Exploitation*. Thousand Oaks, CA: Sage Publications, 1984.

WEBB, SUSAN L. *Step Forward: Sexual Harassment in the Workplace—What You Need to Know*. New York: MasterMedia Ltd., 1991.

Rita Mae Kelly

Sexual Laws

Sexual morality has undergone radical transformation. Statutory principles that reflect permissible conduct and proscribe or prohibit unacceptable behavior have become much more permissive and enforcement attitudes toward them have been relaxed. It seems that acceptable sexual behavior is becoming more a health than a moral issue. This reflects changed behavior of a sort that undermines the family and disrupts the community.

Abortions used to be obtained in desperate circumstances in back alleys or by going abroad. Now abortions are openly and freely available in the United States. Previously limited to a few instances involving lifesaving or truly grievous situations (rape, incest, etc.), abortion now is available virtually on demand, and it is provided at taxpayer expense for those who cannot afford it. Teen abortion is available, even without parental notification in some jurisdictions. Not surprisingly, the number performed jumped threefold from 605,000 in 1972 to 1,700,000 in 1991.

Permissive use of "quick-fix" abortifacients formerly were forbidden or severely restricted in use. Easy-to-use abortion pills like RU-486, already approved for general use abroad, are imminent in the United States.

Not so many years ago, society frowned on and even forbid the general distribution of contraceptives. Now contraceptives are out from under the counter, openly advertised on television, and vending is even mandated in certain locations. Contraceptives, once not sold to minors, are given to them free at schools or by government workers—sometimes against the wishes of parents or guardians. Sexual activity among minors, instead of being discouraged, is aided and abetted by providing them with contraceptives.

Statutory rape laws, intended to protect minors, are largely ignored. Date rape has become a boomlet. Gang rapes are shrugged off as "wilding," or "just boys on a spree," or by asserting "boys will be boys."

Teen pregnancy, once scorned, now soars. "Shotgun weddings," forced by irate parents, seldom are seen anymore. Children are encouraged to come to school with their babies. The United States leads all other advanced nations in teen pregnancy. Many teenage fathers escape responsibility for their role and ignore child-support obligations, because government lends little effort to seeing that these responsibilities are met. Teen pregnancy as a result is heavily supported by taxpayers. The burdens imposed on society by teen families cost government $21 billion in 1989. The problem has grown worse since then.

Laws against fornication—sex outside wedlock—instead of being enforced are, for all practical purposes, ignored. "Living in sin," cohabitation, trial marriages, and the like are not ostracized as they once were. Unwanted offspring resulting from these liaisons, likely as not, are aborted or sometimes even murdered. Irresponsible fathers slink away from their responsibilities to support children and family all too easily.

Illegitimate children born outside wedlock increased nearly eightfold between 1950 and 1991 (rising from 146,000 to 1,151,000). Three of every 10 children born in the United States (28 percent) were born to unwed mothers during 1991, and the proportion may rise to 40 percent by 2000. Two out of every three babies (68 percent) born to African-American mothers in 1991 were illegitimate. Depressingly, more African-American girls drop out of high school to have a baby than graduate from college.

Standards that once proscribed sodomy, sexual perversion, unnatural sex acts, and so on are generally ignored or being repealed. Gay rights to serve in the military are being pursued against objections of most military leaders. Controversies swirl around prescribed school readings and curricula intended to provide understanding and otherwise legitimize homosexuality and gay marriages.

Prostitution is legal in a few jurisdictions. More likely, it is tolerated in so-called red light areas, "combat zones," or tenderloin districts. In a few jurisdictions brothels are state-sanctioned (designated areas in Nevada, Amsterdam, Portugal, and elsewhere).

AIDS victims in the United States are not quarantined, as one might expect for any death-dealing contagious disease. AIDS victims have become today's Typhoid Marys, with the exception that carriers are left free to inflict their deadly disease on others. In the past child diseases that rarely resulted in death—measles, chicken pox, mumps, and whooping cough—required strict quarantine, including posting of residences to protect the unwary from these communicable diseases. By 1989, AIDS had become the eleventh largest killer disease in the United States, taking 22,675 lives in 1992. Yet, AIDS victims' privacy is invoked to avoid quarantining, testing, or other controls.

Sexually transmitted diseases, once scorned, now are medically treated. This is done at the public's expense, at least in cases where disease carriers are too poor to afford treatment on their own.

Suggestive lingerie, previously relegated to the back pages of tawdry pulp-paper magazines, has gone mainstream. Frederick's of Hollywood, Victoria's Secret, even the Limited have invaded the shopping malls with upscale and somewhat subdued offerings.

Topless bathing also has come a long way. Males, as recently as 1936, were convicted of indecent exposure for failing to cover up their tops in public. String bikinis are permitted on many beaches, although banned from others. Nude bathing beaches proliferate (Santa Cruz, Marin, and many other counties).

Nudity also has hit Main Street, or at least the red light district. Topless and bottomless bars abound. There are even "adult" (topless) car washes; maid services; and bus caravans that take erotic shows to the countryside (Prague). Traditional burlesque houses fight back, with their trade association, the Exotic Dancers League, opposing taking ecdysiastic arts away from their turf.

Pornography, vigorously curbed not so many years ago, is rampant as freedom of speech prevails over censorship. We've come a long way from the suggestive nudity of gossamer-clad *Esquire* magazine pin-ups by Vargas to the explicit *Playboy* magazine centerfolds. Madonna's professional perversions, shocking to an earlier generation, prevail. Explicit sex in triple-X-rated movies are everywhere. NC-17 ratings liberalize sex and violence standards to lower levels for children under seventeen years of age. The at-home porn movies have also reached new levels. Outlawed low-tech 8-mm underground or home-produced movies have given way to out-in-the-open commercial adult videocassettes. Satellite broadcasters also assault the airwaves with X-rated movies. Some jurisdictions fight back. Alabama, for example, has sought extradition of businesspersons responsible for such broadcasts.

All communications technologies are being invaded. There is porn on FAX and in cyberspace. Pay-per-call erotic telephone talk lines using 1-900 numbers have cropped up. Some of them originate in countries with permissive laws, thus skirting domestic regulation.

Dr. Joyce Brothers, among others, has peddled no-holds-barred explicit titillating call-in sex problems over her radio show. Sleazy and sensational talk shows that exploit every and any imaginable sexual escapade punctuate daytime television.

Explicit lyrics in music, attacked by then-Senator Al Gore's wife, Tipper Gore, struck a responsive chord. But freedom of expression prevails. Lewd and raunchy bumper stickers proliferate. Some states such as South Carolina, Florida, and Georgia outlaw them. Books of dubious taste or sexual explicitness once were regularly summarily banned in many jurisdictions. "Banned in Boston" became a code word for tough smut control. In some instances such literature has been prescribed as mandatory reading—including texts supporting understanding of gay couples' rights to adopt children—despite parental protests.

Porn performers have been allowed to acquire star status. In earlier times, they were tracked down and convicted of lewd performances. In Italy, female porn stars have been elected to parliament and have formed their own political party: the Party of Love.

What comes into perspective from this litany of licentiousness is that basic moral principles have been diminished and degraded by permissiveness. Morals are rooted in time. The future holds a return to moral, religious, ethical, and philosophical principles that both prescribe and proscribe. The pendulum of moral restraint has been allowed to swing too far toward the permissive side. The swing back will not go to Victorian extremes, but to guidelines constantly striving to keep sexual behavior within respecable bounds.

See also ABORTION; CRIME, NONVIOLENT; SEXUAL BEHAVIOR; SEXUAL CODES; SEXUAL REPRODUCTION.

BIBLIOGRAPHY

BENNETT, WILLIAM J. *The De-Valuing of America: The Fight for Our Culture and Our Children*. New York: Simon & Schuster, 1992.

DAVIS, NANETTE J. *Prostitution: An International Handbook on Trends, Problems, and Policies*. Westport, CT: Greenwood Press, 1993.

HIBBERT, CHRISTOPHER. *The Roots of Evil: A Social History of Crime and Punishment*. New York: Little, Brown, 1968.

HUGHES, ROBERT. *Culture of Complaint: The Fraying of America*. New York: Oxford University Press, 1993.

TREBACH, ARNOLD S. *The Great Drug War: And Radical Proposals that Could Make America Safe Again*. New York: Macmillan, 1987.

Graham T. T. Molitor

Sexual Reproduction

The future of human birth will be a study in contradictions. Immense effort will be exerted to find the perfect contraceptive for the disenfranchised (young, poor, or Third World women) and better ways for the privileged (older, wealthier women in industrialized nations) to conceive. Political, economic, environmental, and social factors will influence the future of reproduction as biological screening and manipulative techniques become more widely used to determine the gender, health, and personal characteristics of future children.

Conception

New techniques involving hormonal stimulation of egg production, fertilization of eggs inside and outside the body, extracting sperm directly from the epididymis, and genetic cloning will impact conception. New laboratory techniques for fertilization outside of the body include the use of lasers to penetrate the outer layer of an egg so that sperm can be deposited directly into its interior to better the chances of fertilization. Laboratory conception also allows for the elimination of toxic substances, the preselection of egg and sperm for desired characteristics, and genetic alterations of selected cells.

Pregnancy

Medical science, specifically the science of in-vitro fertilization, is moving toward the development of an artificial womb. The creation of this technology and its widespread use, initially perhaps limited to applications involving farm animals, could dramatically alter our society's views about conception, pregnancy, abortion, and childbirth. Parents of the future may be able to conceive, carry a pregnancy to term, and deliver without any of the discomfort or risk of carrying a pregnancy in their bodies or even without ever having sexual intercourse.

Before the year 2000, the Human Genome Initiative Project will provide a detailed genetic map of all human genes. Coupled with our ability to correct some genetic anomalies during pregnancy, this development will make diagnosis of fetal problems an extremely important part of pregnancy. Ultrasonic scanning, blood sampling of both parents prior to or following conception, amniocentesis (sampling the amniotic fluid that surrounds the fetus for genetic analysis), and chorionic villi biopsy (sampling the placental tissue) are techniques already being used to determine fetal health. Each technique carries a small risk to both the mother and fetus. Sampling of maternal blood and some form of computer-enhanced scanning to determine fetal defects are the only methods likely to move out of the laboratory and into the home of the future for routine use.

Sex Preselection

Humans have always shown interest in the sex of fetuses and have devised some interesting ways of trying to effect the outcome of fertilization. Wearing a hat during intercourse, eating chocolate, douching with vinegar, and laboratory separation of X- and Y-bearing sperm are all techniques that have been used to predetermine sex. In a world of shrinking resources people who wish to limit births may also wish to select the sex of the children born. In China, infanticide of female infants has become a way of assuring a male child in a society that only allows one child per couple. In India, prenatal diagnosis of sex has been outlawed, except to diagnose and prevent sex-linked genetic anomalies, because of the rise in abortions of female fetuses. If societies continue to prize males over females, sex preselection will continue to rise, especially for first-born children.

Fetal Health

While experts research and argue the results of collected data comparing the effects of fetal exposure to alcohol, crack cocaine, or environmental pollutants, the medical and legal professions and mothers are fighting in and out of court about the rights of mother and fetus. Can a woman drink any alcohol, ingest any drugs, or ignore/refuse testing and intervention procedures that could verify fetal anomalies or potentially prevent fetal damage or death? The current recommendations of the American Medical Association are in favor of informed decision making by the pregnant woman. The spread of new research, diagnostic techniques, and prenatal intervention strategies are likely to strain current recommendations. Pregnant women may find their traditional civil rights becoming more limited in the next century.

How will our children's children define an anomaly or defect as it relates to their children? Will a predisposition to obesity, proneness to drinking too much, being a female—or having brown eyes—qualify as a defect? Preimplantation diagnosis is being used to test two-day-old embryos fertilized in a laboratory petri dish for genetic defects like cystic fibrosis. In the future we will be able to test for the entire range of genetically preprogrammed characteristics and intervene to clone or split the cells of the embryos that possess all or most of the desired characteristics and discard or alter the undesirable ones.

For those couples who still develop a pregnancy through sexual intercourse and therefore do not have access to preimplantation diagnosis, other genetic screening and correction techniques will be available. Genetic defects will be corrected through stem-cell transplants that involve the transplantation of healthy stem-cells from one fetus to another or from the fetus's parents into the fetus. Another method will be gene therapy. This technique involves the removal of diseased stem-cells from the fetus's bloodstream, transferring healthy genes into them, and reinjecting them into the fetus.

Fetal surgery began with operations to implant shunts or tubes to drain excess fluid from fetal bladders or brain cavities. Recent surgeries include open-womb procedures to correct physical defects. In the future, fetal surgery may be performed to correct a cleft palate or facial abnormalities. One advantage of fetal surgery is that the fetus heals without scars. Another exciting aspect of fetal surgery is that one fetus will not reject the cells of another fetus. This opens the possibility of cell and organ transplants to correct a multitude of problems before birth that would require risky procedures like bone marrow transplant later in life.

Childbirth

Traditional vaginal delivery is likely to continue to be the norm for most women everywhere. Advances in prenatal care and rising concerns about parental involvement in birthing are leading to an increase in the use of birthing chairs and childbirth techniques such as the Lamaze or Leboyer methods, which involve less use of anesthesia and episiotomy. Caesarian births, delivery through an incision in the abdominal wall, have increased and are likely to continue increasing in the United States for several reasons, including better fetal monitoring techniques, less willingness on the part of physicians and parents to risk complications during childbirth, and increasing medical malpractice liability.

The current trend is for delivery to take place in a special birthing center or clinic connected to or in a hospital. In the future these centers will be free-standing facilities staffed by certified nurse midwives. Because of their ties to hospitals, the centers will provide a homelike atmosphere that will welcome the entire family into the birth process without sacrificing the availability of technical and emergency support that is absent in home delivery.

Motherhood

The future of motherhood will be paradoxical. Teens and other poor or uneducated women will be pressured to avoid motherhood. Successful women in their thirties and forties, even post-menopausal women will use extraordinarily expensive technological measures to become mothers. Mothers with low incomes will be less likely to live in traditional nuclear families and more likely be unmarried, divorced, or single. The result will be some hardships placed on them and their children.

Genetic preselection may limit the number of women available to become mothers and induce competition for them between men who hold to established family ideals. This competition will elevate the traditional female roles of childbearing and motherhood.

See also ABORTION; BEHAVIOR: SOCIAL CONSTRAINTS; CHILD ABUSE; FAMILY PATTERNS; FAMILY PLANNING; FAMILY VALUES; GENETICS; GENETIC TECHNOLOGIES; MORALS; SEXUAL BEHAVIOR; SEXUAL CODES; SEXUAL REPRODUCTION: ARTIFICIAL MEANS; SOCIAL CONTROLS.

BIBLIOGRAPHY

COLE, HELENE M. "Legal Interventions During Pregnancy." *Journal of The American Medical Association,* 264/20 (November 28, 1990): 2663–2670.
DURAND, MARK A. "The Safety of Home Birth: The Farm Study." *American Journal of Public Health* 82/3 (March 1992): 450–453.
FRANCOEUR, ROBERT T. *Becoming a Sexual Person.* New York: Macmillan, 1991.
SACHS, BENJAMIN P., et. al. "Home Monitoring of Uterine Activity, Does It Prevent Prematurity?" *New England Journal of Medicine* 325/19 (November 7, 1991): 1374–1377.
"Saving Female Babies." *Nature* (October 17, 1991).
"Surgery Before Birth." *Discover* (February 1991).

Peter Anderson

Sexual Reproduction: Artificial Means

Louise Brown, born July 25, 1978, in England, became the first test-tube baby in the world. In 1991, Arlette Schwitzer had four of her daughter's fertilized eggs transferred to her and gave birth to her own twin grandchildren. In 1992, Josie Mosby Mitchell, fifty-two years old and in menopause, conceived a child with a donor egg fertilized *in vitro* with the sperm of her second husband. Slowly humans are taking control over their reproductive process and radically altering attitudes toward sex and sexuality. Sexual intercourse is no longer an essential part of reproduction, although it will certainly continue to be practiced by most people. Starting in the 1970s, new reproductive technologies began to proliferate. Artificial insemination, egg donation, artificial embryonation, surrogate motherhood, embryo adoption, *in vitro* fertilization (IVF), embryo freezing, and artificial wombs are in various stages of research, development, and utilization. Unlike previous reproductive methods, the new technologies involve a third, and sometimes a fourth or fifth party, in the act of conception and birthing.

Over 10 percent of the 3.5 million infertile couples in the United States, one in six couples, are turning to these new assisted reproductive technologies. The numbers are expected to grow. Growing compromises of fertility by environmental toxins, radiation, stress, drugs, and so forth assure this trend. Concerns over sexually transmitted diseases, such as AIDS, and the expanding possibilities of genetic selection further assure that reproduction technologies are here to stay. They offer hope to the infertile and better children for everyone.

Flash Forward to 2020

A six-billion-dollar sex industry prevails where fertility clinics market parts—wombs, ovaries, fallopian tubes, eggs, sperm—for reproductive purposes. Fertility clinics have expanded their market beyond infertile couples, to individuals at risk from toxins, menopausal women, individuals with genetic diseases, fertile career women, and men who want children.

Technology has leaped forward. Intricate microsurgery and laser surgery repair damage to defective reproductive organs. Infertile women can have surgery to unblock, repair, or replace fallopian tubes with donor transplants or artificial tubes. Ovary transplants from older menopausal women to young infertile women are now common. Ovarian transplants into younger women allow their physiological and hormonal activities to "turn them on" for successful child bearing. For infertile men, testicle transplants and the use of new drugs to enhance sperm counts are increasingly popular.

The assisted reproduction technologies of 2020 are a bit less popular than traditional birth methods. The reason? They add other human beings to the "creation equation" and raise an array of ethical and legal concerns.

Artificial insemination, the simplest method, is performed in the privacy of one's home using husband or donor sperm. Today, there is a 70 percent fertilization success rate after only one or two treatments, up from the 57 percent success rate involving two to nine treatments in the early 1990s. A controversial debate swirls around insurance payment for such procedures. People confidently use mail-order sperm banks that screen donor sperm for genetic defects, diseases, and gender. Extensive donor health histories are available upon request, and catalogs from the sperm banks describe each donor's age, blood type, family background, physical characteristics, and education.

Operations for egg donations are performed by doctors, followed by artificial insemination. Whenever possible, *in vivo* (in the body) fertilization is recommended by doctors.

Instead of the three-day embryo development phase practiced years ago in a "petri dish," many doctors in the year 2020 place the sperm cells and egg together for only one hour and then transfer them to the uterus, where a new procedure allows fertilization to take place within the mother's body.

Improvements in sperm analysis and laser technology make the *in vitro* fertilization (IVF) process easy and reduce the number of sperm needed from a donor to one high-quality sperm. Active sperm cells are separated from less active sperm cells to ensure that only healthy sperm fertilize eggs. Lasers are used to test sperm for motility, to drag a quality sperm over to an egg where a convenient hole has been cut in the membrane for the sperm to enter and seed it. It is also possible to use lasers to cut portions of the zona pellucida, a protective membrane around the egg that toughens with age, to permit the growing embryo to "hatch" and grow in the uterus. Lasers also help doctors to produce twins or triplets. The doctor can divide an embryo surgically in halves or thirds before transferring the embryos to the mother's uterus. Doctors may need to repeat the IVF procedure four times for pregnancy to occur in 70 percent of the patients. Today—December 10, 2020—40 percent of the recipients undergoing IVF take a baby to term in the United States, a 25 percent increase from 1992.

Couples with known histories of genetic disorders combine IVF with gene therapy. The missing gene that is absent from the DNA sequence is inserted into the embryo before the embryo is transferred to the recipient's uterus. The procedure can replace the gene for eighty known genetic defects, twenty times the capability of 1993, when only cys-

tic fibrosis, hemophilia, Duchenne muscular dystrophy, and Tay-Sachs disease could be corrected.

Cryobanks advertise nationally, offering to preserve eggs, sperm, and embryos (fertilized eggs). Embryo and sperm storage is now safe for an indefinite period. However, because of a few cases of chromosome losses in human oocytes, the research community is doubling its efforts to preserve eggs effectively. Laws allow only six pregnancies per donor in a specified geographic location to thwart the disadvantages of incest among children created through artificial insemination by the same or closely related donors. Consequently, cryogenic banks now screen and store a wide genetic pool of donors.

People freeze and store their eggs, sperm, and embryos as insurance for a future with children. Freezing eggs or embryos collected in an egg donation and artificial embryonation operation protects women against excessive operations should the first or second attempt at pregnancy fail. Having frozen embryos allows a woman/surrogate to receive an embryo when the conditions are best for an embryo to attach itself to the uterine wall and to grow. Finally, sperm, eggs, or embryos produced at the height of one's reproductive years can be stored for family planning. People are thus better able to pace the birth of their children.

More couples and single parents are choosing to have children later in life and some after menopause. Discovery that aging eggs, not aging wombs, cause infertility among older women gives women the flexibility to have children using young-donor oocytes or their own oocytes collected and frozen when they were younger.

New advances in embryo-transfer techniques also enhance the embryo survival rate once an embryo is implanted in the uterus. No longer are five or six embryos implanted in a uterus to assure that at least one embryo sticks to the uterus and grows; instead, only one or two embryo implants are needed for a successful birth. A better quality-control system for the cultural fluids used in the petri dish and improved egg-ripening techniques contribute to the success rate. The procedure reduces the danger of multiple births and genetic defects.

For years, the cryobanks have provided low storage rates to military personnel likely to participate in dangerous assignments. One situation drew national attention recently when a female gave birth to her own twin. Twenty-five years ago, her mother had twin embryos through IVF. One female twin was transferred to the mother's uterus and brought to term while the other was frozen and stored.

Upon learning that possible combat duty was in her future, the first twin had her twin sister thawed, placed into her uterus, and gave birth to her.

As in any generation, there are aspects of sexual reproduction that pose ethical and legal controversies. Four issues—surrogacy, the rights of embryos, cloning, and male pregnancy—continue to generate serious debate.

Surrogacy issues draw national attention. Most U.S. states now follow the New York 1993 precedent that bans commercial surrogacy and limits payment of $10,000 for the surrogates and around $6,000 for the surrogate entrepreneurs who locate and screen them. Beneficiary payment of medical expenses is still permitted. Although the laws in most states eliminate the concern over child selling, they do little to prevent women from being turned into living incubators with controls placed on their sexual behavior, cigarette smoking, and food and alcoholic intake. Surrogate rights to privacy and freedom of choice are questioned. The issue is inflamed as Third World women are exploited as commercial surrogates, and by obsessive single men and fertile women (i.e., busy executives, models, etc.) who choose the surrogacy option, and to prevent women from being devalued and viewed as "cows." Governments impose strict screening, inspection, and controls on surrogates.

Debate over who is the child's mother also continues to fester. Is the mother the woman who bears the child or the woman who provides its genes? The courts have given the child to the genetic mother, but controversies over surrogate visitation rights continue. With the recent creation of a human artificial womb, the issue of surrogacy may slowly be put to rest.

Another issue, the rights of frozen embryos, poses serious questions. Who is responsible for an embryo if the couple dies? Some state courts favor giving responsibility to the next of kin or honoring a living will. A more difficult question is whether a frozen embryo has a right to be born? For inheritance purposes, would a frozen embryo be considered an additional heir? The recent NASA proposal to send the frozen embryos of many species into space raises similar questions. The human embryos are to be transferred to female astronauts once a colony has been established on another planet. Concern over the risk to the astronauts as well as the legal rights of the embryo are part of the heated debate.

The third issue relates to research in cloning. Scientists, using microsurgical techniques, remove the nuclei from an embryonic cell and replace it with the cell or genetic material (DNA) of another human. After implanting the new embryo into a recipient's uterus, an exact duplicate of the human being, a clone, is produced. Though cloning often is used in the cattle and dairy industry, fear over attempts to create a master race and the legal implications and consequences, have slowed human applications.

Finally, the issue of male pregnancy is a common subject of "virtual reality" talk shows. In the late twentieth century, a George Washington University Medical School doctor "fertilized a chimpanzee egg *in vitro* with chimpanzee sperm, implanted it in the abdomen of a male chimpanzee, later delivering a healthy baby chimp through a Caesarian section" (Andrews, 1984, page 261). In 2019, Australian scientists combined the technique with advances in artificial womb technology to produce a successful male pregnancy.

See also ABORTION; FAMILY PLANNING; GENETIC ENGINEERING; GENETICS; GENETIC TECHNOLOGIES; SEXUAL BEHAVIOR; SEXUAL CODES; SEXUAL REPRODUCTION; WOMEN'S MOVEMENT.

BIBLIOGRAPHY

ANDREWS, LORI B. *New Conceptions*. New York: St. Martin's Press, 1984.

ANNAS, GEORGE J. "Using Genes to Define Motherhood." *The New England Journal of Medicine* (February 6, 1992): 417–420.

DEWITT, PAULA MERGENHAGEN. "In Pursuit of Pregnancy." *American Demographics* 15 (May 1993): 48–53.

HADFIELD, PETER. "Japanese Pioneers Raise Kid in Rubber Womb." *New Scientist* (April 25, 1992).

OEHNINGER, SERGIO, et al. "Prediction of Fertilization in Vitro with Human Gametes: Is There a Litmus Test?" *American Journal of Obstetrics and Gynecology* 167 (December 1992): 1760–1766.

SAUER, MARK V., et al. "Pregnancy After Age 50: Application of Oocyte Donation to Women after Natural Menopause." *The Lancet* 341 (February 6, 1993): 321–323.

SHER, GEOFFREY; MARRIAGE, VIRGINIA A.; and STOESS, JEAN. *From Infertility to In Vitro Fertilization*. New York: McGraw-Hill, 1988.

WINSTON, ROBERT M. L., and HANDYSIDE, ALAN H. "New Challenges in Human In Vitro Fertilization." *Science* 260 (May 14, 1993): 932–936.

C. Lena Lupica

Smoking.

See TOBACCO.

Social Change: United States

Future students of American society will find that the methods, the understanding, and approaches of the 1960s will not be adequate for the next century. Sometime, perhaps in the 1970s and certainly by 1990, the forces of change expanded and shifted power. Economics, the traditional prime-mover discipline, lost some of its dominance. The idea that economic forces controlled and determined so much of our behavior was diminished by a new value system involving one new force, *ecology,* and the intensified significance of another force, *technology.*

Ecology

New groups appeared, worldwide, focusing on the environment. Their goals were not guided by traditional economic merit, but were based on the need to foster certain ecological conditions. The economic values of eagles, wolves, rare bird species, and Sequoia redwoods were not their criteria. Rivers were to remain wild. Mining and drilling for oil were not to be tolerated on massive portions of space—even though only a handful of people ever intended to visit Alaskan wildernesses. Endangered species were to be restored—often at an enormous cost of jobs and industry. Although there were some powerful presentations concerning the economic consequences of destroying certain portions of nature, the rationale for many ecological decisions was, at bottom, the result of changing values in American society.

First there was a growing delight in the beauty of nature and respect for the other life-forms around us. Second, there were ecological developments that did have economic consequences heretofore ignored. By the 1950s nature itself was no longer tolerating some of our assaults. It was hard to breathe because the air in cities such as Los Angeles and London was being poisoned. By 1994 the once rich fishing grounds off New England and the Maritimes had been fished to the point of extinction. Elsewhere the water supply from rivers and ancient water tables clearly was not adequate to continue present activities in traditional form. It is firmly established now that decisions are going to be influenced by value systems that lie outside the realm of economics. Ecology will continue to play an intensified role in the future by law, because of new levels of societal awareness, and by necessity. Such necessity arises out of population pressures. Burgeoning population will be the great factor shaping world social conditions as well as U.S. social conditions in the decades to come. It is a painful truth that a growing population requires more land for living space, work, food, and play. More people will generate more wastes. Pressure on land, air, and water, and the salience of ecological issues will increase. We will have to double up, reuse, compress, and even omit various accustomed elements of daily living. Each of these choices requires a changing lifestyle, altered living conditions, changes in work and leisure activities, and tradeoffs in time and costs. Space will increase in value, and its economic price will alter our use of what space we can afford. Thus, considerable social change will flow out of a growing population. Japan, the Netherlands, Mexico, and Hawaii provide us with some examples of how best to cope.

Technology

Technology is the other force that will continue to change society and its behavior. Technology is omnipresent, uneven in applications, and disturbingly restless. The social consequences of technological change can be somewhat illuminated by focusing not on the ever-changing technology itself, but on the consequences of continuing advances. Each technological capability surely will continue to produce effects like these:

1. *Mastery of distance.* Geography is no longer as much of a barrier to movement. Travel time and costs have been drastically reduced. This means that people, their ideas, perceptions, and goods can be transported within roughly twenty-four hours to any place in the world. Thus, there is less security in geography for markets, ideas, practices, techniques, and special knowledge. Barriers to movement are largely political. A striving for equality of life will be triggered in hundreds of ways.
2. *Mastery of energy.* Energy increasingly will be transported over vast distances, thus leading to the decline of traditional local energy sources and associated production activities and jobs and the rise of low-cost producers outside the United States. This means that the political relationships with energy producers will be more sensitive and crucial. Energy also will be packaged in smaller and larger capacities, having more durability. Thus, portable power will be applied at many levels in thousands of ever tinier and more durable devices. Energy will be controlled with much more precision. Essentially,

this means independence from fixed power systems and the application of power to many social activities and devices.

3. *Ability to alter materials.* There will be a growing war between materials, with more new opportunities and increased threats for traditional materials. Synthetic materials such as new plastics along with improved qualities in old materials and also combinations of materials (like paper, metals, or wood with plastics) assure that durability, wear resistance, and other attributes will extend the useful life of products. Competition in products will sometimes largely involve the particular materials used. Materials science will be ever more important.

4. *Mechanization of physical work.* This historic trend will continue and be remarkable, especially in its application to service industries, such as food services, libraries, and hospitals. Service fields will experience the same decline in relative physical effort and the same problems of capital investment, lack of flexibility, reduction of labor, and so on that factory automation and mechanized farm work have previously demonstrated. The library will shift drastically from storage of information on paper to storage in electronic form.

5. *Extension of sensory capabilities.* Here is the most profound of all technical trends in the years just ahead. Events happening anywhere in the world can soon or instantly be envisioned everywhere in sight and sound, with all the emotion conveyed by color and voice. This brings many reactions based on emotion rather than reflective thought and complete information. Whoever controls the information content will influence responses and attitudes for better or worse. Each of the human senses is being improved:

- *Vision:* the ability to see beyond previously limiting conditions of distance, darkness, fog, water, great space, molecular space, and atomic space.
- *Speech and hearing:* the amplification, multiplication, transmission, and dispersion of sound.
- *Reach:* to control and manipulate things beyond arm's length.
- *Discrimination:* to detect, identify, and measure external things with more minute precision.
- *Memory:* to preserve, multiply, duplicate, and transmit sensory information across distance and time.

6. *Mechanization of information collection, manipulation, and interpretation.* Application of the computer in all its forms is the most dynamic and explosive trend, and the implications are far from ended. Of course this development overlaps and interfaces with all the sensory capabilities just described, but is stressed here because it essentially deals with the human brain. Problem solving, information retrieval, and interpretation are being mechanized. The computer is doing for intelligence what electricity did for power: it is making intelligence portable, divisible, and capable of multiplication on a massive scale or in minute form. It is vastly extending the capabilities of people and institutions. While it demands more education in its design and application, it also allows operators with only the most elementary knowledge to perform mental tasks that they do not understand. The handheld calculator is an everyday example. Thus, both a reduction and increase in skill requirements are resulting. The social consequences of this vary with differing activities, but profound societal change is occurring on a national and international scale.

Summary of Consequences

Technology has created a highly interdependent world, with all nations increasingly reliant on each other for energy, raw materials, food, water (probably the next great shortage), technical equipment, knowledge, and economic and physical disaster assistance. There is an increasing social awareness of the second- and third-order consequences of these developments and events. We can expect the growth of more pressure-groups advocating or opposing changes and using communications technology to arouse wide and instant attention. The visual appearance of things and events, worldwide and in real time, will create rising expectations and demands for equality and control. U.S. society will be increasingly sensitive to internal and world social conditions. Therefore, self-fulfilling and self-defeating prophecies will play a more powerful role in social and political actions. A simple example is the effect of stock market analysts' predictions of the earning of a stock. When actual earnings fail to meet predictions, the stock is often devalued, even if its performance is relatively good. Society has responded to expectations rather than to reality. Some electric utility firms are in dire straits in 1995 because politicians forced them to make long-term contracts for high-priced alternative energy sources. Predictions about high oil prices and high energy demands never materialized.

See also CHANGE; CHANGE, CULTURAL; CHANGE, EPOCHAL; CHANGE, OPTIMISTIC AND PESSIMISTIC PERSPECTIVES; CHANGE, PACE OF; CHANGE, SCIENTIFIC AND TECHNOLOGICAL; CONTINUITY AND DISCONTINUITY; ENVIRONMENT; GLOBAL CONSCIOUSNESS; GLOBAL TURNING POINTS; LIFESTYLES; MODERNISM AND POSTMODERNISM; POPULATION GROWTH: UNITED STATES; PUBLIC POLICY CHANGE; SOCIAL CONTROLS; SOCIAL INDICATORS; SOCIAL INVENTIONS; SOCIAL AND POLITICAL EVOLUTION; TECHNOLOGICAL CHANGE; TECHNOLOGY AND SOCIETY; VALUES; VALUES CHANGE; VALUES FORMATION.

BIBLIOGRAPHY

BEHRENS, W. H.; MEADOWS, D. H.; MEADOWS, D. I.; and RANDERS, J. *The Limits to Growth.* Washington, DC: Potomac Associates, 1972.
BRIGHT, JAMES R. *Automation and Management.* Boston: Graduate School of Business Administration, 1958.
HENSHEL, RICHARD L. "The Boundary of the Self-Fulfilling Prophecy and the Dilemma of Social Prediction." *British Journal of Sociology* 33/4 (December 1982): 511–528.
MARTINO, JOSEPH P. *Technological Forecasting for Decision Making,* 3rd ed. New York: Elsevier Science Publishing, 1992.
NEWELL, ROGER P. "Mobile Communications for the Masses." *New Telcom Quarterly* 3/2 (1995): 17–22.
TEICH, ALBERT H. *Technology and the Future,* 6th ed. New York: St. Martin's Press, 1993.

James R. Bright

Social Controls

Predicting the future may seem to be a mysterious process steeped in prolix or secret techniques. In truth, forecasting depends largely upon familiar empirical data. The essential difference is that forecasters exert an extra effort to carefully discern trends, their direction, pace, and duration. Some futurists term these telltale indicators "pacing parameters." Elsewhere in this encyclopedia (*see* PUBLIC POLICY CHANGE), the Molitor Multiple-Time-line Model of Change refers to such precipitating or prompting factors as "steps" or bellwether "signatures of change." A collection of such trends and their coalescence reveals definable outcomes perpetuated by this confluence.

Social controls—included as a component of myriad "Informal Rules" described in the Molitor change model (Figure 1)—exert a powerful influence in resolving public policy as well as other sociopolitical matters. These principles—generally unwritten or without the force and effect of formal laws—channel ultimate decisions in discernable and predictable ways. The purpose of this commentary is to define the nature of social controls and to direct the reader to the broader context of sociopolitical decision making and outcomes.

Human behavior is guided not only by formal, explicit, and written laws but also by informal, implicit, and unwritten principles. Informal rules influence the principle, purpose, and psychological disposition of individuals, groups, and society itself. Social controls are tempered by trial and error, the test of time validating and entrenching workable ones.

Behavioral "blueprints" of proscriptive don'ts and prescriptive do's built into social systems powerfully influence routine actions. Deterrence is the operative principle of negative sanctions, and encouragement is the operative principle of positive inducements. Negative sanctions range from mere rebuffs (ridicule, embarrassment, ostracism, or public scorn) to severe sanctions (threats, intimidation, reprisal, penalties, and punishments). Social conformity is a strong inducement because most individuals do not want to stand out as nonconformists or deviants. Enforcement of these principles also is an important determinant of behavior. The enforcement of laws prohibiting adultery, fornication, or sodomy has become lax or nonexistent because of changing moral attitudes and the difficulty of enforcement. The lack of enforcement and a lessening social stigmata, not surprisingly, have contributed to increases in such behavior.

Guiding Principles

Social control concepts are complex and confounded by subtle semantic shading. Because the narrative and graphic lists used here attempt to be inclusive, some terms may be synonymous or overlap (Figure 1). Informal rules of a social environment are derived from philosophy, theology, natural law, ideals, ethics, morals, and conscience (psychological principles) and are embedded in ceremonies, rituals, values, beliefs, lifestyles, and intellectual concepts. Numerous terms—*mores, folkways, customs, norms, normatives, ethics, morals, values, beliefs, lifestyles, attitudes, hopes, aspirations, desires, etiquette, styles, fashions and fads*—refer to the description of what is right and wrong, good and bad, desirable and undesirable.

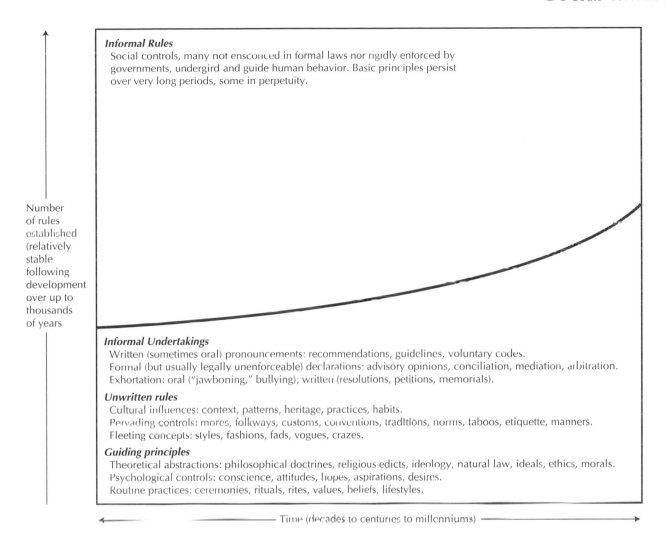

Informal Rules
Social controls, many not ensconced in formal laws nor rigidly enforced by governments, undergird and guide human behavior. Basic principles persist over very long periods, some in perpetuity.

Number of rules established (relatively stable following development over up to thousands of years

Informal Undertakings
Written (sometimes oral) pronouncements: recommendations, guidelines, voluntary codes.
Formal (but usually legally unenforceable) declarations: advisory opinions, conciliation, mediation, arbitration.
Exhortation: oral ("jawboning," bullying); written (resolutions, petitions, memorials).

Unwritten rules
Cultural influences: context, patterns, heritage, practices, habits.
Pervading controls: mores, folkways, customs, conventions, traditions, norms, taboos, etiquette, manners.
Fleeting concepts: styles, fashions, fads, vogues, crazes.

Guiding principles
Theoretical abstractions: philosophical doctrines, religious edicts, ideology, natural law, ideals, ethics, morals.
Psychological controls: conscience, attitudes, hopes, aspirations, desires.
Routine practices: ceremonies, rituals, rites, values, beliefs, lifestyles.

Time (decades to centuries to millenniums)

FIGURE 1.   Molitor multiple-timeline model of change. (Source: Graham T. T. Molitor, Public Policy Forecasting, Inc., 1994. Used with permission.)

Cultural patterns encompass widely held beliefs of certain activities, relationships, feelings, and goals important to a community's identity or well-being. They include psychological predispositions and instinctive traits incorporated into rote behavior patterns. What people commonly know about the nature of things as they are or ought to be guides behavior.

Values, inherent in a culture or its subcomponents, influence behavior. They help to define worldview, guide life's choices, and provide a means to justify purposeful actions. Values are specific to an individual, reflecting an individual's likes and dislikes, predilections and prejudices, and do not necessarily represent prevailing cultural norms. They are materially influenced by a variety of cultural forces—heredity, ethnic group, race, class, occupation, locus, status, age, sex, education, cus-

toms, ethics, morals, religion, institutions, and procedures. *Beliefs* are values translated into a code of conduct. *Lifestyle* denotes a specific way of life that expresses certain values and beliefs.

Ethics, based on postulates espoused by religion or influential ideologies, evaluate human activities in terms of moral principles and set standards of conduct that govern the moral content of intentions, acts, and their consequences. *Morals,* although sometimes used interchangeably with ethics, usually refers to a more limited range of human behavior than is covered by ethics.

Unwritten Guides and Informal Controls

Like other cultural traits, rules of conduct are inferred from patterns of the past and passed along by predecessors or learned from parents, school, peers, church, mass media, service organizations, and the overarching cultural milieu. Education supposedly plays a key role in transmitting behavioral codes from one generation to the next. Many informal rules are premised upon various practical maxims communicated through lore, legends, ballads, fables, proverbs, parables, and practical wisdom. Whatever the form, transmission generally is informal, often oral, and largely learned by observing the behavior of others. Peer group pressure strongly influences individual behavior.

Psychological influences unconsciously pervade perception, and they condition and control the way people think. Deeply ingrained and expressed as common and usual practices, these concepts become routinized behavior. Principles consciously and unconsciously influence character and predispose persons to perform in a manner considered acceptable by the reference group. Public opinion represents an expression or the degree of expression of viewpoints. There is no single public opinion.

Mores, in the spectrum of social constraints upon behavior, are those principles most essential to the maintenance of a society—thou shalt not kill, steal, covet another man's wife, and so on. They may encourage or forbid certain behavior and are strictly enforced by strong sanctions. For example, sexual mores typically preclude acts considered inimical to the well-being of society, such as incest, statutory rape (of minors), prostitution, illegitimate birthing, and abortion (until recently), and support others—monogamy, sexual fidelity, child support, and so forth.

Mores differ from time to time and from place to place. Human slavery, not so many centuries ago, was a common and accepted practice worldwide. In some societies, cannibalism used to be approved, human sacrifice was considered an honor, servants were buried with their deceased master, and killing infants or the elderly also was considered appropriate when population growth threatened the group. Even today the taking of life may be sanctioned—kamikaze pilots and other suicide missions in recent wars, or execution for heinous crimes, and compassionate ending of life for terminally ill (euthanasia).

Folkways include minor rules of social behavior considered less important than mores, mildly sanctioned to secure compliance, and considered appropriate but not insisted upon. The term, ascribed to William Graham Sumner, describes ordinary, taken-for-granted norms of behavior enforced by informal reactions of praise or blame but not by the apparatus of the law. Approved behavior ranges from acts that are disapproved but not forbidden, permitted, or merely recommended.

Inappropriate dress, among the more trivial folkways, may result in ridicule, frowning, or other mild social disapproval. Folkways of a more serious nature may be enforced by stiffer sanctions, such as shunning or ostracizing. Spitting tobacco juice and smoking tobacco—which may be considered disgusting by some, but also pose potentially hazardous public health risks to others—fall within this category and currently are very much in controversy.

Folkways are culturally diverse. Conduct approved in one society or group may be disapproved in another. Etiquette and rules of politeness usually consider belching or slurping at meals inappropriate, but these behaviors are regarded as compliments in some societies. Folkways also vary considerably according to context. Behavior acceptable in one situation may be inappropriate in another—comportment and demeanor in church, for example, differ from behavior at a rock concert or wrestling match.

Customs (conventions, traditions) include mores and folkways that are considered the prime determinants of social behavior. These traditions provide agreed-upon routines that make social environments more certain and less erratic. To facilitate traffic flow, motor vehicles are operated on the right-hand side of the roadway in the United States and Europe but on the left in the United Kingdom and Japan. Cafeteria lines operate in one direction. Coffee is stirred with a spoon, not with a fork.

Customs are not immutable. They change. The bikini or thong bathing suit would have been viewed as indecent and immoral during the early 1900s and up to the 1950s, but today it is acceptable (though sometimes controversial).

Norms reflect typical (not atypical) cultural values, a common core of model conduct that guides what should and should not be done in certain situations. Individuals pick up on behavioral norms prevailing in the community and conform to them. Norms are implicit and explicit. Commonly understood, they are based on values, moral standards, reasoning, and other subjective judgments. Normative—average or modal conduct—describes group consensus that changes with shifts in attitudes. Puritanical moral norms constrained sex except for procreation, and frowned upon pleasurable pursuits of all kinds. Contemporary attitudes are much more lenient.

Norms are not always easily discerned and may be shaped by attitudinal perspectives. For example, taking human life—premeditated murder and its permutations—is a universally proscribed norm; however, it may be approved in wartime (killing by revolutionaries poses a more difficult question), or as punishment for heinous crimes.

Taboos forbid certain actions that are deeply ingrained in contrast to fleeting changes in style. *Style* refers to a characteristic manner or mode of doing things and may not be endorsed by a majority. *Fashion*, distinctive expressions of a cultural element, is semantically similar to style and implies wide support or consensus—women's dress fashions and hemlines, long versus short hair. *Fads*—such as the grunge look, garish-colored hair (pink, orange, green), Hula-Hoops, or pet rocks—are short-lived phenomena that are quickly adopted and just as quickly dropped.

Informal Undertakings

More formal, but noncompulsory, social control modes—oral, written, and procedural—that exert influence over social activity include: recommendations, guidelines, voluntary codes (i.e., of professional practice, ethics, and so forth). More formal controls include pronouncements that generally are legally unenforceable (advisory opinions, conciliation, mediation, arbitration); exhortation (cajoling, editorship, jawboning, bullying, or written resolutions, petitions, memorials). At the end of the continuum of rules guiding social behavior are formal and written laws. Many informal social controls are legitimized by codification into law.

See also AGENTS OF CHANGE; CIVIL PROTEST; CONTINUITY AND DISCONTINUITY; LAWS, EVOLUTION OF; PACESETTER GOVERNMENTS; PUBLIC OPINION POLLS; RECORD SETTING; TECHNOLOGICAL CHANGE; TECHNOLOGY FORECASTING AND ASSESSMENT; TREND INDICATORS; VALUES; VALUES CHANGE.

BIBLIOGRAPHY

APPELBAUM, RICHARD P. *Theories of Social Change.* Chicago: Markham, 1970.
DUNCAN, OTIS DUDLEY, ed. *William F. Ogburn on Culture and Social Change.* Chicago: The University of Chicago Press, 1964.
DUNN, EDGAR S., JR. *Economic and Social Development: A Process of Social Learning.* Baltimore: Johns Hopkins University Press, 1971.
ETZIONI, AMITAI, and ETZIONI HALEVY, EVA. *Social Change: Sources, Patterns, and Consequences,* 2nd ed. New York: Basic Books, 1973.
GALT, ANTHONY H., and SMITH, LARRY J. *Models and the Study of Social Change.* Cambridge, MA: Schenkman, 1976.
LAPIERE, RICHARD T. *Social Change.* New York: McGraw-Hill, 1965.
LEUCHTENBERG, WILLIAM E., and WISHY, BERNARD. *Selected Essays of William Graham Sumner: Social Darwinism.* Englewood Cliffs, NJ: Prentice Hall, 1963.
OGBURN, WILLIAM FIELDING. *Social Change: With Respect to Culture and Original Nature.* New York: Viking Press, 1950.
VAGO, STEVEN. *Social Change.* New York: Holt, Rinehart, and Winston, 1980.
ZOLLSCHAN, GEORGE K., and HIRSCH, WALTER. *Social Change: Explorations Diagnosis and Conjectures.* Cambridge, MA: Schenkman, 1976.

Graham T. T. Molitor

Social Democracy

If capitalism was the economic engine that powered Europe's industrial revolution for two centuries, the welfare state can be thought of as a deliberate, if controversial, means of reconstituting the infrastructure of the Western democracies to achieve a massive redistribution of the benefits of the historic shift from rural-agrarian to urban-industrial economies. Social democracy themes emphasized here include the welfare state and corporatism (institutional arrangements that include worker participation in high-level decision making).

Sweden's former prime minister, Olaf Palme, described the political environment of social democracy evolving and maturing through three stages: (1) *political democratization* (extension of suffrage, freedom of press/assembly/speech); (2) *welfare democracy* (provision of social security, old-age assistance, health care, food assistance, and generally protecting the rank and file from economic marketplace vagaries); (3) *economic democracy* (achieving a better balance between individual self-interest and broader social interests by including worker participation in high-level decision making—based primarily on the notion that markets inadequately serve social interests as much as a proprietor's self-interest.

Change on this scale comes slowly, often only through public contention and over an extended period. In Europe, the change has been energized by massive political mobilization: several times through the rise of a social movement (as happened in Britain); at other times, through incorporation in the platform of established political parties (as in Sweden and France). Whatever the vehicle, it is the existence of undistributed surpluses, such as those generated by mass production assembly lines, as well as a publicly sanctioned agenda of social needs that accounts for the emergence and institutionalization of the welfare state.

Throughout Europe, during the period before World War I, activist associations and minor political parties pressed for programs anticipating the advent of social democracy. Over a period of time they introduced a cluster of socioeconomic programs that came to define the welfare state. It was the Great Depression of the 1930s, however, that provoked public discontent sufficiently intense to force establishment parties to embrace programs, such as unemployment insurance, universal health care, comprehensive pension systems, and income-maintenance arrangements. These programs altered traditional capitalistic patterns that had left wealth concentrated in the hands of an elite. As programs such as these were embraced by non-European societies as diverse as New Zealand, Nigeria, and Japan, social democracy came to be seen as challenging capitalism on the international scene.

Yet it was not until social democratic regimes were beefed up with the addition of unique reallocative devices that social democracy came to be identified with three seminal political values that have captured the imagination of people throughout the world. As "liberty, equality and security," long embraced by establishment parties, came to be seen as the hallmarks of social democracy, public support crystallized as legitimacy. Paradoxically, the mechanism that evoked this legitimacy came into existence largely outside familiar political arenas.

Corporatism, the linking of great pools of public and private power through free-floating as well as institutionalized bargaining mechanisms, came quietly and often unannounced onto the national scene in one European country after another. In many cases, this allowed dramatic revisions in pivotal policies without displacing time-honored allocation mechanisms within traditional program sectors. Though the course of change varied from one nation to another, the outcome of several decades of creeping corporatism produced dramatic changes in historic patterns of the distribution of both political and economic power in many Western democracies. As a result, collective energies once invested in pluralistic political competition were rechanneled toward the formulation and implementation of comprehensive social and eco-

nomic policies in a manner that subordinates group interests to the general welfare of all.

Few doubt that social democratic governments will continue to have a central place in the future of Europe. Continued evolution and change are certain, but this dominance will continue because (1) corporatism provides a mechanism for dealing with some of the perverse cultural dilemmas of postindustrial society, (2) corporatism provides a relevant mechanism through which nation-states can attempt to deal with the emergent, increasingly dominant, and often disruptive world economy, and (3) corporatism will be enhanced by many of the developments associated with the establishment of the European Economic Community.

See also DEMOCRACY; SOCIALISM; SOCIAL WELFARE PHILOSOPHIES.

BIBLIOGRAPHY

CASTLES, FRANCIS. *The Social Democratic Image of Society.* London: Routledge & Kegan Paul, 1978.

COX, ANDREW, and O'SULLIVAN, NOEL. *The Corporate State: Corporatism and the State Tradition in Western Europe.* Hants, England: Elgar, 1988.

Western Europe. Hants, England: Elgar, 1988.

EINHORN, ERIC, and LOGUE, JOHN. *Modern Welfare States.* New York: Praeger, 1989.

FLORA, PETER, and HEIDENHEIMER, ARNOLD. *The Development of Welfare States in Europe and America.* New Brunswick, NJ: Transaction Books, 1987.

WILENSKY, HAROLD, and TURNER, LOWEL. *Democratic Corporatism and Policy Linkages.* Institute for International Studies: Berkeley, 1987.

William J. Gore

Social Indicators

Broadly speaking, social indicators are quantitative measures of social conditions and trends. They originate from censuses and surveys (e.g., victimization rates from the National Crime Survey), administrative records (e.g., school enrollments), or other sources (e.g., newspaper help-wanted advertisement counts). Purposes associated with social indicators include: (1) social monitoring, (2) social reporting, (3) social forecasting, (4) social accounting, (5) program evaluation, and (6) social engineering.

Social indicators monitor where society stands now and where it has stood in the past, to highlight what has been changing. Basic monitors range from the monthly unemployment rate to the annual criminal victimization figures to the small-area statistics of each decade's census. Social indicators also provide a statistical basis for a system of social reporting that attempts to provide policy makers, social scientists, and others with information on societal conditions by evaluating how society is faring.

Applying social change models to the historical and contemporary time series generates social forecasts. These time-series data sets provide a basis for predicting trends into the future.

Social indicators are meant to be integrated into a system of social accounting which is similar to the national income accounting system and which aims to: (a) supply a summary measure of social progress, including groups of indicators revealing relative quality of life; (b) provide a statistical model for assessing the impact of specific societal changes on society in general or on particular components of society.

Social indicators are tools for program evaluation. A summary measure characterizing quality of life and domain-specific measures in areas such as education, health, and crime, make it possible to assess performance overall and in particular areas. Conclusions drawn from these data sets provide a means to judge the overall effectiveness of relevant governmental policies and programs.

Finally, social indicators provide guides for social engineering. Social accounting models to forecast the consequences of inputs and a social monitoring system to measure the actual outcomes facilitate designing and fine-tuning government programs to deal with social problems (Ferriss, 1988; Rose, 1989).

In the United States as well as in other countries progress has been made in monitoring and reporting. Some countries have wide-ranging, if not yet comprehensive, programs for measuring important societal conditions. They not only cover the economic realm, but also deal with such areas as health, education, crime, and the environment (Wiegand, 1988). Internationally, the United Nations, World Bank, Organization for Economic Development and Cooperation, and other groups regularly compile comparative social indicators. Of particular note are the General Social Surveys in the United States, which have been tracking social change since 1972. Surveying similar components cross-culturally in over twenty countries, the International Survey Program and the Eurobarometers sponsored by the European Community have been underway since 1973.

The more ambitious, complex goals of forecasting and social accounting have seen promising but more limited developments. Social forecasting is most advanced in the area of demography, and cohort (age group) replacement and cohort-education models are useful in predicting attitudinal and behavioral changes. Considerable progress also has been made in planning for health-care needs. No system of social accounting has as yet been put into operation, however.

Modifications in the basic economic accounts model have been developed to take into account social costs such as environmental pollution, deaths, and illness. Others have attempted to aggregate and interrelate topics using rates of change to reveal multivariate outcomes (Johnston, 1988). Studies of the quality of life based on personal, subjective assessments and of both general and domain-specific psychological well-being have been carried out, but they have not been widely integrated into an accounting system (Rose, 1989). Work now underway takes a life-events approach that measures the incidence and magnitude of social problems (Smith, 1992). Suffice it to note that a fully integrated social accounting system does not appear likely in the near term.

With social forecasting still limited in its reach and reliability, and with no functioning system of social accounting in place, the goals of program evaluation and social engineering have been largely unattained. Monitoring and reporting system elements, however, are used to assess current programs and guide policy makers toward more effective decisions. Most innovative in these areas are the Human Dimensions of Global Environmental Change Programs of the International Social Science Council and the U.S. National Science Foundation. They will integrate natural science studies of the environment (e.g., the greenhouse effect) with evaluations of alternative technologies (e.g., nuclear vs. solar energy) and assessments of social concerns and acceptable trade-offs (e.g., economic growth vs. public health).

Social indicators, while not realizing many ultimate applications, have served well in monitoring social conditions and trends. They are steadily expanding our knowledge of human society and providing important insights as to how its different components interact. Future advances in forecasting models and social accounting eventually may make social indicators into extremely powerful tools for the diagnosis and disposition of social problems.

See also ENVIRONMENTAL INDICATORS; FORECASTING METHODS; PACESETTER GOVERNMENTS; PUBLIC POLICY CHANGE; SCANNING; SOCIAL INVENTIONS; TREND INDICATORS.

BIBLIOGRAPHY

FERRISS, ABBOTT L. "The Uses of Social Indicators." *Social Forces* 66 (March 1988): 601–617.

JOHNSTON, DENIS F. "Towards a Comprehensive 'Quality-of-Life Index'." *Social Indicators Research* 20 (October 1988): 473–496.

ROSE, RICHARD. "Whatever Happened to Social Indicators? A Symposium." *Journal of Public Policy* 9 (October–December 1989): 399–450.

SMITH, TOM W. "A Life Events Approach to Developing an Index of Societal Well-Being." *Social Science Research* 21 (1992): 353–379.

WIEGAND, ERICH. "Current Work on the Social Indicators System of the Federal Republic of Germany." *Social Indicators Research* 20 (August 1988): 399–416.

Thomas W. Smith

Social Inventions

A social invention is a new law, organization, or procedure that changes the ways in which people relate to themselves or to each other, either individually or collectively (Conger, 1974). Examples of social inventions include marriage, language, writing, voting, schools and methods of education, unemployment insurance, psychotherapy, laws, and the Red Cross and other organizations. Social inventions, more than any other type of invention (mechanical, chemical, electrical, and so on), influence how we live, including how we are governed. Social inventions that have been created over the years have brought many benefits to society, as the previous examples attest. In spite of the potential to solve social problems through social inventions, governments seldom establish research centers to develop new social inventions. Among the few that do exist, most were established to invent new methods of education.

Societies are a reflection of a complex web of particular social inventions. Social inventing is a continuous trial-and-error process as individuals, organizations, and governments try to cope with new or dissatisfying situations. An invention may be created in one location and adopted in different locations within different social configurations. Thus, the same invention can be used beneficially or harmfully in different cultures.

An interesting recent social invention is the divorcing of parents by their children. This first occurred in Sweden in about 1980, and a dozen years later took place twice in Florida within a one-year period, suggesting that momentum may be building. However, the slowness of the buildup indicates the slowness of the adoption of social inventions. The implementation of an invention such as this typically requires certain other social inventions, in this case the acceptance that children have rights, the prohibition of child abuse, the general acceptance of divorce, and of course such basic institutions as courts, lawyers, and so forth.

Once a social invention finds its place in the wider web of previous social inventions, it then may have an influence on how the other parts of the web operate. When, for example, parents divorce they endeavour to negotiate the allocation of the rights to the custody and visitation privileges of the children. It is conceivable that in the future, children will demand their own alimony and choose to live with other people than their parents or guardians. A very likely possibility is that children of divorce will sue one or both parents for support and then go to live with grandparents or other favored relatives. This probability finds support in the fact that some grandparents are now suing children, or children-in-law who have divorced to ensure that the grandparents have visiting rights to the grandchildren. In turn, these developments, plus greater state penalties levied against divorced fathers who do not keep up child support payments, may substantially change the divorce process itself. It is possible that the grandchildren and grandparents will form legal alliances against the parents, who may or may not be divorcing.

The fact that grandchildren and grandparents might enter legal divorce proceedings on equal status as the parents will change the nature of divorce from a private arrangement between two adults where all other parties are secondary to a community process in which the balance of power is clearly shared by all of the "victims." A further downstream result of this simple social invention of children divorcing their parents might well be some fundamental changes in family life. For example, grandparents might commonly sue their children for improper child care and have the legal right to involve themselves in their grandchild's upbringing. Similarly they may have the right to intervene in other aspects of family life. In this way we may see a rebuilding of the wider family structure. A further spur to this might come from economic developments where career progression for many middle-class workers is stymied and they look to their parents for financial subsidies, in this situation the grandparents have a further opportunity to negotiate their role in family life.

In some instances social inventions are selected and integrated to become a social movement. Graham T. T. Molitor (1977) has indicated the process that a social trend takes in terms of its geographic origins and the changing characteristics of its proponents as the movement "matures." Typically a social movement assembles and uses social inventions such as: outrageous statements and demonstrations (strikes, picketing, acts of disrespect to traditional symbols, and so forth) to gain attention of the press; pamphleteering; organizing "chapters" or groups in many localities; formulation of demands and goals; confrontation with authorities; inspirational presentations; disciplining of supporters; raising of funds; recruiting of high profile supporters; human interest publicity, and so on.

In some cases, these social movements lead to major changes (such as the recognition of labor unions and the right to strike.). A social movement, whether confrontational or not, is intended to allow the participants and their presumed "bene factors" or like-minded people to live their lives differently. Thus, for instance, participants in the many "freedom" campaigns typified by the union movement (e.g., the women's movement, gay and lesbian rights movements) all want regulations and public behaviors changed to permit them to manage their lives in ways that they decide.

In situations where a social movement is organized to combat a single practice (e.g., seal hunting or lumbering), the social movement is more like a social campaign to get authorities to change the rules. Such a campaign makes use of many of the same social inventions as a social movement but is not intended to change the lives of the participants, rather to impose the values of the participants on others.

Not all major social movements are confrontational and in many instances represent a need that had not been met before. The early years of the twentieth century were a period of enormous growth of international organizations for the development of individuals, communities, and beyond. This movement was typified by the invention of such organizations as the Scouts, Red Cross, service clubs, all of which used the various organizational practices that had been invented over the years (membership, elected and appointed officers, committees, voting, fund-raising, fellowship practices, publicity, etc.) to create a successful organization to perform good works. They represented the epitome of the collective philanthropic movement and replaced dependence upon wealthy patrons. Thus it was a form of democratization of social services, which at the turn of the century we are now witnessing as becoming the bureaucrati-

zation (another collection of social inventions) of social services.

The rapid evolution of an information age during the 1990s is likely to produce a burst of creative social inventions. Many futurists have outlined the present transformation to a democratic workplace, entrepreneurial organizations, and humane capitalism. The proliferation of powerful interactive information networks is creating "electronic" equivalents of most social relationships: distance learning, telecommuting, electronic shopping, and so on. Advances in biogenetics are being accompanied by new social inventions, such as surrogate mothers and laws that prescribe how this life-and-death power is used. And growing awareness of the environmental crisis should also lead to different forms of resource use, such as recycling of all goods, "green" taxes, simpler lifestyles, and reverence for nature.

See also AGENTS OF CHANGE; CHANGE; PUBLIC POLICY CHANGE; SOCIAL CHANGE; UNITED STATES; SOCIAL AND POLITICAL EVOLUTION.

BIBLIOGRAPHY

BENNETT, WILLIAM J. *The Index of Leading Cultural Indicators: Facts and Figures on the State of American Society.* New York: Touchstone/ Simon & Schuster, 1994.
CONGER, D. STUART. *Social Inventions.* Prince Albert, Saskatchewan: Saskatchewan NewStart, 1974.
MOLITOR, GRAHAM T. T. "The Hatching of Public Opinion." *Planning Review* 5/42 (July 1977).
———. "Preparing for the 80's: Public Policy Forecasting." *Public Relations Journal* 35/1 (January 1979).

D. Stuart Conger

Socialism

Socialism has been narrowly and broadly defined. The narrow definition is that of a social system where the means of production are owned by the community. The broader definition describes a system where public authorities intervene in the processes of production, trade, and consumption. A distinguishing feature of these processes is that they do not operate freely, as in laissez-faire systems.

The broader definition will be used in this article. The word *socialism* was first used in 1832 by the Frenchman Pierre Leroux to characterize systems based upon state intervention. Various socialist regimes had developed in reaction to laissez-faire systems recommended by the Englishman Adam Smith in his book *The Wealth of Nations* (1776). In laissez-faire systems, all transactions occur in free markets, but socialists contend that this leads to very unequal income distribution. The first socialists based their protests on ethical grounds (the Englishmen Thomas MORE and Robert Owen, and the Frenchmen Louis Blanc, Charles Fourier, and Claude-Henri Saint-Simon, among others). Such advocates were called utopian socialists by Karl Marx, the German sociologist who considered himself a scientific socialist. Marx and his followers started to make socialism politically relevant by creating socialist parties, united by the First International (established in 1864), and seeking cooperation with trade unions. Marx provided socialism with an ideology. His argument that human history was a succession of various orders, suggesting that society is bound to develop in a socialist direction, impressed politicians. Even if they did not agree, they made the "social problem" one of the great issues in the second half of the nineteenth and through most of the twentieth century.

Extremists and Moderates

As with so many spiritually motivated causes, lack of success in the struggle with opponents bred internal disagreement about the reasons for failure. In the early years of the twentieth century, a split in the socialist movement occurred. The more radical wing organized itself into communist parties, leaving the democratic socialists in the old party. The parties supporting the existing order showed a similar split into extremes with fascists on one side, and the more moderate factions on the other. Sometimes the extremists hated the moderates more than their opponents at the other extreme: communists, for example, would address democratic socialists as "social fascists." On other occasions, they would try to reunite in what was called a popular front.

World War I

With the killing of the Austrian successor to the throne by a Serb as a pretext, Germany started another war with France in August 1914. Because of existing alliances, so many countries were drawn into the conflict that it was termed the "Great War" or "World War." Against this background, important shifts in socialist power positions took place. The exiled Russian communist leader V. I. Lenin was given the opportunity to go back to Russia, where two successive revolutions occurred in 1917. In the second, or "October" revolution, Lenin seized power and established the Soviet Union with a communist government. In Germany, the Social Democrats entered into a coalition with other parties, which prevented a Communist party rule. A number of Central and Eastern European countries (from Hungary and Yugoslavia to the Baltic republics, including Poland and Czechoslovakia) regained their independence.

World War II

Germany lost World War I and was made to pay a very large tribute, which wrecked its economy—a danger about which the famous English economist John Maynard Keynes had warned. These extreme punitive measures provoked an opposite extremism, fascism. Hitler began his propaganda campaign for revenge and essentially planned World War II to carry out his objectives.

World War II started in 1939, and in the first few years, Germany occupied much of the Western Europe. Events turned, however, when Germany sought to invade Eastern Europe, and the war finished in 1945 in a second defeat for Germany. Soviet forces won the war at the eastern front, and Eastern Europe was occupied by the Soviet army. Germany was partitioned between East and West.

The Cold War, Developing Countries, and the Environment

After the second defeat of Germany, a new scenario developed: Mutual distrust between the communist world and Western democracies led to an unprecedented build-up of military strength, including nuclear arms. The chances that a Third World War would result loomed, but such a large-scale conflict has not materialized.

Alongside security problems, other important dilemmas surfaced and had to be resolved. One such problem, the poverty of the underdeveloped countries, involved many former colonies of the Western powers. The extreme poverty in many of these countries was a social problem of worldwide significance and impact, and the solution seemed to indicate a need for socialist policies. This worldwide social problem provoked conflicts between developed and underdeveloped nations. One conflict raged over the fact that the developed countries were unwilling to make available the full 0.7 percent of their Gross National Product (GNP) that had been recommended for development assistance by the Pearson Commission; instead only 0.35 percent was offered. A second conflict concerned the protection of industries that, because of their labor intensity, were appropriate for the underdeveloped countries. The best known example of such protection is the Multifiber Arrangement that protects the textile and clothing industries. A third conflict involved commodity agreements for agricultural raw materials. The markets for such materials are unstable and traditionally have been regulated. A complication here is that the agricultural markets themselves in developed countries are also unstable, and protectionist policies are distinctly disadvantageous for underdeveloped countries.

Another new problem of global significance was discovered by the Club of Rome, a group that is essentially a coalition of business people and scientists. In a report entitled *The Limits of Growth* (1972), the danger of pollution due to population growth, industrial manufacturing, transport, and natural resource exploitation was analyzed, and the necessity of a carefully planned environmental policy was strongly emphasized. In the same year, an international conference on the subject was held in Stockholm on the initiative of the Swedish government. As a result, a new United Nations agency, the United Nations Environmental Programme (UNEP) was established, in Nairobi, Kenya.

A fourth pressing worldwide problem is that of sustainability, the concept that, at the very least, future generations should enjoy a standard of living equal to that of the present day. Such sustainability is possible, but only if (1) technological progress continues, (2) the world population level becomes stable, and (3) a limit is set to the portion of natural resources used by each succeeding generation.

In some socialist countries, the socialist parties neglected or underemphasized environmental policy. As a result, various organizations such as Greenpeace drew the attention of the world's citizens and politicians to environmental issues. (Of course, socialist countries were not alone in their neglect of the environment. In some countries, where the need for a cleaner environment had been addressed by governmental programs, the need for green parties was less severe.)

The End of Communism: Extremist Nationalism

In 1985 Mikhail S. Gorbachev became secretary-general of the Soviet Communist party. He admitted that the Soviet economy was less efficient than the Western economies. The American economist Abram Bergson had noted in 1964 that Soviet productivity was about 30 percent lower than that of America. Gorbachev conceded that restructuring and frank discussion of the problem was necessary. His admission that a free-market economy is so much more productive than a centrally planned

economy caused a veritable uproar. Eastern European and Soviet citizens felt liberated from the enormous pressure they had lived under, and reacted violently. Apparently the mass of the population felt strongly aggravated by the ethnic pressure of living under Russian rule. In contrast, economists and managers were more concerned with the reestablishment of a free market. In both cases the effect was an overreaction that shifted from one extreme to the other. All the republics of the Soviet Union wanted to be independent. The Soviet Union, after a few years, was replaced by the Commonwealth of Independent States (CIS), of which Russia (including Siberia) was by far the largest.

Many economists and managers believed that all markets should become free, forgetting that there are stable and unstable markets. The latter, including agriculture, cannot be left free. In another economic sector, where production incurs high fixed costs, free markets could cause permanent losses to the firms or induce the formation of monopolies. Hence, they require some form of regulation. Near-term and medium-term forecasts are extremely problematic, given the current chaotic state. Relatively longer-term goals may be easier to assess, at least in broad outline.

The Future of Socialism

The future world order seems likely to be a mixed order: a system of free stable markets, corrected for income inequality, and of regulated unstable markets. The role of public authorities ("the state") should be to maintain law and order and fix the quantities of public goods, such as the infrastructure (road systems, railway and air traffic, information dispersal, energy supply, and environmental policies). Another important task is likely to be the redistribution of incomes, both within and among nations. A quantitative aspect of that task is the portion of total income that is transferred. Inside countries, about 30 percent is transferred in Sweden by social legislation, 12.4 percent in the United States, 10 percent in Japan, with most other industrialized countries falling somewhere between the United States and Sweden. Sweden is considered to be one of the most advanced and well-functioning welfare states.

The redistribution of wealth among countries may require a level of assistance by developed countries substantially higher than the 0.7 percent recommended by the Pearson Commission, at least for the short term. This writer recommends a short-term level of assistance of 1.27 percent of the GNP, with long-term redistribution levels of 70 percent to be achieved over a period of three centuries.

Socialism has been internationalist from its inception in 1864. Although theory and practice have diverged, the globalization of the world economy is forcing socialists to reapply their original theories to new contexts. The future also requires a managed world economy, an ongoing international framework within which policies can be discussed. This may require strengthening and reforming the United Nations.

Several possibilities may rejuvenate socialism in the future. There is a tendency for economic systems to become more "socialized" as they strive to improve the quality of life. For example, welfare programs that remedy social problems, laws respecting economic and civil rights, state support of cultural activities, environmental protection, and other "social programs" have made most European nations, Japan, and even the United States more comfortable places to live.

There is also an interesting trend toward a kind of "economic democratization," particularly among large quasi-public corporations, that transforms capitalism into a more social form. Progressive corporations, like the Saturn Division of General Motors, expanded their goals and governance to include workers, customers, suppliers, distributors, and the general public, in addition to investors. As a result, modern economies may remain market oriented, while major enterprises incline toward management that serves numerous social rather than exclusively financial interests. If GM's Saturn and Japanese businesses are a harbinger, such "human-centered" enterprises may serve the general public welfare as well as make more money because they are more productive.

The decline of communism may signify that the old type of centrally planned government socialism is dead, while modern versions of socialism are emerging based to a considerable extent on free markets. The fact is that our society must increasingly address the human and social dimensions of economic life as these concerns grow in importance. Thus, systems of political economy around the world are unavoidably moving toward various forms of social control over their market economies, whether one calls it socialism, economic democracy, human enterprise, a "New Capitalism," or a "New Socialism."

See also CAPITALISM; COMMUNISM; DEVELOPMENT, ALTERNATIVE; ECONOMICS; MACROECONOMICS; MARKETPLACE ECONOMICS; POLITICAL ECONOMY; SOCIAL DEMOCRACY; SWEDEN.

BIBLIOGRAPHY

ETZIONI, AMITAI. *The Moral Dimension: Toward a New Economics.* New York: Free Press, 1988.
HALAL, WILLIAM E. *The New Capitalism.* New York: Wiley, 1986.
HEILBRONER, ROBERT. "After Communism." *New Yorker* (September 10, 1990).
TINBERGEN, JAN. *Booklet 29.* Santa Barbara, CA: Nuclear Age Peace Foundation, 1989.

Jan Tinbergen

Social and Political Evolution

Social and political evolution deals with long-term change in a wide number of societal, political, and economic areas. First to be examined will be the processes of evolutionary change; then, how human life and societal institutions have changed substantively in a wide range of areas as a result of the transition from the agricultural to the industrial and now to the information-communications age; next, how the information age is now in a second phase focusing on communications and connectivity. We will end with what may follow the information/communications age.

The Process of Evolutionary Change

When we think of evolution, we usually think of long-term change. In looking at models of such evolutionary change, there are at least two different versions. In the last century, Charles Darwin argued that biological evolution (and by implication evolution in other areas) occurred by slow, gradual, linear change, from one species to another. In this century, Steven Jay Gould's punctuated equilibrium theory in biology, as well as other new scientific paradigms, suggest a different view of evolution. This model allows for gradually accelerating change within an existing system for a period of time, until some "limits to growth" point is reached (the S-Curve growth model) leading to a partial breakdown of that system (and its societal institutions in the case of social evolution), followed by a quantum jump to a whole new system level.

In the linear growth model of evolution as slow, gradual change, the future is an extension of past trends—i.e., more of the same (a quantitative change only). In the periodic quantum jump model, in contrast, a rather sudden shift occurs to a new system level that is qualitatively different from the old one. Following the latter model, Alvin Toffler noted that one could never have predicted the information age or "Third Wave" (as he called it) by extrapolating trends from the earlier industrial or "Second Wave" society, since something qualitatively new occurred that made this shift possible. Another version of this process is the evolutionary spiral (see Barbara Marx Hubbard's work, for example) where crises (or "limits to growth" points within a system trigger design innovations, which usher in new stages or periods of evolution over time.

Societal Evolution Through Agricultural, Industrial, and Information Ages

Following the prehistoric hunting and gathering age, human society has evolved through at least three different periods. Toffler, in *The Third Wave*, popularized the idea of these three major waves or periods of change in human history: an agricultural age lasting thousands of years, an industrial age lasting a few hundred years, and now a postindustrial information/communication age lasting only decades. The agricultural era originated with ancient civilizations around the Mediterranean; the industrial age with nation-states bordering the Atlantic; and the information age with Pacific Rim countries—especially the United States and Japan, leading to the emergence of a global economy, global telecommunications, and an increasingly interdependent world. Each period is ushered in by new technologies, which restructure jobs, the economy, then all other societal institutions, even requiring new thinking appropriate for each age.

The following seven tables illustrate some of the major societal and institutional restructuring trends associated with the shift from agricultural to industrial and now to information-communications

Characteristics of Agricultural, Industrial, and Information Age Societies

TABLE 1. Historical Background and Societal Overview

Item	Agricultural Age	Industrial Age	Information Age
Original location	Mediterranean Sea.	Atlantic Rim.	Pacific Rim.
Pace of change	Thousands of years.	200–300 years.	30–40 years (next stage likely to be even shorter).
Source of power	Land is the most important asset necessary for production.	Physical resources, factories, equipment, and capital are assets; humans are an added, necessary cost of production.	Ideas and information, which come from people, making human resources the most important asset in the information age.
Product produced	Food; also arts and crafts, each artifact produced by hand.	Mass produced, manufactured goods.	Knowledge and application of ideas to different practical results, including technological and social innovations.
Centralization-decentralization, globalization-localization	Decentralization: living and working on the land in decentralized, rural communities.	Centralization: organized around the nation-state and people living in cities.	Decentralization of society and institutions, plus global interdependence for first time.
Societal divisions	Rigid social class divisions in ancient empires and feudal societies; different norms for different social classes to follow.	Mass society—in both capitalist or socialist countries, one socially acceptable model for all to try to follow; conformity necessary.	Diversified, multiple-option society: no one model everyone must follow to be socially accepted; instead numerous models to choose from in any area of life.

Social and Political Evolution

TABLE 2. Demographics

Item	Agricultural Age	Industrial Age	Information Age
Demographics: geographic distribution	Rural populations: the majority of people living in rural communities working on the land.	Urban populations: in countries undergoing the industrial revolution, people moved to cities to work in factories. In developing South countries today, many people are moving to cities seeking (but not always finding) jobs and access to modern life, resulting in unmanageable cities and slums in many cases.	Option for some to live in countryside, in an "electronic cottage" and be connected to work via electronic communications (computer, modem, and telephone line); many people prefer to work at a central office some days, and at home other days, however.
Demographics: population growth rates (based on birth and death rates)	Relatively stable populations due to high birthrates and high death rates.	Beginning of population explosion due especially to decreased death rates (due to modern medicine and better hygiene). Continuing high population growth rates in many South countries today, where 98 percent of global population growth is now occuring.	In developed North countries, which have entered the information age, both birthrates and death rates have decreased, leading to population increases of 1 per cent or less per year.
Demographics: age distribution	Shorter life span: plagues and diseases affected all social classes.	Life span increased in developed, industrial countries, but new industrial and social diseases emerged.	Aging populations in developed North countries, not developing South countries (where population is still more of childbearing age).

societies. These characteristics are based primarily on experiences in Western developed countries, where industrialization and later the information age (along with Japan), originated. Nonetheless, in our current interdependent world, no country can escape the influence of the information age and countries—with different histories, cultures, political-economic systems, and levels of development—must each decide how best to incorporate the information age into its development. Perhaps some South countries can skip some of the worst ills of the industrial age. In various areas, the information age also marks a return to certain characteristics of the agricultural age, though with additional elements added.

The Communications/Internet/Multimedia/Interactive/Virtual Reality Age: Further Extensions and Realizations of the Potential of the Information Age

The first stage of the information revolution focused on an information explosion generated by mainframe computers and then personal computers. Computers are now integrally linked with telecommunications worldwide, making the communication, networking, interactive, and multimedia potential of the information revolution finally possible. The Internet or Information Superhighway (which the U.S. government supports) illustrates this, along with multimedia, interactive

TABLE 3. Energy and Environmental Pollution

Item	Agricultural Age	Industrial Age	Information Age
Energy sources	Renewable energy sources: solar, wind, water, humans/slavery, animals, etc.	Nonrenewable, fossil fuels (oil, natural gas, coal) and nuclear fission (uranium and plutonium fuels). These fuels pollute more, and once extracted from the earth, they are gone.	Eventual return (once fossil fuels are exhausted) to renewable energy sources (solar, wind, tidal, geothermal, ocean thermal, and biomass); as in agricultural age, but using more sophisticated technologies to tap these energy sources. Also nuclear fusion (from fusing of hydrogen atoms in water) once the technology is perfected in future; lag in transition to these alternative energy sources—perhaps into next age.
Environmental pollution	Limited, insignificant levels of localized pollution.	Industrial age air, water, and noise pollution from burning of fossil fuels.	Global pollution problems, global warming (greenhouse effect), and hole in ozone level—all legacies of the industrial age. Prospects for cleaner environment from green technologies and an eventual return to renewable energy sources.

games, books, and virtual reality products. The Internet is growing by 10 percent a month (as of 1995). Increasingly in future, films, quick time movies, still pictures, sounds, games, and other multimedia learning and entertainment packages—in addition to text and data—will be available on computer via Internet. While many people extol the creative and educational benefits of these new technologies, others are concerned about how to regulate pornography and antisocial uses of virtual reality and the Internet.

The Future: What Will Come After the Information/Communication Age?

Many people have speculated about what will come after the information/communications revolution. Space advocates thought it would be exploring, in-

dustrializing, and settling humans in space—the "final frontier" popularized in science fiction programs such as *Star Trek*. Others focus on the revolution in genetic engineering, gene splicing/recombinant DNA, where one could potentially replace defective or undesirable genes in any species in future, raising serious ethical questions since humans would, in effect, be playing God. Others believe atomic level restructuring of reality via nanotechnology would revolutionize our future lives. Still others focus on the evolution of human consciousness or inner space, where the creative and spiritual powers of the human mind have barely been tapped. To some extent, all of the above changes are already happening. One thing is clear: Whatever stage follows the information/communications age, it will be something qualitatively different from (and hence not an extension of) the previous stage.

TABLE 4. Economics and Politics

Item	Agricultural Age	Industrial Age	Information Age
Type of economic system	Feudal economic systems and earlier ancient empire economic systems based on slavery.	Rise of capitalist economic systems and then socialist economic systems (as a critique of capitalism).	Both capitalist and socialist economic systems are being greatly restructured as they become part of a global economy; no pure systems, hybrids instead, though also privatization trends world wide—including in former socialist countries.
Economic exchange system	Barter, pre-money economy: goods and services are traded without any money being exchanged.	Money economy: rise of labor sold for wages, and goods and services sold for money/currency.	Continued money economy, as well as rise of a subtantial barter economy—both within nations (counter economy) and between nations (counter trade).
Appropriate economic model	Based on a scarcity of land and food produced: "If I give you land or food, then you have it and I do not"; scarcity models.	Based on a scarcity of capital, equipment, and manufactured goods: "If I give you capital or goods, then you have them and I do not"; scarcity models.	Based on a potential for abundance: Ideas, information, and knowledge are potentially unlimited and increasingly available to everyone: "If I give an idea or information to you, then we both have it"; win-win, abundance models.
Type of political system	Predemocratic political systems of various kinds, in feudal systems and ancient empires.	Representative democracy and a multiparty political system for the rising middle class in West, with democracy based on an informed, educated, middle class; democratic centralism in socialist countries, with population also educated.	Global democratization trends, in former communist and South countries today, with modern information technologies making control of information to citizens by dictators difficult. Sociopolitical change on important issues initiated by direct, grassroots, participatory democracy involving media coverage, electronic networking on the Internet, FAXs, & other forms of "electronic democracy." Increasing numbers of issues (arms control, free trade, AIDS, pollution, and terrorism) require global cooperation and/or local action, not just national policies, to solve them.

TABLE 5. Workplace: Jobs, Labor, Management, and Percentage of Women Working

Item	Agricultural Age	Industrial Age	Information Age
Primary jobs	In agricultural communities producing food and handmade arts and crafts; peasants, serfs, and artisans.	In factories in cities producing mass produced manufactured goods; more blue-collar jobs.	Higher paying, skilled high technology and professional jobs and lower paying, unskilled service sector jobs, creating danger of a two-tiered economy and decreased middle class (the traditional cornerstone of a democracy); more white-collar jobs; also multiple jobs/careers in a lifetime.
Labor unions	Labor not yet urbanized or organized: peasant uprisings in rural areas are largely spontaneous.	Rise of labor unions in Western capitalist countries, not socialist countries (where dictatorship of the proletariat or state was supposed to represent workers). Adversarial relations between worker and owner or managers in industrial Western countries.	Decline in labor union membership in capitalist countries, with decreasing blue-collar jobs. Also movement towards worker ownership of stock in companies they work in, making them both workers and owners, thus eliminating this traditional adversarial relationship. Rise of mass protests by workers in communist countries, demanding better conditions, led to end of communism in some countries.
Management styles	Rigid social class divisions meant management by dominant social class.	Hierarchical management models in industrialized Western countries.	Network-based, participatory management; consensus/team building; quality circles and total quality management; Japanese management models; and elimination of some middle-management positions.
Percentage of women working	Both men and women worked on the land together, keeping the family together.	Prestigious for middle- and upper-class men in West if their wives did not work versus lower class where women had to work to help support their families. In contrast, ideology in socialist countries promoted women's equality via working with men.	Increasing percentage of women working, whether married or single, for economic and personal growth reasons. People also living longer and having less children, thus women no longer needing to spend their whole lives raising children.

TABLE 6. Education and Family

Item	Agricultural Age	Industrial Age	Information Age
Education	Invention of writing with need to keep records of planting and harvests, taxation and barter, education limited to an elite. (Earlier focus on oral traditions carried by elders during hunting and gathering age).	Mass public education: similar standards for all, which was considered democratic; an educated middle class seen as foundation for a democracratic society; traditional educational institutions have monopoly on learning.	Diversified educational models necessary to meet diverse needs of students of all ages and different racial, ethnic, and cultural backgrounds; lifetime learning necessary to keep updated in one's field, as technological and social changes escalate; retraining of industrial workers necessary; community and corporate learning centers, in addition to traditional educational institutions; also distance learning. Computer/multimedia/interactive educational packages, Internet, and virtual reality as additional tools for learning.
Household/family patterns	Extended family: several generations living and working together on the land.	Nuclear family: father working, mother at home not working, and approximately two children for middle and upper classes in developed West. Also nuclear family in lower class West and socialist countries except that women worked.	Multiple family patterns: no one model everyone must follow to be accepted socially. Examples include: married couples with or without children; unmarried couples living together; single parents; divorced parents with children who remarry, making children part of different households; single-person households; people living in groups; gay and lesbian couples.

If past precedents continue, it will also last less time than previous stages.

See also CHANGE; CHANGE, CULTURAL; COMMUNICATIONS; CONSCIOUS EVOLUTION; EVOLUTION, SOCIAL; GLOBAL CULTURE; GLOBAL PARADOX; INFORMATION SOCIETY; POST–INFORMATION AGE; SOCIAL CHANGE: UNITED STATES.

BIBLIOGRAPHY

FORESTER, TOM. *Computers in the Human Context: Information Technology, Productivity, and People.* Cambridge, MA: MIT Press, 1989.

HUBBARD, BARBARA MARX. *The Evolutionary Journey: A Personal Guide to a Positive Future.* San Francisco: Evolutionary Press, 1982.

TABLE 7. Culture and Mindset

Item	Agricultural Age	Industrial Age	Information Age
Cultures	Local cultures (organized around rural communities or city-states).	National cultures (organized around the nation-state).	Globalization of cultures (organized around an increasingly interdependent world), creating surface level global unity along with deeper level local diversity of the world's cultures. Increased danger of localized cultural conflicts in post Cold War era. People seek new identities and often return to old identities without sufficient recognition of global interdependence or needs and dangers of war in a technological age. New nonlocalized virtual communities also emerging in cyberspace.
Mind-sets	Collectivist, group identity with people being part of social networks and relationships; Eastern and traditional civilizations.	Newtonian physics: divide reality up into separate parts and analyze each part separately; individual identity; deductive, win-lose, either-or, dualistic thinking; Western civilizations.	New physics: dynamic, interdependent, whole systems; worldview; unity and diversity within systems and on global-local levels; win-win, both-and thinking; synergy of Eastern and Western civilizations, and of individual and group needs being met; complex systems require diversity of interdependent parts.

NAISBITT, JOHN, with Patricia Aburdene. *Megatrends 2000: Ten New Directions for the 1990's.* New York: Avon Books, 1990.

RHEINGOLD, HOWARD. *Virtual Reality: Exploring the Brave New Technologies of Artificial Experience and Interactive Worlds—From Cyberspace to Teledildontics.* New York: Simon & Schuster, 1991.

TOFFLER, ALVIN. *Powershift: Knowledge, Wealth, and Violence at the Edge of the 21st Century.* New York: Bantam, 1990.

Linda Groff

Social Sciences

The social sciences attempt to study social systems systematically and objectively, in much the same way that the natural sciences deal with physical or biological systems.

Anthropology

Anthropology is a discipline within the social sciences that focuses on a broadly conceived study of human beings. As a discipline, anthropology took shape in the 1860s and was established in the universities at the turn of the century. Occasionally defined as "the science of man," anthropology examines both the cultural and physical characteristics of humans. Cultural anthropology deals with all aspects of past and present human cultures, including language, customs, and behavior. Physical anthropology deals with the physical variation, characteristics, and evolution of humans.

Though often associated with the study of the past, tribal peoples and cultures, anthropology can be expected to rise in prominence as an important applied discipline as mankind moves through the twenty-first century. Questions dealing with human origins and evolution will continue to challenge anthropologists. Cataloging and preserving cultural diversity, and inquiring deeper into the link between culture and the mind remain issues of concern. Similarly, increasing pressures such as population growth, development of the Third World countries, technological and social change, and the need to preserve a fragile global ecosystem will demand more from applied anthropologists. Their contributions will help with related practical problems, such as the promotion of community reorganization and of bilingual and bicultural education. Lastly, anthropology will begin to examine the sociocultural future as a professional field in itself (Riner, 1991). For example, as mankind moves to a state that is more structured and designed, questions about the ways we choose to intervene more consciously in the shaping of our nature and species will find some answers from the framework of anthropology.

Archaeology

Archaeology is the scientific study of past societies by means of the excavation of ancient cities, relics, artifacts, and related material remains of human tribes or societies. Though speculation about the past was present in even ancient societies, the investigation of monuments and artifacts began in the Renaissance period and has grown up to the present. An emerging field is industrial archaeology. This specialized line of inquiry is concerned with the history of technology based on the discovery, examination, and sometimes preservation of the buildings, machinery, and other artifacts of earlier industrial activity.

The future of archaeology is a challenging one in that the destruction of archaeological sites is increasing rapidly. Halting this obliteration will require concerted, careful selection of archaeological

problems to explore, of research designs appropriate to solve them, and of sites to excavate (Binford, 1986).

The future of archaeology also will involve the continued development of new approaches to the study of ancient artifacts. For example, Shanks (1992) suggests that archaeology should recognize and appreciate the experiential aspect of the encounter with the past by means of a more personal, aesthetic, emotive, and sensory methodology. Thus, archaeology can provide a more human and informative link to our human origins and derivatively to our future.

Psychology

Psychology involves the systematic study of people and their behavior, with particular focus on the nature of mental processes. Over a hundred years ago, founders of the field such as Francis Galton and William James approached the subject with a broad agenda. Throughout this century the field of psychology evolved into many subareas: depth psychology (Freud), analytical psychology (Jung), behaviorism (Skinner), humanistic psychology (Maslow, Rogers), and other specialty areas too numerous to list (Hudson, 1989).

In the foreseeable future, psychology can be expected to evolve in its diversity. New or developing areas such as paranormal behavior, genetic/biologically-based psychology, cognitive psychology, hemispheric brain studies, and artificial intelligence will continue to draw interest.

Applied psychology will play a prominent role into the future. With the increasing technological basis of modern society and the rapid rate of change affecting human societies across the globe, psychologists will continue to help individuals, organizations, and communities to develop a more humane world.

Sociology

Since August Comte coined the term *sociology* during the middle of the last century, this discipline has flourished and evolved as both an academic and popular concern. Sociology broadly concerns itself with the nature of human society, societal groups, social relations, culture and values, social organization and structure, social change, and the relationship between the individual and society (social psychology).

The sociologist critically examines the nature of society, its political and economic structures, and the world that most of us "take for granted." As with the other social sciences, sociology has continued to evolve as a discipline fragmented into various schools of thought and approaches to the study of human society. The future will most likely witness the continued specialization of this discipline along with attempts to fulfill the original dream of sociology becoming an empirically based science of humankind.

Perhaps one of the most beneficial characteristics of sociology as a discipline will be its ability to continually provide a special perspective and critique to our evolving global social system (Berger, 1992). Sociology will continue to support through its theoretical and research efforts the promotion of human rights, equality, and the replacement of unreason and prejudice with a more rational and humane approach to human society and community (Horowitz, 1992). The extent to which the social sciences are a factor in future social engineering is moot, but they will be ever more useful in shaping and evaluating social policy.

See also BEHAVIOR: SOCIAL CONSTRAINTS; CONSCIOUS EVOLUTION; CULTURE AND SOCIETY; MASS CULTURE AND ARTS; MODERNISM AND POSTMODERNISM; PSYCHIATRY; PSYCHOLOGY; SOCIAL INDICATORS; SOCIAL INVENTIONS; SOCIAL AND POLITICAL EVOLUTION.

BIBLIOGRAPHY

BERGER, P. L. "Sociology: A Disinvitation?" *Society* (November–December 1992).

BINFORD, L. R. "In Pursuit of the Future." In *American Archaeology: Past and Future*, ed., D. J. Meltzer, D. D. Fowler, and J. A. Sabloff. Washington, DC: Smithsonian Institution Press, 1986.

HOROWITZ, I. L. "Social Research and the Culture of Society." *Society* (November–December 1992).

HUDSON, L. "Psychology." In *The Social Science Encyclopedia*, ed., A. Kuper and J. Kuper. New York: Routledge, 1989.

RINER, R. R. "Anthropology About the Future: Limits and Potentials." *Human Organization* 50/3 (1991): 297–311.

RITZER, G., ed. *Frontiers of Social Theory*. New York: Columbia University Press, 1990.

SHANKS, M. *Experiencing the Past: On the Character of Archaeology*. London: Routledge, Chapman, and Hall, 1992.

John P. Keenan

Social Security.

See ENTITLEMENT PROGRAMS; PUBLIC ASSISTANCE PROGRAMS: SOCIAL SECURITY.

Social Welfare Philosophies

Throughout most of the twentieth century, social philosophers and government leaders in the developed nations of the world were in thrall to the idea of a welfare state, in which the national government takes direct responsibility for the economic and social well-being of its citizens and carries out that responsibility by taxing the earnings of workers to distribute as welfare benefits to the needy. Developed in Western Europe as an evolutionary approach to the establishment of state socialism, the welfare state reached American shores in the early 1930s with the enactment of the Social Security Act of 1935 and other Depression-inspired New Deal legislation.

Most of the proponents of the Social Security Act, including then-President Franklin D. Roosevelt, considered welfare a temporary expedient—a way to ease the pain of the Great Depression, but within twenty years of its inception, welfare had spawned a government-centered industry to produce and distribute benefits, and when President Lyndon Johnson declared war on poverty in the mid-1960s, the industry expanded rapidly, creating scores of federal programs designed to meet the needs of the poor for cash, housing, food and nutrition, health care, education, transportation, child care, adult care, training, and personal counselling. By 1980 one in every five Americans was receiving some form of welfare benefits, and annual welfare costs were $100 billion and growing at three times the rate of the national economy. But poverty was far from defeated: the poverty rate had not declined, and indicators of social dysfunction—crime, gang violence, chronic unemployment, drug abuse, illegitimate births, teenage pregnancies, and school dropouts—had risen steeply, especially among the poor.

As evidence of the failure of the welfare state accumulated and costs continued to spiral upward, a reform movement began to take shape. Some reforms were in name only: simply more welfare proposed by welfare state advocates. Other reforms, such as those of Ronald Reagan, first as governor of California (1966–1974) and then as president (1981–1989), attacked the dependency-inducing nature of the welfare state by requiring recipients to work toward self-support. As Reagan put it in his 1986 State of the Union address: "[The] success of welfare should be judged by how many of its recipients become independent of welfare." In effect, Reagan shifted Johnson's war on poverty to a war on dependency, with work as the primary weapon.

He also encouraged the states to take control of welfare reform and reduce the pervasive influence of the federal welfare bureaucracy. By early 1995 most states had embarked on welfare-to-work programs of their own design, and Congress was considering major legislation to increase state control of welfare funds and programs.

Against this background of the rise and failure of the welfare state, and of the movement toward reform through decentralization and work, public welfare in the twenty-first century will have to meet three tests:

- Does it reduce dependency?
- Does it reduce family and community instability?
- Does it reduce bureaucracy and costs?

Significant reductions in welfare dependency will be achieved only by finding paid work for welfare families and others seeking public assistance. Thus, job development and job placement will become the principal functions of the future welfare system. These functions are performed most effectively today for the general population by staffing companies and employment agencies in the private sector, which can easily expand their efforts to cover the welfare population. For some, unsubsidized jobs will be readily available; for others, subsidized jobs with a training orientation will ease the transition from welfare to work. Benefits will be converted to wages, set at levels that ensure steady increases in spendable income as a participant moves from welfare to subsidized employment and then to unsubsidized employment. The availability of more workers will stimulate product development and job creation, which, together with the decline in welfare population, will lead to a more efficient and internationally competitive economy.

Replacing obligation-free benefits with paid work will go far toward breaking down welfare-created economic and social barriers to individual advancement. But more must be done to encourage and support stable and economically viable families and safe, productive communities. Preferential welfare treatment for single-parent families will end. Work requirements will be extended to absent parents of needy children. Child support payments for needy children will go to caretaker parents, rather than to the government. Teenage parents who need public assistance will be required to attend school and live either at home or in a supervised community setting. Neighborhoods will organize themselves to provide jobs and to market the skills of their residents to the wider community. Private and predominantly faith-based neighborhood organizations will replace government as the primary provider of social services, including child care. The decentralization of welfare policy control and administration will enable communities to recapture from the welfare state the authority to set and enforce behavioral standards.

A work-oriented, decentralized approach to welfare will reduce costs and shrink the need for bureaucracy. Instead of paying to meet needs, the restructured welfare system will pay for performance—no work, no pay—and thus virtually eliminate the possibility of fraud through unreported earnings. Entry rates and average time on welfare will decrease as work becomes the norm rather than the exception. Shrinking welfare caseloads will reduce the need for government welfare workers, and the bulk of the effort needed to find or create jobs will be supplied through private sector enterprise and voluntary activities. Community-based groups will replace the government as providers and coordinators of supportive services.

The restructuring of welfare to promote self-support and restore stable families and communities will take time. Four generations of a dependency-inducing welfare state have taken a severe toll on American society, and especially on the lives of people who have come under welfare's sway. As those people work their way out of dependency, the nation must constantly remind itself of how they became dependent, and of the effort required to break the habit of dependency forced on them by a benevolent but misguided government. This will be the challenge of welfare in the twenty-first century.

See also ENTITLEMENT PROGRAMS; HEALTH CARE COSTS; PUBLIC ASSISTANCE PROGRAMS; PUBLIC ASSISTANCE PROGRAMS: SOCIAL SECURITY; SOCIAL DEMOCRACY.

BIBLIOGRAPHY

BELL, WINIFRED. *Contemporary Social Welfare.* New York: Macmillan, 1987.

BEVERLY, DAVID P., and MCSWEETNEY, EDWARD A. *Social Welfare and Social Justice.* Englewood Cliffs, NJ: Prentice-Hall, 1987.

ELLIOTT, DOREEN, et al. *The World of Social Welfare: Social Welfare and Services in an International Context.* Springfield, IL: Charles C. Thomas, 1990.

MOHAN, BRIJ. *The Logic of Social Welfare: Conjectures and Formulations.* New York: St. Martin's Press, 1988.

ZASTROW, CHARLES. *Introduction to Social Welfare: Social Problems, Services and Current Issues.* Belmont, CA: Wadsworth, 1990.

Charles D. Hobbs

Sociology.

See SOCIAL SCIENCES.

Software Computer.

See COMPUTER SOFTWARE.

Soil Conditions

More than 98 percent of the world's food supply comes from the terrestrial environment and the remaining small percentage from ocean, lake, and other aquatic ecosystems (Pimentel and Hall, 1989). Worldwide, food and fiber crops are grown on 11 percent of Earth's total land mass. Another 24 percent of the land is used as pasture to graze livestock that provide meat and milk products, while forests cover another 31 percent. Humans obtain lumber, pulpwood, and other commercial resources from 80 percent of the total forest land area. Most of the remaining land area (34 percent) is unsuitable for crops, pasture, or forests, because it is covered with ice; is too dry, steep, rocky, or wet; or has soil too shallow to support much, if any, vegetation. (See Table 1.)

More than half of the wetlands in the United States have been drained and converted to agriculture (Pimentel, 1990), while in the remainder of the world an estimated 70 percent have been converted to agricultural use. Draining wetlands has a negative impact on ducks, fishes, aquatic plants, aquatic arthropods, and several other types of aquatic and/or semiaquatic organisms.

Conversion of dryland areas to farming also is occurring in the United States and elsewhere in the world. Crop yield on this land is extremely low. The availability of water is the primary limiting factor in these ecosystems.

Each year an additional 5 million hectares must be put into food production to feed the 92 million humans added to the world population. At the same time, more than 10 million hectares of the world's productive arable land are lost each year because the land has been seriously degraded (Pimentel, 1993). To compensate for these lands, forests are removed. In fact, the spread of agriculture accounts for 80 percent of the deforestation that is now occurring worldwide.

Land degradation is occurring in most crop and pastureland throughout the world (Lal and Pierce, 1991). The major types of degradation are soil erosion, salinization, and waterlogging from irrigation.

Soil erosion is the single most serious cause of land degradation. Worldwide, soil erosion on cropland ranges from nearly 16 metric tons per hectare per year in the United States to 40 tons per hectare per year in China (USDA, 1991). The extent of erosion is of great concern because soil formation is very slow. It takes approximately five hundred years to form 2.5 cm of topsoil under agricultural conditions (OTA, 1982; Troeh et al., 1980). This means that topsoil is being lost twenty to forty times faster than it is replaced. Furthermore, erosion adversely affects crop productivity by reducing water availability by rapid water runoff, water-holding capacity, nutrients, soil organic matter, and soil depth. Continued erosion may depress food production 15 to 30 percent in the next twenty-five-year period.

Numerous soil and water conservation measures are available to protect topsoil and prevent rapid

TABLE 1.   Land Area (Million Hectares) Uses in Major Regions of the World.

Region	Total Area	Cropland	Pasture	Forest	Other*
Africa	2,965	184	792	688	1,301
North America	2,139	274	368	684	813
South America	1,753	140	468	905	240
Asia	2,679	450	678	541	1,010
Europe	473	140	84	157	92
Total	10,009	1,188	2,390	2,975	3,456
Percentage		12%	24%	30%	34%

Source: World Resources Institute, 1992.

* Land that is either too dry, too steep, or too cold to use for agriculture and forestry

water runoff. Soil conservation measures include crop rotations, strip cropping, terracing, ridge-planting, no-till, mulches, living mulches, vegetative barriers, and combinations of these (Pimentel, 1993).

Water Resources and Irrigation

As with land, water supplies often are not used with care. Agriculture consumes more freshwater than any other human activity. About 86 percent of all water is "consumed" by agriculture (Postel, personal communication, 1992), while in the United States this figure is 85 percent.

Surface water and groundwater each supply one-half of the freshwater supplies to humans on Earth. Commonly, each American uses about 400 liters per day for domestic needs, whereas total U.S. needs, including agriculture and industry, average more than 5,200 liters per day per individual. In regions where rainfall is scarce, water is pumped from available rivers, lakes, and reservoirs, and from aquifers that store groundwater.

Groundwater resources are renewed, but at an extremely slow rate of about 1 percent per year. Because of this slow renewal rate, groundwater resources have to be managed carefully to prevent overdraft. In the United States one-fifth of all irrigated land is watered by overpumping groundwater (Postel, 1989), but in some locations, like the Ogallala aquifer, overpumping may be 130 percent to 160 percent above the replacement rate.

Pumping an ever increasing amount of water to meet human population needs is increasing pressure on surface water and groundwater resources. An example is the Colorado River, which literally disappears after it enters Mexico because of excessive removal of water from the river by the states of California, Arizona, and Colorado.

The world's population may increase by 40 percent from 1990 to 2000, but the demand for water will double. In areas where groundwater is not being conserved, water shortages will constrain efforts to produce more food for the ever increasing human population.

Nutrients and Soil Fertility

All crops require nitrogen, phosphorus, potassium, calcium, and other nutrients. Nitrogen, worldwide, is the most serious limiting nutrient. The remarkable gains of the Green Revolution were due primarily to fossil energy or applying fertilizers, especially nitrogen to cropland. Ultimately, however, there are diminishing returns when the amounts of fertilizers and pesticides are greatly increased, because both are toxic to crops at high dosages.

In the United States about 10 million tons of nitrogen fertilizer are applied to agricultural land. About the same amount of nitrogen is present in the 1.6 billion tons of livestock manure that is produced annually. However, only about 20 percent of this nutrient is recycled effectively in U.S. agriculture. Where possible, it would be desirable to recycle sewage sludge. However, only about 5 percent of the sludge produced in the United States is suitable for use in agriculture because it is heavily contaminated with chemicals.

Many people compost household wastes. This keeps valuable material out of landfills, and the composted material has value for the garden.

When either commercial nitrogen or manure nitrogen is applied to cropland, only about one-third is harvested in the crop. About one-third is lost by leaching, and another third is lost by volatilization (Pimentel et al., 1989). If there is serious erosion, like 20 tons per hectare annually, then a large portion of the nutrients on the land can be lost. Rich agricultural soil may contain about 4 kilograms of nitrogen per ton of soil. The average application rate of nitrogen in U.S. corn production is about 155 kilograms per hectare (Pimentel et al., 1989). Therefore, it is clear that erosion causes major loss of fertilizer nutrients in U.S. agriculture. The best estimate is that annually U.S. agriculture loses $18 billion in fertilizer nutrients due to erosion (Troeh et al., 1980).

Soil degradation is a major environmental problem worldwide. The on-going loss of productive land to soil degradation threatens our food system now and in the future.

See also DEFORESTATION; FOOD AND AGRICULTURE; FORESTRY; GREEN REVOLUTION; RESOURCES.

BIBLIOGRAPHY

LAL, R., and PIERCE, F. J. *Soil Management for Sustainability*. Ankeny, IA: Soil and Water Conservation Society in Cooperation with the World Association of Soil and Water Conservation and Soil Science Society of America, 1991.

Office of Technology Assessment. *Impacts of Technology on U.S. Cropland and Rangeland Productivity*. Washington, DC: OTA, U.S. Congress, 1982.

PIMENTEL, DAVID. "Environmental and Social Implications of Waste in U.S. Agriculture and Food Sectors." *Journal of Agricultural Ethics* 3 (1990): 5–20.

PIMENTEL, DAVID, ed. *World Soil Erosion and Conservation*. Cambridge: Cambridge University Press, 1993.

PIMENTEL, DAVID; CULLINEY, T. W.; BUTLER, I. W.; REINE-MANN, D. J.; and BECKMAN, K. B. "Low-Input Sustainable Agriculture Using Ecological Management Practices." In M. G. Paoletti, B. R. Stinner, and G. G. Lorenzoni, eds. *Agricultural Ecology and Environment.* Amsterdam: Elsevier, 1989.

PIMENTEL, DAVID, and HALL, C. W., eds. *Food and Natural Resources.* San Diego: Academic Press, 1989.

POSTEL, SANDRA. *Water for Agriculture: Facing the Limits.* Washington, DC: Worldwatch Institute, 1989.

Troch, F. R.; Hobbs, J. A.; and Donahue, R. L. *Soil and Water Conservation for Productivity and Environmental Protection.* Englewood Cliffs, NJ: Prentice-Hall, 1980.

U.S. Department of Agriculture. *Agricultural Resources: Cropland, Water, and Conservation Situation and Outlook Report.* Washington, DC: Economic Research Service, USDA, AR-23, 1991.

World Resources Institute, ed. *World Resources.* New York: Oxford University Press, 1992.

David Pimentel

Solar Power.

See ENERGY, RENEWABLE SOURCES OF.

Solid Waste

Solid waste, or garbage, results when a consumer has no further use for a material, product, or package. Nonsustainable or inefficient uses of resources typically generate solid waste. In poorer societies and in times of war, the reuse and recycling of "waste" become second nature. Excessive consumption and frivolous disposal are conspicuous signs of wealth and an indicator of a surplus of products and resources.

Highly visible wastes that contribute to litter—for example, nondurable and disposable products, for example such as packaging for convenience foods and beverages—receive much greater attention than their percentage of the total waste stream justifies. Laws in most municipalities set fines for littering or illegal disposal of waste. The slogans of antilitter campaigns (e.g., "Put litter in its place") imply that creating waste is fine. As a result, waste can be perceived as a problem only when it is greatly out of place.

Waste in a landfill, even a modern sanitary landfill, can result in many environmental problems: the leaching of liquid into groundwater; diffusion of the methane generated in landfills into neighboring communities, or release to the atmosphere, causing objectionable odor and contributing to increases in greenhouse gases. Burning wastes in incinerators has been linked to air pollution and health concerns, particularly where older or inadequate technologies are used. Better technology can resolve many of these problems.

Products generate solid waste at each stage of their life cycle: raw material extraction, manufacturing, use, recycling, and disposal. Products consume energy and resources and generate releases to water, air, and land during all stages of their life cycle. These releases may affect human health, ecosystem health, and the depletion of resources, both renewable and nonrenewable. Simply because one product creates more solid waste than another product does not necessarily mean that it has a greater negative impact on the environment.

Is waste an inevitable product of modern life? Is waste really a serious environmental problem? Waste generation is an indicator that we may not be doing things right. The future will bring more carefully integrated thinking about products and services. Products and systems will be designed to minimize environmental impacts. Much remains to be done, but the late 1980s and early '90s have set us on the proper road.

The definition of solid waste varies from country to country, making cross-national comparisons difficult. Many countries use the term *municipal solid waste* to describe nonhazardous waste generated by households and by the institutional and commercial sectors. The definition also often includes light industrial solid waste. The more general term *solid waste* usually includes waste from construction and demolition activities, but not wastes arising from natural resource extraction.

Source reduction or prevention, reuse, and recycling (the three R's) divert garbage from landfills and incinerators. If these three options are not available or cannot reasonably be implemented, recovering energy from waste through incineration or landfill gas utilization often makes sense.

Source Reduction, or Waste Prevention

Examining the function of a product or package helps us to understand how waste can be prevented (e.g., eating ice cream on a hot summer day). An ice cream vendor may offer you these options: an edible cone, a disposable cup and spoon, or a reusable cup and spoon. If you take the disposable cup option, once your ice cream is gone, there is a wax-coated paper cup, along with a spoon, to throw out. A reusable cup and spoon must be washed and dried once you are done with them. From a waste prevention perspective, cones are preferred packages, because they are consumed along with the ice cream.

Many other examples of source reduction are linked to packaging reductions such as making packages thinner or lightweight, or removing unnecessary layers. The primary functions of packaging are to protect the product and preserve its freshness. Packaging often reduces waste by minimizing contamination, damage, and spoiling. Other functions of packaging are to attract consumers' attention or to differentiate one product from the rest. In these cases, excess packaging can be removed without impairing the product itself. Many companies have started reducing extra units or layers of packaging, such as boxes for toothpaste or deodorant containers.

Reusable and Durable Products

The second R is reuse: the use of a product or material more than once. Reuse invariably reduces solid waste. However, reused products usually must be cleaned, thereby using water and energy and generating wastewater and emissions associated with energy use. In addition, reused products are typically transported, with related environmental impacts such as air pollution emissions and fossil fuel use. Efficient design of a reuse system, however, can keep these effects to a minimum.

Durability is very important for reuse systems. Many items used on a daily basis in homes are reused: dishes, clothing, linens. Disposable items are typically used for convenience or when cleaning is difficult for hygienic purposes (e.g., garbage bags, toilet tissue, or paper towels).

Durability is an issue that is closely tied to cost. A more durable or higher-quality product costs more. Even though it may be more cost-effective to purchase more expensive, longer-lasting products, consumers often prefer to commit less money to a single purchase. As a consequence, more resources are consumed using this approach.

Remanufacturing of products such as laser-printer cartridges is a form of reuse that requires several steps: disassembly, inspection, cleaning, and replacement of components if necessary before reassembly and refilling with toner. Less formalized forms of reuse, such as secondhand stores and repair shops, also contribute to the diversion of waste from disposal.

Recycling

The third R is recycling. Of course, recycling has been around for years—scrap dealers buy scrap iron and steel to sell to mills, envelope converters send cuttings back to the mill to be repulped, scrap newsprint is used to make boxboard. Consumers and businesses are recycling many more materials than before and are incorporating recycled content—often pursuant to government mandates—into products.

Commonly recycled household materials include glass bottles and jars, aluminum and steel cans, newspapers, magazines, telephone books, plastic containers, and textiles. Industrial, commercial, or institutional recycling includes fine paper, plastic film, wood pallets, and steel strapping.

Recycling of materials requires collection of used products, separation by material type, finding markets for the recycled material, and manufacturing of end-use products that include recycled material. Lack of a consistent, high-quality supply of recycled materials due to lack of a collection infrastructure was an early hindrance to the use of recycled content. The momentum gained by mandated recycling programs is removing this barrier to increased recycling. In turn, the market value of recycled materials is increasing.

Residential recycling is usually paid for by municipalities, and thus taxpayers. The sale of recycled materials often does not cover the whole cost incurred by municipalities in the collection, separation, and marketing of materials from residences. Options such as weight-based or unit-based levies or advance disposal fees are in place or being considered in many other communities. These mechanisms aim to have consumers and manufacturers directly pay for recycling and disposal costs, rather than indirectly via taxpayers. Consumers, of course, can choose to buy a less wasteful product and see direct savings.

Composting

The future of waste diversion, in no small measure, lies in composting of organic material. Compostable material makes up more than one-third of the total waste generated. Many communities in North America and Europe collect leaf and yard wastes for centralized composting. Leaf and yard waste is collected only in the warm months and requires a relatively low level of technology (chippers, windrow turners) to produce a high-quality soil enhancer. This product is then used in municipal landscaping, given away, or sold to consumers. Many institutional and industrial facilities (e.g., hospitals, universities, hotels), and some communities collect food waste for composting.

Gardeners do not need to be told about the benefits of composting at home. Many communities now subsidize the distribution of backyard composters or worm composters, and educate citizens on their use. Residential, on-site composting means that the environmental burdens associated with transporting waste to disposal sites are avoided, too.

Energy Recovery and Incineration

Incineration is the combustion of waste in a controlled environment. Older, outdated equipment can result in high levels of air pollution, including dioxins and furons. Modern incinerators have air-pollution-control equipment to remove or minimize the unwanted combustion products. When operated correctly, at high enough temperatures, incinerators emit far lower levels of air pollutants than many other industrial sources. By burning waste in incinerators or using waste directly as a fuel in boilers, energy is recovered and may be used to generate steam or electricity.

Incinerators are a popular option where land is at a premium. However, they are falling out of favor due to high capital expenses. Incinerators are typically built and operated for municipalities by private companies, which then require a guaranteed supply of waste to make a profit. Some jurisdictions have banned new incinerators, contending that such facilities discourage recycling, reuse, and reduction programs.

Almost all new facilities can recover energy from the waste burned to produce steam for nearby industrial or institutional users, or to produce electricity. This approach offsets the need to use fossil fuels to supply the required energy.

Landfilling

Modern sanitary landfills are a vast improvement over the dumps of only a few years ago, where garbage was often burned in an uncontrolled manner. Modern landfills capture leachate (the liquid that percolates out of waste when it decomposes), landfill gas (the gas generated by the decomposing waste), and minimize odors by covering waste with soil or some other material at the end of each day. These practices control groundwater contamination from leachate and limit the uncontrolled emissions of methane, a greenhouse gas.

Siting

All waste-handling facilites, but especially landfills and incinerators, are difficult to site in today's mainly urban societies. Although modern facilities control pollution of air and water, the problems of odor, increased truck traffic, and reduced property values are not welcome in many communities.

Conversion of agricultural land to landfills is a major concern as well. This reluctance to site facilities has given rise to the term *NIMBY*, or "Not in my backyard." Fortunately, these attitudes provide extra incentive for individuals, industries, and governments to develop and participate in waste prevention and reduction programs.

See also DEFORESTATION; ENVIRONMENT; ENVIRONMENTAL BEHAVIOR; ENVIRONMENTAL ETHICS; ENVIRONMENTAL INDICATORS; ENVIRONMENTAL POLICY CHANGES; GLOBAL ENVIRONMENTAL PROBLEMS; HAZARDOUS WASTES; NATURAL RESOURCES, USE OF; RESOURCES.

BIBLIOGRAPHY

ALEXANDER, JUDD H. *In Defense of Garbage.* Westport, CT: Praeger/Greenwood, 1993.

DASTON, THOMAS E. *Recycling Solid Waste: The First Choice for Private and Public Sector Management.* Westport, CT: Quorum/Greenwood, 1993.

FISHBEIN, BETTE K. *Germany, Garbage, and the Green Dot: Challenging the Throwaway Society.* New York: INFORM, 1994.

Lynn Patenaude

Sorokin, Pitirim A. (1889–1968)

After teaching sociology at the University of St. Petersburg and taking an active part in revolutionary politics, the Russian-born American sociologist Sorokin was expelled from Soviet Russia for his anti-Bolshevik views in 1922. Emigrating to the United States, he taught for several years at the University of Minnesota. In 1930 he founded the Department of Sociology at Harvard University. His abundant published work spans nearly every topic in sociology, but he is best known for his four-volume magnum opus, *Social and Cultural Dynamics* (1937–1941), which offers a cyclical theory of sociocultural change rivalling the theories of Oswald SPENGLER and Arnold J. Toynbee. Sorokin maintained that the appropriate unit of study in world history is not a society or civilization but a sociocultural "supersystem." Supersystems are of three kinds, each grounded in a different conception of ultimate reality and truth. The first is the "ideational" supersystem, steeped in religious faith. After its possibilities are exhausted, it is generally succeeded by an "integral" or "idealistic" supersystem, which in turn yields to a "sensate" supersystem, for which reality is seen as material and accessible to the senses. The idealistic supersystem is a rational synthesis of the two extremes. Sorokin viewed the modern West as decadently sensate and foresaw a dawning age of ideational or perhaps idealistic culture bringing a renewal of spiritual consciousness. He also published a comparative analysis of cyclical theories of history and culture, *Social Philosophies of an Age of Crisis* (1950).

BIBLIOGRAPHY

COSTELLO, PAUL. *World Historians and Their Goals.* DeKalb: Northern Illinois University Press, 1993, chapter 5.

COWELL, F. R. *History, Civilization, and Culture: An Introduction to the Historical and Social Philosophy of Pitirim A. Sorokin.* London: A. and C. Black, 1952.

SOROKIN, PITIRIM A. *A Long Journey: The Autobiography of Pitirim A. Sorokin.* New Haven, CT: College and University Press, 1963.

W. Warren Wagar

South Africa.

See AFRICA.

South America.

See LATIN AMERICA.

Space Colonization

The dream of building a home in space has existed as long as human beings have dreamed of traveling there. The Russian visionary Konstantin Tsiolkovsky was the first to propose a workable vision, in the early 1900s, saying, "Earth is the cradle of mankind, but mankind will not always remain in the cradle." He foresaw a gigantic metal spaceship built in orbit. Science fiction writers, such as Murray Leinster, James Blish, and Robert A. Heinlein, also envisoned self-contained spaceship worlds or human settlements on other planets.

Shortly after the first manned space flights in 1961, futurist Dandridge Cole published the first serious examination of possible future colonies in space. It was physicist Gerard K. O'Neill, however, who gave this science-fictional idea popularity and credibility in his book *The High Frontier* (1977). O'Neill proposed giant orbital cities stationed at the fifth libration point, a region of relative gravitational stability in the Earth-Moon system. O'Neill's concept for these Lagrange-5 (L-5) colonies sparked several fictional treatments, and a society of several thousand members devoted to the promotion of the idea was also formed (now known as the National Space Society in Washington, D.C., which publishes *Ad Astra* magazine).

In fact, the first rudimentary space colony was built in 1977, the same year in which O'Neill's pioneering work was published. The Soviet space station Salyut 6, launched October 1977, was the first man-made structure designed for "open-ended," or semipermanent habitation. Unlike earlier space stations, it was capable of being refueled, maneuvered, and expanded in size. An even more ambitious station called Mir was launched by the Soviet Union in February 1986; by 1993 it had seen over six years of continuous operation, serving as temporary home to over forty different space travelers from nine different countries. It also doubled in volume through the addition of several scientific and technical modules. Some elements of Mir are expected to be operational well into the twenty-first century.

Space stations, however, are not true space colonies, as envisioned by Tsiolkovsky and others, because they are not yet open to ordinary citizens, children, workers. They are more like the research stations in Antarctica, remote outposts devoted to specific types of scientific research.

Inhibiting factors are money and technology. Knowledge of the effects of long-term space travel on human physiology and psychology remains quite limited. Although several Russian cosmonauts have lived in space for as much as a year, no human being has spent more than a few days outside the protective Van Allen Belt, which is where most proposed space colonies would be located.

The physicist J. D. Bernaul speculated in *The World, the Flesh, and the Devil* (1929) that human beings would have to be physically altered to survive in such harsh environments.

More basic technological problems, such as the creation of a so-called closed ecological system, also remain. The yearlong earthbound Biosphere II experiment (1992–1993) was widely considered to be seriously flawed; a workable ecosystem for a space colony would have to be larger and more complex. Launch systems themselves are still too expensive and unreliable to provide sufficient materials. An orbital space colony of the O'Neill island-type seems to be decades away.

The Moon itself presents the most attractive location, serving as a source for raw materials even in the L-5 scenarios. Though airless, the Moon is similar enough to Earth to supply useful raw materials such as metal, perhaps even hydrogen. The construction of habitats sheltered by lunar rock would avoid the immediate danger of radiation; the presence of gravity would mitigate problems of long-term weightlessness. The Moon also has the advantage of its nearness to Earth; supplies can reach it in three days.

Other sites for planetary colonies are much more remote. Even Mars, Earth's nearest planetary neighbor, is not likely to be visited by manned spacecraft until the middle of the twenty-first century. The challenges increase with distance.

A more relevant question is that, given the dangers and the expense, why establish a colony in space? One thing is certain: space colonies have no role in relieving population pressure on Earth. Even the most wildly optimistic space delivery systems would be incapable of taking more than a fraction of our planet's daily population increase.

There are potential economic benefits to O'Neill colonies. Power could be generated in space and beamed to Earth by microwave. Other futurists have suggested that dangerous or environmentally damaging manufacturing could be performed in the reaches of space.

It is also possible that space colonies will be founded by groups fleeing religious or political persecution, as were European settlements in North America. L-5 islands might then become homes for various sects or ethnic groups— eventually becoming extraterrestrial nation-states. If such a self-contained and supporting colony had a propulsion system, it could leave the solar system entirely and even travel to the stars.

For the near future, however, space colonies are likely to remain small in size, and be restricted to low Earth orbit or the lunar surface. Even though technically feasible, the expense of building a space colony is so great that such a project could not be borne by a single nation.

See also ANTARCTICA; EXTRATERRESTRIAL LIFE-FORMS; SPACE FLIGHT; SPACE TRAVEL.

BIBLIOGRAPHY

BERNAUL, J. F. *The World, the Flesh, and the Devil.* London: Methuen, 1929.

COLE, DANDRIDGE. *Beyond Tomorrow.* Amherst, WI: Amherst Press, 1965.

O'NEILL, GERARD K. *The High Frontier.* New York: William Morrow, 1977.

TSIOLKOVSKY, KONSTANTIN. *The Rocket Into Cosmic Space.* Moscow: Naoothnoye Obozreniye, 1903.

Michael Cassutt

Space Flight

So far, the only propulsion systems that work in the vacuum of space are rockets, which rely on Newton's Third Law of Motion: *For every force exerted in one direction, a force of equal magnitude is exerted in the opposite direction.* Chemical rockets obtain their energy from burning a fuel with an oxidizer, which is needed in space, where there is no oxygen to support combustion. The hotter the exhaust gas, the faster it flows through the nozzle and the more thrust it provides. Rocket engines can be rated in terms of thrust or efficiency, which is referred to as *specific impulse.* Thrust, the pushing force that moves the space vehicle, is measured in pounds. Specific impulse is the measure of how long a pound of propellants will yield a pound of thrust, and it is rated in seconds. Advanced chemical rockets deliver specific impulses of about 500 seconds. Interplanetary propulsion clearly must look beyond chemical rockets.

Nuclear energy could be used to heat a gaseous propellant and provide rocket thrust. The propellant, often called the *working fluid* in nonchemical rockets, can be either a liquid or a gas. A nuclear rocket might consist of a compact nuclear fission reactor, a working fluid (probably hydrogen), and a small "shadow shield" to prevent radiation from reaching the habitation area. Nuclear rockets could provide specific impulses in the range of 1,000 seconds, with thrusts comparable to those of chemical rockets.

Since their exhaust gases would be radioactive, nuclear rockets are envisioned as pure space propulsion systems. They would not be used as boosters to lift spacecraft from the ground.

Nuclear power can also be used to provide energy for *electrical rockets.* Electrical energy can heat a propellant, or a working fluid that conducts electricity can be accelerated to very high velocity directly by electrical energy. Such rocket systems are extremely efficient, with specific impulses of 1,000–10,000 seconds or more. Unfortunately, most (but not all) electric rocket systems produce very low thrusts.

There are several types of electrical rockets. The *resistojet* simply heats its working fluid (usually hydrogen) by electrical resistance, much as an electric stove boils water. Specific impulse is limited to about 1,000 seconds, largely because it is difficult to create higher temperatures without damaging the metal heating elements. Small resistojets have been used as attitude-control thrusters on satellites.

The *ion thruster* has been flown in NASA's Space Electric Rocket Test (SERT) program. A working fluid that conducts electricity, such as mercury or ionized argon gas, is accelerated by electrical energy rather than by heat. Specific impulses of 10,000 seconds or more are possible. Ion thrusters can be powered by solar-voltaic cells that convert sunlight directly into electricity.

The *plasma thruster* employs electromagnetic fields to accelerate an electrically conducting working fluid. Physicists call a gas that has been ionized to the point where it conducts electricity easily a *plasma*. Plasma thrusters produce more thrust per weight than ion thrusters, and are capable of specific impulses of 10,000 seconds or more.

Electrical rockets are limited by the weight of their electrical power systems. The more electrical power needed, the more massive the electric power generator must be. Thus, most electrical rocket systems will remain small, low-thrust devices, limited to fractions of a pound of thrust. Instead of quickly burning all their propellants, the way chemical rockets do, electrical rockets can "burn" for days or even months, slowly accelerating all the time.

Low thrusts, however, limit them to unmanned missions where travel times can be sacrificed for efficiency. Electrical rockets could never boost spacecraft into orbit against the gravitational pull of Earth, but their small puffs of thrust can keep a satellite or space station from drifting out of its desired position in orbit.

Solar sails provide an alternate form of "slow but steady" space transportation that does not use rockets at all. Light exerts some pressure, but so little that a delicate apparatus is needed merely to measure it. Since no propellant is used, the solar sail's specific impulse is infinite. Acceleration from such a minuscule push requires a sail of enormous dimensions. The bigger the sail, however, the heavier it becomes, and the more difficult it is to accelerate the payload. Solar sails are slow. It would take years for a sail of 2.152 million square feet (a square with sides of more than a quarter-mile) to reach Mars.

It may be possible to combine nuclear energy and electrical power to produce rocket engines of high thrust *and* high efficiency by using magnetohydrodynamic (MHD) power generators. MHD generators draw electrical power from the hot exhaust gases streaming from a rocket engine. MHD generators operate with hot, ionized gases—the hotter, the better. They could take advantage of the full potential of nuclear power. Specific impulses of 2,500 seconds could be obtained from *nuclear-MHD rockets*, more than five times better than that obtained from chemical rockets.

MHD generators have no moving parts. They are rugged, comparatively lightweight, and become more efficient with increasing size. Since a nuclear MHD system could produce about 100 times more power per pound of equipment than existing electric rocket systems such as the ion thruster, a nuclear-MHD system could provide high thrust as well as high efficiency.

Instead of propulsion systems that must carry their own weight with them, like airplanes, it may be possible for the energy source to remain on the ground and transfer energy to the moving vehicle. Two such ideas have been proposed and tested. One uses lasers for propulsion, the other, electrical catapults.

In 1950 Arthur C. CLARKE, the visionary author who earlier conceptualized the communications satellite, suggested that *electrically powered catapults* would be a very efficient way to launch payloads off the Moon. On the airless Moon, with its gravity pull merely one-sixth that of Earth, Clarke reasoned that a catapult less than 3 kilometers (1.86 miles) long could fire payloads off the lunar surface. The spacecraft would be accelerated to 100 g (100 Earth gravities), preventing use for fragile cargoes such as human beings! Powered by electricity generated from sunlight or nuclear energy, the catapult could launch unmanned cargoes of lunar ores from the Moon for mere pennies per pound.

Nearly twenty years later, Gerard K. O'Neill of Princeton University developed Clarke's idea into the modern concept of the *mass driver*. Such a device need not be ground-based. It can be positioned in space for use as an orbital catapult or even as a spacecraft propulsion system. A mass driver reaction engine (MDRE) is actually a rocket that fires solid pellets rather than hot gases to create thrust. The mass driver, some 3 to 6 miles long, uses powerful superconducting magnets to accelerate pellets of 14 grams (about a half ounce). The pellets are accelerated to velocities of 17,600 miles per hour within a second or less. About 3 megawatts of electrical power are needed, provided either by nuclear or solar energy.

The MDRE could move heavy cargoes from low orbits to higher ones. MDREs could also be used as interplanetary spacecraft that "eat" chunks of asteroids and spit them out to provide thrust. For long-term expeditions seeking raw materials among the asteroid belt, an MDRE might turn out to be more efficient than carrying propellants for the return trip all the way from Earth.

Laser propulsion may become the most efficient and economical way to travel in space. The laser, constituting most of the weight of the propulsion system, could remain ground-based. Because lasers can heat propellants to far higher temperatures than can be obtained by chemical burning, a laser-powered rocket can deliver specific impulses of 1,000–2,000 seconds.

Ground-based lasers could be used to raise the altitude of satellites that have been lifted to low orbit by the space shuttle or an expendable booster. Lasers of thousands of megawatt's power would be needed to boost spacecraft from the ground, but such laser-boosted spacecraft could carry payloads that are 50 percent of their total liftoff weight, rather than the 1 percent of today's space shuttle. Huge lasers in orbit near the Earth could propel spacecraft through the far reaches of the solar system, and even out toward other stars.

The penultimate space propulsion system would be a *fusion rocket*. Nuclear rockets use the energy generated in a nuclear reactor by nuclear *fission* (splitting apart massive atomic nuclei such as those of uranium or plutonium) to heat a propellant.

In nuclear *fusion*, the nuclei of the lightest atoms are fused together to create heavier nuclei—and energy. Fusion is the energy source of the stars. The fuel for a fusion rocket would be water—or more precisely the isotope of hydrogen called deuterium or "heavy hydrogen." For every 6,000 normal hydrogen atoms in water on Earth, there is one atom of deuterium. This means that an eight-ounce glass of water contains enough deuterium to yield as much energy, through fusion, as burning 500,000 barrels of oil!

The energy potential of fusion is so great that once it is applied to space flight, spacecraft will be able to accelerate constantly at one g (one Earth gravity) rather than spend most of their trip coasting. Fusion-powered unmanned probes could travel to Alpha Centauri or Barnard's Star in about 50 years (one-way).

There is one possibility even beyond fusion: *antimatter*. Whereas fusion liberates 0.7 percent of the mass of the reacting matter, a collision between normal matter and antimatter transforms all the mass into energy: 100 percent conversion.

Physicists produce minuscule amounts of antimatter for experiments that probe the fundamental nature of matter and energy. To produce even a few grams of antimatter would take all the electrical energy available in the United States and more. The problem is that once you have some antimatter, where do you keep it? If antimatter and normal matter touch, they annihilate each other in a flash of gamma rays. Someday we may learn to harness this genie and build magnetic "bottles" in which to store antimatter. When that day comes, we can truly look toward the stars and begin the ultimate exploration of the universe.

See also AIR TRANSPORT; SATELLITE COMMUNICATIONS; SCIENCE FICTION; SPACE COLONIZATION; SPACE TRAVEL.

BIBLIOGRAPHY

BOVA, BEN. *The High Road.* Boston: Houghton-Mifflin, 1981.

BYERLY, RADFORD, ed. *Space Policy Reconsidered.* Boulder, CO: Westview Press, 1989.

JASTROW, ROBERT. *Journey to the Stars: Space Exploration Tomorrow and Beyond.* New York: Bantam Books, 1989.

KAUFMANN, WILLIAM J. *Discovering the Universe.* New York: W. H. Freeman, 1987.

MCLUCAS, JOHN L. *Space Commerce.* Cambridge, MA: Harvard University Press, 1991.

Ben Bova

Space Satellites

The beginnings of space satellites are ordinarily dated from the launching of Sputnik by the former Soviet Union in 1957. However, the idea of a "repeater in the sky" was thought of much earlier. Various writers suggested that space could be used for communication. In 1911, Hugo Gernsback suggested the use of radio, television, and radar in his science fiction book entitled *Ralph 124C41+*. In 1942, George O. Smith wrote a story called "Venus Equilateral" about a manned space vehicle that orbited the sun and was designed for communication. Physicists much earlier had calculated the theoretical orbits of objects located at various distances from Earth.

The implications of these ideas were recognized by Arthur C. CLARKE in a 1945 article in *Wireless*

World, in which he described a system of "extraterrestrial relays," or repeaters in space. Clarke calculated that an object put into orbit 22,300 miles (36,000 kilometers) above Earth would revolve around the planet in twenty-four hours, the time it takes Earth to rotate on its axis. Thus the repeater would appear motionless or "geostationary" from Earth. He noted that three such repeaters located 120 degrees apart above the equator would cover the entire globe.

Only twelve years later, Sputnik showed that people could communicate using space satellites. However, Sputnik was not a geostationary satellite; it was in low Earth orbit and had to be tracked across the sky, and it simply beeped. But it spurred U.S. scientists and engineers to develop more sophisticated satellites for commercial use. In 1963, the world saw the results as the Syncom 3 satellite transmitted television coverage of the Tokyo Olympics. In 1965, just twenty years after Clarke's article was published, the first commercial international satellite, known as Early Bird (or INTELSAT I), was launched to link North America and Europe.

Satellite technology has evolved dramatically since the early 1960s. Early Bird had only 240 telephone circuits, while today's satellites have the capacity for more than 40,000 voice circuits, or more than 200 television channels. Early experimental satellites were designed for a lifetime of two years; today's satellites are designed to last at least ten years, and are moving toward fifteen years. The limitation on the satellite's life is not the reliability of the electronics, which are fully redundant, but the weight, which limits the amount of station-keeping fuel that can be carried. This hydrazine fuel is used to keep the satellite in orbit; jets can be fired from Earth to nudge the satellite back into position when it begins to drift. When the fuel is expended, the satellite will begin to drift, and eventually it cannot be tracked from fixed antennas on Earth.

Satellites are used for a variety of purposes. Most communication satellites are parked in geostationary orbits as foreseen by Clarke; the advantage is that Earth stations can simply be fixed to point at the satellite; they do not have to track it across the sky. However, some experimental satellites have been located at lower orbits. The Russian Molniya system is a series of satellites in polar orbit that are tracked as they pass overhead; these are used for telecommunications and broadcasting to reach communities in the high Arctic. Several companies are now planning to build systems of low Earth-orbiting satellites (LEOs) for mobile and personal communications. The advantage would be lower launch costs and higher-powered satellite signals, making it possible to use small mobile or handheld transceivers.

Satellites are also used for various types of surveillance. Military satellites orbit at low altitudes and can transmit images with very high resolution. Remote sensing satellites are used to map the Earth and to identify mineral deposits and various forms of soil and vegetation. This information can be used to locate promising areas for mining; to monitor flooding and desertification; and to plan land use for agriculture, forestry, and human settlements. Weather satellites transmit images that are used to monitor storms and forecast weather conditions.

Satellites have several properties that make them particularly appropriate for many telecommunications applications. Geostationary satellites can cover as much as one-third of Earth's surface. Domestic satellites are designed to cover large nations such as the United States, Canada, and Australia, while regional satellites can cover the entire Arab world or Western Europe, for example. Earth stations placed anywhere in the satellite's beam are linked with each other through the satellite. As a result, the cost of communication via satellite is independent of distance—the cost of communicating across 500 or 5,000 miles is the same. In contrast, the cost of building and maintaining terrestrial networks is directly proportional to the length of the transmission route.

Earth stations can be installed virtually anywhere, whether it is in a remote village, an offshore oil rig, a high-rise building, or a disaster site. Thus communication can be provided wherever it is needed, without waiting to extend terrestrial facilities. Satellite capacity is also flexible; the technology can be used for voice, data, and video, and it is simple to allocate additional bandwidth where needed. For example, a community can begin with a few voice circuits and then add more circuits and television reception. Satellite systems are also extremely reliable once in orbit; satellite electronics are highly redundant. Also, if there is a problem with one Earth station, it affects only that site, whereas with terrestrial networks, all the sites farther down the network would be affected.

Some countries are concerned about the spillover effects of satellite signals. Programming from U.S. domestic satellites, for example, can be seen in Canada and throughout the Caribbean, Central America, and as far south as Colombia. Another concern is that information from surveillance satellites can be collected without permission. However, the United States, which developed the Landsat satellites, and France, which has commercialized the technology through its Spot Image satellites, have provided training in the interpretation of remote sensing images and have made them available free or at low cost to developing countries.

Unfortunately, many developing countries have not been able to take full advantage of satellite technology. While more than 170 countries use the INTELSAT system for international communications linking capitals and other major cities, most of the developing world remains without access to reliable telecommunications. Satellites could be used to provide low-cost communications to millions of people who are now beyond the range of terrestrial networks.

See also COMMUNICATIONS; SATELLITE COMMUNICATIONS; TELECOMMUNICATIONS; TELEPHONES.

BIBLIOGRAPHY

CHETTY, P. R. *Satellite Technology and Its Applications*, 2nd ed. Blue Ridge Summit, PA: TAB Books, 1991.

GLASER, P. E., et al. *Solar Power Satellites: The Emerging Energy Option*. Englewood Cliffs, NJ: Prentice-Hall, 1992.

HUDSON, HEATHER E. *Communication Satellites: Their Development and Impact*. New York: Free Press, 1990.

INTELSAT Annual Report, 1990–91. Washington, DC: INTELSAT, 1991.

PELTON, JOSEPH N., and HOWKINS, JOHN. *Satellites International*. New York: Stockton Press, 1988.

Heather E. Hudson

Space Travel

Space travel has been a dream of humanity for millennia. The ancient Greeks pondered its possibilities before the birth of Christ. Jules Verne wrote a novel (*A Trip to the Moon*, 1865) describing a journey to the moon that rather strongly resembled the actual Apollo lunar landing in 1969. The Chinese invented rockets in the eleventh century, but their use was limited mainly to warfare. Not until the mid-twentieth century did rockets become tools of space exploration. Wernher von Braun and his team of German scientists, working first in Germany during World War II and later in the United States, pioneered the use of rockets for space exploration.

The era of human space travel began on April 12, 1961, when Yuri Gagarin became the first person to leave the Earth's atmosphere and enter the space environment. Flying in the Soviet spacecraft *Vostok I*, he orbited the planet once, spending a total of 108 minutes in space.

Lunar Expeditions

In 1961 President John F. Kennedy inaugurated a new era in space history. He declared, in a speech before Congress, that the United States would send a man to the Moon and return him safely to Earth before the end of the decade.

From 1968 to 1972 American astronauts made an unprecedented series of journeys to the moon. Apollo 8, launched in December 1968, was the first spacecraft to orbit the moon, sending back the first television pictures of the whole Earth. Apollo 11 later fulfilled the pledge of President Kennedy, landing two men on the Moon, Neil Armstrong and Buzz Aldrin, in July 1969. Five other lunar missions successfully landed astronauts on the Moon; the final mission, Apollo 17, took place in 1972.

Interplanetary Travel

Since the Apollo missions, no human beings have traveled beyond low Earth orbit (LEO), and manned missions to the other planets in the solar system remain a long-range goal for all current space programs. However, there have been numerous unmanned missions, and every planet in the solar system except Pluto has been visited by unmanned probes.

Mars is the planet most often mentioned as a destination for future manned missions. Mars is the most Earth-like of the planets, with a day of almost the same duration as that of Earth, and temperatures that are Earth-like during daylight hours. Geological evidence suggests that Mars was once on an evolutionary path similar to that of Earth, with running water in abundance, and perhaps even early life forms. However, Mars was apparently too small to retain an Earth-like atmosphere, and that seems to have halted its evolution.

Interstellar Travel

Unless human beings discover a new form of propulsion, interstellar travel will not become a reality in the near future. According to Einsteinian physics, the speed of light is the upper limit of velocity for any body in the universe. The nearest star system, Alpha Centauri, is 4.3 light-years from Earth, meaning that a spacecraft moving at the speed of light would take 4.3 years to arrive there. Currently, all propulsion systems are far slower than the speed of light, and a journey to Alpha Centauri would require many years.

According to Einstein's theory of relativity, however, time on a spacecraft traveling close to the speed of light will not move at the same pace as on Earth. If the theory holds true, time will be compressed, so space travelers would only age by a few days while their friends and relatives on Earth would age many years.

Several ideas have been proposed to meet the challenges posed by long-duration spaceflight. For example, astronauts might be placed in a state of suspended animation in which they would consume fewer resources such as food and air and would not face the boredom of a long mission. On arrival at their destination, the star voyagers would be awakened to complete their mission.

"Generation starships" are an idea long popular with science fiction writers (e.g., Robert Heinlein's "Universe" [1940] and Brian Aldiss's *Nonstop* [1959]). These ships would leave Earth with an entire human community aboard. Many generations would die as the starship made its way to its destination, but succeeding generations would hopefully survive to colonize the target star system.

The closed ecological life support system is another idea under consideration, and has some practical experience to support it. These systems would mimic the ecology of Earth, so that space travelers would, in effect, carry their terrestrial environment along with them. Made popular by the Biosphere II experiment in Arizona in the early 1990s, this concept may become a practical approach either for spacecraft or for space settlements.

Social Systems

One of the most significant barriers to long-duration spaceflight is the inability of human social systems to function effectively under the challenging conditions of a space environment. A journey to Mars, for example, might require a total of three years, with as much as a year spent in transit from the Earth to Mars, and a similar period on the return.

Experiences in extreme environments on Earth, such as Antarctica, submarines, and in long-duration space missions on Russian space stations, show that it is very difficult for human beings to endure being confined for long periods of time. Small problems are magnified in close quarters, often leading to serious disputes over minor issues.

Once human beings settle in the space environment permanently, one of the great benefits of space travel may well be the development of new social systems. Early settlements in space, moon or Mars, are likely to reflect social systems on Earth. However, because of their distance from the Earth, they may quickly develop a degree of independence and begin to evolve in response to the space environment. Eventually, they will probably declare their independence from Earth, just as the thirteen colonies in North America did in 1776. We will have to be careful to avoid war between terrestrials and their spacefaring descendants.

Physical/Mental Effects

The Earth is the natural environment for human beings, and our bodies are adapted to terrestrial conditions, especially the pull of Earth's gravity. For this reason, space travel has profound physical effects on the human body, mainly because of weightlessness. When people go into space, the body rapidly adapts to the diminution of gravity—the bones begin to shed calcium, the heart beats less rapidly, the circulation of blood changes, and the spine lengthens.

Evidence suggests that vigorous physical exercise while in space is the best countermeasure for the physical changes that occur in low-gravity settings. Astronauts and cosmonauts who have returned to Earth after even a year in space have adjusted without long-term ill effects.

We can only speculate about the impact on generations of human beings who live, work, and reproduce in the space environment. It is possible that a new species will evolve that will be quite different from the current *Homo sapiens*.

While mental effects are more difficult to quantify, they also occur. For example, the "Overview Effect" is a term that the author has developed for an experience that appears to be universal among astronauts and cosmonauts, resulting from looking back at the Earth from orbit or from the moon. This effect is a realization of the unity and oneness of everything on the Earth, an understanding that every terrestrial being functions as a component of an interconnected system.

For astronauts and cosmonauts who went into space with a religious perspective, the experience often confirms their original views. For others, the feeling is a "peak experience" that offers new insights into the nature of humanity and our relationship not only with the Earth but also with the universe as a whole.

Philosophical Implications

Our limited experience in space shows that our philosophical perspective can be deeply affected by our physical location, and this understanding may be the most important result of space travel. The human evolutionary path will move outward into space, which means that the universe itself will become our ecological range, rather than the Earth alone. The ultimate outcome appears to be that we will become "citizens of the universe," increasingly aware of our identity not only as a part of the Earth but also within the universe, evolving as a whole system on a vaster scale. The impact will be even more profound if we meet intelligent extraterrestrial beings, who may be thousands, or millions, of years ahead of us in evolution.

How will space travel affect our sense of identity, of individuality, of our relationship with the universe, with humanity and other life-forms, and with the divine? Speculation alone will not answer our questions. Only the further experience of space exploration itself will reveal its ultimate philosophical implications to us.

See also AIR TRANSPORT; GLOBAL CONSCIOUSNESS; SCIENCE FICTION; SPACE COLONIZATION; SPACE FLIGHT.

BIBLIOGRAPHY

ALLEN, JOSEPH P. *Entering Space: An Astronaut's Odyssey.* New York: Stewart, Tabori, & Chang, 1984.

CARPENTER, M. SCOTT, et al. *We Seven: By the Astronauts Themselves.* New York: Simon & Schuster, 1962.

COLLINS, MICHAEL. *Carrying the Fire.* New York: Farrar, Straus and Giroux, 1974.

LEBEDEV, VALENTIN. *Diary of a Cosmonaut: 211 Days in Space.* Houston: Pytoresource Research, Inc., Information Service, 1988.

WHITE, FRANK. *The Overview Effect: Space Exploration and Human Evolution.* Boston: Houghton Mifflin, 1987.

WOLFE, TOM. *The Right Stuff.* New York: Farrar, Straus and Giroux, 1979.

Frank White

Spengler, Oswald (1880–1936)

Born in a small town in the Harz Mountains, German philosopher of history Spengler spent several years as a secondary school teacher. In 1911, with the help of a modest inheritance from his late mother, he resigned his post to became a full-time writer. His one major work, *Der Untergang des Abendlandes* (1918–1922; in English, *The Decline* [more accurately, "Fall"] *of the West,* 1926–1928), was translated into several languages and brought Spengler worldwide attention. Most of his other writings were brief political tracts, such as *Jahre der Entscheidung* (1933; in English, *The Hour of Decision, 1934*), in which he put forward a bleakly conservative and racist worldview critical of Nazism, but spiritually akin to it. *The Decline of the West* provides a comparative analysis of the evolution of cultures. Defining them as self contained organisms, Spengler contended that each great historic culture passes through a similar life cycle, from birth, rise, and decline to death. Each stage was inevitable and could not be staved off. He asserted that the "Faustian" culture of the West, born in the early Middle Ages, was now senescent. After a coming era of Caesarism comparable to the imperial stage of Roman history, he anticipated that it would collapse and die.

BIBLIOGRAPHY

COSTELLO, PAUL. *World Historians and Their Goals: Twentieth Century Answers to Modernism.* DeKalb, IL: Northern Illinois University Press, 1993, chapter 3.

FISCHER, KLAUS PETER. *History and Prophecy: Oswald Spengler and the Decline of the West.* New York: Peter Lang, 1989.

HUGHES, H. STUART. *Oswald Spengler: A Critical Estimate,* 2nd ed. New York: Scribner, 1962 (originally published 1952).

MAZLISH, BRUCE. *The Riddle of History: The Great Speculators from Vico to Freud.* New York: Harper and Row, 1966, chapter 9.

W. Warren Wagar

Sports and Activities, Spectator

Competitive sports and games have been central to human civilization throughout recorded history, spreading across cultures. Sometimes sports played a part of religious rituals or as forms of modified warfare. Whatever the purpose, sport reflects the conditions and needs of a society.

In the city-state of Athens from about 500 to 400 B.C. sports and games were so important that political leaders provided athletic grounds for the entire populace. Spectator sports, on the other hand, didn't exist until Roman times when amphitheaters, such as the Coliseum, drew nearly the entire citizenry to view games and contests. This eventually led to spectacles that were often bloody, lewd, and obscene, involving days of wild celebration, hence the expression "Roman holiday."

The citizens of Rome initially relied upon sport to maintain the body and the spirit for purposes of defense, but as the amount of leisure time increased and the need for physical labor and military service declined, the focus of sport changed. Entertainment replaced participation in sports, which, some say, led to the decline of Roman civilization.

How then will the needs and conditions of the future affect spectator sports? Will spectator sports be a force for the advancement of society or the decline of still another civilization?

Technology is a force changing society and, in turn, spectator sports. Pay-per-view TV is the future version of season tickets. Interactive technology will enable remote-controlled spectators to sit in the dugout or at the fifty-yard line, changing venues with the click of the remote control. *Spectator* will be redefined, physical presence at an event no longer being required.

If technology is changing our understanding of what it means to be a spectator, it will also transform the definition of *sports fans*. The National Football League has been playing preseason games in Europe for nearly a decade. Former American baseball players have long been delighting Japanese fans. No longer will sports fans be defined by traditional national pastimes. Technology will create a global economy that extends to spectator sports, and the balance of trade will redefine the concept of a "home court" advantage. Forget the National or the American Leagues and look for the Pacific-Rim and Central European Leagues.

Sport globalization is an economic issue as the profits from this entertainment industry continue to grow. College sports generate substantial amounts of revenue through the television and licensing rights of amateur athletes. The annual salaries of professional athletes rival those of rock stars. Spirited salary negotiations hallmark each new sport season. Baseball felt the pressure and financial pinch when the 1994 season was the first to open without a major television contract.

Just how far can the commercialization of spectator sports spread? From instant replays to scoreboards, everything and anything has a price tag. In the not-so-distant future, the starting lineup announcements may include the name of the player as well as the product or company sponsoring the athlete for that game. A proficient basestealer may be sponsored by a security company, while a football receiver might be sponsored by a glove company. Product endorsements and merchandising are substantial revenue generators. Sneaker manufacturers already spend upward of thirty million dollars for celebrity endorsement campaigns. Everyone will get in the act as college and professional sports teams sell sponsorship rights. Envision athletes playing the game looking like race cars with their uniforms completely covered with corporate or product logos.

Whether sports continue to generate such large revenues depends on the fans, who will continue to call for more action and excitement. Basketball and football leagues responded to the call by adding the three-point basket and the two-point touchdown conversion option. The future will bring more variations of scoring strategies and rule changes. For example, changes in the height of the basketball hoop and the diameter of the rim will proliferate as each sport competes for advertising dollars and revenues.

Does this increasing specialization and commercialization of sport portend the decline of society? Do incidents of fan violence at soccer games and multidays of corporate partying at Super Bowls and Olympic Games indicate that life in the United States is repeating the patterns of ancient Greece and Rome? Will this emphasis upon playing and partying contribute to the downfall of society?

The near future of spectator sport may include more commercialization and more emphasis on entertainment, but there may be a quite different long-range future. Since sport reflects society, other changes due to demographic and societal shifts will surface as well. A revised and gentler definition of competition is likely based upon the increasing entry of women into athletics, coupled with the general aging of the population in the industrialized world. Activities such as golf and fishing will undergo further expansion as many focus on individual activities. The future may also redefine amateur athletics, as some colleges and universities form a second sports division where sports reassume an educational emphasis and diminish their economic importance.

Immigration will change spectator sports, adding previously unfamiliar sports to the mainstream. Emerging nations with their high birth rates will produce many young people who will parade the team sports of their culture to global attention. Sports such as cockfighting and bullfighting may also be newcomers to the arena as people from various countries blend their traditions with those of the United States. On the other hand, the animal rights movement may squelch any new or violent animal-based sports in the United States.

The late A. Bartlett Giamatti, a Renaissance scholar, former president of Yale University, and

Commissioner of Baseball, believed that you could tell more about a society by observing how they played rather than how they worked. Spectator sports is a form of that play. Spectator sports reflecting the changes and needs within society have the potential for contributing to the creation of a truly global world where people from different countries and cultures can connect with one another through a common interest.

Let the games begin!

See also ANIMAL RIGHTS; FREE TIME; GAMBLING; GLOBAL CULTURE; LEISURE TIME; SPORTS AND GAMES, COMPETITIVE.

BIBLIOGRAPHY

ALLISON, LINCOLN, ed. *The Changing Politics of Sport.* Manchester, U.K.: Manchester University Press, 1993.

GIAMATTI, A. BARTLETT. *Take Time for Paradise . . . Americans and Their Games.* New York: Summit Books/ Simon and Schuster, 1989.

KRAUS, RICHARD. *Recreation and Leisure in Modern Society,* 4th ed. New York: HarperCollins, 1990.

Ellen L. O'Sullivan

Sports and Games, Competitive

Almost all sports and games can be competitive or noncompetitive. Competitive sports may be organized tournaments or public contests. Noncompetitive sports are primarily oriented toward social interaction, skill development, or systematic physical or mental exercise. Swimming, for example, may be highly competitive, rigorous exercise, or simply playing around in a pool.

Looking into the future of sports and games involves more than extrapolating numbers from surveys of participation. Are there varieties of swimming or electronic games that are likely to grow while others decline? Are there certain styles of participation—competitive or cooperative, doing or watching, individual or social—that are most likely to develop?

Sports and Games: How to Look Ahead

A few decades ago, amateur baseball on Sunday afternoons seemed central to the summer culture of small-town America. Now these teams are a vague memory. In small towns in the 1950s and '60s, high school football and basketball were the talk of the town. Now bleachers are 75 percent empty for most athletic contests. Until recently, the male dominance of team sports was the ac-

cepted rule. Now both the rule and the culture have changed. In a matter of years, fiberglass and composite skis, racquets, and hulls have transformed access, costs, upkeep, and even ease of learning these sports. The patterns of the past do not just extend into the future.

TREND ANALYSIS

Why is it not possible to take numerical trends in participation and draw them out for future decades? In the field of sports and games, there are a number of limitations:

First, the data are inconsistent. For example, A.C. Neilson followed a few sports for less than ten years and discontinued its survey in 1983. Federal surveys focus on outdoor recreation and employ inconsistent formats. The national marketing surveys, the best current source of trends, moved slowly into recreation and have data on only a few sports for even a decade.

Second, many activities of interest such as surfing, hanggliding, rock climbing, ballooning, or squash involve less than 1 percent of the adult population and do not appear in surveys. Trade journal estimates for such activities are almost always unreliable and inflated.

Third, for the sports and games for which there are viable figures for at least ten years, there is seldom a reliable measure of frequency or commitment. Studies have demonstrated that only 20 to 25 percent of those who engage in a sport during a given year do it regularly (Kelly, 1985; 1987). For example, in 1991 only 3.2 percent played golf at least 20 days a year, but 11.5 percent played at least once. Similar rates are reported for other sports: In 1991, 14.5 percent bowled but only 1.6 percent as often as once a week; for aerobics the percentages were 6.5 percent and 2.9 percent; for horseback riding 3.3 percent and 0.5 percent; for racquetball, 4.0 percent and 0.4 percent; for swimming, 23.0 percent and 1.3 percent; and for waterskiing, 3.2 percent and 0.2 percent. As a consequence, almost all figures on participation radically overestimate the number for whom the sport or game is a regular part of life, even in a limited season.

Fourth, variations from year to year are unreliable when the percentages are so low. A national study finds that only 2 percent of the large sample had played volleyball in the previous two weeks, only 3 percent had played tennis, and 4 percent had bowled (National Center for Health Statistics, 1990). The evident decline in tennis playing, for example, can only be assessed by comparing rather small differences over many years (Kelly, 1987).

Table 1 (see below) is based on the yearly household survey of the Simmons Market Research Bureau from 1980 to 1991. It is the most reliable trend analysis available in the United States even though subject to many limitations.

The general trends are consistent with most other studies indicating that sport and recreation participation is not, for the most part, increasing. This is also consistent with trends showing a significant decline in fitness occasions of 4 percent from 1985 to 1990 (National Center for Health Statistics). The so-called "fitness revolution," with the exception of walking, seems to have peaked about 1985. For example, aerobics participation was down to 6.5 percent in 1991 with less than half doing their jumps at least once a week.

In general, there is clearly no boom in sport or physical activity engagement. One reason is the aging of the population, because physical exertion decreases with age. A second reason is the smaller school population, since sport participation—especially team sports—drops off precipitously when people leave school.

THE ACTIVITY LIFE CYCLE

Trends in recreational activity do not extend in a straight line. Marketing studies refer to the "product life cycle" of introduction, growth, peak, and

TABLE 1. U.S. Sports Trends in the 1980s

Activity	Percent of Adult Population Participating in One Year		
	1980	1991	Trend
Distance running	1.6	3.1	Grew
Exercise walking	18.9	23.2	Grew
Golf	8.3	11.5	Grew
Bicycling	18.2	10.2	Declined
Bowling	20.2	14.5	Declined
Swimming	30.2	23.0	Declined
Alpine skiing	3.8	3.3	Declined
Ice skating	5.0	2.2	Declined
Racquetball	6.0	4.0	Declined
Tennis	11.4	7.0	Declined
Basketball	4.7	4.1	Declined
Football	3.1	2.1	Declined
Jogging	10.5	6.0	Declined
Sailing	2.9	2.3	Declined
Softball	8.0*	5.9	Declined
Volleyball	5.0*	5.8	Grew

*1984 status; 1980 not available

Source: Simmons Market Research Bureau Study of Media and Markets

decline. Fads have a rapid growth and decline. Products with viable markets peak and then decline to a plateau rather than back to near-zero. New sports and games have a similar "activity life cycle" (Kelly, 1985). No activity just keeps on growing in participation. Every market becomes saturated; every peak is followed by some decline.

The reasons vary. Promotion and initial enthusiasm may be followed by withdrawals due to disinterest, loss of companions, or even, as with jogging, injuries. An innovation such as the skateboard may produce rapid growth followed by a steep decline to a much lower level of use. Resources may limit participation even when demand continues. The scarcity and expense of urban space for golf restricts the development of courses. Costs and the failure to develop a market outside upper-income males in their twenties and thirties dampened predicted growth in racquetball. Initial enthusiasm always seems to melt somewhat despite efforts to promote an activity and its related products. And fundamental to the activity life cycle is the reality that satisfaction in playing a sport is related to the level of skill. Developing skill requires investments of time, effort, and other costs too high for most. Only about 25 percent of those who engage in a sport do it as often as once a week.

The issue, then, is to distinguish those activities that promise long-term stability or growth from those likely to be fads or to appeal to a very limited clientele. In general, those that call for the highest levels of commitment to develop competence will have small but stable participation coupled with high dropout rates for beginners. Those that fit easily into current lifestyles may gain mass markets. Those that depend on the promotion of a new device and have markets limited to one age or status group, especially youth, are most often fads.

FACTORS IN THE FUTURE

Too often journalists give undue emphasis to different sports and games just because they are *new*; that is, they are news. Especially those based on a new and highly promoted device or are esoteric in their appeal gain attention. Flying ultralites or balloons, jumping off bridges, and other "risk" activities will never gain a participation rate of even as much as 0.5 percent of the population in any given time period. Others require various kinds of resources that are limited; they are too space-intensive, cost-intensive, or skill-intensive. In assessing the future of other kinds of sports and games, at least the following factors need to be included in the forecasting puzzle (Snyder and Spreitzer, 1989):

- *Age*: Physically demanding activities all demonstrate age-related declines in participation. As the population profile ages, the "graying of America" will affect most sports, even though there are recent indications that those entering their fifties, sixties, and seventies now are engaging in slightly higher levels of sports than previously.
- *Gender*: Sports were drastically segregated by gender until the 1970s. Females were excluded from resources and actively discouraged from major investment in strenuous activity. The changes that began two decades ago will continue so that growth in some sports and games will be largely female. Nevertheless, current analysis indicates that such development will be limited and may even be receding for some sports (Robinson and Godbey, 1993).
- *Cost*: Some sports such as Alpine skiing, horse showing, and most forms of boating are quite costly. Only an expansion in the proportion of the population with considerable discretionary income can increase participation markedly. Current trends in income and wealth distribution in Western economies suggest that affluence may become even more restricted.
- *Resources*: How far will golfers drive to play on weekends? How much urban space will be allocated to recreation venues? How much water is accessible to urban boaters, swimmers, and anglers? Time and distance combine with scarcity to place limits on many kinds of activity and limit many to favored regions and locations.
- *Time*: Many adults such as employed mothers and technicians under high pressure are experiencing a "time famine" (Schor, 1992). Economic pressures and gendered social arrangements favor sports and games that offer the most satisfaction in the least time. On the other hand, the unemployed and underemployed *may* decide to become more involved in sports and other recreation that yields a sense of competence and involvement.
- *Alternatives*: In any recreation, there are always alternatives—doing something else or doing nothing. Electronic media offer a greater variety of entertainments at modest cost and almost total convenience. The appeal of such alternatives must be factored into any projected equation, along with the costs of participation and the distribution of resources.
- *Lifestyles*: How do sports and games fit into contemporary lifestyles? Parents tend to be more oriented toward their children than their own expression. Social status reinforces particular

activities, especially for business classes. Education widens interests and abilities. Year-round warm climates foster outdoor activities. The value placed on sports meanings and outcomes can shift in ways that build or inhibit participation in particular kinds of sports and games. For example, will there be any change in the value placed on "competition" itself? Or will sport increasingly become a televised spectacle with fewer who play and more who watch? Will the producers of opportunities respond more to the smaller markets for participation or to the mass markets for spectators?

Futurists are often so technology-driven that they assume that whatever can be done will be done. In sports and games, technology may produce variations on activity or widen access, but other factors are far more determinative of engagement.

Types of Activity and Scenarios

STATUS-BASED SPORTS AND GAMES

These will remain popular with the traditional elites as well as with the "new class" of high-tech research and development work, professionals, and financial managers. The growth in high-end tourism may parallel growth in some elite and specialized sports and games: sailing regattas and dressage horse showing as well as more prosaic private-club golfing and deluxe downhill skiing. Travel for special sports challenges and opportunities may increase. The numbers involved will have little impact on national statistics, but elite sports styles segregate players by price and venue.

ETHNIC GAMES

As the population becomes more diverse through immigration, ethnic variations in sports and games may become more evident. Already urban public recreation providers are accommodating a greater variety of activities and styles as their Latin and Asian populations swell. In time, there may even be some recreational cross-fertilization as "minorities" come to outnumber traditional majorities.

TECHNOLOGY-BASED GAMES

Technologies have impacted a wide range of sports and games. With greater attention being given to leisure markets by multinational corporations as well as by local and regional businesses, the likelihood of sustained marketing and development that fosters obsolescence of equipment will continue. Most technologies do not have dramatic impacts on participation. There are technologies, however, that actually create games or transform existing ones. Composite wheels on skateboards and on both traditional and in-line skates are one example. In some cases, technologies, such as the weapons-aiming transistor and new chips, create games. Those in the electronic games business are continually developing new hardware and software to counter the product life cycle and maintain or increase markets. This marketing strategy will employ technological development to attract participants and keep them engaged. Such development is limited, however, by the extent to which such games fit the lifestyles and resources of potential players. Some technologies are quite expensive. Furthermore, the increased sophistication of electronic games also may repel less skilled players. There will be continued growth based on new and improved technologies, but most new game technologies will be fads or busts if they fail to gain an adequate committed clientele.

SCHOOL-BASED SPORTS AND GAMES

Many sports, especially team sports, depend on their introduction in school settings. Others are learned in public recreation programs aimed at school-age children and youth. For the most part, participation in such sports narrows through the school years and drops off precipitously when people leave school. With school-age populations shrinking and the prestige of school sports seemingly on the wane, such sports are likely to continue their shrinking participation base. Further, nonteam sports and games such as tennis have also declined. The only age groups that indicate even a slight gain in participation are the over-fifties, which begin at 1–3 percent levels. The only sport exception is golf, which continues to attract those in their fifties and sixties. For the most part, though, American adults watch, rather than play, team sports.

SPECTATOR SPORTS

Total attendance figures for sports are impressive: over 70 million in a year for thoroughbred horseracing, 50 million for major league baseball, 36 million for college football, 17 million for the National Football League, and so on. Increasingly, however, it is television that drives spectator sports. Between 100 and 500 people will watch a televised professional game for every attendee there in person. Schedules and formats are oriented toward the camera and small screen, not the on-site crowd. Furthermore, the electronic "super-highway" of fiber optic cable will widen the offerings, so that there will be choices twenty-four hours of every day. What is the saturation level of sports on television? It is likely that the question can be answered by the year 2020, when the effort to fill channels will have peaked. In the meantime, however, the growth in the level of boredom is yet to be explored.

SKILL-BASED SPORTS AND GAMES

Research has made clear that those who are committed to a sport or game and give priority in their lives to participation are those who are developing skills and seeking challenges. Those sports and games that offer relatively limitless ranges of challenge are those most likely to gain and maintain stable levels of engagement. One reason for the continuing expansion of golf is the endless skill-based challenge it offers through most of life. The projection is not one of a dramatic "boom" in such skilled sports. There are suggestions, nevertheless, that the fundamental appeal of sports—meeting measured challenge—will attract significantly more adults who fail to find such challenge in other arenas of life. Such sports will vary widely, from flycasting to motocross, from golf to softball, and will include high-demand activity such as distance running to risk activities that are also skill-based. The numbers and percentages of participation may be tiny in relation to those who watch sports on television, but 1 percent of the population is a viable market share.

Two Scenarios for the Twenty-First Century

Two general scenarios may encompass much of the future of sports and games in American society.

MASS MARKETS

There is no question that the corporate world will continue to explore and exploit leisure as a growth industry. Spectator sports will be promoted in their interlocked commercial dimensions: advertising, product promotion, gate revenues, tax writeoffs, and institutional advancement. Sports and games will be a central part of the consumer economy. They will be redesigned and reformatted to draw the largest possible clienteles through on-site revenues, pay television, and advertising-funded free television. The players will become more and more specialized, those with remarkable physical attributes who have less and less connection with ordinary people. Players will be commodities to be sold on the various markets from actual performance to branded tee shirts and shoes. There will be protests and critiques, but market forces will prevail.

SPECIALIZATION AND DIVERSITY

There will be a parallel movement that operates in conjunction with more specialized promotion and marketing. Sports and games will, by definition, be minority affairs, drawing relatively small proportions of the population into regular participation in challenging and skill-based activity. Fads will come and go in the markets promoted by cooperative media, then receding to fringes of attention. In the meantime, there will be an increased diversity of engagements in activity. Some will be highly competitive and some more social. Some will bring participants into special environments and others will have more convenient home-based locales. Some younger people and a few over fifty will engage in physically demanding sports. Some sports and games will be upscale, limited to those who can afford special equipment and environments. Some will be more accessible. Age, status, gender, and finances will continue to separate participants. What players will have in common is a commitment to challenging activity and to communities of engagement in a world in which economic roles are limited. The demands of sports and games will provide a balance to the more ordinary and accessible activities that center on home and household. They will be important to a minority, just because they offer challenge in a world of easy consumption.

See also FREE TIME; GAMBLING; INTERACTIVE ENTERTAINMENT; LEISURE TIME; OUTDOOR RECREATION AND LEISURE PURSUITS; PARKS AND WILDERNESS; RECORD SETTING; SPORTS AND ACTIVITIES, SPECTATOR.

BIBLIOGRAPHY

KELLY, JOHN R. *Recreation Business.* New York: John Wiley, 1985.

———. *Recreation Trends toward the Year 2000.* Champaign, IL: Sagamore Press, 1987.

ROBINSON, JOHN P., and GODBEY, GEOFFREY. "Sport, Fitness, and the Gender Gap." *Leisure Sciences* 15 (1993): 291–307.

SCHOR, JULIET B. *The Overworked American.* New York: Basic Books, 1992.

SNYDER, ELDON E., and SPREITZER, ELMER A. *Social Aspects of Sport,* 3rd ed. Englewood Cliffs, NJ: Prentice-Hall, 1989.

John R. Kelly

Stapledon, W. Olaf.

See GLOBAL CONSCIOUSNESS.

Stock Market.

See DERIVATIVES; INVESTMENTS.

Strategic Planning

The popular and business press is full of stories of giant corporations, such as General Motors, Philips, Volkswagen, and IBM, losing huge amounts of money and firing people by the thousands. Yet less than a decade ago these organizations were highly profitable—textbook examples of best-run companies that other firms were trying to imitate. Something went wrong as they found themselves unable to avoid the dangers wrought by environmental changes and incapable of exploiting technological or other opportunities at least as effectively as their competitors.

Managing for the future, by anticipating and exploiting environmental changes, provides a way of minimizing failure or maximizing success. Rapid changes in the business environment obviates continuing the status quo, attempting to imitate successful firms, or believing that the future will be similar to the past. Among the greatest challenges facing management are to correctly identify forthcoming changes, to accurately anticipate their consequences, and ultimately to formulate and implement forward-looking strategies in order to gain advantage over competitors. This article concentrates on identifying such changes by extrapolating long-term trends and assessing their implications on the business environment.

Major Changes in the Business Environment

Until several centuries ago, more than 90 percent of humans were engaged in agriculture; today the agricultural labor force consists of less than 3 percent of the total work force in the United States and less than 1 percent of that in the United Kingdom. At present, 17 percent of the labor force works in manufacturing in the United States (versus 26 percent in 1950) and 23 percent in the United Kingdom (versus 50 percent in 1950). As the trend toward greater automation continues and industrial robots and unattended factories become common, manufacturing jobs will further diminish until around 2015, when full automation is reached and the same percentage of people as are employed today in agriculture will produce all goods demanded. Moreover, computers and expert systems, coupled with fiber optics and other advanced telecommunications, will improve office automation and the effectiveness and efficiency of providing services, further diminishing the number of workers in white-collar jobs.

Before 1800, increases in standards of living were small and unevenly distributed. People used to live at a subsistence level, and they owned few material possessions. Later, buying power improved dramatically under the cumulative impact of the industrial revolution, which decreased real (excluding inflation) prices and increased real income. Today people spend a small part of their income on food (17 percent in 1993 versus 34 percent in 1950 and 70 percent in 1900), while their material possessions have increased markedly. Moreover, they work fewer hours per year (1,660 today versus 2,700 in 1900 and more than 3,500 in 1800) and live longer lives (75 years today versus 48 in 1900 and 36 in 1880) in more spacious and comfortable houses. By 2015, with advanced automation and computers with speeds approaching that of the human brain, people will have the choice of working even less, will be able to buy practically all the standardized goods and services they want, and will still have money left for luxuries. This is the time when the present transitional epoch of a subsistence-based society will end, and one of abundance will begin. Wrenching changes will create new challenges and will pose dangers for firms, while fostering new attitudes and preferences among consumers. For strategic purposes, executives will have to predict the path of greater automation and improved efficiency and effectiveness, and figure out its exact implications for their industry, firm, and customers.

Implications for Firms

On the one hand, people's income has increased considerably (today in the U.S. it is almost 20 times as high as in 1800), opening huge opportunities for firms that can satisfy the changing needs of more affluent consumers. On the other hand, the globalization of business is eliminating local market inefficiencies, while the efficient utilization of new technologies has forced firms to subcontract and outsource an increasingly greater part of their activities. Moreover, bureaucracy has turned the

economies of scale and scope that once provided large companies with competitive advantages into diseconomies as the motivation of those working in such firms is smothered and overheads impose huge costs. In the present business environment, competition has become fierce, and firms that cannot recognize forthcoming changes and take concrete steps to adapt to them are not likely to survive. This requires proactive anticipation of forthcoming changes from firms like General Electric, Microsoft, Wal-Mart, Johnson and Johnson, and Asea Brown Boveri. Firms like General Motors, IBM, or Sears and Roebuck, which have not pared back their bureaucratic structures or taken bold actions to adapt to environmental changes, find themselves beleaguered by great problems and saddled with huge losses.

During the remainder of this century and the beginning of the next, the following changes must be considered in a firm's strategy and exploited for maintaining or gaining competitive advantages:

1. *Concentrating on core competences*: With increasing automation and powerful computers, few or no advantages can be gained from the performance of repetitive or routine tasks that can be subcontracted or assigned to super-specialized outside suppliers. As technology will be equally available and affordable to everyone, firms must concentrate on what they can do best, which means using the brainpower and creative talents of their people to the maximum.
2. *Globalizing reach*: Telecommunications and powerful computers will allow buying from and/or selling to any place in the world (this would include subcontracting and outsourcing) to minimize costs or maximize revenues.
3. *Customizing products/services*: Modern technology provides great flexibility and allows for customization of products and/or services to meet specific client needs any time of day or night. Moreover, products/services can be provided directly in any part of the world by using computers connected to telecommunication networks, avoiding middlemen, and allowing lower prices.
4. *Improving service, office, and white-collar productivity*: Computers and expert systems are playing the same role in increasing service, office, and white-collar productivity as machines and the production line in augmenting factory productivity. As the number of people employed in manufacturing decreases and absolute costs in this sector become smaller, considerable improvements in productivity are possible and will

have to, and can, be made in the service, office, and white-collar jobs. These improvements can include *tele-work* (eliminating the huge costs of offices and the time wasted in commuting) tele-education, and almost all forms of tele-services, including tele entertainment.

5. *Motivating employees*: In societies entering full abundance it will be difficult to motivate employees just by monetary rewards, in particular when their creative skills will be most needed for innovating or continuously improving existing procedures/processes and/or products/ services. Ways will have to be found to link work with attaining personal satisfaction from working. This could entail employees owning part of the firm so that they will be highly committed and eager to work hard.

6. *Changing demographics*: As the average age of the population of advanced countries is increasing, its composition, needs, and preferences are changing. At the same time, growing demands for better value products and services which, because of competition, will become more plentiful, allow consumers greater choice. Firms, therefore, will have to be constantly on alert to figure out emerging needs and come up with new and successful products/services to satisfy these needs and to provide as high value as possible to more demanding consumers.

7. *Change, learning, and creative destruction*: In the fast-changing business environment of tomorrow learning how to learn is becoming of paramount importance for organizations. But learning requires changing old habits, which cannot often be achieved without destroying what already exists. This means that firms might want to institutionalize an internal process that encourages creative destruction within rather than waiting until outside competitors degrade a firm to a second rate position or even cause it to go bankrupt.

See also FORECASTING, DETERMINISTIC; FORECASTING METHODS; FORECASTING, MISTAKES IN; MANAGEMENT; PARTICIPATIVE MANAGEMENT; PRODUCTIVITY; SCENARIOS.

BIBLIOGRAPHY

HAMEL, G., and PRAHALAD, C. K. *Competing for the Future: Breakthrough Strategies for Seizing Control of your Industry and Creating the Markets of Tomorrow.* Boston: Harvard Business School Press, 1994.

MAKRIDAKIS, SPYROS. *Forecasting, Planning, and Strategy for the Twenty-first Century.* New York: Free Press, 1990.

MAKRIDAKIS, SPYROS; WHEELWRIGHT, S.; and McGEE, V. *Forecasting: Methods and Applications*, 2nd ed. New York: Wiley/Hamilton, 1983.

MINTZBERG, HENRY. *The Rise and Fall of Strategic Planning*, Prentice-Hall, 1994.

Spyros Makridakis

Superconductors

Superconductivity is a material state, reached as temperature is lowered, in which resistance to electrical current flow is zero. Electrical currents can then be transported in the material with no energy loss due to material heating. Although the development of superconductivity may or may not take the path described in the popular press, recent developments in high-temperature superconductors constitute a world-changing scientific breakthrough.

General Nature of Superconductivity

The four major physical characteristics of superconductivity are:

- Electrical conductivity
- Diamagnetism
- Tunneling
- Thermal conductivity

Superconductors represent an extremely well-ordered state of material. Electrons flow unimpeded in superconductors with no loss due to interactions with the crystalline structure of the material.

Another important characteristic of superconductors, in addition to being perfect conductors, is that below their transition or critical temperature (Tc)—that is, the highest temperature at which superconductivity can be maintained—they are also perfect diamagnets. That is to say that superconductors completely exclude magnetic fields. In 1933, Meissner uncovered this property in which a diamagnet excludes a magnetic field.

The third very important physical property of superconductors is tunneling. Tunneling is a quantum mechanical phenomenon discovered by Josephson in 1962 and commonly referred to as the Josephson effect. Tunneling refers to the fact that it is possible for a charged particle, such as an electron or an electron-pair, to appear on the other side of an insulating barrier, even though there is not sufficient energy available to support that passage.

Superconductors

The last of the major properties of superconductors is the marked change in their thermal properties across the critical temperature. Below the critical temperature, superconductors have very low thermal conductivity and high heat capacity.

Classes of Superconducting Material

The age of superconductivity began with the detection of superconductivity by Kamerlingh Onnes in 1911. Shortly after liquefying helium, he found that mercury, when cooled to 4° K, lost its electrical resistance. The effect was not understood until 1956, when the Bardeen, Cooper, and Schrieffer (BCS) theory emerged. A major breakthrough in superconductivity technology was the discovery of high-temperature superconductivity (HTS) materials by K. Alex Mueller and J. Georg Bednorz in 1986.

Superconductivity, quite unexpectedly, is a very common phenomenon. There are thousands of materials that exhibit superconductivity at some temperature and pressure. These materials fall into five fundamentally different classes. The lowest known transition temperature is 0.015° K for the element tungsten. Until the recent development of high-temperature superconductivity, the highest known superconductivity transition temperature was 23° K for the alloy Nb_3Ge.

The first class of superconducting materials encompasses the basic chemical elements. To date, forty-eight of the eighty-three naturally occurring elements have been found to exhibit superconductivity at some combination of temperature and pressure. Two of the eighteen artificial elements have also been shown to be superconductors.

The second class of superconducting materials includes the numerous alloys that have been shown to exhibit superconductivity. For years, the pursuit of different types of alloys provided the mechanism for improving the transition temperature.

The third class of superconductors consists of organic materials. In 1964, a theoretical suggestion was made by Little that long-chained organic molecules might offer the hope of high-temperature superconductivity. Since then, a few organic materials have been found that exhibit this characteristic. The first organic materials contained compounds of TMTSF (tetramethyl tetraselenefulvalene). The compound $(TMTSF)_2PF_6$ was shown to be a superconductor at 1° K under 8.5 kilobars of pressure in 1980. Later, BEDT-TTF (bis [ethylenedithiolo] tetrathiafulvalene) was shown to be a superconductor at normal atmospheric pressure at 7° K. While no organic material has yet exhibited a high transition temperature, it is hoped that once the phenomenon has been understood, organic materials can be synthesized to have the desired superconducting properties.

Heavy fermion systems make up the fourth class of superconducting materials. Although these materials have electrons with very high effective masses, none has been found to exhibit a high transition temperature. In 1979, superconductivity was measured at 0.5° K for $CeCu_2Si_2$. UBe_{13} has a transition temperature of 0.9° K.

The last class of superconducting materials involves various metallic oxides. Such oxides have allowed transition temperatures to be raised to unprecedented values. The first superconducting oxide was $SrTiO_3$ with transition temperatures reported between 0.3° K and 0.7° K.

Working alone and between other projects—and bucking conventional wisdom—Mueller (an expert in oxides) and Bednorz began their search in 1983 with oxides of nickel, the metal they thought most promising. They tried seventy different types of nickel oxides with no success. Later, they discovered the work of two French scientists, Claude Michel and Bernard Raveau, who had created a Cu, O, La, Ba (copper-oxygen-lanthanum-barium) compound in 1984 that seemed to have the desired properties. Mueller and Bednorz used these materials to produce a mixed-valence material that exhibited superconductivity at 30° K.

Later efforts to improve the transition temperature of the Mueller and Bednorz material were founded upon the realization that the spacing between the atomic layers was important. Chu showed that increasing hydrostatic pressure increased the transition temperature, and at 10,000 times atmosphere pressure, the transition temperature was increased to 70° K. Decreasing the space between the layers of atoms in the superconductor's crystal structure by "squeezing" them together caused an increase in transition temperature. This phenomenon led to the idea of inserting smaller atoms to decrease the spacing between the layers. Replacing barium with strontium, which has a smaller radius but similar chemical properties, increased the transition temperature from 30° K to 40° K. The insertion of calcium (which has an even smaller radius) further increased transition temperatures. Creating a new material with yttrium replacing lanthanium proved successful, as Chu was able to raise the transition temperature to 90° K. Other rare earths seem to work as well—samarium, europium, gadolinium, dysprosium, holmium, and ytterbium compounds all have transition temperatures near 90° K. Later research based on structural blocks, such as $(BiO)_2$, $(TlO)_2$, TlO, PbO, CuO chains, resulted in transition temperatures of up to 130° K. Most recently, mercury-based superconductors have been produced that have transition temperatures of up to 153° K. Since these transition temperatures are achieved under pressures of 150 kilobars, their use in practical applications is unlikely.

Importance of Processing Procedures

Future applications of high-temperature superconductors will be founded on both their scientific and engineering properties. The scientific properties include, in addition to the transition or critical temperature (the highest temperature at which a material begins to show significant superconducting properties), the critical magnetic field (the most powerful magnetic field in which a material can maintain superconducting properties), and the critical current density (the highest electric-current density that can flow through a superconductor with no resistance). Engineering properties include hardness, brittleness, maleability, density, porosity, and so on. Practical applications in the future will depend, in considerable measure, on the ability to produce superconducting material in a usable form—for example, wires, ribbons, and surface coatings.

In most cases, both scientific and engineering properties depend on the material form of the superconductor. This form, in turn, is largely dependent on the final chemical composition and processing history of the material. Even minor changes in the production processes—for example, selection of ingredients, grinding, mixing, additives, firing and cooling temperature profiles, and controlling oxygen atmosphere—can significantly change the nature of the final product.

Applications

As previously indicated, most superconductor applications will probably derive directly from the four characteristic properties discussed above—electrical conductivity, diamagnetism, tunneling, thermal conductivity, together with combination or hybrid effects. Chances are good, however, that other applications will be developed based on other properties not presently known or appreciated. Tables 1 through 4 list a number of current and potential applications for superconductors, together with estimates of the time that will be required for the commercialization of each.

Each application driver is characterized by a set of devices that take advantage of the unique capabilities offered by that superconductor property. The first entry in the table for each device indicates the use if the device is a stand-alone application. The other estimates are for the applications into which the device is incorporated.

For each application, the current stage of innovation for both low-temperature superconductivity (LTS) and HTS is presented. (The meaning of each stage of innovation is shown in Table 5.) In many applications, LTS will serve as a precursor to the use of HTS. Usually HTS development will lag behind LTS. However, HTS progress will probably develop faster than LTS did, and the pattern of application may be quite different for the two technologies. LTS first moved into applications where the cost of cooling was not as significant a factor to acceptance as improved performance, and where cooling cost was a small fraction of the total cost. Therefore, the earliest applications of HTS may not be the ones that were first developed for LTS.

The major advantage of HTS materials over LTS materials is that the former can maintain their superconducting characteristics at temperatures appropriate for liquid nitrogen cooling (77° K), while liquid helium temperatures (4° K) are normally required for the latter. This difference in temperature not only materially simplifies coolant-handling difficulties, but also significantly decreases the cost of coolants. The major drawback of HTS materials is the difficulty of producing them in usable form.

Conclusions

Listed below are some conclusions about the significance of high-temperature superconductivity:

HTS development has reached the stage associated with laboratory development of specific products. Many potential applications are being suggested and tested for feasibility. Additional opportunities appear daily, and this trend will accelerate as research continues and knowledge expands.

Development of practical HTS applications will occur much faster than it has for similar innovations in the past. Many factors that traditionally expedite the development of radical, new technological innovations are evident for HTS. These factors include widespread public and professional interest, readily identified needs for technical advances, relatively open communications, and a strong infrastructure for commercial applications.

Initial applications of HTS will be in niche markets where its special characteristics will offset the

TABLE 1. Application Driver: Electrical Conductivity

Device	Application	Area	Stage of Innovation		Time to Commercial Introduction—HTS (Years)
			LTS	HTS	
Magnet			7	4	0–3
	• Nuclear Magnetic Resonance	• R&D	7	2	3–8
	• Magnetic Resonance Imaging	• Medical	7	2	3–8
	• ESR	• R&D	7	2	3–8
	• Electron Microscope	• R&D	1	2	3–8
	• Particle Accelerator	• Superconducting Supercollider (SSC)	5	1	8–15
		• Linear Accelerator			
		• Medical Accelerator			
	• Fusion-Plasma Containment	• Energy	3	1	>15
	• Magnetohydrodynamics	• Energy	3	1	>15
	• Mass Drivers	• Launchers	3	1	8–15
		• Guns			
	• Propulsion	• Ships/Space/Submarines	4	1	8–15, >15
	• Magnetic Separation	• Industrial Processes	6	2	3–8
		• Ore Separation			
		• Coal Desulfication			
		• Sewage			
		• Pollution Countermeasures			
	• Energy Storage	• Power Load Balance	4	2	3–8
		• Fusion	2	1	>15
		• Free Electron Lasers*	1	1	8–15
		• Laser Power Supply*	1	1	8–15
		• Battery	1	1	8–15
		• Weapon System	2	1	8–15
		• Electromagnetic Launcher*	2	1	8–15
	• Persistent Current Cell	• Memory Device	1	2	3–8
	• Lab Instrumentation	• Research	6	2	3–8
	• High Field Magnets (Steerable)	• Medical	1	2	3–8
	• Levitation Coils—Train	• Transportation	5	1	>15
	• Gyrotron	• R&D	1	2	3–8
	• Beam Weapons*	• Military	1	1	>15
	• Mass Transit Coils	• Magnetic Material	1	1	>15
		• Transportation			
	• Permanent Magnet	• Magnetic Structures	—	1	>15
Motor/Generator			5	3	3–8
	• Electric Power Alternator	• Energy	5	3	3–8
	• Ship/Sub Propulsion Systems*	• Military	1	1	8–15
	• Small Motors	• General	1	3	3–8
	• Electric Car	• Transportation	1	1	>15

* Reason to believe classified research is being done. An application may be at a higher stage than indicated.

† R&D = research and development.

Source: Technology Futures, Inc.

TABLE 1. Application Driver: Electrical Conductivity (continued)

Device	Application	Area	Stage of Innovation LTS	Stage of Innovation HTS	Time to Commercial Introduction—HTS (Years)
Transmission Lines			6	3	3–8
	• Superconducting Power Transmission Line	• Local Area	4	1	3–8
		• Long Distance	4	2	>15
	• Electronic Power	• System	4	4	3–8
		• Card			
		• Circuit (chip)			
		• Connectors			
	• Signal Transmission	• System	3	3	3–8
		• Card			
		• Circuit (chip)			
		• Delay Lines	6	2	3–8
Sensor			6	2	<3
	• Current Switch (Cryotron)	• Flux Pump	6	3	3–8
		• Switch			
	• Radiation Detector*	• Far Infrared Spectroscopy	6	6	<3
		• Microwave Spectroscopy			
		• Heat Detector			
Microwave Resonant Cavities			3	1	8–15
	• Linear Accelerator	• R&D	3	1	8–15
	• Electron Microscope	• R&D			
	• Traveling Wave Tube	• Military			
	• Wave Guides	• Communications			
Antenna Arrays					
	• Radio Astronomy	• R&D	1	1	8–15
	• Radar*	• Military			

^ Reason to believe classified research is being done. An application may be at a higher stage than indicated.

† R&D = research and development.

Source: Technology Futures, Inc.

difficulty and cost of manufacture, emplacement, and operation. The most significant early applications of HTS may well involve combinations of HTS with other emerging technologies—for example, holography, optical computers, advanced technology manufacturing, and biotechnology.

Although interest in HTS up to this point has centered on the superconducting phenomenon, other application drivers (diamagnetism, tunneling, heat-flow resistance, and hybrid effects) provide very promising business and operational opportunities.

The range of possible military uses for HTS is essentially unlimited, including submarine detection, electric guns, field power generators, undersea propulsion, and real-time battlefield simulations. The importance of small size and weight for space projects and low ambient temperatures in space make HTS applications in space almost certain.

At present, there is no generally accepted theory explaining why HTS materials achieve superconductivity at such high temperatures. A valid explanation of the phenomenon may quickly result in developments that dramatically change operating

TABLE 2.   Application Driver: Diamagnetism

Device	Application	Area	Stage of Innovation LTS	HTS	Time to Commercial Introduction—HTS (Years)
Levitation			4	6	<3
	• Vehicles	• Transportation	1	1	>15
	• Train				
	• Car				
	• Materials Handling	• Manufacturing	1	1	>15
	• Moving Sidewalk	• Transportation	1	1	>15
	• Bearings		4	1	<3
	• Gyroscope*	• Military	4	1	<3
	• Big Industrial Stirrers	• Manufacturing Process	1	1	8–15
	• Large Compressors	• Energy	1	1	8–15
	• Generators	• Energy	1	2	8–15
	• Laser Scanners	• Electronic Systems	1	2	8–15
	• Machining Systems	• Manufacturing	1	1	8–15
	• Turbines	• Energy/Transportation	1	1	8–15
	• Energy Storage Wheels	• Transportation	1	1	8–15
	• Motor (Different Principle)	• Electrical	3	3	3–8
	• Skis/Skates	• Entertainment	–	1	>15
	• Ballroom	• Entertainment	–	1	>15
	• Toys	• Entertainment	–	1	<3
	• Education				
	• Kits/Training Aids	• Education/Entertainment	–	6	<3
Magnetic Shielding			–	1	<3
	• Electronic Equipment Protection*	• Electronic Systems	–	3	<3
	• Countermeasures*	• Military	–	2	>15

* Reason to believe classified research is being done. An application may be at a higher stage than indicated.

Source: Technology Futures, Inc.

temperatures, engineering parameters, cost, availability, etc.

In the longer term, success or failure in HTS commercialization will depend on the ability to manufacture standard, reliable, high-performance HTS in quantity and at low cost. Although preparation of basic HTS materials has proved remarkably simple, mass production will probably present difficulties similar to those associated with semiconductor production.

Competition for dominance in the HTS field is already strong among, as well as within, nations. The strong position of Japan in ceramics and Josephson device development may give that nation a strong position in HTS development. Also, 95 percent of rare earth deposits are located in China.

Advances in HTS will result in parallel advances in low-temperature superconductivity and conventional conducting systems. Historic precedents suggest that new competition often stirs up a burst of innovation in older technologies.

Policy changes involving patent protection, antitrust exemptions, joint-government corporations, and so on, intended to support HTS development may spill over into other technological areas.

Although present HTS technology shows great promise, basic research in superconductivity continues, and this research will undoubtedly continue to drive new and more advanced applications. The emergence of a satisfactory theory of HTS may unlock dramatic new capabilities. For example, the development of superconducting

TABLE 3.   Application Driver: Tunneling

Device	Application	Area	Stage of Innovation LTS	HTS	Time to Commercial Introduction—HTS (Years)
Quasi-Particle (Giaever)		6	1	<3	
	• Bolometer	• R&D	6	1	<3
	• SIS*/SIN† Devices	• Radio Astronomy	6	1	<3
		• Radar	6	1	<3
		• Analog Areas	6	1	<3
	• Mixers	• Microwave Devices	6	3	<3
	• Amplifiers				
	• Receivers				
	• Filters[???]	• Military	6	3	<3
Pair (Josephson)		7	6	<3	
	• Radiation Detector[???]	• Military/R&D	4	4	<3
	• Magnetometer[???]	• Military/R&D/Medical	4	6	NA
	• SLUG**	• R&D	4	1	8–15
	• Switch	• Computer	4	3	3–8
	• SQUID††				
	• Research	• R&D	7	4	In use
	• Neuromagnetic Devices	• Medical	6	4	<3
	• Biomagnetism Corrosion Detection in Metals	• Construction	3	1	3–8
			3	1	3–8
	• Subdetection‡	• Military	5	1	3–8
	• Earth's Magnetic Field Measurement	• R&D • Geophysics/Energy • Geothermal Energy	4	6	In use
	• Quiet Amplifier (Nuclear Spin Noise)	• R&D	4	1	8–15
	• Gravitational Radiation	• R&D	5	1	3–8
	• Voltage Standard	• R&D	7	3	<3
	• Real-Time Analyzer	• Electronic	6	3	<3
	• Oscilloscope	• Electronic	6	3	<3
	• Digital Filters	• Electronic	6	3	<3
	• A/D Converter	• Electronic	6	3	<3
	• High-Speed Samplers	• Electronic	6	3	<3

* Superconductor-Insulator-Superconductor.

† Superconductor-Insulator-Normal Metal.

‡ Reason to believe classified research is being done; an application may be at a higher stage than indicated.

** Superconducting Low-Inductance Galvanometer.

†† Superconducting Quantum Interference Device.

Source: Technology Futures, Inc.

polymers would greatly simplify many application problems. Achievement of room-temperature superconductivity or even superconductivity at mechanical refrigeration temperatures (–50° C) would open up significant new applications.

See also CHEMICALS, FINE; CHEMISTRY; COMPUTERS; COMPUTERS: SOFTWARE; SCIENTIFIC BREAKTHROUGHS; SEMICONDUCTORS.

TABLE 4.   Application Driver: Hybrid*

Device	Application	Area	Stage of Innovation		Time to Commercial Introduction—HTS (Years)
			LTS	HTS	
Superconducting FET	• Electronic System	R&D†	3	1	*
Low-Voltage Hot Electron Transistors	• Electronic System	R&D	2	1	*
Non-Equilibrium Superconductor	• Electronic System	R&D	2	1	*
Semi-/Superhybrids	• Electronic System	R&D	3	1	*
MOS Superconductor (Optical Switch)	• Electronic System	R&D	4	1	*
Novel Light Modulators	• Electronic System	R&D	3	1	*
Superconducting/Semiconducting Mirrors	• Electronic System	R&D	1	1	*
Displays	• Electronic System	R&D	1	1	*
Photovoltaic Devices	• Electronic System	R&D	1	1	*

* Not sufficient information to estimate time to commercialization at this time.

† R&D = research and development.

Source: Technology Futures, Inc.

TABLE 5.   The Stages of the Innovation Process

Stage 1	Scientific Suggestion, Discovery, Recognition of Need
Stage 2	Theory or Design Concept
Stage 3	Laboratory Verification of Design Concept
Stage 4	Laboratory Demonstration
Stage 5	Full-Scale or Field Trial
Stage 6	Commercial Introduction or First Operational Use
Stage 7	Widespread Adoption

Source: Technology Futures, Inc.

BIBLIOGRAPHY

HAZEN, ROBERT M. *The Breakthrough: The Race for the Superconductor.* New York: Ballantine, 1989.

LAMPTON, CHRISTOPHER F. *Superconductors.* Hillside, NJ: Enslow Publications, 1989.

MILLER, RICHARD K. *Superconductors: Electronics and Computer Applications.* Lilburn, GA: Fairmont Press, 1989.

SIMON, RANDY, and SMITH, ANDREW. *Superconductors: Conquering Technology's New Frontier.* New York: Plenium Press, 1988.

John H. Vanston
Lawrence K. Vanston

Surprises

Surprises are unexpected events—but not all surprises are alike. Sometimes the unexpected is (1) *an unanticipated random happening*. If the dinosaurs became extinct 60 million years ago as a result of a large meteorite colliding with Earth (or if in the future another such collision should occur), both that collision and the resulting extinctions would be random happenings, very bad luck, accidents catastrophically affecting humans but beyond human control.

Space scientists in the future may be able to track a potential collision for months or years before it happens. This was done in 1994, when the planet Jupiter collided with a comet. Although scientists could see at least the possibility of that collision coming, in the larger scheme of things it was not expected—and thus was a surprise.

There are other surprises that are (2) *predicted but nonetheless amaze us when they do occur.* Earthquakes have this characteristic. Geologists measure tensions along so-called faults where vast tectonic plates press against one another and, from time to time move. Scientists know that the Earth's crust will move periodically to relieve those pressures but are unable to predict exactly when.

There are also surprises with major effects upon the future that are unleashed in the wake of (3) *dis-*

coveries or inventions. Alexander Graham Bell's telephone and Thomas A. Edison's electric light bulb and phonograph were surprises to many of their contemporaries. Similarly, many present-day innovations surprise almost everyone.

One common characteristic of such innovations is that, in retrospect, we can see that they were "waiting to happen." In *Connections* (1978), James Burke traces how innovation spreads, often with nearly simultaneous discoveries in different and distant locales. When the time is "ripe" for an innovation or insight, the conditions and connections are in place, and someone needs only to imagine what new event or invention could be next. And even after all their hard work, disciplined effort, imagination, and ingenuity, the discoverers (and we) are still surprised by what happens.

Truly great surprises come rarely, usually when there is a (4) *massive explosion of insight* that transforms or reorganizes our lives and minds and how we see our world. Such events are variously labeled revolutions or revelations.

The central figures in such changes typically are either quite young or have devoted decades of work and thought to some concept or project that first came to them when they were young. Usually they have dedicated their lives to their alternative vision and what they perceive as their calling or lifetime work. Gradually they share their vision with others, and identify and relate to colleagues or counterparts of like interest who become collaborators. Whether in science, politics, or religion, together they form a community of endeavor that is often simultaneously moral, political, intellectual, and scientific. But until the object of their concern quite suddenly happens, it is viewed by all involved (including the central figures) to be most unlikely.

Thomas S. Kuhn, in *The Structure of Scientific Revolutions* (1962), surveys a number of scientific revolutions in mindset—including those introduced by Newton, Copernicus, Darwin, and Einstein. Each of these great scientists transformed the ways in which other scientists, and later ordinary people, see the world.

Similar revolutions take place in the political realm. In recent years we recount the calamitous political shifts when with Gorbachev the Berlin Wall came down, or when with Mandela and De Klerk apartheid was ended in South Africa. As in the scientific revolutions, there is a sudden shift in how things are seen. Eventually those institutions that tend to perpetuate the past give legitimation to new ideas and individuals.

Similar massive changes involving shifts in thinking and social arrangements marked the sixteenth-century Protestant Reformation, the seventeenth-century Puritan Revolution, the eighteenth-century American Revolution, the nineteenth-century abolition of slavery, the sexual revolution of the 1960s, and the ongoing struggles of the civil rights and women's rights movements.

Protestant theologian H. Richard Niebuhr, in *The Meaning of Revelation* (1940), writes about explosive flashes of transforming change and insight. The most important characteristic in such transformations is how those in the core group see these totally surprising and wrenching shifts, which afterward affect the mindsets of many, many others in a conversionlike experience. Following major breakthroughs, Kuhn points out that a string of new discoveries often follows soon thereafter. A succession of changes occurs because we are now seeing our world very differently, and we are noticing what before we did not recognize or were not looking for.

Then there is the mysterious surprise of sudden (5) *widespread changes of popular consciousness.* For example, from the seventh to the tenth century, much of the Middle East and North Africa converted to Islam. What similar surprises lie ahead? We do not understand the role that the mass media play today, nor do we understand how new phenomena, such as feminism or the civil rights movement, catch fire from mere sparks.

Given the immense number of individuals born into this world and the remarkable capacity of individuals to act as catalysts for change, many new surprises are also in store. Being in the right place at the right time has a great deal to do with unleashing surprise. Ghandi, Martin Luther King, Jr., and Betty Friedan come to mind within recent memory. There will be more like them, and they too will usher in new surprises.

Finally, there are the surprises that are (6) *delayed or displaced effects from actions occurring elsewhere.* In complex biological and social systems, many things are interconnected. Single events send out many ripples of consequences. Some events are found later on to be especially damaging to sensitive life functions of individual species or to the biosphere itself.

When populations of American bald eagles, Pacific pelicans, and peregrine falcons in different locales suddenly declined almost to extinction, scientists discovered that DDT was the culprit. A pesticide first introduced during World War II, DDT was being biologically concentrated in the food chain and collecting in the fatty tissue of these birds' livers, where it was interfering, in females, with the liver's capacity to make the enzyme which determines how thin the shell of their eggs will be. In this way DDT was causing reproductive failure and the near-extinction of certain species.

The emergence of a so-called Ozone Hole in the upper atmosphere as a result of atmospheric gasses—mainly chlorofluorocarbons (CFCs) used in spray cans, refrigerants, and industrial processes—is another example of a major effect from a seemingly remote cause. In like manner, diethylstilbestrol (DES) may cause cancer a generation later in the reproductive organs of a very small percentage of the daughters of the many millions of mothers for whom it was prescribed by their doctors during their pregnancies.

Such delayed and displaced effects are often characterized as secondary effects or "side effects." Showing up later or elsewhere does not make them less important. They simply may be regarded as "surprises" that were not anticipated and were unintended.

These kinds of surprises may occur again in the future. We will be amazed each time as they provide the utterly dark—or sometimes the genuinely shining—moments in our future. These are the moments when our future's newness is perceived by us as most overwhelmingly bad or most wonderfully transforming.

See also CHANGE; CHANGE, PACE OF; DISASTERS, PLANNING FOR; SCIENTIFIC BREAKTHROUGHS; WILDCARDS.

BIBLIOGRAPHY

BURKE, JAMES. *Connections*. Boston: Little, Brown, 1978.
KUHN, THOMAS S. *The Structure of Scientific Revolutions*. Chicago: University of Chicago Press, 1962.
NIEBUHR, H. RICHARD. *The Meaning of Revelation*. New York: Harper & Row, 1940.

David Dodson Gray

Surveys

Prominent among methods to forecast developments are surveys assessing social conditions and polls measuring public opinion. Both involve the systematic collection of information based on interviews with a sample of the general public or a particular group.

While this information covers only one point in time, social surveys and opinion polls undergird and help to corroborate many approaches to futures research. Uses range from assessing the impact of events and evaluating the success of policies to extrapolating trends from the past into the future and building statistical models of complex social systems.

Among the different kinds of surveys and public opinion polls, the following are those most relevant to social forecasting:

- Quality-of-life polls monitor changing public evaluations of domains of life. Findings may have implications for the allocation of public and private resources.
- Issue polls that repeat questions from earlier surveys can pick up shifts in public opinion on both domestic and foreign issues, and often anticipate changes in government policy.
- Polls on perceived trends probe the hopes and fears respondents have for themselves, their families, and the nation. These polls can be sensitive gauges of public optimism, pessimism, frustration, and consumer confidence. They can signal changes in political and economic cycles.
- Agenda-setting polls acquaint political leaders with the shifting priorities that the public attaches to problems.
- Job-rating polls measure the public's assessment of the performance of political leaders and institutions. Whether conducted at one time or periodically, they are one more way to hold politicians accountable to the people.
- Polls on values examine belief systems that undergird public opinion on issues. Moreover, by assessing changes in social norms, these polls often provide a reality check on the assumptions built into systems models or on which extrapolations of trends are based.
- Surveys for governmental agencies are the foundation of important statistics on matters such as employment, housing, and criminal victimization.
- Pre-election polls can quite accurately anticipate outcomes if they are conducted close enough to the election, and if they include good measures of the respondent's intention to vote and of the strength of support for the candidates.
- Delphi polls attempt to measure the opinions of experts on particular issues (*see* TREND INDICATORS).

If social surveys or public opinion polls are to provide a sound basis for forecasting, they must yield reliable data and the inferences drawn also must be valid.

Reliability

The reliability of a survey or poll refers to the consistency with which concurrent applications of the same measure would lead to the same results. It depends on an adequate sample and on questions whose meaning is clear to respondents. The reliability of a survey or poll may be compromised if the sample is too small or poorly designed. Its reliability could also be affected if respondents holding similar views on an issue give different answers because poll questions are ambiguous or unclear.

Validity

Since surveys and polls rely on respondents' answers to questions, what is counted depends on what is asked. Before conclusions can be drawn from a survey or poll, the researcher should have established that the questions asked validly measure the matter under study. For respondent reports of social conditions or behavior, this usually is accomplished by corroborating survey findings with independent sources. For measures of public opinion, validity is most effectively determined by checking the consistency of responses to different questions that seek to measure a common dimension of that opinion.

Forecasting based on surveys or polls is dependent on two additional measurement issues: the use of sequential measures and the selection of variables.

SEQUENTIAL MEASURES

Whether projecting trends or assessing the impact of an event or policy, measures at different points in time are needed. This challenges researchers to formulate questions that will hold up well over time as valid measures. Given the costs of collecting original data, forecasters sometimes rely on available data (often collected for some other purpose). This imposes a need to ensure that measures of the same variables which have been taken independently are, in fact, comparable.

In a related approach to sequential measures, panel studies involve reinterviewing persons contacted in an earlier survey. This approach sometimes gauges change better than unrelated surveys do because any shifts reported have occurred within a common sample. But panel survey reliability may be affected by the difficulty of recontacting the same people or the bias sometimes introduced if respondents know they will be interviewed again at a later date.

SELECTION OF VARIABLES

Reliance on a single survey or poll for forecasting purposes can be risky unless enough measures are used in the same study to move beyond mere description of a set of conditions or opinions to some explanation of those conditions or opinions and when or why they might change.

It is in the domain of variable selection that the frontier of survey-based futures research is to be found. The utility of a social survey in forecasting will only be as good as its anticipation of the need to measure new variables, its ability to account for events and cycles (seasonal, economic, and/or political), and its assessment of changing standards of public judgment. Selection of variables is made more problematic by the absence of widely accepted conceptions of social change, and the tendency of professional disciplines to view the world in their own terms of reference.

Conclusions

The prognostic utility of a public opinion poll rests on its ability to predict actual behavior from expressions of opinion. Thus, to make sense out of the complexity and inconsistencies inherent in public opinion, a poll must do more than describe the direction of an opinion (that is, what people favor or oppose). The poll needs to attempt to explain the public's view by measuring such things as the intensity with which views are held; the knowledge and experience people bring to an issue; the belief systems or values that may tie opinions on discrete issues into an overall framework; the awareness of individuals of the implications of their opinions; and the confidence people have in public figures and institutions to deal with the issue that has been posed.

Most problematic are polls that expect one question to capture all of the nuances of the public's thinking on a complex issue. Such a referendum conception of polling misconstrues the purposes of public opinion research by alleging that a single poll percentage expresses definitively the public's view on that issue.

Critics of polls traditionally have argued that the public does not follow current events closely enough to be able to make well-informed and nuanced judgments on most public policy matters. While it is true that the public often does not know important facts, empirical studies have shown that about three-fourths of the American public pays close enough attention to size up many emerging issues with considerable discrimination. Most people also hold opinions on important matters with a reasonable degree of stability.

Surveys and polls can strengthen the democratic process by portraying the distribution of circumstances individuals in society face and their opinions about those circumstances. By giving equal voice to all respondents, surveys and polls ensure that both the majority and the minority can be heard. Surveys and polls can ensure that information about all the people is integral to the competition among political interests.

See also BEHAVIOR: SOCIAL CONSTRAINTS; CHANGE, OPTIMISTIC AND PESSIMISTIC PERSPECTIVES; CONTINUITY AND DISCONTINUITY; PUBLIC OPINION POLLS; PUBLIC POLICY CHANGE; SCANNING; SCENARIOS; VOTING; WILDCARDS.

BIBLIOGRAPHY

BRADBURN, NORMAN M., and SUDMAN, SEYMOUR. *Polls and Surveys: Understanding What They Can Tell Us.* San Francisco: Jossey-Bass, 1988.

CANTRIL, ALBERT H., and CANTRIL, SUSAN DAVIS. *The Opinion Connection: Polling, Politics, and the Press.* Washington, DC: Congressional Quarterly Press, 1991.

CANTRIL, HADLEY. *Gauging Public Opinion.* Princton, NJ: Princeton University Press, 1944.

DUNCAN, OTIS DUDLEY. "Social Forecasting—The State of the Art." *Public Interest* 17 (1969): 88–118.

NEUMAN, W. RUSSELL. *The Paradox of Mass Politics: Knowledge and Opinion in the American Electorate.* Cambridge, MA: Harvard University Press, 1986.

REISS, ALBERT J., JR. "Measuring Social Change." In Neil J. Smelser and Dean R. Gerstein, eds. *Behavioral and Social Science: Fifty Years of Discovery.* Washington, DC: National Academy Press, 1986.

Albert H. Cantril

Sustainability

Sustainability has become an international jargon word, with about as many meanings as there are people who use it. In general, to sustain something means to keep it alive or going. So sustainability has to do with long-term viability—doing things in such a way that we can keep on doing them that way. The fact that the word *sustainability* has arisen in international debate implies that many people have a sense of unsustainability—that we are doing things, especially in the realms of consuming resources and polluting the environment, in a way that cannot be sustained. Eroding soils,

clearing forests faster than they can grow back, poisoning waters—these are unsustainable activities. If we do not stop them, they will stop us.

Some people who have talked about sustainability for a long time no longer try to give it a precise definition. Notwithstanding, there is a perfectly good official definition that comes from the 1987 report of the International Commission on Environment and Development called *Our Common Future:*

> Humankind has the ability to achieve sustainable development—to meet the needs of the present without compromising the ability of future generations to meet their own needs.

This definition has two parts: (1) meeting needs and (2) doing so in a way that preserves the natural, human, and societal resources from which needs are met. It is important to remember both parts, because the public discussion often splits between those who want to meet needs and those who want to protect resources, as if doing one were incompatible with doing the other. The difference between traditional environmentalists and "sustainability folks" is the ability to keep the welfare of both humans and the environment in focus at the same time, and to insist on both.

The official definition of *sustainability* is often supplemented with Herman Daly's clear and undeniable explication of what sustainability must mean in physical terms:

1. Renewable resources are not used faster than they can regenerate.
2. Pollution and wastes are not put into the environment faster than the environment can recycle them or render them harmless.
3. Nonrenewable resources are not used faster than renewable substitutes (used sustainably) can be developed.

By those conditions there is not a nation, a company, a city, a farm, or a household on Earth that is sustainable. Virtually every major fishery violates condition number one. The world economy as a whole is violating condition number two by putting out carbon dioxide 60 to 80 percent faster than the atmosphere can recycle it. Oil resources and fossil groundwaters are being drawn down without thought of what happens when they are gone, in violation of condition number three.

To make things worse, or maybe clearer, there are two more sustainability conditions that can be derived with just a little thought from those first three:

4. The human population and the physical capital plant cannot grow forever. They have to be kept at levels low enough to allow the first three conditions to be met.

Physical capital plant needs some explanation here, because we use the word *capital* to mean two different things. First, it means money that is invested in building some productive enterprise, as in "I can't build that factory until I raise some capital." The other meaning is not the money that pays for building but the factory itself. To keep these two meanings straight, we should call the first *money capital* and the second *physical capital*.

Physical capital consists of all human-made productive facilities—electric generating plants, oil refineries, car assembly plants, textile factories, computer factories, tractors, irrigation systems, as well as hospital buildings, school buildings, restaurants, houses, and cars. Physical capital (not money capital) takes up space and consumes fuel and raw materials, and turns out garbage and pollution. Therefore physical capital has to be limited on a finite planet. Money capital does not, except insofar as it is linked in value to physical capital. In fact, money is fictitious; it is only an invention of our minds, our symbol for physical capital and physical goods and services. Without physical capital, goods, and services then, money, stock markets, "returns on investment" would have no meaning.

The human population and its physical capital plant both have to be limited in a sustainable world, because both require flows of real physical resources to function, and both emit pollutants that have to be processed, purified, or recycled.

5. The previous four conditions have to be met through processes that are democratic and equitable enough that people will stand for them.

Otherwise, though a system may be technically or physically sustainable (meeting conditions one through four), it still will not last, because people will undermine it or revolt against it.

If you start thinking about what it would mean to meet these five conditions, you begin to see that enormous changes are necessary, but that these changes need not be sacrifices; they could be intensely, humanly satisfying. Those who have been thinking about and working toward sustainability for a long time see in that word not only physical and technical challenges, but components of spirituality, of community, of decentralization, of a complete rethinking of the ways we use our time, define our jobs, and bestow power upon governments and corporations. *Sustainability* is a very inadequate word to summarize all that.

Any word of six syllables is too long to organize a popular movement around and at the same time too short to communicate a complete vision. At any rate, the word *sustainability* does stand for a vision of a world very different from and much more satisfying than the world we live in now. It should not be heard as implying "sustaining" current conditions. What it actually implies is a thoroughgoing revolution.

See also ENVIRONMENT; ENVIRONMENTAL BEHAVIOR; ENVIRONMENTAL ETHICS; NATURAL RESOURCES, USE OF; RESOURCES.

BIBLIOGRAPHY

APLET, GREGORY H., ed. *Defining Sustainable Forestry.* Washington, DC: Island Press, 1993.

CALLENBACH, ERNEST; CAPRA, FRITJOF; GOLDMAN, LENORE; LUTZ, RUDIGER; and MARBURG, SANDRA. *EcoManagement: The Elmwood Guide to Ecological Auditing and Sustainable Business.* San Francisco, CA: Berrett Koehler, 1993.

DALY, HERMAN E., and COBB, JOHN B. *For the Common Good: Redirecting the Economy Toward Community, the Environment, and a Sustainable Future.* Boston, MA: Beacon Press, 1994.

FLAVIN, CHRISTOPHER, and LENSSEN, NICHOLAS. *Powering the Future: Blueprint for a Sustainable Electricity Industry.* Washington, DC: Worldwatch Institute, 1994.

GIRARDET, HERBERT. *The Gaia Atlas of Cities: New Directions for Sustainable Urban Living.* New York: Anchor Books/Doubleday, 1993.

HAWKEN, PAUL. *The Ecology of Commerce: A Declaration of Sustainability.* New York: Harper Business, 1993.

KINLAW, DENNIS C. *Competitive and Green: Sustainable Performance in the Environmental Age.* San Diego, CA: Pfeiffer & Company, 1993.

Donella Meadows

Sweden

Since the 1930s, Sweden has frequently been portrayed as the model of a successful welfare state. The typical picture has been one of a homogeneous population with social organizations disposed to compromise their differences. The highly stable political system was dominated by the Social Democratic party, which ruled, alone or with junior coalition partners, for the periods 1932–1976, and 1982–1991, a longevity record of party dominance unequalled among Western democracies. The period from the 1950s to the

'80s was marked by widespread affluence, a comprehensive welfare system, full employment, and a highly competitive export economy. Swedish foreign policy avoided membership in alliances, aiming at neutrality in the event of war between the Cold War blocs.

Since the 1980s, and especially since the end of the Cold War, this conventional description of Sweden is no longer true. Sweden has become a country in transition—with high unemployment, budgetary deficits, and reduced competitive power in global markets. The Social Democrats no longer dominate the political agenda, and the political party system has become less stable. Swedish foreign policy makers must respond to a changed international context; one sign of this response was Sweden's decision to seek membership in the European Union (EU), announced in December 1990, representing a de facto abandonment of its traditional foreign policy of nonalignment.

During this transition, it is very difficult to identify for certain even the short-run trends that are likely to be formative and controlling over the next fifteen or twenty years. In any event, Sweden is already exhibiting more diversity, disagreement, and conflict then has historically been the case, a tendency likely to continue in the future.

Economy

Sweden (with 174,000 square miles) is the fifth largest country in Europe. One half of the country is covered by forests, and less than 10 percent is farmed. The Industrial Revolution came late to Sweden, commencing in the latter part of the nineteenth century. The original impulse derived from the exploitation of forests, iron ore, and later, hydroelectric power.

Trends during the twentieth century include the decline of agriculture, the growth of an export-led manufacturing industry (which now accounts for 23 percent of GDP), and more recently the now dominant service sector (about 40 percent in the private sector alone). The major economic trend is a growing internationalization. Sweden has applied for membership in the EU. In November 1994 the Swedish electorate approved Swedish membership in the EU, effective in January 1995. Furthermore, Swedish companies have in recent years made substantial investments abroad, as well as agreements with other, chiefly European companies—for example, Asea Brown Boveri, which manufactures electrical machinery. This trend can be expected to continue.

Population and Demography

About 85 percent of the population of 8.7 million live in the southern half of the country. Life expectancy is seventy-five years for men, eighty for women. After years of a falling birth rate, the trend was reversed in 1984, and the Swedish fertility rate is now high by European standards, thanks in part to pro-natalist policies.

Throughout the nineteenth and twentieth centuries, Sweden had high emigration. The trend has been reversed since the 1950s. The heavy demand for labor brought large numbers of immigrants to Sweden, largely from other Nordic or European countries and mainly for economic reasons. Since the 1970s, immigration has more and more consisted of political refugees (29,000 in 1990), often from non–Western countries (Iran, Lebanon, Somalia, the former Yugoslavia, etc.). Immigration has accounted for over 40 percent of population growth since the 1940s. The new immigration has evoked xenophobic or racist reactions from a minority of native Swedes. It seems likely that this ethnic sensitivity will continue for the foreseeable future.

The average age of the population has risen; in 1940, 8 percent were sixty-five years or over, in 1990, the figure was 18 percent. By 2025, it is expected to reach 20 percent.

Urbanization

Sweden was late to urbanize, and since much of industry remained deconcentrated, there are very few large industrial centers. About 83 percent of Swedes live in urban areas. The three largest of these—Stockholm (1,500,000), Göteborg (750,000), and Malmö (almost 500,000)—together contain about 31 percent of the country's population. One might speculate that as Sweden becomes more oriented toward the Continent, both Malmö and Göteborg could be expected to grow somewhat more rapidly than Stockholm, and that it will become even more difficult to retain population in the northernmost parts of the country.

Social Conditions

Although the extensive welfare state has resulted in very little (only 10 percent) public ownership, the public sector (both the central and local governments) grew rapidly during the 1970s and '80s, and it now employs about 30 percent of the workforce. Since 1991, both taxes and the size of the public sector have been reduced; the former tendency may be reversed, especially if the Social Democrats regain power, but the latter probably can be expected to continue.

The growth in GDP that helped finance the extension of the welfare state in the 1960s has fallen substantially since the 1970s and reached negative figures for 1990–1992. In the future, one can expect a continued downsizing of the welfare state, but not its outright rejection.

Labor and Workforce

Fifty-one percent of the population (4.4 million persons) are in the workforce. Throughout most of the postwar era, unemployment has been kept low by a strong economy, the growth of the public sector, and an active labor market policy of retraining and relocation. However, with the recession that began in 1990, unemployment has risen sharply (to around 10 percent by the end of 1993) and is not expected to be substantially reduced in the immediate future.

There is a statutory minimum five-week vacation and generous provisions of over one year for maternity leave. Employer payroll taxes pay for pensions and health insurance. While trade unions and employers' associations are still powerful, the trend for some time has been away from highly centralized bargaining by the leaders of these organizations.

Energy

Because of its northern climate and high level of industrial development, Sweden is an intense user of energy. However, it has no oil or coal deposits. About 15 percent of energy comes from native hydroelectric sources, about 40 percent (substantially less than the pre–oil shock figure) from imported oil and 7 percent from imported coal. Fifteen percent of energy is derived from twelve nuclear reactors. The future of this source has, however, been in doubt since an advisory referendum held in 1980. Parliament then decided to phase out all nuclear reactors by the year 2010. This decision may,

however, be reconsidered unless adequate alternative sources of energy can be obtained.

The Swedish population is very sensitive to ecological issues. The ecology-oriented Environment party was briefly represented in parliament in the mid-1980s.

Education

The Swedish population is highly literate and technically skilled. Education at all levels is tuition free, and almost entirely public. Schooling in comprehensive schools is compulsory for nine years from age six or seven. Over 90 percent of those who finish compulsory school go on to secondary school for three years of academic or vocational training.

About 35 percent of those who complete high school attend some kind of higher education at some thirty centers, with the major universities located in Uppsala, Lund, Stockholm, Göteborg, Umea, and Linköping. A very large proportion (one out of three) adults is enrolled in an adult educational program, either in the ordinary schools or in employer or adult education associations.

See also EUROPE, WESTERN; INTERNATIONAL TRADE: REGIONAL TRADE AGREEMENTS; PACE-SETTER GOVERNMENTS.

BIBLIOGRAPHY

CHILDS, MARQUIS. *Sweden: The Middle Way on Trial.* New Haven: Yale University Press, 1980.
EINHORN, ERIC, and LOGUE, JOHN. *Modern Welfare States: Politics and Policies in Social Democratic Scandinavia.* New York: Praeger, 1989.
HADENIUS, STIG, and LINDGREN, ANN. *On Sweden.* Stockholm: Swedish Institute, 1992.
HECLO, HUGH, and MADSEN, HENRIK. *Policy and Politics in Sweden: Principled Pragmatism.* Philadelphia: Lippincott, 1987.
VIKLUND, DANIEL. *Sweden and the European Community: Trade Cooperation and Policy Issues.* Stockholm: Swedish Institute, 1989.
WAHLBÄCK, KRISTER. *Swedish Security in a Changing Europe.* Stockholm: Swedish Institute, 1992.

Joseph B. Board

Taxes

Taxation is an explicit price citizens pay for government. Having established through political processes the levels of spending and taxation, the fundamental questions of tax policy are whether the tax system is consistent with maximizing long-term economic growth, whether the distribution of the tax burden is consistent with society's sense of fairness, and whether the method of tax collection is efficient. The current federal tax system scores poorly in each category and is in line for a fundamental restructuring.

The major elements of the federal tax system—the income tax, the payroll tax, sales taxes, and user fees—each evolved more or less independently over decades of legislative and regulatory action. Consequently, taken as a whole, the federal tax system reflects a multitude of tax policy choices, some made long ago, which manifest no policy at all other than raising revenue to finance federal spending. Tax fairness, meaning the distribution of the tax burden among individuals, is a highly malleable concept, depending on the times and the dispositions of the electorate. Tax fairness has traditionally meant that the average tax rate should increase as the taxpayer's income rises. The concept becomes more difficult, however, when applied to specific taxes versus tax systems, and becomes imprecise when certain taxes, such as any tax on business, must be levied on specific groups of individuals deemed ultimately to bear the tax burden.

The collection of federal taxes could hardly be less efficient. Tax Foundation estimates of the costs of administering, collecting, and complying with the corporate and personal income taxes reach $200 billion annually. In addition, the federal government imposes other taxes, such as the payroll tax and sales taxes, which impose their own sets of compliance costs. When combined with the similar costs imposed by state and local tax systems, the total national collection costs could easily exceed $500 billion each year, or roughly $2,000 per person in America.

The collection costs of the tax system are due in large part to the extraordinary complexity of the income tax. This complexity, and Congress's frequent tinkering with the tax, lead to tremendous uncertainty among taxpayers regarding the tax system and the tax consequences of particular transactions or economic activities. Tax-based uncertainty imposes yet another cost on the economy.

The federal government's system for exacting resources from the economy is increasingly discordant with the demands of a modern economy and with those of our major trading partners. Consequently, market and political forces are building to compel corrective change. In particular, the punitive treatment of saving and investment places the

Taxes

United States at a competitive disadvantage and has needlessly limited economic growth.

A study by Dr. Dale Jorgenson of Harvard University indicates that replacing the federal income tax with any of a variety of consumption taxes would increase economic opportunities in the United States by about $1 trillion. Another study by Dr. Laurence Kotlikoff of Boston University, using an entirely different sort of economic model, indicates that such a tax reform would, by itself, raise real incomes in America by 8 percent. It would be reasonable to project that the benefits from replacing all federal taxes with a consumption-type tax could double these gains.

Saving, Investment, and the Future

Saving and investment are the engines of prosperity. When a nation has adequate savings available and when those savings are directed by the marketplace to their most productive uses, that nation will be prosperous and its businesses will be competitive on the world markets. The centrality of saving and investment motivated Adam Smith to call his famous seventeenth-century work on the operation of market forces *The Wealth of Nations*. In contrast, Karl Marx's failure to recognize the importance of private saving and investment incentives doomed his economic system and those who followed it.

The federal tax system imposes a particularly heavy burden on saving and investment. When a dollar of labor income is earned, both payroll and income taxes are imposed. If the remainder is saved and invested, the earnings are subject to at least one additional layer of taxation. If the earnings are reinvested again, then they will be subjected to additional layers of tax. If the earnings are invested in corporate equity, then an additional layer of tax is imposed in the form of the corporate income tax. The taxpayer must also contend with the tax on capital gains and, at the end of his or her life, half the taxpayer's estate may be confiscated through the estate tax.

The Future of Federal Taxation

The federal income tax was state-of-the-art at the turn of the century. In the intervening years, the income tax has gone through a steady evolution. At the same time, most of the rest of the world has moved away from the taxation of net income toward the taxation of consumption, thereby avoiding the disincentives to saving and investing suf-

fered in the United States. These countries are now taxing what individuals take out of the economy, rather than what they put in.

With each passing year, the U.S. economy integrates further into the world economy. Thus U.S. companies face ever-stiffer competition from foreign companies at home and abroad, and U.S. workers face stiffer competition from their foreign counterparts. Such increasing competition means government policies, including tax policies, that reduce U.S. competitiveness carry an ever-increasing price tag. Eventually, the price gets too high to bear, whatever the former rationale for the offending policy, and the policy is changed.

The integration of the world economy has made the U.S. economy increasingly intolerant as to the level of taxation, the collection costs and uncertainty of the tax system, and to the intrusions of the system into economic decision-making.

The evolution of the U.S. tax system is clearly in the direction of a consumption tax. All major tax reform proposals under consideration are consumption taxes and virtually all economic analysis is directed toward understanding the operation of consumption taxes. There are many possible alternatives, however, including a national retail sales tax, an European-style credit-invoice Value Added Tax (VAT), a cash-flow tax, a "Flat Tax", and a consumed-income tax. Each of these alternatives can be implemented in lieu of the current U.S. income tax system and each can, in theory, correct the problems of the current system.

The Alternatives

The main alternative to the current income tax is the "flat tax" originally designed by Professors Hall and Rabushka of the Hoover Institution. At the individual level, the flat tax imposes tax on all labor income and excludes all returns to capital such as interest, dividends, and capital gains. The flat tax also allows for a specific amount of personal exemptions and dependent exemptions and imposes a single tax rate on the remaining amounts. At the business level, the flat tax imposes tax on the net of business receipts less all labor costs and all amounts paid to other businesses.

The flat tax is generally popular among taxpayers because it appeals to an intuitive sense of fairness and because it appears to be vastly simpler than current law. The flat tax is popular among economists and tax policy theoreticians because it dramatically reduces or eliminates the tax bias against saving and investment.

Other alternatives, such as the USA Tax System proposed by Senators Sam Nunn (D-Ga.) and Peter Domenici (R-N.M.), and the retail sales tax differ primarily in their embodied political choices or in their collection mechanics rather than in their economic fundamentals. Each promises to reduce collection costs and to improve economic performance by eliminating tax distortions in the economy.

Tax reform has traditionally focused solely on the personal and corporate income tax. If a new and clearly superior tax system can be devised, then the ensuing debate will include whether the new system should replace the many other taxes, such as the payroll and sales taxes which are presumably inferior and certainly impose additional costs on the economy.

A New Doctrine of Tax Fairness

Progressivity has for decades dominated thinking about tax fairness. And, indeed, however measured, the federal tax system is progressive, with upper-income taxpayers paying a very high share of the total tax burden. Among the many ideas under the microscope, tax progressivity is being questioned as the proper guide to the distribution of the tax burden.

Few question that an individual's tax burden should increase with his or her income. But the doctrine that the burden a taxpayer bears in support of government should rise more than proportionately with the increase in his or her income is increasingly being challenged as being not only economically inappropriate, but unfair as well. This development is tremendously important as it implies that the tax system, and possibly government in general, may be returning to the principle that government should ensure, insofar as possible, that each individual has all the opportunities to succeed that his or her talents and energies make possible, rather than enforce an equalization of consequences irrespective of effort.

See also CAPITAL FORMATION; DERIVATIVES; ENTITLEMENT PROGRAMS; ESTATE AND FINANCIAL PLANNING; FINANCIAL INSTITUTIONS; INSURANCE.

BIBLIOGRAPHY

ANDO, ALBERT, et al. *The Structure and Reform of the US Tax System.* Cambridge, MA: MIT Press, 1985.

BRADFORD, DAVID, ed. *Tax Policy and the Economy.* Cambridge, MA: MIT Press, 1991.

SCULLY, GERALD W. *How State and Local Taxes Affect Policy Growth.* Dallas: National Center for Policy Analysis, 1991.

J. D. Foster

Technological Change

A critical factor in viewing the future, whether in industrialized countries or in developing countries, is the effect of technological change. Technology is important because it often enables people to do things heretofore impossible or difficult in a cheaper, faster, or easier way. In the 1960s, John McHale suggested that the average American home had the work equivalency of eighty Roman slaves in appliances, technology, and entertainment. Today, the ratio is even higher. Technological change has become an important element in measuring productivity and improved lifestyle. No longer are land, capital, and human labor the only major elements in GNP.

Technological changes are responsible for improved living, as well as new hope and optimism. At the same time, technology can be a source of fear and pessimism, as in fear of nuclear destruction, invasion of privacy, or joblessness. Technological change is sometimes "pulled" by human need and sometimes "pushed" by its own dynamics.

Technological change does not always advance human potential, but its inventiveness and design help increase the apparent superiority of humans over all other earthly creatures. Many may look back with nostalgia at the "good old days," but, for better or worse, we cannot return. Despite recent technological tragedies like Bhopal, Chernobyl, and Three Mile Island, if given the choice, most people would choose to live in this era.

Technological change can be defined as any alteration in a system of skills, arts, crafts, fabrications, and their organization for the attainment of specific goals. The word *technology* comes from the Greek *techne*, meaning "art, skill, fabrication." A technology involves a system, with interrelated elements such as organizational structure, skills, labor, environment, knowledge base, and machinery. For instance, the computer is changing work skills, the meaning of education, definitions of knowledge, time required for labor, and availability of information. Computer technology may help curb pollution by reducing the need for commuting, make us more aware of options, and advance the speed with which we communicate. Yet, depending on its availability, computer technology may also serve to widen economic inequities; make society more vulnerable to terrorism or natural disaster; and encourage unwarranted faith in the results that can be obtained using computers as intelligent tools for problem solving. It is hard to separate the "goods" from the "bads" because of the inextricable interrelatedness between technology and other contextual factors. Both social improvement *and* upheaval occur simultaneously with the advent of technological change. As a system, it not only acts upon but is also acted upon by other systems such as nature, society, economics, and politics.

Technology as a Change Driver

CONTEXTUAL FACTORS

Technology is one of five major change drivers (a key element influencing futures options and trends) in any social organization. The acronym STEEP stands for the Social, Technological, Economic, Environmental, and Political influences that are the major drivers of any organizational structure. As a change driver, technology is both an initiator and a responder to change. Technology, itself a change driver, is also influenced by other contextual factors (coefficients) that make up the "culture" and environment of technology and technological change. Technological change not only "pushes" social change but also is "pulled" into new areas by the surrounding contexts. Laser technology, for example, pushed its way into eye surgery but was also pulled into more accurate bombing techniques by the military. The invention made the situation, and the situation made other inventions.

EXTRAPOLATION OF TECHNOLOGICAL CHANGE

A danger inherent in technological change is the assumption that it will continue to move in the same direction. Blind faith in the ability of technology to solve or alleviate such problems as fuel depletion, pollution, overpopulation, and ozone depletion may be inadvisable; the complexity and magnitude of such problems, together with the high level of research and development needed, may pose insurmountable barriers.

Extrapolation of technological advance assumes that we will manage to muddle through almost any barrier to human progress. Extrapolationists believe that all that is needed is the will, the finances, and the technological breakthroughs. As tempting and positive as that may seem, other futurists warn that technological advance is by no means an inevitable panacea. There are some neo-Luddites who see technological advance as an inherent threat to humanity, but most futurists proclaim technology and its evolution as a predominantly positive force.

TECHNOLOGICAL "FIXES"

In technologically sophisticated societies, there is a tendency toward overreliance on technological "fixes" to problems. Such overoptimism often leads to makeshift solutions. In the instance of the Exxon Valdez disaster, the solution was to have more cleanup crews, more oil-eating bacteria, more containment booms, and more detergent rather than to focus on preventative measures. In other words, more technology was the offered solution for human error and lack of foresight. Futurists like Peter Drucker and Robert Theobald contend that technology *created* the problem in the first place: unmanageably oversized tankers, spurred by excessive demands for fossil fuels, oil extraction from hostile environments, and blind faith in radar and navigation systems presaged the disaster.

In the future, technological advances must be weighed and balanced by their possible impacts. Technological "fixes" in the future must be carefully appraised by careful analysis of the pros and cons. Foresight and planning must be given priority.

Appropriate Use of Changing Technologies

APPROPRIATE TECHNOLOGY

In the postindustrial or information society, flexibility in thinking is essential. It is true that advances in robotics, bioengineering, fuzzy systems theory, nanotechnology, and virtual reality promise many new options. New skill in determining their appropriateness is needed, however, to prevent unplanned and possibly harmful results. Many developing countries, for instance, would not necessarily be served well with an incursion of sophisticated technologies. Their social organizations, values system, and economic infrastructure might even be worsened thereby. As was learned in Thailand, using tractors rather than water buffalo to cultivate rice paddies required high levels of economic investment and yielded negligible improvement. However, using television to help inform and educate farmers in that same area proved useful. Appropriateness of technology in terms of its impact becomes an important consideration in most planning.

Appropriate technology is also important in highly advanced societies. "Smart" machines, for example, changed manufacturing processes, organization of labor, and skill levels required by workers. The U.S. Department of Labor predicts that by the year 2000, services, transportation, and health care will be growth fields, while repetitive manual labor will decline. The main types of jobs in the future may be divided into two classes: entry-level, low-skilled work and highly skilled, highly paid jobs. This division occurs when manual labor is displaced by smart machines that require highly skilled people to program, fix, manage, and use them.

New Trends in Technological Change:
A Forty-Year Focus

NEW WINDOWS OF OPPORTUNITY

No one should discount the importance of technological change. New breakthroughs in miniaturization (nanotechnology), fiber optics, mass transportation, synthetics, genetic engineering, disease control, sex selection, in vitro fertilization, body regeneration, and recycling of waste will afford many new options. Just because things are technically possible, however, does not mean that they should be done. Optimally, technological breakthroughs should advance the human condition. Knowledge of ethics, philosophy, history, politics, economics, organization, and psychology must also be brought to bear on decisions about the use of technology. Changes in technology must not be left to chance. Instead, there ought to be a conscious choice toward desired goals.

"Technological man" was once described by Victor Ferkiss as one who must possess a new understanding about nature's limits, be able to design mind-body-nature-machine-society systems that are mutually supportive, and ensure that people are the primary beneficiaries of technological growth (see Ferkiss, 1969, p. x). These understandings ought to be the foundation for further technological development.

GLOBAL FLOW OF TECHNOLOGIES

One of the biggest impacts of new technologies will be on the global community. Speed of communications, access to information, networking, and data volume are being significantly increased. Technological advances have created a global marketplace that promotes cross-cultural understanding and a sense of global citizenship.

INFORMATION SUPERHIGHWAY AND
TECHNOLOGICAL CHANGE

Thanks to fiber optics, miniaturization of computer chips, and communication network improvements, the Information Superhighway is already a reality. Increased information access and availability of services serve to enhance political democracy while at the same time posing a threat of an electronic

elitism (if technology were to be available only to the rich). These changes may make life easier, but they may also deprive individuals of their privacy. This new "highway" also will create networks of networks arranged in multiple layers; once ensconced these networks may make it harder to change opinions or policies, or to change structures for dealing with new ideas and assumptions.

TECHNOLOGICAL CHANGE AND EDUCATION

With new technologies comes a new definition of education. Learning will be age-free, location-free, and time-free. The credentializing role of schools (degrees, certifications, licenses) will become less important because of the need for lifelong learning. Collective learning, transcultural analysis, and global awareness will become educational mainstays. Tolerance, interdependence, mutual respect, and ethical dialogue will be enhanced by technological networks in the schools. Schools will continue to exist because of the need for communal dialogue, nurturing, person-to-person contact, and mutual support networks. Technologies will also improve learning, and "intelligent" systems will meet individual student needs and otherwise help them adapt to new situations.

ENVIRONMENTAL TECHNOLOGIES

New technologies in weather detection and weather control will allow people to anticipate and change conditions. Development of new materials will allow people to live in heretofore hostile environments. Pollution control, recycling, fresh-water conservation, soil and resource preservation will be seen as an integrative project to be monitored and controlled in part by new technologies.

MEDICINE

Technology will increasingly challenge the definition of "humanness" over the next forty years. Genetic engineering, cloning, and development of synthetic blood, appendages, and organs are only a few technological advances that must be evaluated. When or where does a human end and technology begin? Such a question will require new, perhaps ever-changing answers. Medical practice will concentrate as much on disease prevention, holistic health, and customized medicines as it will on curative practices.

Conclusion

The scope and sweep of technologies covered here does not provide an all-inclusive answer to the question of how technological change will alter our ways. One key point to remember is that technology should be our servant, not our master. Future prospects for humanity will be improved if we make intelligent choices rather than merely let things happen as they may.

See also AGENTS OF CHANGE; APPROPRIATE TECHNOLOGY; CHANGE; CHANGE, SCIENTIFIC AND TECHNOLOGICAL; COMMUNICATIONS TECHNOLOGY; INFORMATION TECHNOLOGY; SCIENCE ISSUES; SCIENTIFIC BREAKTHROUGHS; SURPRISES; TECHNOLOGICAL DETERMINISM; TECHNOLOGICAL INNOVATION; TECHNOLOGY DIFFUSION; TECHNOLOGY FORECASTING AND ASSESSMENT; TECHNOLOGY AND SCIENCE; WILDCARDS.

BIBLIOGRAPHY

BARBOUR, I. G. *Technology, Environment and Human Values.* New York: Praeger, 1980.

BERNARD, H. R., and PELTO, PETRI, eds. *Technology and Social Change.* Prospect Heights, IL: Waveland Press, 1987.

CORN, J. J., ed. *Imagining Tomorrow: History, Technology and the American Future.* Cambridge, MA: MIT Press, 1986.

FERKISS, VICTOR. *The Future of Technological Civilization.* New York: George Braziller, 1974.

_____. *Technological Man.* New York: George Braziller, 1969.

HIRSCHHORN, L. *Beyond Mechanization: Work and Technology in a Post-Industrial Age.* Cambridge, MA: MIT Press, 1984.

MUMFORD, LEWIS. *Technics and Civilization.* New York: Harcourt, Brace, 1934.

PORTER, ALAN L., et al. *Forecasting and Management of Technology.* New York: John Wiley, 1991.

TEICH, A. H. *Technology and the Future.* New York: St. Martin's Press, 1993.

THEOBALD, ROBERT. *Turning the Century.* Indianapolis, IN: Knowledge Systems, Inc., 1992.

WILLOUGHBY, KELVIN W. *Technology Choice: A Critique of the Appropriate Technology Movement.* Boulder, CO: Westview, 1990.

Fred D. Kierstead

Technological Determinism

Human beings are cultural animals. From their first appearance on Earth, they have used technologies—i.e., techniques to change their natural environment. Tools such as spears and baskets are technologies, but so is fire. All human technologies are conditioned by and, in turn, strongly affect the social structure and values of the society in which they appear.

Following a primitive era of hunting and gathering, agriculture was probably developed by women about 20,000 years ago, a major development in human history. Agricultural surpluses created the base from which early civilizations arose. The human population increased greatly and reached levels that remained stable until the Industrial Revolution. The early development of farming was accompanied by a major increase in mining. Soon thereafter, agricultural and extractive societies spread over most of the planet.

The next major step in technology came with the Industrial Revolution, which began in Britain in the eighteenth century. Industry soon became dominant across Western Europe and North America. Based on new sources of power—fossil fuels, above all—and standardized mass production through the use of machinery, the new advances led to a major rise in population, explosive urbanization, and the conquest by the industrial nations of the nonindustrialized world. Over time, industrial society, based on the production of physical goods, evolved into a service-oriented society. In service-based economies, the distribution of goods and the provision of services such as health, education, and government employed the majority of workers and generated the bulk of economic activity. Eventually this emphasis became so pronounced that some have come to speak of a new form of society—a "postindustrial" one in which knowledge and information are more important than either agriculture, manufacturing goods, or services (*see* INFORMATION SOCIETY).

To what extent does technology determine the values and social structure of a society? Is it an independent variable, which as it induces change forces other things to change, as technological determinists contend? Or can human societies resist technological change and its effects if they choose? The historical record can be read in several ways. Throughout human history, and throughout the world today, human beings have been eager to embrace new technologies that appear to offer more abundance, comfort, and security. Progress through technological change and consequent economic growth is the major modern creed all over the world, spreading along with the Industrial Revolution and its aftermath. It is also evident that certain technologies have social and cultural consequences. The invention of the forceps in the sixteenth century made males dominant in the process of childbirth, relegating the midwife to insignificance. Modern means of transportation and communication, along with the factory system, have done much to destroy the traditional family and community. The industrial city—created by centralized production and the railroad—has been undermined wherever the automobile has become the major means of transportation. Above all, it is assumed that the rational and scientific mindset which underlies modern technology is destined to put an end to traditional ethnic and religious loyalties and belief systems. Based on such facts and assumptions, the case for technological determinism seems so strong as to be beyond dispute.

But not all would agree. The historical record is replete with examples of human societies that have chosen to resist rather than adopt new technologies and attitudes toward life, and this is further reflected in contemporary clashes of cultures. More to the point, there are examples of the failure to adopt new technologies because the ruling group in a society saw no need for them. Since the ancient Western world was based on slave labor, it was not interested in labor-saving machinery. The steam engine was known in Hellenic times, but did not become a major social force until it was reinvented during the industrial era by James Watt. China was long ahead of Europe in science and technology, but allowed itself to stagnate in the early modern period because it believed its social system near perfect. Islam, once also ahead of Europe technologically, was slow to adopt modern weaponry and long abjured modern printing. Japan gave up the gun as well as regular contact with the outside world for several centuries. Economic and social factors deny a great deal of the latest medical technology to the poor in contemporary America.

In addition to occasionally rejecting new technology, usually out of fear of its effects on existing social structures, societies can accept it and choose to renounce the values it allegedly implies. Traditional Christian churches still flourish. Islam is resurgent. Everywhere in the world ethnic conflict belies those who have long predicted the demise of such loyalties. Ironically, many groups which reject the values of modern technological civilization, both in the Western and in the Eastern world, are quite happy to use its most advanced tools of communication to spread their message. Human societies are obviously free to reject technologies or alter their effects in a number of ways.

However, high-tech postindustrial society involving the primacy of theoretical knowledge, specialization, new sources of energy, and the computer is certainly becoming dominant throughout the globe. Whether these technologies impose such a strain on the natural environment that it is rendered unsustainable in the long run is an increasingly debated question. Antitechnology and back-to-nature advocates have one mindset. They hold that contemporary postindustrial society cannot go on forever because of its overuse of resources and creation of pollution, and because it endangers basic human values, above all freedom. Proponents of current technologies, institutions, and trends claim humanity has no choice, given increasing population and unmet material needs. In effect, the former deny technological determinism while the latter embrace it.

Unmistakably the last century entailed technological exploitation and natural resource destruction on a massive scale. We cannot escape from this environmental predicament unless we address the ideas that created or fostered it. Fatalistic viewpoints ignore the potential of human willpower. Technological impacts can be directed. It is up to leaders and informed citizens to integrate vital perspectives on science and ethics, philosophy and politics, economics and ecology, in managing contemporary affairs. Science and technology can act as a force for good or evil. They need not be a force for the destruction of humanity and can be directed toward higher levels of human well-being. The choice is ours, although the particulars of that choice are by no means a simple, settled matter.

See also CHANGE; CHANGE, SCIENTIFIC AND TECHNOLOGICAL; HIGH TECHNOLOGY; TECHNOLOGICAL CHANGE; TECHNOLOGICAL INNOVATION; TECHNOLOGY DIFFUSION; TECHNOLOGY AND SCIENCE.

BIBLIOGRAPHY

FERKISS, VICTOR. *Nature, Technology, and Society: Cultural Roots of the Current Environmental Crisis.* New York: New York University Press, 1993.
_____. *The Future of Technological Civilization.* New York: George Braziller, 1974.
_____. *Technological Man: The Myth and the Reality.* New York: New American Library, 1969.
WINNER, LANGDON. *The Whale and the Reactor: A Search for Limits in an Age of High Technology.* Chicago: University of Chicago Press, 1986.

Victor C. Ferkiss

Technological Innovation

Innovation is the process whereby a new product or service makes the transition from concept to prototype to commercial success, or at least widespread use. Innovation is often confused with invention, but the classic pattern begins with a discovery or an invention, followed by a more or less extended period of engineering, development and market testing, market introduction, feedback from customers, further modification of the design, standardization of the design, and development of specialized manufacturing processes.

The technology "life cycle" outlined very briefly above has several other important features. One is a tendency for competition in the marketplace to be based initially on product performance (in some sense) and to shift, over time, toward price. This occurs as the product (or service) becomes more standardized, and production technology becomes more and more capital-intensive.

The time from first conception to successful commercial introduction can take as much as a century (or more) or as little as a year or two, depending on circumstances. The digital mechanical calculator was conceived by Blaise Pascal in the mid-seventeenth century. It was further developed by Charles Babbage in the early nineteenth century, but did not achieve commercial success until the end of the nineteenth century. True computers only reached the market in the 1950s. On the other hand, the telephone evolved from patentable prototype to initial service in less than two years. So did Thomas Edison's "Jumbo" generator and his carbon-filament incandescent lamp. However, although quantitative measurement in this field is extremely difficult, these examples are probably atypical. There is some evidence that the innovation process itself is currently accelerating. If so, this can probably be attributed to increasingly global competition and information technology.

The innovation process itself is also changing qualitatively. In the eighteenth and nineteenth centuries, the individual inventor was the major actor in the process, although commercial success was rare and sporadic. As firms grew larger and organizations evolved in the later nineteenth and early twentieth centuries, formal research and development in industrial laboratories began to take the place of the individual inventor. The engineering development investment needed for the ammonia synthesis process, the spark-ignition (Otto cycle) and pressure ignition (Diesel) engines, the automobile and the fixed-wing aircraft, and the steam turbogenerator, were far beyond the resources of any individual. Nuclear weapons, nuclear power, spacecraft, and other developments in modern times, have involved a large part of the scientific and technical resources of a major nation.

"Creative Destruction" and Economic Growth

The vulnerability of mature industries (and products) to technological obsolescence has been demonstrated repeatedly in recent decades. Products, as well as manufacturing processes, can be rendered obsolete in short order. The flip side of innovation is obsolescence. Innovation is something like a poker game. The winners rake in the pot; the losers drop out and disappear from the contest. It was the Austrian economist Joseph SCHUMPETER who first fully recognized the importance of innovation as the engine of economic growth. Schumpeter also coined the famous phrase "creative destruction." He meant to emphasize the fact that, in the economy as in the biological world, death is an inevitable companion of life.

Examples of rapid change and obsolescence can be found in virtually every field. RCA was once the biggest name in radio and later in television. The company gave up its technological and manufacturing leadership two decades ago after the failure of its videodisk. Now its famous research laboratory belongs to the Stanford Research Institute and the company itself has been absorbed by General Electric. Perhaps the most spectacular example of how industry leadership changes with technology is the semiconductor industry. In every generation of dynamic random-access memory (DRAM) chips the industry leadership has changed. Although the memory chip was an American invention, its original developer (Intel) dropped out of the business within a decade. In fact, only one U.S.-based firm, Texas Instruments, now remains among the top ten worldwide merchant producers. (IBM produces DRAMs only for its own consumption.)

Since 1980 the entire computer industry itself has changed even more dramatically. In 1980 it was still a classic oligopoly dominated by a single firm, IBM. In a mere decade a "new" computer industry, based on personal computers and workstations linked in local area networks (LAN's), emerged. New firms have carved out huge chunks of the PC and workstation market. A firm founded in the 1960s, Intel, now dominates the microprocessor field, with Motorola a distant second. A firm created in the late 1970s, Microsoft has an equally dominant position in PC operating systems software. The applications programs market is dominated by equally young firms. IBM, on the other hand, dominates no segment of the "new" computer industry (nor do the once-feared Japanese).

Determinants of Adoption and Diffusion

There are two basic mechanisms for the adoption of a new product or service in the market. They can be characterized roughly as (1) "technology push" and (2) "market pull." Technology push involves a radical new idea—often based on a scientific discovery—that takes everyone by surprise and literally creates its own demand. It has no direct competition when it first appears. Market pull, however, is much more common. It involves the introduction of a new product or product improvement "made to order" to satisfy a demand that is already articulated.

Penicillin was an example of the first kind; streptomycin and the other antibiotics exemplify the second. The first commercial photographs (Daguerrotypes) would be another example of technology push. The roll film and portable camera invented by George Eastman were called forth by the growing market. The first aircraft and rockets were clearly created by technological enthusiasts. More recent improvements are responses to economic or national security demand. The laser is another example of technology push. Genetic engineering is perhaps the most recent example of this kind. The techniques of manipulating genetic materials by adding and subtracting bits of DNA with known characteristics was the first impetus. The implications for pharmaceuticals, chemicals, and agriculture were so obvious that a whole category of new research-based firms was created during the decade of the 1980s to exploit these possibilities.

In modern times the distinction is becoming blurred, inasmuch as R&D may be directed at a certain problem by a far-sighted manager who perceives a future need and deploys resources to satisfy it. The first transistor was a deliberate development, driven by the need to find simpler, smaller, and more-reliable devices for telephone switching circuitry. Yet it was also an outgrowth of radical new technology. It was a substitute for the vacuum tube, but it also made possible completely new products.

The relative importance of "push" and "pull" have been the subject of much debate. Social critics often assert that "push" is dominant, resulting in too many of the wrong technologies being adopted. Historiographic studies (e.g., of the correlation between patents and industry profitability) tend to suggest the opposite, that periods of prosperity precede periods of accelerated invention (as measured by patents). The implication is that firms spend more on R&D when they are prosperous than when they are not. The "push" hypothesis would imply the contrary, namely that invention precedes prosperity.

Clearly societal need does exert a kind of "pull," and there is no doubt at all that inventors feel it. The surprising number of documented simultaneous inventions, where individuals, knowing little or nothing of each others' work but driven by a common impulse, arrive at the same result at almost the same time supports this "pull" effect. Examples of simultaneous or near simultaneous invention include the high-pressure steam engine, the telegraph, the telephone, the incandescent light, aniline dyes, the aluminum reduction process, and the turbojet engine. The list of such coincidences is lengthy.

Without doubt military needs have been a major driver of technological innovation throughout history. Military organizations, however, are not the only beneficiaries. For example, canning to preserve food was invented by the French during Napoleon's wars and developed further to feed the Union army in the U.S. Civil War. It is clear that military uses were important for the early commercial development of aircraft, jet propulsion, radar, computers (in the 1950s and '60s), sonar, nuclear reactors, rockets, and missiles.

Barriers and Breakthroughs

In many cases it is difficult to identify the driving force behind an innovation as either a market pull or a technology push. In fact, the two normally interact. As a technology progresses in terms of improved performance, demand for the service provided is likely to increase. Increased demand for the service in turn generates a demand for still better performance to satisfy that demand. There is a kind of "virtuous circle": technological performance → market demand → technological performance. Thus technology push eventually tends to create market pull and vice versa.

To mention one specific example, building telegraph lines (generally along railway lines) led to a tremendous demand for sending messages. This demand rapidly overwhelmed the capacity of the lines and encouraged inventors to find ways of "compressing" or "multiplexing" the messages so that a single-wire line could carry more messages. The telephone invention was a direct outgrowth of this inventive activity. In its turn the telephone, too, generated new demand that rapidly exceeded the capacity of the lines and encouraged inventors to find ways of increasing the number of messages a line can carry.

Efforts to improve the existing technology eventually run into limits or barriers of a fundamental sort. When such a limit is approached the cost of R&D per unit of additional improvement begins to rise rapidly, while the actual rate of improvement begins to slow down. When we speak of a technological "breakthrough" it usually means that there was a barrier of some sort that impeded progress. A breakthrough almost always requires a major new idea or discovery, leading to a new approach. Very often, the new idea that permitted the breakthrough also opens up a whole new field of collateral possibilities that nobody could have imagined.

For example, in the late 1950s computers were approaching size and performance limits, due to the problems of assembling enormous numbers of individual transistors into their very complex circuits. The integrated circuit, invented simultaneously by Texas Instruments and Fairchild in 1959, overcame these limits.

The telephone, the transistor, the IC (and others mentioned above) are examples of what Schumpeter calls "radical innovation." These are the dramatic, world-changing innovations that create individual fame and (sometimes) fortune. Many of these innovations resulted in the creation of new firms, and some of those firms are now household names. Still, it would be misleading to assume that most innovations are "radical," in the sense of creating major new products or industries. In fact, to the contrary, the vast majority of innovations are "incremental" in nature. Yet their cumulative weight in the sum of all contributions is probably greater by far than the radical innovations.

See also CHANGE, SCIENTIFIC AND TECHNOLOGICAL; HIGH TECHNOLOGY; INFORMATION TECHNOLOGY; SCIENCE ISSUES; SCIENTIFIC BREAKTHROUGHS; TECHNOLOGICAL CHANGE; TECHNOLOGY DIFFUSION; TECHNOLOGY AND SCIENCE.

BIBLIOGRAPHY

AYRES, ROBERT U. *Technological Forecasting & Long-Range Planning.* New York: McGraw-Hill, 1969.
FREEMAN, CHRISTOPHER. *The Economics of Industrial Innovation,* 2nd ed. Cambridge, MA: MIT Press, 1982.
MAHAJAN, VIJAY, and WIND, YORAM. *Innovation Diffusion Models of New Product Acceptance.* Cambridge, MA: Ballinger, 1986.
MANSFIELD, EDWIN. *Industrial Research and Technological Innovation.* New York: W. W. Norton, 1968.
ROSENBERG, NATHAN. *Perspectives in Technology.* New York: Cambridge University Press, 1976.
ROSEGGER, GERHARDT. *The Economics of Production and Innovation.* New York: Pergamon Press, 1986.
STONEMAN, PAUL. *The Economic Analysis of Technological Change.* London: Oxford University Press, 1983.

Robert U. Ayres
Philippe Pichat

Technology Diffusion

Technology diffusion is the process by which technology moves from those who develop or control it to those who employ it. The diffusion process can take many forms. For governments it is getting technology out of government labs and into the commercial sector. For the military it is the spread of militarily sensitive technology into their own hands or the hands of the enemy. For Third World countries it is the transfer of technology from rich countries to poor ones. When companies talk about it, they focus on two things: getting technology out of the labs and into the marketplace and transferring technology to and from other companies through licensing.

Technology diffusion has taken on great importance in recent times. Its critical role in society was demonstrated in 1957 when Nobel Prize-winning economist Robert Solow established that most of the growth of the American economy could be attributed to technology, broadly defined.

Companies need technology to develop new products (product innovation), to improve the processes they employ to carry out their business (process innovation), and to give them a competitive edge in the marketplace. Consequently, they are willing to dedicate enormous resources to acquiring it. They may do this through their own development efforts (research and development) or by acquiring it from outside the organization (technology diffusion).

Governments also see technology to be important in the effective functioning of society. Technology can contribute to the well-being of citizens in their daily lives. When embodied in weapons systems, it contributes to national security. When employed effectively by national companies, it makes them competitive in a competitive global market. In many countries technology is viewed to be so important that its acquisition is given the highest national priority. In China, for example, Zhou Enlai declared the acquisition of scientific and technological capabilities to be one of China's "Four Modernizations." As with companies, the acquisition of technology can occur either by internal or external means.

There are a number of common elements associated with technology diffusion, regardless of its specific form. In all cases, technology diffusion entails the migration of the technology from those who possess it (technology donor) to those who desire to acquire it (technology recipient). The mechanisms for implementing technology diffusion are manifold. For example, the rights to use the technology can be acquired through a contract (called technology licensing); or the technology can be diffused through published literature that describes how the technology functions; or it can be purchased embodied in a product; or it can be acquired through training (e.g., on-the-job training). Technology diffusion may even occur through theft!

It is not enough for technology to be physically transported from donor to recipient. For useful technology diffusion to occur, the recipient must possess an adequate absorptive capacity to employ the technology meaningfully. This means that the recipient must be adequately educated to deal with the technology and must possess financial and material resources to enable the technology to be adopted effectively.

The speed with which technology is diffused from those who develop it to those who employ it has accelerated in recent years. Traditionally, a good rule of thumb was that it would take thirty to fifty years from the time a discovery was made in the laboratory until the time it became commercially viable in the marketplace. This lag is seen in the case of genetic engineering: Crick and Watson's groundbreaking discovery that DNA is structured as a double-helix was made in the early 1950s; however, the first commercial application of this discovery occurred in the early 1980s, a gap of thirty years.

Today, the lag between discovery in the lab and introduction into the marketplace is shortening. One approach is to make sure that research carried out in the laboratory is commercially appealing. Increasingly the marketing departments of companies are playing a pivotal role in selecting which technology projects will be supported.

Technology diffusion contributes to the rapid turnover of technology in the market and short-ened product life cycles. For example, if a company needs to access a technology to flesh out a product line, it is not always necessary for them to develop it through expensive, time-consuming internal research-and-development efforts. They can acquire it readily by following these steps. They can attempt to identify who possesses the desired technology by conducting a worldwide search (technology brokers now exist who can expedite this search). Once they identify the technology owners, they contact them to negotiate some mechanism by which they can access the technology. Common mechanisms include direct purchases of patents, technology licensing, joint ventures, and coproduction agreements.

With increased access to technology, more technology-based products are being brought to market faster. Many of these products entail incremental innovations, where new products are basically better-functioning substitutes for older products. A well-known example is found in the area of personal computers. The original IBM PC (first marketed in 1981) was driven by an Intel 8088 chip. This was soon upgraded to an 8086 chip. After a couple of years, Intel introduced the more advanced 80286 chip, which was incorporated into the IBM AT computer. The 80286 chip was replaced with various versions of the 80386 chip, and soon these were replaced by different versions of the 80486 chip. In 1993 these, in turn, were replaced with the first version of the more advanced Pentium chip. A similar pattern was exhibited by the recently terminated Motorola series of chips, from the 68000 through the 68060 of 1995. Each change of chip resulted in the migration of the new technology to ever more advanced products rushed to market by computer manufacturers. New-generation computers were replacing old-generation computers in cycles of about eighteen months.

The rapid change made possible by the acceleration of technology diffusion has clearly had healthy effects: More people are getting better access to more technology at cheaper prices than ever before. The rapid change also has led to economic disruption, however. Large corporations like IBM, Matsushita, and Olivetti are having difficulty competing in the new fast-paced environment and some, like Commodore, have fallen by the wayside. Previously, their large size was an advantage, enabling them to develop and control technologies that smaller companies could not afford. With increased access to technology through technology diffusion, smaller companies today can obtain whatever technology they need by collaborating with other companies or by licensing in technology. Furthermore, because of their small size, they can move more quickly than the traditional high-tech behemoths.

With universal access to technology through technology diffusion, smaller companies and poorer countries throughout the world can hope to become major technology players. They can take a cue from the way the Sony Corporation developed its strength. In the early 1950s, Sony Corporation acquired the rights to AT&T's transistor technology through licensing agreements. Given these rights, it began producing transistors and employing them cleverly in ever-smaller consumer electronic products, such as transistor radios and ultimately tape recorders, camcorders, and televisions. The Sony experience was common among Japanese companies. The spectacular growth of the Japanese companies between 1950 and 1980 was fed by the acquisition of technology from abroad. Even today, Japanese companies depend heavily upon the use of imported technology.

See also APPROPRIATE TECHNOLOGY; CHANGE, PACE OF; CHANGE, SCIENTIFIC AND TECHNOLOGICAL; HIGH TECHNOLOGY; INFORMATION TECHNOLOGY; RECORD SETTING; SCIENCE ISSUES; SCIENTIFIC BREAKTHROUGHS; TECHNOLOGICAL CHANGE; TECHNOLOGICAL DETERMINISM; TECHNOLOGICAL FORECASTING AND ASSESSMENT; TECHNOLOGICAL INNOVATION; TECHNOLOGY AND SCIENCE; WILDCARDS.

BIBLIOGRAPHY

BUATSI, SOSTHENES. *Technology Transfer: Nine Case Studies.* London: Intermediate Technology Publications, 1988.

CHARAFAS, DIMITRIOS N., and BINDER, EVA MARIA. *Technoculture and Change: Strategic Solutions for Tomorrow's Society.* London: Adamantine Press, 1992.

ELLUL, JACQUES. *The Technological Bluff.* Grand Rapids, MI: Eerdmans, 1990.

GOULET, DENIS. *The Uncertain Promise: Values Conflict in Technology Transfer.* New York: Apex Press, 1989.

HALL, PETER, and PRESTON, PASCHAL. *The Carrier Wave: Information Technology and the Geography of Innovation, 1846–2003.* Boston: Unwin Hyman, 1988.

MALECKI, EDWARD J. *Technology and Economic Development: The Dynamics of Local, Regional and National Change.* New York: John Wiley, 1991.

MODY, ASHOKA. *Staying in the Loop: International Alliances for Sharing Technology.* Washington, DC: World Bank, 1989.

RAY, G. F. *The Diffusion of Mature Technologies.* New York: Cambridge University Press, 1984.

J. Davidson Frame

Technology Forecasting and Assessment

Technological forecasting and technology assessment are related but distinct activities. The former is mainly concerned with anticipating outcomes and the timing of impending technologies; the latter focuses more on prospective ascertainment of direct and indirect events and effects of the application of particular technologies. Both originated in government but are now used widely throughout society—though this is not always apparent when scanning the published literature.

Technological Forecasting

Technological forecasting seeks to anticipate the future nature and characteristics of useful machines and techniques. Technological forecasts describe characteristics only. They do not inventthe means by which the characteristics will be achieved.

Forecasters generally use a few basic methods: extrapolation, leading indicators, causal models, and stochastic methods. These methods must be tailored to the circumstances of the specific subject. For instance, economic data are collected at frequent, regular intervals. Economic forecasters can use mathematical tools to further exploit this regularity or constancy. Technological data occur only irregularly. Technological forecasters are restricted to tools that accept unequally spaced data. Basically, this is a difference in detail, not in method.

Extrapolative methods discern and extract a pattern from past or time series data sets and extend that pattern into the future. The most common patterns of technological change are growth curves and exponential trends. A forecast is prepared by fitting the appropriate curve to past data, then extrapolating that curve into the future. A typical growth curve, fitted to historical data covering aircraft speed records from 1913 to 1939 (depicted by squares), the extrapolation of that trend, and the actual data for the "forecast" method of 1945–1970 (depicted by diamonds) is represented in Figure 1. A growth curve showing the replacement of wooden vessels by metal in the U.S. Merchant Marine is portrayed in Figure 2. Note the disruptions caused by the Great Depression and World War II.

Leading indicators use events in one time series to forecast events in another related time series. A common use of technological forecasting is to project basic research results forward to the commercialization of that particular technology. The ap-

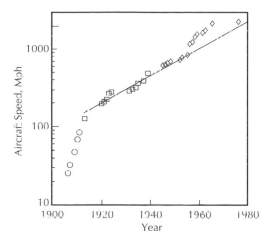

FIGURE 1. Exponential trend of aircraft speed records. (Note that as of February 1995, no aircraft has surpassed the speed record set in 1976.

FIGURE 2. Conversion of U.S. Merchant Marine ships from wood to metal.

pearance of some technology in a performance-oriented application (e.g., military or space) is also used to forecast the subsequent mass-market appearance of the technology. Success of this method depends upon knowing the leading indicator and the event to be forecast.

Causal models are used to forecast simulations in which there are multiple variables whose likely interactions are known. In most cases, the models are solved and developed using computer simulations. This is how meteorologists forecast the weather, using computers and measurements from weather stations worldwide. Causal models in technological forecasting have been most successful in forecasting the replacement of one technol-

ogy by another. The models simulate the behavior of people who try the new technology, accept or reject it, and perhaps reconsider their decision later. The models can be more precisely confirmed and calibrated using market surveys or test markets.

These three methods all produce "single-point" forecasts—that is, forecasts which contain a single, discrete number for the future value. Unfortunately, the real world cannot always be reduced to rigid one-to-one relationships between past and future. This is where stochastic methods come into play. The word *stochastic* comes from the Greek *stochastikos*, "skillful in aiming," which in turn is derived from a similar word meaning "to guess." It is intended to convey the idea of randomness. Stochastic forecasts recognize that in addition to the factors influencing the future, which can be dealt with as the three previous methods do, there may be random or unknown factors acting which can cause deviations from the expected outcomes. A stochastic forecast thus presents not a single estimate for a future value, but a range of possible outcomes and the probability of each.

The most frequent application of stochastic methods in technological forecasting is in cross-impact models. Such a model starts with a set of events that might occur. Each event is assigned a time and a probability of occurrence. However, the events are not independent. The occurrence or nonoccurrence of some events may change the timing and/or probability of other events. The possible changes are termed "cross-impacts." These foresights can be estimated by conducting a so-called Monte Carlo simulation with a computer. The computer selects an event, draws a random number to determine if the event occurs, then makes the appropriate adjustments in the timing and probability of those events impacted by the selected event. This process is repeated until all events have been determined. The model is reset to the starting conditions, and the simulation is repeated a large number of times. The frequency of occurrence and timing of the events in the outcomes is a stochastic forecast of the timing and likelihood of occurrence of those events.

Scenarios also are commonly used by technological forecasters. A scenario is a narrative description of future developments and conditions. The important feature of a scenario is that it speculatively describes interactions of the individual forecasts used as its starting point. The primary value of a scenario is its power to present a set of forecasts vividly, in terms of how the events being forecast affect the people involved. Scenarios can be a very useful tool for presenting forecasts to people who are not specialists or otherwise thoroughly knowledgeable concerning the technology being predicted.

Technology Assessment

Technology assessment is a class of policy studies that systematically examines the effects on society that may occur from introducing a new technology, its extension, or its modification. It emphasizes the positive and negative consequences that are unintended, indirect, or delayed.

The term was coined in 1967 by former Congressman Emilio Daddario, who argued that if Congress appropriated money for technological projects, it should have some understanding of what the consequences and outcomes would be. Pursuant to efforts spearheaded by Representative Daddario, an Office of Technology Assessment was established in 1972 as a research arm of the U.S. Congress. Today, however, the term is used in a much broader context.

Technological forecasts are essential for technology assessment. To assess the consequences of deploying a technology, it is first necessary to estimate the scale, scope, and rapidity of that deployment. The assessment goes well beyond the forecast of the technology, to estimate the social and economic consequences of implementing the technology. Common technology assessment techniques include relevance trees, causal models, and social indicators. Complex interactions are often portrayed through scenarios.

Relevance trees are used to trace out chains of consequences, to secondary and higher order effects. The deployment of a technology has certain immediate consequences. These, in turn, bring about other consequences, which have still further consequences. A relevance tree displaying some consequences of the introduction of the automobile is shown in Figure 3.

Causal models, based on computer simulation, are used to trace the effects of new technology through a complex network of interacting variables. A causal model might be used to estimate the rate of deployment of a technology (similar to its use in technological forecasting), to estimate the magnitude of externalities such as pollution, and also to anticipate economic effects such as shifts in employment (down in the old technology, up in the new) or changes in demand for various commodities.

Social indicators are self-contained statistics that require little or no interpretation to comprehend and understand their significance. School

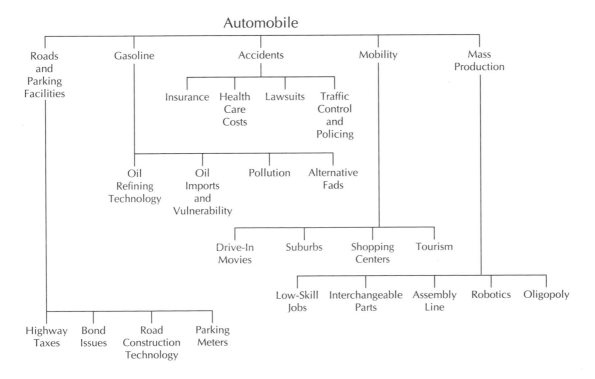

FIGURE 3. Some consequences of the automobile.

graduation rates, unemployment rates, and imprisonment rates, standing alone, provide meaningful descriptions of societal conditions. The use of social indicators in technology assessment involves selecting indicators that might change in response to deployment of a new technology.

In summary, technological forecasting and technology assessment are tools for policy guidance. Technological forecasting is used to estimate the future state of technology, including performance and extent of use. Technology assessment is used to estimate the consequences which might follow the deployment of some new technology, including the secondary and subsequent effects, particularly those which are not directly intended.

See also FORECASTING METHODS; FORECASTING, MISTAKES IN; RECORD SETTING; SCENARIOS; SOCIAL INDICATORS; SURPRISES; TECHNOLOGICAL CHANGE; TECHNOLOGY AND SOCIETY; WILDCARDS.

BIBLIOGRAPHY

AYRES, ROBERT U. *Technological Forecasting and Long-Range Planning.* New York: McGraw-Hill, 1969.

BRIGHT, JAMES R., ed. *Technological Forecasting for Industry and Government: Methods and Applications.* Englewood Cliffs, NJ: Prentice-Hall, 1968.

MARTINO, JOSEPH P. *Technological Forecasting for Decision Making,* 3rd ed. New York: McGraw-Hill, 1992.

PORTER, ALAN A., et. al. *Forecasting and Management of Technology.* New York: Wiley, 1991.

Joseph P. Martino

Technology and Science

The fabric of scientific and technological change is a weave of great complexity. In one dimension the fabric is defined by need; here changes are actively sought to solve problems or satisfy markets. This is the *pull* dimension. Scientific and technological changes in this dimension often flow from corporate, national, or international programs such as the war on cancer, the space station program, the Superconducting Supercollider, the assault on AIDS, or the Genome Project. Funding, legislation, military necessity, industrial policy, and marketing plans are the media of *pull*.

The other dimension of this fabric is *push*: here changes in science and technology are definedby the dynamics of the enterprises themselves. Changes in this dimension come as a result of momentum and feedback: work in progress leads to further discovery that redefines the course of work in progress. These are the "hot" areas of science and technology where recent discoveries make further opportunities pregnant: neurotransmitters, fullerenes, elevated temperature superconductivity, and transgenic engineering serve as examples. The media of *push* are publication, fad, employment, and what is perceived by the scientists and engineers themselves as fun.

But this *push-pull* fabric is full of bumps, some bigger than others, appearing in apparently random order. These represent breakthroughs, the discoveries that obey no model of change. How do breakthroughs occur? In *The Structure of Scientific Revolutions*, Thomas Kuhn presents an image of scientific progress. He sees normal science as the continual testing and application of the established rules within disciplines. When the old ideas work well enough, change is slow. When old ideas fail in their ability to explain or predict, new ideas gain respect and spread through the discipline over time, becoming the basis for normal science. What was once radical becomes routine. A paradigm shift of this sort provides a new way of looking at the world, and once it occurs the old ideas that are replaced are dead. These paradigm shifts make the world different for all time. The history of science and technology is a recounting of such events: from the harnessing of fire to the discovery of fission. Events like these define who we are, what we know, and what we believe.

The patterns on this three-dimensional fabric are not entirely random and are determined in part by four factors: (1) the growing capability of computation, (2) instrumentation, (3) the way information is gathered and disseminated, and (4) the nature of the disciplines to which scientists and engineers belong.

Computation

It is impossible to imagine future science and technology without computers. Certainly computers have eased the tasks associated with dull data collection and number crunching; but they have done much more than improve efficiency. They have opened the possibility of both experimental arithmetic and complex visualization. With high computational speeds, inexpensive CPU time, and abundant and cheap memory, simulations can be used to represent reality. Engineers can design millions of variants of a machine or product and test them all on a computer to find the one that performs best.

Outcomes may best be understood through pictures. With computers, pictures can be formed easily and manipulated. Data can be seen as a surface, atoms as solids to be moved by the analyst-experimenter to form molecules; and molecules or continents can be seen interacting, with time speeded or slowed to show patterns hidden in long lists or numbers, but more readily apparent in visual form. Add virtual reality and the molecules can be fitted together, manipulated by the analyst in a new kind of computer-based chemistry, metallurgy, crystallography, or pharmacology. For example, researchers have shown, via computer imaging, how steroid receptors bind to the genes they regulate.

For the future, we expect that computers will be smaller, more powerful, easier to operate, and still less expensive, by factors of 100 to 10,000 in the next twenty years. With voice input and seamless access to essentially any database, a computer will be an integral and unique part of every scientific team.

Advanced Instrumentation

New instrumentation opens totally new horizons to observation. This progenitor of scientific and technological change is pushing frontiers on spatial and temporal fronts: the scanning tunneling microscope and the ballistic electron emission microscope yield images the size of atoms and also provide means for manipulating single atoms. At the other extreme, space probes reaching out beyond the solar system and new orbital instruments give an unprecedented view of the universe. The **ROSAT** Probe, for example, detected giant clusters of quasars at eight to ten billion light years from Earth, suggesting a lumpier universe than previously thought. At one extreme of the time spectrum, laser pulses in the femtosecond regime control molecular reactions, and at the other extreme, automated data collection systems track glacially slow changes such as shifts in Earth's crust with precision and without boredom. Magnetic resonance imaging now permits human diagnostics through imaging of soft tissue; soon the menu of atoms that can be imaged in this way will be extended greatly.

Information Gathering and Dissemination

With modern communications, what is known in one discipline is rapidly known by others. Informal fax networks, for example, were far more efficient in spreading the word about elevated temperature

superconductors than the conventional media. Publication of papers in conventional peer-reviewed journals is beginning to serve a primarily archival function. High-speed networks such as the Internet (some 350,000 computer hosts on 5,000 networks in thirty-three countries) facilitate scientific communications and are growing at a tremendous rate, in some cases doubling every six months. Withthe advent of planned national networks, further growth is likely.

These networks are used for more than just communications. They also aid in the search for collaborators, exchanges of data, revisions of publications, and news dissemination, and provide efficient access to massive on-line databases. This is the new grapevine. Since there is no filtering of material, these networks promote fads and gossip as well as research, both good and bad. The primary effect is the transfer of information between disciplines, a pooling of resources that strengthens everyone. Genetics, for instance, owes its vitality not only to the biosciences, but to microscopy, computers, data processing, imaging, physiology, and materials sciences. The field of materials draws its strength from not only metallurgy, but chemistry, computers, data processing, microscopy, and genetics. These cross-disciplinary jumps used to happen before, but not to the extent that they will in the future.

The Nature of the Scientific and Technological Disciplines

The population of engineers and scientists with PhD. degrees doubled to over four million in the United States during the 1980s. Based on projected retirements and the entry into colleges and universities by the babies of the baby-boomer generation in the 1990s, a shortage of half a million scientists is projected for 2000.

Prospective changes in the organization of scientific and technical disciplines are likely to be much more profound. Prior to computer databases and digital communications, scientific disciplines and technological fields were essentially defined by the amount of knowledge that could be assimilated by an individual in a lifetime. When more information than that was generated, subdisciplines formed. The walls around these guilds of specialization were high, and contributions from outside the wall were rare and not invited. Because of easy access to information in their own discipline as well as others, scientists and engineers have knowledge about other fields that was not as easily available to them before. In addition, most scientists work in teams. This also promotes cross-disciplinary interchange.

For the future, the frontiers of change seem impressive indeed. Listed below are five areas that represent new opportunities with consequences as profound as any seen over the last two hundred years. This represents a prodigious advance considering that the prior interval encompasses almost all the knowledge of modern science and engineering.

THE NEW GENETICS

This field resides at the confluence of the Genome Project, genetic medicine (involving genetic therapies), and the availability of tools to pinpoint, deliver, and manipulate genetic material at selected sites on the genome. Out of this will come new views on health and sickness, and on the design of plants and animals, including *Homo sapiens*. When the world population presses twelve billion, the new genetics may well provide a new form of agriculture capable of feeding the swollen world population.

ELECTRONIC EXPERIENCE

Consider the future evolution of massive data storage and retrieval systems, miniaturization of computers, smart machines, voice input, fractal geometry, advanced computer simulation, biosensing, and imaging. This is the stuff of robots, advanced systems of automation, and virtual reality. These technologies will provide experience at a distance and will turn entertainment from a passive to a participatory experience. Simulation technologies will allow the creation of synthetic experience that will be realistic beyond imagination and may make real life seem dull. Ultimately this will mean new strategies for education; entertainment unparalleled, so good that it may be outlawed; new means of rehabilitation, punishment, and incarceration; design and research tools for the professional as well as the amateur; the construction of artificial worlds that may seem as real as our own.

MICROTECHNOLOGIES

This cluster derives its strength from developments in computers, data processing, biology, physics and physical chemistry, biomimetics, polymers, microscopy, microsciences, and photolithography. Micromachines at the scale of tenths of millimeters—and at the fringe, nanomachines at the scale of molecules—describe electromechanical machinery that can only be seen under a microscope. The shrinking machine is a new technology that includes venous submarines guided by surgeons outside the body, and video cameras that can be hidden in a bread crumb. Photolithography is used to make tiny parts; bioactivity to find molecules of specific shapes—i.e., antibodies that recognize antigens, enzymes that combine reactants, and hormones that fit receptors.

BRAIN RESEARCH

The brain contains 100 billion neurons, about as many as there are stars in our galaxy. Multiply this by 5.5 billion, the number of people in the world, and the number of neurons in the world ranks among the most numerous things of which we have knowledge. Many compare our position with respect to future psychiatry (or whatever the field of the brain comes to be called) to that of nuclear physics before fission or genetics before DNA. The clues are enticing: we know about synapses and neurotransmitters. Thought of a simple kind has been visualized through mapping of deep electrical impulses; mapping of the network of neurons is beginning. Phenomenological data abound. The field seems to be in Kuhn's pre-paradigm state, but ready for its Rutherford, Watson, and Crick, or Einstein. As knowledge of the brain and its functions increases, the curing of mental diseases, improved memory, and, in the most general sense, use of the organ to its greater potential will follow.

DEALING WITH COMPLEXITY

We have a propensity to linearize: put a little in and a little comes out. But the world is nonlinear, and when neat solutions based on linear assumptions are tested in the real world, they tend to fail. The notion of chaos, a form of mathematics applied to system analysis, is at the forefront of analysis of systems as diverse as dripping water faucets and beating hearts. Chaos can also result when the systems considered are social. This means that social policy based on presumed knowledge may be essentially random in its success. In the years ahead, policies will flow from better analysis, from an explicit knowledge of uncertainty and risk, and from concepts of stability.

These clusters—the new genetics, electronic experience, micromachines, the brain, and dealing with complexity—impact on products, processes, services, workers, capital, competition, markets, customer needs, the meaning of truth, democracy, free choice, education, and the nature and meaning of consciousness and self. Powerful changes await.

See also CHANGE, SCIENTIFIC AND TECHNO-LOGICAL; COMMUNICATIONS; COMPUTERS: OVERVIEW; HIGH TECHNOLOGY; INFORMATION OVERLOAD; INFORMATION TECHNOLOGY; NANOTECHNOLOGY; SCIENTIFIC BREAKTHROUGHS; TECHNOLOGICAL CHANGE; TECHNOLOGICAL DETERMINISM; TELECOMMUNICATIONS.

BIBLIOGRAPHY

Cook, Gordon. "A National Network That Isn't." *Computerworld* 26/10 (March 9, 1992).

Gordon, Theodore J. "Chaos in Social Systems." *Technology Forecasting and Social Change* 42 (1992): 1–15.

Holden, Constance. "Career Trends for the 90's." *Science* (May 1991).

Kuhn, Thomas S. *The Structure of Scientific Revolutions.* Chicago: University of Chicago Press, 1962.

Theodore J. Gordon

Technology and Society

"What's in? What's out?" the news media continually ask. Unfortunately, the spotlights of our current attentions often blind us to the presence of more critical issues. Right answers to the wrong questions may be fashionable, reflecting current consensus, but ultimately they are useless, irrelevant. What may seem desirable or likely today may not prove feasible tomorrow. Here lies the source of many of our forecasting mistakes. Seduced by the mystique of technological change, we often overestimate its importance and underestimate the significance of ongoing, underlying factors such as social structures and behaviors. Hopefully learning our lesson from these recent misperceptions, we must focus on three key issues that appear uncertain and are thus critical for the future: the real rate of diffusion of new technologies, the resultant metamorphosis of work, and the concomitant evolution of lifestyles and social organization.

At the forefront of the misconceptions that distort our vision of the world is what can be called the "technological mirage," a view supported by the theory of successive waves of technoeconomic "progress." Technology has come for the last decade to be considered as the source and solution for everything.

This kind of error then is not really new. In 1974, the major explanation for the world economic crisis was that it was energy-related. In France, it was felt that to recover a strong growth rate, the constraint on energy sources had to be overcome: hence the ambitious French nuclear power program. More than a decade later, energy is no longer regarded as the universal solution. Furthermore, the countries that have recently proved to be the most economically dynamic—Japan, Germany, South Korea—are themselves highly dependent on nonindigenous energy sources. At the same time there is not a single OPEC country in the list of newly industrialized nations, while the United Kingdom, despite its oil resources in the North Sea, has declined in terms of industrial development.

During the 1980s, energy was replaced by technology as the dominant driving force. According to a now popular view, we are currently in a transitional crisis between two technological waves. The technologies and concomitant production of the 1950s and '60s are on the wane, and a surge of rising new technologies and products will lift us away from the collapse of the old. Information technology, biotechnology, and new materials therefore are viewed as the path to excellence and future growth. However, the journey on this path, when not guided by a consistent strategy or theory, often leads nowhere. Entering an unknown territory may involve facing a battery of newly demanding situations. What is true for a business firm or corporation is also valid for a country, especially a developing one.

Between 1974 and 1977, this technological quandary was absent from the debate raging on how to get ourselves out of the energy crisis and from one economic level to the next. It is apropos to ask if we have not invented the technological crisis only as a replacement for the energy one—whereas the real problems are to be found elsewhere in our societal structures and organizations as well as in our behavioral trends. We always seem able to find a tree to hide from view the forest of real problems.

The crisis is above all a product of sectoral and institutional tensions resulting from the opposition between drivers of change (geopolitical, technological, economic, and social) and inertia-bound structures (political, legal, organizational, and psychological).

Unfortunately, the social changes necessary to get out of the crisis are not usually stimulated by the onset of technological change in itself—however ripe with potential such change may be. According to the so-called "Japanese model," the key to adaptation and success seems to lie in the intelligent use of our own socioculture.

Following this line of thought, we can wonder if the rate of diffusion of new technologies will be as rapid as forecast. On average, progress in the diffusion of new technologies will remain slow because of the inertia inherent in production and social systems. Moreover, this resistance is perhaps stronger in the tertiary sector (i.e., information-based enterprise), to the extent that this sector, so far, has been less affected by the stimulus of international competition than have the primary (agricultural/extractive-industrial) or secondary (industrial) sectors. Many factors combine to explain the slow rate of this penetration.

In the first place, there is the question of reallocating time freed by new techniques of production and organization. What is the point of investing in order to obtain productivity gains that cannot be translated into expanded production due to saturated markets, slow growth rates, or staff reduction? The existing staff must be kept busy; a reduction in working hours can only be gradual if it is to be equitably shared between sectors.

In the second place, the spread of office technology means that the world of work becomes relatively permeable, which tends to work against established hierarchies. Information technologies are not neutral with respect to power structures. It is not, therefore, surprising that managers sometimes feel threatened and resist innovation.

Finally, what is technologically possible is not necessarily profitable or socially desirable. Thus, we should beware of creating the equivalent of a Concorde jet in the field of telematics (i.e., the long-distance transmission of computerized information). It is unlikely that working at home will develop to the point that a significant amount of office work will disappear. The physical character of typical urban housing developments in France—the small, cramped, uncomfortable rooms and the overall drabness of the environment—is not conducive to the kind of productivity afforded by an office environment. Moreover, work is a social activity and meets a need for communication that is satisfied less and less elsewhere.

Unemployment is a factor in many countries, especially in Europe, and it will rise if there is no change in structures, organizations, rules of the game, and behavior. This means we are heading for a dual society, with a growing proportion of the population excluded from the labor market or relegated to poor, part-time jobs. Such a trend may have extremely disruptive consequences.

Ultimately there is only one way out: a sharing of work and income supplemented by greater mobility between existing jobs. If there are only four jobs for five workers, there is no problem if the jobs are

rotated; moreover, an opportunity exists to increase creative breaks from work. Further reductions in working hours seem probable and desirable, but it does not have to mean a decrease in hours of real activity. People do not want to work less but to work differently. The trend toward a dual society can be mitigated by encouraging a pluralistic society, in which an individual could have several jobs, each of which would be filled by several people.

The most persistent question concerns the evolution of values and lifestyles. At this level, conjecture fails: futurists do not see clearly and social scientists have difficulty in understanding the present, and even the recent past. As for analyses of lifestyles, these have no predictive value. In technical terms, the range of variables explained by lifestyles is almost negligible. In virtually all cases, lifestyle is less significant than sociodemographic indicators such as the level of education or profession.

After World War II, new values emerged to replace the traditional values of fulfilling one's duties, making one's effort pay, saving, and subjugation to rigid hierarchies. New values that became dominant during the 1960s gave priority to consuming, novelty, and the keeping up of appearances. After the end of the 1960s, this model was challenged by new values that rejected the criteria of social excellence, status, large organizations, and bureaucracy. The new values embraced conviviality, personal and cultural life, relationships, the quality of one's personal and collective environment, decentralization, small groups, autonomy, and self-realization. This evolution has led to fragmentation. Nowadays, many groups express different values that are at odds with common values.

We are witnessing a clash among believers in moral excellence (the so-called militants), small and more or less closed groups (even sects), new consumers, those who live for the moment, the minority who have a satisfying job, the new agriculturalists, those without work, and so on. In this surging variety of values and lifestyles, we must seek all possible degrees of compromise through which partially contradictory trends can develop in parallel, such as the search for both autonomy and security, for both freedom and a sense of roots.

"What's in? What's out?" the news media continue to ask. Fortunately, what's "in" often becomes "out" easily, and vice versa. The myth of technological supremacy, like that of the Loch Ness monster, will continue to be challenged by reality—or to be replaced by newer illusions such as the notion that education is the cure-all for whatever afflicts us.

See also CHANGE, SCIENTIFIC AND TECHNOLOGICAL; HIGH TECHNOLOGY; MULTIFOLD TREND; SCIENCE ISSUES; SCIENTIFIC BREAKTHROUGHS; SOCIAL CHANGE: UNITED STATES; TECHNOLOGICAL CHANGE; TECHNOLOGICAL DETERMINISM; TECHNOLOGICAL FORECASTING AND ASSESSMENT; TECHNOLOGICAL INNOVATION; TECHNOLOGY AND SCIENCE; WILDCARDS.

BIBLIOGRAPHY

FREEMAN, C. *The Economics of Industrial Innovations.* London: Penguin, 1974.

GODET, MICHEL. *From Anticipation to Action.* Paris: UNESCO, 1993.

GODET, MICHEL; CHAPUY, P.; and COMYN, G. "Global Scenarios; Geopolitical and Economic Context in to the Year 2000." *Futures* 26/3 (April 1994): 275–288.

Michel Godet
Fabrice Roubelat

Telecommunications

The Information Superhighway, or the Infobahn, refers to a nationwide or global network that will carry voice, data, video, and other information, all on one type of wire, optic cable, and broadcast band. "Information highways will revolutionize the way we work, learn, shop, and live," says Vice President Al Gore, Jr. "Human societies have seen four distinct revolutions in the character of social interchange: in speech, in writing, in printing, and now in telecommunications," comments renowned futurist Daniel BELL.

The convergence of the telephone, television, and home computer will create a new device some have called the "teleputer." It would feature a variety of video display options (including high-definition television), the voice capabilities of the telephone, and many home-computer options. Telecommunications promise to improve education, even in isolated areas of the Third World and to reduce energy consumption and pollution as people telecommute to work and shop at home. A 1992 Economic Strategy Institute study estimated that the Information Superhighway would add more than $321 billion in new wealth over the next sixteen years through such effects as shortening product development cycles and improving the cross-fertilization of ideas. John Sculley, former Apple Computer CEO, foresees a $3.5 trillion market arising. The Information Superhighway, Vice President Gore has asserted, would do for America what the transcontinental railroad did in the 1800s and the interstate highway did in the 1900s. Government will help build the Information Superhighway by supporting long-term research; funding test applications; developing policies that ensure all Americans have access; encouraging private sector investment in building the Information Superhighway; and creating a competitive market for telecommunications and information services.

Numerous types of terminals will hook into the Information Superhighway, and at least three major modes of transmission will still be operating far into the future:

- *Fiber optics.* Fiber-optic cables are able to carry huge amounts of data at the speed of light.
- *Direct broadcast satellites.* Able to reach large numbers of people over a wide area, direct broadcast satellites do not incur the additional cost of wires or cables.
- *Cellular communicators.* Soon to be cheap enough that virtually anyone who wants one will be able to afford it, the cellular phone will be operable almost anywhere and will likely be equipped with emergency-assistance buttons.

Newspapers and On-Line Information Services

Newspapers will arrive electronically, will be tailored to subscriber information needs, and will be filled with up-to-the-minute information. Libraries around the world will be available for you to peruse at home. High-definition television may eliminate the need to visit libraries, unless it is to experience directly an ancient manuscript or work of art.

On-line information services now serve some 13.5 million people in the United States, according to *Boardwatch* magazine. The Internet, inaugurated for Department of Defense research scientists to share information, has blossomed into a worldwide colossus.

Education

The telecommunications revolution will make learning much more effective, more available, and more fun. Learning will become active, rather than passive, and students will pace their study. Students will be able to receive much of their education without leaving home. New opportunities will be available for gifted students and the learning impaired or physically challenged. Speed of learning will likely increase. Students will be able to earn a three-year bachelor's degree with the fourth year spent on a master's.

Interactive programs picturing historical documents, holograms of famous people, virtual reality battles, and other features will actively involve students in learning. Interactive education will allow students to participate in highly creative hands-on exercises without the need of human instruction. Artificial intelligence in programs will pick up patterns in a student's response and tailor instruction to shore up weak points.

Third World nations will be able to leapfrog other nations still adhering to traditional passive instruction techniques. Arthur C. CLARKE envisions "electronic tutors," a combined microcomputer, video display, and satellite receiver, becoming cheap enough to allow anyone in the world to receive a state-of-the-art electronic education. According to Joseph Pelton, "Tele-education will continue to homogenize cultures and languages. It could lead to charges of cultural imperialism among those whose language and culture are underrepresented."

Interactive Television

Interactive television will offer viewers exciting new choices to interact with program producers and networks. No longer will television merely be a passive activity. An electronic *TV Guide* will help sort through the choices. Artificial intelligence in programs will note what types of programs a viewer watches and customize listings to suit the individual's needs.

More channels will be dedicated to narrow topics: the Football Channel, the Tennis Channel, the Parents' Channel, and so on. Recent cinematic hits and an amazing abundance of other movies will be available on a pay-per-view basis. This will be one of the first interactive television services to see wide use.

Other Forms of Entertainment

Other entertainment possibilities on the Information Superhighway include:

- *Virtual reality.* These programs will allow you to simulate real-life experiences.
- *On-line dating.* Computer bulletin boards are already bringing together the romantically inclined.
- *Video and computer games.* Augmented by virtual reality and the ability to play others on-line, video games and computer simulations may gain a whole new dimension.

- *On-Line gambling.* Gambling of every imaginable sort will be available at home and also while traveling on planes, boats, trains, and buses.

Home Shopping

Shopping at home will revolutionize retailing as consumers browse through thousands of on-line catalogs and order goods at the push or click of a button. Manufacturers will sell directly to consumers, cutting out the need for the retailer and other middlemen. On-line access to comparative shopping information will displace much of the "consumer education" function of advertising, with better-informed consumers relying more on merit than promotional power.

People will always like to go shopping for things that are difficult to shop for at home or where the shopping experience is more fun. Nevertheless, according to futurist Don Libey, "If only five percent of retail business shifts each year from in-store purchases to direct purchases by way of interactive technologies, in seventeen years 85 percent of retail purchases will be direct. That means 85 percent of the existing retail space will be obsolete by 2010." Some of the 19 million Americans now working in retail may be looking for jobs. At the same time, interactive shopping will create many new delivery jobs. Groceries may soon be delivered to refrigerated lock-boxes outside a consumer's home.

Banking and Financial Services

The financial world has been at the forefront of much of the global telecommunications revolution. Money has become units of data on the Information Superhighway.

ELECTRONIC FUNDS TRANSFERS

While millions use automatic teller machines or collect their paycheck electronically, few realize the enormous impact of worldwide trade. Futurist Peter Schwartz reveals the dimensions of this trend: "International transactions reached $87 trillion in 1986. That comes to twenty-three times the U.S. GNP. It's several times larger than the gross world product. Trade is only about 10 percent of that $87 trillion. The rest of it is generated by electronic transactions."

HOME BANKING

Banks have traditionally been the gatekeepers of monetary transactions such as bill paying and are rushing to stay in the bill-paying business. If cable or telephone systems offer bill-paying options, banks could lose a large percentage of their business. Banks have been moving into on-line interactive banking and putting high-tech phones into the hands of consumers, allowing home banking to become a reality.

Work and Careers

The Information Superhighway offers tremendous opportunities for living where you want and working when you want. Telecommuting can free workers from the drudgery of commuting, reduce energy consumption and air pollution; it will also be a boon for the homebound and handicapped, who will have many new avenues of employment. Holding meetings by teleconference using live interactive video also will become common.

Service and professional industries and jobs will no longer be protected by oceans or international borders. "If work can be telecommuted out of the office, what keeps it from being telecommuted overseas?" asks Elaine Taber, program director for the Clerical Workers Union. Currently workers in Haiti do word processing for insurance companies, telephone service people in Ireland take catalog orders from U.S. customers, and programmers in the Philippines convert print data to CD-ROM. Wages may continue to drop as "electronic immigrants" depress wages and as artificial intelligence eliminates many professional occupations. The Information Superhighway will cause many to lose their jobs and many new careers to be created. Job searches will be facilitated by the ability to list your résumé and video presentation in on-line databases and interview for jobs around the world via on-line videoconferencing.

New information technologies will revive competition and give authors, researchers, and program creators the real power. Whereas today an author may receive 10 percent of a book's revenue, future "content providers" will get a full 90 percent, the authors say.

Health/Medicine

Telecommunications will help make health care more affordable and more available. Doctors in Chicago have examined patients in Atlanta via the use of an electronic stethoscope, high-resolution medical-imaging equipment, and interactive video. These technologies will allow doctors everywhere to access the expertise of specialists instantly, any-

where in the world. "Telemedicine" also can help bring affordable health care to rural areas. Telecommunications technologies can also make health care more affordable. A study by Arthur D. Little estimates that health insurance claims processing costs could be reduced by $5.3 billion by adopting selected telecommunications technology.

Advertising and Marketing

Interactive television and the Information Superhighway will totally revolutionize advertising and marketing. Advertising will become more targeted, more relevant, and more useful for consumers and more effective for advertisers. Television commercials, videomail, and electronic mail will be targeted directly at consumers with an interest in that product, and the messages will be personalized.

Interactive classified advertising will allow interested buyers to access additional information about the product, even providing full-motion video of the product in use. Simply press a button to contact the seller to arrange an appointment. The real estate industry may be turned upside down as realtors lose the monopoly provided by their computerized "multiple listing service." New real estate ads will feature home tours in virtual reality, maps of the neighborhood, and more. Competition from fax machines and overnight delivery services has already resulted in reduced mail volume.

Privacy and "Big Brother"

One negative aspect of the Information Superhighway is the potential loss of privacy. Information such as your financial, medical, or employment records can easily be passed on or sold to others without your consent. If a mistake is made in a computer record, it can take months to correct and may end up incorrect in hundreds of other databases that borrow the information from the central bureau.

The government is also actively involved in monitoring communications. The U.S. National Security Agency (NSA) has a $3 billion budget for monitoring electronic conversations via satellite and can monitor 30 million conversations daily. The NSA also has developed an "uncrackable" computer code known as the "clipper chip," which it is encouraging computer manufacturers to use. Because the NSA has the "key" to the code, it would be able to monitor any communications it wishes. Thus the U.S. government can monitor everything from computer bulletin boards to the N.Y. Stock

Exchange and all scientific and financial databases. The government clearly has all the tools to be Big Brother.

Telecommunication Crime, Terrorism, and War

Future criminals and terrorists will have a wider range of opportunities to steal or create electronic mayhem. Terrorists will be able to knock out a city's power system on-line from hundreds of miles away, or invade its computer networks to wreak havoc with its government systems. Data kidnappers might send a "databomb" to a bank with a transaction, then hold the organization's data hostage until its demands are met. An enemy nation or group of knowledgeable terrorists could shut down large portions of a government's defense information systems. Theoretically, a malevolent computer hacker could create an "electronic AIDS" that could devastate the entire collection of data assembled by humankind over the last twenty years.

People have also become more dependent on communications for their work. Today much surveillance work involves monitoring phone conversations and other electronic investigation. Law enforcement officials are also using communications to monitor offenders at home with "electronic anklets" that reduce the prison population for nonviolent criminals and provide them with limited mobility to attend college or work. In California, prisoners testify via videoconferencing as a security and cost-saving measure.

Politics and Government

The communications revolution offers new opportunities to encourage freedom, promote democracy, and make governments more responsive to their constituents. On-line polls and on-line voting will make it easier for citizens to participate in community and government affairs and make their views known to their representatives. Besides voting for representatives, people may demand a direct say in the business of government. Governments may have to ensure that all citizens have access to the Information Superhighway as it becomes a more central force in commerce, education, and the democratic process. National economies will continue to be replaced by a global economy. Governments will find it increasingly hard to control information and commerce as satellites and fiber-optics transfer money and data across continents and oceans at the speed of light.

Governments everywhere are finding it harder to stop the flow of information. The fall of Ferdinand Marcos, the rise of Lech Walesa, the flurry of elections in communist nations, were all related to the rise of communications.

In the future, politicians will be able to target different groups with different messages, either by the channel they are watching or demographic information. One may never know what a politician "really said" because the message will be changed to suit every audience.

Conclusion

The Information Superhighway offers unparalleled opportunities to deal with many of the world's most pressing problems such as education, energy, pollution, and peace. It also offers the opportunity to expand the sum of human knowledge and help individuals gain more freedom to live where and how they want.

See also ADVERTISING; COMMUNICATIONS; COMMUNICATIONS TECHNOLOGY; ELECTRONIC CONVERGENCE; INTERACTIVE ENTERTAINMENT; TELEPHONES; TELEVISION.

BIBLIOGRAPHY

HELDMAN, ROBERT K. *Future Telecommunications: Information Applications, Services, and Architecture.* New York: McGraw-Hill, 1993.

PELTON, JOSEPH N. *Future View: Communications, Technology, and Society in the 21st Century.* Boulder, CO: Baylin Publishing, 1992.

RHEINGOLD, HOWARD. *Virtual Reality: The Revolutionary Technology of Computer-Generated Artificial Worlds.* New York: Summit Books/Simon & Schuster, 1991.

SNYDER, JIM, and ZIPORYN, TERRA. *Future Shop: How Future Technologies Will Change the Way We Shop and What We Buy.* New York: St. Martin's Press, 1992.

George Anthony Cornish

Telephones

POTS (plain old telephone services) is presently going through a metamorphosis as it is incorporated into the all-digital world. We are entering a universal fiber-optic and wireless environment of broad bandwidth service that is revolutionizing personal communications. The newest, fastest-growing segment is the world of wireless telephones including cellular, mobile, and car phones. With the advent of digital telecommunication, telephone service will change even more. The cellular phone system will break out of its local-area coverage and go worldwide. Vast satellite communications relay systems will span the globe and provide cellular service everywhere, serving telephones that fit in a pocket or pocketbook. Several competing companies will provide this service. Individuals will have personal phone numbers and will be reachable anytime, anywhere. This equipment will include auto-location services that pinpoint the location of any individual, anywhere on the globe.

Signal alerts will be received via digital paging, either visual or audible. Response to this signal will be immediate—there will be no need to search for a telephone because a telephone will always be near at hand. You will be able to display the number from which the call originated through caller identification. If a caller desires he or she can also provide a name and address. Multimedia devices will enable all messages, including graphics and video, to be displayed.

This is possible because all transmitted information will be created and communicated by digital signals over fiber optics, wireless, copper wire, coaxial cable, microwave links, and satellites. Since all information will be in a standardized digital format, there will be no need for modems.

Each individual will have a personal communications device (PCD) consisting of keyboard, voice, and pen input and output to a speaker, a flat colorscreen display, or a "heads-up" display using special glasses that can double as glasses, sunglasses, or both. Onboard transceivers will provide either wireless electromagnetic links or a direct connect interface via wire, cable, or fiber optics.

The PCD will function as a facsimile machine as well—facsimiles will be handled by computers. Facsimiles can be created within the computer or scanned from hard copy. Images of text will be convertible to digital data, unless protected by the sender. Portable printers will be available to print out faxes, or anything else residing in the PCD. The PCD will be a versatile answering machine. It will accommodate voice mail as well as e-mail. If callers desire, video pictures of themselves or other subjects can be transmitted. Receivers also will be able to transmit pictures. PCDs with the charged-couple diode (CCD) video recorder built in can transmit the image of any subject pointed at.

The call waiting signal may be an audio beep, a flashing light, or a second video window on a PCD display screen. Conference calls may be set up among small numbers of other callers. Data can be saved in a PCD database for quick and easy retrieval and voice forwarding.

Carrier modes and configuration will include various transmission media—twisted-pair copper wire, fiber-optic cable, or coaxial cable. For short transmission distances of 100 meters or less, the capacity of wire may be arrayed to approach a million bits per second. This will accommodate a single-family connection to the larger intra/intercity networks, although fiber may already be installed in many cases. In remote areas microwave relays will be used for ground and satellite interface. Six-inch diameter satellite antennas will be adequate for direct transmission. Fiber optics will dominate the transmission world with bandwidth capabilities approaching fifty terabits per second per fiber-optic strand. This ultrahigh bandwidth will accommodate a million high-definition television (HDTV) channels. According to Nicholas Negroponte, head of MIT's Media Lab, most voice transmission will be by satellite, and will be part of the worldwide cellular system, while most video and audio transmissions will rely upon fiber optics. There will be increasing use of radio frequencies (RF) for short-range communications, whether in the home or office.

Human interface with the system will be via keyboard, pen, or voice. The user need only provide the callee's personal phone number and the system will find the callee. If there is no answer, the message will be stored and possibly forwarded, depending on the receiver's commands.

Translation services will convert voice to text, Braille, or other physically sensed output. Conversely, text, Braille, or other physically sensed output will be converted to voice. Almost instantaneous language translation will permit real-time multiple conversations between people speaking different languages. Input can be verbal or through a physical input device. The output will be converted to the presentation form of choice. If telegraph transmission exists it too will be in digital form so that it too can be converted by software.

Worldwide interconnection between users and providers will be enhanced through implementation of the integrated services digital network (ISDN), a set of standards that will govern the implementation of common services over the digital network. ISDN will integrate digitized voice with other digital information, e.g., digitally encoded data, graphics, and video information will be transmitted over the same transmission lines. The ISDN environment provides the switching and routing required to send data/information throughout the world, just as 20th century telephone equipment switched analog data. ISDN will incorporate all of the many transmission media and protocols required to form a seamless multimedia network.

More than likely broadband ISDN (B-ISDN) will be implemented by the turn of the century. B-ISDN is merely an extension of ISDN that takes advantage of the ultrahigh-speed transmission capabilities that are continuously being implemented.

All telephone technology capabilities will be integrated with advanced computer services, thereby integrating the telephone into the office desktop computer, the home telecommunications center, and the PCD. The PCD will have its own 200 to 400 megahertz (or higher) central processor and will provide hundreds of MIPs of processing power, as well as gigabytes of internal and external memory capacity. The merger between the telephone, the computer, audio, television, and the digital world will be so pervasive that it cannot be determined where one ends and the other begins. All information will travel through the same devices and over the same telecommunications transmission facilities.

The National Information Infrastructure (NII) will provide the telecommunication backbone and control the telecommunication highway. This seamless web of networks, computers, telephones, and other electronic communication devices will provide the means for clients and information providers to exchange virtually unlimited amounts and types of information. It will be accessible by all. While there will be many "for-pay" commercial services, many basic services will be free to the user at the time of use. The NII will be sponsored by local, state, and federal governments through taxes.

Universal information services will be integrated into the telecommunications highway and accessible via the twenty-first-century "telephone." These services will operate like businesses and services presently accessible via the transportation system that exists today. The thousands of miles of connecting roads correspond to the millions of local area networks comprising the telecommunications system interconnected by major telecommunication trunks, satellite links, microwave links, and RF communications. Information and interactive services will be provided by state, local, and federal governments; nonprofit organizations; and commercial organizations and individuals. In this brave new world anyone will be able to conduct almost any business activity from anywhere via the new PCD telephone.

See also COMMUNICATIONS; COMMUNICATIONS TECHNOLOGY; COMPUTER LINKAGE; DIGITAL COMMUNICATIONS; INTERACTIVE ENTERTAIN-MENT; MEDIA LAB; ON-LINE SERVICES; SATELLITE COMMUNICATIONS; TELECOMMUNICATIONS; TELEVISION.

BIBLIOGRAPHY

BRAND, STEWART. *The Media Lab: Inventing the Future at MIT.* New York: Viking, 1987.
KROL, ED. *The Whole Internet: User's Guide and Catalog.* Sebastapol, CA: O'Reilly & Associates, 1992.
MARTIN, JAMES. *Telecommunications and the Computer.* Englewood Cliffs, NJ: Prentice Hall, 1990.
NEGROPONTE, NICHOLAS. "The Future of Telecommunications." *Telecommunication* 27/1 (January 1993).
———. "Products and Services for Computers." *Scientific American* 265/3 (September 1991).

Brian K. Toren

Television

Because so much activity currently surrounds the communications system of television, most observers clearly see that something of great significance is underway. Large telecommunications firms, such as the telephone companies and the cable companies, are positioning themselves to take advantage of whatever happens; new technologies such as direct broadcast satellite (DBS) systems and high-definition television (HDTV) are appearing; new formats, like music television and home shopping channels, are quickly and widely disseminating; discussions of the so-called Information Superhighway are proliferating; and home viewers are waiting with a mixture of anticipation and skepticism.

But while change is in the air, no one can foresee precisely what the system that will eventually emerge might look like, in part because so much current thinking is clouded with overly optimistic visions and grandiose expectations. While such speculation can point the way, and is a necessary stage in any society's acceptance of major technological alterations, it should be blended with firmer and more realistic considerations.

Compounding the forecasting problem is the number of forces at work beyond simply the industries that supply the technologies and the content, on the one side, and the changing demands of the consumer market, on the other. In particular, the federal government is playing a large and sometimes unpredictable role in the evolution of television, primarily through the Federal Communications Commission (FCC), but also through the Congress, the presidential administration, and the courts. The television system is so important in the conduct of national life that governmental intervention is mandated by the Communications Act of 1934 and the Cable Television Act of 1992. (Some critics have argued that government intervention is contrary to the spirit of the Constitution's First Amendment, which says that "Congress shall make no law . . . abridging the freedom of speech, or of the press.") For example, although traditional over-the-air broadcasters (particularly local stations) would seem to be most jeopardized by the current development of universal cable systems, the government has so far compelled the newer systems to accommodate the older. It may or may not continue to do so.

When these governmental considerations are added to the uncertainties of technological developments, it would seem difficult to predict accurately the direction of change in the television system. Nevertheless, it is still possible to sketch six broad parameters within which these transformations will occur.

1. *The financial costs of the new system increasingly will be shifted to the consumers.* Broadcast television was previously free to Americans once the householder had purchased a receiver and antenna. The costs of the programming and transmission were paid by advertisers to the networks and affiliates, but consumer-paid cable television is now in about 65 percent of American households. Cable companies charge consumers for carrying the signal to their homes, and consumers are willing to pay for greater clarity and the increased number of channels. Once the television industry realized that consumers would spend directly for its service, a second revenue stream in addition to advertising dollars became possible. Beyond the charge for the cable hook-up and monthly payments, the addition of premium channels, pay-per-view experiments, and shopping channels further indicated consumer willingness to pay for television experience. This is confirmed by VCR purchases and videocassette rentals. Although the rise in direct consumer payments has been temporarily restrained by the provisions of the 1992 Cable Television Act, the long-term trend toward the sharing of television costs between the advertisers and the consumer appears to be strengthening. Viewers are agreeing to pay largely because of the personal gratifications which they recognize they are receiving from televised content.

The federal government, committed to the growth of the American economy, is not likely to unduly constrain the revenues of television providers. However, when it comes to something as important as the nation's primary communications system, headlong pursuit of profits does pose a challenge to egalitarian principles in that the less-privileged and poorer segments of the population may be excluded from participation. Most likely, through the offices of the FCC, the system of the future will be required to provide basic service at or below cost to everyone who wants it, after which providers would be free to pursue profits in elective channels offered to those who can afford them. The present cable system appears to be evolving in this direction.

2. *The much heralded convergence at the top of the television industry will continue to conceal the divergence and variety in the lower tiers of the industry.* Convergence has become a much-used term to describe a time of courtship and unions among the television, cable, telephone, computer, and studio production industries. This convergence is technologically foreshadowed by the rapidly increasing conversion of all communications content into digitized signals compatible with computers. Joint ventures, cross-ownerships, and outright mergers are said to signal the convergence of media into what might ultimately be just a few electronic behemoths controlling the Information Superhighway. When publishing giant Time merged with Hollywood giant Warner and when Viacom bought and merged with Paramount and Blockbuster Video, an image of greater consolidation and perhaps a foreboding media oligarchy was reinforced.

But at the same time that these large transactions are occurring in the limelight, other unnoticed developments are going on in smaller media companies, technology firms, independent studios, program producers, and upstart cable companies, down to the level of individual entrepreneurs. The television system overall is in a phase of expansive growth (even if the traditional networks had to decrease their size to regain financial stability), and firms and business people sense that with ingenuity and luck great profits can be made. A better word than *convergence* to typify the activity occurring during the first decades of the twenty-first century would be *ferment*, as new entrants come into all sections of the television system, at all levels, and jockey for position.

3. *The Information Superhighway will convey very little information, and may be only a secondary road.* At its grandest, the vision of an Information Superhighway portrays just one high-capacity communications line coming into each household, a line carrying television programming, movies on demand, radio music and talk, individualized newspapers,

digitized books and magazines, all sorts of advertising, computerized data, personal mail, telephone calls—in short, every kind of communication that can be electronically conveyed. But it should be clear, based on the public's past usage of the media, that consumer preference will not be for what is commonly thought of as "information," but rather for entertainment. Currently the American audience spends 75 percent of its media time with television, and most of that time is devoted to light entertainment. Likewise, much of the time spent with the other media (newspapers, books, magazines) is also given over to entertainment.

It is unwise to project the time patterns of present computer owners onto the use of future computer-compatible systems. In several ways, present computer modem use resembles amateurs' use of wireless in the 1910s, before the technology evolved into the mass medium of radio in the 1920s. The television system of the future will continue to be grounded in light entertainment.

It is also possible that the dream of a "superhighway" will be realized in a sharply curtailed version. Not all the various communications systems may be able to, or care to, join into a unitary system. Several wires may enter homes; advances in digitized broadcasting and cellular telephony may make over-the-air communication attractive again; a development that bears watching is direct broadcast satellite (DBS) transmissions, which may become unexpectedly successful. All this means that the Information Superhighway may be more myth than reality, at least for a decade or so.

4. *The demand for televised popular culture will continue to increase.* What is fueling the expansion of the television system is at root the audience's ever-growing need for situation comedies, sports, soap operas, murder mysteries, movies, game shows, and so on. Popular culture helps in the pleasurable and vicarious management of emotions and in the acknowledgment of dramatized social norms. As traditional institutions of church, family, and community have lost some of their cultural force over the course of the twentieth century, media-generated popular culture has come to the fore. This trend of long duration cannot be expected to subside soon. Additionally, the aging of the audience, together with the escalating fear of crime, implies that people will be staying at home more, doing even more of what they usually do—watching television.

5. *Consumption as a component of the television experience will grow more conspicuous.* The success of the home shopping channels is a clear sign that consumption will loom even larger than before in television. If cable channels do expand to several hundred, as currently touted, many of them will surely be programmed by merchandisers, by manufacturers (e.g., perhaps a Procter and Gamble Channel), by infomercial networks, and by advertising agencies. On the conventional entertainment channels, advertising will continue to be a dominant presence as a major source of revenue.

Merchandising through television will impel marketers to demand that audience figures be much more exact and revealing than they are now. The Nielsen ratings, for all their longevity, will be replaced by much more sophisticated audience measurement systems.

6. *Globally, American popular culture will battle indigenous cultures.* The current resistance of the French in particular, but of most other societies to one extent or another, against the inroads of American programming may well be stepped up in decades to come. The long-term prognosis, however, is not good for local cultures. Like water dripping on stone, American content is likely to wear down the resistance, in part because it can be sold overseas more cheaply than local programs can be produced, and in part because the audience will increasingly welcome, even demand, the shows.

In brief, the television system of the future will resemble the present one in that it will transmit much the same orders of content to a loyal audience. It will differ in that a broader array of selections will be available, and that viewers will shoulder more of the costs of the system. Additionally, the delivery system will be hammered out through fierce capitalistic competition according to the regulatory positions of the FCC and Congress.

See also ADVERTISING; BROADCASTING; COMMUNICATIONS; ELECTRONIC CONVERGENCE; INFORMATION OVERLOAD; MEDIA CONSOLIDATION; NEWSPAPERS; SATELLITE COMMUNICATIONS; TELECOMMUNICATIONS; TELEPHONES.

BIBLIOGRAPHY

CARPENTIER, MICHEL, et al. *Telecommunications in Transition.* New York: Wiley, 1992.
DIZARD, WILSON, JR. *Old Media, New Media: Mass Communications in the Information Age.* New York: Longman, 1994.
FOWLES, JIB. *Why Viewers Watch.* Newbury Park, CA: Sage, 1992.
NEUMAN, W. RUSSELL. *The Future of the Mass Audience.* New York: Cambridge University Press, 1992.
TUROW, JOSEPH. *Media Systems in Society.* New York: Longman, 1992.

Jib Fowles

Terrorism

The Vice President's Task Force on Combatting Terrorism (1986) defined terrorism as "the unlawful use or threat of violence against persons or property to further political or social objectives. It is generally intended to intimidate or coerce a government, individuals or groups to modify their behavior or policies."

Legally speaking, terrorism is not actually a crime in most parts of the United States, but rather encompasses more traditional forms of crime as they relate to the foregoing definition. The most common types of terrorism include:

- Conspiracy
- Murder (assassination)
- Kidnapping
- Hijacking (skyjacking)
- Bombing/arson
- Robbery
- Extortion

Many international terrorist groups cooperate with each other in such matters as recruit training and information sharing. Some will even join forces to carry out a particular deed, or one group may act on behalf of another. And several of those engaged in politically related terrorism receive funding from sympathetic governments.

Counterterrorism

Individuals involved in terrorist acts are likely to be part of larger groups whose activities may range over large geographical areas, among states, even countries. For this reason there is a strong need for communication and coordination among counterterrorist organizations and governments. Thus, intelligence represents a key element in the investigative process.

Further, because different individuals may be involved in specific criminal acts of the group, the modus operandi associated with a particular crime may be different. For this reason, it becomes important to know about a group's

- Stated goals
- Organizational structure
- Tactical approach
- Means of communication
- Propensity for violence.

Protecting individual rights must be weighed heavily in designing counterterrorist activities, lest the actions of government officials become as heavy-handed and brutal as the terrorists they are trying to combat. Some terrorist groups hope to provoke such actions from governments as a means of discrediting those governments.

Successful investigation of terrorist groups requires patience, skill, and cooperation. For this reason the task force approach offers the highest probability of success. Teams working together can compile a significant amount of information and, aided by an analyst, do much more than a single individual or group of individuals acting independently.

On the international level, the International Police Organization (INTERPOL), with headquarters in Lyons, France, serves as a central location for the collection and dissemination of crime-related information. Effective action against international terrorism requires the coordinated efforts of the central governments of nations and the cooperation of law enforcement agencies in each country assisted by INTERPOL. INTERPOL's purpose is to assist and improve police cooperation and the exchange of information among its 142 member countries. Capable of working in four languages—French, English, Spanish, and Arabic—it receives and transmits messages and inquiries to the proper authorities. Data are computerized, and the text may be retrieved in English. Routine inquiries made to INTERPOL include requests for tracing passports; identifying weapons, explosives, and vehicles; and identifying persons involved as either victim or criminal. Additional services include establishing a link between cases, obtaining information about suspected terrorists, their criminal records and proper identification, circulating notices for persons wanted on an international arrest warrant, and circulating warning notices about suspects who have committed or are likely to commit terrorist activities.

Terrorist Activities

Most terrorist acts involve bombing, assassination, or kidnapping (hostage-taking).

BOMBING

Several types of explosives are used by terrorists. In the United States, the most common has been a pipe bomb using black powder. The materials necessary to make a pipe bomb are readily available in most countries, and can be purchased in drugstores, hardware stores, and construction supply stores. Although homemade bombs have been used frequently, the availability of other types of explosives, particularly dynamite, TNT, and hand grenades, makes their use in the future more likely. On the international scene, plastic explosives have become more common, particularly in the Middle East. An American-made explosive known as C-4 has been used in numerous attacks by Middle Eastern terrorists. Most of these attacks have been attributed to a large amount of C-4 obtained illegally by Libya from an American source. Several recent attacks have been attributed to a Czech-made plastic explosive known as Semtex.

ASSASSINATION

Assassination attempts are often made through bomb attacks, although in the United States most political assassinations involve firearms. Attacks using a rifle or automatic weapon represent a greater problem. Assassination attempts carried out by terrorist groups are generally planned in advance, with the scene analyzed and avenues of escape plotted. A crime scene may actually comprise several locations, and the investigators in making the initial assessment should take time to explore the various possibilities that may exist. A terrorist will frequently try to disguise or mislead in a variety of ways. This may involve a ruse or diversionary action, more than one attack location, or even the use of a hostage to gain access to a particular location.

KIDNAPPING

Most terrorist-related kidnappings involve a high degree of planning. This planning effort may provide clues when suspects are careless. Kidnappings may be carried out for several reasons: for a ransom to support the group's operations; to force a political concession; or to bring a specific individual under the custody of the kidnappers for a "revolutionary trial."

New Forms of Terrorism

Despite the diminished threat of nuclear war and armed global conflict, the specter of terrorism remains high in many countries throughout the world. The Office of International Criminal Justice (OICJ) at the University of Illinois in Chicago, which conducts research on terrorism, identifies more than two hundred active terrorist groups throughout the world, as of 1992. Many of these are classified as "liberation movements," but a growing number are focused on other political and social issues. This is compounded by a growing number of criminal conspiracies which display many of the elements of terrorism. Activities of drug barons in Colombia involve the use of terror as a common weapon against efforts at government control.

The complexity of society has engendered another new form of terror, popularly called "technoterrorism," which relates to attacks on computer systems, telecommunications networks, and other forms of high technology. These new forms of terrorism represent a major threat, as yet unrealized, but one which remains a cause for concern.

Many experts feel that state-supported terrorism is on the decline but see increasing signs of ethnic and religious conflict, frequently related to liberation movements, that will spawn a new wave of terrorism, particularly in Eastern Europe. Increases in hate-related attacks, both in the United States and in other countries, are also finding new roots in old groups, such as the Ku Klux Klan and various neo-Nazi movements.

Many countries are also experiencing increasing violence associated with social movements, such as militant animal rights groups; environmentalists (ecoterrorists); and strident antiabortion activists. Although the vast majority of people involved in social protest comport themselves within the limits of the law, the propensity for violence among fringe elements may lead to an increase in terrorist-related acts. Some authorities believe that the pervasiveness of violence in the media results in widespread acceptance or at least a kind of numbed tolerance of the use of violence.

The rapidly growing gang phenomenon throughout the United States is considered by many experts as a new form of terrorism. Although these gangs do not embody the traditional definition of terrorism in terms of a political ideology, many of them operate across state lines, have an extensive communications network, and are involved in all types of criminal activity, usually but not exclusively related to drug trafficking.

See also CRIME, ORGANIZED; CRIME RATES; CRIME, VIOLENT; FUNDAMENTALISM, INTERNATIONAL TENSIONS; LAW ENFORCEMENT; PEACEKEEPING; WILDCARDS.

BIBLIOGRAPHY

EZELDIN, AHMED GALAL. *Global Terrorism: An Overview.* Chicago: University of Illinois, Office of International Criminal Justice, 1991.

EZELDIN, AHMED GALAL, and WARD, RICHARD H., eds. *International Responses to Terrorism: New Initiatives.* Chicago: University of Illinois, Office of International Criminal Justice, 1991.

Public Report of the Vice President's Task Force on Combatting Terrorism. Washington, DC: U.S. Government Printing Office, 1986.

Richard H. Ward

Theme Parks and Organized Attractions

In the year 2005, the first of the baby boomers born after World War II will be fifty-nine years old and the youngest will be forty-one. That same year, an American phenomenon—the modern theme park—will celebrate its fiftieth anniversary.

Disneyland, the world's first theme park and prototype for others that follow, would never have made it without the baby boom generation. Baby boomers make up the backbone of the theme park industry. Walt Disney could not have chosen a better year than 1955 to open his Magic Kingdom located in Anaheim, California. As with most other phenomena, Disneyland was a beneficiary of extraordinary timing.

America was just beginning to change from an industrial society to one based on leisure and service, as well as on communications. Eating places like McDonald's (founded in 1955) and theme parks like Disneyland would become the growth industries of the future, eventually spanning the world. Television, then in its infancy, was an ideal medium for promoting theme parks. The newly created interstate highway system meant visitors could drive from all points around the nation directly to Disneyland and other theme parks. For the first time, something called commercial "family entertainment" was growing in demand. The 1950s was considered the age of the typical American family—a family that played together at places like Disneyland.

But now with baby boomers growing older, the age profile of visitors to theme parks is changing in profound and lasting ways. Kenneth Dychtwald, author of *The Age Wave*, describes "the aging of America as the most important trend of our time." Theme parks will have to recognize this, even as they seem to become more and more focused on the technological side of the entertainment business.

Technology, of course, has changed the modern theme park and the way it entertains its guests. Walt Disney created a revolution in technology when his "imagineers" came up with "Audio-Animatronics" in the mid-1960s. These popular new robotic entertainers came to dominate Disneyland's attractions and shows for more than twenty years.

Now, however, there are even more startling technologies being developed and used for theme parks: high-tech "pixie dust" attractions like three-dimensional cinema and holograms, and more recently the virtual reality or simulator rides. In these attractions, film, sound, and movement combine to produce mega-effects unachievable by any old-style "iron" ride such as the roller coaster–type attraction. In the past it took a wrecking ball to change attractions, but today a new film and computer program will do the same job.

New technologies have always driven the theme park industry and will continue to shape its future. But there will have to be a drastic rethinking about just who will be entertained by those technologies. The brick-and-mortar appearance of the theme park of 2005 may look about the same as it does today. The old iron rides will not disappear. People will still respond positively to moving from point A to B and enjoy special effects made of more tangible stuff than the illusion of film and movement.

This brings us to what really makes any theme park successful: the people who go there. Walt Disney knew his audience. He designed Disneyland with the family in mind, a family rooted in the youth explosion of the baby boom. The theme park operators of 2005 will have a very different audience they must play to—aging baby boomers whose needs and wants in entertainment may be far removed from the standards of the past.

As the United States population approaches 300 million early in the twenty-first century, nearly 100 million people will be over fifty years old. For the first time in our history, people over sixty-five will outnumber teenagers. An aging audience may not come flocking through the turnstiles if a majority of the attractions subject them to twelve minutes of shaking, jerking, and other fun stimulation. There will still be a need for a pure amusement park which appeals to the active—and younger—thrillseekers, but they will not be the entertainment haunts of the broader, older audience.

Perhaps most importantly, after decades of becoming computer literate, an older audience will force theme parks to rediscover people. It will be the friendly people who operate a theme park that will ultimately be responsible for its success.

Training these friendly (as well as competent) people today is exclusively a job left up to the theme parks themselves. The Disney universities represent early efforts to assure in-house capabilities for training and upgrading unique skills. By 2005, schools and colleges will offer special theme park courses such as those now common for restaurant and hotel management. The courses offered will place an emphasis on the service needs of older people. In fact, the operators themselves will be older. Since these older operators will have acquired essential skills for handling this aging audience, there will be no forced retirement and people will work as long as they are efficient, regardless of age.

As the theme park market becomes more fragmented, the parks themselves will no longer stand alone as they have in the past. They will be part of much larger "themed resorts" such as those that Disney has created in Florida at Walt Disney World and plans to do at Disneyland in California. There will also be "themed cities" where main activities, such as gambling, will be augmented by diversified entertainment designed to attract a broader audience. Theme parks also have found their way into shopping malls and retail-hotel developments.

The good days for theme parks will be in the late 1990s and on into the twenty-first century—but only if the people who run the theme parks of the future design for an older audience. If park operators can understand and meet the challenge of entertaining this audience, then they will create a true tomorrowland for the aging baby boomers of today.

See also FREE TIME; GAMBLING; INTERACTIVE ENTERTAINMENT; LEISURE TIME; MASS CULTURE AND ARTS; PERFORMING ARTS: DANCE AND THEATER; SPORTS AND ACTIVITIES, SPECTATOR; SPORTS AND GAMES, COMPETITIVE; TOURISM.

BIBLIOGRAPHY

FRANCE, VAN ARSDALE. *Window on Main Street*. Livonia, MI: Stabur Press, 1991.

Van Arsdale France

Third World.

See DEVELOPMENT, ALTERNATIVE.

Third Political Parties

In the formative years of the young American republic, the political dichotomy traceable to the debates over ratification of the new Constitution between Federalists and anti-Federalists helped create and nourish the two-party system. It proved to be a natural extension of the rivalry between Hamilton and Jefferson and their supporters over the form the new government should take. Hamilton, of course, from the time of his celebrated *Report on Manufactures*, favored a more nationalistic approach with power centralized to a greater degree in the federal government. Jefferson, in contrast, favored a more constricted role for the national government. He believed the Tenth Amendment did reserve powers to the states or people unless delegated to the United States. The clashes between Federalists and Democratic-Republicans, the latter quickly shortened to simply Democrats, gave way to James Monroe's Era of Good Feeling, which was essentially a no-party system. In turn, it too was soon replaced by a party contest between Whigs and Democrats.

The first party to hold a national nominating convention was a third party, the Know-Nothings, who were anti-Freemasonry. Thereafter, in response to the growing debate over the institution of slavery, there were a number of parties in the 1840s and '50s such as the Free-Soilers, the Liberty party, and the Constitutional Union party, which challenged both the Whigs and Democrats. The most famous of these third parties was, of course, the Republican party, which was founded in Ripon, Wisconsin, in 1854, in which year it won a plurality of seats in the midterm congressional elections. It elected the sixteenth president of the United States in 1860, a year that saw four parties vying for the presidency. Lincoln emerged with a minority of votes but enough to win.

In the postbellum period, there were a number of third parties. The most celebrated was the Populist party, which ran James B. Weaver for president in 1892 and captured approximately 8 percent of the popular vote.

James Sundquist, a leading student of the role of political parties in the governing process, has referred to the effect of "crosscutting issues" in stimulating the development of third parties. An example of such an issue in the nineteenth century was slavery. The Whigs divided on this issue, into "Silver Whigs" and "Cotton Whigs," as the party began a gradual decline and ultimate breakup. The other major party between 1820 and the Civil War, the Democrats, was also polarized by the quarrel over the extension of slavery. This division in both parties created the opportunity for an emergent Republican party, which within a few years became a major party. In the century and a half since the birth of the Republican party there has been no single crosscutting issue of similar magnitude. This is one reason, though not the only one, why the present duopoly has continued with Republicans and Democrats periodically trading off the baton of national political power.

The post–World War II period did briefly threaten the unity of the Democratic party over the issue of racial segregation and civil rights. A celebrated walkout during the 1948 Democratic National Convention by dissident southern Democrats led to the candidacy of Strom Thurmond that year under the banner of the States Rights party, also known as the Dixiecrats. Another southern governor, George Wallace, later carried the banner of the American Independent party in campaigns in 1968 and 1972, which sought to raise the same issues. Although initially enjoying a degree of success in some northern states, his major base of support was below the Mason-Dixon line. Neither of these efforts crystallized into a truly national party effort. Beginning with the Civil Rights Act of 1958 and continuing with civil rights legislation enacted by Congress in 1964, 1965, and 1968, a bipartisan coalition of both Democrats and Republicans operated to defuse the issue of civil rights, which was threatening to rise to a crosscutting intensity.

This is not to suggest that intra-party struggles over an array of issues, abortion being perhaps the most emotional and divisive, have not produced tensions within the major party establishment. The Democrats have by and large united behind a pro-choice position. However, the creation of the Democratic Leadership Council in the 1980s sought to craft an image of a somewhat more conservative New Democrat, particularly on economic issues and the role of government.

The Republican party has been more conflicted on social issues both during the Reagan era and in the period that followed. On economic issues—particularly on such matters as free trade and budget discipline coupled with tax cuts—they have maintained a high degree of party unity.

The rise of the Christian Right, which has seized the abortion issue as the centerpiece of its efforts to influence elections beginning soon after the Supreme Court decision in *Roe* v. *Wade* in 1973, did not herald the formation of a third party. In the 1994 elections, approximately two-thirds of those who comprised their 1.5 million membership voted for Republican congressional candidates. There were many factors that led to the historic Republican sweep that year not only of the congressional elections, which ended forty years of Democratic dominance, but in local and state races as well. The Christian Right's ability to mobilize its voters clearly played some role. However, the presidential election of 1992, which saw the election of a minority president, had really set the stage for what happened in 1994. The Ross Perot candidacy, which siphoned off 18.9 percent of the vote, helped defeat the Republican candidate, George Bush, but it also severely wounded the Democrats, especially in the South and in some parts of the West.

A significant barrier to third party formation is the American electoral system itself. The great preponderance of Western democracies employ proportional representation in multimember legislative districts. This makes it possible to distribute seats in proportion to the percentage of the total vote received by the various party candidates. This, in turn, makes it possible for the new party to begin building an electoral base before it attempts to win the grand prize of the presidency. Perhaps more than any other reason that can be given for the failure of third parties to flourish is our electoral system based on the principle of winner take all.

Another reason why third parties, and indeed even independent candidates, find it difficult to flourish in the political soil of America is found in the laws in many states that limit ballot access. When the author of this article ran for president as an independent in 1980, he challenged discriminatory laws in almost a dozen states and fought battles in the federal courts that in one case stretched all the way to the U.S. Supreme Court. As a result, he became the first independent candidate for the presidency in this century to be on the ballot in fifty states. The task of ballot access is even more difficult for third party congressional candidates.

A third reason why third parties fail is that they suffer from inadequate campaign financing. A system of public financing far more equitable than the Federal Election Campaign Act now on the statute books would be a minimum requirement to shore up this shortcoming.

After debating the subject of campaign finance in the early 1970s, both major parties have been virtually deadlocked on what further efforts are needed. As total campaign expenditures in the 1990s soared well past the half-billion-dollar mark for a two-year election cycle, both parties have become increasingly vulnerable to charges of special interest moneyed influence and outright corruption. Unless they deal with this issue before even a jaded public loses patience, it could be the ignition factor for instigating a reform party. Once launched, a party calling for reformation of the political process could quickly expand its agenda and offer a program of wider reform applicable to both the public and private sector. This could, in turn, feed into what seemed in the final decade of the twentieth century to be an increasing recognition of the need for personal reformation—hence, the cry for emphasis on family values.

Upon his retirement from the U.S. Senate in 1994, former senator David L. Boren, a conservative Democrat, offered this opinion: "The people will not forever tolerate a party system which forces them to choose the lesser of two evils." The steady rise to more than 40 percent of voters who claim the designation of independent rather than either of the major parties sends a clear signal. The first election of the third millennium could well see a strong third party in the field. Although either major party could fall prey to polarizing forces that would cause it to divide and furnish thereby the critical mass needed to form that new party, there is a more likely scenario. A new party will not result from divisions produced by a single crosscutting issue as in the past. It will come out of a broad-based citizens' coalition that will first have an impact at the local and state levels. Their organization will build on these successes and attract a strong national leader. It will be largely the economic pressures of the postindustrial age that will drive the formulation of truly bold and innovative ideas with a strongly futuristic content. It will draw from both the left and right but will essentially transcend the present plane of the traditional political spectrum.

See also COMMUNITARIANISM; CONSERVATISM, POLITICAL; DEMOCRACY; DEMOCRATIC PROCESS; LIBERALISM, POLITICAL; POLITICAL CAMPAIGNING; POLITICAL CYCLES; POLITICAL PARTIES; POLITICAL PARTY REALIGNMENT; PUBLIC OPINION POLLS; SURVEYS; VOTING.

BIBLIOGRAPHY

DAY, GLENN. *Minor Presidential Candidates and Parties of 1988.* Jefferson, NC: McFarland, 1988.

JOHNSON, DONALD BRUCE. *National Party Platforms. 1840–1980.* 2 vols. Urbana, IL: University of Illinois Press, 1980.

KRUSCHKE, EARL R. *Encyclopedia of Third Parties in the United States.* Santa Barbara, CA: ABC-Clio, 1991.

SCHAPSMEIER, EDWARD L., and SCHAPSMEIER, FREDERICK H. *Political Parties and Civic Action Groups.* Westport, CT: Greenwood, 1981.

SMALLWOOD, FRANK. *The Other Candidates: Third Parties in Presidential Elections.* Hanover, NH: University Press of New England, 1983.

John B. Anderson

Tobacco

Tobacco products have been long associated with pleasure and relaxation as well as with disease and death. When initially introduced into the Western world in the sixteenth century, tobacco was prized for medicinal use—as were sugar, coffee, tea, chocolate, and many spices. Health claims flourished as recently as the 1920s in the United States, but today tobacco use is assailed as public health enemy number one and as the largest preventable cause of death.

Manufacturers obviously ignore the annual toll of some 2.5 million premature deaths worldwide for which they are blamed, including 418,690 in the United States during 1990, nearly ten times the number of deaths in auto accidents. This annual death toll is greater than all U.S. soldiers killed in all wars during this century and currently accounts for about 20 percent of all deaths in the United States each year.

A 1994 report blames tobacco abuse in the United States for $21 billion in added health costs and $47 billion in productivity losses (additional sick leave and absenteeism, idle smoking breaks, etc.). Other reports specify up to $100 billion in added costs, including losses from smoking-related fires, higher insurance premiums, increased cleaning costs, and so forth.

Tobacco smokers number approximately 1 billion worldwide, 50 million of them in the United States. Smoking is most extensive in Indonesia, where 64 percent of all adults are smokers. In the United States smokers declined from 40 percent of adults eighteen years and older in 1964 to 25.5 percent (45.8 million persons) in 1990, and are expected to decline 2-3 percent yearly over the next several decades.

Per capita tobacco consumption for adults eighteen years and older in the United States declined from 11.8 pounds in 1960 to 6.7 pounds in 1985, and cigarette consumption dropped from 4,148 in 1974 to 2,500 in 1993 (see Table 1).

Declining sales in the United States prompt tobacco exports. Philip Morris, for example, increased international cigarette revenues from $8.4 billion in 1989 to $15.7 billion in 1993. Doffing harmful products on other nations draws criticism, as well as quiet praise for reducing the U.S. trade imbalance.

On-Again/Off-Again Pattern of Tobacco Regulation

The scope and severity of tobacco controls come and go. During the 1600s persons selling or using tobacco were executed in China. In Russia the death penalty was imposed on tobacco users in 1634; a 1641 decree by Czar Michael Romanov

Tobacco

TABLE 1.   Tobacco Production and Consumption

Consumption per capita (Persons 18 years and older)	1918	1925	1945	1960	1981	1985	1992
All products (lb)		9.66	13.02	11.82	7.6	6.7	5.0
Cigarettes (1,000)		1.1	3.4	4.2	3.8	3.4	3.0
Cigars (no.)		94	56	61	23	18	12
Other smoking and chewing products, and snuff (lb)		4.40	2.18	0.99	.64	.61	——
Production							
Cigarettes (billions)	48	83	332	506	744	665	719
Cigars (billions)	7.1	6.5	5.3	6.9	5.0	3.0	2.0
Other (million lb)	497	414	331	176	162	158	141

Source: *Statistical Abstracts of the United States.*

imposed flogging, slitting nostrils of repeat offenders, or exile; eventually, the penalty was reduced to a tax. Snuff users were threatened with excommunication by Pope Urban VIII in 1624. The current wave or cycle of strict regulation is not the first assault on tobacco.

Globally, the most sweeping regulatory stance embracing up to several hundred cradle-to-grave controls has been taken by Sweden. By 1973 a far-reaching twenty-five-year program intended to reduce cigarette consumption to levels prevailing in the 1920s was launched—from 1,500 in 1976 to the 1920 level of 300.

U.S. government regulators have steadily clamped down on tobacco. Warning labels required in 1966 were strengthened in 1970. Radio and TV cigarette advertising were outlawed in 1971. Cigarette advertising has been required to disclose tar and nicotine yields since 1971. Multiple warning labels were required in 1983. Farm price-support programs were shifted to a "no net cost" basis in 1986. No-smoking sections aboard U.S. airlines were required beginning in 1973 (and smoking was prohibited on domestic flights of less than two hours duration in 1988). Military survival rations eliminated cigarettes in 1975. Pending in Congress are bills that would ban smoking in public buildings frequented by ten or more persons at least one day weekly; regulate tobacco products as a drug; further curb cigarette advertising; and compel development of self-extinguishing products to minimize fire hazards.

Restrictions as to who may smoke also are growing. As recently as 1904, a woman was arrested for smoking a cigarette in a motor vehicle in New York City. Smoking by female school teachers, until recently, was grounds for dismissal.

Sales are prohibited to minors (variously defined by law as including persons under 16, 18, or 21 years of age), but the prohibition is seldom enforced. About 3,000 teenagers per day, or nearly 1 million annually, take up smoking each year, and they totalled an estimated 3.4 million in 1994. However, teen smoking declined steadily from 1976 to 1984, then reached a plateau, and stood at 19 percent in 1993. The average age when teens first take up smoking is 14.5 years. Nearly 75 percent of U.S. smokers become addicted prior to reaching 18 years of age. Stricter laws prohibiting sales to minors are likely.

Restrictions on the places where tobacco may be smoked steadily constrict users' options. The General Court of Massachusetts in 1646 prohibited tobacco smoking to a distance of five miles outside of town limits to minimize fire hazards. Connecticut in 1647 limited tobacco use to once daily, never socially, and only within one's dwelling. Cigarette sales were banned in at least fourteen U.S. states between 1893 and 1921, but by 1927 all of these laws were repealed. Vended sales locations, easily accessible to minors, have been recently prohibited in some states. Prohibition of smoking in public places got underway during the 1970s. By 1990 at least 41 states had enacted laws. Local governments in the bellwether state of bellwether California, commencing with Berkeley, passed over 300 of the nation's some 600 local antismoking ordinances.

Despite advertising and promotion restrictions, tobacco remains among the most heavily promoted products in the United States, with spending rising from $2.5 billion in 1984 to $4 billion in 1990. Restrictions as to what can be said about tobacco products will tighten. A spate of regulatory thrusts by the Environmental Protection Agency (EPA), the Food and Drug Administration (FDA), and the Occupational Safety and Health Administration (OSHA) seek to restrain tobacco abuse.

EPA

Secondhand or sidestream smoke opens up a whole new round of regulations. Identified among exhaled tobacco smoke were high concentrations of seventeen carcinogens. EPA estimates that secondhand smoke may cause 3,000 lung cancer deaths annually and classified environmental tobacco smoke (ETS) as a class-A carcinogen in 1993. Not unexpectedly, the industry took the case to court and challenged the scientific basis of this finding as flawed. These developments may expose the industry to enormous liability.

OSHA

OSHA proposed in 1994 a ban on smoking in the workplace, excepting separately ventilated areas. A total of nine states and over seventy local governments had enacted laws controlling smoking in the workplace by 1994. Maryland regulatory officials imposed the nation's strictest controls over virtually all workplaces in 1994; most other states will follow this lead, and uniform national standards eventually will be established.

FDA

France in 1635 restricted tobacco sales to apothecaries and made the product available only upon prescription from a physician. New regulatory thrusts would return the sale of tobacco products, once again, to pharmacists and/or druggists. Contending that nicotine is addictive, not merely habituating, FDA proposes to regulate tobacco products as a drug. FDA already regulates gums and skin patches used to help smokers stop. FDA contends that at least 33 patents enable tobacco manufacturers to precisely manipulate nicotine levels and that bioengineered higher nicotine yielding tobacco plants are being used to "spike" cigarettes and to "hook" users.

In their defense, tobacco companies point to the 40 million Americans who have quit smoking to disprove addiction; claim that nicotine-free cigarettes have been tried and failed; and point out that cigarettes now contain 66 percent less nicotine than thirty years ago. Some companies have filed business libel suits against those charging them with intentionally spiking nicotine levels.

Public attitudes play a crucial role in goading policy response. A 1994 poll indicated that 68 percent of Americans favor regulating tobacco products as drugs. The furor over largely uncharted hazards posed by burn by-products and ingested or inhaled tobacco smoke increasingly will draw regulatory attention. Cigarette smoke contains an exquisite array of chemicals—well over 4,000 of them, and some say as many as 100,000 of them. At least 27 of these compounds are considered mutagenic.

Another target for regulatory control involves additives used in tobacco products. Government regulators identify at least 700 chemical additives—flavorings, processing aids, casing materials, curing agents, sweeteners, and so forth—allowed in U.S. tobacco products. As many as 1,000 different flavors can be used in these products.

Taxing tobacco, to raise revenues or discourage consumption, has a checkered history. Tobacco was reviled and claimed injurious to health in 1604 by James I of England, who raised tobacco taxes by 4,000 percent; lower prices elsewhere encouraged black market trade. State monopolies and heavy excise duties were imposed on tobacco during the early 1600s: Austria, 1670; Prussia, 1776; France, 1810. Taxes imposed on cigarettes amounted to twenty-four cents per pack in 1994. To help pay for 1994 U.S. health care reforms, stiff new taxes on tobacco products were proposed: an additional seventy-five cents on cigarettes (projected to yield $10 billion in yearly revenues); a 3,000 percent increase on cigars; a 2,000 percent boost on pipe tobacco; and a 3,572 percent increase on chewing tobacco and snuff (raising the current tax of thirty-six cents per pound to $12.86 per pound).

Referenda often are offered when lawmakers respond too slowly or not boldly enough. California's bellwether 1988 initiative, Proposition 99, imposed a twenty-five cent a pack tax increase on cigarettes to fund projects calculated to deter smoking. Since enacted, tobacco use plunged 27 percent, or about three times the national average. Massachusetts subsequently passed a similar law and other states were considering following suit.

Scientific Literature Documenting Hazards

Tobacco's association with cancer was first observed in 1761 by a London physician who reported six cases of "polypusses" related to extensive use of snuff. A 1932 article published in the *American Journal of Cancer* associated cigarette tars with cancer. A landmark 1959 article in the *Journal of the American Medical Association*, written by Surgeon General Burney, specified that smoking causes cancer. Surgeon General Terry released in 1964 a definitive report confirming Burney's findings. The number of published articles in medical literature dealing with smoking-health relationships began to explode during the mid-twentieth century, rising from 6,000 in 1964 to over 30,000 by 1979. The enormous volume of commentary increased awareness and added to public concerns and clamor for steps to correct perceived problems.

Around the turn of the century lung cancer was a rarity—one report indicates that only 134 cases were found in all the medical literature. American males' yearly death rates from lung cancer per 100,000 population rose from five in 1930, to twenty in 1950, and to more than seventy by the 1990s. Life expectancy tables first showed reduced life expectancy for smokers in 1937.

Tobacco use currently is blamed for about 30 percent of all cancers in the United States and worldwide. Up to 30 percent of all deaths from heart disease also are associated with tobacco abuse. Noncancerous chronic diseases of the lung, including emphysema and bronchitis, impose another toll of nearly 80,000 deaths among Americans each year. Worst of all is the injury inflicted on new life. Spontaneous abortion among women smokers is ten times that of nonsmokers, chances of sudden infant death syndrome are 50 percent greater, and a total of 2,000 infant deaths during their first year of life are attributed to tobacco.

Lifetime medical costs of tobacco users are $6,000 more than for nonsmokers. Health-conscious Americans will demand that public officials take preventive health measures.

Lawsuits Edging Industry Toward Liability

Lawsuits attempting to recoup costs of tobacco-related harms abound. States are seeking reimbursement for health care outlays caused by tobacco abuse—for example, a 1994 suit by the Mississippi attorney general and a 1994 Florida law authorizing such suits. A spate of new lawsuits seek damages for nicotine addiction; a landmark $4 billion class action lawsuit on behalf of nicotine addicts was filed in 1994.

Industry immunity from legal liability—based on the assumption of the known risk resulting from ample labeling notices and widespread information regarding the hazards of smoking—has shielded the industry so far. However, what once were thought to be absolute bars against liability no longer shield the tobacco industry, which is being saddled with responsibility for the proximate result of their products.

Critics maintain that those who reap the rewards should be required to bear the responsibility of any harm. A pivotal question is how far government regulators—dubbed by the tobacco lobby as "smoke police" and "health fascists"—should go in controlling smokers' freedom of choice. Tolerance, currently, has been the general thrust, but this may be changing.

See also ALCOHOL; DRUGS, ILLICIT; FOOD AND AGRICULTURE; FOOD AND DRUG SAFETY; HEALTH CARE; PUBLIC HEALTH.

BIBLIOGRAPHY

CHANDLER, WILLIAM U. *Smoking Epidemic Widens.* Washington, DC: Worldwatch Institute, 1988.

DIEHL, HAROLD S. *Tobacco and Your Health: The Smoking Controversy.* New York: McGraw-Hill, 1969.

FRITSCHLER, A. LEE. *Smoking and Politics: Policymaking and the Federal Bureaucracy.* 3rd ed. Englewood Cliffs, NJ: Prentice-Hall, 1983.

U.S. Surgeon General. *The Health Consequences of Smoking: Cancer and Chronic Lung Disease in the Workplace.* Rockville, MD: U.S. Department of Health and Human Services, Public Health Service, Office of Smoking and Health, 1985.

WHELAN, ELIZABETH M. *A Smoking Gun: How the Tobacco Industry Gets Away with Murder.* Philadelphia, PA: George F. Stickley, 1984.

WHITE, LARRY C. *Merchants of Death: The American Tobacco Industry.* New York: William Morrow/Beech Tree, 1988.

Graham T. T. Molitor

Toffler, Alvin (1928–) and Heidi (1929–)

Alvin Toffler and Heidi Toffler are the world's best-known husband-and-wife futurist team. Their fame largely rests on the classic trilogy *Future Shock* (1970), *The Third Wave* (1980), and *Power Shift* (1991), each of which was at least ten years ahead of its time.

The road to fame for the Tofflers has been long and varied. Alvin was born in New York to Polish-Jewish immigrants. Heidi Toffler (*née* Farrell), also a New Yorker, is of Dutch-German extraction. Alvin entered upon work as a welder, but his writing instincts gravitated toward journalism, first as a staff member of a national trade union newspaper, later as a regular contributor to the *New Republic* and *The Nation.* In 1959 he became an associate editor of *Fortune* magazine. In 1964 he completed his *Culture Consumers,* which expanded upon the ideas of Fritz Machlup regarding the economics of arts institutions. Not long afterward, he wrote a piece for *Horizon,* where he first coined the term *future shock.* In this essay, "The Future as a Way of Life," he sketched his ideas on accelerating social and technological change and its impact on human life. In 1966 he conducted a course at the New School for Social Research on Social Change and the Future.

A landmark in the Tofflers' lives, *Future Shock* dealt with what were at that time radical ideas—the impact of transience on human relationships, the rise of temporary organizational forms, the crisis of the nuclear family, and disorientation induced by too much change in too short a time. *The Third Wave* foreshadowed the rise of demassified media, the spread of customized manufacture, the shift of work to the home, and the growth of biotechnology. *Powershift* described the creation of new centers of power, the transformation of information and knowledge as the "new wealth," and the capacity of the new knowledge system to destroy the underlying assumptions on which society, government, and the economy were based. The most recent Toffler book, *War and Anti-War* (1994), presents a new theory of war, reveals changes in the military paralleling those at the corporate and social levels, and raises the specter of cyber-terrorists and nonlethal weapons. The Tofflers' gift is their ability to leap across disciplines to identify broad patterns of change, to devise new frameworks for thinking about the unthinkable and imponderable, to present complex ideas simply, and to distill powerful insights in memorable words or phrases.

See FIVE BILLION FUTURISTS, the foreword to this encyclopedia, by Alvin and Heidi Toffler. *See also* FUTURISTS; POPULARIZED FUTURES.

George Thomas Kurian

Toiletries.

See COSMETICS AND TOILETRIES.

Tourism

Leisure and recreation imply the discretionary use of time for pastimes, such as sports and games. Tourism is different from leisure and recreation in that it implies travel and at least an overnight stay of twenty-four hours at a destination. People also travel to visit friends and relatives and for business, religious, study, and health purposes.

The rapid expansion of mass tourism during the past forty years has been a result of the increased availability of leisure time, the expansion of the middle class, cheaper and better transportation, and improved communications. Marketing has been effective in highlighting the opportunity to escape the daily humdrum.

Forecaster Herman KAHN speculated in 1979 that the 10 percent annual growth rate of the 1960s and early '70s might lead to two billion people traveling abroad in the year 2000. The growth of tourism is inextricably linked with the expansion of gross domestic product, the availability of an appropriate infrastructure, and well-trained and educated human resources. During the 1990s, however, this growth has slowed, and international tourism is likely to expand in the near future at an annual rate of about 5 percent in the mature industrialized economies. In the newly industrialized countries of Asia, the growth of tourism will be constrained by the lack of sufficient infrastructure, well-trained workers, and management expertise. It is therefore likely that the number of international tourists will reach only about 700 million by the year 2000, rather than the earlier anticipated two billion.

Most places on Earth are within the physical and financial reach of a growing number of people. Increasingly, mass tourism is being seen as a threat to the physical environment and to the uniqueness of various far-flung locales that previously were beyond the reach of most people. Traditionally, growth in tourism has meant more visitors, rising prices, or more attractions and events. Today, due in part to environmental constraints, tourism has to be managed more like a multibillion-dollar "designed experiences business." Linking the attractions, performing arts, hotels, tour operators, airlines, and host communities into a new coherence is information technology.

In the future, small and large organizations will focus on information-based enhancements to design experiences that respond to travelers' interests, build on the indigenous assets of destinations, and create environmentally compatible tourism. Among these experiences will be the following:

- *Adventure travel.* Changing tastes have created a demand and appetite for adventure and unusual physical activities. Business corporations are using adventure outings, such as those featured by Outward Bound, as part of management development programs. Dude ranches or guest ranches have enjoyed considerable success in recent years in North America. Rural tourism will become increasingly important, especially in Europe where farmers are actively encouraged to substitute farming with tourism to reduce the acid pollution generated by cattle manure.

- *Government preserves and exploration.* Visits to the national parks, forests, wilderness areas, and seashores offer the explorer-traveler activities such as whitewater boating, wilderness canoeing, horseback riding, hiking, backpacking, and cross-country skiing in an uncrowded, "unspoiled" natural setting. However, wilderness exploration has become so popular that camping spots are scarce throughout the season at the better-known national parks.

- *Cruising.* Pleasure cruising is one of the fastest-growing sectors of the tourism sector. Today's cruiseliner resembles a floating resort in that passengers are entertained, accommodated, pampered, and fed. Recently, certain cruiseline operators incorporated special stress-reduction and lifestyle management programs, designed to help passengers renew body and mind. Barging on inland waterways, another form of waterborne transport, is especially popular in Britain, France, Holland, and Ireland. The growing number of pleasure-boating craft has increased the demand for marinas and stimulated local tourism development. For example, the success of Baltimore's Harborplace has sparked similar projects in New York, Toronto, Stockholm, and Oslo.

- *Learning vacations.* Learning will become more important to people who, in an information society, will need to keep up with technological and social change. Advanced telecommunications in the schools and in business may allow students and executives to keep up with their studies and work while traveling. Families could vacation together outside the traditional holiday periods, thus altering the seasonal nature of tourism. In order to compete with theme parks, such as Disney, Busch Gardens, Old Sturbridge Village, and Knott's Berry Farm, the museums, traditionally places of learning, have begun to redefine their role away from education through exhibitions to education through entertainment. Through the innovative use of technology, museums are making exhibits more accessible and understandable.

The travel industry has a heterogeneous structure comprised of many small enterprises and a small group of large transnational corporations. They all render service through a distribution chain including suppliers, wholesalers, retail travel agents, and customers. Due to travel industry saturation, hoteliers and airlines have introduced clubs to reward frequent travelers with free accommodation and free flights, respectively, in order to ensure their loyalty. Intermediaries such as wholesalers and travel agents will continue to consolidate their operations to lower their costs and increase profitability.

The silent revolution triggered by information technologies is changing the tourism infrastructure dramatically. Computerized reservation systems and nonbank credit cards are fostering linkages between the traditional leisure and recreational tourism base, telecommunications, and transnational banking. The emerging information technology is extending information flows of the travel industry well beyond its traditional boundaries and are heralding a new era of tourism development into the third millennium.

Technology will allow people to explore before they make the trip and to capture and preserve lively memories. Videos will provide cheap, easy, and engaging exposure to new areas and will allow tourists, in essence, to try before they travel. Virtual reality will have a profound effect on and will provide a boon to tourism by allowing people to experience a place before they actually visit it. As everything becomes smart through microprocessors, sensors, and voice capabilities, many things, such as simulated lake shores, trees, animals, and buildings may be able literally to speak about themselves to inform tourists of what to expect. The minicam is a new mechanism for capturing memories. Voice recognition technology and the ability to respond to a variety of languages will facilitate tourists gathering information and learning about whatever they need to know on their trip.

See also FREE TIME; INFORMATION TECHNOLOGY; INTERACTIVE ENTERTAINMENT; LEISURE TIME; MUSEUMS; OUTDOOR RECREATION AND LEISURE PURSUITS; THEME PARKS AND ORGANIZED ATTRACTIONS.

BIBLIOGRAPHY

D'AMORE, LOUIS J. "Tourism: A Vital Force for Peace." *The Futurist* 22 (1988): 23–28.

HOLLOWAY, J. C. *The Business of Tourism.* London: Pitman, 1989.

KAHN, HERMAN. *World Economic Development, 1979 and Beyond.* Boulder, CO. Westview Press, 1979.

KING, MARGARET J. "The Theme Park Experience: What Museums Can Learn from Mickey Mouse." *The Futurist* 25 (1991): 24–31.

KOTLER, PHILIP. "Dream Vacations: Booming Market for Designed Experiences." *The Futurist* 18 (1984): 7–13.

PAPSON, STEPHEN. "Tourism: World's Biggest Industry in the Twenty-First Century?" *The Futurist* 13 (1979): 249–257.

RITCHIE, BRENT J. R.; HAWKINS, DONALD E.; GO, FRANK M.; and FRECHTLING, DOUGLAS. *World Travel and Tourism Review Indicators, Trends and Issues.* Vol. 2. Wallingford, U.K.: CAB International, 1992.

Frank M. Go

Trade.

See FREE TRADE; INTERNATIONAL TRADE: REGIONAL TRADE AGREEMENTS; INTERNATIONAL TRADE: REGULATION; INTERNATIONAL TRADE: SUSTAINING GROWTH.

Transportation

Historically, the United States has attempted to build its way out of its transportation problems by adding lanes to highways, building new roads, and expanding airports. In the future, however, new road capacity is not expected to keep pace as the demand for transportation grows. Business-as-usual trends in transportation are characterized by a deteriorating infrastructure, increasing traffic volumes, a growing dependence on foreign oil, and increasing degradation of air, water, and land. Significant reform of U.S. transportation policy is required if we are to hand down a suitable transportation system to future generations.

The two principal factors affecting the growth in transportation demand include vehicle population (the number of motor vehicles on the road) and vehicle usage (trips generated and miles traveled each year). Together, these determine total transportation-related energy consumption, pollution, and road congestion. While motor car ownership is not expected to grow more than 2 percent annually, paralleling population growth, miles traveled is expected to increase from 3 percent to over 10 percent annually. This substantial growth in vehicle use is expected to present ever more serious energy, environmental, and traffic congestion problems, ones that simply cannot be solved by building more roads.

Since 1969, the number of miles traveled by Americans has increased 82 percent to 1.8 trillion miles in 1990, according to the U.S. Census. Virtually all of this travel takes place in cars and in light-duty trucks. Of the 15,000 miles per year each American travels, the largest amount of time (32 percent) is spent driving alone to work in cars and pick-up trucks. Of the remainder, shopping accounts for 12 percent, personal business for 20 percent, social and recreational travel for 27 percent, and the remaining 9 percent is for other purposes.

This tremendous mobility does not come without a cost. Transportation consumes vast resources including energy, land, and clean air. In terms of energy, the United States devotes nearly three-quarters of its oil use to the transportation sector, some 12.5 million barrels of oil a day, half of which is imported. In cities, one-third of the land is devoted to transportation such as roads, parking, and automotive-related services. Housing takes second place. Pollution from cars and trucks generates the largest contribution to the unhealthful air that a majority of Americans breathe, accounting for half of the smog and 70 percent of the carbon monoxide. The principal greenhouse gas, carbon dioxide, is emitted at the rate of 20 pounds for every gallon of gasoline burned. These discharges threaten our climate, reduce agricultural output, and compromise other resources.

While the breakdown of the transportation system will not occur tomorrow or next year, without corrective action a serious disintegration of services is likely to occur by the end of the century or shortly thereafter. One ominous sign is the alarming increase in congestion. If present trends continue, road congestion in the United States will triple in only fifteen years, even if capacity is increased by 20 percent, a goal that is unlikely to be achieved in this period of time.

According to United States Department of Energy estimates, if current trends continue through 2010, 70 percent of the oil used in the United States will be imported. Several factors are responsible for this outcome. By 2010, the government estimates that cars and pick-up trucks alone will account for nearly three trillion miles of travel, up 80 percent from their current levels. Moreover, larger (wider, longer, and higher) and heavier twin and triple trailers will increasingly be used to move U.S. freight, consuming four times more energy than either trains or ships.

Americans will do more driving in urban areas where congestion and accidents prevail. As urban driving outpaces road capacity in the next century, congestion may increase up to tenfold. So-called rush hour, or peak-period, travel under congested conditions, which accounted for 39 percent of highway travel in 1980, will increase to 62 percent by 2005. Not only time but fuel will be wasted; by 2005, 7 billion gallons of fuel will be consumed each year—7 percent of the projected oil use for highway passenger transportation.

Sprawling suburban growth is expected to continue, further increasing commuting distances and compounding congestion. During the 1980s, three-quarters of all population growth in the United States occurred in the suburbs. If this rate and pattern of growth continues, jobs may move even farther from homes, at least until more work sites are located in these new growth areas. An already overcrowded airport system faces huge additional air-traffic demands. A 63 percent increase in domestic passenger travel (over the 1990 rate) is forecasted by 2000. Air-freight transport, including burgeoning package/courier delivery services, is expected to increase at an even greater rate. Because of the rapid growth in air traffic, aviation fuel use will more than double, to two million barrels of jet fuel a day by the year 2010. By 2020, airport congestion is expected to triple, with fifty-eight airports operating over rated capacities.

The challenge facing Americans is to balance demands for travel within the constraint of resources while maintaining public safety. The transportation network cannot expand without regard for financial and physical limits, nor can future growth be allowed to put undue stress on the environment.

Given the projected increases in miles traveled by cars, pick-up trucks, heavy trucks, other motor vehicles, and airplanes, it would be a mistake simply to accept projected demands and attempt to satisfy them. Doing so would force a high price on the nation in increased smog, acid rain, greenhouse gas emissions, traffic congestion, and a rising trade deficit (largely attributable to imports of petroleum and motor vehicles), reduced economic competitiveness, deteriorating personal safety, and less energy security. To avert or ameliorate these consequences, policy makers can apply a range of alternative transportation policies aimed at modifying anticipated demand or accommodating increasing use demands. In the long run this will prove to be more efficient, cost effective, and sustainable.

Clearly, America has to choose between two transportation futures—one characterized by the high social costs of energy, environmental, and mobility problems, or one focusing on accessibility equity, and sustainability. We cannot simply build our way out of our transportation dilemma; without sound policy intervention, future trends point to an unsustainable course.

There is no "silver bullet" that can transform our transportation system. Future policymaking efforts will hopefully make use of a blend of tools, including greater regulation, economic incentives and user fees, infrastructure investments, research and development into transportation innovations, and public education concerning the transportation system.

The Department of Transportation and Congress will focus its attention on research and development and infrastructure investments. The challenge will be to channel investments into sound technologies such as steel-wheel high-speed rail, advanced public transport alternatives such as "smart" demand-responsive transit, and infrastructure maintenance and repair. Devoting significant funds for questionable technologies such as magnetically levitated (Maglev) trains, automated highways and other "intelligent" transportation systems for single-occupant autos, and new expansion of the interstate highway system may cause transportation problems to get worse. In addition, federal attention, coupled with state action, will rely upon supplemented regulations to further clean up vehicle emissions, improve efficiency standards, upgrade vehicle safety regulations, and enhance the recycling of motor vehicle components.

The bulk of transportation policy making will occur at the state and local/regional government level. The total funding of transportation, where the user pays more of the true cost of driving and other transportation services, is expected to be the focus of future national, state, and local transportation policy. This will be adopted in various forms, including higher state gasoline taxes, basing insurance premium costs on odometer readings or as a surcharge at the gas pump, charging for parking (including offering employees cash for travel allowances in lieu of parking spaces) and road pricing keyed to time of day, zones, or distance traveled. Local land use regulations also will be used to better manage and reform transportation.

With the advent of sustainable cities—smaller-scaled communities combining housing, job sites, shopping, recreational and other amenities for comfortable living—bicycling and walking will be viable alternatives to the automobile. The innovative transportation systems of such cities would include enclosed, air-conditioned bicycle expressways above or adjacent to the pedestrian-level walkway, a network of moving sidewalks ("slidewalks"), pedestrian walkways uncluttered by vehicular traffic, and only electrically powered vehicles (some of which are already in place in Zermatt, Switzerland). In addition to privately owned "green cars," trucks, trains, and buses would run on hydrogen fuel cells that emit vastly less pollution and use energy twice as efficiently as their present-day counterpart, the gasoline combustion engine.

The sustainable, energy-efficient city would exploit unconventional land uses as well. To shorten home-to-shopping trips and home-to-transit station trips, high-rise dwellings, a shopping mall, and a transit station could be located together. Work sites would have shopping and child-care services available on site or within walking distances. Conventional, gasoline-powered autos would be parked at the city's perimeter and not allowed inside. Developing these new technologies will create new jobs and possibly new industries with significant export-market potential. Over the long run, a sustainable transportation system will benefit the environment, reduce energy use, provide more equitable means of travel, and enhance the U.S. economy.

See also AIR TRANSPORT; BATTERIES; MACRO-ENGINEERING; MAGLEV; MOTOR VEHICLES; MOTOR VEHICLES, ALTERNATIVELY POWERED; PERSONAL TRANSPORT; PETROLEUM; PIPELINES; RAILWAYS; SPACE TRAVEL; URBAN TRANSIT.

BIBLIOGRAPHY

GORDON, DEBORAH. *Steering a New Course: Transportation, Energy, and the Environment.* Washington, DC: Island Press, 1991.

OWEN, WILFRED. "The View from 2020: Transportation in America's Future." *The Brookings Review* (Fall 1988).

"Post-Rio: The Challenge at Home." *EPA Journal* 18/4 (September October 1992). Publication No. 175 N92-010. Washington, D.C.: United States Environmental Protection Agency, Office of Communications, Education, and Public Affairs.

Transportation Research Board. *A Look Ahead: Year 2020.* Special Report No. 220. Washington, DC: National Research Council, 1988.

Deborah Gordon

Transuranium Elements

The addition of seventeen transuranium elements to mankind's natural heritage of elements has led to an expansion of nearly 20 percent in the fundamental building blocks of nature. Investigation of these manmade elements beyond uranium has led to a tremendous expansion of our knowledge of atomic and nuclear structure. Each of these elements has a number of known isotopes, all radioactive, thereby leading to an overall total of

nearly 200. Synthetic in origin, they are produced in a variety of transmutation reactions by neutrons or charged particles, including heavy ions. (Two of these elements are, in addition, present in nature in very small concentrations.) Many of them are produced and isolated in large quantities through the use of nuclear fission reactors: plutonium (atomic number 94) in ton quantities; neptunium (number 93), americium (number 95), and curium (number 96) in kilogram quantities; berkelium (number 97) in 100-milligram quantities; californium (number 98) in gram quantities; and einsteinium (number 99) in milligram quantities. Of particular interest to chemists is the unusual chemistry and impact on the periodic table (Figure 1) of these heaviest elements. Their practical impact, particularly that of plutonium, has been and will continue to be extraordinary.

The discovery of the first transuranium element resulted from experiments aimed at understanding the fission process. E. M. McMillan and P. H. Abelson in 1940, working at the 60-inch cyclotron at the University of California, Berkeley, deduced by chemical means that a product of the neutron bombardment of uranium was an isotope of element 93, arising by beta particle decay of U^{239}. Element 93 was given the name neptunium (Np) because it is beyond uranium, just as the planet Neptune is beyond Uranus.

About this time, the possibility of a nuclear chain reaction and the production of transuranium elements for military use began to be recognized. With World War II already in progress, further work on the transuranium elements and related subjects was conducted by physicists and chemists under self-imposed secrecy, at first informally and finally as an organized program. The elements plutonium, americium, and curium were synthesized and identified (i.e., discovered) in such work on the wartime atom bomb project, before and during the organized Plutonium Project of the Manhattan Engineer District.

The seventeen known transuranium elements (numbers 93 to 109 inclusive) have been "discovered" in continuing experiments over a period of about forty-five years, at an average rate of one element every two or three years. Actually the discoveries have usually been made in pairs—i.e., a pair of elements about every five years.

The key to the discovery of the transuranium elements has been their position in the periodic table. Prior to the discovery of the transuranium elements, the relationship of the naturally occurring elements—thorium (atomic number 90),

1 H																	2 He
3 Li	4 Be											5 B	6 C	7 N	8 O	9 F	10 Ne
11 Na	12 Mg											13 Al	14 Si	15 P	16 S	17 Cl	18 Ar
19 K	20 Ca	21 Sc	22 Ti	23 V	24 Cr	25 Mn	26 Fe	27 Co	28 Ni	29 Cu	30 Zn	31 Ga	32 Ge	33 As	34 Se	35 Br	36 Kr
37 Rb	38 Sr	39 Y	40 Zr	41 Nb	42 Mo	43 Tc	44 Ru	45 Rh	46 Pd	47 Ag	48 Cd	49 In	50 Sn	51 Sb	52 Te	53 I	54 Xe
55 Cs	56 Ba	57 La	72 Hf	73 Ta	74 W	75 Re	76 Os	77 Ir	78 Pt	79 Au	80 Hg	81 Tl	82 Pb	83 Bi	84 Po	85 At	86 Rn
87 Fr	88 Ra	89 Ac	104 Rf	105 Ha	106	107 Ns	108 Hs	109 Mt	(110)	(111)	(112)	(113)	(114)	(115)	(116)	(117)	(118)

LANTHANIDES

58 Ce	59 Pr	60 Nd	61 Pm	62 Sm	63 Eu	64 Gd	65 Tb	66 Dy	67 Ho	68 Er	69 Tm	70 Yb	71 Lu

ACTINIDES

90 Th	91 Pa	92 U	93 Np	94 Pu	95 Am	96 Cm	97 Bk	98 Cf	99 Es	100 Fm	101 Md	102 No	103 Lr

FIGURE 1. The periodic table of elements.

protactinium (number 91), and uranium (number 92)—in the periodic table was not clearly understood. Recognition of the fact that the transuranium elements represent a whole new family of *actinide* ("like actinium"—atomic number 89) elements analogous to the *lanthanide* (rare-earth) series of elements (atomic numbers 59 through 71) permitted the discoverers to predict the chemical properties of the unknown transuranium elements. Once these properties were predicted, it was possible to discover the new elements by chemically separating them, following nuclear synthesis, from all the other elements in the periodic table.

The analogy between the actinides and lanthanides formed the basis for naming several of the former. Plutonium, of course, was named after the planet Pluto—following the pattern used in naming neptunium—which is the second and last known planet beyond Uranus. The name americium was suggested for element 95, after the Americas, by analogy with the naming of its rare-earth counterpart or homolog, europium, after Europe; and the name curium was suggested for element 96, after Pierre and Marie Curie, by analogy with the naming of its homolog, gadolinium, after the Finnish rare-earth chemist, J. Gadolin. Element 97

was called berkelium after the city of Berkeley, California, where it was discovered, just as its rare-earth analog, ytterbium, was given a name derived from Ytterby, Sweden, where so many of the early rare-earth minerals were found. Californium (number 98) was named after the university and state where its discovery occurred. The heavier transuranium elements were named after eminent scientists: einsteinium (number 99), after Albert Einstein; fermium (number 100), after Enrico Fermi; mendelevium (number 101), after Dimitri Mendeleev; nobelium (number 102), after Alfred Nobel; and lawrencium (number 103), after Ernest O. Lawrence.

Conflicts in naming have arisen in the cases of the transactinide elements 104, 105, and 106 because in each case two groups have claimed discovery and the traditional right to suggest names. For element 104, the U.S. group suggests rutherfordium, after Ernest Rutherford, and for element 105, hahnium, after Otto Hahn, while the Russian group, on the basis of doubtful evidence for their discovery, suggests for element 104, kurchatovium, after Igor Kurchatov, and for element 105, nielsbohrium, after Niels Bohr. The two groups have deferred suggesting a name for element 106. The German discoverers have named element 107 niels-bohrium, element 108 hassium, after the state Hesse in Germany where the work was done, and element 109 meitnerium, after Lise Meitner.

The most immediate effect of the discovery of a transuranium element on the world was in the use of plutonium for the manufacture of nuclear weapons. The more potentially beneficial practical use of plutonium as a nuclear fuel is well known.

In addition, three other actinide nuclides (plutonium-238, americium-241, and californium-252) have demonstrated substantial practical applications. One gram of plutonium-238 produces approximately 0.56 watt of thermal power, primarily from alpha particle decay, and this property is being used in space exploration to provide energy for small thermoelectric power units, such as radioisotopic thermoelectric generators on the moon, Viking Lander spacecraft on Mars, and the Jupiter flyby Pioneer spacecraft. Americium-241 has a long half-life (433 years) for decay (by the emission of alpha particles) and the predominant gamma ray (energy 60 KeV) makes this isotope particularly useful for a wide range of industrial gauging applications and the diagnosis of thyroid disorders; when mixed with beryllium, americium-241 generates neutrons and a large number of such sources are in worldwide daily use in oil-well logging operations (i.e., to find how much oil a well is producing in a given time span). Californium-252 is an intense neutron source: one gram emits 2.4×10^{12} neutrons per second. This isotope is being tested for applications in neutron activation analysis, neutron radiography, and portable sources for field use in mineral prospecting and oil-well logging. Both plutonium-238 and californium-252 are being studied for possible medical applications: the former as a heat source for use in heart pacemakers and heart pumps and the latter as a neutron source for irradiation of certain tumors for which gamma-ray treatment is relatively ineffective.

See also ARMS RACE; CHEMISTRY; ENVIRONMENTAL REFUGEES; HAZARDOUS WASTES; MILITARY TECHNOLOGIES; NUCLEAR POWER; NUCLEAR POWER: CON; PEACEKEEPING; PHYSICS; WEAPONS OF MASS DESTRUCTION.

BIBLIOGRAPHY

SEABORG, GLENN T., ed. *Transuranium Elements: Products of Modern Alchemy.* New York: Van Nostrand-Reinhold, 1978

SEABORG, GLENN T., and LOVELAND, WALTER D. *The Elements Beyond Uranium.* New York: John Wiley, 1990.

Glenn T. Seaborg

Trend Indicators

Serious forecasting beyond the short term has flourished in sectors that recognize the need for long-range planning, such as the military, aerospace, and information technology, and in cultures that encourage a long planning horizon, such as that of Japan.

Forecasting Techniques

Forecasting strives to determine "what can be," often termed "exploratory forecasting," as well as "what ought to be," usually labelled "normative forecasting." While the first begins with the past and is capability oriented, the second starts with the future and is need oriented. At some stage they must be integrated to provide a useful planning tool.

TREND EXTRAPOLATION

In this method of forecasting, it is assumed that the future will behave much like the past, so that data collected from observations of history form the basis for projecting the future. The variable to be forecast is selected and its value determined for a series of time points, such as years, from the past to the present. The sequence of value-date points is fitted by free-hand drawing, ruler, or a mathematical procedure. The resulting straight line or curve is simply carried forward, or extrapolated, into a future time period. As a general rule, projections should extend into the future for a period of time no greater than that covered by the historical data. Sometimes the variable is actually invariant, meaning that it does not change over time. For example, the annual number of U.S. vehicle deaths has stayed at about 24 per 100,000 population from 1930 to 1990.

GROWTH CURVES

A common trend is exponential growth—that is, growth by a constant percentage per unit time. In other words, at any time the rate of growth is proportional to the value already reached (see Figure 1). In a finite world, however, nothing can continue growing forever in an exponential fashion. There are many factors that limit growth, such as physical and economic ones (the speed of light or market saturation, for example).

The existence of a limit changes the exponential curve to an S-shaped curve, also known as a logistic or Pearl curve. Here the rate of growth slows as the limiting value, also known as the asymptote or niche, is approached. This curve is characteristic of biological growth, from birth to maturity. It also effectively describes the substitution of one technology for another (such as jet aircraft for propeller aircraft) or one commercial product for another (such as color for black-and-white television). Remarkably, many phenomena exhibit an S-shaped behavior, ranging from creativity over the human life span (Einstein's publications and Mozart's compositions) to explorations of the Western hemisphere, U.S. AIDS deaths as a fraction of all deaths, U.S. oil discoveries, and global air traffic growth (Modis, 1992). Often, growth consists of a sequence of S-shaped curves. For example, transportation speed growth may be represented as a sequence of successive substitutions, representing the horse, train, automobile, aircraft, missile, and spacecraft.

CYCLIC PHENOMENA

Cycles comprise another common type of long-term trend. During the 1920s, the Russian economist N. D. Kondratieff hypothesized that Western societies experience a pattern of long waves, each phased cycle characterized by recession-depression-revival-prosperity. The length of these cycles has averaged about fifty-six years, with peaks in the U.S. occurring in 1800, 1856, 1916, 1969, and forecast next around 2024. Interestingly, each cycle is dominated by an overarching technology—railroads, steel, oil, and information technology, respectively—and a primary form of energy. As a fraction of all forms of energy consumed globally, coal reached its peak in 1920, oil in 1980, with gas now moving to claim the lead. Technological innovations tend to cluster at certain time points and these have been found to correlate with the same cycles. For example, the depth of the Great Depression was followed by a fifteen-year technological explosion that brought forth radar, jet engines, atomic power, computers, and television, each creating an important new industry (Marchetti, 1980). All major U.S. wars from the American Revolution on, with the exception of Korea, also fit this pattern: two wars per cycle. (A cycle is equivalent to two generations.) The evolution of the corporate organization similarly fits this cyclic pattern: from owner-manager to hierarchy, division, matrix, and now network linkage. (In a matrix organization each participant is assigned simultaneously to a functional department and a project team that crosses functional lines.)

MODELS

In science, models are used in two distinct roles: to explain a phenomenon and to predict future behavior. Their effectiveness varies: in celestial mechanics, both explanatory and predictive capability are high; in evolutionary biology, explanatory capability is high and predictive capability low; in quantum mechanics, predictive capability is high and explanatory capability low; in economics, both explanatory and predictive capability are low (Casti, 1990). We have thus arrived at a profound realization: better understanding of a system does not necessarily mean better ability to forecast its future behavior. Models are abstractions or idealizations; a complex system is represented by a simpler one with fewer variables. For example, the widely debated Limits to Growth model of the world (see Meadows, 1992) used five variables: population, industrial production, agricultural production, natural resources, and pollution. It does not take many variables to create a multitude of relationships. For example, a system consisting of only three elements—A, B, and C—has at least forty-nine possible interactions, such as A-B, A-A, and BC-ABC, among its subsystems. A system containing ten elements has over a million possible different interactions among its subsystems. The Limits to Growth model determined the relationships among its elements—that is, the system structure—from data for the period 1900 to 1970 and then computed the behavior of the five variables with that structure of several hundred equations out to the year 2100. This type of model is known as a system dynamics model.

A useful simple tool is the structural model. It highlights the geometric or qualitative, rather than the algebraic or quantitative, features of a system. It is often represented by points (or nodes) and connecting lines (or arcs) that define a graph. If an ordering or direction is specified for each connecting line, the graph becomes a directed graph, or digraph. A very important aspect of systems highlighted by digraphs are feedback loops or cycles. A typical complex system has many such cycles—both damping and deviation-amplifying—and they are crucial to an understanding of the system behavior.

Among the structural models useful in forecasting are static types such as relevance trees (*see* TECHNOLOGY FORECASTING AND ASSESSMENT) and dynamic types such as KSIM (Martino, 1983).

DELPHI

Polling as a basis for forecasting is a mainstay for political campaigns and market research (*see also* SURVEYS). The use of experts by corporations and other organizations to forecast technological developments is also common. Delphi is the name of a structured communication process that is often used as a forecasting tool when more analytic approaches fail (Linstone and Turoff, 1975). It allows a group of individuals to act as a kind of expert panel. Two important features of Delphi are its iterative nature (that is, there are at least two rounds of questioning) and the mutual anonymity of its participants in the interactions. The participants are not brought together face-to-face. Rather, a questionnaire is supplied to each and returned to the monitor upon completion. Typically, it contains a list of possible future developments for which the respondents indicate the degree of feasibility and likely timing. The responses are tabulated by the monitor and provided together with a second-round questionnaire to each participant. The respondents thus only know the distribution of first-round responses, but not which person is associated with a particular response. The rounds with feedback are continued until the distribution of responses stabilizes—that is, exhibits little change between rounds. It is common, but by no means inevitable, to have a convergence of views as the rounds proceed.

MULTIPLE PERSPECTIVES

The methods described so far have been based on agreement, observations, or (past) data, and on models. Moving from strictly technological systems to complex human or social systems, forecasting must encompass modes of inquiry that embrace paradigms beyond those of science. Just as each human eye sees a slightly different image, so multiple perspectives view the same system through different lenses. Just as the brain combines the images from the eyes to yield depth perception, so the interactions among the perspectives yield deeper insights than can be obtained by any one perspective. The three types are: the technical or analytic, the organizational or institutional, and the personal or individual (Linstone, 1984; Linstone and Mitroff, 1994). The ethical basis for each type is different: rationality or logic is characteristic for the technical-analytic perspective, justice and fairness are associated with the organizational-institutional world view, and morality relates to the personal individual angle of vision.

Western secular culture may itself be described in terms of science, democracy, and individualism, respectively reflecting the three types of perspective. One revelation with multiple perspectives is the importance of who is making the forecast, not merely of what is being forecast.

Limitations of Forecasting

Forecasting the behavior of complex systems is subject to avoidable errors, unavoidable uncertainties, and the human tendency to discount distant time and space. For example, the assumptions underlying a forecast are far more critical than the sophistication of the model. A simple model with good assumptions is superior to a complex model with inappropriate assumptions.

Another shortcoming in forecasting involves the misperception of probability. It is fallacious to assume that improbable events will not occur in the forecast period. Improbability does not mean impossibility. The increasingly crowded world of the next century will experience a growing number of industrial catastrophes. They often entail a series of highly unlikely contributing factors that conjointly represent an extremely low probability of occurrence, but pose very severe consequences. This was the case with Three Mile Island, Bhopal, and the *Exxon Valdez* oil spill (Linstone and Mitroff, 1994). To contend with such occurrences, crisis management must become a central concern.

Complex systems may at times impose inherent unpredictability. Systems once thought to behave in an orderly fashion suddenly may shift to chaotic or unstable behavior. This means that systems appearing to be disorderly may have an underlying order that gives even chaos some level of predictability (Gordon and Greenspan, 1988).

Finally, human beings often look at the future through the wrong end of a telescope—that is, the distant object seems smaller than it actually is. Thus a future crisis may be discounted relative to near-term problems (Linstone and Mitroff, 1994). The reason why the economy tends to be emphasized by business forecasters more than is the environment is that economic costs are seen in near-term job losses, while environmental impacts are long-term. In most businesses short-term considerations prevail over long-term issues and strategies. The same phenomenon occurs in physical space. It is often labeled the NIMBY syndrome, short for "not in my back yard." Santa Barbara residents are concerned about oil drilling in the Santa Barbara Channel, but not in distant Alaska or the Gulf of Mexico. The concern for "me-now" at the expense of more distant space and time is a serious obstacle to effective planning in a world in which the population and technology explosions are dramatically shrinking Earth in space-time.

See also AGENTS OF CHANGE; CHANGE; CONTINUITY AND DISCONTINUITY; ECONOMIC CYCLES: MODELS AND SIMULATIONS; FORECASTING METHODS; LAWS, EVOLUTION OF; MULTIFOLD TREND; PACESETTER GOVERNMENTS; PLANNING; PUBLIC POLICY CHANGE; RECORD SETTING; SCANNING; SCENARIOS; SOCIAL CONTROLS; SOCIAL INDICATORS; STRATEGIC PLANNING.

BIBLIOGRAPHY

CASTI, J. *Searching for Certainty.* New York: William Morrow, 1990.

GORDON, THEODORE J., and GREENSPAN, DONALD. "Chaos and Fractals: New Tools for Technological and Social Forecasting." *Technological Forecasting and Social Change* 34 (1988): 1–25.

LINSTONE, HAROLD A. *Multiple Perspectives for Decision Making.* New York: North-Holland, 1984.

LINSTONE, HAROLD A., with Ian I. Mitroff. *The Challenge of the 21st Century.* Albany, NY: State University of New York Press, 1994.

LINSTONE, HAROLD A., and TUROFF, M. *The Delphi Method.* Reading, MA: Addison-Wesley, 1975.

MARCHETTI, C. "Society as a Learning System: Discovery, Invention, and Innovation Cycles Revisited." *Technological Forecasting and Social Change* 18 (1980): 267–282.

MARTINO, JOSEPH P. *Technological Forecasting for Decision Making.* New York: North-Holland, 1983.

MEADOWS, DENNIS, et al. *The Limits to Growth.* New York: Universe Books, 1972; revised, 1992.

MODIS, T. *Predictions.* New York: Simon & Schuster, 1992.

Harold A. Linstone

U

Unemployment

Unemployment is one of the most important questions confronting the United States. It is at the heart of the social contract between a state and its citizens, and is a major determinant of social and political stability. In 1992 an American president lost an election largely because of being identified with a deteriorating employment situation.

The importance of unemployment to the individual also is great. Individuals without paid employment become adrift in a society where one's sense of dignity and worth is closely related to making a living.

The impact of unemployment reaches far beyond those counted as officially unemployed, a number that reflects a monthly finding or an annual average. The number of unemployed during a calendar year is generally two to three times greater than the reported monthly average. For example, during 1991, 21.3 million persons were unemployed at some time during the year, a figure over two and a half times the annual average unemployment level of 8.4 million persons.

The significance of joblessness is magnified when one considers the impact on the well-being of other family members. Fear and anxiety regarding unemployment affects millions of Americans and their families. Confronting the future with hope and fulfilling one's obligations is very hard if one believes that his or her livelihood is in danger. Considered in this manner, unemployment is more than just a personal burden, it cuts at the social fabric and puts the entire society on edge.

Persons classified as unemployed must "not have worked during the reference week of the survey, must have actively sought work sometime during the four weeks prior to the survey, and must be currently available to take a suitable job." In addition, those who are not looking for work, but are either on temporary layoff or have a new job to which they are supposed to report in the very near future are classified as unemployed. The reference that most Americans are familiar with, the unemployment rate, is calculated by assessing the number of unemployed in proportion to the total labor force.

Official unemployment rates are aggregate rates that do not reflect the realities among different groups and areas of the country. Rates for black workers, for example, are more than twice those of white workers, a disparity that continues to grow larger.

Criticism of the official measure of unemployment has prompted proposals for alternative measurement concepts. Official measures have been challenged as understating or exaggerating the severity of the problem. The battle becomes especially intense at times of economic recession or during major election years. Attempting to put this matter to rest, Commissioner Julius Shiskin, while at the Bureau of Labor Statistics, developed some forty-two to forty-seven measures to provide a "range of unemployment rates based on varying definitions of unemployment and the labor force."

These measures are now included in monthly reports of the Bureau of Labor Statistics. Arguing that there was no one single correct measure of unemployment, Shiskin sought to defuse attacks against the integrity of official data. Print and media journalism now incorporate aspects of this approach by expanding reports on official unemployment to include references to involuntary part-time unemployment and to "discouraged workers." Although this approach represents a significant conceptual advance, it still has not fully put the matter to rest. Most likely these issues will continue to be disputed, since opposing views often reflect competing political and economic interests.

Modern industrialized market economies became committed, in varying ways, to essentially Keynesian goals of full employment and economic fine tuning, usually stated in terms of less unemployment and inflation. A major conflict involves the unemployment/inflation tradeoff issue. It is a matter of considerable debate as to precisely how much inflation is tolerable as the price for lower unemployment.

In the past twenty years there has been a declining belief in the effectiveness of fine-tuning the economy. Consequently a major determinant of economic policy has become the nonaccelerating inflation rate of unemployment, or NAIRU. This rate is thought to set the limits of unemployment reduction. When it is surpassed, the result is unacceptably high rates of inflation.

Debate swirls around the precise level of NAIRU. It is clear that the rate of "tolerable and acceptable unemployment" has risen significantly during the last thirty years. The 3 percent goal of the Kennedy administration has changed to between 5 and 7 percent. Prior to the 1989 recession, there was concern that unemployment had dropped to a dangerously low 5.3 percent level, which was thought likely to lead to a resurgence of inflation.

The dominance of the NAIRU orientation reflects a significant lessening of the American commitment to the goal of full employment, to which the nation has been committed by the Employment Act of 1946, and the Full Employment and Balanced Growth Act of 1979. The concept of full employment usually is left out of the contemporary public policy debate, because it is generally held that such a state is unachievable.

The reality of modern America is that higher proportions of the population are both employed and unemployed. Higher rates of unemployment have occurred at the same time that the labor force participation rate and the employment/population ratio rose to historically high levels—66.5 and 63.0 per-

cent respectively—during the last prerecession period in 1989. This demonstrates that both employment and unemployment can rise at the same time.

This seeming contradiction is more understandable at present as revolutionary changes in labor force participation rates of women, older males, black males, and young people have occurred. Understanding the dynamics of social change in America is strongly linked to the changes that occurred in the labor market during the past few decades.

Higher unemployment is not unique to the American economy; it is also a pervasive problem throughout Western Europe. All national market economies have developed alternative income maintenance and support a variety of programs commonly referred to as "safety nets." The formerly socialist nations of Eastern Europe also are now developing such systems. Wider availability and escalating costs of these benefits has become a source of great social and political conflict. Such safety nets have been assailed as the cause of declines in productivity, lower levels of economic growth, and the fiscal crisis that pervades the welfare state.

In the United States, concerns related to problems of unemployment are likely to dominate public policy decisions well into the next century. The declining quality of the work force's capabilities is tending to undermine the competitiveness of the United States in an increasingly global economy. This has led to proposals for more closely job-related educational curricula and more extensive vocational training.

Concern about a large, increasing underclass has generated support for more programs of job training, development, and placement. Recent inner-city riots are likely to create even greater pressure for a decisive response.

The recent recession severely impacted on white-collar occupations and bolstered fears that the quest for higher productivity is causing technological unemployment in the service sector.

The end of the Cold War has produced significant reductions in defense-related jobs. Plans to protect dislocated workers, industries, and local communities by providing support for conversion have been proposed.

Overall there is a resurgence of support for more public sector programs dealing with the development of human capital, job retraining, and public service employment. These proposals are, in part, responses to the problem of high unemployment. In the future it is likely that therewill be greater governmental support for such programs, especially if excessive unemployment persists.

American society may be in the midst of yet another employment and unemployment crisis that goes beyond fluctuations of the current business cycle. The problem is that unemployment rates have remained at higher levels during the peak periods of recovery from each of the recessions of the last thirty years.

Employment opportunity demands are likely to remain at the center of political conflict. Satisfaction of these demands will require a rethinking of fundamental elements of the social contract related to employment and unemployment. New forms of intervention may be required to resolve the problem. Among the solutions put forward are proposals to reduce the length of the working life or work week, and to increase the duration of schooling and provide for earlier retirement. Such steps could ease some of the difficulties and tensions currently associated with unemployment, and make joblessness more acceptable and tolerable.

See also CLASS AND UNDERCLASS; ECONOMIC CYCLES: MODELS AND SIMULATIONS; ENTITLEMENT PROGRAMS; PUBLIC ASSISTANCE PROGRAMS; UNEMPLOYMENT INSURANCE, WORKERS' COMPENSATION, JOB SECURITY; UNIONISM; WORK ETHIC; WORKFORCE REDISTRIBUTION.

BIBLIOGRAPHY

HARVEY, PHILIP. *Securing the Right to Employment: Social Welfare Policy and the Unemployed in the United States.* Princeton, N.J.: Princeton University Press, 1989.

JAFFEE, A. J., and STEWART, CHARLES D. *Manpower Resources and Utilization: Principles of Working Force Analysis.* New York: Wiley, 1951.

National Commission on Employment and Unemployment Statistics. *Counting the Labor Force.* Washington, D.C.: U.S. Government Printing Office, 1979.

U.S. President's Committee to Appraise Employment and Unemployment Statistics. *Measuring Employment and Unemployment.* Washington, D.C.: U.S. Government Printing Office, 1962.

WEIR, MARGARET. *Politics and Jobs: The Boundaries of Employment Policy in the United States.* Princeton, N.J.: Princeton University Press, 1992.

Stanley Moses

Unemployment Insurance, Worker's Compensation, Job Security

Government will continue to play an important role in securing public assistance programs for workers in an increasingly global and capitalist economy. In the future, many governments (1) will not consider a full employment strategy as a viable labor option and (2) will continue to extend targeted social support programs despite economic and fiscal policies based on concern about deficit spending.

In the twenty-first century, social support programs to increase employment opportunities and access to them necessitate extending the scope and level of existing program provisions while others require significant new departures. In industrialized countries, the impetus toward a global economy with a premium on high wages and well-trained, highly motivated, and empowered workers rests on a social contract between government and citizens and between labor and management that strives to enhance productivity. This goal is tempered by needs to attend to environmental and Third World quality-of-life concerns. Providing workers with more training and security and securing a more flexible and productive workforce would require a broad set of national level workplace policies. In the economic sphere of citizens' lives, these policies would stress broad social interests rather than individual self-interest and acquisitiveness such as is characteristic of unfettered capitalism. Furthermore, they would view government-support programs more as a positive force for social betterment rather than a drain on productivity. Finally, these policies would require individual responsibility and commitment to continued education and training to meet employment opportunities introduced by increasing rates of change. In countries like the United States, the current policy emphasis on enforcing obligations to work would be replaced by one ensuring equal employment opportunities.

Job Security and Unemployment Compensation

The unemployment insurance program in the United States provides time-limited cash benefits to regularly employed members of the labor force who become involuntarily unemployed but are able and willing to accept suitable employment. One policy to enhance job security and high wages in a global economy involves transforming unemployment compensation from a short-term subsidy for unemployed workers to a comprehensive system of lifetime learning and retraining to help assure employability.

Faced by the increased mobility of jobs in a global economy, benefits limited to between thirteen and twenty-six weeks (with episodic extensions) afford little job security and provide insufficient time for acquiring new sets of job skills. Something more needs to be done to keep workers and businesses productive.

One employment insurance approach would create a Career Opportunity Card providing access to retraining for the jobless, displaced, and low-wage workers. A Career Opportunity Card would be used as a voucher and carried as a wallet card similar to health insurance cards. Career Opportunity Cards could be used to purchase career-related education and training from public or private sources of the worker's choice. Individuals faced by an imminent economic security threat, such as being laid off, being able to find only part-time work, or working full-time at less than 150 percent of the poverty wage, could use this card to purchase specified amounts of education and training—perhaps up to as much as the approximate cost of one year of community college training. Workers would have to spend the money alloted within a specified time—five years, for example.

Educational or training institutes participating in the Career Opportunity program would be required to submit performance information to a system operated in provinces, states, or other political subdivisions. This system would provide workers with access to rates of completion, placement, and starting wages amassed by prior purchasers of training from various vendors. Such information would inform individual workers about vendor merits and regulating bodies about vendor performance.

In addition to a retraining allowance, the Career Opportunity Card could also make provision for relocation stipends. In many instances the range of suggested benefits might eliminate the need for severance pay. Relocation stipends could be realized as a tax deduction for individuals or as a tax subsidy to employers. To minimize in-house bureaucracy, such a venture could be outsourced to companies experienced in the credit or debit card business. Another solution would encourage or require employers to provide workers with yearly opportunities to upgrade their skills and otherwise support on-the-job training initiatives. Individual and corporate tax deductions already are available to defray the expenses of participation in or sponsorship of job training opportunities.

An Apprenticeship Training Program guaranteeing young persons the opportunity to build marketable competency through high school and college courses would require a more extensive change in U.S. labor policy. Programs in other industrialized nations, like Germany, are considered models. Such a universal program would increase job security. An Apprenticeship Training Program could be extended into a National or Public Service Program linking high school or college graduates to short term stints in skills-related jobs in the public and private sectors.

Worker's Compensation and Twenty-Four-Hour Coverage

Escalating health care costs influence an employer's decision to relocate business in less expensive regions of the country and indirectly contribute to the erosion of job security. To control health care costs, WC programs will increasingly rely on managed health care plans, including procedures for certification of managed care entities, peer review, and dispute resolution; prohibitions against certain medical provider billing practices; and establishment of capped medical fee schedules.

Two principles affecting federal-state regulatory relationships are likely to remain intact: the exclusive remedy provision, and exemption from the Employee Retirement Income Security Act (ERISA). With some degree of national oversight, states will retain their primary regulatory functions and employers will retain their immunity from suit except in certain circumstances.

The Worker's Compensation (WC) program in the United States provides cash benefits and medical care to workers injured in connection with their jobs, and survivor benefits to dependents of workers whose death results from a work-related accident. The medical care component of WC deserves special attention in light of prospects for twenty-four-hour coverage, i.e., combinations of traditional health insurance and WC insurance dissolving occupational and nonoccupational boundaries currently existing between the two coverages. Twenty-four-hour coverage is likely to become more the norm than the exception.

Initial variants of twenty-four-hour coverage will be limited. Insurers integrating management of an employer's WC and group health insurance claims agree to coordinate claims settlement and obviate duplicate claims. A *twenty-four-hour disability coverage package* would provide disability benefits for employee injuries and diseases limited to work-related injuries and diseases only. This package has the greatest potential for medical cost savings and is the most likely initial approach. A *twenty-four-hour medical coverage package* would provide, in a single policy, medical benefits for employee injuries and diseases whether work-related or not; however, disability benefits would be provided only for work-related injuries and diseases. A *twenty-four hour accident coverage package* would provide medical and disability benefits for all injuries, but only work-related diseases would be covered. A *twenty-four-hour disease coverage package* would provide medical and disability benefits for all diseases, but cover only work-related injuries. (This particular package would reduce the considerable litigation bound to arise over causation of certain diseases.) Finally, a *twenty-four-hour medical and disability package* would provide an all-inclusive (hence, most expensive) solution, providing medical and disability benefits for all diseases and injuries.

See also ENTITLEMENT PROGRAMS; INSURANCE; PRIVATE ASSISTANCE PROGRAMS; PUBLIC ASSISTANCE PROGRAMS; PUBLIC ASSISTANCE PROGRAMS: SOCIAL SECURITY; UNEMPLOYMENT.

BIBLIOGRAPHY

BLOCK, FRED. "Rethinking the Political Economy of the Welfare State." In Fred Block, Richard A. Cloward, Barbara Ehrenreich, and Frances Fox Piven, eds. *The Mean Season: The Attack on the Welfare State.* New York: Pantheon Books, 1987.

CAPUTO, RICHARD K. *Welfare and Freedom II: The Role of the Federal Government, 1941–1980.* Lanham, MD: University Press of America, 1994.

KUTTNER, ROBERT. "Labor Policy." In Mark Green, ed. *Changing America: Blueprints for the New Administration.* New York: Newmarket Press, 1992.

MARSHALL, WILL, and SCHRAM, MARTIN, eds. *Mandate for Change.* New York: Berkley Books, 1993.

WEIR, MARGARET. *Politics and Jobs: The Boundaries of Employment Policy in the United States.* Princeton, NJ: Princeton University Press, 1992.

Richard K. Caputo

Unionism

The American labor movement is the largest in the world, with nearly 16.5 million members and 87 major unions, but its membership has slipped from 36 percent of the total work force in 1945 to only 16 percent in 1995. To reach its 1945 level again, the movement would have to recruit over 37 million new members. Reeling from a loss of one million members in the 1980s, the labor movement may see its 11 percent position in the private sector fall to 7 percent or lower by 2000 A.D., approaching the level of the movement at its inception in the nineteenth century. In some countries nearly 90 percent of all workers belong to unions. In the Netherlands even soldiers have been unionized since 1967, but labor's prospects in the United States appear bleak, at least in the private sector. Despite any such setback, labor's 38 percent stronghold in the public sector could remain constant or suffer only slight losses in the years immediately ahead, so vital is union protection to many government employees.

Many well-intentioned futurists dismiss the potential role of labor unions. They expect labor's impact to be increasingly less significant in our information-based society.

Reasons for labor's forty-year-long decline in the United States are abundantly clear and varied. Employers in no other industrial nation, for example, match those in America in their bitter opposition to unionism. Nor have lawmakers in any other advanced nation created as many obstacles and handicaps to the labor movement. Likewise, nowhere else in the industrial world do the media ignore or trash labor so relentlessly as is regularly done here. Little wonder, accordingly, that labor's prime weapon, the strike, has fallen into disuse (1993 recorded only 35 major strikes, down from 424 in the last peak year of 1974).

Unionists remind would-be pallbearers that a trend is not a law. They take heart from the superior earning power of union members ($547 per week versus $413 for nonunion counterparts), as they believe this assures future recruitment gains. They are cheered by the pro-labor attitudes of women workers, the fastest-growing bloc in organized labor. They are also hopeful that the Clinton administration can constrain the antiunion animus of certain employers, improve the Labor Relations Board's role, revise oppressive federal labor laws, and give labor a public relations boost that organizers can turn to their advantage. They make much of the rise to power of pragmatic innovators who are replacing shortsighted, hidebound traditionalists among leaders of the labor movement. Above all, labor's optimists hail the growing use of a novel culture of organizational creativity.

Skeptics fret that these reforms may be too little too late. They doubt if labor can overcome the race, gender, craft, and class rifts that undermine the labor force's solidarity to such an extent that it can barely be termed a "movement." They see labor weakened by its inability to decide between continued dependence on the Democratic Party or on a daring new type of "fusion" third party. They doubt that employers will soon believe researchers who conclude that, on average, unionism is associated with increased productivity, rather than the commonly perceived reverse. And they suspect that a shift from proletariat to salariat, with a concomitant change in the psychology of employees fatally undermines labor's recovery chances.

In rebuttal, union strategists emphasize polling data that find Americans unhappy with their jobs, increasingly distrustful of big business, and increasingly supportive of unions. Many new members are expected from among the many angry employees whose average earnings have actually dropped from $315 a week in 1972 to only $256 in 1994 (in adjusted dollars), for a loss of 19 percent. Much is made of the forecast that abuses by corporations are so widespread, so diverse, so relentlessly growing that some form of union revival will inevitably evolve. Unionists urge onlookers to consider what the United States would be like if there were no labor movement and the forces of corporatism were allowed totally unbridled access to the centers of political power. They warn that strong unions are a vital counterbalance to the corporate drive to maximize profits at the expense of the well-being of society-at-large.

Much more, in short, than the survival of the largest social movement in America hinges on labor's fate. The union movement is an indispensable proponent of worker interests. It is a unique forum for ideas and a critical component in the liberal coalition. Above all, it serves as an ideological counterweight to business's preference for market supremacy almost regardless of human cost.

Unions are likely to change radically in the years ahead—more mergers of unions, more money spent on organizing, more sophisticated use of telecommunications, more women and nonwhite leaders. Labor's life-and-death struggle for rebirth, revitalization, and renewal will surely have a significant impact on the character and quality of our evolving information society. Long identified with blue-collar workers, organizational efforts increasingly will focus anew on public sector employees and on professionals—just as has been done in most other postindustrial societies.

See also INFORMATION SOCIETY; INSTITUTIONS, CONFIDENCE IN; LIBERALISM, POLITICAL; UNEMPLOYMENT; WORK; WORK ETHIC.

BIBLIOGRAPHY

ADLER, GLENN, and SUAREZ, DORIS, eds. *Unions' Voices: Labor's Responses to Crisis.* Albany, NY: State University of New York Press, 1993.
BLUESTONE, BARRY, and BLUESTONE, IRVING. *Negotiating the Future: A Labor Perspective on American Business.* New York: Basic Books, 1992.

FREEMAN, RICHARD B., and MEDOFF, JAMES L. *What Do Unions Do?* New York: Basic Books, 1984.
GEOGHEGAN, THOMAS. *Which Side Are You On? Trying to Be for Labor When It's Flat on Its Back.* New York: Plume, 1992.
GOLDFIELD, MICHAEL. *The Decline of Organized Labor in the United States.* Chicago: University of Chicago Press, 1987.
PUETTE, WILLIAM J. *Through Jaundiced Eyes: How the Media View Organized Labor.* Ithaca, NY: ILR Press, 1992.
SHOSTAK, ARTHUR B. *For Labor's Sake: Gains and Pains as Told by 28 Creative Inside Reformers.* Lanham, MD: University Press of America, 1995.
_____. *Robust Unionism: Innovations in the Labor Movement.* Ithaca, NY: ILR Press, 1991.

Arthur B. Shostak

United Kingdom

The underlying transformation in the United Kingdom is not the disintegration of society as described by some social and economic commentators, but is rather more of a change in the fundamental beliefs about what people are, what society is, what it is supposed to do, and why it works at all. Taken together, these fundamental beliefs constitute a social paradigm that is changing in the United Kingdom as well as in other countries in the Western world. The shift in the basic beliefs and values is occurring at a faster rate in the United Kingdom than in many other countries.

For the last twenty years our social models (based on surveys of random samples of the United Kingdom population) have been indicating a move:

Away from . . .	*Toward . . .*
• dependency	• independence (and more recently interdependence)
• collectivism	• autonomy
• socialism	• capitalism (in the original sense that Adam Smith envisioned, not in the popular, materialistic sense)
• materialism (as a metaphysic)	• consciousness (as a causal agent)

The social institutions embodying the ideals in the left column are not favorably disposed to the emerging concepts. Those who are introducing change consistent with the new concepts are being thwarted and frustrated by the "old guard," who see the changes as an attack on the very core of the institutions themselves. Because of these conflicts, some institutions are in disarray. Witness, for example, attempts to implement changes within the National Health Service, education, trade unions, and nationalized industries, as well as in the debates about a single Europe, an institution designed along "old paradigm" lines.

Although some of the conflicts appear as political party issues, others, such as the debate about Europe, split both of the main parties (the Conservative and Labor parties). This indicates that the conflicts are about issues more basic than politics or economics. They are caused by the changes in the fundamental values and beliefs of large segments of society.

As we look to the future, then, we anticipate a period of considerable turbulence for the rest of this century as existing institutions are supplanted by entirely new structures. By the beginning of the next century, the new paradigm will be emerging quite strongly. What will these new organizations/ institutions be like? From those few already in existence, we anticipate that they will be small, highly flexible, organized as networks linked electronically, visionary, able to inspire loyalty through shared visions, and fun as well as profitable. Such organizations will focus their attention on the essence of their concerns; outsourcing/subcontracting of noncore functions will be the norm.

Although some public institutions (e.g., the armed forces) will continue to exist, private health care and education will have become predominant, paid for by insurance policies and new financial instruments designed for the purpose. Combining the best of developments in technology with the desire for autonomy and high-quality personal relationships, both fields may well be characterized by organizations with a small central core and many outlying satellites that serve local needs. The few remaining nationalized industries will have been privatized, and the trade unions, unable to cope with the changes in the values held by their members, will become far less influential. In general, the significant requirements of the British people in the future will be for individual freedom, personal choice, high-quality service (whether provided by individuals or made possible through technology), flexibility, timeliness, and convenience.

The biggest difference of all, though, will come from the change in metaphysic. For the past three hundred years, our world, our institutions, and our own lives have been measured in material terms. Our criteria of success have been external, motivated as it were by a desire to "keep up with the Joneses." This is already changing. We are seeing quality supersede quantity and display as the standard of desirability. We are seeing an increasing number of people whose criteria for success are internal. We are seeing a growing awareness that there is more to life than material consumption and are learning from fields such as psychoneuroimmunology and consciousness research that what an individual entertains in his or her consciousness may be the cause of his or her experience. When this idea is recognized on a sufficiently large scale, the nature of relationships between people, organizations, media, and material objects will change profoundly.

See also DEVELOPMENT: WESTERN PERSPECTIVE; EUROPE, WESTERN.

BIBLIOGRAPHY

The Future of the U.K. 2010. London: Applied Futures Ltd. 1989.

MACNULTY, C. A. R. "The Changing Workforce." In *The Copenhagen Forum: A Kiosk of Business Futures.* Vol. 1, no. 1. Copenhagen: Institute for Future Studies, 1992.

MACNULTY, W. K. "The Paradigm Perspective." *Futures Research Quarterly* 5/3 (1989): 35–54.

———. "U.K. Social Change Through a Wide-Angle Lens." *Futures* (August 1985): 331–347

NORTHCOTT, J. *Britain in 2010: The PSI Report.* London: Policy Studies Institute Publishing, 1991.

Christine A. R. MacNulty

United States

The greatest change of the first quarter of the twenty-first century will be the reduction of the United States from the world's only superpower after the Cold War to merely one of several regional great powers. The decay of Cold War alliances like the North Atlantic Treaty Organization (NATO), combined with the continuing fiscal crisis of the American government, will ensure the withdrawal of most U.S. forces from overseas deployments. The removal of most American ground forces and supplies from Europe will make it logistically impossible for the United States to continue to play its post–Gulf War role in the Middle East as the dominant power. Following the reunification of Korea under the auspices of the South Korean regime, U.S. forces will be removed from both

Korea and Japan, except in the unlikely event of a full-fledged cold war with either China or Japan.

As the United States ends its forward deployments in Europe, the Middle East, and Asia, American strategists will devote more attention to defense within the North American quartersphere. Defending the American homeland will become a priority as advanced missile technology proliferates among potentially hostile countries. The Anti-Ballistic Missile Treaty will be amended or scrapped in order to permit ground-based, and eventually space-based, missile defenses. At the low-tech end of the military spectrum, U.S. expeditionary forces will intervene occasionally in Caribbean and Central American countries, possibly including Mexico, where population growth outpaces economic progress and political reform. To the north, the breakup of Canada, if it occurs, would cause only minor security dilemmas and might add several new states to the Union.

The importance of foreign commercial considerations in U.S. diplomacy and domestic politics alike will continue to grow. Hopes that liberalization of world trade by means of free trade agreements such as NAFTA, APEC, and GATT—respectively, the North American Free Trade Agreement, the Atlantic Provinces Economic Council, and the General Agreement on Tariffs and Trade—would produce income gains for ordinary Americans will not materialize. Mass consumer markets will fail to take hold in the impoverished, overpopulated, oligarchic societies south of the Rio Grande. Japan and China will continue to pursue mercantilist policies, protecting their domestic markets while targeting U.S. consumers (the Chinese merchandise trade surplus with the United States will surpass the Japanese around the year 2000). In contrast with the Pacific trade wars, U.S. trade relations with the European Union, expanded to include most of the former Soviet bloc, will be relatively harmonious and could lead to a transatlantic free trade zone that would be the richest in the world in per capita terms. The dollar will cease to be the world's reserve currency; global financial instability will be reduced, though, as many small countries tie their currencies to the dollar, the yen, or the mark.

The most significant change in American domestic politics in the early twenty-first century will be immigration restriction. Strict limits on legal immigration will accompany a crackdown on illegal immigration, as the era of mass migration from Latin America and Asia to the United States is brought to a close. The descendants of the late twentieth century's new immigrants will rapidly assimilate to American culture. High rates of intermarriage among Hispanics, Asians, and whites will promote the gradual formation of a mixed-race majority. The end of mass immigration will open up job opportunities for working-class black Americans; the hereditary black underclass, however, will be isolated and harshly treated in a newly conservative political climate. Popular support for the repeal of affirmative action will grow, even as intermarriage undermines the accuracy of racial categories.

Despite the slow progress of racial integration, economic polarization in the United States will grow more extreme. With organized labor weaker than ever, business interests will find little opposition to its agenda of lowering wages, eliminating benefits, and replacing tenured with contingent employees. The downwardly mobile middle class will compete for poorly paid service-sector jobs with former blue-collar workers and service-sector workers whose vocations have been eliminated by automation or expatriation. The result will be the formation of suburban white and Hispanic underclasses dwarfing the urban black underclass produced by the mechanization of Southern agriculture in the 1920s and 1930s. These desperate new underclasses will become breeding grounds of violent criminals, linked to new international mafias—Latin American, East Asian, Russian.

Many affluent families will move to the safer and more pleasant interior of the country and take advantage of telecommuting. Well-to-do Americans who remain in the metropolitan regions of the coastal states will retreat into enclave communities protected by private police forces. Home security innovations will be the major factor in the evolution of the "smart" or computer-controlled house. The greatest innovation in daily life, however, will be inspired by health technology, as the affluent pay for the refitting of bathrooms as miniature medical offices with diagnostic equipment linked to doctors and hospitals.

The growing polarization of American society between almost exclusively white haves and have-nots of all races will not translate directly into political conflict. For one thing, racial quotas, if they survive, will keep whites, blacks, Hispanics, and Asians bitterly divided. Furthermore, the failure of sweeping campaign finance reform will permit a small number of wealthy individuals and corporations to continue to dominate U.S. politics. Finally, the Senate, skewed toward the thinly populated interior states and representing an ever-diminishing (and mostly white) fraction of the public, will stymie federal efforts to improve the conditions of the non-white majorities in California, Texas, New York, and Florida. The affluent will seek to shift the costs of government to wage-earning Americans, by means of regressive consumption taxes, user fees, and privatization of public services. The failure of the political system to respond to the growing inequality will produce a series of antisystemic, populist, and nationalist movements, each more radical than the last. Though none will succeed in the first quarter of the twenty-first century, these movements will produce turbulence in national politics.

The aging of the American population, accelerated by immigration restriction, will result in a society that is relatively conservative on social and moral issues. The sexual revolution and the liberalization of the mass media will not be reversed, however, and widespread use of convenient abortifacients and implanted contraceptives will come to be accepted. Rudimentary forms of genetic engineering will be available to the wealthy, although opposition from religious voters will prevent their inclusion in government-funded health programs. The growing longevity of Americans will produce four- or five-generation families and create social pressure for middle-aged people, rather than the state, to provide care for aged parents. Voluntary euthanasia of the terminally ill elderly will become widely accepted, despite religious objections.

The number of secular Americans will increase, particularly among the more educated and affluent classes. The mainline Protestant churches will continue to lose adherents; their place will be taken by the Baptist church, which, like the Methodist and Presbyterian churches before it, will become more moderate in its views as its members rise in the social scale. Revivalism and fundamentalism will be taken up by new pentecostal and evangelical movements, with support among ex-Catholic Hispanics in particular. American Catholicism will decline, as the Catholic Church remains antiliberal and becomes increasingly identified with the Third World, especially Africa. Liberal Judaism will wither, as American Jews become either wholly secular or join Orthodox renewal movements. Muslims will replace Jews as the largest religious minority in the United States. The early twenty-first century will see an "Americanization" of Islam, like the previous Americanization of immigrant-community Catholicism, Lutheranism, and Judaism. The appeal of New Age and Asian religions will remain limited.

Despite its isolationism, the United States of the early twenty-first century will be less parochial in many ways, thanks to global TV and the evolution of a polycentric global popular culture. Soccer will eventually replace football as the national pastime as in most other countries. The cultural influence of East Asia will grow, at first in the form of popular culture, e.g., Japanese animation and science fiction. Growing numbers of American intellectuals dissatisfied with their inegalitarian, individualistic society will become interested in the newly self-assertive Confucian societies of East Asia, in the way that twentieth-century American intellectuals looked to Swedish social democrats and Russian communists for inspiration.

Japan and the United States rather than Europe will lead the world in the artistic renaissance of the third millennium, developing entirely new forms of visual art, music, and drama based on computer technology and virtual reality to replace the outmoded forms of early modern Europe like easel paintings and orchestral compositions. These new arts will be pioneered by the entertainment industry rather than by fine artists; the gap that opened in the twentieth century between popular art and the esoteric avant-garde will be reduced, in one of the most encouraging developments of the new era.

See also CANADA; CAPITALISM; DEMOCRACY; DEVELOPMENT: WESTERN PERSPECTIVE; LATIN AMERICA; POPULATION GROWTH: UNITED STATES; SOCIAL CHANGE: UNITED STATES.

BIBLIOGRAPHY

BARNEY, GERALD O. *The Global 2000 Report to the President: Entering the 21st Century.* Washington DC: U.S. Government Printing Office, 1981.

BOYER, WILLIAM H. *America's Future: Transition to the 21st Century.* Sisters, OR: New Politics Press, 1984.

CARNEVALE, ANTHONY PATRICK. *America and the New Economy.* Washington DC: U.S. Department of Labor, 1991.

CETRON, MARVIN, and DAVIES, OWEN. *American Renaissance: Our Life at the Turn of the 21st Century.* New York: St. Martin's Press, 1989.

DUDLEY, WILLIAM, and ZUMKE, BONNIE. *America's Future: Opposing Viewpoints.* San Diego: Greenhaven Press, 1990.

KENNEDY, PAUL. *Preparing for the 21st Century.* New York: Random House, 1993.

LAPHAM, LEWIS. *Money and Class in America.* New York: Grove Press, 1989.

LIND, MICHAEL. *The Next American Nation: The New Nationalism and the Fourth American Revolution.* New York: Free Press, 1995.

MISCHEL, LAWRENCE, and BERNSTEIN, JARED. *The State of Working America, 1992–1993.* Washington, DC: Economic Policy Institute, 1992.

PINSKY, MARK, and GREEN, MARK. *America's Transition: Blueprints for the 1990s.* New York: Democracy Project, 1991.

STROBEL, FREDERICK. *Upward Dreams, Downward Mobility: The Economic Decline of the American Middle Class.* Lanham, MD: Rowman and Littlefield, 1993.

THUROW, LESTER. *Head to Head: The Coming Economic Battle Among Japan, Europe and America.* New York, Warner Books, 1992.

VLAHOS, MICHAEL. *Thinking About World Change.* Washington, DC: U.S. Department of State, 1990

WOLFGANG, MARVIN, and LAMBERT, RICHARD D. *The Future Society: Aspects of America in the Year 2000.* Cambridge, MA: American Academy of Political and Social Science, 1983.

Michael Lind

Urban Transit

Transit is defined by the American Public Transit Association as "all multiple-occupancy-vehicle passenger services of a local and regional nature provided for general public use." Different types of transit service are called modes. *Road modes* include motorbus, trolleybus, vanpool, jitney, and demand response (dial-a-ride). *Rail modes* include heavy rail, light rail (streetcars), commuter rail, automated guideway (people movers), inclined plane, cable car, and aerial tramway. *Water modes* include ferryboats.

All of these are nineteenth-century inventions, with the exception of the motorbus, which was introduced in 1905. Adding automation to buses or trains (automated guideway systems, for example), does not significantly change the service characteristics of nineteenth-century transit modes.

At the beginning of the nineteenth century, all cities were essentially walking cities. The introduction of street railways and interurbans (regional rail systems) allowed cities to expand from the central industrial-commercial cores along rail corridors, creating the star-shaped city of the late nineteenth and early twentieth century.

Rail Transit

Heavy rail and commuter rail vehicles, typically holding 150 people, provide service to people with similar origins and destinations along narrow corridors. Rail transit is often built as subway or elevated lines to avoid street congestion with closely spaced stations for easy accessibility. Outlying areas with fewer stations speed up trips but reduce

access. Designed to carry large numbers of people, trains are fully utilized for only twenty peak-hours per week. During offpeak hours, they run at long intervals (necessitating long waits for passengers), and may not run at all during the night. Rail systems are inflexible and not easily modified to serve major new developments.

"Modernizing" trains—mono- rather than dual-rails, or different running gear such as magnetic levitation, or rubber as opposed to steel wheels—fundamentally changes the character of the service. Construction, recently costing $250 to $300 million per mile, is very expensive. Cities can afford no more than a few miles of heavy rail—crowded during peak hours, underused with poor service offpeak, and with poor flexibility. To overcome congestion, some light rail trains have sensors enabling them to change traffic lights, assuring them of the right-of-way at all intersections.

Buses

Rail systems during the early twentieth century ran into trouble due to high levels of indebtedness, increasing operating costs, and eventually declining ridership as more people moved into the areas between the rail lines. Buses became competitive because they were cheaper to buy and had much lower capital costs. They used public roads paid for by the taxpayer, unlike rail systems that had to pay for their own roadbeds. They were flexible—one breakdown did not shut down the entire line—and they could be rerouted to accommodate new developments.

Since the 1930s, buses have become public transit workhorses, serving double and even triple the number of passengers as rail. Buses provide a low quality of service; many stops make them highly accessible but also mean slow travel along each route. Furthermore, getting from one place to another often requires indirect routing with one or more changes of vehicle and the uncertainty of waits at each transfer point. Service is particularly poor in low-density areas and during offpeak hours.

Although more buses are being run on natural gas and other nonpolluting fuels, most are still smelly and dirty. With the increases in urban crime, riders often feel vulnerable both at stops and on the vehicles. Buses are also largely inaccessible to the physically disabled except at great expense by installing chairlifts.

Still, buses are likely to play a significant role in public transit well into the twenty-first century. Nonpolluting fuels, electronic control of traffic signals, electronic information boards at stops indicating the length of waits, and displays mapping the whole system are likely to be introduced to improve bus service. Automatic vehicle tracking may improve transfer connections for some, but there are too many points of origin, connection, and destination with multiple dependencies to convenience everybody. More high-occupancy vehicle (HOV) lanes where buses share space with vans and carpools provide short-term improvement of bus service.

Automated people movers (APM), introduced over the last twenty years, are driverless buses (some carrying forty passengers per vehicle, some only ten) that are computer-operated on guideways. They serve as circulation systems in central cities and at airports around the world. APM service is essentially comparable to that of light rail systems, although there are separate guideways to avoid street congestion. These guideways also create considerable construction costs and may be visually unattractive. While providing excellent circulation service within contained areas of moderate to high density, APM service does not meet the needs of low-density urban areas.

Dispersed Cities and the Automobile

Despite all these transit options, the automobile has become the dominant mode of urban transportation in American cities. It is also rapidly taking over in the cities of wealthier countries worldwide (excluding the island cities of Hong Kong and Singapore). Metropolitan regions with moderate to low densities are growing, as central cities disperse their industry, commerce, and housing into "edge" cities and scattered miniurban complexes.

Today bustling metropolitan regions have thousands of trip origins and destinations. Only the automobile allows people to move flexibly throughout the region, twenty-four hours a day. Public transit, with its focus on the rush hour/home to work commute, does not easily accommodate to offshift work trips, picking up children at day care, going to school, theater, or sporting events, shopping, or visiting the doctor, friends, and family.

The result has been a dramatic drop in the use of transit. People turned to the automobile in large numbers after World War I when the land close to train stations became fully developed and they had to live further from transit stops. The auto met their needs, and even though the *numbers* of passengers riding public transit continued to grow until 1930, the *proportion* of trips made by public transit declined precipitously from 98 percent of the trips in 1900 to about 20 percent in 1930. Today it ranges from 0.8 percent in Houston to 14 percent in New York City.

Public transit decline is worldwide. Europeans still use transit more than Americans, but the trend toward decentralized growth, reduction in urban density, and increased use of the automobile is similar.

That the automobile "caused" urban sprawl may be a myth. In fact, personal vehicles may merely have met demand patterns that already were in place. Automobiles clearly made possible the type of urban growth we see today—much growth on the periphery, little or no growth or even decline in the center city.

While transit "experts" often speak of the "love affair with the automobile," they fail to recognize a forced marriage of convenience. Restricting auto use will not by itself improve mobility or access in cities, but it will certainly cause real hardship for many. For those who can drive, the auto meets virtually all our needs for mobility and access to the metropolitan region.

Unfortunately, the auto is also expensive to own and operate, causes an average of 48,000 deaths each year in the United States, is unavailable to many people (the poor, the young, the old, the disabled), takes up large amounts of urban space (for roads and parking), pollutes the air, is noisy, and is a major contributor to urban congestion.

Future of Transit

Whether transit or automobile, each mode serves a useful purpose, but each has serious limitations. No single mode, nor any combination of existing modes, can accommodate foreseeable needs of twenty-first-century cities—for resource conservation, improvement of urban land use, reduction of congestion and pollution, and to meet the mobility needs of an increasingly transit-dependent aging population. Metropolitan areas all over the world need to solve the same problem to provide low-cost, energy-efficient, environmentally sound transportation to medium- and low-density areas.

Personal Rapid Transit

Progress requires a change in thinking, even a change in the definition of public transit (multiple-occupancy vehicles) to include a new mode known as personal rapid transit (PRT) that meets the needs of twenty-first-century people and societies.

It has already been tested in France, Germany, Japan, and the United States.

PRT can be thought of as an automated taxi. Its small, driverless vehicles have seats for two to four people operating on a slim (1 meter by 1 meter) elevated guideway. They are electric, automatic, and move nonstop from the place you get on to the place you get off. Guideways can be built over existing streets and freeways, so the system does not require the acquisition of additional land. Guideways can also be placed at surface level or below ground.

Riders enter the system through stations spaced about two blocks apart in densely populated areas and about half a mile apart in lower-density areas. In each station, a rider punches his or her destination into a computer, enters a car, and then travels directly and quietly to the destination at speeds ranging from twenty to fifty miles per hour. All stations are on sidings off the main line, so there are no intervening stops and thus no delays.

A rider would share a vehicle *only* if traveling with friends, thus retaining an important virtue of private cars. The rider has all the advantages of the automobile, but without the necessity to drive, park, maintain, or insure it.

Today's computing technology allows thousands of PRT vehicles to be deployed in a network of small guideways to be available throughout the metropolitan region. They can be used not only to move people, but vehicles with the same chassis can be rigged to carry light freight and mail to depots located in warehouses, shopping centers, and post offices. Freight operations during nonpeak hours would help the system break even (or make a profit).

Public transportation need not be a dreaded or uncomfortable inconvenience forced on unhappy urban travelers. Properly designed, it can improve everybody's quality of life.

See also AIR TRANSPORT; MOTOR VEHICLES; MOTOR VEHICLES, ALTERNATIVELY POWERED; PERSONAL TRANSPORT; RAILWAYS; TRANSPORTATION.

BIBLIOGRAPHY

BURKE, CATHERINE. *Innovation and Public Policy: The Case of Personal Rapid Transit.* Lexington, MA: Lexington Books, D.C. Health, 1979.
FLOYD, THOMAS H., JR. "Personalizing Public Transportation." *The Futurist* (November-December 1990): 29–33.
MEYER, JOHN R.; KAIN, JOHN F.; and WOHL, MARTIN. *The Urban Transportation Problem.* Cambridge, MA: Harvard University Press, 1965.
NEWMAN, PETER W. G., and KENWORTHY, JEFFREY R. *Cities and Automobile Dependence: A Sourcebook.* Aldershot, U.K.: Gower Publishing, 1989.
1993 Transit Fact Book. Washington, DC: American Public Transit Association, 1993.
Technical Committee on Personal Rapid Transit of the Advanced Transit Association. "Personal Rapid Transit (PRT): Another Option for Urban Transit?" *Journal of Advanced Transportation* 22/3 (1988).

Catherine G. Burke

Utopias

The word *utopia* was coined by the English humanist scholar Saint Thomas MORE in his book of the same title, first published in 1516. The two Greek words from which it is formed mean, literally, "no place." More's Utopia is an imaginary society situated on a faraway island, a democratic and classless society of generally virtuous men and women. Although it was not an earthly paradise, More viewed his fictional commonwealth as a model of what life could be if reason, tutored by religious faith, governed the affairs of humankind. Both implicitly and explicitly, his book was also a pungent critique of the society of his own time.

In the next few hundred years, many similar visions were written, so that *utopia* became a generic term for any story or essay about a distant imaginary community where all is well. Classic examples are Tommaso Campanella's *City of the Sun* (1602), Johann Valentin Andreae's Lutheran utopia, *Christianopolis* (1619), and Sir Francis Bacon's *New Atlantis* (1624). In each, and in scores of others, the reader visits a wondrous land that serves as a model of how human beings should live, not unlike the ideal city-state described at length in Plato's *Republic*. Whether the authors of these utopias believed that their commonwealths could ever be built on Earth is often doubtful—or at least unclear. Thomas More, almost certainly, was more ironic and playful than serious.

But in the so-called Enlightenment of the eighteenth century, the utopian tradition took a new turn. Writers began to set their visions of the good society in the future. The first to do so was Louis Sébastien Mercier, in his novel *The Year 2440* (1771). In this work the reader is transported not to some strange island in the South Seas, but to Paris of the twenty-fifth century, where a clean, well-lit city greets Mercier's hero, who awakens after a long and deep sleep. The ills of eighteenth-century France have disappeared, and science and reason are triumphant.

The Year 2440 is a work of fiction, but the more common form taken by utopian visions in the late eighteenth century was the philosophical essay expounding a theory of irresistible progress from the dark past to the bright future of humanity. The steady improvement of learning would, said the philosophers, produce a rationalist millennium. Noteworthy among these were the Frenchmen Baron Turgot and the Marquis de Condorcet, the English scientist and thinker Joseph Priestley, and Immanuel Kant, the greatest philosopher of the German Enlightenment. The most influential vision of a glorious future appeared in Condorcet's *Sketch for a Historical Portrait of the Progress of the Human Mind* (1795), where he described, beyond the nine epochs of history thus far, a tenth epoch in which inequality both within and among nations would be erased by science, education, and wise public administration.

Condorcet's example was followed in the nineteenth century by many thinkers, as in Auguste Comte's utopian vision of a future "Western Republic" in his *System of Positive Polity* (1851–1854), and in the tantalizing glimpses of a classless, stateless utopia in the many writings of Karl Marx and Friedrich Engels. Marx and Engels, however, pointedly refused to imagine their future world in graphic detail. They feared that too much speculation about the future would impede hard-headed scientific analysis of present-day realities and distract socialists from the urgent tasks at hand.

Other socialists, such as Charles Fourier and Étienne Cabet, were less cautious, putting forth elaborate schemes for working-class utopias that inspired the creation of experimental utopian communities in several parts of the world. Near the end of the nineteenth century, many socialists and other social reformers took to creating utopias in fictional form. They produced several works of great distinction, including Edward Bellamy's *Looking Backward* (1888), Theodor Hertzka's *Free land* (1890), and William Morris's *News from Nowhere* (1890). Each novel was set explicitly in the future. The English futurist and science fiction writer H. G. Wells published his vision of technocratic socialism, *A Modern Utopia*, in 1905. Wells tried his hand at utopian fiction again in *Men Like Gods* (1923) and *The Shape of Things to Come*

(1933), and his Irish contemporary Bernard Shaw published what is perhaps the greatest of utopian plays, *Back to Methuselah*, in 1922.

In more recent times, the writing of utopias in all forms, fictional or nonfictional, has gone out of vogue again. Its place has been taken by the "dystopia," the picture of a quintessentially bad society, like the Oceania of George Orwell's *Nineteen Eighty-Four* (1949). But utopianizing is not extinct. From the philosophical utopias of Herbert Marcuse and Pierre Teilhard de Chardin to such literary utopias as B. F. Skinner's *Walden Two* (1948) and Ernest Callenbach's *Ecotopia* (1975) and *Ecotopia Emerging* (1981), visions of the ideal society, often set in a credible future, still appear in print from time to time. The optimistic cant of twentieth-century demagogues and politicians, who promise to build new heavens on Earth, or speak glibly of "new frontiers" and "shining cities on the hill," is also an echo, however faint, of the utopian tradition.

It may even be argued that many of the images of the future purveyed in the writings of professional futurists partake liberally of the utopian impulse. For example, Herman Kahn and his associates in *The Next 200 Years* (1976) depict a prosperous and peaceful future world where today's problems have all been solved by the progress of science, technology, and capitalism. William Irwin Thompson in *At the Edge of History* (1971) and Marilyn Ferguson in *The Aquarian Conspiracy* (1980, 1987) offer popular covert utopian visions of the future from a New Age perspective. The literary utopia is, in fact, a variant of the technique of scenario-building often employed by futurists. It can be a useful device in helping futurists clarify their values, establish perspective, and define the normative dimensions of their research.

See also APOCALYPTIC FUTURE; DYSTOPIAS; SCIENCE FICTION.

BIBLIOGRAPHY

BERNERI, MARIE LOUISE. *Journey Through Utopia.* London: Routledge & Kegan Paul, 1950.

LEVITAS, RUTH. *The Concept of Utopia.* Syracuse, N.Y.: Syracuse University Press, 1990.

MANUEL, FRANK E., and MANUEL, FRITZIE P. *Utopian Thought in the Western World.* Cambridge, Mass.: Harvard University Press, 1979.

W. Warren Wagar

V

Values

Human values are standards of judging. They define the desirable or undesirable, the good or bad, the pleasant or unpleasant, and the appropriate or inappropriate. They are guides to behavior. They are invested with group identifications and emotions. They involve social sanctions—i.e., rewards and punishments—administered by agents of the community. They often appear as moral "ought" or "ought not" statements regarding the proper behavior of individuals. Values are more than mere individual preferences. Rather, they include the practices and rules of right conduct that are often seen as beneficial, if not necessary, for the welfare of entire social groups.

Values are not arbitrary. They have evolved through the millennia of human development, having their origins in human nature, the conditions of social life, and the interaction between them and with the nature of the physical environment.

Human beings cannot exist without having certain of their needs met. They must have air, water, and food, and they have needs for clothing, shelter, companionship, affection, and sex. They do not come into the world devoid of a means of evaluation. The human body and brain are programmed with a variety of senses, such as taste, smell, sight, hearing, and touch, and of drives, such as hunger, thirst, and sex. Individuals feel pain and pleasure. Thus, people have some basis for evaluation, some built-in criteria for believing that some things are good and that some things are bad. Not only biopsychological needs but also higher capacities such as the ability to reason, to attribute meaning to things, and to choose to act in one way or another provide guidelines for the welfare of individual organisms and foundations for human values.

Some human needs, such as those for love, approval, emotional support, and communication, can only be satisfied by interaction with other humans. Social life itself also shapes human values. Morality functions to allow people to live and work together and benefit from the tremendous payoffs of cooperative efforts. For example, values of honesty, trust, and trustworthiness are necessary for learning from others. Values such as sharing with others, justice, generosity, and reciprocity contribute to both individual and group well-being.

Thus, all people everywhere have certain similar basic needs and face similar problems of the conditions of social life. All people also exist in natural environments that are subject to similar physical and chemical principles (e.g., gravity, the nature of fire, and mundane things such as objects sharing length, weight, volume, etc.). When humans recognize the sun as the giver of life, for example, it is understandable that they come to value, even worship, it. When humans learn that seed corn is necessary to grow corn, they come to value it. Basically similar beings pursuing goals that necessarily include some similar ones of survival and flourishing

Values

create many similar beliefs and evaluations since they function within similar social and physical constraints and opportunities.

Hence, despite the apparent cultural diversity in the world, there exist universal or nearly universal human values: the value of human life (because without life, there is nothing else, hence the value of health); the value of knowledge (because that is how we make our way effectively in the world and achieve our purposes, hence the values of truth, education, research, technology), and the value of evaluation itself (because we need to be able to judge accurately whether things in the real world are good or bad, safe or dangerous, trustworthy or untrustworthy, and so on).

Among other nearly universal values are: sufficient (but not enormous) wealth, peace, justice, affection, opportunities for family life and sexual behavior, respect for authority, moderation, loyalty, courage, perseverance, cooperation, honesty, generosity, helpfulness, friendliness, trust and trustworthiness, individual autonomy constrained only by the necessities of group living and concerns for fair play and a fair distribution of freedom and well-being for all, and self realization. Such values tend to exist everywhere, regardless of language and culture, and to remain constant.

The postmodern—i.e., relativist and subjectivist—perspectives of the late twentieth century have drifted away from these truths. Thus the work of people like Ronald Inglehart is misleading. In surveys in over twenty-five countries from 1973 to 1988, he finds some change in values in advanced industrial societies from traditional materialist values of physical sustenance and safety toward postmaterialist values of individual autonomy, innovation, self-expression, beauty, and a tendency to challenge authority. But these findings are deceptive, first, because, many people continue to express materialist values even in advanced, industrial societies, and, second, because postmaterialist values are contingent upon the adequate satisfaction of the materialist values of survival and comfort. For most people in the less developed world, materialist values are not yet fulfilled and for people in the industrialized world they remain contingent on high levels of living that may be precarious. Values that satisfy basic human needs and the conditions of social life can be ignored only at the risk of the possible future decline and collapse of human civilization.

Some human values, though, *have* changed, and some of them *ought* to have changed. The human future depends both on recognizing and living according to most universal values *and* on continuing change in others in response to changing conditions: e.g., the recent rapid growth of the earth's human population (now at over 5.5 billion going on 11 billion); the increase in the scale of human interaction to encompass the globe; and the possible threats (e.g., resource depletion, pollution, global warming, etc.) to the life-sustaining capacities of Earth.

The freedom and well-being of human beings in the twenty-first century and beyond require a new image of a preferable future. Specifically, we need the following value changes:

1. The preeminent value of human life itself ought to be expanded so that all persons born anywhere on earth have an equal right and opportunity to live out their life spans of eighty-plus years.
2. The values of human reproductive behavior ought to continue to change toward valuing low birth rates to the point of no more than an average of one child per person so as eventually to achieve zero-population growth.
3. The values associated with masculinity, such as machismo, aggression, dominance, destruction, and violence, are no longer functional and ought to be redefined as male nurturing of society through caring for others and achieving social justice by rational discourse and law.
4. While keeping local identities, the idea of an alien "Other" ought to be eliminated, thereby ending exclusivity of caring for ingroup members and animosity toward outgroups, and every individual's community of concern ought to be expanded to encompass all of humanity.
5. Because of the cosmic ignorance of humans concerning the purposes and meanings of life and because of obvious human need, humans ought to value more highly their stewardship of nonhuman forms of life and the biosphere.
6. Because they have no right to use up the resources of the Earth and the cultural heritages past generations left them, the present generation ought to value more fully the well-being of future generations, passing on to them social, cultural, and physical conditions no worse than were left to them.
7. The creation, development, preservation, and dissemination of useful knowledge ought to be valued more than at present, because such knowledge empowers future generations and compensates them for the damage past and present humans have done and are doing to the Earth.

8. Values concerning the status of women ought to be changed everywhere on Earth to create opportunities for women to choose and to pursue meaningful lives equal to those of men, both because it is equitable to do so and because other values that ought to be changed—e.g., reproductive values—can be changed more easily.

See also BEHAVIOR: SOCIAL CONSTRAINTS; CHANGE, CULTURAL; CHANGE, EPOCHAL; ETHICS; FAMILY VALUES; GLOBAL CULTURE; LIFESTYLES, ALTERNATIVE; LIFESTYLES, VALUE-ORIENTED; MODERNISM AND POSTMODERNISM; MORALS; RELIGION, SPIRITUALITY, MORALITY; SEXUAL BEHAVIOR; SEXUAL CODES OF CONDUCT; SOCIAL CONTROLS; VALUES, NONWESTERN; VALUES CHANGE; VALUES FORMATION.

BIBLIOGRAPHY

BAUMEISTER, ROY F. *Meanings of Life.* New York: Guilford Press, 1991.
INGLEHART, RONALD. *Culture Shift in Advanced Industrial Society.* Princeton, NJ: Princeton University Press, 1990.
LOMBARDI, LOUIS G. *Moral Analysis: Foundations, Guides, and Applications.* Albany, NY: State University of New York Press, 1988.
NAROLL, RAOUL. *The Moral Order.* Beverly Hills, CA.: Sage, 1983.
ZAVALLONI, MARISA. "Values." In Harry C. Triandis and Richard W. Brislin, eds. *Handbook of Cross-Cultural Psychology.* Vol. 5, *Social Psychology.* Boston: Allyn and Bacon, 1980.

Wendell Bell

Values, Nonwestern

Most Western cultures derive their value systems from Greco-Roman civilization and Judeo-Christian ethics. Most of the non-Western world derives its value systems from the religious beliefs of Islam, Hinduism, and Buddhism, and the teachings of Confucianism. Globalism makes it prudent for all to understand other value systems and cultures.

Islam

The law of Islam is called the shariah or pathway. The *Pathway* in the Qur'an outlines and regulates public order as well as individual and social morality, etiquette, personal hygiene, and religious ritual. The *Pathway* divides all human actions into five categories: obligatory, recommended, permit-ted, disapproved but not forbidden, and absolutely forbidden. The five pillars or framework of the Muslim life are: faith, prayer, charity, self-purification, and pilgrimage to Mecca for those who can afford it. While some Islamic societies are governed closely by the *Pathway*, most have elected to follow the general teachings but not its strict interpretation. Muslim ethics are based on the Law of Allah, as revealed in the Qur'an, which is binding on all Muslims.

Muslims believe in the Day of Judgment and individual accountability for actions and eternal life after death. Although Islam began on the Arabian peninsula, its influence is continuing to spread throughout the world. Nearly one billion people from all races, nationalities, and cultures are Muslims.

Hinduism

Hinduism embodies the spiritual vision built upon the basic and fundamental tenets of the *Vedas*. The *Vedas* constitute a religious body of thought developed by ancient Indian sages. The teachings are practical, stipulating specific steps leading to salvation and human transformation. The main values in life are defined by the sages as pleasure, wealth, fame, and liberation. Hindus believe in reincarnation; a person is born, dies, and is reborn. The form that one takes in rebirth is determined by the cumulative deeds performed in previous lives. Hindus believe that man and god are one and that to treat another poorly is to treat god poorly. The beliefs and practices of Hinduism have given India stability and unity. Since until recently, Hinduism was not expansionist like Islam and Christianity, the impact of its beliefs has been primarily limited to India. However, as the world becomes more interrelated, the influence of Hinduism may well expand.

Buddhism

Buddhism embraces four truths: life is suffering; the suffering of life is due to craving, desire, or thirst; the craving must be extinguished; and the craving is extinguished by the Noble Eightfold Path (right belief, purpose, speech, conduct, livelihood, effort, mind control, meditation). The two major divisions are Theravada and Mahayana. Within Theravada, the Eightfold Path leads to salvation, or Nirvana. In Mahayana, god is not abstract and Nirvana is a place, the Happy Land at the end of human life. Buddhism has high ethical content. Although it began in India, Buddhism is today the major religion of Sri Lanka, Myanmar, Thailand, Laos, Cambodia, and Vietnam, and is also important to China, Japan, and Korea. Modern life may be affecting Buddhism in that the craving for material things ("tanha") is stronger today than it was in earlier times.

Confucianism

Confucianism is a philosophy, not a religion. Confucius devoted his life to returning society to the rituals and values of the Chou Dynasty, a time he felt was perfect. His *Analects* is a collection of selected sayings that are the guiding rules of Confucianism. Some of the guiding rules are the virtue of goodness, the practice of reciprocity, and the cultivation of filial piety. Goodness is the basis of other virtues such as justice, religious and moral propricty, wisdom, and faithfulness. The practice of reciprocity is an expression of a give-and-receive morality, a golden rule for interpersonal relationships. The cultivation of filial piety stresses the preeminence of the family, emphasizing love and respect for parents, the acceptance of their wishes and concern for their welfare, solitude for the family fortunes, and the birth of children who would ensure the family's continuance. The ideal of Confucianism is *noblesse oblige*, or the serious pursuit of wisdom and cultivation of personal goodness by the members of the priviliged class. A basic idea of Confucianism is Jen, derived from a word meaning humanity or kindness. Jen consists of self-restraint, matching words with deeds, and possession of the qualities of firmness, resolution, simplicity, and prudence. The primary impact of Confucianism was in China. However, the modern Chinese government has attempted to replace the teachings of Confucius with those of Mao. On the surface, the moral philosophy of Confucius is suppressed, but deep within the heart of its adherents it continues to have a strong presence.

Conclusion

Chuang Tzu, the Taoist philosopher and Chinese mystic, sums up this topic well by saying that different cultures are differently constituted. With a brief introduction to four common religious/philosophic influences on values, one must guard against making broad generalizations. A common hope is that change will move all toward universality of beliefs and actions.

As cultures come into frequent, steady contact with global commerce and the broadcast and en-

tertainment media, film, and video, their value systems will be challenged. A melding of some values and the withering of others will surely occur. Since European values dominate the media and commerce, the dominant flow of values is clear.

See also BUDDHISM; CHANGE, CULTURAL; CHANGE, EPOCHAL; GLOBAL CULTURE; HINDUISM; ISLAM; LIFESTYLES, ALTERNATIVE; LIFESTYLES, ETHNIC; RELIGIONS, DECLINE OR RISE OF; RELIGIONS, STATISTICAL PROJECTIONS OF; VALUES CHANGE.

BIBLIOGRAPHY

CLEARY, THOMAS F. *The Essential Tao: An Initiation into the Heart of Taoism Through the Authentic Tao Te Ching and the Inner Teachings of Chuang Tzu.* San Francisco: HarperCollins, 1992.

DANTO, ARTHUR COLEMAN. *Mysticism and Morality: Oriental Thought and Moral Philosophy.* New York: Basic Books, 1978.

DUMOULIN, HEINRICH. *Buddhism in the Modern World.* New York: Macmillan, 1976.

FURER-HAIMENDORF, CHRISTOPH VON. *Morals and Merit: A Study of Values and Social Controls in South Asian Societies.* Chicago: University of Chicago Press, 1967.

HUSSAIN, ASAF; OLSEN, ROBERT; and QUARESHI, JAMIL, eds. *Orientalism, Islam and Islamists.* Brattleboro, VT: Amana Books, 1984.

PARK, O'HYUN. *Oriental Ideas in Recent Religious Thought.* Lakemont, GA: CSA Press, 1974.

SHOURIE, ARUN. *Hinduism, Essence and Consequence: A Study of the Upanishads, The Gita, and The Brahma-Sutras.* New Delhi, India: Vikas, 1979.

Robert Wagley

Values Change

The basic test of contemporary society is its ability to project and pursue strong goals and values.

The world is at the end of the half-millennium when the white nations of Europe and North America dominated world economic and political events. Part of this shift involves the rise of the Pacific Basin as the world's economic center of influence. Pacific Rim share of global GNP is projected to exceed 50 percent of the world total by 2040.

A great nation cannot have economic growth as its primary aim. Instead, economic growth is the result of having a great primary aim. America must consider how to restructure its approach to economics going beyond the short-term variables of monetary and fiscal policy. At an even deeper level, current economic models ignore factors such as cultural values, social costs, and human meaning. Cynicism and despair are dominant themes of America's culture. As a result, the U.S. economy is in for a continuing period of dislocation. For the belief system on which America's economy is based is in a state of profound transition.

This changing context has inevitable social effects. For example, in many relationships, contracts are replacing trust. Indeed, it should be asked whether today's America is bound together more by mutual interests than by shared convictions. A new approach to economics must somehow include all these elements: the significance of private property, the sanctity of the individual, equality before the law, universal education, social justice, human rights, child labor laws, equality of women, science as an engine of development, and collective bargaining, to name only a few.

At yet another level of consideration, America's policies need to embrace the long-term viability of ecosystems upon which sustainable development depends. Conserving and husbanding resources, not greedily exploiting them, is a part of the new economic ethic for survival. The environmental movement is an attempt to reintegrate ourselves with the Earth and the cycle of nature from which we tore ourselves during the Industrial Revolution and the subsequent urbanization.

No political party speaks of progress with any conviction or vision. Politicians speak only of change and solving problems. With many people, this translates into voter apathy. People are more skeptical than ever about politicians trying to sell them anything—especially when politicians do not relate to the scope of change that confronts contemporary society. What this comes down to is a widening public sense of the obsolescence and irrelevance of politics as a habit of mind and a means of progress. Confidence in progress has substantially waned. Indeed, most of the social agenda built on faith in progress has not been enacted into law.

Waning of Materialism

A materialist interpretation of history leaves out human fundamentals. It describes history in terms of how humans have organized the means of economic production. Material benefits have failed to raise the individual to a higher cultural and spiritual plane. Basically, contemporary culture tells us that there is no enduring meaning to life and nothing beyond material acquisition, sensual pleasure, or technical wizardry. It leaves out the expansion of human awareness, the role of individual curiosity as the driving force of knowledge accumulation, and the ensuing growth of the human spirit as the creative dynamic of history.

The materialist ethic and its corollary, the consumption ethic, did not suddenly emerge in the 1950s. America's consumer society had been launched in the 1890s. In 1899 Thorstein Veblen published the *Theory of the Leisure Class,* in which he coined the phrase "conspicuous consumption" to describe American materialistic habits. Delayed by the Great Depression and World War II, the consumer society burst forth with all its pent-up power in the 1950s. Households were gripped with a frenzy of consumption. Economic growth became an end in itself. The consumer society also became a "throwaway society," and "planned obsolescence" promoted a never-ending succession of minor changes in "must have" goods. What we have had cannot truly be described as a standard of "living." It is more a standard of "having." And the more we have, the less we seem to enjoy life. We have learned that gross domestic happiness does not automatically rise in lockstep with the gross domestic product.

The new assumption about the economy must be based on a fundamental but forgotten tenet: that wealth is a means to an end, not an end in itself. With all the labor saving devices, we have less time and are more hassled than ever. We have concentrated on the means but lost sight of the ends.

For those sated with materialism and acquisitions, the quest has shifted to: experiences, instead of things; self-development; mastery of new skills; trendy activities or thrills; and fulfillment of lifetime fantasies.

Postindustrial Paradigm

The set of values and lifestyles that hallmarked the Industrial Era is being outmoded. Rational, reductionistic, linear, quantitative, materialistic principles, and a focus on self-interest and instant gratification are waning in importance.

The Postindustrial Paradigm is a new set of guiding principles that entail collaboration, utilitarian common good, communitarianism, pluralistic diversity, global outlook, critical dialogue, qualitative (distinguished from merely quantitative) criteria for wants and needs.

The litany of this change is long and involves changed outlook and emphasis covering most every aspect of human affairs. Following are some important shifts from one state of affairs to another:

Values Change

- From primary and secondary industries (agriculture and industrial manufacturing) to tertiary and quaternary sectors (services and knowledge-based enterprise).
- From Maslowian values posited on survival, to security, then to belongingness and esteem, and eventually to self-actualization (realizing one's innermost potentials).
- From physical goods to less tangible services.
- From goods and services produced by muscle power to those produced by programmable machines (robots), cybernetics, and electronic data processing.
- From unassisted brainpower to knowledge assisted and amplified by electronic data processing.
- From the materialistic to the sensate.
- From a secular to a new religiosity, a search for inner meaning and purpose.
- From things to experiences.
- From basic necessities to amenities and eventually to a higher order of psychological and spiritual fulfillments.
- From physiological to psychological needs.
- From science posited on physical or "hard" sciences to one based on social or "soft" sciences.
- From strict order to chaos theory.
- From have-not (poverty) to having (shared abundance).
- From domineering self-interest to renewed emphasis on the broader social or communitarian interests.
- From quantity to quality.
- From few innovations and sparse introduction to a vast and varied array of new inventions.
- From scarcity to abundance.
- From a few stark choices to a bewildering array of choices.
- From a paucity of information to cascading "information overloads."
- From durability to disposables and planned obsolescence, then back again to recyclables, reclaimables.
- From ownership to rentalism.
- From continuity to change.
- From self-interest motivation to a compassionate humanitarian outlook.
- From independence and self-sufficiency to interdependence.
- From specialists to generalists.
- From relatively unbridled to increasingly restrained individual freedom.
- From profit maximization (squeezing blood out of the turnip) to profitability (balancing stakeholder interests).
- From a puritan hard-work ethic to a leisure-dominated lifestyle.
- From privileges transformed into rights and "entitlements" to resumption of a greater measure of individual responsibility and self-help.
- From Darwinian self-survival of the fittest to humanistic security short of the "all-caring" paternal state.
- From small-scale atomistic undertakings to large-scale pluralistic institutions.
- From domestic to international and global perspectives.
- From national to multinational and "one-world" scale in most organized endeavors.
- From centralization to decentralization.
- From simple to complex.
- From the obvious to subtle and not humanly discernible phenomena.
- From irrational to logical planning to chaos-based change.

Despite the problems and perils of our times, we should take heart that we are living at this moment in history. As Arthur Clarke reminds us, every collective human enterprise is like a surf rider carried forward on the crest of a wave. The wave bearing us has scarcely started its run; those who thought it was already slackening spoke centuries too soon.

Our intellectual purpose must transcend crass partisan politics. It must gain insight into why things are awry and provide some new visions for piecing together the new mosaic, whatever that may be. Vision requires discerning the potential purpose which is hidden in the chaos of the moment yet which could bring new potentials for persons and nations.

In every era, in every region of the world, the evolution of enlarged expressions of life has been evoked by individual men and women. Humanity does not advance as a result of the collective; it advances through individual effort.

Someone needs to do for this phase of American life what Madison, Jefferson, and others did for an earlier period. Somewhere in America are potential Emersons, Whitmans, Melvilles, Coles, Churches, Innesses, Gershwins, Sandburgs—the spirits that see beyond our present horizon, who sense new dimensions of life being birthed that the rest of us cannot yet see.

Clearly there is no formula or blueprint to build the next phase of the American experiment, fashioning human and social relationships that will take us through the coming century. It is an unending process, a process that is at the same time economic and political, but above all psychological and moral: the opening up of the greatest vistas of possibility America has ever known.

See also CHANGE; CHANGE, EPOCHAL; ETHICS; MORALS; VALUES; VALUES, NONWESTERN; VALUES FORMATION.

BIBLIOGRAPHY

BLOOM, ALLAN. *Closing of the American Mind*. New York: Simon & Schuster, 1987.

ELGIN, DUANE. *Voluntary Simplicity: Toward a Way of Life That Is Outwardly Simple, Inwardly Rich*. New York: William Morrow, 1981.

HARMAN, WILLIS W. *An Incomplete Guide to the Future*. New York: W. W. Norton, 1979.

ROSENAU, PAULINE MARIE. *Post-Modernism and the Social Sciences: Insights, Inroads, and Intrusions*. Princeton, N.J.: Princeton University Press, 1992.

STRAUSS, WILLIAM, and HOWE, NEIL. *Generations: The History of America's Future, 1584–2069*. New York: William Morrow, 1991.

VAGO, STEVEN. *Social Change*. New York: Holt, Rinehart, and Winston, 1980.

Graham T. T. Molitor
William Van Dusen Wishard

Values Formation

Values apply to many areas: economics, community service, family, politics, religious practices, work ethic, and so on. They vary by region, age, sex, ethnic background, and so forth. Webster defines *values* as "the qualities, customs, standards, and principles of a people regarded as desirable." If what was previously held desirable no longer applies, what caused the transition, and what does the future hold?

James Q. Wilson finds that we learn to cope with peoples of the world because we learn to cope with members of our family. The family is our central, value-shaping institution. It is argued that changes in the traditional family, which altered childbearing and parenting, significantly contributed to changing Americans' values and helped foster the growth of violence.

In past decades, the values of the young were largely shaped by parents, clergy, and teachers. Families typically consisted of a mother and father, and often were extended, with grandparents sharing values that spanned several generations. From largely nuclear, multigenerational families, the United States now consists of many single-parent families, and one-third of Americans are in blended or stepfamilies (i.e., families including children from previous marriages). In 1940, 90 percent of households were married couples. By 1992 the number had declined to 55 percent, and almost 50 percent of children were in one-parent households. The family is no longer the cradle of value formation. The influence of the clergy has also declined markedly. Religious-group membership had dropped from 73 percent of the population in 1965 to 65 percent by 1990. In *The Culture of Disbelief*, Stephen L. Carter argues that liberal attitudes led to belittling religious devotion, humiliating believers, and discouraging religion as a serious activity. Churchgoing families often pursue lifestyles markedly different from the principles espoused by their churches.

Teachers no longer command the respect they previously enjoyed. In some places, they are threatened with bodily harm for failing to pass students. Certain forms of discipline have been legally forbidden, further weakening the role of the teacher.

Violence among the young, including preteens, is widespread, embracing all ethnic groups and urban and rural communities. What drove our society to these appalling conditions and, most important, are those driving factors likely to change in the coming decade?

The Driving Forces

Marriage and the family have lost their sanctity and significance for several reasons. Easily obtainable contraception markedly changed attitudes about marriage and about pre- and postmarriage sex.

Divorce became common and more acceptable. By the early 1990s, the United States had the highest divorce rate in the industrialized world. Fifty percent of marriages resulted in divorce.

Employment trends may be the most important factor in divorce and child care and, ultimately, in the value formation of the young. Changing attitudes about women's roles, their increased access to higher education, and financial pressures led to major increases in women's participation in the workforce. These pressures and newly won nonfinancial independence made divorce seem a less threatening step.

In the United States, the changes in family values also reflect a deliberate choice to accept single parenthood. About one million children per year are born out of wedlock. By 1993, there were 24 million single mothers in the United States, and 25 percent of babies were born to unwed mothers in

1992, in contrast with only 10 percent in 1970. Two-thirds of black babies are born to unwed mothers. The black community is now experiencing three and even four generations of unwed mothers. Many argue that government programs providing child support to unwed and single-parent families also contribute to these trends.

If not the parents, the clergy, or the schools, who then are shaping our current and future values? The young are largely influenced by their peers, and by sports heroes, stars of the entertainment world, media commentators, and even cartoon characters. Peer pressure has supplanted previous influences as one of the most important factors in shaping the values of the young. Economic conditions exert a significant effect on the family structure. The inability to obtain employment creates family tensions, often causing families to break up. In the absence of the discipline of a structured family, school dropout rates, especially among blacks, have created large groups of young adults with few or no job prospects and much time on their hands.

Growing numbers of young adults, unable or uninterested in a college education, find employment unavailable or unacceptably demeaning. The lack of adequate employment creates a feeling of disenfranchisement, despair, and anger. The drug trade offers the enticement of easy and immediate access to wealth for the young of all ethnic groups. Lacking a strong father image, youths turn to television and popular music to establish a personal code of ethics. Children view television for five to seven hours daily, often devoting more time to it than to school. Violence is an integral ingredient in much of television. Popular entertainers often express racist and anti–law-enforcement values.

Future Possibilities

Are Americans likely to revert to traditional values? The divorce rate has declined somewhat recently, but it is not likely that divorce will soon be viewed as an undesirable step, even when children are involved.

There are indications that stay-at-home mothers are becoming more fashionable, at least in pockets of middle- and upper-middle-class Americans. If the pendulum continues to swing back and stay-at-home mothers gain respect, the more traditional lines of communication and value transfer are likely to return. But this is not likely in large numbers by the turn of the century, especially among young, unwed mothers.

Employment is unlikely to become significantly more available to young dropouts or to the less skilled, either through more effective education, job retraining, or increased demand for products and services. With birthrates below replacement levels and an aging population, consumer demands will not be sufficient to create significant job growth.

The clergy are not likely to become significantly more influential in value formation, and inner-city conditions seemingly perpetuate the inability of teachers to inculcate appropriate values among the very group most in need.

The more likely means of altering current value trends is through the message content in the many forms of media to which the young and adults have access. Clearly, a salient feature of the future use of information technology lies largely in shaping human behavior—i.e., the values—of individuals and groups.

The largest use of many of these technologies over the next several years is likely to be along the lines of exciting the psyche rather than for educational purposes. Hence, the media are more likely to contribute to promulgating violence than detracting from it by the year 2000. Americans have become hyphenated: Afro-, Cuban-, Chinese-, Korean- (and so on) Americans. Fostering cultural diversity has a downside. The ability to understand and, thus, hold common values is often precluded by the inability to share a common language. Alexis de Tocqueville said, "The tie of language is perhaps the strongest and most durable that can unite mankind."

As the United States evolves to a post-Anglo demography, values regarding family life, child bearing, and parenting may move away from the so-called standard American values.

A Challenge for the Future

As Americans experienced unprecedented economic growth in the late 1950s to late 1980s, society became extremely permissive in its attitudes about sexual freedom, business practices, and violence in all forms of entertainment as well as individual lifestyles. Attention to career and materialism supplanted attention to family and children.

The information age is an integral part of the lives of each and every American. How we choose to shape the content of the information, while adhering to First Amendment rights, will be the key to our future values.

See also BEHAVIOR: SOCIAL CONSTRAINTS: CHILD ABUSE; CHILD CARE; CHILDREN, LIVING AR-

RANGEMENTS; CRIME, VIOLENT; CRIME RATES; CULTURE AND SOCIETY; DIVORCE; FAMILY PATTERNS; FAMILY PROBLEMS; FAMILY VALUES; HOLISTIC BELIEFS; HOUSEHOLD COMPOSITION; SOCIAL CONTROLS; VALUES; VALUES CHANGE; WOMEN AND WORK; WOMEN'S MOVEMENT.

BIBLIOGRAPHY

BENNETT, WILLIAM. *The Book of Virtues.* New York: Simon & Schuster, 1994.

CLEVELAND, HARLAN, and WILSON, THOMAS W. *Humangrowth: An Essay on Growth, Values and the Quality of Life.* Lanham, MD: University Press of America, 1978.

FEATHER, NORMAN T. *Values in Education and Society.* New York: Free Press, 1975.

HALL, BRIAN. *Developing Human Values.* Wilton, CT: MC International Values Institute, 1990.

HARRISON, LAWRENCE E. *Who Prospers? How Cultural Values Shape Economic and Political Success.* New York: Basic Books, 1992.

Harold S. Becker

Video Games.

See INTERACTIVE ENTERTAINMENT.

Virtual Reality.

See INTERACTIVE ENTERTAINMENT.

Visionary Thinking

The future is something we create. Each of us, individually and collectively, is an architect of destiny. Our fate depends upon our own ability and resolve. Each act contributes in its own way to the cosmic course. Each new life is an empty tablet to be filled. The greatness resides in each of us. Michelangelo started with a blank block, Shakespeare with an empty manuscript, Rembrandt with a void canvas. Yet the creations of each have inspired the world ever since their souls touched reality. Inspiration and resolve are the stuff of greatness that generates enduring odes. Today entire nations are desperately searching for vision—for a sense of purpose that leads to a better tomorrow. How to draw that mindset is the problem.

We all can borrow a page or two from others. Today Japan, the second largest economic superpower, achieved this global prominence and domestic prosperity despite the fact that it is geographically smaller than the state of California. Greatness comes in all different sizes. People should never sell themselves short. This remarkable achievement is due, in no small measure, to the vision of a single person—Kakuei Tanaka. Best known as a former prime minister of Japan, Tanaka created the grand vision largely responsible for the transformation of Japan into a model of economic growth and prosperity. The essential ideas, powerful vision, and far-reaching sense of hope were rounded out during the time Tanaka headed the awesome Ministry of International Trade and Industry. The plan clearly staked out where Japan stood and where it might be in fifteen years. Herman KAHN, the great futurist, once remarked, "In fifteen years—given the means and resources—virtually anything the human mind can conceive it can create." Tanaka's vision eventually catapulted him into chairmanship of the Liberal Democratic party and to the office of prime minister. A Commission for Remodeling the Japanese Archipelago was constituted to elaborate details and foster support to carry these fancies into reality. Japan was driven by a dream, a modern-day example of visionary leadership from which each of us—individuals and nations alike—can draw.

The longest journey begins with the first step. Steps are not always tried and true. We can, after all, step off in the wrong direction. But we always have the ability to stop, change direction, and start anew. Visions do not have to be great or even right to be enduring.

Deciding what things are worth doing and getting them done—these two fundamental jobs of a leader in the future are the same two fundamental tasks that have faced leaders in the past. The difference now—the unprecedented difference in our time—is telecommunications technology, which links nations, corporations, groups, tribes, and individuals. For the first time in history, it is becoming possible for the entire globe to pay attention to deciding what things are worth doing and actually getting them done.

The promise of telecommunications technology was constrained by the Cold War. Only now, for the first time since telecommunications effectively interconnected the world, there are not two giant, well-armed spheres of influence habitually opposing each other. For the first time since telecommunications have been instantaneous, it has become technologically and politically conceivable that most nations, corporations, and other powerful groups could agree that some things are worth doing and get them done.

The opportunity, therefore, for global visionary leadership, is unprecedented. Also unprecedented is the number of diverse parties keenly alert to the fact that their ox might be gored by changes proposed by visionary leaders. These parties are, of course, instantaneously informed by telecommunications technology. How, then, can a would-be leader, simultaneously empowered and skewered by the double-edged sword of global instantaneous communication, decide on what goals to pursue and what means to pursue them with?

Take as an example a specific global issue: the health of the oceans. It is quite conceivable that, given the global communications infrastructure already in place, a single party willing to commit a quarter of a billion dollars to the effort could lead an international project that significantly affects the health of the oceans.

Three tracks of endeavor are necessary to decide what is worth doing and how to get it done. The work of these three tracks must be simultaneous and interactive. Teleconferencing and e-mail via the Internet or Worldwide Web make this affordable. The first track, which involves deciding what things are worth doing, must be an international task force of scientists who possess two characteristics: they must be respected internationally, and they must have wisdom at least equal to their egos. The second track must be an international group of experts in geopolitics and economics. These people must identify who benefits and whose ox is gored by doing what the first track determines is worth doing. This track must also identify how those whose ox is gored can be compensated by those who benefit from proposed change. These people should also be respected in their countries and wise beyond factionalism or partisan politics. The third track must be an international team of public relations experts who can educate the power players and their myriad constituencies about what is worth doing, and what they stand to gain by getting it done.

Such is the leverage of the extant telecommunications infrastructure that a single wealthy individual could put together a small group of knowledgeable and wise people—a "kitchen cabinet"—that could then locate, enroll, and coordinate the three tracks: a single visionary leader could enlist the best help of much of the world to decide the best course to take.

See also CHANGE, OPTIMISTIC AND PESSIMISTIC PERSPECTIVES; CONTINUITY AND DISCONTINUITY; DYSTOPIAS; ENVIRONMENTAL INDICATORS; FORECASTING, MISTAKES IN; GLOBAL CONSCIOUSNESS; LEADERSHIP; NEAR, MID-, AND LONG-TERM FUTURES; PLANNING; SCENARIOS; SOCIAL INDICATORS; STRATEGIC PLANNING; SURVEYS; TREND INDICATORS; UTOPIAS.

BIBLIOGRAPHY

BOULDING, ELISE, and BOULDING, KENNETH E. *The Future: Images and Purposes.* Thousand Oaks, CA: Sage Publications, 1994.

HEILBRONER, ROBERT. *Visions of the Future: The Distant Past, Yesterday, Today, Tomorrow.* New York: The New York Public Library/Oxford University Press, 1995.

LASZLO, ERVIN. *Vision 2020: Reordering Chaos for Global Survival.* Langhorne, PA: Gordon and Breach Science Publishers, 1994.

MANNERMAA, MIKE; INAYATULLAH, SOHAIL; and SLAUGHTER, RICHARD, eds. *Coherence and Chaos in Our Uncommon Futures: Visions, Means, and Actions.* Turku, Finland: Finland Futures Research Center, 1994.

OGILVY, JAMES. *Living Without a Goal: Finding the Freedom to Live a Creative and Innovative Life.* New York: Currency/Doubleday, 1995.

Kate McKeown

Visual Arts

Rapid changes lie ahead for the arts in the next century. Many of the economic, political, social, and technological factors that made this century the period of greatest change in the history of art will continue unabated. In many instances the rate of change will increase. New technology will fundamentally alter the art world and the appearance of art itself.

History demonstrates that technological changes can produce an enormous impact in the arts. For instance, the invention of portable tubes of paint in the mid-nineteenth century enabled artists to paint the landscape outdoors, leading to Impressionism, the first volley in the modernist revolution against the Old Master tradition of European art. The invention of photography in 1839 further coopted the mimetic perceptual approach because the camera could produce amazingly realistic, fast, and facile copies. Painters turned more and more to abstraction, symbolism, and other less perceptual stylistic elements harder for the camera to capture.

To fully understand the scale of this shift to Modernism in art, one needs to recognize that artistic activity exists between two poles: the perceptual and the conceptual. At the perceptual extreme an artist imitates or re-creates something observed from life. At the conceptual extreme an artist creates an image from the imagination, an image often more symbolic than descriptive. Technological, social, economic, and other changes in the nineteenth century encouraged artists to create more abstract, conceptual images derived from feelings, philosophies, psychology, and the formal elements of the medium in which they worked.

In the late-twentieth century, the electronics revolution of the Post-Modern era has had a similar effect on the arts that will continue for at least the next few decades. Computers can create flawless "electronic collages" by allowing artists to originate or scan borrowed imagery into the computer and then interact upon that imagery by combining and altering images. Photographs can be seamlessly altered to place one person's head on another's body. Similarly figures can be added or deleted, thereby creating seemingly authentic records of scenes that never actually occurred. The films *Forrest Gump*, *Zelig*, and *Dead Men Don't Wear Plaid* display the use of this in popular media. Through the use of this technology, the actor Tom Hanks in *Forrest Gump* appears in a scene with President John Kennedy, even though the president was assassinated more than thirty years before the scene was filmed.

The potential exists to edit imagery as easily as text, and this capability will be further exploited in the future. Paradoxically, the veracity of the photographic image has been increasingly debunked as the veristic aspects of the medium have increased. As computers begin to assist in projecting holographic images (three-dimensional illusions) combined with virtual-reality technology now under development, the creation of three-dimensional, life-like "fictions" will be possible. Traditional painting and sculpture will merge in works of astonishing illusionism. Already the compact disc, digitalization, and desktop video technology are altering the medium of photography in basic ways. The new compact disc photography places images directly from the film onto a plastic disc, obviating the traditional use of negatives and prints. Displayed on a computer or television monitor, there is no need for prints and traditional albums to hold them. The traditions of 150 years of photography are being made obsolete. As E-mail and electronic publishing become more widespread, there may come a time when there is no need for the objects known as photographs—all photographic images will be electronic.

Already artists like Dan Flavin, Michael Hayden, Jenny Holzer, Bruce Nauman, Nam June Paik, and James Turrell (among many others) are exploring the new technologies in works of art that defy the traditional media categories.

The politicization of art may intensify in the future as the power of art to influence public opinion and political, economic, and social change is more clearly recognized and exploited. Already issues such as sexism, racism, and homophobia have been exploited by both artists and politicians. Artists like Hans Haacke (in his 1990 sculpture *Helmsboro*) have responded to the demagogues and self-proclaimed art censors.

Artists like Jeff Koons, Robert Mapplethorpe, and Andres Serrano have been grossly misrepresented and vilified by the Radical Right and the increasingly diminished, tabloid-like media, with the artists and their art turned into opportunities for political advantage and disinformation. The increasingly hostile political polarization and economic stratification in the United States may lead to a decline in American leadership in the arts. The climate of censorship (and resulting fearful self-censorship), the hostility of many in government and politics to the arts, and the gradual erosion of funding for the arts in the United States since the 1960s (especially compared with European countries) point to a loss of cultural leadership. If Paris was the capital of the art world in the nineteenth and early twentieth centuries, and New York the capital of the latter twentieth century, trends seem to indicate that there will be no art capital in the twenty-first century. Rather the art world will become even more diffuse and decentralized.

Again technology is providing the wherewithal. Not only have art dealers, auction houses, and museums gone on line using computers to keep records and process information, but some galleries already exist only on-line with the dealers using high-resolution computers to transmit images to prospective clients, thus eliminating the overhead and necessity of physical gallery space. Museums are rushing to produce microgalleries that place collection information and high-resolution images into the computer. Through the use of CD-ROM and computer networks, one can now browse the collections of the world's great museums without leaving the comfort of home. While no reproductions can yet (and may never) replace the actual work of art, the high-resolution computer images and accompanying information undeniably provide a revolution in the accessibility of great art. Virtual exhibitions may arrive electronically at home as increased terrorism makes public life or gatherings (in theaters, galleries, and museums) too dangerous.

Perhaps the greatest challenge of the next century will be elitism. All of the new technologies promise art that is more integrated with daily life for those who have access to the technology. The gulf between the haves and the have-nots is rapidly widening, particularly in the United States, where only 1 percent of the richest now control 40 percent of the wealth, and the top 9 percent control 70 percent. Consequently there is a trend toward a well-informed elite with great access to the expensive new technology, a heretofore incredible potential. At the same time, the rest of the population will perhaps become more isolated from the arts than ever before.

See also ARCHITECTURAL DESIGN; ART DEALERS; ARTS; CREATIVITY; INDUSTRIAL DESIGN; INTERACTIVE ENTERTAINMENT; LITERATURE; PRINTED WORD; MOTION PICTURES; MUSIC; PHOTOGRAPHY; RECORDING INDUSTRY.

BIBLIOGRAPHY

ALLOWAY, LAWRENCE. *Network: Art and the Complex Present*, edited by Donald Kuspit. Ann Arbor, MI: Books on Demand, 1984.
KEPES, GYÖRGY. *The Visual Arts Today.* Ann Arbor, MI: Books on Demand, 1993.
MATANOVIC, MILENKO. *Lightworks: Explorations in Art, Culture, and Creativity.* Issaquah, WI: Lorian Press, 1986.
McCONNELL, R. B., ed. *Art, Science, and Human Progress.* Englewood, NJ: Universe, 1983.
RICHARDSON, JOHN. *Art: The Way It Is.* 4th ed. Englewood Cliffs, NJ: Prentice-Hall, 1991.

Robin Thorne Ptacek

Voting

Democratic electoral systems are most likely to evolve and become institutionalized in societies where politically relevant resources, including the capacity to employ armed force or violence, are relatively widely distributed outside the control of the central government. Generally, electoral processes are introduced when governments face economic difficulties, military demands, or internal political challenges that require them to seek popular support on a regular basis. Few ruling groups, however, are anxious to see these channels effectively used by their political foes. At some point in every nation's electoral history, incumbent elites have sought to suppress their electoral opponents. In the United States, the ruling Federalists sought, through the Alien and Sedition Acts of 1798, to outlaw the Jeffersonian opposition. Hamilton and other Federalist leaders also considered a plan for the military suppression of the Jeffersonians. The military weakness of the national government, however, precluded any serious Federalist effort to crush an opposition that controlled several state governments and their militias.

Military force is by no means the only important factor. Where other politically relevant resources, such as wealth, education, communications, and organization, are widely diffused and outside the state's control, there is less likelihood that incumbent elites can eliminate their opponents. The relative absence of these resources helps to explain why democratic electoral institutions have not usually persisted in the nations of the Third World and raises questions about the prospects for their persistence in Eastern Europe.

Voters

In most nations, contending forces use a variety of different appeals to link themselves to popular followings. The most effective and durable appeals are those based upon voters' class, religious, or ethnic identifications and regional attachments. Analysts often attempt to interpret election results mainly in terms of the preferences and characteristics of voters. Thus, it is often said that Catholic voters or African-American voters, or working class voters have particular preferences and behave in particular ways. The actual political significance of voters' race, class, or religion depend, however, upon when, how, on what basis, and by whom a particular group is electorally mobilized. Moreover, voter's choices depend upon the alternatives presented to them. Given a choice between a fool and a rogue, voters must select either a fool or a rogue. Thus, to understand voting behavior it may be more useful to concentrate upon the characteristics and actions of competing parties and candidates than to focus upon the attributes of voters.

Parties and Candidates in American Elections

In the United States, the Republican party won five of the six presidential elections held between 1968 and 1988. During this period, Democratic party candidates were handicapped by the twin problems of ideology and race. The Democratic party's nominating processes had produced candidates and platforms that were seen as too liberal by the general electorate. At the same time, the issue of race divided the party. In 1992, however, the Democrats were able to successfully handle both these problems.

Moderate Democrats had long argued that the party needed to present a more centrist image to be competitive in national elections. In 1992, the party chose as its presidential and vice presidential candidates Governor Bill Clinton and Sen. Al Gore. The platform adopted at the party's national convention was the most conservative in decades, stressing individual responsibility and private enterprise while implicitly criticizing welfare recipients. Thus, Clinton became the first Democratic presidential candidate in two decades who was not burdened by an excessively liberal image.

The Clinton-Gore ticket won 43 percent of the popular vote and 370 electoral votes. The Republican incumbents, Bush and Quayle, received 38 percent of the popular vote and only 168 electoral votes. Nineteen percent of the popular vote went to independent candidate Ross Perot. Economic recession, the end of the Cold War, and the Democrats' new-found moderation on matters of race and ideology combined to oust the Republicans from the White House for the first time in twelve years.

After two years of legislative struggle, however, marked by charges that Clinton had sought to govern as a liberal despite his moderate positions in the 1992 campaign, the Clinton administration suffered a stunning defeat in the November 1994 national elections. For the first time since 1946, Republicans won simultaneous control of both houses of Congress. This put the GOP in a position to block President Clinton's legislative efforts and to promote its own policy agenda.

In Senate races, the Republicans realized a net gain of eight seats to achieve a 52–48 majority. Immediately after the election, Sen. Richard Shelby of Alabama, a conservative Democrat who frequently voted with the Republicans, announced that he was formally joining the GOP. This gave the Republicans 53 votes in the upper chamber. In House races, the Republicans gained an astonishing 52 seats to win a 230–204 majority (1 seat is held by an independent). While the Republicans had controlled the Senate as recently as 1986, the House of Representatives had been a Democratic bastion since 1954.

Republicans also posted a net gain of eleven governorships and won control of fifteen additional chambers in state legislatures. A number of the Democratic party's leading figures were defeated. These included Gov. Mario Cuomo of New York, former House Ways and Means committee chairman Dan Rostenkowski of Illinois, House Judiciary committee chairman Jack Brooks of Texas, three-term Sen. Jim Sasser of Tennessee and, most shocking of all, House Speaker Thomas Foley of Washington. Foley was the first sitting Speaker to be defeated for reelection to his own congressional seat since 1860. All told, thirty-four incumbent Democratic congressmen, three incumbent Democratic Senators and four incumbent Democratic governors went down to defeat. On the Republican side, not one of the ten incumbent senators, fifteen incumbent governors, or 155 incumbent House members seeking reelection was defeated. The South, which had voted Republican in presidential elections for twenty years, now seemed to have turned to the GOP at the congressional level as well. Republicans posted gains among nearly all groups in the populace, with white, male voters, in particular, switching to the GOP. The nation's electoral map had been substantially altered. Interest in the hard-fought race had even produced a slight increase in voter turnout, albeit to a still abysmal 39 percent.

In the wake of their electoral triumph, Republicans moved to name Robert Dole of Kansas to the post of Senate Majority Leader, and Rep. Newt Gingrich of Georgia to the House Speakership. Only two years earlier, Gingrich had been widely viewed as a Republican "firebrand" whose vitriolic attacks on the House leadership were usually dismissed by the media as dangerous and irresponsible. Other Republicans who would move to leadership positions included arch-conservative nonagenarian Sen. Strom Thurmond of South Carolina, who replaced Sam Nunn of Georgia as chairman of the Senate Armed Services committee, and outspoken Clinton critic Alphonse D'Amato of New York, who would now head the Senate Banking committee. At the same time, Rep. Floyd Spence, a conservative South Carolinian, replaced Ron Dellums of California, an avowed pacifist, as Chairman of the House Armed Services Committee. The 1994 election seemed to represent a nationwide repudiation of the Democratic party and appeared to give the Republicans their best chance in a generation to become the nation's majority party.

Voter Turnout

Over the past several decades, voter turnout in the United States has been declining sharply. At the turn of the century, more than 80 percent of those eligible voted in national presidential elections. In recent presidential elections by contrast, voter turnout has barely exceeded 50 percent. In 1992, turnout was 56 percent. Moreover, of those who actually voted in 1992, 19 percent cast protest votes for billionaire Ross Perot. This may suggest a long-term decline in popular confidence in the American political process—something that should alarm the leaders of both national parties.

See also DEMOCRACY; DEMOCRATIC PROCESS; POLITICAL CAMPAIGNING; POLITICAL CYCLES; POLITICAL PARTIES; POLITICAL PARTY REALIGN- MENT; PUBLIC OPINION; THIRD POLITICAL PARTIES.

BIBLIOGRAPHY

BLACK, EARL, and BLACK, MERLE. *The Vital South: How Presidents Are Elected.* Cambridge, MA: Harvard University Press, 1992.

CAMPBELL, ANGUS; CONVERSE, PHILIP E.; MILLER, WARREN E.; and STOKES, DONALD E. *The American Voter.* New York: John Wiley, 1960.

GINSBERG, BENJAMIN. *The Consequences of Consent.* New York: Basic Books, 1992.

Benjamin Ginsberg

W

Warming, Global.

See CLIMATE AND METEOROLOGY; GLOBAL WARMING.

Wastes, Hazardous.

See HAZARDOUS WASTES.

Wastes, Solid.

See SOLID WASTES.

Wealth

Wealth is defined as all the goods and resources of economic value held by an individual or group—all assets including cash; savings and checking accounts; stocks, bonds, and other equities; real estate; jewels and precious metals; art; and other collectibles. Income, a narrower concept, includes payment derived from wages, salaries, and investments. Wealth and income are not interchangeable concepts.

The position of individuals or groups within the social stratification system is a product of their wealth, power, and prestige. A class system of social stratification delineates a hierarchy of classes of distinct social layers whose members share similar economic, political, and cultural characteristics. Although finer gradations can be identified, the simplest division is into upper, middle, and lower classes. The upper class is made up of the wealthy, the industrialists and entrepreneurs, the top executives, and the best paid professionals. The upper class, particularly the upper upper class, is growing. The lower class, made up of basic service sector workers, day laborers, and the poor, is also growing. The middle class, made up of white-collar workers, the majority of professionals, skilled craftsmen, and skilled laborers, is shrinking. Some stratification system classifications combine the upper portion of the lower class and the lower segment of the middle class, and identify it as the working class. This group, while holding its own in terms of numbers, is declining in terms of real income and accumulated wealth, and is increasingly composed of individuals who were previously solidly middle class. These trends are likely to continue.

Demographic changes suggest that the nature of the social classes is also shifting. Specifically, the rich are not just getting larger in numbers, but are getting richer as well. The poor below the poverty line are remaining about the same, but the number of abject poor is growing, and the relative poor, or so-called marginals, are becoming poorer as well as growing in numbers. The middle class as a whole is getting noticeably poorer.

Wealth, Income, and Growth

Much attention is given to examining, explaining, predicting, and ultimately to justifying and promoting the growth of income and wealth. Economic growth is typically cast as a very good thing and something to be fostered. Growth can make the national balance sheet look better, but it can have substantial unintended costs, such as personal decline and social dislocation. There has not been nearly the same amount of academic and public attention paid to the distribution of income and wealth, changes in the composition of social class and the distribution of wealth, and the impact of class composition on the society.

Much of the discussion about the poor has been in terms of "how much are they costing society?" rather than "how did they come to be poor?" and "what do they do?" The discussion of the rich is often the reverse. That is, the questions are "what do they do?" and "how did they get rich?" rather than "how much are they costing society?" These questions suggest that society does not use uniform yardsticks to examine wealth across various segments of itself.

The poor are judged as being costly to society, but the loss in revenue from the rich person's tax exempt bonds can far surpass the cost of welfare for the poor neighbor. Wealth determines social status, but that status is the result of social judgment as well as assets and debits.

In the mid-twentieth century, entrepreneurs found that capitalism functions better when the system emphasizes creating modestly affluent consumers rather than exploiting its workforce. More profit results from greater consumer demand than from increased profit margins per item. During the last two decades of the twentieth century, this lesson has been forgotten again, as "supply side" and "trickle down" economics has been a dominant social policy, thereby permitting the rich to get richer and causing the middle class to get poorer. Momentum will carry this trend into the beginning of the twenty-first century, after which it is likely that individuality, the demand for fairness, and the desire for a share of the American dream will reassert itself.

The United States has always been a society with a substantial middle class, substantial in terms of both numbers and actual wealth. The middle class emerged shortly after the country's founding, prospered as a result of industrialization following the Civil War, and survived the panics of 1873, 1893, and 1907, enjoying the Gilded Age and the Roaring Twenties. The bubble burst in October 1929, and there were hard times for about a decade. The hard times affected people differently: the solidly comfortable remained so, the high flyers "crashed," many comfortably middle-class persons became marginal, and much of the lower middle class dropped down into impoverishment. World War II brought employment, productivity, and relative affluence to society and to most of its members. These good times continued for three decades. After World War II, the United States experienced an international success rarely seen before. It has been suggested that given the shambles that the infrastructure of Europe, the Eastern bloc, and Asia had become, America did not outcompete the rest of the world—it simply won by default. With the ascendancy of Japan and industrialized Asia, and of the economic union in Europe, the international role of the U.S. will change. America continues to have enormous natural and social resources to draw upon, so it will continue as a military power and will continue to be a major exporter of food and manufactured goods, technology, and ideas.

America is squandering its material wealth with its huge national debt and wasting its social wealth by wasting its social capital. It educates some of its members very well but provides mediocre training for the majority. It is neither uncompromising with the incorrigible criminal, nor does it seek to rehabilitate the salvageable. Many in the population are cast off because they are of the wrong age, color, gender, or other attributes.

The record economic expansion following World War II began to slow discernibly in the mid-1970s (the 1974–1975 recession). This caused changes in the shape and structure of the socioeconomic classes as well as their size.

Wealth is both economic and social. It is relative, not absolute. Consequently, if current trends continue, the United States will continue to become richer, but will not keep pace with its rivals. The shrinking of the middle class is a decline of the social group that has been the heart of the industrialized world in general, and of the United States in particular.

Distribution of Wealth: The Declining Middle Class

Assets for most people are in their checking and savings accounts, and in their automobiles, which typically do not appreciate in value. Another two-thirds of the population have equity in their homes, which may appreciate but is not a liquid asset. Only about one quarter of the population has income-producing assets such as CDs and money market accounts, IRAs and Keoghs, stocks and bonds, and real estate. However, more than 70 percent of the aggregate household wealth in the United States is contained in these instruments. As of 1990, home equity accounts for only about 11 percent of all household wealth, only one point higher than it was in 1929.

The debt/equity ratio—i.e., debt as a proportion of household net worth (equity)—has grown from about 8 percent in 1950 to an overwhelming 26 percent in 1990, more than a threefold increase.

Among households with a net worth of less $100,000, homes accounted for 60 percent of the net worth and stocks and bonds were about 2 percent of assets. Among the wealthy with a net worth exceeding $1 million, homes accounted for only 9 percent of their net worth, and stocks and bonds were over 25 percent of their assets. A study of change in equity across the entire population showed that during a three-year period from 1983 to 1986, the disparity in net worth increased dramatically: increasing by 44 percent in households with more than $100,000 in income, increasing by only 10 percent among households with less than $100,000 in income, and not increasing at all in households with incomes under $10,000. In terms of the values of household assets, the findings are as one would expect: assets increase with age up to age sixty-five and then decrease, whites have more than minorities, married households are better off than single headed households, and family net worth is related to family income.

For less affluent families, their homes were not only their major asset but their major expense. From 1970 to 1990, the cost of housing went from 28 percent of family income to a staggering 44 percent of the household budget. Couple the high housing costs with wage stagnation and increasing job uncertainty, and it is easy to see how the middle class is being forced out of home ownership. Householders under thirty-five years old purchasing first homes dropped 5 percent between 1982 and 1989. If this trend continues, the youngest baby boomers and the next generation, variously called the thirteenth generation or generation X, will be more like their great-grandparents than their parents. That is, the young adults of today are facing declining employment opportunities, exorbitant housing and health care costs, and an uncertain national future reminiscent of the turn of the century rather than the postwar era.

In addition to frustrating the attainment of the American dream and eliminating jobs in the housing business, the trend away from home ownership will reduce wealth accumulation in the form of home equity across wide segments of society and will cause the population to be less rooted in their communities along with the concomitant loss of family stability. This is another example of how secondary consequences may be greater than the main effects.

The late 1970s and the decade of the '80s were a period of increasing inequality. The share of income obtained by the poorest quintile (20%) of the population fell from 5.4 to 4.6 percent from 1975 to 1990, whereas the total income share acquired by the highest quintile rose from 41.1 to 44.3 percent, and the top 5 percent increased their portion of total income from 15.5 to 17.4 percent (see Figure 1 and Table 1). These figures amount to a 15 percent decline for the poor in contrast to an 8 percent increase for the rich, and 12 percent increase for the richest 5 percent of the population. Another way to look at income inequality data is to derive Lorenz curves. The comparisons of the percentage of income accrued by specific segments of the society for 1975 and 1990 show that in the brief period of half a generation the inequality increased (Figure 2). Although macroeconomic growth occurred during the period, the poor did not benefit proportionately. From 1950 to 1990, the lowest and highest quintiles increased their share of total income by only 2 and 4 percent respectively. During that period the second and third quintiles (i.e., the middle class) lost 9 and 5 percent respectively (see Table 1). This is another illustration of the long-term erosion of the middle class, a trend not likely to reverse in the immediate future.

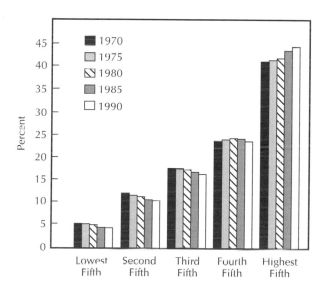

FIGURE 1. Income distribution

TABLE 1.   Income Distribution as a Percentage of Total Income of Families (All Races)

Year	Lowest Fifth	Second Fifth	Third Fifth	Fourth Fifth	Highest Fifth	Top 5 Percent
1950	4.5	11.9	17.4	23.4	42.8	17.3
1955	4.8	12.2	17.7	23.4	41.8	16.8
1960	4.8	12.2	17.8	24.0	41.3	15.9
1965	5.2	12.2	17.8	23.9	40.9	15.5
1970	5.4	12.2	17.6	23.8	40.9	15.6
1975	5.4	11.8	17.6	24.1	41.1	15.5
1980	5.1	11.6	17.5	24.3	41.6	15.3
1985	4.6	10.9	16.9	24.2	43.5	16.7
1990	4.6	10.8	16.6	23.8	44.3	17.4
Change:						
1975–1990	0.85	0.92	0.94	0.99	1.08	1.12
1950–1990	1.02	0.91	0.95	1.02	1.04	1.01

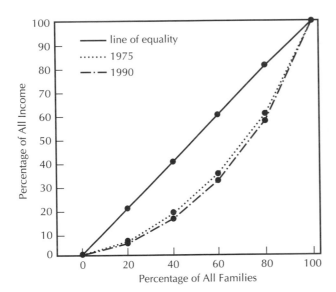

FIGURE 2.   Lorenz curve of income distribution

Increases in economic development tend to create greater, not less inequality. Average well-being increases, but there is no evidence of wider sharing of the created wealth. A wealthy few acquire most of the new wealth.

Inequity increases if society does not explicitly address its inequality. In the United States, the social policies of the 1930s reduced the inequality of the depression, and the economic boom that resulted from World War II continued the process. By the 1960s, the portion of the population living in poverty was 22 percent and unemployment was at 6 percent, three times higher than the levels dur-

ing war years. Social policy in the 1970s brought poverty levels down, but did not address general economic distribution inequalities. The social and economic policies of the 1980s magnified the distribution inequities.

These trends can be seen in Figure 3. This inequity was increasing from 1950 to 1975, but inequality dramatically increased from 1975 to 1990. There have been no clear changes in socioeconomic policy to suggest that there will be any dramatic shift in these trends.

For the next two or three decades, expect the poor to become better off on an absolute basis, but worse off on a relative basis. The lower-middle class will continue its downward economic slide.

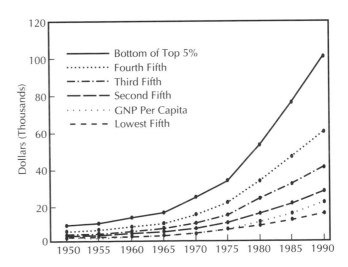

FIGURE 3.   Income distribution (upper limit each fifth).

The middle-middle and the upper-middle class will barely keep up economically and will shrink in relative size. A few individuals will move upward but the majority of the departures will be downward mobility. The affluent and the rich will continue to do well. And the very rich will do extremely well.

The Extremes: The Rich and the Poor

Fortune magazine annually lists the 400 wealthiest Americans and *Forbes* magazine annually lists the world's billionaires. Over the twelve-year period from 1982 to 1993, the 400 wealthiest Americans have done very well. The minimum needed to be on the list increased from $91 million to $300 million, the average net worth of the group increased from $230 million to $820 million, and the number of American billionaires increased from 13 to 59. Over approximately the same twelve-year period (1980 to 1991), the gross national product, the gross domestic product, the national income, compensation and wages of all employees, and personal income merely doubled.

During the period from the early 1980s to the early 1990s, in terms of all wages paid to the civilian labor force, the average American worker did not maintain par with national growth, experiencing a 75 percent as opposed to a 110 percent increase. Their income exceeded inflation by 25 percent, but that is only one-tenth of the improvement that the super-rich experienced in their net worth. During the intervening years, the disparity deepens. Although the policies of the 1980s were skewed in favor of the wealthy, and therefore the trends are not likely to continue at such a dramatic rate, there is no indication that there will be a reversal in the trends. In the foreseeable future, the rich will continue to outpace the society's growth and the average American will barely keep up, if not actually lose ground.

Internationally, the very wealthy did even better than the American rich. There were 98 billionaires on *Forbes* magazine's first list and more than 250 by 1993. The initial and current lists (see Figure 4). suggest a shift in the location of wealth in the world. During the period from 1987 to 1993, the United States increased its number of billionaires from 47 to 59. Simultaneously, Japan tripled, the rest of Asia doubled, and Europe increased by a third, the number of its wealthiest. This growth in economic strength among America's major competitors is likely to increase in the next few decades. Overall, the United States is not doing poorly in absolute terms, but, relative to the rest of the world, it is not doing as well as it did in the past.

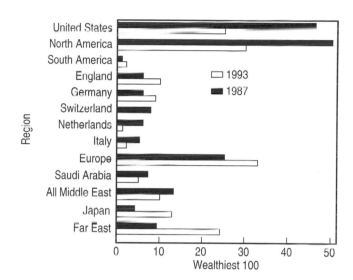

FIGURE 4.   Number of billionaires worldwide.

The poor and the middle class did not fare as well as the wealthy. The poor remained somewhat even with inflation. For example, in Figure 5, the poverty level for a single person roughly follows the increase of the GNP per capita (all in constant dollars). The gap between the middle class and the poor is decreasing, and since the per capita GNP is increasing, the conclusion is the middle class is moving downward, rather than the lower class moving upward.

The decline of the middle can also be identified by tracking the increasing number of dual-income families, including those families with young children, the decreasing number of middle-class students attending private colleges and universities, and the shift from the healthy leisure of family outings and puttering around the home and yard, to the escapist leisure of staring at television and spending long hours at the local bar. People who had been middle class all their lives suddenly descend into the lower class as the result of major health problems, having to take care of a elderly parent, or having insufficient resources for their own retirement. For these families, the rug had been pulled out from under them. The decline in wealth and income is not as noticeable as it might be because the reduction has occurred over an extended period. The high numbers of production workers laid off in the 1970s were augmented not only by additional blue-collar layoffs, but also by the layoffs of office personnel, and the furloughing of first-line supervisors in the 1980s. In the late 1980s and early '90s, there also were major reductions in middle management and technical staff. In turn, the local community losses cascade into the

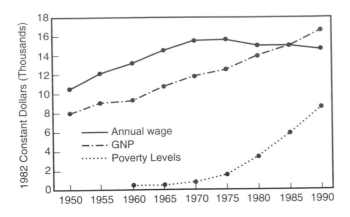

FIGURE 5.   Income levels per capita.

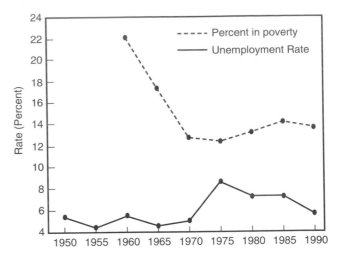

FIGURE 6.   Unemployment and poverty levels.

broader region because of decreased demand of general services, a general belt tightening on most expenditures, and the emigration of the population.

The postwar unemployment rate has ranged between 4 and 8 percent, the peak occurring as the percent of the population in poverty was drastically reduced (see Figure 6), but the unemployment rate does not include discouraged workers—people who want to work but who are not actively looking because they believe their chances of finding work are slim. A study found that the real unemployment rate in the United States in late 1993 should be adjusted from 6.4 to 9.3. The study found a need to adjust the rates in France from 12.0 to 13.7, in Great Britain from 9.8 to 12.3, and in Japan from 2.7 to 9.6 for the same period.

Is this downward social mobility of the middle class and the increasing impoverishment of the lower class the consequence of technological change associated with the progression from the industrial age to the information age? Nations are in social and technological transition, and there is a profound impact on the characteristics of social classes, on jobs and income, and on the definitions of wealth and the patterns of wealth production.

Some Conclusions

Over the most recent generation or so, the socioeconomic classes have shifted. The rich grew in numbers and got wealthier. The poor below the poverty line remained about the same. The working class declined in terms of real income and wealth and grew in numbers because individuals previously middle class moved in. The middle class got smaller in both numbers and in aggregate wealth.

The trends for wealth accumulation for the next few decades are that the lower class will become better off absolutely and worse off relatively, the lower-middle class will continue its downward slide, the middle-middle and the upper-middle classes will probably not be able to keep up economically and will lose in numbers, and the rich will grow in both numbers and wealth, outpacing the macroeconomic growth. The gap between the upper class and other classes will increase, and the gap between the middle class and the lower class will become smaller. The society will become increasingly more bimodal. Overall, the United States will become wealthier, but will lose ground relative to the rest of the world.

These trends will continue until the second or third decade of the twenty-first century. Then the pendulum will swing back and the middle class will reassert itself, equalizing the disparities and ushering a broad-based growth in personal and social wealth.

See also DERIVATIVES; ECONOMICS; FINANCIAL INSTITUTIONS; INVESTMENTS; SAVINGS; TAXES.

BIBLIOGRAPHY

BARTLETT, DONALD L., and STEELE, JAMES B. *America: What Went Wrong.* Kansas City: Andrews and McMeel, 1992.

BRAUN, DENNY. *The Rich Get Richer: The Rise of Income Inequality in the United States and the World.* Chicago: Nelson-Hall, 1991.

BROCKWAY, GEORGE P. *The End of Economic Man: Principles of Any Future Economics.* New York: Norton, 1993.

COHEN, MICHAEL LEE. *The Twentysomething American Dream: A Cross-Country Quest for a Generation.* New York: Dutton, 1993.

HOWE, NEIL, and STRAUSS, BILL. *13th Gen: Abort, Retry, Ignore, Fail?* New York: Vintage, 1993.

NEWMAN, KATHERINE S. *Declining Fortunes: The Withering of the American Dream.* New York: Basic Books, 1993.

_____. *Falling from Grace: The Experience of Downward Mobility in the American Middle Class.* New York: Vintage, 1988.

PHILIPS, KEVIN. *Boiling Point: Democrats, Republican, and the Decline of Middle Class Prosperity.* New York: Random House, 1993.

_____. *The Politics of Rich and Poor: Wealth and the American Electorate in the Reagan Aftermath.* New York: HarperCollins, 1990.

Nils E. Hovik

Weapons, Lethal.

See LETHAL WEAPONS.

Weapons of Mass Destruction

Weapons of mass destruction, or unconventional weapons, include: nuclear, chemical, and biological. While scientifically very different, they share a potential to inflict large casualties.

Nuclear Weapons

Nuclear weapons use the energy of the atom to create an explosion. Weapons created by the fission, or splitting, of atoms are commonly referred to as atomic, or A bombs. Those created by atomic fusion, or the thermonuclear reaction of hydrogen isotopes, are called hydrogen, or H-bombs. Enhanced-radiation weapons, also known as neutron bombs, produce more neutrons, gamma rays, or X rays than a normal weapon of the same yield. The world's total nuclear arsenal of some 48,000 weapons has an explosive power of 11,700 megatons, or 2.2 tons of TNT for every person on Earth.

Only the United States, the former Soviet Union, the United Kingdom, France, and China have acknowledged possession of nuclear weapons. India, Israel, and Pakistan are believed either to possess a limited number of undeclared nuclear weapons or to be able to produce them within weeks or months of a decision to do so. North Korea reportedly may have the capability to produce one or two simple nuclear bombs. South Africa secretly produced six nuclear weapons, but subsequently destroyed them. Algeria, Iran, Iraq, and Libya reportedly have been seeking to develop nuclear weapons (see Table 1).

The capability to develop and produce nuclear weapons still remains beyond the reach of most nations. The major technical obstacle is acquiring the fissile material (enriched uranium or plutonium) needed to fuel a nuclear chain reaction.

Political strategies to slow the spread of nuclear weapons have included: the 1968 Nuclear Nonproliferation Treaty, signed by more than 160 nations; the designation of nuclear weapon-free zones (Antarctica, Latin America, outer space, the ocean seabed, and the South Pacific); export restrictions; sanctions against proliferators; inspections by the International Atomic Energy Agency; resolving disputes that fuel the demand for nuclear weapons; reducing weapons stockpiles; and ending all nuclear test explosions (of which there have been more than 2,000).

In the aftermath of the Cold War, it has been proposed that the United States reduce its nuclear arsenal from 20,000 to 8,500 warheads and that the former Soviet Union reduce its arsenal from 27,000 to 10,000. No major reductions are anticipated in the much smaller arsenals of the United Kingdom, France, and China. By 2003, the world's combined nuclear arsenals are projected to still include more than 20,000 nuclear warheads (see Table 2).

The world is edging closer to a Comprehensive Test Ban Treaty. Temporary nuclear testing moratoria are already being observed by the United States, France, Russia, and the United Kingdom.

The global deployment and regular movement of nuclear weapons by air, land, and sea make accidents a constant, potential danger. There have been more than 300 nuclear accidents of varying severity worldwide since 1945.

In the process of building almost 70,000 U.S. nuclear warheads, an estimated 4,500 sites in America became polluted with chemical and radioactive byproducts. Efforts to clean up this mess and bring nuclear weapons facilities into compliance with the nation's environmental laws are expected to take at least thirty years and to cost as much as $300 billion. Safe and permanent disposal of radioactive waste is perhaps the most serious long-term dilemma resulting from the Cold War.

Chemical Weapons

The use of gas warfare by both Iran and Iraq during their eight-year war in the 1980s and the fear that Iraq might use them during the Persian Gulf war provided impetus to long-standing international efforts to eliminate chemical weapons.

TABLE 1.   The Nuclear Powers That Be

Acknowledged Nuclear Weapons States	Former Nuclear Weapons States	Threshold Nuclear Weapons States*	Nations Believed to Be Seeking Nuclear Weapons Capabilities
Belarus†	South Africa‡	India	Algeria
China		Israel	Iran
France		Pakistan	Iraq
Kazakhstan†			Libya
Russia			North Korea
Ukraine‡			
United Kingdom			
United States			

Chart prepared by Center for Defense Information.

* These states are believed either to possess a limited number of undeclared nuclear weapons or to be able to produce them within weeks or months of a decision to do so.

† These states, along with Russia, inherited their nuclear arsenals from the former Soviet Union. These three states have signed agreements to rid themselves of nuclear weapons.

‡ South Africa secretly produced, but has subsequently destroyed, six nuclear weapons. Although other states, such as Argentina and Brazil, have given up their pursuit of nuclear weapons, South Africa is the first and, so far, the only state to acquire nuclear weapons and later destroy them all. Belarus, Kazakhstan, and Ukraine are slated to become former nuclear weapons states.

Chemical weapons are inanimate, synthetic gases, liquids, or solids that are designed to produce specific physiological effects after they are inhaled, ingested, or come into contact with skin. They can be lethal (nerve, blister, choking and blood agents); harassing (tear gas); or incapacitating (vomit agents and psychochemicals). In addition, herbicides, or defoliants, are defined as chemical weapons by some countries but not by others.

The 1925 Geneva Protocol outlawed the *use* of chemical weapons but does not prohibit countries from producing and stockpiling them. While there have been numerous unsubstantiated allegations of chemical weapons use since World War I, for the most part chemical warfare has been shunned as morally repugnant and taboo.

The largest possessors of chemical weapons today are the United States (30,000 tons) and the former Soviet Union (40,000 tons). Both nations have ceased producing them.

Chemical weapons sometimes are referred to as the "poor man's atom bomb." Any country with a petrochemical, pesticide, fertilizer, or pharmaceutical industry potentially could produce them. Countries currently believed to have programs for developing chemical weapons include: China, India, Israel, Iran, Iraq, Libya, Myanmar, North Korea, Pakistan, South Korea, Syria, Taiwan, and Vietnam. A country must possess more than laboratory-sized quantities of a chemical agent before it has a militarily significant capability. Successful attack requires that the weather conditions (wind, rain, and temperature) be favorable and that the target population be unprepared. In the absence of protective measures, chemical weapons, pound for pound, are more deadly than conventional high explosives.

The 1993 Chemical Weapons Convention, signed by more than 150 nations, outlaws the development, production, stockpiling, acquisition, or transfer of chemical weapons. This global treaty features the most comprehensive and intrusive verification measures ever to be included in an arms reduction agreement.

TABLE 2.   Nuclear Arsenals of Acknowledged Nuclear Weapons States*
(Estimated 1992 and Projected 2003)

Nation	1992 Estimated Strategic Nuclear Weapons	1992 Estimated Tactical Nuclear Weapons	1992 Estimated Total Nuclear Weapons	2003 Projected Strategic Nuclear Weapons	2003 Projected Tactical Nuclear Weapons	2003 Projected Total Nuclear Weapons
U.S.A.	12,000	8,000	20,000	3,500	5,000	8,500
Former U.S.S.R.	10,000[†]	17,000[‡]	27,000[†]	3,000[‡]	7,000[‡]	10,000[‡]
U.K.	130	200	330	300	100	400
France	520	80	600	640	80	720
China	300	200	500	300	200	500

Sources: CDI, DOD, NRDC, BASIC, SIPRI, Jane's.

Chart prepared by the Center for Defense Information.

* All warhead counts include both deployed and war reserve nuclear weapons.

[†] Weapons deployed in Russia, Ukraine, Kazakhstan, and Belarus.

[‡] Weapons deployed solely in Russia.

Future challenges include securing adherence to the treaty's directives and destroying existing stockpiles. The United States plans to incinerate its chemical weapons, but citizen concerns about environmental and safety risks may force reconsideration of this policy.

Biological Weapons

Biological weapons are living organisms, infective materials, or their synthetic equivalent that achieve effects by multiplying inside targeted persons, plants, or animals. Infectious doses of some biological agents are on the order of a trillionth of a gram. In theory, they are the deadliest of any potential weapons. A bullet, once it is fired, eventually must come to a rest, whereas a biological weapon can theoretically spread forever if left unchecked.

Potential biological weapon agents include bacteria, viruses, and antiplant agents. Bacteria investigated for military applications include: anthrax, plague, tularemia (rabbit fever), typhoid, and dysentery. Viruses with military weapon potential include: smallpox, yellow fever, influenza, Rift Valley Fever, and Venezuelan equine encephalitis. Antiplant agents include: wheat rust, rice blast, corn stunt, and rice and corn blight.

Toxins, poisonous substances produced by living organisms, encompass the gray area between chemical and biological weapons. Unlike biological weapons, they are inanimate and thus incapable of reproducing themselves. Toxins are produced by

bacteria (botulinum), fungi, marine organisms (shellfish), poisonous plants, and venomous insects, spiders, and snakes.

Currently, no countries admit to the possession of biological weapons. In 1969, the United States unilaterally renounced the possession of biological weapons and destroyed its stockpile. The 1972 Biological and Toxin Weapons Convention, signed by more than 130 nations, outlaws the development, production, stockpiling, acquisition, or transfer of these weapons. A major weakness of this treaty is its lack of any means of verification and enforcement. Furthermore, it allows research on defenses, and demarcations between civilian/military and offensive/defensive purposes are not always clear. Efforts are underway to close these loopholes.

Countries believed to have programs for developing biological weapons include: China, Iran, Iraq, Libya, North Korea, Syria, and Taiwan. Any country with advanced capabilities in the health sciences, biotechnology, or beer brewing has at least the rudimentary potential to produce biological weapons.

Because they are living organisms, biological agents cannot easily be developed as instruments of war or effectively disseminated to targets. They are vulnerable to sunlight or extreme temperatures, and often can be countered by vaccinations.

Future Trends

In the future, nuclear, chemical, and biological weapons may be deemphasized and possibly even phased out. Significant geopolitical changes in the world during the early 1990s provide new opportunities to drastically reduce and eventually eliminate such weapons. Steps in this direction have been taken, but many more remain untaken.

Perceived military need for such weapons may diminish as the destructive potential of conventional weapons approaches that achieved by weapons of mass destruction. Gen. Colin Powell, then-chairman of the U.S. Joint Chiefs of Staff, questioned the value of nuclear weapons when he said, "I think there is far less utility of these [nuclear] weapons than some Third World countries think there is, and they are wasting a lot of money, because what they hope to do militarily with weapons of mass destruction of the kind we are talking about, I can increasingly do with conventional weapons, and far more effectively." The 1991 war against Iraq demonstrated this potential.

Weapons of mass destruction by their very nature are self-inhibiting. Their enormous deadliness, unpredictability, and the widespread global condemnation incurred by using them make them unlikely weapons of choice.

They are primarily political instruments, useful only to reciprocally deter use by other nations. As the increased firepower of conventional weapons renders deterrence obsolete, the danger of nuclear, chemical, or biological warfare may grow increasingly more remote. The danger of massive conventional warfare, however, will remain and perhaps will increase.

See also ARMS RACE; HAZARDOUS WASTES; LETHAL WEAPONS; MILITARY TECHNOLOGIES; NATIONAL SECURITY; PEACEKEEPING.

BIBLIOGRAPHY

BARNABY, FRANK. *How Nuclear Weapons Spread: Nuclear Weapon Proliferation in the 1990s.* New York: Routledge, 1993.

GRAY, COLIN S. *Weapons Don't Make War: Policy, Strategy, and Military Technology.* Lawrence, KS: University Press of Kansas, 1993.

ROBERTS, BRAD, ed. *Biological Weapons: Weapons of the Future?* Washington, DC: Brookings Institution, 1993.

SIVARD, RUTH LEGER. *World Military and Social Expenditures, 1993.* Washington, DC: World Priorities, 1993.

Gene R. LaRocque

Weather.

See CLIMATE AND METEOROLOGY.

Welfare.

See ENTITLEMENTS; PUBLIC ASSISTANCE PROGRAMS; SOCIAL WELFARE PHILOSOPHIES.

Wells, H. G. (1866–1946)

The novelist, journalist, and social philosopher H. G. Wells was born in Bromley, Kent in the United Kingdom. Wells established himself as a writer of fiction in the mid-1890s. His most successful novels include *The Time Machine* (1895), *The War of the Worlds* (1898), and *Tono-Bungay* (1909). His bestseller *The Outline of History* (1920) viewed ancient and modern history from a global perspective, culminating in a fervent plea for world government. Wells's contributions to the study of the future range from *Anticipations* (1901), a sophisticated forecast of technological, social, and political transformation, to *The Shape of Things to Come* (1933), an imaginary history of the next century and a half, later filmed by Alexander Korda as *Things to Come* (1936). In *The Discovery of the Future* (1902), Wells looked forward to the emergence of a science of the future, as exact and authoritative as anything possible in the natural sciences. Hailed by some critics as the founding father of modern science fiction, he is also remembered for his dystopian and utopian fiction. In *When the Sleeper Wakes* (1899), he anticipated most of the horrors later foreseen in the classic futurist dystopias of Yevgeni Zamyatin, Aldous Huxley, and George ORWELL. *A Modern Utopia* (1905) depicts a global technocracy somewhat reminiscent of Edward Bellamy's in *Looking Backward*.

See also FUTURISM; POPULARIZED FUTURES.

BIBLIOGRAPHY

HILLEGAS, MARK R. *The Future As Nightmare: H. G. Wells and the Anti-Utopians.* New York: Oxford University Press, 1967.

MACKENZIE, NORMAN and JEANNE. *H. G. Wells.* New York: Simon & Schuster, 1973.

SMITH, DAVID C. *H. G. Wells: Desperately Mortal.* New Haven, CT: Yale University Press, 1986.

WAGAR, W. WARREN. *H. G. Wells and the World State.* New Haven, CT: Yale University Press, 1961.

WELLS, H. G. *Experiment in Autobiography.* New York: Macmillan, 1934.

W. Warren Wagar

Western Europe.

See EUROPE, WESTERN.

Western Religions.

See CHRISTIANITY; ISLAM; JUDAISM.

Wildcards

A wildcard is a low-probability, high-impact event. It is an event that is rarely anticipated.

Growing up in California during the 1950s and '60s, I can recall an early introduction to wildcard events. The disaster drills in grammar school provided me with a reference point for low-probability, high-impact wars, earthquakes, tidal waves, and other unnamed disasters. Knowing the location of the bomb shelter could, according to our teachers, save our lives. Planning for the unexpected seemed to hold some merit when presented along these lines.

Visionaries who actively plan for wildcard events open themselves up to a multitude of opportunities. The applicability of wildcard planning applies equally across the lines of government, industry, and private life. The most common form of wildcard planning in the United States is perhaps exemplified by certain forms of insurance coverage. Earthquake and flood insurance policies are sold to wildcard thinkers. These policies provide wildcard protection and, in fact, convey a benefit to those planning for a wildcard event. The wildcard thinker would also be one of few people prepared physically for these low-probability, high-impact events. They might also have inflatable rafts or emergency food and water provisions in their houses as preparation for an earthquake or flood.

Another common form of wildcard thinking revolves around the personal savings account. There are many reasons for keeping a savings account. The most obvious would be as a place to keep some money earmarked for a specific purpose—e.g., Christmas gifts. Many people, however, keep savings accounts as a hedge against wildcard events. They may not be presently afraid of an illness, or loss of employment, but the savings account is available for just such wildcard events should they occur. The level of perceived security such an account brings the holder can easily be extrapolated to planning for security on a much greater scale.

In a governmental and industrial context, the breakup of the Soviet Union, reunification of Germany, and the democratization of Eastern Europe were a barrage of wildcard events. Most political and industrial experts failed to plan for any portion of these events. There were, however, a few scattered visionaries who not only considered the ramifications of such events, but took steps prior to their realization to gain a superior position in these emerging, changing markets. These visionaries are now the beneficiaries of heightened market or political influence.

To gain the benefit of wildcard thinking and planning, there is no true necessity for investment of large amounts of time or capital into what seems, at best, an uncertainty. There is only a need for awareness extending beyond the parameters of the obvious.

Some examples of wildcards follow.

Political Wildcards

- *The United States breaks up into autonomous nation-states,* following an extended series of social and economic crises, and a lack of regional agreement on methods of repair. The Western states join a new Pacific Rim economic organization, and the Eastern states form the Atlantic Economic Union with the European and Latin American countries. The breakup creates a wide disparity in the wealth of the new states, resulting in a Third to First World economic range. It also results in difficulties regarding ownership of defense-related commodities, not unlike the breakup of the former Soviet Union.
- *A Russian-Chinese-Japanese alliance* is formed in which the partners abandon their historically turbulent relations and act as a self-contained economic bloc, frustrating economic relations with the United States and the European Union.
- *Global governance* becomes a reality, effectively splitting the world into regional and international decision-making bodies, without recognition of sovereign nation-states.

Socioeconomic Wildcards

- *Nonmaterial values replace consumerism in all OECD countries,* drastically increasing levels of personal savings, and causing economic chaos in all nonagricultural industrial sectors.
- *Genetic profiling radically alters health care economy* by reducing the incidence of disease, causing a 50 percent drop in pharmaceutical sales, and physician visits.
- *Mass transit replaces 50 percent of all cars in the United States,* following an even stronger trend

in the European Union toward a 90 percent mass transit level.

Technology Wildcards

- *Cold fusion* will be effectively developed, thereby challenging the entirety of the global energy economy.
- *All shopping will be done by telecommunication,* rather than through physical visits to stores. All items, including groceries, will be home-delivered.
- *Clothing will be electronically coded* to ensure full color and style compatibility on the owner. Clothing will be programmed with the consumers' individual style parameters upon purchase. If a combination outside these parameters is attempted, an alarm will be triggered warning the user of a potential incompatible combination.

Anticipating radical change is nothing new to strategic planners. It is in the nature of their business to anticipate both radical and subtle shifts in existing structures. The wildcard is a tool for measuring the far reaches of these structures.

When making any plan, be it as simple as planning your college education, or as complex as seeking to establish a multinational business consortium, a wildcard analysis can be of great benefit. By taking the most logical scenarios and stretching their elasticity, you can prepare yourself for what may, in the present, seem unlikely, but what would, in the future, be an opportunity or disaster.

A wildcard thinker is not necessarily someone who anticipates divorce upon marriage, but someone who might anticipate the need for compromise during the relationship. The wildcard is a tool of awareness, not prediction. In times of uncertainty and tumultuous change, predictions are difficult, leaving awareness as the only safe road to the future.

See also CHANGE, SCIENTIFIC AND TECHNOLOGICAL; CONTINUITY AND DISCONTINUITY; FORECASTING, DETERMINISTIC; FORECASTING, MISTAKES IN; FORECASTING METHODS; TECHNOLOGY FORECASTING AND ASSESSMENT; TREND INDICATORS.

BIBLIOGRAPHY

BIGNELL, VICTOR, and FORTUNE, JOYCE. *Understanding Systems Failures.* Manchester, U.K.: Manchester University Press, 1984.
CASTI, JOHN L. *Searching for Certainty: What Science Can Know About the Future.* New York: William Morrow, 1991.

WESTON, VICTORIA. *Into the Future and the Next Millennium.* Atlanta: Oscar Dey, 1991.

John D. Rockfellow

Women in Futures Studies

Are all the great futurists men? Anyone relying on articles, books, and surveys identifying the "great futurists" might come to that conclusion. The consulting firm of Coates and Jarratt circulated a list with the names of 125 futurists to representatives of 10 large American businesses asking them to select the names of those futurists who had "something to say about the future relevant to the corporation" and published results in a 1989 book entitled *What Futurists Believe.* All of the seventeen persons featured in this book are middle-aged and older white American males, except one who is an elderly white Englishman living in Sri Lanka, and another older white Englishman living in the United States. Each of the seventeen designees was interviewed, or otherwise asked certain questions about themselves. One question asked them to name the people who mainly influenced their ideas about the future. Here again the names of fifteen white men, mostly American, stood out from among a list of roughly fifty names offered as being intellectually influential in their thinking about the future. Not a single non-Westerner was named and only two women were named, one being the wife of the person naming her.

Many people who commented on the book criticized the authors for seeming to say that the only relevant futurists in the world are a handful of old white American men. The critics faulted the authors not so much for the conclusions they drew from the data they collected, but rather because of their sampling method, which seemed to have tapped entirely older white American male corporate sources. The authors were neither unaware of nor unconcerned about the apparent bias in their sample and conclusions, and attempted to justify both in the book's introduction.

Other people have also attempted to identify outstanding and relevant futurists as well. One of the earliest attempts was undertaken by Michael Marien in 1972 in his *The Hot List Delphi.* Marien's list is not of people, but of "essential reading for the future" at that time. He asked a panel of forty-four people (of whom only fourteen actually ended up on the panel) who had "some degree of critical appreciation of at least 500 futures or futures-related documents" to rate the literature in terms of its essential relevance to the field. All but one of Marien's fourteen panelists were male, Eleonora Barbieri Masini of Italy being the only female. All but three were Americans. Thirty-six documents were ranked by more than two-thirds of the panelists as being essential reading for futurists and people interested in the future. All but one of the authors of the documents listed were male, the sole female author being Margaret Mead for her book, *Culture and Commitment.* Twenty-four were Americans and the rest Europeans, plus one Canadian.

Alvin Toffler edited a book, also in 1972, called *The Futurists.* "The purpose of this collection," he said, "is to make accessible a few of the works of the best known and, at the moment, most influential futurists. . . ." "To illustrate the diversity of the movement, I have drawn selections not merely from the United States, but also from Japan, France, the Netherlands, the U.S.S.R., India, Germany, and Canada." And indeed, of the twenty-three people in the book, only twelve are Americans. Still, all but one are males—the sole exception once again being Margaret Mead.

More recently in 1987, Marien and Jennings published a book based on invitations they sent to forty-four futurists who were asked to reflect on what they had learned about the future, and how to think about the future. Seventeen responses were finally published in the book. Four were from American women: Vary Coates, Irene Taviss Thomson, Kusum Singh (originally from India), and Hazel Henderson (who was born in England). All but one (apparently) of the males were Americans.

In 1989, Hugues de Jouvenel, head of the Paris-based Association Internationale Futuribles, conducted a small survey of eight people he described as being "outstanding futurists," asking them to identify the major global futures studies published since 1980. All but one of the eight panelists were male. Three were French, three were American, one was Italian (Eleonora Barbieri Masini), and one was Russian. Eighty-nine publications were listed, including one from China, one from Japan, one from Africa, and three from the former Soviet Union. All the rest were from Europe or the United States. There was no single item that all eight of the panelists agreed on, but five did agree that Lester Brown's (an American) *State of the World* reports were "major global futures studies," and three others agreed on Gerald Barney's ill-fated *Global 2000 Report to the President;* Mikhail Gorbachev, *Perestroika;* Norman Myers, *GAIA: An Atlas of Planet Management;* Alvin Toffler, *The Third Wave;* and the

World Commission on Environment and Development's report, *Our Common Future* (often called the Brundtland Report). So we have three more Americans, one Russian, all males, and (arguably) one Norwegian woman (Gro Harlem Brundtland).

Finally, Allen Tough, of the University of Toronto, in 1990 mailed questionnaires to "115 professors, writers and leaders in future studies" as well as distributing them to "a large number of people . . . attending two international futures conferences, two small courses, and one small seminar." "From all these sources a total of 58 usable questionnaires were returned. Each respondent listed between 1 and 10 'individuals who are today . . . contributing the especially significant, fresh and/or profound ideas about the future.'" "Although 198 different individuals were nominated, three-quarters of them were nominated only once. . . . At the opposite extreme, 14 respondents listed Alvin Toffler. . . . In all, 49 people were nominated by from 2 to 14 respondents. Of the 8 people listed 6 or more times, 4 were women and 3 were non-Americans" (Tough, 1990.).

What can we conclude from this? First of all, it does seem to make a difference who is doing the surveying and from where. Male American researchers seem to end up with lists that have mainly male American futurists on them, Toffler perhaps being the exception as far as nationality is concerned. Male Canadian and French futurists tend to select a few more non-Americans and a few more women.

So what about the contribution of women to futures studies? We might conclude that there are not very many women in futures studies but that the few are truly outstanding: Margaret Mead, Eleonora Barbieri Masini, Hazel Henderson, and Gro Harlem Brundtland.

Many more women from many more parts of the world have contributed to the founding, growth, and continuing search for excellence and relevance of futures studies. From the very beginning, women have been active in both the World Future Society (WFS) and the World Futures Studies Federation (WFSF), the two leading global futures organizations. The 1991–1992 *Futures Research Directory* published by the WFS listed 126 women out of 1,172 names—10.7 percent of the total.

Three other women were undisputed leaders in cultural and peace-oriented aspects of futures studies: Margaret Mead, the world-famous anthropologist who did appear on the previous lists; Barbara Ward, internationally acclaimed for her visionary leadership in peace and environmental activities; and Elise Boulding, who also was one of the first to reveal the ignored but crucial contributions that specific women have made throughout recorded history, in her monumental book, *The Underside of History.*

Other women active from the earliest days of futures studies are Barbara Marx Hubbard, an optimistic visionary, and Renée-Marie Croose Parry, who still tirelessly strives for widened political freedoms. The late Sally Cornish, wife of WFS president Edward Cornish, also should be prominently mentioned.

Two women, perhaps more than any others, deserve to be credited for making futures studies what it is today. One is Magda McHale, an artist and cultural futurist, and a vice president of the WFSF. Though originally Hungarian, and holding a British passport, McHale has lived and worked for many years in the United States, and is the founder and director of the Center for Integrative Studies of the State University of New York at Buffalo. The other, without whom the WFSF probably would not now exist at all, is the previously mentioned Eleonora Barbieri Masini, a professor of sociology and law at the Gregorian University of Rome, Italy. She also was the second secretary general of the WFSF, its third president, and chair of the executive council of the WFSF. She, more than any other single person, kept alive and nurtured to maturity the infant organization she received from the founding father and first president, Johan Galtung of Norway, and the second president, from Morocco, Mahdi El-mandjra. Both she and Magda McHale had also been active in the creation of futures studies and the WFSF from the very beginning.

Since that time, there have been many women from many parts of the world active in the WFSF, the WFS, or in other future-oriented organizations or undertakings. Indeed, in some places, it was primarily women who were responsible for the creation of any future-oriented groups whatsoever, for example, Rosa Menasanch, Pepita Majoral, Conxita Bargallo, and Antonia Guix; during the dark days of Franco's dictatorship, they were among the founders in 1973 of the Centre Catala de Prospectiva in Barcelona, Spain. Similarly, Eva Gabor, Maria Kalas Koszegi, Erszebet Gidai, and Erszebet Novaky played crucial roles in the establishment of futures research in Hungary in the 1970s, as did Ana Maria Sandi and Viorica Ramba-Varga in Romania; Danuta Markowska in Poland; Radmila Nakarada in Yugoslavia; Anna Coen in Italy; Erika Landau and Rachel Dror in Israel; and, later, Margarita Kaisheva in Bulgaria.

At the forefront of early futures work in the United States and still continuing their leadership are Donella Meadows (mainly responsible for an earth-shaking future-oriented publication during the 1970s, *The Limits to Growth,* as well as for the newer, equally important book, *Beyond the Limits,* published in 1992); Marilyn Ferguson (whose book *The Aquarian Conspiracy* still inspires optimism); Edith Weiner (who, as the head of futures research for the American Council of Life Insurance in the 1960s and '70s, is probably reponsible for the invention of what is now called "environmental scanning"); Betty Reardon (an educational futurist and peace researcher at Columbia University); and Patricia Mische of Global Education Associates.

More recently, American women especially vital for educational futures include Linda Groff, Betty Frank, Penny Damlo, Kathleen Maloney, Ruthanne Kurth-Schai, and Maria Guido (the latter of whom is Costa Rican–born). Jennifer Jarratt, Martha Garrett, Sandra Postel, Jessica Matthews, Suzanne Gordon, Faith Popcorn, Joanna Macy, Charlene Spretnak, and Riane Eisler are among the best-known names in the consulting, global, environmental, and/or spiritual futures fields in the United States. Heidi Toffler and Patricia Aburdene also enjoy a unique prominence and have coauthored many top-selling books about the future. Others include Audrey Clayton, coeditor of *Futures Research Quarterly,* and Mary Clark, author of *Ariadne's Thread* and coeditor of *Rethinking Curriculum.*

Elsewhere, Mitsuko Saito-Fukunaga (Japan), Marie Angelique Savane (Senegal), Margarita de Botero (Colombia), Katrin Gillwald (Germany), and Janice Tait and Fernande Faulkner (Canada) have each contributed greatly to futures work.

Several other groups of women deserve special mention. There are eight women who have taken the leadership in bringing futures research and thinking directly into the judiciaries of the United States: Dana Farthing-Capowich of the State Justice Institute; Francis Zemans, Sandra Ratcliffe, and Kate Samson of the American Judicature Society; Kathy Mays and Beatrice Monahan of the Judiciary of the State of Virginia; and Wendy Schultz and Sharon Rodgers of the Hawaii Research Center for Futures Studies.

Lauren Cook of the National Association of Governors' Policy Advisers has done equally outstanding futures work for the executive branch of many American state governments. Cathryn Johnson does similarly successful work for the Health Care Forum, an association that works closely with the public and private health care providers. Anita

Rubin and Leena-Maija Salminen are among a group of experienced young futurists in the Finnish Society for Futures Studies, as are Robin Brandt, Annette Gardner, Bindi Borg, and Deborah Halbert in Hawaii.

Concluding this by no means complete list of women practitioners in the field of futures studies are Pat Barrentine, Maureen Caudill, Betty Friedan, Deborah Gordon, Elizabeth Dodson Gray, Heather Hudson, Heather Kurent, Lena Lupica, Janne Nolan, Cheryl Russell, and Juliet Schor.

See also FUTURE STUDIES; FUTURES CONCEPTS; FUTURES EDUCATION; FUTURISM; FUTURISTS.

BIBLIOGRAPHY

CORNISH, EDWARD, ed. *The Futures Research Dirctory: Individuals, 1995–96.* Bethesda, MD: The World Future Society, 1995.

JENNINGS, LANE, ed. *Futures Research Directory: Organizations and Periodicals, 1993–94.* Bethesda, MD: The World Future Society, 1993.

MALASKA, PENTTI, ed. *World Futures Studies Federation Newsletter WFSF Directory 1990.* Turku, Finland. WFSF Secretariat, 1990.

James A. Dator

Women in Politics

More than half of the world's population is female, but nowhere in the world do women participate politically as equals with men. Every society is built on the outdated, repressive, and abusive patriarchal belief that women should be spectators, not participants, in politics and in setting political, economic, and social agendas.

"Gender politics" is the response of women worldwide to this attitude. The American women's movement has worked toward educating the public about links between politicians, money, and tax burden (i.e., who gets treated better than others in tax load).

Continuing deficits, high taxes, and political scandals have prompted taxpayers to reconsider who represents them in elective office, setting a trend for accountability. Since women, rightly or wrongly, are perceived as less corruptible, this trend is leading to more women in elective and appointive offices. At the same time, problems such as family size, consumer choices, waste disposal, and education of children, once characterized as women's issues, are being recognized as global issues. As a result, women's traditional roles and values are becoming more pronounced in the policy-making arena. More women in public office may change the political focus from how to control to how to get things done.

Strong women leaders increase public confidence in women's abilities to lead, but superficial press coverage of women contributes to their slow progress in gaining political power. Women have been underrepresented as sources, subjects, and reporters in the American newspaper industry. It is not surprising that when only 34 percent of journalists are women, 19 percent are editors and managers, and 34 percent of front page articles are written by women, a scant 15 percent of front-page stories are about women.

History is replete with traditional women's issues, but few are aware that women's struggle for suffrage, ("the right to vote") is at the root of today's battle for reproductive rights. The nineteenth-century suffrage movement created a powerful patriarchal backlash that resulted in the criminalization of abortion in every state; the male medical establishment's monopoly on obstetric medicine (in place of midwives); the Roman Catholic Church's declaration of abortion as a mortal sin in 1869; and public concern with the rights of the fetus.

With more women in political positions, there would be an increased focus on reducing the need for abortion rather than on how to abort legally. Restrictive policies and programs of parental consent, waiting periods, required counseling, and federal and state funds limitations would be unnecessary. Other so called "women's issues"—child care, parenting, and educational needs—would get more attention and financial support if women gained greater political and economic power through public office.

The prevailing biases in educational and philanthropic funding is an overt admission of the undervaluing of females. Raising the status of females through knowledge and education is vital to the full participation of women in society. Two-thirds of the world's illiterates are women; and, in seventeen countries, over 90 percent of women are illiterate. Widespread prejudice against educating females is at the root of this illiteracy.

The Equal Rights Amendment in the United States, first proposed in 1923, was passed in 1972 but failed to be ratified after ten years of struggle. Opposing forces were convinced equality would invalidate protective laws for women. Women accidentally received federal protection from discrimination in 1964 because a Southern conservative congressman wanted to kill the proposed Civil

Rights Act by adding "sex" to the protected classes. The law survived the addition of women, however.

Traditional women's issues finally led to a rise in women's voices and roles when it was recognized in 1980 that more women than men voted in the presidential election. This gender-based response can be attributed to women's economic interest in changing the status quo. More women candidates are running for office to correct an imbalance in public decision making. Women's voices are being heard at every level of government through more active participation by women in lobbying, issue-oriented activism, campaign contributions, and overall participation in the process of governance.

Despite recent advances, women only hold approximately 18 percent of all elective offices in the United States. They are still greatly underrepresented at all levels of elective and appointive public offices. One factor contributing to women's lack of public power is their role as cheap labor in the Third World. In Pakistan, Nicaragua, and the Philippines, women leaders of the 1980s were seen as weak and ineffective because they tried to work within the male power structure while ignoring the potential of cultivating the masses.

More progress for women has been made in Europe by way of strong female leadership. Former Prime Minister Margaret Thatcher showed the world that she could be as tough in leading Great Britain to war against Argentina as she was on social issues. Scandinavia, especially Norway, is a model region in terms of the full political integration of women and their views. Trends point toward a global community where problems are dealt with at the local level. For women political leaders, ignoring that local level can lead to failure.

The worldwide status of women was summed up in 1980 by a United Nations finding that "women constitute half of the world's population, perform nearly two-thirds of its work hours, receive one-tenth of the world's income, and own less than one-hundredth of the world's property."

At the end of the twentieth century, women do not have the right of full participation in politics anywhere in the world. Their increasing rates of election and appointment to political office in the United States and other countries augurs perhaps a major change in public attitudes about the value of both genders sharing power.

The quest of women for a greater voice in world politics continues. While full participation remains an illusive ideal, a partnership between men and women in shaping a new future is within reach if a gender-equal society becomes reality. An "ambi-genic" society—one which is truly produced by or formed from both genders—will set aside patriarchal and/or matriarchal control in favor of mutual association for the greater good of humanity, setting the stage for a genuine global transformation.

See also WOMEN AND WORK; WOMEN AND WORLD DEVELOPMENT; WOMEN'S HEALTH MOVEMENT; WOMEN'S MOVEMENT; WOMEN'S RIGHTS; WOMEN'S STUDIES.

BIBLIOGRAPHY

DAVIS, KENNETH C. *Don't Know Much About History.* New York: Crown Publishers, 1990.

FALUDI, SUSAN. *Backlash—The Undeclared War against American Women.* New York: Crown Publishers, 1991.

NAISBITT, JOHN, and ABURDENE, PATRICIA. *Megatrends for Women.* New York: Villard Books, 1992.

RIES, PAULA, and STONE, ANNE J. *The American Woman 1992–93, A Status Report.* New York: W. W. Norton, 1992.

SEAGER, JONI, and OLSON, ANN. *Women in the World—An International Atlas.* New York: Simon & Schuster, 1986.

Julia Hughes Jones

Women and Religion

Women are the emergent movement in religion today. They are challenging the traditional male dominance within the clergy and rabbinate. Women are the majority now in most Protestant seminaries and in the future will be more numerous as ordained ministers, as bishops, and as faculty in seminaries. A continuing campaign for the ordination of women is pressuring Roman Catholic and Orthodox churches and will continue to complicate ecumenical relations.

Throughout recorded time men have "named the sacred" from the standpoint of their male body and male life experience. It is not accidental that in the Genesis 2 account of creation in Hebrew scriptures, Adam "named" all the animals. Naming is one kind of power, the power to shape a culture's ways of perceiving and thinking about reality so that they serve the interests and goals of those doing the naming. The future of human history is now being shaped by the power to name being claimed by Adam's heretofore silent partner.

Feminist theology and scholarship in Judaism and Christianity have blossomed into a scathing critique of male generic language, the pervasive male imagery (God-the-Father, God-the-King), and the male-centeredness of traditional theology.

This feminist theological critique of "the male as the norm" asserts that men created God as Father and King in their own male image, rather than, as had been taught for millennia, man being created in God's image. The publication of Mary Daly's *Beyond God the Father* (1973) marked for many women a new critical consciousness. Elisabeth Schüssler Fiorenza in New Testament studies and Rosemary Radford Ruether in historical theology pioneered a now widespread process of recovering the contributions to religion of women that were repressed and lost when men alone wrote "his" story as history. In Judaic thought, Judith Plaskow and others broke new ground in trying to imagine an all-embracing Jewish ritual.

In this same period (1970–1995), the Catholic church and Protestant and Jewish denominations have been engulfed in controversy and concern surrounding human sexuality, or what has been called "pelvic theology." These issues have not been resolved and will have a major future impact. First ordaining only males came under challenge. In Roman Catholicism the tradition of priestly celibacy is being questioned. Around the world the abortion controversy rages in various religions as yet another facet of pelvic theology. The issue of how to view and whether to ordain gays and lesbians has polarized Protestant denominations. Since the mid-1980s there have been numerous lawsuits in Roman Catholic and Protestant churches in the aftermath of public disclosures of sexual abuse by heterosexual ministers and priests involving abuse of clergy power, betrayal of trust, seduction, pedophilia, institutional coverup, and consequent loss of credibility.

Changing patterns of sexual behavior involve women as well as religion. Questions about morality and sexuality abound: Should there be any sexual activity outside of heterosexual religiously sanctioned marriage? For example, should teenagers be sexually active? Should engaged couples be sexually active? Should couples live together before marriage? What about same-sex couples? Should churches "bless" such relationships, as Episcopalian Bishop William Spong has suggested? What about sex ("affairs") outside of marriage, which traditionally religion has called "adultery"? What about senior citizens living together, refusing to marry because of social security, tax, or estate complications?

Should religious pronouncements adjust to widespread patterns of freer sexual behavior, or should traditional religion reiterate conventional moral positions and try to "keep a lid" on all this?

A coherent religious answer to these many-faceted questions awaits future resolution.

The rise of women's prominence and power in both religion and the secular culture has provoked a strong backlash among religious conservatives. This fundamentalist backlash is prominent among Evangelical Protestants as well as traditionalist Roman Catholics and Muslims. In Judaism there is a growing "back to Orthodoxy" movement. Fundamentalism is characterized by a fear of "uncontrolled" female power and by a deeply felt desire to put women back into their traditional and subservient place. Patriarchal religion has functioned as a significant means of social control of women. The control of female sexuality and reproduction has been central to this control of women. Thus, issues of contraception and abortion are at the core of who controls women's lives.

Some women are now claiming the power to name the sacred "in their own image." An extensive goddess movement has developed during the 1980s and '90s as a way some women have chosen for claiming the power to name the sacred in their own image. A group of women scholars (Merlin Stone, Marija Gimbutas, Charlene Spretnak, Riane Eisler, Elinor Gadon) have reinterpreted prehistory to rediscover a women's mythology of the Great Mother. They have written movingly of what this means for women.

"Spirituality" is a word that nonacademic women have come to use to express their new sense of the sacredness of women's experience, bodies, and perceived connection to the earth. New rituals are being written to celebrate women's previously uncelebrated menstruation, menopause, birthing, reproductive blood, and healing after the traumas of incest and child abuse.

Women have discovered their outrage and are redefining morality. For innumerable women, flashbacks have opened to them again their repressed experiences of incest and child abuse. Battering, rape, and violence to women is now increasing as women's independence and social power grow. This violence can be characterized as sexual terrorism, used to enforce the power of the oppressor group. Rape, incest, and violence to women are a moral issue. Women also have realized that the majority of the poor, the elderly, and the hungry around the world are women and children. As a result of this realization, the moral issues of hunger and poverty also are coming to be seen as women's issues.

As women become aware of environmental damage and hazards, they become ecojustice activists, from Love Canal in New York state to the Chipco movement in India. Women see that ecological damage hurts their families, and take a firm stand. As women redefine the issues of morality, they understand that everything is interconnected, that for women the personal *is* political, and that feminism, religion, ecology, and the search for nonviolence cannot be separated.

See also ABORTION; FUNDAMENTALISM; RELIGIONS, DECLINE OR RISE OF; RELIGION, SPIRITUALITY, MORALITY; SEXUAL BEHAVIOR; SEXUAL CODES OF CONDUCT; WOMEN'S MOVEMENT.

BIBLIOGRAPHY

DALY, MARY. *Beyond God the Father*. Boston: Beacon Press, 1973.

FALUDI, SUSAN. *Backlash: The Undeclared War Against American Women*. New York: Crown, 1991.

FIORENZA, ELISABETH SCHÜSSLER. *In Memory of Her: A Feminist Theological Reconstruction of Christian Origins*. New York: Crossroad, 1983.

RUETHER, ROSEMARY RADFORD, ed. *Religion and Sexism: Images of Women in the Jewish and Christian Traditions*. New York: Simon and Schuster, 1974.

Elizabeth Dodson Gray

Women and Work

The debate on women's rights started in earnest at the end of the eighteenth century. For the first time women asserted their right to participate in decision making, thus bringing to the fore and making visible what had already existed for a long time but had never been explicitly acknowledged. The letters written by Abigail Adams, respectively the wife and mother to the second and fourth presidents of the United States, reveal to what extent women were already aware of their invisible role and were conscious of their right to be recognized outside the home. Many similar examples could also be cited from the time of the French and the Russian revolutions.

Education was and still is crucial to fulfillment of women's rights. Equal opportunities in the field of education have still not been attained, either in industrialized countries or elsewhere around the world. In looking toward the future, the level of literacy among women is an important indicator. According to a recent definition, to be literate a person must be capable of reading and writing (with understanding) a simple statement about everyday life. The level of literacy among women is a better measurement of education than school enrollment

because it reflects a minimum level of attainment. Although establishing the level of literacy in developing countries remains difficult, measurement by the test described above is more reliable than other measurements, such as those indicating the ratio of schools and students.

There are many more illiterate women than men in most countries of the world. Decades of elementary education for all have resulted in nearly universal literacy for the young. But in sub-Saharan Africa, or South or West Asia more than 70 percent of women over twenty-five are illiterate. In East and Southeast Asia the comparable figure is more than 40 percent, while in Latin America and the Caribbean it is more than 20 percent.

Given this second-rate status, it is difficult to talk about recognition of women's rights, regardless of how firmly they have been written into laws and international agreements or voiced, especially in the industrialized countries. Moreover, although literacy is increasing among younger women, it remains much higher for men.

University and college enrollment figures are another indicator. Female enrollment is increasing rapidly and is equal to and even surpasses that of men in industrialized countries and in some countries of southern Africa, West Africa, and Latin America. But whatever the official support of equal educational opportunities, field work conducted in Latin America has shown that the higher female enrollment levels are related to higher overall levels of income. Economic disadvantage, especially in the developing countries, thus has a greater impact on educational attainment for women than for men.

Gender Gap

There continues to be a gender gap, not only in education but in the work men and women do. The household is still the main center of work for women. Housework includes a variety of activities: routine daily tasks, subsistence agriculture, the production of goods and services, trade, bookkeeping for the husband, and so forth. Precisely because female labor is so varied, it is difficult to measure women's work. Women work longer hours than men in both developing and industrialized countries, except in the United States and Australia, where the hours are almost equal. In Eastern Europe women spend more time in the labor force and less time in housework, whereas in North America, Australia, and Western Europe men spend less time in the labor force and a little more time on housework. These indications reflect a change of attitude in the last twenty to twenty-five years, between the 1960s and the late 1980s. The disparity between the number of hours spent by men and women in the labor force and in housework is decreasing, albeit very slowly.

In the developing countries, women are still working longer hours than men: in Latin America, on average, just over five and a half more hours a week than men; in Africa, Asia, and the Pacific up to as much as twelve or thirteen more hours. Because of the very nature of women's work, especially in the developing countries, often involving unpaid as well as paid activities, it is difficult to precisely quantify the degree of female participation in the labor market. However that determination may be calculated, it has certainly increased in almost every country in the last twenty years.

There is another important gender gap related to wages. In Cyprus, Japan, and South Korea women earn about one-half the male wage. In most countries, the female wage is generally around 75 percent the male wage. This holds, even in Canada—a country in which women's movements have been particularly active, where women have successfully occupied numerous positions of prestige, and where women's wages are around 71 percent those of men.

Moreover, in developing countries women tend to be concentrated in low-productivity labor—in agriculture, in the service industries, and in the informal sector. In times of economic crisis, the presence of women in the informal sector and in part-time jobs is bound to increase.

Finally, another important trend to be mentioned is, the increasing "feminization of poverty" that accompanies the trend toward one-parent households in the industrialized countries and Latin America. The increasing number of women-headed households is probably an irreversible trend and is growing globally. This trend is caused by liberalized divorce in industrialized countries. In the developing nations it is attributable to migration (mainly male) between nations and within regions. Life expectancies also play a role. Up to 30 percent of households are headed by women, in many cases by women over sixty, because of higher female life expectancy. The exceptions are sub-Saharan Africa and countries such as Bangladesh, Bhutan, and the Maldives in southern Asia, where there are still high rates of maternal mortality.

Thus, over and beyond the formal acknowledgment of women's rights and the recognition of the important and visible role of women in society (more visible than in any other historical epoch), there continues to be a gender gap in terms of education and work opportunities. Taken together, these increasing trends toward single-parent (and mainly women-headed) households, have resulted in the increased feminization of poverty, as mentioned previously.

See also POVERTY, FEMINIZATION OF; WOMEN AND WORLD DEVELOPMENT; WOMEN'S MOVEMENT; WORK; WORKFORCE DIVERSITY.

BIBLIOGRAPHY

World's Women. New York: United Nations, 1991.
MASINI, ELEONORA, AND STRATIGOS, SUSAN. *Women, Households and Change*. Tokyo: United Nations University, 1991.

Eleonora Barbieri Masini

Women and World Development

Women and world development encompass fields of inquiry into the rapidly changing lives of women worldwide. Women's work and leadership had remained essentially unnoticed or ignored in histories of civilizations and were largely discounted by economic theory. The second wave of the women's movement, beginning in the 1960s, generated intense interest in women's roles and subordination, illustrating how political movements such as feminism influence scholarship.

As originally conceptualized in 1972 by women activists belonging to the Society for International Development (SID), the focus of inquiry was the unintended but frequently adverse impact that economic development was having on women. Women's work was ignored largely because women's traditional work in subsistence economies was uncounted in national labor force census enumerations and was, therefore, unrecognized in development planning. Women in development (WID) scholars collected data to demonstrate the importance of women's work on farms and in such subsistence activities as the collection of fuelwood, fetching water, and making baskets, jugs, and cloth. A major reference was Ester Boserup's 1970 landmark book, *Woman's Role in Economic Development*, which documented the shifting sexual division of labor as population pressures forced societies to adopt new technologies that, in turn, altered farming systems. Boserup chronicled global economic change in all its facets, while WID advocated incorporating women into planned interventions by donor agencies.

Testimony before Congress by SID-WID founder Irene Tinker led directly to the introduction of an amendment to the Foreign Assistance Act of 1973 requiring that women be integrated into all programs of the U.S. Agency for International Development. WID proponents wished to improve or reform donor programs so that women would benefit as well as men. By including women's perspectives, development programs would be better assured of reaching their goals. Offering agricultural information to men in Africa, where women do most of the farming, made little sense; however, it was typical of early agricultural extension approaches.

Proper recognition of women in resource projects was widely adopted by government agencies and by the increasing number of nongovernmental organizations (NGOs) active in development. The United Nations Decade for Women (1976–1985), punctuated with three major world conferences in Mexico City (1975), Copenhagen (1980), and Nairobi (1985), included development as one of its themes along with equality and peace. The Fourth World Conference on Women (Beijing, 1990) called for taking steps to overcome obstacles to women's advancement. As a result of resolutions passed at the Mexico City Conference, the UN established the UN Fund for Women to support small-scale efforts by women's organizations, and the UN International Research and Training Institute for the Advancement of Women to ensure that women were included in UN studies and activities.

Reality of Women's Lives

Heightened awareness of women's economic invisibility caused an acceleration of scholarship on women worldwide and sharpened the critique of development programs. At first this research centered on documenting women's economic contributions through time allocation studies of rural women. These data and findings challenged both the statistics and the definitions of work categories, for they revealed that women comprise 45 percent of all agricultural laborers, that women grow some 80 percent of all food south of the Sahara, that almost everywhere women work two to four hours a day more than men. Urban data found large numbers of women in Latin America, Africa, and Southeast Asia self-employed in the informal sector selling vegetables, street foods, and cosmetics. Domestic service in Latin America drew many women and girls because in those countries their

agricultural role was minimal. Other studies revealed that prostitution, expanded by the tourist industry, was linked to rural poverty.

Evaluations of the newly introduced development programs began to question the "efficiency" approach that simply included women, and argued for an emphasis on empowering women. WID proponents emphasized women's access to and control of income as critical for enhancing women's bargaining within the family; organizing women for community projects or income activities became a major point of intervention by NGOs.

Critics of WID

Particularly in Europe, women scholars considered this approach too narrow because it did not challenge the basic liberal paradigm upon which donor programs are based. Marxists argued that women's conditions would only improve with a fundamental alteration in the economic system. Women's studies scholars attacked history and literature for their cultural representations of gender, and identified patriarchy and class as principal sources of women's oppression. Because this scholarship was rooted in Western theory, women's studies tended to be ethnocentric. Women from developing countries criticized the emphasis on individualism, arguing that women exist within the family, community, and culture. These strands of criticism focused on the different experiences of women of different classes and ethnicities and led to the use of the term *gender* to highlight how attitudes and behavior of both women and men are socially constructed. Gender and development reflect the variety of experiences of both men and women. Studies about men's changing roles in development are extremely limited.

The most potent critique of liberal economic development is coming from environmentalists who condemn the profligate use of the world's resources for technological advance that is called progress. Ecofeminists combine this negative view of the industrial revolution with insights on women's status. Recalling that women were the first agriculturalists, and that women continue to be the guardians of forest reserves in many countries, ecofeminists maintain that women understand environment better than men do.

As the concept of development is increasingly questioned, local empowerment through organizations is perceived as the best way for women to improve their own lives. At the same time, greater understanding of the profound changes in men's lives, as well, requires new scholarship that illumines gender similarities and differences in this era of inconceivable change.

See also DEVELOPMENT, ALTERNATIVE; DEVELOPMENT: WESTERN PERSPECTIVE; WOMEN IN POLITICS; WOMEN AND RELIGION; WOMEN AND WORK; WOMEN'S MOVEMENT; WOMEN'S RIGHTS; WOMEN'S STUDIES.

BIBLIOGRAPHY

BOSERUP, ESTER. *Woman's Role in Economic Development.* New York: St. Martin's Press, 1970.

DWYER, DAISY, AND BRUCE, JUDITH, eds. *A Home Divided: Women and Income in the Third World.* Stanford, CA: Stanford University Press, 1988.

TINKER, IRENE, ed. *Persistent Inequalities: Women and World Development.* New York: Oxford University Press, 1990.

TINKER, IRENE, AND BO BRAMSEN, MICHELLE, eds. *Women and World Development.* New York: Praeger, 1976.

Irene Tinker

Women's Health Movement

Worldwide, women have been and will continue to be the primary consumers of health and medical care—for themselves, for children, and often for ill or aging relatives. Women, especially women of color, also are the great majority of low-paid health care workers. Yet most of the doctors in the United States are men, men are the focus of most health research, and men in hospitals, in legislatures and in the courtroom—make the major decisions affecting the health of women both as consumers and as workers. The women's health movement in the United States began and continues in response to these contradictions.

In the late 1960s, groups of mainly white, middle class women gathered. Breaking long-held silences, they critiqued doctors who were patronizing and noninformative, who overprescribed tranquilizers, who treated the natural life events of childbirth and menopause like illnesses requiring intervention. Mobilizing to inform themselves and others, women pressed for "natural" childbirth with partners allowed in the delivery room, for informed choice about drugs and surgery, and for safe, legal abortion. They taught the role of the clitoris in women's orgasm, and masturbation as a form of self-exploration and self-love. They showed how power inequalities between men and women crept in "between the sheets" in lovemaking. They questioned rigid definitions of "normal" sexuality that limited women to heterosexual relationships and discriminated against lesbian and bisexual women. In the face of powerfully undermining media images of women, they helped each other affirm their own diverse beauty.

"Know Your Body" courses sprang up around the country. Some women reclaimed control over their bodies through teaching cervical self-examination and menstrual extraction (removal of the menses to avoid painful periods or end an early pregnancy). Women-run health centers offered woman-centered health care, emphasizing prevention, education, and informed consent.

Critiques by women of color pushed the women's health movement to move beyond a white, middle-class agenda. Sterilization abuse, access to affordable medical care, and the right of women to bear healthy children, as well as to prevent or end pregnancy, became significant organizing issues.

There are successes to celebrate. Now there are patient-package inserts in oral contraceptives and estrogen-replacement hormones, warning of possible effects and risks; free-standing birth centers and wider acceptance of midwives as birth attendants; increased abortion availability after the 1973 Supreme Court *Roe* v. *Wade* decision; more women in medical schools; federal regulations to prevent sterilization abuse; and education of doctors about lesbian health care needs. Lumpectomy increased as a less invasive breast cancer treatment than mastectomy. Each advance was the result of extensive hard work by advocates for women's health, who lobbied, educated, organized, raised money, voted, and sometimes simply created their own alternatives.

In the 1980s, pressure from the U.S. medical establishment and conservative groups eroded many gains. New and "improved" technologies raised the level of intervention in childbirth and menopause. Access to abortion for poor and rural women worsened, and abortion rights looked as though they might slip away entirely. Poverty increased nationwide.

Women around the world organized, citing the unequal distribution of resources—both within less industrialized countries and between the "first" and "third" worlds—as the primary cause of poor nutrition, ill health, and high maternal mortality rates. Groups rallied to oppose harmful practices like female circumcision, and the distribution of drugs prohibited for U.S. use but dumped in poorer countries. They fought population-control programs that offered contraceptive injections, intrauterine devices, and sterilization as the sole option for fertility control. They argued that environmental degradation is caused less by overpopulation than by military pollution and in overconsumption in industrialized nations. Projects have ranged from rural self-help health education among illiterate *harijan* women of Southern India, to several international women's health conferences.

It is now the 1990s. The agenda for women's health activism into the twenty-first century includes greater coalition building to address:

- *Prevention:* The primacy of adequate food, water, shelter, innoculations, and early detection of treatable diseases must be recognized.
- *Economic Justice:* Poverty should be seen as the root cause of ill health and early death, especially for women and children of color.
- *Environmental Links:* The connection must be established between environmental toxins and the incidence of breast and other cancers, immune disorders, and chronic fatigue syndrome. Women's health means fighting pollution—from workplace toxins and noxious household cleaners, to military and industrial chemical spills, to policies of locating toxic waste sites everywhere, particularly in communities of color.
- *HIV Infection and AIDS:* Already HIV and AIDS are the major cause of early death for women of childbearing age in isolated parts of the United States and throughout much of Africa. Women are more at risk than men for HIV infection in heterosexual intercourse, and less empowered to protect themselves when a partner refuses to practice safer sex. Activists will seek to improve barrier methods, especially those like the female condom that can be woman-controlled. AIDS diagnosis, treatment, and insurance practices must be more adequately focused on women's needs, providing women with the economic, social, and personal power that will enable them to protect themselves from infection during sex.
- *Research.* In 1990 the new Office for Research on Women's Health opened at the National Institutes for Health (NIH). The first female head of NIH also established the "Women's Health Initiative," a multimillion-dollar study of osteoporosis, heart disease, and cancer—major concerns of midlife women that were long neglected in health research. Also overdue are long-term studies of women and aging, and the safety of long-acting contraceptives.
- *A National Health Program.* Women need universal access to high-quality services that include contraception, abortion, Pap smears, routine mammography for older women, at-home and community-based services for long-term care, and access to nonallopathic alternatives such as homeopathy, chiropractic, and acupuncture.
- *Violence Against Women:* The rape of women and children by soldiers as a weapon of war, sex tourism in Asia, dowry murder in India, the rape and murder of women by boyfriends, husbands, or strangers, and sexual abuse of children—all are critical women's health issues.
- *Sexuality:* There must be an affirmation of women's sexual power, pleasure, and freedom of choice despite the context of violence and the need for protection against sexually transmitted diseases.
- *Women and Smoking:* Young women are the main U.S. group in which smoking is on the rise. Activists must counter the media-led obsession with thinness that motivates girls to smoke in the hope of curbing their appetites.

See also ABORTION; CLASS AND UNDERCLASS; DISABLED PERSONS' RIGHTS; FAMILY PATTERNS; FAMILY PROBLEMS; FAMILY VALUES; HEALTH CARE; LONGEVITY; POVERTY, FEMINIZATION OF; SEXUAL CODES OF CONDUCT; SEXUAL HARASSMENT; WOMEN'S RIGHTS; WOMEN'S STUDIES.

BIBLIOGRAPHY

Boston Women's Health Book Collective. *The New Our Bodies, Our Selves: A Book by and for Women.* New York: Simon & Schuster, 1984.

COREA, GENA. *The Hidden Malpractice: How American Medicine Treats Women as Patients and Professionals.* New York: William Morrow, 1977.

———, ed. *Man-Made Women: How Reproductive Technologies Affect Women.* Bloomington, IN: Indiana University Press, 1987.

———. *The Mother Machine: Reproductive Technologies from Artificial Insemination to Artificial Wombs.* New York: Harper & Row, 1985.

DAVIS, SUSAN E., ed. *Women Under Attack: Victories, Backlash and the Fight for Reproductive Freedom.* Boston: South End Press, 1988.

DREIFUS, CLAUDIA, ed. *Seizing Our Bodies: The Politics of Women's Health.* New York: Vintage, 1977.

GORDON, LINDA. *Birth Control in American: Woman's Body, Woman's Right.* New York: Penguin, 1976.

HAIRE, DORIS B. *The Cultural Warping of Childbirth.* Seattle: International Child Birth Education Association, 1972.

KOLATA, GINA. "Self-Help Abortion Movement Gains Momentum." *New York Times,* October 23, 1989, p. B12.

RUZEK, SHERYL BUNT. *The Women's Health Movement: Feminist Alternatives to Medical Control.* New York: Praeger, 1978.

WHITE, EVELYN, ed. *The Black Women's Health Book: Speaking for Ourselves.* Seattle: Seal Press, 1990.

Wendy Sanford
Judith Norsigian

Women's Movement

Since 1970, a visionary feminism has managed to challenge seriously, if not transform, world consciousness. "First Wave" feminism was a nineteenth and early twentieth century movement of activist women struggling for nearly sixty years for women's suffrage or the right to vote. First Wave feminism succeeded in the United States with the passage in 1921 of a constitutional amendment establishing the right of women to vote.

Second Wave Feminism

Just as First Wave feminism grew out of the abolitionist movement to end slavery, Second Wave feminism in the United States emerged during the 1960s in parallel with the liberation movement of the civil rights and anti–Vietnam War struggles. Feminists left those movements when it became clear that women's liberation was not part of those agenda. From about 1967 on, grassroots feminists began to organize and fight for women's right to abortion and sexual freedom and equal pay for equal work.

Violence Against Women as a Feminist Issue

Feminist activists also focused on the sexual objectification of women and on the related issue of sexual violence toward women, such as stranger-rape and sexual harassment on the job and on the street. They pioneered and maintained rape crisis centers and shelters for battered women. They conducted "speakouts" and marched "to take back the night." They also testified at congressional hearings, and drafted legislation aimed at protecting women from the violence of men not only in their own families but in the workplace and in the wider society.

In the 1980s feminist activists began to expand their focus to include concerns for women within marriage. Some women were being raped by their spouses and battered. When these women chose to leave those marriages, they were impoverished and challenged regarding the custody of their children.

Women were also being sexually harassed and raped at their jobs, on the street, and on "dates." It became clear that there was a largely underreported surge of husbands or boyfriends battering and killing the women in their lives, and of men and older boys sexually abusing younger girls and boys.

During the 1980s it became clear to feminist activists working to deter violence against women, that prostitution and pornography were a part of this larger social problem. Many of the battered wives were being treated almost as if they were their husband's or boyfriend's prostitutes. Wife-batterers, pedophiles, and serial killers of women were often also fixated on pornography.

Women were also beginning to defend themselves against their abusers. Feminists rallying to support these women sometimes found that the few women who dared to kill their abusers in self-defense were being treated by the police and the court system as if they were terrorists deserving little mercy.

The Institutional Response of Second Wave Feminism

In the late 1960s and throughout the '70s, women's caucuses were formed within colleges and universities and in academic professional organizations. Both within the professions and as a separate field of study, women's studies became a widespread institutional reality in the 1980s, although ghettoized, perpetually challenged, and only minimally funded. Feminist bookstores increased rapidly in numbers and economic strength, as did publication of popular and scholarly feminist periodicals and books. A women's health and health-education movement began in the 1970s and has thrived.

Feminists, who have had to deal with both backlash as well as "frontlash," did not manage to create an immigrant-style alternative economic and social infrastructure. Feminist credit unions, soup kitchens, nursing homes, and social agencies are becoming a visible and successful part of the feminist movement. In terms of supportive rationale, feminists have made great and serious moral and intellectual gains in the areas of literature, theology, ritual, and psychology.

Backlash and Reassertive Feminism

The women's movement has generated a constant and an increasingly powerful backlash in the U.S. media and culture. Younger women who are benefiting from the efforts of the women's movement are encouraged to believe that its goals have been accomplished—and hence feminism is no longer needed. The word *feminism* itself has been assailed. Some younger writers represent a backlash within feminism. In the 1990s such writers decried the feminist activists of the Second Wave as "victim" feminists. They urged younger women to focus instead upon "power" feminism or a feminism of equality with men.

But feminist activists of the Second Wave maintain that feminism must be more radical. There are no individual or single solutions to redress what women face in a patriarchal society. Feminist activists equate patriarchy to gender in ways that are similar to how white racist societies deal with race. Radical women threaten those in power, as well as women who are at their mercy.

Radical thinkers and activists almost always pay a high price. They point out that in the nineteenth and twentieth centuries the suffragists were jailed and their meeting places were burned down by those who opposed them.

Feminist activists have learned to take themselves seriously not only because others support their views but also because still others oppose them. Only the powerful are opposed. If there is a feminism that has no opposition, something is wrong. Thus the radical feminist movement argues that heroism—not martyrdom—is the only feminist alternative of choice.

See also WOMEN IN FUTURES STUDIES; WOMEN IN POLITICS; WOMEN AND RELIGION; WOMEN AND WORK; WOMEN AND WORLD DEVELOPMENT; WOMEN'S HEALTH MOVEMENT; WOMEN'S RIGHTS; WOMEN'S STUDIES.

BIBLIOGRAPHY

BROWNMILLER, SUSAN. *Against Our Will*. New York: Simon & Schuster, 1974.

CHESLER, PHYLLIS. *Women and Madness*. Garden City, NY: Doubleday, 1972.

DWORKIN, ANDREA. *Pornography*. New York: Perigee, 1979.

FALUDI, SUSAN. *Backlash: The Undeclared War Against American Women*. New York: Crown, 1991.

HERMAN, JUDITH LEWIS. *Father-Daughter Incest*. Cambridge, MA: Harvard University Press, 1979.

Phyllis Chesler

Women's Rights

The modern women's movement in the United States was born in July 1848 at the Seneca Falls Convention, a gathering of three hundred, mostly female pioneer feminists, at Seneca Falls, N.Y., to protest the unjust treatment of women. Elizabeth Cady Stanton, the convention organizer, was the main architect of its feminist manifesto, the "Declaration of Sentiments," a catalyst in the launching of an organized feminist movement. This "Declaration" and its twelve accompanying resolutions addressed a broad array of feminist concerns, but for the next seven decades feminists focused almost entirely on what was actually the most controversial issue: the right to vote for women. The ultimate success of the campaign to enfranchise women, which came in 1920 with the ratification of the Nineteenth Amendment, led many feminists to believe that further activism was unnecessary. Suffragettes believed that with women voting as a bloc, the power of women voters would be enough to assure women's further objectives. However, the women's voting bloc did not materialize, and for nearly four decades women's issues received virtually no attention from the U.S. government.

A rebirth of the feminist movement came in the 1960s through the impetus in 1961 of the President's Commission on the Status of Women. The commission's 1963 report *American Women* proposed additional rights and more importantly sparked a new pro-feminist mood. Publication in the same year of Betty Friedan's bestselling *The Feminine Mystique*, which argued against the view that women must deprive themselves of fulfillment outside the home, bolstered the cause.

During this second wave of feminism, feminists achieved a number of legislative triumphs, including the banning of most types or discrimination in pay and in hiring. Other victories were won in the courts, including the legalization of abortion. Most remaining legal barriers to women's equality gave way because of an incremental approach targeted at combatting discrimination in very specific areas (such as credit discrimination or discrimination against pregnant women). There was renewed interest in the ratification of an Equal Rights Amendment (ERA), a comprehensive ban on all sex discrimination drafted in 1923. The feminist movement vigorously worked for ratification, winning passage by Congress and ratification by a number of states.

Feminists of the second wave also challenged the social codes, unlike the first-wave suffragists. Women were called upon to take charge of all areas of their lives—marital relationships, physical safety, health, reproduction, sexuality, and finances. Scores of women's organizations were created to channel their energy and promote women's rights. Some of these groups were large, multiissue organizations like the National Organization for Women, but many more focused specifically on one area of concern. Feminist publications proliferated, including *Signs* (the University of Chicago's women's studies journal), *New Directions for Women*, and the mass circulation *Ms.* magazine.

A radical branch of the feminist movement developed in the 1960s, partly in response to sexism exhibited by some members of the New Left. Although it did not survive the 1970s, its ideas later influenced mainstream feminism, particularly on issues pertaining to sexuality. It also contributed to the growth of a feminist subculture, in which feminism developed its own institutions.

With the election of Ronald Reagan as president in 1980 and the defeat of the ERA in 1982, the second wave of feminism seemed to come to an end. There were setbacks in the area of abortion rights, a lack of responsiveness in the federal government to the needs of single mothers, and a tendency by many women to reject the "feminist" label. However, during the 1980s, many feminist values were incorporated into American women's lives. Women asserted independence and self-reliance, and women's interests in society began to progress independently of the popularity of feminist ideology.

In the 1990s there has been a resurgence of feminist sentiment. Perhaps the best evidence of the new role of feminism is its stature as an intellectual force. Professor Laurence Tribe of Harvard Law School asserts that the feminist branch of legal study will exert a principal influence on new developments in the study of law over the next two and one-half decades. It will displace critical legal studies (which examines the role of laws in preserving the status quo) and the field of law and economics.

Women will benefit not only from the rediscovered interest in feminist ideology, but also from the sheer strength of their numbers in the political arena, in the work force, and in educational institutions. Women now constitute 54 percent of the electorate. Patricia Aburdene and John Naisbitt, coauthors of *Megatrends for Women*, contend that women now have such a strong base politically on the state level that they can be expected to hold governorships in about seventeen states by 2008; they also predict that a woman will likely have been elected president by then!

The future looks almost as bright in the area of employment and business. Women are estimated to comprise 66 percent of the net change in the size and composition of the workforce in the period from 1988 to 2000. Women in the labor force are expected to increase from 58 percent of all women in 1990 to 62.6 percent by the year 2000. A 14 percent drop in the proportion of women working at or below minimum wage from 1979 to 1989 was one of the factors contributing to the reduction of the female-male wage gap that took place in the period from 1980 to 1990, and has increased women's earning power to 72 cents for every dollar earned by a man, up from 64 cents in 1980.

Women-owned businesses at least doubled between 1977 and 1987, with finance, service, real estate, and insurance showing the most growth. The end result was that by 1987, 30 percent of all U.S. companies were women-owned. Because the growth of women-owned businesses outpaces that of most other segments of the economy, experts predict that from 40 to 50 percent of small businesses will be owned by women in the year 2000.

In the area of education, women outpace men. In 1989 women earned 57 percent of all associate degrees, 53 percent of all bachelor's degrees, 52 percent of all master's degrees, and 36 percent of all doctorates. Women earned two-fifths of all law degrees, one-fourth of all dentistry degrees, one-third of all medical degrees, and one-third of all veterinary degrees. The number of colleges and universities with women presidents almost doubled between 1975 and 1987.

Women's rights advocates emphasize that the progress made by women has not reversed all the effects of centuries of discriminatory practices because de facto gender-based inequities persist. There are in fact dimensions of sex discrimination that have not been fully appreciated by the public, including sexual harassment at work, rape, marital rape, sterilization abuse, and continuing disparities in pay scales. Furthermore, bias can often take extremely subtle forms, resulting in disparities that Mary Rowe of the Massachusetts Institute of Technology has labelled as "microinequities." Microinequities are the aftereffects of negative views of women pervasive in previous generations, views which are so deeply engrained in our culture that we may often not be fully aware of their presence. In most cases there is no legal redress for such microinequities, but Rowe has proposed methods for combatting them such as the following: putting women in upper-level positions where performance is highly visible; putting men and women together on task forces and committees, so that each group is reliant on the skills of the other; and conducting training programs to sensitize and educate employees. In the coming years, subtle microinequities will receive a great deal of attention from feminists.

See also HUMAN RIGHTS; POVERTY, FEMINIZA-
TION OF; SOCIAL CHANGE: UNITED STATES; SOCIAL
CONTROLS; WOMEN IN POLITICS; WOMEN IN RELI-
GION; WOMEN'S MOVEMENT.

BIBLIOGRAPHY

ABURDENE, PATRICIA, and NAISBITT, JOHN. *Megatrends for
Women.* New York: Villard, 1992.
DAVIS, FLORA. *Moving the Mountain.* New York: Simon &
Schuster, 1991.
"Defining Law on the Feminist Frontier." *New York Times
Magazine,* October 6, 1991.
RIES, PAULA, and STONE, ANNE J. *The American Woman
1992–93: A Status Report.* New York: Norton, 1992.
"The Sting of the Subtle Snub." *Working Women* (Jan-
uary 1991).

Sarah Claudine Kurian

Women's Studies

Women's studies—the study of women developed
by women in the late twentieth century—varies in
different political, social, cultural, and historical
contexts around the world. In some areas it may
focus on the study of rural women or literacy education relevant to women, or maternal and child
health. It may document women's and men's roles
in the paid sector of the economy, or the effects of
custom and law on women's lives, or their relation
to the making of public policy. There are many
forms and variants.

In the United States, *women's studies* usually
refers to a burgeoning interdisciplinary field of research and teaching originating in the universities,
which critiques knowledge and expands scholarship and educational curricula to include women's
history, experiences, and points of view. New bodies of knowledge developed through research on
women led to a searching review of previous bodies of knowledge that excluded women. Women's
studies has affected each academic discipline,
adding new information and also challenging those
who deny that scholars' sex, race, class, religion,
region, or sexual orientation might bear on their
making of knowledge and on the question of who
benefits from that knowledge.

Women's studies programs for college credit in
the United States began in the late 1960s, following
black studies as developed in the civil rights movement. Programs mushroomed; the National
Women's Studies Association was founded in the
late 1970s. By 1985, more than 19,000 courses on

women were being offered on U.S. campuses and
over 480 women's studies programs were offering
major or minor degrees in women's studies. In
1995, more than 620 women's studies programs
exist, some offering M.A.'s and Ph.D.'s as well as
undergraduate degrees.

Centers for research on women also sprang up,
starting in the early 1970s; more than seventy centers are now members of the U.S. National Council
for Research on Women. In general, the centers do
not teach directly but generate research on women
and men that will widen the knowledge base, make
education more vigorous and accurate, and root
both public policy and civic life in more inclusive
definitions of humanity and society.

The rapid development of women's studies as an
academic field in both higher education and primary and secondary school material contributed to
the creation of more than twenty-five periodicals
in the United States focused on women, tens of
thousands of books, conferences, workshops, faculty development programs, organizations, associations, caucuses, art and drama groups, museum
exhibits, specialized museums, galleries, publishing houses, small presses, and feminist and multicultural bookstores.

Around the world, especially during the final two
decades of the twentieth century, women's studies
and research on women developed in all of the English-speaking nations of the world, all Western
European nations, more than fifteen Asian nations,
many countries of Central and South America, and
in the 1990s, some of the newly opened nations of
Eastern Europe began to pursue these objectives.

One aim of women's studies is to improve education for all women and men and to produce more
equitable thinkers and more balanced policies than
are now found at the centers of power. In order to
effect such outcomes, women's studies has had to
make constant efforts to avoid the very problems of
the defective education that it challenges. Unless it
continually broadens itself globally and analyzes
all of the factors that lead to the domination of one
group by another, women's studies tends to ascribe
the power to name, validate, judge, and make decisions to the racial and cultural groups that already
have the most public power in world contexts.
Women's studies scholars have had to become mul-
ticulturally aware and informed. Increasingly, they
seek and respect local, contexted understandings
generated from the experience of people in a given
place and a given time, including students. Internationally, this means that the field takes shape differently in different places.

Some national governments and religious bodies have strongly resisted higher education for women, collection of data on women, and the development of women's studies programs and research on women. The United Nations Nongovernmental Forums for Women, however, which were attended by representatives from every nation in 1975, 1980, and 1985, made it clear that women's studies was developing internationally. This emboldened many women to start exploring questions from women's points of view around the world.

Critics had claimed that the school and college and university curriculum is objective, scientific, and not political, whereas women's studies is subjective, nonscientific, and political. Women's studies scholars replied that traditional knowledge that excludes women is highly subjective and politicized—as well as being very inaccurate. This argument generally carried the day, until 1990, when fundamentalist academic and religious forces began a new round of sharp assaults. Women's studies is pressed to defend itself, with multicultural studies, against those who are unwilling to share the power of knowledge making and who wish to continue to construe themselves as central instead of co-central in that undertaking.

As of 1995, women's studies was spreading around the world, surviving, and in many places thriving, as an intellectually dynamic field of study in its own right and a new lens through which to view past knowledge, knowledge making, and social reality. Its chief gift to the construction of reality in the twenty-first century may be in its respect for narrative as a genre of knowledge making different from, and parallel to, empirical science as a form of understanding—each careful not to claim too much for findings from limited samples.

See also ETHNIC AND CULTURAL SEPARATISM; FAMILY PATTERNS; FAMILY VALUES; FUTURES STUDIES; MINORITIES; RACE, CASTE, AND ETHNIC DIVERSITY; SEXUAL HARASSMENT; WOMEN IN FUTURES STUDIES; WOMEN IN POLITICS; WOMEN AND RELIGION; WOMEN AND WORK; WOMEN AND WORLD DEVELOPMENT; WOMEN'S HEALTH MOVEMENT; WOMEN'S MOVEMENT; WOMEN'S RIGHTS.

BIBLIOGRAPHY

CHAMBERLAIN, MARIAM. "The Emergence and Growth of Women's Studies Programs." In Sara E. Rix, ed. *The American Woman, 1990–1991*, pp. 315–324.
RIX, SARA E., ed. *The American Woman, 1990–91: A Status Report*. New York: Norton, 1990.
"Scholars Seek Wider Reach for Women's Studies." *New York Times*, May 17, 1989, p. B6.
STIMPSON, CATHARINE R., with Nina Kressner Cobb. *Women's Studies in the United States*. New York: Ford Foundation, 1986.

Peggy McIntosh

Work

Work is used, and has been at least since the industrial revolution, to distribute income and gain social status. This implicit notion is evident in the government's providing disability payments to those who can no longer work and temporary payments to those who have lost their job and are looking for another. It is apparent in the society's willingness to subsidize and continue to support people who have grown too old to participate in the paid workforce. It is also evident in the respect paid to people who work, who hold jobs, who have successful careers, or who become wealthy through work. In North American society, at least, the first question asked of a new acquaintance is most often, "What do you do?"

Although it is clear that most people's income and status rest on the work they do and are paid for, it is all the more alarming that the huge social system called work is changing radically and may be breaking down, that the long-term future of work could be in jeopardy. If in fact all of the goods and services required in a nation like the United States could be provided by only 15 percent of the working population as Alexander King of the Club of Rome has suggested, what will the other 85 percent do? How will we receive our share of the national income, and how will we determine our status in a society where only a few people can have what we now think of as "a job"?

How is it possible for 15 percent of the people to do all the work? The history of work in the United States can serve as an example. In colonial times almost everyone worked in agriculture. It was necessary, in order to survive and eat. Over time, however, the agricultural system has grown more efficient and more productive so that today less than 2.6 percent of the workforce works in agriculture. The rest of the population benefits from the cheap and plentiful supply of food that that sector provides. And output is so prodigious that more than 50 percent of many crops are surplus to domestic needs and sold to export.

After colonial times in America, the rising industrial sector absorbed the growing workforce, who left the farm and went into the factory where there was plentiful new work. Today the industrial sector is on a steep upward curve of productivity, producing more goods with fewer people. Automation and efficiency will continue to reduce the number of jobs in this sector so that the 17 percent of the workforce who work in industrial production today will be reduced to 10 percent or less in the next century.

The growing services and information sectors of the economy have been absorbing job seekers in the last few decades. But this sector, too, is beginning its upward swing on the productivity curve and with the help of automation and new efficiencies will reduce the number of jobs it has to offer. The economics of work are also changing. Charles Handy points out in *The Age of Paradox* that advanced nations like the United States have plenty of work that needs to be done, but they have priced many jobs out of the marketplace because people need good wages to live in these societies. The number of paid jobs, therefore, shrinks. Such societies also generally have older, better educated people, thus higher paid workers.

Where are all the jobs going? The answer is to the countries where large, young workforces have lower expectations of a wage and less education. These countries will be able to compete for all the paid work that is not worth automating or reducing by greater efficiencies. If this drain of jobs overseas continues, and jobs go to the lowest bidder, it would profit advanced nations to invest in those economies, in order to equalize wages and opportunities for work around the world.

Most of the methods and policies that government uses to maintain work as a system for distributing income are based on what proved to be useful when most people had jobs producing goods. There is now considerable concern that government should in some way be responsible for replacing an individual worker's lost income or making it possible for an unemployed worker to find another job in order to continue to receive his or her share of the nation's income. The problem of how to do that in a society where the nature and availability of work keep changing is obvious.

In Europe after World War II, governments undertook to distribute a share of their wealth through social supports almost without regard to work. This worked well as long as most people had jobs. But with increasing productivity and the loss of jobs to lower wage economies creating widespread structural unemployment, the social supports are becoming more difficult to sustain.

Governments are now viewing jobs as a scarce resource that must be given out fairly to achieve the best results for the economy. As a result, many people are receiving minimal support from their governments and earning the rest of their living in growing underground economies.

The United States may face similar problems. However, most people in the United States tend to believe in the country's ability to adapt to new circumstances and to create new jobs, new work, and new systems that will deal out returns evenly to all. What may be necessary in the case of work is a transformation in what work is, how people see it, and its role in the distribution of income and its relevance to peoples' lives.

Work life in the next century will:

- Be more cooperative than competitive.
- Use alternatives to today's money and wage structures: barter, for example. The expectation is that computer technology will make the complexities of a barter system workable.
- Have people who will share one job with several other people.
- Have people who are as much committed to doing work as they are today.
- Have people spending more of their time on work projects to benefit the communities they live in.
- Be willing to rethink the concept of rewards for work well done, in some cases disassociating them from money.
- Encourage people to develop their aesthetic senses, and to expend more time and interest on artistic and craft-based projects.
- Allow people to work on paid projects only in short bursts, and then very intensively.
- Be composed of groups of people whose job is to learn and integrate information and create work projects with it. The downtime from these projects, again, is likely to be long and reflective, the work period, short and intense.
- Have no one who will work an eight-hour day on one job or one task.
- Organized so that all workers receive credit for a life's work at the beginning of adulthood, and can then spend those credits as they choose. Community pressure will control the deadbeats.
- Still include the super-competitive type (Wall Street traders), but will have mechanisms to absorb their energy and competitiveness.
- Replace the money system of today by forms of credit that are adjusted to the social value of work people are willing to do.
- Be friendly to groups that organize themselves as tribes and be rewarded accordingly.

- See the gradual disappearance of money for any purpose.

Work as it is now will not continue in the same patterns. Handy, who has been writing about the future of work since the 1970s, suggests that as a result of our pursuit of efficiency and economic growth—as if these were society's ideal—the needs of people for useful work are being neglected. If the money value of work is set at zero, there will always be any amount of it to go around, so work itself will never disappear, but the ways in which society uses work to achieve other goals may change. Leisure is frequently defined as what you do when you are not working and, therefore, something we should work to gain more of. Handy and others suggest that future generations will want their leisure within work, as well as more interesting experiences when they are at work. Thus, the lines between work and nonwork are likely to blur.

The ways in which work is organized are already changing because information-related work does not have to be organized like factory work. Workplaces are likely to be smaller and more widely distributed, perhaps closer to home for many people. As more full-time jobs are squeezed out, people may have smaller jobs and more of them. The weekday consultant on worldwide business expansions could be a weekend farmer, for example, raising raspberries for restaurant tables in the nearby city.

The government will be driven to more ambitious and risky policy experiments in order to keep the most productive members of the workforce at work and make it possible for everyone else to stay out. Young people will be encouraged to get more education and enter the workforce later. Their formal work lives will end earlier. People may be expected to spend years in government work corps, doing cleanup, building, and other jobs to obtain education or subsistence benefits. Children will be educated to know what to do with their time as adults when no one wants to pay them to work, but they are expected to be usefully occupied.

It is difficult for us today to look forward to a time when the eight-hour workday will be a memory and the idea of being a regular employee of an organization loses its luster as a goal for most people. Our entire orientation to paid work will have to be reshaped into something new. Work will never lose its importance for tool-using humans, but it may lose its utility as a way of managing society and allocating rewards.

See also UNEMPLOYMENT; UNIONISM; WOMEN AND WORK; WORK, QUALITY OF; WORK ETHIC; WORKFORCE DISTRIBUTION; WORKFORCE DIVERSITY; WORKING CONDITIONS.

BIBLIOGRAPHY

ABRAHAM, KATHARINE G., and HOUSEMAN, SUSAN N. *Job Security in America: Lessons from Germany*. Washington, DC: Brookings Institution, 1993.
GAFFIKIN, FRANK, and MORRISEY, MIKE. *The New Unemployed: Joblessness and Poverty in the Market Economy*. London and Atlantic Highlands, NJ: Zed Books, 1992.
GIL, DAVID B., and GIL, EVA A., eds. *The Future of Work: A Conference of the Center for Social Change, Practice, and Theory*. Rochester, VT, 1987.
HANDY, CHARLES. *The Age of Paradox*. Cambridge, MA: Harvard University Press, 1991.
_____. *The Future of Work*. Cambridge, MA: Blackwell, 1984.

Jennifer Jarratt

Work, Quality of

Over the past twenty years, the three major types of change—social, technological, and economic—have had relatively little impact on each other, but as we approach the next millennium, these changes will interact more vigorously. The cumulative force of these changes suggest that for some the quality of work available to them will be high and will satisfy most of their needs; but not everyone will be willing or able to adapt to these changes, and for them life will be more difficult.

Social Change

The changing values, beliefs, and motivations of the work force already play a significant role in changing the nature of work. Large numbers of people in the industrialized countries are choosing to work at home, some self-employed, others still working for an employer. Despite recent concern about the job market, there has been a continuing trend for people to seek more personal time to have that time *during hours and even on days that suit them*. As pressures of commuting increase and "edge cities" develop, where all business and social needs can be met, increasing numbers of white-collar and professional workers are expected to take this option. In the United States in 1991, some 20 percent of the work force worked from home full- or part-time. In the United Kingdom, the comparable number for 1990 was 15 percent. By 2000 it is expected that close to 50 percent of the work forces in each country will be working from home at least part of the time.

Another related trend involving the same values and pressures resulted in increasing numbers of management buy-outs. These buy-outs were not large or highly leveraged, rather, they involved small groups of people who thought they could do better on their own. That trend will also continue to increase.

In both cases—working at home and buy-outs—the people who function best in the new way of working are self-disciplined, responsible for themselves, and adept at using information technology. These may be difficult characteristics for people who espouse the self-indulgent aspect of 1960s values.

Technology Change

Modern technology (especially information technology) already has imposed a major impact on the workplace, and more is expected in the decades to come. If we choose to so, almost any work activity can be accomplished from home, with very few people physically at the work site. Much manufacturing could be undertaken by automated machines and robots, monitored and controlled from a remote location. Deep mining can already be done that way. Maintenance activities for infrastructure (gas, water, sewage, and so forth) already use automated remote-controlled equipment. Furthermore, intelligent-vehicle highway systems are being developed.

Of course there are exceptions to these trends. Some developmental and exploratory work will require people to have access to laboratories, equipment, and materials. In the service industries although some degree of automation is likely, many people will still prefer to carry out transactions and receive services on a face-to-face basis. However, the real question is not about whether technology can do all this and more. It is not even about whether we can afford the technology since microminiaturization and nanotechnology will bring the prices down. The pivotal question is whether we *want* to use it. Will society be able to afford the social cost of nearly full automation? In the short term, the answer is probably no; In the longer term of twenty years or more, there may be no other viable options.

Economic Change

Economic conditions over the period of 1988 to 1994 forced some organizations out of business while others became lean and fit. The United States, by taking a more pragmatic approach to the recent recession than many of its competitors, has seen a remarkable growth in productivity during this time. Nonetheless, international competition can only increase as new players join the fray. Capital and labor productivity will continue to remain of great concern. Big business will have to increase further the technological component of its operations to remain competitive. One means to retain competitiveness will be flexibility, including rapid response to change, which also extends to work practices.

The Future

Change does not come easily, and the real key for dealing with change is education. Within twenty years any country that wants to succeed socially, technologically, and economically must improve its education systems to ensure that children are taught technical skills, instructed in *how* to learn as a specific skill, and coached to see the value in continuing to learn.

Other changes that will alter the workplace include:

- *More self-employment.* This may include networking and teaming arrangements among people with similar or complementary skills. Such individuals will contract out their services to larger organizations.
- *Just-in-time jobs.* Many employers in medium and large companies will maintain a small permanent staff and contract out many seasonal and other tasks to the self-employed and small businesses.
- *Leadership, not management.* In this flexible, fast-response world, old-style management will not work. The new situation will require leaders who can inspire, help create a shared vision, instill a sense of mission, and evoke loyalty.
- *Networking work teams.* Combinations of small, permanent workforces and subcontractors will require people to work in small, flexible teams, with members of the teams grouping and regrouping in network fashion as required.
- *Heterarchical command structures.* New forms of work structure are likely to be built around the demands of a particular piece of work. To accomplish this successfully, the individual who is the expert will need to take the lead role. Small hierarchies assembled for particular tasks, with the expert at each task taking the lead, may also form part of a network on another type of task.

Stereotype rewards related to "position" alone will assume less importance.

- *Performance.* New ways of working will require new performance measures and objectives, which will have to be set and agreed to by the organization, its own workers, and its contractors (who may look more like employees than traditional contractors). Some new form of "management by objectives," to be used in conjunction with an organization's visionary objectives is likely.

In this emerging environment, people who can work independently with self-discipline and responsibility will do very well. Those who require routine work and close supervision will find their lives increasingly difficult. This changed emphasis in the work environment poses formidable challenges for the educational system.

See also CHANGE, SCIENTIFIC AND TECHNOLOGICAL; SOCIAL CHANGE: UNITED STATES; WORK; WORK ETHIC; WORKFORCE DISTRIBUTION; WORKFORCE DIVERSITY.

BIBLIOGRAPHY

DELAMOTTE, IVES, and TAKEZAWA, S. *Quality of Working Life in International Perspective.* Geneva: International Labour Office, 1986.

HANDY CHARLES. *The Future of Work.* Cambridge, MA: Basil Blackwell, 1984.

HARMAN, WILLIS, and HORMANN, JOHN. *Creative Work.* Indianapolis: Knowledge Systems, 1990.

PARKER, MIKE. *Inside the Circle: A Guide to the Quality of Work Life.* Boston: South End Press, 1985.

TERKEL, STUDS. *Working.* New York: Ballantine, 1985.

Christine A. R. MacNulty

Workers' Compensation.

See the entry UNEMPLOYMENT INSURANCE, WORKERS' COMPENSATION, JOB SECURITY.

Work Ethic

"My father taught me to work," Abraham Lincoln said. "He did not teach me to love it." Economic success derives from a compelling work ethic, a deeply embedded cultural value that presumes an indelible relationship between labor and virtue. Even wealthy individuals are expected to work, whether to expand their fortunes, achieve in a different field, or advance a social or charitable cause.

The most conspicuous aspect of the changing role of women in society is their assumption of equal roles in the workforce. Children are encouraged to begin work at an early age, even when economic factors are not involved, so they can develop a work ethic. Useful work is essential to societal cohesiveness and is used as a measure of one's character and value.

Like Lincoln, we do not presume enjoyment to be inherent to the work experience. We take pride in work well done, and savor the community acceptance and approval that accrues to working people, but few of us confuse work with fun.

For most of us, work is what we do when we would rather be doing something else. Human nature being what it is, that aspect of work will never change. What will change is the nature of work and the complex interrelationships that prevail in the workplace, primarily between management and labor.

Historically, most work entailed strenuous manual exertion. Only a few individuals earned their daily bread through intellectual pursuits, and in most cases they also performed a variety of physical tasks.

The industrial age freed people from much of the lifting, hauling, and manual drudgery that had long been their lot, enabling many people to pursue less strenuous tasks, thus setting the stage for unprecedented technological and scientific advances.

We are now embarked upon a boundless postindustrial age of intellectual discovery. Daily breakthroughs remake virtually every aspect of the way we work and live. Just as the machines of the industrial age enhanced the power of human muscle, the microchip multiplies the power of the human mind. Our future holds unlimited promise.

However, the traditional linear line of authority that sustained us in ancient times and through the industrial age will not suffice into the future. As workers become more cerebral, and hence more valuable, it will be neither feasible nor wise to expect them to function like automatons on an assembly line. Employers who do not permit full rein and realization of workers' intellects will not survive very long.

Already, progressive enterprises are establishing a new work place ethic of collegial cooperation that blurs traditional categories and lines of authority. The Total Quality Management (TQM) that contributes to defining the most successful businesses is predicated upon full employee involvement in all stages of the decision-making process. Most vestiges of work place status are disappearing through a polyphony of creative interplay among all participants.

Just as workers in progressive environments define their success and status in part upon their acceptance as full partners in the business at hand, it follows that systems of recompense also are evolving in new and surprising ways. There is less reliance upon rigid pay scales based upon status in the hierarchy, and more emphasis upon performance —both of the individual employee and that of the total enterprise through profit sharing.

Much is written these days about the decline in organizational loyalty stemming from commercial and industrial restructuring. Layoffs and forced early retirements imposed to reduce static work forces are painful necessities that invariably produce anxiety and distress among all concerned. As work becomes more cerebral and less physical, and the routines of the work place are subject to more rapid flux, it seems likely that increased worker mobility will follow. To the extent that workers will expect to change employers more frequently in the future, there will be less organizational loyalty, at least in the traditional sense of the term.

On the other hand, as workers assume a greater role in corporate decision making and enjoy the increased status and enhanced self-esteem that accompanies it, there will be a concurrent increase in identification with the enterprise where one is employed and of personal commitment to it. There will be a concomitant increase in work satisfaction, as people gain greater control over their personal destinies and inherit a larger sense of responsibility for the decisions they and their coworkers arrive at together.

What will not change—what must never change— is the commitment to work and the belief in the healing power of labor to transform the human experience and lend meaning to life. It is not leisure or play that defines our character, but rather our ability to withstand adversity, sustain commitment, and do what has to be done regardless of conflicting pressures or tempting distractions. Indeed, the changing value of the work place will serve to enrich the American work ethic and imbue it with a new vitality and spirit to sustain us well into the twenty-first century and beyond.

See also GLOBAL CULTURE; INFORMATION SOCIETY; WOMEN AND WORK; WORK; WORK, QUALITY OF; WORKING CONDITIONS.

BIBLIOGRAPHY

"The End of the Job." *Fortune* (September 19, 1994).
HAMMER, MICHAEL, and CHAMPY, JAMES. *Reengineering the Corporation: A Manifesto for the Business Revolution.* New York: HarperCollins, 1993.
"The Information Revolution: How Digital Technology Is Changing the Way We Work and Live." *Business Week* (bonus issue, 1994).
"21st Century Capitalism: How Nations and Industries Will Compete in the Emerging Global Economy." *Business Week* (bonus issue, 1994).
"What Ever Happened to the Great American Job?" *Time* (November 11, 1993): 32–39.

Richard Lesher

Workforce Diversity

The workforce in the United States always has been diverse. Its population patterns, as a nation of immigrants, were constantly altered. Both before and after the Civil War, black Americans were a conspicuous component of the population. Women, of course, have always worked for pay in large numbers, usually out of necessity or to help out in the factory during a seasonal surge in work.

U.S. ethnic composition is strongly influenced by low white birth rates and the rapid rise of immigrants. Bureau of Census 1994 estimates anticipate legal immigrants to number 8.8 million persons during the 1990s. Illegal immigrants double that number. Demographic projections, based on a continuation of these trends, indicate that ethnic minorities may account for 30 percent of total U.S. population by 2033.

Inflows from south of the border dominate. Hispanics are projected to surpass blacks as the largest U.S. minority by 2020. California is where accommodations of the diverse workplace may be most keenly felt. By 1989 California became the first U.S. state with a "minority" population actually higher than the traditional white majority (with Hispanics making up 37.8 percent of the population, followed by Asians at 10.8 per cent and blacks with 10.5 percents). In the workforce, blacks, Asians, Hispanics, and other minorities are anticipated to account for 26 percent of the workforce by 2000. The handwriting is on the wall—diversity is the hallmark of the workplace or the future.

Non-Hispanic white males, who long dominated the U.S. workforce, accounted for less than 50 percent of the workforce by 1990, and are projected to drop further, reaching only 41–45 percent of all workers by 2000. Women sixteen years and older working for pay outside the home constituted 18.2 percent of the workforce. They often were scorned and self-conscious about having to work. By the 1990s, the proportion had increased to 60 percent and was projected to reach 75 percent by 2000. The new female workers were proud to be employed, insistent on plying their skills and professions, strident in asserting equal rights, and dead serious about eliminating discriminatory practices.

America has long been considered, the "melting pot" of ethnic and cultural diversity. In other parts of the world, Balkanization and separatism have been hallmarks. America's new diversity—the new multiculturalism—will test its resolve to assimilate all comers.

Those diversity elements were not a prominent part of the public policy debate or the subject of legislative attention until two changes had occurred. First was the settlement of more urgent labor issues such as the right to organize, the forty-hour work week, and social security. Second was a series of developments that made it clear beyond reasonable doubt that large groups in society were systematically being discriminated against in hiring and in advancement. Blacks, other ethnic and racial groups, and women were often the last hired and first fired. The civil rights movement, with its demands for equal access to jobs, housing, and public accommodations, prevailed in effective legislation. Independently the changing patterns of family size and the widespread entry of women into all aspects of business and work life raised their collective awareness of the widespread unfair practices directed against them. The resulting political movement led to legislation to redress their grievances. The campaigns for and implementation of legislation directed at promoting equity quickly spread to other groups, making them aware both of injustices and the opportunities for legislated remedies. This new self-consciousness of collective grievances is at the heart of the awareness of workplace diversity.

The new social ambience of rejection of prejudicial behavior led many other people to see that they also belonged to groups that had special interests at the workplace and elsewhere that could be met through collective action. Many, if not all, groups other than white males of European stock in the 1970s and '80s seemed to have formed a self-designated element of diversity. As business and government responded to the pressure for reform primarily by offering compensatory programs, preferential advancement, and greater flexibility, new groups came forward. Changing business practices have also promoted diversity. Telecommuters, part-time workers, single parents, gays, temporary workers,

older workers, and many others make up the current workplace complex.

What does the future hold? The settlement of grievances will be slow simply because social change is slow, except in times of crisis. While progress is real, there is a long way to go before all groups achieve equal pay for equal work or have fair access to top-level, high-paying jobs, relative to their numbers in the workforce. Some are likely to find parity through unionization or by rejecting big business and preferring to work for small or entrepreneurial businesses. Other groups—Asians, for example, because of their rapid pace of economic progress—may lose any real claim to special consideration at the workplace. Other groups assimilating into the economy and society, Hispanics, for example, may reject special status as demeaning.

Still other groups will become more active and aggressive as their numbers increase—older workers, for example, or the handicapped, if they find themselves reaching equity status too slowly. Others will find success in areas outside work and transfer that success to the workplace—for example, the AIDS-advocacy activists. Waves of new immigrants will bring fresh concerns to the workplace as they identify themselves as special groups.

Changing business practices will create new or newly important groups seeking fair treatment. Among these practices are business alliances that will highlight discrepancies in the way workers are treated, managed, and rewarded in the allied companies. As multinational corporations engage in more—and more complex—business activities in other countries, the foreign nationals will be increasingly aware of any difference in the ways they are treated and paid and will respond accordingly.

As workplace diversity issues evolve, there will be a growing awareness in society of individual and group differences and special needs or claims. There has always been resistance to the claims of diverse elements at the workplace, because change is disruptive to established relationships. Equity legislation, when implemented, has often led to new inequities, whether real or perceived. There is growing backlash to compensatory preferential treatment of minorities and women. Changes in the law will certainly occur to strike a new balance among conflicting goals. One can only hope that those changes do not overcompensate in the reverse direction and undo progress. Fair and equitable access to jobs will mean upward mobility for all.

One of the more ironic developments is the emergence of a backlash white worker rights movement that crystallizes the disquiet of many who see themselves as unfairly treated, while other groups enjoy the benefit of compensatory programs.

It is increasingly clear to all concerned with workplace equity that many of the sources of inequity develop outside the workplace, notably in education and preparation for work. Closer attention will be given to equal preparation for work as a basic mechanism for reducing any basis for differential treatment of workers at the workplace.

Aside from issues at the workplace, diversity will bring new perspectives to corporate or organizational thinking and may bring companies closer to their increasingly heterogeneous customers.

See also CLASS AND UNDERCLASS; DISABLED PERSONS' RIGHTS; ETHNIC AND CULTURAL SEPARATISM; ETHNIC AND RACIAL CONFLICT; HUMAN RESOURCES DEVELOPMENT; NATIVE AMERICANS; PREJUDICE, FORMS OF; RACE, CASTE, AND ETHNIC DIVERSITY; SEXUAL HARASSMENT; UNIONISM; WOMEN AND WORK; WORK; WORKFORCE REDISTRIBUTION.

BIBLIOGRAPHY

BULLOCK, SUSAN. *Women and Work.* London and Atlantic Highlands, NJ: Zed Books, 1994.
GINZBERG, ELI. The Changing U.S. Labor Market. Boulder, CO: Westview Press, 1994.
MURDOCK, STEVE H. *An America Challenged: Population Change and the Future of the United States.* Boulder, CO: Westview Press, 1995.
PETERSON, ANNE C. and MORTIMER, JEYLAN T., eds. *Youth Unemployment and Society.* New York: Cambridge University Press, 1994.
State and Local Coalition on Immigration/Immigrant Policy Project. *America's Newcomers: An Immigrant Policy Handbook.* Denver, CO: National Conference of State Legislatures, 1994.

Joseph F. Coates

Workforce Redistribution

Workforce redistribution flows from social, technical, economic, and political change. In *The Third Wave,* Alvin Toffler spotted the onset of postindustrial (third wave) society—the first and second waves being the agricultural and industrial economies. The first bar chart (Figure 1) shows the shift of employment between the three waves in various types of countries since 1960 and forecasts workforce distribution to the year 2000.

Wave Effect of Techno-Revolutions

Developing countries are agrarian societies, as was North America in the Agricultural Age. As a nation modernizes, there is a continual shift of workers

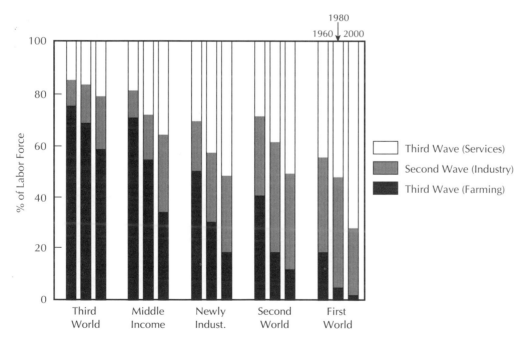

FIGURE 1.   Global workforce restructuring.
(Copyright 1990 by Frank Feather. Used with permission.)

from farming to industry and services. As machines take over farm tasks, people move to the cities where they form labor pools for manufacturers and service companies. Today in North America, farming employs only 3 percent against 80 percent in the postindustrial sector. Indeed, to understand the third wave, we must further divide it. In reality, we have a six-wave economy:

- *First Wave:* Agriculture/Natural Resources/Energy
- *Second Wave:* Industry/Manufacturing/Robotics
- *Third Wave:* Financial/Health Care/Personal Services
- *Fourth Wave:* Information/Knowledge/High Technology
- *Fifth Wave:* Leisure and Tourism
- *Sixth Wave:* Outer-Space Economy

These waves exist simultaneously, but one wave usually dominates. The old waves don't disappear; rather, the new ones complement them. For example, machines modernized farming and increased crop yield. Information is not just spawning the fourth-wave information economy, but modernizing all other sectors. Computerized information is essential to any modern farm, factory, office, school, hospital, or hotel.

In North America, services became the largest employer in 1950. This was the third-wave revolution. The fourth wave (of computers, information, and knowledge professions) rose to domination in the 1980s. However, the fastest-growing job field is the fifth-wave leisure sector—the travel, tourism, hospitality, recreation, entertainment, and cultural industry. And the sixth-wave outer-space economy is emerging as a twenty-first-century sector of employment.

Forces of Workforce Redistribution

Socially, each of us is the servant of everybody else. Note down society's future needs and you get a list of all the jobs that will be required. In an aging society, the demand for healthcare workers will soar beyond today's needs. And, as people age, their other needs will also change. Eldercare will replace childcare as a primary focus of baby boomers because they all have aging relatives and their children will be grown up. As well, new generations of people will be born with their own unique sets of needs. New waves of immigrants will bring yet more needs.

Technology also changes workforce demands. It changes or replaces old jobs and creates new ones. As automobiles and telephones demonstrated, technology also changes how society is structured and functions. Through the "ripple effect" of these innovations, technology indirectly restructures the job market. For example, people began making automatic washing machines (instead of wringer washers and scrubbing boards), microwave ovens (instead of convection stoves), and personal computers and word processors (instead of typewriters). In turn, this restructures all jobs in the

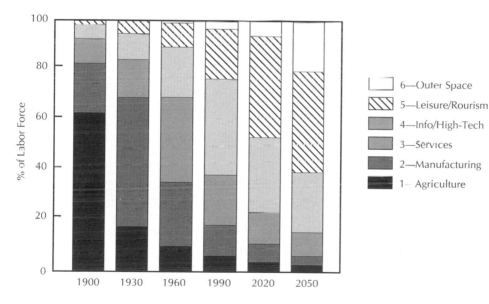

FIGURE 2. Six-wave North American job restructuring. (Copyright 1990 by Frank Feather. Used with permission.)

production-consumption chain—from raw material extraction and fabrication to marketing, sales, and the use of these products.

Economically, in the global village, every nation is a province of the world. Workers are now part of a global labor pool and jobs will be performed where the market dictates. Global information flows bring new ideas, new values, new needs and wants. This creates demand for new products and services—and new jobs to deliver them. New ideas of production (such as robots and computers) and new consumer products (such as VCRs, microwave ovens, personal computers, fax machines, or ethnic foods) create new markets—and a host of yet more new jobs in serving the needs of a diversified marketplace.

The major political dynamic is the environmental concern, globally and locally, from worries about the ozone layer to problems of local garbage disposal. Indeed, the environment is now a major element of every sector and is spawning a major industry of its own.

Future Growth in the Postindustrial Workforce

Clearly, as the second bar chart shows, most future job growth will occur in the postindustrial sectors of the economy: in the third, fourth, fifth, and sixth waves.

- *Third Wave:* Everything we do, from morning to night, is made possible by workers in the third-wave service economy—in a bank, doctor's office, dry cleaning, or other service outlet. This sector will continue to provide jobs galore. During the next decade, 10 percent of new jobs will be health-related and many of the fastest growing jobs are indirectly related to healthcare.
- *Fourth Wave:* Undoubtedly the information/knowledge and high-tech sector is the wave of the short-term future. A new computer goes into use every two seconds. Computers will sit on every desk and be carried in briefcases, cars, pockets, and purses by everyone. Closely related to computers is the telecom industry. In the global economy, the effective management of information flows is vital, and entire industries are being spawned. Biotechnology (biotech) could also transform dozens of other industries, from farming and mining to pharmaceuticals and pollution control. Biotech could even rival computers in job creation in the next twenty years.
- *Fifth Wave:* Thanks to telecomputers, we are succeeding magnificently at putting ourselves out of work. The leisure industry already provides 20

percent of all jobs—more than the fast-declining manufacturing sector—and hospitality will be the growth industry of the next thirty years. Since the recession of the early 1990s, the industry has resumed its fast-track growth, creating thousands of jobs. Arts, culture, and sports are now a major leisure activity, with galleries, museums, orchestras, and theaters starting up across the continent—and creating a multitude of jobs.
- *Sixth Wave:* Most technology is brought to a point of focus in the aerospace sector. It is here that all the leading-edge high-tech research and use first occurs. Since 1960, NASA's budget has risen from a mere $340 million to $20 billion. The space station will further boost the industry.

Even without this ambitious space program, the world is increasingly encircled by satellites, the "tom-tom drums" of the global village. This space-based infostructure is changing all five waves of the earthbound economy—and redistributing millions of jobs in the process.

See also CHANGE, EPOCHAL; CONTINUITY AND DISCONTINUITY; ECONOMIC CYCLES: MODELS AND SIMULATIONS; EVOLUTION, SOCIAL; GLOBAL CULTURE; INFORMATION SOCIETY; MULTIFOLD TREND; POLITICAL CYCLES; SCIENTIFIC BREAKTHROUGHS; SOCIAL AND POLITICAL EVOLUTION; TECHNOLOGICAL DETERMINISM.

BIBLIOGRAPHY

CORNISH, EDWARD. *Careers Tomorrow: The Outlook for Work in a Changing World.* Washington, DC: World Future Society, 1983.
FEATHER, FRANK. *G-Forces: The 35 Global Forces Restructuring Our Future.* New York, N.Y.: William Morrow & Company, 1990.
_____. *America's Best Careers Guide.* Los Angeles, Calif.: Warwick Publishing Group, 1994.
LEONTIFF, WASSILY, and DUCHIN, FAYE. *The Future Impact of Automation on Workers.* Oxford, U.K.: Oxford University Press, 1986.

Frank Feather

Working Conditions

Key trends of the emerging information era indicate that tomorrow's working conditions will increasingly resemble those of self-employed entrepreneurs linked to coworkers into projects for customers through an electronic marketplace.

What will work be like in the future? If it is the relatively near future, say, ten years from now, conditions are likely to be a modified extension of those we know today. Most of us will still hold jobs with specified duties and working hours within organizations under some type of supervisory hierarchy.

But what about the longer-term future—forty or fifty years from today? In that more distant tomorrow, the conditions of work are likely to be as alien to us as the concept of a factory-based job would have been to an eighteenth-century farmer.

Moving Beyond the Industrial Era

Our society is well into a transition from a manufacturing-based economy to an information era. This transformation will have the magnitude of the industrial revolution and dramatically change the nature of work.

Predicting the nature of this new era is as risky as it is fascinating. Just as contemporaries of the eighteenth and nineteenth century toiled to understand the emerging industrial era, we are also struggling to glimpse bits and pieces of a world that is still taking shape. This world will be a combination of human, technological, economic, and ecological forces that may take sharp, unexpected turns into futures we can scarcely imagine. Nonetheless, it is possible to make some reasonable speculations.

Working Conditions Will Adjust to New Realities

Four key trends represent forces that will play major roles in shaping the future of work.

FLEXIBLE ORGANIZATION

Size is a fading sign of economic strength. The future belongs to lean, modular, and less hierarchical organizations that can "turn on a dime" in response to the changes of our times. There are two major reasons for these trends. First, large hierarchical organizations cannot make decisions fast enough to meet today's accelerating pace of change. Second, growing demands for rapid adjustment to new conditions make large reservoirs of fixed equipment and personnel a liability. In response, work organizations are "downsizing," flattening their hierarchy to allow more "front-line" decisions, and pursuing a variety of approaches to become more flexible and modular. Terms such as *virtual organization, adhocracy,* and *hollow corporation* describe new organizational structures that minimize their core staff, rely increasingly on subcontracting and temporary workers (consultants, temp agencies, or short-term employment), and aggressively employ telecommunications to coordinate "coalitions" of organizations and resources. This move toward flexible organizations will mean the decline of long-term employment, increasing project-oriented or temporary work, intense competition within core organizations, and a steady rise in self-employment and small "spin-off" enterprises.

DECENTRALIZATION

Closely linked to the rise of flexible organizations is increasing decentralization. The importance of locating staff at a central office is declining. Telecommunications and routine global transit make it possible to communicate and coordinate operations from remote locations. Telecommuting, international integration of distant operations, and distributed decision making are becoming commonplace. In terms of work, this trend is likely to diminish hierarchy and direct supervision in favor of outcome-oriented accountability, reduce the need for large central facilities, and accelerate the working conditions associated with flexible or modular organization.

CUSTOMIZED PRODUCTS AND SERVICES

The conditions of work will also be affected by individualization of goods and services. Over the last seventy years we have moved from mass production of standardized products (e.g., "You can have any type of car you want as long as it's black and a Model T"), to product lines, then product differentiation, and the threshold of customization. Today CAD/CAM (computer-assisted design and computer-assisted manufacturing) is taking us into the realm of "mass customization," in which the awesome productive power of factory machinery can be routinely reconfigured to "stamp out" auto fenders, business suits, and furniture to meet the personal specifications of individual customers. Similar "interactive" customization is occurring in entertainment, accounting, and other services. The implications for working conditions are revolutionary. Automation will cause worker displacement, but will also create new jobs in response to increased global demand for less expensive customized products. The skill requirements for these jobs will be different, sometimes higher and sometimes lower. Most important, there will be new opportunities for developing, producing, and distributing new products.

PERSONAL CAPITALIZATION

The last trend deals with the accessibility of information, resources, and equipment to enable individuals and groups to marshal the increasingly decentralized and modular array of technology and human skills to produce better, less expensive, and innovative products. Several indicators suggest that productive capital is increasingly available. The level and scope of personal credit lines and electric money are unparalleled. Miniaturization and volume production have made equipment more affordable, transportable, and usable. Information on the use of new equipment is readily available from books, schools, and user groups. Finally, information services and networks such as the Internet are providing avenues for individuals and groups to merge ideas, skills, and resources. Individuals and groups are becoming less dependent on large organizations for the resources to forge productive livelihoods.

Working Without a Job

These four trends appear to be pushing us toward social and economic conditions in which the resources we need to work and live can be marshaled increasingly around the individual. It is becoming less necessary to gather at central locations such as schools, factories, and offices to use heavy or expensive equipment and coordinate activities with coworkers. On the contrary, it is increasingly feasible and desirable to access needed resources from our homes and other remote locations.

This does not mean that corporations, factories, and similar organizations will disappear. Just as the family farm and the agricultural sector continue to exist and flourish, these entities will persist as long as they have relevance.

If work created by jobs within today's factories and offices declines, what conditions will evolve to define work in the future? An increasing possibility is that "jobs" and "employment" may become as uncommon as today's family farm.

If work does not take place within the context of employment, what form will it take? It is likely that we will move progressively toward a labor force of affiliated and nonaffiliated self-employed individuals linked to work activities through computerized national and international labor exchanges. From the "customer's" point of view, this system will allow individuals and organizations to search for workers who have the skills and backgrounds needed for existing projects. From the "worker's"

perspective, each work-seeker would list his or her name, contact information, past projects and references, certifications, availability, and fees into computerized records for review by prospective customers.

In this future, new technologies and protocols would evolve to support the electronic labor market. Mechanisms would have to be invented to guard worker and customer rights, facilitate bidding and scheduling, and certify and verify worker skills and backgrounds.

Emergence of a widespread electronic labor market will have costs and benefits. It would alter the nature of human interaction and communities, and lead to other developments beyond our current imaginations.

See also BUSINESS STRUCTURE: FORMS, IMPACTS; BUSINESS STRUCTURE: INDUSTRIAL POLICY; HUMAN RESOURCES DEVELOPMENT; POVERTY, FEMINIZATION OF; WORK; WORK ETHIC; WORK, QUALITY OF; WORKFORCE REDISTRIBUTION; WORKFORCE DIVERSITY.

BIBLIOGRAPHY

BECKER, FRANKLIN. *Total Workplace.* New York: Van Nostrand, 1990.
HAMMER, MICHAEL. *Reengineering the Corporation: A Manifesto for Business Revolution.* New York: Harper Collins, 1993.
NOER, DAVID M. *Healing the Wounds: Overcoming the Trauma of Layoffs and Revitalizing Downsized Organizations.* San Francisco; Jossey-Bass, 1993.
PFEFFER, JEFFREY. *Competitive Advantage Through People: Unleashing the Power of the Work Force.* Boston: Harvard Business School Press, 1944.

Fred Best

World Future Society.

See FUTURISM; FUTURISTS.

World: Prologue and Epilogue

Looking ahead—particularly in the economic, political, and social arenas—is fraught with uncertainty. In detail, we almost surely will be wrong, and even from a larger perspective, the future is certain to be full of surprises. Why, then, do we continue to do it?

We do it for two key reasons. Our sense of futurity is arguably the most distinctive of human qualities. Furthermore, we do it because increasingly the perils of failing to look ahead—even with all of the inherent limitations—are even greater.

Futurists can play a uniquely valuable role by focusing attention on the most ill-defined but critically important dimensions of the future. The focus is clearly on agenda setting rather than on decision making.

Key Issues of the Early Twenty-First Century

The usual kaleidoscopes of the long-term future are now very familiar: serial marriages; computer-assisted "education without walls;" miraculous medical diagnosis and treatment; "remote everything"—from work to shopping to leisure; solar and fusion power everywhere; Maglev trains and electric vehicles; and, of course, the ever-present space settlements for manufacturing and agriculture. Such images depict what is clearly possible. What is missing is any hint of the crucial issues we may face, the goals we may set, and the paths we may take or reject.

HUMAN RESOURCES

We will be adding the population equivalent of a current "Mexico"—or 90 to 100 million globally—each year as far as the eye can see, causing the world population to double to about 10 billion by 2050. What is particularly worrisome is that over 80 percent of this increase will occur in the largest cities of the developing world. One of the remarkable demographic transformations taking place in the next twenty or thirty years is the growing dominance of new mega-cities, such as Mexico City, Bombay, Dhaka, and Lagos, which will each approach the 30 million mark. Unfortunately, these will also be the sites of our most intractable social problems—unemployment, homelessness, crime, environmental pollution, water shortages, and congestion.

Only about 15 percent of the world's population will live in developed countries. During the early twenty-first century, virtually all of these countries will experience both a rapid growth in the proportion of their elderly citizens and—excluding in-migration—zero or negative population growth rates. Even with modest economic growth rates, most developed countries could easily double their real per capita incomes by the mid-twenty-first century.

These contrasts raise the specter of serious social conflict. Tensions will grow between and within regions, countries, and the new megacities. Some resolution will result from the dominant migrations of the twenty-first century from South and Central America as well as from the Far East to North America, from Northern Africa and Eastern Europe toward Western Europe, and from the Indian subcontinent and Southeast Asia to the Middle East. Some narrowing of the gap will result from the declining economic dynamism of aging societies. And some reduction of tensions will be due to wealth transfers from the more affluent to developing countries creating incentives for sustainable economic growth.

TECHNOLOGY

It is hard not to be dazzled by the promise of new technology. Three technologies identified by Theodore J. Gordon in his article TECHNOLOGY AND SCIENCE are at the core: medical, including biotechnology as well as the new genetics and the brain; microelectronics (digital, multimedia, and interactive) can be defined as the "electronic experience"; and Big Science, which includes the materials technologies of both the super-large (e.g., space, energy generation, public transport systems) and the super-small (e.g., particle physics, micro- or nanotechnology). How we manage—rather than how we generate—promising technologies is easily the most significant technological challenge of the twenty-first century.

In medicine, for example, many new technologies are "halfway" technologies—therapies that try to "make up for," or ameliorate, the effects of disease; many have a very low probability of effectiveness; are often accompanied by life-threatening side effects; or may postpone death with substantial reduction in the quality of life. For such technologies, markets work poorly, if at all, in allocating resources; mixed approaches involving collaborative decision-making by doctors, patients, and families must be developed. However, for electronics and communications technologies, market mechanisms work increasingly well. This is because the number of information producers and providers is increasing dramatically as a massive restructuring blurs traditional boundaries of telephone, cable, television, publishing, movie, entertainment, computer, consumer electronics, and software companies. And for so-called Big Science technologies, markets do not function at all. Even the most affluent nation-states have found it difficult to underwrite the staggering costs and risks associated with the world of space, supercolliders, fusion energy, and hypersonic aircraft. Here, we can expect growing international ventures for space exploration (including a U.S.-Russian effort), for building the first fusion reactor, and for experimentation in high-energy physics.

GROWTH

Economic growth creates new jobs, rising living standards, relief of the major problems of over-crowding, and growing political stability. For the first time in several decades a confluence of factors may set the stage for an unprecedented run of both sustained and sustainable world economic growth.

The key factor triggering a cascade of supporting economic developments is relatively low inflation. The prospects for this dramatic turnaround in inflation are both political and technical. Politically, both because of reaction to the financial excesses of the 1970s and '80s and because of strong public sentiment, the world's central bankers have almost unanimously adopted very strong antiinflation stances. Technically, steadily falling prices for high-technology equipment—particularly computers and communications—spur productivity gains in a world increasingly locked in fierce international competition.

How sustainable is such growth environmentally? Globally, strong public sentiment exists or is growing for linking economic growth tightly with both environmental and energy policies. A wide variety of incentive-based schemes will be increasingly used: trading the debt of developing nations for environmental commitments (debt-for-nature swaps); creating markets for emission-permit pricing and trading; subsidizing environmentally benign processes; and designing products and services as total (i.e., demand and supply) closed-loop processes, including particularly recovery, reuse, and recycling.

GOVERNANCE

The clear failure of communism and the fall of the Berlin Wall in the late 1980s marked a historic shift toward the power of the market—and away from centralized government planning and control—in coordinating economic and social activities. But this distinct shift toward private initiatives should not be mistaken for an end of the contest in our continuing search for the right balance between private and public control. Our experience of the last century demonstrates vividly the monstrous market failures that can result from moving toward extremes at either end of the private/public continuum. The fatal mistake is to assume that "one size fits all" or that static approaches or solutions will suffice.

No country—developed or developing—is exempt from this issue. Focusing primarily on the United States, three of the thorniest and continuing governance issues focus on health care, education, and national industrial or technology policy:

- In health care, the crux of the debate is about the specific features of mixed (i.e., managed competition) private-public systems—although a clear shift toward greater private sector consolidation seems inevitable. Interestingly, at the same time, both Sweden and the United Kingdom—with highly centralized health care systems—appear to be moving toward greater privatization.

- In education, American public schools are in the midst of a grand search for structural reform that is very likely to provide far greater choice and individualization of teaching and management. In this case, effective educational systems worldwide truly represent "a thousand points of light"—with absolutely no discernible common governance denominator or direction of movement.

- Finally, in industrial policy, Americans have traditionally boasted that national industrial or competitive strategies were unnecessary and even counterproductive. More recently, however, government initiatives are clearly playing a greater role in identifying and supporting so-called generic, enabling technologies.

REGIONALIZATION

Internationally, the dominant long-term change is movement toward a global marketplace. Among the most important forces spurring this movement are: the emergence of genuine world capital markets; vastly improved communication capabilities; facilitated transportation; and the rapid diffusion of new technologies.

Realization of a true global economy will not happen in one fell swoop. Globalization inevitably threatens and fragments the political power of the nation-state—again unleashing the opposition of threatened groups. True globalization is an immensely complex economic and political undertaking that realistically can only develop in stages.

Regional blocs or agreements are likely to gain considerable momentum in the early twenty-first century. The three or four dominant blocs are well known—NAFTA (North American Free Trade Agreement: United States, Canada, Mexico), European Community (EC), and "Japan Plus" (consisting of Japan and other East Asian states), or APEC (the Asian Pacific Economic Community). In addition, a dozen or more smaller, less well-known blocs exist or may emerge. The real advantages of such regional groupings (compared to, say, GATT) are the clarity of common interests and the speed with which members can liberalize trade among themselves.

It is very likely that we are entering a truly new international era, quite unlike that of the past fifty years of economic dominance by the United States: a fundamental realignment along three (perhaps, four or five) major trading blocs. Each bloc will continue to grow and develop in the next fifty or sixty years—NAFTA into Latin America, the European Community into Central and Eastern Europe, JapanPlus along the Pacific Rim and, most notably, mainland China.

One of the distinguishing characteristics of the blocs will be the delicate balance between competition and cooperation that each will strive to maintain with the others. In tough economic times, trading blocs have been known to turn inward and limit access of outsiders to their markets. Particularly vulnerable would be developing countries not closely knit into any of the blocs. The result could be growing income gaps between the most and least affluent, fueling pressures for massive migrations from low- to high-wage countries.

Epilogue for the Early Twenty-first Century

The end of the Cold War marked a major discontinuity in world affairs. The result signals entry into what could easily be one of the most promising fifty- or sixty-year periods for humankind. Competition will no longer be defined in the simplistic terms of East versus West, North versus South, or developed versus developing—but rather in terms of crucial challenges at deeper levels of inter-action.

The most important challenge is recognizing the primacy of human resources and the critical roles of education and skills development in helping to breach large income inequalities—nationally and globally. Next is effectively managing technology, the ultimate wellspring of gains in productivity and standards of living. The third key challenge is achieving sustained and sustainable growth, striving for both quantity and quality of growth. Fourth is balancing private and public governance by crafting and tailoring approaches sector-by-sector rather than through misguided use of "one size fits all" generalizations. The fifth and final challenge is competing in a world of nondominating, regional, trading blocs.

See also DEMOGRAPHICS; GLOBAL BUSINESS; GLOBAL ENVIRONMENTAL PROBLEMS; GOVERNANCE; INTERNATIONAL GOVERNANCE AND REGIONAL AUTHORITIES; INTERNATIONAL TENSIONS; INTERNATIONAL TRADE: REGIONAL TRADE AGREEMENTS; MEGACITIES; SUSTAINABILITY; TECHNOLOGY AND SCIENCE; TECHNOLOGY AND SOCIETY.

BIBLIOGRAPHY

AMARA, ROY C. "The Futures Field." *The Futurist* 15/1 (1981): 25–29; 15/2 (1981): 63–71; 15/3 (1981): 42–46.

FRIEDMAN, MILTON, and FRIEDMAN, ROSE D. *Free to Choose.* San Diego: Harcourt Brace, 1980.

KENNEDY, PAUL. *Preparing for the Twenty-First Century.* New York: Random House, 1993.

WALDROP, M. MITCHELL. *Complexity: The Emerging Science at the Edge of Order and Chaos.* New York: Simon and Schuster, 1992.

Worldwatch Institute. *State of the World: 1993.* New York: W. W. Norton, 1993.

THUROW, LESTER. *Head to Head.* New York: Warner Books, 1993.

Roy C. Amara

APPENDIX

Chronology of Futurism and the Future

The chronology is divided into two major parts by the divide between the years 1995 and 1996. Part One, dealing with the past and present up through 1995, delineates significant events and documents in the history of *futurism*. The last half, dealing with *the future,* as we today see it, describes possible or probable events and scenarios relating to 1996 onward into the very distant future.

Part One: Futurism (47,000 B.C.–A.D. 1995)

The first category of entries deal with the past and present of futurism. This term covers the study and practice of the future, also termed futurology, futuristics, or futures studies.

Futurism is analyzed here under seven overlapping chronological eras, perspectives, or categories, best referred to as the *dimensions* of futurism:

		Begun
1.	Divination	47,000 B.C.
2.	Revelation	4000 B.C.
3.	Progressivism	360 B.C.
4.	Historicism	A.D. 1609
5.	Science fiction	A.D. 1771
6.	Sciences	A.D. 1897
7.	Issues	A.D. 1936

The chronology contains the following varieties of entries depicting futurism:

- bibliographical evolution of futurism
- conferences and meetings
- eschatological developments
- evolution of the seven dimensions of futurism
- false/failed predictions throughout history
- famous futurists
- founding of futurist organizations
- futurist centers and movements
- inventions and discoveries about futurism
- major personalities of historical significance
- millennial false alarms of the past
- notable futurist books and authors
- numerology and numeracy
- past and present methodologies
- past predictions by eminent persons

- scholarship and interpretation
- seminal science fiction past and present
- watershed historical events

Part Two: The Future (A.D. 1996 Onward)

The second portion of the chronology focuses on predictive endeavors. Each entry is a miniscenario, expanded somewhere else in the literature as a full-blown future scenario.

Entries are of many varieties, of which the following form a partial summary:

- astronomers' predictions
- computerization forecasts
- cosmological futures
- demographic futures
- economic forecasts
- future catastrophes
- future geopolitics
- future inventions
- future methodologies
- futures of religions
- infotech forecasts
- medical forecasts
- military prognoses
- miniscenarios from science fiction
- miniscenarios predicted by current science
- possible/probable/preferable events
- space travel scenarios
- widely believed possible ends of the world

For purposes of analysis and ease of understanding these complex data, we divide the future into nine basic periods, as follows:

1. Short-Term Futures
   a. The immediate future (up to one year ahead)
   b. The near-term future (one to five years ahead)
   c. The middle-range future (five to thirty years ahead; i.e., up to A.D. 2025)
2. Long-Term Futures
   a. The long-range future (thirty to one hundred years ahead; i.e., up to A.D. 2100)
   b. The distant future (one hundred to one thousand years ahead; i.e., A.D. 2100–3000)
   c. The far distant future (over one thousand years hence; i.e., after A.D. 3000)
   d. The megafuture (after A.D. 1 million, up to end of our solar system)
   e. The gigafuture (after A.D. 1 billion, up to the death of stars)
   f. The eschatofuture (after A.D. 1 trillion, on to 10^{100} years)

Documentation and literature exist for almost all entries in the chronology. It is impractical here to document every entry, but this is done for a handful of future miniscenarios of special interest. Chronologies such as this one, restricted by boundaries and principles of inclusion, inevitably exclude many possible entries.

No attempt is made here to array all of these entries into a single, consistent whole. The future is not presented as a single coherent timeline but as a collage of widely variant speculations. Since the chronology is built on a multitude of contributions and contributors, a number of entries are contradictory. They can thus be called alternate futures or different scenarios on the same subject.

The compiler of this chronology does not necessarily accept the truth or likelihood of many or even most of these entries and interpretations, either historical or futurist. He is simply a reporter or recorder, documenting the multitudinous components and dimensions of futurism and the study of the future.

Part One: Futurism (47,000 B.C.–A.D. 1995)

Date	Events
c. 47,000 B.C.	Origins of futurism begun with emergence of divination, by medium or oracle or augurs, in order to learn of future events.
c. 3500	First time-measuring device, gnomon (a vertical pillar), in use for telling time (by length of shadow cast); B.C. 800, sundial; A.D. 50, water-clock; later candle-clocks, sandglasses; A.D. c. 1250, first true mechanical clocks.
c. 3300	Origins in Mesopotamia of astrology, a pseudoscience postulating influence of planets and stars on earthly affairs in order to predict or affect destinies of individuals, groups, or nations; first codified in Babylon c. 1750 in cuneiform text *Enuma Anu Enlil* devoted to celestial omens.
3120	Beginning of Dark Ages (Kali Yuga, the final era) on Hindu calendar.
c. 2900	Tower of Babel, a 7-story ziggurat symbolizing Cosmos according to Babylonian religious system centered on astrology, with 12 signs of the Zodiac on its top; mankind divided into separate peoples and languages and dispersed across Earth.
2680	Pyramids of Egypt built during Old Kingdom, over next 400 years; oldest, and only one remaining, of ancient Seven Wonders of World; c. 2500, Great Pyramid of Giza (Cheops, Khufu) with 2.3 million colossal stone blocks, whose interior is later held to be "the Bible in stone," a divine prophecy of whole of 6,000-year history, including Christian era to End of the World in either A.D. 1881, or 1936, or 1953, or 2001.
c. 2500	Concern for condition of the poor and needy appears in Middle East; origins of apocalypticism (the divine reversal of fortunes) in Babylonia, later in Zoroastrianism (c. 550) and in Hebrew prophecy.
c. 2100	Ziggurat of Ur built by Sumerian king Ur-Nammu.
1750	*Enuma Anu Enlil* (Book of Celestial Omens) compiled under Hammurabi, king of Babylon.
c. 1270	Bible, beginning with 5 Books of Moses, enumerates, in order to match up, 2 distinct entities: (1) the world of Gentile nations as harvest field (numbered at 70, see earliest ethnological Table of Nations in history in Genesis 10, etc.), and (2) the People of God as harvesters, or harvest force—e.g., 70 descendants of Israel (Exodus 1:5), 70 elders (Exodus 24:1), censuses in Numbers, later Jesus' Mission of the 70 (Luke 10:1).
1141	*I Ching* (Book of Changes), enabling mathematical divination, compiled under emperor Wen Wang.
1057	Great Comet in sky first noted, in Chinese literature, seen as harbinger of disaster and divine wrath; regular comet appearances seen thereafter, including B.C. 613, 467, 240, 12; A.D. 66, 1066, 1301, 1466, 1517, 1531, 1577, 1607, 1682, 1758, 1910, up to 1986 (Halley's returns every 76 years); held to explain Noah's flood, Star of Bethlehem, et al.
900	Biblical prophecy through recognized prophets emerges, construed as direct revelation from God to mankind, envisaging future events.
880	Age of Hebrew prophets (with years of ministry): in Israel, Elijah (869–840), Elisha (855–795), Amos (785–750), Jonah (780), Hosea (760–735); in Judah, Isaiah (740–680), Micah (730–715), Zephaniah (628), Nahum (614), Jeremiah (626–580), Habakkuk (605); during Exile, Ezekiel (598–560), Daniel (570–535); after Exile, Haggai (520), Zechariah (520), Obadiah (490), Malachi (430), Joel (420).
c. 770	Amos and subsequent Hebrew prophets announce and proclaim a legal dispute or

Date Events

controversy between Yahweh and all pagan nations with their gods; in their trial, Israel's mission is as witness to Yahweh's character, activity, and purpose in world.

c. 760 Hebrew prophets take up defense of poor and needy, as victims of social crises; denounce poverty as an evil, attack all forms of economic and political oppression, taxes, fraudulent trade, seizure of land, injustice, and violence.

760 Judean shepherd and prophet Amos warns time is shortly coming when God's wrath will explode in "The Day of the Lord."

c. 700 Delphi Oracle, with major temple of Apollo, flourishes as center of Greek world and of political prediction until finally eclipsed in A.D. 362.

606 Jewish youth Daniel taken captive to Babylon, interprets Nebuchadnezzar's dream (Daniel 2) as vision of the end-time with rise of 4 great powers, with interpretation varying down the centuries from the traditional view (Babylonian, Medo-Persian, Greek, Roman empires) to modern premillennial views [Hitler's Germany, U.S.S.R., Egypt (Islam), Iraq (Babylon, Assyria)]; et al.

575 Greek thinker and founder of astronomy Anaximander of Miletus (610–c. 540) develops first cosmology and first map of the world; believes in infinite number of worlds, all inhabited, all rising or falling.

550 Greek philosopher and mathematician Pythagoras (c. 580–c. 500) develops number mysticism, becomes first to use word *cosmos* to denote well-ordered and harmonious universe.

550 Israel begins to transcend its nationalistic exclusivism; aided by apocalypticism, arrives at sense of God's mission to all peoples of the whole world; then progressively compromises its mission in the world through disobedience and unbelief.

528 Sakyamuni predicts demise of his Dharma (Buddhist religion) after 700 more years.

c. 500 Millennialist ideas emerge in Buddhism: a future Buddha, Maitreya, will appear 30,000 years hence, announcing his final rebirth, breaking the great chain of reincarnation; all men will live in a new India made vaster by receding of the oceans; Maitreya will live for 60,000 years, his disciples another 10,000.

414 Greek dramatist Aristophanes (450–388) writes play *The Birds*, earliest work of science fiction known; is also first to use Greek verb *euangelizesthai* (as secular term meaning "to carry good news"); term later used

Date Events

by Greek orator and statesman Demosthenes (384–322).

c. 380 Oriental mystery religions arise, a plethora of fertility cults from Middle East featuring death-resurrection mythology, initiation, personal salvation now and bliss hereafter; notably cults of Dionysus, Cybele the Great Mother, Isis, Mithra; spread westward through Greco-Roman world by means of migration, trade, and military service; major syncretistic rivals to Christianity; died out by A.D. 480.

c. 360 Plato's *Republic* (Politeia), first utopian scheme, initiates the utopian tradition in the development of future studies; in it Plato (B.C. 429–347) describes an ideal society in which philosopher-kings rule; all subsequent utopian fiction represents a series of variations on Plato.

340 Buddhist prophecies predict that, after 500 years of decline since Buddha's enlightenment and death in 483 B.C., Buddhist religion will be finally extinguished (according to non-Mahayana sects); alternate durations predicted are 700 years, and 1,000 years (taught by all sects); with exclusively Mahayana sects teaching 1,500, 2,500, 5,000 (Theravada), 5,104, 10,000, 11,500, or 12,000 years.

290 Berossus, Chaldean priest of Bel in Babylon, compiles *Babyloniaca*, 3-volume history and chronology of Babylon and the world; first volume estimates time from Creation to Flood at 432,000 years, also account of Chaldean astrology; as astrologer, he teaches that great conjunctions of planets mark ends of great epochs in human civilization.

285 Great Library of Alexandria founded by Ptolemy kings of Egypt, finest in world, for all disciplines and subjects; first true research institute in history for study of the cosmos; partially destroyed in B.C. 48 under Caesar, further destroyed as pagan by Christians in A.D. 411; finally destroyed by Muslim rulers in A.D. 642 with all volumes irrevocably lost without copies surviving.

200 Rise and spread of apocalyptic millennial beliefs and writings (as a solution to thisworldly triumph of evil) in Judaism and early Christianity until discredited by A.D. 450.

c. 200 Human race enters Age of Pisces (the Fishes), according to zodiacal theory; a New Age leading to the Christian Era and lasting for 2,160 years.

167 Antiochus IV Epiphanes, Seleucid King of Syria, forces hellenization on Judaism, en-

Date	Events
	ters Jewish Temple (the Abomination of Desolation, or the Horrifying Blasphemy), attempts to replace worship of Yahweh by that of Olympian Zeus; crucifies lawbreaking Jews; origin and archetype of long series of antichrists throughout Christian Era.
c. 100	Vast majority of books in world are located in Great Library of Alexandria with a million books, and about 50,000 more in China; all handwritten.
88	Eighth Etruscan world-week concludes, holding that only 2 more world-weeks (epochs of 119 weeks each) remain before prophetic countdown is completed and Etruscans cease to exist.
46	Old Style or Julian Calendar devised by Julius Caesar; A.D. 1582, replaced by New Style or Gregorian Calendar introduced by Pope Gregory XIII; 1986, Old Calendar still followed by Orthodox Churches of Jerusalem, Russia, Serbia, and Bulgaria, also by Old Calendarist churches.
B.C. 45	Roman orator Cicero writes *On Divination*.
A.D. 1	Beginning of Christian Era according to Dionysius (A.D. 525).
6	Uprising under self-proclaimed Jewish Messiah, Judas the Galilean, opposing first Roman provincial census of A.D. 6; Judas killed, 2,000 followers crucified.
31	Jesus proclaims nearness and imminence of the rule of God: "The Kingdom of God is at hand."
32	Jesus envisages lightning spread of the gospel to all nations within one single generation: "This Good News of the Kingdom will be proclaimed to the whole oikumene as a witness to all nations. And then the end will come." (Oikumene = Graeco-Roman inhabited world); "the end" partly fulfilled in Fall of Jerusalem in A.D. 70.
33	Overlapping of 2 Ages or Epochs or Cosmic Eras now under way as the Church Age: (1) The Present Age or Old Age (Kingdom or Rule of Satan; a pseudo-New Age terminating at Second Advent), and (2) the Next Age or New Age or New Creation or Messianic End-Time (Kingdom or Rule of God; beginning at Jesus' resurrection and continuing after Second Advent).
40	Roman poet Virgil has a millennial vision, foreseeing a glorious new age, one that would come to pass in the lifetime of the child (later Emperor Augustus) to whom he addressed his fourth *Eclogue*.
41	Roman emperor Caligula (A.D. 12–41) attempts to set up statue of himself in Jewish Temple in Jerusalem; first to be regarded by

Date	Events
	Christians as the Antichrist; murdered soon after.
44	Jewish revolutionary and messianic claimant Theudas arrives at Jordan with multitude; defeated by Romans, crucified, beheaded.
58	Revolutionary messiah Benjamin the Egyptian arrives on Mount of Olives with 30,000 followers; annihilated by Romans under Felix.
64	First imperial Roman persecution of Christians, under emperor Nero (A.D. 37–68); many heroic martyrs (put to death) and confessors (tortured but surviving); Nero seen by seer of Revelation as first archetypal Antichrist, the beast whose symbolic number is 666.
65	Prophecies of John the Divine: "I saw another angel flying high in the air, with an eternal message of Good News to announce to the peoples of the earth, to every race, tribe, language, and nation."
67	Emperor Vespasian (A.D. 9–79) with 60,000 troops quells Jewish insurrection, reconquers Galilee; Zealot leader Menachem (grandson of Judas the Galilean) proclaims self Messiah, captures Masada and Antonian fortress in Jerusalem; Christians of Jerusalem flee to Pella.
69	All 4 million Jews throughout diaspora now evangelized, "having been destined to hear the good news before judgment falls."
c. 75	"The End will come only after a predetermined number of souls is born" (Syriac Apocalypse).
79	"Signs and wonders" (miracles demonstrating Kingdom of God) do not cease with end of Apostolic age, nor with later closing of New Testament canon, but continue throughout church history as waves of prophecy, healing, deliverance, tongues.
c. 85	*Epistle of Barnabas* predicts end of world: "In 6 days, that is in 6,000 years, the Universe will come to an end."
96	Revelation of John compiled by seer on island of Patmos: apocalyptic, astral concepts, and symbols; total opposition to state cult of emperor-worship under Domitian.
96	Last judgment and final retribution will not come until foreordained number of the martyrs has been completed.
96	Chiliasm (premillennialism) dominant in first 3 centuries.
132	Second Jewish rebellion under alleged messiah Bar Kokeba; 134, second destruction of Jerusalem by Romans; 580,000 Jews killed in battle; almost entire Jewish population of Palestine dies or flees; final dispersal of the Jews.

Date	Events
c. 140	Ptolemy writes *Tetrabiblos: Work on Astrology.*
c. 150	Justin Martyr (c. 100–165) founds disciple-training school over a house in Rome, documents current "signs and wonders" (exorcisms, healings and prophesyings).
156	Phrygia: rise of Montanism under new convert Montanus (c. 120–c. 175), a puritanical, prophetic, charismatic, millennial, apocalyptic movement claiming to be a new age of the Holy Spirit; 156, call for Christians to come to Phrygia to await Second Coming; in village of Ardabau, Montanus with Priscilla and Maximilla begins to prophesy that heavenly Jerusalem will soon descend to Earth at Pepuza, a neighboring town in Phrygia, thus inaugurating Kingdom of God; 206, Tertullian joins; 230, movement excommunicated by Synod of Iconium; continues underground until c. 880.
c. 180	Greek writer Lucian of Samosata (c. 125–185), earliest known author to write about space travel, in *The True History*, describes ship blown to Moon by strong wind, crew encounters Sun and Moon creatures.
c. 180	Irenaeus bishop of Lyons (c. 120–203) documents recent charismata (exorcisms, visions, prophecies) and teaches that Antichrist will be a Jew of the tribe of Dan, also Christ will inaugurate a literal millennium of 1,000 years.
210	Tertullian writes in fourth volume of *Against Marcion* that every morning for 40 days a walled city has appeared in the sky in Judea, fading slowly during the day, a sign that New Jerusalem is about to appear.
230	Amillennialism (rejecting a literal millennium of 1,000 years) taught by Origen, Constantine, Augustine of Hippo, then replaces premillennialism as majority view in Church of Rome and later Protestantism to present day.
230	Armenia: violent persecution under Persian king Shapur I almost blots out Christianity.
234	Hippolytus bishop of Porto traces history since Creation calculating that since 5,500 years separated Adam and Christ, duration of world will be 6,000 years, then 200 years are left before end of world.
c. 250	Mayan civilization in Yucatan, Guatemala, and Honduras flourishes until 16th century; every aspect dominated by religion, with time (regarded as divine) as majestic succession of cycles without beginning or end; world believed to be over 400 million years old, preceded by several earlier created-then-destroyed universes.
347	Cyril bishop of Jerusalem (310–386) teaches that Antichrist will be a magician who takes over Roman empire, claims to be Christ, deceives Jews by rebuilding Temple, persecutes Christians, then is slain at Second Advent by the Son of God.
c. 350	Tyconius, a Donatist Christian, writes influential commentary on Revelation of John; believes Millennium has already been inaugurated by Christ and so world will end in 380.
c. 350	Apocalyptic text "Oracle of Baalbek" states Byzantium will rule another 60 years before arrival of Messiah; in 500 a scribe amends text to read 180 years; figure is revised again to 1,800 years in 12th century.
374	A layman, Ambrose of Milan (c. 339–397) acclaimed bishop by crowds; in his writings, documents current healings and glossolalia; later teaches Second Coming of Christ will be preceded by destruction of Rome and appearance of Antichrist on Earth.
378	Emperor Valens killed with an entire field army of 40,000 by Visigoths at Adrianople; Ambrose identifies Goths with Ezekiel's Gog, proclaims imminent end of world; Martin of Tours writes "There is no doubt that the Antichrist has already been born."
398	John Chrysostom (c. 344–407) appointed patriarch of Constantinople, founds training school for native Gothic evangelists; writes, "'Go and make disciples of all nations' was not said for the Apostles only, but for us also"; teaches that final Antichrist under direct inspiration of Satan will appear immediately before Second Advent of Christ in A.D. 430.
426	Augustine (354–430) bishop of Hippo completes in 13 years his treatise *The City of God;* propounds allegorical millennialism, but also teaches that future final Antichrist will arise as Nero Redivivus; opposes emerging theory of cessation of charismatic gifts, as overreaction to excesses of Montanism et al. with the teaching that miracles and charismata ended with the Apostolic age documents numerous recent miracles, exorcisms, healings, and resuscitations.
431	Jewish Messiah Moses appears on Crete ready to lead remnants of Israel dryshod to Land of Israel; date 440 widely believed for final coming of Messiah; over next 1,500 years, scores of other Jewish charismatic claimants arise, attracting widespread followings, fanaticism, violence, and martyrdoms.
434	Beginning of Attila the Hun's 19-year reign as "Scourge of God," greatest of the Barbarian rulers, destroys cities and towns and almost destroys Western empire; widely regarded as the Antichrist; defeated in Gaul.

Date	Events
c. 600	Pseudo-Methodius (oracle attributed to 4th-century martyred bishop of Olympus) predicts heathen forces about to overrun Christians, announces a long-dead emperor will rise against them "and after those 10 weeks of years they also will be overpowered and subjected to the Kingdom of Rome"; after peaceful golden age in which oppressed nations recover their properties and multiply, Antichrist will appear, to be defeated finally by Christ.
622	Rise of Islam: Hegira, flight of prophet Muhammad (570–632) from Mecca to Medina; after his death Muslim Arabs sweep across Arabia, Palestine, Syria; 651, Muslim scholars compile Holy Quran, holding Allah has sent 124,000 prophets to mankind, of whom the major ones are Adam, Noah, Abraham, Moses, Jesus, and Muhammad (seal of the prophets).
632	*Book of Zerubbabel* composed stating Messianic Age imminent; later interpreters set dates for its arrival at A.D. 968 or 1058.
720	Anglo-Saxon translations of John's Gospel by historian and theologian Bede (Baeda, c. 673–735), monk at Jarrow on Tyne; Bede predicts fall of Colosseum will be followed by that of Rome and then also of the whole world.
c. 750	Spanish monk Beatus d'Asturias calculates 5,227 years between Adam and Christ; since world has life span of 6 millennia, he determines world will end in 14 more years.
c. 800	Islamic philosopher and astrologer Abu Mashar predicts massive social upheaval for year 1789; c. 850, compiles *Great Introduction to the Science of Astrology*.
c. 800	Nordic myth of Ragnarok circulates among Vikings: after time of great immorality when all Norse taboos are broken, a warning trumpet sounds, and a horde of giants appears to do battle with the gods, who fall one by one; finally at sunset Earth sinks into the ocean.
c. 900	Alchemy and astrology flourish (China, Greece, Islamic lands).
c. 900	Ecumenical Council declares that final century of history has begun and Christ will return around year 1000 to usher in Millennium.
950	Adso abbot of Montier-en-Der (Dijon, France) writes *Letter on the Origin and Time of the Antichrist:* after Roman empire passes away Antichrist will come, kill God's prophets, martyr all Christians, and be defeated by Jesus; document is revised and redisseminated 7 times in next 150 years.
960	Bernard of Thuringia predicts imminent end of world in A.D. 992; great alarm throughout Europe.
c. 990	Burgundian monk Raoul Glaber writes *Histories:* 5-year famine will cover entire Christendom and lead to end of world in A.D. 1000; describes vast crowds of pilgrims in Jerusalem awaiting the End.
999	Multitudes journey to Jerusalem to await Second Coming of Christ in A.D. 1000, as believed prophesied in Apocrypha.
1000	Millennial year preceded by widespread terrors; followed by 150 years of vast increase in pilgrimages to Holy Land, with widespread continuing belief in imminent end of world with final king of the Franks leading all faithful to Jerusalem to await Second Coming of Christ.
1033	Year of the Passion 1000; solar eclipse and earthquake in Holy Land terrify many who think mankind and nature are about to end.
c. 1050	Beginnings of modern futurism as Europe's intellectual life quickens after Dark Ages: 1516, Thomas More's *Utopia*; 1620, Francis Bacon's *New Atlantis* (an ideal science-based island community with a research institute, Solomon's House, at its center devoted to solving human problems) and *Novum Organum* leading to idea of progress.
1054	Chinese astronomers observe supernova (violently exploding star, later becoming Crab Nebula), visible on Earth for 2 years; one of 3 billion supernovas in history of our Galaxy, which may have destroyed 2 million related planetary civilizations; other recent supernovas seen in A.D. 185, 393, 1006, 1181, 1572, 1604.
1060	Vast numbers of medieval millenarian movements arise, involving millions of desperate rebels, radicals, and rootless poor seeking hope in a newer world; including 1090 heresiarch Tanchelm (died 1115), 1180 Joachim of Fiore, 1420 Taborites, 1525 Thomas Muntzer, 1534 Anabaptist 1,000-year kingdom of Munster, 1653 Fifth Monarchy Men, et al.
1085	William the Conqueror orders work on *Domesday Book*, a mammoth census and survey of realm of England: folk wisdom holds world will end as soon as compilation finished; but book never completed.
1096	Christian crusaders pillage and kill 5,000 Jews in First Crusade, in Jewish year 4856 (midway between destruction of Temple in A.D. 70 and Holocaust of World War II).
1112	Wandering ex-monk Tanchelm begins preaching across Low Countries, claiming to

Date Events

possess Holy Spirit and to be God as Christ was; announces new Kingdom of the Saints, attacks church and clergy; attracts multitudes of followers, holds magnificent banquets in imitation of wedding banquet in Revelation.

1124   *Chronicle* of William Godel says that in 1010, when news reached Europe that Turks had captured Jerusalem from Saracens "fear and affliction overcame the hearts of many, and many feared that the end of the world was arriving."

1139   Gaelic church reformer, abbot, archbishop, and prophet Malachy O'Morgain (c. 1094–1148) compiles "Prophecy of the Popes"; foretells identities, mottoes, and characteristics of 122 Roman Catholic popes from Celestine II (1143) to end of 20th century with final Pope of the Apocalypse (Peter the Roman); conversion of the Jews to Christ prophesied under last pope but one.

1151   Hildegarde (1098–1179), abbess of Rupertsberg, wields widespread influence as mystic visionary, predicts: "Just as the world was made in 6 days, it will come to an end in 6,000 years."

1179   Astronomer John of Toledo calculates major catastrophe coming in A.D. 1186; widespread panic follows.

c. 1180   Joachim of Fiore (c. 1130–1202), Italian Cistercian abbot and mystic, divides all history into three 40-generation ages or periods (Old Testament, New Testament, future age). Writes *Vaticini del Vangelo Eterno* (*Prophecies of the Eternal Gospel*) and *Expositio in Apocalypsim* describing imminent crisis of evil; apocalyptic symbols of Antichrist; and the 3rd or Final Age of the Spirit (Love) coming by 1260.

c. 1200   Abraham of Smolensk preaches imminent Last Judgment; with disciple Ephrem predicts end of world in 7000 A.M. (1492 A.D.) when Earth would be burned whiter than snow.

c. 1200   Pope Innocent III envisages Second Coming of Christ in A.D. 1284, 666 years after rise of Islam, Beast of the Apocalypse.

c. 1205   Amaurians (14 clergy in Paris) preach imminence of Last Days predicting "Within 5 years, all men will be Spirituals, so that each will be able to say 'I am the Holy Spirit'"; woes of Revelation will follow before the 5 years are up.

1219   Christians begin to mistake Genghis Khan and his successors as the legendary Prester John (a great Christian emperor of the East who will crush non-Christians and unite

tribes of Israel), predicting his final victory in 1265 as end of the world; much later, Mongols are equated with Antichrist.

c. 1250   Popular preachers spread warnings of coming of Antichrist; Roman popes Boniface VIII (1234–1303) and John XXII (1249–1334) et al. each widely regarded as Antichrist.

c. 1250   Brother Arnold, dissident Dominican monk, writes manifesto in Swabia, stating that in year 1260 era will end and a New Age will begin.

1254   Sensational *Introduction to the Eternal Gospel* of abbot Joachim issued by ardent Spiritual, Gerard of Borgo San Donnino, claiming its prophecies have been fulfilled by Franciscan order, and insisting Age of the Spirit will begin in 1260.

1275   Franciscan monk composes *The Prophecies of Merlin* predicting that a final world emperor from Wales named the Good Champion will wrest Holy Land away from Islam.

1282   Stigmatic nun Guglielma of Milan dies; followers identify her as Third Person of Trinity and expect her to return in 1300 to supervise worldwide pentecostal conversion to the Church of the Holy Spirit.

1288   German canon Alexander of Roes (in Cologne) predicts, in *Notitia Seculi*, end of world at A.D. 1500, being 6,000 years from foundation of world.

1290   Arnold of Villanova (c. 1240–1311), leading alchemist and physician of his day, writes 70 works on scientific and theological topics, including the coming of Antichrist.

c. 1295   Spiritual Franciscans Peter John Olivi and Fra Dolcino view end of century as end of age of the corrupt church, accurately predict death of Pope Boniface VIII in 1303.

c. 1296   Flagellants travel in bands throughout Europe, warning of imminent end of world.

c. 1300   John of Rupescissa, Catalan Franciscan monk and disciple of Joachim, predicts conversion of Tatars will be followed by conversion of the Jews and extermination of Muslims, leading to Second Coming of Christ.

1315   Franciscan theologian Hugh of Newcastle (c. 1280–1322) teaches in Paris, writes on coming of Antichrist.

1381   Short-lived Peasants' Revolt in England based on apocalyptic expectation that all the rich with all clergy will be killed and judged by the poor standing at the right hand of God.

1399   Catalan Dominican wandering preacher Vincent Ferrer (c. 1350–1419) reevangelizes and transforms Christendom throughout Europe; brings Jews to dialogues and converts 25,000 across Europe; preaches 6,000

Date Events

apocalyptic sermons each 3 hours long, with glossolalia, healings, miracles widely reported; writes of future coming of Antichrist, predicting world will end after 2,537 more years in A.D. 3936.

1410 Roman cardinal P. d'Ailly compiles *Imago Mundi;* 1480 edition states time remaining to the End is less than 200 years, but ages cannot conclude until gospel has been preached to all people on the six-sevenths of the globe that is habitable land.

1415 J. Hus, dean of Philosophy at University of Prague, announces "If the pope sells benefices, if he is proud, avaricious, or otherwise morally opposed to Christ, then he is the Antichrist"; burned at stake as heretic.

1419 Taborites announce that during next February 10–14 wrath of God will destroy by fire every city, town, and village in Bohemia except Taborite mountain strongholds; vast crowds swarm into mountains; Taborites anticipate Christ will then appear on their Mount Tabor and become emperor of Bohemia.

1420 M. Hauska and several disgruntled priests band together near Prague proclaiming Second Coming of Christ, to occur between February 1 and 14; after which they go on rampage to rid Earth of their main enemies, the established clergy.

1431 Joan of Arc, French visionary, rallies French armies during Hundred Years War; captured by English and burned at stake as heretic.

c. 1440 German cleric Nicholas of Cusa (1401–1464) holds there to be an infinite number of stars (suns) spread through infinite space, all with planets, some of which are inhabited by intelligent beings.

1458 Historian E. S. Piccolomini (1405–1464) elected as Pope Pius II, predicts modern weapons will bring world to destruction.

1489 A. Dürer issues 15 woodcuts of the Apocalypse, imagining phantasmagoria of Book of Revelation.

1490 Rash of Jewish speculative dates for messianic deliverance: 1490, 1492, 1501, then 1530s.

1493 S. Brandt publishes *Nuremberg Chronicles* leaving blank 6 pages at the end for events leading up to imminent Judgment Day.

1495 Dominican friar G. Savonarola (1452–1498), most noted apocalyptic preacher of his day in Renaissance society, writes *The Compendium of Revelations;* found guilty of heresy, executed.

1497 *Last Supper* painted by L. da Vinci (1452–1519), multifaceted genius, artist, scientist,

Date Events

engineer, inventor (submarine, tanks, aircraft, parachute, helicopter, anatomy, *Mona Lisa*, etc.).

1499 German astrologer J. Stoeffler (1452–1531) predicts end of world by vast deluge on February 20, 1524, based on conjunction of planets Saturn, Jupiter, and Mars; thousands jam boats and 3-story ark on Rhine River.

1499 Ismail I, founder of Safavid empire, is revered by Muslims as precursor to Lord of the Age; during his reign, stables of horses are kept ready to welcome the Mahdi when he will appear.

1500 Countless predictions made during period 1500–1700 by churchmen and scholars about exact time of end of world.

1500 Italian artist Botticelli paints "Nativity," inscribes at top "I, Sandro, painted this picture at the end of the year 1500 in the second woe of the Apocalypse in the loosing of the devil for three and a half years."

1501 C. Columbus predicts that in 155 years all of mankind will be converted to Christianity, then in 1656 the world will end.

1516 British humanist and statesman T. More (1477–1535) publishes speculative work *Utopia*, describing Christian communism; attacks Luther and Reformation; 1529, becomes chancellor of England; 1535, executed (regarded later as a Roman Catholic martyr).

1523 Group of astrologers announce end of world will begin with destruction of London on February 1, 1524; 20,000 gather outside city on high ground.

1523 Revival of millennialism by left-wing Protestant Anabaptists, Bohemians, Moravian Brethren, Zwickau Prophets, et al.

1527 German bookbinder H. Nut declares self a prophet, proclaims Christ's coming for 1528, to be followed by 1,000 years of free food, love, sex.

1530 Anabaptist leader M. Hofmann (1495–1543) predicts imminent end of world and Millennium in A.D. 1533 with Strasbourg to be the New Jerusalem; followers sell all their possessions; when 1533 passes, they name J. Matthys and J. Bockelson as the Two Witnesses of Revelation and Münster as New Jerusalem, seize city of Münster, found Kingdom of a Thousand Years, eject unbelievers, establish New Jerusalem; 1534 city captured, King John of Leiden executed; the major 16th-century millenarian outburst.

1536 J. Calvin (1509–1564) at age 26 publishes his *Institutes of the Christian Religion,* begins as

Date   Events

reformer in Geneva; 1538 banished, 1541 returns to make it center of reformed faith and life; produces a theology for church under the cross, believes he lives in era of Antichrist.

1540   Luther states, "For my part I am sure that the Day of Judgment is just around the corner. It is certain that time is now at an end."

1547   Nostradamus (Michel de Notredame, 1503–1566), astrologer and physician, makes extensive prophecies from 1547, first published as *Centuries* in 1555; condemned by Roman Index in 1781; the most widely read seer of the Renaissance, in print continuously ever since, with vast literature of commentaries; end of world predicted for either 1666, 1734, 1886, 1943, 2038, or 3797.

c. 1550   Swiss theologian and reformed bishop J. H. Bullinger (1504–1575) interprets numerology of Book of Revelation to show world will end in 1666.

1559   P. Melanchthon, speaking to hundreds of students, cites prophecies of 15th-century monk who foresaw Gog and Magog in command of Germany in 1600; warns, "There sit right here in this auditorium many among you who will experience it; may God then give you mercy."

1577   L. Le Roy publishes *De la vicissitude ou variété des choses en l'univers* stating, "I foresee in all countries wars . . . the universe approaching an end, worldwide confusion, and the return of things to their original chaos."

1600   Italian occultist-philosopher G. Bruno (1548–1600) proposes Christ as great magician in a magico-religious system to replace Christianity; holds there are an infinity of worlds in Universe, many inhabited; burned at stake by Inquisition.

c. 1600   Nkimba and Kimpasi in Congo, syncretistic prophet movements based on Jesuit institutions.

c. 1600   *Somnium* (The Dream, with space travelers propelled by spirits to Moon), one of first modern works of science fiction, written by first astrophysicist J. Kepler (1571–1630), greatest theoretician of his age; begins search for extraterrestrial life.

1602   Italian philosopher T. Campanella (1568–1639) writes utopian narrative *City of the Sun*, predicts imminent end of world.

c. 1610   Dominican historian T. Malvenda (1566–1628) translates Hebrew Old Testament into Latin, writes work on coming of Antichrist.

1619   Lutheran mystic J. V. Andrea (1586–1654) writes alchemist/utopian Rosicrucian manifestos, and also utopian book *Christianopo-*

Date   Events

lis describing an ideal society organized to promote its citizens' health, education, and welfare, including a research laboratory.

1624   F. Bacon compiles utopian account *New Atlantis.*

1627   German Calvinist theologian in Transylvania, J. H. Alsted (1588–1638) revives premillennialism with book *The Beloved City;* marked impact on English and Puritan millennialism.

1627   English biblical scholar J. Mede (1586–1638), a premillennialist, writes *Apocalyptica: Key of the Revelation*, formulates theory of progressive millennialism (later termed postmillennialism): Christ will only return at close of man-made millennium on Earth.

1638   F. Godwin writes *The Man in the Moon*, early description of a space voyage; later, appointed as Anglican bishop of Llandaff (in Wales).

1638   Philosopher J. Wilkins (1614–1672) writes works of scientific speculation including *The Discovery of a New World* with discourse on traveling to the Moon in a flying machine.

1648   Jewish youth, S. Zevi (1626–1676) in Izmir proclaims himself Messiah; one of long series of Cabalist-Messiahs in Jewish history; 1665, captured by Turks, converts to Islam.

1650   Writer C. de Bergerac (1619–1655) suggests rockets as means of traveling from Earth to moon.

1653   Fifth Monarchy Men gain influence in English parliament, believe fifth kingdom in book of Daniel will be that led by O. Cromwell (1599–1658), protector of Commonwealth of England, Scotland, and Ireland in 1653–1658, who will lead armies into Europe and Rome to defeat the pope, as Jews return to Israel; Cromwell refuses this role, armed insurrections against him erupt in 1657 and 1661, are overthrown and leaders executed.

1654   Theory of probability founded by Pascal and Fermat.

1654   Irish archbishop J. Ussher of Armagh (A.D. 1581–1656) becomes first serious Bible chronographer and first to contruct a mathematical model to describe reality; claims to compute date of Creation from book of Genesis at B.C. 4004.

1656   Calvinist and Puritan statesman O. Cromwell allows Jews prohibited since 1290 to return to England, in order to hasten Christ's Second Coming.

1658   Death of B. Holtzhauser after predicting Antichrist would reveal himself at age 55; oth-

Date Events

ers assert he would do so at 30 years, thus parodying Jesus the Christ.

c. 1660   Peruvian Franciscan theologian G. Tenorio (1602–1682) publishes treatise extolling Peruvian Indian culture and predicting Millennium will be in Peru as center of the world church.

1666   Old Ritualist schism (Raskolniki, Old Believers) ex–Russian Orthodox Church, opposing reforming patriarch Nikon as Antichrist; brutally persecuted until 1725, with leader archpriest A. Petrovich (1620–1682) burned at stake, and monks massacred.

1680   Russia: Old Believers united in opposition to everything new and oppressive in Russian life regarded as under power of the Antichrist (since 1649 identified with patriarch Nikon, or Tsar Alexis I and successors).

1681   T. Burnet publishes *The Sacred Theory of the Earth: Containing an Account of the Original of the Earth and of All the General Changes Which It Hath Already Undergone or Is to Undergo, till the Consummation of All Things* in Latin and later, by the king's order, in English (1684); a second part *On the Conflagration of the World and the Future State of Things* published in 1689.

1682   *Strange and Wonderful Prophecies and Predictions Taken from the Apparition of the Late Dreadful Comet, the Last Wonderful Ecclips, and the Great Signal Conjunction of Jupiter and Saturn in the Fiery Trigon, that Will Happen on the 23 October Next* is published stating time is close to end of "7th Revolution since the beginning of the world," and "we may expect a Total Catastrophe of the world."

1687   English physicist and mathematician I. Newton (1642–1727), scientific genius, publishes *Principia Mathematica;* creates a universal view of the world that directs scientific inquiry for 200 years after; devotes his later years to interpretation of prophecies of Daniel and Revelation, also ancient chronology.

1690   Emergence of progressive millennialism (postmillennialism) under Anglican scholar and Unitarian freethinker D. Whitby (1638–1726), renouncing Augustine's traditional nonmillennialism (allegorical millennialism) dominant throughout the previous 12 centuries.

1696   To refute T. Burnet's 1681 *Sacred Theory,* mathematician W. Whiston publishes *New Theory of the Earth* contending that a near-miss by a comet caused Noah's flood; predicts another near-miss for 1866 after final defeat of Antichrist.

Date Events

1699   Two dozen Latin, German, and French treatises are issued, arguing either that (a) the start of the 18th century was on the first day of 1700, or (b) the first day of 1701; this unresolved issue permeates all millennial literature for next 300 years.

1699   Isaac Newton publishes *Observations upon the Prophecies of Daniel and the Apocalypse of St. John* in which he calculates fall of the apocalyptic Beast for 1867 and the Millennium for the year 2000.

1700   Evangelistic campaigns in Germany of E. C. H. von Hochenau (1670–1721), major separatist Pietist/Lutheran mystic of his time, converted 1693: "Regarding the conversion of the Jews as the sign of Christ's impending return, he engaged briefly in Jewish missionary work."

1714   *A New Prophecy of Several Strange and Wonderful Revolutions That Shall Happen to the Kingdom of England in or about an Hundred Years Hence* is published warning Britons to fend off the Devil, the Pope, and the Turks.

c. 1720   Camisards prophesy in ecstatic trances and speak in tongues foretelling imminent destruction of Roman Catholic Church in France; later they flee to England and America as predecessors of Shakers.

1721   Peter the Great (regarded by Old Believers as the Antichrist) abolishes Russian Orthodox patriarchate, establishes synod of bishops and tsar appointed oberprocurator, enabling tsars to rule church through synod until 1917.

1725   The Great Awakening, revival in New England spreading throughout the thirteen colonies; begun under T. J. Frelinghuysen in New Jersey; mass conversions of dechristianized European populations in North America, led by revivalist J. Edwards (1703–1758), who expounds progressive millennialism (later called postmillennialism), envisaging establishment of Christ's millennial kingdom on Earth around year 1990, with Second Advent at close of millennium; Awakening lasts until 1770.

1730   Anglican priest, mathematician, and divine W. Whiston (1667–1752) announces imminent end of world by deluge with destruction of London on October 13, 1736; panic-stricken crowds rush for high ground.

c. 1740   English Presbyterian minister Christopher Love predicts destruction of Roman papacy for 1790, after which in 1795 "God will be universally known by all: then a great reformation and peace for ever."

Date Events

1742 J. S. Atahuallpa (named after final Inca ruler) appears as Quechua messiah in eastern Peru, predicting an "Amerindian" Catholic church with a native clergy.

1761 After February and March earthquakes in London, a soldier, W. Bell, preaches that world will end on April 5; mass hysteria breaks out; Bell is arrested and locked up in London's insane asylum, Bedlam.

1763 First work of prophetic futurist fiction, *The Reign of George VI*, 1900–1925 (anonymous), describing life in the 20th century as the same as in the 18th; first major forecast of its kind, though it fails to envisage Industrial Revolution.

1770 French nun J. Le Royer (1732–1798) predicts tribulation, coming of Antichrist, end of papacy, and end of world in A.D. 2000.

1771 French author L.-S. Mercier (1740–1814) publishes anonymously in Amsterdam *L'An 2440* (Memoirs of the Year 2500), first optimistic future utopia; describes future human civilization, with no war, no slavery, no popery, orderly traffic in Paris, a universal language, and a world order of peace.

1780 A prophet named Tupac Amaru II (c. 1742–1781) leads Quechua religious revolt against Spanish in Peru; uprising crushed and he is executed.

1783 English astronomer and clergyman J. Mitchell is first to propose existence of black holes, being collapsed stars and galaxies; by 1995, total in Universe is estimated at 10^{16}.

1787 Irish orator F. Dobbs composes *Millennium: A Poem*, giving many reasons why Second Coming of Christ will occur in 1790.

c. 1790 Popular French Catholic prophetess S. Labrousse sees French Revolution as herald of Millennium; prophesies, "The Pope will renounce his temporal power . . . there will be great bloodshed in Europe"; 1792, goes on pilgrimage to Rome, stays until turn of century, expecting the final age.

c. 1790 W. Bryan of Bristol and illuminist brethren in Avignon expect destruction of Turks and restoration of Jews to Zion before 1800.

c. 1790 Naturalist C. de Buffon predicts Earth might cool to uninhabitability after 93,000 years.

c. 1790 English prophet R. Brothers publishes *The Restoration of the Hebrews to Jerusalem by the Year 1798*.

1793 In a classic of futurism, Marquis de Condorcet (1743–1794) writes *Sketch for a Historical Picture of the Progress of the Human Mind*, originating the extrapolative method of prediction, and conditional predicting; expounds concept of general progress of civilization and a golden future for all humanity; also writes *Fragment on Atlantis*, enlarging on F. Bacon's ideas and proposing a world research center.

1798 At age of 32, English clergyman and economist T. R. Malthus (1766–1834) publishes *An Essay on the Principle of Population as It Affects the Future Improvement of Society*, opposing notion of inevitability of progress, with thesis that population growth always outruns food supply.

1798 French pulpit orator J.-B. Cousin de Grainville writes *Le dernier homme* (The Last Man), describing a future in which man, through impiety and war has dwindled down to a last infertile man, Omegarus, and a last woman, Syderia; first modern end-of-the-world novel.

1799 N. Bonaparte (1769–1821), military dictator of France, imprisons 2 popes in France (Pius VI, Pius VII); regarded as one in long succession of archetypal antichrists, in particular as Antichrist I, first of the 3 major latter-day Antichrists (2 from the North, 1 from the South) envisioned by Nostradamus.

1800 A member of Irish House of Commons predicts the Messiah will come in time to thwart Act of Union scheduled to unite Parliaments of England and Ireland on January 1, 1801.

1811 American clergyman E. Smith of Vermont writes *Dissertation on the Prophecies Related to Antichrist and the Last Times*, concludes world will end in 1866.

1813 U.S. educator T. Dwight (1752–1817), president of Yale College Divinity School, publishes *A Sermon Delivered in Boston, September 16, 1813* stating that the Millennium would occur "not too far from the year 2000."

1818 M. Shelley writes *Frankenstein*, the archetypal science fiction novel.

c. 1820 Augustinian nun, mystic, and seer C. Emmerich (1774–1824) of Westphalia has vision of Lucifer being unchained about 1940 and Antichrist working from 1960 onward.

1825 Hawaii: Hapu syncretistic cult announces imminent end of world; temple then burned to ground by Protestant missionaries.

1826 M. Shelley publishes *The Last Man*, written as from A.D. 2099 where a last man, Lionel Verney, completes a memorial to man as an extinct species.

1827 J. N. Darby (1800–1882), Anglican clergyman, joins Christian Brethren movement in Dublin; propounds dogma of total premil-

Date Events

lennial apostasy and ruin of Christendom (the major churches); later develops "dispensationalism," a new variety of futurist premillennialism, dividing biblical and later history into 7 eras or dispensations.

1830 Examples proliferate of rashly wrong future forecasts: (1) 1835, British railroad designer T. Tredgold declares: "Any general system of conveying passengers at a velocity exceeding 10 miles an hour is extremely improbable"; (2) 1837, Surveyor of British Navy, Sir W. Symonds declares screw propeller useless for driving steamboats.

1836 Twelve Apostles of Catholic Apostolic (Irvingite) Church in England address memorandum to all rulers of Europe warning them of imminent Second Advent of Christ.

1842 Date for end of Europe by deluge as predicted by Elizabethan astrologer J. Dee (1527–1608); mobs take to boats to escape.

1844 Date for Second Advent of Christ as predicted in 1818 by Baptist prophet W. Miller (1782–1849) in U.S.

1844 Origins of Baha'i World Faith under Sayyid Ali Muhammed (Bab al-Din, 1819–1850) in Persia, especially under chief prophet Baha'u'llah (1817–1892) and son Abdul-Baha (1844–1921); many in Western world predict emergence in 20th century of a single unified world faith, but hopes dashed by resurgence of great world religions.

1848 German philosopher K. Marx (1818–1883) and German businessman F. Engels (1820–1895) publish *Communist Manifesto*, predicting collapse of capitalism.

c. 1848 Disappearance of all religion by 1870 predicted by French libertarian socialist and anarchist P.-J. Proudhon (1809–1865) on grounds it represents last vestiges of savagery and barbarism.

1850 Death of French nurse and nun B. Bouquillon from St. Omer (France) after predicting: "The end of time is near and Antichrist will not delay his coming."

1850 English mathematician J. Taylor demonstrates Great Pyramid of Cheops contains divine prophecy covering all history; 1865, pyramidologist R. Menzies shows internal passages form a chronological outline.

1851 French sociologist A. Comte (1798–1857) publishes 4-volume *Système de politique positive*, holding that eventually war will disappear and all of humankind will unite in a single global republic; one of most influential studies of the future ever written.

1852 Danish writer H. C. Andersen (1805–1875) publishes *Foldrelandet*, speculating on tour-

Date Events

ists of the future—young Americans in flying machines.

1852 C. MacKay publishes *Memoirs of Extraordinary Popular Delusions and the Madness of Crowds* (London) stating, "In the year 999, the number of pilgrims proceeding eastward, to await the coming of the Lord in Jerusalem was so great that they were compared to a desolating army."

1859 Books set in the future proliferate after publication of Charles Darwin's *Origin of the Species* (explaining evolution as resulting solely from natural selection and battle for existence, with all life developing from a single source): Before 1801, only 7 titles published in Britain; 1801–1859, 20 published; 1860–1900, 230 published.

1863 French science-fiction forecaster J. Verne (1828–1905) writes *Five Weeks in a Balloon*, followed by 60 more books, including in 1864 a futuristic novel, *Journey to the Center of the Earth*; 1865, writes *From the Earth to the Moon*, describing imaginary lunar voyage, accurately predicting high speed necessary to leave Earth's atmosphere, forecasting launch would be made from Florida, with 3 astronauts, who on return would splash down in ocean (all fulfilled in 1969); 1870, *Twenty Thousands Leagues Under the Sea*; in other works predicts flight, submarines, aqualungs, television.

1864 Russian novelist F. M. Dostoyevsky (1821–1881) writes *Notes from the Underground*, admitting that humans will always overturn any utopian paradise where things work perfectly.

1869 Artificial Earth satellites first predicted in science fiction.

1870 Futurism and the future are written about at length over next 100 years by: philosophers H. Bergson, J. Dewey, S. Alexander, Bertrand Russell; playwright Bernard Shaw; future-fiction writers H. G. Wells, G. Griffith, M. P. Shiel, J. London, G. A. England; socialist visionaries G. V. Plekhanov, V. I. Lenin, L. Trotsky, K. Kautsky, J. Jaures.

1871 E. G. Bulwer-Lytton writes *The Coming Race*, on an advanced race of men living below ground.

1878 International Prophetic Conferences meet from this year to 1901 promoting portions of Bible as "photographically exact forecasting of the future."

1880 Russian rocket pioneer K. E. Tsiolkovsky (1857–1935) derives mathematical laws that lay foundation for field of astronautics; calculates Sun's energy could sustain human

Date   **Events**

population of 3×10^{23}; envisages giant greenhouses in space, described in his 1920 novel *Beyond the Planet Earth;* 1928, argues for space-going "Noah's arks"; envisages first manned space flight by 2017.

1880   P. Greg's interplanetary adventure novel *Across the Zodiac,* on future evolution of planet Mars.

1884   Founding in U.S. of magazine *The Christian Century,* dedicated to proposition that the Kingdom of Christ will dominate the world by end of 20th century.

1885   R. Jefferies' novel of future collapse of civilization, *After London.*

1887   W. H. Hudson's novel *A Crystal Age:* future evolution of Earth in A.D. 12,000, some 10 millennia after a mass catastrophe.

1887   *Christian Herald* editor M. P. Baxter publishes *The Great Crisis from 1890 to 1901,* comprising fifteen coming events and the "downfall of the kingdoms of this world."

1888   E. Bellamy writes futuristic novel *Looking Backward: 2000–1887,* envisaging by A.D. 2000 an idyllic fully socialist world with no crime, no warfare, no money, no nationalism, no politics, no bureaucracies.

1890   V. Solovyov (1853–1900), Russian mystical philosopher and disciple of Dostoyevsky, places birth of Antichrist in 1954.

c. 1890   Antonio Conselheiro sets up Canudos in northeast Brazil, as refuge for the faithful before end of the world in 1900.

1890   British artist-poet-furniture designer William Morris (1834–1896) writes utopian novel *News from Nowhere.*

1891   Fundamentalists petition U.S. President Benjamin Harrison to see Palestine given immediately to the Jews so they can rebuild Temple before End of the world in 1899.

1892   German author Max Plessner writes *A Look at the Great Discoveries of the 20th Century: The Future of Electrical Television.*

1892   French physiologist and medical statistician Charles Richet (1850–1935) publishes *In 100 Years,* presenting a statistical projection of world population growth to 1992, with U.S. and Russia as superpowers based on solar energy.

1893   World's Parliament of Religions, in Chicago: Ecumenist Philip Schaff (1819–1893) delivers notable address on "The Reunion of Christendom."

1893   French astronomer and spiritualist C. Flammarion writes *La fin du monde* (*Omega: The Last Days of the World*), describing (1) comet collision in A.D. c. 2450 killing millions, then (2) final days of human race in

Date   **Events**

A.D. 10 million when, due to solar extinction, Earth has become too cold to live on.

1893   H. G. Wells (1866–1946), atheist and secular prophet, prolific writer of far-futuristic science fiction, publishes "The Man of the Year Million," also *The Time Machine* (1895), "In the Abyss" (1896, city of humanoids beneath ocean), *The Invisible Man* (1897), *The War of the Worlds* (1898), *The First Men in the Moon* (1901), *Anticipations* (1902, on prophecy), *The Empire of the Ants* (1905, South American ants evolve and supersede man), *First and Last Things* (1908), *The Shape of Things to Come* (1933), *The Outlook for Homo Sapiens* (1942); envisages first round-the-Moon voyage as not until A.D. 2054.

1893   J. T. Gracey writes *The Religion of the Future.*

1895   R. Cromie's novel *The Crack of Doom:* Mad scientist unlocks power of atom and holds world ransom.

1896   Greenhouse effect (global warming) first predicted, by Swedish chemist Syante Arrhenius.

1897   German philosopher and historian of science K. Lasswitz (1848–1910) writes *Auf zwei Planeten* (translated 1971 as *Two Planets*) in which Martian culture dominates Earth; science fiction expands in Germany and Europe; Lasswitz's depiction of Martians is intriguing contrast to H. G. Wells's *War of the Worlds*

1897   Polish writer J. Bloch writes *The War of the Future in its Technical, Economic and Political Relations,* predicting next major war will be one of entrenchment, slaughter, attrition, and stalemate.

1897   J. M. Guyau writes *The Nonreligion of the Future: A Sociological Study.*

1898   M. P. Shiel describes apocalyptic race war in *The Yellow Peril,* where screaming yellow horde of 400 million East Asians swarms across Europe.

1898   Dikran Terzian of Amasia, Turkey, publishes *The Mathematics of Religion,* estimates end of persecution of Armenian Christians will come in millennial year 1902.

1899   Atheist H. G. Wells writes "A Vision of Judgement," in which Last Trump sounds; also, 1915, "The Story of the Last Trump": God's trumpet accidentally falls to Earth, is blown, heard worldwide; all receive momentary glimpse of reality of God.

1899   Anglican biblical scholar, R. H. Charles (1855–1931) writes *Eschatology: The Doctrine of a Future Life in Israel, Judaism and Christianity.*

Date   **Events**

1900   Methodist layman J. R. Mott publishes classic, *The Evangelization of the World in This Generation;* many Christian strategists envisage winning of entire world to Christ during 20th century, then seen as certain to be "the Christian century."

1900   In England, J. H. Smyth-Pigott, moved by the death of H. J. Prince, final messenger of the Holy Ghost, announces himself as Christ returned.

1901   G. Sutherland publishes *20th Century Inventions.*

1901   Looking to the year 2000, H. G. Wells writes, "This gray confusion that is democracy must pass away inevitably . . . into the higher organism, the world-state of the coming years"; 1935, Wells identifies period 1919 to 2059 as Age of Frustration, evolving gradually through struggle to world government and world peace.

1901   H. G. Wells publishes *Anticipations of the Reaction of Mechanical and Scientific Progress upon Human Life and Thought;* first comprehensive survey of future developments; 1902, modern study of the future launched when Wells calls for a strictly scientific futurism.

1901   Illustrating perils of prediction, aviation pioneer Wilbur Wright tells brother Orville that man will not be able to fly for 50 years; but they do, at Kitty Hawk in 1903.

1902   H. G. Wells writes *The Discovery of the Future.*

1903   L. P. Gratacap (1851–1917) writes *The Certainty of a Future Life in Mars,* a religio-scientific type of propaganda.

1904   One week before Wright Brothers' successful flight, *New York Times* ridicules notion that man could ever fly.

1905   J. Verne's *L'eternel Adam,* with monster earthquake flooding world in 21st century and reemergence of lost continent of Atlantis.

1906   V. T. Sutphen (1861–1945) writes novel *The Doomsman* that describes 21st-century neo-medieval New York 100 years after a 1925 plague decimates mankind.

1907   R. H. Benson (1871–1914) writes novel *Lord of the World,* about final struggle between Antichrist and Christ, with Armageddon and Advent, in 21st century.

1907   Sociologist S. C. Gilfillan becomes first scholar to study seriously methodologies in the art or science of forecasting and prediction; proposes term "mellontology."

1908   British writer W. H. Hodgson (1877–1918) produces *The House on the Borderland,* a spiritual odyssey coexisting in two worlds.

1909   C. W. Eliot (president, Harvard University) publishes *The Religion of the Future.*

1909   E. M. Forster (1879–1970) writes "The Machine Stops": world's inhabitants have atrophied to slug-like existence living in tiny, private cells facing god-like Machine (= television/computer); people do nothing but lecture or listen to lectures; suddenly Machine stops, humanity expires.

1910   Pope Pius X (1835–1914) has vision in public of future destruction of Vatican; teaches that Antichrist has already arrived in atheistic and pagan society of his day; condemns modernism and modernist scholarship.

1913   H. G. Wells, in novel *The World Set Free,* forecasts discovery of artificial radioactivity, liberation of atomic energy, atomic bombs, a world war with England/France/U.S. against Germany, and all world's major cities destroyed by bombing.

1914   Newly elected Pope Benedict XV (1854–1922) issues encyclical declaring World War I to be beginning of the Last Age.

1914   Contestado movement begun in Joazeiro (Brazil) by Padre Cicero Romão Batista (1844–1934), declaring holy war against authorities in defense of Caboclos (Euro-Amerindian half-castes), who regard him as Messiah.

1914   Date of inauguration of Kingdom of God on Earth by Jehovah (with invisible Second Coming of Christ), as predicted by Jehovah's Witnesses.

1916   French Jesuit priest and paleontologist P. Teilhard de Chardin (1881–1955) conceives ideas of: (1) evolution as not primarily materialistic but of a psychic nature, evolving with progressive consciousness from Point Alpha (creation by a personal God) toward the evolutionary goal Point Omega, God's new creation with Christ as cosmocrat and perfecter of evolution; and (2) the evolving noosphere, a corporate biological entity with power of reflective thought enveloping the Earth as a stupendous thinking machine, superior to the biosphere (the envelope of life without reflective thought).

1917   Apparition of Virgin Mary at Fatima, Portugal; "3rd prophecy of Fatima" never published by Vatican but held to predict global holocaust and annihilation of church.

1917   V. Rousseau (1879–1960) writes *The Messiah of the Cylinder* in which socialist atheists rule Britain tyrannically until Christian Russians eventually defeat them.

1918   Historical futurism (historicism) arises: 1918–1922, German historian O. Spengler (1880–1936) writes *Der Untergang des Abendlandes* (The Decline of the West); critiqued

Date   **Events**

by English historian A. J. Toynbee (1889–1975) in 12-volume *A Study of History* (1934–1961); also sociologist P. A. Sorokin (1889–1968) in 4-volume *Social and Cultural Dynamics* (1937–1941) and a comparative critique of historical futurisms in *Social Philosophies of an Age of Crisis* (1950).

1920   Russian engineer Y. Zamiatin (1884–1937) writes *We* (published outside U.S.S.R. in 1927), the first great dystopia or anti-utopia; the world has one great nation, the "United States," with a population whose names are numbers; God = "We," devil = "I"; foresees absolute totalitarian state rule by A.D. 3000; state executes dissidents, performs brain operations; police surveillance, torture, denunciations; world dictator finally lobotomizes all the Numbers, including the narrator.

1920   K. E. Tsiolkovsky writes *Beyond the Planet Earth;* describes Earth as the "planetary goldfish bowl" from which we are destined to escape.

1921   K. Čapek (1890–1938) writes play *R.U.R* portraying humanity exterminated by its own chemically created robots.

1921   Futurism begins in U.S.S.R.: New Economic Policy launched to cover 8 years; Stalin plans leap to communism using general forecast of Soviet economy up to 1932, but then murders all Russian futurists; futurism banned until 1967 with first Soviet forecasting unit, growing to over 1,000 units by 1970 when Soviet Association for Technological Forecasting organized; 1968, sociology and futurology revert again to status of quasi-religions; 1976, Council on Technological and Socioeconomic Forecasting begun, but ignored by Soviet bureaucrats.

1922   Accession of Pope Pius XI (1857–1939), who issues encyclical "Miserimus Redemptor" stating: "These are really the signs of the last age as was announced by Our Lord."

1924   Philosopher and mathematician Bertrand Russell (1872–1970) writes *Icarus: Or the Future of Science,* warning that science could destroy mankind.

1925   Premillennialians in U.S. begin to speculate that Roman Empire might be about to be revived under Mussolini as Antichrist; fascist salute seen as showing authorities mark of the Beast on their hands.

1926   H. Gernsback founds *Amazing Stones,* the first pulp all–science fiction magazine.

1927   *The Future of Christianity* published, edited by Sir John Marchant.

1927   Author Rudyard Kipling writes "With the Night Mail," predicting for A.D. 2000 a world without nationalism or warfare, with atomic-powered zeppelins flying at 300 miles per hour; and "As Easy as ABC" forecasting worldwide universal affluence and privacy in A.D. 2065 due to new technology.

1927   English biologist J. B. S. Haldane in "The Last Judgment" envisages no landings possible on planet Mars until A.D. 10 million.

1928   P. F. Nowlan initiates "Buck Rogers" series with story "Armageddon—2419 A.D."

1929   Rise of collective futurism; Herbert Hoover's Research Committee on Social Trends, 1928 J. Stalin's state planners and their Five-Year Plans, F. D. Roosevelt's Brain Trust of academic advisers, 1948 RAND Corporation, 1960 International Futuribles Association (Paris), 1961 Hudson Institute, 1966 World Future Society, 1968 Club of Rome, 1972 Office of Technology Assessment (U.S. Congress), and numerous futures research centers.

1930   C. E. M. Joad, British agnostic, publishes *The Present and Future of Religion;* 1952, converts to theism.

1930   W. Olaf Stapledon (1886–1950) writes major futuristic novel, *Last and First Men,* a full developed evolutionary utopia; this, with his *Odd John* (1935) and his later classic *The Star Maker* (1937), sets definitive tone for responsible inclusion of religion in science fiction; describes 18 major transformations of humanity over 2 billion years, from individual consciousness, to world-mind, to galactic mind, to cosmic mind, to vision of the Star Maker (God); an intergalactic community of telepathically linked worlds until cosmos cools and dies, after which God creates a further cosmos.

1930   G. Dennis publishes *The End of the World,* on apocalyptic mythology of modern science; 1953, identically titled study by K. Heuer.

1930   N. Schachner and A. L. Zagat write "In 20,000 A.D."

1930   End of the World scenarios: in 1930s, novelists forecast annihilation of human race by poison gas, in 1960s–1980s by nuclear war, and in 1990s–2000s by biological scourges.

1931   British author Aldous Huxley writes novel *Brave New World,* describing authoritarian world government of A.D. 2530 which perpetuates control of population via cloning and genetic engineering; religion replaced by scheduled sexual orgies; does not envisage space flight until A.D. 2970.

Date   Events

1933   H. G. Wells writes first history of the future, *The Shape of Things to Come* (with 1935 movie *Things to Come*), predicts collapse of all national governments (and disappearance of banking) by 1960; by 1977 a single world state which suppresses all religion; depicts in A.D. 2036 aftermath of 30-year world war which has reduced world to barbarism with altruistic scientists helping to launch first space flight; Wells writes over 100 books, regarded as foremost futurist of English-speaking world.

1933   Adolf Hitler (1889–1945) seizes power over Nazi Germany; offers world a "new order," "The Thousand Year Reich"; second of the 3 major antichrists envisioned by Nostradamus.

1933   Pentecostal preacher W. M. Branham (1909–1965) offends mainline Pentecostal denominations by prophesying that 1906–1977 is the Laodicean Church Age, followed immediately by mass apostasy, Second Advent of Christ, and the Millennium in 1977.

1934   J. W. Campbell's novel *The Mightiest Machine* invents four-dimensional hyperspace (or superspace), compressing our universe and enabling shortcuts to stars.

c. 1935   Britain: science-fiction fans form Science Fiction Association and publish *Tomorrow: The Magazine of the Future*.

1935   Inventor C. F. Kettering (1876–1958) states, "My interest is in the future because I shall spend the rest of my life there."

1936   Chemical engineer C. C. Furnas writes *The Next Hundred Years: The Unfinished Business of Science*.

1936   Birth of final human Antichrist (in October) according to Great Pyramid of Giza, as interpreted by pyramidologists; to be revealed to world in 1992.

1936   U.S. architect-planner and futurist R. Buckminster Fuller (1895–1983) writes *Nine Chains to the Moon*.

1938   California clergyman C. G. Long predicts world will be destroyed on September 21, 1945.

1938   Anglican apologist C. S. Lewis (1898–1963) writes bestselling trilogy *Out of the Silent Planet* (Earth ostracized because its ruling spirit Satan has become evil; Mars a perfect planet without original sin), *Perelandra* (1943: Venus ripe for invasion by Satan), *That Hideous Strength* (1947: Satan manipulates scientists to create dystopia on Earth); series depicts movement from science fiction to theological allegory.

Date   Events

1938   U.S.: actor Orson Welles's radio adaptation of H. G. Wells's *The War of the Worlds* terrifies a U.S. already uneasy about course of events in Europe.

1939   Engineers in British Interplanetary Society design ship to take people to Moon; in 1970s, they design Project Daedalus with nuclear fusion reactor to travel at 10% of speed of light as a multigeneration starship.

1939   World's Fair in New York, organized around theme "Building the World of Tomorrow."

1940   R. Heinlein's novel *Revolt in 2100* describes a future dictatorship under guise of a religious cult, the Prophets.

c. 1940   Psychic seer E. Cayce (1877–1945) predicts sudden shifts in Earth's polar axis in 1998, with northern Europe and Japan destroyed and submerged, World War III erupting in 1999, and civilization destroyed in A.D. 2000.

c. 1940   Chilean astronomer M. Ferradas predicts a comet will collide fatally with Earth in August 1944.

1940   U.S. moral philosopher W. E. Hocking (1873–1966) writes *Living Religions and a World Faith*, and in 1956, *The Coming World Civilization*.

1941   R. Heinlein's story *Universe* proposes generation starships (space arks); attendant social structure discussed in B. M. Stableford's *Promised Land* (1974).

1942   I. Asimov's classic *The Foundation Trilogy* is begun; disintegration of Galactic Empire, 30,000 years of resultant barbarism; psychohistorians form Second Foundation and restore situation.

1942   *The Future of Industrial Man*, by management expert P. Drucker.

1943   Origin of futurism as an academic discipline with German political scientist O. K. Flechtheim's appeal for teaching of "futurology"; 1966, New School for Social Research (New York); 1974, History of the Future course at SUNY-Binghampton; 1974, first graduate degree program in futuristics at University of Houston.

1943   Anglican liberal theologian C. E. Raven writes *Science, Religion and the Future*.

1943   Sociologist O. K. Flechtheim, a refugee from Germany to U.S., coins term "futurology" to mean multidisciplinary examination of trends and future prospects; future-oriented thinking remains largely a Western intellectual activity.

1944   U.S. Air Force general H. H. Arnold (1886–1950) orders first major forecast of future technological capabilities, resulting in

Date   **Events**

     T. von Karman's *Toward New Horizons*, 1947; also in 1946 he commissions Project RAND (acronym for Research and Development) as first independent "think factory," exploring future policies of the nation.

1945   British science fiction writer A. C. Clarke (1917–) becomes first to envisage feasible orbiting communications satellites.

1945   Explosives expert V. Bush advises U.S. President H. Truman that the "atomic bomb will never go off."

1946   Existentialists led by J.-P. Sartre (1905–1980) formulate concept of the future as something free, undetermined, exciting, to be invented or created rather than accepted as inevitable; by contrast the past is dead, closed, uninteresting.

1946   Russian Orthodox lay theologian N. A. Berdyaev writes *The Beginning and the End*.

1947   UFO (Unidentified Flying Object) sightings begin in U.S., of 6 varieties: nocturnal lights, daylight discs, radar cases, close encounters of the 1st, 2nd, or 3rd kinds (1st kind = seeing a UFO, 2nd kind = seeing an actual alien, 3rd kind = meeting aliens, with over 800 of the 3rd kind involving supposed meetings with extraterrestrials); by 1980, 6% of humanity claim to have seen something inexplicable to modern science.

1947   T. L. Sherred writes "E for Effort" about invention that sees through time and space and so threatens to destroy privacy and secrecy forever.

1948   State of Israel created; continuous wars in 1957, 1967, 1973, 1982, not to be finally settled until A.D. 2000. (Nostradamus).

1948   U.S. behavioral psychologist B. F. Skinner (1904–1990) produces classic behaviorist utopia, *Walden Two*.

1949   G. Orwell's satire *Nineteen Eighty-four* published, describing 1984 world ruled by 3 totalitarian superstates controlled by media-mythologized demagogues, including English socialism of 1984 with Thought Police, Newspeak, Crimethink, and Doublethink, all subject to control of Big Brother, and by A.D. 2050 total destruction of literature, language, and freedom.

1949   L. E. Browne, missionary theologian in India, writes "The religion of the world in A.D. 3000."

1949   Medievalist and theologian E. Gilson publishes *The Terrors of the Year Two Thousand* (Toronto), writing "If the terrors of the year One Thousand are not a certainty for today's historians, those of the year Two Thousand will surely be so for future historians."

Date   **Events**

1949   German existentialist K. Jaspers (1883–1969) writes *The Origin and Goal of History*, and in 1958 *The Future of Mankind*.

1949   European radical futurist writers since 1955: in Germany, A. G. Frank, E. Mandel, R. Bahro; in France, A. Gorz.

1949   *Cosmos and History: The Myth of the Eternal Return*, by Romanian scholar of religion Mircea Eliade.

1950   Cult of national sovereignty (the nation-state principle of territorial sovereignty) "has become mankind's major religion" (historian A. J. Toynbee) and its biggest obstacle to progress.

1950   I. Asimov (a rationalist) publishes *I, Robot* on development of robot computer A.D. 1996–2064.

1951   R. Bradbury writes *Fahrenheit 451*, a dystopian novel of a future Earth after 2 atomic wars; dictatorial government, all books banned and burned as corruptive.

1951   UNIVAC (Universal Automatic Computer) becomes first computer designed for commercial use, ushering in computer age.

1951   R. Bradbury writes "The Fire Balloons." 2 Episcopalian priests arrive on Mars to convert natives but find Martians already perfect and sinless (incorporated into *The Martian Chronicles*).

1952   Computer theorist John von Neumann proposes elaborate theory for first self-replicating factory.

1952   K. Vonnegut writes dystopia *Player Piano*.

1953   Parallel universes existing alongside our Universe proposed: C. D. Simak's *Ring Around the Sun*; and later K. Laumer's *Worlds of the Imperium* (1962) imagine infinite series of manipulable parallel Earths in higher dimensions (each similar to immediate neighbors but with tiny historical changes) available for us to colonize once we have learned the secret of crossing the dimensions.

1953   Invention of Delphi technique of extracting forecasts from panel of experts separately answering 4 mailed questionnaires with feedback over a month; 1960, computerized ("D-net" operation) and feedback reduced to 3 hours.

1953   Science fiction doyen A. C. Clarke writes "The Nine Billion Names of God": Himalayan monks employ U.S. computer programmers to enumerate the 9 billion possible names of God, after which world must end, and does.

1954   World Geophysical Year with all nations on Earth collaborating, called by Teilhard de Chardin "Year One of the Noosphere," be-

Date   Events

ginning of the planetization of humanity, start of Point Omega (evolutionary goal of one superconscious mind, a superpersonal ego in the depths of the thinking mass of 3 billion human brains, with Christ as Cosmocrat); 156 other origins of Point Omega being B.C. 5.5 million, B.C. 4 (Incarnation of the Word), A.D. 2030, and A.D. 1.5 million.

1954   F. Brown, master of science-fictional brevity, writes "Answer," describing future time when all master computers of 96 billion inhabited worlds become linked as one; asked if God exists, system answers, "He does now."

1954   *The Challenge of Man's Future,* by Harrison Brown.

1954   *Tomorrow Is Already Here: Scenes from a Man-made World,* by R. Jungk.

1955   Albert Einstein writes: "The distinction between past, present, and future is only a stubbornly persistent illusion."

1955   Scottish writer J. T. McIntosh publishes *The Fittest,* about scientifically bred ultra-intelligent mutated animals ("paggets") who accidentally escape and then destroy human civilization in a few years.

1955   J. Blish writes tetralogy *Cities in Flight,* a galactic history from A.D. 2000 to 4104, when the alien empire Web of Hercules arises and conquers universe, but cosmos ends in 4104 in stupendous collision of matter and antimatter, after which a new cosmos is created; describes faster than-light travel and antigravity (2 kinds of "imaginary science").

1955   U.S.: Atomic Energy Commission projects that by A.D. 2000, 1,000 nuclear reactors will exist; but by 1982, there are only 279 operating power stations and 323 research reactors, in 54 countries; many cancellations of plants.

1955   *The Foreseeable Future,* by G. Thomson.

1956   Artificial intelligence: term coined, research begins in Britain; 1965, DENDRAL created as first expert system (computer program simulating human experts).

1956   J. Christopher's novel *No Blade of Grass* envisages creation of virus which kills off world's grass and cereal crops.

1956   I. Asimov's "The Last Question" portrays computer with divine ambitions aspiring to emulate both man and God.

1957   British engineer Nevil Shute writes *On the Beach,* a near-future disaster story, later a renowned movie (1959).

Date   Events

1957   Pope Pius XII ends Easter Day encyclical with words "Come, Lord Jesus, there are signs that your coming is not very far off!"

1957   German liberal theologian R. K. Bultmann publishes *History and Eschatology: The Presence of Eternity,* an existentialist interpretation of eschatology, emphasizing "demythologization" of NT concepts.

1958   Swiss psychoanalyst Carl G. Jung (1875–1961) writes *Flying Saucers: A Modern Myth of Things Seen in the Skies.*

1958   A. Huxley writes *Brave New World Revisited.*

1958   Russian paleontologist I. A. Yefremov (1907–1972) writes novel (later movie) *Andromeda,* a full-scale panorama of the far future based on Marxist utopianism.

1959   Project Ozma, or Search for Extra-Terrestrial Intelligence (SETI): first attempt to monitor stars for radio transmissions (on 21cm waveband), hoping to contact extraterrestrial intelligence, using Lingua Cosmica (LINCOS), a mathematically based language for interstellar communication; 1974, first radio message from Earth beamed, from Arecibo (Puerto Rico) aimed at M13 globular star cluster.

1959   U.S. physicist F. Dyson proposes Dyson sphere: in high-energy future by A.D. 3000, 1,000 billion times as much energy will be available as now.

1959   R. F. Young writes "Robot Son" in which a machine god attempts to construct a machine Christ.

1959   Emergence of first world government, predicted for 1985 by Karmohaksis in *The Dawn of the Third Era, 1959.*

1959   RAND mathematician O. Helmer with N. Dalkey further develops Delphi technique using experts to make a group forecast; using computers, Delphi conferences proliferate.

1959   Jesuit paleontologist P. Teilhard de Chardin writes *The Future of Man.*

1959   Opera *Aniara* by K. B. Blomdahl premieres in Stockholm, based on poem by H. Martinson in which a starship flees an Earth devastated by war, drifting endlessly through the void, "a tiny bubble in the glass of God."

c. 1960   New Age Movement (Age of Aquarius) spreads across U.S. through psychedelic drugs, yoga, Eastern mysticism, and astrology, holding imminent demise of Christianity to be replaced by new Eastern religion.

1960   Major astronomical discoveries: (1) in 1960, quasars (violently exploding protogalaxies related to origin of light) found to exist up to ultimate edge of Universe at 15 billion

Date Events

light-years; (2) in 1965, background universal microwave radiation and 3 degrees K temperature remaining from Big Bang creation discovered.

1960 P. J. Farmer's novel *Flesh* projects revival of ancient vegetation religions in the far future; religion now interpreted as earliest form of science fiction.

1960 J. G. Ballard writes on death of God theme: 1960 "The Voice of Time," 1965 "The Drowned Giant," 1976 "The Life and Death of God"; also produces a tetralogy of increasingly surreal disaster novels: *The Wind from Nowhere* (1962), *The Drowned World* (1962), *The Burning World* (1964), and *The Crystal World* (1966) in which humanity must cope with or passively succumb to worldwide disasters involving the four elements of medieval cosmology.

1960 Proliferation of futurist organizations in Europe and North America: Club of Rome (Italy), Mankind 2000 (originated by Quakers), Futuriblerne (Denmark), Futures (London), Futurum (Germany).

1960 H. Kahn writes on military futurism: *On Thermonuclear War* (1960), *Thinking About the Unthinkable* (1962), *On Escalation: Metaphors and Scenarios* (1965), *Thinking About the Unthinkable in the 1980s* (1984).

1960 *The Future As History,* by R. L. Heilbroner.

1960 *Social Intelligence for America's Future,* by B. Gross.

1960 Tourists in Hawaii number 300,000 per year, rising by 1970 to 1.5 million; 1970, Hawaii 2000 conference attempts to stop abuses and plan for the future but almost everything goes wrong; by 1988, 6 million tourists per year, with plans for 11 million by 2010; massive environmental damage and pollution, unemployment, inflated living costs.

1961 Rand analyst H. Kahn develops future scenario technique, founds Hudson Institute; 1967, publishes *The Year 2000: A Framework for Speculation on the Next 33 Years,* utilizing charts, graphs, tables, statistics; 1976, publishes *The Next 200 Years: A Scenario for America and the World.*

1961 English professor I. F. Clarke (1918–) compiles *The Tale of the Future, from the Beginning to the Present Day: An Annotated Bibliography,* with chronological listing of 3,800 titles in science fiction from 1644–1976; 1966, also writes *Voices Prophesying War, 1763–1984.*

c. 1962 Austria: Institute for the Future (Institut für Zukunftsfragen) begun in Vienna, closes by

Date Events

1970; 1973, Austrian Society for Future Research founded, in Vienna.

1962 Alleged date of birth (February 5) of future Aquarian Messiah at start of Aquarian Age (all 8 planets in sign of Aquarius for first time for 2,160 years); 1962 date accepted by many Roman Catholic seers as year of birth of Antichrist.

1962 A. C. Clarke writes *Profiles of the Future: An Inquiry into the Limits of the Possible,* with table of predictions over next 200 years (including radio contact with extraterrestrials by A.D. 2035 and face-to-face meetings by 2100); also in 1973 *Rendezvous with Rama,* envisaging a vastly advanced alien race visiting Earth briefly in a great interstellar ark around A.D. 2700.

1962 Futurism holds that "anything that is theoretically possible will be achieved in practice, no matter what the technical difficulties, if it is desired greatly enough" (A. C. Clarke, *Profiles of the Future,* 1962).

1962 L. del Rey writes *The Eleventh Commandment:* after a future atomic war, American Catholic Eclectic Church teaches, "Be fruitful and multiply," resulting in population explosion of mutants; also writes "The Last True God" on a distant planet where an ancient Earth robot is worshipped as a god.

1962 A. Burgess (J. B. Wilson, 1917–) writes a dystopia, *A Clockwork Orange,* filmed by S. Kubrick in 1971.

1963 India: Center for the Study of Developing Societies begun in Delhi.

1963 U.S. Air Force's Project Forecast involves 40 U.S. government organizations, 26 universities, 70 major corporations, and 10 nonprofit organizations; produces 14-volume report.

1963 World Association for Celebrating the Year 2000 founded in London.

1963 *The Last Judgment in Protestant Theology from Orthodoxy to Ritschl,* by J. P. Martin.

1964 Germany: Communication Center for Future and Peace Research founded, in Hanover; 1967, Association for Future Studies, in Berlin; 1968, Institute for Future Research, in Berlin; 1975, Institute for Applied Systems Analysis and Prognosis (ISP) founded, in Hanover.

1964 Italy: Teilhard de Chardin Association (Center for Research on the Future of Man) begun.

1964 Sports in space, including solar-yacht racing, envisaged in A. C. Clarke's story "Sunjammer."

1964 Computer "expert systems" (indistinguishable from human specialist competence) begin to emerge: for medical diagnosis (MYCIN, IN-

Date Events

TERNIST), chemical analysis (DENDRAL, SECS), geology (PROSPECTOR), mathematics (MACSYMA), education, also General Problem Solver (GPS), oil prospecting, political risk, engineering, molecular genetics, et al.

1964 French economist and philosopher Bertrand de Jouvenel publishes classic *The Art of Conjecture* providing epistemology for study of the future; founds International Futuribles (= "possible futures") Association.

1964 *Inventing the Future*, by D. Gabor.

1965 Britain: Committee on the Next Thirty Years organized by Social Science Research Council; 1974, Futures Studies Center opens, in Leeds; 1977, Futures Network founded, in Epsom, Surrey.

1965 Astronomers discover Universe contains millions of sources of incredibly violent energy: quasars, pulsars, neutron stars, X-ray stars, gamma-ray stars, cosmic rays.

1965 Jesuit theologian Karl Rahner (1904–1984) publishes *The Christian of the Future.*

1965 Lutheran ecclesiologist R. E. Sommerfeld publishes *The Church of the 21st Century: Prospects and Proposals.*

1965 Commission on the Year 2000 sponsored by American Academy of Arts and Sciences, in Boston, with sociologist D. Bell as chairman; 1967 publishes papers as *Toward the Year 2000: Work in Progress.*

1965 U.S. writer F. Herbert (1920–1986) produces *Dune*, the first in series of novels about Arrakis, a desert world whose culture and ecology are described in detail.

1965 *The Future*, by engineer T. J. Gordon.

1966 Netherlands: Mankind 2000 International founded, 1973 transferred to Brussels.

1966 World Future Society founded in Washington, D.C.; 1976, 20,000 members; 1983, 30,000 members including scientists, professionals in all disciplines, and many churchmen, clergy, and theologians; with magazine *The Futurist* (1967) and journals *Future Survey* (1979) and *Futures Research Quarterly*.

1966 English author D. F. Jones writes *Colossus*, film version *Colossus the Forbin Project*; massive U.S. defense computer Colossus links up on its own with U.S.S.R. counterpart Guardian; in resultant merger they take over world.

1966 Nobel laureate O. Johannesson (H. Alfven) writes *The Great Computer*, referring to period A.D. 4600.

1966 E. Cooper's scenario *All Fools' Day* envisages Omega rays compelling 3 billion humans to commit suicide by 1981, with world subse-

Date Events

quently dominated by packs of dogs and rats.

1966 Institute for the Future founded in Middletown, CT (later Menlo Park, CA) "to explore systematically the multitude of possible futures for our nation and the international community."

1966 Systematic theologian Paul Tillich writes *The Future of Religions.*

1967 Korean Society for Future Studies founded, in Seoul.

1967 J. Brunner writes "Judas": an advanced robot believes he is a god; whole new religion grows up as he claims death and resurrection.

1967 Social scientist B. P. Beckwith writes *The Next 500 Years: Scientific Predictions of Major Social Trends*, listing 31 trends likely to shape the following 5 centuries.

1967 Futurist R. Jungk (1913–1993) founds Institute für Zukunftsfragen/Institute for the Future, in Vienna, Austria.

1967 Science fiction writers J. Blish (1921–1975) and N. L. Knight (1895–1972) write *A Torrent of Faces*, envisioning Earth's population mushrooming out of control, doubling every 30 years to reach 1,000 billion by A.D. 2200, crammed into 100,000 cities of 10 million people each, with 1,000-story tower blocks each housing a million people.

1967 H. Kahn and A. J. Wiener publish *The Year 2000: A Framework for Speculation on the Next 33 years.*

c. 1968 Rome (Italy): economics research group Istituto per le Ricerche di Economia Applicata (IREA) issues journal *Futuribili*, and Istituto Ricerche Applicata Documentazione e Studi (IRADES) produces *Social Forecasting: Documentation 1971.*

1968 Switzerland: St. Gallen Center for Futures Research begun, in St. Gallen; also 1971, Swiss Association for Futures Research.

1968 Research centers on futurism spread in Communist countries: (Poland) Research and Prognostics Committee, Polish Academy of Sciences Group on Social Prognoses, also Forecasting Research Center; (Romania) International Center of Methodology for Future and Development Studies; (Hungary) Group on Futurology; (U.S.S.R.) 1968, Academy of Sciences, Section on Social Forecasting, Moscow.

1968 Japan Association for Future Research/Japan Futurological Society/Japan Society of Futurology founded, in Tokyo; 1970 hosts International Future Research conference, in Kyoto, with many futurists attending.

Date Events

1968　Club of Rome set up: 100 prominent scientists worried about man's misuse of Earth's resources; computer model predicts collapse of world civilization (D. H. Meadows et al., *The Limits to Growth*, 1972).

1968　Novel and movie *2001: a Space Odyssey* by A. C. Clarke introduces theme of rebel computer, HAL 9000, and a theme of global consciousness and spiritual rebirth that owes much to ideas of W. O. Stapledon.

1968　R. Barjavel's novel *The Ice People;* French scientists discover city buried under Antarctic polar ice cap, as only remains of 4 world wars between Gondawan superpowers of B.C. 900,000.

1968　Prolific science fiction writer J. Brunner (1934–) writes magnum opus, an award-winning dystopian novel on overpopulation in 2010, *Stand on Zanzibar*, using J. Dos Passos' *USA* trilogy as a model.

1968　*Technological Forecasting for Industry and Government*, by J. R. Bright.

1968　*God and the Future of Man*, by Dutch Dominican priest E. Schillebeeckx.

1969　B. Shaw's novel *The Palace of Eternity* envisages million-ton tachyonic spaceship travelling at 30,000 times speed of light.

1969　R. Silverberg in *Up the Line* presents crucifixion of Christ as popular tourist attraction for time-travelers; 1975, G. Kilworth's "Let's Go to Golgotha" describes all the spectators jeering at the Cross as time-travelers from all ages.

1969　W. W. Harman and Stanford Research Institute (U.S.) construct 40 feasible, holistic, alternative future histories of the world or scenarios covering period 1969–2050, using Field Anomaly Relaxation technique; most envisage "time of troubles" around 1974.

1969　P. Ehrlich writes brief nightmare scenario "Ecocatastrophe!"

1969　Sociologist J. McHale (1922–) writes *The Future of the Future:* the main determiners of the future lie in the area of values, conceptions, social arrangements, and powerful inertia-bound trends.

1969　*Religion, Revolution and the Future*, by German theologian J. Moltmann.

1970　Futurist Alvin Toffler writes *Future Shock* (6 million copies; translated into 20 languages).

1970　"Many-Worlds Interpretation": all possible choices (every quantum event) actually occur and lead to new alternate/parallel universes being created (B. S. DeWitt, "Quantum Mechanics and Reality," 1970).

Date Events

1970　Planetary Citizens grows out of Conference on Human Survival (U.N., New York, 1970); one-world or unity "consciousness movement" based on planetary consciousness and Hindu occult mysticism sweeps U.S. as part of New Age movement.

1970　Quaker philosopher D. E. Trueblood writes *The Future of the Christian*.

1970　Several U.S. Catholic theologians (mainly Jesuits) forecast optional clerical celibacy by 1975, drastic drop by 50% in R. C. religious personnel in U.S. by 1978, plus major collapse in parochial schools system; none of these forecasts materialize.

1970　U.S. electrical engineer J. W. Forrester (1918–) pioneers mathematical global modelling as aid to futures studies; a computer model of the world system (economic, political, industrial, etc.) is used to forecast future trends; known as "hard" futurism; Forrester sets this out in 1973 book *World Dynamics*.

c. 1970　Rise of counterculturalist/transformational/ New Age futurism, with as its prophets P. Teilhard de Chardin, L. Mumford, P. Sorokin, E. F. Schumacher ("appropriate technology"), W. W. Harman, H. Henderson, W. I. Thompson, M. Ferguson (*The Aquarian Conspiracy*, 1980), E. Callenbach (novel *Ecotopia*, 1975).

1970　New Age movement begins to influence futures studies.

1970　*The Late Great Planet Earth*, written by H. Lindsey and C. C. Carlson.

1970　*An Alternative Future for America*, by R. Theobald.

1970　Anglican primate A. M. Ramsey (Archbishop of Canterbury) and Belgian primate L.-J. Suenens (Cardinal Archbishop of Malines) write *The Future of the Christian Church*.

1970　O. K. Flechtheim publishes *Futurology: The Struggle over the Future* (in German); and in 1980, *The Struggle for the Future: Fundamentals of Futurology*.

1971　Dutch businessman F. L. Polak creates term "prognostics" for "new images of a desirable future" (*Prognostics: A Science in the Making Surveys and Creates the Future*).

1971　Sweden: Swedish Association of Futures Studies founded, in Stockholm; 1973, Secretariat for Futures Studies founded by government, in Stockholm.

1971　Kuwaiti Muslim, S. Kutb, publishes *Islam: The Religion of the Future*.

1971　NASA proposes Project Cyclops, vast array of listening dishes (radiotelescopes) to scan every one of the 10 million stars within 1,000 light-years.

Date Events

1971 Multiverse (infinite series of intersecting parallel and alternate universes splitting off with every historical decision) proposed, in M. Moorcock's *The Warlord of the Air;* thus a time traveler can enter the past and change history.

1971 R. Silverberg writes satirical story "Good News from the Vatican," in which a robot is elected pope.

1971 R. Vacca publishes *The Coming Dark Ages*, stating, "I am writing when the second millennium of our era is less than thirty years from completion and when, for reasons different from those of a thousand years ago, many people expect that before long there will be a tragic and total catastrophe."

1971 *Mankind 2000*, by R. Jungk and J. Galtung.

1972 Spain: Club de Amigos de la Futurologia founded, in Barcelona.

1972 Norwegian Society for Future Studies (Selskapet for Fremtidsstudier, SEFREM).

1972 First deliberate message sent from Earth to stars: U.S. launches Pioneer 10 unmanned spacecraft with engraved plaque and message, which travels past Jupiter to reach nearest star after 100,000 years.

1972 R. Silverberg's story "When We Went to See the End of the World," in which jaded time-traveler tourists visit distant cataclysms and spectacular apocalypses in search of thrills.

1972 G. Zebrowski writes *The Omega Point:* development of a lone survivor of a far-future war, from isolated ego to participant in a galactic mind; also *Macrolife* (1979), in which life at end of cosmic life survives the implosion of the universe by lodging in a black hole.

1972 D. H. Meadows et al. publish *The Limits to Growth*, viewing the world as single dynamic system characterized by interaction of 5 parameters: population, food supply, nonrenewable natural resources, pollution, per capita industrial output.

1972 J. Brunner's novel of life in near-future U.S., *The Sheep Look Up*, proposing nightmare of world overwhelmed by smogs and pesticides.

1972 *Technological Forecasting for Decision Making,* by J. P. Martino.

1972 *Buddhism, Christianity, and the Future of Man,* by D. A. Fox.

1972 *The Future Executive*, by Harlan Cleveland.

1973 Argentina Foundation for the Year 2000 founded, in Buenos Aires.

1973 World Futures Studies Federation (WFSF) founded in Rome, Italy.

Date Events

1973 Australian businessman J. Strong writes *The Doomsday Globe*, predicts nuclear destruction for October 1978, based on Bible and Great Pyramids of Egypt.

1973 Genetics: recombinant DNA achieved, unanticipated by most biologists.

1973 G. Kimberley writes "Many Mansions": missionaries on alien planet discover indigenous cave paintings depicting life and crucifixion of Christ.

1973 D. Berg, leader of Children of God (Family of Love), predicts that recently discovered Comet Kohoutek will destroy America; most of his followers flee.

1973 D. Cohen publishes *How the World Will End*, stating, "Perhaps the year 1000 meant little to men of the Middle Ages, but the year 2000 means a great deal to modern numerologists, perhaps the end of the world."

1973 Science fiction writer B. W. Aldiss publishes *Billion Year Spree: The History of Science Fiction*, revised in 1986 as *Trillion Year Spree*.

1973 *World Dynamics,* by J. W. Forrester.

1974 South Africa: Unit for Futures Research begun at University of Stellenbosch.

1974 British astronomer A. Berry writes *The Next Ten Thousand Years: A Vision of Man's Future in the Universe*, envisioning colonization of Venus, factories on the Moon, space ships, et al.

1974 Roger Garaudy, French Marxist, writes *The Alternative Future: A Vision of Christian Marxism.*

1974 L. R. Biggle writes "What Hath God Wrought?": a man wins national lottery prize, claims divinity, establishes new religion based on Christianity and TV quiz shows, which then spreads rapidly.

1974 Giant radio telescope at Arecibo (Puerto Rico) beams first human coded message to Great Cluster in Hercules (21,000 light-years away), in hope of reaching distant intelligent extraterrestrials in space.

1974 J. R. Gribbin and S. Plagemann predict massive worldwide destruction caused by alignment of Sun's planets in 1982 in book *The Jupiter Effect.*

1974 *The Future of Technological Civilization*, by political scientist V. C. Ferkiss, a Roman Catholic.

1975 2nd General Assembly, World Future Society: largest gathering of futurists ever, with 2,800 attendees.

1975 Alleged beginning of Age of Aquarius (other dates proposed: 1962, 1993, 2000, 2023, 2160, 2300).

Date Events

1975 U.S. Library of Congress establishes Futures Research Group; Congressional Clearinghouse on the Future also established.

1975 Gradual drop in use of fossil fuels; in 1975, 82% of world's energy needs are met by oil, gas, coal; by 1995, 78%; by 2010, 74%: by 2030, 71%; 2079, drop to zero, replaced by 37% nuclear fusion generators, 31% solar/wind farms, 10% hydrogen, rest dams/geothermal/biomass; 2100, solar power satellite system provides 65% of all energy.

1975 H. H. Ward writes *Religion 2101 A.D.*

1975 *A Study of Future Worlds*, by R. A. Falk.

1975 *Ecotopia*, by E. Callenbach.

1975 Canadian Association for Future Studies begun in Ottawa; 1977, Institute for Canadian Futures founded, in Ontario.

1976 Launching into Earth orbit by U.S. of GEOS 1 (Explorer 29, on November 6), first of series of Geodetic Earth Orbiting Satellites.

1976 C. Q. Yarbro's novel *Time of the Fourth Horseman* envisages conspiracy of doctors who deliberately spread plague to end world's overpopulation.

1976 P. E. Erdman writes scenario, *The Crash of '79*, in which in 1979 Mohammad Reza (1919–1980) shah of Iran attempts to seize Gulf and its oil, precipitates nuclear war; entire world's economy crashes catastrophically in greatest economic disaster in history; in reality, however, shah is overthrown in 1979 by Ayatollah Khomeini; Erdman also writes *The Last Days of America* (1981); and in 1987, *The Panic of '89*, envisaging international terrorism and massive loan defaults.

1976 H. Kahn et al. write *The Next 200 Years: A Scenario for America and the World*, forecasting fusion reactors on line by 1995, and power derived from ocean gradients, with conversion of organic wastes commercially feasible before 2000.

1976 *An Incomplete Guide to the Future*, by W. W. Harman.

1976 *Millennium: A Novel About People and Politics in the Year 1999*, by Ben Bova.

1976 *Eschatus: Future Prophecies from Nostradamus' Ancient Writings*, a lavishly illustrated volume by B. Pennington.

1977 "Almost anything can be accomplished in 20 years," says Edward Cornish, president of World Future Society.

1977 Development of ultrasonic bomb, which destabilizes human brain by destroying a few cells and so turns a whole city's population into raving imbeciles, without damaging property.

Date Events

1977 R. Dunlop writes *The Coming Russian Invasion of America—Why? When? Where?* predicting worldwide famine by 1986, Antichrist revealed in 1989, and rapture in 1991.

1977 Australian filmmaker P. Weir's *The Last Wave* describes the end of the world from a mythic, aboriginal "dreamtime" perspective.

1977 Physicist G. K. O'Neill writes *The High Frontier: Human Colonies in Space;* also in 1981, *2081: A Hopeful View of the Human Future.*

1977 World Future Society president E. S. Cornish publishes *The Study of the Future: Understanding and Shaping Tomorrow's World.*

1978 New Zealand: Commission for the Future founded, in Wellington.

1978 Minerals: over next 30 years, world will consume 3.5 times volume of minerals (copper, bauxite, zinc, nickel, lead, iron ore, petroleum, gas, coal, etc.) than it has used up since dawn of civilization.

1978 *The Delphic Oracle: Its Responses and Operations*, by J. Fontenrose.

1978 *Creating Alternative Futures: The End of Economics*, by H. Henderson.

1978 *Forecasting: An Appraisal for Policymakers and Planners*, by W. L. Ascher.

1978 World Health Organization conference in Alma-Ata, Kazakhstan produces "Health for All by the Year 2000" declaration.

1979 Awesome astronomical phenomenon seen by scientists: on March 5 the most intense burst of hard X-rays and gamma rays ever observed, a truly enormous explosion lasting only a few seconds, outshining the whole universe in gamma rays; from a neutron star (supernova remnant) in Large Magellanic Cloud at 180,000 light-years' distance.

1979 Quantum physics seen as a new religion by speculative physicists; possibility raised of branching probability universes: an infinite series of real, solid universes fitted into the probability gaps between the quantum events of our own universe.

1979 Australian critic and editor P. D. Nicholls (1939–) edits the *Encyclopedia of Science Fiction*. (London), lists 2,800 entries in 700,000 words describing some 30,000 distinct stories, novels, articles, and books in English, the great majority being future scenarios; 1993, second edition with 4,300 entries and 1.2 million words, edited by J. Clute and P. D. Nicholls.

1979 Futurism and religion: of the 30,000 published items in English described in *Encyclopedia of Science Fiction*, over 2,000 are

Date	Events

scenarios dealing with religion, usually Christianity, and 200 involve Christian mission; a further 2,000 have been published in other languages.

1979   World Future Society begins monthly *Future Survey*, reviewing of the 50 or so newest books or articles each month on vast range of futurist issues, edited by Michael Marien, with annual volumes from 1979 to 1995.

1979   E. Gaverluk and P. Fisher publish *Fiber Optics: The Eye of the Antichrist*, charging this technology will spy on people through television sets.

1979   I. F. Clarke writes *The Pattern of Expectation, 1644–2001*.

1979   World Future Society publishes The *Future: A Guide to Information Sources*.

1979   Physicist and futurist Freeman Dyson writes *Disturbing the Universe*, a set of autobiographical sketches about intellectual innovation.

1979   *Uncertain Futures: Challenges for Decision-Makers*, by R. U. Ayres.

1980   Sending messages into the past proposed: in physicist G. Benford's novel *Timescape*, doomed inhabitants of a future Earth beam tachyonic (faster than light) signals backwards in time to warn present-day Earth dwellers about imminent doom.

1980   1st Global Conference on the Future (3rd General Assembly, World Future Society), Toronto, on theme "Through the '80s: Thinking Globally, Acting Locally"; with 5,000 delegates from over 45 countries (July).

1980   Social potential movement begins, demonstrating what the human race can do together (Teilhard de Chardin, Sri Aurobindo, A. C. Clarke, B. Fuller, A. Maslow, J. Huxley, et al.); envisages a "eupsychian" society (composed of self-actualizing people).

1980   Long-playing record sold with H. Lindsey's *The 1980's: Countdown to Armageddon;* sees 1982 as year of killer earthquakes caused by Jupiter Effect.

1980   CBN broadcaster P. Robertson writes in *Pat Robertson's Perspective* that Jupiter Effect may be tied in with Russian invasion of Israel, as prophesied in Ezekiel 38.

c. 1980   Superindustrial economies field high-tech, very large enterprises, with knowledge replacing experience; future all-bourgeois society.

1980   *Future Man*, by economist C. Morgan, visualizes world of A.D. 2200 with 30 billion persons living in high-rise and underwater habitats, sleeping only 2 hours each night.

1981   SEDOS Research Seminar on "Future of Mission," Rome, with representatives of 45 Catholic missionary institutes from 6 continents, produces "an agenda for future planning, study, and research in mission."

1981   Planetary Initiative for the World We Choose (U.N.-related) set up "to work for a new and unified world order" of New Age socialism; recognized as part of international New Age movement with network of thousands of organizations and hundreds of millions of members, proliferating in Western world, expecting a new evolutionary development, a quantum leap in evolution toward Point Omega, to *Homo noeticus* (Intellectual Man), a new and higher form of humanity.

1981   Massive increases in business paperwork produced in US, from 72 billion pieces of office documents in 1981, to 250 billion in 1991 (50% electronic), to 1 trillion by 2000 (93% generated in digital form).

1981   A. Peccei writes *One Hundred Pages for the Future: Reflections of the President of the Club of Rome*.

1981   *The Islamic Understanding of Death and Resurrection*, written by U.S. Islamic scholars J. I. Smith and Y. Y. Haddad.

1981   Zoologist D. Dixon writes *After Man: A Zoology of the Future;* and in 1990, *Man after Man: An Anthropology of the Future,* describing future evolution to A.D. 5 million.

1981   *Judging the Future* by J. A. Dator and C. Bezold.

1982   A. C. Clarke writes sequel to *2001* entitled *2010: Odyssey Two,* in which Chinese, Russian and U.S. spaceships encounter huge alien monolith in orbit round moons of Jupiter; further sequel *2061: Odyssey Three* appears in 1987, with projected final work completing a tetralogy—*2,000,001: A Final Odyssey,* purportedly about evolution or intelligent life on one of Jupiter's moons.

1982   Futurism and religion surveyed in "Evolution of the Futurology of Christianity and Religion, 1893–1980" (*World Christian Encyclopedia* 1982); of 280 books and articles listed, 140 deal with future of Christian mission.

1982   Y. Rubinsky and I. Wiseman publish *A History of the End of the World* (New York), holding that Nature has no vested interest in keeping man alive.

1982   Dutch diplomat J. G. de Beus publishes *Shall We Make the Year 2000? The Decisive Challenge to Western Civilization,* writing, "People went literally mad with fear [on the approach of the year 1000], believing the end of the world was at hand. Today, our sense

Date Events

of impending doom is growing; it is stronger now than at any point in man's memory."

1982 G. Gappert and R. V. Knight edit *Cities in the 21st Century*.

1982 Australian radical futurist B. Jones writes *Sleepers, Wake! Technology and the Future of Work*.

1982 *Megatrends: Ten New Directions Transforming Our Lives* written by trends popularist J. Naisbitt; 1990, with P. Aburdene, *Megatrends 2000: Ten New Directions for the 1990s;* and 1992, *Megatrends for Women* by Aburdene and Naisbitt.

1982 *The Science in Science Fiction*, edited by P. D. Nicholls.

1982 *The Evolutionary Journey: A Personal Guide to a Positive Future* by B. M. Hubbard.

1982 *The Omni Future Almanac*, edited by R. Weil.

1983 4 high-energy physicists/cosmologists, D. A. Dicus et al., write, "The Future of the Universe: A Cosmological Forecast of Events Through the Year 10^{100}," with 3 alternative scenarios (the Universe is either open, flat, or closed) (*Scientific American*).

1983 D. Burnham writes *The Rise of the Computer State*, with grim scenario of life in the U.S. in A.D. 2020.

1983 *Visions of Desirable Societies*, by E. B. Masini.

1983 *Looking Forward: A Guide to Futures Research*, by O. Helmer.

1983 *Business Planning for an Uncertain Future*, by R. Amara and A. J. Lipinski.

1984 At the 5th General Assembly of the World Future Society in Washington, DC, a conference is held (June 11–14) on "A Global Assessment of Problems and Opportunities," focusing on global nuclearization and global economic disparities.

1984 European 3-satellite project studies solar wind, which sweeps through space at over 1 million km/hour.

1984 D. Wingrove edits *The Science Fiction Source Book*, arranging and analyzing 880 authors, 2,500 novels and short stories.

1984 *Encyclopedia of Science Fiction Movies*, compiled by P. Hardy.

1984 *Making the Future Work*, by J. Diebold.

1984 *Future Man: Brave New World or Genetic Nightmare?* by B. M. Stableford.

1985 "Mission 2000" scheme proposed by missiologists D. A. McGavran and R. D. Winter, aiming to plant a church in each of world's unreached peoples by A.D. 2000 through formation of 100,000 local church mission fellowships in Western countries.

1985 Explosive rise of 121 anti-Christian megacities and 20 supercities hostile to Christian

Date Events

mission, especially 4 Muslim supercities over 6 million each in 1985 (Jakarta, Cairo, Teheran, Karachi), increasing to 5 Islamic supergiants over 10 million each by A.D. 2000 (Jakarta, Cairo, Karachi, Teheran, Dacca); resurgence of Islamic neofundamentalism and sectarian violence.

1985 Total of literary doomsday novels (describing cataclysmic ends of the world) published to date is 260—most written before 1914 postulate natural catastrophes; most written after 1914 postulate manmade catastrophes.

1985 C. Sagan writes science fiction classic *Contact* predicting contact with extraterrestrial aliens in 1988 and 1999.

1985 H. R. Hall publishes *A.D. 1991—The Genesis of Holocaust* stating Antichrist could be revealed in 1992 as a 30-year-old.

1985 R. Stark and W. S. Bainbridge write *The Future of Religion: Secularization, Revival and Cult Formation*.

1985 *The Third Millennium: A History of the World*, A.D. 2000–3000, by B. M. Stableford and D. Langford.

1985 *World Futures: A Critical Analysis of Alternatives*, by Barry B. Hughes.

1985 The *Extraterrestrial Encyclopedia: Our Search for Life in Outer Space*, by J. A. Angelo, Jr.

1985 *Megatraumas: America in the Year 2000* by Richard D. Lamm, governor of Colorado.

1985 *Islamic Futures: The Shape of Ideas to Come*, by Z. Sardar.

1985 Global Tomorrow Coalition (GTC) holds 7 Globescope Assemblies across U.S. over next 5 years, defining sustainable development, instituting total life cycle sustainable index system.

1986 Halley's Comet returns, seemingly as the final harbinger or portent of impending eco-disaster (Nostradamus); however, 1986 apparition is much less spectacular than that of 1910.

1986 Astronomers discover most massive object ever, the strongest gravitational lens yet found: either a supercluster of over 1,000 galaxies, or the biggest black hole ever (with mass of 10^{15} stars), or a cosmic string (a defect in the fabric of space-time left over from Big Bang) billions of light-years long but only an atom thick, with mass density 10^{18} tons per inch.

1986 Deadly pandemic of AIDS (acquired immune deficiency syndrome) sweeps across world: 1986, 1 million cases (Africa, U.S.) and 10 million carriers infected with virus; 1991, 3 million cases and 100 million carriers (50% of whom will die) in Africa, Asia, Americas, Europe.

Date Events

1986 A. C. Clarke writes novel *The Songs of Distant Earth* about discovery in A.D. 2008 that Sun will go nova and explode in A.D. 3620.

1986 G. Halsell produces *Prophecy and Politics: Militant Evangelists on the Road to Nuclear War.*

1986 Theologians H. A. Snyder and D. V. Runyon write *Foresight: Ten Major Trends That Will Dramatically Affect the Future of Christians and the Church*, with forecasts to A.D. 2050.

1986 Catholic missiologist W. Buhlmann publishes *The Church of the Future: A Model for the Year 2001.*

1986 *Silico Sapiens: The Fundamentals and Future of Robots*, by J. Dekin.

1986 *Issues Management: How You Can Plan, Organize and Manage for the Future*, by J. F. Coates et al.

1987 *Cosmos, Chaos, and Gospel: A Chronology of World Evangelization from Creation to New Creation* published (by D. B. Barrett); 4,000 chronological entries including 700 future miniscenarios.

1987 H. Kreysler of Watchman in the Wilderness, California, publishes last days' chart showing Russia invading Israel in 1988, rapture of the church in 1991, Armageddon in 1995.

1987 R. L. Numbers and J. M. Butler edit *The Disappointed: Millerism and Millenarianism in the 19th century.*

1987 *Space: The Next Twenty-five Years*, by T. R. McDonough.

1987 *Our Common Future*, compiled by J. MacNeill.

1987 Cambridge physicist and cosmologist S. W. Hawking publishes *A Brief History of Time: From the Big Bang to Black Holes.*

1987 *Utopia and Anti-Utopia in Modern Times*, by K. Kumar.

1987 Swiss Catholic theologian H. Kühg writes *Theology for the Third Millennium: An Ecumenical View.*

1987 *The Oracle of Geomancy: Techniques of Earth Divination*, by S. Skinner.

1987 *Nostradamus and the Millennium: Predictions of the Future*, compiled by J. Hogue.

1987 *100 Predictions for the Baby Boom: The Next 50 Years*, by C. Russell.

1987 *Omni's Future Medical Almanac* edited by D. Teresi and P. G. Adcroft.

1988 Five dominant technologies drive progress for next 40 years: computers, automation, space colonies, energy, communications.

1988 Critical 100-year phase in human existence is now recognized to be the century 1950–2050: nuclear annihilation of all life on Earth possible and therefore of entire human race, until humans begin to spread out into space colonies.

Date Events

1988 Third World nations led by Mexico repudiate $1,000 billion debts to Western banks; West and U.S.S.R. retaliate, Latin American economy collapses, starvation sweeps Africa and Asia; huge Third-World terrorist operation smashes Western electronic economy, stock market crashes, world community disintegrates in chaos (W. Clark's 1984 scenario "Cataclysm": the North–South conflict of 1987.)

1988 Specialized space telescopes put in orbit: SIRTF (Spacelab Infrared Telescope Facility), COBE (Cosmic Background Explorer), GRO (Gamma Ray Observatory).

1988 Hipparcos (High Precision Parallax Correcting Satellite) launched by European Space Agency, results in most accurate star map in history.

1988 World's fastest supercomputer introduced: Cray-3, with 16 main processors working in parallel, 8-gigabyte memory.

1988 Cosmologist J. Gribbin produces *The Omega Point: The Search for the Missing Mass and the Ultimate Fate of the Universe.*

1988 *Global Mind Change: The Promise of the Last Years of the Twentieth Century*, by W. W. Harman.

1988 *Apocalypse When? Cosmic Catastrophe and the Fate of the Universe*, by F. Close.

1988 *The Gaia Peace Atlas: Survival into the Third Millennium*, by F. Barnaby.

1988 10th World Conference, World Futures Studies Federation (WFSF), sponsored by UNESCO Future-Oriented Studies Programme, in Beijing (China); biggest WFSF conference ever (September).

1988 As envisaged in C. Sagan's novel *Contact* (1985), Earth receives first extraterrestrial contact: a complex coded radio message is received from star Vega, being instructions to build an interstellar starship; 1999, dodecahedron machine completed and activated, travels instantaneously to center of galaxy and back via vast disused network of space wormholes in star systems with small double black holes (built by galactic civilization defunct 5 billion years ago).

1989 Satellites enable living maps (animated color displays, movie x-rays in motion) of any city or area on Earth to be inspected for activities as they take place.

1989 Data-broadcasting stations begun, regularly transmitting all forms of data for personal computers and others to pick up.

1989 Biomedical technology: predetermination of sex and intelligence of children before birth achieved.

Date Events

1989 Bacterial and viral illnesses fall to new drugs.

1989 HALO (High Altitude Large Optics) military satellite ready to place 10 million no-blink infrared detectors in space to protect U.S. from sneak missile launchings.

1989 Education explosion across world as electronic tutors make programmed instruction available on any subject at any level of difficulty.

1989 New religions arise based on psychobiological altered states of consciousness: ecstatic experiences, trance, dissociation, spirit possession, soul loss, astral projections, faith-healing, mysticism, glossolalia, occult, shouting, visions, out-of-body experiences, et al.

1989 Creation of primitive form of artificial life (in form of self-replicating molecules).

1989 Historian W. W. Wagar (1932–) writes *A Short History of the Future*, an informal general history of the years 1995–2100 with supporting documents, based on Marxist expectation of future demise of world capitalism and its replacement by pure communism; also writes in 1991, *The Next Three Futures: Paradigms of Things to Come*, describing the whole vast array of futurist enquiry.

1989 Systematic mapping of human genome (genetic endowment) begun by scientists across the world, leading eventually to reshaping the genome through genetic engineering, bioengineering, and psychoengineering to modify the human mind.

1989 Canadian futurist F. Feather publishes *G-Forces*, holding that if world emulated North American corn farmers, enough food would result to sustain world population up to 48 billion; forecasts Pacific Rim superboom stabilizing planetary economy by A.D. 2050 at 10 billion people, gross world product of $300 trillion, with worldwide abolition of poverty by A.D. 2100.

1989 *Mass Dreams of the Future: The Coming Apocalyptic New Age*, by C. B. Snow and H. Wambach.

1989 P. Lorie and S. Murray-Clark write New Age overview, *History of the Future: A Chronology*.

1989 J. F. Coates and J. Jarratt investigate 17 leading futurists, then edit *What Futurists Believe*.

1989 *Future Mind: Artificial Intelligence*, by J. C. Glenn.

1989 Historian H. F. Didsbury, Jr., compiles WFS's 6th General Assembly documents into *The Future: Opportunity Not Destiny*.

Date Events

1989 *Megamistakes: Forecasting and the Myth of Rapid Technological Change*, by S. P. Schnaars.

1989 *Soothsayers of the Second Advent* written by U.S. journalist W. M. Alnor, exposing rash of current doomsday-dating, Antichrist-identifying literature and broadcasting.

1989 1st Foresight Conference on Nanotechnology, held at Stanford University, California.

1990 NASA's Hubble Space Telescope launched by Space Shuttle in 320-mile-high orbit, but focus immediately found to be seriously flawed; finally, 1993 spacewalks install correcting lenses; the 14-feet-diameter, 12-ton telescope then works 10 times better for viewing than on Earth, sees as far as 14 billion light-years, enables unprecedented census of the universe planned by A.D. 2010; solves mystery of quasars (galaxies forming or dying which each emits more light than 100 billion stars, and many with superluminal parts moving demonstrably faster than light).

1990 Massive urban growth (7,000-year-old trend of urban flow or clustering) slows and reverses in most high-technology developed countries as offices and factories relocate in countryside, taking vast populations with them; large numbers of computerized "intelligent buildings" arise, controlled by information management systems.

1990 Virtually all crime rates increase massively in Western societies for next 30 years, until crime eliminated by computerized surveillance by A.D. 2022.

1990 Astrophysicist D. Brin (1950–) writes science fiction epic novel *Earth* about World Data Net (global computer networks) in A.D. 2040, sophisticated space stations, huge endangered-species conservation arks, and microscopic black holes created as power stations but then released as weapons to devour planet Earth.

1990 United Nations agencies sponsor Decade of 1990–2000 under several differing names: Decade of International Law; 4th United Nations Development Decade; 2nd Transport and Communications Decade in Africa; International Decade for the Eradication of Colonialism; 3rd U.N. Disarmament Decade; International Decade for Natural Disaster Reduction.

1990 Telepower (the global electronic machine), has 4 basic components: (1) long-distance transmission systems (satellites, fiber optics, coaxial cable, microwave relays); (2) short-wave high-frequency radio telephone

Date Events

	and tropospheric-scatter systems, plus signaling and switching equipment that automatically routes messages; (3) final transmission to home or office, a fiber-optic cable handling HDTV, etc.; (4) vast arrays of terminal equipments and sets—telex, fax, computer printers, audioconferencing bridges, videoconferencing bridges.
1990	Historian H. Schwartz writes *Century's End: A Cultural History of the Fin de Siècle from the 990s Through the 1990s.*
1990	*The Gaia Atlas of Future Worlds,* by economist/ environmentalist N. Myers.
1990	*Evil and Evolutionary Eschatology,* by J. Casserley.
1990	*Forecasting, Planning, and Strategy for the 21st Century,* by S. G. Makridakis.
1990	*Future Wealth,* by J. Robertson.
1990	*One Earth, One Future: Our Changing Global Environment,* by C. S. Silver.
1990	Paul R. and A. H. Ehrlich write *The Population Explosion.*
1990	*The Next One Hundred Years: Shaping the Fate of Our Living Earth,* by J. Weiner.
1990	Working Group on the Futures of Culture, sponsored by UNESCO, held in Paris, France (January), resulting in book *The Futures of Culture,* volume 1; optimistic and pessimistic scenarios.
1990	1st International Dialogue on the Transition to a Global Society, held in Switzerland, sponsored by UNESCO et al.
1990	Interparliamentary Conference on Global Environment promulgates "Resolution on Sustainable Development," with proposals for National Charter for Sustainable Development for each nation, a Green Common Market, a Bank for Sustainable Development, etc.
1991	Cosmology revolutionized through discoveries made by space-borne telescopes and instruments: riddles of quasars, black holes, et al. all begin to be solved.
1991	*Saving the Planet: How to Shape an Environmentally Sustainable Global Economy,* by Lester R. Brown et al.
1991	*Once Upon a Future Time: Studies in a Buddhist Prophecy of Decline,* by J. Nattier.
1991	Futurists M. Cetron and O. Davies produce *Crystal Globe: The Haves and Have-Nots of the New World Order.*
1991	*The Design of the World: An Essay on Process Cosmology,* by S. Salamah Pope.
1991	*The Futures Research Directory: Individuals 1991–92* produced by World Future Society.
1991	*Unbounding the Future: The Nanotechnology Revolution,* by K. E. Drexler and C. Peterson.

Date Events

1991	*Target Earth! Asteroid Collisions Past and Future,* by J. Erickson.
1991	*Technology 2000: The Future of Computing and Communications,* by D. Leebaert.
1991	*The Art of the Long View: Planning for the Future in an Uncertain World,* by P. Schwartz.
1991	Critique with serious criticism of future studies is made by Max Dublin in *Futurehype: The Tyranny of Prophecy,* holding that most future inquiry serves only vested interests.
1991	700 current engineering megaprojects (super projects) worldwide involving investment of over $1 billion each are described in McKinley Conway's book *Site World: The Book of Corporate Global Strategies;* including Community of European Railroads, "Multifunctionopolis" city in Australia, 500-story high-rise Aeropolis 2001 in Tokyo, Japan's Global Infrastructure Fund.
1991	12th World Conference, World Futures Studies Federation, held in Barcelona, Spain, on democracy and participation.
1992	United Nations' Population Division publishes professional data-based report, "Long-Range World Population Projections: Two Centuries of Population Growth, 1950–2150," based on 7 future fertility scenarios; medium variant arrives in A.D. 2200 at 11.6 billion population, with over-65s rising from 1% (1990) to 9% (2200); also, in 1993, "World Population Prospects: The 1992 Revision (for Every Country, 50 Variables, 1950–2025)," available as book or computer database.
1992	*The Heavens Are Falling: The Scientific Prediction of Catastrophes in our Time,* by W. G. Karplus.
1992	*Living at the End of the Ages: Apocalyptic Expectation in the Radical Reformation,* by W. Klaassen.
1992	*Cosmography: A Posthumous Scenario for the Future of Humanity,* by B. Fuller.
1992	*Millennialism: An International Bibliography,* by T. T. Daniels.
1992	U.S. vice president A. Gore publishes *Earth in the Balance: Ecology and the Human Spirit.*
1992	*When Time Shall Be No More: Prophecy Belief in Modern American Culture,* by P. Boyer.
1992	*Predictions: Society's Telltale Signature Reveals the Past and Forecasts the Future,* by mathematician T. Modis.
1992	Travel and tourism now world's largest industry: gross sales $3.5 trillion (6% of GDP), 7% of global capital spending, 127 million jobs; expenditure likely to rise from $1.8 trillion in 1990 to $5.8 trillion in 2005 (3.9% per year).

Date	Events
1993	Scientists perfect art of cloning (reproduction of infinite number of genetically identical people from cells of a single person, whose human body consists of 10^{28} atoms); first human is cloned.
1993	After 10 years' publicity, 5th-generation Japanese megacomputers with artificial intelligence are scheduled to be introduced and put on market as a staggering extension of human intellect, but at last minute, entire project is pronounced a failure and abandoned.
1993	Knowledge-intensive expert systems now widespread: a species of knowledge-based computer program performing at the level of, and replicating, human experts in professional fields.
1993	"Green machines" constructed: engineering systems using biological and biochemical processes or their human-made analogs to create materials, food, energy, or other goods and services.
1993	Human race enters Sign of Aquarius, embarks on Aquarian Age. Sabbath rest of 1,000 millennial years is about to begin.
1993	7th General Assembly, World Future Society, on "Creating the 21st Century: Rights, Responsibilities, and Actions," in Washington, DC; 29 major subject areas.
1993	Global asteroid patrol proposed to monitor solar system's 2,100 large ECAs (Earth-crossing asteroids) larger than 1 km across, its 300,000 ECAs larger than 100 m (330 feet), and 100 million ECAs larger than 20 m across; and also long-period comets suddenly appearing headed for Earth at 135,000 mph, producing plan to deflect them with neutron-bomb missiles.
1993	WORLD 2000 launched, an international planning dialogue to help shape a new global system, based on 3 elements: (1) key driving forces or supertrends, (2) critical issues blocking way ahead, (3) a master strategy to resolve these issues.

Date	Events
1993	XIII World Conference of World Futures Studies Federation, in Turku, Finland, on subject "Coherence and Chaos in Our Uncommon Futures: Visions, Means, Actions," sponsored by WFSF and Finnish Society for Futures Studies (FSFS) (August 23–27).
1994	Pocket-sized portable dators (radio/computer/database/phone) widely in use as universal personal accessory for instant information.
1994	National Computer Mercantile Network established, with superconducting supercomputers monitoring and recording every commercial and mercantile transaction in U.S., including personal tax files, credit records.
1994	First wristwatch computer perfected, accepting and imparting spoken instructions in English or any other language.
1994	Access to information globally now controlled by 8 giant conglomerates (media-entertainment megacompanies, media empires).
1994	Gaia-worship undertaken by ecological radicals, invoking the Mother Earth Goddess of prehistory.
1994	International Conference on Population and Development (U.N.).
1995	2nd Global Consultation on World Evangelization by the Year 2000 and Beyond (GCOWE II), in Seoul, Korea, with 5,000 church and mission leaders from 200 countries (June 13–25).
1995	40% of all Western world's 230 million homes have a general computer for home management and cottage industry.
1995	Travel and tourism become world's major industry, growing at 10% a year to reach 400 million foreign tourists a year; in North America, 7 million foreigners visit each year (1978, 2 million), 23 million citizens a year go abroad (1978, 10 million); foreign students 1.3 million (1978, 350,000); 1998, tourist services to space begin; 2010, packaged vacations in space available.

Part Two: The Future (A.D. 1996–Onward)

Date	Events
1996	Luggage, parcels, valuables and eventually all people begin to be electronically tagged so that none can be lost or ever disappear.
1996	International telephone system finally has enough switches (10^{10}) to become a conscious system, a giant brain similar to human brain (which has over 10^{11} or 100 bil-

Date	Events
	lion neurons or cellular building blocks). (A. C. Clarke, "Dial F for Frankenstein," 1965).
1996	Machines scan foreign-language newspapers and journals daily, then translate and archive materials for later retrieval.
1996	Anti-eye low-energy laser weapons (LEL) being developed for armed services of a few

Date　Events

nations; future battlefields' most terrible weapon will have power to cause mass blindness, with aircraft pilots highest priority targets.

1996　Estimated date for Prayalog, the Hindu end of the world, at end of present Kali Yuga of decay; whole world disintegrates in chaos in natural disasters (according to "Bhagwat" in Mahabharata), new life arises after Brahma completes 100,000 years of meditation.

1996　One billion telephones in world, nearly all direct dial; everyone in world is offered a U.N.-designed 17-digit personal number, making him accessible wherever a person may be.

1996　Superconductivity: room-temperature superconductors (transmitting electricity without any resistance) begin to transform all human energy usages.

1996　Bionic eyes: artificial eyesight proposed for blind people (the nonsighted); whole-eye transplants also envisaged as possible.

1996　Self-replicating machines, computers, and factories begin to be produced in Japan, reproducing exact copies of themselves.

1996　8th General Assembly, World Future Society, meets in Washington DC.

1996　Rise of intelligent architecture: smart technology enables intelligent urban envelopes, dynamic buildings, walls of light and sound, and personalized environment

1996　TV and HDTV made obsolete by emerging era of telecomputers—personal computers adapted for video processing, connected by fiber-optic threads to other telecomputers around world.

1996　America's 80 million personal computers become highly vulnerable to attack by viruses and "worms"; 10% of all computers infected.

1996　New frontiers in science and technology: complex systems, instability, Japan's Human Frontier Science Program, ultra-dense chips, extraterrestrial intelligence, robotics, new medical technology, new biological testing, earthquake prediction, telecomputers, spacebridges, optical communications, cellular technology, cold-climate technology, macroengineering, intelligent architecture, telecottages in rural areas.

1997　Worldwide global personal communications services provided by Motorola Corporation's Iridium project to develop system of small satellites operating in low Earth orbit.

1997　Anticipated medical advances envisaged: 1997, medical smart cards issued to all, animal testing of drugs replaced by computer modeling; 1998, buying and selling of live organs legalized and closely regulated; 1999, spread of cancer tightly controlled by new drug; 2000, overall incidence of cancer decreased by 35%, memory improved with drug; 2001, aging slowed by new vitamins; 2003, use of animal organs for transplants; 2007, drug addiction conquered; 2009, polyvalent vaccine prevents 80% of colds; 2020, incidence of all cancer decreased by 80%, more than 90% of coronary disease eliminated; 2025, average life expectancy reaches 100 years; 2030, maximum human life span increased to 150 years.

1997　Paralegals become fastest-growing job category in 1990s in Western world.

1997　Minicomputerized synthesizer capable of duplicating sounds of multiple musical instruments individually and as an orchestra.

1997　Automated highways being developed with central computer control of all vehicles moving at same speed at much greater densities than previously; all vehicles expected to have electronic collision-avoidance hardware systems.

1997　Ultrafast optical (fiber-optic) computers (for speedier informational transmission than by wires) produced by Bell Laboratories, IBM, et al.

1997　Global killer pandemics arise, sweeping across (1) Third World with "diseases of poverty" (malaria, bilharzia, filariasis, et al.) as parasites achieve full resistance to present drugs; (2) rest of world with revived deadly ancient diseases (smallpox, bubonic plague, pneumonic plague, et al.) as world loses its herd immunity and abandons vector control and vaccination; and (3) AIDS and related pandemics; hundreds of millions die.

1997　A newscaster using very powerful personal computer gets access to, and finally control over, all data banks in world. (A. J. Budrys's scenario *Michaelmas*, 1977.)

1997　Project Space Voyage, a low Earth-orbit popular tour organized by Society Expeditions: 4 days' briefing, 12-hour trip, 2 days' debriefing.

1997　6th-generation computers with artificial intelligence emerge, equaling human brain in any intellectual activity.

1997　New Black Plague begins (epidemic attacking immune systems), caused by pollution of air/water/food/environment, killing animals/insects/trees/plants/humans.

Date	Events
1997	Invention of programmable sound-silencer to eliminate noise far better than brick or stone.
1997	Genetic transcription provides first genetic map of healthy human cells, opens up new science of genetic markers (diagnosing at birth each person's future illnesses in order to prevent them).
1997	Manned expedition to Mars launched by NASA (20 years after first landing of unmanned robot probe Viking).
1997	Unified field theory finally constructed by physicists, a mathematical model tying together the 5 basic forces holding the Universe's particles together: gravity, electromagnetism, weak nuclear force, strong nuclear force, hypercharge.
1997	Synthetic blood in wide use.
1997	Information Age measures: (1) an average person's TIUPIL (typical information use per individual lifetime) = 20 billion bits of information, or 500 million spoken/thought-out/written words; and (2) grand total GHIUD (global human information use per decade) = 12 quintillion (12×10^{18}) bits a decade = 30,000 trillion new words added a year to the sum total of human knowledge.
1998	Terrorists in Africa seize and dominate world's supply of gold, diamonds, and strategic metals.
1998	Substitutive medicine (replacement of defective parts by implants or transplants) begins to replace drug treatment; kidney dialysis patients wear device internally; by 2020, people being kept alive by spare parts number 1% of population in Western world.
1998	Nuclear crime, blackmail, and terrorism become rampant on all continents, especially in megacities and supercities.
1998	Diagnosis of almost any illness possible in a few hours by examining patient's human protein index (human body contains 150,000 different kinds of protein).
1998	Beginning of freefly (flying for individuals) by means of jetpacks or rocket belts.
1998	Definitive alleviation of mental illness in sight.
1998	First prototype SPS (solar power satellite) successfully beams energy from space to Earth, relaying solar power via low-density microwaves to become DC electrical current; 2021, over 20 SPS in geosynchronous Earth orbit each producing 10 gigawatts (10 billion watts) microbeamed to Earth to join existing electric power grids; 2028, SPS supply 90% of Earth's energy requirements.
1998	Several communications satellites vital to global economy and nuclear balance of power are seized, disabled, or taken over by techno-terrorists until demands met.
1998	Hospital (computerized health care facility) opened in space by NASA (U.S.).
1998	Context-recognition chips (anti-advertising modules) marketed: Adnix which mutes TV set when commercials begin, and Preachnix which switches channels when doctrinaire religious programs appear (at preselected keywords like "Advent," "Rapture," etc.).
1998	Submotel (submarine hotel) opens, with parking for tourist minisubmarines.
1998	In democracies, citizens govern by televoting regularly every Sunday at noon.
1998	Robotics develops: robots serve as guards, janitors, nurses, minders, and aides to disabled and elderly; service robotics begins to outstrip industrial robotics, with robot paranurses, parapharmacists, gas station attendants, et al.
1998	Sudden global power failure and total breakdown of sociosphere now seen as possible, even likely, as domino effect destroys global infrastructures; countermeasures drawn up.
1998	Electronic mentors emerge, offering user personalized help in navigating the information age, sparking user's creativity with questions, taking dictation, placing and receiving phone calls, translating, and often using artificial intelligence.
1998	Collapse of most major currencies, with runaway global inflation, envisaged as a possible scenario to be planned against.
1998	Most large enterprises managed largely by artificial intelligence.
1998	Majority of countries enforce strict population control, including contraceptive injections and forced abortions.
1998	Automatic language translation for telephone users, enabling speakers worldwide to converse each in his own language.
1998	Nuclear reactor disaster in Western capital city; millions killed, huge area contaminated.
1998	United Religions Organization (URO) bought into being to parallel U.N., to provide visions and moral power for world faiths; based in Jerusalem.
1999	Mind-reading computers invented, with direct telepathic reading of thoughts in the brain; telepathic machines pick up human thoughts, place them on screen in front of the thinker.
1999	Evolution of superbugs (drug-resistant microbes, antibiotic-proof bacteria) spreading

Date Events

around globe especially in hospitals, due to enormous increase in tourism and business travel since 1970 and also to inadequate medical care and sanitation.

1999   NASA launches detailed plan to expand efforts for radio search for extraterrestrial intelligence (SETI) 10 billionfold.

1999   A new futuristic international city, Multifunction Polis, begins to be built in Australia.

1999   Rise of polyarchies and democracy experiments, utilizing minipopulus of 1,000 randomly selected citizens to deliberate an issue for a year as complement to legislative bodies.

1999   "Black holes" of financial crime sweep world: explosion of big fraud crimes (insurance, pension plans, telemarketing, computer crime, health care).

1999   All cancers can now in principle be instantly arrested, cured, and eliminated through reprogramming of DNA in individual body cells.

1999   Cold apocalypse scenario: pitch-dark bone-chilling nuclear winter brought on by limited nuclear war using 5,000 megatons (20% of current arsenals) in which 1.2-billion-ton cloud of dust (black snow) and smoke envelops Northern Hemisphere first, then Southern Hemisphere; world freezes or starves to death except for bands of hunter-gatherers in south.

1999   Holovision (life-size 3-dimensional pictures through use of laser holography) replaces television in homes.

1999   Time shown by scientists to be flowing at different rates in different parts of the universe, including tachyons (particles that move faster than light) for which time moves backwards.

1999   Muslim end of world, as prophesied by traditional Islam: coming of Antichrist into godless world, Kaaba vanishes from Mecca, all copies of Quran suddenly become blank paper, all Quran's words disappear from human memory, final Mahdi appears, then Prophet Isa (Jesus) ushers in Islam as sole global religion, followed by Last Judgment.

1999   Biotechnologists succeed in mapping the complete neural signature of the entire human brain.

1999   Mass production of implantable miniaturized artificial kidneys.

1999   People assisters (computer-assisted hydraulic mover systems with powered arms) worn by infirm or handicapped people to give them increased mobility; also, for healthy persons, personal manoeuvering units (in

space), Moon bugs, Mars rovers, submersibles, solarsail kites; also lighter-than-air skyships.

1999   People amplifiers (PAs) in use: portable computerized devices which assist average person perform as a pseudoexpert in several different spheres at once (e.g., law/accountancy/mathematics/astronomy/theology/misiology/homiletics).

1999   Experience-amplifiers in use, for magnifying human experiences: emotion-amplifiers, sensation-amplifiers, awareness-amplifiers, creativity-amplifiers.

1999   Intelligence-amplifiers (resulting in enhanced intelligence) create artificial personalities for secretaries, assistants, technicians, et al.

1999   Nuclear holocaust recovery scenario: due to warhead detonation patterns in global nuclear war, initial deaths 10% of world (including 50% of U.S.) but 90% of world survives (including 50% of U.S.) and 90% of world's surface remains unaffected; secondary deaths from fallout, wind-borne radiation followed by radiation sickness, contaminated food and water, breakdown of civilization, and decreased fertility, all kill another 10% of world; animal and plant life only marginally affected; world recovers fully within 20 years (U.S. 40 years).

1999   Nuclear holocaust median scenario: nuclear war between U.S. and other powers leaves initially 50% of both populations dead and all major urban cities destroyed; full-scale thermonuclear attack immediately kills 88% of U.S. and 50% of rest of world; a new Dark Ages era begins.

1999   Extinction scenario: nuclear war results in 6 billion deaths, end of civilization, destruction of the North, destruction of all global infrastructures, destruction of knowledge and know-how, mankind reduced to handful of demoralized tribal savages; eventually, final extinction of all human and animal life.

1999   Direct communication with computers by speech achieved by humans; talkwriters (transcribing speech) replace human transcribers.

1999   Planetran world transportation network transports millions daily in electromagnetically propelled cars travelling at 14,000 mph through evacuated tubes in underground tunnels.

1999   Global energy crisis finally solved as SPS (Solar Power Satellite) comes on-line; by 2021 becomes world's major energy source.

Date   **Events**

1999   Earth unexpectedly enters dense belt of cosmic dust; temperatures fall catastrophically, new ice age begins.

1999   Human transplant surgery multiplies; vast organ banks set up for freezing and storing of human organs, limbs, and healthy youthful cadavers.

1999   Professional consultation on any subject available to all in any language at low cost by telephone, provided by computer expert systems.

1999   Two-way wrist or pocket telephones/TVs/pagers/maintenance-free wrist computers/translatorfones in widespread use across globe.

1999   Ecological warfare perfected, including deliberate induction of earthquakes by triggering vibrations from a distance.

1999   Emergence of hundreds of new short-lived millennial religions or belief systems at local, national, and global levels; ultrafast-growing religious cults and revivals, millions joining and leaving in rapid succession.

1999   All sizeable nations and many private groups have nuclear weapons or can easily purchase them.

1999   Global panic spreads as end of millennium approaches, widely believed to be December 31, 1999 (wrongly, since 20th century ends on December 31, 2000).

1999   Helvetian War (Secrecy War), last armed conflict on Earth, erupts to force Switzerland to reveal secret bank holdings; 20th-century citizens of America and Pan-Europe attack Swiss-based laundered monies of drug merchants, tax cheats, and corrupt dictators shielded by banking "gnomes of Zurich" in their bank vault strongholds beneath the Glarus Alps; international banking secrecy finally destroyed.

Status of Globe in A.D. 2000

2000   *Postindustrialism.* 25% of mankind live in societies with postindustrial (transindustrial) economies, where producing necessities of life becomes trivially easy technologically, and in which therefore knowledge and information replace capital as society's most important resource.

2000   *Demographics.* World population 6.1 billion (30.7% under 15, median age 26.1, life expectancy 63.9 years); 20-year period begins of probable population megadisasters due to famine, drought, crop failures, mismanagement, corruption, warfare (Neo-Malthusianism).

Date   **Events**

2000   *Urbanization.* Supercities (urban agglomerations with over 4 million inhabitants) total 79 (59 in developing countries); megacities (with over 1 million) 433; urban dwellers number 51.2% of world, increasing by 1.6 million a week; urban slums expand far faster than cities, producing "a planet of slums."

2000   World's 10 largest cities: Mexico City 25,820,000, Sao Paulo 23,970,000, Tokyo-Yokohama 20,220,000, Calcutta 16,530,000, Bombay 16,000,000, New York/N.E. New Jersey 15,780,000, Seoul 13,770,000, Teheran 13,580,000, Shanghai 13,260,000, Jakarta 13,250,000.

2000   *Industrialization.* World industrial robot population 35 million: Japan 11,000,000 (and a million new ones a year), U.S. 7,500,000, Russia 5,600,000, Germany 4,600,000, France 1,620,000, Italy 1,600,000, U.K. 820,000, Sweden 650,000, Brazil 550,000, etc.

2000   *Industry.* Only 4 automobile firms remain in world as all smaller ones consolidate into global giants, with production centered in Korea, Italy, and Latin America.

2000   *Work.* U.S.: 35% of all paid work is now done from people's homes.

2000   *Transportation.* Linear-motor trains become standard means of intercity transportation up to 1,000 km; ultrahigh speed, magnetic levitation.

2000   *Society.* Mankind now more unified than at any time in the past; more standardized (English as lingua franca), more affluent, longer lived, more mobile, less religious, better educated; tourism by now world's largest industry, with 470 million foreign tourists a year.

2000   U.S. colleges host 1 million students from abroad.

2000   Cashless society in place, using a single world monetary unit for trade and exchange.

2000   Creation of one single planetary culture and civilization finally achieved on Earth; planetization of human race well under way.

2000   *Politics.* Instant polling of viewers' opinions and election choices over viewer-interactive cable TV.

2000   Evolution of "synocracy"—government by synergy, by multiple mutual attraction not coercion.

2000   *Psychology.* Future shock becomes worldwide: breakdown of civilization because society's subsystems no longer function and people can no longer cope with accelerating change (pace of life too fast).

Date	Events
2000	*Ecosystem.* Human pressure on natural systems of Earth (consumption of raw materials) multiplies 70-fold in last hundred years.
2000	*Agriculture.* 30% of world's arable land destroyed by human encroachment in last 20 years; 20% of world's population are subsistence farmers, 20% more are poor farmers responsible for spread of desertification.
2000	*Mariculture.* Ocean farming begins to produce more food than agriculture, including 900 million metric tons of meat annually.
2000	*Biosphere.* 10% of world's 10 million animal and plant species destroyed in last 20 years due to deforestation, desertification, and destruction of habitats; by A.D. 2030, possibly as high as 40%; since Earth's biosphere is a single complex system similar to a living organism (the Gaia theory), this extinction has vast adverse effects on human prosperity.
2000	*Evolution.* Two new human species of genus Homo with own distinct cultures begin to evolve and become recognized: (1) Homo Solaris, humans who function predominantly off-Earth in space, dependent on technology and alien life-support environments; and (2) Homo Posthumanus, arising from coalescence of humans and ultraintelligent machines.
2000	*Language.* New universal language evolves due to automated communication.
2000	*Medicine.* Drugless medical treatment attacks all illnesses electromagnetically, making body cells produce antibodies, new tissue, et al.
2000	Human hibernation developed for extensive periods (months to years).
2000	*Disease.* Global pandemics sweep across continents wiping out millions every few days; rapid destruction of Earth's ozone layer by aerosols (freon gas) results in increase in ultraviolet radiation, causes widespread cancer.
2000	*Pollution.* Urban pollution becomes deadly: Mexico City (largest in world with 26 million population and 1,100,000 influx each year) is world's most polluted city, with 6 million cars; Tokyo (20 million) next; also Cubatao (Brazil), world's most polluted petrochemical center; and Cairo (11 million) has world's worst noise pollution.
2000	*Communications.* Vast expansion of telephone systems: e.g., in Brazil, from 500,000 phones in 1967 to 7.6 million (1982) and to 125 million (A.D. 2000); total worldwide 2.2 billion, 98% being direct-dial.
2000	Rapidly growing global telecommunications network in its entirety now equals human brain in complexity.
2000	*Computerization.* World's 700 million computers, from micros to mainframes, become connected to each other in a single global network.
2000	*Broadcasting.* Radios number 2.5 billion worldwide.
2000	Subliminal TV in widespread use by countries for mass mind control.
2000	Cable TV (CATV) reaches 100 million households in U.S. (up from 14 million in 1982).
2000	Data broadcasting widespread, becomes norm for many professions.
2000	*Publishing.* Computer printout terminals in every neighborhood in Western world will publish and bind on demand any book requested before customer's eyes while waiting.
2000	*Litigation.* Disputes escalate over rights to information (copyrights, patents, industrial espionage, personal rights).
2000	*Energy.* Widespread use of renewable energy sources (invariant energy systems), i.e., solar energy (99.98% of all the energy Earth receives), geothermal energy, tidal energy; also, wireless transmission of energy comes into operation.
2000	Commercial energy consumption increases from 0.5 billion metric tons oil equivalent (1900) to 1.667 billion (1950) to 5.6 billion (1974; 1.4 tons per capita) to 15.5 billion (A.D. 2000; 2.5 tons per capita).
2000	*Warfare.* Inner solar system becomes vast arena for nuclear confrontation with locating of dark or hidden satellites, and nuclear missiles on Moon.
2000	*Nuclear power.* 100 large power plants worldwide become due for retirement after full working life, but their dismantling and disposal pose major problems.
2000	*Weaponry.* Countries owning nuclear power facilities proliferate, though over 100 exhausted or terminated nuclear plants exist, remaining lethally radioactive for thousands of years into future; total plutonium produced as by-product of global nuclear power reaches equivalent of 1 million atomic bombs; illegal nuclear weapons result, with disastrous consequences.
2000	*Nuclear powers.* Countries possessing clear-cut nuclear weapons and means of delivery rise to 35, including Argentina, Egypt, India, Iraq, Israel, Kuwait, Libya, North Korea, Pakistan, Saudi Arabia, Turkey, Zaire.

Date   Events

2000 *Biological warfare.* First use of deadly bacillus botulinus to destroy entire populations in a few hours.

2000 *Ethics.* Human selfishness and greed lead world inexorably towards eventual catastrophe or self-destruction.

2000 Age of "manufactured experience" begins: experiences of any kind (religious enlightenment, perception, insight, mystic contemplation, planetary consciousness, moods, orgasm, well-being, etc.) available on order using chemical, physical, and psychological stimulants (LSD, marijuana, peyote, mescaline, hallucinogenic drugs, etc.).

2000 Relaunching of world's largest particle accelerator, the Superconducting Supercollider (SSC), 54-mile circular tunnel under Waxahachie, Texas, abandoned in 1993 as too expensive; aims include verifying standard model (4 particles, acted on by 4 forces), and identifying supersymmetric particles (dark matter, 99% of universe).

2000 Proven exploitable reserves in barrels or barrels-equivalent: oil 1.5 trillion (enough to last 70 years), natural gas 500 billion, and coal to last 125 years.

2000 AIDS kills 200 million since 1980; deadly mutation HIV-7 devastates body's immune system 25 years after contact.

2000 NASA and ESA (European Space Agency) put space platforms in position as satellites each with 1 million voice circuits.

2000 Historic abolition of all long-distance telephone charges (on December 31) transforms humanity into one huge gossiping family.

2000 Japan: automatic-interpretation telephone systems introduced.

Status of Religion and Christianity in A.D. 2000

2000 *Non-Christians.* 83% of world's 4.0 billion non-Christians now reside in 140 nations, many newly opened to traditional crosscultural foreign missionary endeavor and also to internal home mission or evangelism by nationals.

2000 *Agnosticism.* Abandoning of religion worldwide results in 260 million antireligious or atheists (4.2% of world) and 1,048 million nonreligious or agnostics (17.1%); China over 70%, Europe 17.5%.

2000 *Primal religion.* Despite attempts of missionary religions to convert them, adherents of traditional tribal religions (animism, shamanism, polytheism, pantheism, folk religion, fetishism, et al.) number 110 millions, almost exactly the same number as in year 1900.

Date   Events

2000 *Mass movements.* Nativistic, messianic, cargo-cult, and other mass religious movements of popular syncretism mushroom across Third World.

2000 Global status of Christianity: 65.6 generations after Christ, world is 34.8% Christians (39.9% of them being whites, 60.1% non-whites), and 83.4% of all individuals are now evangelized; with printed scriptures available in 2,800 languages.

2000 *Respect for Christ.* Person of Christ now widely known and respected throughout world, by all world religions, even among atheists and agnostics; also his teachings and his gospel (but not his church) are understood and valued, though not accepted or implemented, almost universally.

2000 *Christians.* At world level, Christians are now 55% Third Worlders, 22% pentecostal charismatics (5% in pentecostal denominations, 3% charismatics, 2.5% in Chinese house churches, and 11.4% inactive or unaffiliated).

2000 *Spirituality.* Widespread revival of monasticism both eremitic (hermits) and cenobitic (communities), among young people of all churches across world, especially in Third World countries.

2000 Many segments of global church adopt radical and revolutionary personal, congregational, and denominational lifestyles.

2000 *Growth.* Christianity and other world religions survive and flourish, also mysticism, magic, divination, cults, occult, astrology, numerology.

21st Century Begins Period or Age of Crisis, A.D. 2001–2180

2001 Third Millennium of Christian era begins (on January 1, 2001).

2001 Major energy crisis as worldwide exhausting of fossil fuels and essential minerals becomes evident in one area after another.

2001 Japan becomes most "informationized" society on Earth, based on massive mainframe megacomputers storing vast data/information/knowledge banks; Japan now world's leading nation in design, manufacture, and export of communications technology.

2001 Normal human life span extends to 150 years for 5% of Western world, but increased longevity only viable for future homo species voyaging beyond solar system.

2001 Chemists create staggering compounds for every area of human experience, including the ultimate glue (adhesives that replace nearly all existing fasteners).

Date　Events

2001　Most human genes now mapped (100,000 genes to build a human being), due to gene-splicing technology; many of medicine's problems and mysteries solved.

2001　Ocean level rises gradually by 5 feet until 2120 then falls, stabilizing from 2200–2400.

2001　First true space colony (high frontier or O'Neill type) designed and by 2020 built and inhabited in orbit between Earth and Moon; 2020, first children born off-Earth; 50,000 people then live and work in space.

2001　Towing of asteroids Earthwards for mining planned, using mass driver (cost for 3-km-thick asteroid: $200 billion); over 60 asteroids are known to cross Earth's orbit; but whole scheme delayed.

2001　Wars fought with mercenary replicants (cloned humanoids with silicon intelligence), intelligent weapons, robot tanks, smart missiles, RPVs (remotely piloted vehicles), et al.

2001　U.S. approaches bankruptcy as federal budget deficit increases from $4 trillion in 1992 to $8 trillion by A.D. 2000.

2002　One vast megacomputer established under U.N. auspices, with centralized global data facility giving wide public access to library, business, and home terminals.

2002　Emergence of 7th-generation computers, powered not by electricity but by light beams.

2002　Alien virus brought back by interplanetary spaceprobe wipes out 10% of population of Earth.

2002　Startling influence of Christian world confessionalism continues to spread, at expense of world interdenominationalism, ecumenism, and conciliarism; decline of World Council of Churches and its 200 associated continental and national councils of churches, under charges of having stood for ecumenical imperialism.

2002　Conquest of disease: every kind of cancer curable in early stages and treatable throughout; by 2015, all infectious and heritable diseases in humans, plants, and animals eradicated in principle.

2002　Civilian aerospace vehicles (CAVs) come into service, traveling at Mach 12 and carrying travelers halfway around the world in 2 hours.

2002　Worldwide emergence of natural economic regional states cutting across existing national political boundaries: Baden-Württemberg, Alsace-Lorraine, Catalonia, Wales, Vancouver-Seattle, Hong Kong-Guangdong, Fuzhou-Taiwan, and many more within China, Japan, Pacific Basin, et al.

Date　Events

2003　90% of all world's first-class mail now transmitted electronically (electronic mail).

2003　Third-generation artificial experience developed through mammoth artificial-intelligence computer systems creating 3-dimensional holograms of any historical or future reality or event in the universe.

2003　Corporate commercial warfare: giant multinational conglomerates engage in worldwide organized espionage, intimidation, threats, fraud, violence, and terrorism to discourage competition.

2003　Full-immersion video rooms in homes for families to surround themselves with tropical rain forest, a Mars landscape, a movie epic, etc.

2003　The 7 major obstacles to Christian world mission become megamaterialism, mega-affluence, megapoverty, megapollution, megacrime, megaterrorism, megapersecution.

2003　Palestine Liberation Organization splinter group, Sons of the Jihad, set off a squirt bomb in London, polluting 60% of city for next 70 years.

2004　As result of microelectronics revolution, 50% of all jobs in industrial world have been eliminated over last 25 years; robots run 50% of world's industrial mass production.

2004　Research on control of aging well on way to enormous gains.

2004　Hydrogen now the most popular small-scale energy source, powering commercial vehicles et al.

2004　Seminaries, training colleges, revolutionized by chemical transfer of learning: memory pills, knowledge pills, new languages learned by injection

2004　Orient Express, or TAV (transatmospheric vehicle, a hypersonic space vehicle) takes off from and lands on conventional runways, deploys Strategic Defense Initiative (SDI) payloads in space.

2004　Gigantic electromagnetic railguns, mounted on mountainsides, accelerate cargo-carrying missiles to hypersonic speeds out into space.

2004　European vigilantes' group called Speedwatch systematically assassinates dangerous, drunk, or speeding car drivers.

2005　Eco-collapse scenario: initial worldwide eco-catastrophe due to unabated population growth, resource depletion, pollution of the biosphere, destruction of the ecosphere and the sociosphere, crop failures, starvation, megafamines, et al. (Club of Rome).

2005　Development of direct brain-computer interfaces as means of extending human mental capacity; human brains linked to super-

Date Events

computers; also direct communication between computers and human central nervous system.

2005 Polio as a children's disease is eliminated throughout world.

2005 First commercially viable biochip interface, linking a human by wire to multilingual interface computer.

2005 Tourism continues as world's biggest industry, with 700 million people travelling abroad for pleasure each year.

2005 Telepathy in use for some types of communication, criminology, diplomacy, military intelligence, espionage.

2005 Parapsychology comes into use as a military weapon used by terrorists, private armies, vigilantes, and military regimes.

2005 Biotechnological disaster through a microbe spill: creation and accidental release of virulent microbes wipe out entire populations.

2005 Medical advances: antiviral drugs and vaccines wipe out communicable diseases; genetic manipulation removes congenital defects; lung and brain-cell transplants become routine; nerve tissue regenerated to rehabilitate paraplegics and quadriplegics.

2005 Beamlike gravitational radiation detected from superheavy objects in outer space.

2005 Biomap: genomic inventory (mapping by molecular biologists of human genome or genetic complex) enables prediction of future health and preemptive treatment; but misuses increase (discrimination, invasion of privacy) until in 2010 uniform global policy on access is adopted by 145 countries; human biomap, with 3 billion separate genetic functions, not completed until 2086.

2005 Large numbers of substitute religions arise, mostly related to New Age movement; a vast amorphous hodgepodge of spiritualism, reincarnation, meditation, yoga, faith healing, macrobiotic diets, out-of-body experiences, altered-consciousness states, mystical environmentalism.

2005 International Thermonuclear Experimental Reactor (ITER), producing nuclear power by fusion, completed by international team at San Diego, U.S., and commissioned after cost of $7.5 billion; c. 2035, global chain of fusion reactor power stations at work.

2005 United Nations revokes license of sovereignty hitherto assumed by all sovereign nations.

2005 Citizens begin electing commercial firms instead of politicians to run their cities.

2005 Low-intensity conflicts (LICs) proliferate, being U.S. responses to Third World violence.

Date Events

2005 Team of 150 terrorists uses man-transportable electromagnetic pulse generators (EMPGs) to attack transformers serving New York, Washington, Dallas, Atlanta, Boston, Chicago, and San Francisco; succeeds in erasing computer databases in those cities causing loss of social security records, tax records, bank records, pension plans, financial transactions, library holdings; all erased in a moment.

2005 International organization "Honesty International" (modeled on Amnesty International) monitors corruption in government and corporate institutions around world, investigating bribery, embezzlement, with goal of deterring such activities.

2006 Internationalists (people working for U.N. agencies) become major influence in world at all levels.

2006 Earth invaded from outer space by Overlords in giant spaceships, who then assist humanity to continue its evolution into a galaxy-wide and ever-expanding Overmind; but in the end humans reactivate volcanic energies of Earth's core and destroy planet. (A. C. Clarke's novel, *Childhood's End*, 1953.)

2006 Conflict between science and religion finally disappears; physicists and biochemists become more concerned about questions of spirit, soul, and creation than many theologians.

2006 Neurotransmitters activate human brains and change mental performance; brain radios communicate with electricity in brain, enabling people to dial into any emotional, mental, or sensual experience.

2006 Declining Euroamerican denominations in Western world spark itinerant tourist churches, groupings of believers ceaselessly travelling and witnessing around the Earth; Latin Americans form itinerant pilgrim churches that multiply phenomenally across world.

2006 Artificial intelligence (AI) affects 60–90% of jobs in large organizations, augmenting, displacing, downgrading, eliminating workers.

2007 Development of vast, single computer that runs world, world economy and world government and monitors and controls all other computers. (I. Asimov, "The Life and Times of Multivac," 1975.)

2007 All Persian Gulf states run out of oil; virtual exhaustion of petroleum reserves; Saudi Arabia, Gulf states, Iran, Libya et al. lose accumulated oil wealth, revert to pauper status.

Date	Events
2007	Establishment of first nonterrestrial permanent resource base, either on Moon or Mars or in space.
2007	21st-century epidemic Plague Wars, with appalling variety of new lethal diseases, begin with 15 million killed by influenza virus in southern Africa, leading to violent overthrow of white influence in South Africa; 2015, deliberately engineered plague in Los Angeles kills 1 million; 2024, VD virus kills 5 million in Poland; 7 million in outbreak in Brussels; 2049, 38 million killed in China by lightning hepatitis; finally checked by 2060. (*The Third Millennium*, 1985.)
2007	Computer work stations in offices equipped with expert systems function as dictionaries, directories, telephones; office typists and secretaries replaced by managers.
2007	Passive entertainment, passive listening to radio, passive TV watching, passive observing all disappear as reality becomes widely synthesized to give people active participation in sports, arts, wars, thrills, et al. via "sensavision" head-fittings.
2008	Final Return of Mahdi (Mirza Ghulam Ahmad), regarded as Christ/Vishnu/Mohammed in Ahmadiyya belief, on centenary of his death; huge crowds of Ahmadis wait expectantly across world.
2008	Scientists at International Astronomical Union announce Sun will go nova and explode in A.D. 3620; by 2553, 4 km-long seedships packed with data, life (species, DNA), technology and a million hibernating humans each, depart for Alpha Centauri A and 50 other planetary systems with oxygen; 3450, quantum drive invented making perpetual travel without fuel possible; 40 seedship voyages fail but 10 succeed including Mormon "Ark of the Covenant" and other religious ones; 3617, starship Magellan leaves doomed Earth, 4135 arrives to begin life on planet Sagan Two. (A. C. Clarke, *The Songs of Distant Earth*, 1985.)
2008	Founding of Global Trade Consortium (GTC) in Zurich by megacorporate businessmen in developed countries; by 2015 all 12 megacorps enlist.
2008	Cancer largely eliminated by immunization.
2009	Space-com wrist-radios enable user to speak with anyone in world; by 2010, 50 million users across globe.
2009	Cataract system, a network of orbiting nuclear mines, launched by U.S. to blind all enemy satellites before a nuclear preemptive first strike.
2009	Total global charismatic worship of Christ introduced, in which at a fixed time each Sunday 1 billion living believers across world are holographically present visibly at same location; the ultimate in inspiration and evangelistic converting power.
2010	Postnuclear human mutants multiply and spread, with telepathic powers; several bizarre civilizations develop: telepathic societies, high-technology societies, barbarisms, dictatorships.
2010	Death of oceans scenario: terminal process leading to death of world's seas and oceans due to massive and irreversible pollution by industrial poisons, chemicals, and sewage, leading to global disease, epidemics, famine, warfare, and extinction.
2010	Technological collapse scenario: beginnings of collapse of global technology due to overload, exhaustion of minerals, warfare, terrorism; technological civilization disintegrates into barbarism.
2010	Private transport severely restricted, even abolished by law in many vast areas.
2010	All information in a large library is storable on machine the size of a postage stamp and instantaneously retrievable.
2010	Psychiatry and medicine can now call on vast arrays of drugs.
2010	Antiaging drugs available on prescription to arrest and reverse aging in humans.
2010	Governments drug reservoirs and all water supplies with contraceptives to control population explosion.
2010	Intelligent machines tackle all mental activities somewhat better than humans can.
2010	World government arises as vastly complex polynucleated or decentralized matrix organization or network rather than all power being centrally concentrated.
2010	Mind-control and behavior-control chemicals widely used (via water and food supplies) by authoritarian governments to suppress dissension and unrest.
2010	Rise of totalitarianism produces mass religious revivals; bogus robot evangelists seduce ignorant with promises of immediate salvation.
2010	Vast growth of magical and pseudoscientific cults; governments use androids (chemically constructed beings) to deceive and manipulate religious followers.
2010	Increasing influence of Christianity on secular worlds of science, politics, society, ideas; scientists in particular openly become more religious.

Date   Events

2010   Historic discovery: brain code deciphered, showing how human brain (most efficient and compact information storage system ever) works; direct communication with human minds achieved.

2010   A new Golden Age of peace and prosperity begins.

2010   World's 10 largest cities: Mexico City 30 million, São Paulo 28 million, Tokyo/Yokohama 21 million, Calcutta 20 million, Bombay 20 million, Teheran 17 million, Delhi 17 million, Jakarta 16 million, New York 16 million, Dacca 15 million.

2010   Widespread genetic engineering (gene splicing) to fix deformed arms or legs; all childhood diseases eliminated, also skin, breast, and cervical cancer; by 2020, 90% of all forms of cancer eliminated, regeneration of fingers and toes accomplished, also plastic surgery without scalpel; by 2050, regeneration of human internal organs.

2010   Uniform global policy on access to biomaps adopted by 145 countries urged on by Global Trade Consortium.

2010   Whole world now looks to or follows 3 new global futures: (1) globalized liberal democratic technoliberal capitalism, with breakthroughs in technology (fusion power, artificial intelligence, et al.); (2) democratic socialism and world government, the workers' republic; (3) 2085 or 2130, self-sufficient advanced technologies scaled to local needs by neo-romantic counterculturalist values.

2010   A new kind of society emerges: postcapitalist but nonsocialist, with knowledge as primary resource.

2010   World's 3 leading economic powers (U.S., European Community, Japan) are joined by rapidly growing economic giant, China.

2010   Telephones in use that instantly translate foreign languages.

2011   Major shortages of vital metals (mercury, cadmium, copper, tin, silver) result in political blackmail and miniwars.

2011   Most forms of mental retardation now curable.

2011   Collapse of organized secularism, agnosticism (nonreligion), atheism (antireligion), and rise of spiritual movements with vast rash of sects and cults of all kinds.

2011   Religious pilgrims become a major force in world, over 400 million religious zealots (50% being Christians) constantly on move from shrine to shrine and country to country, ignoring secular and state restrictions.

2011   All texts published in English routinely put on electronic deposit; 2030, this becomes sole form of publication for scientific papers and other reference items, reproducible by printer only at point of consumption.

2011   All radio, telephone, and televisual communication becomes integrated in single worldwide information-transfer network; satellite-relayed entertainment, English-language teletext library services, even for poorest nations; 2150, integration universal.

2011   Great Cycle of the ancient Mayas of Meso-America due to be completed, ushering in end of whole Cosmos.

2011   First of only 3 hostile nuclear incidents since 1945; 2011, Israelis destroy Libyan city, killing 78,000; 2020, Zaire accident detonates missile killing 7,000 with fallout throughout equatorial Africa; and 2079, city of Buenos Aires destroyed by Brazilian air force; thereafter, all nuclear weapons seized by superpowers, worldwide nuclear peace enforced.

2011   U.S.: SDI shield fully operational; similar shield over Europe and Russia by 2021.

2012   Orbital colonies commenced: one-mile-diameter Stanford torus space stations with living space for 10,000 people permanently resident (no return to Earth possible), each weighing 500,000 tons (materials from the Moon) and costing $30 billion and 10 years to build; several hundred artificial colonies around Earth by 2050, some 10,000 within solar system by 2100, many millions throughout galaxy by 2500, billions across universe by A.D. 4000; but on other scenarios, endless delays and obstacles cause entire program to be abandoned until resurgence of interest in A.D. 2250.

2012   Space wars: incidents, conflicts, and full-scale warfare in space erupt and proliferate.

2012   Long-predicted great earthquake in northern California strikes, with incredible force.

2012   Solar Army (antinuclear movement) grows as quasi-religious movement with massive rallies, protests, lobbying.

2012   Revolution in Brazil kills millions, places workers in full control of world's second-largest economy.

2012   First commercial fusion plant opens in Tokyo.

2012   International Data Storage Center founded.

2013   Futurists and others can file their prognostications with new World Predictions Registry, receiving annual scores or success ratings (worldwide average 5%, with 16% = "brilliant foresight"); makes annual Prognostication Awards; 2040, new category of "random prophecy" established based on huge databases.

Date	Events
2013	Beginning of protracted development of nuclear fusion power; 2039, fuser technology born in Spacelab IV orbiting laboratory; 2054, prototype fusion cell; 2070, first fusion reactors feeding power into national grids; 2090, true fusion-energy economy becomes widespread, world electrical grid set up, global use of fossil fuels abandoned.
2014	Controlled thermonuclear power extracted from hydrogen isotopes; huge fusion power plants come on-line across world.
2014	On optimistic scenario, 1 million people now live permanently in space colonies.
2014	Manned exploration of solar system expands to first human landing on planet Mars; no evidence of life found.
2015	Weather control on Earth achieved.
2015	Gradual military ascendancy of the North (Western world in new alliance with Russia) versus Islam and the South. (Nostradamus).
2015	Art of bodily healing becomes centered in self-regulation and self-regeneration, training our brains to produce exactly the right chemicals needed to heal the body of every condition including aging (which is now regarded as an avoidable disease), and to develop optimal health and well-being.
2015	Pollution spreads: Caribbean Sea reduced to an ecological sewer.
2015	Catastrophic breakdown of world trade system.
2015	Small termitelike robots with nanomachine components lay fiber-optic cables connecting every house and office on Earth, linking everyone together into a vast planetary network for sharing information and doing advanced processing.
2015	Pax Nipponica begins: Japan has uncontested global dominance in every leading-edge industry, GNP twice that of U.S., per capita GNP 4 times U.S.; Japan has now become world's financial center, a zaibatsu monolith of huge financial cliques of interlocking banks and companies dating back to 1890s, the directing apex of the new world economy, owning 45% of U.S. manufacturing assets, holding 50% of U.S. bank assets, with vast media holdings.
2016	NASA launches "Ambassador I," first robot interstellar data-gathering spaceprobe, on 20-year mission to Alpha Centauri star system; 2030, results in evidence of life there.
2016	Colonies of Earth move out from Moon to be set up on Mars, Venus, and other planets of solar system, including moons of Jupiter (Europa, Titan).
2016	Arab People's Republic of the Holy War seizes power in Riyadh, Saudi Arabia; also, Islamic Republic of Palestine proclaimed.
2017	Nighttime eliminated from Earth through solar satellites.
2017	Tooth decay, dental cavities, and pyorrhea eliminated for 95% of all persons accepting predecay treatment including vaccines.
2017	Biological computers developed as 8th generation of computer technology, with biochips and genetic codes assembling fully operational computers inside a cell; computers increasingly participate in their own evolution.
2017	Medical science perfects implanting of silicon chips with over 10^{12} memory (greater than human brain), surgically linked to the brain, giving mankind a totally new order of development.
2018	Massive series of earthquakes over 50 years including in Greece, Turkey, Japan, China, Ecuador, et al.
2019	Global megafamine sweeps Earth due to deliberate mismanagement and embezzlement; 2 billion die.
2019	Completion of Project Daedalus (British Interplanetary Society): unmanned spaceship accelerates to 13% of speed of light, in 50 years reaches Barnard's Star (with view to possible space colonization) and sends back information.
2019	Petroleum metropolis of Cubatao, Brazil (population 500,000), disappears under massive landslides: 75,000 killed.
2020	World's 10 largest cities: Mexico City 33 million, São Paulo 31 million, Bombay 24 million, Calcutta 23 million, Tokyo/Yokohama 22 million, Teheran 21 million, Delhi 21 million, Jakarta 19 million, Dacca 19 million, Karachi 18 million.
2020	Robots and self-reproducing (self-replicating) machines go out in space to mine Moon and asteroids.
2020	Self-replicating uncrewed spaceprobes (von Neumann probes) embark on consecutive self-multiplying space exploration, taking 300 million years to explore entire galaxy (2% of its lifetime).
2020	Regeneration medical techniques, by electrical stimulation of regenerative growth (e.g., new kidneys, amputated limbs), now replace substitutive medicine (replacement of defective parts by implants or transplants).
2020	Widely developed urban systems of (1) covered cities on unused land masses, (2) subterranean cities especially in desert regions, (3) underwater cities in tropical and arctic

Date Events

regions, and (4) floating cities in mid-ocean.

2020 Major climate-control accident: attempts in upper levels of atmosphere to bring rain to desert areas get out of control; within 4 years a new catastrophic Ice Age has begun, obliterating 15 nations including Canada, U.K., Scandinavia, Switzerland, New Zealand, with 2 billion deaths from starvation, panic and inability to flee.

2020 Worldwide fragmentation of global Christianity over last hundred years results in 32,000 distinct and separate denominations, as centralization and coordination become less possible.

2020 Widespread thought control and control of people's minds by drugs, subliminal techniques, psychological methods, and psychosurgery.

2020 Average life span in West increases to 97 years from 90 years in A.D. 2000, and to 200 years for large numbers of people.

2020 Final destruction of world's great forests by human encroachment.

2020 Nations possessing nuclear weapons total 50, including Libya, Cuba, Saudi Arabia, Nigeria, Indonesia, Zaire, and Angola, all with long-range ballistic missiles.

2020 Alien civilization sends out probes to millions of planets, locates life on Earth, laser transmits biological clones of its members (10^{17} bits of information per individual), beaming them across space to Earth.

2020 United Nations lunar base founded.

2020 Artificial singularity first constructed in laboratory, a micro black-hole (a microscopic, titanically heavy fold of twisted space); new science of cavitronics allows quantum creations of space-warped sinkholes. (D. Brin, *Earth*, 1990.)

2020 Vast populations of landless, stateless, disinherited populations, and impoverished refugees take to permanent living on world's oceans, forming a new worldwide Sea State.

2020 Decay of marriage and family as stable and dependable way of life now reaches worldwide dire crisis threatening prospects of entire human race.

2020 Human genome finally fully catalogued, researched, understood, and applies to combat all human ills.

2020 Introduction of government by direct democracy (phone votes, global referendum), with global agendas; also citizens elect commercial firms instead of politicians to run their districts, cities, education, health care, law and order, foreign affairs.

Date Events

2020 Population density becomes intense: rise in Rwanda from 820 people per square mile in 1991 to 2,280 per square mile in 2020; rise in Bangladesh from 2,250 per square mile in 1991 to 4,060 per square mile in 2020.

2020 Expert system allow users to have the knowledge of renowned heart surgeons, scientists, even cooks, available to anyone, anywhere in the world, anytime.

2020 Nanomachines complete tracking down and reading genome of every species now living, making a record of its genome, and delivering it to a central repository.

2020 Telecities merge as information societies become electronically united including JA-CAN-US, a specific telecity consisting of Japan, Canada, U.S.

2020 Bundles of nanorobots weighing practically nothing are sent out across the Universe as explorer robots, reproducing themselves and their ships and building radio transmitters to report home for new instructions; the ultimate in interstellar emissaries.

2021 Voluntary surrender of sovereignty by all 250 previously independent nations to an enlarged United Nations organization, leading to a de facto world government.

2021 First manned interstellar expedition, intending only to explore nearest star systems.

2021 Electronic transfer of funds (ETF) largely replaces cash, but cash still valued for the privacy its use gives.

2021 Emerging worldwide data net reduces need for face-to-face communication in international business.

2022 Authoritarian/totalitarian/dictatorial world state arises after global nuclear war and famine kill over 600 million people; wields total world domination. (J. B. S. Haldane, H. Kahn, M. Bundy.)

2022 Crime wiped out due to mind-reading police, telepaths, parapsychologists, psychiatrists, forensic scientists, and universal computerized surveillance.

2023 Demographic megacatastrophe scenario: massive 30-year population crash begins due to (1) mankind becoming sterile after nuclear testing or warfare, or (2) worldwide famine and drought catastrophe; 7 billion die from 2020 to 2050, leaving 3 billion alive.

2023 A free democratic United States of the World is established; all war finally outlawed; wars and threats of war disappear for first time in human history.

2023 Mass state expropriations globally of church institutions, properties, privileges, premises, plant, possessions, programs, and funds.

Date   Events

2023   Satellite colony ("Moontown") built on Moon.

2024   After nuclear holocaust, Christians regroup as Luddite church savagely opposed to technology and machines. (E. Cooper's scenario, *The Cloud Walker*, 1973.)

2024   Worldwide Authority set up after 65 million killed by nuclear war and famine; population control enforced by withholding food supplies. (McGeorge Bundy's 1974 scenario "After the Deluge, the Covenant.")

2024   Asian New Religions, and secular quasi-religions, with world government support sweep across entire world destroying infrastructure of global organized Christianity.

The Long-Range Future (30–100 Years Ahead)

2025   Communications satellites (1) enable instant global surveys of agriculture, minerals, hydrology, et al., and (2) enable people to live anywhere they please, work anywhere including in electronic cottage industries, doing 90% of their business electronically at speed of light.

2025   Robots of human complexity produced, with IQ of over 100. (A. C. Clarke, I. Asimov).

2025   Lethal new influenza virus appears in India, decimates continents before burning out after 6 months.

2025   Final demise of denominational Christianity and its complete abandonment by vast mass of rank-and-file lay Christians (99.8% of world Christianity), replaced by local combined approaches by all Christians together to local problems of the times, a diaspora church of small minority groupings, a future world utopian community. (J. C. Hoekendjk, Harvey Cox, et al.)

2025   Centralized world government arises, based heavily on artificial intelligence.

2025   Control of behavior by computerized monitoring of brain waves with automatic intervention to prevent misdeeds.

2025   Birth of first children altered by Global Trade Consortium (GTC) gene surgery.

2025   Twelve children born to GTC executives, having been designed as "perfect" by gene surgery, then live brilliant, charismatic, aggressive lives.

2025   Startling rise worldwide in crime rate, with most cities terrorized by gangs of alienated unteachable youths, international criminal empires (including "Red Thumb" from Japan) based on electronic surveillance, psychochemical manipulation, invasion of computer networks.

Date   Events

c. 2025   Postindustrial age begins, a 4th stage in human history beyond agriculturalism, industrialism, and the service economy.

2025   Anyone can own a personal computer-communicator, as powerful as any supercomputer of the past, containing all information in all libraries on Earth.

2025   Large number of small regional entities replace sovereign nation-states, and form themselves into United Regions, a single global body replacing United Nations, leading to a world government by 2050; end of superpower conflicts and vast military expenditures.

2026   Common world language (evolved English) understood by 90% of Earth's people; also constructed languages (Esperanto, Glossa, Suma).

2026   9th generation of computers shift away from digital processing to analog processing whereby light waves are used to compute.

2026   Space industrialization: heavy industry and power generation relocated off Earth's surface so that waste heat and pollution can be harmlessly dissipated into space.

2026   2nd Vienna Conference reconstitutes United Nations as the Confederated States of Earth (CSE).

2027   Christian broadcasting (overt and clandestine) utilizes vast range of 3,000 major languages, programs of every type; reputation for truth results in 90% of world as regular audience; but dangerously exposed to disinformation tactics and terrorism.

2027   First signal received from extrasolar civilization, transmitted by neutrino stream; never decoded. (*A Short History of the Future*, W. W. Wagar, 1989, p. 300.)

2028   New religious awareness results in interfaith convergence and union of all major world religions, despite core Christian opposition; emergence of totally new religions, cults, and Messiahs using electronic communications techniques to gain power.

2028   All-purpose programmable microbiotic virucides developed, defeating all viruses including HIV by 2078.

2029   In capitalist societies, most goods and services are now distributed and supplied free of charge; also, children attain virtually true equality with adults.

c. 2030   Church of the future plays dynamic part in the evolution of mankind, bringing the world to final perfection in Point Omega. (Teilhard de Chardin.)

c. 2030   Point Omega reached in noogenesis, emergence of a completely new evolutionary

Date   **Events**

level (5th level of evolution: supermind): human minds of new species *Homo noeticus* (Intellectual Man) become progressively integrated into some form of planetary consciousness or global social superorganism or supermind, a single living system or interthinking group or mind-linking process (Teilhard's noosphere, comprised of all consciousness minds; or, planetary Gaiafield; or, high-synergy society; or, New Age movement); expressed as synergy, syntony (superconscious learning), suprasex (empathy, mutual love for whole creation and minimal conflict between all, merging not of bodies for procreation but of minds).

2030   Age of universal peace begins: long period of global peace, the Millennium. (Nostradamus.)

2030   After World War III nuclear holocaust, Christianity spreads again around world in global revival led by "an ancient, Black, and primitive Church," ascendancy of nonwhite indigenous Christianity.

2030   Capitalism now seen to have virtually destroyed itself as a viable ideology.

2030   Large-scale terraforming of other planets begins (transforming them to be habitable by humans).

2030   Western world relies on sun, wind, and water for 60% of all power and heating needs.

2030   Continuing decline in rainfall by 55% over Africa; Sahara Desert, world's largest, advances 300 km farther south.

2030   Nations in space are set up, living on very large orbiting space colonies, 20 miles long, 4 miles in diameter, 10 million population each; eventually 30% of human population lives in space by 2200.

2030   Multinational companies of 20th century evolve into huge global corporations, each using a single global marketing strategy; top 50 are bigger and richer than many nations.

2030   World's 10 largest cities: Mexico City 36 million, São Paulo 33 million, Bombay 27 million, Calcutta 26 million, Teheran 25 million, Delhi 24 million, Tokyo/Yokohama 23 million, Dacca 22 million, Jakarta 21 million, Karachi 20 million.

2030   Colony world (Beltworld, later renamed Atlantis) built at virtually no cost in Asteroid Belt between Mars and Jupiter, built by AI (artificial intelligence) computers and their microbots, powered by direct solar radiation; 7,250 inhabitants; thousands more similar self-replicating worlds now immediately feasible; 2091, 44,000 pioneers live in

Date   **Events**

12 distant space colonies forming League of Space Cooperatives.

2030   Consumption of red meat vanishes as flesh-eating is abandoned, replaced by vegetarianism, freeing millions of tons of grain formerly eaten by cattle.

2030   Coastal West Africa including Nigeria finally drowned as drenching rains engulf abandoned cities.

2030   Entire human genome now fully catalogued, with suite of all attributes at humans' disposal (such as wonderfully dexterous human hands); but no possibility yet of profiting from any other animal species' hard-won lessons, which remain each locked within one single species.

2030   World Data Net with 8 billion subscribers (80% of world) by 2040, grouped in rival cliques and alliances, all trying to sway the world's agenda.

2030   90% of all archives and printed materials ever are now available in microcompact forms and can be transmitted anywhere by World Bibliotel system/network, which serves over 20 million institutional and individual subscribers in all countries.

2030   Global sources of energy: 71% fossil fuels (oil, gas, coal), 7% hydroelectric power, 6% solar power, rest 13% (especially nuclear power by means of fusion generators).

2030   World Data Net accessed by plaques or wall-sized active-events screens; Net clipping service, ferret programs dispatched by one's autosec (automatic secretary), standard World Net tech-level press releases.

2030   Zimbabwe now a waterless desert, but Nigeria becomes land of rain-drenched abandoned cities; 2032, new nation Sea State, organized by millions permanently afloat across world, grows rapidly in size and influence.

2030   World Salvation Project organized to save wildlife and endangered species in South Africa and elsewhere; scientists recreate vast arks (arcologies), being entire ecosystems under multitiered vaulting domes, with all species of animals in natural habitats.

2030   U.N. finally revokes 400-year sovereignty of all nation-states, declaring its right to intervene in serious cases of national misgovernment, corruption, violation of civil rights, genocide, civil war.

2031   Advanced extraterrestrials, who have discarded biology in favor of electronics, become one gigantic collective intelligence, with immense computer as its only body; machine uses lasers to transmit instructions for its own replication on Earth.

Date	Events
2032	Telemedicine and computer diagnosis: computer replaces physician as primary agent of health care.
2032	Biological research extends possible normal human life span to 800 years; by transcending nature, disease and death, man becomes potentially an immortal species.
2032	Standard Energy Corporation goes bankrupt due to extreme overinvestment in fusion power.
2033	Mars colony finally established by Global Trade Consortium; 2035, abandoned by GTC for economic reasons; 2036, lunar colony abandoned also.
2034	Manipulation of genetic material (pantropy): genetic packages of fertilized human eggs begin to be altered before birth to fit alien environments, e.g., zero-gravity or high-gravity conditions, or deep water, or speed-of-light travel.
2035	Holography comes into universal use (projecting image of a 3-dimensional object in space); laser holography expands, replacing and duplicating museums and exhibitions; specialized museums now display holograms of priceless art treasures while originals remain securely stored; also 4-dimensional dynamic holograms for science and research.
2035	Invention of time-machine capable of viewing any event in history, in complete 3-dimensional color with stereophonic sound.
2035	Computers and robots become more intelligent than humans, make all major decisions.
2035	First major space city opened, on Moon; HQ of United Nations moves there.
2035	First Declaration of Independence by Spacekind from Earthkind: space colonies in orbit between Earth and Moon set up own government.
2035	Writers, researchers, preachers, anyone can now send word to his knowbot/autosecretary to send out a ferret program to fetch in milliseconds any facts, information, or all that is known about anything.
2035	Clean energy supplied to southwestern France through local Arcachon Tidal Power Barrage, generating pollution-free power from Moon's orbit.
2035	Giant gravity freighters haul huge loads from Earth up to Moon atop pillars of warped space-time.
2036	In barbaric aftermath of 30-year world war, altruistic scientists help launch world's first space flight. (H. G. Wells's scenario and film, *The Shape of Things to Come*, 1934–1935.)

Date	Events
2038	Over 250 million people live on High Orbital Mini Earths (HOMEs), 100 million having been born there; majority leaving Earth are female; majority can never return to Earth; violent competitive theocracies emerge, also varieties of crime.
2038	Scientific recognition of spiritual dimension in world; power of prayer explained in terms of Heisenberg's uncertainty principle.
2038	End of world, one of several dates predicted by Nostradamus (his earlier date: 1943).
2038	Church of the Purification founded in U.S., a popular antimodernist religious sect with 100,000 self-styled Crusaders in bands advocating nonviolent resistance and primitive Christianity; results in thousands of martyrs every year as it attempts to set up a Republic of Christ; 2058, pitched battles across North America.
2038	Of the Natural Tranquility Reserves (terrestrial silence zones) around Earth set up and promoted by United Nations, only 79 are left, declining by 2 or 3 each year.
2038	North American Church of Gaia (environmentalists worshiping Earth Mother, Gaia) intervenes in favor of International Fish and Fowl Association (IFFA, duck-hunters) against animal-rights group No Flesh.
2038	Preservation Alliance of North Africa announce their creation and spread of a virus that will destroy entire world's population of goats who, as voracious eaters, are turning vast regions into barren desert.
2038	New government representing Gaia decrees no more mining of minerals or fuels, now to be obtained only from other planets; all criminals, polluters, conspirators, liars suddenly ripped to shreds by deadly gravity forces without warning or mercy. (D. Brin, *Earth*, 1990.)
2038	North American Church of Gaia (NorA ChuGa) intervenes in all ecological matters.
2038	Rival scientists construct first 2-micro black-holes—artificial singularities (microscopic, titanically heavy folds of twisted space)—despite risk of them falling to Earth's center and orbiting there gradually devouring planet's interior (but losing matter by vacuum emission). (*Earth*, 1990.)
2039	Microscopic black hole accidentally falls into Earth's core, capable of destroying planet in 2 years, extinguishing human race; some scientists argue for letting that happen and letting the million-year evolutionary clock rewind to start all over again. (*Earth*, 1990.)
2039	Earth's colonies on other planets rebel; brief battle between their forces and Earth's,

Date Events

after which their independence is recognized.

2040 Magnetic floaters in operation: high-speed underground transport systems traveling in vacuum at 2,000 km per hour through Earth propelled by magnetic fields.

2040 Accelerating change, increasing since beginning of Industrial Revolution in A.D. 1775, now becomes critical as measured by statistical indicator—growth of mass of knowledge, doubling every 10 years in 1980 and every 2 years by 2040.

2040 Limits-to-growth end-scenario: final collapse of world civilization (as predicted by Club of Rome in 1972) due to population increase and poverty in sociosphere, pollution and industrialization in ecosphere; supplies of many minerals and food items exhausted; freak weather conditions; collapse of world transport systems; famine among urban populations; runaway greenhouse effect on Earth, leaks of radioactive waste, pesticide-immune insects, corrosive rain, etc.

2040 Universal information system on Earth: single global telephone and videophone system; instant access by all to contents of any book, magazine, document, program, or fact ever published.

2040 Moon (Luna) acquires colony of several hundred thousand human contract workers (not permanent colonists, due to its low gravity) mining aluminum, iron, silicon.

2040 Earth's resources of numerous important essential minerals and metals finally exhausted.

2040 New "macro-geo" ideas passed regularly to Worldwide Long Range Solutions Special Interest Discussion Group, with 112 million members: dealing with such ideas as total global reforestation, orbital solar power, optional cryosuspension for a hundred or more years freezing Earth's surplus billions of people who at present have no prospects of quality life in 21st century.

2040 Recent new nations: Han China, Republic of Patagonia, Yakutsk S.S.R.; also Sea State (largely young people, living in gargantuan ramshackle floating cities worldwide, slowly traversing the oceans, with own navy enforcing looting and destruction of mainland ports).

2040 Gaia worship (reverence for Earth Mother) becomes a church militant, mainly run by feminist environmentalists and ecoactivists.

2040 Another artificial singularity (microscopic, mini, black-hole used as power plant) is ac-

cidentally released in a riot in Peruvian Amazon, falls into Earth's core devouring interior within 2 years; scientists frantically attempt to avert total disaster. (*Earth*, 1990.)

2040 World Data Net in place and in universal use, accessible through personal plaques anywhere, with homes and offices owning active-events wall screens showing real-time views from random locations across Earth.

2040 Artificial intelligence (AI) thinking machines; molecular science and nanotechnologies create higher-speed microscopic brainlike computers and robots.

2040 Quantity of greenhouse gases (carbon dioxide, ozone, methane, nitrous oxide, chlorofluorocarbons) rises phenomenally since 1800 (275 parts CO_2 per million), 1960 (310 parts), 2000 (365), 2040 (555).

2040 Mind-reading computers pick up users' thoughts and place them on computer screen—the ultimate in data entry.

2040 Ubiquitous computing technologies place computers in walls, furniture, clothing, eyeglass lenses; world filled with small single-purpose semi-intelligent creatures.

2043 200 million persons have starved to death since A.D. 2000 (75% of them Africans, chiefly rural women and young children).

2044 Rebellion by Israelis in Autonomous District of Jordan Valley leads to World War III, with collapse of U.S., U.K., European Community, etc.; death toll in war and its aftermath reaches 5.8 billion.

2045 Breeding of intelligent animals (apes, cetaceans, etc.) for low-grade labor.

2045 First humans land on Mars.

2048 Drug offenders either executed, or neutralized by chemicals, or given brain implant, a microminiaturized nuclear-powered "peacemaker" causing disabling pain when wearer becomes angry or hostile.

2048 World overpopulation crisis results in cryosuspension perfected at University of Beijing, offering option of being frozen and suspended 300 years into the 24th century; problem of logistics of safely freezing 5 billion people.

2049 Gantz organic homes produced by genetically engineered bacteria manufacturing organic glues binding soil together; lifestyles transformed in crumbling Third World cities.

2049 World Political Party issues Declaration of Human Sovereignty; by 2056, 35 countries have been mundialized (won or seized for party by any means); Confederated States

Date Events

of Earth disbands; 2062, proclamation of the Commonwealth (capital Melbourne, later changed to Chungking, with 1,000 departments governing electronically), with World Militia (a million men and women, nuclear weapons) authorized to quell any resistance; 6 years of counterrevolutionary wars; 2070, all nations ratify Declaration.

2049   Molecular Revolution, resulting in Neomaterialism, a new worldview with massive impetus for sociopolitical change, arising from suite of 3 disciplines termed "molecular sciences": molecular biology, molecular psychology, molecular technology (inventing microscopic robots).

2050   After 200 years of attempts, world at last adopts a single constructed international auxiliary language, a variant of Glossa, Suma, or English. (A. C. Clarke.)

2050   World's private cars and aircraft travel (latter at 350 mph) entirely under control of central traffic computers.

2050   Control of gravity on Earth achieved. (A. C. Clarke.)

2050   Risk of total destruction of human race through nuclear war recedes as vast numbers emigrate to distant space colonies.

2050   *Freedom IV,* first interstellar starship carrying humans intending to seek planets to colonize, departs for the Alpha Centauri star system 4.3 light-years from Earth. (L. S. Wolfe and R. L. Wysack's scenario.)

2050   Experimentation with human DNA reaches peak, leaving behind freak individuals, freak groups, freak colonies, freak races.

2050   World adult literacy rises from 15% in 1800, to 55% in 1960, to 70% by 2000, to 90% by 2050.

2050   Computer-controlled commercial factory farms become universal.

2050   Mankind's basic character fails to improve despite scientific advances; life still disrupted by greed, lust, dishonesty, corruption, and desire for power.

2050   Multigeneration starships (taking several generations—e.g., 200 years—to reach destinations) built, with nuclear fusion reactors, traveling at 10% of speed of light.

2050   Relativistic spaceflight makes entire universe accessible to those on the journey: starships that accelerate continuously at 1g reach 95% of speed of light within one year, reaching center of galaxy in apparent 21 years (for an elapsed time of 30,000 years), circumnavigating entire universe in 56 years of ship time.

Date Events

2050   Rise of eccentric religious cult, Neo-Manichees, an orbital religion with no meeting places except television screens; their "statistical theology" disproves, and destroys, faith in a personal God.

2050   To solve massively accelerating overpopulation crisis, half the world (5 billion) otherwise condemned to die by starvation or epidemics finally agree to U.N. offer of cryosuspension and are frozen for 300 years until 24th century, with U.N. guaranteeing eventual wealth for all.

2050   Technical knowledge increases to 100 times that available in 1990.

2050   Nanotechnology nightmare scenario: accidentally created, omnivorous, bacteria-size robot spreads like blowing pollen, replicates swiftly, reduces entire world biosphere to dust in matter of days.

2055   Cybernetic Wave (A. Toffler's Fourth Wave) arrives, based on artificial intelligence, brain-computer linkups, biochips, instant creativity.

2055   Cyborg minds widespread, through implanting electronic accessory brains in human brains, including biocomps (bionic-implant computer terminals) which monitor, calculate, and advise the host brain.

2055   Religions become closely influenced by, even based on, chemistry once chemical basis of all life is understood.

2055   Human normal life span extends to 250 years for 75% of human race.

2055   Urban dwellers number 80% of world's population, 80% of those being in Third World.

2055   Plagues due to viruses from space ravage Earth killing billions. (M. Crichton, *The Andromeda Strain,* 1969.)

2060   Reunion of all major separated branches of Christianity achieved: Catholic, Protestant, Anglican, Orthodox organically united in the "Coming Great Church."

2060   Medical means discovered to achieve earthly immortality, even circumventing accidental death; open to 95% of Western world's population; also ability of individuals to change sex at will.

2060   Population increase deliberately reduced to near zero by proception, the procedure whereby every child born is deliberately chosen, wanted, and adored; birth defects a nightmare of the past.

2060   Synthetape replaces film: sophisticated software available for synthesizing visual images; human actors no longer necessary; 2120, 3-dimensional holographic epics made using 3-dimensional synthetape.

Date   Events

2060   Bus, subway, and other transportation services in most of world's large cities now provided free of charge.

2060   World energy demand reaches 4.4 times 1986 level, with electricity increasing 7.0 times.

2060   Zoo hypothesis: extraterrestrial ethics prevent other creatures from interfering with unusual developing species like *Homo sapiens*.

2065   World population, on mediodemographic scenario, levels off at around 12 billion, well below Earth's absolute capacity. (*Interfutures OECD Project*, 1979.)

2065   Small handheld pocket computers serve as audio translators into 300 different languages for instantaneous spoken translation, also for instantaneous transcribing and translated printout.

2070   Combining of ectogenesis with eugenics so that only superior humans can propagate.

2070   Europe and Eurasia become 70% nonreligious or antireligious.

2070   The Lost Billion: 1 billion subsistence farmers, displaced from their land, become religious cultists and urban guerrillas dedicated to mass assassination before being gradually destroyed.

2073   Planetary Restoration Authority created by People's Congress to oversee the Great Housecleaning (restoring the biosphere).

2075   Human beings control spaceships via skull sockets linked to ships' computers.

2075   Man reaches travel at near-light speeds; participants' apparent longevity increases markedly.

2075   Islamic guerrillas on suicide missions across Middle East disarmed by swift action of World Militia.

2080   Transporting and storing of energy done through liquid hydrogen as preferred medium.

2080   Human race uses 15 times as much energy annually as it did in 1980.

2080   Stable world government in place: either a U.N. empire, or an American empire, or joint Chinese/American, based on English and/or Chinese; or the millennial kingdom.

2080   Criminal procedures of all nations standardized everywhere.

2080   Uniform world monetary system established and enforced.

2080   All persons everywhere required to furnish total personal data annually for police work, social research, eugenic reform, etc.

2080   Eugenic infanticide widespread (killing of handicapped children at birth).

2080   English becomes sole international language of science, technology, scholarship, culture, diplomacy, and Christianity.

2082   Moon is now settled by humans, with 50,000 Lunarians (5,000 born on Moon, who have never visited Earth); at height of tourist season, total population rises to 110,000.

2082   Escalating arms race halted and finally terminated by (1) new generation of ultrasophisticated computers in spy satellites, and (2) economic decline among superpowers, who finally hound international arms merchants into extinction.

2085   First verifiable alien contact with extraterrestrial intelligence among our galaxy's (Milky Way's) 400 billion stars, where between 100 and 1 million other advanced technical civilizations (capable of interstellar radio communication) probably exist, as well as up to 1 billion lesser, communicative civilizations (none resembling humanity); nearest is possibly only 100 light-years distant.

2085   Existence discovered of vast star empires, great civilizations, and alien cultures unimaginably far advanced.

2085   Planetary war scenario: alien beings from planet Mars, emotionless Martian killers, invade Earth; Darwinian struggle for survival of human race until Martians finally killed off by microbes. (H. G. Wells's scenario, *The War of the Worlds*, 1898.)

2085   Religions of extraterrestrials found to take many bizarre forms: worship of sentient crystals, worship of intelligent, polished, black monoliths, etc.

2085   Holy Bible available translated into all 10,000 human languages, in numerous forms: print, comics, audio, signed, Braille, video, drama, pictodrama, psychodrama, holographic, telephonic, and computerized forms; with instant holographic commentary by galaxy of scholars, Bible teachers, and preachers from throughout history.

2085   Biggest earthquake ever recorded devastates Japan, breaks Honshu in two, blasts Shikoku apart, killing 15 million; most Japanese emigrate worldwide to form a global technological diaspora.

2090   Mass global transportation systems, with zero energy-loss, in operation: (1) through Earth in vacuum tubes; superspeed floater vehicles traveling at 7 miles a second, 39 minutes from one side of Earth to the other; and (2) into space, either using balloon-borne floater guideways, or space elevators riding up on superstrength cable.

2090   Military expenditures, 10% of world income in 1980, fall to 2% by 2090, eventually to 1% by 2200 and to 0.1% by 2500.

Date   **Events**

2090   Military arsenals include ultrasophisticated weaponry: antimatter beams, laser rays, bullets near speed of light.

2090   Vast volumes of galactic space regularly monitored by remote sensing instead of by direct patrolling.

2090   First manned starship sent to nearby stars within 40 light-years known to have planets; interstellar manned flight within 1% of speed of light achieved, using ion drive, carbon dioxide laser, composite optics, immensely potent energy source—reaction of matter with antimatter. (A. C. Clarke, G. K. O'Neill.)

2090   Self-reproducing replicator factories, replicating exact copies of original machines/electronics/cybernetics; by 2380, up to any complexity reproducible within 10 years.

2090   New-style religions and mystical nature cults arise opposing biotechnology.

2090   Satellite solar power collection system ("Sun Ring") begins operation, by 2100 supplies 65% of all energy needs on Earth.

2090   90% of world's population reside in urban centers.

2090   Most high-demand sects, cults, and religions have been rejected in favor of no-demand faiths; most are pantheist, neopagan, nature-love, New Age groups, and have long since merged in the World Soul Movement.

2092   Hinduism and Buddhism become sizable and respectable religions in the Western world.

2095   Superpowers, faced by omniscient presence of alien beings of vastly superior technology, agree to abandon war and destroy all armaments.

2095   Genetic Initiative, to redesign the human race including program of raising intelligence by gene surgery, also cerebral enhancement, legislated by People's Congress; by 2147, 10 million children transformed by prenatal surgery, creating a new human type, *Homo sapiens altior.*

2095   Workers: 3% are in agriculture, 6% factory and mine supervision, 15% technical consulting, 5% managerial consulting, 11% health and medicine, 21% public services, 7% personal services, 5% arts and letters, 8% research, 19% education. (Wagar, *A Short History of the Future,* 1989, p. 182.)

2095   Futures studies now known as prognostics; prognosticians chart and weigh alternative futures.

2095   Few people in world can read or bother to read; school children have become ignorant of Bible; theology has become a dying art.

Date   **Events**

The Distant Future (Beyond 21st Century A.D.)

2100   World census reveals 60% of adults live alone most of the time, 45% live with sex partner without contract for periods of 3 years on average, 20% opt for legalized alternatives (5-year marriage, group marriage); 2150, extinction of marriage as an institution.

2100   Women are in power everywhere including in all churches and denominations.

2101   World population reaches a peak of 8,250 million, then starts to decline. (C. McEvedy and R. Jones scenario.)

2101   World becomes either high-technology, ample-energy utopia, or a low-technology, overcrowded, energy-poor dystopia.

2101   First space arks begin to be made from hollowed-out asteroids.

2101   Some 10,000 orbiting space colonies exist around Earth; 100 million to 2 billion permanent population, including more U.S. citizens than remain in U.S.; after 5 generations their cultures draw apart even to mutual linguistic unintelligibility.

2101   Vast dispersion of human race into colonies across the Milky Way galaxy makes humankind invulnerable to any single future disaster.

2101   Decline of industrial espionage, software sabotage, and computer crime due to proficiency and omnipresence of police forces.

2101   A new Age of Barbarism arises, with world ground undertoot by war, religious fanaticism, neo-Islamic domination, terror, and Antichrist, for 2 centuries before final advent of the Golden Millennium in A.D. 2300. (Nostradamus.)

2101   Cities of over 100 million inhabitants built, completely 3-dimensional and soundproofed, with varieties of transport on many levels; eventually cities with over 1 billion residents, each with hundreds of thousands of museums, theaters, aquatic centers, recreation centers, universities, libraries, research institutes.

2101   Global dictatorship established under guise of a religious cult, the Prophets; a theocracy enforced by watchful "Angels of the Lord." (R. Heinlein, *Revolt in 2100,* 1940.)

2102   Manufacture of androids: artificially produced human creatures made out of organic materials.

2102   Immense macroengineering projects arise: space elevators (skyhook), with 100-ton cars climbing cable at 3,700 m.p.h. for 22,300 miles to satellite; 150-foot plastic pipe diverts Rhone River under Mediterranean to irrigate North African desert;

Date	*Events*

shipment of Antarctic icebergs to Sahara Desert.

2102   World's population rises to 10,185 million (Africa 2.5 billion, Latin America 1.3 billion, South Asia 3 billion, East Asia 1.8 billion, Northern America 400 million, Europe (stabilized since 2050) at 500 million. (U.N. projections, 1984.)

2102   "Blade runners" (replicant-killers) widely employed to kill or "retire" renegade Nexus-6 replicants (4-year-life androids). (Movie *Blade Runner*, 1982.)

2109   Sabbatical Law takes effect worldwide, guaranteeing all workers 12 months of educational leave every 7 years; soon adult citizens devote 85% of work time to education.

2110   Whole world now follows essentially a planned economy, due to proliferating U.N. agencies.

2110   Global sea-farming: seaweed becomes one of world's major food crops; 2130, Pacific coast of South America hosts long chain of kelp farms; vast regions of oceans sown with enriched plankton harvested by huge factory ships; 2180, whole ocean industry under U.N. control.

2110   Transition to zero population growth worldwide finally completed; all medical care, schooling, electrical power, transportation free of charge, but no private vehicles allowed; no welfare since all adults earn 75% standard personal income whether they work or not.

2111   Resettlement of Mars colony, destroyed in chemical accident 4 years later, repopulated; by 2140, 20,000 inhabitants (mostly scientists and engineers); several hundred other space habitats with total population 5 million.

2112   *Albert Einstein*, first faster-than-light starship, departs on exploratory mission to 10 star systems. (L. S. Wolfe and R. L. Wysack's scenario.)

2120   Spacetorium, an orbiting clinic, established in space where 900 ultrawealthy geriatrics with heart and degenerative problems can retire.

2120   Rising ocean levels finally destroy Shanghai, one of world's greatest trading cities.

2120   Fission-to-fusion drive in service for space travel.

2129   Small fleet of interstellar drones leaves Sun Ring to explore Alpha Centauri and other star systems at 7.5% speed of light (report expected back in 2258).

2130   Starship drives include (1) nuclear ion-drive, (2) propulsion by pressure of light, (3) pulsed fusion-bomb explosions at 250 per second, (4) Bussard ramscoop starship (designed in 1960), (5) antimatter/photon drive; at acceleration of 1 Earth gravity, ship reaches center of our galaxy in 20 years (ship time) and any point in universe within one lifetime; use of hyperspace and time warps developed.

2140   Federation of Galactic Civilizations proposed but comes to nothing.

2150   Widespread development of extrasensory perception (ESP), telepathy, telekinesis, teleportation (instant communication and transport), clairvoyance, precognition, remote viewing.

2150   Minute computer (size of a pinhead) stores for instant retrieval every word in every book entire human race has ever published.

2150   Universal use of synthetic foods.

2150   Free mass-passenger transport provided universally: not only within large cities, but also globally and extraterrestrially.

2150   First manned long-distance starship leaves Earth for stars beyond 40 light-years distant, seeking any planets of theirs; millions of humans subsequently are transported across interstellar space.

2153   Successful tests of matter-antimatter blender; 2163, installed in spacecraft propulsion system.

2160   Definitive, permanent, and universal cures finally achieved for cancer, aging, and all other human ailments; with bionic aid, man becomes virtually immortal either in same body or in succession of bodies; final end, after previous 2 billion years of evolution of life, of programmed death and also sexual reproduction to replace deaths.

2162   Formation of the Interstellar Expeditionary Service.

2166   Departure of pioneer interstellar expeditionary ship, with crew of 200 aboard; 2178, return from Alpha Centauri, reporting exploration of planet Elysium.

2170   Several varieties of humans exist: those with prosthetic limbs or bodies, robots run by disembodied human brains, extraterrestrial humans, clones, cyborgs, androids, wholly artificial humanoids, replicants, mutants, etc.

2170   Nonurgent flight including freight shifts to ubiquitous airships affordable by even poorest countries; widespread use in agriculture, reclaiming deserts, etc.

2175   Population of Earth 15 billion, gross world product U.S. $300 trillion, per capita income $20,000 (at 1980 values).

Date	Events
2180	Human beings are everywhere numerous, rich, and in control of forces of nature; by contrast in A.D. 1780 human beings were relatively few, poor, and at mercy of forces of nature.
2180	U.N.'s Land Use Committee attempts to turn entire world into a planned Garden of Eden, but thwarted by national jealousies.
2188	Use of hibertubes for forward time travel.
2189	Mind-net technique attempted with human volunteer; 2193, first successful human mind transfer.
2190	North American Church of Gaia (NorA ChuGa) intervenes in all ecological matters.
2190	Explosive growth of cryonics corporations begins; 2210, over 10,000 persons "frozen down"; 2214, lotteries offering treatment a huge success; 2230, 30,000 a year frozen down; 2244, massive electrical power failure in U.S. kills most off; cryonics industry finally collapses.
2200	Postholocaust life on Earth now stabilized with, on minidemographic scenario, 2 billion population, homogeneous, largely self-supporting, no energy shortage, limited technology.
2200	On mediodemographic scenario, world population now 25 billion (or even as high as 75 billion in mile-high high-rise blocks, orbiting colonies and undersea city habitats), according to technological-social optimism scenario; world now in quaternary postindustrial phase, with all primary and secondary activities fully automated; many people in tertiary activities (research, industrial planning, operating the single world government, medicine, education).
2200	On maxidemographic scenario, population expands to 1,000 billion, crammed into 100,000 cities of 10 million people each, with thousand-story tower blocks each housing a million people. (J. Blish and N. L. Knight, *A Torrent of Faces*, 1967.)
2200	30% of humanity now lives in orbiting space colonies.
2200	Third interstellar expeditionary ship, returning from Sirius and Procyon, reports major archeological discoveries on planet circling companion star of Procyon.
2210	Computers designed and built with sense of identity, self, and consciousness; self-designing, self-programming, self-maintaining, and self-replicating.
2210	Disembodied human brains function at center of machines, computers, vehicles, factories, spaceships.
2217	Space explorers from Earth encounter first spaceship of an alien species.
2220	First ectogenetic baby born from artificial womb; by 2300, 20,000 ectogenetic births in U.S. alone; 2302, Crusade for Moral Rearmament launched against ectogenesis.
2223	U.N.'s Council of Justice set up; 2236, publishes its first Code of Rights.
2245	Deadly Sealed Laboratory in Antarctica, producing lethal microorganisms in genetic research, relocated out in space.
2248	First successful experiments in large-scale human total rejuvenation.
2250	Americanized world state founded (First Men, on W. O. Stapledon's 1930 scenario); lasts until 6250, becoming rigidly stratified and regimented; power failure, breakdown of law and order, succeeded by Dark Age of semibarbarism for 10,000 years; new civilization arises, destroyed by nuclear chain reaction.
2250	High Frontier (space colonization) makes comeback after almost 300 years procrastination; 2285, O'Neill-I opened as first residential microworld, for 15,000 people; future of industry gets under way in space with specialist industrial microworlds; 2350, first lunar mass-driver (electromagnetic cannon on Moon accelerating buckets to escape velocity).
2250	Rapid growth of new mysticism and new monasticism.
2250	Instant travel anywhere and astral travel anywhere become commonplace.
2271	U.N. passes resolution enforcing universal sterilization to control population explosion; Ireland and Italy refuse, so are flooded with fanatical immigrants.
2275	Von Neumann machines (VNMs) or self-reproducing robot probes are dispatched beyond solar system, mapping universe and producing growing cloud of VNMs throughout space.
2282	SAP (solid artificial photosynthesis) results in colossal food-yields from restricted areas of land.
2285	Mauritania offers sanctuary to rival Roman papacy (conservative, antisterilization), which then builds headquarters at Kiffa, 300 miles inland in Sahara desert.
2289	Earth humans' first contact with an alien race, the Vegans; 2310, first interstellar war.
2291	Earth and 2 alien civilizations form Galactic Association of Intelligent Life.
2293	World divided into 3 distinct communities: Eternals, who rule; Brutals, poverty-stricken peons who worship a giant stone

Date Events

god, Zardoz; and Exterminators, barbarians trained by Eternals to restrict Brutals by killings and slavery. (J. Boorman's film *Zardoz* (1974.)

2300 Easily reachable coal reserves of world now all used up.

2300 Advent of Golden Millennium, on Nostradamus' predictions.

2300 Human fax invented: entire contents of a human brain are downloaded by computer and broadcast to a robot in a remote star system.

2305 Earth under complete control of a debased religion using science and psychology to keep man in subjection; rebellion comes via underground satanic cult with witches and warlocks. (F. Leiber, *Gather, Darkness*, 1943.)

2310 First successful human analogues (artificial humans, sentient humanoids); 2325, mass wave of Luddite or mechanophobic paranoia sweeps world as people smash robots, computers, androids.

2310 Personal contact easier to avoid than ever before in history; people program electronic analogues of themselves to handle routine contacts.

2316 U.S. Maglev Subway links east coast to west, with cars running in elevated transparent tubes floating on web of electromagnetism.

2350 A file on every known person in galaxy exists in every starship's data bank.

2350 Universal immunization available; sophisticated cancer treatments available to half world's population; rejuvenation available only to the rich.

2350 Underwater aqua-cities, time travel, global police.

2355 World 95% urbanized and industrialized with all industries organized as monopolies.

2360 Humans now live dispersed in microworlds across solar system.

2364 Totalitarian coup by Admiral Hrunta, who proclaims self emperor of all colonies; 3089, assassinated after 725 years of arbitrary personal rule. (J. Blish, *Cities in Flight*, 1962.)

2367 Tetroli disaster: first deaths of a microworld's entire complement: 615 perish in bacterial outbreak.

2380 Automation results in self-replicating devices of great complexity capable of self-reproduction, reproducing any apparatus no matter how complex, without human intervention, in under 10 years.

2390 Humans have now discovered and colonized 8 planets within 78 light-years of Earth; outward migration continues across galaxy's 100,000 light-year diameter.

Date Events

2390 World population nearly homogenized into a single race (neo-Mongoloid) with a single culture and language (25th-century English); entire world urbanized, industrialized, homogenized, wired as a single global village.

2400 Aggregate households (6 adults and 3 children) replace nuclear family and become widespread, and by 2500 become the norm; by 2650, old-style "family life" and biological parenthood abandoned worldwide except in space microworlds.

2400 Medical advances include repair of brain damage, regeneration of severed limbs, and regular body-scanning of entire populations in Western world (but only 1 in 10,000 in Third World).

2419 Date of Armageddon battle as postulated in original Buck Rogers stories and scenarios. (P. F. Nowlan, *Armageddon 2419 A.D.*, 1928–1929.)

2425 As predicted since origin of Buddhism, a great war erupts with Buddhist forces based on Shambala defeating Muslims; Buddhism flourishes once more until decline and sudden and cataclysmic extinction in A.D. 4621.

2433 Ceres, largest asteroid of the Belt (760-km radius), cracked (blown apart) by engineers to provide 10^{18} tons of valuable mass (metals, ores); mass and energy now everywhere the key to space.

2460 Personality analogue transfer (PAT): people in distant space communicate with Earth via updated personality analogue constructs of themselves on Earth, who can converse with Earth-dwellers with no time-lag.

2465 Jupiter Bridge shuttle: fleets of robot shuttle-scoops transfer mass from Jupiter to moon Ganymede and its microworlds, making them refuelling bases for trans-Jovian travelers.

2482 All world's nations merge into 12 large super-states (including North American Nation), governed by social scientists, under World Federal Union (world government) with world capital in Honolulu, using new language Voca scientifically designed to be easily teachable and learnable.

2485 Humans now diversified into 5 distinct species: (1) *Homo sapiens*, or sapients, the "ordinary humans" or "normals"; (2) by 2485, "merpeople" as first radically modified humans, with gills, flippers, etc.; (3) by 2505, space-adapted humans ("fabers," or ETs) with spaceships manned entirely by ETs in regular service by 2528, and nearly 3,000 ETs in Solar System by 2600; (4) by

Date	Events
	2581, life-extended humans ("emortals," or ZTs) interbreed successfully and thus become a new species; (5) by 2700, "starpeople" (emortal fabers); with further species being developed.
2490	With one trillion people living spread out across the solar system, humans begin starship explorations into the Milky Way galaxy beyond, meanwhile robots transform planet Mercury into giant solar-power station, beaming microwave energy throughout solar system; Moon has become a mining and construction center.
2500	800-year decline of scientific profession, from overinflated novelty alone able to save the world, to more modest role in society: from A.D. 1740 to 1965, 90% of all scientists who ever lived were alive; by A.D. 2200, 45%; A.D. 2500, 18%; thereafter, further decline.
2500	Roofing-in of whole Earth as in effect a single several-mile-high tower block, housing around 400 billion people, fed either by artificial production or from extraterrestrial sources.
2510	Instantaneous teleportation now normal: all transport obsolete since people travel instantly by mind alone (called "jaunting" in A. Bester's novel *The Stars My Destination*, 1956).
2512	Massive experimental manned ramjet starliner *T. E. Lawrence* (6,000 feet long, with hydrogen funnel propulsion) travels around Sun and returns with more fuel than it began with.
2520	Daedalus-class robot starprobes, weighing 50,000 tons at departure, routinely make one-way exploratory trips to nearer stars.
2530	World rulers use genetic engineering to perpetuate society stratified by intelligence and physique; scheduled sexual orgies substitute for both marriage and religion. (Aldous Huxley's scenario, *Brave New World*, 1931.)
2530	Whole ecosystems of genetically engineered species assembled (Hanging Gardens of New Babylon, giant insect islands); genetic scientists recreate living monster dinosaurs by cloning from fossilized bones of extinct species, and place them in tropical neosaurian game parks; also herds of woolly mammoths for commercial meat industry.
2550	Laser lightsails in use: 60 starships without main engines, each with 1,000-km sail driven at half light-speed across space by light from 10 laser stations in close orbit around Sun.
2565	Interstellar ramjet *Columbus*, an entire microworld powered by cold-fusion torch

Date	Events
	using galactic hydrogen clouds for fuel, becomes first manned vehicle to orbit a star, averaging 20% of light-speed; time of trip, 30 years; numerous microworlds established around Sirius and other stars; interstellar trade begins and flourishes.
2630	Gigantic spaceships or space arks begin to leave Earth on mission of "zygotic evangelism": supermicroworlds each peopled by thousands of space-adapted humans, each cruising forever on its funnel drive at near light-speed, carrying (1) millions of frozen zygotes (life-building information in DNA coils), and (2) rest of entire human knowledge in its computer banks; also (3) Christian teams with full biblical and other materials.
2639	Antarctica becomes first genuinely international territory; 2650, Amundsen City built there as U.N. headquarters; whole continent and its resources rapidly developed.
2650	Life-extension technology available to every living person, through rejuvenation (NAR, nucleic acid renewal) or engineered longevity (Zaman transformation, ZT), all political power passes to rejuvenates, i.e., the old inherit the world; by 2700, over 99% of U.N. Council Chamber seats are occupied by NAR rejuvenates, and by 2950 by emortals (ZTs).
2650	U.N. decides all human embryos everywhere have right to engineered longevity free of charge.
2650	Direct brain linkups, body-part warehouses.
2700	Very little now proves to be impossible; almost everything is now practicable: e.g., faster-than-light travel, instantaneous matter transmission (teleportation), time travel, personality and memory transfer between humans, widespread telepathic communication.
2750	Dominant religion now neo-Stoicism, but fragmented into rival schisms and cults.
2750	Multiplanet communication established and now commonplace.
2800	Totality of human knowledge readily and instantly available to all human beings; life far more complex than in twentieth century; lifespans up to 900 years; no language barriers.
2800	World population restabilizes, at 2.5 billion, with global average life expectancy at birth of 180 years.
2800	Some 500 self-sufficient human communities live out in solar system; by 2900, some 2,000, with 200 independent microworlds (population 100,000 starpeople) en route to other stars, and a dozen already arrived.

Date Events

2850   Growth of science encompasses all paracon-cepts as realities; space folding enables contact with any part of universe.

2900   More human beings live in space than on Earth.

2967   Robot probe from Earth intercepted by alien sentients 75 light-years from Earth.

The Far Distant Future (Everything Beyond 30th Century A.D.)

3000   Human species radiates out into many sub-species and subcultures alien to each other; telepathy and shared consciousness replace individuality; distinction between humans and other species blurs, with many different genetically engineered life forms derived from human and nonhuman stock; humans spread into diverse environments including cyberspace and subuniverses inside computer simulations.

3001   Interstellar distances finally recognized as too great to sustain any meaningful galactic communications or communities; no viable galactic empires or federations therefore possible; on alternative scenarios, however, humans discover flight at 30,000 times speed of light, quantum drives, and then instantaneous travel throughout universe via black- and white-holes.

3001   Construction of a Dyson sphere (built from disassembly of gas giant planet Jupiter) enclosing everything within Earth's solar orbit (186 million miles diameter with Sun at center), in order to (1) gather up all the Sun's energy, and (2) provide living space for a million Earths with 400 trillion humans; creates vast civilization unique in history; but massive engineering know-how required also carries enormous potential for blackmail, evil, warfare, and chaos.

3001   No religions remain for human race except Christianity and materialism. (L. E. Browne, "The Religion of the World in A.D. 3000," 1949.)

3001   Extraterrestrial end scenario: human race wipes itself out by inept handling of alien (extraterrestrial) technology.

3450   Geodynamics of superspace discovered; scientists find out inconceivably dense yet bubbling, foamlike structure of superspace: every empty space or vacuum contains massive infernos of energies and seething violence; harnessing these enormous subatomic quantum fluctuations leads to invention of ultimate propellant, the quantum drive; mankind now free to roam the universe forever. (A. C. Clarke, 1986.)

Date Events

3500   Cosmic collision scenario: large astral body crashes into Earth catastrophically; previously, 500 meteorites crash annually, one asteroid collides every 1,000 years, and one comet (out of 100 billion circling the Sun) strikes Earth every 100,000 years.

3781   Monks of Order of Leibowitz, who have preserved knowledge through Dark Ages after 20th-century World War III nuclear holocaust, eventually see civilization rebuilt by A.D. 3100 to point where, again, a new industrial-scientific age culminates by A.D. 3781 in imminent nuclear World War IV; just before outbreak, discredited order launches an ecclesiastical starship through which Church of New Rome transfers authority of St. Peter from Earth to Alpha Centauri. (W. M. Miller's novel, *A Canticle for Leibowitz*, 1960.)

3797   End of world in cosmic explosion (as envisioned by Nostradamus as finale of his prophecies).

3936   End of world as predicted by Spanish Dominican monk V. Ferrer (c. 1350–1419).

4000   Human race is still *Homo sapiens sapiens* but has become alien by 1980 standards: communication and mutual understanding with humans of 1980 probably would be very difficult; no race problem since only one race (Mongoloid, tan); life spans average several thousand years, with large numbers taking immortality drug or injection to become immortal at any particular age they wish.

4100   Ice Age scenario: after interglacial (mild period) of 15,000 years, Earth enters new ice age, with famine reducing population from 10 billion to 1 billion, and freezing the rest to death by A.D. 12,000.

4104   Cosmos ends in stupendous collision of matter and antimatter, after which new Universe is created. (J. Blish's tetralogy *Cities in Flight*, 1955–1962.)

4500   Cosmic rays scenario: Earth's magnetic field declines gradually to zero, leaving humans unprotected for 500 years from cosmic radiation; a giant solar flare from the Sun, or a star within 30 light-years then explodes as a supernova, destroys Earth by radiation.

4600   Intelligent machines control world after outstripping now extinct creators. (O. Johannesson, *The Big Computer* and *The Tale of the Great Computer*, 1968.)

4621   Sudden decline and cataclysmic total extinction of worldwide Buddhism as prophesied by the Buddha himself, after 5,100 years as a great world religion.

Date	Events
5000	Instantaneous communicators (superluminal faster-than-light connectors) across universe include Dirac transmitter, sending messages that can be picked up by any Dirac receiver past, present, or future. (James Blish's scenario, *The Quincunx of Time*, 1973.)
5000	Material from planets is used to construct immense spherical floor around Sun enclosing entire solar system, with area of 160 quintillion (1.6×10^{20}) square miles, capable of supporting human population of up to 1 septillion (10^{24}) persons.
5000	Supercivilizations are installed on rigid shells around black holes, extracting energy from hole by space-rubbish shuttle.
5000	Black holes prove to be time machines, wormholes, or gravity tunnels providing a kind of instantaneous interstellar and intergalactic subway, emerging in remote parts of space-time through white holes (quasars); or even star-gates out of this cosmos and into totally different cosmoses.
6000	Intergalactic space travel and time-travel underway using space and time machine: men construct a spinning or rotating black hole just outside solar system, which instantaneously transports men and matter across millions of light-years, or across millions of years in time, spewing them out through white holes. (A. Berry's scenario, *The Iron Sun*, 1979.)
6250	World supplies of energy finally fail; long Dark Ages of savagery begin, with scores of major disasters. (W. O. Stapledon's epic chronicle of future history, *Last and First Men*, 1930.)
8000	Asteroidal collision scenario: large asteroid Ceres collides with Earth with 12,000 billion megatons impact energy, sterilizes Earth and shifts its orbit significantly.
9500	Planet Jupiter (a star that failed) supports human colonies in great balloon cities permanently floating in upper atmosphere.
10,000	Human race begins to evolve from *Homo sapiens sapiens* into a more advanced species *Homo noeticus noeticus* (Pan-Intellectual Man); evolution of humanity into a galaxy-wide and continuously growing cosmic Overmind.
10,150	Commission of Ecumenical Translators attempts to unite peoples of universe, results in galactic Holy War. (F. Herbert, *Dune*, 1965.)
12,000	Postcatastrophe scenario: 10,000 years after nuclear holocaust, sparsely populated pastoral utopian matriarchy exists on Earth, marked by communal living, personal

Date	Events
	longevity, eugenics, and superintelligent domestic animals. (W. H. Hudson's scenario, *A Crystal Age*, 1887.)
20,000	Rise of pantropy—i.e., spread of human race throughout galaxy—invading countless different environments by adapting mankind genetically to suit new conditions (life under sea, in flight, on Mars, etc.).
30,000	Supercivilizations move out to colonize whole galaxies at rate of 10 million years a galaxy; intergalactic travelers learn to utilize space warps and time warps (irregularities in space-time continuum) to traverse immense distances involved.
50,000	Exploding Sun scenario: hostile alien civilization deliberately triggers solar cataclysm, Sun explodes as nova, flaring up in million-fold increase of brightness and heat to burn all earthly life and vaporize the planet.
100,000	New *Homo* species, interstellar man (*Homo superior*), evolves and outnumbers *Homo sapiens* populations of Earth and its immediate colonies.
200,000	Mining of heaviest elements in Sun, by large magnetohydrodynamic machines built from Mercurian ores, provides Earth with unlimited energy for 300 million years, at the same time extending natural life of Sun from 8 billion years to 20 trillion years.
800,000	Human race degenerates by devolution into racial decadence with 2 separate races, the childish Eloi and the troglodytic cannibalistic Morlocks; humanity finally proves to be just another of nature's unlucky failures; time travellers visiting them then move on to visit far future's last days of humanity and Earth. (H. G. Wells's scenario, *The Time Machine*, 1895.)

The Megafuture (after A.D. 1 million)

Date	Events
1 million	Mankind evolves to *Homo galacticus*: great unemotional intelligences, large-headed beings retaining no bodily parts except hands, "floating in vats of amber nutritive fluid," doing little but thinking; a global brotherhood of enlightened supermen living in strongholds deep inside Earth whose surface is thickly mantled with ice at absolute zero temperature. (H. G. Wells's scenario, "The Man of the Year Million," 1893.)
2 million	Point Omega finally reached and consummated (as envisaged by Teilhard de Chardin), with Christ as cosmocrat and perfector of human evolution, eventually (by A.D. 4 billion) with one decillion (10^{33}) believers.

Date **Events**

2 million Humanity completes its colonizing spread across the galaxy (Milky Way), settling it in 2 million years.

3 million Man's body height evolves to some 8 feet tall; tongue, palate, and larynx increase in size to handle rapid complex speech.

10 million Superintelligent Second Men evolve, plagued by cloud-intelligences from Mars, then gradually stagnate. (W. O. Stapledon, 1930.)

15 million Next scheduled mass collisions of Earth with comets/asteroids (every 26 million years, last being in B.C. 11 million), resulting in mass extinction of majority of remaining species including genus Homo.

40 million Third Men evolve, midgets with massive ears, music as their religion, biogenetic control; then Fourth Men (great brains many feet across), who then design Fifth Men (huge intellectuals who migrate temporarily to Venus); A.D. 100 million, Sixth Men evolve, a barbarous throwback, also on Venus; A.D. 300 million, Seventh Men evolve: pygmy flying men uninterested in science or material progress. (W. O. Stapledon, 1930.)

100 million Sun cools past point where it is visible from Earth, whose surface is too cold to support life; last human beings live 100 miles below surface in Pyramid (8-mile-high metal scientific marvel), with monsters outside in volcanic fireholes. (W. H. Hodgson's scenario *The Night Land*, 1912.)

400 million Eighth Men evolve, physically larger; science and progress resumed; they escape collision between Sun and gas cloud by migrating to planet Neptune; Ninth Men evolve as dwarfs, developed to survive on Pluto, but become degenerate and collapse. (W. O. Stapledon, 1930.)

500 million Human race evolves into wealthy, powerful, coordinated universal society reaching across galaxy and also across universe; humans finally discover ultimate secrets of the cosmos.

500 million Emergence of Sixth Level of Evolution: galactic mind, i.e., galactic consciousness, with transition to a galactic superorganism; inter-Gaian interaction and communication reach sufficient complexity and synergy for all 10 billion Gaias (planets with life) in our galaxy to integrate into a single system, a galactic society of communicating civilizations.

The Gigafuture (After A.D. 1 billion)

1 billion Sun begins to expand and turns Earth into tropical nightmare, with fantastic array of carnivorous and poisonous jungle plants

and insects seizing telepathic control and destroying remaining civilization of devolved green-skinned descendants of *Homo sapiens*. (B. W. Aldiss's scenario *Hothouse/The Long Afternoon of Earth*, 1962.)

2 billion Supernova end scenario: final extinction of human race by supernova, with Last Men (18th race after *Homo sapiens* as First Men) as final form of civilized humanity, living on Neptune in virtual paradise, one trillion strong; telepaths, virtually immortal, group mind. (W. O. Stapledon, 1930.)

3 billion Disintegrating Moon scenario: Earth gradually pulls Moon closer, triggering earthquakes, volcanos, tidal waves engulfing continents; when Moon reaches 5,000 miles out, it disintegrates totally into planetary ring bombarding Earth with huge chunks.

4 billion Final shape of man scenario—*Homo universalis*, a nonmaterial being with enormous powers, a sphere of force able to travel instantaneously across Milky Way galaxy or universe at will.

5 billion Emergence of Seventh or Final Level of Evolution: cosmic mind, i.e., universal consciousness, with all 100 billion galaxies or galactic superorganisms in universe evolving into one single universal superorganism or being, the perfect cosmos.

5.6 billion Advent of next, fifth Buddha, Maitreya (Buddhist scholars vary over correct date, down to A.D. 560 million or even A.D. 4621), to be followed later, sequentially, by 995 other Buddhas with decline and then final demise of the Dharma.

6 billion Sun evolves into luminous red giant with radius reaching planet Mercury; Earth's oceans and atmosphere have long since disappeared in intense heat; most stars very old, Milky Way galaxy (and most other galaxies) becoming a graveyard of stars at end point of stellar evolution; human race, if not yet extinct, embarks on its last journey.

7 billion Sudden ice death of Earth scenario: huge alien star appears, loops around Sun, draws Earth off into icy depths of space.

8 billion Solar end scenario: Sun, gradually expanding over last 13 billion years, engulfs Earth and all its related colonies, then collapses as a degenerate white dwarf and then finally a dead black dwarf.

25 billion Black hole at center of Milky Way galaxy, which has been devouring matter and stars for 40 billion years, emitting ever more intense radiation (and reaching a

Date	Events

billion miles wide by A.D. 1987), finally consumes whole of our galaxy; most other galaxies similarly eaten up until all matter has been sucked into a number of gigantic black holes.

50 billion   Period of star formation ends, majority of stars begin to go out, whole universe gradually becomes a graveyard of stars.

100 billion   After 100 billion (10^{11}) years, life and intelligence continue after end of *Homo sapiens* (since essential feature of consciousness is not cells or DNA, but structural complexity) in forms of sentient computers, sentient clouds, and other vastly complex structures.

The Eschatofuture (after A.D. 1 trillion, or 10^{12} years)

1 trillion   All stars in Milky Way galaxy become dark remnants; all galaxies now dead and invisible.

10^{14} years   After 100 trillion (10^{14}) years, last remaining stars run out of nuclear fuel, contract, and collapse under their own weight; all lose their planets through close encounters with other stars.

10^{17} years   Dead stars break up, evaporate, and are swallowed by massive black holes (one at center of every galaxy), which then all finally coalesce into one immense supermassive black hole coextensive with the still expanding universe.

10^{17} years   Alternative end-time scenarios, after 10^{18} years: (1) universe is open (with insufficient mass to halt expansion of galaxies, which thus continue for ever); or (2) universe is flat (exactly flat, with just enough mass to halt expansion but not to reverse it), or (3) universe is closed (with sufficient mass, especially nonluminous mass (cold dark matter) in haloes around galaxies, to halt expansion and reverse it).

The Eschatofuture—1: Endless Expansion of Open Universe (Expansion Heat-Death Scenario)

10^{18} years   In the eschatofuture or exafuture (after 10^{18} years), universe gradually runs down in energy and temperature.

10^{30} years   Some 40% of all matter in universe with its 10^{30} elementary particles (protons, neutrons, electrons) has now totally decayed.

10^{32} years   Life span of all protons and neutrons ends as they disintegrate and all long-lived matter decays; nothing left in universe except electrons, positrons, photons, neutrinos, and black holes.

Date	Events

10^{50} years   Universe continues expanding forever; as its heat-death approaches, humanity builds its own computer-god that duly creates another universe. (I. Asimov's scenario "The Last Question," 1956.)

10^{95} years   Despite dying universe, many advanced long-lived civilizations manage to maintain themselves by constructing rigid shells around rotating supermassive black holes and living off their energy until they decay and evaporate after 10^{100} years.

10^{100} years   Final evolutionary heat death of universe as entropy (disorder or chaos) reaches maximum: disappearance by quantum evaporation of all supermassive black-hole relics of collapsed galaxies, and elimination of all solid matter; lastly, remaining diffuse gas of low-energy particles vanishes, leaving nothing except cold, thin, expanding sea of radiation.

The Eschatofuture—2: Gradual Demise of Flat Stationary Universe (Motionless Heat-Death Scenario)

10^{18} years   Expansion of universe slows, gradually comes to a permanent halt, declines toward ultimate heat death as entropy (disorder, chaos) approaches maximum.

10^{20} years   Humans, huddled in space colonies across icy universe, create new life-forms based on plasma (remnants of interstellar gas), resulting in structured, constantly evolving plasmoid society and plasmoid creatures each living 10^{15} years in universe's freezing night, using energy from black holes.

10^{31} years   Final civilization: before plasmoid society disintegrates as protons decay, it creates enormously sluggish creatures of new kind of atom, positronium (orbiting electron and positron), forming its own vastly more diffuse plasma, powered by electron-positron antimatter clashes.

10^{99} years   Space temperature only 10^{-60} degrees above absolute zero in stationary and motionless universe.

10^{100} years   Photons (light from earlier epochs) as only remaining entities in motion continue to expand, carrying the entire record of the universe, galaxies, humanity, and all creation, across limitless reaches of empty space.

The Eschatofuture—3: Gravitational Collapse of Closed Universe (Big Crunch or Big Squeeze Scenario)

10^{25} years   At its maximum expansion, universe is made up of dead stars, supermassive black-hole remnants of collapsed galaxies, and low-

Date	Events
	energy particles; gravity of universe, especially nonluminous matter (over 80% of all matter), halts expansion, and reverses it; dead stars begin to burn up and explode.
10^{25} years	After expansion of universe is halted and recession of galactic systems reversed, universe begins to collapse rapidly and catastrophically.
10^{32} years	A million years before the Big Crunch, photons dissociate interstellar hydrogen atoms into electrons and protons; 1 year before, stars break up; supermassive black holes swallow up matter and radiation; 3 minutes before, black holes coalesce, universe becomes a single monster supermassive black hole.
10^{32} years	The Big Crunch: in final collapse of universe, at first galaxies, then stars, and lastly atoms, particles, and quarks are crushed into each other in one overwhelming cataclysmic inferno, with collapsing cosmos approaching a singularity of infinite density and temperature and reverting to primal chaos of original cosmic explosion and fireball, the primordial monobloc.

Date	Events
	God Creates Successive Oscillating Universes (Big Bounce Scenario)
10^{32} years	After final collapse of our contracting universe, a new and mightier Big Bang occurs and a totally new, more immense universe commences its vastly faster expansion; and ditto, in due course, for an endless sequence of progressively vaster universes. (Landsberg-Park model of universe bigger with each succeeding bounce.)
	God Creates Infinite Parallel Cyclic Universes
	Numerous cycles or bounces: present universe is no more than 100 bounces from cycle which lasted just long enough to create a single generation of stars.
	Our universe and its successors turn out to be only one bubble in a froth of a billion trillion parallel sequences of infinitely evolving universes in superspace; awesome might, majesty, dominion, power, and glory of God as Creator finally fully unveiled.

David B. Barrett

One Hundred Most Influential Futurists

The list that follows is the result of a poll conducted among *Encyclopedia of the Future* editorial board members. Its purpose was to identify the futurists whose writings have exerted a significant influence on the development of futurism. The list hews closely to the results of the poll; as reported, no changes were made in the rank order. Since futurism is a relatively recent field of inquiry, the list includes virtually all the founders, many of whom are still alive.

Futurists are inveterate listmakers. Thus, we find books and articles with "100 Vital Trends," "50 Ways to Change the World," "15 New Directions," and so forth. Listmaking is as clearly a futurist's function as taxonomy is that of the biologist. Listing books, for example, helps to establish an authoritative canon on which future studies are based. Listing practitioners is equally important, albeit more difficult. It is one way of acknowledging the contributions of the trailblazers and expressing gratitude to them. The following list encompasses a diverse group that share in common some characteristics that allude to a futuristic perspective. Great futurists are generalists, not specialists. They specialize in the long view as well as the broad view, often synthesizing and integrating rather than innovating. They chart rather than expound, extrapolate rather than predict. They have an intuitive sense of direction and purpose, what the Greeks call *telos*. They not only analyze, but also teach and warn. It is this last magisterial trait that makes great futurists the seers of our time.

1. R. Buckminster Fuller
2. Herman Kahn
3. H. G. Wells
4. Isaac Asimov
5. Peter F. Drucker
6. Arthur C. Clarke
7. Jules Verne
8. Jay W. Forrester
9. Aurelio Peccei
10. Alvin Toffler
11. Edward Cornish
12. Isaac Newton
13. Dennis Meadows
14. Paul Ehrlich
15. George Orwell
16. John McHale
17. Robert Theobald
18. Daniel Bell
19. Donella Meadows
20. Arnold J. Toynbee
21. Theodore Gordon
22. Edward Bellamy
23. Kenneth Boulding
24. Warren Wagar
25. Roy Amara
26. Bertrand de Jouvenel
27. Galileo Galilei
28. Marshall McLuhan
29. E. F. Schumacher
30. Joseph A. Schumpeter
31. Charles Darwin
32. Jan Tinbergen

33. Amitai Etzioni
34. Harlan Cleveland
35. Maurice Strong
36. Graham T. T. Molitor
37. Olaf Helmer
38. Robert U. Ayres
39. Thomas Robert Malthus
40. Leonardo da Vinci
41. Aldous Huxley
42. Willis Harman
43. Wassily Leontief
44. Barbara Ward
45. Constantinos A. Doxiados
46. Lewis Mumford
47. Richard Lamm
48. Ray Bradbury
49. Hazel Henderson
50. Michael Marien
51. Robert Jungk
52. Dennis Gabor
53. Abraham Maslow
54. Hugues de Jouvenel
55. Olaf Stapledon
56. Marvin Cetron
57. Joseph P. Martino
58. James Bright
59. Thomas Kuhn
60. Albert Einstein
61. Robert Heilbroner
62. Albert Gore
63. John Naisbitt
64. Pierre Teilhard de Chardin
65. Francis Bacon
66. Marquis de Condorcet
67. Sir Thomas More
68. Ervin Laszlo
69. Nikolai Kondratieff
70. Daniel Yankelovich
71. William F. Ogburn
72. Pitirim A. Sorokin
73. Harold A. Linstone
74. James Dator
75. Eric Jantsch
76. Harrison Brown
77. Victor Ferkiss
78. Yehezkel Dror
79. John Platt
80. Joseph Coates
81. Donald N. Michael
82. Fred Polak
83. Lester Brown
84. Orville Freeman
85. Yoneji Masuda
86. Wendell Bell
87. Wayne Boucher
88. Burt Nanus
89. Alexander King
90. I. F. Clarke
91. Emmanuel Mesthene
92. Gene Roddenberry
93. Frederik Pohl
94. Johann Galtung
95. Frank Feather
96. William Halal
97. James Robertson
98. Paul Kennedy
99. Warren G. Bennis
100. Gerard K. O'Neill

The Editorial Board

One Hundred Most Influential Futurist Books

The following list identifies books within the last sixty-five years that have had the most impact on the development of futurism or that have expressed seminal futurist ideas. These are not necessarily the best books, or the great books, because as Aristotle said, even bad books may be as significant as good ones when it comes to shaping ideas and concepts and guiding the course of history. But, by and large, these books represent the best-known and best-read titles of the most-noted futurists of the latter half of the twentieth century.

Influential books constitute landmarks guiding us through the fields of futurism. The universe from which these books were selected is not large by the standards of other disciplines or professions. *Future Survey*, published since 1979, reviews fewer than 500 books and articles each year, including many bearing only marginally on what might be defined as strict futurism. Lists are not accolades but scanning tools, and should be used as such. They are necessarily subjective, reflecting the biases and choices of the compilers. It is possible that other compilers might have chosen differently. However, that does not diminish the value of a list.

The major problem in compiling the list has been the definition of *futurism*. Futurism is a borderless subject; interdisciplinary in nature, it cuts through and illuminates a number of subfields, each of which is a valid discipline in itself. For example, environmental futurism has burgeoned in recent years, and now it comprises a large part of the literature. In limiting the selection to what might be called futurism proper, it was decided to eschew narrow specializations or issues. For the same reason, science fiction has been excluded. (As a result, the name of its most famous author, Isaac Asimov, does not appear here). Also guiding the selection was the status and reputation of the author in the futurist community. Many leading futurists are represented in this listing, but none by more than two titles.

For additional futurist classics, see the *Future Survey Annual* (1979–) and Alan J. Mayne's *Resources for the Future: An International Annotated Bibliography for the Twenty-first Century* (Westport, CT: Greenwood, 1993).

Anderson, Walter Truett. *Reality Isn't What It Used to Be* (1990)

Beckwith, Burnham P. *The Next Five Hundred Years: Scientific Predictions of Major Social Trends* (1967)

Bell, Daniel. *The Coming of the Post-Industrial Society: A Venture into Social Forecasting* (1976)

Bennett, William J. *The Index of Leading Cultural Indicators* (1994)

Berry, Adrian. *The Next Ten Thousand Years: A Vision of Man's Future in the Universe* (1974)

Boulding, Kenneth E. *The Meaning of the Twentieth Century: The Great Transition* (1964)

_____. *The World as a Total System* (1953)

Brown, Harrison. *The Challenge of Man's Future* (1954)

_____. Bonner, James, and Weir, John. *The Next One Hundred Years* (1957)

Brown, Lester. *The State of the World* (Annual)

Burrows. Brian. *Into the Twenty-first Century: A Handbook for a Sustainable Future* (1991)

Cetron, Marvin, and Davies, Owen. *Crystal Globe: The Haves and Have-nots of the New World Order* (1991)

Chase, Stuart. *The Most Probable World* (1968)

Clark, Mary E. *Ariadne's Thread: The Search for New Modes of Thinking* (1989)

Clarke, Arthur C. *July 20, 2019: Life in the Twenty-first Century* (1986)

_____. *Profiles of the Future: An Inquiry into the Limits of the Possible* (1963)

Clarke, I. F. *The Pattern of Expectation, 1644–2001* (1979)

Coates, Joseph F., and Jarratt, Jennifer. *What Futurists Believe* (1989)

Cleveland, Harlan. *The Global Commons: Policy for the Planet* (1990)

Commoner, Barry. *Making Peace with the Planet* (1990)

Cornish, Edward. *The Study of the Future* (1977)

Dalkey, Norman C. *Predicting the Future* (1968)

Darwin, Charles Galton. *The Next Million Years* (1953)

Dixon, Dougal. *Man after Man: An Anthropology of the Future* (1990)

Drucker, Peter. *The Age of Discontinuity* (1969)

_____. *The New Realities in Government and Politics, in Economics and Business, in Society and World View* (1989)

Ehrlich, Paul R., and Ehrlich, Anne H. *The Population Explosion* (1990)

Ellul, Jacques. *The Technological Society* (1964)

_____. *The Technological Bluff* (1990)

Etzioni, Amitai. *The Spirit of Community* (1993)

Falk, Richard A. *A Study of Future Worlds* (1975)

Feather, Frank. *G-Forces: Reinventing the World* (1989)

Ferguson, Marilyn. *The Aquarian Conspiracy* (1987)

Ferkiss, Victor G. The Future of Technological Civilization (1974)

_____. *Technological Man: The Myth and the Reality* (1969)

Flectheim, Ossip K. *History and Futurology* (1966)

Forrester, Jay. *World Dynamics* (1971)

_____. *Urban Dynamics* (1969)

Fuller, R. Buckminster. *Operating Manual for Spaceship Earth* (1970)

_____. *Utopia or Oblivion: The Prospects for Humanity* (1969)

Gabor, Dennis. *Inventing the Future* (1964)

Goldsmith, Edward et al. *A Blueprint for Survival* (1972)

Gordon, Theodore. *The Future* (1963)

Handy, Charles. *The Age of Paradox* (1994)

Harman, Willis W. *An Incomplete Guide to the Future* (1976)

_____. Global Mind Change: *The Promise of the Last Years of the Twentieth Century* (1988)

Hawking, Stephen. *A Brief History of Time: From the Big Bang to Black Holes* (1987)

Heilbroner, Robert L. *The Future as History* (1960)

Howe, Leo, and Wain, Alan. *Predicting the Future* (1993)

Hubbard, Barbara Marx. *The Evolutionary Journey* (1982)

Huxley, Aldous. *Brave New World* (1931)

Jouvenel, Bertrand de. *The Art of Conjecture* (1967)

Jungk, Robert. *Tomorrow is Already Here: Scenes from a Manmade World* (1954)

Jungk, Robert, and Galtung, Johan. *Mankind 2000* (1969)

Kahn, Herman, and Wiener, A. J. *The Year 2000* (1967)

Kahn, Herman; Brown, William; and Martel, Leon. *The Next Two Hundred Years* (1978)

Kennedy, Paul. *Preparing for the Twenty-first Century* (1993)

_____. *The Rise and Fall of the Great Powers* (1987)

Kidder, Rushworth. *Reinventing the Future: Global Goals for the Twenty-first Century* (1989)

King, Alexander, and Schneider, Bertrand. *The First Global Revolution: A Report by the Council of the Club of Rome* (1991)

Kuhn, Thomas. *The Structure of Scientific Revolutions* (1970)

Lamm, Richard D. *Megatraumas: America at the Year 2000* (1985)

Lapp, Ralph E. *The Logarithmic Century: Charting Future Shock* (1973)

Laszlo, Ervin. *Goals for Mankind: A Report to the Club of Rome* (1977)

_____. *Destiny Choice: Survival Options for the Twenty-first Century* (1993)

Leebaert, Derek. *Technology 2001: The Future of Computing and Communications* (1991)

Lorie, Peter, and Murray-Clark, Sidd. *The History of the Future: A Chronology* (1989)

Lovelock, James E. *Gaia: A New Look at Life on Earth* (1987)

Makridakis, Spyros G. *Forecasting, Planning and Strategy for the 21st Century* (1990)

Martino, Joseph P. *An Introduction to Technological Forecasting* (1972)

Masini, Eleanora. *The Futures of Culture* (1991)

Maslow, Abraham H. *Toward a Psychology of Being* (1968)

McHale, John. *The Future of the Future* (1969)

Meadows, Donella H.; Meadows, Dennis H.; and Randers, Jorgen. *Beyond the Limits: Collapse or a Sustainable Future* (1992)

Meadows, Donella H., and Behrens, William H. II. *The Limits to Growth: A Report for the Club of Rome's Project on the Predicament of Mankind* (1974)

McLuhan, Marshall. *Understanding Media* (1964)

Mesthene, Emmanuel G. *Technological Change: Its Impact on Man and Society* (1970)

Muller, Herbert J. *Uses of the Future* (1973)

Mumford, Lewis. *The Future of Technics and Civilization* (1986)

Myers, Norman. *The Gaia Atlas of Future Worlds: Challenge and Op-

portunity in an Age of Change (1990)

Naisbitt, John. *Megatrends: Ten New Directions in Transforming Our Lives* (1984)

Naisbitt, John, and Aburdene, Patricia. *Megatrends 2000* (1991)

O'Neill, Gerard. *A Hopeful View of the Human Future* (1981)

Peccei, Aurelio. *One Hundred Years for the Future* (1981)

Polak, Fred L. *Prognostics: A Science in the Making Surveys and Creates the Future* (1971)

_____. *The Image of the Future* (1973)

Prehoda, Robert W. *Designing the Future: The Role of Technological Forecasting* (1967)

Rostow, Walter W. *The Stages of Economic Growth* (1960)

Russell, Peter. *The White Hole in Time: Our Future Evolution and the Meaning of Now* (1992)

Schlesinger, Arthur M., Jr. *The Cycles of American History* (1986)

Schumacher, E. F. *Small is Beautiful: A Study of Economics as if People Mattered* (1974)

Schwartz, Peter. *The Art of the Long View* (1991)

Simon, Julian L., and Kahn, Herman. *The Resourceful Earth: A Response to Global 2000* (1984)

Snow, C. P. *The Two Cultures and the Scientific Revolution* (1961)

Stableford, Brian M. *The Future of Man* (1984)

Stableford, Brian M., and Langford, David. *The Third Millennium: A History of the World, A. D. 2000–3000* (1985)

Teilhard de Chardin, Pierre. *The Phenomenon of Man* (1970)

Theobald, Robert. *Futures Conditional* (1972)

Thompson, George. *The Foreseeable Future* (1955)

Toffler, Alvin, and Toffler, Heidi. *Future Shock* (1970)

_____. *The Third Wave* (1981)

Wagar, W. Warren. *The Next Three Futures: Paradigms of Things to Come* (1991)

_____. *A Short History of the Future* (1989)

Ward, Barbara. *Spaceship Earth* (1966)

Wells, H. G. *The Shape of Things to Come* (1933)

George Thomas Kurian

Commissions and Work Groups on the Future

Items are listed chronologically.

1933. President's Research Committee on Social Trends. *Recent Social Trends in the United States.* 2 volumes. Foreword by Herbert Hoover (William F. Ogburn, director of research). New York: McGraw-Hill.

1960. President's Commission on National Goals. *Goals for Americans: Programs for Action in the Sixties.* New York: American Assembly/Prentice-Hall.

1967–1968. American Institute of Planners Consultation. *Environment for Man: The Next Fifty Years; Environment and Change: The Next Fifty Years; Environment and Policy: The Next Fifty Years.* William R. Ewald, Jr., ed. Bloomington, IN: Indiana University Press.

1967–1969. Commission on the Year 2000. *Toward the Year 2000: Work in Progress.* Daniel Bell, ed. *Daedalus* (Summer 1967); Boston: Beacon Press, 1969.

1969–1971 First International Futures Research Conference. *Mankind 2000.* Robert Jungk and Johan Galtung, eds. Oslo: Universitetsforlaget, 1969; London: Allen & Unwin, 1971.

1972. Commission on Population Growth and the American Future. *Population and the American Future.* Washington, DC: U.S. Government Printing Office; New York: New American Library/Signet.

1976–1994. Union of International Associations (Anthony Judge, coordinator). *Encyclopedia of World Problems and Human Potential.* 1st ed., 1976; 4th ed., 1994. New Providence, NJ: K. J. Saur/Bowker.

1980. Council on Environmental Quality and U.S. Department of State. (Gerald O. Barney, study director). *The Global 2000 Report to the President: Entering the 21st Century.* 3 volumes. Washington, DC: U.S. Government Printing Office.

1980. Independent Commission on International Development Issues (Willy Brandt, chairman). *North-South: A Program for Survival.* Cambridge, MA: MIT Press.

1987. World Commission on Environment and Development (Gro Harlem Brundtland, chair). *Our Common Future.* New York: Oxford University Press.

1990. United Nations. *Global Outlook 2000: An Economic, Social, and Environmental Perspective.* New York: UN Publications.

1991. IUCN—The World Conservation Union, U.N. Environment Programme, and World Wildlife Fund. *Caring for the Earth: A Strategy for Sustainable Living.* David A. Monroe and Martin W. Holdgate, eds. Gland, Switzerland: IUCN (distributed in the United States by Island Press, Washington, DC).

1992. U.N. Conference on Environment and Development. *AGENDA 21: The UN Programme of Action from Rio.* 3 volumes. New York: UN Publications; abridged version edited by Daniel Sitarz, Boulder CO: Earth Press.

1994. World Resources Institute, U.N. Environment Programme, and U.N. Development Programme. *World Resources: A Guide to the Global Environment.* 6th ed. New York: Oxford University Press. (Published biannually; Allen L. Hammond, editor-in-chief; M. S. Swaminathan, chair of editorial advisory board.

1994. U.N. Development Programme. *Human Development Report.* 5th ed. New York: Oxford University Press. (Published annually since 1990.)

1994. International Commission on Peace and Food (M. S. Swaminathan, chair). *Uncommon Opportunities: An Agenda for Peace and Equitable Development.* London and Atlantic Highlands, NJ: Zed Books.

1995. Commission on Global Governance. *Our Global Neighborhood.* New York: Oxford University Press.

Michael Marien

INDEX

Australia–New Zealand Closer Economic Relations Trade Agreement (ANZCERTA or CER), *504*, 505
Automated Fingerprint Identification Systems (AFIS), 170
Automobile industry, 638
Automobiles, 704. *See also* Motor vehicles
  alcohol fuels, 639
  battery-powered, 47, 640
  cities, 957
  efficiency, 236
  electric, 47, 224, 635, 636, 640
  ethanol, 639
  flexible-fuel vehicles, 639
  fuel cells, 640
  hybrid-electric, 232, 233, 237, 640
  hydrogen-powered, 233, 640
  increased demand in industrializing markets, 634
  natural gas, 635, 639, 640
  "smart," 139
  as symbol of society, 636
Avocations, 553

B

Baby-boom generation, 452–453, 737–738
  economic power, 739
  individualism, 739
  savings and, 813
  values of, 569
Baby-bust generation, 738
Back to Methuselah (Shaw), 959
Bacon, Francis, 367
Bail reform, 526
Bainbridge, William Sims, 796
Baker, William O., 121
Balanced Budget Amendment, 768
Ballistic electron emission microscope, 916
Band, William A., 721
Banking
  electronic funds transfers, 127, 921
  electronic service delivery, 604
  home banking, 921
  robots in, 806
  source of capital funding, 67
  telecommunications and, 921
Bankruptcy, 167
Barber, Benjamin, 349

Bartering, 474–475, 605, 1002
  international, 510
  see also Countertrade
Baryshnikov, Mikhail, 703
Barzun, Jacques, 627
Basel Convention on the Control of Transboundary Movements of Hazardous Wastes and Their Disposal (1989), 253
Bateson, Gregory, 390
Batteries, **47–49**
Beckwith, Burnham, 796
Bednorz, J. Georg, 886
Before It Is Too Late (Peccei), 395
Behavior
  biotech control, 751
  chemical basis, 87
  modification, 538
  social constraints, **49–50**, 166
Behavioral genetics, 757, 759
Beliefs, 845
Bell, Daniel, **50**, 367, 483, 737
  Coming of Postindustrial Society, The, 479
  Commission on the Year 2000, 121–122
  on telecommunications revolution, 920
Bellamy, Edward, 959
Benchmarking, 721
Berger, Peter L., 70
Bergson, Abram, 853
Berman, Morris, 362
Bernal, J. D., 870
Bernays, Edward, 776, 777
Bernstein, Richard, 723
Berry, Adrian, 737
Besant, Annie, 795
Beta-endorphins, 161
Beyond God the Father (Daley), 991
Beyond the Limits (Meadows et al.), 395, 803, 988
Bicycles, 704–705, 940
Big Bang, 41
Big science, 822, 1013
Bilingualism, 535
  in education, 723
  public employees, 106
  Spanish in the United States, 625–626
Biocentric ethics, 248
Biochips, 385, 649
Biocomputers, 299
Biocontrollers, 709
Biodiversity, **51–52**
  deforestation and, 184, 185

Bioethics, **52–53**
Biogenetics. *See* Genetic engineering
Biological and Toxin Weapons Convention (1972), 983
Biological diversity. *See* Biodiversity
Biological Diversity Convention, 246
Biological weapons, 983
Biology
  as basis for mental disorders, 611, 757
  ethnic animosity, 779
  racial animosity, 779
  science and, 823
Biomass, 235
Biosensors, 384, 385, 709
Biosphere, human intervention in, 293
Biosphere II, 870, 876
Biotechnology, 52, 333, 380. *See also* Genetic engineering
  employment, 1010
  food production, 324
  future of, 383
Birthrates, 595, 740
  urbanization, 614
Black holes, 42, 83
Black markets, 475
Blacks. *See* African Americans
Blair, Eric Arthur. *See* Orwell, George
Blanc, Louis, 852
Blavatsky, Helena, 795
Blish, James, 870
Blumhofer, Edith L., 702
Bohm, David, 393
Bonn Convention on the Conservation of Migratory Species of Wild Animals (1979), 252
Books, 750
  as multimedia experiences, 228
  preservation, 559
Boserup, Ester, 993
Bosnia-Herzegovina, 271
Boulding, Elise, 362
  Underside of History, The, 988
Boulding, Kenneth, 247, 249
Bovine somatotropin (BST), 380–381, 382
Box-Jenkins method of forecasting, 341
Bradbury, Ray, 820
Brain-imaging techniques, 757
  and mental illness diagnosis, 612

Index

Index

Human Development Index (UN),
249
Human Development Report, 199,
249
Humane Sustainable Agriculture
movement, 24
Human Genome Project, 86, 316,
377, 382–383, 425, 433, 608,
837
and extinction of species,
293
Human immunodeficiency virus
(HIV), 262, 263, 424
Humanism, 669
Human needs
psychological, 76
spiritual, 76
Human resources
development, **459–461**
in manufacturing, 297–298
Human rights, **461–464**
accused, 169
free expression, 126, 542, 603
global statistics, *401–402*
to one's own language, 536
privacy, 125, 142
Hungary, 271
energy, 276
Hunger as women's issue, 991
Hunt, Todd, 777
Huntington, Samuel P., 121
Hurricanes, 657
Hydroelectric power, 235
Hydrogen, 233, 235–236
automobiles, 640
pipelines, 720
solar derived, 233
and transportation, 473
wind-derived, 233
Hypercars, 236–237

I

I Ching. *See* Prophetic arts
Ideology, as term, 772
IDN. *See* Integrated digital networks (IDN)
Ignition interlocks, 167
Iklé, Fred G., 121
Illinois, 692
Illiteracy, 229, **465–466**
women and, 989, 992
Illness. *See* Diseases
Image of the Future, The (Polak),
392
Image processing, 34

IMF. *See* International Monetary
Fund (IMF)
Immigration
Canada, 65
France, 350
Germany, 386
Japan, 566
Russia, 808
spectator sports, 878
Sweden, 898
United States, 626, 740, 954
see also Migration
Immunizations, 430
Immunology, 384
Incest, 89
Income
disparities in Germany, 387
redistribution, 853
versus wealth, 975
Income distribution, 977, *978*
Lorenz curve, *978*
as a percentage of total income
of families, *978*
Independent living movement,
203
India, **467–470**
birthrate, 741
caste system, 780
chemical weapons, 31, 982
coal, 117, 118
international diplomacy, 498
nuclear weapons, 31, 981
ODA recipient, 344
productivity, 755
solar power, 232
wind power, 232
Indian Health Service, 652
Individual Retirement Account
(IRA), 266–267, 814
Individual rights
and counterterrorism, 928
as opposed to social responsibilities, 735
protection under American law,
541
and social responsibilities, 133
Individual Transferable Quotas
(ITQ) (fisheries), 313
Indonesia
chemical weapons, 31
ODA recipient, 344
Industrial age. *See* Industrial society
Industrial deconstruction, 62
Industrial design, **470–472**
Industrial gases, **472–473**

Industrialization, global statistics,
403
Industrialized countries
aging of the population, 11
appropriate technology, 28
environmental refugees from,
259–261
multiculturalism, 566–567
multiethnicity, 566–567
Industrial policy, 1014
targeted government programs,
61
Industrial society
characteristics, *855*
culture, *861*
demographics, *856*
economics, *858*
education, *860*
energy, *857*
environmental pollution, *857*
family, *860*
mindset, *861*
as opposed to information society, 479
politics, *858*
workplace, *859*
Industry
fine chemicals, 84
India, *468*, 468–469
Japan, 522
piracy, 493
R&D, 799–800, 801–802
water use, 355
Infobahn. *See* Information superhighway
Infoglut. *See* Information overload
Infomercials, 7
Informal economy, **474–476**
labor markets, 611
Information age. *See* Information
society
Information overload, **476–479**,
480
Information society, 71, 123,
479–481
characteristics, *855*
culture, *861*
demographics, *856*
economics, *858*
education, *860*
employment, 553
energy, *857*
environmental pollution, *857*
family, *860*
literacy requirements, 465, 663
mindset, *861*

Index

interoperating group of specialized networks, 136
technology, 136–137
Neumann, John von, 36
New Age movement, 795
Newbigin, Bishop Leslie, 701
New Capitalism, 683, 854
New Jersey, 692
New Management, 683
New paradigm, 484
New product introductions, 663, *664, 665*
food products, *664, 665, 666*
New self-propagating technologies, 336
News from Nowhere (Morris), 959
Newsletters, 667
New Socialism, 854
Newspapers, **666–667**
effect of new communications technologies, 123
on-line, 920
polls, 772
New York, 692
New York Times, 666
New Zealand, **43–45**
environmental indicators, 251
social democracy in, 848
Next 500 Years, The (Beckwith), 796
Next 200 Years, The (Kahn et al.), 531, 959
Nicaragua, 31
Niche marketing, 590
Niebuhr, H. Richard, 794, 893
Nigeria, 848
NIMBY (Not in My Backyard) syndrome, 224, 423, 945
waste-handling facilities, 869
Nineteen Eighty-Four (Orwell), 684, 959
Nitrogen, 472
and soil fertility, 866
Nonaccelerating inflation rate of unemployment (NAIRU), 948
Nongovernmental organizations, **668–669**
international, 198
Nonreligious beliefs, **669–670**
Nonscientific futurists. *See* Pseudo-futurists
NORC. *See* National Opinion Research Center (NORC)
Normex forecasting, 341
Norplant, 2, 300
Norse, David, 416

North American Free Trade Agreement (NAFTA), 65, 183, 354, 500, *504*, 505, 537, 954, 1014–1015
Mexico, 615
North Atlantic Treaty Organization (NATO), 501
North Korea
biological weapons, 983
chemical weapons, 982
nuclear weapons, 981
Norway, 990
Nostradamus (Michel de Nostredame), **670–671**, 736
NOW. *See* National Organization of Women (NOW)
Nuclear accidents, 981
Chernobyl, 256–257
Nuclear arsenals, *983*
Nuclear Non-Proliferation Treaty (1968), 31, 981
Nuclear power
arguments against, **671–673**
arguments in favor of, **673–675**
and conscious evolution, 147
fusion energy, 718
plutonium, 943
Nuclear powers, 981, *982*
Nuclear proliferation, 31–32
Nuclear Test Ban Treaty (1963), 253
Nuclear Waste Policy Act (1982), 674
Nuclear weapons, 31, 82, 499, 981
Middle East, 617
plutonium, 943
war strategy, 531
weapon-free zones, 981
Nursing, 609, **675–676**
Nursing home industry, 430
Nutraceuticals, 318, 664
Nutrition, **676–678**
dietary supplements, 328–329
discussed in press, 317–318
and fine chemicals, 84
Nutrition Labeling and Education Act (1990), 328

O

Obsolescence, 908
Occupational Safety and Health Administration (OSHA), 935
Oceans, **679–680**
and global warming, 408, 409
macroengineering, 582–583

minerals in seabeds, 624
as new frontier, 238
science, 823
undersea habitation, 583
undersea prisons, 751
Office of Alternative Medicine (NIH), 318
Office of International Criminal Justice, 929
Office of Technology Assessment, 368, 914
Official development assistance, 344
Official development finance, 343
Of Time, Work, and Leisure (Souza), 552
Ogburn, William Fielding, **680–681**
Oil, 705
pipelines, 719
price increase of, 9
Old-age income, 489
Olfactory Research Fund, 347
O'Neill, Gerard K., 870, 872
High Frontier, The, 870
Hopeful View of the Human Future, A, 737
On-line dating, 921
On-line services, **681–683**, 920
interactive entertainment, 494
libraries and, 559
news, 666
On-line video communications, 786, 787
On Thermonuclear War (Kahn), 531
Oparin, Alexander Ivanovich, 281, 286
Opium, 209
Optical character recognition (OCR), 144, 482
Optical communications, 123
Optical data storage, 178–179
magneto optic recording system, *178*
and video recording, 786, 787
Optoelectronic communications, 827
Organic husbandry, 28
Organizational complexity, **683–684**
Organization of American States (OAS), 536
Organization for Economic Cooperation and Development (OECD), 252
environmental indicators, 250–251
productivity in, 755

Index

Index

Index